To Sarah

Have a wonderful
time. many thanks for
your help!

KT-156-474

# New England

**Tom Brosnahan**

**Kim Grant**

**Steve Jermanok**

Lynne

30 June, 2000

LONELY PLANET PUBLICATIONS
Melbourne · Oakland · London · Paris

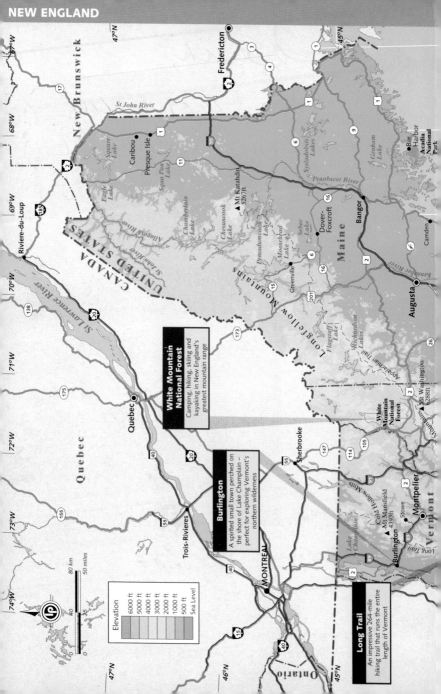

**White Mountain National Forest**

Camping, hiking, skiing and kayaking in New England's greatest mountain range

**Burlington**

A spirited small town perched on the shore of Lake Champlain – perfect for exploring Vermont's northern wilderness

**Long Trail**

An impressive 264-mile hiking trail that runs the entire length of Vermont

Fredericton

New Brunswick

St John River

Riviere-du-Loup

CANADA

UNITED STATES

Quebec

Trois-Rivieres

MONTREAL

Ontario

Caribou
Presque Isle
Square Lake
Eagle Lake
Squa Pan Lake
Allagash River
St John River
Chamberlain Lake
Chesuncook Lake
▲ Mt Katahdin 5267ft
Pemadumcook Lake
Moosehead Lake
Sebec Lake
Greenville
Longfellow Mountains
Flagstaff Lake
Richardson Lakes
Appalachian Trail
Dover-Foxcroft
Bangor
Maine
Penobscot River
Sysladobsis Lakes
Graham Lake
Bar Harbor
Acadia National Park
Camden
Kennebec River
Augusta
Sherbrooke
White Mountain National Forest
▲ Mt Washington 6288ft
Green Mtns
Cold Hollow Mtns
▲ Mt Mansfield 4393ft
Stowe
Lake Champlain
Burlington
Montpelier
Vermont
Long Trail

St Lawrence River

Elevation

6000 ft
5000 ft
4000 ft
3000 ft
2000 ft
1000 ft
500 ft
Sea Level

80 km
50 miles

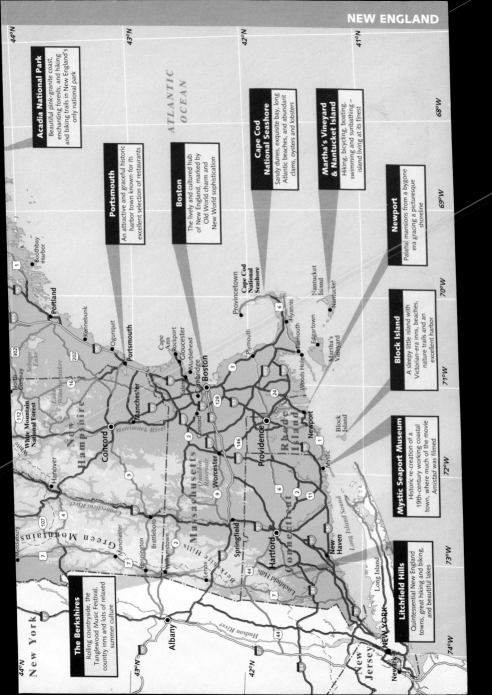

**Acadia National Park**
Beautiful pink-granite coast, enchanting forests, and hiking and biking trails in New England's only national park

**Portsmouth**
An attractive and graceful historic harbor town known for its excellent selection of restaurants

**Boston**
The lively and cultured hub of New England, marked by Old World charm and New World sophistication

**Cape Cod National Seashore**
Sandy dunes, exquisite bay, long Atlantic beaches, and abundant clams, oysters and lobsters

**Martha's Vineyard & Nantucket Island**
Hiking, bicycling, boating, swimming and sunbathing – island living at its finest

**Newport**
Palatial mansions from a bygone era gracing a picturesque shoreline

**Block Island**
A sleepy little island with Victorian-era inns, beaches, nature trails and an excellent harbor

**Mystic Seaport Museum**
Historic re-creation of a 19th-century working coastal town, where much of the movie Amistad was filmed

**Litchfield Hills**
Quintessential New England towns, great hiking and biking, and beautiful lakes

**The Berkshires**
Rolling countryside, the Tanglewood Music Festival, country inns and lots of relaxed summer culture

ATLANTIC OCEAN

Boothbay Harbor
Portland
Kennebunk
Ogunquit
Portsmouth
Cape Ann
Rockport
Gloucester
Marblehead
Salem
Cambridge
Boston
Plymouth
Provincetown
Cape Cod National Seashore
Hyannis
Falmouth
Woods Hole
Edgartown
Martha's Vineyard
Nantucket Island
Nantucket

North Conway
White Mountain National Forest
Hanover
New Hampshire
Manchester
Concord
Merrimack River
Sebago Lake
Lake Winnipesaukee

Massachusetts
Quabbin Reservoir
Worcester
Providence
Rhode Island
Newport
Block Island
Mystic

Green Mountains
Middlebury
Manchester
Brattleboro
Williamstown
Bennington
Lenox
Berkshire Hills
Springfield
Hartford
Connecticut
New Haven
Litchfield Hills
Long Island Sound

New York
Albany
Hudson River
New Jersey
Newark
NEW YORK
Long Island

Connecticut River
White Mountains

44°N
43°N
42°N
41°N
68°W
69°W
70°W
71°W
72°W
73°W
74°W
44°N
43°N
42°N

New England
**2nd edition** – November 1999
**First Published** – September 1996

**Published by**
**Lonely Planet Publications Pty Ltd** A.C.N. 005 607 983
192 Burwood Rd, Hawthorn, Victoria 3122, Australia

**Lonely Planet Offices**
**Australia** PO Box 617, Hawthorn, Victoria 3122
**USA** 150 Linden St, Oakland, CA 94607
**UK** 10a Spring Place, London NW5 3BH
**France** 1 rue du Dahomey, 75011 Paris

**Photographs**
Barrett & MacKay, Bob & Suzanne Clemenz, Jon Davison, Lee Foster,
Kim Grant, Robert Holmes, Andre Jenny/International Stock,
Markham Johnson/Robert Holmes Photography, Jerry & Marcy
Monkman, David Noton/International Stock, Joanne Pearson, James
P Rowan, Sylvia Stevens, Stephen Trimble, Randy Wells

Some of the images in this guide are available for licensing from
Lonely Planet Images.
email: lpi@lonelyplanet.com.au

**Front cover photograph**
Portsmouth, New Hampshire (Jerry & Marcy Monkman)

ISBN 0 86442 570 8

Printed by The Bookmaker Pty Ltd
Printed in China

# Contents

# AROUND BOSTON

# CAPE COD

# MARTHA'S VINEYARD & NANTUCKET ISLAND

# CENTRAL MASSACHUSETTS & THE BERKSHIRES

# RHODE ISLAND

# CONNECTICUT

# VERMONT

## NEW HAMPSHIRE

## MAINE

## NEW YORK CITY

## GLOSSARY

## TOLL-FREE NUMBERS

## ACKNOWLEDGEMENTS

## INDEX

# MAP INDEX

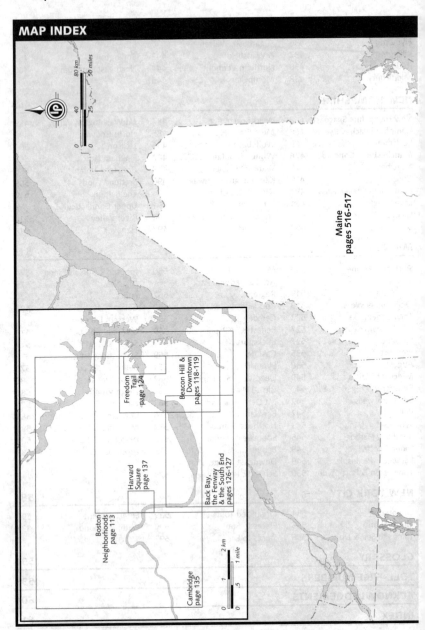

Maine
pages 516-517

Boston
Neighborhoods
page 113

Freedom
Trail
page 124

Beacon Hill &
Downtown
pages 118-119

Harvard
Square
page 137

Back Bay,
the Fenway
& the South End
pages 126-127

Cambridge
page 135

80 km
40
0

50 miles
25
0

2 km
1
0

1 mile
.5
0

# MAP INDEX

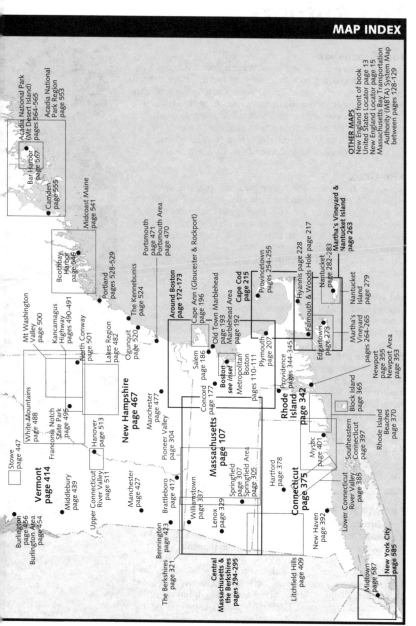

**OTHER MAPS**
New England front of book
United States Locator page 13
New England Locator page 15
Massachusetts Bay Transportation
Authority (MBTA) System Map
between pages 128–129

Acadia National Park
(Mt Desert Island)
pages 564–565

Acadia National
Park Region
page 553

Bar Harbor
page 567

Camden
page 555

Midcoast Maine
page 541

Boothbay
Harbor
page 546

Portsmouth
page 471
Portsmouth Area
page 470

Portland
pages 528–529

The Kennebunks
page 524

Mt Washington
Valley
page 500

Kancamagus
Highway
pages 490–491

North Conway
page 501

Lakes Region
page 482

Ogunquit
page 520

**Around Boston**
**page 172–173**

Cape Ann (Gloucester & Rockport)
page 196

Old Town Marblehead
page 193
Marblehead Area
page 192

Salem
page 186

Concord page 177

**Boston**
*see inset*

Metropolitan
Boston
pages 110–111

Plymouth
page 207

Provincetown
pages 254–255

Hyannis page 228

**Cape Cod**
**page 215**

Falmouth & Woods Hole page 217

**Martha's Vineyard &**
**Nantucket Island**
**page 263**

Nantucket
page 282–283

Nantucket
Island
page 279

Martha's
Vineyard
pages 264–265

Edgartown
page 273

Providence pages 344–345

**Rhode**
**Island**
**page 342**

Newport
page 355
Newport Area
page 353

Block Island
page 365

Rhode Island
Beaches
page 370

White Mountains
page 488

Franconia Notch
State Park
page 495

Hanover
page 513

**New Hampshire**
**page 467**

Manchester
page 477

Stowe
page 447

**Vermont**
**page 414**

Upper Connecticut
River Valley
page 511

Middlebury
page 439

Manchester
page 427

Pioneer Valley
page 304

Concord page 177

**Massachusetts**
**page 107**

Springfield
page 307
Springfield Area
page 305

Hartford
page 378

Burlington
page 456
Burlington Area
page 454

The Berkshires
page 321

Bennington
page 423

Brattleboro
page 417

Williamstown
page 387

Lenox
page 329

**Central**
**Massachusetts &**
**the Berkshires**
**pages 294–295**

**Connecticut**
**page 375**

Mystic
page 401

Southeastern
Connecticut
page 397

New Haven
page 392

Lower Connecticut
River Valley
page 385

Litchfield Hills
page 409

**New York City**
**page 585**

Midtown
page 587

# The Authors

### Tom Brosnahan

Tom Brosnahan was born and raised in Pennsylvania but took a trip to New England during his high school years and fell in love with the region. He returned to attend Tufts University near Boston, and, after Peace Corps service and graduate study, he came to New England to live. Tom has been writing guidebooks about New England since 1975. Though he travels frequently as coauthor of Lonely Planet's *Turkey*, *Mexico* and *Guatemala, Belize & Yucatán* guides, he's always happy to return back home to Concord, Massachusetts.

### Kim Grant

Kim Grant grew up in the Boston area and graduated from Mt Holyoke College in western Massachusetts in 1984. After 900 (or so) days of traveling on $10 a day throughout Europe, the only satisfying lifestyle and work she could envision through retirement was exactly what she'd just done: travel, write and photograph. Determined not to find herself wondering 'What if...?' at age 50, she convinced enough editors and publishers to let her try. Currently, she is the author of *Cape Cod, Martha's Vineyard & Nantucket: An Explorer's Guide*, coauthor of *Best Places to Stay in New England* and editor of *Insight New England*. Her photos appear in many Lonely Planet, Insight and Explorer's guides, as well as regional and national travel magazines. Kim's been working with Tom since the late 1980s.

### Steve Jermanok

Steve Jermanok was born and raised in upstate New York, a mere hour's drive from his boyhood stomping grounds of Vermont and the Berkshires. Now a father of two young children, he makes his home just outside of Boston in Newton, Massachusetts. He is the author of *Frommer's Great Outdoor Guide to New England* and coauthor of *Outside Magazine's Family Vacation Guide*. Steve is also a frequent contributor to many publications, including *National Geographic Adventure*, *Men's Journal*, *Sports Afield*, *Outside*, *Outdoor Explorer*, *Arthur Frommer's Budget Travel* and the *Boston Globe*.

## FROM THE AUTHORS
**Tom Brosnahan** My thanks to the ever-cheerful Larry Meehan of the Greater Boston Convention & Visitors Bureau and to Glenn Faira of Destinnations for their valuable advice and support.

**Kim Grant** I never refuse a chance to work with or learn from Tom. He's been my mentor since I met him; no one writes a better book or runs a better business. After I returned from Turkey in 1986 and declared it the most fascinating place I visited during my lengthy Euro sojourn, Tom invited me over for dinner and ended up offering me a job researching part of a New England guidebook. Somewhere along the line, after years of mentoring and numerous cups of coffee, he became my friend. He has always graciously called me his colleague.

Thanks to the whole LP contingent in Oakland, California, for creating the world's best guidebooks. In particular, the diligence of editor Susan Charles deserves special mention. I would be remiss not to thank Scott Summers, who, although on a 'paternity homestay' during production, was initially responsible for my gaining access to LP's new stock photo agency. And to the cartographers: you have no equal.

For Lisa, who, although thrilled that Tom and LP are in my life, needs no reminder (especially when I am on deadline) why she chose to be a prisoner civil-rights lawyer rather than a guidebook author.

**Steve Jermanok** I am delighted to have this opportunity to work with Tom Brosnahan, an icon in the annals of travel guidebook writing. Few travel writers take their job as seriously as Tom and even fewer can convey their thoughts on a piece of paper so effortlessly. Thanks to Maria Donohoe and Susan Charles at LP for going over my manuscript with a fine-tooth comb. I'd like to thank Steven Ziglar for his help with the Berkshires section. The Vermont chapter owes much of its existence to the diligent work of Emily Case. And in Maine, kudos go to my 'Maine' gal, Nancy Marshall. Thanks, once again, to Dad, Jim, Fawn, Jack, Julie, Neil and Fran for their unyielding support. Lastly, this book is dedicated to my wife, Lisa, who miraculously raises two children, ages one and three, when I'm on the road doing research.

# This Book

The 1st edition of New England was written by Tom Brosnahan and Kim Grant. This 2nd edition was updated by Tom, Kim and Steve Jermanok. Tom was the coordinating author and wrote the introductory chapters, Rhode Island, Connecticut and New York City. He coauthored Around Boston with Kim and Central Massachusetts & the Berkshires, New Hampshire and Maine with Steve. Kim wrote and updated Boston, Cape Cod and Martha's Vineyard & Nantucket Island in addition to the chapter she coauthored with Tom. Steve updated the Vermont chapter in addition to the three chapters he coauthored with Tom. The New York City chapter was updated and condensed from material in LP's *USA* that was written by Tom Smallman, Michael Clark, David Ellis, Eric Wakin and Brad Wong.

## FROM THE PUBLISHER

This 2nd edition of New England was produced in Lonely Planet's Oakland office. Susan Charles was the coordinating editor. Text and maps were edited by Maria Donohoe, Julie Connery, Valerie Sinzdak and Susan, with help from senior editor Laura Harger. Rebecca Northen, Valerie, Maria, Karen O'Donnell Stein, Don Root, Doug Lloyd and Kevin Anglin (map proofer extraordinaire) proofed the text and maps. Lead cartographer Andy Rebold and cartographer Chris Gillis drew and corrected the maps, with guidance from Amy Dennis and Alex Guilbert. Shelley Firth and Richard Wilson designed the book with guidance from Margaret Livingston. Laura, Valerie and Maria helped out with layout review. Hayden Foell, Hugh D'Andrade, Wendy Yanagihara, Shelley Firth, Jennifer Steffey and Jim Swanson drew the illustrations. Hayden also drew the chapter ends. Rini Keagy designed the cover.

Many thanks to Carolyn Hubbard, the first senior editor on the project, and to Laura Harger, who competently took over, for providing editorial supervision and support throughout the project.

**THANKS**
Many thanks to the travelers who used the last edition and wrote to us with helpful hints, advice and interesting anecdotes. Your names appear in the back of this book.

# Foreword

## ABOUT LONELY PLANET GUIDEBOOKS

The story begins with a classic travel adventure: Tony and Maureen Wheeler's 1972 journey across Europe and Asia to Australia. Useful information about the overland trail did not exist at that time, so Tony and Maureen published the first Lonely Planet guidebook to meet a growing need.

From a kitchen table, then from a tiny office in Melbourne (Australia), Lonely Planet has become the largest independent travel publisher in the world, an international company with offices in Melbourne, Oakland (USA), London (UK) and Paris (France).

Today Lonely Planet guidebooks cover the globe. There is an ever-growing list of books, and there's information in a variety of forms and media. Some things haven't changed. The main aim is still to help make it possible for adventurous travelers to get out there – to explore and better understand the world.

At Lonely Planet we believe travelers can make a positive contribution to the countries they visit – if they respect their host communities and spend their money wisely. Since 1986 a percentage of the income from each book has been donated to aid projects and human-rights campaigns.

**Updates** Lonely Planet thoroughly updates each guidebook as often as possible. This usually means there are around two years between editions, although for more unusual or more stable destinations the gap can be longer. Check the imprint page (following the color map at the beginning of the book) for publication dates.

Between editions, up-to-date information is available in two free newsletters – the paper *Planet Talk* and email *Comet* (to subscribe, contact any Lonely Planet office) – and on our website at www.lonelyplanet.com. The *Upgrades* section of the website covers a number of important and volatile destinations and is regularly updated by Lonely Planet authors. *Scoop* covers news and current affairs relevant to travelers. And, lastly, the *Thorn Tree* bulletin board and *Postcards* section of the site carry unverified, but fascinating, reports from travelers.

**Correspondence** The process of creating new editions begins with the letters, postcards and emails received from travelers. This correspondence often includes suggestions, criticisms and comments about the current editions. Interesting excerpts are immediately passed on via newsletters and the website, and everything goes to our authors to be verified when they're researching on the road. We're keen to get more feedback from organizations or individuals who represent communities visited by travelers.

Lonely Planet gathers information for everyone who's curious about the planet – and especially for those who explore it firsthand. Through guidebooks, phrasebooks, activity guides, maps, literature, newsletters, image library, TV series and website, we act as an information exchange for a worldwide community of travelers.

**Research** Authors aim to gather sufficient practical information to enable travelers to make informed choices and to make the mechanics of a journey run smoothly. They also research historical and cultural background to help enrich the travel experience and allow travelers to understand and respond appropriately to cultural and environmental issues.

Authors don't stay in every hotel because that would mean spending a couple of months in each medium-size city and, no, they don't eat at every restaurant because that would mean stretching belts beyond capacity. They do visit hotels and restaurants to check standards and prices, but feedback based on readers' direct experiences can be very helpful.

Many of our authors work undercover; others aren't so secretive. None of them accept freebies in exchange for positive write-ups. And none of our guidebooks contain any advertising.

**Production** Authors submit their raw manuscripts and maps to offices in Australia, the USA, the UK or France. Editors and cartographers – all experienced travelers themselves – then begin the process of assembling the pieces. When the book finally hits the shops, some things are already out of date, we start getting feedback from readers and the process begins again....

## WARNING & REQUEST

Things change – prices go up, schedules change, good places go bad and bad places go bankrupt – nothing stays the same. So, if you find things better or worse, recently opened or long since closed, please tell us and help make the next edition even more accurate and useful. We genuinely value all the feedback we receive. Julie Young coordinates a well-traveled team that reads and acknowledges every letter, postcard and email and ensures that every morsel of information finds its way to the appropriate authors, editors and cartographers for verification.

Everyone who writes to us will find their name in the next edition of the appropriate guidebook. They will also receive the latest issue of *Planet Talk*, our quarterly printed newsletter, or *Comet*, our monthly email newsletter. Subscriptions to both newsletters are free. The very best contributions will be rewarded with a free guidebook.

Excerpts from your correspondence may appear in new editions of Lonely Planet guidebooks, the Lonely Planet website, *Planet Talk* or *Comet*, so please let us know if you *don't* want your letter published or your name acknowledged.

Send all correspondence to the Lonely Planet office closest to you:

**Australia:** PO Box 617, Hawthorn, Victoria 3122
**USA:** 150 Linden St, Oakland, CA 94607
**UK:** 10A Spring Place, London NW5 3BH
**France:** 1 rue du Dahomey, 75011 Paris

Or email us at: talk2us@lonelyplanet.com.au

**For news, views and updates, see our website: www.lonelyplanet.com**

## HOW TO USE A LONELY PLANET GUIDEBOOK

The best way to use a Lonely Planet guidebook is any way you choose. At Lonely Planet, we believe the most memorable travel experiences are often those that are unexpected, and the finest discoveries are those you make yourself. Guidebooks are not intended to be used as if they provided a detailed set of infallible instructions!

**Contents** All Lonely Planet guidebooks follow the same format. The Facts about the Country chapters or sections give background information ranging from history to weather. Facts for the Visitor gives practical information on issues like visas and health. Getting There & Away gives a brief starting point for researching travel to and from the destination. Getting Around gives an overview of the transport options available when you arrive.

The peculiar demands of each destination determine how subsequent chapters are broken up, but some things remain constant. We always start with background, then proceed to sights, places to stay, places to eat, entertainment, getting there and away, and getting around information – in that order.

**Heading Hierarchy** Lonely Planet headings are used in a strict hierarchical structure that can be visualized as a set of Russian dolls. Each heading (and its following text) is encompassed by any preceding heading that is higher on the hierarchical ladder.

Although inclusion in a guidebook usually implies a recommendation, we cannot list every good place. Exclusion does not necessarily imply criticism. In fact, there are a number of reasons why we might exclude a place – sometimes it is simply inappropriate to encourage an influx of travelers.

**Entry Points** We do not assume guidebooks will be read from beginning to end, but that people will dip into them. The traditional entry points are the list of contents and the index. In addition, however, some books have a complete list of maps and an index map illustrating map coverage.

There may also be a color map that shows highlights. These highlights are dealt with in greater detail later in the book, along with planning questions. Each chapter covering a geographical region usually begins with a locator map and another list of highlights. Once you find something of interest in a list of highlights, turn to the index.

**Maps** Maps play a crucial role in Lonely Planet guidebooks and include a huge amount of information. A legend is printed on the back page. We seek to have complete consistency between maps and text, and to have every important place in the text captured on a map. Map key numbers usually start in the top left corner.

# Introduction

The English explorer Captain John Smith, while cruising the coast of North America in 1614, christened the land New England. The name came to be used when referring to the four early British colonies of Massachusetts Bay, Rhode Island and Providence Plantations, Connecticut and New Hampshire.

In the 18th century, the states of Maine and Vermont were included. Since that time, the six states have preserved their character as a unique region.

'Early America' is alive and well in New England as in no other part of the USA. The heavily forested region is scattered with picture-perfect villages and towns, small farms, granite mountain ranges and thousands of glacial lakes and ponds. New England's dramatic rockbound coast – 6000 miles long – is cut by innumerable coves and bays and punctuated by sandy beaches.

New Englanders are proud of their history, secure in their regional identity and welcoming – if sometimes reserved – to visitors.

Americans from other regions of the country come to New England for its history, culture and cuisine, and to feel as though they're 'almost in Europe.' Europeans and other foreign visitors come to beautiful, refined, stable New England in search of something different from the brash energy of New York City, for example, or the machismo of Texas and the good-natured but bewildering trendiness of the West Coast.

Though New Englanders feel a common regional identity, the six states are also quite different in character.

Massachusetts is the powerhouse, with the regional capital, Boston, the major industrial and commercial base, and the lion's share of the vacation resorts.

Rhode Island, the smallest state in the Union, is, like Switzerland, enhanced rather than diminished by its size.

Connecticut's cosmopolitan feel comes from its several important coastal cities as well as from its proximity to New York City.

Vermont has unspoiled mountains and forests, lakes and towns, and far more cows than people, which is why 'flatlanders' (non-Vermonters) flock here for summer hiking and winter skiing.

New Hampshire, the Granite State, is famous for its right-wing, less-government, pro-commercial policies and for the majesty of the White Mountain National Forest.

Maine is New England's last frontier, the largest of the six states, with vast forests, 3500 miles of beautiful coastline, popular Acadia National Park and innumerable potato fields.

A traveler setting out to see most of the USA must think of distances in continental terms. Not so in New England. Like its namesake, New England packs a lot of beauty and interest into a relatively small space. From Boston, most points can be reached in a morning's drive, and no point in the region is more than a day's drive away.

Other parts of America may be exciting, brawny, dramatic, breathtaking, sordid, bland or dangerous. New England, however, is beautiful, historic, dignified, romantic, self-satisfied and, many visitors say, simply delightful.

# Facts about New England

## HISTORY
### Early Times

The first human inhabitants of the Western Hemisphere are thought to have been a Mongolian race who crossed the Bering Strait over a land bridge from east Asia to Alaska sometime between 12,000 and 25,000 years ago. They reached present-day New England about 10,000 or 9000 BC. The history of these people has been lost, and archaeologists are not certain if they were the ancestors of the Algonquian peoples who inhabited the region when the first European settlers arrived.

The first peoples of New England developed an agrarian tradition, raising corn, beans, pumpkins and tobacco. They also hunted turkey, deer, moose, beaver, squirrel and rabbit, and harvested clams, lobsters and fish from coastal waters.

Unlike the tribes of New York's Iroquois confederacy, these tribes were not allied as a single power. Intertribal warfare wasn't uncommon here, making a united defense against the European settlers impossible.

See Native Americans under Population & People, later in this chapter, for more information on Native American tribes.

### The Explorers

Many European countries claim that their early explorers were the first to cross the Atlantic and land in America. Most historians believe the Vikings arrived first, exploring New England around 1000 AD and calling it Vinland. But the Spaniards, Irish and Portuguese all claim the honor as well, some pointing to strange inscriptions on Dighton Rock, near the Taunton River in Berkeley, Massachusetts, as proof.

Even assuming the Norse came first, their colonies failed, leaving it to subsequent explorers to put down permanent roots in the New World. The next Europeans who stumbled across the continent were the Spaniards; Christopher Columbus, an Italian mariner in the service of the Spanish Crown, reached landfall in the Caribbean in 1492.

Upon Columbus' return to Europe, his supposed confirmation of the tales of 'western islands,' or 'Indies,' sent explorers from many nations racing across the ocean in search of adventure and glory. John Cabot (actually Giovanni Caboto, another Italian mariner) claimed the land of New England for his patron, King Henry VII of England, in 1497. In 1534, Jacques Cartier claimed the land for France by setting a cross on the Gaspé Peninsula. However, despite these early claims, little progress was made in exploiting the discovery of land in the following years.

## New England

### State Abbreviations

| | |
|---|---|
| Massachusetts | MA |
| Rhode Island | RI |
| Connecticut | CT |
| Vermont | VT |
| New Hampshire | NH |
| Maine | ME |

15

The French were the first to send settlers to the North American continent, first to Quebec in 1604 and then to Nova Scotia in 1608. The English followed with the ultimately unsuccessful settlement at Jamestown, Virginia, established in 1607. In 1621, the Dutch West India Company received a huge but ill-defined land grant from the government of Holland and soon sent settlers to the Hudson River valley.

But it was the English explorers and settlers who most successfully colonized New England. In 1602, British mariner Bartholomew Gosnold, in command of the *Concord*, explored the New England coast from Maine to Rhode Island. Three years later, George Weymouth took a Pawtuxet man named Tisquantum (Squanto) prisoner and sailed back to England to show him at court.

## Pilgrim Founders

English Captain John Smith – the man whom Pocahontas saved from execution near the Jamestown colony – arrived in the region in 1614 and coined the name 'New England' for the area. Upon his return to London, Smith praised New England's possibilities for settlement. His recommendation was soon acted upon by a group of religious dissenters in search of a place where they could practice their Congregationalist beliefs unhindered by government.

The small ship *Mayflower* set sail from Plymouth, England, in the late summer of 1620. The boat carried 102 passengers, some animals, tools, seed, household goods and foodstuffs, all bound for New England. After a tedious two-month voyage, these English 'Pilgrims' made landfall at Provincetown, on the tip of Cape Cod, in November, when the winds of winter had already begun to blow.

Having left England in disagreement with their financial backers, the Virginia Company, the Pilgrims now found themselves without a governing charter. They composed the Mayflower Compact, which defined 'majority rule' as their fundamental law.

Unhappy with the exposed position and sandy, unproductive soil of Cape Cod, they spent some time searching the coasts for a more suitable place. They finally decided on Plymouth, Massachusetts, and the Pilgrims arrived there in December.

Though the local people were not bitterly hostile, the New England winter was. The Pilgrims hastily built shelters, but about half of them perished of scurvy, exposure and other privations during the winter of 1620-21. Their first governor, John Carver, died within a year. But the Pilgrim Founders, as this first group is called, had indeed established a colony.

## Prosperity

In the spring of 1621, things began to get better for the struggling people of the 'Plimoth Plantation.'

Squanto, the Pawtuxet who had been taken to England in 1605 by George Weymouth, had returned to the New World in 1615. Hearing of the new English settlement, he sought out the Pilgrims. Speaking both languages, Squanto facilitated a 50-year treaty of peace between the Pilgrims and Massasoit, the *sachem* (chief) of the Wampanoag people in whose territory the Pilgrims had settled. Though the Narragansett (who lived farther inland) remained hostile, the Pilgrim-Wampanoag alliance secured basic peace.

Squanto also taught the new arrivals essential survival skills: how to plant corn, and how and where to hunt deer and other game.

The late John Carver was succeeded as governor by William Bradford, a born leader of strong character and great resourcefulness who continued to lead the colony's development until his death in 1657.

In the summer of 1621, the new colony grew its first modest corn crop, but this had to be shared with a boatload of new arrivals from England. Even so, at harvest time that autumn, the colonists celebrated their survival with a three-day feast of Thanksgiving, inviting their Wampanoag neighbors to join them.

This first English toehold at Plymouth was followed by the foundation of the Massachusetts Bay Colony in 1628. Soon the region boasted several thousand English settlers, with more coming every year.

In 1643, New Englanders attempted a political union; Massachusetts Bay Colony, Plimoth Plantation, Connecticut and New Haven all joined together as the 'United Colonists of New England' to promote mutual welfare and defense. Though this confederation broke down a decade later, it was an early example of political solidarity in the region.

## Growth of a Nation

From the mid-1600s to the mid-1700s, both the population and wealth of the New England colonies grew rapidly. The region's forests and fields produced food and natural resources in abundance, and New England's numerous excellent natural ports provided a springboard for the lucrative maritime trade.

As the new colonists flooded into New England, the indigenous peoples retreated and died – victims of war, of European diseases against which they had little natural immunity, and of alcoholism, to which they were genetically susceptible. Within only three generations, the native peoples of the region were reduced to small, relatively powerless groups of survivors.

Though New Englanders still considered themselves subjects of the English Crown, they had no representation in Parliament. Nor did they think they needed it. From the first days of settlement in New England, the colonists had governed themselves by majority rule in their own legislative councils, with oversight by governors appointed from London. The colonists saw their affairs as largely separate from the concerns of the old country.

But after the Restoration of 1660, English monarchs began to assert more control. The wars fought between 1689 and 1763, including the French & Indian War, were echoes in the New World of continental French and English rivalries that cost the colonists dearly. Besides the local battles and Indian depredations brought on by the wars, the expenses of colonial defense provided a rationale for direct taxation of the colonies from London: If the English government was going to spend money defending the colonists, then the colonists could help to pay the bill for their defense.

The problem the colonists saw in this reasoning was that they had no voice in the deliberations over these new taxes. The taxes were decided in Parliament, which meant taxation without representation.

King George III (reigned 1760-1820) and Great Britain's Prime Minister Lord North pursued taxation of the colonies vigorously. In 1764, Parliament passed the Sugar Act, requiring colonial subjects to pay duties on sugar. And in 1765, the Stamp Act imposed a tax on all public and legal documents, such as newspapers, licenses and leases. This presumption of authority by the British government was met first with resistance, and ultimately with revolution.

## War & Independence

Tensions mounted, resulting in several inflammatory incidents. An angry crowd in Boston taunted and threatened a small number of Royal Army sentries in March of 1770. The British sentries, afraid for their lives, fired into the crowd and killed five colonists, giving the nascent revolution its first martyrs in this 'Boston Massacre.'

In response to the Boston Massacre, a number of the repressive Townshend Acts, passed in 1767, were repealed by Parliament, but the tax on tea was retained as a symbol of London's right to tax the colonists directly. The colonists' response was the Boston Tea Party: in the dead of night on December 16, 1773, a band of colonials masquerading as Africans and Native Americans forcibly boarded HMS *Dartmouth* and two other ships and dumped their cargoes of taxable tea into Boston Harbor.

The response from London was to tighten the screws even further. Parliament passed what were known in the colonies as the 'Intolerable Acts,' and the colonists, who had traditionally maintained militias against the possibility of Indian attack, began arming and training for war with their erstwhile motherland.

**Battles of Lexington & Concord** In April 1775, a British spy posing as a carpenter from Maine in search of work discovered that the colonials were stockpiling arms and munitions at Concord, about 18 miles west of Boston. Secret orders were given for a British expeditionary force to march under cover of darkness to Concord on the night of April 18, and to make a surprise search of the town at dawn.

American spies learned of the plan, and three riders – Paul Revere, William Dawes and Samuel Prescott – sped into the countryside to spread the word: 'The British are coming!' Members of the local militias, called 'minutemen' because of their ability to be ready for battle at a moment's notice, proved true to their name, turning out, matchlocks in hand, to face the 'aggressors.'

The small local militia, with little training and no experience, was about to face a sizable force of the world's best professional soldiers, and no one knew what might happen. Word went out beyond Lexington and Concord for minuteman reinforcements.

The rhythmic crunch of 1400 British boots in the streets of Lexington must have terrified the 70 minutemen who had lined up in defensive formation on Lexington Green at dawn, but they did not disperse when ordered to do so by Major Pitcairn, the British commander. Tension mounted, and finally a shot rang out. Many more followed as the redcoats overwhelmed the colonial force. Eight minutemen died in the melee.

If the Lexington minutemen had been apprehensive, those assembled at Concord had reason to be scared stiff. Joined by the minutemen from surrounding towns such as Acton and Bedford, the Concord group mustered on a hill with a view of the town across the Concord River.

Having been warned well in advance of the British expedition, the colonists had spirited away their Concord arms caches and hidden them elsewhere. Thus the British search for arms turned up only a few wooden gun carriages, which the redcoats set afire.

Seeing smoke rising from the town, the minutemen assumed their town was being put to the torch. 'Will you let them burn the town down?' shouted one. Emboldened,

they advanced down the hill and engaged the British at the North Bridge. The British, having marched to the far side of the bridge to disperse the minutemen, were forced to retreat across it when met with salvos from colonial muskets.

The ranks of the minutemen continued to swell as reinforcements poured in even from distant towns. By noon, now seriously outnumbered, the British force began its retreat from Concord to Boston. But minutemen harried and sniped at them all along the way, inflicting a shocking number of casualties.

News of the battles of Lexington and Concord spread like wildfire through the colonies, enflaming revolutionary fervor among most colonists, and terrifying those Loyalists who still supported the Crown.

**Ticonderoga & Bunker Hill** The battles of Lexington and Concord resulted in the gathering of the Second Continental Congress in Philadelphia on May 10, 1775, to decide on defensive measures. On the same day, Ethan Allen led his Green Mountain Boys from Vermont in a successful assault against the British outpost at Fort Ticonderoga (for details, see the 'Ethan Allen & Vermont' boxed text). The Revolutionary War was well under way.

Boston itself was held by the British. As a challenge, the Americans fortified Breed's Hill, next to Bunker Hill, right across Boston Harbor. The British response was to throw wave after wave of troops up the hill, only to see them mowed down by murderous American fire.

With his troops' ammunition running low, Colonel Prescott, the American commander, shouted the famous order, 'Don't fire until you see the whites of their eyes!' His troops obeyed, and when their ammunition was finally exhausted they retreated, leaving more than a thousand royal soldiers wounded or dying on the slopes of Breed's Hill.

Though it was a British victory, it was an inordinately costly one. As it was being fought, the Continental Congress selected George Washington to lead American forces against those of the Crown.

## Ethan Allen & Vermont

Far from Boston, New York and Hartford, rural Vermont was the last corner of New England to be extensively settled. In 1749, Benning Wentworth, royal governor of New Hampshire, issued land grants to Vermont territory for the settlement of towns. This infuriated New York, which also claimed the land (as did the French Crown).

In 1764, King George III upheld New York's claim, and in 1770, Vermont farmer Ethan Allen organized the Green Mountain Boys to carry out attacks against New York claimants. His exploits became so well known that the governor of New York offered a reward of £100 for Allen's capture.

At the beginning of the Revolutionary War, Allen's Green Mountain Boys and a small force from Connecticut laid siege to Fort Ticonderoga in a surprise attack, forcing the fort's astonished British commander to surrender in a bloodless victory.

During the war, the residents of the 'New Hampshire Grants' organized a constituent assembly and, in 1777, declared Vermont an independent state. The new state petitioned Congress for admission to the US, but was refused (because of competing land grants), whereupon Ethan Allen and others plotted to have Vermont come under the aegis of the British Crown as an independent state. In 1791, however, Vermont was admitted to the Union.

Colonial society was torn by divided loyalties. Many colonists remained loyal to the British monarchy despite its injustice; others saw independence as the only solution. All of colonial life was in turmoil, and society broke down in many areas.

**Declaration of Independence** On May 4, 1776, the colony of Rhode Island and Providence Plantations formally renounced allegiance to King George III, provoking the British to occupy the area. By this time it was clear to the colonists what needed to be done, and on July 4, 1776, colonial leaders met in Philadelphia to sign the Declaration of Independence.

The Revolutionary War raged throughout the colonies. Although many decisive battles, such as Valley Forge and Yorktown, did not take place in New England, this is where the war began. April 19 (Patriots' Day), the date of the battles at Lexington and Concord in 1775, is a holiday in Massachusetts, and the battles are reenacted each year.

## Early USA

'After the revolution,' as they say, 'the real work begins.' The Revolutionary War freed the American colonies from governance by Great Britain, but it did not guarantee America's survival as an independent nation. Americans had no strong, effective central government. It took most of the 1780s to work out the details, but by 1789 the US Constitution had been written, amended and ratified as the basic law of the land.

Freed at last from the restrictions imposed by Great Britain, New England's mariners and merchants built up the young nation's trade in fishing and commerce, to be followed soon after by manufacturing.

## 19th Century

In the 19th century, New England prospered from another sort of 'water power.' Designs for textile machinery powered by river flow were smuggled out of England and brought to America. Soon New England's many rivers were bordered by vast brick mills turning out a wealth of clothing, shoes and machinery.

Only the War of 1812 got in the way of New England's progress. While most of the US saw the war as a chance to grab Canada from the British, New Englanders saw it as an interruption of their very profitable maritime trade – even though the War of 1812 was ostensibly fought to stop Britain from blockading French ports against neutral ships (including American vessels) and to protect American seamen from being forced into service on British ships under the pretext that they were deserters from His Majesty's Navy. There was even talk of New England concluding a separate peace with Great Britain.

After the war, local prosperity quickly returned. The wealth generated by the Industrial Revolution, added to that from the fishing, whaling and maritime trades, made up for the region's relatively modest agricultural endowments and allowed 19th-century Boston to become the country's most highly educated and literary-minded city, earning it the nickname 'Athens of America.' The boom in textile weaving turned Vermont into one huge sheep farm, as the state's forests were felled in great swaths to make grazing land.

Perhaps because of their strong traditions of self-reliance, self-government and religious morals, New Englanders were in the vanguard of numerous 19th-century reform movements, including temperance (ie, abstinence from the use of alcoholic beverages), improvements in prisons and insane asylums, the prohibition of child labor and the abolition of slavery.

The notable flowering of literature that took place in mid-19th-century New England (see Literature under Arts, later in this chapter) included many important abolitionist works, such as Harriet Beecher Stowe's *Uncle Tom's Cabin*. The Underground Railroad (see boxed text) had many overnight 'stations' in New England, and during the Civil War (1861-65), the Union army's 54th Massachusetts Regiment distinguished itself as the first body of African American troops from a free state.

As the century drew to a close, New England saw its prosperity threatened on all sides. With the advent of steam engines, the great textile factories no longer needed river power. The unorganized labor was being organized and agitating for better pay and working conditions. In response, factories were moved to the South where the wages were lower. Steel-hulled, steam-powered ships replaced New England's renowned wooden, wind-powered clipper ships. Petroleum, natural gas and electricity did away with the need for whale oil.

Millions of immigrants who had come from abroad to share in New England's commercial boom – many fleeing Ireland's potato famine – had only minimal skills in a diminishing job market. As the new settlers moved westward across North America, they opened up vast new farming and grazing lands, producing far greater agricultural riches than the rocky soil and northerly climate of New England would allow.

## 20th Century

The treaty ending the Russo-Japanese War was signed at Portsmouth, New Hampshire, on September 5, 1905. The New England economy was boosted by the wartime spending of WWI, but was then dealt a staggering blow by the stock market crash of 1929.

The labor needs of WWII (1941-45) benefited New England's economy in some ways. The shipyards in Maine and Massachusetts, the firearms factories of Connecticut and the naval ports of all the coastal states all redoubled their business as the Allies required additional labor and materials. The brainpower of New England's universities also contributed to the war effort.

The war was followed by recession as New England's defense-related businesses found themselves with far fewer orders for their goods. During the 1960s, when John F Kennedy of Massachusetts was president of the US and John McCormack of Massachusetts was Speaker of the House of Representatives (to be succeeded in that office by Thomas P O'Neill, also of Massachusetts), money from government defense contracts flowed into New England. Also pouring in at that time were children from the postwar baby boom, who crowded the region's hundreds of colleges and universities. Enchanted by New England's beautiful towns, villages and livable cities, many industrious college graduates remained in the region to pursue careers in high technology, which became the new basis for the region's prosperity.

During the 1980s, the boom in computers, biotechnology and defense spending brought renewed prosperity to the region. Boston housing prices soared as well-educated engineers and technicians were recruited by the

## The Underground Railroad

Before the Civil War (1861-65), those in favor of abolishing slavery formed a secret network of guides and safe houses to escort runaway slaves to the 'free' (nonslavery) states of the American union. Called the Underground Railroad, it was extended into Canada in 1851 upon passage of the Fugitive Slave Act, which required escaped slaves to be returned to their owners even from free states.

**Frederick Douglass**

The Underground Railroad had important 'stations' in many New England towns, including Farmington, Connecticut; Burlington, Vermont; Canaan, New Hampshire; Portland, Maine; and Plymouth, Massachusetts, to name a few. Many abolitionists risked imprisonment for guiding and sheltering escaped slaves on their way to freedom.

Among the more prominent abolitionists was orator William Lloyd Garrison (1805-79) of Newburyport, Massachusetts, who published the antislavery newspaper *The Liberator* and introduced Frederick Douglass (1817-95) to the world. Born into slavery in Maryland, Douglass became a spokesperson for the cause throughout New England. He wrote three autobiographies, was the country's first African American publisher, and served as government minister to Haiti.

Harriet Beecher Stowe (1811-96), of Litchfield, Connecticut, was from a family of abolitionists that included her brother, Reverend Henry Ward Beecher. Stowe's novel *Uncle Tom's Cabin, or Life Among the Lowly*, published in the early 1850s, told the heartrending story of a slave family's flight and quest for freedom along the Underground Railroad. It sold an astounding 500,000 copies in the US and abroad and is counted among the factors leading to the Civil War and the abolition of slavery.

Harriet Tubman (circa 1820-1913), known as 'Moses the deliverer,' escaped from slavery in Maryland, only to risk recapture by returning to the slave state and rescuing her brethren and parents, whom she brought to Boston. Her motto was 'I can't die but once.' When she finally did, many years later, she was a free woman.

Charles L Blockson's book *The Underground Railroad: Dramatic Firsthand Accounts of Daring Escapes to Freedom* has more information.

region's fast-growing companies. Meanwhile, the 'clean' industry of tourism (with no industrial pollutants) brought wealth into unspoiled Vermont.

When recession hit the computer industry in the late 1980s, New England's fortunes again turned down, but not for long. The subsequent continuation of the country's longest stock-market boom poured money into the coffers of Boston's banks and money management firms, and venture capital produced a bumper crop of successful high-tech startup companies. At the end of the 20th century, New England's fundamental strengths in education, finance, high technology, health care, tourism and sophisticated manufacturing remain intact.

## GEOGRAPHY

New England's topography is glacial, but its geology dates from long before the glaciers covered this part of North America. Several billion years ago, as the earth's crust shrank and wrinkled, towering mountain ranges rose here. Friction and pressure from the clash of rock masses turned sand to marble and formed the distinctive gneiss and schist, flecked with shiny mica, seen throughout the region.

Magma (molten rock) from the earth's core crept into crevasses and cracks in the earth's crust and filled huge air bubbles hidden beneath the surface. Magma that cooled quickly near the surface became fine-grained stone called trap. Rock that cooled slowly deep within the earth became New England's distinctive granite, which was later thrust to the surface, or exposed by erosion. You can readily 'read' New England's geology in the dikes (rock veins) and batholiths (huge granite mounds) found here.

Beginning several hundred million years ago, the bedrock of New England was thrust upward into a spine of craggy mountains running roughly from northeast to southwest. Over the ages, erosion and geologic pressures reduced these early Alps to lower heights, so that 8 million years ago they looked much as they do today.

A scant million years ago, the earth's temperature dropped, and the polar ice caps built and spread toward the equator. This last Ice Age blanketed New England with a river of ice a half mile thick.

Pushed slowly southward by the pressure of ice buildup at the North Pole, these glaciers dredged up millions of tons of soil and rock and carried them southward. At the glaciers' southernmost extent, this soil and rock was deposited to form New York's Long Island, a glacial moraine.

Throughout New England, the retreat of the ice 10,000 to 20,000 years ago scooped out holes which became glacial ponds (Thoreau's Walden Pond, for example); deposited rock and debris in oblong hills called drumlins (Bunker Hill); and left huge granite boulders called erratics in fields and streams.

The resulting landscape has an appealing variety: verdant, winding valleys; abundant forests; and a rocky coastline sculpted into innumerable coves and sprinkled with sandy beaches. The mountains lack dramatic height, but that makes them all the more accessible. Farmers may complain that New England's rock-strewn soil 'grows boulders' (they're actually pushed up by the succession of freezing winters), but outdoors enthusiasts will find the New England countryside a perfect place for bicycling, hiking, canoeing, kayaking and boating.

## CLIMATE

In 1838, the author Harriet Martineau wrote, 'I believe no one attempts to praise the climate of New England.'

New England's weather conforms to that humorous dictum, 'If you don't like the weather, just wait a minute.' It is not at all impossible to have hot, muggy 90°F days in July followed by a day or two of cool 65°F weather. And the January thaw – when the temperature rises from below freezing to 50°, 60° or even 70°F, is a fervently awaited – if not always dependable – anomaly.

The best weather is in spring and autumn, when the days are warm and the nights are cool.

### Spring

Spring can be very short: 'Last year it was on a Tuesday' is the typical joke. If the spring weather, usually occurring at some point between late April and early June, lasts awhile, the season can be glorious, with apple and cherry trees in bloom and farmers out tapping maple trees for sap. But if spring is short, it may just come on a Tuesday, to be followed on Wednesday by the heat and humidity of summer.

### Summer

Depending on the year, June can be late spring, with some cold, rainy days, or early summer, with balmy temperatures. July and August are warm to hot, with temperatures above 90°F – occasionally above 100°F – and high humidity. Water temperatures, however, never get really high even in the dog days of summer. The good weather typically lasts into early September.

### Autumn

This is New England's finest season, a pleasant period with daytime temperatures

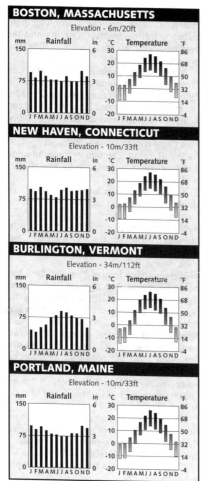

**BOSTON, MASSACHUSETTS**
Elevation - 6m/20ft
Rainfall · Temperature

**NEW HAVEN, CONNECTICUT**
Elevation - 10m/33ft
Rainfall · Temperature

**BURLINGTON, VERMONT**
Elevation - 34m/112ft
Rainfall · Temperature

**PORTLAND, MAINE**
Elevation - 10m/33ft
Rainfall · Temperature

weekend a time when everyone goes out 'leaf-peeping.'

The color depends upon rainfall and temperature patterns, however, and its timing is not predictable until a few weeks before it happens. It is also uneven; you may travel in late October through country bare of foliage, only to turn into a valley where the trees are ablaze with color.

Inns and tourist resorts normally stay open through mid-October; those open in the winter often close in late October or November for staff vacations.

Harvest time includes fresh cranberries on sale in the markets and 'pick-your-own fruit' days and cider making at orchards throughout the region.

By November most of the leaves have fallen from the trees, but a brief period of 'Indian Summer' often brings back a week or so of warmer daytime temperatures. By the end of November it's clear that winter is approaching, and by mid-December the bitter, icy winds have begun to blow.

## Winter

Winter can be severe or moderate; it is rarely mild. Though the snow can start in November, this is considered early. It's expected in December. Total snowfall may be anywhere from a few inches to the 9 feet recorded in the winter of 1995-96. When it's not snowing, however, it's likely to be bright and sunny, with temperatures between 15°F and freezing (32°F), with occasional days below 0°F in severe winters. On cold, clear days without wind, the sun warms you, and winter sports such as ice skating, snowshoeing, skiing and snowboarding are delightful.

## FLORA & FAUNA

For the last 10,000 to 20,000 years, the region has been covered in thick forests of beech, birch, hemlock, maple, oak, pine and spruce. The forest floor harbors many flowers and mushrooms suited to the northerly climate.

The thick forests are populated with white-tailed deer, moose, black bears, raccoons, beavers, woodchucks (groundhogs), rabbits and porcupines. Visitors comment on the legions of squirrels (mostly gray, but some

above 60° or 70°F, and cool, sometimes chilly, nights. As the weather gets steadily cooler in late September, the foliage begins to change color, and by early October the color of the maples and beeches reaches its peak in northern New England. The wave of color spreads south through mid-October, with Columbus Day (the second Monday in October) making the holiday smaller red) that hop about on the lawns and paths and leap from tree to tree in the forest canopy. Chipmunks, smaller and with characteristic stripes, stay closer to the ground.

Wild turkeys are native to New England, as are pheasant, grouse and a variety of songbirds. Hawks and even some eagles favor the mountain areas. The seacoast is crowded with numerous types of gulls. Many Canada geese, which once flew over New England on their way south for the winter, have come to stay in recent years.

Whales, dolphins and seals play in New England's coastal waters, and ecotourism provides an alternative livelihood for some of the fishing and lobstering crews put out of work by the closing of fishing grounds. The whales seem truly to enjoy sporting for the boats; the captains of whale-watching cruises know their 'regulars' by name, and even expect the whales at certain maritime rendezvous.

## GOVERNMENT & POLITICS

The six New England states – Connecticut, Maine, Massachusetts, New Hampshire, Rhode Island and Vermont – are separate governing entities that each send representatives and senators to Congress in Washington, DC. The governors of the six states, elected by their respective populations, meet as the New England Governors' Council to solve common problems, but this body is unofficial.

New England towns and villages are famous for their 'town meetings,' a form of direct democracy descended from simple beginnings in the rough-and-ready settlements of religious congregations.

In the classic town meeting, the entire adult population of a town is invited to congregate once or twice a year, often in the spring, to approve ordinances and budgets. Anyone can speak, and many do. Most towns have made practical modifications to the town meeting scheme so that for most of the year, town business is carried out by an elected council and a professional town manager. But important, and especially budgetary, questions are decided at town meetings.

## ECONOMY

Electronic and medical technology, light industry, fishing, tourism, farming and the service sector all fuel the New England economy.

New England Yankees have always been famous for their technical prowess. In the 19th century, Connecticut was renowned for the gadgets, gizmos and firearms turned out in its workshops and its factories. Today, MA 128, Boston's ring road, is famed as the East Coast counterpart to California's Silicon Valley. Research, computer programming and electronics manufacturing are all carried out here.

Though the region has a long history of shipbuilding, much of the industry's business has moved to northern Europe and Asia. Sophisticated ships (including nuclear submarines), however, are still built in Connecticut's Groton-New London area and in Bath, Maine.

Farming New England's rocky land has never been easy, but the soil itself can be rich. Some native crops introduced by Native Americans to the first European settlers still have an important role in New England's commercial agricultural economy. Tart, sour, ruby-red cranberries are still harvested from the bogs and wetlands of Massachusetts and Rhode Island for juice, sauces, jellies and pies. Blueberries are an important cash crop in Maine and several other states.

New England farmers grow apples, cherries, grapes, lettuce, peaches, pears, plums, rhubarb, strawberries, sweet corn, tomatoes and many other vegetables and fruits.

Though Vermont is famous for its maple syrup, all of the New England states produce excellent maple syrup from the sap of the sugar maple tree (see the 'Maple Sugaring' boxed text).

Dairy and sheep farming are important throughout the region, but especially in Vermont, which is – not surprisingly – noted for its cheese and premium ice cream.

The legendary New England fishing industry is now on its knees. Overfishing has nearly exhausted the once-inexhaustible fishing grounds, and the lobster industry may be in for a similar fate. During the 1980s, easy bank loans encouraged by certain government programs led to investment in more efficient boats and equipment, which in turn led to larger seafood harvests. In 1994, the government belatedly changed its policies and closed the fishing grounds of Georges Bank, a mainstay of the New England economy since colonial times. Overfishing has also led to serious imbalances in the food chain, which means that any recovery will be long in coming and its ultimate success uncertain. Meanwhile, tens of thousands of fishing crews are out of work.

## POPULATION & PEOPLE

New England is home to about 13,423,000 people, or about 5% of the US population. The following figures represent the states' populations, ranked by size from largest to smallest:

| | |
|---|---|
| Massachusetts | 6,147,100 |
| Connecticut | 3,274,100 |
| Maine | 1,244,300 |
| New Hampshire | 1,185,100 |
| Rhode Island | 988,500 |
| Vermont | 590,900 |

## Native Americans

The New England landscape is dotted with long Native American names such as Connecticut, Massachusetts, Narragansett, Pemigewasset, Penobscot and Winnipesaukee, testifying to the peoples who lived here before the arrival of the Europeans.

Reporting on his discoveries along the New England coast, Captain John Smith wrote of 'large fields of corn (maize), and great troops of well-proportioned people.'

The Native American population at the time might have been somewhere between 25,000 and 75,000, but an Indian census wasn't taken until 1890. It is thought that 10 major Algonquian tribes, often divided into clans, inhabited the present New England area when the Pilgrims arrived. Among these tribes were the Abenaki, Malecite, Micmac, Narragansett, Passamaquoddie, Penobscot, Pequot and Wampanoag. They lived in villages of about 100 people each, migrating between summer camps on the coast and winter quarters inland.

Today, New England is home to about 36,000 Native Americans, some of whom live on reservations of ancestral land such as those on Martha's Vineyard and in Mashpee, Massachusetts, and on Indian Island, Maine.

### Maple Sugaring

During New England's spring thaw (late March to early April), when nights are still cold but days are warm, the sap of the sugar maple tree (*Acer saccharum*) rises. Farmers go out to the sugar bush (grove of sugar maples), tap little metal pipes into the tree trunks, and collect the sap in buckets or through a network of plastic tubing.

The collected sap is transferred to big vats, where it is simmered for hours and reduced to a thick, amber-colored syrup with a distinctive flavor. Grade A Light Amber and Medium Amber are the finest grades, traditionally used on pancakes or waffles, or crystallized and molded into maple sugar candy. Dark Amber has a heartier, stronger flavor good for cooking. Grade B, very dark and coarse, is used in some baking recipes and in commercial food preparation.

Because of the time and labor required for harvesting and preparation, maple sugar is not cheap. Nevertheless, for its devotees there is no substitute.

If you're interested in learning more about maple sugaring, check out the website for the Massachusetts Maple Producers Association (www.massmaple.org), a nonprofit organization dedicated to the preservation and promotion of maple sugaring.

## Immigrants

The British and French made the first European claims to this land, and they have left their mark throughout New England. The French presence is most obvious in northern and eastern Maine and in the northern reaches of Vermont and New Hampshire, where many residents are bilingual. But colonies of French-speakers can also be found in some Massachusetts' industrial towns, where French Canadians often went in search of work.

In the mid-19th century, many black Africans and Caribbean islanders ended up in New England after fleeing Southern slavery on the Underground Railroad (see the 'Underground Railroad' boxed text).

In the 19th and early 20th centuries, Armenian, Greek, Irish, Italian and Portuguese immigrants flooded into the region to provide labor for its factories and fishing boats. Many neighborhoods in the region's cities still hold fast to these century-old European ties.

In recent years, immigrants have come from around the world to study at New England's universities, work in its factories or manage its high-tech firms. You can hear Caribbean rhythms in Hartford, smell Vietnamese and Cambodian cookery in Cambridge and see signs in Brazilian Portuguese in Somerville, Massachusetts.

## EDUCATION

Many students from other regions of the USA come to New England to take advantage of its hundreds of excellent schools, colleges and universities.

New Englanders' desire for religious education inspired the founding of many of the great colleges and universities in the region. Although today secular in outlook, Amherst, Bowdoin, Brown, Dartmouth, Harvard, Tufts, Williams and Yale were all founded to train candidates for the ministry.

The Boston Latin School, the country's oldest school (founded in 1635), has always been supported by public taxes and has accepted applicants from all social classes. It sets an example for excellence in public education in the USA. (Today, Boston Latin is considered an elite public school.)

New England also has many highly regarded private preparatory schools, including Phillips Academy Andover (in Andover, Massachusetts), Phillips Exeter Academy (in Exeter, New Hampshire), Groton Preparatory School (Groton, Massachusetts), Deerfield Academy (Greenfield, Massachusetts) and Choate Rosemary Hall School (Wallingford, Connecticut).

## ARTS

New England looks upon itself as the birthplace of North American culture, and it has a lot of evidence to prove the point. Many of the greatest early US architects, painters, silversmiths and other artisans were from New England.

## Crafts

In colonial times, popular arts such as sewing, quilting, glassblowing and ironmongery were most common, though furniture making, painting and other more sophisticated artistic pursuits developed in a fairly short time.

Perhaps the region's most famous early artisan was Paul Revere. Remembered mostly for his midnight ride to warn the minutemen that the redcoats were coming, Revere was in fact a master silversmith. His famous design for the Revere bowl is still followed today.

**Scrimshaw** The best-loved New England art from past centuries is undoubtedly scrimshaw, the carving and engraving of ivory. Ivory teeth and whalebone were readily available byproducts of the whaling trade, and whaling voyages allowed for long hours of inactivity for sailors. Many sailors became expert scrimshanders, turning out remarkably fine, delicate carvings. Some objects were utilitarian, such as kitchen utensils, buttons, letter openers and corset stays. Other objects, like cameos, brooches and pins, were made for gifts, and to exhibit the artisan's abilities. The scenes etched on scrimshaw pieces were often of ships and other nautical subjects. Though scrimshaw is still done, most pieces are replicas on imitation ivory (plastic). The antique pieces are very valuable.

**Furniture** The Shakers were among the finest New England artisans in the 19th century (see the Religion section near the end of this chapter). At their communal settlements in Maine, New Hampshire and western Massachusetts, the Shakers equated work with prayer, and each object was made as a tribute to the Almighty. The Shakers worked hard, carefully and well, and their harmonious, pleasant designs continue to be reproduced by artisans today.

## Painting

For all its wealth, 19th-century New England society could not fully nurture its renowned artists, most of whom sought training and artistic fulfillment abroad. These included Henry Sargent (1770-1845), of Gloucester, Massachusetts, who was a student of Benjamin West's, and James Abbott McNeill Whistler (1834-1903), of Lowell, Massachusetts, who challenged the tradition of representational painting by blurring lines and emphasizing the play of light in his work.

An exception was Winslow Homer (1836-1910), who pursued a career as an illustrator for the popular press but later dedicated his talents to painting. Though a Bostonian, Homer is most famous for his accurately depicted scenes of the Maine coast.

By the 20th century, however, New England – Boston in particular – was capable of supporting its world-class artists. John Singer Sargent (1856-1925) painted his telling portraits of Boston's upper class, and Childe Hassam (1859-1935) used Boston Common and other New England cityscapes and landscapes as subjects for his impressionist works.

Norman Rockwell (1894-1978), perhaps New England's most famous artist, reached his public mainly through his magazine illustrations, particularly the covers he painted for the *Saturday Evening Post*. His evocative, realistic pictures of common men,

women and children involved in the small triumphs, tragedies and comedies of daily life cemented US popular culture and helped define the nation's concept of what it meant to be an American. Rockwell lived and worked in Arlington, Vermont, and Stockbridge, Massachusetts, both of which now have major museums of his work.

Highly regarded for her 'American primitive' paintings of rural life, Anna Mary Robertson Moses (1860-1961) didn't begin painting until her late seventies. See Bennington in the Vermont chapter for information on 'Grandma Moses.'

## Sculpture

New England has produced its share of sculptors. Daniel Chester French (1850-1931) designed the minuteman memorial in Concord, Massachusetts, and the seated Lincoln in Washington, DC's Lincoln Memorial. Augustus Saint-Gaudens (1848-1907) was born in Ireland and worked in New York, London and Rome, but he finished his career in Cornish, New Hampshire. His evocative memorial statue of Colonel Robert Gould Shaw stands in Boston's Public Garden. Alexander Calder (1898-1976) made many of his world-famous mobiles and stabiles at his studio in Roxbury, Connecticut.

## Architecture

Though not as eager to break with architectural tradition as some US regions, New England has its share of dramatic modern structures, from the glass-sheathed, airfoil skyscrapers of Boston and Hartford, Connecticut, to the radical IM Pei-designed John F Kennedy Library & Museum just outside of Boston (see the Boston chapter for details).

New Englanders carefully preserve their historic buildings, and the well-protected historic cores of the cities are good examples of the many architectural styles that flourished here. At the time of settlement, the Pilgrims in Plymouth built simple thatched-roof log huts – and were glad to have them. As the Pilgrims prospered, wood-frame clapboard houses followed.

The simple life of colonial settlers gradually gave way to a life of greater comfort and worldliness. Clapboard houses were followed by more beautiful and elaborate Georgian structures inspired by the Palladian architecture of Inigo Jones and the English baroque style of Christopher Wren during the latter half of the 17th century. Called Georgian after the reigning British monarchs, the style was – and still is – used extensively: Harvard, Dartmouth and many other New England schools boast a riot of red brick and white cornices in Georgian style. Cambridge, Massachusetts, even has a Georgian firefighters' station built only a few decades ago. The typical tall-steepled New England meetinghouse (church) is a variation on the Palladian design.

When European taste moved on to the classic revival aesthetic in the late 18th and early 19th centuries, American taste followed. The updated Roman temple design Thomas Jefferson used for Monticello influenced New Englanders as well, and soon Greek- and Roman-style temples appeared as college halls, courthouses and bank buildings. Boston's Quincy Market echoes the neoclassicism of London's Haymarket.

State capitols built in the 19th century typically featured neoclassical domes, colonnades and arcades. Perhaps the best example of this style is the Massachusetts State House, designed by Charles Bulfinch (1763-1844). Even when the rest of New England and the nation had succumbed to a fascination with Gothic Revival, Boston architect Henry Hobson Richardson (1838-86) continued to build romantic Romanesque structures like Trinity Church (erected between 1872 and 1877), in Copley Square, Boston.

New England's fascination with European styles continued into the 20th century, but was diluted by a blossoming of local creativity. While modified Cape Cod cottage styles were exported to the Midwest and California, ranch-style houses started popping up in New England.

The lyrical art nouveau style of the early 20th century left little impression on the region, and most modern art deco buildings have fallen to the wrecker's ball. However, one exceptional example, the Fleet Bank Building, still stands in Providence, Rhode Island.

In the 1950s and '60s, cold, modern monumentalism produced huge sterile building complexes such as Boston's Prudential Center and the graceless blocks in the city's West End, which, in later years, had to be softened and humanized with gardens and clusters of shops. Also during this era, the sturdy granite warehouses along Boston's waterfront were slated for destruction, to be replaced by a dull modern shopping center; the old buildings were eventually saved by the efforts of preservationists.

In the following decade, new sleek skyscrapers added contrast to the local skyline. Richardson's Trinity Church was soon reflected in the glass wall of the John Hancock Tower, designed in 1976 by IM Pei.

## Literature

Literature has always been the lifeblood of New England culture. The region's traditional reverence for literature was brought by the Puritans, who believed that through religious education one came to know God. American literature, therefore, was initially ecclesiastical.

The New Englanders' passion for literacy was evident as early as 1828, when Noah Webster (1758-1843) published his *American Dictionary of the English Language*. It sold hundreds of thousands of copies in edition after edition – an astounding achievement considering the country's small and mostly rural population at the time.

New England is distinguished by producing the first African American female poet of note, Phyllis Wheatley (1753-1784). Sold from a slave ship in Boston, she impressed her master, merchant John Wheatley, with her intelligence and was encouraged to get an education. She began writing poetry at the age of 14, and her later work was celebrated in both North America and Europe.

By the late 19th century, the preoccupation with theological education had lessened as the region developed a passion for secular letters. New England's colleges became magnets for literati of all beliefs and opinions. Some New England towns – most notably Concord, Massachusetts – nurtured the seeds of 19th-century America's literary and philosophical flowering.

This transition is epitomized in the writings of Ralph Waldo Emerson (1803-82), a founder of Transcendentalism (see the Religion section, later in this chapter) who believed in the mystical unity of all creation. Emerson gained a nationwide – even worldwide – audience for the teachings he promulgated from his home in Concord.

Emerson's friend and fellow Concordian, Henry David Thoreau (1817-62), was among the first Americans to advocate a life of simplicity, lived in harmony with nature. Such beliefs were a radical departure from the prevailing industrial and commercial Protestantism of the time, but they gained a wide and impassioned following. Thoreau is best remembered for *Walden, or Life in the Woods* (1854), his journal of observations written during his solitary sojourn from 1845 to 1847 in a log cabin at Walden Pond, on the outskirts of Concord. He also wrote a treatise on 'Civil Disobedience' in 1849, long before this moral position was put to good use by Mahatma Gandhi. Less well known but equally engaging are Thoreau's travelogues, *The Maine Woods* (1863) and *Cape Cod* (1865).

Another Concord author was Nathaniel Hawthorne (1804-64), America's first great short-story writer and author of *The Scarlet Letter* (1850), *Twice-Told Tales* (1837 and 1842) and *The House of the Seven Gables* (1851).

Louisa May Alcott (1832-88), although born in Pennsylvania, lived much of her life in Concord, too, and wrote to contribute to the family income. She knew Emerson and Thoreau well. Her largely autobiographical novel *Little Women* (1868-69) is her best-known work, but its several sequels – *Little Men* (1871) and *Jo's Boys* (1886) – are also still read with pleasure by many Americans.

Among New England's classics are many dealing with its maritime past, including *Moby-Dick* (1851), by Herman Melville (1819-91), and *Two Years Before the Mast* (1840), by Richard Henry Dana (1815-82).

Altogether different are Henry James' *The Bostonians* (1886) and John P Marquand's *The Late George Apley* (1937), novels of Boston parlor society.

Few New England authors were more prominent than Mark Twain (born Samuel Clemens, 1835-1910), who reached a worldwide audience. Born in Missouri, Twain settled in Hartford, Connecticut, and there wrote *The Adventures of Tom Sawyer* (1876) as well as *The Adventures of Huckleberry Finn* (1884). He also wrote *A Connecticut Yankee in King Arthur's Court* (1889).

Several New England writers were instrumental in the battle against slavery preceding and during the Civil War. Among them were William Lloyd Garrison (1805-79), John Greenleaf Whittier (1807-92) and Harriet Beecher Stowe (1811-96). Stowe's best-selling fictionalization of life on a slave-holding plantation, *Uncle Tom's Cabin* (1852), received acclaim both in the USA and abroad and helped to hasten the end of American slavery. More information on Stowe is given in the 'Underground Railroad' boxed text, earlier in this chapter.

In 1903, Harvard graduate and sociologist Dr William Edward Burghardt Du Bois (1868-1963), of Great Barrington, Massachusetts, wrote *The Souls of Black Folk*, an

**Harriet Beecher Stowe**

influential book that sought to change the way blacks dealt with segregation, urging pride in African heritage.

*The Last Puritan* (1936), by George Santayana (1863-1952), explores what it might be like for someone with 17th-century Puritan ideals to be attending Harvard in the 20th century.

Henry Wadsworth Longfellow (1807-82) wrote *The Song of Hiawatha, Paul Revere's Ride*, 'The Village Blacksmith,' 'Excelsior' and 'The Wreck of the Hesperus.' Emily Dickinson (1830-86), 'the Belle of Amherst,' wrote beautifully crafted poems that were largely published following her death. Edgar Allen Poe (1809-49) wrote *The Raven* (1845) while wooing his beloved in Providence, Rhode Island. Edna St Vincent Millay (1892-1950) wrote poetry that reflects her native Maine.

New England's signature poet is, of course, Robert Frost (1874-1963). Though born in California, Frost returned to his New England roots and attended Dartmouth and Harvard. He tried farming at various places in Vermont and New Hampshire (with very limited success). His many books of poetry use New England themes to explore the depths of human emotion and experience.

Stephen Vincent Benét (1898-1943), the author of *John Brown's Body*, about the abolitionist, lived in Stonington, Connecticut.

Pulitzer prize-winning novelist Edith Wharton (1862-1937) was born in New York, but she married a Boston banker. Her best-known novel, *Ethan Frome* (1911), gives a grim but accurate picture of emotional entanglements on a New England farm. It's based on observations that Wharton made while in residence at her grand summer mansion at Lenox, in Massachusetts' Berkshire hills.

Playwrights from New England include Eugene O'Neill (1888-1953), author of *Long Day's Journey into Night*. O'Neill's house in New London, Connecticut, has become a museum. Arthur Miller (1915- ), though from New York, wrote *The Crucible*, successfully dramatizing the Salem, Massachusetts, witch trials.

**Modern Fiction** Many of today's books written by New England authors are less political and ethical than their forebears, but are usually more enjoyable.

For up-to-date thrills set in Boston and elsewhere in New England, pick up any of the 'Spenser' thrillers written by Robert B Parker. It's interesting that Maine resident Stephen King, author of horror novels such as *Carrie* (1976), *The Shining* (1977) and many more, was strongly influenced by pioneering gothic/sci-fi novelist HP Lovecraft (1890-1937) of Rhode Island.

*Jaws,* by Peter Benchley, set on Martha's Vineyard, is the novel from which the popular motion picture (1975) was made. Little known is that Benchley's grandfather was humorist Robert Benchley (1889-1945), born in Worcester, Massachusetts, and a member of New York's famous Algonquin Round Table.

Annie Proulx, award-winning author of *The Shipping News* (1994), describes rural Vermont in her novel *Postcards* (1992). John Irving, a New Hampshire native, wrote *Hotel New Hampshire, The World According to Garp, Cider House Rules* and *A Prayer for Owen Meany*, all of which are set in New England.

John Knowles, who wrote the affecting *A Separate Peace* (1960), went to Yale. The book is set in a New England prep school.

More recently, Donna Tartt wrote *The Secret History* (1993), whose characters commit murder at a college modeled on her alma mater, Vermont's Bennington College. Jay McInerney of Connecticut attended nearby Williams and is memorable as the author of *Bright Lights, Big City* (about making the grade in New York City). His virtually unnoticed 1996 novel, *Last of the Savages,* is about two very different students who become friends at a New England prep school.

## RELIGION

New England began its modern history as a haven for religious dissenters, and the tradition of religious freedom and pluralism continues today. Today, the region is home to large numbers of Christian Protestants and

Roman Catholics, and smaller numbers of Jews, Muslims, Hindus, Buddhists and many other faiths.

The Pilgrims who arrived at Plymouth in 1620 were 'Puritans,' believers in a strict form of Calvinism that sought to 'purify' the church of the 'excesses' of ceremony and decoration acquired over the centuries. The Bible was to be interpreted closely, not to be subjected to elaborate theological interpretation. Their strict and rigorous adherence to religious law gave them the strength to survive the harsh, unforgiving conditions of early colonial life.

The Pilgrims disagreed early and often on the details of religious belief and church governance. Presbyterians believed in a central governing body for the church, while Congregationalists wanted autonomy for each church community. A common solution to theological disagreements was for the minority group to shove off into the wilderness and establish a new community where they could worship as they wished. Human nature and theology being what they are, this resulted in new communities popping up throughout the region. Thomas Hooker and his followers abandoned Cambridge, Massachusetts, to found Hartford, Connecticut; and Roger Williams and his flock split to found Providence, Rhode Island. In many cases the new colonial towns, having more recently suffered intolerance, were more tolerant themselves. Newport, Rhode Island, although founded by Puritans, soon had a Quaker meetinghouse and a Jewish synagogue.

## Shakerism

Shakerism originated among members of the Society of Friends ('Quakers') in Manchester, England, in the mid-1700s. The sect's early leaders were Jane and James Wardley, but its leadership was soon taken over by Ann Lee (1736-84), a convert to Shakerism imprisoned by the English government for her zeal. 'Mother Ann,' as she came to be known, had a religious epiphany in 1770 and came to believe that she was the manifestation of Christ's 'female nature.'

In order to pursue her beliefs freely, she emigrated to the New World in 1775 and established a community with her followers in Watervliet, New York. In later years, Shaker communities were founded throughout New England. At its height, New England Shakerism could boast some 6000 members.

The name 'Shakers' was given to the members of the sect because their religious ceremonies involved a trembling dance to symbolize being possessed of the Holy Spirit. The tenets of Shakerism called for closed communities, set apart from the world, in which men and women lived in separate quarters, coming together only for prayer, dining and work. Shakers were admonished to 'put their hands to work and their hearts to God.' Work was looked upon as an act of worship, and the result an offering to God. The Shakers' craft items such as quilts and furniture possess a timeless beauty and flawless quality.

The combined strictures of separation from the world and separation of the sexes spelled the end to Shakerism. Cut off from the world there could be no proselytization, and cut off from the opposite sex there could be no procreation, so the Shakers died out. Their exquisite crafts survive, however, in museums throughout the USA and in the four former Shaker communities that now survive as museums in Hancock and Harvard, Massachusetts; Sabbathday Lake, Maine; and Canterbury, New Hampshire.

## Christian Science

The 19th century saw the birth of another religion in New England. Mary Baker Eddy (1821-1910) of New Hampshire experienced a miraculously speedy recovery from an accident in 1866. She attributed her cure to the healing powers of God as lived and taught by Christ. After a thorough and devoted study of the Bible and its teachings on the matter of medical science and health, she formulated the tenets of Christian Science. Her findings and beliefs were embodied in the Church of Christ, Scientist, headquartered at The Mother Church in Boston, with its 'daughter' churches now spread throughout the world in 70 countries. In the 20th century, the sect's fame has spread

## Mary Baker Eddy

The Women's National Book Association recently named Mary Baker Eddy's *Science and Health* as one of the 75 books by women 'whose words have changed the world.'

Mary Baker Eddy (1821-1910), the founder of Christian Science, was born in Bow, New Hampshire. Sickly as a child, she grew into a pious young woman noted for her stubbornness and love of study. She married in 1843, but her husband died four months before the birth of their son. Left with no resources and in poor health, she had no choice but to allow her son to be raised by others. She married again in 1853 and, preoccupied with questions of health, studied alternative therapeutic methods such as homeopathy, arriving finally at the belief that the roots of physical illness were mental and spiritual.

According to her own account, as she lay bedridden and alone one day in 1866, she opened the Bible and began to read an account of how Jesus had healed the sick. By the time Eddy put down the book, she herself was healed.

For three years thereafter, Eddy retreated from society to contemplate her miraculous cure and to formulate the principles of Christian Science, a system of belief based less on traditional faith than on a rational understanding that the mind is an inalienable part of the greater goodness that is God.

Mary Baker Eddy taught that by consciously working to gain 'the mind of Christ,' normal humans can enter into a state in which spirit is seen to be more powerful than – and in command of – material things, including the human body. Gaining this spiritual state is not easy. It involves patience, humility, repentance and tribulation and includes among its tasks the cure of human illness through prayer – as Christ had done.

*Science and Health,* which details her philosophy, was published in 1875 to mixed reviews. 'Critics took pleasure in saying that the book was wholly original, but would never be read,' Eddy noted wryly. To date, the book has sold more than 9 million copies.

In 1879, Eddy and a small group of adherents founded the Church of Christ, Scientist, which, unusual among sects at the time, encouraged the full equality of men and women. In 1881, Eddy founded the Massachusetts Metaphysical College in Boston to train practitioners in Christian Science healing arts. Men and women were equally welcome, and the training provided hundreds of women with careers, allowing them a measure of financial self-sufficiency – something Eddy prized. Even as she discussed retirement, Eddy continued to write and publish, founding the respected *Christian Science Monitor* newspaper at the age of 88.

Mary Baker Eddy is remembered as a person of rare achievements. 'In natural law and in religion the right of a woman to fill the highest measure of enlightened understanding and the highest places of government is undeniable,' she wrote. 'This is woman's hour, with all its sweet amenities.'

Her voice continues to echo through American culture.

**Paige R Penland**

through its excellent daily newspaper, the *Christian Science Monitor*. See the 'Mary Baker Eddy' boxed text.

## Congregationalism

The basic beliefs of Congregationalists are that each Protestant Christian community should have full control of its own affairs, and that there should be no hierarchy of bishops or a popelike head of the church, because Jesus is the only head needed. When the movement began in England in the 1500s, early proponents, called Independents, were persecuted by the Church of England.

Congregationalism flourished in New England, where conditions were right for its practice. New England's noted early preachers, including Jonathan Edwards, were all Congregationalists, and the region's most prominent colleges, including Amherst, Harvard, Williams and Yale, were founded by Congregations, though the colleges were nonsectarian.

Unitarianism (see below) and Congregationalism had many points of mutual attraction, and during the 19th century some Congregations adopted Unitarian beliefs.

Self-government does not preclude association, however, and Congregational churches have long formed associations of equals, including the United Church of Christ (1957).

## Transcendentalism

Emerson, Thoreau, Bronson Alcott and other prominent thinkers in Concord, Massachusetts, during the mid-1800s refined the tenets of Unitarianism into a belief called Transcendentalism. They believed not just that God was inherent in all people, but that each person could 'listen' to that Godlike part for ethical, moral and spiritual guidance. Furthermore, they believed that humans must seek to understand nature and to live in harmony with it. This was no doubt the inspiration for Thoreau's retreat at Walden Pond from 1845 to 1847.

Other Transcendentalist thinkers went even further. In 1841 they purchased Brook Farm in West Roxbury, Massachusetts (now an affluent Boston suburb), as a living laboratory for their beliefs. Hawthorne, Melville and other Transcendentalists both famous and unknown lived together at Brook Farm until 1847, when the experiment came to an end. Though it must be counted a failure, the Brook Farm experiment identified an ideal that is perhaps more meaningful today than it was a century and a half ago.

## Unitarianism

In its earliest forms, Unitarianism declared the unity of God, which was blasphemy to Christians who believed in the Trinity (ie, that God was made up of God the Father, Jesus Christ the Son, and the Holy Spirit). In its American incarnation, Unitarianism became a religion based on reason, compassion, self-government and community service. It has no doctrine; members declare only that 'in the love of truth and in the spirit of Jesus, we unite for worship of God and service to Man.' Unitarian beliefs were advocated most forcefully by William Ellery Channing (1780-1842), by Ralph Waldo Emerson (1803-82) and by Theodore Parker (1810-60).

Unitarianism became popular among the Congregational churches of New England, and today most Unitarian churches have a Congregational structure.

In 1825, the American Unitarian Association was formed, and in 1865 it held a national convention. In 1961, the American Unitarian Association joined with the Universalist Church of America to form the Unitarian Universalist Association, based in Boston.

## Universalism

John Murray (1741-1815) arrived in New Jersey from England in 1770 to preach the Universalist belief that God's purpose was to save every person from sin through the divine grace of Jesus. John Murray settled in Gloucester, Massachusetts, and here he founded the first Universalist church in America.

Universalism spread throughout New England, with each congregation being independent, though all accepted a common doctrine. Early on, it had a Calvinist cast, but Universalism distanced itself from strict

Calvinism in the 19th century and later allied itself closely with Unitarianism. The Universalist Church merged into the Unitarian Universalist Association in 1961.

## LANGUAGE

Though the principal language of New England is English, various other languages thrive as well. Northern Maine is home to communities of French-speakers descended from the *voyageurs* (early explorers) of Quebec. Gloucester, New Bedford and other coastal towns harbor significant communities of Portuguese-speakers from Portugal and the Azores who came to New England to work the rich fishing grounds. In Boston's North End, many older people still speak only Italian, and in Hartford you may hear the musical patois of the Caribbean islands. Legal notices in the Boston area are frequently printed in English, Portuguese, Spanish, Vietnamese and Cambodian in recognition of immigrants who arrived during the 20th century.

New Englanders, and especially Bostonians, are well known for abbreviating many words. Massachusetts Avenue becomes 'Mass Ave'; the Harvard Business School becomes 'the B School'; Cape Cod is 'the Cape' and Martha's Vineyard is 'the Vineyard.' Boston's subway system, officially the MBTA Rapid Transit System, becomes 'the T' in local parlance.

But the region is most famous for the broad-voweled English that's commonly called the Boston accent. 'Pahk the cah in Hahvahd Yahd' (Park the car in Harvard Yard) is the common joke sentence satirizing the peculiar 'r' that is also common to some dialects in England. During John F Kennedy's presidency, his speech was satirized for the 'r's that would disappear in some places ('cah' for car) and pop up in others ('Cuber,' pronounced 'KYOO-berr,' for Cuba).

To the north, the people of Maine and New Hampshire are kidded for often punctuating their speech with the meaningless sound 'ayuh' (uh-YUH).

See the Glossary at the end of this book for the meanings of some additional regional colloquialisms.

# Facts for the Visitor

## HIGHLIGHTS
### Boston
Among cities, Boston comes first. Explore the Freedom Trail, major art and science museums, parks and gardens, and neighboring Cambridge, home of Harvard University and its museums. Historic Lexington and Concord, Salem, Marblehead, Gloucester, Rockport and Plymouth all make great day trips.

### Cape Cod & Islands
Next top sights, at least in summer, are Cape Cod and the islands of Nantucket and Martha's Vineyard.

### Central Massachusetts & the Berkshires
In central Massachusetts, the prime attraction is Old Sturbridge Village, the re-created 17th-century town populated by 'interpreters' wearing period dress. In western Massachusetts, visit one of the Berkshires' fine old summer vacation resorts or attend a performance at the Tanglewood Music Festival, Jacob's Pillow Dance Festival or Williamstown Theater Festival.

### Rhode Island
In Rhode Island, Newport is a must-see. Tour the palatial mansions and enjoy the seaside ambience. Spend at least an afternoon on one of the great beaches or take a day trip to Block Island.

### Connecticut
Visit Hartford to see Mark Twain's mansion at Nook Farm. New Haven has Yale University and several excellent museums. Mystic and New London are the centers of the state's maritime activities. Mystic Seaport Museum is a re-created maritime town of the 19th century. New London is the home of the US Coast Guard Academy, and neighboring Groton has a navy submarine base.

For the prettiest Connecticut scenery, go to the picturesque towns of Essex, Old Lyme and Ivoryton at the mouth of the Connecticut River or to the Litchfield Hills in the northwestern corner of the state.

### Vermont
In northern New England, drive and walk in the Green Mountains, preferably along VT 100, which threads its way from south to north through the center of the state. The most charming towns are Bennington, Dorset, Grafton, Manchester, Middlebury, Stowe and Woodstock. The city of Burlington, which is a day trip from Stowe, is also worth a stop. Be sure to see the vast Shelburne Museum south of Burlington.

### New Hampshire
In New Hampshire, you should see Portsmouth and the restored historic Strawbery Banke on the coast, and perhaps make brief stops at Manchester (for the Currier Gallery of Art) and Concord (the state capital) on your way to Lake Winnipesaukee for water sports and the White Mountain National Forest for hiking and camping. Check out the beauties of Franconia Notch State Park north of Lincoln, and then don't miss the scenic drive along the Kancamagus Hwy (NH 112) between Lincoln and Conway. North Conway is the outdoor-activity center of the region.

### Maine
Enjoy the beach resort towns along the southern coast and then head to Portland. Go 'Downeast,' stopping in several of the wonderful coastal towns and villages (Blue Hill, Boothbay Harbor, Camden, Castine, Pemaquid Point) before reaching Bar Harbor and Acadia National Park. Those looking for outdoor adventure should consider an excursion to the lakes and mountains of north-central Maine.

## SUGGESTED ITINERARIES
There's no 'right' way to see New England, but it can help to have sample itineraries.

Modify and combine these to suit your interests. Try to visit cities on weekends and country towns and resorts on weekdays in summer or foliage season. This gets you lower prices and fewer crowds.

## Less than a Week

With only three to five days, use **Boston** as your base. Plan to spend at least a half day walking the Freedom Trail (you may spend most of a day, though) and another half day at the Museum of Fine Arts and the Gardner Museum.

Any number of other excellent attractions can fill another half day: The Museum of Science, the New England Aquarium and the Children's Museum are top picks.

If you're a shopper, schedule at least a half day at Downtown Crossing or spend the time strolling past the boutiques on Newbury St. Harvard Square requires a half day for a stroll through Harvard Yard with some shopping, or a full day if you include a visit to Harvard's excellent museums.

For excursions, go west to Lexington (by car) and Concord (car or train), or north to Salem (car, bus or train) and Marblehead (car or bus). You could even do a day trip to Plymouth (preferably by car or bus tour). In summer, excursion boats sail from Boston to Provincetown and back in a day, and these are definitely the best way to go to the tip of Cape Cod on a day trip if you want to avoid the long drive.

## A Week or More

If you have a week or 10 days, you can (after spending several days in Boston) really get a good taste of New England. Your itinerary will change depending upon the season, but consider these high points.

Stay at least one night in a fine old **Cape Cod** town. If you can stay two or three nights, spend one day on an excursion to one of the islands, Martha's Vineyard or Nantucket, or better yet, overnight there. Stop in Plymouth on the way to or from the Cape.

If it's summer or autumn, drive to the **Berkshires** and stay at least one night, stopping midway to tour Old Sturbridge Village.

If you have two nights, that's even better. With three nights to spend, take in Williamstown or the Litchfield Hills of northwestern Connecticut.

In **Rhode Island**, spend a long half day in Providence, and at least one night in Newport touring the mansions and strolling the Cliff Walk. With another night to spend, you can take in some sun on the Rhode Island beaches. Block Island requires at least a day of its own.

Drive north to New Hampshire's **White Mountains** for a few days of sightseeing, hiking, canoeing, white-water rafting or skiing, spending the nights in campgrounds or country inns. Two nights is the minimum to see central New Hampshire. With three, you can tour Lake Winnipesaukee as well.

**Portsmouth**, New Hampshire, **Portland**, Maine, and the towns of the southern Maine coast are only a few hours' drive or bus ride from Boston, making them accessible for an overnight excursion. With two nights to spend, you can take in Boothbay Harbor and even Camden, though you'll want at least a full day, and preferably three or five days, for a windjammer (sailing) cruise along the Maine coast.

## Two Weeks

With two weeks to spend, you'll have the time to see Boston and other top sights and to venture to some of the more remote parts of New England, which are of special interest to outdoor enthusiasts.

In **Downeast Maine**, spend two nights on Mt Desert Island exploring Acadia National Park, a night or two (or more) on a windjammer and the rest of your time in any of the beautiful small coastal towns.

Spend three or four days in the wilds of **northern Maine** on a canoe or kayak excursion, on a white-water rafting expedition, or hiking and camping. Rafting is most exciting in the springtime when the rivers are at their highest and whitest.

Though southern **Vermont** is only a few hours' drive from Boston, it takes several more hours to get to the northern part of the state. With four or five days to devote to

Vermont, spend a day and a half exploring Bennington, Brattleboro and a few of the pretty southern towns such as Newfane and Grafton. Then drive north along VT 100 through the center of the state, camping or staying at inns. There are lots of organized activities at Killington: in winter, downhill skiing, snowboarding and cross-country skiing; in summer, hiking and mountain biking.

Make a detour to beautiful Woodstock and then continue north via Waitsfield to Stowe for a hike on the Long Trail or for skiing in winter. Finish with a visit to friendly Burlington and the Shelburne Museum.

Take a day or two to visit New Haven and the historic towns of the **Connecticut** coast. After at least a day at Mystic Seaport Museum, head up the Connecticut River Valley. Stop at Hartford for a half day on your way to Lake Waramaug and the Litchfield Hills or go on via Sturbridge, Massachusetts, and Old Sturbridge Village.

## PLANNING

New England is principally a summer destination, with another busy season when the fall foliage reaches its full color. From mid-July through August, the summer resort areas are very busy, accommodations are fully booked and restaurants are crowded. Perhaps the best time to travel here is between the weekend of Memorial Day (the last Monday in May) and mid-June, before the local schools close and families hit the road; and the early part of September, after the big summer rush but before the 'leaf peepers' (foliage tourists) arrive. Especially during the week at these times, hotels and inns are likely to have rooms available, vacant campsites can be found easily and the hottest restaurants have tables ready without a long wait.

Because New England entertains a dense tourist population in the summer and fall, the opportunity for special events, festivals and celebrations is endless – and therefore only a few are detailed in this part of the book. For more information on them, refer to the state or city's website (see Tourist Offices, later in this chapter).

## When to Go

New England has many events and festivals throughout the year, and it may be worthwhile to plan your itinerary around some of them. See the regional chapters for more information on the ones listed here.

**January** New Year's Day (January 1) is a legal holiday. (See December, below, for New Year's Eve and 'First Night' celebrations.) Transportation services are crowded several days before and after New Year's Day, but from January 4 to 14, travel services are not heavily used, and traveling is easy and relatively cheap. The weather is usually bitterly cold and snowy, though often there is a welcome 'January thaw,' a few days of surprisingly mild temperatures.

The third Monday is Martin Luther King Jr Day, a holiday celebrating the civil rights leader's birth (January 15, 1929). This is the unofficial opening of the busy skiing season.

Chinese New Year begins at the end of January or the beginning of February and lasts two weeks. In cities with a significant Chinese population (such as Boston), the first day is celebrated with parades, fireworks and lots of food.

Contact ski areas for local snow festivals and ski/snowboard/snowmobile competitions in January and February, especially in Maine and New Hampshire. Stowe, Vermont, has a popular winter carnival in mid-month.

**February** The weather remains quite cold, and skiing is the big activity this month. Many New Englanders fly off to warm southern islands for a respite.

February 14 is Valentine's Day (not a legal holiday).

The third Monday is Presidents' Day, a legal holiday commemorating the birthdays of George Washington (February 22, 1732) and Abraham Lincoln (February 12, 1809). Ski destinations are particularly busy.

In New Hampshire, Hanover's Dartmouth Winter Carnival has been celebrated since 1911 with games, drink and cultural activities.

In Maine, the Annual US National Toboggan Championship takes place the first week in Camden. Kennebunk, Houlton, Caribou, Searsport, Greenville and other towns celebrate Winter Carnival.

**March** Cold and snow continue at least until mid-March. Late March brings the beginning of 'mud time,' when the earth thaws. When days are warm and nights cold, farmers tap the maple sap from their 'sugar bushes' (maple tree groves) to make maple syrup (see the 'Maple Sugaring' boxed text in the Facts about New England chapter).

St Patrick's Day (March 17 or the Monday closest to it) is celebrated in Boston and other cities with large Irish American populations. Parades, speeches and drinking parties are the order of the day. In Boston, it's a local public holiday accomplished by means of a subterfuge: Officially, the day off is for celebrating Evacuation Day, the day the British pulled out of Boston Harbor in 1775.

In some years, Easter (see April) falls in late March.

**April** Mud time continues, and the chance of a major snowstorm disappears. By Patriots' Day (April 19), nights are still chilly but days can be relatively warm and pleasant. The Monday nearest Patriots' Day is a holiday in Massachusetts, with parades and speeches taking place (state government offices and some local businesses close). In Lexington and Concord, Massachusetts, the opening battles of the Revolutionary War fought on April 19, 1775, are reenacted, and the parades feature troops of 'British redcoats,' colonial minutemen, fire engines and politicians seeking publicity. Celebrations in the year 2000, the 275th anniversary of the battles, will be particularly lavish.

Also in April is the Boston Marathon, which celebrates its 104th anniversary in 2000. In Vermont, the Vermont Maple Festival is held in St Albans near the start of the month.

Easter often falls in April. New England's hundreds of colleges empty out and close down for 'spring break.' Some businesses are closed Good Friday (not a holiday) and transportation services are crowded. Many businesses are closed on Easter Sunday.

In April, ski season is winding down and spring has not really arrived, so many country inns and other vacation lodgings are closed for all or part of the month.

**May** Weather in May is usually delightful, with cool nights and warm days, though cold rain and even a short freak snowstorm aren't impossible.

Mother's Day, the second Sunday in May, is a commercial celebration that has become the busiest restaurant day of the year – reservations are required everywhere.

The weekend of Memorial Day (the last Monday in May) signals the official start of the summer vacation season. The holiday commemorates US veterans with patriotic parades and ceremonies. Many festivals are held during the three-day weekend. Campgrounds, theme parks, seasonal museums and attractions are all open – and very busy. Make advance reservations for any tourist services (hotel, restaurant, transport) that you may need.

The Brimfield Outdoor Antiques Show near Sturbridge, Massachusetts, is a mile-long strip featuring more than 1000 dealers it is also held in July and September in Brimfield itself.

In Connecticut, Mystic's Lobsterfest is an outdoor old-fashioned lobster bake on the banks of the Mystic River, held on Memorial Day weekend.

During the entire month, Greenville, Maine, celebrates Moosemania with 'moose-related activities and events.'

**June** Early June is an excellent time to travel in New England. Because schools are still in session, local families do not crowd resort areas except on the weekends. Everything's open, but prices are not yet at the high level they will reach in late July and August. The weather is completely unpredictable: A breathlessly hot few days may be followed by a surprising chill, but mostly the weather is quite fine.

After mid-June, when schools adjourn, resorts become much busier on weekdays as well as weekends. You may need to make advance reservations as summer festivals hit their stride.

June 17 is Bunker Hill Day, a Boston holiday that closes some local businesses. The third Sunday in June is Father's Day, a commercial celebration similar to Mother's Day (see May) but without the restaurant crowds.

In Massachusetts, Provincetown's Blessing of the Fleet features family events and a religious celebration honoring fisherfolk. The ACC Crafts Fair in West Springfield brings together more than 350 of the nation's artisans to show and sell their work in the Eastern States' Exhibition.

In Connecticut, the Taste of Hartford festival is one of New England's largest outdoor food fests; it's held near the start of the month. Around the same time, Farmington Antiques Weekend is the largest antique event in the state, with over 600 exhibitors.

In Providence, Rhode Island, the second weekend brings the Festival of Historic Homes, when private gardens and buildings are open to the public.

Vermont has the Annual Vermont Dairy Festival in Enosburg Falls in the early part of the month, as well as Burlington's Discover Jazz Festival. Waterbury hosts free Concerts in the Park (with free ice cream!) every Thursday night from mid-June to mid-August. Ethan Allen Days – 'Fun with the Green Mountain Boys' – features historical reenactments in Arlington during the middle of the month.

In New Hampshire, the second weekend in June brings Portsmouth's Old Market Square Days, which mostly celebrates food. The last weekend of the month brings Portsmouth's Jazz Festival, which is on the waterfront.

In Maine, Rockport celebrates with an Annual Down East Jazz Society Festival. At the end of the month, Boothbay Harbor has its Annual Windjammer Days, which includes a parade, concerts and more. More unusual is Caribou's Midsomer Dagen, a Swedish-American celebration of midsummer, with a maypole and traditional Swedish dancing.

**July** Independence Day (July 4) is the USA's biggest patriotic holiday, commemorating the signing of the Declaration of Independence on July 4, 1776. It is celebrated on the actual day with parades, cookouts and fireworks in every town, ranging from the smallest village to large cities.

In Boston, the Boston Pops give an evening performance of Tchaikovsky's *1812 Overture*, complete with brass cannons and synchronized fireworks, to a gigantic crowd. When the Fourth of July falls on a Friday or a Monday, resorts and transport are particularly busy as everyone takes off for a long weekend. The weather at the beginning of July is warm to hot.

Other notable Fourth of July celebrations take place at Old Sturbridge Village, Massachusetts; Hartford, Connecticut; and Burlington, Vermont. In Maine, you can find a good one anywhere, but especially in Bar Harbor (plus a Seafood Fest the same weekend), Bethel, Boothbay, Greenville, Kennebunk, Millinocket, Ogunquit and Rangeley.

The eight weeks between the Fourth of July and Labor Day (the first Monday in September) are New England's high season for tourism. Everything is crowded and reservations are required for many services: lodgings, campsites, car ferries, etc.

In the month's second week, Boston's Harborfest celebrates maritime history with fireworks, concerts, food festivals and historic reenactments. In New Bedford, Massachusetts, the Annual Feast of the Blessed Sacrament is the largest Portuguese festival in the USA, with a parade, entertainment and a giant fair with rides and amusements.

Near the start of the month, in Bridgeport, Connecticut, the Barnum Festival culminates with a giant parade honoring the circus king. In Litchfield, Connecticut, an Open House Tour lets you inside the town's private historic homes and gardens. In Connecticut, the Guilford Handcrafts Exposition, a show featuring items from more than 100 artisans nationwide, is held toward the end of the month.

In the first week of July, in Brandon, Vermont, you can take a self-guided tour of the cellars and hiding places once used by slaves fleeing to Canada on the Underground Railroad. The Manchester Music Festival and the Marlboro Music Fest are held from July through August, as is the Champlain Shakespeare Festival in Burlington, Vermont, at the University of Vermont's Royal Tyler Theatre.

July is a busy month for Maine: The second weekend of the month, Crawford has an Annual Breakneck Mountain Bluegrass Festival; Rockland has the Annual Great Schooner Race; and Fort Kent has Summerfest, with an arts and crafts fair, barbecue and more. Mid-month brings Camden's Annual Arts and Crafts Show, with more than 100 professionals attending, and Bar Harbor has a Native American Festival, with crafts, dancing and food. Yarmouth has an Annual Yarmouth Clam Festival good for everyone in the family. Running for two weeks near the end of the month is the Bangor State Fair, the largest in the state, complete with agricultural exhibits, rides, entertainment and down-home fun.

**August** The weather is at its hottest in August, often with a week or so of 'dog days,' when the temperature exceeds 90° or 95°F in high humidity and, despite prevalent air-con, everyone except those at the beach complains. Tourism is at its busiest in August, with prices at their highest.

In Massachusetts, the Gloucester Waterfront Festival has a Yankee lobster bake, pancake breakfast, whale watching and more.

In Connecticut, mid-month brings the Volvo International Tennis Tournament to New Haven, where international stars of men's tennis compete.

In Newport, Rhode Island, the JVC Jazz Festival and the Ben & Jerry's Folk Festival are held on alternate weekends near the start of the month.

August 16 is Bennington Battle Day in Vermont, a state holiday that might close some businesses. The battle is reenacted in Bennington.

In Maine, Rockland has its long-running Annual Lobster Festival near the start of the month. Wilton has a Blueberry Festival

with many activities for the whole family, and Rangeley and Machias have blueberry festivals toward the end of the month. Mid-month, Perry has 'The Gathering, Passamaquoddy Tribe,' which includes traditional dance and the lighting of the sacred fire.

**September** Labor Day, the first Monday of the month, honors workers and signals the official end of the summer tourism season. It's the busiest vacation weekend of the season and everything is crowded, so advance reservations are essential.

The two weeks after Labor Day are an excellent time to travel in New England. School is in session, so the crowds disappear, but almost all services are still open and prices drop somewhat. The weather is summer-like, but without the intensity of heat and humidity.

Mid-September brings the beginning of foliage season. Days are still pleasantly warm, but nights are cool. Prices for tourist services rise a bit and inland resorts see a new surge of visitors. The fall foliage color spreads southward from Canada, often reaching its peak in southern New England by mid-October.

In Massachusetts, in mid-September, the Eastern States Exposition (the Big E) is a New England 'state fair' in West Springfield. A Taste of the Berkshires, in Great Barrington, is an outdoor event celebrating the bounty of the area; restaurants offer samples and you can tour local farms. In Pittsfield, the Hancock Shaker Village has the Autumn Farm Weekend, a harvest festival.

Mid-month in Somers, Connecticut, the Four Town Fair is the state's oldest fair, with exhibits, rides, amusements and fireworks. At the end of the month, the Connecticut Antiques Show takes place in West Hartford.

The biggest Vermont fall festival is probably the Stratton Arts Festival, held near Manchester. More than 200 artisans participate from mid-month to mid-November. There's also the Vermont State Fair early in the month in Rutland.

In New Hampshire, the White Mountain Jazz and Blues Crafts Festival is held early in the month in North Conway.

In Maine, the annual Fiddle Contest and Old Time Country Music Show takes place the second weekend of the month in Kennebunk. Farmington has a Leaf Peeper Festival at the end of the month.

**October** The first half of October usually finds fall foliage blazing throughout New England. Beach resorts may be open but are not particularly busy. Columbus Day, celebrated on the second Monday of the month, commemorates the landing of Christopher Columbus in the Bahamas on October 12, 1492. On Columbus Day weekend, country inns and other inland lodgings are all booked up well in advance, at high-season prices. Conventioneers often fill many city hotels.

Sunny days are pleasantly warmish ('sweater weather'), but rainy days are chilly; nights are very brisk, with frost likely in northern New England. After Columbus Day, many resorts, attractions and small local museums close for the winter, but enough services stay open to make travel possible. In fact, with a bit of luck, late October can be a wonderful time to travel. Prices for all services are low, the weather is usually brisk but agreeable, and blazing pockets of fall foliage can be found everywhere except in extreme northern regions.

On Halloween (October 31, not a public holiday), children dress in costumes and go from house to house 'trick-or-treating,' looking for sweet treats and (rarely) playing tricks if the treats aren't forthcoming. In Salem, Massachusetts, Haunted Happenings is a celebration of Halloween (make reservations for accommodations at least a year in advance) that includes events such as the Psychic Fair.

Elsewhere in Massachusetts, look for harvest festivals in Westport, South Carver (cranberries!), Plimoth Plantation in Plymouth, and Old Sturbridge Village. In Cambridge and Boston, the Head of the Charles Regatta is the world's largest single-day rowing event, with championship events and races for all ages. In Lexington, it's Colonial Weekend at Minuteman National Historic Park.

In Southington, Connecticut, the Apple Harvest Festival is celebrated over two weekends, with entertainment and a carnival.

Vermont also has an Applefest, held in South Hero the first weekend in October. The annual Festival of Vermont Crafts in Montpelier is held the first weekend of the month, with good foliage and outdoor fun. The Springfield Annual Vermont Apple Festival & Craft Show is held the first weekend of the month; Brattleboro also celebrates Apple Days then.

In Maine, Boothbay, York, Machias, Sunday River and Camden all have annual Fall Foliage Festivals throughout the month, with outdoor activities, craft fairs and all sorts of entertainment.

**November** Early November is much like late October for travel in New England. With fall foliage color gone, the New England countryside shows a limited palette of gray shades. Many inns close, as foliage season has passed and ski season has yet to begin. Thus, hotel rates and transport fares are often quite reasonable.

Veterans Day (November 11) is a national holiday honoring war veterans. This long weekend marks the opening of the ski season at resorts with snowmaking capabilities.

Thanksgiving, the fourth Thursday in November, is the busiest holiday of the year for travel throughout the US. Millions of people crowd highways, buses, trains and airplanes in order to be with relatives and friends for the dinner that recalls the feast the Pilgrims and their Wampanoag Indian neighbors shared in Plymouth, Massachusetts, in 1621. Peak travel times are the Wednesday just before Thanksgiving Day and the Sunday following it. Avoid traveling on those days if possible. If not, make advance reservations and allow plenty of time for delays.

In Massachusetts, Plimoth Plantation and Old Sturbridge Village celebrate Thanksgiving Day in traditional costume with traditional food, and everyone is invited.

The Friday after Thanksgiving marks the beginning of Christmas shopping season – shopping districts and malls are packed.

By late November, days are chilly and nights cold. The ground in northern New England is frozen hard, and there may be snowfalls anywhere in the region.

**December** By mid-December, the weather can be bitterly cold, with snowfalls from an inch or two to a foot. If there's freezing weather but no snow, the ice skating can be wonderful on the region's many glacial ponds.

Shopping districts in cities and towns are hectic, thanks to the annual pre-Christmas shopping spree. Shops may do as much business in December as they do in all the other 11 months of the year. Transportation is crowded during the few days before and after Christmas (December 25), which is a national holiday. Between Christmas and the New Year, many New Englanders take short vacations to New York City.

In Massachusetts, Boston has two Christmas tree lightings: one at the Prudential Center downtown and another on Boston Common. There's also a reenactment of the Boston Tea Party on or near December 16, the date of the original event. Cape Ann, Nantucket, Stockbridge and Worcester County celebrate a month-long Christmas Festival.

In Rhode Island, Newport's Christmas celebrations start the first week of the month with decorated mansions, festivities and food.

In New Hampshire, Portsmouth's Strawbery Banke Museum celebrates Christmas the first two weekends of the month with activities and music.

On New Year's Eve (on December 31), Boston; Burlington, Vermont; Providence, Rhode Island; Stamford and Hartford, Connecticut; and other cities and towns hold First Night celebrations – winter festivals featuring parades, ice- and snow-sculpture exhibitions, concerts and other performances. New Year's Day (January 1) is a national holiday.

## Maps

The most detailed state highway maps are those distributed – usually for free – by state governments. You can call or write the state tourism offices in advance (see Tourist Offices, later on in this chapter) and have the maps sent out, or you can pick up the maps at highway tourism information offices ('welcome centers') when you enter the state on a major highway (see Tourist Offices for details).

Other highway maps, with sufficient detail to be useful for driving, are for sale in fuel stations, bookstores, newsstands and some shops and lodging places.

Local chambers of commerce usually hand out simple maps of their towns. These vary from useless advertisements to very detailed street maps.

The US Dept of the Interior Geological Survey (USGS) topographical maps cover the USA at a scale of 1:24,000, showing every road, path and building (though some of these may be out of date). They are superb close-up maps for hiking or intensive exploration by car. USGS also publishes a variety of other maps, including metropolitan and resort-destination maps at scales between 1:24,000 and 1:100,000, and state topographical maps at 1:500,000.

Information on ordering USGS maps is now available on the USGS website (www .usgs.gov) or by writing: USGS Information Services, Box 25286, Denver, CO 80225. When you order maps, also request the folder describing topographic maps and the symbols used on them. For faster, easier service, you may order maps by mail from Boston's Globe Corner Bookstore (☎ 617-523-6658, 800-358-6013, fax 617-227-2771, info@gcb.com, www.globecorner.com), at 3 School St, Boston, MA 02108 (see the boxed text 'Bookstores' in the Boston chapter for other bookstore addresses).

Hiking trail maps are available from outdoors organizations (see Guidebooks, later in this chapter).

## Atlases

If you plan to do a lot of traveling – especially hiking or biking – in a particular state, you may want to get a state atlas.

The Delorme Mapping Company (☎ 207-846-7100, www.delorme.com), PO Box 298, Yarmouth, ME 04096, sells atlases for all New England states, except Connecticut and Rhode Island, for $17. The Massachusetts atlas is done at an impressive 1:80,000 scale.

Arrow Map Company (☎ 508-279-1177, 800-343-7500, www.arrowmap.com), 50 Scotland Blvd, Bridgewater, MA 02324, has atlases to all the New England states and to many cities and towns as well.

## What to Bring

If you take prescription medicines regularly, bring a supply of the medicine, not a prescription for it. Doctors are licensed by state, and their prescriptions are not normally accepted in any state except the one in which they are licensed.

From mid-June through early September in southern New England, have cool summer clothing plus a sweater or jacket for evenings. A windbreaker and sweater will be necessary for the mountains of northern New England and the windy coast. If you plan to dine in fancy restaurants in Newport, Boston or other cosmopolitan centers, you'll need to dress up (skirt, dress, or coat and tie). An umbrella or raincoat and hat are good to have any time of year.

In spring (April to May) and autumn (mid-September to late October or mid-November), there can be chilly mornings and afternoons followed by cold nights approaching freezing, so have warmer clothes, especially in the northern New England states.

For the winter (mid-November through March), have cold-weather gear: fleece, woolens, waterproof footwear, a warm hat, scarf and gloves. From mid-December through February, Boston can have several weeks when the temperature does not go above freezing and even a few days when it does not reach 0°F. In northern New England, the cold lasts even longer and is more bitter.

## TOURIST OFFICES
### Local Tourist Offices

State tourism offices will send you excellent detailed road maps, lists of lodgings, festivals and special events, and other materials before your trip.

They also maintain 'welcome centers' at major highway entrances to their states. Typically, you drive across the state line into a new state, and one of the next exits will have a welcome center with toilets, a picnic area, vending machines for hot and cold drinks and snacks, and an information desk dispensing maps, brochures, and camping, lodging and restaurant lists.

Here are the main addresses for state-run tourist offices:

Massachusetts Office of Travel & Tourism
(☎ 617-727-3201, 800-227-6277 ext 300,
fax 617-727-6525, www.mass-vacation.com)
100 Cambridge St, 13th floor,
Boston, MA 02202

Rhode Island Tourism Division
(☎ 401-222-2601, 800-556-2484,
fax 401-222-2102, www.visitrhodeisland.com)
7 Jackson Walkway,
Providence, RI 02903

Connecticut Office of Tourism
(☎ 860-270-8080, 800-282-6863,
fax 860-563-4877, www.state.ct.us/tourism)
505 Hudson St, Hartford, CT 06106

Vermont Dept of Tourism and Marketing
(☎ 802-828-3236, 800-837-6668,
fax 802-828-3233, www.travel-vermont.com)
6 Baldwin St, Montpelier, VT 05633-1301

New Hampshire Office of Travel &
Tourism Development
(☎ 603-271-2666, 800-386-4664 ext 145,
fax 603-271-2629, www.visitnh.com)
172 Pembroke Rd, PO Box 1856,
Concord, NH 03302-0856

Maine Office of Tourism
(☎ 207-623-0363, 800-533-9595,
fax 207-623-0288, www.visitmaine.com)
325B Water St, Hallowell, ME 04347

## Chambers of Commerce

Sometimes called convention and visitors' bureaus (CVBs), these are membership organizations for local businesses: hotels, restaurants, shops and any other commercial establishment. Although they often provide maps and other useful information, they usually don't tell you about establishments that are not chamber members, and these nonmembers are often the smallest or cheapest establishments.

A local chamber of commerce usually maintains an information booth at the entrance to the town or in the town center, usually open only during tourist seasons (summer, foliage season, ski season). It may also have a separate business office (ie, not an information office) elsewhere. Some chamber information offices will help you make reservations at member lodgings.

In this book, the addresses and telephone numbers of local chambers of commerce and other tourist offices are given in the Information sections under town headings.

## Tourist Offices Abroad

US embassies and consulates abroad may have some tourist information (see Embassies & Consulates, later in this chapter).

In Montreal, Quebec, contact the New England Tourism Centre (☎ 514-731-4898, nengland@portal.net), 4270 Sere St, Laurent.

In the UK, contact Discover New England (☎ 0173-274-2777, sylvia@admail4.co.uk), Vestry Rd, Seven Oaks, Kent TN14 5XA. Include two letter stamps.

## VISAS & DOCUMENTS
### Passport & Visas

To enter the USA, Canadians must have proof of Canadian citizenship, such as a citizenship card with photo ID or a passport. Visitors from other countries must have a valid passport, and most visitors also require a US visa. Check out the US State Dept's website (travel.state.gov/visa_services.html) for visa information.

However, there is a reciprocal visa-waiver program in which citizens of certain countries (26 at present) may enter the USA without a US visa for stays of 90 days or less. Currently these countries include Andorra, Argentina, Australia, Austria, Belgium, Brunei, Denmark, Finland, France, Germany, Iceland, Ireland, Italy, Japan, Liechtenstein, Luxembourg, Monaco, the Netherlands, New Zealand, Norway, San Marino, Slovenia, Spain, Sweden, Switzerland and the UK. Under this program you must have a roundtrip ticket that is nonrefundable in the USA, and you are not allowed to extend your stay beyond 90 days.

Other travelers need to obtain a visa from a US consulate or embassy. In most countries the process can be done by mail.

Your passport should be valid for at least six months longer than your intended stay in the USA, and you'll need to submit a recent photo (37mm by 37mm) with the application. Documents of financial stability and/or guarantees from a US resident are sometimes required, particularly for those from developing countries.

Visa applicants may be required to 'demonstrate binding obligations' that will ensure their return home. Because of this requirement, those planning to travel through other countries before arriving in the USA are generally better off applying for their US visa while they are still in their home countries rather than while on the road.

The most common visa is a Non-Immigrant Visitors Visa, B1 for business purposes, B2 for tourism or visits to friends and relatives. A visitor's visa is good for one or five years with multiple entries, and it specifically prohibits the visitor from taking paid employment in the USA. If you're coming to the USA to work or study, you will probably need a different type of visa, and the company or institution to which you're going should make the arrangements. Allow six months in advance for processing the application. For information on work visas and employment in the US, see the Work section, later in this chapter.

The validity period of your US Visitors Visa depends on your citizenship. The length of time you are allowed to stay in the USA is ultimately determined by US immigration authorities at the port of entry.

**Visa Extensions** If you want to stay in the USA past the date stamped in your passport, contact the local office of the Justice Dept's

## HIV/AIDS & Entering the USA

Anyone entering the USA who is not a US citizen is subject to the authority of the Immigration & Naturalization Service (INS). The INS can keep someone from entering or staying in the USA by excluding or deporting them. This is especially relevant to travelers with HIV (human immunodeficiency virus) or AIDS (acquired immune deficiency syndrome). Though being HIV-positive is not a ground for deportation, it is a 'ground for exclusion,' meaning that the INS can invoke this rule and refuse to admit an HIV-positive visitor to the country.

Although INS officers don't test people for HIV or AIDS at the point of entry into the USA, they may try to exclude anyone who answers 'yes' to this question on the non-immigrant visa application form: 'Have you ever been afflicted with a communicable disease of public health significance?' An INS officer may also stop someone who seems sick, is carrying AIDS/HIV medicine or appears to be from a 'high-risk group' (ie, gay), though sexual orientation itself is not legally a ground for exclusion. Visitors may be deported if the INS later finds that they are HIV-positive but did not declare it. Being HIV-positive is not a 'ground for deportation,' but failing to provide correct information on the visa application is.

If you can prove to consular officials that you are the spouse, parent or child of a US citizen or legal permanent resident (green-card holder), you are exempt from the exclusionary law, even if you are HIV-positive or have AIDS.

Immigrants and visitors who may face exclusion should discuss their rights and options with a trained immigration advocate within the USA before applying for a visa. For legal immigration information and referrals to immigration advocates, contact the National Immigration Project of the National Lawyers Guild (☎ 617-227-9727), 14 Beacon St, suite 506, Boston, MA 02108, or the Immigrant HIV Assistance Project, Bar Association of San Francisco (☎ 415-782-8995), 465 California St, suite 1100, San Francisco, CA 94104.

---

Immigration & Naturalization Service (INS) *before* the stamped date. In Boston, call the INS at ☎ 617-565-3879 for information or ☎ 800-870-3676 for forms. The Boston office is in the John F Kennedy Federal Office Building, 5th floor, Government Center, Boston, MA 02203; take the subway to the Government Center station.

If you remain more than a few days past the expiration date, the INS may assume you want to work illegally. At an interview with the INS, you will need to explain why you didn't leave by the expiration date, and you will have to convince the officials you're not looking for work and that you have enough money to support yourself until you do leave. It's a good idea to bring a US citizen with you to vouch for your character, and to bring some sort of proof that you have enough currency to support yourself.

## Travel Insurance

A travel insurance policy to cover theft, loss and medical problems is a good idea. This should cover you not only for medical expenses and luggage theft or loss, but also for cancellations or delays in your travel arrangements, and everyone should be covered for the worst possible case, such as an accident that requires hospital treatment and a flight home. Coverage depends on your insurance and type of ticket, so ask both your insurer and your ticket-issuing agency to explain the finer points.

Many travel agencies sell medical and emergency repatriation policies, but these can be relatively expensive for what you get. You'd be well advised to discuss the matter of travel insurance with your health care provider or regular insurance agent for comparison of coverages and costs.

## Embassies & Consulates

### US Embassies & Consulates Abroad
US diplomatic offices abroad include the following:

**Australia**
Embassy:
(☎ 02-6214-5600,
www.usis-australia.gov
/embassy.html)
21 Moonah Place,
Yaralumla, ACT 2600
Consulate:
(☎ 02-9373-9200,
www.usconsydney.org)
Level 59 MLC Center,
19-29 Martin Place,
Sydney, NSW 2000
Consulate:
(☎ 03-9526-5900,
www.usis-australia.gov
/melbourne)
Level 6, 553 St Kilda Rd
(PO Box 6722),
Melbourne, VIC 3004
Consulate:
(☎ 08-9231-9400,
www.usis-australia.gov
/perth)
St George's Court, 13th floor,
16 St George's Terrace,
Perth, WA 6000

**Austria**
Embassy:
(☎ 1-31339-0,
www.usembassy-vienna.at)
Boltzmanngasse 16,
A-1090, Vienna

**Canada**
Embassy:
(☎ 613-238-4470,
800-283-4356,
www.usembassycanada.gov)
100 Wellington St,
Ottawa, ON K1P 5T1
Consulate:
(☎ 902-429-2485)
2000 Barrington St,
Cogswell Tower, suite 910,
Halifax, NS B3J 3K1

Consulate:
(☎ 514-398-9695)
1155 rue St-Alexandre,
Montreal,
Quebec H2Z 1Z2
Consulate:
(☎ 416-595-1700)
360 University Ave,
Toronto ON M5G 1S4
There are also consulates
in Calgary, Quebec City
and Vancouver.

**Denmark**
Embassy:
(☎ 35-55-31-44,
www.usembassy.dk)
Dag Hammarskjölds Allé 24,
2100 Copenhagen

**Finland**
Embassy:
(☎ 9-171-931,
www.usembassy.fi)
Itäinen Puistotie 14,
00140 Helsinki

**France**
Embassy:
(☎ 01 43 12 22 22,
www.amb-usa.fr)
2 rue Saint-Florentin,
75382 Paris Cedex 08

**Germany**
Embassy:
(☎ 228-339-1,
www.usembassy.de)
Deichmanns Aue 29,
53170 Bonn
Embassy:
(☎ 030-832-9233)
Clayallee 170,
14195 Berlin
There are consulates in
Dusseldorf, Frankfurt, Ham-
burg, Leipzig and Munich.

**Greece**
Embassy:
(☎ 1-721-2951,
www.usisathens.gr)
91 Vasilissis Sophias Blvd,
10160 Athens
There is a consulate general
in Thessaloniki.

**Ireland**
Embassy:
(☎ 01-688-7122, www
.indigo.ie/usembassy-usis)
42 Elgin Rd, Ballsbridge,
Dublin 4

**Israel**
Embassy:
(☎ 3-519-7575,
www.usis-israel.org.il)
71 Hayarkon St, Tel Aviv
There is a consulate in
Jerusalem.

**Italy**
Embassy:
(☎ 6-46-741, www.usis.it)
Via Vittorio Veneto 119/A,
00187 Rome

**Japan**
Embassy:
(☎ 3-224-5000) 1-10-5
Akasaka Chome,
Minato-ku, Tokyo

**Mexico**
Embassy:
(☎ 5-209-9100,
www.usembassy.org.mx)
Paseo de la Reforma 305,
Colonia Cuauhtémoc,
06500 México, DF
There are consulates in
Ciudad Juárez, Guadalajara,
Hermosillo, Matamoros,
Mérida, Monterrey, Nuevo
Laredo and Tijuana.

## Embassies & Consulates

**Netherlands**
Embassy:
(☎ 70-310-9209,
www.usemb.nl)
Lange Voorhout 102,
2514 EJ The Hague
Consulate:
(☎ 20-575-5309)
Museumplein 19,
1071 DJ Amsterdam

**New Zealand**
Embassy:
(☎ 9-303-2724)
General Bldg,
29 Shortland St,
Auckland

**Spain**
Embassy:
(☎ 1-906-421431 from
Spain only, fee payable;
US passport holders call
91587-2251)
Calle Serrano 75,
28006 Madrid

**Sweden**
Embassy:
(☎ 08 783 53 00, fax 660
58 79, www.usis.usemb.se)
Strandvägen 101,
S-115 89 Stockholm

**Switzerland**
Embassy:
(☎ 31-157-51-54, 357-72-34,
fax 357-73-98)

Jubiläumsstrasse 95,
3005 Bern

**UK**
Embassy:
(☎ 020-499-9000,
www.usembassy.org.uk)
24 Grosvenor Square,
London W1A 1AE
Consulate:
(☎ 31-556-8315,
fax 557-6023)
3 Regent Terrace,
Edinburgh EH7 5BW
Consulate:
(☎ 028-90328-239,
fax 90248-482)
Queens House, 14 Queen St,
Belfast BT1 6EQ

### Embassies & Consulates in the USA

Embassies are in Washington, DC. Some countries maintain consulates, honorary consuls
or consular agents in Boston and/or New York City. To get the telephone number of an
embassy or consulate not listed below, call the directory assistance number for the city in
which you hope to find a consulate (Boston: ☎ 617-555-1212; New York: ☎ 212-555-
1212; Washington: ☎ 202-555-1212).

**Australia**
Embassy:
(☎ 202-797-3000, fax 797-
3168, www.austemb.org)
1601 Massachusetts Ave NW,
Washington, DC 20036
Consulate:
(☎ 617-542-8655)
20 Park Plaza, 4th floor,
Boston, MA 02116
Consulate:
(☎ 212-245-4000)
International Bldg,
636 Fifth Ave,
New York, NY 10111

**Canada**
Embassy:
(☎ 202-682-1740,
www.cdnemb-washdc.org)
501 Pennsylvania Ave NW,
Washington, DC 20001

Consulate:
(☎ 617-262-3760)
3 Copley Place, suite 400,
Boston, MA 02116
Consulate:
(☎ 212-768-2400,
fax 768-2440)
1251 Ave of the Americas
(Sixth Ave), 16th floor,
New York, NY 10020-1175

**France**
Embassy:
(☎ 202-944-6200)
4101 Reservoir Rd NW,
Washington, DC
20007-2171
Consulate:
(☎ 617-542-7374)
31 St James Ave, suite 750,
Boston, MA 02116

Consulate:
(☎ 212-606-3699)
934 Fifth Ave,
New York, NY 10021

**Germany**
Embassy:
(☎ 202-298-4000,
fax 298-4249,
www.germany-info.org)
4645 Reservoir Rd NW,
Washington, DC
20007-1998
Consulate:
(☎ 617-536-4414,
fax 536-8573)
3 Copley Place, suite 500,
Boston, MA 02116
Consulate:
(☎ 212-308-8700)
460 Park Ave,
New York, NY 10022

## Embassies & Consulates

**Ireland**
Embassy:
(☎ 202-462-3939,
www.irelandemb.org)
2234 Massachusetts Ave NW,
Washington, DC 20008
Consulate:
(☎ 617-267-9330)
Chase Bldg, 535 Boylston St,
Boston, MA 02116
Consulate:
(☎ 212-319-2555)
515 Madison Ave,
New York, NY 10022

**Israel**
Embassy:
(☎ 202-364-5500,
fax 364-5423,
www.israelemb.org)
3514 International Drive NW,
Washington, DC 20008

**Italy**
Embassy:
(☎ 202-328-5500,
fax 462-3605,
www.italyemb.nw.dc.us
/italy)
1601 Fuller St NW,
Washington, DC 20009

Consulate:
(☎ 617-542-0483)
100 Boylston St, suite 900,
Boston, MA 02116
Consulate:
(☎ 212-737-9100)
690 Park Ave,
New York, NY 10021

**Japan**
Embassy:
(☎ 202-238-6700, fax 238-
2187, www.embjapan.org)
2520 Massachusetts Ave NW,
Washington, DC 20008

**Mexico**
Embassy:
(☎ 202-728-1600,
www.embassyofmexico.org)
1911 Pennsylvania Ave NW,
Washington, DC 20006

**Netherlands**
Embassy:
(☎ 202-244-5300,
fax 362-3430,
www.netherlands-embassy
.org)
4200 Linnean Ave NW,
Washington, DC 20008

Consulate:
(☎ 617-542-8452)
6 St James Ave, Boston,
MA 02116

**New Zealand**
Embassy:
(☎ 202-328-4800,
fax 667-5227,
www.emb.com/nzemb)
37 Observatory Circle NW,
Washington, DC 20008

**UK**
Embassy:
(☎ 202-588-6500,
fax 588-7850,
britain-info.org)
3100 Massachusetts Ave NW,
Washington, DC 20008
Consulate:
(☎ 617-248-9555,
fax 248-9578)
Federal Reserve Plaza,
25th floor, 600 Atlantic Ave,
Boston, MA 02210
New York British
Information Services:
(☎ 212-745-0444,
752-5747)
845 Third Ave,
New York, NY 10022

### Your Own Embassy

As a tourist, it's important to realize what your own embassy – the embassy of the country of which you are a citizen – can and can't do.

Generally speaking, it won't be much help in emergencies if the trouble you're in is remotely your own fault. Remember that you are bound by the laws of the country you are in. Your embassy will not be sympathetic if you end up in jail after committing a crime locally, even if such actions are legal in your own country.

In genuine emergencies you might get some assistance, but only if other channels have been exhausted. For example, if you need to get home urgently, a free ticket home is exceedingly unlikely – the embassy would expect you to have insurance. If you have all your money and documents stolen, it might assist in getting a new passport, but a loan for onward travel is out of the question.

Embassies used to keep letters for travelers or have a small reading room with home newspapers, but these days the mail-holding service has been stopped and even newspapers tend to be out of date.

Companies offering various sorts of travel insurance, including health insurance, include the following:

Access America, Inc
 (☎ 212-490-5345, 800-284-8300,
 www.accessamerica.com)
 600 Third Ave, New York,
 NY 10116

Tripguard Plus
 (☎ 800-423-3632, fax 818-892-6576,
 www.tripguard.com)
 16933 Parthenia St, North Hills, CA 91343

In the UK, apply to Europ Assistance (☎ 0181-680-1234, www.europassistance.com), 252 High St, Croyden, Surrey CR0 1NF, for insurance.

Make sure you have a separate record of all your ticket details or, better still, a photocopy of the ticket. Also make a copy of your policy, in case the original is lost.

Buy travel insurance as early as possible. If you buy it the week before you fly, you may find, for instance, that you're not covered for delays to your flight caused by strikes or other industrial action that may have been in force before you took out the insurance. Insurance may seem very expensive, but it's nowhere near the cost of a medical emergency in the USA.

## International Driving Permit

An International Driving Permit is a useful accessory for foreign visitors in the USA. Local traffic police are more likely to accept it as valid identification than an unfamiliar document from another country. Your national automobile association can provide one for a nominal fee. It's usually valid for one year.

## Automobile Association Card

If you plan on doing a lot of driving in the USA, it might be beneficial to join your national automobile association. Members of the American Automobile Association (AAA) or an affiliated automobile club can get lodging, car rental and sightseeing admission discounts with membership cards. See the Useful Organizations section in this chapter for more information.

## Hostel Card

Most hostels in the USA are members of Hostelling International/American Youth Hostels (HI/AYH). For more information on HI/AYH, see the Useful Organizations and Hostels sections, later in this chapter.

## Student & Youth Cards

In college towns such as Amherst, Boston, Cambridge, Hanover or New Haven, your student ID card can sometimes get you discounts. Museums and attractions outside these cities may also give small discounts to students, and you'll need a card to prove you are one.

## Photocopies

It's a good idea to make photocopies of your important travel documents (passport data page and visa page, credit cards, travel insurance policy, air/bus/train tickets, driver's license, etc). Keep the copies in a different, safe place from the documents themselves. If your documents are lost or stolen, replacing them will be much easier.

## CUSTOMS

The US Customs Service allows each person 21 years of age or older to bring 1 liter of liquor and 200 cigarettes duty free into the USA. US citizens are allowed to import, duty free, $400 worth of gifts from abroad, while non-US citizens are allowed to bring in $100 worth. Should you be carrying more than $10,000 in US and foreign cash, traveler's checks, money orders and the like, you need to declare the excess amount. There is no legal restriction on the amount that may be imported, but undeclared sums may be subject to confiscation.

## MONEY
## Currency

Most of the world knows that the US currency is the dollar ($), divided into 100 cents (¢). Coins are in denominations of 1¢ (penny), 5¢ (nickel), 10¢ (dime), 25¢ (quarter), 50¢ (half dollar – rare) and $1 (silver dollar – rare). Notes ('bills') are in denominations of $1, $2 (rare), $5, $10, $20, $50 and $100.

## Exchange Rates

At press time, exchange rates were as follows:

| country | unit | | dollars |
|---|---|---|---|
| Australia | A$1 | = | US$0.66 |
| Canada | C$1 | = | US$0.68 |
| euro | €1 | = | US$1.04 |
| Germany | DM1 | = | US$0.53 |
| Hong Kong | HK$10 | = | US$1.28 |
| Japan | ¥100 | = | US$0.84 |
| New Zealand | NZ$1 | = | US$0.53 |
| UK | UK£1 | = | US$1.60 |

## Exchanging Money

**Cash & Traveler's Checks** Only a few banks, mostly in Boston, are prepared to exchange foreign cash. If you are coming to the US from abroad, you should plan on using your bank cash card (ATM card, cashpoint card, etc) to obtain cash most easily at the most advantageous rate of exchange. Also plan to use your major credit card (Visa, MasterCard, EuroCard, Access, Diners Club, American Express) often. If you don't have credit cards or a cash card, plan to buy US-dollar traveler's checks before leaving home or upon arrival in the US.

Many banks in small vacation towns frequented by Canadian tourists will buy and sell Canadian currency; some businesses near the border will offer to accept Canadian dollars 'at par,' meaning that they will accept Canadian dollars as though they were US dollars, in effect giving you a substantial discount on your purchase.

There are Fleet Boston foreign currency exchange booths at Boston's Logan Airport in Terminals C (☎ 617-569-1172) and E (☎ 617-567-2313). Fleet Boston has 10 other exchange locations in Boston and Cambridge, including its International Personal Banking office in Harvard Square (☎ 617-556-6050) at 1414 Massachusetts Ave, Cambridge. It also has more than 400 other locations throughout New England that can exchange foreign currency. Call ☎ 800-788-5000 for locations.

**ATMs** Cash (cashpoint, debit) cards from many banks may be used to pay at hotels, restaurants, shops, fuel stations, etc, and to obtain cash from automated teller machines (ATMs). Look for ATMs in or near banks, shopping malls, large supermarkets, airports and train stations, and on busy streets. Most are available for use 24 hours a day. In urban settings, use caution at ATMs after dark. In order for your card to be useful in New England, the bank that issued it must be a member of one of the large interbank card systems such as Cirrus, Interlink, Plus Systems or Star Systems. Before leaving home, ask your bank whether your card can be used in New England.

**Credit Cards** Major credit and charge cards are accepted by car rental agencies and most hotels, restaurants, fuel stations, shops and larger grocery stores. Many recreational and tourist activities can also be paid for by credit card. The most commonly accepted cards are Visa, MasterCard (EuroCard, Access) and American Express. However, Discover and Diners Club cards are also accepted by a fair number of businesses.

You'll find it hard to perform certain transactions without a credit card. Ticket-buying services, for instance, won't reserve tickets over the phone unless you offer a credit card number, and it's difficult to rent a car without a credit card (you may have to put down a cash deposit of several hundred dollars). Even if you prefer traveler's checks and ATMs, it's a good idea to have a Visa or MasterCard for emergencies.

Note that some inns, B&Bs and restaurants in the most popular resorts (Nantucket, Martha's Vineyard, etc) and also in rural areas (inland Maine, northern New Hampshire, etc) do not accept credit cards. Luckily, there are ATMs everywhere, so you can always get cash. Carry copies of your credit card numbers separately from the cards. If you lose your credit cards or they are stolen, contact the company immediately. The following are toll-free numbers for the main credit card companies:

| American Express | ☎ 800-528-4800 |
|---|---|
| Diners Club | ☎ 800-234-6377 |
| Discover | ☎ 800-347-2683 |

MasterCard          ☎ 800-826-2181
Visa                ☎ 800-336-8472

## Costs

New England is among the more expensive regions in the USA for travel, but it is worth the cost. You can travel quite cheaply here if you know how.

What you spend depends upon several factors: when and where you travel, how you travel and your age.

**Seasonal Costs** New England's busiest travel seasons are July and August (high summer or in-season), and late September through mid-October (foliage season, also considered in-season). Prices for hotels, transportation and attractions are generally highest at these times. (See the Planning section, earlier in this chapter, for more details.)

**City vs Country** Generally speaking, accommodations in cities are more expensive during the week, less expensive on Friday, Saturday and sometimes Sunday nights. In small towns, resorts and the countryside, inns and motels are cheapest during the week, more expensive on weekends. Thus you should plan to visit cities on weekends, and venture out into the country during the week, if possible.

**Budget Ranges** The most inexpensive way to see New England is to camp with a tent, share a rental car among four people, and have picnics for lunch. Traveling this way, your daily budget for food, lodging and transport can be as low as $25 to $35 per person; figure $10 to $15 more per person per day if you plan to spend lots of time in the big cities or resorts. Remember that it's only practical to camp from May through mid-October.

Traveling on a mid-range budget, a couple staying in budget motels, eating breakfast and lunch in fast-food places or lunchrooms and dinner in moderately priced little restaurants, and getting around by rental car can expect to spend between $60 and $80 per person per day. If you spend lots of time in resorts and cities, your costs might be $80 to $100 per person.

For more luxurious accommodations, two people touring in a rental car, staying at luxury-class hotels, motels and inns, and dining as they please should expect to spend $125 to $175 per person per day.

## Discounts

At some state tourism information centers are racks of brochures for hotels, motels, inns, restaurants, tours and attractions. Some of these accommodations offer discounts to travelers who present handbills or coupons given out at the information centers. For some lodgings, you must call and make a reservation from the information center to obtain the discount. Also, call the state tourism office for publicity materials, which will be mailed to you and may contain discount coupons for savings on car rentals, lodgings and meals.

If you are a member of a local or regional auto club affiliated with the American Automobile Association (AAA; ☎ 407-444-8000, 800-222-4357, fax 407-444-8030, www.aaa.com), 1000 AAA Drive, Heathrow, FL 32746, many roadside motels and some inns and hotels may offer you room rate discounts of 10% to 20%. Contact AAA for more information; a local affiliate in New England is AAA of Southern New England (☎ 800-222-7448, www.aaasne.com).

**Students** Some museums and attractions offer slightly lower rates to college students. Though there are many special student deals available in college towns like Boston, often these special rates for cultural attractions are available only through individual colleges and universities. You must buy your tickets through the university, not at the attraction itself.

**Families** Virtually all hotels and motels allow one or two children to share their parents' room at no extra charge. If a roll-away bed is needed, there may be a charge (often $10 to $20). Usually, children must be younger than 18 years of age. At country inns and B&Bs, however, this policy does not usually apply. In fact, many country inns do not allow young children as guests.

Most activities and attractions – including museums, theme parks, whale-watching expeditions, etc – offer reduced admission charges for children. Some offer special family rates; always ask if they do.

Some outdoor attractions (concerts, state parks, beaches, etc) charge admission by the car: Whether there's one person or seven inside, the charge is the same.

**Seniors** Older travelers are eligible for discounts at attractions, museums, parks and many hotels, on car rental and train and bus fares, and on other items. The age at which discounts apply varies and you must have photo identification as proof of your age. See Senior Travelers, later in this chapter, for more information.

## Tipping

Tipping is expected in restaurants and better hotels, and by taxi drivers, hairdressers and baggage carriers. Americans tend to be liberal tippers. (Not giving the appropriate tip may even earn you scorn from the un- or under-tipped service provider.)

If you sit down in a restaurant, bar or lounge, be prepared to tip 10% for mundane service, 15% for good service or up to 20% for exceptional service. If you leave less than 10%, it will be interpreted as foreign ignorance or a purposeful insult (which may be what you intend). Tip in cash on the table, or add it to your credit card slip in the appropriate space.

At take-out food counters, there may be a jar or other container labeled 'tips' into which you may throw a few coins if you like. Never tip in fast-food restaurants such as McDonald's, Burger King, etc.

Most hotels and inns allow you to carry your bags and find your room by yourself if you prefer, instead of having to tip the staffperson accompanying you. See the 'Tipping Guidelines' boxed text.

## Taxes

There is no national sales tax (such as VAT) in the USA. Some states levy sales taxes, and states and cities/towns may levy taxes on hotel rooms and restaurant meals. Room

| Tipping Guidelines |
| --- |
| Bartenders |
|    10% to 15% of the bill |
| Cinemas, theaters |
|    no tip |
| Coat checkrooms |
|    75¢ to $1 per coat |
| Doorman (hotel or restaurant) |
|    $1 at top hotels for calling a cab, getting your car from the parking lot or other direct service |
| Drivers who handle your luggage |
|    $1 (not required) |
| Fast-food restaurants |
|    no tip |
| Fuel station attendants |
|    no tip |
| Hairdressers, barbers |
|    about 15% |
| Hotel housekeepers |
|    $2 to $3 per day at inexpensive hotels |
| Luggage porters |
|    75¢ to $1 per piece |
| Restaurant or nightclub servers |
|    15% to 20% of the bill |
| Taxi drivers |
|    12% to 18% of the fare |
| Valet parking |
|    75¢ to $1 if attendant brings your car to you |

and meal taxes are not normally included in prices quoted to you, even though (or perhaps because) they may increase your final bill by as much as 11% or 12%. Be sure to ask about taxes when you ask for hotel room rates.

Taxes on transport services (bus, rail and air tickets, gasoline, taxi rides) are usually included in the prices quoted to you. See the 'Taxes' boxed text for more details.

## POST & COMMUNICATIONS

There's a post office in virtually every town and village, providing the familiar postal services such as parcel shipping and international express mail. For 24-hour postal information, call ☎ 800-275-8777 or check www.usps.gov. For hours of operation, see Sending Mail, below. Private shippers such as United Parcel Service (UPS; ☎ 800-742-5877) and Federal Express (FedEx; ☎ 800-463-3339) ship much of the nation's load of parcels and important time-sensitive documents to both domestic and foreign destinations.

## Postal Rates

US postal rates are fairly cheap and fairly stable, changing every few years. As of January 1999, rates for 1st-class mail within the USA were set at 33¢ for letters up to 1oz, 22¢ for each additional ounce and 20¢ for postcards.

International airmail rates (except Canada and Mexico) are 60¢ for a half-ounce letter and 40¢ for each additional half ounce. International postcard rates are 50¢.

Letters to Canada are 46¢ for a half-ounce letter and 72¢ for a letter up to 2oz. Postcards are 40¢. Letters to Mexico are 40¢ for a half-ounce letter, 46¢ for a 1oz letter and 35¢ for a postcard. Aerogrammes are 50¢.

## Sending Mail

If you have the correct postage, you can drop your mail into any blue mailbox. However, to send a package 16oz or heavier, you must bring it to a post office. Addresses of towns' main post offices are given in this book. For the address of the nearest, call the main post office listed under 'Postal Service' in the US Government section of the white pages telephone directory.

Usually, post offices are open 8 or 8:30 am to 5 pm weekdays; some major post offices

| Taxes | | | |
|---|---|---|---|
| state | meal | lodging | sales |
| Massachusetts | 5% | 5.7% | 5% |
| Rhode Island | 6% | 11% | 6% |
| Connecticut | 8% | 8% | 8% |
| Vermont | 6% | – | 6% |
| New Hampshire | 8% | 8% | – |
| Maine | 5% | 5% | 5% |

in cities stay open until 5:30 or 6 pm. Weekend hours are normally 8 am to noon or 2 pm on Saturday, closed Sunday. In the USA, the post office does not provide telephone service.

Packages must be securely wrapped in sturdy containers to be accepted for international shipment, especially if you expect to insure them. If you want to send a letter or parcel by US Registered Mail, be sure it is sealed with glue or paper tape (not cellophane or masking tape) so that the seams can be stamped with the postmark of the originating postal station.

## Receiving Mail

*Poste restante* is called 'general delivery' in the US. If you're sending (or expecting) mail to be held at the post office in a certain city or town, it should be addressed as follows:

Your name
c/o General Delivery (*Optional:* Station Name)
Town, State, ZIP Code
USA

Mail is usually held for 10 days before it's returned to the sender; you might request your correspondents to write 'hold for arrival' on their letters.

In large cities, it's a good idea to add the optional station name if you know it. If you do not add the ZIP code or station name, your mail will be held at the main station (central post office). It may not be the most convenient one for you, but it will have the longest hours of operation.

When you pick up your mail, bring some photo identification. Your passport is best.

Alternatively, have mail sent to the local representative of American Express or Thomas Cook, which provide mail service for their clients.

## Telephone

Telephone service is good, convenient and not particularly expensive, but the plethora of private companies, policies and rates is very confusing, even for Americans. Some smaller companies charge much higher rates than the large companies; some charge lower rates.

**How to Place a Call** All phone numbers within the USA consist of a three-digit area code followed by a seven-digit local number. If you are calling locally, just dial the seven-digit number. From a town in one area code to a town in another, dial ☎ 1 + area code + the number. This method is used, for example, to call from Boston to nearby Lexington, or to California, or to Bermuda or Canada. (To call a nearby city or town within the same area code, you may be able to dial only the last seven digits, or you may have to also dial ☎ 1 + area code.)

For calls to other countries from a public phone, dial ☎ 0 (zero) for an operator and ask for an international operator.

For local directory assistance, dial ☎ 411. For directory assistance outside your area code, dial ☎ 1 + the three-digit area code of the place you want to call + 555-1212. If you don't know the area code, dial ☎ 0 for operator assistance (free of charge).

Area codes for places outside the region are listed in telephone directories. Be aware that due to skyrocketing demand for phone numbers (for faxes, cellular phones, etc), some metropolitan areas are being divided into multiple new area codes. These changes are not reflected in older phone books. When in doubt, ask the operator.

The 800, 888 and 877 area codes designate toll-free numbers within the USA and sometimes from Canada. These calls are free. For toll-free directory assistance, call ☎ 800-555-1212.

It is important to note that toll-free numbers may be limited to calls from within a given region; ie, New England establishments may designate that calls from outside New England will not be received on their toll-free numbers. In addition, as of this writing, toll-free numbers are not accessible from outside North America.

Some area codes, including 550, 554, 900, 920, 940, 976 and others beginning with 5 and 9 designate information services (sports scores, phone sex, horoscopes, chat lines, etc) for which charges – sometimes as much as $2 or $3 per minute – may be levied.

Massachusetts has five area codes: 617, 508, 978, 781 and 413 – with three more to be added soon. Connecticut has two area codes: 860 for most of the state, including Hartford, and 203 for Fairfield and New Haven Counties, which include Bridgeport and New Haven.

Each of the other New England states has only one area code: 401 for Rhode Island, 802 for Vermont, 603 for New Hampshire and 207 for Maine.

If you're calling from abroad, the international country code for the USA is 1.

**Cost of Calling** Local calls cost 25¢ to 35¢ for three minutes or more, depending upon the town.

Because of the Byzantine rate structure and plethora of phone companies, regional calls (anywhere from 2 miles to 200 miles) are often the most expensive domestic calls, costing from 60¢ to $1 and up per three-minute call. In some cases, it is cheaper to call from Boston to California than from Boston to Worcester.

Long-distance domestic calls can cost as little as 9¢ per minute if dialed from a home phone, but will be more like 25¢ to 75¢ per minute from a public coin telephone. Telephone company credit card calls may cost several dollars for the first minute, but only 25¢ to 35¢ for subsequent minutes.

Foreign calls vary by the country being called, the telephone used (public or private), the company providing the long-distance service, the time of day and the day of the week. US rates are generally competitive with, and often cheaper than, public-phone rates in other countries.

For specific rate information, call the operator (☎ 0). Don't ask the operator to put your call through, however, because operator-assisted calls are much more expensive than direct-dial calls. Generally, nights (11 pm to 8 am), all day Saturday and 8 am to 5 pm Sunday are the cheapest times to call (60% discount). Evenings (5 to 11 pm Sunday to Friday) are mid-priced (35% discount). Day calls (8 am to 5 pm weekdays) are full-price calls within the USA.

**Paying for Calls** Most public telephones in the USA accept only coins (5¢, 10¢, 25¢);

some accept credit cards instead. For local and short calls to other points in the USA, using coins is easy enough. However, there are ways to pay for calls that are more convenient than feeding a stack of quarters into the phone.

Some telephones in airports and large hotels allow payment by credit card. There may be a slot to slide your card into, or you may have to punch in your credit card number.

An alternative is phone debit cards that allow purchasers to pay in advance. However, compared to the easy-to-use debit card systems in many other countries, those in the USA are confusing, cumbersome and often expensive.

Purchase a telephone debit card from a convenience store, phone company office, post office or tourist information office. Cards are usually sold in denominations of $5, $10, $20, $40 or $50, and offer calls in the USA for anywhere from 20¢ to 60¢ per minute; 70¢ to $1.80 per minute to Canada and the UK; $1 to $2.40 per minute to Europe; or $2 to $3 per minute to Asian and Pacific countries.

Unfortunately, it is usually impossible to tell how much a call may cost when purchasing a card. To learn per-minute call costs, you must call a customer service number (on the card) and ask. When dialing, follow the calling instructions on the card, which usually require that you punch in 35 or so digits altogether. As you talk, your time on the line is deducted from your account.

There are some security issues with phone debit cards. The card often has no magnetic stripe or microchip; instead it just has an account number, so when you use your card in a public place, be careful – you are vulnerable to thieves who will watch you punch in the account number. If given the opportunity, they will memorize it and use your card to make phone calls to all corners of the earth.

In addition, when you purchase a phone debit card, the account number should be covered up (by scratch-off paint or a paper wrapper) to keep it a secret. If the number is exposed to view when you buy the card, you

must assume that it has already been used by someone and is worthless.

## Fax & Telegram

Fax machines are easy to find in the USA, at shipping companies like Mail Boxes Etc, hotel business-service centers and photocopy services, but be prepared to pay high prices (over $1 a page). Telegrams can be sent from Western Union offices. Call for information (☎ 800-325-6000).

## Email & Internet Access

If you want to surf the Net or send the occasional email message, most public libraries have a computer with Internet access. Other options are an Internet cafe (for worldwide lists of cybercafes, browse www.traveltales .com or www.netcafeguide.com); a copy center (such as Kinko's, which charges about $10 per hour); or a hotel that caters to business travelers. Some hostels even offer Internet access to their guests. The cheapest way to have email access while traveling is to get a free web-based email account from Hotmail (www.hotmail.com), Yahoo (www .yahoo.com) or Netscape (www.netscape .com) that you can access from any online computer with a browser.

If you're traveling with a computer and modem, you may be able to connect to the Internet from your hotel room. Many hotel phones now have standard RJ-11 jacks labeled 'Data' into which you can safely plug your modem cord. Before you plug into a regular wall-mounted phone jack, ask if it's connected to a PBX (ie, a private branch exchange; found mainly in big hotels and office buildings). If it is, it may fry your modem. What you want is a normal 'analog' phone jack.

Then you have to program your computer to dial an Internet service provider (ISP) – this can be difficult if the ISP is not a local or 800 number, because most cheap and mid-range accommodations won't let you direct-dial a long-distance number. If you're using a phone card, you (or the computer) will have to dial at least two numbers and supply a personal identification number (PIN).

If you can get access to a direct-dial long-distance phone connection, set your modem to make an international call to your ISP at home. You can upload or download a big bunch of email at your regular address within a minute or so, but if you want to stay online for a while, the phone call gets expensive.

The best solution is probably to sign up with a big US service provider that has local access throughout the country (eg, Earthlink, AOL, Compuserve). You can do this before you leave home or when you arrive in the USA. If you have a credit card, the ISP should have you up and running in a few days, with a user name, password and email address for about $30 for the first month.

With a little technical savvy, you can access your home email on the road from any online computer. Change the POP3 email settings on the computer to connect to your home ISP (before you leave, ask your ISP what settings to use). Just be sure to switch the settings back to the defaults, or the next person to use the computer will download your email.

Cities and most larger towns – especially college towns – have cybercafes where you can retrieve and send email.

## INTERNET RESOURCES
The World Wide Web is a rich resource for travelers. You can research your trip, hunt down bargain airfares, book hotels, check on weather conditions or chat with locals and other travelers about the best places to visit (or avoid!).

There's no better place to start your Web explorations than the Lonely Planet website (www.lonelyplanet.com). Here you'll find succinct summaries on traveling to most places on earth, postcards from other travelers, and the Thorn Tree bulletin board, where you can ask questions before you go or dispense advice when you get back. You can also find travel news and updates to many of our most popular guidebooks, and the sub-WWWay section links you to the most useful travel resources elsewhere on the Web.

Website addresses are given throughout this book for many state and city informa-

tion services and for many other helpful organizations and businesses.

## BOOKS
Most books are published in different editions by different publishers in different countries. As a result, a book might be a hardcover rarity in one country while it's readily available in paperback in another. Fortunately, local bookstores and libraries can search by title or author, so these are the best places to find out about the availability of the following recommendations.

For literature, see that section in the Facts about New England chapter.

### Lonely Planet
Lonely Planet's *New York City*; *New York, New Jersey & Pennsylvania*; and *Washington, DC & the Capital Region* are good supplemental guides for travelers exploring the East Coast. Lonely Planet's *Canada* is useful for those who intend to continue their journey north.

### Guidebooks
It is hoped that the guidebook you have in your hands can provide you with all of the information you may need on a first, second or later tour through New England. But obviously, no single book can tell all travelers everything they want to know.

For exploring New England's several states in greater detail, you may want to consult the Explorer's Guide series by The Countryman Press. *Cape Cod and the Islands: An Explorer's Guide*, by Kimberly Grant, has 390 pages on that area alone. These guides are available at bookstores in New England or from The Countryman Press, PO Box 175, Woodstock, VT 05091-0175.

A guide specific to Boston's historic and modern architecture is Susan and Michael Southworth's *The Boston Society of Architects' AIA Guide to Boston*, 2nd edition. It details general walking tours as well as specific buildings not only in the city, but also in Charlestown and Cambridge.

For those who want to spend their New England vacation pursuing outdoor activities such as biking, fishing, hiking and skiing,

*Frommer's Great Outdoor Guide to New England,* by Stephen Jermanok, has information on everything from where to go to what gear to take.

Excellent, detailed trail guides (with maps) of the Appalachian Trail and the White Mountain National Forest trail system are published by the Appalachian Mountain Club (AMC; ☎ 617-523-0636, www.outdoors .org), 5 Joy St, Boston, MA 02108.

The Green Mountain Club (☎ 802-244-7037), RR1, Box 650, Waterbury Center, VT 05677, publishes some excellent hikers' materials, including the *Guide Book of the Long Trail* ($10), complete with 16 color topographical maps. The Long Trail is a primitive footpath that follows the crest of Vermont's Green Mountains 265 miles from Canada to Massachusetts, with 175 miles of side trails and more than 62 rustic cabins and lean-tos for shelter.

For more on hiking, see the Activities section later in this chapter.

## History

*The Flowering of New England,* by Van Wyck Brooks, is a Pulitzer Prize-winning work on New England writers, such as Hawthorne and Thoreau, who shaped contemporary ideas.

*Literary New England,* by William Corbett, is a guidebook to the historic literary sites of New England.

*Inside New England,* by Judson Hale, is a witty combination of anecdotes, history and highly opinionated satire.

*How New England Happened,* by Christina Tree (Little, Brown and Co), is the definitive traveler's history of the New England region.

## FILMS

*Little Women* (1994), Louisa May Alcott's wonderful book about girls growing up in 19th-century Concord, Massachusetts, has been made into a movie starring Susan Sarandon as Marmie.

*Jaws* (1975), the improbable but still terrifying story of a great white shark attacking swimmers on New England beaches, is widely available on video.

*On Golden Pond* (1981), the story of two lovers in their declining years, was filmed at New Hampshire's Squam Lake and features fine performances by Henry Fonda and Katharine Hepburn.

John Huston's classic *Moby Dick* (1956), with Gregory Peck and Orson Welles, is a wonderful introduction to New England maritime life in the 19th century.

*School Ties,* the story of a working-class scholarship student at an elite New England prep school, was filmed at the Middlesex School in Concord, Massachusetts. *The Witches of Eastwick* was filmed in Duxbury, Massachusetts.

*Housesitter,* with Steve Martin and Goldie Hawn, is a light romantic comedy set in a fictional New England town somewhere west of Boston, but it was filmed in Concord and Duxbury, Massachusetts.

*The Crucible,* with Daniel Day-Lewis and Winona Ryder, is a 1996 film adaptation of Arthur Miller's play about the Salem witch trials.

## NEWSPAPERS & MAGAZINES

More than 1500 daily newspapers are published in the USA, with a combined circulation of about 60 million. The newspaper with the highest circulation is the *Wall Street Journal,* followed by *USA Today,* the *New York Times* and the *Los Angeles Times,* which are all available in major cities.

The region's major newspaper, on sale throughout New England, is the highly regarded *Boston Globe,* followed by the more popular tabloid *Boston Herald.*

Many smaller cities and large towns have their own local newspapers, published daily or weekly.

Boston and Cambridge have newsstands that sell many foreign publications; see the 'Bookstores' boxed text in the Boston chapter.

For the frequent traveler to New England, *Yankee Traveler* (nine issues a year – $36 for a subscription or $5 per copy; write to PO Box 37021, Boone, IA 50037-0021) is a helpful newsletter from the travel editors of *Yankee Magazine* (www.newengland.com, PO Box 523, Dublin, NH 03444). It has an ideal format for those living in and around New England, offering destination recommendations and reviews for the coming months, but it isn't available at newsstands. *Yankee Magazine* is available at stores throughout New England.

## RADIO & TV

All rental cars have radios, and travelers can choose from hundreds of radio stations. Each station follows a format, which may be to play classical music, country and western, rock and roll, jazz, easy-listening, or 'golden oldies.' FM stations mainly carry popular music. On the AM (middle wave) frequencies, 'talk radio' rules: A more or less intelligent or outrageous radio host receives telephone calls from listeners, makes comments and expresses opinions.

National Public Radio (NPR) features a more level-headed approach to news, discussion, music and more. NPR normally broadcasts on the lower end of the FM dial.

Most hotel and motel rooms have color TVs that receive perhaps several dozen channels, including the major broadcast networks: Public Broadcasting System (PBS), the American Broadcasting Company (ABC), National Broadcasting Company (NBC), FOX and Columbia Broadcasting System (CBS), as well as the many cable stations, including CNN.

## PHOTOGRAPHY & VIDEO
### Film & Equipment

All major brands of film are available at reasonable prices. Every town of any size has at least one photo shop that stocks a variety of fresh film, cameras and accessories.

In most towns and tourist centers, some shops can develop your color print film in one hour (that can end up being two or so), or at least the same day, for an extra charge. Processing a roll of 100 ASA 35mm color print film with 24 exposures will typically cost about $7 for regular service.

Film can be damaged by excessive heat, so don't leave your camera and film in the car on a hot summer's day and avoid placing your camera on the dashboard while you are driving.

It's worth carrying a spare battery for your camera to avoid disappointment when your camera dies in the middle of nowhere. If you're buying a new camera for your trip, do so several weeks before you leave and practice using it.

### Video Systems

Overseas visitors should remember that the USA and Canada use the National Television System Committee (NTSC) color TV and video standard, which is not compatible with the PAL and SECAM standards used in Africa, Europe, Asia and Australia unless converted. If you buy an NTSC video movie and put it in your PAL or SECAM videocassette player, you'll get only garbled images and sound.

### Restrictions

There are virtually no restrictions on photography, except within museums and at musical and artistic performances.

### Airport Security

All air passengers must pass their luggage through X-ray machines, which are said to pose no danger to most films. If you'd like to bypass the X-ray scanner, prepare: Unpack your film from boxes and plastic film cans and have all the film canisters readily visible in a plastic bag. You really only need to do this for very high-speed film (1600 ASA and above).

## TIME

The USA (excluding Alaska and Hawaii) spans four time zones.

New England is on US Eastern Time, five hours earlier than GMT/UTC, and three hours later than US Pacific Time. When it's noon in Boston, it's 5 pm in London and 9 am in San Francisco.

New England observes daylight saving time. Clocks are set ahead one hour on the first Sunday in April and back one hour on the last Sunday in October.

## ELECTRICITY

Electric current is 110 to 120 volts, 60-cycle. Appliances built to take 220- to 240-volt,

50-cycle current (as in Europe and Asia) will need a converter (transformer) and a US-style plug adapter with two flat pins, or three (two flat, one round) pins. Plugs with three pins don't fit into a two-hole socket, but adapters are easy to buy at hardware shops and drugstores.

## WEIGHTS & MEASURES
The USA uses a modified version of the traditional English measuring system of inches, feet, yards, miles, ounces, pounds and gallons. See the inside back cover of this book for a conversion chart.

Here are some easy-to-remember rules of thumb: A yard is slightly less than a meter, and a mile is about 1.6km; a pound is slightly less than half a kilogram; a normal 12oz soft-drink can or bottle holds slightly more than a third of a liter, and a quart of liquid is slightly less than a liter.

More precisely, distances are measured in inches (1 inch equals 2.54cm), feet (1 foot is equal to 30.48cm), yards (1 yard equals 0.9144m) and miles (1 mile equals 1.609km). Twelve inches equal 1 foot; 3 feet equal 1 yard (.914m); 1760 yards, or 5280 feet, equal 1 mile (1.61km).

Dry weights are in ounces (1oz equals 28.35g), pounds (1lb equals 453.592g) and tons (1 ton equals 1016kg). Sixteen ounces equal 1lb; 2000lb equal 1 ton.

Liquids are measured by the fluid ounce (1oz equals 29.573ml), the cup (8oz equal 0.237 liter), the pint (1 pint equals 16oz or 0.473 liter), the quart (1 quart equals 32oz, 2 pints or 0.946 liter) and the gallon (1 gallon equals 4 quarts or 3.784 liters). Note that the US pint equals 16 fluid oz, not 20 as in the Imperial (British) system. The US gallon, at 64oz, is 20% less than the Imperial gallon (it takes 1.2 US gallons to make an Imperial gallon). Wine bottles tend to be 70 centiliters or 750 milliliters. Gasoline is dispensed by the US gallon.

The metric system is used in certain situations in the USA. Most commercial products have labels giving their weight, volume or length in metric measure as well as the traditional one. Cars sold in the USA usually have speedometers that are marked in kilometers per hour (kph) as well as miles per hour (mph).

## LAUNDRY
Pricier hotels and motels usually provide laundry and dry-cleaning services, but it is often faster, and certainly cheaper, to find the nearest laundromat (self-service coin-operated laundry) or dry cleaners yourself. Ask a local, search in the nearest shopping center (but *not* in a shopping mall), or check the local yellow pages under 'Laundries – Self-Service' and 'Cleaners.'

## RECYCLING
It is illegal to litter highways, streets, sidewalks or other public spaces. Fines can be stiff, though enforcement is usually lax. Litter clean-up costs governments millions of dollars annually.

Virtually all commercial beverage containers sold in the USA are recyclable. In Connecticut, Maine, Massachusetts and Vermont, containers for soft drinks, beer, etc, are subject to a deposit fee of 5¢ or 10¢ each, payable at purchase and refundable when you redeem the container at a recycling center. Supermarkets, liquor stores and some other places where beverages are sold in these states are usually required to redeem beverage containers, so you can get your nickel or dime back.

In New Hampshire and Rhode Island, beverage containers are not subject to deposit, although they are of course recyclable.

Whether you get your deposit back or not, please recycle your containers. Many highway rest stops and other public facilities (such as airports and bus and train stations) have trash and recycling bins side by side; the recycling bins are usually labeled 'cans and bottles.' In places where many newspapers may be discarded, such as airports and train stations, there are newspaper recycling bins.

Wine bottles are not subject to deposit but are recyclable, as are most sanitary paper drink containers, such as milk and juice boxes.

Many other packaging materials made of plastic, metal, paper or cardboard are recyclable but are collected by towns according to local recycling plans.

By the way, it is a serious legal offense in most states to dispose of hazardous materials such as petroleum fuels or lubricants (eg, used motor oil) in any way other than through an establishment licensed to accept them, such as an auto repair shop or town recycling center.

## TOILETS
Americans have many names for public toilet facilities. The most common name is 'rest room.' Other names include 'ladies'/men's room,' 'comfort station,' 'facility' and 'sanitary facility.'

You will find relatively clean public toilets in airports, bars, large stores, museums, state and national parks, restaurants, hotels and tourist information offices. The ones in bus, train and highway fuel stations and rest stops might be clean or might not, but most are still usable. Not all fuel stations have toilets; among those that do, the quality varies considerably. Public toilets in city parks and other public places have mostly been closed due to criminal and sexual misuse.

## HEALTH
In an emergency, dial ☎ 911 from any telephone for assistance.

Boston is among the world's most highly regarded centers for medical care and research, with a dozen major hospitals and a half dozen medical schools. The quality of care is generally very high, as are its costs.

All other cities in New England – even small ones – have hospitals. To find one, look on the highways and roads for the standard hospital symbol, a white 'H' on a blue background. Many cities also have walk-in clinics where you can show up without an appointment, see a nurse, nurse-practitioner or doctor for a minor ailment or preliminary diagnosis, and pay for it in cash or by credit card.

Make sure you're healthy before you start traveling. If you are embarking on a long trip, make sure your teeth are in good shape. If you wear glasses, take a spare pair

and your prescription. You can get new spectacles made up quickly and competently for around $100, depending on the prescription and frame you choose. If you require a particular medication, take an adequate supply. Bring a prescription as well, although the dispensing of prescription medicines is regulated by each state, and a prescription written by a doctor licensed to practice medicine in one state may not be accepted by a pharmacy in another state.

No immunizations are needed, unless you are coming to the USA from a country that has experienced a recent cholera or yellow fever epidemic.

### Health Insurance
Be sure that you have some form of health insurance that will pay your US medical bills in full should you need medical care while in the USA. Bills for an illness that requires hospitalization can easily exceed $1000 or even $2000 per day, and you will be expected to pay even at publicly supported government hospitals unless you can show that you are destitute.

Some policies specifically exclude 'dangerous activities' such as scuba diving, motorcycling and even hiking. If these activities are on your agenda, avoid this sort of policy.

You may prefer a policy that pays doctors or hospitals directly, rather than making you pay first and claim later. If you have to claim later, keep all documentation. Some policies ask you to call collect (reverse charges) to a center in your home country for an immediate assessment of your problem.

Check whether the policy covers ambulance fees or an emergency flight home. If you have to stretch out, you will need two seats, and somebody has to pay for them! (For more on insurance, see Travel Insurance under the Visas & Documents section, earlier in this chapter.)

### Travel Health Guides
For comprehensive health information and advice for travelers, browse the US Centers for Disease Control and Prevention's website (www.cdc.gov/travel). Lonely Planet's website has lots of good travel health advice

(www.lonelyplanet.com/health), and many other travel health sites are listed. Visit dir.yahoo.com/Health/Travel.

Books on travel health include *Travelers' Health*, by Dr Richard Dawood, a comprehensive, easy to read, authoritative and highly recommended book, but rather large to lug around, and *Travel with Children*, by Maureen Wheeler, which offers basic advice on travel health for younger children.

## Heat Exhaustion

Dehydration or salt deficiency can cause heat exhaustion. Heat exhaustion is characterized by fatigue, lethargy, headaches, giddiness and muscle cramps. Always carry – and use – a water bottle on long trips.

## Hypothermia

If you plan to camp, hike or ski in New England, remember this: Changing weather can leave you vulnerable to exposure. After dark, autumn temperatures can drop from balmy to below freezing, while a sudden soaking and high winds can lower your body temperature rapidly. On Mt Washington, it can be summer at the base and deep winter at the summit. If possible, don't travel alone; partners are more likely to avoid hypothermia successfully. If you must travel alone, especially when hiking, be sure someone knows your route and when you expect to return.

## Motion Sickness

New England lives by the sea. You should take advantage of this by enjoying ferry and whale-watching cruises, but follow these guidelines:

- Go to a pharmacy or health-food store before your trip and buy some ginger capsules (a natural motion-sickness preventive). Take several about a half-hour before boarding a boat. If you prefer commercial anti-motion sickness preparations, remember that these must also be taken before the trip commences. They can cause drowsiness.

- Eat lightly and avoid alcohol before and during a trip to reduce the chances of motion sickness. If you are prone to motion sickness, try to find a place that minimizes disturbance, for example,

near the wing if you are on aircraft or near the center on boats or buses.

- Fresh air usually helps; motor exhaust hurts. When you're feeling sick, it's too late.

## Jet Lag

Jet lag occurs because many of the body's functions (such as temperature, pulse rate and emptying of the bladder and bowels) are regulated by internal 24-hour cycles called circadian rhythms. When we travel long distances rapidly, it takes our bodies time to adjust to the 'new time' of our destination, and we may experience fatigue, disorientation, insomnia, anxiety, impaired concentration and loss of appetite. These effects begin to fade within three days of arrival, but there are ways of minimizing the impact of jet lag:

- Rest for a couple of days prior to departure; avoid late nights and last-minute dashes for traveler's checks, passport, etc.

- Select flight schedules that minimize sleep deprivation; arriving late in the day means you can go to sleep soon after you arrive. For very long flights, try to organize a stopover.

- Avoid excessive eating and don't drink alcohol during the flight. Instead, drink plenty of noncarbonated, nonalcoholic drinks such as fruit juice or water.

- Make yourself comfortable by wearing loose-fitting clothes and perhaps bringing an eye mask and ear plugs to help you sleep.

## Sexually Transmitted Diseases

Sexual contact with an infected partner spreads these diseases. While abstinence is the only 100% effective preventive, practicing safe sex and using latex condoms can reduce the chance of infection by diseases such as gonorrhea and syphilis (the most common STDs) and HIV/AIDS.

Gonorrhea and syphilis can be cured but can be debilitating if left untreated. Herpes can be treated but not cured. If you suspect that you've caught an STD, have an examination and explore your options.

### HIV/AIDS

Any exposure to blood, blood products or bodily fluids may place you in danger of contracting HIV/AIDS. In addition to unprotected sex, infection can come from sharing contaminated needles, including needles re-used for acupuncture, tattooing or body piercing (a clean-looking needle or tool, or a healthy-looking person, may be carrying HIV). HIV/AIDS can also be spread through infected blood transfusions, though the blood supply in the USA is screened and presumably safe. Symptoms may appear only months after infection, so it is impossible to detect a person's HIV status without a blood test.

A good resource for help and information is the US Centers for Disease Control AIDS hotline (☎ 800-342-2437, 800-344-7432 in Spanish, www.cdc.gov). See the 'HIV/AIDS & Entering the USA' boxed text, earlier in this chapter.

### Ticks & Lyme Disease

Ticks are parasitic arachnids that may be present in brush, forest and grasslands, where hikers often get them on their legs or in their boots. Adult ticks suck blood from hosts by burying their heads in the skin but are often found unattached and can simply be brushed off.

Deer ticks, which can carry and spread a serious bacterial infection called Lyme disease, are found throughout New England. The ticks are usually very small (some as small as a pinhead) and thus are not likely to be noticed casually – you must look carefully for them. A bite from a Lyme disease-infected deer tick may show a red welt and circular 'halo' of redness within a day or two, or there may be no symptoms beyond a minor itch. Also, mild flu-like symptoms – headache, nausea, etc – may follow or may not.

Lyme disease can be treated successfully, but early treatment is essential. If left untreated, Lyme disease causes mental and muscular deterioration.

The best preventive measures are to wear clothing that covers your arms and legs when walking in grassy or wooded areas, apply insect repellent containing DEET on exposed skin and around ankles and trouser leg openings, and always check your body

(and especially your child's and pet's bodies) for ticks after outdoor activities.

If one has attached itself to you, use tweezers to pull it straight out – do not twist it. If a small chunk of skin comes out along with the head, that's good – you've got it all, and no part of the tick will be left to cause infection. Do not touch the tick with a hot object like a match or a cigarette, because this can cause it to regurgitate noxious gut substances or saliva into the wound. And do not rub oil, alcohol or petroleum jelly on it. If you get sick in the next couple of weeks, consult a doctor.

## WOMEN TRAVELERS

If you are traveling alone, maintain a little extra awareness of your surroundings. People are generally friendly and happy to help travelers. The following suggestions should reduce or eliminate the chances of problems, but the best advice is to trust your instincts.

In general, you might want to ask for advice at your hotel or telephone the visitors' center if you are unsure which areas are considered unsafe, especially when making room reservations.

Avoiding vulnerable situations and conducting yourself in a common-sense manner will help you to avoid most problems. You're more vulnerable if you've been drinking or using drugs than if you're sober; and you're more vulnerable alone than if you're with company. If you don't want company, most men will respect a firm but polite 'no thank you.'

Don't pick up hitchhikers. At night, avoid getting out of your car to flag down help; turn on your hazard lights and/or display a white cloth outside the driver's-side window or from the radio antenna and wait for official help to arrive. Leaving the hood (bonnet) of your car raised is also a signal that you need assistance.

Some women protect themselves with a whistle, pepper spray or self-defense training. If you decide to purchase a spray, ask which sprays are legal at a local police station. Laws regarding sprays vary from state to state. It is a federal felony to carry defensive sprays on airplanes.

If despite all your precautions you are assaulted, call the police (☎ 911). Many cities have rape crisis centers established to aid victims of rape. For the telephone number of the nearest center, call directory information (☎ 411 or 1 + area code + 555-1212).

The headquarters of the National Organization for Women (NOW; ☎ 202-331-0066, now@now.org, www.now.org), 1000 16th St NW, suite 700, Washington, DC 20036, is a good resource for a variety of information and can refer you to state and local chapters. Planned Parenthood (☎ 212-541-7800, communications@ppfa.org, www .plannedparenthood.org), 810 Seventh Ave, New York, NY 10019, can refer you to clinics throughout the country and offer advice on medical issues. Check the yellow pages under 'Social & Human Services,' 'Clinics' and 'Health Services' for local resources.

## GAY & LESBIAN TRAVELERS
Gay communities are most visible in the major coastal cities, such as San Francisco and New York, which have the largest gay populations, and where it is easier for gay men and women to live their lives with a certain amount of openness. When you travel outside of large cities, it is much harder to be open about your sexual preferences. Gay travelers should be careful – holding hands in public might get you bashed.

Larger US cities often have a gay neighborhood or area. One example is the South End in Boston. Provincetown, on Cape Cod, happens to be a small-town gay mecca. Most cities have a gay or alternative newspaper that lists current events or at least provides phone numbers of local organizations.

Some good national guidebooks are *The Womens' Traveller*, providing listings for lesbians; *Damron's Address Book*, for men; and *Damron Accommodations*, with gay-owned/gay-friendly hotel, B&B and guest-house listings nationwide. All three books are published by the Damron Company (☎ 415-255-0404, 800-462-6654, www.damron.com), PO Box 422458, San Francisco, CA 94142-2458. Ferrari's *Places for Women* and *Places for Men* are also useful, as are guides to specific cities (check out *Betty & Pansy's Severe*

*Queer Reviews* to various cities, available in some bookstores; it's also available online from www.gaymart.com).

Another good resource is the *Gay Yellow Pages* (☎ 212-674-0120, gayyellowpages .com), PO Box 533, Village Station, NY 10014-0533, which has a national edition as well as regional editions.

National resource numbers include the National AIDS/HIV Hotline (☎ 800-342-2437), the National Gay/Lesbian Task Force in Washington, DC (☎ 202-332-6483), and the Lambda Legal Defense Fund in New York City (☎ 212-995-8585) and Los Angeles (☎ 213-937-2727).

## DISABLED TRAVELERS
Travel within the USA is becoming easier for people with disabilities. Public buildings (including hotels, restaurants, theaters and museums) are now required by law to be wheelchair accessible and to have available rest room facilities. Public transportation services (buses, trains and taxis) must be made accessible to all, including those in wheelchairs, and telephone companies are required to provide relay operators for the hearing impaired. Many banks now provide ATM instructions in Braille. Curb ramps are common, and some of the busier roadway intersections have audible crossing signals.

Larger private and chain hotels have suites for disabled guests. Major car rental agencies offer hand-controlled models at no extra charge. All major airlines, intercity buses and Amtrak trains allow guide dogs to accompany passengers and frequently sell two-for-one packages when seriously disabled passengers require attendants.

Airlines also provide assistance for connecting, boarding and deplaning the flight – just ask for assistance when making your reservation. (Note: Airlines must accept wheelchairs as checked baggage and have an onboard chair available, though some advance notice may be required on smaller aircraft.) Of course, the more populous the area, the greater the likelihood of facilities for the disabled, so it's important to call ahead to see what is available.

Global Access: A Network for Disabled Travelers (www.geocities.com/Paris/1502/index.html) provides trip advice, lists of guidebooks for the handicapped and an excellent variety of links to other websites with similar information.

A number of organizations and tour providers specialize in the needs of disabled travelers. The Society for the Advancement of Travel for the Handicapped (SATH; ☎ 212-447-7284), 347 Fifth Ave, suite 610, New York, NY 10016, publishes *Open World* magazine.

## SENIOR TRAVELERS

When retirees leave the time clock behind and the myriad 'senior' discounts begin to apply, the prospect of rediscovering the USA exerts a magnetic pull for foreigners and the native-born alike. Though the age when the benefits begin varies with the attraction, travelers from 50 years and up can expect to receive cut rates and benefits. Be sure to inquire about such rates at hotels, museums and restaurants *before* you make your reservation.

Visitors to national parks and campgrounds can cut costs greatly by using the Golden Age Passport, a card that allows US citizens age 62-plus (and those traveling in the same car) free admission nationwide and a 50% reduction on camping fees. You can apply in person for any of these at any national park – the only one in New England is Acadia, in Maine – or regional office of the US Forest Service (USFS) or National Park Service (NPS). Or call ☎ 800-280-2267 for information and ordering.

Some national advocacy groups that can help in planning your travels include the following:

American Association of Retired Persons
(☎ 800-227-7737, www.aarp.org) 601 E St NW, Washington, DC 20049. The AARP is an advocacy group for Americans 50-plus and is a good resource for travel bargains. Annual membership for US residents is $8.

Elderhostel
(☎ 617-426-8056, 877-426-8056, www.elderhostel.org) 75 Federal St, Boston, MA 02110-1941. Elderhostel is a nonprofit organization that offers seniors the opportunity to attend academic college courses throughout the USA and Canada. The programs last one to three weeks, include meals and accommodations and are open to people 55-plus and their companions.

Grand Circle Travel
(☎ 800-248-3737, www.gct.com) 347 Congress St, Boston, MA 02210. This organization offers escorted tours aimed at travelers age 50 and older in a variety of formats and distributes a free useful booklet, *Going Abroad: 101 Tips for Mature Travelers.*

## TRAVEL WITH CHILDREN

Many establishments and services offer discounted fees and fares for children. Age limits for discounts vary. Hotels and motels may count anyone under 18 as a child, though B&Bs rarely offer discounts and may not welcome children at all. At museums, a child may be someone aged three to nine, or five to 12. You'll have to ask at each establishment.

Some restaurants offer a limited selection of inexpensive child-friendly foods; ask for the children's menu. Airlines sometimes discount international fares for children's tickets, but these are often more expensive than the cheapest APEX adult tickets. Many buses and tours have discounted children's prices (often 50%). Car rental companies provide infant seats for their cars on request.

Various children's activities are mentioned in appropriate places in this book. For information on enjoying travel with the young ones, read *Travel with Children*, written by Lonely Planet cofounder Maureen Wheeler.

## USEFUL ORGANIZATIONS
### American Automobile Association

AAA ('Triple-A'; ☎ 800-222-4357, www.aaa.com) is an umbrella organization uniting a variety of local and regional auto clubs that use the AAA name. Members belong to a certain club and also may use the facilities of any other AAA club in the USA. Clubs have offices in all major cities and many resort towns where they provide useful information, free maps and routine road services such as tire repair and towing (free within a limited radius).

AAA members often receive discounts on attraction admission fees and on lodgings. The annual membership fee depends upon the particular club you join, but may range from $30 to $60; there may also be a smaller one-time initiation fee. Members of its foreign affiliates, such as the Automobile Association in the UK, are entitled to the same services. See the Car section in the Getting Around chapter for more details.

## Appalachian Mountain Club

The AMC (☎ 617-523-0636, www.outdoors .org), 5 Joy St, Boston, MA 02108, sells hiking guides and maps to the White Mountains and other New England backcountry. See the Activities section, later in this chapter, for more details on hiking.

## Appalachian Trail Conference

The Appalachian National Scenic Trail is administered by the Appalachian Trail Conference (☎ 304-535-6331, www.nps.gov/aptr), PO Box 807, Harpers Ferry, WV 25425-0807, in cooperation with the National Park Service (see below). See the Activities section, later in this chapter, for details on the trail

## Hostelling International/ American Youth Hostels

HI/AYH (☎ 202-783-6161, fax 783-6171, hiayhserv@hiayh.org, www.hiayh.org), PO Box 37613, Washington, DC 20013, is the successor to the International Youth Hostel Federation (IYHF). For hostel listings in the USA and Canada, get HI/AYH's *Hostelling North America*, the official guide. For a list of New England hostel locales and organizations by state, see the Accommodations section, later in this chapter.

## National Park Service & US Forest Service

The NPS and USFS administer the use of national parks and forests. National forests are less protected than parks, allowing commercial use of some areas (usually logging or privately owned recreational facilities).

National parks most often surround spectacular natural features and cover hundreds of square miles. A full range of accommodations can be found in and around national parks. In New England, there's only one national park, Acadia National Park in Maine, but the NPS also administers the Freedom Trail in Boston and other frequently visited historic places in the area.

Contact the NPS for national park campground information and for reservations (☎ 800-365-2267, www.nps.gov), National Park Service Public Inquiry, Dept of the Interior, 18th and C Sts NW, Washington, DC 20013.

Current information about national forests can be obtained from ranger stations or at www.recreation.gov. National forest campground and reservation information can be obtained by calling ☎ 800-280-2267 or writing to the NPS address listed above.

## DANGERS & ANNOYANCES

The USA has a widespread reputation, partly true but also propagated and exaggerated by the media, as a dangerous place because of the availability of firearms. New England's cities – Boston, Burlington, Hartford, New Haven, Portland, Providence, Springfield, Worcester – are among the safer ones, but all suffer to some degree from the crimes of pickpockets, muggers (robbers), carjackers and rapists.

As in other cities throughout the world, the majority of crimes takes place in the poorest neighborhoods among the local residents. The signs of a bad or dangerous neighborhood are obvious, and pretty much the same as in any other country. Observe the following standard common-sense urban safety rules and you should have no trouble:

- Street people and panhandlers may approach visitors in the larger cities and towns; nearly all of them are harmless. It's an individual judgment call as to whether it's appropriate to offer them money or anything else.

- Carry valuables such as money, traveler's checks, credit cards, passport, etc, in a money belt or pouch underneath your clothing for maximum safety from pickpockets. This is usually only necessary in crowded areas such as airports, subways, city buses, markets or concerts, but it doesn't hurt to do it all the time.

- Lock valuables in your suitcase in your hotel room or put them in the hotel safe when you're not there.
- Don't leave anything visible in your car when you park it in a city, particularly at night. Always lock your car when you leave it.
- Avoid walking or driving through poorer neighborhoods, especially at night. Don't walk in parks at night. Avoid walking along any empty street at night. Aim to use ATMs in well-trafficked areas. Well-lit streets busy with other walkers are usually all right.

As for rural dangers, avoid forests – or indeed anywhere where game and hunters roam – during the November hunting season, especially at dawn and dusk, when game is most active. 'No Hunting' signs are widely ignored and are not a guarantee of safety.

## EMERGENCY

Most states, cities and towns in New England are connected to the emergency notification system reached by dialing ☎ 911 from any telephone (no money required). Operators who answer 911 calls can fill your need for help from the police, firefighters, emergency medical response teams or other emergency services.

In areas without 911 service (or if dialing 911 does not work), dial ☎ 0 for the telephone operator, who will connect you to the necessary local emergency service.

The Travelers Aid Society (☎ 617-542-7286, www.travelersaid.org), 17 East St, Boston, MA 02111, is an organization of volunteers who do their best to help travelers solve their problems. Volunteers are on duty at Boston's Logan International Airport (☎ 617-567-5385) and at Boston's Amtrak South Station (☎ 617-737-2880). For offices in other large New England cities, look in the local yellow pages or call directory assistance at ☎ 411 and ask for the Travelers Aid Society.

## LEGAL MATTERS

If you are stopped by the police for any reason, bear in mind that there is no system of paying fines on the spot. For traffic offenses, the police officer will explain your options to you. Attempting to pay the fine to the officer is frowned upon at best and may lead to a charge of bribery to compound your troubles. Should the officer decide that you should pay up front, he or she can take you directly to a magistrate instead of allowing you the usual 30-day period to pay the fine.

If you are arrested for more serious offenses, you are allowed to remain silent, entitled to have an attorney present during any interrogation and presumed innocent until proven guilty. There is no legal reason to speak to a police officer if you don't wish. All persons who are arrested are legally allowed (and given) the right to make one phone call. If you don't have a lawyer or family member to help you, call your embassy or consulate. The police will give you the number upon request.

The minimum age for drinking alcoholic beverages is 21. You'll need a government-issued photo ID (such as a passport or US driver's license) to prove your age. Stiff fines, jail time and penalties can be incurred if you are caught driving under the influence of alcohol or providing alcohol to minors. During festive holidays and special events, roadblocks with breathalyzer tests are sometimes set up to deter drunk drivers. Be aware of your alcohol consumption and drive responsibly.

## BUSINESS HOURS

Public and private office hours are normally 8 or 9 am to 5 pm weekdays.

For post office business hours, see Post & Communications, earlier in this chapter.

### Banks

Customary banking hours are 9 am to 3 pm weekdays, but most banks have extended customer service hours until 5 pm (or even 8 or 9 pm on Thursday) and on Saturday from 9 am to 2 pm or later. No banks are open on Sunday except the currency exchange booths at international airports.

### Fuel Stations

Fuel stations on major highways are open 24 hours a day, seven days a week. City fuel stations usually open at 6 or 7 am and stay open until 8 or 9 pm. In small towns and villages, hours may be only from 7 or 8 am to 7 or 8 pm.

## Museums

Most museums open at 10 am and close at 5 pm Tuesday through Sunday (closed on Monday), but there are variations, so call to be sure.

Some smaller museums and exhibits are seasonal and open only in the warmer months.

Many museums and attractions close on Thanksgiving Day (the fourth Thursday in November), Christmas Day and New Year's Day.

## Stores & Markets

Most stores are open Monday through Saturday 9:30 or 10 am to 5:30 or 6 pm (usually later in big cities). Many stores are also open 11 am or noon until 5 pm on Sunday.

All cities, and many large towns, have at least a few 'convenience stores,' open 24 hours a day, which sell food, beverages, newspapers and some household items. Many highway fuel stations, also open 24 hours a day, have small shops selling snacks, beverages and frequently needed items.

Most city supermarkets stay open from 8 or 9 am to 9 or 10 pm, with shorter hours on Sunday, but some in large cities remain open 24 hours a day, closing only from Sunday evening to Monday morning for maintenance.

## PUBLIC HOLIDAYS & SPECIAL EVENTS

National public holidays are celebrated throughout the USA (though in fact they are mandated by state laws). Banks, schools and government offices (including post offices) are closed and transportation, museums and other services operate on a Sunday schedule. Many stores, however, maintain regular business hours. Holidays falling on weekends are usually observed the following Monday.

| | |
|---|---|
| New Year's Day | January 1 |
| Martin Luther King Jr Day | 3rd Monday in January |
| Presidents' Day | 3rd Monday in February |
| Memorial Day | Last Monday in May |
| Independence Day (the Fourth of July) | July 4 |
| Labor Day | 1st Monday in September |
| Columbus Day | 2nd Monday in October |
| Veterans' Day | November 11 |
| Thanksgiving | 4th Thursday in November |
| Christmas Day | December 25 |

Special events happen all the time throughout New England, including holiday celebrations, harvest celebrations and craft fairs. See Planning, earlier in this chapter, for a month-by-month description of such events.

## ACTIVITIES

New England's mountains may not be as high as the Rockies, but the region has many virtues as an outdoor paradise. With its hundreds of colleges and universities, and cutting-edge research and technology companies, New England has a large population of young, eager outdoor enthusiasts who support efforts to expand recreational opportunities and preserve natural resources.

New Hampshire's White Mountains, Vermont's Green Mountains and the dense forests of northern Maine offer good mountain hiking and rock climbing, camping, canoeing and white-water rafting. The Appalachian Trail runs through several New England states. The thousands of miles of rugged coastline are good for sailing, canoeing, sea kayaking, windsurfing, whale watching and even scuba diving. Swimming, canoeing, boating, fishing and water skiing are available on many of the region's thousands of lakes and ponds. Though the waters of the Atlantic are usually chilly, swimming and other beach sports are popular in summer, particularly in the warmer, sheltered waters of Rhode Island and Cape Cod Bay.

Last but not least, New England is relatively small and manageable: It is entirely possible to begin the day with a climb in New Hampshire's White Mountains and finish it by watching the sunset on a Rhode Island beach.

## Hiking & Walking

The Appalachian National Scenic Trail (☎ 304-535-6331, www.nps.gov/aptr), PO Box 807, Harpers Ferry, WV 25425-0807, usually just called the Appalachian Trail, runs through New England from its northern terminus at Mt Katahdin (5267 feet) in Maine, heading southward through the Maine woods, New Hampshire's White Mountain National Forest, Vermont's Green Mountains and Massachusetts' Berkshire hills. It then crosses into Connecticut and passes north of New York City before continuing south to Springer Mountain in Georgia, 2158 miles away from Mt Katahdin. A full 98% of the trail is on public land (parks, national forests, etc).

Shorter but still challenging, Vermont's Long Trail starts at Jay Peak (3861 feet) in the Northeast Kingdom and follows the Green Mountains south to Bennington. For more on these trails, see the boxed text 'A Month in the Woods' in the Vermont chapter. See also the Guidebooks and Useful Organizations sections, earlier in this chapter.

If you're seeking a shorter trek, Acadia National Park in Maine has a good system of hiking trails as well as a unique, easier (and bikeable) system of unpaved 'carriage roads.'

Most of the region's hundreds of state forests, parks and reservations have walking or hiking trails of varying levels of difficulty. Even many cities and towns have simple trail systems meandering through woodlands, parks and city reservations.

**Mountain Hiking** For mountain hiking and rock climbing, by far the most popular area is the White Mountains' Presidential Range, with Mt Washington (6288 feet) at its apex. Though hardly a challenger to the Rockies or the Alps, Mt Washington has the severest weather in the region, and – please note – at least a few hikers perish or are badly injured on its slopes each year.

Mt Katahdin in Maine's north country is for the serious outdoors types who want wilder country, more adventure and fewer people around. It has remained remote backcountry because it is a considerable distance from New England's cities.

In Vermont's Green Mountains, the best hikes are near Stowe and up Mt Mansfield along the Long Trail.

Mt Greylock (3491 feet), the highest mountain in Massachusetts, is an excellent goal for a day's walk from Williamstown in the northwest corner of the state.

New Hampshire's accessible Mt Monadnock (3165 feet), near Jaffrey just a short distance north of the Massachusetts state line, is the 'beginners' mountain,' a relatively easy climb up a bald granite batholith.

**Organized Hikes** Should you want to see nature with an organized group, Country Walkers, Inc (☎ 802-244-1387, 800-464-9255, www.countrywalkers.com), PO Box 180, Waterbury, VT 05676, organizes four- to five-day walking trips in Vermont and Maine, as well as other parts of the world. Tour participants range from eight to 80 years old and are matched so that they keep about the same pace during each day's 4- to 9-mile trek, covered in three to five hours. Luggage is transported by van, not carried. Lodgings are usually at country inns in rooms with private baths. The four-day weekend trips cost about $1400, five-day trips about $1500. Lodging and all meals are included.

Another company, New England Hiking Holidays (☎ 603-356-9696, 800-869-0949, www.nehikingholidays.com), PO Box 1648, North Conway, NH 03860, runs similar two- to five-day hiking trips throughout New England and other areas, with lodgings and meals at country inns ($625 to $2125).

## Camping

Tent camping is popular in New England and is done mostly in state and national forests and parks. Private campgrounds usually have a few places for tents, but they make their money catering to huge, plush recreational vehicles (RVs) that require facilities such as water, sewer and electricity hookups.

For details on camping, see the Accommodations section, later in this chapter, and the Useful Organizations section, earlier in this chapter.

# Bicycling

New England's varied and visually interesting terrain makes it good for bicycle touring and mountain biking.

Thousands of miles of back roads wander through handsome villages and red-brick towns, far enough apart to give cyclists a sense of being in the country but close enough to provide needed services. Bicycle parts and supplies are available in the larger cities and towns, particularly in college towns.

Rubel Bike Maps (☎ 617-776-6567, www.bikemaps.com), PO Box 1035, Cambridge, MA 02140, publishes good topographic bike maps of the Boston area, Massachusetts' North Shore and Cape Cod.

**Bicycle Touring** The Minuteman Bikeway goes from Boston and Cambridge through Lexington and Bedford almost to Concord, making for a fine getaway from the city (see the Around Boston chapter).

Cape Cod is among the region's best biking areas, with several special bike paths (Shining Sea Bike Path between Falmouth and Woods Hole; Cape Cod Rail Trail from Dennis to Wellfleet; and the paths in the Cape Cod National Seashore near Province-

town). *Cape Cod Bike Book*, by William E Peace, with maps and information on bike rentals, bike paths, rest stops and other necessities, is sold in bookstores on the Cape, and may also be ordered by mail from Cape Cod Bike Book, PO Box 627, South Dennis, MA 02660, for $4.

Getting your car to the islands of Martha's Vineyard, Nantucket or Block Island is expensive (and often, without reservations, impossible). But bicycles move easily and cheaply on the ferries (no reservation needed), and each island has a network of bike paths. The flat terrain and fine sea views make these among the best areas for biking. If you don't have a bike, rent one there.

**Mountain Biking** Many of the region's forest and mountain trails are open to mountain bikers. Be sure you know the rules before heading down the trail. If you plan a mountain-bike tour during the autumn foliage season, probably the best time of the year, reserve your accommodations well in advance.

Many companies operate mountain-bike tours in New England. The Mountain Bike School (☎ 802-464-333, 800-245-7669, www.mountsnow.com), at Mt Snow in Vermont, operates on summer weekends, offering tours of varying difficulty.

Craftsbury Outdoor Center (☎ 802-586-7767), PO Box 31, Craftsbury Common, VT 05827, offers mountain-bike programs at a variety of prices. Bring your own bike, opt for an inn room with shared bath and provide your own meals, and you pay less; if you prefer all the comforts, you pay more.

# Leaf Peeping

Touring by bicycle, car, bus, train, boat or on foot to enjoy the spectacular colors of the region's fall foliage is one of the glories of New England. Special tours are organized by many commercial and nonprofit organizations. The tourist information offices for the New England states can give you names and contact information; see the Tourist Offices section earlier in this chapter.

The easiest way to pinpoint where the peak autumn foliage is on any given September or October day is to call the states' Autumn Foliage Hotlines at these numbers:

| | |
|---|---|
| Massachusetts | ☎ 800-227-6277 |
| Rhode Island | ☎ 800-556-2484 |
| Connecticut | ☎ 800-252-6863 |
| Vermont | ☎ 802-828-3239 |
| New Hampshire | ☎ 800-258-3608 |
| Maine | ☎ 800-533-9595 |

## Swimming & Beaches

The Rhode Island seacoast has excellent beaches. Also, Cape Cod and the islands of Martha's Vineyard and Nantucket, all in Massachusetts, sport that state's best beaches. Cape Cod National Seashore is a glorious array of dunes making their way to the Atlantic.

Maine has a scattering of beaches in its coastal towns, including Ogunquit, Old Orchard Beach, Kennebunkport and Bar Harbor. It also has a few inland lakes, including Rangeley Lake. Swimming in New England's lakes (such as Lake Winnipesaukee in New Hampshire) and ponds can be warmer and more enjoyable than a dip in the chilly ocean.

## White-Water Rafting: How Difficult Is It?

White-water rafting trips are classed according to difficulty:

**Class I** – slow current, no obstructions in the river, very small rapids and low waves
**Class II** – faster current, frequent rapids of medium difficulty, but few obstructions in the river
**Class III** – numerous rapids and large, irregular waves up to 4 feet in height; the raft needs to be maneuvered by an experienced leader
**Class IV** – fast current along a course that is not always easy to maneuver; numerous and often dangerous obstacles and powerful waves
**Class V** – extremely fast and difficult course through long and violent rapids and large, unavoidable and irregular waves
**Class VI** – maximum difficulty, approaching the unnavigable, with significant risk to life and limb

## Canoeing, Kayaking & Rafting

Canoeing is popular in summer throughout New England on ponds, lakes, rivers and along the sheltered parts of its coastline. The heart of riverine canoe activity is undoubtedly North Conway, New Hampshire, but there are many canoe outfitters in Maine as well.

Saco Bound & Downeast Whitewater (☎ 603-447-3002, 800-677-7238, fax 603-447-6278, www.sacobound.com), PO Box 119, Center Conway, NH 03813, can take you on canoe, white-water rafting and inflatable kayak trips in Maine and New Hampshire.

New England Outdoor Center (☎ 207-723-5438, 800-634-7238, www.neoc.com), PO Box 21, Caratunk, ME 04925, leads guided canoe, raft and kayak trips on Maine's Kennebec, Upper Kennebec, Penobscot and Dead Rivers.

Either in rigid or inflatable boats, kayaking is popular wherever there's water, from the quiet ponds of Rhode Island and Connecticut to the Boston waterfront and the wilds of northern Maine. Many outfitters provide rentals and instruction. Perhaps the ultimate New England kayak experience is along the rocky, pine-fringed coasts of Maine.

Only 20 minutes by ferry from Portland, Maine Island Kayak Co (☎ 207-766-2373, 800-796-2373, www.maineislandkayak.com), 70 Luther St, Peaks Island, ME 04108, runs half- and full-day kayak tours ($55/90) among the Diamond Islands in Casco Bay, and more ambitious weekend and five- to 10-day expeditions covering the best reaches of the Maine coast. Nights are spent at low-impact campgrounds on islands along the way. The guides welcome beginners. 'If you can walk a few miles,' they say, 'you can paddle between camps.'

White-water rafting is mostly done in the northern New England states, particularly on New Hampshire's Saco River and on Maine's Kennebec, Upper Kennebec, Penobscot and Dead Rivers. For adventures closer to Boston, contact Zoar Outdoor (☎ 413-339-8596, 800-532-7483, fax 413-337-8436), PO Box 245, Charlemont, MA 01339.

In addition to the companies mentioned above, you can obtain rental craft (canoes,

kayaks, rafts) and equipment, instruction and guide service from these companies:

Magic Falls Rafting Co
(☎ 800-207-7238, www.magicfalls.com)
PO Box 9, West Forks, ME 04985

Maine Whitewater
(☎ 207-672-4814, 800-345-6246,
www.mainewhitewater.com)
PO Box 633, Bingham, ME 04920

North Country Rivers
(☎ 207-923-3492, 800-348-8871, fax 207-923-3850, www.ncrivers.com)
PO Box 47, East Vassalboro, ME 04935

Northern Outdoors
(☎ 207-663-4466, 800-765-7238, fax 207-663-2244, www.northernoutdoors.com) PO Box 100, Route 201, The Forks, ME 04985

Professional River Runners of Maine
(☎ 207-663-2229, 800-325-3911,
www.proriverrunners.com)
PO Box 92, West Forks, ME 04985

Wilderness Expeditions
(☎ 207-534-2242, 800-825-9453, fax 207-534-8835, www.birches.com)
PO Box 41, Rockwood, ME 04478

## Windjammer Cruises

The Maine coast in summer is among the world's finest sail-cruising areas. Tall-masted craft use Camden, Rockport and Rockland as their home ports. A cruise of a few days along the gorgeous Maine coast is a perfect way to forget your daily worries and concentrate on nature for a while. For details, see the Camden section in the Maine chapter.

Cruising isn't limited to Maine. Day cruises are available in many coastal towns, such as Gloucester and Rockport, Massachusetts. They're also available on the islands: Block Island, Rhode Island; and Nantucket and Martha's Vineyard, Massachusetts.

## Whale-Watching Cruises

Once known for their prowess in seeking out whales for slaughter, New England's sea captains now follow the whales with boatloads of camera-carrying summer tourists.

Craft vary from small and old-fashioned fishing vessels to posh, modern, double-hulled speedboats. Whale-watching cruises depart from South County, Rhode Island;

Barnstable, Provincetown, Boston and Gloucester, Massachusetts; Portsmouth, New
Hampshire; and Portland, Boothbay Harbor
and Bar Harbor, Maine, among other coastal
towns.

The captains, equipped with electronic
sounding gear, radios and long experience in
New England waters, usually have little
trouble finding marine behemoths such as
minke whales, finbacks, right whales and
dolphins. If for some reason they fail to sight
a whale, most boats will give you a pass for
another cruise.

When you go whale watching, be prepared. Unless you're an experienced sailor,
pick a day when the sea is calm; stormy days
and the day immediately following a storm
are usually uncomfortably choppy. If you
think you might get seasick (on choppy
seas, most people do), take ginger capsules
(sold at health-food stores) before boarding
the boat. In addition, don't eat a big meal
right before you sail, and avoid alcoholic
beverages.

Some whale-watching necessities include
a sweater or windbreaker, even on hot days,
and a hat, sunglasses and sunblock to protect you from the harsh sunlight from the
sky and sea.

For a detailed description of whale watching, see the Gloucester section in the Around
Boston chapter.

## Skiing

Virtually all ski resorts in New England have
substantial snowmaking capacity, and the
many gladed trails provide a memorable
experience. Smaller, local hills are often
cheaper to ski, less crowded and ideal for
beginners. Before making reservations at a
big resort, check for motels around the
smaller hills, which might save you a significant sum.

Snowboarding has invaded the New
England ski areas as it has others; most of
the larger ski resorts offer rental equipment, lessons, and special 'snow parks' with
bumps and jumps for boarders.

New England's best skiing is in Vermont
at Killington, Mt Snow, Stratton and at
Stowe; and in New Hampshire's White
Mountains at Waterville Valley, the Franconia Notch area (Loon Mountain) and the
Mt Washington Valley. In Maine, Sugarloaf
and Sunday River are excellent. Connecticut and Massachusetts' Berkshires have
smaller ski areas

Cross-country (Nordic) skiing is also
popular and especially pleasing in the
forests or traveling from village to village or
inn to inn. Every town seems to have at
least a few marked cross-country trails. Out
in the countryside, resort towns such as
North Conway, New Hampshire, and Stowe,
Vermont, have elaborate systems of well-
groomed cross-country trails.

For more details on particular resorts, see
the Activities sections in the appropriate
state chapters.

## Snowmobiling

Snowmobiling is offered in a number of
state parks during the winter. Use of the
noisy machines is regulated: You must be at
least 16 to operate one, and you must stay on
approved snowmobile routes and tracks. If
you haven't ridden a snowmobile before,
you should definitely take a safety training
course beforehand, as there are special cau-
tions and dangers associated with them.
Maine and New Hampshire are particularly
good places to pursue the sport.

## WORK

There are lots of summer jobs at New
England seaside and mountain resorts.
These are usually low-paying service jobs
filled by young people (often college students) who are happy to work part of the
day so they can play the rest. If you want
such a job, contact the local chambers of
commerce or businesses well in advance.
You can't depend on finding a job just by
arriving in May or June and looking around.

In winter, contact New England's ski
resorts, where full- and part-time help is
often needed.

Foreigners entering the USA to work
must have a visa that permits it. Apply for a
work visa from the US embassy in your
home country before you leave. The type of
visa varies, depending on how long you're

staying and the kind of work you plan to do. Generally, you need either a J-1 visa, which you can obtain by joining a visitor-exchange program (issued mostly to students for work in summer camps), or a H-2B visa, which you receive when sponsored by a US employer.

The latter can be difficult to procure unless you can show that you already have a job offer from an employer who considers your qualifications to be unique and not readily available in the USA. There are, of course, many foreigners working illegally in the country. Controversial laws prescribe punishments for employers employing 'aliens' (foreigners) who do not have the proper visas. The Immigration & Naturalization Service (INS) officers can be persistent and insistent as they enforce the laws.

## ACCOMMODATIONS

New England provides a comfortable array of choices in accommodations. In the countryside, the choices range from simple campsites to lavish country inns. In the cities, both mid-range and top-end hotels abound, but truly inexpensive accommodations are rare. The most comfortable accommodations for the lowest price are usually found in that great American invention, the roadside motel.

In order to keep the cost of accommodations down, observe this rule: Visit cities on weekends and the countryside during the week. Most city hotels offer low weekend rates for Friday, Saturday and Sunday nights; most country and resort lodgings reduce their rates by 20% to 45% Monday through Thursday.

At the busiest times (July, August and late September through mid-October), you may have to reserve accommodations well in advance. This is particularly true of B&Bs and inns. When you reserve a room in advance, be conscious of the terms and requirements. Here are some key questions to ask:

- Is smoking allowed? Most B&Bs and inns are 'smoke free,' meaning you must go outside to smoke.

- Are children allowed? Many inns do not welcome children under a certain age, perhaps as old as 12 years.
- Are pets allowed? In most cases, they are not.
- Is a minimum stay required?
- Are meals included or required?
- Can you reserve precisely the sort of room you want ('in the main inn, not in the annex,' 'with private bath,' 'with water view'), or must you take whatever is available when you arrive?
- Are there additional charges for service, activities or facilities? How much is the tax?
- Are credit cards accepted? Personal checks? Only cash?
- Is a deposit required? How much? Under what circumstances can the reservation be canceled and the deposit refunded?

## Camping

If you don't bring your own camping equipment, you can buy good supplies at good prices at many places in New England. Refer to the Shopping section in the Boston chapter and to the Freeport section in the Maine chapter.

You cannot plan to just stop by the road and camp. With few exceptions, you will have to camp in an established campground. Luckily, New England has lots of them. Unfortunately, most of them are full on weekends in July and August, and many fill up during the week as well. You must reserve in advance or arrive early in the day to give yourself the best chance of getting a site.

Rough camping is permitted in the backcountry of some national forests, but often it must be at established sites; these may have simple shelters and are usually free. Excellent trail guides and maps exist that show and describe these sites; see the Guidebooks section, earlier in this chapter, for details.

An inexpensive option is the primitive forest site with only basic services: pit (ie, waterless) toilets, cold running water (perhaps from a pump) and fireplaces. These are generally found in national forests and cost about $6.

Standard campsites in state and national parks usually have flush toilets, hot showers (for a fee) and often a dump station for RVs.

Tent sites are usually shaded and are sometimes on wooden platforms or grass, with plenty of space between sites. These sites cost between $6 and $20. Most government-run campgrounds only stay open during the summer season, from mid-May to early September or late October. For reservations information, see the Useful Organizations section, earlier in this chapter.

Private campgrounds are usually more expensive ($18 to $40) and less spacious, with sites closer together and less shade, but with lots more entertainment facilities. Most of the sites are for RVs and have water and electric hookups and perhaps sewage hookups. A small grassy area without hookups is usually set aside for tent campers, who are distinctly in the minority and pay the lowest rate. Sometimes hot showers are free, sometimes not. Private campgrounds usually have small shops and snack bars for essentials. Recreation facilities are usually elaborate, with playgrounds, swimming, game rooms and even miniature golf courses. Some private campgrounds are open from late May to early September, some from mid-April through November; a few are open all year.

## Hostels

Hostelling is not nearly as well developed in New England as in Europe. But some prime travel destinations, including Maine's Bar Harbor and Massachusetts' Boston, Cape Cod, Martha's Vineyard and Nantucket, have hostels that allow you to stay in $100-per-night destinations for $12 to $17. Needless to say, advance reservations are essential, and may often be made by phone if you have a credit card.

US citizens/residents can join Hostelling International/American Youth Hostels (HI/AYH; ☎ 202-783-6161, fax 783-6171, hiayhserv@hiayh.org, www.hiayh.org), PO Box 37613, Washington DC, 20013, by calling and requesting a membership form or by downloading a form from their website and mailing or faxing it. Membership can also be purchased at regional council offices and at many (but not all) youth hostels. Non-US residents should buy a HI/AYH membership in their home countries. If not, you can still stay in US hostels by purchasing 'Welcome Stamps' for each night you stay in a hostel. When you have six stamps, your stamp card becomes a valid one-year HI/AYH membership card valid throughout the world.

HI/AYH has its own toll- and surcharge-free reservations service (☎ 800-444-6111), but not all hostels participate in the service, and you need the access codes for the hostels to use it. The HI/AYH card may be used to get discounts at some local merchants and services, including some intercity bus companies.

Two hostelling councils cover New England (there aren't any hostels in Rhode Island). HI/AYH Eastern New England Council (☎ 617-779-0090, fax 779-0904), 1105 Commonwealth Ave, Boston, MA 02215, is the office for hostels in Maine, Massachusetts and New Hampshire. The HI/AYH Yankee Council (☎ 860-683-2847), PO Box 87, Windsor, CT 06095, is the office for hostels in Connecticut and Vermont.

Here's a list of New England hostel locations – get in touch with the appropriate hostelling council for more information on these:

Massachusetts
  Boston (two), Dudley, Eastham and Truro (Cape Cod), Littleton (near Concord), Martha's Vineyard, Nantucket
Connecticut
  Hartford, Windsor
Vermont
  Burlington, East Jamaica (north of Brattleboro), Ludlow (near Plymouth), Middlebury, Montpelier, White River Junction, Woodford (near Bennington)
New Hampshire
  Conway
Maine
  Bar Harbor, Portland, Searsport, South Hiram

## Motels

Motels range from small, homey, cheap, 10-room places in need of paint and wallpaper to lavish resorts with manicured lawns and gardens, vast restaurants and resort-style facilities. Prices range from $30 to $100 and up. On the highway or on the outskirts of any but the largest cities, you can get a very comfortable motel room for $50 to $75. The cheapest places are invariably the small local ones that are not members of a national chain, which makes it more difficult to find out about them.

Motels offer standard accommodations: a room entered from the outside, with private bath, color cable TV, heat and air-con. Though some smaller, older places may have only twin beds, most motels now have two double beds (or larger beds) or perhaps a queen-size bed and a single bed. In other words, it's easy for a small family (parents and two children) to find one room to accommodate them all. Whether you all want to sleep together in the same room is another matter.

Motel rooms often have small refrigerators, and motels always provide free ice for drinks and usually have vending machines for soft drinks and snacks. Many motels have restaurants attached or nearby; if not, most provide a simple breakfast of muffins or rolls, fruit and coffee, often at no extra charge. Many motels without restaurants keep menus from local restaurants on hand, and you can study them to decide where to go for dinner. Most motels (excluding the very cheapest) have swimming pools. Most also provide toll-free reservations lines. See the Toll-Free Numbers directory at the back of this book.

## Efficiencies

An efficiency (or efficiency unit), in New England parlance, is a hotel, motel or inn room, or a small one-room cabin, with cooking and dining facilities: stove (cooker), sink, refrigerator, dining table and chairs, cooking utensils and tableware. Efficiencies usually cost slightly more than standard rooms, but the difference can be negligible for a family that prepares its own meals rather than buying them in restaurants.

## Hotels

City hotels are mostly large and fairly lavish, and there are few of the small, inexpensive 'boutique' hotels found in London or Paris.

Hotel rooms provide similar services to motel rooms but are usually a bit more inclusive. Standard hotel services include restaurants and bars, room service for meals and beverages, and exercise rooms ('health clubs'). Many city hotels set aside several floors as special 'executive' sections, with more elaborate decoration and a central lounge with an attendant.

Prices range from $80 to $200 and up per night, with most between $100 and $150. Weekend discounts and special weekend packages offer significant savings. Be sure to ask about them when you call to inquire about prices and make reservations. Virtually all large hotels have numbers for reservations, but you may find better savings by calling the hotel directly, as some discounts are aimed only at local callers. See the Toll-Free Numbers directory at the back of this book.

Usually, children under 18 may stay for free in their parents' room. In a room with two double beds, then, a family of four could stay for the same price as a couple. If you are 55 or older, ask about senior citizen discounts; AAA members (see the Useful Organizations section, earlier in this chapter) may be entitled to discounts as well.

## B&Bs

Between the two world wars, before large-scale automobile production, American resorts had 'tourist homes,' private residences with several simple rooms to rent to travelers. The tourist home was often the main source of income of the single woman, retired couple or widow who ran it. After WWII, tourist homes were largely replaced by motels.

In the 1960s, young American tourists flooded Europe and discovered the convenient, congenial and, above all, inexpensive B&Bs, *pensions, gasthofen* and *pensioni*. They took the experience home to America, and the tourist home came to life again. But, as with most imports to America, it was thoroughly Americanized.

European visitors should be aware that North American B&Bs are often not the casual, inexpensive sort of accommodations found on the continent or in the UK. While they are usually family-run, most B&Bs are like small inns, and they usually require advance reservations. Some are relentlessly charming, with abundantly frilly decor and theatrically adorable hosts (and pets). Some have the services and amenities of minor resort hotels, and prices to match.

The simpler B&Bs in smaller towns and resorts may charge $60 to $85 for single or double rooms with shared bath, breakfast included. Fancier B&Bs in or near the more popular resorts charge $75 to $150 per night for a room with private bath. At peak times, from mid-July through early September and late September through mid-October, as well as on holiday weekends, prices at the fanciest B&Bs in the most popular resort towns may rise to $175 or even above $200.

B&B rooms vary in size, appointments and conveniences. Most have private bathrooms. Some have air-con and TVs; most do not.

Breakfast may be store-bought cake or muffins and instant coffee; fresh-baked pastries and a selection of fresh-brewed stimulants; a full American-style breakfast of bacon or ham and eggs, toast or muffins, fruit, cereal and milk; or any variation of the above. Usually it's pretty good.

In the most popular resort towns, B&Bs may have restrictive policies: A minimum stay of two or three days may be required on weekends; bills may have to be paid in advance by check or in cash (not by credit card); and cancellations may be subject to a processing fee, or worse.

## Inns

New England has more than 1500 country inns. They vary in size and amenities from small B&Bs (see above) to large, rambling old inns that have been sheltering travelers for several centuries. Many inns are historic and authentically furnished, with modern services. Others aspire to historicity. Many large mansions and summer houses, built by wealthy families a century ago, are now comfortable, even sumptuous, inns.

The charm and character of New England's inns are famous throughout the country.

New Englanders and those from neighboring regions (such as New York City, Philadelphia and Montreal) look upon them not simply as lodgings, but as weekend resorts or good places for a one- or two-week summer vacation. Many inns have excellent dining rooms and taverns, and they may also have such amenities as swimming pools, gardens, hiking trails or associations with local golf courses or tennis clubs.

Inn rooms are often decorated in antique styles. Most have private baths but may not have air-con or TV.

Prices range from $85 to $250 and up, depending upon the inn, the particular room, the town, the season and the day(s) of the week. A room priced at $85 Sunday through Wednesday in Lenox, Massachusetts, may cost $150 on Thursday, Friday or Saturday night. To this price you may have to add a $5 obligatory maid's fee, $10 if you use that romantic fireplace in your room, and the 10.7% state and local lodging taxes, making your final bill $181.

As with B&Bs, inns may require minimum stays or payment in advance and may have other restrictions.

Destinnations (☎ 508-790-0577, 800-333-4667, fax 508-790-0565, destinn@capecod.net, www.destinnations.com) is a reservations service for inns and an itinerary-planning service for visitors staying in New England more than a few nights. Ask for their free color catalog showing the inns and resorts they represent. If you have them plan your itinerary, you'll receive driving directions and recommendations for sights to see and restaurants to try, as well as the comfort of a toll-free number to call should you have any questions en route.

## Rental Accommodations

Renting a cottage or condominium for a week or two is popular in New England but not particularly easy for those who do not live in the region. There is no central registry of vacation rental properties. The best you can do is contact the local chamber of commerce and ask for listings of available properties. Chamber of commerce phone numbers are listed in the Information sections for the larger towns that are discussed throughout this book.

A condominium (or condo) is a small multi-room apartment with kitchen and dining facilities; it's larger, more elaborate and more expensive than an efficiency. Condos are usually capable of accommodating more people than an efficiency unit – some condos can sleep six, eight or even 10 people. Rates vary greatly, from $70 to $700 per night, depending upon the location, season and size. Condos are especially popular with skiers, but they're also available – and much cheaper – during the warmer months

## FOOD

A hundred years ago, Boston was famous for baked beans (white/navy beans, molasses, salt pork and onions cooked slowly in a crock) and New England boiled dinner (beef boiled with cabbage, carrots and potatoes). Though these dishes regularly show up in nostalgic and tourist accounts of the region, they are not common on menus anymore.

Some traditional foods are still common, and for good reason. New England's seafood is outstanding. Maple syrup is produced in all the New England states. Vermont dairy products – milk, cream, yogurt and cheese – are only slightly less famous than that state's most famous edible: Ben & Jerry's ice cream.

It is possible to spend anywhere from $2 to $200 per person for a meal. The major cities and the more sophisticated country inns have excellent restaurants serving refined American, continental and international cuisine. Except deep in the forest, you are never far from some place serving food. Some fast-food restaurants (offering hamburgers, pizza, doughnuts and coffee) are open 24 hours a day in cities and on highways. The food is often bland, but prices are low.

Breakfast is served in restaurants from 6 or 7 to 11 am or noon, and in lodgings from about 7 to 9 or 10 am. Some restaurants advertise that they serve breakfast all day. The meal can be a muffin and coffee for less than $2, a hearty meal of fried eggs, or an omelette, bacon, ham or sausage, toast, fruit juice and coffee for $6 or $7.

Lunch is served from 11:30 am to 2 or 3 pm, and in fact, many luncheon items are served until the evening closing time. A good simple lunch can cost $3 to $12, a fancy one up to $25. If you like good restaurants but can't afford their dinner prices, go for lunch. Portions are somewhat smaller, but prices may be significantly lower.

Dinner is served in restaurants from 6 to 10 pm. Normally, a good dinner can be had in a pleasant, though not fancy, restaurant for $16 to $35 per person, drinks included. In posh big-city restaurants and resorts, it is possible (but unusual) to see a bill of $100 per person. Portions are usually large. Some restaurants continue serving from a lighter, less formal ('bar' or 'tavern') menu until midnight or 1 am. Some restaurants close on Monday; a very few close on other days of the week.

In almost all restaurants, sections are designated as 'smoking' and 'nonsmoking.' You normally are asked which section you want. A growing number of restaurants are completely nonsmoking, meaning that you must step outside for a puff. See the 'Smoking' boxed text under Entertainment, later in this chapter.

### Fruit

New England produces excellent fruit in abundant variety. Orchard farmstands are the best places to buy fruit.

Strawberries come early, from mid-June through July. Local rhubarb is also ripe then, and if you come across a strawberry-rhubarb pie, grab two pieces at least. Late June to mid-July is blueberry season, when pies of fresh blueberries (huckleberries) appear. September brings peaches, plums and apples, as well as fresh-squeezed apple cider.

Cranberries, a Massachusetts specialty, are harvested in the autumn. The bright-red berries grow in shallow ponds called bogs and are harvested by amphibious machines. The berries are very tart and sour, but when sweetened they make good juice, jelly, sauce, muffins and pies. Tart cranberry sauce is the traditional garnish for a Thanksgiving turkey.

## Seafood

**Fish** New England's early commerce was built on fish. It is thought that Scandinavian fishing boats found bounteous harvests in the fishing grounds of Georges Bank even before the arrival of Columbus. In colonial and early American times, the trade in codfish was so important that a stuffed codfish was put in a place of honor in the Massachusetts State House. It's still there.

Both intensive and illegal fishing, however, have depleted stocks here as in other oceans, raising seafood prices. Still, if you enjoy seafood, you'll enjoy eating in New England.

Fish chowder is whitefish, potatoes, corn and milk. It usually takes second place to the more popular clam chowder (see Oysters, Mussels & Clams, below).

Boston scrod is any bland whitefish. The term 'scrod' is said to have originated at a local hotel restaurant. The chef could never be sure which whitefish (cod, haddock, etc) would be freshest in port that day, so he invented the word 'scrod' and served the catch of the day sautéed in butter or covered with a cheese sauce. Patrons happily ordered the bland fish filets and didn't notice any difference. Today, scrod usually refers to young codfish.

Bluefish, a full-flavored fish, can be fried, baked, broiled, grilled, or smoked and made into a pâté appetizer.

Monkfish is a large-flaked whitefish. When sautéed in butter it tastes a bit like lobster.

Halibut, swordfish and tuna steaks are excellent charcoal-grilled and drizzled with lemon juice.

**Oysters, Mussels & Clams** Oysters are available on many restaurant menus. Those harvested in Wellfleet on Cape Cod are the region's choicest. They're best eaten raw on the half shell but may come grilled, fried, baked and stuffed, or in rich, creamy oyster stew.

Attached to the rocks and sea floor, dark-purple saltwater mussels are abundant along the New England coast. Their flavor is coarser than that of oysters or clams.

New England clams are of two types: soft-shell, with chalky, easily breakable shells; and hard-shell clams, with shells that resemble porcelain.

The most popular soft-shell clams are 'steamers.' They're cooked in steam, which opens the shells. Extract the clam meat, shuck off the wrinkled membrane from the black 'neck,' wash off any sand by dipping the clam in the thin clam 'broth' provided, dip in melted butter and eat. After about five clams, you'll be shucking those membranes easily. The clam broth, by the way, is just the water the clams have been steamed in. It's used for dipping, not drinking.

The most common hard-shell clams are littlenecks and cherrystones. They're best eaten raw on the half shell with a few drops of lemon juice, tomato sauce or horseradish, but they may be steamed or stuffed and baked as well.

Quahogs (pronounced 'KO-hogs') are sea clams larger than your fist. They're usually cut into strips, deep-fried and served as fried clams in seaside clam shacks or chopped and used to make clam chowder. New England clam chowder is made of sliced or chopped quahogs, potatoes, milk, cream and perhaps a bit of seasoning. (Manhattan clam chowder, by the way, is made with a tomato base, not milk or cream, and is rarely found in New England.)

The traditional New England clambake is a feast of steamed clams, boiled or roasted corn on the cob and steamed or boiled lobsters. The closest you can easily get to enjoying a traditional clambake is to order a 'shore dinner' (lobster, steamers and corn) at one of the many summer-only seaside restaurants mentioned in this guide.

**Lobster** Though lobster has a reputation as a luxury food, it was not always so. In colonial times, a governor of the Massachusetts Bay Colony was forced to apologize to an important visitor because he had only lobster to serve him, as the cod boats could not go out. Lobsters were then so common that they were harvested in great quantity from shallow waters and used as fodder and fertilizer.

Today Maine lobster is perhaps the most famous seafood dish. In fact, the same kind of lobster is also caught off the coasts of

## How to Eat a Lobster

Lobster is messy to eat. In early summer, your lobster may come with a bone-hard shell, and you have to use a cracker to break the claws. In mid- to late summer, they have their new shells, which are soft and easily broken with the fingers. Purists believe (perhaps rightly) that spring hard-shell lobsters have the sweetest meat and that soft-shell lobsters are not quite as good.

The best place to eat lobster is in a beachfront shack called a lobster 'pound' or 'pool.' Here you can tear the beasts apart with abandon, using your fingers, which is the only way it can be done. To eat only the tail meat is looked upon by New Englanders as a terrible waste of good body and claw meat.

At lobster pounds or pools, live lobsters are cooked on order. They range in size from 1lb ('chicken lobsters' or 'chicks') to those weighing 1¼ to 1½lb ('selects') to 'large' lobsters from 2 to 20lb in weight. 'Culls,' those missing a claw, are sold at a discount, as the claw meat is considered choice. 'Shorts,' smaller than chicks, do not meet the legal minimum size for harvesting. Do your part to discourage illegal lobstering and question any lobster that looks very small.

When you order lobster, you'll be brought some special tools: a plastic bib, a supply of napkins, a cracker for breaking the claws, a small fork or pick for excavating claws and other tight places, a bowl in which to throw shells, a container of melted butter, a slice of lemon and an alcohol-soaked towelette to wipe your hands after the mess is over.

The lobster may be very hot, with hot water inside the shell. Start by twisting off the little legs and sucking or chewing out the slender bits of meat inside. Go on to the claws: Twist the claws and knuckles off the body, break the claws and knuckles with the cracker and dip the tender claw meat in butter before eating. Each knuckle also has a large, succulent bit of meat in it. Use the cracker and pick to get it, but beware the sharp spines.

Next, pick up the lobster body in one hand and the tail in the other. Twist the tail back and forth to break it off. Break off each of the flippers at the end of the tail and suck out the meat. Then use your finger or an implement to push through the hole at the end of the tail where the flippers were, and the big chunk of tail meat will come out.

There is delicious meat in the body as well, though it takes work to get it. Tear off the carapace (back shell), then split the body in two lengthwise. Behind the spot where each small leg was attached is a chunk of meat, best gotten with pick and fingers.

Massachusetts, Maine and the Atlantic provinces of Canada and is shipped around as demand requires. Purists – which means most New Englanders – demand live lobsters cooked to order, usually steamed for 10 to 20 minutes (depending upon size) in a large pot with a few inches of water. Steaming or boiling in seawater gives a distinctive flavor and salty tang. Lobsters may also be split from head to tail and grilled. Many restaurants serve baked stuffed lobster: The meat is removed and mixed with other ingredients, and the shell is refilled. Most New Englanders look upon this as a tourist dish for the uninitiated.

Store prices for live lobster range from $4 to $8 or more per pound, depending upon the season; restaurant prices can be as low as $10 for a whole small lobster with salad, corn on the cob, and bread and butter, or $15 to $20 for 'twin lobsters' (two small 'chicken' lobsters).

Summer sees the lowest prices for live lobsters. After summer, they're kept alive in seawater tanks ('pounds') for sale in other seasons and are consequently more expensive. Prices are highest in spring.

For tips on eating one of these creatures, see the boxed text 'How to Eat a Lobster.'

## Groceries & Markets

Many bakeries, snack shops, cafes and small restaurants in resort areas prepare food to take away. Most supermarkets have delicatessen counters where you can buy cold meats, cheeses, salads, pâtés, dips, spreads and other picnic and quick-meal items.

Vacation cottages and condominiums have kitchens or kitchenettes, as do 'efficiencies' – motel rooms equipped for light cooking.

## DRINKS
## Nonalcoholic Drinks

The familiar soft drinks – such as Coca-Cola, Pepsi, 7-Up, fruit-flavored fizzy drinks, root beer and ginger ale – are readily available and are sometimes called 'tonic' or 'pop' rather than soda or soft drinks. Also popular are bottled fruit juices, iced tea and spring water. Maine's own Poland Spring water is the local favorite. Most drinks are served in cups or glasses filled with ice, so you're paying mostly for frozen water. You might want to order your drinks 'without ice' or 'with just a little ice.'

Tap water is safe to drink virtually everywhere and usually is quite palatable.

Americans are among the world's most frequent drinkers of coffee. Traditionally, American coffee is brewed from a light-brown roasted bean and is weaker than that preferred in Europe. In some parts of New England, 'regular' coffee means coffee with sugar and milk or cream, so specify 'black coffee' if that's what you want.

Espresso is readily available, as are American versions of other European favorites such as café au lait, cappuccino and caffè latte. True to form, the American versions are often elaborate concoctions with endless variations – vanilla, raspberry or cinnamon flavoring, for instance – but little regard for the quality of the underlying coffee. Still, cities and most larger towns have specialty coffee shops where beans are roasted frequently, ground shortly before brewing and brewed by bean variety or origin, to order.

Tea likewise comes in bewildering variety. Tea is often served with lemon, unless milk is specified. Herbal teas of many kinds are readily available; decaffeinated tea is also available. Iced tea with lemon is a popular summer drink

## Alcoholic Drinks

New England has vineyards, wineries and craft breweries producing palatable, even excellent, regional vintages and beers.

**Beverage Laws** Alcoholic beverage use is governed by federal, state and local laws. In Maine, New Hampshire and Vermont, liquor may only be bought in state government-operated stores; in Connecticut, Massachusetts and Rhode Island, liquor stores are private, and some supermarkets are licensed to sell wine and beer. Retail liquor stores are not permitted to sell alcohol on Sunday, though most restaurants and bars with liquor licenses may serve liquor by the drink on Sunday. The minimum age for drinking is 21 years, and anyone who looks younger than that is 'carded' – that is, asked to produce a photo ID card bearing their birthdate. A driver's license or a passport is accepted in virtually all cases.

A restaurant may have a 'full liquor license' (for liquor, wine and beer), a 'wine and beer' license or no license. Some small or new restaurants without liquor licenses allow you to 'BYO' (Bring Your Own alcoholic beverages). Such restaurants typically offer 'set-ups' (ice buckets for wine, glasses, corkscrews, mixers for mixed drinks, etc). A few New England towns (Cape Ann's Rockport and Vineyard Haven on Martha's Vineyard, both in Massachusetts, come to mind) are 'dry': no shop, restaurant or hotel can sell you alcohol, but you can buy wine or beer in another town, bring it into the dry town and drink it legally.

You are not allowed to drink alcohol, even beer, in most fast-food restaurants, such as hamburger, doughnut, pizza or sandwich shops. When in doubt, look for beer advertisements, such as a neon sign in the window, or ask inside.

Public drinking is also prohibited outdoors – you may not take alcoholic beverages to the park, beach or forest trail, or drink on a sidewalk – though if you are discreet and keep bottles out of view, you can usually get away with having wine or beer with your picnic.

Do not have any open alcoholic beverage containers in your car. In some states, the driver may be prosecuted for drunk driving (a serious offense) if any open alcoholic beverage container is found in a car he or she is operating – even if the alcohol is being drunk exclusively by the passengers.

**Wine** Grapes grow wild in New England. The Concord grape, a labrusca variety developed in Concord, Massachusetts, is used for grape juice, sweet and ceremonial wines, jellies, jams and fillings. Even so, the short growing season and rocky soil are not optimal for fine wine grapes.

Modern growing methods and careful study of microclimates have allowed vintners in the southern New England states to produce drinkable table wines, white, red and 'blush' (the favored euphemism for rosé). Some vintage wines from hybrid and even vinifera grapes are of respectable quality and interesting flavor. Eastern Massachusetts, southeastern Rhode Island and northwestern Connecticut have vineyards. Try wines made by Sakonnet Vineyards, Rhode Island; the Chicama Vineyards on Martha's Vineyard, Massachusetts; Haight Vineyards near Litchfield, Connecticut; and Hopkins Vineyard on Lake Waramaug, Connecticut.

Wines made from other fruits – apples, blueberries, pears, peaches, raspberries, etc – are produced at a few wineries. Though lacking the complexity and body of grape wines, they can be tasty. Nashoba Valley Winery, near Concord, Massachusetts, makes good fruit wines, and you may find drinkable blueberry wine in Maine.

**Beer** New England's craft or microbreweries produce interesting and often fine brews. The smallest microbreweries are really brewpubs, serving their beers in only one or two local establishments. Slightly larger microbreweries may distribute throughout their home

## Culinary Terms

Here are some culinary terms common or unique to New England:

**boiled dinner** – a one-dish meal of boiled beef, cabbage, carrots and potatoes

**bread pudding** – baked pudding made with bread, milk, eggs, vanilla, nutmeg and diced fruit such as dates, nuts or raisins

**clam chowder** (in New England style) – chopped sea clams, potatoes and perhaps corn in a base of milk and cream

**clambake** – a meal, usually steamed, of lobster, clams and corn on the cob

**cranberries** – very tart, sour, water-grown berries, sweetened and used in juice, sauces, muffins, etc

**frappe** – pronounced 'FRAP,' whipped milk and ice cream; called a milkshake in other regions

**fried dough** – deep-fried pastry dough sprinkled with powdered sugar; served at snack stands and fairs

**grinder** – large sandwich of sliced meat, sausage, meatballs, cheese, etc, and salad on a long bread roll; called a hoagie, sub(marine), po' boy or Cuban in other regions

**Indian pudding** – baked pudding made of milk, cornmeal, molasses, butter, ginger, cinnamon and raisins

**johnnycake** – Rhode Island-style pancakes, made with cornmeal

**milkshake** – a thin frappe

**oven grinder** – a heated grinder (see grinder)

**raw bar** – place to eat fresh-shucked live (raw) oysters and clams

**tonic** – soda; sweet carbonated ('fizzy') beverage

states. A few, such as Boston Brewing Company's famous Samuel Adams dark lager and Harpoon Lager (another Boston beer), are shipped to other states and even to other countries.

Liquor stores stock a bewildering variety of 'coolers,' flavored sparkling wines and beers, which might be best described as alcoholic soda pop.

**Liquor** Strong liquors of all kinds, both domestic and imported, are widely available. Favorite mixed drinks on hot days are gin, rum or vodka and tonic water, and drinks made with liquor and fruit or fruit juice, perhaps beaten or blended with ice.

If you're visiting from abroad and you like whiskey, be sure to try some Kentucky bourbon. Representative brands are Old Granddad, Wild Turkey and Maker's Mark. Perhaps the best-known American whiskeys are Jack Daniels and Jim Beam, sour mash whiskeys distilled in Tennessee. The premium brand is Knob Creek, well aged, smooth as cognac and nearly as expensive.

## ENTERTAINMENT
New England is rich in opportunities for entertainment in music, dance and theater. Local newspapers often have a section with entertainment listings.

### Classical Music
The most famous symphony orchestra in the area is the Boston Symphony Orchestra (BSO), but New England's other large cities have their own orchestras as well. The winter season runs from September to March and is followed in the spring by a 'Pops' season of informal concerts held indoors in a music hall atmosphere. (See Boston's Entertainment section for information on tickets.)

In summer, the orchestras move outdoors: The BSO heads for its season at the Tanglewood estate in Lenox, Massachusetts, where it performs along with guest and student artists and ensembles. There are other good chamber music series at Tanglewood as well as in Great Barrington, Massachusetts; Stowe and Marlboro, Vermont; and

Blue Hill, Maine, among other venues. (See the Tanglewood Music Festival section in the Central Massachusetts & the Berkshires chapter.)

There is no major opera house in New England. It is surprising that Boston, with such a rich cultural life and many distinguished musical performance halls, does not have a proper opera house, although satisfying opera performances are given in several large theaters.

### Popular Music
Several cities, including Boston, Burlington, Hartford, New Haven, Newport, Portland, Providence and Worcester, are on the circuit for rock, pop and jazz performers year-round. Warm-weather concerts are held outdoors in several cities and resorts, especially in Boston, in Massachusetts' Berkshire hills, on Cape Cod and in Newport, Rhode Island. Ticket prices vary widely, from a few dollars for standing room to $50 to $100 for the best seats. Sunday band or ensemble concerts are given, usually for free, in many towns.

### Theater
Boston is a proving ground for Broadway plays and musicals. (See Boston's Entertainment section for information on tickets.) Many of New England's universities have good theater departments. In summer, local theater companies in resort areas provide good entertainment at low prices, often with well-known stars.

If you love theater, it's worth making a special trip to the summer Williamstown Theater Festival in Williamstown, Massachusetts. See the Williamstown section in the Berkshires chapter for more details.

An evening of Shakespeare at The Mount, the late Edith Wharton's mansion in Lenox, Massachusetts, is a delight as well. (See The Mount section in the Central Massachusetts & the Berkshires chapter for information.)

### Dance
Boston has many wonderful dance companies, including the Boston Ballet Company and a number of modern and experimental dance companies. In summer, the Jacob's

## Smoking

The USA, which gave the world tobacco, is now mostly a huge no-smoking zone. Government regulations have banished smokers from virtually all public spaces except the out-of-doors and have also banished most tobacco advertising from the media. Several state governments banded together and sued tobacco companies in order to reclaim the millions of public-health dollars they have had to spend dealing with tobacco-related ill-

nesses. The trial revealed that the tobacco companies had indeed designed their products to be particularly addictive and had suppressed evidence that tobacco use causes various diseases. In short, tobacco products, their manufacturers and their users are now in high disrepute.

Many Americans find smoking unpleasant and know that heavy or habitual smoking is unhealthful and harmful not only to the smoker, but also to those nearby (particularly children and people with asthma or other pulmonary impairments). If you are a smoker from a country that permits smoking in public places, you should be aware of American regulations and social customs.

Smoking is prohibited in most public buildings, such as airports, train and bus stations, offices, hospitals and stores, and on public conveyances (subways, trains, buses, planes, etc.). Except for the designated smoking areas in some restaurants, bars and a few other enclosed places, you must step outside to smoke. (It's now common to see office workers standing outside near a door to their building, puffing away.)

Most cities and towns require restaurants to have nonsmoking sections. There is no requirement that there be smoking sections, and indeed some restaurants are completely 'smoke-free.' Many hotels offer 'nonsmoking' rooms – that is, rooms used only by nonsmoking guests so that the rooms have no stale tobacco smell.

If you are in an enclosed space (a room or car, for example) with other people, it's polite to ask permission of all others before you smoke and to refrain from smoking if anyone protests.

Pillow Dance Festival in Lee, Massachusetts, in the Berkshires, is the region's premiere dance festival, presenting ballet, jazz and modern dance. (See the Jacob's Pillow section in the Central Massachusetts & the Berkshires chapter for more information.)

## Clubs

Every city and town has at least a few clubs, lounges or bars providing live entertainment such as pop music, jazz, rock and roll or stand-up comedy. In the larger cities and summer resorts, the choice and variety are great. Many places require you to pay a cover (admission) charge of a few dollars or spend a minimum amount on food or drinks, if you're there when the entertainment is on.

## Coffeehouses & Bars

In the cities and in college towns, many coffeehouses and bars (which are usually more downscale than clubs) have live entertainment several nights per week. The groups are usually local but are sometimes regional or even national talent. Prices, which may be a cover charge of $3 to $10 or a minimum order of drinks or food, are reasonable. Look in local newspapers and free tourist handouts, in the cafes and bars themselves, or on their websites for programs of events.

## Cinemas

Boston, Cambridge and New Haven, being university towns, have the most cinemas with the widest range of offerings. Most towns of any size have at least one cinema, usually a 'multiplex' or 'cineplex' holding several small cinemas showing different movies. Admission ranges from a few dollars for some of the student shows to $6 to $8 for first-run flicks at the big-city cinemas.

## SPECTATOR SPORTS

In the fall, regardless of the temperature or class of play, an American football game is an exhilarating, fun experience. The same goes for baseball in the spring, summer and fall. Minor-league and college team games are sometimes significantly less expensive and yet more fun than those of professional teams, with their blazing egos and contract disputes.

Boston has major-league teams in baseball (Boston Red Sox), ice hockey (Boston Bruins), soccer (New England Revolution) and basketball (Boston Celtics). For information on the Basketball Hall of Fame, see the Springfield section in the Central Massachusetts & the Berkshires chapter. Also, Boston's colleges and universities support some excellent National Collegiate Athletic Association (NCAA) sports. See the Boston chapter for details.

Massachusetts' New England Patriots football team plays in Foxboro Stadium, Foxboro, about 50 minutes south of Boston (see the Boston chapter).

In Rhode Island, the Pawtucket 'Paw-Sox' are a big minor-league Triple-A baseball draw.

In Vermont, Burlington has a Triple-A baseball team and the University of Vermont (UVM) has a good hockey team. In Connecticut, Hartford has the University of Connecticut's excellent basketball team (1999 NCAA champions) and the major-league Hartford Whalers hockey team, and Yale in New Haven has an athletic rivalry with Harvard in Cambridge, Massachusetts. In Cape Cod, the Cape Cod Baseball League (established 1885) has teams in Brewster, Chatham, Falmouth, Harwich, Hyannis, Orleans and Yarmouth-Dennis.

## SHOPPING

Regional gifts and souvenirs include maple syrup and maple sugar candy, silver or pewter items in designs originally made by Paul Revere, and scrimshaw (carved whale ivory – but today it's plastic 'imitation ivory'). The Bull & Finch Pub, inspiration for the popular television series *Cheers*, is Boston's most prolific souvenir factory, selling everything from T-shirts to buttons to beer mugs.

Discounted clothing, shoes, accessories, china, jewelry and all manner of other items are offered at Filene's Basement in Boston and at factory outlet stores in Fall River and Worcester, Massachusetts; and in Freeport, Maine and along US 1 in Kittery, Maine.

See the Shopping sections in regional chapters for more details on things to buy.

# Getting There & Away

The two most common ways to reach New England are by air and by car, but you can also get there by train and by bus.

## AIR

From the mid-Atlantic states or the Midwest, it may make sense to drive your own car to New England. But from elsewhere in the USA, it makes sense to fly, then rent a car or get around by a combination of bus, plane or train once you arrive.

### Airports

**New England** Boston's Logan International Airport (www.massport.org) is the major gateway to the region and is easily accessible – usually by nonstop or direct flight – from other major airports in the USA and abroad.

Several other airports in the region receive limited national and international flights: Albany, New York; Bradley International Airport in Windsor Locks, Connecticut (serving Hartford, Connecticut, and Springfield, Massachusetts); Burlington, Vermont; and Bangor and Portland, Maine. See the Getting Around chapter for more information on these airports.

**New York City** See the New York City chapter at the back of this book for detailed information on New York's airports.

The greater New York City area has seven airports. There are numerous flights daily to Boston from each of New York's three major airports – John F Kennedy International, La Guardia and Newark International – and even some commuter flights from New York's smaller airports, such as MacArthur and Islip.

US Airways and Delta operate hourly shuttle flights between La Guardia (LGA) and Boston (BOS); although no advance reservation is required, it's good to have one in order to avoid disappointment. Continental operates similar flights between Newark (EWR) and Boston. One-way fares range between $60 (weekends, with advance purchase) and $205 (weekdays, without advance purchase) for the 40-minute flight.

Scheduled flights connect New York City with these regional airports: Albany, in New York; Hyannis, Martha's Vineyard, Nantucket and Worcester, Massachusetts; Bridgeport, New Haven, New London and Hartford, Connecticut; Providence, Rhode Island; Burlington, Vermont; Lebanon and Manchester, New Hampshire; and Bangor, Portland and Presque Isle, Maine.

**Chicago** Chicago is served by four airports: O'Hare International, Midway, Palwaukee and Merrill C Meigs. As one of the country's major air hubs, it has many daily flights to New England and nearby destinations, including Albany; Bangor and Portland;

## Air Travel Glossary

**Baggage Allowance** This will be written on your ticket and usually includes one 44lb item to go in the hold, plus one item of hand luggage.

**Bucket Shops** These are unbonded travel agencies specializing in discounted airline tickets.

**Bumped** Just because you have a confirmed seat doesn't mean you're going to get on the plane (see Overbooking).

**Cancellation Penalties** If you have to cancel or change a ticket you purchased at a discounted rate, there are often heavy penalties involved; insurance can sometimes be taken out against these penalties. Some airlines impose penalties on regular full-fare tickets as well, particularly against 'no-show' passengers.

**Check-In** Airlines ask you to check in a certain time ahead of the flight departure (usually one to two hours on international flights). If you fail to check in on time and the flight is overbooked, the airline can cancel your booking and give your seat to somebody else.

**Confirmation** Having a ticket written out with the flight and date you want doesn't mean you have a seat until the agent has checked with the airline that your status is 'OK' or confirmed. Meanwhile you could just be 'on request.'

**Courier Fares** Businesses often need to send urgent documents or freight securely and quickly. Courier companies hire people to accompany the package through customs and, in return, offer a discount ticket that is sometimes a phenomenal bargain. In effect, what the companies do is ship their freight as your luggage on regular commercial flights. This is a legitimate operation, but there are two shortcomings – the short turnaround time of the ticket (usually not longer than a month) and the limitation on your luggage allowance. You may have to surrender all your allowance and take only carry-on luggage.

**ITX** An ITX, or 'independent inclusive tour excursion,' is often available on tickets to popular holiday destinations. Officially it's a package deal combined with hotel accommodations, but many agents will sell you one of these for the flight only and give you phony hotel vouchers in the unlikely event that you're challenged at the airport.

**Lost Tickets** If you lose your airline ticket, an airline will usually treat it like a traveler's check and, after inquiries, issue you another one. Legally, however, an airline is entitled to treat it like cash, and if you lose it, then it's gone forever. Take good care of your tickets.

**MCO** An MCO, or 'miscellaneous charge order,' is a voucher that looks like an airline ticket but carries no destination or date. It can be exchanged through any International Association of Travel Agents (IATA) airline for a ticket on a specific flight. It's a useful alternative to an onward ticket in those countries that demand one, and is more flexible than an ordinary ticket if you're unsure of your route.

## Air Travel Glossary

**No-Shows** No-shows are passengers who fail to show up for their flight. Full-fare passengers who fail to turn up are sometimes entitled to travel on a later flight. The rest are penalized (see Cancellation Penalties).

**On Request** This is an unconfirmed booking for a flight.

**Onward Tickets** An entry requirement for many countries is that you have a ticket out of the country. If you're unsure of what your next move may be, the easiest solution is to buy the cheapest onward ticket you can find to a neighboring country or a ticket from a reliable airline that can later be refunded if you do not use it.

**Open-Jaw Tickets** These are return tickets on which you fly out to one place but return from another. If available, these can save you backtracking to your arrival point.

**Overbooking** Airlines hate to fly with empty seats and since every flight has some passengers who fail to show up, airlines often book more passengers than they have seats. Usually excess passengers make up for the no-shows, but occasionally somebody gets bumped. Guess who it is most likely to be? The passengers who check in late.

**Point-to-Point Tickets** These are discount tickets that can be bought on some routes in return for passengers waiving their rights to a stopover.

**Reconfirmation** At least 72 hours prior to departure time of an onward or return flight, you must contact the airline and 'reconfirm' that you intend to be on the flight. If you don't do this, the airline can delete your name from the passenger list and you could lose your seat.

**Restrictions** Discounted tickets often have various restrictions on them – such as advance payment, minimum and maximum periods you must be away (eg, a minimum of two weeks or a maximum of one year), and penalties for changing the tickets.

**Round-the-World Tickets** RTW tickets give you a limited period (usually a year) in which to circumnavigate the globe. You can go anywhere the carrying airlines go, as long as you don't backtrack. The number of stopovers or total number of separate flights is decided before you set off, and they usually cost a bit more than a basic roundtrip flight.

**Standby** This is a discounted ticket on which you only fly if there is a seat free at the last moment. Standby fares are usually available only on domestic routes.

**Travel Periods** Ticket prices vary with the time of year. There is a low (off-peak) season and a high (peak) season, and often a low-shoulder season and a high-shoulder season as well. Usually the fare depends on your outward flight – if you depart in the high season and return in the low season, you pay the high-season fare.

Boston and Worcester; Burlington; Hartford; Manchester; New York City; and Providence.

Its most active airlines are American, Midway, Northwest, United and US Airways.

**Canada** Montreal's Dorval airport, 14 miles southwest of the city center, handles Canadian domestic flights and flights to the USA. Mirabel, 34 miles northwest of Montreal, handles intercontinental flights. Delta Air Lines operates routes from Dorval airport to Boston and Hartford. When flying to the USA from Toronto or Montreal, you clear US customs and immigration right in the Canadian airport before departure.

## Airlines

These major airlines serve Boston and/or New York City:

| Aer Lingus | ☎ 800-223-6537 |
|---|---|
| Air Canada | ☎ 800-776-3000 |
| Air France | ☎ 800-237-2747 |
| Air New Zealand | ☎ 800-262-1234 |
| America West Airlines | ☎ 800-235-9292 |
| American Airlines* | ☎ 800-433-7300 |
| British Airways | ☎ 800-247-9297 |
| Canadian Airlines | ☎ 800-426-7000 |
| China Airlines | ☎ 800-227-5118 |
| Continental Airlines* | ☎ 800-523-3273 |
| Delta Air Lines* | ☎ 800-221-1212 |
| El Al Israel | ☎ 800-223-6700 |
| Japan Air Lines | ☎ 800-525-3663 |
| KLM Royal Dutch | ☎ 800-374-7747 |
| Lufthansa German Airlines | ☎ 800-399-5838 |
| MetroJet | ☎ 888-638-7653 |
| Midwest Express | ☎ 800-452-2022 |
| Northwest Airlines* | ☎ 800-447-4747 |
| (Domestic) | ☎ 800-225-2525 |
| Scandinavian Airlines | ☎ 800-221-2350 |
| Southwest Airlines | ☎ 800-435-9792 |
| Swissair | ☎ 800-221-4750 |
| TWA* | ☎ 800-221-2000 |
| United Airlines* | ☎ 800-241-6522 |
| US Airways* | ☎ 800-428-4322 |
| Virgin Atlantic Airways | ☎ 800-862-8621 |

* denotes major domestic carriers

A dozen smaller domestic airlines, such as Midway Airlines (☎ 800-446-4392), have route systems concentrated in a particular region, with some national flights. Several of these are discount airlines that offer lower fares and fewer restrictions on their flights but usually have fewer flights than major carriers. Southwest Airlines (☎ 800-435-9792) offers discounted fares to and from Warwick, Rhode Island's TF Green State Airport, south of Providence, and the Manchester airport.

Small regional commuter airlines shuttle passengers from large and intermediate-size local airports, such as Bradley International Airport, TF Green State Airport and Albany, to the airports of smaller cities. Others make short hops across bodies of water, such as from Massachusetts' New Bedford to Nantucket, or Warwick to Block Island, off Rhode Island. See the Getting Around chapter and the Getting There & Away heading under individual destinations for information on these commuter airlines.

## Buying Tickets

Airfares in the US range from incredibly low to heights that enter the realm of fantasy. At the time of this writing, there were 105 separate roundtrip fares between Boston and Washington, DC, ranging from $92 to $2082. That means some people are paying $92 while others are paying $2082 to fly on the same airplane.

To get an idea of fares, try these online reservations services:

www.1travel.com
www.atevo.com
www.bestfares.com
www.counciltravel.com
www.previewtravel.com
www.statravel.com
www.travelocity.com

Keep in mind that your local travel agent, who is an expert in finding fares, may be able to find you the best deal of all. Because of cuts in airline commissions, many travel agents have been forced to charge small fees for making reservations and issuing tickets.

## Sample US & Canadian Airfares

Here are sample discount roundtrip fares from various US and Canadian cities to Boston:

| From | Roundtrip Excursion Fares |
| --- | --- |
| Atlanta, GA | $220 to $395 |
| Chicago, IL | $154 to $337 |
| Dallas-Fort Worth, TX | $230 to $507 |
| Denver, CO | $294 to $456 |
| Indianapolis, IN | $194 to $310 |
| Los Angeles, CA | $536 to $724 |
| Miami, FL | $210 to $351 |
| Minneapolis-St Paul, MN | $238 to $449 |
| Montreal, Canada | $145 to $426 |
| New York, NY | $ 98 to $171 |
| Phoenix, AZ | $420 to $538 |
| San Francisco, CA | $347 to $623 |
| Seattle-Tacoma, WA | $328 to $604 |
| Toronto, Canada | $155 to $288 |
| Washington, DC | $ 78 to $218 |

But, for example, if an agent saves you $60 on a fare and charges you $10 for the service, you'll still save $50.

In the USA, the *Boston Globe*, *New York Times*, *Los Angeles Times*, *Chicago Tribune*, *San Francisco Examiner* and other major newspapers have weekly travel sections with many advertisements for discounted airfares. Council Travel (☎ 800-226-8624, www.counciltravel.com) and STA Travel (☎ 800-777-0112, www.statravel.com) have offices in major cities nationwide and may offer good fares.

Travel CUTS (www.travelcuts.com) has offices in all major Canadian cities and often has fare bargains. The *Toronto Globe & Mail* and *Vancouver Sun* carry ads for low fares; the magazine *Great Expeditions* (PO Box 8000-411, Abbotsford, BC V2S 6H1) is also useful.

The travel sections of magazines such as *Time Out* and *TNT* in the UK, or the Satur-day editions of the *Sydney Morning Herald* and *The Age* in Australia, carry ads offering cheap fares. STA Travel, which has been dependable in the past, also has offices worldwide.

The magazine *Travel Unlimited* (PO Box 1058, Allston, MA 02134) publishes details of the cheapest international airfares and courier possibilities.

Return (roundtrip) tickets usually work out cheaper than two one-way fares – often *much* cheaper.

**Discount Tickets** If you call a major airline and book a same-day roundtrip flight to Boston from Chicago or Washington, DC, the fare can be as high as $600 or even more. If you purchase a ticket at least a week in advance and stay over a Saturday night before returning, the roundtrip fare can be as low as $78 to $133.

The rules are complex, but buying as far in advance as possible and staying over a Saturday night usually get you the best fare. Also, certain times of the year are cheaper to fly than others – particularly mid-January through March and October through mid-December, except for Thanksgiving (see When to Go in the Facts for the Visitor chapter). Also, flights on certain days (Tuesday, Wednesday, Thursday, Saturday and Sunday) may be cheaper than others, and flights at certain times (10 am to 3 pm and after 8 pm on weekdays; Saturday after noon and Sunday before noon) may be cheaper as well.

The cheapest tickets are what the airlines call 'nonrefundable,' even though you may be able to get your money (or at least some of it) back under certain circumstances. A good strategy to use when buying a non-refundable ticket is to schedule your return flight for the latest possible date you're likely to use it. In many cases, an airline will allow you to fly standby at no extra charge if you return earlier than your scheduled flight; but if you want to fly later, you may have to pay a penalty or buy another ticket entirely.

**Holiday Periods** At holiday times it can be difficult, if not impossible, to get the flights you want unless you plan – and purchase your ticket – well in advance. Holiday times include Christmas, New Year's, Easter, Memorial Day, Labor Day and *especially* Thanksgiving, the busiest travel time of the year. Not only do the planes fill up early during these times, but discount tickets are virtually impossible to find.

**Special Fares for Foreign Visitors** Just about all domestic carriers offer special fares to visitors who are not US citizens. Typically, you must purchase a booklet of coupons in conjunction with a flight into the USA from a foreign country other than Canada or Mexico. Each coupon in the booklet entitles you to a single flight segment on the issuing airline. However, you may have to use all the coupons within a limited period of time, and there may be other restrictions, such as a limit of two transcontinental flights (ie, flights all the way across the USA).

Continental Airlines' Visit USA pass costs $479 for three coupons (minimum purchase) and $769 for eight coupons (maximum purchase) in high summer. Changes of itinerary incur a $50 penalty. Northwest has a similar program.

On American Airlines, you must reserve your flights one day in advance.

Delta has two different programs: Visit USA grants discounts on fully planned itineraries; Discover America allows purchase of coupons good for standby travel anywhere in the continental USA. The minimum purchase is three coupons, the maximum is 10. The price depends upon your home country but averages about $125 per coupon. Children's fares are about $40 less.

When flying standby, call the airline one or two days before the flight and make a standby reservation. This way you get priority over all the others who just appear and hope to get on the flight the same day.

**Round-the-World Tickets** Round-the-world (RTW) tickets can be a great deal if you want to visit other regions as well as the USA. Often they work out to be no more expensive – or even cheaper – than a simple roundtrip ticket to the USA, so you get the extra stops for nothing. They're of most value for trips that combine the USA with Europe, Asia and Australia or New Zealand. RTW itineraries that include stops in South America or Africa can be substantially more expensive.

Official airline RTW tickets are usually put together by a combination of two or three airlines, and they permit you to fly to a specified number of stops on their routes as long as you don't backtrack. Other restrictions are that you must usually book the first sector in advance and cancellation penalties apply. The tickets are valid for a fixed period, usually one year. An alternative type of RTW ticket is one put together by a travel agent using a combination of discounted tickets.

Most airlines do restrict the number of sectors that can be flown within the USA and Canada to three or four, and some airlines even 'black out' a few heavily traveled routes (such as Honolulu to Tokyo). In most cases, a 14-day advance purchase is required. After the ticket is purchased, dates can usually be changed without penalty, and tickets can be rewritten to add or delete stops for $50 each.

From Australia, a RTW ticket that uses United, Lufthansa and Thai, with several stops in the USA, costs about A$2500. A cheap deal with Qantas and Air France flies to Los Angeles, has an open-jaw segment (enabling you to fly into one city and leave from another city) across the USA, then includes flights from New York to Europe, Asia and back to Australia, for A$1880. There are many other possibilities with Qantas and various partner airlines, ranging from A$1500 to A$3200.

From New Zealand, a RTW ticket via North America, Europe and Asia with Air New Zealand and other airlines costs NZ$2300 and up.

**Getting 'Bumped'** Airlines routinely overbook flights, knowing that there are always numerous 'no-shows' (people with reservations who do not take the flight). When no-shows leave empty seats, the seats become available to standby passengers. When there are few no-shows and there are more people than seats, the airline must 'bump' excess passengers onto later flights.

If it appears that passengers will have to be bumped, the gate agent first asks for volunteers. Those willing are booked on the next available flight to their destination and are also offered an incentive, which can be a voucher good for a roundtrip flight on the airline, or at least a discount on a flight, at a later date. In extreme circumstances or when faced with a hard bargainer, the airlines may even offer cash, or both cash and a flight pass.

If your schedule is flexible (the next available flight may not be until the next day), getting bumped can be a bonanza. When you check in at the gate, ask if the plane is oversold and if there may be a call for volunteers. If so, leave your name so you'll get first choice. When it comes time to collect your incentive, keep in mind that you do not have to accept the airline's first offer. You can haggle for a better reward.

## Baggage & Other Restrictions

Baggage regulations are set by each airline but usually allow you to check two bags of average size and weight and to carry at least one smaller bag onto the plane. If you are carrying many pieces of luggage, or pieces that are particularly big, bulky, fragile or heavy (such as a bicycle or other sports equipment), check with the airline about special procedures and extra charges.

Your ticket folder usually gives details of items that are illegal to carry on airplanes, either in checked baggage or on your person. These may include weapons, aerosols, tear gas and pepper spray, camp stove fuel canisters and full oxygen tanks. You may carry matches and lighters on your person, but do not put them in checked luggage.

Smoking is prohibited on all domestic flights within the USA and on most international flights to and from the USA. Most airports in the USA prohibit smoking except in designated areas.

## Travelers with Special Needs

If you have special needs of any sort – a broken leg, dietary restrictions, dependence on a wheelchair, responsibility for a baby, fear of flying – airports and airlines can be surprisingly helpful, but you should let them know as soon as possible so that they can make arrangements accordingly. You should also remind them when you reconfirm your booking (at least 72 hours before departure) and again when you check in at the airport.

Guide dogs for the blind must often travel in a specially pressurized baggage compartment with other animals, away from their owners, though smaller guide dogs may be admitted to the cabin. Guide dogs are not subject to quarantine as long as they have proof of being vaccinated against rabies.

Deaf travelers can ask that airport and inflight announcements be written down for them.

Children under two years of age travel for 10% of the standard fare (or free on some airlines), as long as they don't occupy a seat, but they usually don't receive a baggage allowance. 'Skycots' may be provided by the airline if requested in advance; these will hold a child weighing up to 22lb. Children between the ages of two and 12 can sometimes occupy a seat for half to two-thirds of the full fare and do get a baggage allowance. Strollers must usually be checked at the aircraft door; they are returned to you at the door right after the aircraft lands.

## Departure Tax

There's a $6 airport departure tax charged to all passengers bound for a foreign destination, as well as a $6.50 North American Free Trade Agreement (or NAFTA) tax charged to passengers entering the USA from a foreign country. There may also be smaller airport usage and security fees payable, depending upon which airport you fly to or from. Airport departure taxes are normally included in the cost of tickets bought in the USA. If you bought your ticket outside the USA, you may have to pay the tax when you check in for your departing flight.

## Arriving in the USA

As you approach the USA, your flight's cabin crew will hand out a customs and immigration form for you to fill in.

Arriving from outside North America, you must complete customs and immigration formalities at the airport where you first land, whether or not it is your final destination. Choose the proper immigration line: US citizens or non-US citizens. After immigration, pick up your luggage in the customs area and proceed to an officer, who will ask you a few questions and perhaps check your luggage. The dog sniffing around the luggage is looking for drugs, explosives and restricted agricultural and food products.

If the airport where you enter the country is not your final destination, you must re-check your luggage.

See also the Customs section in the Facts for the Visitor chapter.

## Leaving the USA

You should check in for international flights at least two hours early. During check-in procedures, you might be asked for photo identification, and you will be asked questions about whether you packed your own bags, whether anyone else has had access to them since you packed them and whether you have received any parcels to carry. These questions are for security purposes.

## Canada

Boston receives daily direct and nonstop flights from most major Canadian cities, with Toronto, Montreal and Halifax having the most frequent service. Carriers include Air Atlantic, Air Canada, Air Nova, American, Canadian Airlines, Delta, Northwest and United. Roundtrip fares to Boston are reasonable: Halifax for $240, Montreal $255, Toronto $265, Vancouver $613. See Canada under Airports near the beginning of this chapter.

Major Canadian newspapers such as the *Toronto Globe & Mail* carry travel agencies' advertisements. The Canadian Federation of Students' Travel CUTS travel agency (www.travelcuts.com) offers low fares and has offices in major cities throughout Canada.

## The UK

The Globetrotters Club (www.globetrotters .co.uk), BCM Roving, London WC1N 3XX, publishes a newsletter called *Globe* that covers obscure destinations and can help you find traveling companions. Check the free magazines widely available in London – start by looking outside the main railway stations.

**Travel Agents** Most British travel agents are registered with the Association of British Travel Agents (ABTA; www.abta.com). If you have paid for your flight through an ABTA-registered agent who then goes out of business, ABTA will guarantee a refund or an alternative.

Besides the many official fares published by the airlines and sold by them and their travel agencies, there are also 'unofficial' bucket shop (consolidator) fares. These seats are sold by the airlines in bulk at a big discount to wholesale brokers, who then sell them to the public and hope to make a profit. If you deal with a reputable shop or agency, these fares can be a good value on the major airlines. Most such fares are non-refundable (see Discount Tickets under Buying Tickets, earlier in this chapter).

London is arguably the world's headquarters for bucket shops, which are well advertised and can usually beat published airline fares. Two reliable agents for cheap tickets in the UK are Trailfinders (☎ 0171-938-3366, www.trailfinders.co.uk), 46 Earls Court Rd, London W8 6EJ, and STA Travel (☎ 0171-937-9962, www.statravel.co.uk), 74 Old Brompton Rd, London SW7. Trailfinders produces a lavishly illustrated brochure including airfare details.

The very cheapest flights are often advertised by obscure bucket shops whose names haven't yet reached the telephone directory. Many such firms are honest and solvent, but there are a few rogues who will take your money and disappear, only to reopen elsewhere a month or two later under a new name. If you feel suspicious about a firm, don't give them all the money at once – leave a deposit of 20% or so and pay the rest when you receive the ticket. If they insist on cash in advance, go elsewhere. And once you have the ticket, phone the airline to confirm that you are booked on the flight.

**Fares** Virgin Atlantic has a roundtrip in-season fare from London to Boston for £505 (US$838), or to New York for £432 (US$717), allowing a one-month maximum stay and requiring a 21-day advance purchase. Off-season (wintertime) flights from London can be as low as £190 (US$315) to Boston or £200 (US$332) to New York.

British Airways flies nonstop between London and Boston. For flights from London to Montreal, Canadian Airlines International is a good bet, with off-season fares beginning around £215 (US$356).

Aer Lingus offers direct flights from Shannon and Dublin to New York City, but because competition on flights from London is so much fiercer, it's generally cheaper to fly to London first.

## Continental Europe
Virgin Atlantic flights from Paris to New York are substantially cheaper than alternatives; a ticket with seven-day advance purchase ranges from FF4000 (US$673) up to FF4756 (US$800). In Paris, Transalpino (www.transalpino.com) and Council Travel (www.counciltravel.com) are both popular agencies.

Lufthansa has nonstop service to Boston from its Frankfurt hub.

## Australia & New Zealand
In Australia and New Zealand, STA Travel (www.statravel.com) is a major dealer in cheap airfares.

Qantas flies to Los Angeles from Sydney, Melbourne (via Sydney or Auckland) and Cairns. United flies to San Francisco from Sydney and Auckland (via Sydney), and also flies to Los Angeles. Connector flights are available to the East Coast. Fares are generally around A$2500 (US$1575) to A$2777 (US$1750) roundtrip from Melbourne or Sydney to Boston.

## Asia
Hong Kong is the discount-ticket capital of the region, but its bucket shops can be un-reliable. Ask the advice of other travelers before buying a ticket. STA Travel (www.sta-travel.com) has branches in Hong Kong, Tokyo, Singapore, Bangkok and Kuala Lumpur. As long as the Asian economic crisis continues, bargain airfares may be available for as low as $900 roundtrip from Hong Kong to New York or Boston, though normal fares are more like $1200.

## Central & South America
Most flights from Central and South America go via Miami, Dallas/Fort Worth or Los Angeles, though a few go nonstop to New York. American, Continental, Delta, Northwest and United all have routes to Mexico and Central and South America. Aeroméxico, Mexicana and the airlines of the Central American nations (Aeroquetzal, Aeronica, Aviateca, COPA, LACSA and TACA) have flights to either Miami or New York, with connections to Boston. Fares are somewhat expensive: $550 roundtrip to Boston from Mexico City, $767 from Guatemala City.

## BUS
Big, comfortable, air-conditioned buses connect most cities and some towns in the USA. However, as the private auto is king, and air service is faster in this big country, bus service is limited. You can get to New England by bus from all parts of the USA, Canada and Mexico, but the trip will be long and tedious and ultimately won't be dramatically less expensive than a discounted flight. Bus travel usually only makes sense for those traveling alone, as couples and families can travel more quickly, pleasantly and independently by rented car at about the same expense.

As with planes and trains, New York City is the region's major hub for buses, and many routes from around the country come through New York on their way to New England.

The Port Authority Bus Terminal (☎ 212-564-8484, www.panynj.gov/tbt/pabframe .HTM), Eighth Ave and W 42nd St in Manhattan, is the city's main bus terminal.

See the New York City chapter at the back of this book for more information on

New York City's bus stations. See also the Getting Around chapter for details on bus travel within the region.

## Fares

Special travel plans and promotional fares are sometimes offered, and these can reduce fares substantially, especially on the longer trips. Ask about them when you call the bus company.

The table below contains regular fares (one-way/roundtrip) to Boston:

| from | fare | hours |
|------|------|-------|
| Chicago, IL | $95/155 | 20 |
| Montreal, Canada | $45/80 | 8 |
| New York, NY | $30/55 | 5 |
| San Francisco, CA | $159/308 | 67 |
| Toronto, Canada | $80/112 | 12 |
| Washington, DC | $47/88 | 9 |

## Bonanza

Bonanza Bus Lines (☎ 212-564-8484, 800-556-3815, www.bonanzabus.com) operates routes from New York City to Albany via the Berkshires (Great Barrington, Stockbridge, Lee, Lenox and Pittsfield, Massachusetts), and from New York City to Cape Cod (Falmouth, Woods Hole and Hyannis) via Providence. Bonanza also operates buses to Newport and New Bedford.

## Green Tortoise

For travel between the West Coast and New England, Green Tortoise (☎ 415-956-7500, 800-867-8647, www.greentortoise.com) buses are more relaxing than Greyhound and a *lot* more entertaining. Foam mattresses and booths with tables replace bus seats, the maximum number of passengers is 38, and food, music and merriment prevail. Tortoise buses leave about every two weeks from San Francisco and spend either 10, 11 or 14 days winding across the country via New York to Boston, and vice versa. Along the way you visit state and national parks, monuments, forests and anywhere else your fellow passengers agree to stop; flexibility is key. Fares are from $350 to $389, plus a food fund payment of $111 to $121 per person.

## Greyhound

Greyhound Lines (☎ 212-635-0800, 800-231-2222, www.greyhound.com) operates buses from New York City to Hartford, Springfield, Worcester, New Haven, New London and Providence. Service to Cape Cod is provided in conjunction with Bonanza. The Boston service has a few buses daily.

## Vermont Transit

Vermont Transit Lines (☎ 802-864-6811, 212-594-2000, 800-451-3292 in New England, www.vermonttransit.com) serves Montreal, Vermont, Boston, Maine and several points in New Hampshire in conjunction with Greyhound.

## TRAIN

Rail passenger service in the USA is operated primarily by Amtrak (☎ 800-872-7245, 800-USA-RAIL, www.amtrak.com), a quasi-governmental corporation. Service in the 'Northeast Corridor' (connecting Boston with New York and Washington, DC) is some of the most frequent in Amtrak's system.

By the time you read this, Amtrak should be running its new Acela high-speed 'tilt' trains on a fully electrified line at up to 150mph between Boston, New York and Washington, DC, cutting travel time from New York City center to Boston city center to under three hours. The fare is around $135 one way for premium service. It's expensive but cheaper and more comfortable than a plane, and just about as fast if you're going from city center to city center. Travel times for conventional trains will also be improved, to under four hours, and no doubt fares will be raised somewhat.

Several Amtrak routes pass through New York City's Pennsylvania Station (Penn Station), from which about 10 trains depart daily for Boston.

Half the trains that run between Boston and New York are unreserved; the other half are all-reserved trains with somewhat higher fares. Book reservations through Amtrak or a travel agent.

See the New York City chapter at the back of this book for more information on New York City's train stations.

Smoking is not permitted on most routes; however, on some routes smoking is allowed in private rooms and in the lounge car during specific times.

## Fares

Amtrak offers special excursion fares, seasonal discounts and rail passes good for unlimited travel during a certain period of time. Children receive discounts as well. The fares listed below are unreserved, coach class, peak-season fares, one-way/roundtrip, to Boston. They're subject to change and do not include meals. You may buy snacks or meals onboard or take your own food. If you travel 1st class in a club or sleeping car, meals are included.

| from | fare | hours |
|---|---|---|
| Chicago, IL | $82/164 | 22 |
| New York, NY | $45/89 | 4 |
| San Francisco, CA | $159/308 | 72 |
| Washington, DC | $52/98 | 9 |

## Washington, DC to Boston

Boston is the northern terminus of Amtrak's bustling *Northeast Corridor* train service, connecting Hartford, Providence, New Haven, New York City, Philadelphia, Baltimore and Washington, DC.

## New York City to Boston

The main line from New York to Boston, the *Shore Route*, follows the coast for much of the way, stopping in New Rochelle, New York, and Stamford and Bridgeport, Connecticut, before coming to New Haven (Yale University); Old Saybrook, Connecticut (for Old Lyme, Essex and Ivoryton); New London (for the US Coast Guard Academy); Mystic, Connecticut (for the Mystic Seaport Museum); Westerly, Rhode Island (for Stonington and Rhode Island beaches); Kingston, Rhode Island (for Narragansett, Port Galilee and Block Island); and Providence before reaching Boston.

The *Inland Route* itinerary follows the main line from New York City as far as New Haven, then runs west up the Connecticut River Valley, stopping off at Wallingford, Meriden, Berlin (New Britain) and Hartford, then Windsor, Windsor Locks (for Bradley International Airport) and Springfield. One or two trains daily continue past Springfield to Worcester and Framingham, Massachusetts, then to Boston. This route takes much longer than the *Shore Route* via Providence.

## New York City to Connecticut

Metro-North trains (☎ 212-532-4900, 800-638-7646, www.mta.nyc.ny.us) link New York City's Grand Central Station to New Haven (with stops in between) every hour on the hour from 7 am until after midnight on weekdays, with extra trains during the peak morning and evening hours. Service on Saturday, Sunday and holidays is less frequent, but there is a train at least every two hours. The trip from Grand Central to New Haven takes 1½ hours.

## New York City to Cape Cod

During July and August, Amtrak operates special weekend trains from New York City to Hyannis on Cape Cod.

The *Cape Codder* departs from New York City's Penn Station in the late afternoon on Friday, stops at Bridgeport, New Haven, New London and Mystic in Connecticut; Westerly and Providence in Rhode Island; and Buzzards Bay, Sandwich and West Barnstable in Cape Cod, terminating in Hyannis. Return trips from Hyannis depart on Sunday afternoon. This train may also serve parts of New Jersey, Philadelphia, Baltimore and Washington, DC. Contact Amtrak for details.

## New York City to Vermont

The *Vermonter* begins in Washington, DC, and runs to Newark; New York City; Stamford, New Haven and Hartford; Springfield and Amherst; and then on to St Albans in Vermont, near the Canadian border.

## New York City to Montreal

Two Amtrak trains run daily between New York City and Montreal's Central Station (beneath the Queen Elizabeth Hotel), a distance of 450 miles.

The *Adirondack*, a day train (10 hours), runs down the Hudson River Valley along the eastern border of New York, stopping at Port Kent, New York (ferry to Burlington), and Albany-Rensselaer, New York, before terminating at New York's Grand Central Station. Buses connect Albany with southern Vermont and the Berkshires.

The *Montrealer* runs between New York City and northern Vermont along the Connecticut River Valley. At the Canadian border, passengers board a bus for the ride to Montreal. Stops include Essex Junction (for Burlington), White River Junction and Brattleboro, Vermont; Amherst; and New Haven.

## Chicago to Boston

The Amtrak *Lake Shore Limited* departs Chicago's Union Station each evening for Boston, making stops at Toledo and Cleveland, Ohio; Buffalo, Rochester, Syracuse and Albany-Rensselaer; and at Springfield, Worcester and Boston. You can make a connection with a New York-bound train at Springfield.

## CAR

Foreign drivers of cars and riders of motorcycles will need their vehicle's registration papers, liability insurance and an international driving permit, in addition to their domestic driver's license. Canadian and Mexican driver's licenses are accepted.

Though the easiest way to get to New England is by airplane, the best way to get around is by car, so you may want to drive. Below are some route suggestions.

## From New York City

If you're heading to Connecticut's Litchfield Hills, Massachusetts' Berkshires or southern or western Vermont, follow the Henry Hudson Parkway or I-87 north from New York City to the Saw Mill River Parkway, which connects with the Taconic State Parkway North. The Taconic is a beautiful, non-toll road free of trucks.

To reach southwestern Connecticut, Hartford, central Massachusetts, Boston, eastern Vermont, New Hampshire or Maine from the Saw Mill River Parkway, head north to I-684, which connects with I-84 East via Danbury and Waterbury to Hartford and beyond.

For the Connecticut and Rhode Island coasts (New Haven, New London, Mystic, Providence, Newport) and for Massachusetts' New Bedford, Plymouth, Cape Cod, Martha's Vineyard and Nantucket, take the Henry Hudson Parkway or I-87 north to I-287, and then go east on I-287 to the Hutchinson River Parkway North. This leads into Connecticut's Merritt Parkway, a scenic toll road that's closed to trucks. (The alternate route, I-95, has very heavy truck traffic.) The Merritt Parkway in turn leads into the similarly pleasant Wilbur Cross Parkway, which passes New Haven before heading north to Meriden and Hartford.

For points along Connecticut's southern shore, go east from New Haven on truck-filled I-95. The alternative is the much slower, though more interesting, US 1, which goes through all the coastal towns and their traffic lights.

## From Montreal & Toronto

If you're headed for western Vermont, Massachusetts and Connecticut from Montreal, go across the Pont Victoria or Pont Jacques-Cartier east from Montreal and take CN 15 south to the US border and I-87. From Gordon Landing (I-87 exit 39) north of Plattsburgh, New York, you can catch a ferry to Grand Isle and follow US 2 to I-89 and Burlington. An alternate route is via New York's Port Kent, farther south, and the ferry (summer only) across Lake Champlain to Burlington. Ferry service is described in the Burlington section of the Vermont chapter.

For Vermont, southern New Hampshire and the southern New England states, cross the Pont Victoria and follow CN 10 (Auto route des Cantons de l'Est) eastward 22km (13 miles) to CN 35 and QC 133 South. At the US border, follow I-89 south via Burlington and Montpelier to White River Junction and the junction with I-91. Continue on I-89 to reach Concord, Manchester and Boston, or take I-91 south to southern Vermont and

Sunrise over New Castle, NH

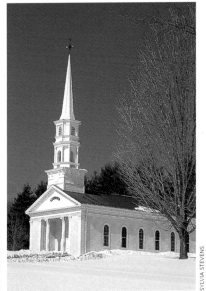

Church steeple in winter, Sudbury, MA

The road beckons on a glorious autumn day near Woodstock, VT.

Two New England symbols: the lighthouse and the clipper ship, York, ME

Ready for the lobster pound, Portsmouth, NH

Repairing the ol' fishing net, Gloucester, MA

JERRY & MARCY MONKMAN

LEE FOSTER

BARRETT & MACKAY

New Hampshire, central Massachusetts and central Connecticut around Hartford.

If you're traveling from Montreal to northern New Hampshire and Maine, take the Pont Victoria and follow CN 10 eastward as far as Magog. Turn south on CN 55 and go to the US border to connect with I-91 and then I-93, which leads straight to New Hampshire's White Mountains. To get to Maine, follow US 2 eastward from I-91 or US 302 from I-93.

Another route from Montreal to Maine – though slower, less scenic and with fewer tourist services – is to continue on CN 10 east from Magog and go through Sherbrooke. Beyond Sherbrooke, QC 112 is a two-lane road. Follow it to St-Gerard and then follow QC 161 through Lac-Mégantic to the US border. In Maine, follow ME 27 through sparsely populated forests and mountains to the capital city of Augusta.

If you're driving from Toronto, follow CN 401 to Hamilton and then to Niagara Falls, Buffalo, Albany and Boston. This is the most direct route unless you're headed for northern New England, in which case you might want to drive via Montreal.

## From Chicago

The most direct route is I-80, though the portion between Chicago and Cleveland has heavy truck traffic and is not particularly pleasant. An alternative is I-94 via Detroit into Canada to follow CN 401 to Hamilton before heading down via Niagara Falls on to Buffalo and I-90, the New York State Thruway, to Albany and Boston.

## Drive-Aways

A drive-away is a car that belongs to someone who can't (or doesn't care to) drive it to a specific destination but is willing to allow someone else to drive it. For example, if somebody moves from Denver to Boston, they may elect to fly and leave the car with a drive-away agency. The agency will find a driver and take care of all the necessary insurance and permits. If you happen to want to drive from Denver to Boston and have a valid driver's license and a clean driving record, you can apply to drive the car. Normally, you have to pay a small, refundable deposit and pay for the gas (though sometimes a gas allowance is given). You are given a set number of days within which to deliver the car – usually based on driving eight hours a day – and a limited number of miles, based on the best route and allowing for reasonable side trips, so you can't just zigzag all over the country. This is a cheap way to get around if you like long-distance driving and meet the eligibility requirements.

Drive-away companies often advertise in the classified sections of newspapers under 'Travel.' They are also listed in the yellow pages under 'Automobile Transporters & Drive-Away Companies.' You will need to be flexible about dates and destinations when you call. If you are going to a popular area, you may be able to leave within two days or less, or you may have to wait over a week before a car becomes available. The most easily available routes are coast to coast, although intermediate trips are certainly possible.

# Getting Around

Without a doubt, the best way to get around New England is by car. The region is relatively small, the highways are good and public transportation is not as frequent or as widespread as in some other countries. Still, there are the alternatives of air, train, bus and boat, which may make sense for some routes.

## AIR
### Domestic Airports

Smaller regional and commuter airlines connect New England's cities and resorts with Boston and New York City. The following airports receive scheduled flights.

The Albany County Airport (☎ 518-869-9611), in Albany, New York, on I-90 across the Massachusetts border from Stockbridge, serves the Berkshires and western Massachusetts as well as Vermont.

Barnstable Municipal Airport (☎ 508-775-2020), in Hyannis, Massachusetts, serves Cape Cod. The Martha's Vineyard Airport (☎ 508-693-7022) serves that island, just as the Nantucket Airport (☎ 508-325-5300) serves Nantucket Island.

Worcester Municipal Airport (☎ 508-792-0610), in Worcester, Massachusetts, serves central Massachusetts.

Bradley International Airport (☎ 860-292-2000), in Windsor Locks, Connecticut, services all of Connecticut and greater Springfield and the Pioneer Valley and the Berkshires in Massachusetts, plus Vermont.

Groton/New London Airport (☎ 860-445-8549), in Connecticut, serves the southeastern Connecticut coast. Nearby Tweed-New Haven Airport (☎ 203-787-8283) and Igor Sikorsky Memorial Airport (☎ 203-576-7498) also serve the coast with commuter flights.

TF Green State Airport (☎ 401-737-4000), in Warwick, Rhode Island (near Providence), is that state's largest airport served by commercial and commuter airlines.

Burlington Airport (☎ 802-862-9286) is Vermont's major airport, but Vermont is also served by the airports in Albany, Boston, Hartford and Montreal, Canada.

Augusta, Bangor, Bar Harbor/Hancock County (which services Acadia National Park), Portland, Presque Isle and Rockland/Knox County Regional Airports in Maine all have regularly scheduled flight service. For more on these airports, see the destination headings in the Maine chapter.

### Domestic Airlines

Business Express Airlines (☎ 800-345-3400, www.flybex.com) is the largest of New England's regional airlines, flying from Boston to Washington, DC; Philadelphia, Pennsylvania; Albany, Islip, Rochester, Syracuse and White Plains, New York; Burlington, Vermont; Bangor, Portland and Presque Isle, Maine; Halifax, Nova Scotia; Ottawa, Ontario; and Quebec City, Quebec. It also runs flights between Providence and New York City's La Guardia Airport.

Smaller airlines offer specialized routes: Colgan Air (☎ 800-523-3273, www.colganair.com) flies from Boston to Augusta, Bar Harbor and Rockland, Maine; Rutland, Vermont; and Hyannis and Nantucket, Massachusetts. It flies from Nantucket to New York's La Guardia Airport.

Cape Air (☎ 508-771-6944, 800-352-0714, www.flycapeair.com) flies from Boston and New Bedford, Massachusetts, and Providence to Hyannis, Martha's Vineyard, Nantucket and Provincetown. Also, Nantucket Airlines (☎ 508-790-0300, 800-635-8787, www.nantucketairlines.com), a division of Cape Air, offers hourly shuttle service from Hyannis to Nantucket.

New England Airlines (☎ 800-243-2460, www.block-island.com/flybi/nea/) flies from Westerly, Rhode Island, to Block Island, Rhode Island.

## BUS

Buses go to more places than airplanes or trains, but the routes still leave a lot out, bypassing some prime destination. Except on the most heavily traveled routes, there may be only one or two buses per day.

The major bus companies, with routes that cover several New England states, are Bonanza, Greyhound, Peter Pan and Vermont Transit.

## Bonanza

Bonanza Bus Lines (☎ 212-564-8484, 401-331-7500, 800-556-3815, www.bonanzabus.com), with its hub in Providence, runs buses from New York City via Danbury and Hartford, Connecticut, to Providence; and via New Milford, Kent and Canaan, Connecticut, to Massachusetts' Berkshire hills and Bennington, Vermont. Other routes connect Providence with Newport, Rhode Island, and with Boston, Fall River, Falmouth, Hyannis and Woods Hole (Cape Cod), all in Massachusetts.

## Greyhound

Greyhound (☎ 212-635-0800, 617-526-1810, 800-231-2222, www.greyhound.com), working in conjunction with Bonanza, Peter Pan and Vermont Transit, runs buses connecting Boston with Albany; Hartford and New Haven, Connecticut; Newark, New Jersey; New York City; and the Berkshire hills, Springfield and Worcester, Massachusetts, with connecting service to many other parts of the country.

Other Greyhound routes run north via Portsmouth, New Hampshire, along the Maine coast, with stops in Portland, Freeport, Brunswick, Bath, Wiscasset, Camden and Bangor. Connecting services can carry you onward to Ellsworth for Bar Harbor and Acadia National Park; and into New Brunswick and Nova Scotia.

## Peter Pan

Peter Pan Bus Lines (☎ 413-781-3320, 800-343-9999, www.peterpan-bus.com), based in Springfield, runs routes connecting Boston with Washington, DC; Baltimore; Philadelphia; Albany (with connections as far as Toronto) and New York City; Amherst, Greenfield, Holyoke, Lee, Northampton, Pittsfield, Springfield, Sturbridge, Williamstown and Worcester, Massachusetts; Bridge-

port, Danbury, Hartford, Middletown, New Britain, New Haven, Norwalk and Waterbury, Connecticut; Bennington, Vermont; and Bangor and Portland, Maine.

Peter Pan buses also run from Springfield and the Pioneer Valley to Bradley International Airport, north of Hartford.

## Vermont Transit

Vermont Transit Lines (☎ 212-594-2000, 802-864-6811, 800-451-3292 in New England, www.vermonttransit.com), based in Burlington, has routes connecting major Vermont towns with New York's Albany and Binghamton and New York City; Boston; Manchester and Portsmouth, New Hampshire; and Bangor, Bar Harbor, Brunswick and Portland, Maine. There are connections via Greyhound to many other points in New England. There are connections at Burlington to Montreal.

### Massachusetts Service

Plymouth & Brockton Street Railway Co (☎ 508-746-0378, www.p-b.com), at Boston's Peter Pan Terminal, goes to Plymouth, Sagamore, Barnstable, Hyannis, Chatham and Provincetown on Cape Cod.

### New Hampshire Service

Concord Trailways (☎ 603-228-3300, 800-639-3317, www.concordtrailways.com), based in Concord, provides most of the bus service in the state, running from Boston up I-91 all the way to Littleton, and also via Laconia and Conway to Gorham and Berlin.

### Maine Service

C&J Trailways (☎ 800-258-7111) serves Newburyport, Massachusetts; Portsmouth, New Hampshire; and lower coastal Maine, including Kennebunkport, Wells and Ogunquit. Greyhound and Vermont Transit also run buses within Maine.

## TRAIN

Amtrak (☎ 800-872-7245, www.amtrak.com) routes in New England are covered in the Getting There & Away chapter. Work is underway to restore train service between Boston and Portland.

Connecticut is served by two convenient rail lines, Metro-North and the Connecticut Commuter Rail Service's Shore Line East service. Metro-North trains (☎ 212-532-4900, 800-638-7646, www.mta.nyc.ny.us) make the 1½-hour run between New York City's Grand Central Station and New Haven. Other branches of Metro-North's service go north to Danbury, New Canaan and Waterbury.

Connecticut Commuter Rail Service's Shore Line East service (☎ 800-255-7433, www.rideworks.com/rwsl.htm) travels along the shore of Long Island Sound. At New Haven, trains connect with Metro-North and Amtrak routes. See the Getting There & Around section of the Connecticut chapter for more details on train travel in the state.

In Boston, North Station serves MBTA Commuter Rail trains (☎ 800-392-6099, www.mbta.com) that travel out of the city to the west and north, making stops at Concord, Rockport, Gloucester and Manchester. See Boston's Getting There & Away section for more information.

## CAR

Driving is the best way to see New England. If you don't have your own transportation, consider renting a car for at least part of your stay.

## Road Rules

Driving laws are different in each of the New England states. Generally, you must be 16 years of age to have a driver's license.

**Speed Limits** The maximum speed limit on most New England interstate highways is 65mph (but you're likely to find traffic moving at 70mph); some of the interstates have limits of 55mph. On undivided highways, speed

---

## Accidents Happen

It's important to know the appropriate protocol when involved in a 'fender-bender.'

Remain at the scene of the accident until you have exchanged information with the police or the other driver(s) involved, especially if there has been substantial damage or personal injury. It may be necessary to move your car off the road for safety's sake, but leaving the scene of an accident is illegal.

Call the police (and an ambulance, if needed) immediately, and give the operator as much specific information as possible (your location, any injuries, etc). The emergency phone number is ☎ 911.

Get the other driver's name, address, driver's license number, license plate number and insurance information. Be prepared to provide any documentation you have, such as your passport, international driving license and insurance documents.

Tell your story to the police carefully. Refrain from answering any questions until you feel comfortable doing so (with a lawyer present, if need be). That's your right under the law. The only insurance information needed is the name of your insurance carrier and your policy number.

If you've hit a large animal, such as a deer or moose, and it's badly injured, call the police to report it immediately. If your car is damaged in any way, report it to your insurance company or rental agency.

If a police officer suspects that you are under the influence of alcohol, he or she may request that you submit to a breath-analysis test. If you do not, you may have your driving privileges suspended until a verdict is delivered in your court case.

If you're driving a rental car, call the rental company promptly.

limits vary from 30 to 55mph. In cities and towns, they are usually 25 to 35mph, lower near schools and medical facilities.

Speed limits are enforced by police patrolling in marked police cars and in unmarked cars and by 'radar traps' placed so that you won't see them until it's too late. One way to avoid a radar trap is to watch the brake lights of the cars ahead of you. If all the drivers ahead put on their brakes as they pass a certain point, it's likely they've seen – too late! – a radar trap.

The fine for a first speeding offense is $350 in Connecticut, and it's similarly expensive in other states.

**Safety Restraints** Some states (such as Rhode Island and Connecticut) require the use of safety belts, fining both the driver and the beltless passenger for riding unsecured. Regardless, your chances of avoiding injury in an accident are significantly higher if you wear a safety belt. Buckle up!

In every state, children under four years of age are required by law to be placed in child safety seats secured by a seat belt. Older children may be required by law to wear safety belts. Child safety seats are available from car rental firms, sometimes at a small extra charge. In any car equipped with a front-passenger-seat air bag, no child should sit in the front passenger seat. Air bags, which inflate at 200mph, are designed to protect a full-size, full-weight adult and can seriously injure or kill a small or light person. Seat children in the back and buckle their seat belts for added safety.

## Rental

You must be at least 21 years of age (in some cases 25) and have a valid driver's license to rent an automobile. A major credit card is a practical necessity as well. Without one, you may have to put down a cash deposit of up to $2000.

Well-known national car rental companies such as Avis, Budget, Dollar, Hertz, National and Thrifty tend to have higher rates but more efficient service. National firms can be a bit cheaper, but it is the small local companies that are the cheapest. Quality, service and car condition are most variable among the local firms, which often specialize in rentals to people whose own cars are under repair.

**National Companies** Reservations can be made with the large rental companies through a travel agent or by calling the company directly; numbers are listed under 'Automobile Renting' in the yellow pages. Here are some numbers, local to Boston and national:

| Alamo | ☎ 617-561-4100 |
| | 800-327-9633 |
| American International | ☎ 800-227-0648 |
| Avis | ☎ 617-534-1400 |
| | 800-831-2847 |
| Budget | ☎ 617-497-1800 |
| | 800-527-0700 |
| Dollar | ☎ 800-800-4000 |
| Enterprise | ☎ 617-742-1955 |
| | 800-325-8007 |
| Hertz | ☎ 800-654-3131 |
| National | ☎ 617-661-8747 |
| | 800-227-7368 |
| Payless Car Rental | ☎ 800-729-5377 |
| Rent-A-Wreck | ☎ 617-576-3700 |
| | 800-535-1391 |
| Thrifty | ☎ 617-569-6500 |
| | 800-367-2277 |

**Local Companies** Some local rental companies and automobile dealerships rent cars as well, often providing good service at cheaper rates than national companies. Most offer free delivery and pickup at the airport or a hotel, unlimited mileage and quality cars.

However, before you rent from a local agency, you might want to check their Reliability Report at Boston's Better Business Bureau (☎ 617-426-9000, www.bosbbb.org), 20 Park Plaza, Boston, MA 02116, which serves eastern Massachusetts, Maine and Vermont. All of the reports are available on the bureau's website. (If you find that one of these companies gives particularly good service, please write to us so that we can recommend it in future editions of this guide.) The following are a few choices:

Americar Auto Rental
(☎ 617-776-4640, 800-540-4642)
265 Medford St, Somerville, MA 02143

Cartemps
(☎ 617-924-7147)
40 Joy St, Somerville, MA 02143

Peter Fuller Rent-a-Car
(☎ 617-926-7511)
43 N Beacon St, Watertown, MA 02172

**Insurance** Rental vehicles come with liability insurance so that if you hit another person or property, the damage will be paid for. What is not covered is damage to the rental vehicle itself. The so-called Collision Damage Waiver (CDW) or Loss Damage Waiver on a rental car may cost between $10 and $16 or more per day, significantly increasing the cost of the overall rental. Though it would be foolish to rent without insuring the vehicle in some way, you do not necessarily have to buy the rental company's inflated CDW.

If you own a car registered in the USA, your own auto insurance may cover damage to a rental car; check with your insurance agent to be sure. Some major credit card companies may provide coverage for any vehicle rented with their cards; check your credit card agreement to see what coverage is provided. Note that in case of damage, rental companies may require that you not only pay for repairs, but also that you pay normal rental fees for all the time that the rental car is off the road for repairs. Your policy should cover this loss as well.

**Saving Money** The cheapest rates are for the smallest cars, from noon Thursday through noon Monday (or for an entire week or more), returning the vehicle to the place of rental (or at least to the city of rental).

Because of airport taxes, a rental is often more expensive if you pick it up at the airport. A taxi ride to the off-airport office of a local firm may result in a lower price.

You may be offered a choice of 'fuel plans': You can pick up and return the car with a full tank of fuel, or you can pay for the gas that's in the car and return it empty. The full tank is always the better choice. As it's virtually impossible to return a car empty of gas, you will end up turning over several gallons of fuel to the rental company, which will then try to sell it to the next renter.

**RV Rental** Most private campgrounds are designed to accommodate recreational vehicles, from camper vans to the largest motorhomes. Rentals can cost anywhere from $75 to $125 per day, and as they are large vehicles, they use lots of fuel. In addition, parking them and sleeping in them overnight outside of campgrounds is not allowed in many areas, so you should expect to spend around $20 to $35 per night for a camping place.

Before you decide on an RV rental, read about camping under Accommodations in the Facts for the Visitor chapter. For further information, contact the Recreation Vehicle Rental Association (☎ 703-591-7130, 800-336-0355, fax 703-591-0734, www.rvra.org), 3930 University Drive, Fairfax, VA 22030. Companies that rent RVs can be found in the yellow pages of the phone book under 'Recreational Vehicles – Renting & Leasing,' 'Trailers – Camping & Travel' and 'Motor Homes – Renting & Leasing.'

## Fuel

Gas stations can be found everywhere – sometimes on each of the four corners of an intersection – and many are open 24 hours a day. Small-town stations may be open only from 7 am to 8 or 9 pm.

At some stations, you must pay before you pump; at others, you may pump before you pay. The more modern pumps have credit/debit card terminals built into them, so you can pay with plastic right at the pump. (The most modern pumps have little TV screens that blast advertisements in your face as you pump the gas.) At more expensive, 'full service' stations, an attendant will pump your gas for you; no tip is expected.

Plan on spending $1.15 to $1.50 per US gallon, more around bigger cities and for higher-octane fuels. Leaded gasoline is not sold in the USA.

## Road Maps

Detailed road maps are printed and distributed by state tourism offices (see Tourist Offices in the Facts for the Visitor chapter), usually for free. Good commercial maps (see Maps in Facts for the Visitor) are sold in gas stations, newsstands, bookstores, convenience shops and drugstores for $2 to $4.

## Parking

Parking is controlled mostly by signs on the street stating explicitly what may or may not be done. A yellow line or yellow-painted curb means that no parking is allowed there. In some towns, a white line is painted along the curb in areas where you may park.

## Safety

To avert theft, do not leave expensive items, such as purses, CDs, cameras, leather bags or even sunglasses, visibly lying around in your car. Tuck items under a seat or, even better, put them in the trunk and make sure your car does not have trunk entry through the back seat; if it does, make sure this is locked. Don't leave valuables in your car overnight.

Some, but not all, US states have laws requiring motorcycle riders to wear helmets whenever they ride. In any case, use of a helmet is highly recommended.

## Breakdowns & Assistance

If your car breaks down and you need help, a few highways in New England have Motorist Aid Call Boxes with emergency telephones posted every few miles along the roadside. On other highways, raise the hood (bonnet) of your vehicle and/or tie a white cloth (such as a handkerchief) to the radio aerial to signal that you need help, and await a police patrol, which often comes within an hour.

The American Automobile Association (AAA; ☎ 800-222-4357, www.aaa.com) provides battery charging, short-range towing, gasoline delivery and minor repairs at no charge to its members and to those of affiliated auto clubs. However, members are still liable for long-distance towing and for major repairs.

## BICYCLE

Bicycling is a common sport and means of transport on both city streets and country roads. Several of the larger cities have systems of bike paths that make bike travel much easier and more pleasant. Some towns have turned disused railroad rights-of-way into bike trails that run for several miles. The Shining Sea Bicycle Path between Falmouth and Woods Hole is a prominent example.

Bicycle rentals are available in most New England cities, towns and resorts at reasonable prices (often $15 to $20 per day). Many rental shops are mentioned in this guide. For others, look in the yellow pages under 'Bicycles.'

## HITCHHIKING

Hitchhiking is not safe, not recommended and often not legal. Smart, law-abiding drivers do not pick up hitchhikers, which means that if you hitch, you are likely to be picked up by a driver who is not smart or law-abiding. Both hitchers and the drivers who pick them up should understand that they are taking a small but potentially serious risk. People who do choose to hitch will be safer if they travel in pairs and let someone know where they are planning to go.

## WALKING

Walking and jogging are very popular in New England. Most cities and resort towns have sightseeing trails marked by signs or shown on brochure maps, and jogging/bike trails along rivers, lakes or the seashore. In the countryside, several extensive trail systems even allow for interstate hikes. The Appalachian Trail, which stretches from Maine to Georgia, is the most famous, but Vermont's Long Trail is also impressive. See Activities in the Facts for the Visitor chapter for more on walking.

## BOAT

Boat service is mostly local, and tends to be more for pleasure excursions than transportation. Ferries offer a few exceptions.

In Massachusetts, you can take a ferry between Falmouth Heights and Edgartown (Martha's Vineyard); Gloucester and Provincetown; Hyannis and Nantucket Island; New Bedford and Woods Hole or Cuttyhunk Island; and Woods Hole and Oak Bluffs or Vineyard Haven (Martha's Vineyard).

In Connecticut, ferries travel between Bridgeport and Port Jefferson (Long Island, New York); New London and Block Island; and New London and Orient Point (Long Island).

In Vermont, there's a ferry running from Burlington to New York state, traversing Lake Champlain.

In Maine, you can travel by ferry between Bar Harbor and Portland and Yarmouth, Nova Scotia; and Port Clyde and Monhegan Island.

## LOCAL TRANSPORT
### Bus & Subway

City buses and, in Boston, the T (a subway/underground), provide useful transportation within the larger cities and to some suburban points. Resort areas also tend to have some useful regional bus lines. These are mentioned in the text.

### Taxi

Taxis are useful and common in the largest cities. In smaller cities and towns, you will probably have to telephone a cab to pick you up. Ask at a hotel, restaurant or tourist office or look in the yellow pages under 'Taxicabs.' Note that a taxi must be licensed by the city in which you board it in order to pick you up, though some companies are licensed to operate in a number of cities.

Taxi drivers are usually willing to take you just about anywhere if you can afford the fare. For longer trips, this may be about $2.50 or $3 per mile.

City taxis have fare meters, which usually begin at $1.90 and then add a certain price per mile. Extra charges may be added for extra passengers or, as in New York City, an extra 50¢ charge may apply for driving after sundown. On top of cab fare, you should add a tip of about 15%. Town taxis may not have meters but will quote you the fare when you call. The same 15% tip is expected.

Standards of service are generally low in big cities, better in smaller towns. Some city drivers speak a limited amount of English. Also, some drivers may not know their city well, but they can usually radio to headquarters and get directions.

Many city taxis are rolling wrecks in which the back seat (where the passenger rides) is separated from the front (driver's) seat by a thick, clear plastic barrier. The passenger can easily be forgiven for feeling as if he/she is in a jail-on-wheels. Cut into the plastic barrier is usually some sort of hole, chute or sliding door so that the passenger can get money to the driver at the end of the ride. Although this arrangement makes it more difficult for the passenger to rob the driver, it does not hamper the driver from 'robbing' the passenger by taking an unnecessarily long route. For longer journeys that you are able to plan in advance (such as trips to the airport), you may want to hire a limo instead (see below). The cost is about the same, the comfort and service far better.

### Limousine

A limousine (limo for short) is either an 'executive sedan' (a luxury car such as a Lincoln Town Car or Cadillac El Dorado, or at least a very comfortable full-size sedan) or a 'stretch limo' (an executive sedan that has been lengthened to provide more interior room). A limo takes you anywhere you like at either a predetermined or an hourly fare. Executive sedans are often not much more expensive than regular taxis, though they cannot be hailed on the street; they must be booked in advance. Standards of service and comfort are far above those of regular taxis. If you can plan ahead and want a more pleasant ride at a modest increase in price, look in the yellow pages under 'Limousine Service.'

Some shuttle van services (see below) use the term 'limo' or 'limousine' for their comfortable – but hardly luxurious – shuttle vans. Ask what you're getting when you reserve.

## Shuttle Services

It's also possible to reserve a seat in a comfortable van or minibus that shuttles passengers between the airport and the city center or suburbs. Shuttles hold anywhere from eight to 25 passengers and may serve cities as much as an hour or two away from the airport. Shuttle fares are often less expensive than taxi fares. The shuttle may pick you up at your hotel (or other point), or you may have to meet it at a predetermined stop or station. For the telephone numbers of airport shuttle companies, look in the yellow pages under 'Airport Transportation Service.'

## ORGANIZED TOURS
### Local Tours

City tours by bus or 'trolley' (actually a bus disguised as a light-rail trolley) are popular in the major cities, tourist towns and resort areas. Most are useful for getting a look at the major sights, though the commentary is often bland.

There are some adventurous exceptions, such as the 'duck' tours in Boston and Gloucester, a 'duck' being a huge military amphibious vehicle that cruises the city streets, then glides into the river or bay for a nautical cruise.

### Regional Tours

Regional tours are the way to go if you don't have time to make reservations in many different destinations or don't have a car. By far the most popular are the autumn foliage tours – they can be a good way to get out of the city. They are often fully booked early on and may be more expensive than normal tours.

In the mountain towns of Maine, New Hampshire and Vermont, tours by bicycle, canoe, raft and kayak are popular. See the Activities section of the Facts for the Visitor chapter for more information.

The company Destinnations (☎ 508-428-5600, fax 420-0565), PO Box 1173, Osterville, MA 02655, tailors individual tours according to budget and interests: You could do a 'Cape and Island Hop,' a B&B & Inns tour, a factory outlet mall tour and more. A five-day seasonal value package could run as low as $500, giving you lodging at B&Bs around New England.

# Boston

Most visitors to Boston come to the same opinion: This city is lively, attractive, interesting and educational, and, perhaps most importantly, it's manageable.

The city's liveliness comes in large part from the huge population of college-age residents. Having 60-odd colleges and universities in greater Boston means that there are always lots of sporting activities, cultural pursuits (cinema, theater, galleries, literary cafes, and bars and musical performances for all tastes), shopping and nightlife.

Boston's attractiveness comes in part from its being a wealthy port and commercial city since colonial times. During the 19th century, Boston prided itself on being the 'Athens of America' because of its many beautiful buildings, its large population of literati, artists and educators, and its varied cultural institutions of the highest standard.

The Atlantic Ocean, Boston Harbor and the Charles and Mystic Rivers vary the cityscape and provide light and a sense of openness. Urban planning, including a long 'emerald necklace' of parks, gardens and verdant thoroughfares designed by the great American landscape architect Frederick Law Olmstead, brings a bit of the country right into the city.

Boston suffers a bit by being within a four-hour drive of New York City, the great American metropolis. When Boston's top professionals and artists reach the pinnacle of success, many of them take that final step up the career ladder to New York City. But Boston is cleaner, safer, friendlier and easier to negotiate. It is a city of vibrant neighborhoods, from working-class Charlestown to staid, old Beacon Hill to the Italian North End. And just 30 minutes outside of town, you'll find yourself among cornfields, gardens, beautiful colonial towns, scenic rivers and country roads ideal for cycling.

## HISTORY

Called Trimountain (for its three hills) in its earliest days, Boston took its permanent name from the English town of that name. The vanguard of English settlers led by Reverend William Blaxton arrived in 1624 – less than four years after the Pilgrims arrived in nearby Plymouth.

The colony of Massachusetts Bay was established six years later in 1630 when the elder John Winthrop, official representative

## Highlights

- Deciding for yourself who makes the best New England clam chowder
- Walking through the Mapparium at the Christian Science Mother Church
- Taking in a Boston Pops concert on the Esplanade
- Walking across the Saltonstall Bridge from Kendall Square at dusk
- Window shopping on Newbury St
- Eating cannoli in the North End
- Finding the oldest tombstone in the Old Granary Burying Ground
- Getting a bird's-eye view of Boston from the John Hancock Tower Observatory

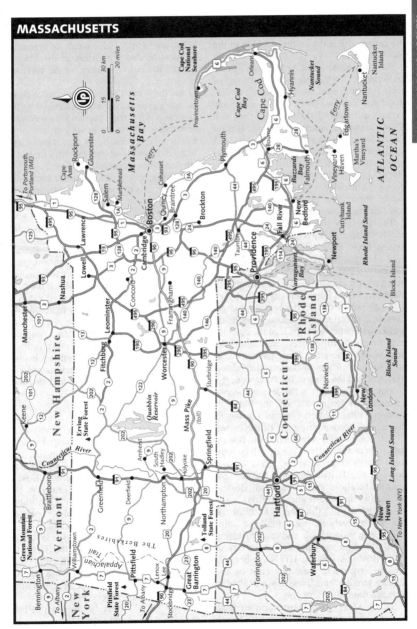

# MASSACHUSETTS

of the Massachusetts Bay Company, took up residence. From the beginning, this was the center of Puritan culture and life in the New World.

Puritanism was intellectual and theocratic, and so the leading men and women of early Boston society were those who understood and followed Biblical law – and could explain in powerful rhetoric why they did. Thus it comes as no surprise that the Boston Public Latin School was established in 1635 (and continues as an elite public high school today). A year later, Harvard College (now Harvard University) was founded in neighboring Cambridge. By 1653, Boston had a public library, and by 1704 the 13 original colonies' first newspaper, the *News-Letter*.

Though the New England coast had many excellent natural ports such as Essex, Plymouth, Providence and Salem, Boston was blessed by geography with the best of all. By the early 1700s it was well on its way to being what it remains today: New England's largest and most important city.

As the chief city in the region, it drew London's attention. When King George III and Parliament chose to burden the colonies with taxation without representation, the taxes were first levied in Boston. When resistance surfaced, it was in Boston. The Boston Massacre and the Boston Tea Party were significant turning points in the development of revolutionary sentiments, and the Battle of Bunker Hill solidified colonial resolve to declare independence from the British crown.

Following the Revolutionary War, Boston suffered economically as the British government cut off American ships' access to other ports in the British Empire. But as new trading relationships developed, Boston entered a commercial and industrial boom which lasted from the late 1700s until the mid-1800s. Fortunes were made in shipbuilding, maritime trade and manufacturing textiles and shoes. Chartered as a city in 1822, Boston's Beacon Hill soon became crowned with fine mansions built by the leading families, and Back Bay was filled in to make room for more.

These same prominent families also patronized arts and culture heavily. Though

typically conservative and traditionalist in their general outlook, Bostonians were firm believers in American ideals of freedom. They were also supporters of the Underground Railroad and were for the abolition of slavery.

As the 19th century drew to a close, Boston's prominence was challenged by the growth of other port cities and the westward expansion of the national borders. New England's economic boom turned into a bust when the textile and shoe factories moved to cheaper labor markets in the South.

The Irish potato famine drove thousands of immigrants to the New World, especially Boston, changing the city's ethnic and economic profiles. The new arrivals were soon to be joined by immigrants from Italy, the Ottoman Empire and Portugal.

In the 20th century, however, Boston managed to remain an important port, becoming a prominent center for medical education, treatment and research, and the premiere university center in the USA. Many graduates have chosen to stay in the Boston area, which has helped to fuel booming local commerce in computer research, development and manufacturing.

As we head into the 21st century, Boston is still poised to continue its preeminent contributions in the technology and financial services sectors.

## ORIENTATION

For a city of its stature, Boston is quite small. The sights and activities of principal interest to travelers are contained within an area that's only about 1 mile wide by 3 miles long. It's bounded on the eastern edge by Boston Harbor and the Atlantic Ocean, on the north by the Charles River and Cambridge. Boston proper has about 600,000 people; 'greater' Boston has over 3 million.

Most of what you'll want to see in Boston is easily accessible by MBTA (the 'T'; ☎ 617-222-3200, 800-392-6100, www.mbta.com) subway trains. Convenient T subway stations are given throughout the text. See the Getting Around section for more information.

The Central Artery (also known as I-93, the John F Fitzgerald Expressway and simply 'the expressway') cuts right through downtown, separating the North End and waterfront from the rest of the city. The Central Artery, currently undergoing the largest public works construction project (also known as the 'Big Dig') in US history, is being widened and rerouted underground to alleviate the persistent traffic nightmares. The construction, of course, is creating its own set of surface-artery problems, which will remain well into the 21st century. Don't let this deter you from visiting; do, though, think twice about driving in Boston. Currently the hardest-hit areas are around South Station and the waterfront. (See the 'Big Dig' text under Car in the Getting There & Away section near the end of this chapter.)

Most of Boston's downtown streets began as simple colonial cow paths. And as such, they're often winding, one way and narrow. Expect to get a bit lost as you wander the downtown neighborhoods of the small but powerful Financial District (and adjacent Downtown Crossing), the primarily Italian North End, the Brahmin Beacon Hill, the no-nonsense Government Center, colorful and aromatic Chinatown and the Theater District. Boston's neighborhoods are quite distinct, and since all the above areas abut one another, they're best explored on foot.

Beacon Hill, its brick streets lit by gas lanterns and lined with patrician townhouses, is one of the loveliest areas for strolling. It is bounded by Charles, Cambridge and Beacon Sts. Two large parks – the Boston Common and Public Garden – lie adjacent to it on the south.

Back Bay, created as a mid-19th century landfill project, is more orderly than the rest of the city. Its streets, lined with lovely brownstones and flowering trees, are laid out east to west in alphabetical order: Arlington, Berkeley, Clarendon and so on to Hereford. Commonwealth Ave (referred to as Comm Ave) is Boston's most grand boulevard, with a grassy promenade running the length of it. The Back Bay ends at Massachusetts Ave (known simply as Mass Ave), which runs northeast across the Charles River and into Cambridge and Harvard Square.

West of Mass Ave lies Kenmore Square and the Fenway area. Kenmore Square is home to a vibrant nightclub scene and lots of university students. The Fenway includes a 4-mile-long grassy byway that leads in one direction to an arboretum, and in the other to two important museums, the Museum of Fine Arts and the Isabella Stewart Gardner Museum. Fenway Park is the home of the much-loved Boston Red Sox baseball team.

The South End is just south of Back Bay. It lies between Berkeley St to the east and Mass Ave to the west, with Huntington and Shawmut Aves to the north and south, respectively. This newly gentrified area, thick with restaurants, artsy shops and renovated Victorian brownstones, is also nice for walking.

The Charles River, with a popular grassy esplanade along both its banks, separates Boston and Cambridge, which is home to Harvard University and the Massachusetts Institute of Technology (MIT). The best views of the Boston skyline and Beacon Hill are from the northern banks of the Charles River near the Longfellow Bridge.

## Maps

You can get good maps of Boston and New England at just about any bookstore (see the 'Bookstores' boxed text). The AAA map of Boston is good, if a bit large. Look for the smaller, laminated 'Streetwise' maps of the city, which are useful for longer stays and cost about $6.

If you plan on doing more bicycling than simply along the banks of the Charles River, get ahold of the fantastic *Boston's Bike Map* produced by Rubel BikeMaps (☎ 617-776-6567, www.bikemaps.com), PO Box 1035, Cambridge, MA 02140. It costs $4.25 and is available from the Globe Corner Bookstore (see the 'Bookstores' boxed text) or directly from Rubel. See also Bicycling later in this chapter for information on their laminated 'Pocket Rides.'

## Observatories

For a bird's-eye view of Boston, head to the 60th-floor observatory of New England's tallest building: the **John Hancock Tower**

(☎ 617-247-1977), 200 Clarendon St. The ticket booth is at Trinity Place and St James Ave. In addition to providing a good overview of your neighborhood walking tour, observatory bonuses include a topographical map of Boston as it appeared in 1775 and an audio presentation of the Revolutionary War battles that took place in and around Boston. It's open 9 am to 11 pm daily; open until 6 pm Sunday November through March. Admission is $5 adults, $3 seniors and children. The last tickets are sold one hour before closing, so plan ahead. Ⓣ Green Line to Copley or Orange Line to Back Bay.

The 50th-floor **Prudential Center Skywalk** (☎ 617-236-3318), 800 Boylston St, offers a spectacular 360° view of metro Boston and Cambridge. (The John Hancock Observatory only has views on three sides.) It's open 10 am to 10 pm daily, and the last tickets are sold 30 minutes prior to closing. Fees are the same as the Hancock. Ⓣ Green Line to Prudential or Hynes Convention Center.

## INFORMATION
### Tourist Offices
Write or call the Greater Boston Convention and Visitors Bureau (GBCVB; ☎ 617-536-4100, 800-888-5515, visitus@bostonusa.com, www.bostonusa.com), 2 Copley Place, suite 105, Boston, MA 02116, in advance of your visit. They'll send an information packet. Ⓣ Green Line to Copley.

Once in Boston, drop in at the GBCVB's year-round Visitor Information Center (☎ 617-426-3115), Tremont and West Sts on Boston Common. You can pick up a subway and bus route map, as well as other maps and information. The center (which has public restrooms) is open 8:30 am to 5 pm daily (Sunday from 9 am). Ⓣ Red or Green Line to Park St.

In Back Bay, the GBCVB has an information booth in the center court of the Prudential Center mall, 800 Boylston St. It's open 9 am to 5 pm daily. Ⓣ Green Line to Prudential or Hynes Convention Center.

The National Park Service Visitor Center (NPS; ☎ 617-242-5642, www.nps.gov/bost/), 15 State St across from the Old State House,

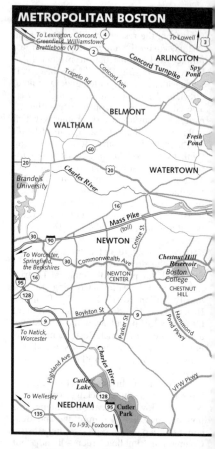

has plenty of historical literature, a short slide show and free walking tours of the Freedom Trail (see the 'Walking Tours' boxed text). The center is open 9 am to 5 pm daily (until 6 pm in summer). Ⓣ Orange or Blue Line to State.

For city and statewide information, write to or stop in at the Massachusetts Office of Travel & Tourism (☎ 617-973-8500, 800-227-6277, vacationinfo@state.ma.us, www.massvacation.com), Transportation Building, 10 Park Plaza, 4th floor, Boston, MA 02116. The office is open 9 am to 5 pm weekdays. Ⓣ Green Line to Boylston.

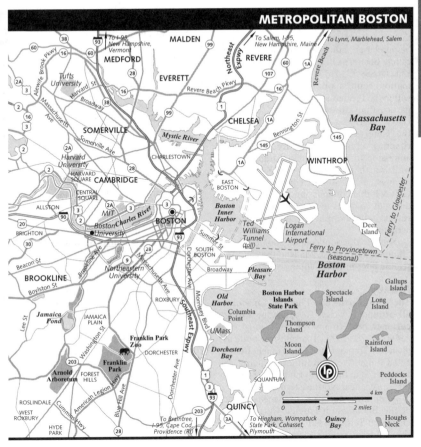

**METROPOLITAN BOSTON**

In Cambridge, the Visitor Information Booth (☎ 617-441-2884, 800-862-5678, www.cambridge.usa.org), in Harvard Square, has plenty of detailed information on current Cambridge happenings and self-guided walking tours. The visitor information kiosk is staffed 9 am to 5 pm Monday through Saturday, 1 to 5 pm on Sundays. Ⓣ Red Line to Harvard.

The Appalachian Mountain Club Headquarters (the AMC; ☎ 617-523-0636, www.outdoors.org), 5 Joy St, is *the* resource for outdoor activities in Boston and throughout New England. AMC Headquarters,

complete with bookstore, is open 8:30 am to 5:30 pm weekdays. Ⓣ Red or Green Line to Park St.

## Discount Tickets

The Boston Citypass, a discount attraction ticket program, provides a great value if you plan on going to most of the following sites: the Museum of Fine Arts, Museum of Science, New England Aquarium, Isabella Stewart Gardner Museum, John F Kennedy Library & Museum and the John Hancock Observatory. The pass costs $26.50 adults, $20.50 for seniors and $13.50 for children.

(Purchased separately, the tickets would cost double that.) Once the pass is purchased, there's no more waiting in line. Passes may be purchased either prior to your arrival by calling Boston's Official Visitors Information Line (☎ 888-733-2678), or at the visitor information centers on Boston Common or within the Prudential Center or at any of the participating attractions.

For $9, Bostix (see Discount Tickets in the Entertainment section later in this chapter) offers a booklet for two-for-one admission to museums and attractions. It's well worth it. Ask for the 'Passport to Savings,' a blue booklet published by the GBCVB that contains almost $200 worth of discount coupons to area attractions, a few restaurants, shopping areas and outdoor activities.

See also discount coupon booklets under Shopping Districts & Malls in the shopping section later in this chapter.

## Money
There are Cirrus and Plus ATM machines all around the city. To exchange foreign currency, head to any BankBoston (☎ 617-434-4275, 788-5000). BankBoston branches include: 6 Tremont St at Government Center; 540 Comm Ave at Kenmore Square; 260 Hanover St in the North End; and 285 Huntington Ave near Northeastern University.

At the airport, you can exchange currency at the BankBoston Foreign Currency Exchange at Terminal C (☎ 617-569-1172), on the 2nd level, open 8:30 am to 10 pm daily, and Terminal E (☎ 617-567-2313), 1st level, open from 8:30 am to 10 pm weekdays, 11:30 am to 10 pm weekends.

## Post & Communications
Boston's main post office, the General Mail Facility (☎ 617-654-5326), 25 Dorchester Ave, Boston, MA 02205, is just one block southeast of South Station. It never closes. Ⓣ Red Line to South Station.

Branch post offices include the following:

Back Bay
  (☎ 617-267-8162)
  800 Boylston St, in the Prudential Center

Beacon Hill
  (☎ 617-723-1951)
  136 Charles St
Cambridge
  (☎ 617-876-0620)
  Central Square, 770 Mass Ave
Faneuil Hall Marketplace
  (☎ 617-723-1791)
  In the original Faneuil Hall; no packages
Financial District
  (☎ 617-720-5314)
  90 Devonshire St, Post Office Square
North End
  (☎ 617-723-5134)
  217 Hanover St

Most of these branches are open 7:30 or 8 am to 5 or 6 pm weekdays and on Saturday morning.

All general delivery (poste restante) mail must be sent to the main post office; branch offices cannot accept it.

## Internet Resources
Websites are listed throughout the text. They are particularly useful in checking up-to-the-minute entertainment offerings.

## Travel Agencies
Budget travel specialists include the Council on International Educational Exchange's Council Travel (CIEE; ☎ 617-266-1926, 800-226-8624, www.ciee.org), 273 Newbury St. They can satisfy just about every travel-related need that arises. The Council's offices are open 9 am to 7 pm daily except Sunday. Ⓣ Green Line to Hynes Convention Center.

Other CIEE offices include Harvard Square, 12 Elliot St, 2nd floor, which is open from 9:30 am to 5:30 pm weekdays, except 10:30 am on Wednesday and 10 am to 2 pm on Saturday; and on the MIT campus at Stratton Student Center, 84 Mass Ave, with the same weekday hours as Harvard Square.

Let's Go Travel (☎ 617-495-9649, www.hsa.net/travel), 53A Church St, is in Cambridge and is open 10 am to 6 pm weekdays. They do not sell air tickets. Ⓣ Red Line to Harvard.

The Vacation Outlet agency at Filene's Basement (☎ 617-267-8100, 800-527-8646,

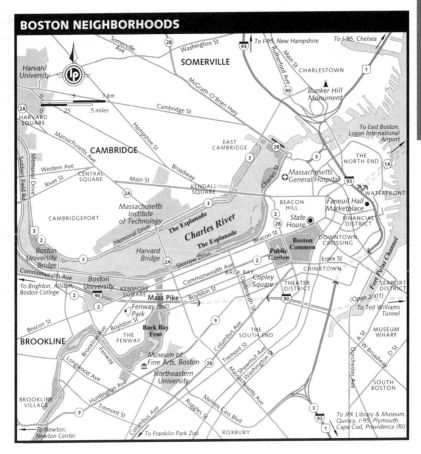

## BOSTON NEIGHBORHOODS

www.vacationoutlet.com), 426 Washington St at Downtown Crossing, offers lots of last-minute deals that tour consolidators could not sell. The idea is that they'd rather sell the package at the last minute for a pretty nominal fee than take a complete loss on it. Their loss could be your gain. ⓣ Red or Orange Line to Downtown Crossing.

### Libraries

The venerable Boston Public Library (☎ 617-536-5400, www.bpl.org), 666 Boylston St, is the country's oldest free city library; it dates

back to 1852. Although more than 2 million people visit annually, most bypass the walled-in tranquil garden courtyard, which has a reflecting pool and trees, where you can read 9 am to 9 pm Monday through Thursday, 9 am to 5 pm Friday and Saturday and 1 to 5 pm Sunday. ⓣ Green Line to Copley.

The grand Boston Athenaeum (☎ 617-227-0270, www.bostonathenaeum.org), 10½ Beacon St, is an impressive, independent library, owned by 1049 shareholders whose shares trace back to 1807. One-hour tours of the neoclassical reading rooms are offered

## Bookstores

Boston and Cambridge are a book lover's paradise. For example, there are entire stores devoted to maps, mysteries, foreign languages or scholarly texts. The Harvard Square Visitor Information Booth hands out a free brochure of Harvard Square's more than 30 bookstores, and the Yellow Pages lists more than 100. Here are a few worth searching out.

The outstanding Globe Corner Bookstore (www.globecorner.com) has two locations: 500 Boylston St (☎ 617-859-8008), Ⓣ Green Line to Arlington or Copley; 49 Palmer St, Cambridge (☎ 617-497-6277), Ⓣ Red Line to Harvard. Specializing in travel books for near and far, Globe Corner also carries hundreds of specialty maps, including topographical maps of New England. (For more topos, check out the AMC Headquarters, listed under Tourist Offices near the beginning of the chapter.)

Another excellent choice for travel guides and maps is the Rand McNally Map & Travel Store (☎ 617-720-1125), 84 State St, near Faneuil Hall Marketplace. Ⓣ Orange or Blue Line to State.

The Glad Day Gay Liberation Bookshop (☎ 617-267-3010), 673 Boylston St, is a well-stocked store dedicated to gay- and lesbian-related titles. The bulletin board outside the 2nd-floor store is packed with useful community information. Ⓣ Green Line to Copley.

In business since the 1930s, the outdoor Copley Square News (no ☎), on Boylston St at Dartmouth St, sells hundreds of magazines and many foreign-language periodicals. Ⓣ Green Line to Copley.

In Cambridge, Out of Town News (☎ 617-354-7777), Harvard Square, is no ordinary newsstand; in fact, it's a National Historic Landmark, open 6 am to 10:30 pm. It sells papers from virtually every major US city, as well as from dozens of cities around the world. Ⓣ Red Line to Harvard.

Schoenhof's Foreign Books (☎ 617-547-8855), 76A Mt Auburn St, in the basement, is a national center for foreign-language materials and books, and dictionaries covering just about any language. Ⓣ Harvard on the Red Line.

The Brattle Book Shop (☎ 617-542-0210), 9 West St, is a treasure, crammed with out-of-print, rare and first-edition books. Ⓣ Orange or Red Line to Downtown Crossing.

Tuesday and Thursday at 3 pm, but you must call 24 hours in advance to reserve. Ⓣ Red or Green Line to Park St.

Also see the John F Kennedy Library & Museum, which has an Ernest Hemingway archive, later in this chapter.

### Newspapers & Magazines

The major daily newspapers include *The Boston Globe* (www.boston.com), which publishes an extensive and useful Calendar section every Thursday, and the competing *Boston Herald* (www.bostonherald.com), which has its own Scene section published every Friday.

The *Boston Phoenix* (www.bostonphoenix.com), the 'alternative' paper that focuses on arts and entertainment, is published weekly. The sassy, bi-weekly *Improper Bostonian* is available free from blue sidewalk dispenser boxes. *Boston Magazine* (www.bostonmagazine.com) is the city's monthly.

### Universities

The greater Boston area has many, many college campuses, too many to mention here. Cultural and sporting events are often open to the public, and this brief listing should help you get further information (see also Spectator Sports later in this chapter). For the Berklee College of Music, see the Entertainment section.

Harvard University (☎ 617-495-1000), founded in 1636, stretches for a few blocks

## Bookstores

One of the most famous poetry bookstores in the USA is near Harvard Square: the Grolier Poetry Bookshop (☎ 617-547-4648), 6 Plympton St. Ⓣ Red Line to Harvard.

The Avenue Victor Hugo Bookshop (☎ 617-266-7746), 339 Newbury St in Back Bay, is one of the best used bookstores in the city. You could browse an entire day away here. Ⓣ Green Line to Hynes Convention Center.

Wordsworth, a good general bookstore, has three locations in Harvard Square within a block of one another on Brattle St: the original Wordsworth (☎ 617-354-5201), 30 Brattle St; Wordsworth Abridged (☎ 617-354-5277), 5 Brattle St; and Curious George Goes to Wordsworth (☎ 617-498-0062), 1 JFK St. Ⓣ Red Line to Harvard.

Known simply as 'The Coop,' the Harvard Cooperative Society (☎ 617-499-2000), 1400 Mass Ave in Harvard Square, carries three floors of books, music and every other 'essential' thing a Harvard student could need. But you don't have to be a student to shop here: Anyone can buy just about anything emblazoned with the Harvard logo.

Barnes & Noble manages the Coop bookstore, but not the Harvard Book Store (☎ 617-661-1515), which is not related at all. In fact, it's been called 'the premiere intellectual bookstore on the Square.'

Barnes & Noble (☎ 617-426-5502), 395 Washington St at Downtown Crossing, is part of a large national chain that offers a 10% discount on hardcover books, 30% off *New York Times* bestsellers.

The Barnes & Noble at Boston University (☎ 617-267-8484), 660 Beacon St, is one of New England's biggest bookstores, with three floors of books. Ⓣ Green Line to Kenmore.

Borders Books, Music & Cafe (☎ 617-557-7188), 10-24 School St at Washington St in Downtown Crossing, has more than 200,000 titles.

The Trident Bookseller & Café (☎ 617-267-8688), 338 Newbury St, in Back Bay, specializes in New Age titles.

Named 'Bookstore of the Year' in 1998, the Brookline Booksmith (☎ 617-325-1512), 279 Harvard St, Brookline, is definitely worth checking out.

east and west along Mass Ave. The main gates leading to the quadrangle of the campus are across the street from the Red Line T stop in Cambridge. Free hour-long historical tours of the Harvard Yard (pronounced locally as 'Hahvahd Yahd') are given at 10 am and 2 pm weekdays (at 2 pm on Saturdays) from the information office (☎ 617-495-1573, www .harvard.edu/news), Holyoke Center, 1350 Mass Ave. There are additional tours in summer. Ⓣ Red Line to Cambridge.

The Massachusetts Institute of Technology (MIT; ☎ 617-253-4795, web.mit.edu/www), a world-renowned scientific mecca founded in 1861, is also spread out along Mass Ave in Cambridge, about 1½ miles east of Harvard Square. Free tours of the campus are given

weekdays at 10 am and 2 pm from 77 Mass Ave, Building 7 lobby. The number of excellent museums and amount of public art on the campus are impressive. Ⓣ Red Line to Kendall.

Northeastern University (☎ 617-373-2000, www.neu.edu), on Huntington Ave, boasts one of the country's largest work-study cooperative programs. Ⓣ Green Line 'E' branch to Northeastern.

Boston University (BU; ☎ 617-353-2000, 353-2169, www.bu.edu), on Comm Ave west of Kenmore Square, enrolls about 30,000 graduate and undergraduate students, and has a huge campus and popular sports teams. Ⓣ Green Line 'B' branch to BU East, BU Central or BU West.

MASSACHUSETTS

The University of Massachusetts, Boston (UMass; ☎ 617-287-5000, www.umb.edu), 100 Morrissey Blvd, is on Columbia Point, surrounded by Dorchester Bay on three sides. It's a commuter campus near the John F Kennedy Library & Museum. Ⓣ Red Line to JFK/UMass, then take a quick shuttle bus.

Other well-established universities on the city's fringe include the following.

Boston College (BC; ☎ 617-552-8000, www.bc.edu) is on Comm Ave (MA 30) in Chestnut Hill. BC boasts a large green campus, Gothic towers, stained glass, a good art museum and excellent Irish and Catholic ephemera collections in the library. Their basketball and football teams are usually high in national rankings. This is also the nation's largest Jesuit community. Ⓣ Green Line 'B' branch to the last stop.

Wellesley College (☎ 781-283-2380, www .wellesley.edu), a Seven Sisters women's college in Wellesley, also sports a lovely green campus and the excellent Davis Museum & Cultural Center. To get to Wellesley, take the MBTA Commuter Rail plus a 10-minute walk, or drive MA 16 to MA 135.

Tufts University (☎ 617-628-5000, www .tufts.edu), in Medford, has about 8500 students and a good basketball team. Ⓣ Red Line to Davis Square, then a five-minute bus ride aboard No 94 or No 96 directly to the campus.

Brandeis University (☎ 781-736-2000, www.brandeis.edu), on South St in Waltham, is a train ride out of Boston. The small campus includes the Rose Art Museum, specializing in New England art. Take the MBTA Commuter Rail from North Station to the Brandeis/Roberts stop.

Massachusetts College of Art (☎ 617-232-1555, www.massart.edu), on Huntington Ave, hosts regular exhibitions at their galleries. The main gallery, 621 Huntington Ave, is open 10 am to 6 pm weekdays. Ⓣ Green Line 'E' branch to Longwood.

## Cultural Centers

The French Library in Boston (☎ 617-266-4351, www.frenchlib.org), 53 Marlborough St, founded in 1946, sponsors regular lectures on travel, cooking and all things French;

receptions often follow. The library sponsors an annual Bastille Day celebration (July 14) during which Marlborough St is closed off. The library is open 10 am to 8 pm Tuesday through Thursday, until 5 pm on Friday and Saturday. Ⓣ Green Line to Arlington.

The Goethe Institute (☎ 617-262-6050, www.goethe.de/uk/bos), at 170 Beacon St, sponsors a cultural program of German events; its library is also well stocked with books, tapes and periodicals. It's open 10 am to 5:30 pm weekdays. They also offer evening classes. Ⓣ Green Line to Arlington.

## Medical Services

Massachusetts General Hospital (MGH; ☎ 617-726-2000) is arguably the city's biggest and best. They can often refer you to smaller clinics and crisis hotlines. The traveler's clinic (☎ 617-724-1934) offers immunization services. Ⓣ Red Line to Charles/MGH.

CVS (☎ 617-876-5519), in the Porter Square shopping mall on Mass Ave, Cambridge, is the area's only 24-hour pharmacy. Ⓣ Red Line to Porter.

## Emergency

The police, ambulances and fire department can be reached by dialing ☎ 911.

Traveler's Aid Society (☎ 617-542-7286), 17 East St (just off Atlantic Ave, across from South Station), is a nonprofit agency that helps stranded travelers in despair. From stolen wallets to practical information to transportation assistance to 'bedless in Boston,' Traveler's Aid is there to help. They also have a booth in South Station (☎ 617-737-2880), open 9 am to 5 pm weekends. The Logan Airport 'Terminal E' Traveler's Aid (☎ 617-567-5385) is open noon to 9 pm daily.

## Dangers & Annoyances

As with most big US cities, there are rundown sections of Boston in which crime is a problem. Avoid parks (such as Boston Common) after dark if there are not many other people around. The same goes for unfamiliar, unpeopled streets and subway stations at night.

## BEACON HILL & DOWNTOWN

Established in 1634, the 50-acre **Boston Common**, bordered by Beacon, Tremont and Charles Sts, is the country's oldest public park. During the Revolutionary War, British troops camped here and until 1830, the Common was used for cattle-grazing. Although there is still a grazing ordinance on the books, today the Common serves picnickers, sunbathers and people-watchers. Colorful characters are often heard spouting off from atop a soapbox near the Park St T station at Tremont and Park Sts. ⓉGreen Line to Boylston, Green or Red Line to Park St.

Adjacent to and southwest of the Boston Common is the **Public Garden**, a 24-acre botanical oasis of cultivated flower beds, clipped grass, ancient trees and a tranquil lagoon. You can't picnic on the lawn like you can on the Common, but there are plenty of benches. Pick one in front of the Swan Boats, pedal-powered boats that ferry children and adults around the pond while ducks swim alongside squawking for bread crumbs. Swan Boat rides cost $1.75 for adults and just under $1 for children. Ⓣ Green Line to Arlington.

The area known as Beacon Hill is Boston's most handsome and affluent residential neighborhood. It lies adjacent to Boston Common and the Public Garden. Beacon Hill extends northward to Cambridge St and west to the Charles River. Charles St, which divides the flat and hilly parts of the neighborhood, is lined with shops and eateries. Distinguished 19th-century brick townhouses, lavender windowpanes, gas lanterns, little courtyards, rooftop gardens and picturesque narrow alleyways – this is the stuff of Beacon Hill. Ⓣ Red Line to Charles/MGH, Blue Line to Bowdoin, Red or Green Line to Park St.

Specifically, seek out the cobblestone **Acorn St** (the city's often-photographed and narrowest street), **Mt Vernon** and **Pinckney Sts** (two of Beacon Hill's prettiest) and **Louisburg Square** (pronounced Lewis-burg), an elegant cluster of million-dollar homes that face a private park owned by the square's residents.

Beacon Hill was never the exclusive domain of blue-blood Brahmins, though. Waves of immigrants, and especially African Americans, free from slavery, settled here in the 19th century.

The **African Meeting House** (☎ 617-723-8863), 8 Smith Court, is the country's oldest African American meeting house. Abolitionists Frederick Douglass and William Lloyd Garrison delivered some passionate speeches here. A ground floor gallery houses changing exhibits. The NPS offers tours 10 am to 4 pm daily late May to early September; call ahead for hours the rest of the year. Admission is free. (The NPS anticipates closing the African Meeting House to the public for restoration beginning October 1, 1999, for approximately a year.) ⓉRed or Green Line to Park St.

The **Museum of Afro-American History** (☎ 617-739-1200, www.afroammuseum.org), 46 Joy St at Smith Court, housed next door in the country's first primary school for blacks (the **Abiel Smith School**), is the best place to learn about Beacon Hill's African American roots. The resource center has an extensive library, CD-ROM collection and permanent exhibits. Same hours as the African Meeting House.

High atop Beacon Hill stands the golden-domed **Massachusetts State House** (☎ 617-727-3676, www.state.ma.us/sec/trs), at Beacon and Bowdoin Sts, where the idiosyncrasies of Massachusetts government and politics are played out like a sporting match. The commanding state capitol building was designed by Boston's beloved Charles Bulfinch and completed in 1798. A free 40-minute tour (10 am to 3:30 pm weekdays) includes a discussion of the history, art works, architecture and political personalities as well as a visit to the legislative chambers when it's in session. Reservations are recommended. Self-guided tours are possible 9 am to 5 pm, when the building is open. Ⓣ Red or Green Line to Park St.

The bas-relief **Robert Gould Shaw Memorial**, at Beacon and Park Sts, across from the State House, honors the nation's first all-black Civil War regiment, which was depicted in the 1989 film *Glory*. The soldiers,

MASSACHUSETTS

# BEACON HILL & DOWNTOWN

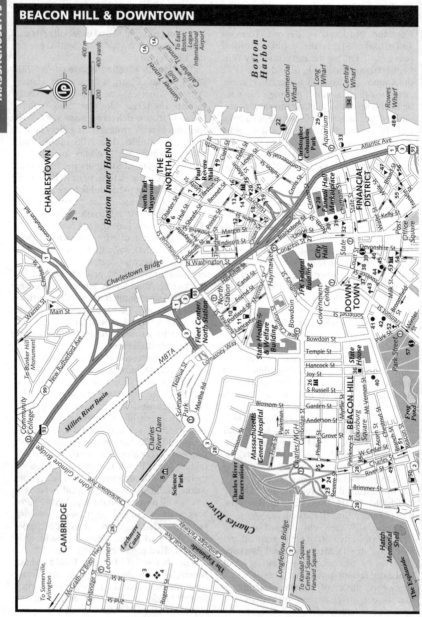

# BEACON HILL & DOWNTOWN

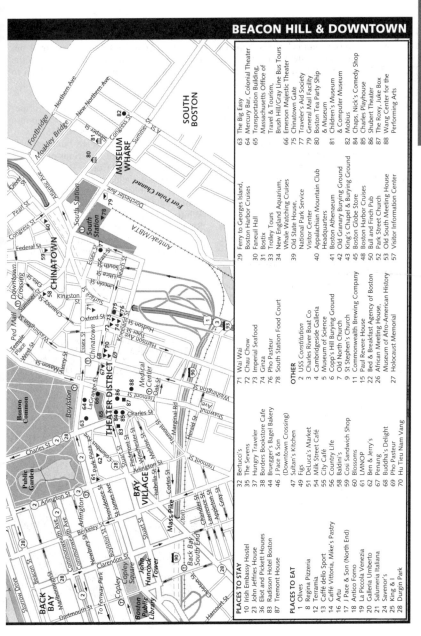

**PLACES TO STAY**
10 Irish Embassy Hostel
23 John Jeffries House
36 Eliot and Pickett Houses
83 Radisson Hotel Boston
87 Tremont House

**PLACES TO EAT**
1 Olives
8 Regina Pizzeria
12 Terramia
13 Caffè dello Sport
14 Caffè Vittoria, Mike's Pastry
16 Artu
17 J Pace & Son (North End)
18 Antico Forno
19 La Piccola Venezia
20 Galleria Umberto
21 Salumeria Italiana
24 Savenor's
25 King & I
28 Durgin Park
32 Bertucci's
35 The Sevens
37 Hungry Traveler
38 Borders Bookstore Cafe
44 Bruegger's Bagel Bakery
46 J Pace & Son
   (Downtown Crossing)
47 Sultan's Kitchen
49 Figs
51 DeLuca's Market
54 Milk Street Café
55 City Café
56 Country Life
58 Baldini's
59 Cosi Sandwich Shop
60 Blossoms
61 LMNOP
62 Ben & Jerry's
67 Penang
68 Buddha's Delight
69 Pho Pasteur
70 Hu Tieu Nam Vang
71 Wai Wai
72 Chau Chow
73 Imperial Seafood
74 Ginza
76 Pho Pasteur
78 South Station Food Court

**OTHER**
2 USS *Constitution*
3 Charles River Boat Co
4 Cambridgeside Galleria
5 Museum of Science
6 Copp's Hill Burying Ground
7 Old North Church
9 St Stephen's Church
11 Commonwealth Brewing Company
15 Paul Revere House
22 Bed & Breakfast Agency of Boston
26 African Meeting House,
   Museum of Afro-American History
27 Holocaust Memorial
29 Ferry to Georges Island,
   Boston Harbor Cruises
31 Bostix
33 Trolley Tours
34 New England Aquarium,
   Whale Watching Cruises
39 Old State House,
   National Park Service
   Visitor Center
40 Appalachian Mountain Club
   Headquarters
41 Boston Athenaeum
42 Old Granary Burying Ground
43 King's Chapel & Burying Ground
45 Boston Globe Store
48 Boston Harbor Cruises
50 Bull and Finch Pub
52 Park Street Church
53 Old South Meeting House
57 Visitor Information Center
63 The Big Easy
64 Mercury Bar, Colonial Theater
65 Transportation Building,
   Massachusetts Office of
   Travel & Tourism,
   Brush Hill/Gray Line Bus Tours
66 Emerson Majestic Theater
75 Chinatown Gate
77 Traveler's Aid Society
79 General Mail Facility
80 Boston Tea Party Ship
   & Museum
81 Children's Museum
   & Computer Museum
82 Mobius
84 Chaps, Nick's Comedy Shop
85 Charles Playhouse
86 Shubert Theater
87 The Roxy, Juke Box
88 Wang Center for the
   Performing Arts

led by Shaw (the son of a notable white family in Boston), refused their $10 monthly stipend for two years until Congress upped it to $13, the amount white regiments were paid. Ⓣ Red or Green Line to Park St.

Walk south on Park St to the **Park Street Church** (☎ 617-523-3383), at the corner of Tremont St. William Lloyd Garrison railed against slavery from the church's pulpit in 1829. This is also where, on Independence Day in 1895, Katherine Lee Bates' hymn 'America the Beautiful' was first sung. The church is noted for its graceful and narrow 200-foot steeple. It's open 9 am to 3 pm daily (except during Sunday services) in July and August, and by appointment the rest of the year. Duck inside to see what musical program is being offered; the schedule is irregular but full. Ⓣ Red or Green Line to Park St.

Adjacent to the church on Tremont St is the **Old Granary Burying Ground**, dating to 1660 and filled with exceptional headstone carvings. Revolutionary heroes including Paul Revere, Samuel Adams and John Hancock are buried here, as are Crispus Attucks (the freed slave who died in the Boston Massacre when British soldiers fired into a group of angry Bostonians in 1770), Benjamin Franklin's parents (he's buried in Philadelphia) and Peter Faneuil (of Faneuil Hall fame). Ⓣ Red or Green Line to Park St.

Continue north to the **King's Chapel & Burying Ground** (☎ 617-523-1749), 58 Tremont at School St. Bostonians were not pleased at all when the original Anglican church was erected in 1688. (Remember, it was the Anglicans – the Church of England – whom the Puritans were fleeing.) The granite church standing today was built in 1754 around the original wooden structure. Then the wooden church was taken apart and tossed out the windows. If the church seems to be missing something, it is: Building funds ran out before a spire could be added. The church houses the largest bell ever made by Paul Revere as well as a lovely sounding organ. An eclectic line-up of recitals is given at 12:15 pm on Tuesdays, year-round. The adjacent burying ground contains the grave of John Winthrop, the first governor of the

fledgling Massachusetts Bay Colony. The church is open 10 am to 2 pm on Saturday mid-October to mid-April; 9 am to 4 pm Friday, Saturday and Monday the rest of the year; additional summer hours are 9 am to 4 pm on Thursday and 1 to 3 pm on Sunday. Ⓣ Red or Green Line to Park St.

Head south on School St to the former Old Corner Bookstore, now converted into the **Boston Globe Store** (☎ 617-367-4000), 1 School St. This circa-1718 building once housed Boston's most illustrious publishing company. As the Old Corner Bookstore, run by Ticknor & Fields, a set of names later used as a publisher's imprint, it produced books by Thoreau, Emerson, Hawthorne, Whittier, Longfellow and Harriet Beecher Stowe. The 19th-century authors often held lively discussions and meetings here. Today you can purchase front-page reprints of historical events covered in the *Boston Globe*. Ⓣ Blue or Orange Line to State, or Red or Orange Line to Downtown Crossing.

You can cross the street to see the **Old South Meeting House** (☎ 617-482-6439),

Samuel Adams,
Old Granary Burying Ground resident

310 Washington St. After a typically feisty town meeting here, colonists decided to protest the British tea taxation (see the entry for the Museum Wharf). The traditional brick-and-wood meetinghouse is open 10 am to 4 pm daily November through March, and 9:30 am to 5 pm daily the rest of the year. Admission is $3 adults, $2.50 seniors and students, $1 children.

Near the intersection of Washington, Summer and Winter Sts, **Downtown Crossing** is a bustling pedestrian-only shopping area that's also home to pushcart vendors and street musicians. Thanks to the volume of nearby office workers, there are plenty of places here for an inexpensive, quick lunch. Ⓣ Orange or Red Line to Downtown Crossing.

The rest of downtown and the **Financial District** lies east of Tremont St and stretches all the way to the waterfront (a 10-minute walk). Bounded by State St to the north and Essex St to the south, this district was once the domain of cows. Their well-trodden, muddy, 17th- and 18th-century paths eventually gave rise to the maze of streets occupied by today's high rises. The buildings are a distinctive blend of modern and historic architecture. The most pleasant place to get a feel for the pace of weekday life in Boston is **Post Office Square** (Congress, Pearl and Franklin Sts). This postage-stamp-size oasis, built atop an underground parking garage, boasts a small cafe (see Places to Eat), a fountain and live music at lunchtime in summer.

To reach the **Old State House** (☎ 617-720-3290, www.oldstatehouse.org), 206 Washington St, from Post Office Square, head north on Congress St to State St. Dating to 1713, this building is perhaps best known for its balcony, where the Declaration of Independence was first read to Bostonians in 1776. One of the best views of the recently restored building, dwarfed by encroaching modern structures, is from a few blocks south on State St. Operated by the Bostonian Society, the museum is definitely worth a visit. It houses Revolutionary memorabilia pertinent to Boston's (and thus the nation's) history. The Old State House is open 9:30 am to 5 pm daily. Admission costs $3 adults,

$2 seniors and students, $1 children. The NPS Visitor Center (see Tourist Offices earlier in this chapter) is across the street. Ⓣ Orange or Blue Line to State.

The site of the Boston Massacre, directly in front of the Old State House balcony, is encircled by cobblestones. It marks the spot where, on March 5, 1770, British soldiers fired upon an angry mob of protesting colonists, killing five of them. This incident inflamed anti-British sentiment, which led to the outbreak of the Revolutionary War.

Heading north on Congress St brings you smack up against a coldly impersonal mass of concrete buildings dating to the 1960s. The **Government Center** is home to the fortresslike Boston City Hall. Although there are plans afoot to create a more inviting and humane City Hall Plaza, city politics tend to slow to a snail's pace even when dealing with the most benign ideas for change. What few vestiges remain of the Old West End, as the neighborhood was once called, are found in the little byways between Merrimac and Causeway Sts. Ⓣ Green or Blue Line to Government Center or Green or Orange Line to Haymarket.

**Faneuil Hall Marketplace** (☎ 617-338-2323, www.faneuilhallmarketplace.com), due east of Boston City Hall, is the granddaddy of East Coast waterfront revitalizations. Pronounced 'fan'l' or 'fan-yool,' the actual hall was constructed as a market and public meeting place in 1740. It's the brick building with the beloved grasshopper weathervane on top. The 2nd floor is still used for public meetings. Behind Faneuil Hall are three long granite buildings that make up the rest of the marketplace, the center of the city's produce and meat industry for almost 150 years. In the 1970s, the **Quincy Market** area was redeveloped into today's colorful, festive shopping and eating mecca. It's quietest here in the morning. For Faneuil Hall restaurants or shops, see the Places to Eat and Shopping sections later in this chapter. Ⓣ Blue or Orange Line to State.

To escape the crowds at Faneuil Hall Marketplace, head to Christopher Columbus Park northeast of the marketplace, on the other side of the expressway. The park, complete with its benches, grassy knolls, moored sailboats and a trellised archway, is a nice place for a picnic.

Northeast of Faneuil Hall on North St, between Union and Congress Sts, are two lifelike bronzes of Boston's former Mayor Curley, a cherished but controversial Irish politician.

Just beyond are the six glass columns of Boston's sobering Holocaust Memorial, erected in 1995. Inside each tower is a pit, representing the major Nazi death camps, with smoldering coals sending plumes of steam up through the glass corridors. It's particularly dramatic at night.

## THE NORTH END & CHARLESTOWN

The North End is physically separated from the city by the I-93 expressway, but psychologically the enclave is more like a continent and a century away. Old-world Italians have held court in this warren of narrow, winding streets and alleys since the 1920s. Walk around and you'll soon hear passionate discussions in Italian by old-timers dressed in black. You'll see children running through the streets. Ritual Saturday morning shopping is done at specialty stores selling handmade pasta, cannoli or biscotti, fresh cuts of meat, flowers, a little of this or that – all within a ¼-mile radius of Boston's oldest colonial buildings. When you get tired or hungry, there are a dozen cafes and more *ristoranti* per block than anywhere else in the city.

From Faneuil Hall walk north on Union St, past the Union Oyster House (the oldest restaurant in the city, established in 1826) and cross under the expressway at Cross St.

Follow the red-brick (or painted red line) **Freedom Trail** north on Hanover St, the principle commercial thoroughfare, to reach the **Paul Revere House** (☎ 617-523-1676, www .paulreverehouse.org), 19 North Square. This small clapboard house, originally built in 1680, is worth a visit – and not just because it's the oldest house in Boston. The hour-long tour also provides a great history lesson. The blacksmith Revere was one of three horseback messengers who carried advance warning on the night of April 18, 1775, of the British march into Concord and Lexington (see those towns in the Around Boston chapter). He lived here for 10 years during the revolutionary period. The house is open 9:30 am to 4:15 pm daily (except Monday November to mid-April), until 5:15 pm mid-April through October. Tickets cost $2.50 adults, $2 seniors and students, $1 children. Ⓣ Green or Orange Line to Haymarket.

At the Paul Revere House you can get a combination ticket (for just $1 or so more) that's also good for the adjacent **Pierce-Hichborn House**, built in 1710 and owned by Revere's cousin. It's a fine example of an English Renaissance brick house. Visitation is by guided tour only, usually at 12:30 and 2:30 pm. It's best to call the morning you want to visit. Contact the Paul Revere House for information.

Retrace your steps to Hanover St. Across the street is the lovely little St Leonard's Church Peace Garden. Head north on Hanover St for a few blocks to reach the 1804 **St Stephen's Church**, at Harris St, the only remaining church in Boston designed by Boston's renowned architect Charles Bulfinch.

Across the street is the shady **Paul Revere Mall** (called 'the prado' by locals), which might as well be in Italy. Not only does it serve as a perfect frame for the Old North Church to the east, but it's also a lively meeting place for locals of all generations. It's also one of the few places in the cramped quarter where you can rest while contemplating the imposing equestrian statue of Revere.

The 1723 **Old North Church** (☎ 617-523-6676, www.oldnorth.com), 193 Salem St, is Boston's oldest church, best known as the place where two lanterns were hung from the steeple on the night of April 18, 1775, as a signal that the British were coming by sea. Tall, white box-pews, many with brass nameplates of early parishioners, occupy the graceful interior. Look for the little terraces and gardens behind the church. It's open from 9 am to 5 pm daily; Sunday Episcopal services are held at 9 and 11 am and 4 pm. A little museum and gift shop are next door. Ⓣ Green or Orange Line to Haymarket.

Paul Revere

Head up Hull St to **Copp's Hill Burying Ground**, the city's second-oldest cemetery (1660), for excellent views of the waterfront and Charlestown Harbor. Look for headstones chipped and pocked by Revolutionary War musket fire.

Across the street at 44 Hull St is Boston's **narrowest house**, which measures a whopping 9½ feet wide. The circa-1800 house was reportedly built out of spite: to block light from the neighbor's house and to obliterate the view of the house behind it.

From the vantage point at Copp's Hill Terrace, which is to the north on Charter St, Charlestown and the last two Freedom Trail sites – Charlestown Bridge and USS *Constitution* – are visible. If you decide to skip them, retrace your steps to **Salem St**, perhaps the most interesting street in the North End for its collection of specialty markets and restaurants. Stop in at the Bova Italian Bakery, 134 Salem St, which is open 24 hours a day; the aromatic Polcari's Coffee, 105 Salem St; and Dairy Fresh Candies, 57 Salem St, for an unsurpassed selection of nuts, chocolates, candies and dried fruit. Around the corner to the north is J Pace & Son (☎ 617-227-9673), 42 Cross St, a friendly neighborhood Italian grocer where you can pick up fresh cheese, olives, bread and pro-

sciutto (there's also a branch near the Financial District; see the Places to Eat section).

To reach the last two Freedom Trail sites, walk a mile or so across the **Charlestown Bridge** from Commercial St and follow the shoreline north to the **USS *Constitution*** (☎ 617-242-5670), Charlestown Navy Yard.

It's the oldest commissioned US Navy ship (1797) and despite its wooden hull was nicknamed Old Ironsides for never having gone down in a battle. Outfitted in period uniforms, Navy personnel give free tours of the top deck, gun deck and cramped quarters. In order to maintain the ship's commissioned status, she is taken out onto Boston Harbor every Fourth of July, turned around and brought back to the dock. Free guided tours are offered 9:30 am to 3:50 pm 365 days a year.

Visit the **Constitution Museum** (☎ 617-426-1812, www.ussconstitutionmuseum.org), across from the ship, which shows an informative film about ship life and the ship's battles. The museum is open 10 am to 5 pm daily November through April, until 6 pm the rest of the year. Admission is free.

The Charlestown Navy Yard was a thriving ship-building center from 1800 until the early 1900s. Although it was closed in 1974, it's been making a slow comeback ever since. Walk around the impressive granite buildings, which have been transformed into shops and residential and office space. There's a good view of Boston from the Navy Yard. Ⓣ Green or Orange Line to North Station and then a 15-minute walk. You can also get here by boat; see Boston Harbor Cruises under Cruises later in this chapter.

Make a short detour through the heart of Charlestown's winding, narrow streets lined with colonial houses and gas lanterns to reach the **Bunker Hill Monument** (☎ 617-242-5641), a 220-foot granite obelisk that rises from atop the hill. Climb the 295 steps for a fine view of Boston. NPS park rangers are on hand in summer to give talks; the obelisk is open 9 am to 4:30 pm daily (admission is free).

Surrounding the Bunker Hill Monument is **Monument Square**, the most impressive spot in Charlestown. It was here, on June 17,

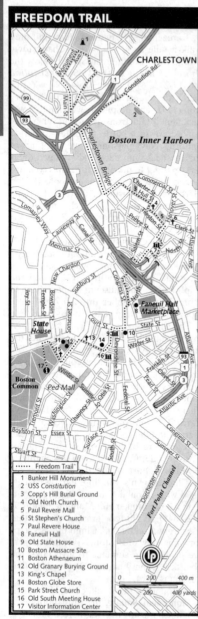

## FREEDOM TRAIL

CHARLESTOWN

*Boston Inner Harbor*

Faneuil Hall Marketplace

State House

Boston Common

Ped Mall

····· Freedom Trail

1 Bunker Hill Monument
2 USS *Constitution*
3 Copp's Hill Burial Ground
4 Old North Church
5 Paul Revere Mall
6 St Stephen's Church
7 Paul Revere House
8 Faneuil Hall
9 Old State House
10 Boston Massacre Site
11 Boston Athenaeum
12 Old Granary Burying Ground
13 King's Chapel
14 Boston Globe Store
15 Park Street Church
16 Old South Meeting House
17 Visitor Information Center

0    200    400 m
0    200    400 yards

1775, that Colonel Prescott told his revolutionary soldiers, 'Don't fire until you see the whites of their eyes.' A reenactment of this event takes place every June.

The narrow streets immediately surrounding Monument Square are picturesque, lined with restored mid-19th century Federal and colonial houses. (Venture four or five blocks beyond it in any direction and you'll see another side of Charlestown. Many of the homes around the square are owned by working-class families who've lived here all their lives. Indeed there is a bit of tension between the 'townies' and the yuppies.)

Charlestown, the monument and the *Constitution* are worth at least a couple of hours. The circa-1780 Warren Tavern (☎ 617-241-8142), 2 Pleasant St at Main St in Charlestown, is an atmospheric place for a late afternoon drink, or a sandwich or burger for lunch or dinner. Ⓣ Green or Orange Line to North Station.

## CHARLES RIVER ESPLANADE

Boston and Cambridge are graced with grassy banks and paved byways along both sides of the curvaceous Charles River. These paths are perfect for bicycling, jogging or walking. On the Boston side, it's about 2 miles from the Museum of Science at the Esplanade's eastern end to the Anderson Bridge (which turns into JFK St and leads into Harvard Square).

For a great view of Boston, walk – or take the T Red Line, between Charles/MGH and Kendall – across the Longfellow Bridge, nicknamed the 'Salt and Pepper' bridge because of its towers' resemblance to the shakers.

From Beacon St near Arlington St, cross Storrow Drive (a noisy but necessary auto way) via the Arthur Fiedler Footbridge to reach the Esplanade. This is its most popular and picturesque portion, which includes the **Hatch Memorial Shell**, the scene of free outdoor concerts and movies (see Entertainment later in this chapter). On warm days, Bostonians migrate here to sunbathe, sail and feed waterfowl gliding along the tranquil riverbank.

With more than 600 interactive exhibits, the **Museum of Science** (☎ 617-723-2500, www.mos.org), in the Science Park at the Charles River Dam, is an educational ball of fun, especially for children. Favorite exhibits include the world's largest lightning bolt generator, a full-scale space capsule, a World Population Meter (a baby is born every second or so) and a 20-foot-tall Tyrannosaurus rex dinosaur model. The Skyline Room Cafeteria offers good food and skyline views. The museum is open 9 am to 5 pm daily, until 9 pm on Fridays, and in July and August until 7 pm daily. The cost is $9 adults, $7 seniors and children. Ⓣ Green Line to Science Park.

The museum also houses the **Hayden Planetarium** and **Omni Theater**; combination tickets to the museum and shows save you about $3. Generally there are shows on the hour, but call the museum for exact times, especially since you can't count on waltzing in and finding tickets available for the next show.

The planetarium boasts a state-of-the-art projection system that puts on a heavenly star show and has programs about black holes and other astronomical mysteries. The Omni, a four-story, wraparound theater, makes you feel as if you're experiencing whatever is projected around you: the Grand Canyon, Antarctica or even the human body.

## BACK BAY

During the 1850s, when Boston was experiencing a population and building boom, Back Bay was an uninhabitable tidal flat. To solve the problem, urban planners embarked on an ambitious and wildly successful 40-year project: Fill in the marsh, lay out an orderly grid of streets, erect magnificent Victorian brownstones and design high-minded civic plazas.

Back Bay is one of Boston's most cherished treasures. You could easily spend a half day here, strolling down shady Comm Ave, window-shopping and sipping a latte on chic Newbury St, taking in the remarkable Victorian architecture or popping into grand churches. Although the neighborhood is home to young professionals and blue-blood Bostonians, Back Bay also has a large student population that keeps it from growing too stodgy.

The area is bounded by the Public Garden and Arlington St to the northeast, Mass Ave to the southwest, the Charles River to the northwest and Stuart St and Huntington Ave to the southeast. Cross streets are laid out alphabetically from Arlington St through to Hereford St.

Back Bay is at its most enchanting during May when magnolia, tulip and dogwood trees are in bloom. Marlborough St, one block north and parallel to Comm Ave, is the most tranquil of Back Bay's shady, patrician streets.

To get an idea of what these opulent mansions were like in the 19th century, visit the **Gibson House** (☎ 617-267-6338), 137 Beacon St near Arlington St, a splendid six-story Victorian brownstone. The house is open Wednesday through Sunday May through October; weekends from November through April. Tours are given at 1, 2 and 3 pm. Tickets are $5 for everyone over age 12. The Victorian Society (☎ 617-789-3927) is headquartered here. Ⓣ Green Line to Arlington.

High-minded **Copley Square**, set between Dartmouth, Clarendon and Boylston Sts, is surrounded by historic buildings. **Trinity Church** (☎ 617-536-0944), 206 Clarendon St, is one of the nation's truly great buildings. Designed by Henry Hobson Richardson in 1872-77, the grand French and Romanesque building still holds Sunday services. It's open 8 am to 6 pm daily. Across the street, the 62-story **John Hancock Tower**, 200 Clarendon St, constructed with more than 10,000 panels of mirrored glass, stands in stark contrast to Trinity Church. Designed in 1976 by IM Pei, the tower suffered serious initial problems: Inferior glass panes were installed and when the wind whipped up, the panes popped out, falling hundreds of feet to the ground. The area was quickly cordoned off and all the panes were replaced. Luckily, no one was ever hurt. There are great views from the observatory; see Observatories under Orientation close to the beginning of the chapter. Ⓣ Green Line to Copley.

MASSACHUSETTS

# BACK BAY, THE FENWAY & THE SOUTH END

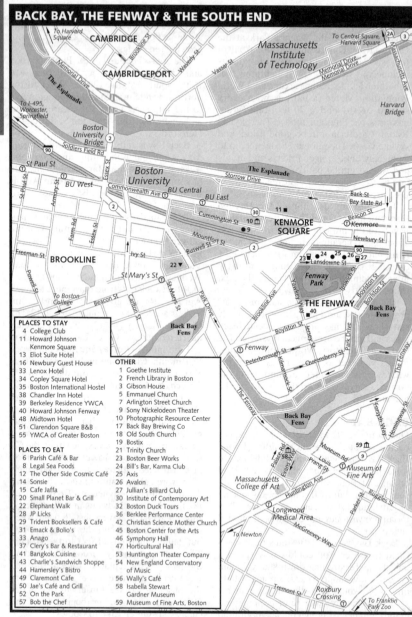

**PLACES TO STAY**
4 College Club
11 Howard Johnson Kenmore Square
13 Eliot Suite Hotel
16 Newbury Guest House
33 Lenox Hotel
34 Copley Square Hotel
35 Boston International Hostel
38 Chandler Inn Hotel
39 Berkeley Residence YWCA
40 Howard Johnson Fenway
48 Midtown Hotel
51 Clarendon Square B&B
55 YMCA of Greater Boston

**PLACES TO EAT**
6 Parish Café & Bar
8 Legal Sea Foods
12 The Other Side Cosmic Café
14 Sonsie
15 Cafe Jaffa
20 Small Planet Bar & Grill
22 Elephant Walk
28 JP Licks
29 Trident Booksellers & Café
31 Emack & Bolio's
33 Anago
37 Clery's Bar & Restaurant
41 Bangkok Cuisine
43 Charlie's Sandwich Shoppe
44 Hamersley's Bistro
49 Claremont Cafe
50 Jae's Café and Grill
52 On the Park
57 Bob the Chef

**OTHER**
1 Goethe Institute
2 French Library in Boston
3 Gibson House
5 Emmanuel Church
7 Arlington Street Church
9 Sony Nickelodeon Theater
10 Photographic Resource Center
17 Back Bay Brewing Co
18 Old South Church
19 Bostix
21 Trinity Church
23 Boston Beer Works
24 Bill's Bar, Karma Club
25 Axis
26 Avalon
27 Jullian's Billiard Club
30 Institute of Contemporary Art
32 Boston Duck Tours
36 Berklee Performance Center
42 Christian Science Mother Church
45 Boston Center for the Arts
46 Symphony Hall
47 Horticultural Hall
53 Huntington Theater Company
54 New England Conservatory of Music
56 Wally's Café
58 Isabella Stewart Gardner Museum
59 Museum of Fine Arts, Boston

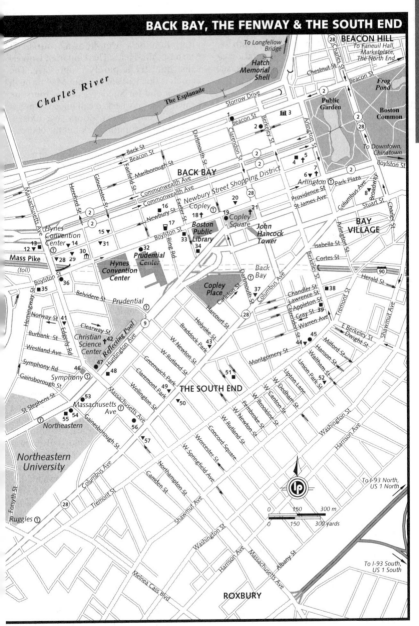

MASSACHUSETTS

The esteemed **Boston Public Library** (☎ 617-536-5400, www.bpl.org), 666 Boylston St, between Exeter and Dartmouth Sts, lends credence to Boston's reputation as the 'Athens of America.' For details, see Libraries under Information, earlier in this chapter.

Adjacent to Copley Square is the enormous and modern **Copley Place**, the largest privately funded development in Boston's history. Another large shopping development, the **Prudential Center**, lies a few blocks southwest of Copley Place. Like the John Hancock Tower, the 'Pru' also has an observatory; see Observatories under Orientation, earlier in this chapter.

On the subject of shopping, **Newbury St** is to Boston what Fifth Ave is to New York City. International boutiques and galleries get tonier and tonier the closer you get to the Public Garden. As you approach Mass Ave in the other direction, you'll see more and more nose rings, platform shoes and dyed hair. Newbury St is also fun to wander at night when shops are closed but the well-lit windows are dressed to the nines, and when the darkness cloaks your less-than-Armani attire. Newbury St is epitomized by its cafe culture and a worldly, haute-couture crowd. ⓣ Green Line to Arlington, Copley Square or Hynes Convention Center.

The Episcopal **Emmanuel Church** (☎ 617-536-3355, 536-3356 concert information), 15 Newbury St near Arlington St, is highly regarded for its musical and cultural offerings. Call or stop in to see what's scheduled.

The **Old South Church** (☎ 617-536-1970), 645 Boylston St, a distinctive Italian Gothic structure, complete with a campanile and multicolored granite, is often referred to as the 'new' Old South Church because up until 1875 the congregation worshipped in their original home, what is now called the Old South Meeting House. You can visit 9 am to 4:30 pm weekdays, on Saturday only when other events are taking place and from about 9 am to 1 pm on Sunday (services are held at 11 am Sunday).

The **Arlington Street Church** (☎ 617-536-7050), 351 Boylston St, was the first public building to be erected in Back Bay. The church features 16 commissioned Tiffany windows, a bell tower and a steeple modeled after London's well-known church St Martin-in-the-Fields. The Unitarian Universalist ministry is purely progressive. The church is open 10 am to 6 pm May through October and for Sunday services. Tours are available but it's best to call ahead. When it gets cold, the great doors are closed, although you can still check out the church's sanctuary.

Beyond the Pru on the southwestern edge of Back Bay, the **Institute of Contemporary Art** (ICA; ☎ 617-266-5152), 955 Boylston St, livens up Boston's often conservative art scene by showing avant-garde art created by well-known national artists as well as unknown regional artists. The ICA's airy galleries, housed within a renovated 19th-century firehouse, are open noon to 5 pm Wednesday through Sunday (Thursday until 9 pm). Tickets are $6 adults, $4 seniors and students over 12, free under 12; it's free 5 to 9 pm on Thursday. ⓣ Green Line to Hynes Convention Center.

The Christian Science Mother Church (☎ 617-450-3790, www.tfccs.com), 175 Huntington Ave at Mass Ave, built in 1894, is the home base for the Church of Christ, Scientist, or Christian Science, which was founded by Mary Baker Eddy in 1866. Tour the grand basilica, which can seat 3000 worshippers, listen to the 14,000-pipe organ or linger on the expansive plaza with its 670-foot-long reflecting pool. Next door are the offices of the internationally regarded daily newspaper, the Christian Science Monitor (www.csmonitor.com), an elegant reading room and the **Mapparium**, one of Boston's hidden treasures. The Mapparium is a room-size, stained-glass globe that you can walk through on a glass bridge. Geo-political boundaries are drawn as the world appeared in 1935. Interestingly, about 170,000 people visited it when it first opened in 1935 and these days, it gets about 150,000 visitors yearly. The acoustics, which were a surprise to the designer, are a wonder: No matter how softly you whisper into the ear of your companion, everyone in the room will hear it perfectly! Hours for the Mother Church

Feast of St Anthony, Boston

Boston's Trinity Church reflected in the John Hancock Tower

Boston's pedal-powered swan boats

Colonial drummer, Boston

The golden-domed State House, Boston

# Massachusetts Bay Transportation Authority

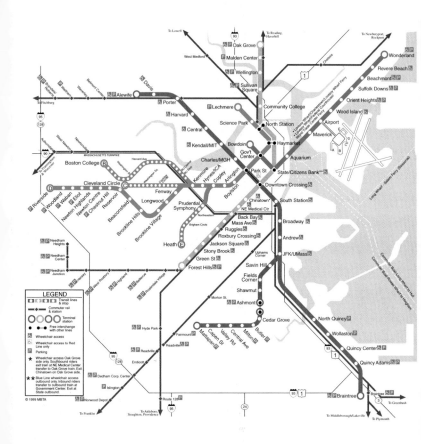

KIM GRANT

(as it's known to adherents) were not set at the time of this writing; the Mapparium is presently closed for renovations, but may be open by the time you arrive. Admission to both the church and Mapparium is free. oT Green Line to Symphony.

Nearby are two architecturally noteworthy buildings. First is **Horticultural Hall**, 300 Mass Ave, home to the Massachusetts Horticultural Society (☎ 617-536-9280). It has the largest independent library devoted to gardening in the world. Head to the 2nd floor for a peek; it's open 9 am to 5 pm weekdays. Across the street is **Symphony Hall** (☎ 617-266-1492, www.bso.org), 301 Mass Ave, the first concert hall in the world to be designed according to acoustic principles. Tours are offered by appointment only. The preeminent Boston Symphony Orchestra plays here; see the Entertainment section later in this chapter. ⓣ Green Line to Symphony.

## KENMORE SQUARE

West of Back Bay, Beacon St and Comm Ave converge at Kenmore Square, the epicenter of student life in Boston. In addition to the behemoth Boston University (see Campuses under Information earlier in this chapter), which stretches along Comm Ave, there are more than a half-dozen colleges in the area. Kenmore Square has more than its share of clubs (see the Entertainment section later in this chapter), inexpensive but nondescript eateries and dormitories disguised as innocuous brownstones. You'll know you're in Kenmore Square when you spot the 60-sq-foot Citgo sign. This mammoth neon sign has marked the spot since 1965. ⓣ Green Line to Kenmore.

One block west of Kenmore Square, the **Photographic Resource Center** (☎ 617-353-0700, www.bu.edu/prc), 602 Comm Ave, is one of the few centers in the country devoted exclusively to this art form. Ever-changing exhibits lean toward the modern and experimental. It is open noon to 5 pm Tuesday through Sunday, until 8 pm on Thursday. Admission is $3 adults, $2 seniors and students and free on Thursday. The well-stocked library is only open on Tuesday, Thursday and Saturday.

## THE FENWAY

South of Kenmore Square is the Fenway, an area wherein the names can be confusing, even to Bostonians. Although the Fenway is a highway and Fenway Park is where the Boston Red Sox play baseball, when people refer to 'Fenway,' they're generally talking about the **Back Bay Fens**, a tranquil and interconnected park system that extends south from the Charles River Esplanade (at Park Drive or Charlesgate East), along a winding brook to the lush Arnold Arboretum and Franklin Park Zoo. It's part of the **Emerald Necklace**, a series of parks throughout the city, linked in the 1880s and 1890s by landscape architect Frederick Law Olmstead. Two renowned museums, the Museum of Fine Arts and the Isabella Stewart Gardner Museum (see below), are in the Fenway. It's not advisable, however, to linger in the Fenway after dark, especially near the tall reeds. In recent years there have been a number of gay-bashing incidents here.

The 265-acre **Arnold Arboretum** (☎ 617-524-1717, www.arboretum.harvard.edu), 125 The Arborway in Jamaica Plain, is a gem. Under a public/private partnership with the city and Harvard University, it's planted with over 14,000 exotic trees, flowering shrubs and other specimens. It's particularly beautiful in the spring. Dog walking, Frisbee throwing, bicycling and general contemplation are encouraged (but picnicking is not allowed). It's free and open daily from dawn to dusk. A visitor center is located at the main gate, just south of the rotary at Rte 1 and Rte 203. ⓣ Orange Line to Forest Hills and walk ¼ mile northwest to the Forest Hills gate.

The 70-acre **Franklin Park Zoo** (☎ 617-541-5466, www.zoonewengland.com), on Peabody Circle at Blue Hill Ave and Columbia Rd, boasts a Tropical Forest pavilion, complete with lush vegetation, waterfalls, lowland gorillas, a leopard and warthogs. It's a well-designed ecosystem with nearly invisible barriers between you and the animals. The mixed-species Bongo Congo features zebras, ostrich and ibex. There's also an Australian Outback Trail, with wallabies, emus and kangaroos. The zoo is open 10 am to

## Fenway Park

Boston's most cherished landmark? Site of Boston's greatest dramas and worst defeats? To many Bostonians it's not Bunker Hill or the Freedom Trail, not Harvard or MIT, but tiny Fenway Park, home of baseball's Red Sox, where names like Babe Ruth, Ted Williams, Carl Yastrzemski, Jim Rice and Roger Clemens are uttered and remembered as reverently as any heroes from Boston's colonial history.

Fenway Park has earned the reputation of baseball's mecca, the class of the major leagues. Only Wrigley Field in Chicago can rival Fenway's age and uniqueness.

Nestled between the Back Bay Fens and the Mass Pike, Fenway Park is truly an integral part of downtown Boston. The park is little more than a hundred yards from Kenmore Square, and adjoining Lansdowne St (also known as Ted Williams Way), which sports many of Boston's most popular nightclubs. Even closer to the park are the hearts of the Red Sox fans, who have remained loyal (the Red Sox are a top draw in the major leagues) despite the team's failure to win a World Series in close to 80 years.

Much of the team's ill fate is attributed to the 'Curse of the Great Bambino,' the sale of their best young pitcher Babe Ruth to the hated rival New York Yankees in 1918. The Red Sox have not won a World Series since that season, while Babe Ruth and the Yankees went on to achieve legendary success and fame. Many believe the sale of Ruth to be among the worst transactions in professional sports history.

Baseball played in Fenway is made special by the unique geometry of the park. Thanks to its downtown location, an economy of space gives the fans an intimate proximity to the playing field. The Fenway Faithful claim to feel more a part of the ball game than might be possible in larger, more modern parks. Fenway also has the one and only 'Green Monster,' a towering wall in left field that compensates for the relatively short distance from home plate. The Green Monster consistently alters the regular course of play – what appears to be a lazy fly ball could actually drop over the Monster for a home run, and what appears to be a sharp double into the gap may be played off the wall to hold the runner to a single.

So fabled and important a site as Fenway Park certainly should have protection against urban development. However, that's not the case. There are plans afoot to move the park to a nearby site or to unceremoniously move it to South Boston so that it can abut the 'historic' World Trade Center and Expressway areas. The debate continues, as Boston is slow to decide anything.

For more information on attending a game at Fenway, see Spectator Sports, later in this chapter.

5 pm April through September (until 6 pm on weekends) and until 4 pm October through March. Tickets costs $6 adults, $5 seniors, $4 children. The lovely park is surrounded by one of the city's less safe neighborhoods, but the zoo is fine. Take the Ⓣ Orange Line to Forest Hills, then ride the No 16 bus, which departs every 15 minutes and takes about four minutes to reach the Franklin Park Zoo.

The collections at the **Museum of Fine Arts** (MFA; ☎ 617-267-9300, www.mfa.org), 465 Huntington Ave in the Fenway, are second in this country only to those of New York's Metropolitan Museum of Art. Particularly noteworthy are its holdings of American art, which include major works by John Singleton Copley, Winslow Homer, Edward Hopper and the Hudson River School; American decorative arts are also well represented. The museum has more Asian treasures, including a full-scale Japanese Buddhist temple, than any other collection in the world. European paintings from the

11th to the 20th centuries, including a huge collection of French impressionists, are outdone by only a handful of museums around the globe.

When it's time to rest your feet, there is a very good indoor cafe, a ground floor cafeteria, an outdoor cafe and a tranquil Japanese Garden (also known as Tenshin-en, which means 'Garden of the Heart of Heaven'). The museum is open 10 am to 4:45 pm weekdays, 10 am to 5:45 pm Saturday and Sunday, until 9:45 pm Wednesday (when admission is 'voluntary donation' after 4 pm); only the West Wing, where special shows are held, stays open until 9:45 pm on Thursday and Friday. Admission costs $10 for adults, $8 for seniors and students, and is free for those under 17. ⓣ Green Line 'E' branch to Museum.

The **Isabella Stewart Gardner Museum** (☎ 617-566-1401, www.boston.com/gardner), 280 The Fenway, is a magnificent Venetian-style palazzo built to house 'Mrs Jack' Gardner's collection, but it was also her home until her death in 1924. A monument to one woman's exquisite taste for acquiring unequaled art, the Gardner, as the museum is called, is filled with almost 2000 priceless objects, primarily European, including outstanding tapestries and Italian Renaissance and 17th-century Dutch paintings.

Since her will stipulated that her collection remain exactly as it was at the time of her death, nothing in the museum will ever change. That helps explain the few empty spaces on the walls: In 1990, the museum was robbed of nearly $200 million worth of paintings, including a rare and beloved Vermeer. The walls on which they were mounted will remain barren until the paintings are recovered (highly unlikely). The palazzo itself, with a four-story greenhouse courtyard, is a masterpiece, a tranquil oasis alone worth the price of admission.

The Gardner has a lovely cafe that's open for lunch. The museum is open 11 am to 5 pm Tuesday through Sunday. Admission is $11 adults, $7 seniors, $5 students ($3 on Wednesday for students), free under 17. ⓣ Green Line 'E' branch to Museum.

## THE SOUTH END

Not to be confused with South Boston ('Southie'), which is still remembered for its violent opposition to integrating the Boston public schools in the 1970s, the South End is a study in ethnic, racial and economic diversity. The South End doesn't have any sights per se, but it's worth exploring to get a sense of the vibrancy Boston still holds. Huge portions have been claimed by artists, gays, architects and young professionals, but other parts are less gentrified. Housing projects and halfway houses rub elbows with converted condos. ⓣ Orange Line to Back Bay/South End.

South of Back Bay and to the west of the Theater District, this neighborhood is bounded by Huntington, Mass and Shawmut Aves and the Mass Turnpike to the north. Columbus Ave and Tremont St are the principal commercial streets, lined with trendy restaurants.

Almost 5 miles long, the **Southwest Corridor** is a one-way, paved and landscaped walkway, running between and parallel to Columbus and Huntington Aves. Walk north from Mass Ave for rewarding views of the Back Bay skyline.

The side streets of the South End, which boast the country's largest concentration of Victorian row houses, have a more British feel to them than other parts of the city. Particularly quaint and tranquil is the tiny, elliptical **Union Park Square** between Tremont St and Shawmut Ave. Visit the lovely Rutland Square, just north of Tremont St, as well. ⓣ Orange Line to Back Bay/South End.

## THE THEATER DISTRICT

Although the area is tiny by New York standards, Boston has long served as an important pre-Broadway staging area for shows. Thanks to the building boom in the 1980s, many of the landmark theaters received long-needed face-lifts. Little more than a square block, the district is bounded by Boylston St, Stuart St, Tremont St and Charles St South. Don't overlook the smaller venues (see Entertainment later in this chapter) where better value is often found. ⓣ Orange Line to NE Medical Center or Chinatown.

Off Boylston St is **Boylston Place**, a pedestrian-only alleyway that is lined with nightclubs (see Entertainment later in this chapter). As suburban theater patrons spill out of the theaters, the youth of America are just beginning to make their way here.

Much of the daytime action takes place within the drearily named **State Transportation Building**, 10 Park Plaza, where you'll find an atrium-like space with eateries, free lunchtime concerts and art exhibits.

Wedged inside Stuart, Arlington, Marginal and Charles St South, **Bay Village** is an often overlooked but charming neighborhood that's certainly worth a stroll. The tiny, early 19th-century brick houses were built and occupied by those who built the Beacon Hill mansions. Today, the tight-knit neighborhood is more gay and bohemian than most neighborhoods. ⓣ Green Line to Arlington.

## CHINATOWN

Adjacent to the eastern edge of the Theater District, the most colorful part of Chinatown is bounded by Tremont, Essex, Kneeland and Kingston Sts. This tiny area is overflowing with authentic restaurants (many open until 4 am), bakeries, markets selling live animals, import and textile shops, and phone booths topped with little pagodas. Don't miss the enormous gate that guards Beach and Kingston Sts. In addition to the Chinese, who began arriving in the late 1870s, the community of 8000 also includes Cambodians, Vietnamese and Laotians. ⓣ Orange Line to Chinatown.

## NEW ENGLAND AQUARIUM

Teeming with sea creatures of all sizes, shapes and colors, the **New England Aquarium** (☎ 617-973-5200, www.neaq.org), on Central Wharf off Atlantic Ave, is equally popular with adults and children. Harbor seals and sea otters within an outdoor enclosure introduce the main indoor attraction: a three-story, cylindrical saltwater tank. It swirls with over 600 creatures great and small – including turtles, sharks and eels. Leave a little time to be mesmerized by the

*Echo of the Waves* sculpture, not to mention the 'Coastal Rhythms,' which explores animals who live on the edge and their habitats. You can have a quick meal here and catch whale-watching cruises as well; see Whale-Watching Cruises under Cruises later in this chapter. The aquarium is open 9 am to 5 pm weekdays, until 6 pm on weekends and until 8 pm on Wednesday and Thursday in summer. Sea lion presentations take place every half hour beginning at 11 am. Admission is $12 adults, $10 seniors, $6 children. Seniors are free Monday afternoons from January to late May. ⓣ Blue Line to Aquarium.

## MUSEUM WHARF

South of the aquarium and across Fort Point Channel (a waterway separating Boston proper from South Boston) is a district of old brick warehouses, part of which includes Museum Wharf. The Fort Point Channel district also contains many artists' lofts, design studios and waterfront businesses such as seafood markets and shipping docks. Museum Wharf is where you'll find the Children's Museum, Computer Museum and Boston Tea Party Ship & Museum (see below). Walk to Northern Ave, then east for a few blocks and turn around for a great view of the Boston skyline. ⓣ Red Line to South Station plus a 10-minute walk.

Boston's delightful **Children's Museum** (☎ 617-426-8855, www.bostonchildren.org), 300 Congress St, can entertain preschoolers to teenagers for an entire day with interactive educational exhibits. There are bubble exhibits, dress-up areas, a two-story climbing gym and an exhibit on what it's like to be a teen in Tokyo. The museum is open 10 am to 5 pm Tuesday through Sunday and on Monday when school is not in session. Every Friday from 5 to 9 pm year-round, the admission is reduced to $1 for everyone. (Be forewarned; it's crowded then!) Otherwise, admission is $7 adults, $6 seniors and children (two to 15), $2 for one-year-olds.

The most popular exhibit at the **Computer Museum** (☎ 617-426-2800, www.tcm .org), 300 Congress St, is the enormous, functional Walk-Through Computer. The

250-foot keyboard is linked to a 108-foot monitor. There are over 35 other hands-on exhibits where you can explore state-of-the-art devices and pay homage to PC precursors: the abacus, slide rule, punch card and calculator. Virtual reality rears its head in the Virtual Fishtank, a compelling – albeit simulated – undersea world. The museum is open 10 am to 5 pm Tuesday through Sunday and on Monday when school is not in session. Admission is $7 adults, $5 seniors and children over age two.

The **Boston Tea Party Ship & Museum** (☎ 617-338-1773, www.historictours.com), at Congress St Bridge, stands as testimony to the spirited colonists who refused to pay the levy imposed on their beloved beverage. In 1773, they left a town meeting at the Old South Meeting House and donned Native American garb as a disguise before boarding the *Beaver* (the *Beaver II*, which you board today, is an approximate replica) and dumping all the tea overboard in rebellion. Costumed guides tell the story, while the adjacent museum offers multilingual information and a complimentary cup of tax-free Salada tea. The ship and museum are open 9 am to 5 pm daily March through November (until 5:45 pm from late May to mid-September); admission to both is $8 adults, $7 students, $4 children.

## BOSTON HARBOR ISLANDS

Until recently, Boston Harbor had the unenviable distinction of being the dirtiest harbor in the country. After a massive, multimillion-dollar clean-up in the mid-1990s, the harbor is well on its way to regaining a healthier

## Walking Tours

Boston is a walker's paradise and is best explored by foot. There are several special-interest maps you can pick up at the Visitor Information Center on Boston Common that make navigating easier.

The 2½-mile **Freedom Trail** (☎ 617-242-5642) is the granddaddy of walks. Sixteen historically important sites, including colonial and Revolutionary-era buildings, are linked by a double row of red sidewalk bricks (or a painted red line) that begins near the MBTA Park St station, winds through downtown Boston and the North End and ends in Charlestown at the USS *Constitution*. In addition to each site being marked by a bronze medallion in the sidewalk, directional signposts and kiosks have been installed along the route.

The NPS (☎ 617-242-5642, www.nps.gov/bost), 15 State St, offers six, free ranger-led walking tours (on the hour from 10 am to 3 pm) along the Freedom Trail from June through August. From mid-April through November, it's reduced to twice daily on weekdays (10 am and 2 pm), four on the weekends (10 and 11 am, 1 and 2 pm). Ⓣ Orange or Blue Line to State.

The Boston Park Rangers (☎ 617-635-7383), at Tremont St on Boston Common, offer free naturalist-led and historical walks around the Emerald Necklace, Boston Common and the Boston Public Garden. The extensive schedule varies so it's best to call ahead; there's something going on at least once a weekend throughout the year. Ⓣ Green or Red Line to Park St.

The **Black Heritage Trail**, about 1.6 miles long, encompasses more than a dozen 19th-century sites, most of which are on Beacon Hill. Pick up a map at the African Meeting House, 8 Smith Ct (☎ 617-742-5415, 723-8863). Or take a guided walk from late May to early September, daily at 10 am, noon and 2 pm; it departs from in front of the Shaw Memorial on Beacon St, in front of the State House, and takes about two hours.

Maps for the **Women's Heritage Trail** (☎ 617-734-6947) are available from the NPS. There are four walks (downtown, in the North End, Chinatown and on Beacon Hill) detailed in an inexpensive booklet sold at the NPS.

reputation. Good thing, too, since it has more than 30 large and small islands that offer plenty of history, picnic spots, nature walks and fishing.

**Georges Island**, the jumping-off spot for all the other islands, features a 19th-century fort. **Lovell Island** is the largest, good for walking along dunes, marshes and meadows. Look for wild raspberries on **Bumpkin Island** and for a variety of birds on **Grape Island**.

To get to the islands, Boston Harbor Cruises (☎ 617-227-4320), 1 Long Wharf off Atlantic Ave, offers regular ferry service from early May to mid-October. Purchase a roundtrip ticket ($8 adults, $7 senior, $6 children) to Georges Island where you then catch a free water taxi (another five to 10 minutes) to the smaller islands. Boats run on the hour.

For information on camping on the islands, see Camping under Places to Stay.

## JOHN F KENNEDY LIBRARY & MUSEUM

The library and museum (☎ 617-929-4500) are set on dramatic Columbia Point, in Dorchester, near the UMass, Boston campus. Designed by architect IM Pei (who is also responsible for the dramatic John Hancock Tower in Back Bay), the stark white structure successfully blends cylindrical elements with strong pyramid-like lines. Together, they take up most of the peninsula, which is nice for strolling.

The JFK museum is the repository for memorabilia related to the 35th US president: papers, videotape, speeches and photographs. Check out the good introductory film about JFK. The museum is open 9 am to 5 pm daily. Admission is $8 adults, $6 seniors and students, $4 children.

Interestingly, the library has an archive of writer Ernest Hemingway's manuscripts and papers. About 95% of his works can be accessed if you're interested in research, but there is no exhibit space. What's the connection? Kennedy was key in helping Mary Hemingway, Ernest's fourth wife and widow, get the manuscripts and papers out of Cuba during the first and most intense days of the embargo. When she died, she willed them here, because the library offers the public better access than most archival libraries.

The **Commonwealth Museum** (☎ 617-727-9268, www.state.ma.us/sec/mus) exhibits documents dating back to the first days of colonization. Exhibits are drawn from the Massachusetts Archives (☎ 617-727-2816), a research facility and depository for Massachusetts' history. The museum is open 9 am to 5 pm weekdays, 9 am to 3 pm Saturday. Admission is free.

Take the ⊤ Red Line to JFK/UMass, and then catch a free shuttle bus to the museum or to the university campus.

## CAMBRIDGE

Cambridge is known around the globe as the home of the intellectual heavyweights Harvard University and MIT; see Universities under Information earlier in this chapter for details. With thousands of students, Cambridge is a diverse and youthful place, to say the least.

Founded in 1638, Cambridge was home to the country's first college (Harvard) and first printing press, virtually putting an early lock on its reputation as a hotbed for ideas and intellectualism.

Cambridge has always been known for its progressive politics, much of it centering around Harvard Square. Cantabrigians, as residents are called, vehemently opposed the Vietnam War before others did; they embraced the environmental movement before recycling became profitable; and they were one of the first communities to ban smoking in public buildings. And when gays were excluded from marching in South Boston's traditional St Patrick's Day parade in the mid-1990s, Cambridge immediately pledged to hold its own inclusive parade.

You'll find **Harvard Square** overflowing with cafes, bookstores, restaurants and a lot of street musicians. Although many Cantabrigians complain that the 'Square' has lost its edge – once-independently owned shops are continually gobbled up by national chains – Harvard Square is still worth an afternoon.

The Square isn't a square at all, but rather a triangle of brick pavement above the

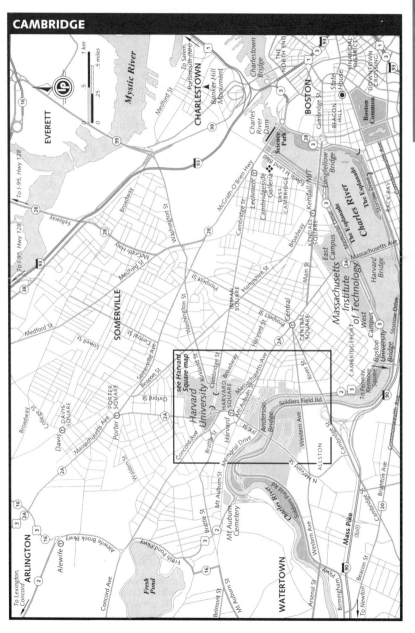

Harvard T station. When people refer to the Square, they are referring to the four or five block area that radiates from the Mass Ave and JFK St intersection. Ⓣ Red Line to Harvard. The newspaper and periodicals shop Out of Town News (see the Bookstores boxed text) and an information kiosk are located here (for kiosk hours, see Tourist Offices under Information earlier in this chapter).

Most of **Harvard University** lies east of JFK St and east of Mass Ave after it jogs north out of the Square. The gates to famed **Harvard Yard**, a quadrangle of ivy-covered brick buildings, are just across Harvard St from the T station. Informative campus tours are offered from the Holyoke Center, 1350 Mass Ave, although the guides probably won't tell you tell you tidbits like the fact that the university's multibillion endowment is easily the world's largest.

Harvard operates four distinct museums (archaeology, botany, minerals and zoology) that seem to be more devoted to teaching than they are geared to visitors. Under the aegis of the **Museum of Natural History** (☎ 617-495-3045, www.mcnh.harvard.edu), 24 Oxford St, you'll find the Museum of Comparative Zoology, with impressive fossil collections. The multicultural Peabody Museum of Archaeology and Ethnology boasts a strong collection of North American Indian artifacts. The Botanical Museum, perhaps the most well-known of these museums, houses over 800 life-like pieces of handblown-glass flowers and plants. The museums are open 9 am to 5 pm Monday through Saturday, Sunday 1 to 5 pm. Tickets, good for all four, cost $5 adults, $4 seniors and students, $3 children. Admission is free from 9 am to noon on Saturday.

The **Fogg Art Museum** (☎ 617-495-9400, www.fas.harvard.edu/~artmuseums), at 32 Quincy St, concerns itself with no less than the history of Western art from the Middle Ages to the present. There is also a good selection of decorative arts. It is open 10 am to 5 pm Monday through Saturday, 1 to 5 pm on Sunday. Free tours are given at 11 am weekdays (except during summer when they are only given on Wednesday). Tickets,

which include admission to the Busch-Reisinger and Arthur Sackler Museums (see below), cost $5 adults, $4 seniors, $3 students, free to those under 18. It is also free every day at 4:30 pm, 10 am to noon on Saturday and all day Wednesday.

The **Busch-Reisinger Museum**, entered through the Fogg, specializes in Central and Northern European art. Hours are the same as the Fogg, except that free tours are given weekdays at 1 pm.

Across the street, the **Arthur Sackler Museum** (☎ 617-495-9400), 485 Broadway, is devoted to Asian and Islamic art. It boasts the world's most impressive collection of Chinese jade as well as fine Japanese woodblock prints. Hours are the same as the Fogg, except that free tours are given weekdays at 2 pm.

One of Cambridge's most distinctive and humorous buildings is the **Harvard Lampoon Castle**, on Mt Auburn at Plympton St. The namesake student humor magazine, which has its offices here, was said to have inspired the creation of the *National Lampoon* magazine.

Two blocks north of Harvard Square is **Christ Church**, on Garden St near Mass Ave, designed by Peter Harrison who designed Boston's King's Chapel.

Next door is **Radcliffe Yard,** between Brattle and Garden Sts, and Appian Way and Mason St. Radcliffe College was founded in 1879 as the sister school to the then-all-male Harvard. The two colleges merged in 1975. Across the street to the east is **Cambridge Common**, where George Washington pitched camp from 1775 to 1776.

The western boundary of Radcliffe Yard is **Brattle St**, one of the area's most prestigious residential addresses, lined with magnificent 18th- and 19th-century homes. In the early 1770s, Brattle St, dubbed Tory Row, was generally home to British loyalists. But in 1775, Washington got his revenge by appropriating most of these houses for his patriots.

The stately home now known as the **Longfellow National Historic Site** (☎ 617-876-4491, www.nps.gov/long), 105 Brattle St, was no exception to the appropriation.

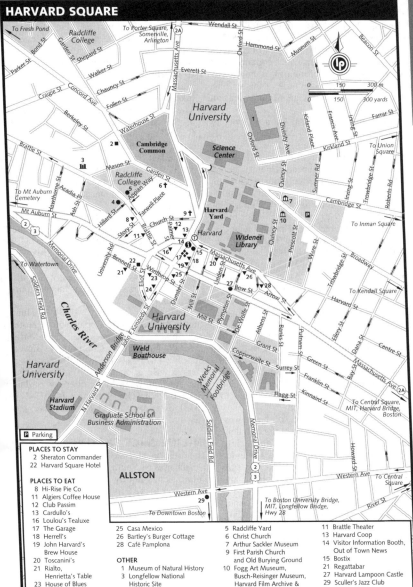

# HARVARD SQUARE

**PLACES TO STAY**
2 Sheraton Commander
22 Harvard Square Hotel

**PLACES TO EAT**
8 Hi-Rise Pie Co
11 Algiers Coffee House
12 Club Passim
13 Cardullo's
16 Loulou's Tealuxe
17 The Garage
Herrell's
19 John Harvard's
Brew House
20 Toscanini's
21 Rialto,
Henrietta's Table
23 House of Blues
24 Bombay Club

25 Casa Mexico
26 Bartley's Burger Cottage
28 Café Pamplona

**OTHER**
1 Museum of Natural History
3 Longfellow National
Historic Site
4 American Repertory Theater

5 Radcliffe Yard
6 Christ Church
7 Arthur Sackler Museum
9 First Parish Church
and Old Burying Ground
10 Fogg Art Museum,
Busch-Reisinger Museum,
Harvard Film Archive &
Film Study Library

11 Brattle Theater
13 Harvard Coop
14 Visitor Information Booth,
Out of Town News
15 Bostix
21 Regattabar
27 Harvard Lampoon Castle
29 Sculler's Jazz Club

Washington liked it so much that he moved his headquarters here during the siege of Boston. Henry Wadsworth Longfellow lived and wrote here for 45 years from 1837 to 1882. Now under the auspices of the NPS, the Georgian mansion, which contains many of Longfellow's belongings, is being elegantly restored. At the time of this writing, the site was closed. Call for information about the site's hours.

On a sunny day, the **Mt Auburn Cemetery** (☎ 617-547-7105), 580 Mt Auburn St, is worth the 30-minute walk west out of Harvard Square. Developed in 1831, its 170 acres were the first 'garden cemetery' in the US. Until then, the colonial notion of moving a body and grave marker around a cemetery was commonplace. Pick up a self-guided map of the rare botanical specimens and of the notable burial plots, including those for Mary Baker Eddy (founder of the Christian Science Church), Isabella Stewart Gardner (of the Gardner Museum), Winslow Homer (19th-century American painter extraordinaire) and Oliver Wendell Holmes (US Supreme Court Justice). The cemetery is open 8 am to 5 pm daily (until 7 pm during daylight saving time).

In East Cambridge, **Kendall Square** at Main St has come alive in recent years thanks to the high-tech industry and the takeover of the neglected brick warehouses. The One Kendall Square complex, at Hampshire and Broadway Sts, is its nucleus (see Places to Eat). Ⓣ Red Line to Kendall.

The **MIT** campus extends south and west of Kendall Square. Join one of the excellent guided campus tours to best appreciate MIT's contributions to the sciences. Wander around the East Campus (on the east side of Mass Ave), bejeweled with public art. The nearby **List Visual Arts Center** (☎ 617-253-4680, web.mit.edu/lvac/www), Weisner Building, 20 Ames St, mounts rewarding and sophisticated shows. A $5 contribution is suggested, and the galleries are open daily (except Monday) noon to 6 pm (Friday until 8 pm).

From the East Campus, make your way one block south to the Charles River for a great view of Boston.

## BICYCLING

More than 50 miles of bicycle trails originate in the Boston area. One of the most popular circuits runs along both sides of the Charles River, but you can also ride for miles out to the Arnold Arboretum or out to nearby Watertown and back. Although you have to be something of a kamikaze to take to the inner-city streets, people do it. You can take your bike, by the way, on any of the MBTA subway lines, except the Green Line, during off-peak weekday hours (anytime on the weekends). Be sure to get on the last train car. Permits to carry bikes on the subway are required ($5, for 3 years) and available from the Back Bay Orange Line train station at Dartmouth and Columbus Sts.

Rubel BikeMaps (☎ 617-776-6567, www.bikemaps.com) produces little laminated 'Pocket Rides,' 30 different rides ($1.95 each) in greater Boston or from area commuter rail stations. The rides are incredibly detailed and worth every penny. See also Maps under Orientation near the beginning of the chapter.

Earth Bikes (☎ 617-267-4733), 35 Huntington Ave next to the Copley Square Hotel, rents bikes and organizes tours from March through November. Community Bicycle Supply (☎ 617-542-8623), 496 Tremont St at Berkeley St, is open year-round for sales, and April through September for rentals. Back Bay Bicycles & Boards (☎ 617-247-2336), 336 Newbury St at Mass Ave, has year-round rentals.

## IN-LINE & ICE SKATING

The Beacon Hill Skate (☎ 617-482-7400), 135 Charles St South, in Bay Village, rents in-line skates hourly ($5) and daily ($15). Glide over to the Esplanade or, better yet, to Memorial Drive on the Cambridge side of the Charles River, which is closed to auto traffic from 11 am to 7 pm on Sunday in warm weather.

Ice skating on the human-made 'Frog Pond' on Boston Common is a very popular winter activity. Skate rentals, lockers and restrooms are available at the kiosk next to the pond.

## BOATING & KAYAKING

The Charles River Canoe and Kayak Center (☎ 617-965-5110), at 2401 Comm Ave in Newton (near the intersection of MA 30 and I-95), rents boats from mid-April through October. Canoes cost $9 per hour, rowboats $10, double kayaks $12, kid's kayaks $5. Rowing shells are available for $25 per session. The center is across from a tranquil stretch of the Charles River. Ⓣ Green Line 'D' branch to Riverside and then a 20-minute walk. It's best to call for directions.

Community Boating (☎ 617-523-1038), at the Charles River Esplanade near the Charles St footbridge, offers experienced sailors unlimited use of 140 sailboats, kayaks and windsurfers for $50 for two days, from April through October. You'll have to take a little test to demonstrate your ability. Ⓣ Red Line to Charles/MGH.

## ORGANIZED TOURS

See the Cruises section, below, for information on cruise tours in the Boston Harbor. For organized walking tours, see the 'Walking Tours' boxed text.

If you're only going to be in town a couple of days, trolley tours offer great ease and flexibility because you can hop on and off as you like, catching the next trolley that comes along. Trolley operators include the red-colored Beantown Trolleys (☎ 617-236-2148), operated by Gray Line. Tours are year-round and last just over two hours if you don't get off; tickets cost $20 adults, $16 seniors and students, $6 children. The last tour leaves at 4:30 pm.

The blue Minuteman Trolley (☎ 617-269-3626) runs Friday through Monday year-round. In summer, trolleys depart every 45 to 60 minutes daily. Of all the tours, this is the only one that goes into Cambridge. Tickets cost $23 adults, $9 children.

The orange-and-green Old Town Trolley (☎ 617-269-7150) operates daily year-round; tickets are $21 adults, $8 children.

All three trolleys originate across from the New England Aquarium, at Atlantic Ave and State St, but you can also purchase tickets at trolley booths on Tremont St next to the Visitor Information Center. You must purchase a ticket before boarding. Ⓣ Blue Line to Aquarium.

The Brush Hill/Gray Line bus tour (☎ 617-236-2148, 800-343-1328) offers a 3½ hour motor coach tour of Cambridge, Lexington and Concord for $25 adults, $13 children from late March through November. Buses depart from the Transportation Building, 14 Charles St South at Stuart St, near the Public Garden.

## CRUISES

Boston Harbor Cruises (☎ 617-227-4320, www.bostonharborcruises.com), at 1 Long Wharf off Atlantic Ave near the Aquarium, operates a number of harbor cruises. Ⓣ Blue Line to Aquarium.

There are 90-minute narrated sightseeing trips around the outer harbor from May through October for $15 adults, $12 seniors, $10 children. There are sunset cruises (7 pm May through September) and boats that go to the John F Kennedy Library & Museum on Columbia Point in Dorchester and USS *Constitution* in Charlestown.

Boston Harbor Cruises also operates ferry service to Georges Island in Boston Harbor; see Boston Harbor Islands earlier in this chapter for details. For details on its whale-watching tours, see Whale-Watching Cruises below.

Or, if you just want to see the Boston skyline from the water, take its inexpensive ($2 per person) 30-minute weekday lunchtime cruise at 12:15 pm in summer. Ⓣ Blue Line to Aquarium.

Boston Duck Tours (☎ 617-723-3825, www.bostonducktours.com), at the Prudential Center between Huntington Ave and Boylston St, offers unusual land and water tours using modified amphibious vehicles from WWII. Rain or shine, the narrated tour splashes around the Charles River for about 25 minutes, and then competes with cars on Boston city streets for another 55 minutes. The ticket booth within the Prudential Center opens at 9 am but people are in line before then. Tickets sell out by noon on weekends. Boats depart (on the Boylston St side of the Pru) every 30 minutes from 9 am to one hour prior to sunset daily from early April through November. Tickets cost $21 adults, $18 seniors and students, $11 children, and come with a coupon booklet for Prudential Center shops and restaurants. Ⓣ Green Line 'E' branch to Prudential for tickets, Green Line to Copley for tours.

The Charles River Boat Co (☎ 617-621-3001), at the Cambridgeside Galleria, in Cambridge, runs an hour-long narrated trip of the Charles River Basin for $8 adults, $7 seniors, $6 children. The boat cruises upstream to Harvard and downstream to the Boston Harbor locks. Trips depart on weekends in May and September, and noon to 5 pm daily late May to early September. Meet at the ticket counter near the food court in the mall or at the riverside back doors of the Galleria.

Bay State Cruises (☎ 617-748-1428), at the Commonwealth Pier on Northern Ave next to the World Trade Center, offers a three-hour Music on Board harbor cruise on Friday and Saturday evenings, June through September, for $16 to $18 per person. DJs and bands provide the entertainment.

The AC Cruise Line Inc (☎ 617-261-6633, 800-422-8419), 290 Northern Ave in South Boston, operates boats to Gloucester from late May to early September. Tickets are $14 adults; up to four children are permitted free when accompanied by two adults. The boat docks at the Rocky Neck Artists' Colony and includes a 2½-hour layover to walk around town.

The AC Cruise Line also offers a similar family-style trip to Salem. The boat departs at 10 am and arrives at Salem Willows Park by noon, where you'll have 4½ hours to picnic on the beach before taking the boat back to Boston. Ⓣ Red Line to South Station and then a 15-minute walk.

## Whale-Watching Cruises
Whale sightings are practically guaranteed at Stellwagen Bank, a fertile feeding ground 25 miles out to sea. The big humpback whales are most impressive, breaching and frolicking, but in the spring and fall, huge pods of dolphins making their way to and from summering in the Arctic are also impressive. Trips take about 4½ to 5 hours, with onboard commentary provided by naturalists. Dress warmly even on summer days.

The AC Cruise Line (see above) offers family-friendly trips: Up to four children are free when accompanied by two paying adults ($19 adults, $14 seniors). The trips depart at 10:30 am on weekends from mid-April to mid-October, and daily (except Monday) from late June to early September. Ⓣ Red Line to South Station and then a 15-minute walk.

Tickets for the New England Aquarium Whale-Watching Tour (☎ 617-973-5277), at the Central Wharf off Atlantic Ave, cost $26 adults, $21 seniors and students, $19 children (no children under three permitted). Boats depart at 9:30 am and 3:30 pm on weekends in April and mid-October to early November, and at 10 am weekdays May to mid-October. An additional boat is added on weekdays in summer. The trip takes about 4½ to 5 hours. A new catamaran, however, cuts the trip time by one hour. Ⓣ Blue Line to Aquarium.

Boston Harbor Cruises (☎ 617-227-4320) also has daily whale-watching tours that depart from Rowes Wharf and Long Wharf May through October. Tickets are $28 adults, $24 seniors, $22 children.

## SPECIAL EVENTS
Once in town, Thursday's *Boston Globe* Calendar section has up-to-the-minute details on all events. Prior to your arrival, check with the GBCVB (see Tourist Offices earlier in this chapter). Remember that accommodations are much, much harder to secure during big events.

**January to March**
An outstanding wine festival is held at the Boston Harbor Hotel (☎ 617-439-7000).

**January/February**
Chinese New Year is celebrated with a colorful parade in Chinatown in late January or early February.

**March**
The large and vocal South Boston Irish community hosts the St Patrick's Day Parade on W Broadway St in mid-March. Since the mid-1990s, the St Patrick's Day Parade has been

marred by the council's decision to exclude gay and lesbian Irish groups from marching.

**April to May**
The Big Apple Circus comes to town. The exact location changes from year to year. Call ☎ 212-268-2500 for information.

**April**
On the third Monday in April, Patriot's Day is celebrated with a reenactment of Paul Revere's historic ride from the North End to Lexington. Also in April, thousands of runners compete in the Boston Marathon (www.bostonmarathon .org), a 26.2-mile run that has been an annual event for more than a century. Starting in Hopkinton west of the city, the race finishes on Boylston St in front of the Boston Public Library. April also is when the Swan Boats return to the lagoon in the Public Garden.

**May**
Magnolia trees bloom all along Newbury St and Comm Ave. Lilac Sunday at Arnold Arboretum celebrates the arrival of spring when more than 400 varieties of fragrant lilacs are in bloom. It is the only day of the year that visitors can picnic on the grass at the venerable arboretum. The Boston Kite Festival is held in Franklin Park. A lively Street Performers Festival is held at Faneuil Hall Marketplace.

**June**
Bunker Hill Weekend includes a parade and battle reenactment at Charlestown's Bunker Hill Monument. The Gay Pride March in Boston draws tens of thousands of participants and spectators; the parade culminates in a big party on Boston Common.

**July**
The Fourth of July weekend (www.july4th.org) extends to a weeklong Harborfest. This is very big in Boston. The Boston Pops gives a free concert on the Esplanade, attended by hundreds of thousands of people. Fireworks cap off the evening. During Chowderfest, you can sample dozens of fish and clam chowders prepared by Boston's best restaurants.

**July to August**
In the North End, Italian festivals honoring patron saints are celebrated with food and music on the weekends.

**August**
The August Moon festival takes place in Chinatown while the Caribbean-American Carnival takes place around Boston.

**September**
The Cambridge River Festival takes place along the banks of the Charles River. The Boston Film Festival screens a variety of movies at dozens of venues all over the city.

**October**
The mid-month Head of the Charles Regatta (www.boston.com/head_of_the_charles) draws more than 3000 collegiate rowers, while cheering fans line the banks of the river, lounging on blankets and drinking beer (technically illegal). It's the world's largest rowing event.

**November**
The Boston Ballet's *Nutcracker* at the Wang Center is staged until early January.

**December**
Trees that ring Boston Common and the huge Prudential Center Christmas tree are lit in early December and remain lit throughout the month. The mid-month Boston Tea Party reenactment involves costumed actors who march from downtown to the waterfront and dump bales of tea into the harbor. First Night celebrations begin early on the 31st and continue past midnight, culminating in fireworks over the harbor. Buy a special button that permits entrance into many events.

**December to Mid-March**
Ice skating takes place on the Boston Common Frog Pond; weather permitting, there is more natural skating on the Public Garden lagoon (bring your own skates).

## PLACES TO STAY

Although it's certainly more convenient to stay in downtown neighborhoods like Back Bay, Kenmore Square and Beacon Hill, especially considering Boston's notorious traffic problems, if you're willing to spend a little bit of time getting into the city from neighboring suburbs like Brookline, Braintree or Newton, you'll have plenty of moderately priced options. A few of these require a car; most don't. You will need reservations months in advance. Remember that it's usually less expensive to stay in city hotels on weekends, when packages are offered.

Boston hotels experienced an astounding 80% occupancy rate during 1998, ranking it in the top three US cities for occupancy. In fact, lodging can be so difficult to secure in Boston that the GBCVB has set up a Hotel Hot Line (☎ 800-777-6001). The service is available 9 am to 8 pm weekdays, 10 am to 4 pm on Saturday and 11 am to 4 pm on Sunday.

Hotel prices are generally lowest between mid-November and mid-March with the exception of major holidays. Many hotels refer to prices during this time as their 'winter' or 'off-season' rates ('summer' constituting the rest of the year!). Regardless of what they call it, if occupancy is tight, the off-season rates may fly out the window.

Price ranges for budget, mid-range and top-end accommodations are generally as follows: budget, less than $100; mid-range, $100 to $180; top end, $200 and up.

## PLACES TO STAY – BUDGET
### Camping
The **Boston Harbor Islands State Park**, managed by both the Department of Environmental Management *(DEM; ☎ 877-422-6762 for reservations only, www.state.ma .us/dem/forparks.htm)* and the Metropolitan District Commission *(MDC; ☎ 617-727-7676, www.state.mass.us/mdc)*, consists of almost 30 islands. There are about 50 campsites on four islands: Peddock's, Lovell's, Grape Island and Bumpkin. Bring your own water and supplies; facilities are limited to primitive sites and composting toilets. You must obtain a camping permit in advance. Free permits are available for Peddock's and Lovell's (MDC-managed), late May to mid-October. Lovell's has a lifeguard-attended swimming beach.

The DEM-managed islands, which also require a permit ($6 nightly), include Grape Island and the more remote and less populated Bumpkin. Both are wooded and open for camping early May to mid-October.

Phone the DEM for Grape Island and Bumpkin for permits or, for Peddock's and Lovell's, write to the Metropolitan District Commission, 98 Taylor St, Dorchester, MA 02122.

Regular ferry service is provided by Boston Harbor Cruises (☎ 617-227-4320, 1 Long Wharf), off Atlantic Ave, from early May to mid-October. Purchase a roundtrip ticket ($8 adults, $7 senior, $6 children) to Georges Island where you then catch a free water taxi (another five to 10 minutes) to the smaller islands. Boats run on the hour.

*Wompatuck State Park (☎ 781-749-7160, 877-422-6762, Union St, Hingham, MA 02043)* offers 400 relatively undeveloped campsites on almost 3000 acres; it's about 30 minutes south of Boston by car. There is an excellent network of paved paths and mountain bike trails here. Open late May to early September, sites cost $6 to $9 for two people. Take I-93 south out of Boston to MA 3 south to MA 228 (exit 14). Go 7 miles north on Free St to Union St.

*Normandy Farms Campground (☎ 508-543-7600, 72 West St, Foxboro, MA 02035)* is a fully developed campground that caters more to RVs than tenters. It's open year-round, with a big recreation room and four pools (one indoor), and 450 open and wooded sites on more than 100 acres. It's about 50 minutes from Boston by car; take I-93 south to I-95 south to MA 1 south for 7 miles; go east on Thurston St to West St. Rates for two in a tent are $28 to $44 nightly.

*Boston Hub KOA Kampground (☎ 508-384-8930, 800-562-2173, 1095 South St (MA 1A), Wrentham, MA 02093)* is another developed campground about the same distance from Boston. It has 145 tent sites ($25 to $32.50 a night) on 22 acres as well as 15 one- and two-room Kamping Kabins that rent for $39 to $46 for two people. It's open mid-April through October.

### Hostels
*Boston International Hostel (☎ 617-536-9455, fax 424-6558, www.tiac.net/users/hienec, bostonhostel@juno.com, 12 Hemenway St, Boston, MA 02115)* is very well run and conveniently located near the Museum of Fine Arts and Kenmore Square. In addition to offering discount tickets to museums and whale-watching cruises and selling MBTA passes, the hostel also offers daily walking tours, slide shows, free or cheap lectures and coffeehouses with musicians. Its dorm-style bunk rooms hold four to six people each (same sex), plus there are some rooms for coed couples. Beds cost $20 members, $23 nonmembers, nightly, with a 14-night maximum. You can become a member for $25 on the spot. Try to reserve a month ahead of

time in summer; make reservations with a credit card either by phone, fax or email. If the hostel is full, they'll guide you elsewhere. Ⓣ Green Line to Hynes Convention Center or Orange Line to Mass Ave, and then a 15-minute walk.

Near the North End and Faneuil Hall, the *Irish Embassy Hostel* (☎ 617-973-4841, fax 720-3998, 232 Friend St, Boston, MA 02114) rents 54 beds (with four to 10 people per room) above its very lively eponymous pub. For $15, you get a very tidy place; free sheets; free admission to hear live bands in two pubs (McGann's Pub is around the corner at 197 Portland St); free barbecue on Tuesday, Friday and Sunday; a pub lunch for $3.95; dinner specials for $4.95; and $1.50 beers. It just can't be beat, but don't get too comfortable; there's a six-night maximum stay. There's no lockout. The hostel is full by 9 am in summer, so it's best to make reservations as far in advance as possible. Ⓣ Green or Orange Line to North Station.

The nearby *Beantown Hostel* (☎ 617-723-0800, fax 720-3998, 222 Friend St), operated by the Irish Embassy Hostel, has an additional 56 beds. Prices and information are the same as at the Irish Embassy.

The *Berkeley Residence YWCA* (☎ 617-482-8850, fax 482-9692, 40 Berkeley St, Boston, MA 02116), on the edge of the South End and Back Bay, rents over 200 small rooms out to women. Singles ($48), doubles ($74) and triples ($84) are available and include breakfast. Guests can use the library, TV room and garden. Some guest rooms overlook the garden. Ⓣ Orange Line to Back Bay/South End.

The *YMCA of Greater Boston* (☎ 617-536-7800, fax 267-4653, 316 Huntington Ave, Boston, MA 02115), near the Fenway and the Museum of Fine Arts, rents 39 rooms to both men and women, though only men are allowed from September through May. Shared-bath singles cost $41, doubles $61; breakfast is included. There are also a couple of suites for four people. Use of the excellent gym and pool is included. Reserve by mail two weeks prior to your visit or walk in after noon; otherwise the rooms will be taken.

Take the Ⓣ Green Line 'E' branch to Northeastern University.

## Motels

Although this *Motel 6* (☎ 781-848-7890, 800-466-8356, fax 781-843-1929, 125 Union St, Braintree, MA 02184) is 15 miles south of Boston, you can be whisked hassle-free into Boston in 30 minutes via public transportation, which stops 50 feet away. Singles rent for $70, doubles $76. Ⓣ Red Line to Braintree.

## PLACES TO STAY – MID-RANGE
## Motels & Hotels

*Susse Chalet Lodge* (☎ 617-287-9100, 800-886-0056, fax 617-265-9287, info@bostonhotel .com, 800 Morrissey Blvd, Dorchester, MA 02122) and the *Susse Chalet Inn* (☎ 617-287-9200, fax 282-2365, 900 Morrissey Blvd) are next door to each other right off the I-93 Expressway, 5 miles south of the city. Between the two there are 310 standard rooms that rent for $70 to $110 single, $78 to $117 double (about $10 less in winter). To get the lowest rates, ask for 'sure saver' rooms (they're smaller) at the lodge, which also boasts a pool. Inn rooms are newer and more hotel-like. Next door there is a family bowling center that's enjoying a resurgence in popularity, and a restaurant. Every 30 minutes a van shuttles guests to and from the JFK Red Line T station.

Across from the Chestnut Hill shopping mall and near the Boston College campus, the *Newton Susse Chalet* (☎ 617-527-9000, 800-524-2538, fax 617-527-4994, 160 Boylston St (Route 9), Newton, MA 02467) is about 8 miles (30 minutes) west of downtown Boston on public transportation. Its 144 simple rooms rent for $77 double in winter and $96 double in summer, including free parking and cable movies. There's also an outdoor pool. Ⓣ Green Line 'D' branch to Chestnut Hill, and then a 10-minute walk.

The *Holiday Inn Express* (☎ 617-288-3030, 800-465-4329, fax 617-265-6543), exit 16 off I-93, Dorchester, is about 3 miles south of Boston. Parking is free and public transportation on the Red Line is eight blocks away on a well-lit street. A 24-hour grocery store is around the corner. The 118 standard motel-style rooms with air-con rent for $159 to $169 March through November, $99 to $129 the rest of the year. (T) Red Line to Andrew.

The *Howard Johnson Fenway* (☎ 617-267-8300, 800-654-2000, fax 617-267-2763, 1271 Boylston St, Boston, MA 02215) is within a 15-minute walk of the Museum of Fine Arts and Gardner Museum, and about 10 minutes from downtown on the trolley. The 94 standard rooms rent for $130 to $190 (single or double) from mid-March to mid-November, $100 to $130 off season, including parking. (T) Green Line to Kenmore.

The *Best Western Terrace Inn* (☎ 617-566-6260, 800-528-1234, fax 617-731-3543, 1650 Commonwealth Ave, Brighton, MA 02135), 3 miles west of Kenmore Square, is about 20 minutes from Boston Common via public transportation. Some of the 72 rooms have kitchenettes; all have TV, refrigerator and air-con. Rates are $89 to $129 single or double, including parking. (T) Green Line 'B' branch to Mt Hood.

The no-nonsense *Susse Chalet Cambridge* (☎ 617-661-7800, 800-524-2538, fax 617-868-8153, www.sussechalet.com, 211 Concord Turnpike (Route 2 East), Cambridge, MA 02140) has 78 rooms. It's more remote than other Susse Chalets, but the rooms are similar and you can still reach Harvard Square in 10 minutes by car. Otherwise, walk 10 minutes to the Alewife T station and be in Harvard Square in another five minutes. Parking is free; rooms are $93 to $109 March to mid-November (about $20 less off season).

The central *Chandler Inn Hotel* (☎ 617-482-3450, 800-842-3450, fax 617-542-3428, inn3450@ix.netcom.com, 26 Chandler St, Boston, MA 02116) has 56 clean, albeit nondescript, rooms. From June to mid-November they rent for $109 to $129 double, $10 less for singles, about $10 less off season. The hotel is popular with Europeans and gays. (T) Orange Line to Back Bay/South End.

The four-floored *John Jeffries House* (☎ 617-367-1866, fax 742-0313, 14 David Mugar Way, Boston, MA 02114), at the base of Beacon Hill and across Storrow Drive from the Charles River, has 46 rooms and suites in an early-20th-century building owned by the Mass Eye and Ear Infirmary. (You don't have to know someone having an operation to stay here.) Rooms are nicely decorated, and some still have original molding and hardwood floors; most have a kitchenette. From April through November, you'll pay $90 single, $110 double, $130 to $150 suites; off season it's $10 to $15 less. (T) Red Line Charles/MGH.

## Inns & B&Bs
The Bed & Breakfast Agency of Boston (☎ 617-720-3540, 800-248-9262, 0800-895128 from the UK, fax 617-523-5761, bosbnb@ aol.com, 47 Commercial Wharf, Boston, MA 02110) lists about 150 B&Bs and apartments, most of which are located downtown. Some are in historic Victorian-furnished brownstones, some are waterfront lofts; one is even in a docked wooden boat. The agency will give you all the details of what's available at any given time. Expect to pay from $70 to $100 nightly for a double with shared bath, $100 to $160 with private bath. From mid-November to mid-February, stay two nights and get the third night free, based on availability.

The *College Club* (☎ 617-536-9510, fax 247-8537, cclub@javanet.com, 44 Comm Ave, Boston, MA 02116), originally a private club for women college graduates in the 1940s, has just 11 rooms, open to both sexes, renting for $75 single with shared bath, $120 double with private bath, continental breakfast included. Some furnishings are a bit shabby, but most rooms are enormous. The location couldn't be better: one block from the Public Garden and Newbury St, just three from the grassy Charles River Esplanade. (T) Green Line to Arlington.

The *Newbury Guest House* (☎ 617-437-7666, 800-437-7668, mbknghl@aol.com, 261 Newbury St, Boston, MA 02116) has 32 rooms with private bath in a four-story, circa-1882 renovated brownstone. Expect to pay $115 to $145 double ($5 to $15 less for a single), including a continental breakfast.

It's hard to beat the location; there is limited parking for $15. ⓣ Green Line to Hynes Convention Center.

Adjacent to the State House atop Beacon Hill, the ***Eliot & Pickett Houses*** (☎ 617-248-8707, fax 742-1364, e&p@uua.org, 6 Mt Vernon Place, Boston, MA 02108) has 20 rooms with shared and private bath in two adjoining brick townhouses. There's a great deck for resting and it has comfortable living rooms. The kitchen is stocked with all the supplies you'll need for making breakfast or lunch. Some rooms have two four-poster beds, and families are reasonably accommodated. Doubles cost $85 with shared bath, $110 to $150 with private bath; from December through March the most expensive room drops to $125 but the low-end rooms don't move. ⓣ Green Line to Park St.

The brick townhouse ***Clarendon Square B&B*** (☎ 617-536-2229, 198 W Brookline St, Boston, MA 02116) has only three rooms (with private bath) but they're very stylish. Staying at the B&B, complete with airy living room and a small back deck, will give you a great idea of what chichi South End living is all about. Doubles are $125 to $185. ⓣ Orange Line to Back Bay/South End.

## PLACES TO STAY – TOP END
### Motels
The older ***Howard Johnson Kenmore Square*** (☎ 617-267-3100, 800-654-2000, fax 617-424-1045, 575 Comm Ave, Boston, MA 02215) has 180 comfortable rooms, free parking and an indoor pool. Rates hover around $210 double March through October, $99 to $145 the rest of the year. ⓣ Green Line to Kenmore.

The ***Holiday Inn Brookline*** (☎ 617-277-1200, 800-465-4329, fax 617-734-6991, 1200 Beacon St, Brookline, MA 02146) is just over the Boston city line, a 25-minute trolley ride from downtown. The 225 rooms rent for $179 to $209 in high season, $119 to $139 off season. Rates include an indoor pool and parking. ⓣ Green Line 'C' branch to St Paul.

### Hotels
Built in 1891, the modest seven-story ***Copley Square Hotel*** (☎ 617-536-9000, 800-225-7062, fax 617-236-0351, www.copleysquare.com, 47 Huntington Ave, Boston, MA 02116) attracts a low-key European crowd. The 143 refurbished rooms vary considerably in size and boast windows that open. Rates are fairly reasonable considering the convenient Back Bay location; doubles start at $245 March through October, or $179 November through February. Ask about special packages. The hotel's Original Sports Saloon has all-you-can-eat ribs for $15 on Wednesday. ⓣ Green Line to Prudential.

The two-story ***Midtown Hotel*** (☎ 617-262-1000, 800-343-1177, fax 617-262-8739, 220 Huntington Ave, Boston, MA 02115) is on the edge of the South End, just two blocks from the 4½-mile-long Southwest Corridor Park (great for walking). The 159-room hotel fills up with families, business people and tour groups alike. Free parking and use of the outdoor pool are included for $189 to $209 April through October, or $99 to $189 the rest of the year. ⓣ Green Line to Symphony.

Although the ***Radisson Hotel Boston*** (☎ 617-482-1800, 800-333-3333, fax 617-482-0242, www.radisson.com, 200 Stuart St, Boston, MA 02116) is popular with business travelers, tourists also appreciate its proximity to Boston Common. This 24-story hotel has 354 rooms that rent for $229 to $279 double ($119 December to mid-March), including parking. Added bonuses include private balconies, free movie channels, a fitness center and an indoor swimming pool. ⓣ Green Line to Boylston.

Right in Harvard Square, the ***Harvard Square Hotel*** (☎ 617-864-5200, 800-458-5886, fax 617-492-4896, www.theinnatharvard.com, 110 Mt Auburn St, Cambridge, MA 02138) has 73 rooms that rent for $149 to $219 year-round. ⓣ Red Line to Harvard Square.

In the Theater District near Chinatown and a favorite among actors and stagehands, the ***Tremont House*** (☎ 617-426-1400, 800-331-9998, fax 617-338-7881, www.wyndham.com, 275 Tremont St, Boston, MA 02116) has 322 smallish guest rooms nicely decorated with early American reproduction furniture and prints from the Museum of Fine Arts.

The 1925 hotel retains an ornate and elegant lobby, complete with chandeliers and a marble stairway and columns. Rooms rent for $129 to $322 March through October, $99 to $199 the rest of the year. ⓣ Green Line to Boylston or Orange Line to NE Medical Center.

In Cambridge, the *Sheraton Commander* (☎ 617-547-4800, 800-535-5007, fax 617-868-8322, www.sheraton.com, 16 Garden St, Cambridge, MA 02138) is a few minutes' walk from Harvard Square. The 175 rooms on six floors are comfortably decorated; suites have refrigerators. A multilingual staff caters to many foreign guests. Rates are $160 to $324 March through October, or $119 to $209 November through February. ⓣ Red Line to Harvard.

The European-style, nine-story *Eliot Suite Hotel* (☎ 617-267-1607, 800-443-5468, fax 617-536-9114, www.eliothotel.com, 370 Comm Ave, Boston, MA 02215) offers 85 suites and 10 regular rooms on the edge of Back Bay near Kenmore Square. The hotel dates to 1925, but the rooms were elegantly remodeled in the mid-1990s with marble tubs, antiques and French doors separating the living room and bedrooms. It's all quite low-key and inviting. Rates are $195 to $325 April through November, $195 December through March. ⓣ Green Line to Hynes Convention Center.

*Lenox Hotel* (☎ 617-536-5300, 800-225-7676, fax 617-236-0351, www.lenoxhotel.com, 710 Boylston St, Boston, MA 02116) is another early-20th-century hotel that's undergone recent extensive renovations. A fancy Old-Worldish lobby (complete with crackling fireplace) gives way to sound-proofed guest rooms with classical furnishings, high ceilings, big closets and sitting areas. The 213 rooms rent for $288 to $308 mid-March to mid-November, $197 to $250 off season. ⓣ Green Line to Copley.

## PLACES TO EAT

Since the early 1990s, the Boston restaurant scene has exploded with great places to eat. Most restaurants are concentrated in Chinatown, the North End, around Newbury St and Harvard Square in Cambridge. The places that seem a bit more difficult to reach are also worth seeking out.

In Boston, eating cheaply doesn't have to mean eating badly. Conversely, if you want to splurge a bit, there are memorable places to enjoy an evening.

See the Entertainment section for breweries, pubs and music venues that offer dining as well. (Also see the North End & Charlestown section for North End specialty markets.)

### Farmer's Markets

Touch the produce and you risk the wrath of pushcart vendors at *Haymarket*, between the I-93 expressway and Blackstone St. No one else in the city matches their prices on ripe-and-ready fruits and vegetables. The spectacle takes place every Friday and Saturday, with the best bargains on Saturday afternoon. ⓣ Green or Orange Line to Haymarket.

Cambridge might seem ripe for a farmer's market, but the plaza at the ritzy *Charles Hotel*, 5 Bennett St in Harvard Square, hardly seems the obvious site. Nonetheless, there is a great market there on Sundays (from 10 am to 2:30 pm) mid-June through mid-November. ⓣ Red Line to Harvard.

There is also an almost-daily produce market in *Downtown Crossing*, on the corner of Washington and Summer Sts. ⓣ Red or Orange Line to Downtown Crossing.

### Health Food Stores

Organic produce is sold by weight at the *Harvest Co-Op* (☎ 617-661-1580, 581 Mass Ave) in Cambridge's Central Square. There's a good community bulletin board there. ⓣ Red Line to Central.

*Bread & Circus* (☎ 617-492-0070, 115 Prospect St), two blocks north of Mass Ave in Central Square, is a whole-food supermarket. Although you can find organic produce and other goods in many grocery stores these days, Bread & Circus sells the best (but often priciest). ⓣ Red Line to Central.

### Delis & Bakeries

For assembling a picnic on the Common or the Esplanade, there are two gourmet shops at the foot of Beacon Hill, one at either end of Charles St. (Remember when assembling a picnic that drinking alcoholic beverages in public is illegal.)

*Savenor's* (☎ 617-723-6328, *160 Charles St*) and *DeLuca's Market* (☎ 617-523-4343, *11 Charles St*) are not cheap, but they both have a fine selection of cheeses and deli meats, fresh-baked bread and pastries, and fruit and vegetables. DeLuca's is open 7 am to 10 pm daily. Savenor's opens at 9 am daily and closes at 8:30 pm weekdays, 8 pm on Saturday and 7 pm on Sunday. Ⓣ Red Line to Charles/MGH.

*LMNOP* (☎ 617-338-4220, *79 Park Plaza*), across from the Park Plaza Hotel, bakes for the posh restaurant next door, but luckily also sells crusty loaves and delectable baked pastries retail. At lunchtime there are also sandwiches, soups and pasta dishes ($4 to $5.50) for take-out. It's open from 7:30 am to 6:45 pm daily except Sunday. Ⓣ Green Line to Arlington.

*J Pace & Son* (☎ 617-227-4949, *2 Devonshire Place*), in the Financial District, is both an Italian grocery and trattoria, featuring hot pasta dishes, salads, soups and sandwiches. It's open 6 am to 7 pm weekdays, 8 am to 4 pm on Saturday. Ⓣ Orange or Blue Line to State.

At *Salumeria Italiana* (☎ 617-523-8743, *151 Richmond St*), in the North End, you can assemble an Italian-style picnic complete with prosciutto, salami, cheese, bread and olives. It's open 8 am to 6 pm daily except Sunday. Ⓣ Orange or Green Line to Haymarket.

Before heading off to the waterfront to enjoy your sandwich from Salumeria Italiana, stop at *Mike's Pastry* (☎ 617-742-3050, *300 Hanover St*), North End's favorite bakery. Muscle your way through the crowds and grab the attention of one of the staff as they scurry to and fro. Order a ricotta cannoli, which they will make fresh in the back room, rather than opting for an already-filled pastry shell. It's open 9 am to 9 pm weekdays, to 10 pm on Friday and Saturday and until 6 pm on Tuesday. Ⓣ Orange or Green Line to Haymarket.

In Cambridge, *Cardullo's* (☎ 617-491-8888, *6 Brattle St*) carries an impressive assortment of international goods, but more importantly they make sandwiches-to-go. It's open 8 am to 8 pm weekdays, 11 am to 9 pm on Saturday, with shorter Sunday hours. Ⓣ Red Line to Harvard.

Nearby, *Hi-Rise Pie Co* (☎ 617-492-3003, *56 Brattle St*) is well known for wonderful scones, cookies and crusty loaves. You can also get light meals (sandwiches and soups) in the cafe. Outdoor tables are popular in warm weather; indoors is cozy. The cafe and pastry counter are open 8:30 am to 5 pm weekdays, 9 am to 5 pm on Saturday. Ⓣ Red Line to Harvard.

## Tea & Coffeehouses

Cambridge's decidedly European *Café Pamplona* (no ☎, *12 Bow St*), located in a cozy cellar on a backstreet near Harvard Square, is *the* choice among highbrow intellectuals who still enjoy a good face-to-face conversation and who relish the feel of books, pencils and paper. In addition to espresso, they have light snacks like gazpacho, sandwiches and biscotti. The tiny outdoor terrace is delightful in summer. It's open 11 am to 1 am daily (2 pm to 1 am on Sunday). Ⓣ Red Line to Harvard.

*Loulou's Tealuxe* (☎ 617-441-0077, *Zero Brattle St*) is in Harvard Square and worth stopping in simply for the aroma. It is preferred by lovers of steeped leaves rather than brewed beans. The tiny storefront dispensary has only a few tables, but if you're lucky, you can take in the ever-engaging *passeggiata* (passers-by) while you sip. It's open 8 am until 11 pm daily (until midnight Thursday through Saturday). Ⓣ Red Line to Harvard.

In Cambridge's Central Square, *1369 Coffee House* (☎ 617-576-4600, *757 Mass Ave*) is a bohemian place with good music, serious coffee, a laudable selection of tea, a limited snack list and a friendly waitstaff. What more could you want? It's open 7 or 8 am to 10 or 11 pm daily. Ⓣ Red Line to Central.

The *Caffé Vittoria* (☎ 617-227-7606, *296 Hanover St*), in the North End, is the most atmospheric and Old-Worldly of the many area Italian cafes. It's been here since the 1930s and a few of the Italian-speaking patrons have been coming here as long. To get the full effect, don't get herded with the tourists into the modern expansion rooms; wait for a table in the original dining room. It's open 8 am until midnight daily. ⓣ Orange or Green Line to Haymarket.

*Caffé dello Sport* (☎ 617-523-5063, 308 Hanover St) is the primo place to watch just about any sporting event, especially soccer. It's open 6:30 or 7 am to 11:30 pm or midnight daily. ⓣ Orange or Green Line to Haymarket.

The 'other side' in *The Other Side Cosmic Café* (☎ 617-536-9477, 407 Newbury St) refers to the other side of Mass Ave, which few strollers crossed before this place opened. The 'cosmic' alludes to its funky, Seattle-inspired style. The 1st floor is done in cast iron, while the 2nd floor is softened by velvet drapes, mismatched couches and low ceilings. Vegetarian chili, sandwiches, fruit and veggie drinks and strong coffee are the order of the day. Some of the twentysomething clientele hang out here all day and night. The cafe is open 10 am to midnight daily (from noon on Sunday). ⓣ Green Line to Hynes Convention Center.

*Sonsie* (☎ 617-351-2500, 327 Newbury St), near Mass Ave, is perhaps the most hip place to be seen drinking a cappuccino. Europeans descend on the place wearing basic black and dark sunglasses. In warm weather, a wall of French doors is flung open, making the indoor tables seem al fresco. During busy mealtimes, cafe tables are reserved for diners. Pizza, pasta and other light dishes are available. Although full-fledged dining here is pricey, the French and Asian fusion menu is worth it. It's open 8 am to 1 am daily. ⓣ Green Line to Hynes Convention Center.

*Borders Bookstore Café* (☎ 617-557-7188, 10-24 School St), near Downtown Crossing, is a favorite among those for whom book-browsing, punctuated by a few coffee breaks, is an all-day affair. It's open 7 am to 9 pm Monday through Saturday, 10 am to 8 pm Sunday. ⓣ Orange or Red Line to Downtown Crossing.

Every time you turn around, another *Starbucks* coffee shop pops up on another corner in Boston and Cambridge. As of this writing, there are more than 30 branches of the Seattle-based java suppliers in the area, including: 222 Cambridge St near Government Center; 1 Charles St on the northwestern corner of Boston Common; 443 and 745 Boylston St; 75-101 Federal St, 211 Congress St, 655 Atlantic Ave and 10 High St, all in the Financial District; 31 Church St and 36 John F Kennedy St, both in Harvard Square; and at 1662 Mass Ave, between Harvard and Porter Squares.

## Ice Cream

Regardless of the weather, Bostonians never lose their appetite for the frozen treat. Sample from among the city's favorites and you'll understand why.

*Toscanini's* has two branches in Cambridge: 899 Main St (☎ 617-491-5877), between Central and Kendall Squares, and 1310 Mass Ave (☎ 617-354-9350), in Harvard Square. Two yummy flavors to try are gingersnap molasses and Vienna finger cookie.

At *Herrell's* (☎ 617-497-2179, 15 Dunster St), in Harvard Square, and (☎ 617-236-0857, 224 Newbury St), in Back Bay (ⓣ Green Line to Copley), favorites include malted vanilla and chocolate pudding.

*Emack & Bolio's* (☎ 617-247-8772, 290 Newbury St), between Hereford St and Gloucester St, takes pride in its status as an old-timer on the Boston gourmet ice cream scene. Many consider their Oreo cookie ice cream definitive; nonfat yogurt creations like latte espresso chip are also good. ⓣ Green Line to Hynes Convention Center.

At *JP Licks* (☎ 617-236-1666, 352 Newbury St), near Mass Ave and adjacent to Tower Records, it's a toss-up between white coffee and chocolate turtle. ⓣ Green Line to Hynes Convention Center.

Vermont's own *Ben & Jerry's* (☎ 617-426-0890, 20 Park Plaza) and (☎ 617-536-5456, 174 Newbury St) has ever-changing choices, including triple caramel chunk and chocolate mint patty. ⓣ Green Line to Arlington for the Park Plaza branch; ⓣ Green Line to Copley for Newbury St.

*Wai Wai* (☎ 617-338-9833, 26 Oxford St), in Chinatown, is probably Boston's most offbeat choice. Although the tiny basement eatery exudes an aroma of roasting chickens, don't be scared. In addition to quick meals, Wai Wai offers five or six homemade tropical ice-cream flavors including ginger, coconut and banana. (If you're feeling down and out after a long day, you can medicate yourself with the Wong Lo Kat 'medical' tea for 85¢.) ⓣ Orange Line to Chinatown.

At the South Station Food Court, *JB Scoops* (☎ *617-443-0500)* dishes out homemade ice cream in old-fashioned flavors like maple walnut and pumpkin pie ($2 for one scoop, $3.15 for three); it's open 9 am to 9 pm daily. ⓣ Red Line to South Station.

## Fast Food

*Faneuil Hall Marketplace,* (☎ *617-338-2323)*, or Quincy Market as it's also known, northeast of Congress and State Sts, offers the greatest number and variety of places under one roof: There are about 20 restaurants and 40 food stalls. You'll find chowder, bagels, Indian, Greek, baked goods and ice cream. The center rotunda has tables. The food court is open 10 am to 9 pm Monday through Saturday, noon to 6 pm on Sunday. Breakfast stalls (for a coffee and bagel) open earlier. ⓣ Green or Blue Line to Government Center.

*Hungry Traveler* (☎ *617-742-5989, 29 Court Square)*, near Government Center, is a little-known gem for budget travelers. Hidden on a small side street, this cafeteria serves eggs and sausage and other breakfast staples, as well as cold sandwiches and hot entrees like meatloaf and pot pie at lunchtime for about $5. This place is neither vegetarian nor gourmet. And the service is brusque, so you'd better know what you want before getting to the head of the line. Phone ahead to hear the daily recorded menu. It's open 6:30 am to 4 pm weekdays. ⓣ Blue or Orange Line to State.

In the *Downtown Crossing*, at Summer St between Washington and Chauncy Sts, lunch cart vendors offer tasty and inexpensive fast food such as meat and bean burritos, sandwiches, sausages, hot dogs and veggie wraps. ⓣ Red or Orange Line to Downtown Crossing.

Within the grandly renovated train terminal, the *South Station Food Court,* on Atlantic Ave at Summer St, offers a range of fast food, but hidden among the usual suspects are a few gems. *Rosie's Bakery* (☎ *617-439-4684)* satisfies the most demanding sweet tooth and challenges the most determined dieter; try a pecan sticky bun ($2.25) or a savory foccacia ($3). Rosie's is open 7 am to 7 pm weekdays, until 6 pm on Saturday. *The Boston Coffee Exchange* brews flavorful espresso and cappuccino. It's open 5 am to 7:30 pm weekdays, 6 am to noon on Saturday. ⓣ Red Line to South Station.

*Bruegger's Bagel Bakery* (☎ *617-367-4702, 7 School St)*, near Downtown Crossing, has a dozen kinds of bagels and 10 varieties of cream cheese. They'll also slap some deli meat and veggies on a bagel if you want a bagel sandwich. ⓣ Red or Orange Line to Downtown Crossing. Bruegger's has numerous locations, including in the Financial District (☎ *617-261-7115, 64 Broad St)*; Kenmore Square (☎ *617-262-7939, 644 Beacon St)*; and Harvard Square (☎ *617-661-4664, 85 Mt Auburn St)*. All are open from early morning to late afternoon daily.

*The Garage* (*36 John F Kennedy St)*, in Harvard Square, has about a dozen places to eat under one roof. You're bound to find something fast, filling and cheap here. ⓣ Red Line to Harvard.

## Seafood

There are few rivals to *Legal Sea Foods* (☎ *617-426-4444, 26 Park Square)*, near the Theater District, which has built its reputation and a local empire on the motto: 'If it's not fresh, it's not Legal.' The menu is simple: Every kind of seafood, it seems, broiled, steamed, sautéed, grilled or fried. Freshness comes at a price: Lunch is about $10, while dinner runs $15 to $25 per entree. The servings are generous; depending on your appetite, the fried calamari appetizer ($8) could be a main dish. The clam chowder ($4) is justifiably considered the best in New England. ⓣ Green Line to Arlington. There are branches at Prudential Center (☎ *617-266-6800, 800 Boylston St)*, at the Copley Place shopping mall (☎ *617-266-7775)* and in

Kendall Square (☎ 617-864-3400, 5 Cambridge Center) in Cambridge. All are open from about noon to 10 pm daily, until 9 pm on Sunday.

## Vegetarian

**Country Life** (☎ 617-951-2534, 200 High St), in the Financial District, is worth seeking out for its all-you-can-eat lunch buffet ($7), served 11:30 am to 3 pm weekdays. You'll find tasty lasagna, pot pies and lots of different soups, but no meat, dairy or refined grains. The decor is pleasant enough and the self-service keeps the prices reasonable. It also serves dinner on Sunday and Tuesday, and brunch on Sunday. Ⓣ Red Line to South Station.

## Pizza

**Bertucci's** (☎ 617-227-7889, 22 Merchants Row), next to the Faneuil Hall Marketplace, is one of the most popular places for sit-down, brick-oven pizza ($9.25 for a large cheese, $13 for a large 'specialty'). Try not to fill up on the tasty, piping-hot rolls, because they also have salads, pasta dishes and calzones. Ⓣ Blue or Green Line to Government Center. This ever-expanding chain now also has branches in Harvard Square (☎ 617-864-4748, 21 Brattle St); between Kendall and Central Squares (☎ 617-661-8356, 799 Main St); and near Copley Square (☎ 617-247-6161, 43 Stanhope St). It's open 11 am to 11 pm daily, until midnight on Friday and Saturday.

The North End wouldn't be what it is without the legendary **Regina Pizzeria** (☎ 617-227-0765, 11½ Thatcher St). The crispy, thin-crust pizza – $12.50 for a large with two toppings – is best consumed with a pitcher of beer (about $9). It's open from about 11 am to 11 pm daily. Ⓣ Green or Orange Line to Haymarket. There's also a branch in Faneuil Hall Marketplace (☎ 617-227-8180), but hard-core devotees say it's not as good as the original.

**Galleria Umberto** (☎ 617-227-5709, 289 Hanover St) certainly rivals its North End counterpart in quality, but its crust is as thick and chewy as Regina's is thin and crispy. Furthermore, the 75¢ slices are usually gone by 2 pm, at which time the place closes; it opens at 11 am daily except Sunday. Ⓣ Green or Orange Line to Haymarket.

**Figs** (☎ 617-742-3447, 42 Charles St), on Beacon Hill, excels in fancy pasta dishes, salads and creative pizzas (with whisper-thin crusts) topped with goat cheese, prosciutto, portabella mushrooms and the like. Pizzas run from $11 to $17. Although it's pricier than most, it will also feel more like a night out than most pizza joints. It's open 5:30 pm to 10 pm weekdays, noon to 9 or 10 pm on weekends. Ⓣ Red Line to Charles/MGH.

Figs has another branch in Charlestown (☎ 617-242-2229, 67 Main St), perfect after a late afternoon spent climbing the Bunker Hill Monument. It's open daily for dinner. Ⓣ Green or Orange Line to North Station.

**Baldini's** (☎ 617-695-1559, 71 Summer St), in the Downtown Crossing area, is an inexpensive, self-service Italian place where you can get hefty, if uninspired, pizza-by-the-slice ($2.35), calzones (about $4) and pasta with meatballs and red sauce ($5.25). It's mobbed at lunchtime, but there is seating upstairs, too. It's open until 7 pm Monday through Thursday, until 4 or 4:30 pm on Friday and Saturday. Ⓣ Orange or Red Line to Downtown Crossing. There are a number of other locations, including near Copley Square (☎ 617-262-2555, 549 Boylston St); in Kenmore Square (☎ 617-267-6269, 532 Commonwealth Ave); and near the Arlington T station (☎ 617-338-0095, 304 Stuart St). It's open for lunch and dinner daily.

## American

**The Sevens** (☎ 617-523-9074, 77 Charles St) is a popular and friendly Beacon Hill neighborhood pub that's crowded from 11:30 am to 2 am. Sit at the bar or in a booth and order a sandwich and beer ($6) or anything else off the menu for about $8.50. Ⓣ Red Line to Charles/MGH.

If you think 'Boston, books and breakfast' go together, head to **Trident Booksellers & Café** (☎ 617-267-8688, 338 Newbury St), in Back Bay. The shelves are primarily filled with New Age titles, while the tables are crowded with decidedly down-to-earth salads, soups, sandwiches ($5 to $7), pasta entrees ($8 to $12) and desserts; breakfast is served all day. Vegetarians rejoice with the vegan cashew chili. It's open 9 am to midnight daily. Ⓣ Green Line to Hynes Convention Center.

***Parish Café & Bar*** (☎ 617-247-4777, 361 Boylston St), next to the Public Garden, is known for creative and hearty sandwiches, each designed by a local celebrity chef. Try the one by Rialto chef Jody Adams: prosciutto and buffalo mozzarella with pesto and a touch of basil oil on grilled white bread ($12) – not your average sandwich. Some are accompanied by a salad. Other draws include an outdoor patio, a stylish interior, 70 different brands of beer and 20 wines by the glass. It's open 11:30 am or noon to 2 am, daily. Ⓣ Green Line to Arlington.

***Milk Street Café*** (☎ 617-542-3663, 50 Milk St) is popular with the Financial District suit crowd, but don't let that deter you from large servings of above-average lunch fare ($6 to $8) such as pastas, salads, soups, sandwiches and pastries. The dairy is kosher. It's open 7 am to 3 pm weekdays. The Post Office Square location (☎ 617-350-7275) is pleasant in summer, when cafe tables are set out and diners spill out onto the little park; it's open 7 am to 5 pm weekdays. Ⓣ Red or Orange Line to Downtown Crossing, or Blue Line to State.

***Blossoms*** (☎ 617-423-1911, 99 High St), in the Financial District, is actually a catering operation that doubles as a self-service lunch spot. The creative salads, soups, wraps, and hot and cold sandwiches ($4.50 to $6.50) are a cut well above other area options. Blossoms does mostly take-out business, so there are usually plenty of tables. Ⓣ Red Line to South Station.

Open for weekday lunches, the ***City Café*** (☎ 617-261-7458, 274 Franklin St), in the Financial District, is a bustling New York City-style, self-serve cafeteria-deli. Selections include hot Italian pasta dishes, cold salads, Chinese entrees and sushi. You can get a full meal to go for about $5. Join the local business folks and take your food to the Post Office Square park. Ⓣ Red Line to South Station.

***Cosi Sandwich Shop*** (☎ 617-292-2674, 133 Federal St), the latest import from Paris by way of New York, has taken the Boston lunch crowd by storm. Line up behind the suits and select from 20 fillings to be sandwiched between pieces of crusty, fresh, hearth-baked flatbread. Possibilities include cranberry roasted turkey, tandoori grilled chicken and roasted red pepper with eggplant feta spread. 'Cosi One' (one filling) goes for $5.75, 'Cosi Two' for $6.50 and so on. The price may seem steep, but one sandwich is big enough to share. It is open from 6:30 am to 5 or 5:30 pm weekdays. Ⓣ Red Line to South Station.

***Durgin Park*** (☎ 617-227-2038), in Faneuil Hall Marketplace, is known for no-nonsense service, sawdust underfoot on the old floorboards and family-style dining at large tables. The bill of fare hasn't changed much since the restaurant was built in 1827: huge slabs of prime rib, fish chowder, chicken pot pie, Boston baked beans, and strawberry shortcake and Indian pudding for dessert. It's open 11:30 am to 10 pm daily; expect to pay $7 to $16 for lunch or dinner. Ⓣ Orange or Blue Line to State, or Green Line to Government Center.

***Charlie's Sandwich Shoppe*** (☎ 617-536-7669, 429 Columbus Ave), a classic South End coffee shop, is frequented by both lawyers in suits and laborers in work boots. It's been serving creative omelettes ($6 to $8 with a salad), cranberry french toast and other breakfast platters ($3.50 to $5 with meat) since 1927. For lunch, it's turkey hash with two eggs ($5.75), hot pastrami and homemade pies at a few shared tables or the counter. It's open 6 am to 2:30 pm weekdays, 7:30 am to 1 pm on Saturday. Ⓣ Orange Line to Back Bay/South End or Green Line to Prudential.

***Bob the Chef*** (☎ 617-536-6204, 604 Columbus Ave), in the South End, serves Boston's best down-home soul food: We're talking barbecue ribs with a hunk of cornbread or fried chicken with collard greens or black-eyed peas. Sit at the long counter or in a booth. Most meals cost about $10; sandwiches are half that. It's open 11 am to 10 pm Monday through Thursday, 8 am to

11 pm on Friday and Saturday, 11 am to 9 pm on Sunday. The Sunday jazz brunch ($15), served from 11 am to 3:30 pm, is a local favorite; reservations are recommended. ⓣ Orange Line to Mass Ave.

*Bartley's Burger Cottage* (☎ 617-354-6559, 1246 Mass Ave) is *the* primo burger joint, offering at least 40 different burgers. But if none of those suits your fancy, create your own 7oz, juicy masterpiece topped with guacamole or sprouts. They do make a veggie burger (for vegetarians who don't mind being surrounded by all that red meat). French fries and onion rings complete the classic American meal. Bartley's is packed with small tables and hungry college students from 11 am to 10 pm daily, except Sunday. You can get out of here for about $10. ⓣ Red Line to Harvard.

A popular haunt for Harvard students, *Henry's Diner* (☎ 617-783-5844, 270 Western Ave), at N Harvard St, has basic American food so cheap it could compete with a grocery store. It's out of the way but worth seeking out. Just pronounce Henry's (on-REES) as the French do, order the chicken parm (chicken parmesan) dinner ($6) and you'll fit right in. Henry's is open 6 am to 7:30 pm daily, until 6 pm on Saturday and Sunday. ⓣ Red Line to Harvard Square, and then a 20-minute walk.

In Cambridge, *Henrietta's Table* (☎ 617-864-1200, 1 Bennett St), in the Charles Hotel, features a New England regional menu highlighting locally grown produce. The creative and 'fresh and honest' preparations, country inn decor and friendly service make it *the* choice for better-than-home cooking. Main dishes cost $11.50 to $15, sides about $3.50. You'll need an appetite to get your money's worth out of the abundant and deservedly popular Sunday brunch ($32 per person), from noon to 2:45 pm. The restaurant serves all three meals daily. ⓣ Red Line to Harvard.

## Italian

In the North End, *La Piccola Venezia* (☎ 617-523-3888, 263 Hanover St) provides consistently great values with huge portions of old-fashioned dishes: eggplant parmagiana ($11 at dinner, less at lunch), spaghetti and meatballs drenched with red sauce ($11) and more unusual but authentic dishes like tripe and gnocchi. It's open 11 am to 10 or 11 pm daily. ⓣ Green or Orange Line to Haymarket.

Although *Artu* (☎ 617-742-4336, 6 Prince St) looks small, its menu of country-style Italian dishes is ambitious and successful. At lunch you can get roasted chicken or pork sandwiches ($5) and a dozen different pasta dishes for under $7, while at dinner and lunch you can also order more sophisticated dishes like the *gamberi arrabbiata* (spicy shrimp over linguini) or roast leg of lamb with peppers and marinated eggplant (both for $14.50). ⓣ Green or Orange Line to Haymarket. The branch on Beacon Hill (☎ 617-227-9023, 89 Charles St) is also open from 11 am to 11 pm daily. ⓣ Red Line to Charles/MGH.

*Antico Forno* (☎ 617-723-6733, 93 Salem St) is named for its beehive, wood-burning brick oven, the source of all that's warm and wonderful in this North End Neapolitan place. It specializes in pizza ($7 to $13); try the *vesuvio* (spicy sausage, cherry tomatoes, roasted peppers, mozzarella and ricotta). Southern Italian home cooking ($15 to $18 per entree) and roasted meats aren't slighted either though. It's open 11:30 am to 11 pm daily. ⓣ Green or Orange Line to Haymarket.

Antico Forno's sibling, *Terramia* (☎ 617-523-3112, 98 Salem St) is the creation of impresario Mario Nocera, who hand-selects every mushroom that enters the kitchen. The creative menu changes seasonally and showcases the essential beauty of vintage balsamic vinegars and rare Italian cheeses from the country. Dishes could be pasta-and rice-based ($11 to $18) or centered around seafood and meat ($17 to $30). You'll have to go elsewhere for dessert and coffee – not a problem in the cafe-filled North End. Terramia serves dinner 5 to 10:30 pm daily, and lunch and dinner from 1 pm on Sunday. ⓣ Green or Orange Line to Haymarket.

# Asian

At their two Chinatown locations, **Pho Pasteur** (☎ *617-482-7467, 682 Washington St;* ☎ *617-451-0247, 8 Kneeland St)* serves hearty, hot and cheap meals in a bowl. Although there are other Vietnamese dishes from which to choose, most people come for *pho*, the sometimes exotic, always fragrant and flavorful noodle soup ($5.50 for extra large). Both shops are open from about 9 or 10 am to 9 or 10 pm daily. Ⓣ Orange Line to Chinatown. There are also branches in Back Bay (☎ *617-262-8200, 119 Newbury St)* and in Harvard Square (☎ *617-864-4100, 35 Dunster St)*.

**Penang** (☎ *617-451-6373, 685 Washington St)* serves creative Malaysian fare in a festive atmosphere. Although you can test your fortitude with fish heads, intestines and pig's feet, it's not required. There are several vegetarian options for the less than intrepid. Some items come with the admonition 'Ask your server for advice before you order!!!' Appetizers range from $3.50 to $7; entrees are $8 to $15. Penang is open from 11:30 am to 11:30 pm daily. Ⓣ Orange Line to Chinatown.

**Hu Tieu Nam Vang** (☎ *617-422-0501, 7 Beach St)*, in Chinatown, serves authentic Vietnamese specialties, from pho to vermicelli dishes; they're all delicious. For a great value ($6.50), try a hot pot – a crock of rice, vegetables and any combination of meat, seafood or tofu, cooked together in a spicy aromatic sauce. It's enough for two people. There are over 40 kinds of cold drinks and fresh fruit shakes. It's open 8 am to 10 pm daily. Ⓣ Orange Line to Chinatown.

Nearby, **Buddha's Delight** (☎ *617-451-2395, 3 Beach St)* thrills vegetarians with noodle soups, tasty tofu dishes and imitation meat dishes like soybean 'roast pork.' Try a fruit and milk drink for dessert. It's open 11 am to 10 or 11 pm daily. Lunch specials are about $5, dinners are around $10. Ⓣ Orange Line to Chinatown.

Down the street and highlighting various regions in China, **Chau Chow** (☎ *617-426-6266, 52 Beach St)* has excellent, daily seafood specials, ample portions and renowned ginger and black bean sauces. Try the garlicky sautéed pea pod stems and the crispy, chewy fried squid. The same delicious food is served in newer and bigger digs across the street at **Grand Chau Chow** (☎ *617-292-5166, 45 Beach St)*. Both are open for lunch and dinner until 2 am daily; lunch will cost you about $5 or $6, dinner $8 to $10. Ⓣ Orange Line to Chinatown.

**Imperial Seafood** (☎ *617-426-8439, 70 Beach St)* is well known for dim sum. These little treats are ferried around the room on carts; you pick what looks good and pay based on the number of empty plates at the end of your meal. Classic choices include pork dumplings, quail eggs, duck's feet, tofu and shrimp balls. Dim sum is best shared among a few people; this way you can sample many things and pay about $10 to $15 per person. Dim sum is available 8:30 am to 3 pm daily, but the restaurant is open until midnight. Ⓣ Orange Line to Chinatown.

**Ginza** (☎ *617-338-2261, 16 Hudson St)*, a hip Japanese restaurant in Chinatown, serves some of the best sushi and maki in Boston. For those who prefer their fish hot, there's always tempura. It's open for lunch and dinner until midnight daily. All this excellence doesn't come cheap, though; expect to spend $25 to $30 per person for dinner. Ⓣ Orange Line to Chinatown.

**Bangkok Cuisine** (☎ *617-262-5377, 177A Mass Ave)*, near the Boston International Hostel, was the first Thai restaurant in Boston, and it's still one of the best. The conventional choices of satay (grilled or broiled for $4) and pad Thai ($4.75 at lunch, $6.50 at dinner) are very good. When the menu says hot, it means it. Bangkok Cuisine is open 11:30 am to 3 pm and 5 to 10:30 pm weekdays, noon to 11 pm on Saturday and 5 to 10 pm on Sunday. Ⓣ Green Line to Hynes Convention Center.

A good choice for Thai food on Beacon is the **King & I** (☎ *617-227-3320, 145 Charles St)*, which is a bit more expensive than Bangkok Cuisine at dinnertime, but you'll get good service and ample portions. Seafood dishes and pad Thai ($7.25) are good bets. Vegetables and tofu can be substituted for meat in any of the dishes. Lunch specials are $6.25. It's open for lunch and dinner Monday through Saturday, for dinner on Sundays. T Red Line to Charles/MGH.

In the South End, *Jae's Café and Grill* (☎ 617-421-9405, 520 Columbus Ave) specializes in Korean food but they have a full pan-Asian menu. Order sushi, satay, pad Thai or vegetarian noodle dishes in this cozy spot. Expect to wait for dinner unless you arrive by 6 pm. Lunch specials are $8 or $9, dinner entrees range from $8 to $15. It's open daily. T Orange Line to Mass Ave. There is also a larger branch (☎ 617-451-7788, 212 Stuart St) near the Theater District, which is also open daily. T Green Line to Arlington.

*Elephant Walk* (☎ 617-247-1500, 900 Beacon St), in Brookline just west of Kenmore Square, is highly regarded for its dual menus of classic French and traditional Cambodian cuisine. The large dining room is open for lunch 11:30 am to 2:30 pm Monday through Saturday and for dinner from 4:30 pm nightly. Lunch is $8 to $10; a Cambodian dinner costs $9 to $15.50, French $8.50 to $23. T Green Line 'C' branch to St Mary's.

### Middle Eastern

The storefront eatery of *Café Jaffa* (☎ 617-536-0230, 48 Gloucester St) is a surprising bargain in the middle of blue-blood Back Bay. When was the last time you had authentic Turkish coffee, shwarma or falafel in a place with polished wooden floors and exposed brick? The servings are large and the prices more than reasonable ($3.50 to $10). You can take out or eat in for lunch and dinner daily. T Green Line to Hynes Convention Center.

*Sultan's Kitchen* (☎ 617-338-7819, 72 Broad St), in the Financial District, is a real find. Line up with the crowds at the fast-moving self-service counter, and take your plate upstairs to dine. You'll be rewarded with sizable portions of complex and delicately flavored Turkish dishes. Standbys include baba ghanoush, stuffed grape leaves, falafel, shish kebobs, salads and baklava. If

you can't decide, get the sampler plate ($7.50). Save room for arguably the best rice pudding in the world ($2.50). Too bad it's only open for lunch weekdays (11 am to 5 pm) and Saturday (until 3 pm). T Red Line to South Station.

Although the service at Harvard Square's *Algiers Coffee House* (☎ 617-492-1557, 40 Brattle St) can be glacial, the palatial Middle Eastern decor makes it a comfortable rest spot. Head to the airy 2nd floor and order a falafel sandwich ($7.25), a bowl of lentil soup ($4), *merguesa* (lamb sausage) for $12 or a kebab ($11). Algiers is open 8 am to midnight daily. The one good thing about the relaxed service is that you won't be rushed to finish your pot of Arabic coffee ($3.75) or mint tea ($3). T Red Line to Harvard.

### Indian

In Harvard Square, the *Bombay Club* (☎ 617-661-8100, 57 John F Kennedy St) is a good choice for lunch because of the $7 bargain buffet (11:30 am to 3 pm on weekends). Dinner also features authentic northern Indian dishes such as chicken *tikka masala* ($11). T Red Line to Harvard.

Cambridge's Central Square offers a number of good Indian restaurants. You can't go wrong at *India Pavillion* (☎ 617-547-7463, 17 Central Square), at Western Ave. The decor is simple and the dining area tiny, but the excellent and authentic dishes more than make up for it. It's open for lunch ($4.50 to $6) and dinner ($9 to $12) daily. There is a $6 lunch buffet Friday through Sunday. T Red Line to Central.

Another prime choice is the *Tandoor House* (☎ 617-661-9001, 569 Mass Ave), where the dishes are distinctive tandoori and the waitstaff is particularly friendly. It's open for lunch and dinner daily. Expect to spend $6 for the lunch buffet and about $15 for a complete dinner. T Red Line to Central.

Nearby, *Shalimar of India* (☎ 617-547-9280, 546 Mass Ave) is known for its hot-and-spicy dishes, vegetarian selections and daily all-you-can-eat lunch buffet ($6). It's open for lunch and dinner. T Red Line to Central.

Always quite crowded, **Kebab-N-Kurry** (☎ 617-536-9835, 30 Mass Ave), near Beacon St in Back Bay, is a small basement place boasting consistently good dishes sold at consistently good prices ($7 lunch, $13 dinner). The lunch menu is only offered weekdays. ⓣ Green Line to Hynes Convention Center.

## Mexican

**Casa Mexico** (☎ 617-491-4552, 75 Winthrop St), in Harvard Square, is the best place for inexpensive and authentic Mexican on either side of the Charles River. The basement dining room is usually crowded with patrons who come for rich *mole* sauce (as in chicken *mole poblano*), tostadas and enchiladas. It's been around since the 1970s, so it must be doing something right. Expect to spend about $6 for lunch, double that for dinner. It's open noon to 2:30 pm and 6 to 10 pm, daily except Sunday. ⓣ Red Line to Harvard.

## Eclectic

In the South End, **On the Park** (☎ 617-426-0862, 1 Union Park) is a friendly little neighborhood place that feels a bit like it belongs in New York's Greenwich Village. It's bright and funky, with lots of local art on the walls. The food tends towards creative American: marinated pork chops, gingered lamb stew or whole wheat pasta for $10 to $17. It's open for dinner Tuesday through Saturday. The weekend brunch ($6.50 to $12), with mimosas, is particularly popular. ⓣ Orange Line to Back Bay/South End.

**Small Planet Bar & Grill** (☎ 617-536-4477, 565 Boylston Sts), between Clarendon and Dartmouth Sts, is a lively spot for lunch, dinner or late night drinks and snacks. The international menu (quesadillas, black bean soup, braised Cuban pork and hamburgers), relaxed atmosphere (à la tropical rain forest decor) and reasonable prices ($6 to $16 for a full meal) attract a youthful crowd. It's open 11:30 am to midnight daily (from 5 pm on Monday). ⓣ Green Line to Copley.

**Claremont Café** (☎ 617-247-9001, 535 Columbus Ave), in the South End, is a tiny, romantic place that offers large portions of its South American- and Mediterranean-inspired cuisine. Rice dishes, paella and roast chicken dishes go for $12 to $20. The cafe draws an artsy group of neighborhood residents, especially in the morning for terrific scones. It's open for all three meals Tuesday through Saturday, and Sunday brunch 9 am to 3 pm. ⓣ Orange Line to Mass Ave.

## Worth a Splurge

**Hamersley's Bistro** (☎ 617-423-2700, 553 Tremont St), consistently at the top of every 'best restaurants' list, serves French/country American cuisine. The seasonal menu might include grilled filet of beef or hot-and-spicy grilled tuna. Roasted chicken with garlic, parsley and lemon ($23) is a house specialty. The ambiance is urban and cool, but not too cool. It's open nightly for dinner; you could spend $100 for two, but you only 'have' to spend $60 for two. Reservations are highly recommended. ⓣ Green Line to Copley or Orange Line to Back Bay/South End.

**Rialto** (☎ 617-661-5050, 1 Bennett St), within the Charles Hotel in Cambridge, is another top-notch restaurant. You'll pay handsomely ($100 for two, all inclusive) for dining in this understated, Euro-chic elegance, but it will be romantic and memorable. Good Mediterranean-inspired dishes include creamy mussel and saffron stew with leeks or seared beef tenderloin with cognac sauce and shellfish paella. The vegetarian main course is always equally creative. Reservations are advised; dinner is served nightly. ⓣ Red Line to Harvard.

**Anago** (☎ 617-266-6222, 65 Exeter St), in the Lenox Hotel, serves a hearty blend of Mediterranean and New American cuisine. Entrees like pan-seared salmon ($23) and rack of lamb ($27) are creatively prepared and artfully presented. Appetizers ($12 to $18) are uniformly exceptional, albeit pricey. It's open for lunch weekdays, dinner nightly (make reservations) and Sunday brunch ($28 adults, $14 children). ⓣ Green Line to Copley.

Just over the Charlestown Bridge from the North End, **Olives** (☎ 617-242-1999, 10 City Square) also draws some rave reviews. The creative Mediterranean-New American menu, all of which is prepared in the exposed kitchen, includes spit-roasted meats and an open-face roasted lamb sandwich. Entrees are in the $16 to $30 range. You can expect to blow $100 for two people here. There are two drawbacks associated with these prices: It's quite noisy and you'll have to wait unless you arrive very early (at 4:45 pm) or very late. It's open nightly except Sunday, and doesn't accept reservations. T Green or Orange Line to North Station.

## ENTERTAINMENT

The breadth and depth of cultural offerings in Boston and Cambridge is impressive. There's no doubt that much of it is fueled by the vital university scene. For up-to-the-minute listings of cultural events, entertainment and nightlife, check out Thursday's *Boston Globe*, Friday's *Boston Herald* and the weekly *Boston Phoenix*.

Note: The drinking age for alcoholic beverages in New England is 21, and in most cases you must be 21 to enter a drinking establishment. Some clubs offer '19-plus' nights; check the papers for details. Bars usually close at 1 am, clubs at 2 am. The last Red Line trains pass through Park St at about 12:30 am (depending on the direction), but all T stations and lines are different. To reliably count on catching the last train, head to the nearest T station at about midnight. Otherwise, plan ahead by budgeting for a cab if you think it'll be a late night. At press time, the MBTA was planning to temporarily extend service until 2:30 am on weekends. The pilot service may or may not be continued; if you're going to rely on it, please call the MBTA (☎ 617-222-3200, 800-392-6100).

## Discount Tickets

Half-price tickets to same-day performances are available beginning at 11 am at Bostix (☎ 617-723-5181), on the south side of Faneuil Hall Marketplace. (You can always buy full-price tickets here, too.) Another kiosk is located in Back Bay's Copley Square (☎ 617-723-5181), at Dartmouth and Boylston Sts. Both kiosks are open 10 am to 6 pm Tuesday through Saturday, 11 am to 4 pm on Sunday; the Copley Square kiosk is also open 10 am to 6 pm on Monday. In Harvard Square, Bostix has a kiosk at the Holyoke Arcade, just 100 yards east of the T station.

## Cinemas

Art and foreign films are alive and well in Boston and Cambridge. The **Kendall Square Cinema** (☎ 617-494-9800, 1 Kendall Square), in Cambridge, opened with great fanfare in 1995. It has nine screens as well as espresso machines that can churn out a cup of java in 10 seconds. T Red Line to Kendall, and then a 10-minute walk.

In Harvard Square, the **Brattle Theater** (☎ 617-876-6837, www.beaconcinema.com /brattle, 40 Brattle St) is a film lover's 'cinema paradiso.' Film noir, independent films and series' that celebrate directors or periods are shown regularly in this no-frills, 1890 repertory theater. You can often catch a classic double feature for $6. (Outstanding Toscanini's ice cream is sold at the concession stand.) T Red Line to Harvard.

The **Coolidge Corner Theater** (☎ 617-734-2500, 290 Harvard St), in Brookline, is the area's only not-for-profit movie house. Documentaries, foreign films and first-run movies are shown on two enormous screens in this grand art deco theater. T Green Line 'C' branch to Coolidge Corner.

The **Somerville Theater** (☎ 617-625-5700), in Davis Square in Somerville, is another classic theater that has survived the megaplex movie house invasion. Second-run films alternate with live musical performances. Before or after a show, you might appreciate the funky coffeehouse next door or the ice-cream shop directly across the street. T Red Line to Davis.

In Boston, the **Sony Nickelodeon Theater** (☎ 617-424-1500, 606 Comm Ave), behind Boston University's College of Communications, shows independent and foreign films. Most screens at 'the Nick' are on the smallish side. T Green Line 'B' branch to the first above-ground stop.

At Harvard University in Cambridge, the **Harvard Film Archive & Film Study Library** (☎ 617-495-4700, 24 Quincy St) screens at least two films per day at the Carpenter Center for the Visual Arts. Directors and actors are frequently on hand to talk about their work. ⓣ Red Line to Harvard.

The *Museum of Fine Arts, Boston* (☎ 617-369-3306 information, 369-3770 tickets, 465 Huntington Ave), at the West Wing entrance, screens a wide variety of films – silent, avant-garde and local – in the Remis Auditorium. ⓣ Green Line 'E' branch to Museum.

The *French Library in Boston* (☎ 617-266-4351, 53 Marlborough St), in Back Bay, shows classic and contemporary French films on Thursday and Friday at 8 pm. ⓣ Green Line to Arlington.

The City of Boston's 'Free Friday Flicks,' under the stars at the *Hatch Memorial Shell* (☎ 617-727-9547), at the Charles River Esplanade, are shown on Friday at dusk late June through August. You'll be sitting on the lawn, so bring a blanket and picnic. Many movies are family-oriented. ⓣ Green Line to Arlington.

## Performing Arts

The following venues host big production and pre-Broadway musicals and plays, as well as excellent nonprofit performances.

The opulent 1925 *Wang Center for the Performing Arts* (☎ 617-482-9393, 800-447-7400 tickets, 268 Tremont St), an enormous hall, has one of the largest stages in the country. The Boston Ballet performs here, but the Wang also hosts extravagant music and modern dance productions, as well as movies on a giant screen. (The center was originally built as a movie palace.) ⓣ Green Line to Boylston or the Orange Line to NE Medical Center.

Across the street, the *Shubert Theater* (☎ 617-482-9393, 800-447-7400 tickets) is another illustrious venue. The Boston Lyric Opera and smaller ballet productions are staged here. ⓣ Green Line to Boylston or Orange Line to NE Medical Center.

Although the lavish *Colonial Theater* (☎ 617-426-9366, 931-2787 tickets, 106 Boylston St) is now enveloped by an office building, it is still resplendent with all the gilded ornamentation, mirrors and frescoes it had in 1900. ⓣ Green Line to Boylston.

The beaux-arts-style *Emerson Majestic Theater* (☎ 617-824-8000, 219 Tremont St) is owned by Emerson College, a private performing arts school. Since the theater's majesty and luster were restored, it's a fitting space for the excellent nonprofit dance, opera and theater groups that perform here. ⓣ Green Line to Boylston.

**Classical & Jazz** The *Berklee Performance Center* (☎ 617-266-7455 professional shows, 747-8820 faculty and student shows, 747-2261 box office, 136 Mass Ave) hosts jazz concerts given by the Berklee College of Music's renowned faculty members and exceptional students for a mere $4 during the school year. The center also hosts big-name performers at big-buck prices. ⓣ Green Line to Hynes Convention Center.

The *New England Conservatory of Music* (☎ 617-585-1122 concert line, 536-2412 box office, Jordan Hall, 30 Gainsborough St), at Huntington Ave, also hosts professional and student chamber and orchestral concerts in the acoustically superlative hall. Many free student and faculty concerts are held Monday through Thursday. ⓣ Green Line to Symphony or Orange Line to Mass Ave.

The *Hatch Memorial Shell* (☎ 617-727-9547), at the Charles River Esplanade, has lots of free jazz and classical concerts in summertime. Check the newspapers for its evening shows (midweek) and midday shows (on weekends). There are public restrooms and an inexpensive snack bar here. ⓣ Green Line to Arlington.

The near-perfect acoustics at *Symphony Hall* (☎ 617-266-1492, 266-1200 tickets, www.bso.org, 301 Mass Ave), at Huntington Ave, match the ambitious programs of the world-renowned Boston Symphony Orchestra (BSO). The BSO performs from October through April. The Boston Pops plays popular classical music and show tunes from May to mid-July, and again in December for a popular holiday show. A cafe (open 5:30 to 7:30 pm) offers buffet-style dining prior to all evening concerts. Tickets cost $25 to $80.

For same-day discounted 'rush' tickets (one per person, you don't have to be a student), line up at the box office on Tuesday and Thursday at 5 pm for the 8 pm show, Friday at 9 am for the 2 pm show. (No rush tickets are sold for the Saturday show.) The only other way to beat the high cost of the BSO is to get lucky by catching one of its sporadic (once-monthly) open rehearsals on Wednesday at 7:30 pm or on Thursday at 10:30 am. These $14 tickets can be purchased in advance. Ⓣ Green Line to Symphony.

**Dance** The *Boston Ballet* (☎ 617-695-6950, www.boston.com/bostonballet) performs modern and classical works at the Wang Center, 275 Tremont St. Tickets cost $25 to $69, but students can get 'rush' tickets for $12.50 one hour before the performance. Ⓣ Green Line to Boylston or Orange Line to NE Medical Center.

*Dance Umbrella* (☎ 617-482-7570, 824-8000 tickets), responsible for holding the Boston alternative dance scene together, sponsors renowned international touring companies as well as local contemporary dance troupes. The original shows often end with question-and-answer periods with the diverse troupe. Tickets start at about $15 (unless it's a huge name dance company), but again, students can get half-price 'rush' tickets to many performances 30 minutes prior to curtain time.

**Theater** Boston University's very highly regarded *Huntington Theater Company* (☎ 617-266-0800, www.bu.edu/huntington, 264 Huntington Ave) performs five modern and classical plays annually in its Greek Revival theater. Rear balcony seats are usually available for $10; tickets go up to $49. Student 'rush' tickets for $10 are available two hours prior to curtain call. Ⓣ Green Line to Symphony.

Harvard University's *Loeb Drama Center* (☎ 617-547-8300, 64 Brattle St) is home to the prestigious American Repertory Theater (the ART), which stages eight new plays and experimental interpretations of classics. There isn't a bad seat in the small theater; tickets cost $23 to $55. There's another way to get in, too: Every Monday morning the theater sets aside 50 tickets for the following Saturday matinee. You liter-

ally 'pay what you can.' Student 'rush' tickets are sold 30 minutes prior to the curtain call for $12. Ⓣ Red Line to Harvard.

In the Theater District, the two-stage *Charles Playhouse* (☎ 617-426-5225, 74 Warrenton St) has presented *Shear Madness*, a comical murder mystery with audience participation, since 1980. It holds the record for the world's 'longest-running nonmusical play.' Tickets cost $34 nightly. Ⓣ Green Line to Boylston or Orange Line to NE Medical Center.

Since 1996, *Blue Man Group* (☎ 617-426-6912) has occupied the other stage with a mixed-media performance art piece that pokes fun at the arts community. Music and percussion are heavily relied upon, as is the tactic of plucking members from the audience. Tickets are $39 and $49 Wednesday through Sunday. Remaining tickets are released one hour before showtime to students for $25. Ⓣ Green Line to Boylston or Orange Line to NE Medical Center.

The *Boston Center for the Arts* (BCA; ☎ 617-426-7700, 539 Tremont St), at Clarendon St, has three distinctive performance spaces (as well as the Mills Gallery, a contemporary art space) perfect for the unusual productions it stages. There's rarely a dull moment at the BCA. Ⓣ Orange Line to Back Bay/South End or the Green Line to Copley.

The avant-garde performance artists who belong to *Mobius* (☎ 617-542-7416, www.mobius.org, 354 Congress St, 5th floor) present experimental dance, music and other art-in-progress almost every weekend. You might catch something like this: a performance artist crawling around the studio on her hands and knees for three days (on and off) picking up little grains of rice and placing them into tiny pinch pots. As one bowl fills up she moves to fill another. Could this say something about the way we conduct our lives, they posit? Tickets are sometimes free, but usually about $5 to $12. Ⓣ Red Line to South Station.

## Comedy Clubs
The *Comedy Connection* (☎ 617-248-9700), at the Faneuil Hall Marketplace, on the

2nd floor above the food court, is one of the city's oldest and biggest comedy venues. Go mid-week when tickets are about $8, rather than on weekends when tickets range from $14 to $25. ⊤ Green or Blue Line to Government Center.

***Nick's Comedy Stop*** *(☎ 617-482-0930, 100 Warrenton St)*, in the Theater District near Chinatown, is another place featuring local as well as nationally known jokesters. Tickets are $10 to $14; shows are Thursday through Saturday only. ⊤ Green Line to Boylston.

***Improv Boston*** *(☎ 617-576-1253, www .improvboston.com, 1253 Cambridge St)*, at the Back Alley Theater, is actually in Inman Square, in Cambridge. This long-running ensemble makes things up as they go along; audience members throw out ideas and the cast is off and running. Sunday afternoon (2 pm) shows are family-oriented. Other shows ($12) run Thursday through Saturday at 8 pm and 10:30 pm. ⊤ Red Line to Central, then walk 5 minutes up Prospect St.

## Dance Clubs

The thriving club scene is fueled by the constant infusion of thousands of American and international students. Clubs are fairly stable, although the nightly line-up often changes. Check the *Boston Phoenix* for up-to-the-minute information. Most clubs are along Lansdowne St near Kenmore Square and The Fenway, but there are also some near the Theater District and in Cambridge. Cover charges vary widely, from free (if you arrive early) to $15, but the average is more like $10 on weekends. Most clubs are open 10 pm to 2 am.

***Man Ray*** *(☎ 617-864-0400, 21 Brookline St)*, in Cambridge's Central Square, is the area's most 'underground' club. It encourages creative attire (when in doubt wear black; fetishware is suggested on Friday). Wednesday is '19-plus' night with industrial rock; Thursday is predominantly gay, with high-energy dance tunes; Friday is industrial techno; and Saturday features campy, classic disco trash and '80s new wave. It's open 10 pm to 2 am. ⊤ Red Line to Central.

The decor at ***The Big Easy*** *(☎ 617-351-7000, 1 Boylston Place)*, in the alley, in the Theater District, plays off the New Orleans Mardi Gras style. In addition to dance bands on Friday and Saturday, a DJ spins R&B, funk and disco. You can just watch from the 2nd-floor balcony if you prefer. 'Proper dress' is required; the crowd is a bit older here. It's open 9 pm to 2 am Thursday through Saturday; cover is $5 to $7. ⊤ Green Line to Boylston.

***The Roxy*** *(☎ 617-338-7699, 279 Tremont St)*, in the Tremont House hotel, plays salsa and merengue on Thursday, swing on Friday and Top-40 dance tunes on Saturday. Cover varies from $10 to $15. ⊤ Green Line to Boylston.

On Friday and Saturday nights, the ***Juke Box*** *(☎ 617-542-4077)*, below the Tremont House hotel (see The Roxy, above), plays classic rock and roll (from the '50s to the '80s) on one side and disco on the other; Sunday is Latin night.

***Avalon*** *(☎ 617-262-2424, 15 Lansdowne St)* is a huge dance club featuring international house music on Thursday and Friday, progressive bands on Saturday. Thursday and Friday are '19-plus' nights; the cover charge is $10 to $15. Sunday night is gay night when the club connects to ***Axis*** *(☎ 617-262-2437, 13 Lansdowne St)*, which generally attracts a younger crowd, has two dance floors and also hosts hard rock bands. It's open Thursday through Saturday; Monday is anything but 'Static,' as it's called, when drag queens and the cross-gendered community are summoned into this artsy scene. ⊤ Green Line 'D' branch to Fenway.

Also on Lansdowne St, the smaller ***Bill's Bar*** *(☎ 617-421-9678, 9 Lansdowne St)* is open nightly and packed with BU students. Alternative music rules here, except on Tuesday (devoted to hip hop) and Thursday (swing). Cover is $6 to $10. ⊤ Green Line 'D' branch to Fenway.

More formal and upscale, ***Karma Club*** *(☎ 617-421-9595, 9 Lansdowne St)* is a different sort of place, decorated with Indian tapestries and Tibetan and Nepalese wooden carvings. What would Krishna think of the hip hop and house beat? The cover charge is $10 to $15. ⊤ Green Line 'D' branch to Fenway.

## Live Music

**Rock & Roll** Plenty of nationally known alternative and rock bands got their start in Boston clubs; there are more than 5000 bands registered here.

Over in Somerville, *Johnny D's (☎ 617-776-2004, 17 Holland St)* is one of the best and most eclectic venues, with a different style of music every night. Cover charges average $7 to $8. There's everything from blues and Cajun to swing and rock and roll. Sunday night blues jams are popular. The weekend jazz brunches are mellow. Ⓣ Red Line to Davis Square.

In Cambridge, *The Middle East (☎ 617-354-8238, www.mideastclub.com, 472 Mass Ave)* usually has three different gigs going on simultaneously every night. Local bands cost $6 to $7, national acts are more like $7 to $12. There's always a free jazz show in the 'corner.' The Middle East also serves pretty good (well-priced) food until midnight. Ⓣ Red Line to Central Square.

*The Paradise (☎ 617-562-8800, 967 Comm Ave)*, a small club known for its acumen in booking groups from all walks of the musical spectrum, has shows throughout the week. Tickets are $8 to $20 depending on the act. On Wednesday, Friday and Saturday (from 11 pm to 2 am) the club becomes *M-80* as the dance beat turns into Euro house music. Ⓣ Green Line, 'B' branch.

**Jazz & Blues** Gritty, smoky and storied, *Wally's Café (☎ 617-424-1408, 427 Mass Ave)*, at Columbus Ave, is the kind of place that burns into your imagination. The music rests squarely on up-tempo traditional jazz and fusion. Monday is blues; Tuesday and Wednesday are fusion; Thursday is Latin jazz; Friday and Saturday are traditional; and Sunday sees afternoon jam sessions and evening fusion. It's crowded from 9 pm to 2 am every night, which has nothing to do with the fact that there's no cover charge here. Ⓣ Orange Line to Mass Ave or Green Line to Symphony.

In Harvard Square, the original *House of Blues (☎ 617-491-2583, 96 Winthrop St)* was opened by 'Blues Brother' Dan Akroyd in 1992 and has since become a major force on

the national blues scene. The music begins at 9 or 10 pm nightly; tickets cost $10 to $25. It's free during lunch on Friday from 12:30 to 2:30 pm and Saturday 2 to 4 pm. The all-you-can-eat-and-listen-to Sunday gospel brunch ($26, or $14 for just the food) is a downright religious experience for some. Reservations are required. Ⓣ Red Line to Harvard.

*Marketplace Café (☎ 617-227-9660)*, in the North Building of Faneuil Hall Marketplace, near Congress St, has live music: blues on Tuesday, calypso on Wednesday and jazz on Thursday. The musical line-up often changes, so it's a good idea to call ahead. Listening is free; all you have to do is buy a drink. Ⓣ Blue or Green Line to Government Center.

*Ryles (☎ 617-876-9330, 212 Hampshire St)*, in Inman Square, is one of a few great places in Cambridge to hear jazz. It's open from 9 pm nightly except Monday (tickets are usually in the $7 to $10 range), and for a jazz brunch on weekends (when the music is free). Ⓣ Red Line to Central.

The *Regattabar (☎ 617-661-5000, 876-7777 tickets, www.concerttix.com)*, in Harvard Square on the 3rd floor of the Charles Hotel, is an upscale club with a yacht-club atmosphere that books internationally known groups, including some of the best jazz acts in town. A limited number of general seating tickets go on sale one hour before show time. It's open Tuesday through Saturday. Tickets are $10 to $26, depending on the fame quotient. Ⓣ Red Line to Harvard.

*Scullers Jazz Club (☎ 617-783-0811, 931-2000 for tickets, www.scullersjazz.com, 400 Soldier's Field Rd)*, in the Doubletree Guest Suites Hotel, is the other big-name jazz club, but this one is cozier. There are shows Tuesday through Saturday. Tickets range from $9 to $24, but often you can stay for both sets. You'll have better luck getting tickets to the weekday shows. Ⓣ Red Line to Central, then a 15-minute walk.

**Folk** Although other clubs occasionally book folk acts, two Cambridge places are devoted to giving struggling folk singers a venue. Venerable *Club Passim (☎ 617-492-7679, www.clubpassim.com, 47 Palmer St)*, in Harvard Square, is known around the country for supporting the early careers of such notables as Jackson Browne, Tracy Chapman, Nanci Griffith and Patty Larkin. The small club has only 125 seats; call ahead for the nightly programs and show times. Tuesday is open-mike night. Tickets are about $5 to $15. Passim is also open daily for all three meals. They serve lots of rice and vegetable dishes (with a choice of beef or chicken), with a Middle Eastern emphasis; a full dinner will run you about $11. ⓣ Red Line to Harvard.

*Nameless Coffeehouse (☎ 617-864-1630, 3 Church St)*, in Harvard Square within the First Parish Church (Unitarian Universalist), is a low-key place, run by volunteers, that sponsors acoustic singer-songwriters on most Saturday nights. The suggested donation is $3 to $4.

## Bars & Pubs

*Mercury Bar (☎ 617-482-7799, 116 Boylston St)*, in the Theater District, is well known for Spanish tapas, and is the kind of place where you wear black and watch people watching others. They also have a small dance space ($6 cover, with DJ) in the back of the bar, with plush seats, open Thursday through Saturday. The bar is open 5 pm to 2 am daily. ⓣ Green Line to Boylston.

Although the three-story *Jullian's Billiard Club (☎ 617-437-0300, 145 Ipswich St)*, near Fenway Park and Kenmore Square, has more than 50 billiards tables, people also come here to play darts, black jack, snooker, table tennis and virtual reality games. There are five bars and a full-service menu in this enormous place. It's open 11 am to 2 am daily. Jullian's also sports a dance club, *Atlas*, open on Friday and Saturday with DJ-spun '80s and '90s tunes. ⓣ Green Line to Kenmore.

In the South End, *Clery's Bar & Restaurant (☎ 617-262-9874, 113 Dartmouth St)*, at Columbus Ave, is a nice neighborhood place, though it gets pretty boisterous on weekends. It's open daily for lunch and dinner, serving simple pub grub. Draughts go for $3.50, Guinness for $4.25. ⓣ Orange Line to Back Bay/South End.

*Plough & Stars (☎ 617-441-3455, 912 Mass Ave)*, between Central and Harvard Squares in Cambridge, is a friendly Irish bar with the requisite Guinness and Bass on tap, as well as live rock and roll bands 9 pm to 1 am nightly. There's a $3 cover charge on weekends. ⓣ Red Line to Central.

In Charlestown, the circa-1780 *Warren Tavern (☎ 617-241-8142, 2 Pleasant St)*, at Main St, is an atmospheric place for a drink. ⓣ Orange or Green Line to North Station.

*Chaps (☎ 617-695-9500, 100 Warrenton St)*, in the Theater District, is one of the most popular gay bars and dance clubs. Parts of the line up can be wild: Monday it's a quiet piano bar (complimentary pizza is served); Tuesday there's retro disco with a DJ; Wednesday features Latino music; Thursday starts out quiet as a piano bar then picks up the pace with a rap, hip hop and new wave mix; Friday has techno and house; Saturday begins with quiet piano and ends with serious dance music; and Sunday tea dances start at 7 pm. You'll find male go-go dancers Friday through Sunday. ⓣ Green Line to Boylston.

Although the *Bull and Finch Pub (☎ 617-227-9605, 84 Beacon St)*, across from the Public Garden, is an authentic English pub (it was dismantled in England, shipped to Boston and reassembled inside this Beacon Hill townhouse, the Hampshire House), that's not why hundreds of tourists descend on the place daily; the pub served as the inspiration for the TV sitcom *Cheers*. (However, if there was ever a reason to go here, it's gone.) ⓣ Green Line to Arlington.

South Boston's *L Street Tavern (☎ 617-268-1155, 108 L St)*, at E 5th St, the neighborhood hangout for characters in the movie *Good Will Hunting*, is popular with those wanting a closer connection with Hollywood.

**Brewpubs** Near North Station, *Commonwealth Brewing Company (☎ 617-523-8383, 138 Portland St)*, with the requisite gleaming copper kettles and pipes, was Boston's first microbrewery in 1986. This airy meeting place produces over 10 kinds of English-style suds on the premises. And true to tradition, the pints are served up at various temperatures. The menu includes appetizers such as nachos, ribs and buffalo wings, as well as pub standards such as fish and chips. The basement is comfortably 'clubby,' with cushy couches and pool tables, while the ground floor is more of a restaurant. The place is packed when the Bruins and Celtics play at the nearby Fleet Center. Food is served until 10:30 pm; the bar closes at midnight. T Green or Orange Line to North Station.

*Boston Beer Works* (☎ *617-536-2337, 61 Brookline Ave)*, near Fenway Park and Kenmore Square, also has seasonal brews and exposed tanks and pipes. About eight different kinds of beer, including Boston Red and Buckeye Oatmeal Stout, are available at any given time. The appetizers and munchies are pretty good too. If you don't like crowds, avoid this place after a Red Sox game. The kitchen closes at 12:45 am, the bar at 1:30 am. T Green Line to Kenmore.

*Cambridge Brewing Company* (☎ *617-494-1994, 1 Kendall Square)*, in Cambridge, has reputable seasonal ales and pizza, but beyond the burgers, you'd do better eating somewhere else. This is a convenient place to go after a movie, but it's packed on weekends. T Red Line to Kendall.

The *Back Bay Brewing Co* (☎ *617-424-8300, 755 Boylston St)*, a more sophisticated joint with high ceilings and rich paneling, has more intimate seating on the 2nd floor. The IPA is full-bodied, the seasonal brews are fresh and the burgers are good. T Green Line to Copley.

The subterranean *John Harvard's Brew House* (☎ *617-868-3585, 33 Dunster St)*, in Harvard Square, smells and feels more like an English pub than the others and has perhaps the best beer among the crowded microbrewery field. Ale, lager, pilsner and stout: You'll find them all here (plus a sampler rack of all of them). Above average pub grub is available daily at lunch ($6 to $10) and dinner ($10 to $15). A pub menu is served until 11 pm on weeknights, up until 12:30 am weekends. T Red Line to Harvard.

Although the massive *Mass Bay Brewing Co* (☎ *617-574-9551, 306 Northern Ave)* is not a brewpub, the Harpoon Brewery is the largest facility in the state. Free hour-long tours and tastings of their popular Harpoon Ale and India Pale Ale are offered on Friday and Saturday at 1 pm. T Red Line to South Station, and then a 20-minute walk over the Northern Ave Bridge to the Marine Industrial Park.

## SPECTATOR SPORTS

Boston is a big sports town, and emotions run high during the various sporting seasons. Be prepared for an impassioned conversation with a local by simply asking, 'Hey, what do you think of the Sox this season?'

The *Boston Red Sox* (☎ *617-267-1700 for tickets, www.redsox.com)*, 4 Yawkey Way, play in Fenway Park, the nation's oldest ballpark, built in 1912, and certainly one of the most storied (see the 'Fenway Park' boxed text). The season runs from mid-April to late September. Sit with the 'common fan' in outfield bleacher seats for $12 or $14 versus about $16 to $26 for regular seats. During sold-out games, there are often first-come, first-served standing-room-only tickets sold at 9 am for same-day games; head to the ticket windows on Lansdowne St. Game times are at 1:05 pm, 4:05 pm and 7:05 pm. T Green Line to Kenmore.

The *Boston Celtics* (☎ *617-523-3030 information, 931-2000 tickets, www.celtics .com)* play basketball from late October through April at the Fleet Center, across from North Station. Tickets start at $10, if you're lucky enough to get one, and go up to $85; the Celtics have won more championships (16 as of 1999) than any other NBA team. T Orange or Green Line to North Station.

Watch the *Boston Bruins* (☎ *617-624-1900 information, 931-2000 tickets, www .bostonbruins.com)* play hockey in the Fleet Center from mid-October to mid-April. Tickets go for $20 to $75. You can also buy Bruins and Celtics tickets in person at the box office, at the western end of the Fleet Center, 150 Causeway St. T Orange or Green Line to North Station.

The *New England Patriots* (☎ *508-543-8200, 800-543-1776, www.patriots.com)*, on Route 1 in Foxboro, play football in Foxboro

Stadium, about 50 minutes south of Boston. The season runs from late August to late December, and tickets begin at $39, if you can get one. There are direct trains ($8 roundtrip) and buses ($6 roundtrip) from South Station to and from the stadium; contact the MBTA (☎ 617-222-3200) for exact times.

Many colleges also have teams worth watching, and spirited, loyal fans. In April, look for the annual Bean Pot Tournament: college hockey's premier event.

***Boston University*** *(☎ 617-353-3838)* has a good hockey team that plays at Case Athletic Center on Babcock St, off Comm Ave. Tickets start at $12 adults, $6 children. Ⓣ Green Line 'B' branch to Bleasant St.

***Boston College*** *(☎ 617-552-3000)* has a tough hockey team that plays at Conte Forum. Tickets are $10 to $12 adults, half-price for children. BC football fans are devoted, so tickets are nearly impossible to get. Basketball is also good here. Ⓣ Green Line, 'B' branch to the end.

Tickets for ***Harvard University football*** *(☎ 617-495-2211)*, North Harvard St and Soldiers Field Rd, across the Anderson Bridge south of Harvard Square, go for $10, unless the match is a famous rivalry with another Ivy League school (in which case all the tickets get snatched up quickly). Ⓣ Red Line to Harvard.

## SHOPPING

Stores are generally open Monday through Saturday from 9 or 10 am until 6 or 7 pm, unless otherwise noted. Most are also open on Sundays from noon to 5 pm.

### Shopping Districts & Malls

Many malls offer free discount coupon books, most easily obtainable prior to your arrival. The 'Spree Value Card' (☎ 800-697-7733, www.myspree.com) is valid at select shops at Copley Place. Cambridgeside Galleria has a similar 'Passport Coupon Book' (www.mallsUS.com/cambridgeside), as does Faneuil Hall with its 'Passport to Shopping & Dining' (www.bostonian.com/faneuil).

Faneuil Hall Marketplace (☎ 617-338-2323, www.faneuilhallmarketplace.com), or Quincy Market, as it's also known, northeast of Congress and State Sts, is perhaps the most well-known shopping area; about 14 million people visit annually. The five buildings are filled with 100 or so one-of-a-kind shops (catering mainly to tourists), pushcart vendors and national chain stores such as The Gap, The Body Shop and Crate & Barrel. (Shops are generally open until 9 pm daily, except until 6 pm on Sunday.) It's expensive and crowded, especially on the weekends, but it's rather festive too. There are lots of fast-food outlets (see Places to Eat, above), street performers and outdoor benches to rest your weary feet.

Nearby, in the historic Faneuil Hall (as opposed to the adjacent marketplace), is the nonprofit Boston City Store (☎ 617-635-2911). Proceeds from authentic Boston keepsakes, such as retired street signs ($30) and memorabilia from the yesteryear's running of the Boston Marathon, benefit local youth organizations. Ⓣ Green or Blue Line to Government Center or Orange or Blue Line to State.

Downtown Crossing, an outdoor pedestrian mall at Winter, Summer and Washington Sts, has more practical shops geared to everyday Bostonians. You'll find two department stores, Filene's (☎ 617-357-2100), 426 Washington St, and Macy's (☎ 617-357-3000), 450 Washington St, as well as smaller retail outlets for clothing, jewelry, shoes, books, and electronic equipment; see also the Clothing section later in this chapter. This area is enlivened by street musicians, food and souvenir pushcart vendors, a few outdoor cafes and benches for people-watching. (Look for the cart aptly named Boston's Best Burritos.) Ⓣ Red or Orange Line to Downtown Crossing.

Newbury St (see www.newbury-st.com), between Arlington St (the western boundary of the Boston Garden) and Mass Ave, is filled with chic boutiques, cafes and galleries. These eight high-rent blocks are great for strolling and window shopping. Fashionable clothiers here include Akris (☎ 617-536-6225), 16 Newbury St; Giorgio Armani Boutique (☎ 617-267-3200), 22 Newbury St; and Louis, Boston (☎ 617-262-6100), 234 Newbury St.

Don't get too discouraged about the high prices; as you walk west you'll find that prices begin to drop back into this stratosphere as shops get more youth oriented. Check out Loulou's Lost and Found (☎ 617-859-8593), 121 Newbury St, for an eclectic inventory of retro objects for the home, some from the early 20th century. The Hempfest (☎ 617-421-9944), 207 Newbury St, sells all manner of products made from hemp, the botanical cousin of marijuana: items to wear, to furnish one's home and even to eat. Shoes at John Fluevog (☎ 617-266-1079), 302 Newbury St, are more fun to look at than comfortable to walk in. Condom World (☎ 617-267-7233) is located at 332 Newbury St. Patagonia (☎ 617-424-1776), 346 Newbury St, carries the finest outdoor fleecewear. At the corner of Mass Ave, Tower Records (☎ 617-247-5900), 360 Newbury St, has the city's largest selection of music, and Urban Outfitters (☎ 617-236-0088), 361 Newbury St, the latest in trendy clothing and housewares. Ⓣ Green Line to Arlington (for the eastern end of the street) or Hynes Convention Center (for the western end).

The Shops at the Pru (☎ 617-267-1002, www.prudentialcenter.com), 800 Boylston St, an upscale indoor mall, includes about 70 stores and eateries within an atrium-like space. One of the few inner-city grocery stores, Star Market, is on the ground level. Ⓣ Green Line to Prudential.

Copley Place (☎ 617-369-5000, www.myspree.com), 100 Huntington Ave, an enormous indoor shopping mall, encompasses two hotels, a first-run cineplex, glass walkways, restaurants and dozens of very pricey shops. American consumerism is alive and well here. Ⓣ Green Line to Copley or Orange Line to Back Bay/South End.

Over in Cambridge, Harvard Square (www.harvardsquare.org) boasts about 150 shops within a few blocks. Although there used to be many more independent stores in the square, most have been replaced by national chains. However, there's still a spirited street life with plenty of musicians and performance artists. Of course it's still the favored place to buy Harvard University insignia and related items. You'll find the best selection at J August (☎ 617-864-6650), 1320 Mass Ave, and at the Harvard Coop (☎ 617-499-2000), 1400 Mass Ave.

For those who prefer unique Harvard-related gifts without the Harvard name and seal emblazoned all over them, browse through Harvard Collections (☎ 617-496-3532). The store has fine reproductions and original works inspired by the immense holdings of the various University museums, from African masks and carvings to jewelry crafted from ancient coins. There is also a cluster of shops within The Garage, 36 John F Kennedy St. Head northwest out of the square on Mass Ave and you'll find an interesting array of shops all the way to Porter Square (about a 30-minute walk).

The Cambridgeside Galleria (☎ 617-621-8666), 100 Cambridgeside Place, just beyond the Science Museum, is a three-story mall comprised of about 100 shops, including the big and moderately priced department store Sears (☎ 617-252-3500). Ⓣ Green Line to Lechmere.

## Art Galleries

While Newbury St has the most expensive and dense concentration of galleries, there are also a number of avant-garde galleries in the Leather District, an area near South Station bounded by South, Lincoln, Essex and Kneeland Sts.

There are galleries throughout the city that allow you to support local and national artists and artisans without losing your shirt. The prestigious, nonprofit Society of Arts and Crafts (☎ 617-266-1810), 175 Newbury St, between Dartmouth and Exeter Sts in Back Bay, was founded in 1897. Within the exhibition and retail space are high-quality weaving, leather, ceramics, furniture and other handcrafted items. Ⓣ Green Line to Copley. There's also a branch in the Downtown Crossing area at 101 Arch St (☎ 617-345-0033).

The Bromfield Art Gallery (☎ 617-451-3605), 560 Harrison Ave, at Union Park St in the South End, is one of the more accessible, affordable and reputable galleries on the Boston art scene. It also happens to be the city's oldest cooperative. ⓣ Orange Line to Back Bay, and then a 15-minute walk.

Craftspeople double as salespeople at the Cambridge Artists' Cooperative (☎ 617-868-4434), 59A Church St in Harvard Square, which has handcrafted objects ranging from $3 to $1000.

Barbara Krakow Gallery (☎ 617-262-4490), 10 Newbury St, provides an elegant venue for contemporary artists. It's worth a look even if you can't afford to buy anything. ⓣ Green Line to Arlington.

## Antiques

Antiques in Boston are extremely pricey, but if you want to do some window shopping, head to Charles and River Sts on Beacon Hill. ⓣ Red Line to Charles/MGH.

Or try the five floors of the Cambridge Antique Market (☎ 617-868-9655), 201 McGrath-O'Brien Hwy, where you might find a little something – furniture, glass, clothing, pottery, jewelry – to take home. ⓣ Green Line to Lechmere.

For a more intimate shopping experience, try Justin Tyme (☎ 617-491-1088), 91 River St, a shop specializing in antiques, collectibles, costume jewelry and vintage clothing. ⓣ Red Line to Central Square, and then head west on Western Ave for one block until River St forks to the left.

## Camping Supplies

Although it's dusty and musty, Hilton's Tent City (☎ 617-227-9242), 272 Friend St near North Station, boasts four floors of tents (most of which are set up to test out) and all the camping and backpacking accessories, equipment and clothing you'll ever need – all at the lowest prices around. ⓣ Orange or Green Line to North Station.

Eastern Mountain Sports (EMS; ☎ 617-254-4250), 1041 Comm Ave in Brighton, is another good source for hiking and camping gear, books and maps. If you can't find it at Hilton's, you'll find it here. ⓣ Green Line 'B' branch to Babcock.

## Clothing

The granddaddy of Boston bargain stores, Filene's Basement (☎ 617-542-2011), at 426 Washington St in Downtown Crossing, carries overstocked and irregular items at everyday low prices. But the deal gets better: Items are automatically marked down the longer they remain in the store. With a little bit of luck and lots of determination you could find a $300 designer jacket for $30; but be forewarned, the chances of finding something perfect (ie, that is well made, undamaged, your size and in a color other than neon purple or fire-engine red) are pretty slim. Patience is a prerequisite since customers rip through piles of merchandise, turning the place upside down as if a tornado hit it. Even so, it's a sight to see, an experience unique to Boston; don't miss it. ⓣ Red or Orange Line to Downtown Crossing.

Also in Downtown Crossing, the Eddie Bauer Outlet (☎ 617-227-4840), 252 Washington St, offers irregulars of their popular outdoor wear for 30% to 70% off.

The Gap Outlet (☎ 617-482-1657), 425 Washington St in the Corner Mall at Downtown Crossing, sells jeans and ubiquitous everyday clothing for half of the regular retail prices. Banana Republic, owned by the same company, sells its clothing here too. ⓣ Red or Orange Line to Downtown Crossing.

The Original Levi's Store, which sells nothing but the real thing, is located within the Prudential Center (☎ 617-375-9010), 800 Boylston St at Fairfield St. ⓣ Green Line to Prudential.

## Thrift Shops & Vintage Clothing

Bertha Cool (☎ 617-247-4111), 528 Comm Ave in Kenmore Square, is a shop as hip as its name. Come for the vintage clothing, including a large inventory of leather jackets and '50s collectibles, all in great condition. ⓣ Green Line to Kenmore.

Boomerangs (☎ 617-723-2666), 60 Canal St near North Station, stocks new department store surplus and private donations, so inventory ranges from the banal (new toasters) to someone's version of the ultimate in style (lime-green patent leather go-go boots). It's fun and all proceeds from the shop go to the AIDS Action Committee of

Massachusetts. Ⓣ Green or Orange Line to Haymarket or North Station.

The Garment District (☎ 617-876-5230), 200 Broadway near Kendall Square, boasts a huge collection of '60s and '70s clothing. If your memories of these fashion-conscious decades have faded like that old pair of jeans, entering this store will bring it all back with a vengeance. Ⓣ Red Line to Kendall.

Also at 200 Broadway, Dollar-a-Pound Plus (☎ 617-876-5230), shares an owner but has different merchandise and pricing methods. Like a flea market gone berserk, piles of clothing are dumped on the warehouse floor and folks wade through it looking for their needle in the haystack. Upon checkout, your pile is weighed and you pay 'by the pound.' The price per pound is usually $1.50, but on Friday it's lowered in order to move the merchandise faster. There are also books, records and cassettes, and kitchen supplies, all individually priced to move. Hours are irregular, so call ahead. Ⓣ Red Line to Kendall.

## GETTING THERE & AWAY
### Air
Logan International Airport (☎ 800-235-6426), MA 1A, East Boston, is served by most major national and international carriers. Its five separate terminals are connected by a frequent shuttle bus (No 11). The nonprofit Traveler's Aid Society (☎ 617-567-5385), an agency that assists travelers in need, maintains a booth at Terminal 'E,' where all international flights arrive and depart; the booth is open noon to 9 pm daily.

### Bus
Boston has a modern, indoor, user-friendly bus station (no ☎) at 700 Atlantic Ave at Summer St, conveniently adjacent to the South Station train station and above a T stop for the Red Line.

Greyhound (☎ 617-526-1800, 800-231-2222, www.greyhound.com) buses depart for New York City throughout the day. Express buses only take 4½ hours, but others take up to two hours longer. Adult

fares are $34 one way, $60 roundtrip (children are half-price). Other sample destinations and adult one-way fares from Boston include the following:

| destination | fare | duration |
|---|---|---|
| Albany, NY | $25 | 3¾ to 4¾ hours |
| Hartford, CT | $20 | 2½ hours |
| New Haven, CT | $25 | 3½ hours |
| Newark, NJ | $34 | 6 to 7 hours |
| Providence, RI | $7 | 1 hour |
| Springfield, MA | $18 | 2 hours |

Inquire about special offers like buying one roundtrip ticket with a three-day advance purchase and getting a companion ticket free.

Bonanza Bus Lines (☎ 617-720-4110, 800-556-3815, www.bonanzabus.com) serves Falmouth, Woods Hole and Hyannis on Cape Cod, as well as Providence, Hartford, Albany and New York City.

Plymouth & Brockton (☎ 508-746-0378, 778-9767, www.p-b.com) provides frequent service to most towns on Cape Cod, including Hyannis and Provincetown.

Peter Pan Bus Lines (☎ 800-343-9999, www.peterpan.com) serves Northampton and Williamstown in western Massachusetts (the Berkshires), Hartford, New Haven and New York City.

Concord Trailways (☎ 617-426-8080, 800-639-3317, www.concordtrailways.com) plies routes from Boston to New Hampshire, and Boston to Portland and Bangor in Maine.

C&J Trailways (☎ 800-258-7111, www.cjtrailways.com) provides daily service to Newburyport, Massachusetts, and Portsmouth, New Hampshire.

Vermont Transit (☎ 800-451-3292, www.vermonttransit.com) operates its buses to White River Junction and Keene, New Hampshire; Portland (year-round) and Bar Harbor (seasonal), Maine. In Vermont, buses go to Burlington, Brattleboro, Bennington and lots of small towns in between.

### Train
Amtrak (☎ 617-482-3660, 800-872-7245, www.amtrak.com) trains stop at the South

Station terminal, at Atlantic Ave and Summer St (on the T Red Line), as well as Back Bay Station, at Dartmouth St (on the T Orange Line). Express service (four hours) to New York City costs $45 to $66 one way, depending on the day and time. Service to Manhattan on a new high-speed train (under three hours) should be running by the time you read this. Amtrak's online 'Rail Sale' program offers substantial discounts on many reserved tickets.

When it was built in 1900, South Station was the world's largest railroad station. Decades of heavy use took their toll, though, but a renovation in the late 1980s brought the magnificent gateway back up to par. Today, the curved, five-story building is alive with pushcart vendors, fast-food eateries, cafe tables, a newsstand and live concerts on many summer afternoons.

By contrast, North Station (☎ 617-222-3200), 150 Causeway St, is a dowdy younger sibling terminal that serves MBTA Commuter Rail trains (☎ 800-392-6099, www .mbta.com) to the west and north of the city, including Concord. Catch the 'beach trains' to Salem, Gloucester and Rockport here. North Station is on the T Green and Orange Lines.

## Car

From western Massachusetts, the Massachusetts Turnpike ('Mass Pike' or I-90, a toll road) takes you right into downtown. After paying a toll in Newton, drive east 10 more minutes on the pike and pay another 50¢; then the fun begins.

There are three exits for the Boston area: Cambridge, Copley Square (Prudential Center) and Kneeland St (Chinatown). Then, the turnpike ends abruptly. At that point you can head north or south of the city on the I-93 Expressway (the Central Artery; see the Orientation section at the beginning of this chapter) or right past South Station, into downtown.

From New York and other southerly points, take I-95 north to MA 128 to I-93 north, which cuts through the heart of the city. From northerly points, take I-93 south

across the Tobin Bridge, which merges into the Central Artery.

The 'Big Dig,' the combined construction of the Ted Williams Tunnel and the depression of the Central Artery, is scheduled for completion in 2004 (with a little luck). Approaching the city, you'll feel its greatest impact from the south. Once in the city, there are serious traffic problems along the entire waterfront area, South Station and the North End. Although the project managers have done a commendable job rerouting auto and pedestrian traffic, snarls are inevitable. Admittedly, it's fascinating to watch the around-the-clock phalanx of workers, the enormous cranes and the convoys of trucks hauling away mega-tons of earth.

Driving details for Boston are as follows:

| destination | mileage | hr:min |
| --- | --- | --- |
| Bar Harbor, ME | 269 miles | 6:30 |
| Burlington, VT | 220 miles | 4:35 |
| Hartford, CT | 108 miles | 2:13 |
| Lenox, MA | 138 miles | 3:10 |
| New Haven, CT | 141 miles | 3:25 |
| New York, NY | 227 miles | 4:30 |
| Portland, ME | 108 miles | 2:15 |
| Portsmouth, NH | 57 miles | 1:10 |
| Providence, RI | 45 miles | 1:00 |

## Boat

Boston Harbor Cruises (☎ 617-227-4320) operates boats to Georges Island from Long Wharf; see the Boston Harbor Islands section for details.

Bay State Cruises (☎ 617-748-1428) operates boats from Commonwealth Pier in South Boston to Provincetown at the tip of Cape Cod; see the Getting There & Away section for Provincetown in the Cape Cod chapter for details. For information on its summertime evening cruises, see Cruises earlier in this chapter.

The AC Cruise Line (☎ 617-261-6633), 290 Northern Ave, across the Fort Point Channel in South Boston, operates boats to Gloucester and Salem on the North Shore; see Cruises earlier in this chapter.

## GETTING AROUND
### To/From the Airport

Downtown Boston is just a few miles from Logan International Airport, and is accessible by subway (the 'T'), water shuttle, van shuttle, limo, taxi and rental car (see Getting There & Away, above).

The T, or the MBTA subway (☎ 617-222-3200, 800-392-6100, www.mbta.com), is the fastest and cheapest way to reach the city from the airport. From any terminal, take a free, well-marked shuttle bus (No 22 or No 33) to the Airport T station on the Blue Line, purchase an 85¢ token and you'll be downtown within 30 minutes, including waiting. The subway operates daily from about 5:30 am to about 12:30 am.

Taxis are plentiful but pricey; traffic snarls can translate into a $20 fare to downtown.

If you are driving to downtown from the airport, take the Sumner Tunnel ($2 toll) downtown to Government Center and the North End, where there are immediate on-ramps for the I-93 Expressway (Central Artery) north and south. When you're going *from* Boston *to* the airport, take the Callahan Tunnel (no toll). The new Third Harbor Tunnel (Ted Williams Tunnel; $2), a mile south of the city off I-93, is open to buses, taxis and limos every day, but to noncommercial vehicles (that's you) only on weekends. There's a hefty fine for going through it when you're not supposed to. When it's open, it saves travelers approaching from the south a great deal of time.

The Airport Water Shuttle (☎ 617-330-8680, 800-235-6426), also accessible via free shuttle buses from each terminal, whisks passengers to downtown Rowes Wharf (Atlantic Ave) in seven minutes. Once downtown, though, you'll probably still have to take the subway. (The closest T station to Rowes Wharf is Blue Line to Aquarium, a five-minute walk.) However, the water shuttle across Boston Harbor provides a great view of Boston's skyline. Purchase tickets onboard; one way is $10 adults, $5 seniors, free for children under 12. The shuttle runs every 15 minutes from 6 am to 8 pm weekdays, until 11 pm on Friday; every

30 minutes from 10 am to 11 pm on Saturdays and from 10 am to 8 pm on Sundays.

There is a direct bus connection (☎ 800-235-6426) from Logan airport to the South Station Transportation Center, bay No 25. Participating bus companies include Bonanza, C&J Trailways, Concord Trailways and Plymouth & Brockton. Buses depart every 15 to 30 minutes from about 7:15 am to 10:15 pm daily (from 8:45 am on weekends) and cost $6 adults, free for children under 12. Buy tickets onboard or at South Station.

### Bus

The MBTA also operates bus routes within the city, but these can be difficult to figure out for short-term visitors. The subway goes to 95% of the places you'll want to go.

### The T

The MBTA (☎ 617-222-3200, 800-392-6100) operates the USA's oldest subway, built in 1897, known locally as 'the T.' Stops are easily spotted in this guide by the Ⓣ. There are four lines – Red, Blue, Green and Orange – that radiate from the principal downtown stations. These are Park St, which has an information booth, Downtown Crossing, Government Center and State. When traveling away from any of these stations, you are heading outbound.

Tourist passes with unlimited travel are available for periods of one week ($18), three days ($9) and one day ($5). Passes may be purchased at the Visitor Information Center on Tremont St and at the following T stations: Park St, Government Center, Back Bay, Alewife, North Station, South Station, Hynes and Airport. For longer stays, monthly unlimited-travel passes are available from around the first of the month to the 15th; subway-only passes are $27, subway-plus-bus passes are $46.

Otherwise, purchase tokens at all stations (85¢ adults, 40¢ children) except those west of Symphony ('E' branch) and Kenmore ('B', 'C' and 'D' branches) on the Green Line, which are above ground. You must have exact change to board these trains. No fare is collected when heading outbound from an above-ground Green Line station. Some fares heading inbound, though, are higher than 85¢.

The T operates from about 5:30 am to 12:30 am.

## Car

With any luck you won't have to drive in or around Boston. Not only are the streets a maze of confusion, choked with construction (see the 'Big Dig' text under Car in the Getting There & Away section, above) and legendary traffic jams, but Boston drivers use their own set of rules. Driving is often considered a sport – in a town that takes its sports very seriously.

Two highways skirt the Charles River: Storrow Drive runs along the Boston side and Memorial Drive (more scenic) parallels it on the Cambridge side. There are exits off of Storrow Drive for Kenmore Square, Back Bay and Government Center. Both Storrow Drive and Memorial Drive are accessible from the Mass Pike and the I-93 Expressway.

All major rental car agencies are represented at the airport; free shuttle vans will take you to their nearby pick-up counters

(see also Car Rental in the main Getting Around chapter). Rental car companies with offices downtown include:

Avis
(☎ 617-534-1400, 800-331-1212)
3 Center Plaza at Government Center
Budget
(☎ 617-497-1800, 800-527-0700)
24 Park Plaza
Enterprise
(☎ 617-262-8222, 800-736-8222)
Prudential Center, 800 Boylston St
Hertz
(☎ 617-338-1500, 800-654-3131)
Park Square near the Public Garden
National
(☎ 617-661-8747, 800-227-7368)
1663 Mass Ave, between Harvard Square and Porter Square
Rent a Wreck
(☎ 617-576-3700, 800-535-1391)
McGrath-O'Brien Hwy, Cambridge
Thrifty
(☎ 617-330-5011, 800-367-2277)
125 Summer at High St, near South Station

Hertz has installed its 'Never Lost' navigational system in its Boston cars. With road

---

## Pahking the Cah

If you must drive into the city, park at one of the following centrally located garages and walk or take the T from there. It's unnecessary (and incredibly expensive) to move from one lot to another. Since on-street parking is limited and the meters finicky, you could end up paying as much as $27 daily to park. When you make lodging reservations, ask if parking is available and what it costs.

There are parking lots beneath Boston Common (access via Charles St South) and Post Office Square (access is via Pearl St in the Financial District); at Center Plaza (access off Cambridge St) for Faneuil Hall and Government Center; in Back Bay at the Prudential Center (via Boylston St) and Copley Place (via Huntington St); and in Cambridge off JFK St. Look for the blue 'P' sign around town. Keep an eye out for the numerous small lots too.

configurations in Boston that literally change overnight, the system will surely be put to a test. Regardless, these cars cost an additional $6 daily.

## Taxi

Taxis are plentiful (although you'll have to walk to a major hotel to find one with any degree of assurance), but expensive. At press time, the initial rates were $1.50 plus 25¢ per quarter-mile. If you miss the last subway, expect to spend about $10 from Harvard Square to Copley Square in Back Bay. From the North End or Faneuil Hall to Kenmore Square, it'll cost you about $7 without much traffic.

You'll have lots of trouble hailing a cab during bad weather and between 3:30 and 6:30 pm weekdays. Again, head to major hotels or Faneuil Hall.

Recommended taxi companies include the following:

| | |
|---|---|
| Checker Cab | ☎ 617-536-7000 |
| Independent | ☎ 617-426-8700 |
| Metro Cab | ☎ 617-242-8000 |

## Bicycle

Daredevil Bostonians cycle around town, but there are no bike lanes, so use caution if you take to the Boston city streets on two wheels. For information on biking and renting bicycles in Boston, see the Bicycling section earlier in this chapter. Be sure to get a hold of *Boston's Bike Map*; see Maps under Orientation at the beginning of this chapter.

## Boat

City Water Taxi (☎ 617-422-0392) makes on-demand taxi stops seasonally at 10 waterfront points, including the airport, the Children's and Computer Museums, Long Wharf, Burroughs Wharf in the North End, the USS *Constitution* and the Charlestown Navy Yard. The fare is $5 between any two points, with the exception of the airport ($10 for one person, $8 each for two or more).

Boston by Boat (☎ 617-422-0392) plies the waterfront circuit every day during the summer, making stops at the Children's Museum, the Aquarium, the North End (Burroughs Wharf at Battery and Commercial Sts) and the USS *Constitution*. Hop on and off all day for $5.

For information on the airport water shuttle, see the beginning of the Getting Around section. For information on cruises, see Cruises earlier in this chapter.

# Around Boston

Part of what makes Boston one of the USA's most livable cities is its easy access to the countryside. The beautiful colonial towns founded shortly after Boston and Cambridge, including Lexington, Concord, Salem and others, have attractive historic centers and offer a variety of things to see and do, including museums, hikes, whale-watching cruises, and canoe and bicycle trips. All ot these destinations are reachable by car or bus in under an hour; some are accessible by train as well.

## West of Boston

Lexington, about 18 miles northwest of the city center, has a colonial village green and acres of market gardens where fruits and vegetables are grown for sale. Concord, an easy 40-minute drive or train ride northwest, is an historic colonial town surrounded by rolling fields, forests and beautiful country roads for bicycling.

Lexington can be reached from Boston by bus, Concord by train, and both by bicycle. The **Minuteman Commuter Bikeway** follows an old railroad right-of-way from near the Alewife Red Line subway terminus in Cambridge through Arlington to Lexington and to Bedford, a distance of about 14 miles. From Bedford, ride along MA 4 northwest, then MA 62 southwest, to reach Concord, another 6 miles along. For bike rentals, see the Boston, Cambridge and Lexington sections.

### LEXINGTON
The roads between Lexington and Boston teem with commuters weekday mornings. But two centuries ago, the two towns were a horse ride of several hours apart.

### History
On April 18, 1775, Paul Revere, William Dawes and Samuel Prescott set out on their midnight ride from Boston to Lexington and Concord. They rode to warn these communities and others that General Gage, the British commander in Boston, was sending an expeditionary force to search for arms and matériel rumored to be stockpiled at Concord.

Revere, Dawes and Prescott were part of a colonial intelligence and communications network so efficient that the local troops of militia, the minutemen, turned out long before the tramp of British boots was heard on the dirt road approaching Lexington.

When the advance body of 700 redcoats under Major John Pitcairn marched up to Lexington Green just after daybreak, they found Captain John Parker's company of 77

## Highlights

- Strolling through the gracious, historic villages of Lexington and Concord

- Visiting the picturesque coastal town of Salem

- Touring Gloucester, the region's most famous fishing port

- Spending the day wandering in Rockport or sailing on the bay

171

# AROUND BOSTON

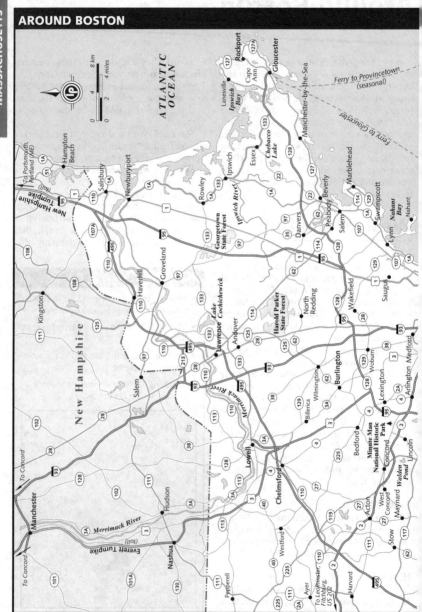

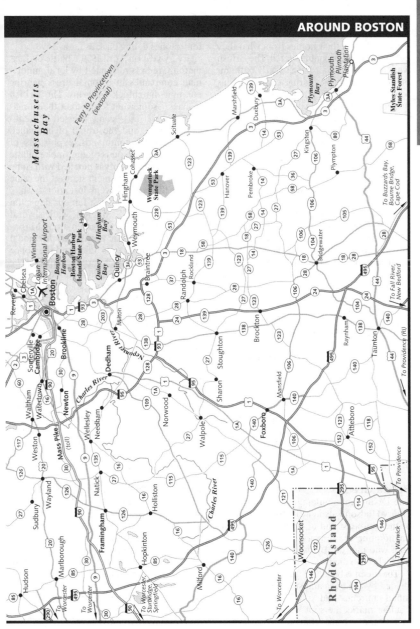

**AROUND BOSTON**

minutemen lined up in formation to meet them. Captain Parker and his men were there to defend their homes from what they deemed an unreasonable search. The British were there to do their duty. Clearly outnumbered and, perhaps, fearing capture of his force, Captain Parker ordered his men to disperse peaceably, which they slowly began to do. But the British took this as capitulation and began trying to arrest the 'rebels' who had raised arms against them.

A shot rang out – from which side has never been clear – and then others, and soon eight minutemen lay dead on the green, with 10 others wounded. Pitcairn regained control of his troops with difficulty and marched them out of Lexington toward Concord.

The skirmish on Lexington Green (now called Battle Green) was the first organized, armed resistance to British rule in a colonial town, and the beginning of the Revolutionary War. Without the bloodshed at Lexington, the Concord minutemen might not have been steeled to offer spirited resistance to the British troops.

## Orientation & Information

MA 4 and 225 follow Massachusetts Ave through the center of Lexington, passing by Battle Green. The green is at the northwestern end of the business district.

The Lexington Chamber of Commerce (☎ 781-862-1450), 1875 Massachusetts Ave, maintains a visitors' center opposite Battle Green, next to Buckman Tavern. Stop in to see the exhibits that recall the 1775 events. It's open 9 am to 5 pm daily (10 am to 4 pm in winter).

## Battle Green

The Lexington minuteman statue (done by Henry Hudson Kitson in 1900) stands guard at the southeast end of Battle Green, commemorating the bravery of the 77 minutemen who met the British here in 1775 and the eight who died.

The green is beautiful and tranquil today, shaded by tall trees and surrounded by dignified churches and stately old homes. A boulder marks the spot where the minutemen faced a force almost 10 times their

strength. Just off the green, by the church, is **Ye Olde Burying Ground**, with some fine tombstones dating back as far as 1690.

Every year on April 19, the battle on Lexington Green is reenacted by local minuteman companies in colonial dress bearing colonial matchlock firearms. The British heavies – somewhat fewer than their original force of 700 – come dressed authentically as well, and the tramp of hobnailed boots, barked commands, explosions of musket fire and clouds of gun smoke fill the air again. Authenticity is pursued with some vigor, so the re-enactment starts at the same time as the original event: just after dawn.

For a look at the most famous depiction of the battle of Lexington, walk several blocks southeast of the green along Massachusetts Ave to **Isaac Harris Cary Memorial Hall**, between the post office and the police station. Sandham's famous painting *The Dawn of Liberty* hangs in an honored spot, flanked by marble statues of patriots John Hancock and Samuel Adams. The hall has no strict hours but is generally open during conventional business hours.

## Historic Houses

Three historic houses are maintained by the Lexington Historical Society (☎ 781-862-1703), 1332 Massachusetts Ave, and are open 10 am to 5 pm (1 to 5 pm Sunday) mid-April through October, until 8 pm in high summer. Admission costs $4 per adult for each house ($1 for children six to 16), or $10 per adult for all three houses ($2 for children).

**Buckman Tavern** Facing the green next to the visitors' center, Buckman Tavern (built 1709; ☎ 781-862-5598), 1 Bedford Rd, was where the minutemen spent the tense hours between the original midnight call to arms and the dawn arrival of the redcoats. It also served as a field hospital that treated the wounded after the fight. Today, it is a worthy museum of colonial life, with instructive tours given by 'interpreters' in period costume.

**Munroe Tavern** Now serving as the Lexington Historical Society's headquarters, Munroe Tavern (built 1695; ☎ 781-674-9238),

1332 Massachusetts Ave, about seven long blocks southeast of the green, was used by the British as a command post and field infirmary. It's now furnished with antiques, mementos of the battle and artifacts from President George Washington's visit in 1789.

**Hancock-Clarke House** This house (built 1698; ☎ 781-861-0928), 36 Hancock St, about a block north of Battle Green, was the parsonage of the Reverend Jonas Clarke in 1775, and the goal of Paul Revere as he rode out to warn the colonials of the British troops' advance. John Hancock and Samuel Adams, 'rabble-rousers' wanted by the British crown, hid themselves here on the fateful day.

## Museum of
## Our National Heritage
The museum (☎ 781-861-6559), 33 Marrett Rd (MA 2A), just off Massachusetts Ave (MA 4 and 225), is over a mile southeast of Battle Green. Founded by the Scottish Rite Masons in 1975, it has four large galleries with changing exhibits of Americana. It's open 10 am to 5 pm (noon to 5 pm Sunday), and is free.

## Places to Stay
The chamber of commerce visitors' center has a list of small local bed-and-breakfast guest houses; see the Orientation & Information section.

The **Battle Green Inn** (☎ 781-862-6100, 800-343-0235, 1720 Massachusetts Ave) is a motel-style lodging right in the center of Lexington's business district. The rooms cost $95 with one double bed and $99 for two beds, with a light self-service breakfast included.

**Sheraton Tara Lexington Inn** (☎ 781-862-8700, fax 863-0404, 727 Marrett Rd), just west of I-95 exit 30B (follow signs for Hanscom Field), has 119 comfortable rooms for $152 to $211 in a full-service facility favored by business travelers. Ask about weekend discounts.

## Places to Eat
More than a dozen eateries lie within a five-minute walk of Battle Green.

**Goodies** (☎ 781-863-1704, 1734 Massachusetts Ave), right by the traffic lights in the center of town, can supply you with deli sandwiches ($2 to $5), soups, salads and hot platters. They're open 10 am to 9 pm. **Via Lago Gourmet Foods** (☎ 781-861-6174, 1845 Massachusetts Ave) is more upscale and pricier.

**Bertucci's** (☎ 781-860-9000, 1777 Massachusetts Ave), in the very center of town, serves pizzas baked in a wood-fired brick oven, pastas, salads and other light meals for $5 to $14. For more elaborate and substantial Italian fare, go to **Vinny Testa's** (☎ 781-860-5200, 20 Waltham St), where huge pasta plates cost $6 to $19, Italian main courses $20 to $30, and alcohol is served.

**Stone Soup Grill & Café** (☎ 781-862-9797, 1709 Massachusetts Ave), at Edison Way, features steaks and more innovative cuisine for lunch ($8 to $12) and dinner ($20 to $45), with wine tasting every Tuesday evening.

For a sit-down meal, you can't beat the luncheon specials at two Chinese restaurants. The **Yangtze River** (☎ 781-861-6030, 21 Depot Square), off Massachusetts Ave just south of Battle Green, features Szechuan and Mandarin cuisine in an all-you-can-eat luncheon buffet for $6 ($7.50 on weekends), or a dinner buffet for $11 ($12 on weekends). **Peking Garden** (☎ 781-862-1051, 27-31 Waltham St), a block south of Massachusetts Ave from the traffic light opposite Vinny Testa's, is similar.

**Lemon Grass Thai Cuisine** (☎ 781-862-3530, 1710 Massachusetts Ave), opposite Stone Soup, has good, huge meal-in-a-bowl soups with noodles for $5 and other delicious Thai dishes for only slightly more. For sushi ($9 to $12), or other Japanese and Korean dishes (for $10 to $15), try **Dabin** (☎ 781-860-0171, 10 Muzzey St), a half block south of Massachusetts Ave.

## Getting There & Away
Take MA 2 west from Boston or Cambridge to exit 54 (Waltham St) or exit 53 (Spring St). From I-95 (MA 128), take exit 30 or 31.

MBTA buses (☎ 800-392-6100) No 62 (Bedford VA Hospital) and No 76 (Hanscom Field) run from the Red Line Alewife subway terminus through Lexington center at least every hour weekdays, less frequently on Saturday; no buses on Sunday.

Bikes can be rented from Bikeway Cycle & Sports Center (☎ 781-861-1199), 3 Bow St, Lexington, off Massachusetts Ave just west of the Arlington town line. A good day's biking excursion is to take the Red Line subway to the end of the line at Alewife, then take bus Nos 62, 76 or 79 to Arlington Heights, walk five minutes farther west along Massachusetts Ave to Bow St, rent a bike at Bikeway Cycle, then ride through Lexington to Concord and back. Hybrid and mountain bikes rent for $6 an hour, $14 a half day and $20 for 24 hours. They rent bike trailers for the children to ride in, too.

## CONCORD

Tall white church steeples rise above huge old trees in colonial Concord, giving the town a dignity and beauty that makes it a favorite goal for those wanting to get out of the city for awhile. The placid Concord River offers canoeing possibilities, the town's scenic roads are excellent for bicycling and the town's colonial and 19th-century literary history attracts visitors from around the world.

### History

**Revolutionary History** On the morning of April 19, 1775, after the skirmish on Lexington Green, General Gage's expeditionary force of 700 British soldiers marched to nearby Concord. The colonial intelligence system preceded them, however, reporting that minutemen had died in Lexington. This strengthened the resolve of the minuteman companies from Acton, Bedford, Concord, Lexington, Stow and other communities who had turned out to face the 'lobsterbacks.'

The British marched into Concord at around 7 am and commandeered the Wright Tavern at the corner of Main St and Lexington Rd as their headquarters. Their commander sent seven companies off to the north to seize arms reported by spies to be stored at Colonel James Barrett's farm, leaving only three of these companies to secure the North Bridge.

The minutemen, outnumbered, mustered on Punkatasset Hill northeast of the town center and awaited reinforcements, which came steadily from surrounding towns. When several hundred had assembled, the minutemen saw smoke rising from the town. The British searchers had found nothing but a few gun carriages, which they burned, but the minutemen assumed the worst.

'Will you let them burn the town down?' shouted their commander. Enraged that the regulars would burn their homes, the minutemen fired on the now-outnumbered British troops, wounding half of their officers and forcing them back across the North Bridge. Soon, the British were on their way out of Concord.

The battle at North Bridge, called 'the shot heard 'round the world' by Ralph Waldo Emerson, was the first successful armed resistance to British rule. But it did not end there.

The British suffered 11 wounded and two dead at North Bridge, but it was only the beginning of the calamity. On their march back to Boston, the British troops were pursued by minutemen who fired at them from behind trees, walls and buildings. Most of this fire did little harm, but occasionally a bullet would find its mark, and in places where the minutemen had defensible positions, British troops fell. They were tired, dispirited and angry when they reached Lexington and encountered 1000 reinforcements.

These guerrilla tactics were unusual for the time and were looked upon as cowardly and unfair by the British troops. Enraged at the locals' resistance, and their ever-mounting casualties, the British rioted and murdered innocent colonials whom they encountered along their line of march. At Menotomy (modern Arlington), 5000 men battled one another. By the time the British regained the safety of Boston, they had lost 73 dead, 174 wounded and 26 missing. The American losses were 49 dead, 40 wounded and five missing.

The die had been cast. The situation in the American colonies was no longer one of political and social resistance to rule from

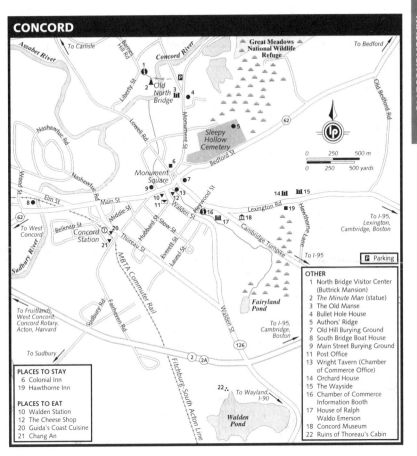

CONCORD

To Carlisle

*Assabet River*

*Concord River*

To Bedford

Barrett's Hill Rd

Liberty St

Old North Bridge

Lowell Rd

Monument St

Great Meadows National Wildlife Refuge

Old Bedford Rd

Nashawtuc Rd

Sleepy Hollow Cemetery

62

Bedford St

0   250   500 m

0   250   500 yards

Nashawtuc Rd

Woods St

Monument Square

Main St

Elm St

Middle St

Walden St

Heywood St

Lexington Rd

Hawthorne Lane

14   15

18   19

16

17

Cambridge Turnpike

To I-95, Lexington, Cambridge, Boston

62

To West Concord

Belknap St

Concord Station

Thoreau St

Hubbard St

Stow St

Everett St

Laurel St

MBTA Commuter Rail

To Fruitlands, West Concord, Concord Rotary, Acton, Harvard

Sudbury River

To Sudbury

Sudbury Rd

Fairhaven Rd

Walden St

Fairyland Pond

To I-95, Cambridge, Boston

126

Fitchburg-South Acton Line

2   2A

22

To Wayland, I-90

*Walden Pond*

To I-95, Lexington, Cambridge, Boston

Parking

PLACES TO STAY
6   Colonial Inn
19  Hawthorne Inn

PLACES TO EAT
10  Walden Station
12  The Cheese Shop
20  Guida's Coast Cuisine
21  Chang An

OTHER
1   North Bridge Visitor Center (Buttrick Mansion)
2   *The Minute Man* (statue)
3   The Old Manse
4   Bullet Hole House
5   Authors' Ridge
7   Old Hill Burying Ground
8   South Bridge Boat House
9   Main Street Burying Ground
11  Post Office
13  Wright Tavern (Chamber of Commerce Office)
14  Orchard House
15  The Wayside
16  Chamber of Commerce Information Booth
17  House of Ralph Waldo Emerson
18  Concord Museum
22  Ruins of Thoreau's Cabin

London, but of armed rebellion against the forces of the British crown.

**19th-Century Literary History** Concord in the 19th century was a very different place. Though still a town of prosperous farmers, it was home to a surprising number of the literary figures of the age, including essayist, preacher and poet Ralph Waldo Emerson (1803-82); essayist and naturalist Henry David Thoreau (1817-62); short-story writer and novelist Nathaniel Hawthorne (1804-64); and novelist and children's book author Louisa May Alcott (1832-88).

Emerson was the paterfamilias of literary Concord, one of the great literary figures of his age and the founding thinker of the Transcendentalist movement. While traveling in Great Britain, he befriended Carlyle, Coleridge and Wordsworth. His Concord house is now a museum.

Thoreau took the naturalist beliefs of Transcendentalism out of the realm of theory and into practice when he left the comforts of the town and built himself a rustic cabin on the shores of Walden Pond several miles from the town center. His memoir of his time spent there, the famous

*Walden, or Life in the Woods* (1854) was full of praise for nature and disapproval of the stresses of civilized life, sentiments that have found an eager audience ever since. Many of his readers visit the site of his cabin at Walden Pond (see Walden Pond, below).

Hawthorne, author of *The Scarlet Letter, Twice-Told Tales* and *The House of the Seven Gables*, was born and raised in Salem, Massachusetts, but lived in Concord at the Old Manse next to the North Bridge for three years just after his marriage. His residence in Concord gave him material for several later stories.

Alcott was a junior member of this august literary crowd, but her work proved more durable than that of the others. *Little Women* (1868-69), her mostly autobiographical novel about women's coming-of-age in Concord, is among the most popular young-adult books ever written. Its several sequels continued her work of portraying family life in Victorian America with keen perception and affection. Her childhood home, Orchard House, is among Concord's most-visited sites (see Historic Houses, below).

Daniel Chester French (1850-1931) was a young sculptor living in Concord when the town asked him to create a bronze sculpture of a minuteman to commemorate the 100th anniversary of the battle at Old North Bridge (1875). French went on to create the marble statue of Emerson now in Concord's public library, the equestrian statue of General George Washington that now stands in Paris, the great marble statue in the Lincoln Memorial (1922) in Washington, DC, and many other works.

Resident Ephraim Bull had a different kind of success altogether. Around 1850, his hybrid Concord grape gave birth to commercial table grape agriculture in the USA. For many years, the Welch's company had its headquarters on Main St.

## Orientation

Concord (population 17,000) lies about 22 miles northwest of Boston along MA 2. The center of the sprawling, mostly rural town is Monument Square, marked by its war memorial obelisk. The Colonial Inn stands on the square's north side.

Main St runs westward from Monument Square through the business district to MA 2. Walden and Thoreau Sts run southeast from Main St and out to Walden Pond some 3 miles away.

The MBTA Commuter Rail train station, the Concord Station ('the Depot'), is on Thoreau St at Sudbury Rd, a mile west of Monument Square.

## Information

The information booth for the Concord Chamber of Commerce (☎ 978-369-3120, www.concordma.com) is on Heywood St between Lexington Rd and Walden St. Approaching Concord from the east via MA 2 and Cambridge Turnpike, look for Heywood St on the left a few blocks before Monument Square. The Chamber's booth, staffed by volunteers, is open on weekends mid-April through May and daily June through mid-October.

The chamber's main office is in the historic Wright Tavern at Main St and Lexington Rd. They'll answer questions here when the booth is not open.

Minuteman National Historic Park's Battle Road Visitor Center (☎ 978-371-2687)

**Ralph Waldo Emerson**

## Transcendentalism

Transcendentalism was a 19th-century American social and philosophical movement that flourished from 1836 to 1860 in Boston and Concord. Though small in numbers, the Transcendentalists had a significant effect on American literature and society.

The core of Transcendentalist belief was that each person and element of nature had within it a part of the divine essence, that God 'transcended' all things. The search for divinity was thus not so much in scripture and prayer, nor in perception and reason, but in individual intuition or 'instinct.' By intuition we can know what is right and wrong according to divine law. By intuition we can know the meaning of life. Living in harmony with the natural world was very important to Transcendentalists.

Bronson Alcott (1799-1888), educational and social reformer and father of Louisa May Alcott, joined Emerson, Thoreau, Margaret Fuller and other Concordians in turning away from their traditional Unitarianism to Transcendentalism.

The Transcendentalists founded a periodical, *The Dial*, to disseminate their views, and established the community of Brook Farm (1841-47) based on Transcendentalist doctrines of community life and work, social reform and anti-slavery. Hawthorne was a resident for a time, and both he and novelist Herman Melville were influenced by Transcendentalist beliefs.

Bronson Alcott was also a founder of Fruitlands, an experimental vegetarian community in Harvard, Massachusetts, established in 1843. He lived here with his family (including 10-year-old daughter Louisa) and others for a year before abandoning the project. Fruitlands is now a museum open to the public (see the Fruitlands section, below).

is on Massachusetts Ave between Lexington and Concord. It's open from mid-April through October. The Concord North Bridge Visitor Center (☎ 978-369-6993), on Liberty St just north of the North Bridge, is open 9:30 am to 4:30 pm daily in summer, until 4 pm in winter; closed Christmas and New Year's Day.

### Walking Tour

The grassy center of Monument Square is a favorite rest and picnic spot for bicyclers touring Concord's scenic roads. It's the best place to start your walk around historic Concord.

If you'd like a guided walking tour, contact the Concord Guides (☎ 978-287-0897, members.aol.com/concordweb). Two-hour walking tours hosted by knowledgeable guides depart daily from early July through October, on weekends from April to July. Adults pay $15, college students and seniors $12, youth (11 to 18) $10, children six to 10 pay $5.

At the southeastern end of the square is **Wright Tavern**, one of the first places the British troops searched in their hunt for arms on April 19, 1775. It became their headquarters for the operation. At the opposite end of the square is the **Colonial Inn** (see Places to Stay, below), the oldest part of which dates from 1716.

Walk northeast out of Monument Square (keep the Colonial Inn on your left) along Monument St. It's a 15-minute walk past some of the town's most beautiful colonial houses to Old North Bridge, site of the first battle of the Revolutionary War. Along the way, watch for the yellow **Bullet Hole House** on the right-hand (east) side. British troops fired at the owner of the house as they retreated from the engagement at North Bridge, and a hole made by one of their bullets can still be seen in the wall of the shed attached to the house.

The wooden span of **Old North Bridge**, now part of the Minuteman National Historic Park, has been rebuilt many times but still gives a good impression of what it must have looked like at the time of the battle. Across the bridge is Daniel Chester French's first statue, *The Minute Man*, which is on the way up the hill to the Buttrick Mansion, the park's visitors' center.

Walking south and east from Monument Square for five minutes brings you to the **Concord Museum** (☎ 978-369-9609, www .concordmuseum.org), 200 Lexington Rd. Among the museum's exhibits are one of the lanterns hung in the steeple of Boston's Old North Church as a signal to Revere, Dawes and Prescott; Ralph Waldo Emerson's study; and the world's largest collection of Thoreau artifacts. It's open in the summer 10 am to 5 pm (1 pm to 5 pm Sunday), in winter 11 am to 4 pm (1 to 4 pm on Sunday). Admission costs $6 for adults, $5 for seniors, $3 for children and $12 for families.

## Historic Houses

Across from the Concord Museum is the **House of Ralph Waldo Emerson** (☎ 978-369-2236), 28 Cambridge Turnpike. The house, where Emerson lived from 1835 until his death in 1882, often hosted his renowned circle of friends and still contains many original furnishings. It's open mid-April through October, 10 am to 4:30 pm Thursday to Saturday and 2 to 4:30 pm Sunday. Admission costs $4.50 for adults, $3 for children seven to 17.

About a mile east of Monument Square is Louisa May Alcott's home, **Orchard House** (☎ 978-369-4118, www.louisamayalcott.org), 399 Lexington Rd, on the left-hand (north) side as you come from the center of Concord. Her father, Bronson Alcott, bought the property in 1857 and lived here with his family until his death in 1888. Louisa wrote *Little Women* here from May to July 1868 and died here twenty years later (two days after her father). The house, furnishings and Bronson's Concord School of Philosophy on the hillside behind the house are open to visitors April through October 10 am to 4:30 pm (1 to 4:30 pm Sunday ) and November through March 11 am to 3 pm (10 am to 4:30 pm Saturday, 1 to 4:30 pm Sunday). You

Louisa May Alcott wrote *Little Women* in Concord.

must take a guided tour: $5.50 for adults, $4.50 for seniors, $3.50 for those six to 17, $16 for families. Call ☎ 978-369-5617 on the day you wish to visit, ask tour times, then get to the house in plenty of time to get your tickets, as the tours fill up, particularly in summer.

A short stroll to the east is **The Wayside** (☎ 978-369-6975), 455 Lexington Rd, another house in which Louisa May Alcott lived and which she described in *Little Women*. At another time, it was Nathaniel Hawthorne's home, but most of the remaining furnishings are those of Margaret Sidney, author of *Five Little Peppers*. The house is open to visitors 9:30 am to 5:30 pm mid-April through October, closed Wednesday and Thursday.

Right next to Old North Bridge, **The Old Manse** (☎ 978-369-3909) was built in 1769 by Reverend William Emerson and was owned by the Emerson family for the following 169 years, until it was deeded to the NPS. Today, it's a museum filled with mementos of the Emerson family, and also of Nathaniel and Sophia Hawthorne, who lived here from

1842 to 1845 following their marriage. A guided tour costs $5 for adults, $4 for seniors and college students, $3.50 for children six to 16 and $13 for families. It's open mid-April through October 10 am to 5 pm (noon to 5 pm Sunday); last tour at 4:30 pm.

## Historic Graveyards

Old Hill Burying Ground, with graves dating from colonial times, is on the hillside at the southeastern end of Monument Square. Main Street Burying Ground, at the intersection of Keyes Rd in the commercial center, has the town's oldest tombstones, dating from Concord's founding in the 17th century. Legend says the town has two burying grounds because in earlier times it was considered bad luck to carry a corpse across a stream (the Mill Brook runs beneath Main St just off Monument Square).

It is in spacious Sleepy Hollow Cemetery (☎ 978-371-6299), however, that the most famous deceased Concordians rest. Though the cemetery is only a block east of Monument Square along MA 62, the most interesting part, Authors' Ridge, is a 15-minute hike (or a shorter drive) further. Enter the gate from MA 62 and follow signs to Authors' Ridge.

Henry David Thoreau and his family are buried here, as are the Alcotts and Nathaniel Hawthorne and his wife. Ralph Waldo Emerson's tombstone is a large uncarved rock of New England marble, an appropriate Transcendentalist symbol. Down the hill a bit is the tombstone of Ephraim Bull, developer of the famous Concord grape.

Nearby is the Melvin Memorial, a beautiful and much-photographed monument to the memory of three Concord brothers who died in the Civil War. It is the work of Daniel Chester French, who is buried in Sleepy Hollow as well.

## Walden Pond

The glacial pond near which Henry David Thoreau spent the years 1845-1847 is about 3 miles south of Monument Square along Walden St (MA 126) south of MA 2. It's now a state park, with a parking fee payable during the summer. There's a swimming beach and facilities on the southern side and a footpath that circles the large pond (about a half-hour stroll). The site of Thoreau's cabin is on the northeast side, marked by a cairn and signs.

## Fruitlands

Thirty miles west of Boston, but just a fast half-hour's drive west of Concord on MA 2, lies the town of Harvard and **Fruitlands Museums** (☎ 978-456-3924, www.ultranet .com/~frutlan), 102 Prospect Hill Rd (MA 2 exit 38A). The original hillside farmhouse, set on spacious grounds with panoramic views, dates from the 18th century and was used by Bronson Alcott and his utopian 'Con-Sociate' (communal) family in 1843. Other museums were moved to the 200-acre estate, including the 1794 Shaker House, an American Indian museum and a picture gallery featuring paintings by 19th-century itinerant artists and Hudson River School landscape painters.

The estate's grounds and nature trails are open 10 am to 5 pm daily. The museums are open mid-May through mid-October (closed Monday, except on holidays) for $4.

The tearoom at Fruitlands offers luncheon ($5 to $10) and beverages 10 am to 4 pm (Sunday brunch is 10 am to 2 pm), with outdoor dining to enjoy the excellent views.

## Canoeing

The South Bridge Boat House (☎ 978-369-9438), 496-502 Main St (MA 62), a mile west of Monument Square, rents canoes for cruising the Concord and Assabet Rivers from April until the first snowfall. The favorite route is downstream to Old North Bridge and back past the many fine riverside houses and the campus of prestigious Concord Academy, a paddle of about two hours. Rental rates are $10 per hour, $40 per day on weekends, with discounts on weekdays and for students.

## Places to Stay

**Motels** The *Concordian Motel* (☎ 978-263-7765, 800-552-7765, 71 Hosmer St), on MA 2 in neighboring Acton, has modern rooms for $69, light breakfast included. Follow MA 2 west from the Concord Rotary and look for the motel on the left-hand side.

The **Best Western Concord Motel** (☎ 978-369-6100, 800-528-1234, 740 Elm St), at MA 2 near the Concord Rotary, charges $99 to $114, with light breakfast. Several good restaurants are right next door.

**Inns & B&Bs** The original building of the **Colonial Inn** (☎ 978-369-9200, 48 Monument Square) dates from 1716 and has 12 guest rooms ($185), a lobby, dining rooms and tavern. The other 48 guest rooms ($149) are in a modern brick annex. The inn's dining room, tavern and front porch are a center of town social life.

The **Hawthorne Inn** (☎ 978-369-5610, www.concordmass.com, 462 Lexington Rd) is about a mile southeast of Monument Square near Orchard House and The Wayside (see Historic Houses, above). The inn has seven rooms with period decor, air-con, private baths and prices from $175 to $215, light breakfast included.

Thirteen miles south of Concord on US 20 lies the town of Sudbury and its **Wayside Inn** (☎ 978-443-8846). The inn, dating from 1700, was made famous by Longfellow's poems entitled *Tales from a Wayside Inn*, and it now boasts that it is the oldest operating inn in the USA. It was restored by Henry Ford in the 1920s and still operates as a restaurant and hostelry, with 10 rooms: Nos 9 and 10 are original to the inn and cost $120, full breakfast included. The newer rooms cost a bit less.

### Places to Eat
For a good, fresh, huge luncheon sandwich for $5 to $7, or for picnic supplies, drop in at **The Cheese Shop** (☎ 978-369-5778, 29 Walden St), a half block southeast of Main St, more or less across from the post office.

Across from The Cheese Shop, **Walden Station** (☎ 978-371-2233, 24 Walden St) is a tavern-restaurant with a full menu of luncheon sandwiches and main courses priced from $6 to $18, with slightly higher prices for larger portions at dinner.

The best restaurant is **Guida's Coast Cuisine** (☎ 978-371-1333, 84 Thoreau St),

upstairs in the Concord Depot (called 'the Depot'). The continental-influenced cuisine is refined, inventive and served daily. Lunch costs about $12 to $20, dinner to $40 or $50 per person.

**Chang An** (☎ 978-369-5288, 10 Concord Crossing), off Sudbury Rd just across the railroad tracks from Thoreau St, has the best Chinese cuisine in town. Lunch usually costs $10 to $16, dinner $16 to $28 per person.

West Concord, several miles southwest of Concord center along MA 62, has a number of restaurants as well. The best value is the **99 Restaurant** (☎ 978-369-0300, 18 Commonwealth Ave), with steak dinners for under $13.

### Getting There & Away
Driving west on MA 2 from Boston or Cambridge, it's 20-some miles to Concord. Coming from Lexington, follow signs from Lexington Green to Concord and Battle Rd, the route taken by the British troops on April 19, 1775.

MBTA Commuter Rail trains (☎ 617-722-3200, 800-392-6100, www.mbta.com) run between Boston's North Station and Concord and West Concord Stations 16 times each weekday on the Fitchburg/South Acton line. The 40-minute ride costs $3.25, half price for children 5 to 11 (under five free). In Concord, buy your tickets at Coggins Bakery (☎ 978-371-3040), 68 Thoreau St, just northwest of the depot building.

### LOWELL
Located at the confluence of the Concord and Merrimack Rivers 25 miles northwest of Boston, Lowell (population 103,000) was the crucible of the Industrial Revolution in America. The painter James McNeill Whistler and Beat writer Jack Kerouac were both Lowell natives and are remembered here with affection.

### History
Though a farming community since its founding in 1653, Lowell took on its modern aspect after 1822 when it was chosen by Boston merchant Francis Cabot Lowell as the site of a new kind of industrial project

Lowell, who had toured England's factories, paid for the development of a new and better power loom. Breaking with the traditional model of a factory that's funded and founded by one investor or family, Lowell assembled a group of investors called the Boston Associates, who pooled all of their capital to fund a huge and complex industrial installation.

Driven by the abundant water power of Pawtucket Falls, Lowell's new factories were soon turning out cloth by the mile. A network of canals and the Boston and Lowell Railroad (after 1835) shipped raw materials in and finished cloth out. In 1834, Anna Mathilda (McNeill) Whistler, wife of Major George Washington Whistler, who was the local agent for the Locks and Canals Corporation, gave birth to James Abbott McNeill Whistler (1834-1903). The coming of the railroad made locks and canals less important, and the Whistlers moved away from Lowell in 1837. Young James went on to the US Military Academy at West Point and, with that superb training as a soldier under his belt, became one of America's greatest 19th-century painters.

The Industrial Revolution in America echoed the one in England: huge amounts of wealth were quickly generated by investment capital leveraging the efforts of low-paid, unorganized laborers working long hours under dangerous conditions. Heroic efforts at labor organization and reform efforts, such as those by Sarah Bagley for the 'mill girls' of Lowell, were often frustrated by new influxes of unskilled immigrants willing to work for any wage, in any conditions. But ultimately, workers' rights were acknowledged in the body of American labor law.

In the 1920s, a century after the birth of modern Lowell and just as workers' rights were being recognized in law, Lowell's textile business began to decline as capital moved to southern states with cheaper labor. By mid-century the city was a wasteland of huge abandoned mills and high unemployment. Beat Generation author Jack Kerouac (1922-1969) was born into this milieu, and used it as the setting for his five novels, most famous of which is *On the Road* (1957). Poet, painter and author, Kerouac is remembered annually during the Lowell Celebrates Kerouac! festival held in early October.

During the 1980s, re-industrialization efforts brought in high-tech and other industries to provide a strong economic base. Restoration of the city's fine 19th-century buildings and the declaration of the city center as a National Historic Park have now made Lowell an attractive place to visit. Walking its streets, the golden age of America's Industrial Revolution comes alive.

## Orientation

From I-495, follow the Lowell Connector to its end at exit 5-C to reach the city center. Signage is excellent, allowing you to find all the attractions easily.

Trains from Boston terminate at the Gallagher Transportation Terminal on Thorndike St, a 15-minute walk southwest of the city center, or take the Downtown Shuttle bus (30¢, every 30 minutes) to the Downtown Transit Center in the heart of the city.

Once in the city center, you can walk to most of the sights. Merrimack St is the city's main commercial thoroughfare, holding the Downtown Transit Center, the chamber of commerce office and several restaurants.

## Information

The National Park Service Visitor Center (☎ 978-970-5000, www.nps.gov/lowe), 246 Market St, is the place to start your explorations of historic Lowell. The Greater Merrimack Valley Convention & Visitors Bureau (☎ 978-459-6150, 800-443-3332, www.lowell.org), 22 Shattuck St, a half block northeast of the visitor center, has maps, pamphlets and answers to questions. Two blocks away, the Greater Lowell Chamber of Commerce (☎ 978-459-8154), 77 Merrimack St, Lowell, MA 01852, in the heart of downtown, can also help with questions.

## Lowell National Historical Park

Lowell National Historical Park consists of several exhibits in neighboring buildings in the city center. The visitor center (☎ 978-970-5000), 246 Market St, at Market Mills, is open for free 9 am to 5 pm (10 am to 5 pm Sunday).

The Boott Cotton Mills Museum includes a working power loom and exhibits chronicling the rise and fall of the Industrial Revolution in Lowell. It's open 9:30 am to 5 pm (11 am to 5 pm Sunday) for $4, or $3 for youth six to 16.

To see how the 'mill girls' lived and worked in Lowell, visit the Working People Exhibit in the Patrick J Mogan Cultural Center (☎ 978-970-5000), 40 French St, open 1 to 5 pm weekends for free.

### Whistler House Museum of Art

James McNeill Whistler's birthplace (☎ 978-452-7641), 243 Worthen St, built in 1823, is now the home of the Lowell Art Association. It contains a permanent collection of his works and hosts exhibits of works by Whistler, his contemporaries and modern New England artists. Whistler's most famous painting, *Arrangement in Grey and Black* (popularly known as 'Whistler's Mother'), is not here, unfortunately, but in the Musée d'Orsay in Paris.

The Whistler House is on the west side of the Merrimack Canal, less than two blocks west of the National Park Service Visitor Center. Call for hours of operation.

### Other Museums

Lowell is also home to the **American Textile History Museum** (☎ 978-441-0400), 491 Dutton St, a block south of the Whistler House; the **New England Quilt Museum** (☎ 978-452-4207), 18 Shattuck St, a half block from the NPS Visitor Center; and the nearby **Sports Museum of New England** (☎ 978-452-6775), 25 Shattuck St.

### Places to Eat

Across the street from the NPS Visitor Center, the *Athenian Corner* (☎ 978-458-7052, 207 Market St), corner of Shattuck, has Greek soups, salads and sandwiches for $3 to $6 and main courses for $7 to $10.

Walk north on Shattuck St for one long block to Merrimack St and turn right to find *Quick Pickin's Deli* (☎ 978-452-8161, 96 Merrimack St), opposite John St, which sells huge sandwiches for less than $4, and even bigger subs (and salads) for little more. Nearby, *Mossie's Sandwich Shop* (☎ 978-454-4463, 72 Merrimack St) is an alternative.

For a fancier meal, try the nearby *La Boniche* (☎ 978-458-9473, 143 Merrimack St), which always has daily special burgers, pastas and seafood, as well as innovative American cuisine. It's closed Sunday and Monday.

Enjoy a bit of old Lowell over at the *Old Worthen House* (☎ 978-459-0300, 141 Worthen St), two blocks northwest of the NPS Visitor Center, built in the 1830s and serving a standard menu of burgers, sandwiches and seafood, with low prices and long hours: 9 am to 2 am daily.

### Getting There & Away

Lowell is at the end of the Lowell Connector, a spur road that goes north from MA 3 and I-495.

MBTA (☎ 617-722-3200, 800-392-6100) trains depart Boston's North Station for Lowell (45 minutes, fare $3.50) 21 times on weekdays, eight times a day on weekends.

### Getting Around

The Lowell Regional Transit Authority (☎ 978-452-6161) operates the bus system, including the Downtown Shuttle buses that link the Gallagher Transportation Terminal and the Downtown Transit Center.

# North Shore

The entire coast of Massachusetts Bay has a rich maritime history, but no part is richer than the shore north of Boston. Salem was among America's wealthiest ports in the 19th century; Marblehead is among New England's premier yachting ports today; and Gloucester is the region's – perhaps the nation's – most famous fishing port.

Trade and fishing brought wealth, which brought sumptuous houses and great collections of art and artifacts.

## Getting There & Around

MBTA Commuter Rail trains (☎ 617-722-3200, 800-392-6100, www.mbta.com) run from Boston's North Station to Salem (30 minutes, $2.50), Gloucester (one hour, $3.75) and Rockport (70 minutes, $4) on the Rockport Line about every 30 minutes during the morning and evening rush hours, hourly during the rest of day, with trains every two or three hours in the evening and on weekends (13 trains on weekdays, seven on Saturday and Sunday). Buy your ticket before you get on the train; there's a $2 surcharge to buy a ticket on the train during the time when tickets are being sold at the station.

If you're driving, note that street signage north of Boston is often confusing, making it easy to get lost here. Be prepared to ask the way.

## SALEM

To anyone familiar with New England's colonial history, this town's very name brings thoughts of witches and witchcraft. The famous Salem witch trials of 1692 are burned into the national memory, and Halloween (October 31) is this city's biggest holiday, with all lodgings booked a year in advance. Sadly, this short-lived and bizarre episode has obscured this beautiful city's true claim to fame: its glorious maritime history.

Today, Salem is a commuter suburb of Boston with some light industry, though not quite enough to make it wealthy. Visit Salem to take in its world-class Peabody Essex Museum, sumptuous 19th-century ship captains' and merchants' homes, the House of the Seven Gables (made famous in Hawthorne's novel of that name) and – particularly for children – some of the kitschy witch museums.

## History

Salem was established in 1626 by Roger Conant and a band of 20 hearty settlers. Within a century, Salem was a port of note and by 1762 it counted among its residents Elias Hasket Derby, America's first millionaire. Derby and his father, Captain Richard Derby, built the half-mile-long Derby Wharf, which is now the center of the Salem Maritime National Historic Site.

During the Revolutionary War, Salem's merchants fitted 158 vessels as privateers – private vessels that preyed on enemy shipping – and held the distinction of sinking or capturing more British ships than all the ships of all the other American ports combined.

After the war, the privateers went into trade. Their traditional British Empire ports abroad being closed to them, they were forced to sail further afield. Elias Derby's ship *Grand Turk* sailed around the Cape of Good Hope, the first Salem vessel to do so, reaching Canton in 1786. Many Salem vessels followed and soon also circumnavigated Cape Horn to the East Indies, China and India to bring back rich cargoes of spices, silks and porcelain.

In 1799, they founded the East India Marine Society to provide warehousing services and a central repository for their ships' logs and charts. The new company's charter required the establishment of 'a museum in which to house the natural and artificial curiosities' to be brought back by members' ships. The collection, grown to a half-million artifacts, was the basis of the Peabody Museum, now combined with the Essex Institute into the Peabody Essex Museum (see below).

Salem's golden age lasted until the mid-19th century, when New England clipper ships emerged onto the scene. These swift new ships that raced around the world – even carrying New England ice to tropical ports – needed harbors that were deeper than Salem's. As the tall masts gradually disappeared from Salem's harbor, the harbor silted up, ending a chapter in colonial and early American maritime history.

## Orientation

The main areas of interest in Salem are the Essex St Mall, a pedestrian way through the heart of historic Salem; Salem Common, adjoining the mall; and the Derby Wharf, a block away (see Salem Maritime National Historic Site, below). All are walkable. The train station is a five-minute walk from Essex St Mall.

MASSACHUSETTS

# SALEM

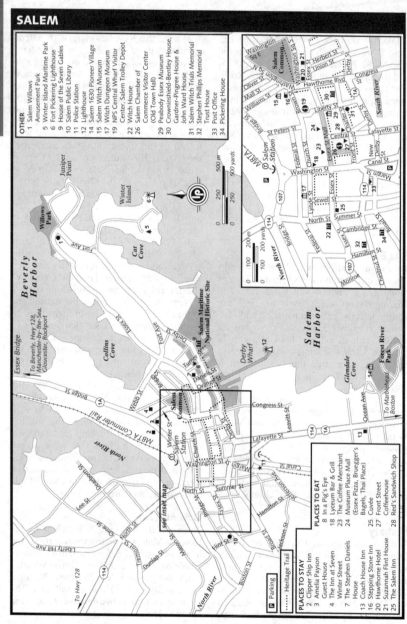

**OTHER**
1 Salem Willows Amusement Park
5 Winter Island Maritime Park
6 Fort Pickering Lighthouse
9 House of the Seven Gables
10 Salem Public Library
11 Police Station
12 Lighthouse
14 Salem 1630 Pioneer Village
15 Salem Witch Museum
17 Witch Dungeon Museum
19 NPS Central Wharf Visitor Center, Salem Trolley Depot
22 Witch House
26 Salem Chamber of Commerce Visitor Center (Old Town Hall)
29 Peabody Essex Museum
30 Crowninshield-Bentley House, Gardner-Pingree House & John Ward House
31 Salem Witch Trials Memorial
32 Stephen Phillips Memorial Trust House
33 Post Office
34 Pickering House

**PLACES TO STAY**
2 Clipper Ship Inn
3 Amelia Payson Guest House
4 The Inn at Seven Winter Street
7 The Stephen Daniels House
13 Coach House Inn
16 Stepping Stone Inn
20 Hawthorne Hotel
21 Suzannah Flint House
25 The Salem Inn

**PLACES TO EAT**
8 In a Pig's Eye
18 Lyceum Bar & Grill
23 The Coffee Merchant
24 Museum Place Mall (Essex Pizza, Bruegger's Bagels, Thai Place)
25 Cuvee
27 Front Street Coffeehouse
28 Red's Sandwich Shop

P Parking
····· Heritage Trail

The Heritage Trail is a 1.7-mile route connecting Salem's major historic sites. Follow the red line painted on the sidewalk.

## Information

The Salem Chamber of Commerce (☎ 508-744-0004, www.salem-chamber.org), at 32 Derby Square, in the Old Town Hall building on Essex St Mall, has a visitors' center open 9 am to 5 pm weekdays. The Salem Office of Business Development & Tourism (☎ 800-777-6848, fax 978-741-7539, SalemMA@cove.com) can also provide you information.

The NPS Visitor Center (☎ 978-744-4323, 741-3648 on weekends), 2 Liberty St, is open 9 am to 6 pm daily.

The North of Boston Convention and Visitors Bureau (☎ 978-977-7760, 800-742-5306, www.northofboston.org), 17 Peabody Square, Peabody, MA 01960, also offers printed materials and can answer questions.

## Peabody Essex Museum

The treasure trove of art, artifacts and curiosities brought back from the Far East by ships out of Salem is housed in the Peabody Essex Museum (☎ 978-745-1876, 745-9500 for taped information, 800-745-4054, www.pem.org), on Essex St Mall at New Liberty St.

This is America's oldest private museum in continuous operation. It has expanded many times since it was first housed in East India Marine Hall in 1824.

The museum includes exhibits from New England's history, including clocks, ceramics, costumes, dolls and toys, military uniforms and weapons, lamps, lanterns and glassware. The town's maritime history is particularly well documented with ship captains' portraits, scale models and paintings of ships, 18th-century navigation instruments, scrimshaw (carved whalebone) and carved ships' figureheads. There's even a reproduction of the main cabin of *Cleopatra's Barge*, America's first oceangoing yacht, built in 1816 for a member of the East India Marine Society.

The Asian collections cover arts and crafts of peoples native to America, the Pacific Islands and East Asia, including porcelain, paintings, silver, furniture and other arts from China, Japan, Polynesia, Micronesia and Melanesia. The collection from pre-industrial Japan is rated the best in the world.

There are also exhibits on the natural history of Essex County. The Museum Café (☎ 978-740-4551) serves lunch and afternoon tea.

The museum is open 10 am to 5 pm daily (noon to 5 pm Sunday) but closed Monday from November through May. Admission costs $8.50 for adults, $7.50 seniors and college students, $6.50 children six to 18, $20 for families.

## Historic Houses

Salem's most famous house is the **House of the Seven Gables** (☎ 978-744-0991, www.7gables.org), 54 Turner St, made famous in Nathaniel Hawthorne's novel (1851) of that name. The novel brings to life the gloomy Puritan atmosphere of early New England and its effects on the people's psyches; the house does the same. It's open 10 am to 5 pm daily (in winter, Sunday hours are noon to 5 pm). Adults pay $7, seniors pay $6, children six to 17 pay $4. That fee allows entrance to the site's four historic buildings, the Gables Garden Café and luxuriant gardens on the waterfront.

Furnished in antiques, **Pickering House** (☎ 978-744-1647), 18 Broad St, is said to be the oldest house in the USA continuously occupied by the same family. It's open 10 am to 3 pm Monday and any other time by appointment, for $4.

House-lovers should also seek out Chestnut St, which, with its beautiful homes, is among the most architecturally lovely streets in the country. It's a block south of western Essex St.

The **Stephen Phillips Memorial Trust House** (☎ 978-744-0440), 34 Chestnut St, is decorated with the family furnishings of Salem sea captains and includes a collection of antique carriages and cars. Visit from late May through mid-October 10 am to 4:30 pm (last tour at 4 pm); closed Sunday. Adults pay $3, seniors, students and youth $2, under six free.

The tour at the **Gardner-Pingree House** (1804) and at the **Crowninshield-Bentley House** (1727) is entitled 'At Home in Salem: 1780-1820.' At the **John Ward House** (1684) it's 'Salem 1692: The Witchcraft Trials.' All three historic houses are operated by the Peabody Essex Museum (see above) and are open 10 am to 5 pm (till 8 pm Friday, noon to 5 pm Sunday). Adults pay $7.50, seniors and students $6.50, children $4, a family $18. Buy tickets at the museum.

## Salem Maritime National Historic Site

The Custom House on Derby Wharf is the centerpiece of this national historic site (☎ 978-740-1660). The Central Wharf Visitor Center is the first place for visitors to go. The

---

## Salem Witch Trials

In the late 17th century, it was widely believed that one could make a pact with the devil in order to gain evil powers to be used against one's enemies. Thousands had been found guilty of witchcraft in Europe in previous centuries. The judges of the Massachusetts Bay Colony had tried 44 persons for witchcraft (hanging three of them) before 1692.

The Reverend Cotton Mather, one of the colony's most fiery preachers, had added his own book on witchcraft to the already considerable literature on the subject. In March 1692, a girl named Betty Parris, who lived in what is now Danvers, and her cousin Abigail began acting strangely. Other children copied their bizarre antics, and their parents came to believe that 'the Devil' had come to their village. (More likely, the girls got hold of a copy of Reverend Mather's book, read how the 'possessed' were thought to behave and acted it out.)

Partly as a prank, they accused a slave named Tituba of being a witch. The accused, a half-black, half-Indian woman, 'confessed' under torture and accused two other women of being accomplices in order to save her own life. Soon, the accusations flew thick and fast as the accused confessed to riding broomsticks, having sex with the devil and participating in witches' sabbaths. They implicated others in attempts to save themselves. The girls, afraid of being discovered as fakes, kept the accusations coming.

Governor Phips appointed a special court to deal with the accusations, but its justices saw fit to accept 'spectral evidence' (evidence of 'spirits' seen only by the witness). With imaginations, superstitions and religious passions enflamed, the situation soon careened out of control.

By September 1692, 156 people stood accused, 55 people had pleaded guilty and implicated others to save their own lives, and 14 women and five men who would not 'confess' to witchcraft had been hung. Giles Corey, who refused to plead either guilty or not guilty, was pressed to death, and at least four people died in jail of disease.

The frenzy died down when the accusers began pointing at prominent merchants, clergy and even the governor's wife. With the powers-that-be in jeopardy, the trials were called off, the jails were opened and the remaining accused were released. Judges and witnesses confessed to having been misled or having used bad judgment, and the families of many victims were compensated for the injustice.

This cautionary tale of justice gone awry and innocents sacrificed to popular hysteria came powerfully to mind in the 1950s during Senator Joseph R McCarthy's destructive career of ill-considered condemnation and character destruction.

Salem never had any witches. The Salem Witch Trials Memorial, a modest monument off Charter St, honors the innocents who died. If their spirits linger here, however, the pervasive 'witch' commercialism and the circus atmosphere of Halloween that today capitalize on the tragedy of 1692 are hardly a fitting epitaph.

site is open 9 am to 6 pm in summer, 9 am to 5 pm in winter, and admission is free.

Nathaniel Hawthorne, a Salem native, was surveyor of the port from 1846 to 1849. Other buildings at the site include the Government Bonded Warehouse, containing cargoes typical of the trade in 1819; the Scale House; West India Goods Store, a working store with many items similar to those sold two centuries ago; Derby House, home of the famous shipping family; Hawkes House, used as a privateer prize warehouse during the Revolutionary War; Narbonne-Hale House, a more modest house owned by artisans and their families; and the lighthouse on Derby Wharf.

## Witchcraft Sights

The tragic events of 1692 have proved a boon to modern operators of witch-related attractions.

Most authentic of the witchy sites is the **Witch House** (☎ 978-744-0180), 310½ Essex St, operated by Salem's Parks and Recreation Department. This was the home of Magistrate Jonathan Corwin, where some preliminary examinations of persons accused of witchcraft were held. It's open 10 am to 4:30 pm (until 6 pm in July and August); closed from December through mid-March. Adults pay $5, seniors $4, children $2.

The **Salem Witch Museum** (☎ 978-744-1692), 19½ Washington Square North, is on Brown St at Hawthorne Blvd. The church-like building holds dioramas, exhibits, audio-visual shows and costumed staff who help you to understand the witchcraft scare. It's open 10 am to 5 pm (until 7 pm in July and August), for $5 for adults, $4.50 seniors, $3 children six to 14.

The **Witch Dungeon Museum** (☎ 978-741-3570), 16 Lynde St, stages re-creations of a witch trial based on historical transcripts. It's open 10 am to 5 pm daily April through November. Adults pay $5, seniors $4, children $3.

## Parks

Salem Common is the broad green space at the town center next to the Hawthorne Hotel. On the west side of the common is Washington Square, marked by the dramatic, brooding statue of Roger Conant (1592-1679), Salem's first settler. If you look closely at 'The Puritan,' as it's usually known, you'll see a number of bullet holes in its bronze skirts.

Less than 2 miles northeast of Salem center is Salem Willows Amusement Park (☎ 978-745-0251), at 171 Fort Ave, with beaches, children's rides and games and harbor cruises. Just south of it is Winter Island Maritime Park, the site of Fort Pickering and its lighthouse, now a public park and campground (see below).

Forest River Park, on West St less than 2 miles south of the center, has beaches, picnic areas and a saltwater swimming pool, as well as **Salem 1630** (☎ 978-744-0991), a replicated Puritan village of the 1600s with costumed interpreters, period buildings, gardens, crafts and animals.

## Places to Stay

A number of the lodging-places described below have web pages, which can be found at www.salemweb.com.

**Camping** *Winter Island Maritime Park* (☎ 978-745-9430, 50 Winter Island Rd), less than 2 miles east of the center of town, is open May through October and has space for 25 tents ($15) and 30 RVs ($18 with electricity). Call them to reserve your space in advance.

**Motels & Hotels** The *Clipper Ship Inn* (☎ 978-745-8022, 40 Bridge St (MA 1A)) has 60 motel rooms for $78 to $99.

The 130-room *Days Inn Boston-Salem* (☎ 978-777-1030, 800-325-2525, 152 Endicott St), in Danvers, is 4 miles from the center of Salem on MA 114 on the northwest side of MA 128 (take exit 24). Rooms with one queen-size bed and light breakfast cost $69 single, $79 double.

Salem's centerpiece is the *Hawthorne Hotel* (☎ 978-744-4080, 800-729-7829, fax 978-745-9842, 18 Washington Square West), at the corner of Hawthorne Blvd and Essex St, right next to the common. This historic (1920s) full-service hotel charges $135 to

$212 for its 89 double rooms, with discounts of 8% to 10% off-season. For dining, there's Nathaniel's, the formal restaurant serving New American cuisine, and the informal Tavern on the Green.

**Inns & B&Bs** Salem has at least 10 nice B&Bs charging from $85 to $200 a night in summer. All are nonsmoking, include breakfast, and virtually all rooms have direct-dial phones and cable TVs.

*The Stephen Daniels House (☎ 978-744-5709, 1 Daniels St)*, at Essex St, two blocks north of the waterfront, must be Salem's oldest lodging, with parts dating from 1667 – before the witch trials – and many period antiques. Several of the four bedrooms adjoin, making them perfect for families, two couples or small groups. Mrs Katherine Gill, the proprietor, charges $85 to $95 single, $115 to $125 double, non-taxable. Be sure to call for reservations.

*Amelia Payson Guest House (☎ 978-744-8304, 16 Winter St)* is within walking distance of Salem's sights and has all the comforts for $95 to $115 double with private bath.

*Stepping Stone Inn (☎ 978-741-8900, 800-338-3022, 19 Washington Square North)*, just off Salem Common facing the statue of Roger Conant, is the beautifully restored house built for naval officer Benjamin True in 1846. Its eight rooms with bath now rent for $80 to $130.

*Suzannah Flint House (☎ 978-744-5281, 888-752-5281, 98 Essex St)* is a beautiful old 1808 Federal house just off Salem Common, with private baths and prices of $80 to $120 double.

*The Inn at Seven Winter Street (☎ 978-745-9520, 800-932-5547, 7 Winter St)* is an 1870 Second Empire Victorian mansion about four blocks from the center. The seven rooms, priced at $95 to $135 double, have private baths, and a few have kitchens.

*The Salem Inn (☎ 978-741-0680, 800-446-2995, 7 Summer St)* offers a variety of accommodations in three historic houses, including the Captain West House, a large brick sea captain's home built in 1834, which now also holds the inn's restaurant; the Curwen House, dating from 1854; and the Peabody House (1874). Double rooms with bath are priced at $129 to $185, with a light breakfast and all the conveniences. There are more expensive Jacuzzi-equipped rooms and suites as well.

The *Coach House Inn (☎ 978-744-4092, 800-688-8689, fax 978-745-8031, 284 Lafayette St)* is about a mile south of the center on MA 1A/114. Built in 1879, its 11 rooms (nine with bath) cost $85 to $135 double.

## Places to Eat

If you're visiting Salem on a day trip, you might just want a sandwich. Try *Red's Sandwich Shop (☎ 978-745-3527, 15 Central St)*, in the old London Coffee House building (1698), with sandwiches and breakfast plates from $2 to $5, hot meals from $6 to $9.

For a blast of gourmet java, it's *The Coffee Merchant (☎ 978-744-1729, 196 Essex St)*, which opens at 7 am weekdays (10 am weekends), serving espresso, lattes, scones and bagels. Also try the *Front Street Coffeehouse (☎ 978-740-6697, 20 Front St)*, currently the cool place for hot joe. Sandwiches are served 11 am to 4 pm.

The *Museum Place Mall (2 East India Square)*, just west of the Peabody Essex Museum along Essex St, has several breakfast and quick-lunch places, including *Essex Pizza*, *Bruegger's Bagels* and the *Thai Place (☎ 978-741-8008)*, where a big plate of regular or vegetarian pad Thai costs $7 and full meals are $10 to $25 per person.

Salem's all-purpose eatery is the historic *Lyceum Bar & Grill (☎ 978-745-7665, 43 Church St)*. A varied menu of luncheon sandwiches, salads and main courses carries prices from $6 to $9; at dinner, hearty traditional main-course favorites with New American accents cost $15 to $23.

*In a Pig's Eye (☎ 978-741-4436, 148 Derby St)*, at Daniels, is a funky place with an eclectic menu of Greek salads, vegetarian dishes, pastas and many steak, chicken and seafood main courses priced below $14. Monday and Tuesday are Mexican nights, and there's live entertainment most evenings (no dinner on Sunday).

*Cuvée (☎ 978-744-0777, 7 Summer St)*, inside the Salem Inn's Captain West House, serves dinners of New American cuisine in elegant surroundings. It's open nightly, except Monday, for $30 to $40 per person.

## Getting There & Away

See Getting There & Around at the beginning of the North Shore section for train information. The MBTA buses (450 or 455) from Boston's Haymarket Square (near North Station) take longer than the train and cost no less.

Salem lies 20 miles northeast of Boston, a 35-minute drive if it's not rush hour. From Boston, follow US 1 north across the Mystic River (Tobin) Bridge and bear right onto MA 16 (Revere Beach Parkway) toward Revere Beach, then follow MA 1A (Shore Rd) north through Saugus, Lynn (Lynnway) and Swampscott to Salem. The MA 1A becomes Lafayette St in Salem and takes you right to Essex St Mall and the common.

Coming from MA 128, take exit 25A and follow MA 114 east, which becomes North St, which intersects with Essex St.

## Getting Around

The Salem Trolley (☎ 978-744-5469), at 8 Central St, runs a figure-eight route past 14 of the town's places of interest with a running commentary, departing on the hour 10 am to 4 pm (last departure) daily. July through October, departures are on the hour and half hour. Your ticket ($8 for adults, $7 seniors, $4 children five to 12, $20 families) is good all day, so you can hop on and off as you like.

## MARBLEHEAD

First settled in 1629, Marblehead's Old Town is a picturesque New England maritime village with winding streets, brightly painted colonial and early-American houses, and sleek yachts bobbing at anchor in its well-sheltered harbor. As the great number of boats indicates, this is the North Shore's premier yachting port, and indeed one of New England's choicest moorings.

It has been so for a long time. Incorporated in 1649, citizens of Marblehead boast that their town was the 'birthplace of the navy' because the Marblehead schooner

*Hannah* (1775) was the first ship to be commissioned by General George Washington in the Revolutionary War.

Marblehead makes a fine day trip from Boston. Wander its narrow streets, admire its historic houses, have a picnic overlooking the ocean in one of its parks, and Marblehead will stay with you for years afterward.

## Orientation

You pass through the modern districts of Marblehead along Pleasant St (MA 114) on the way to the Marblehead Historic District, called Old Town, with its network of narrow, winding streets, many of them one-way. The small directional signs sometimes help, but Old Town is difficult to negotiate by car. Parking is usually a problem in summer, particularly on weekends, so it's best to find a legal parking place inland from the waterfront and explore the town on foot.

Washington St, State St and Mugford St intersect at an open space that is the nearest thing Marblehead's Old Town has to a main square. It's marked by the Old Town House, once the town hall.

Heading southeast of the Old Town House along Washington and State Sts brings you to the State Street Landing, the town's main dock, with views across the harbor to the grand houses on Marblehead Neck. Marblehead Neck is a wooded island east of the town center. It's connected to the mainland by the Ocean Ave causeway.

## Information

The Marblehead Chamber of Commerce (☎ 781-631-2868, fax 639-8582) maintains an information booth on MA 114 (Pleasant St), corner of Essex and Spring Sts. Look for it on the right-hand side as you approach Old Town and pick up a copy of their walking tour brochure and map. The chamber's business office (which serves as its information office during the winter) is in the old Masonic Lodge at 62 Pleasant St, Marblehead, MA 01945, beside the bank.

## Things to See & Do

Every American is familiar with *The Spirit of '76*, the patriotic painting (circa 1876)

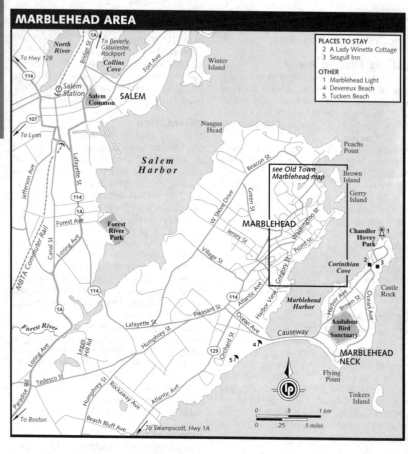

## MARBLEHEAD AREA

PLACES TO STAY
2  A Lady Winette Cottage
3  Seagull Inn

OTHER
1  Marblehead Light
4  Devereux Beach
5  Tuckers Beach

by Archibald M Willard. It depicts three Revolutionary War figures – a drummer, a fife-player and a flag bearer. The painting hangs in the Selectmen's meeting room in the red-brick Marblehead **Abbott Hall** (☎ 781-631-0000), home of the Marblehead Historical Commission on Washington St (look for the lofty clock tower). The painting, as well as the deed given by Marblehead's Native American residents to its European settlers in 1694 and several marine life exhibits, are all on view for free 8 am to 5 pm weekdays, with extended hours from June to October: until 8 pm on Wednesday, 1 to 6 pm weekends, 11 am to 6 pm holidays.

The Georgian **Jeremiah Lee Mansion** (☎ 781-631-1069), near the corner of Hooper and Washington Sts, was built on the order of a prominent merchant in 1768. It is now a museum with period furnishings and collections of toys and children's furniture, folk art and nautical and military artifacts. It's open 10 am to 4 pm (1 to 4 pm Sunday) mid-May through October. Adults pay $4, seniors and students $3, under 10 free.

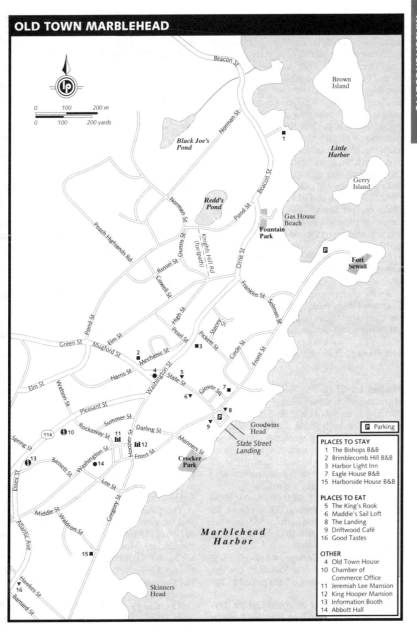

# OLD TOWN MARBLEHEAD

Beacon St

Brown Island

Norman St

Black Joe's Pond

Little Harbor

Gerry Island

Beacon St

Redd's Pond

Pond St

Gas House Beach

Fountain Park

Fort Sewall

Peach Highlands Rd

Norman St

Dunns St

Knights Hill Rd (footpath)

Russel St

Cowell St

Ocine St

Franklin St

Selman St

High St

Pearl St

Elm St

Green St

Mugford St

Pickett St

Steeger St

Circle St

Front St

Pond St

Mechanic St

Harris St

Washington St

State St

Glover Sq

2

3

4

5

6

7

8

9

Elm St

Watson St

Pleasant St

Summer St

Rockaway St

Darling St

Mariners St

Goodwins Head

State Street Landing

P   Parking

114

10

11

12

Hooper St

Front St

Crocker Park

Spring St

Bassett St

Washington St

13

14

Essex St

Middle St

Waldron St

Gregory St

Lee St

Marblehead Harbor

Atlantic Ave

15

Hawkes St

16

Barnard St

Skinners Head

**PLACES TO STAY**
1 The Bishops B&B
2 Brimblecomb Hill B&B
3 Harbor Light Inn
7 Eagle House B&B
15 Harborside House B&B

**PLACES TO EAT**
5 The King's Rook
6 Maddie's Sail Loft
8 The Landing
9 Driftwood Café
16 Good Tastes

**OTHER**
4 Old Town House
10 Chamber of Commerce Office
11 Jeremiah Lee Mansion
12 King Hooper Mansion
13 Information Booth
14 Abbott Hall

The **King Hooper Mansion** (☎ 781-631-2608), 8 Hooper St, more or less across the street from the Jeremiah Lee Mansion, is the home of the Marblehead Arts Association. The historic 1728 house holds four floors of exhibit space, with shows changing monthly. Hours are 10 am to 4 pm (1 to 4 pm Sunday). Exhibits are free (donations are accepted); the house tour costs $1.

Old Town is perfect for a morning's or afternoon's strolling, cafe-sitting, window-shopping, photo-snapping and picnicking.

A block west of State Street Landing, **Crocker Park** has fine views of the harbor and excellent picnic possibilities.

At the eastern end of Front St, the earthworks of **Fort Sewall** also provide a prime venue for picnics. The fort, built in the 17th century, was strengthened during the Revolutionary War and is now a park.

On Marblehead Neck's Ocean Ave is an **Audubon Bird Sanctuary** (access is on the southwest side via Risley St).

At the eastern end of Marblehead Neck, **Chandler Hovey Park**, by Marblehead Light, has marvelous views in all directions.

On the southeastern side of Marblehead Neck, a short walk takes you to **Castle Rock**, with views of open ocean and welcome cool breezes on hot days.

## Places to Stay

Marblehead has two dozen small B&Bs charging from $60 with shared bath to $125 with private bath for a double room; the higher prices are for weekend stays. None have more than a few rooms, so reservations are essential. If you have no luck finding a room, or if you want different accommodations, stay in Salem. Try the following.

*Brimblecomb Hill B&B* (☎ 781-631-6366 daytime, 631-3172 evenings, 33 Mechanic St) has a room with shared bath for $65, another with private bath for $85 and a private entrance for guests.

*A Lady Winette Cottage* (☎ 781-631-8579, 3 Corinthian Lane) is a Victorian cottage with two rooms sharing a bath priced at $80 to $90.

*The Bishops Bed & Breakfast* (☎ 781-631-4954, fax 631-2102, 10 Harding Lane) is right on the water and charges $85 to $135 for its three rooms, with a two-night minimum on weekends.

*Eagle House B&B* (☎ 781-631-1532, 800-572-7335, 96R Front St and 6½ Merritt St) has two suites with sitting room, kitchenette and separate entrance for $125.

*Harbor Light Inn* (☎ 781-631-2186, 58 Washington St) is Marblehead's 'big' hostelry, with 20 rooms priced from $125 to $245. All have private baths, while 11 have working fireplaces and five have Jacuzzis. There's a heated pool as well.

*Harborside House B&B* (☎ 781-631-1032, 23 Gregory St) has two rooms with shared bath for $80.

*Seagull Inn* (☎ 781-631-1893, fax 631-3535, host@seagullinn.com, 106 Harbor Ave), on Marblehead Neck, has luxury suites with kitchenettes, air-conditioning and ocean views for $150 to $200.

## Places to Eat

For picnic supplies – fresh breads, baked goods, take-out sandwiches and main courses – head for *Good Tastes* (☎ 781-639-2897, 32 Atlantic Ave), open daily 7 am to 8 pm (Friday and Saturday until 10 pm).

Four eateries are right near State Street Landing. The most prominent is appropriately named *The Landing* (☎ 781-631-1878, 81 Front St), a full-service restaurant and pub with a long menu (plenty of seafood) and a variety of dining spaces inside and out. Lunches cost $10 to $18, dinners $20 to $40.

Across the parking lot, the inexpensive *Driftwood Cafe* (☎ 781-631-1145, 63 Front St) is a Marblehead fixture, serving hearty mariners' breakfasts to early risers starting at 5:30 am. It closes after lunch at 2 pm (open in summer until 5 pm).

The place for the yachting crowd to see and be seen is *Maddie's Sail Loft* (☎ 781-631-9824, 15 State St), a block inland from the landing. Moderately priced food (sandwiches for $5, fish and chips for $10, lobster pie for $16) is served Monday to Saturday, but the main attractions in this pub are the beverages.

*The King's Rook* (☎ 781-631-9838, 12 State St) is a cafe and wine bar good for a cup of joe while reading the news, or a light lunch or dinner of pizza, pastry, soup and salad, sandwich or rich dessert. Pizzas are priced from $5 to $7, sandwiches, salads and main-course platters from $4 to $7. They serve wine by the glass, specialty beers and liqueurs. It's open noon to 11:30 pm; closed Monday evening.

Another good place for coffee drinks, pastries or a light meal is **Caffe Appassion-ato** (☎ 781-639-3200, 12 Atlantic Ave). Read their newspapers or use their chess- or checkerboards. They open at 6 am on week-days, 7 am on weekends, and stay open until 10 or 11 pm.

### Getting There & Away
From Salem, follow MA 114 southeast 4 miles to Marblehead, where it becomes Pleasant St.

MBTA buses No 441/442 and 448/449 run between Boston's Haymarket Square (near North Station) and Marblehead.

See Getting There & Around at the beginning of the North Shore section for information on MBTA trains to neighboring Salem. From Salem's train station, you can take a taxi to Marblehead.

## GLOUCESTER
Founded in 1623, just three years after the colony at Plymouth, Gloucester is among New England's oldest towns. To Americans, it's synonymous with fishing. It was founded by fisherfolk and until the early 1990s, it made its living at fishing.

But overfishing, by both the boats out of Gloucester and those of other nations, imperiled New England's fish stock. Strict government limits on catches in 1994, fol-lowed by the closing of most of the once-rich fishing grounds in 1995, dealt Gloucester a terrible economic blow. In only two years, up to 20,000 fishermen found themselves out of full-time work.

Gloucester's industrious workers are presently reinventing the town's economy. The big fish-processing plants are converting to process seafood brought in from other regions, and there's an active search for new industries.

You can still see fishing boats, festooned with big nets and winches, motoring into Gloucester Harbor with clouds of hungry seagulls circling above, but it will be a long time before the once-rich fishing grounds of Georges Bank teem with fish again – if they ever do.

### Orientation
Washington St runs from Grant Circle (a rotary out on MA 128) into the center of Gloucester at St Peter's Square, an irregular brick plaza overlooking the sea. Rogers St, the waterfront road, goes east from the plaza; Main St, the business and shopping thoroughfare, is one block inland.

East Gloucester, with the Rocky Neck artists' colony, is on the southeastern side of Gloucester Harbor.

### Information
The office for the Cape Ann Chamber of Commerce (☎ 978-283-1601, 800-321-0133, www.gloucesterma.com), 33 Commercial St, Gloucester, MA 01930, provides informa-tion and maps. Look for it just to the south of St Peter's Square.

In summer, a visitors' information office is open in Stage Fort Park, on the west side of the Annisquam River up the hill (follow the signs). Browse www.cape-ann.com as well.

### Walking Tour
The town has organized a Maritime Trail that you can follow using a brochure from the chamber of commerce or by following signs posted around town. Highlights are the Harbor Cove, Inner Harbor, Fish Pier and Leonarde Craske's famous statue, *The Gloucester Fisherman*, often called 'The Man at the Wheel.' The statue is dedicated to 'They That Go Down to the Sea in Ships, 1623-1923.'

### Rocky Neck Artists' Colony
Cape Ann's natural beauty and seaside visual interest have attracted artists for at least a century. The narrow peninsula of Rocky Neck, jutting into Gloucester Harbor from East Gloucester, offers some of the

MASSACHUSETTS

# CAPE ANN (GLOUCESTER & ROCKPORT)

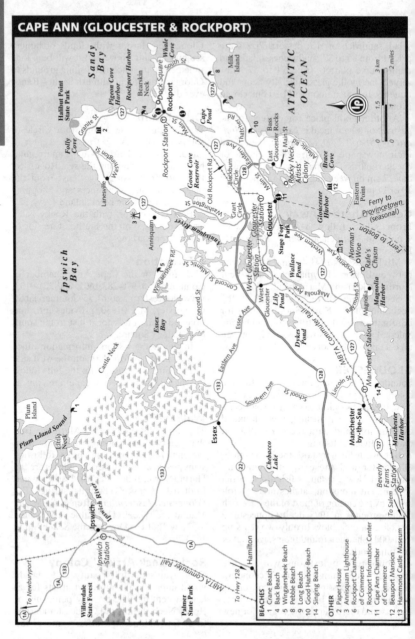

**BEACHES**
1  Crane Beach
4  Back Beach
5  Wingaersheek Beach
8  Pebble Beach
9  Long Beach
10  Good Harbor Beach
14  Singing Beach

**OTHER**
2  Paper House
3  Annisquam Lighthouse
6  Rockport Chamber
    of Commerce
7  Rockport Information Center
11  Cape Ann Chamber
    of Commerce
12  Beauport Mansion
13  Hammond Castle Museum

best views. Between the world wars, artists began renting little seaside shacks from local fishermen, which they used as studios. Today many of these same shanties, considerably gentrified, are quaint galleries displaying the work of local artists.

Follow Main St east and south around the northeastern end of Gloucester Harbor to East Gloucester. Turn onto Rocky Neck Ave and park in the lot on the right (parking farther on in the village proper is nearly impossible in high summer). Parking violation tickets are handed out early and often.

It's only a five-minute walk from the parking lot to the galleries and restaurants. Stroll along enjoying the view, poke your head into a gallery or two, then stop for refreshments at one of the restaurants overlooking Smith Cove (see Places to Eat).

### Beauport Mansion
Beauport (☎ 978-283-0800), the Sleeper-McCann mansion at 75 Eastern Point Blvd on Eastern Point, East Gloucester, is a lavish 'summer cottage' constructed between 1907 and 1934 by Henry Davis Sleeper. Its builder, a prominent interior designer and collector of antiques, worked to make his fantasy palace a showplace of American decor. He toured New England in search of houses about to be demolished and bought up selected elements from each: wood paneling, architectural elements and furniture. In place of unity, Sleeper created a wildly eclectic but artistically surprising – and satisfying – place to live.

Now in the care of the Society for the Preservation of New England Antiquities, Beauport is open to visitors 10 am to 4 pm weekdays from mid-May to mid-October, and also 10 am to 4 pm weekends from mid-September to mid-October. Admission costs $6 for adults, $5.50 for seniors and $3 for children six to 12. Beauport also holds afternoon teas, evening concerts and other special events. Call for schedules.

### Hammond Castle Museum
Dr John Hays Hammond, Jr (1888-1965) was an electrical engineer whose inventions were important to the development of

*The Gloucester Fisherman*, symbol of a once-thriving trade

radar, sonar and radio remote-control systems, including torpedo guidance. Despite his genius with electrical things, it was not Dr John, but rather Laurens Hammond (unrelated), who invented the electric organ.

Defense contracts filled his bank account, and with this wealth Dr Hammond pursued his passion for collecting European art and architecture. His eccentric home is an odd castle of four sections, each epitomizing a period in European history: Romanesque, Medieval, Gothic and Renaissance. Furnishings, including an 8200-pipe organ in the Romanesque Great Hall, are eclectic, quirky, at times beautiful and at other times gimcrackery or even macabre.

The museum (☎ 978-283-7673) is open 10 am to 5 pm daily from late May through October; open 10 am to 4 pm weekends only from November to late May. The 45-minute guided tour costs $6 for adults, $5 for seniors and college students, $4 for children four to 12. For the schedule of concerts and special programs, call ☎ 978-283-2080.

Hammond Castle overlooks several natural features famous in literature. **Rafe's Chasm** is a cleft in the rocky shoreline that is characterized by turgid and thrashing water. Near it is **Norman's Woe**, the reef on which the ship broke up in Longfellow's poem 'The Wreck of the Hesperus.'

## Beaches

Gloucester has several excellent beaches that draw thousands of Boston-area sun and sea worshippers on any hot day in July or August. (See also Ipswich, later.)

**Wingaersheek Beach** Perhaps biggest and best of all is Wingaersheek Beach, a wide swath of sand on Ipswich Bay by the Annisquam River. At low tide, a long sandbar stretches for more than a half mile out into the bay. At its tip, you have a fine view of the Annisquam lighthouse.

On weekends and very hot days in July and August, plan to arrive by mid-morning at the latest. The parking lot fills up by then, and latecomers are turned away. To get there, take the Concord St exit from MA 128 (the exit just before the Grant Circle rotary). Follow Concord St north for several miles, turning at the sign.

Admission costs $15 per car on weekends, $10 on weekdays. There are showers, toilets and refreshments available. If you come too late and the parking lot is full, retrace your route. Several homeowners on the way to the beach rent parking space on their front lawns on busy weekends. The beach is closed at sunset.

**Good Harbor Beach** Another large beach is Good Harbor, east of East Gloucester off MA 127A on the way to Rockport. Fees, facilities and parking policies are similar to those at Wingaersheek Beach. On hot days and weekends, make sure you come early to avoid disappointment.

**Long & Pebble Beaches** A short distance farther east and north along MA 127A are two smaller beaches, Long Beach and Pebble Beach, in the neighboring town of Rockport.

**Stage Fort Park Beach** There is a small, but usually uncrowded, beach down the hill in Stage Fort Park, off Western Ave on the west side of Gloucester. Parking costs $10, but you can park for free on Western Ave; it's a 10-minute walk over the hill to the beach.

## Whale-Watching Cruises

Gloucester has a particularly good selection of whale-watching cruise boats. If you have not yet gone out in search of the denizen behemoths, you can do it here. See 'The New Whalers' boxed text, below.

Cruises out of Gloucester cost about $25 for adults, $20 seniors, $15 for children under 16. You can sometimes find discount coupons at the chamber of commerce or in local publications. Here are some companies:

Cape Ann Whale Watch (☎ 978-283-5110, 800-877-5110) Rose's Wharf, 415 Main St (PO Box 345). Sailings are accompanied by naturalists from the Whale Conservation Institute and depart from Rose's Wharf, east of Gloucester center (on the way to East Gloucester).

Capt Bill & Sons Whale Watch (☎ 978-283-6995, 800-339-4253) 33 Harbor Loop, behind Captain Carlo's Seafood Market & Restaurant. Capt Bill's cruises feature naturalists from the Cetacean Research Unit, Inc.

Seven Seas Whale Watch (☎ 978-283-1776, 800-238-1776) Rogers St (MA 127). Seven Seas vessels depart from Rogers St in the center of Gloucester, between St Peter's Square and the Gloucester House Restaurant. The cruises are narrated by naturalists from the Marine Education Center of Cape Ann.

Yankee Whale Watch (☎ 978-283-0313, 800-942-5464) 75 W Essex Ave (MA 133). The Yankee fleet carries naturalists from the Atlantic Cetacean Research Center. Boats leave from the dock next door to the Gull Restaurant on MA 133 (MA 128 exit 14).

## Special Events

Gloucester's St Peter's Festival, held on a weekend in late June, brings a carnival to St Peter's Square with rides, snacks, musical performances and special events such as a greased-pole-climbing competition and boat races. The main event is the procession through the streets of a statue of St Peter, patron saint of fishermen. Customarily, the cardinal of the Catholic Archdiocese of Boston attends to bless the fishing fleet.

Gloucester's Fourth of July parade takes place on the evening of July 3 and is called the Fishtown Horribles Parade. By tradition, children dress up in fanciful costumes (from horrible to humorous) and march, hoping to win a prize for the best. Politicians and local businesses enter floats, and various bands perform.

## Places to Stay

**Camping** *Camp Annisquam Campground* (☎ 978-283-2992), at Stanwood Point in West Gloucester, has 35 tent and trailer sites going for $18 in high summer. *Cape Ann Campsite* (☎ 978-283-8683, 80 Atlantic St), in Gloucester, has 300 sites priced at $17, or $20 with hookups.

**Motels & Hotels** *Anchorage Inn* (☎ 978-283-4788, 5-7 Hawthorne Lane), in East Gloucester, is two new buildings in traditional style in a great location: close to Rocky Neck, walking distance to the beach and quietly off E Main St. Many rooms ($70 to $115) have balconies with harbor views; the most expensive have kitchenettes.

Follow Eastern Point Ave until it becomes Atlantic Rd to find several sea-view motels. Most of these have a large old mansion as the office and dining room, with guest rooms (priced from $85 to $185) built into new motel-type units facing the sea. Prices depend on the size of the room, number of beds, other amenities and views. Most of these motels close from December through March.

There's the *Ocean View Resort & Inn* (☎ 978-283-6200, 800-315-7557, 171 Atlantic Rd); the *Atlantis Motor Inn* (☎ 978-283-0014, 125 Atlantic Rd); the *Bass Rocks Ocean Inn* (☎ 978-283-7600, 800-528-1234, 103 Atlantic Rd); and the *Back Shore Motor Lodge* (☎ 978-283-1198, 85 Atlantic Rd).

## Places to Eat

**Downtown Gloucester** For a snack, grab a slab of pizza ($1.50) and some cookies at *Virgilio's Italian Bakery* (☎ 978-283-5295,

29 Main St). This is also a good place for picnic supplies. Across the street, *Valentino's* (☎ 978-283-6186, 38 Main St), at Short St, serves whole pizzas for $9.25 to $15 and pasta plates for $7 to $9.25. *Mike's Pastry & Coffee Shop* (☎ 978-283-5333, 37 Main St) has excellent Italian pastries and, in summer, cooling lemon ice. *Café Sicilia* (☎ 978-283-7345, 40 Main St), at Short St, has Italian pastries and also good, strong espresso.

*Halibut Point Restaurant & Pub* (☎ 978-281-1900, 289 Main St) is an authentic Gloucester tavern with good food and drink at reasonable prices. Patronized mostly by locals, it serves chowder, sandwiches and burgers ($5 to $10), lunch and dinner plates ($9 to $13) in cozy, congenial surroundings. It's open daily 11:30 am to 11:30 pm.

*Captain Carlo's Seafoods* (☎ 978-283-6342), on the street called Harbor Loop right on the water, is a seafood market with some picnic tables inside and some on a seaside deck. Seafood salads, cakes and fried fish are fresh and low-priced at $4 to $9, lobster a bit more. The huge fisherman's platter goes for $13.

*Jalapeño's* (☎ 978-283-8228, 86 Main St) has authentic, tasty Mexican food at decent prices. Try the *pollo con mole* or a cactus salad followed by the shrimp chipotle (shrimp in a spicy sauce). Full lunches cost $11 to $17, dinners $20 to $30.

*The Gull* (☎ 978-281-6060, 75 Essex Ave (MA 133)) is a bit out of the way in West Gloucester but is worth the trip. It's a bright, upbeat place with large windows overlooking a busy marina. Seafood is the strong point, from excellent lobster rolls ($10) to grilled tuna and swordfish steaks and clambakes ($14 to $24). There's a bar popular with locals.

*Blackburn Tavern* (☎ 978-282-1919, 2 Main St), at the corner of Washington St, is an upscale tavern with a varied bar menu of sandwiches ($5 to $8), main courses ($9 to $13) and, of course, drinks.

For elegant dining, the *White Rainbow* (☎ 978-281-0017, 65 Main St) serves dinner every day in a cozy brick-lined basement dining room. The menu lists the classic main courses – steak, roast duckling, rack of lamb, grilled shrimp – but the appetizers are more adventurous. Dinner costs $38 to $50.

**Rocky Neck** Parking is tight on E Main St and Rocky Neck Ave, so allow a bit of time to find a place.

*The Studio* (☎ *978-283-4123, 51 Rocky Neck Ave*) is great for lunch or a light dinner or a drink on the deck overlooking the harbor. It's the epicenter of the Rocky Neck dating scene, with a young crowd and a good band. Almost everything on the menu is under $12, and though the drinks are expensive, the view and ambience are worth it.

Just down the street is *The Rudder* (☎ *978-283-7967, 73 Rocky Neck Ave*), known to locals as Evie's. Evie herself, who founded the place four decades ago, shows

## The New Whalers

A century and a half ago, many New England mariners made their livings – if not their fortunes – hunting the great mammals of the sea. With the discovery of petroleum and natural gas, the importance of whale oil faded away, and with it New England's whaling business.

Whaling is still a business, of course. As of this writing, Japan and Norway both have active whaling programs even though the hunting of whales is condemned by most other nations. A kilo of whale meat can be worth up to $400 at retail in Tokyo. For more information, see www.physics.helsinki.fi/whale.

The great whales still produce income for New England mariners, too, but they don't give their lives to do it. Whale-watching cruises are very popular.

### Vessels
The typical whale-watch vessel is a steel-hulled, diesel-powered boat of 80 to 100 feet in length. Boats are equipped with snack bars, toilets, indoor and outdoor seating areas and full safety equipment. Sonar helps track the schools of fish that often indicate where the whales will be feeding that day. A naturalist accompanies the cruise to provide full information on the species of whales, their habits and even, in some cases, their 'names,' as many of the whales are 'regulars' known to the crews.

### Schedules
The typical cruise is a four- or five-hour voyage departing at breakfast-time, mid-morning or just after lunch. Cruises run from late April to late October. From late June through early September, many boats make two cruises daily.

### Preparations
To prepare for your cruise, call ahead and confirm departure times and ticket prices. Ask about maritime conditions: If it's been stormy in the past few days, the seas may still be rough, which means most landlubbers will suffer from seasickness.

Take a warm sweater and/or jacket (a lined windbreaker is perfect) as it will be considerably cooler out on the windy ocean, particularly on morning cruises, even on warm days. Wear rubber-soled shoes.

Sunglasses, sunscreen or sunblock and a hat are also necessary, as you will be exposed to direct sunlight as well as the harsh light reflected off the water.

Take your camera and perhaps binoculars. Though not all whale sightings are photogenic, you may be in luck and should be prepared.

Nonalcoholic beverages, snacks and sometimes even light meals are available onboard. Only a few boats sell alcoholic beverages or allow them to be served. If the sea is not dead calm, and if you are not an experienced mariner, forget the booze.

up nightly around 10 pm to engage in hilarious antics with her colleagues (the menu calls it 'spontaneous entertainment'). If you want one of the few tables on the seaside deck, request it when you make your dinner reservation (a good idea on weekends). The simplest dishes are the best choices here. Expect to spend $25 to $40 per person for a full dinner with drinks.

## Entertainment

During the summer, the *Gloucester Stage Company* (☎ *978-281-4099, www.cape-ann .com/cacc/stageco.html, 267 E Main St*) stages excellent small-theater productions of classics, modern works and new plays by acclaimed playwright Israel Horovitz. Call the theater or surf the web page for current offerings.

## The New Whalers

### Seasickness Prevention

If possible, carry capsules of powdered ginger (from a health-food store) and take one or two before departure. Ginger helps to settle the stomach on rocky voyages. There are also anti-seasickness drugs such as Dramamine (ask your doctor or pharmacist). Bring paper napkins and a plastic bag in case these don't work.

If you feel queasy, sit outside, breathe the sea air deeply and look at land or the horizon until the feeling passes. Don't read for long periods on a rocking boat, as that is the short, fast route to nausea.

### Sightings

Your boat motors out to sea for about an hour to where the whales customarily hunt for food, perhaps at the National Marine Sanctuary of Stellwagen Bank. It will then cruise slowly for about two hours looking for whales. Most boats have enviable records, sighting whales over 99% of the time, not to mention sea birds, dolphins and seals. If your cruise fails to sight a whale, the company usually gives you a pass good for another cruise.

The **humpback** whales are baleen (filter-feeding) whales of up to 50 feet in length and weigh 30 tons, with flippers up to 15 feet long. They're the ones most sought because they're big, playful and they tend to 'breach' (leap out of the water).

The **finbacks,** or fin whales as they're also called, are more slender and longer (up to 70 feet) and heavier (up to 50 tons). They're second only to the great blue whales in size. They don't breach, but roll and spout in the water.

The **minke** (MINK-kee) whales are smaller (23 to 28 feet in length) and lighter and do ʲt breach, but roll on the surface.

You might also see **Atlantic white-sided dolphins**, 8 or 9 feet in length, ʷ have
teeth rather than baleen and feed on fish and squid. The dolphins love to leap ￪air and
sport in boat wakes.

Numerous restaurants and cafes have live entertainment, including the ***Rhumb Line*** (☎ 978-283-9732, 40 Railroad Ave), across from the Gloucester train station; ***Dockside*** (☎ 978-281-4554, 77 Rocky Neck Ave), in East Gloucester; and the ***Blackburn Tavern*** (see Places to Eat).

## Getting There & Away

**Train** See the beginning of the North Shore section, earlier in this chapter, for train information.

**Car** Driving details for Gloucester are as follows:

| destination | mileage | hr:min |
| --- | --- | --- |
| Boston, MA | 33 miles | 0:50 |
| Portsmouth, NH | 50 miles | 1:00 |
| Rockport, MA | 7 miles | 0:15 |
| Salem, MA | 16 miles | 0:30 |

**Boat** There's boat service (☎ 978-283-5110) between Gloucester and Provincetown ('P-town') on Cape Cod on Friday, Sunday and Monday from late June through early September. The boat departs Rose's Wharf, 415 Main St, east of the town center, at 9 am, arriving in P-town at 11:30 am. The return trip departs P-town at 3:30 pm, arriving back in Gloucester at 6 pm. Roundtrip tickets cost $40 for adults, $30 for seniors (60-plus) and $20 for children eight to 15; children under eight ride free. One-way tickets cost 33% less than roundtrip tickets. You may go on Friday and return on Sunday. Call for reservations.

AC Cruise Line (☎ 617-261-6633) sails the *Virginia* daily in summer from Boston to Gloucester (290 Northern). Departure from Boston is at 10 am, in the Seaport district) Rocky Neck (docking in Smith Cove at 12:30 pm. The return (the Studio restaurant) at Neck is at 3 pm, departure from Rocky 5 pm. Roundtrip check in Boston at $15 for seniors; $18 for adults, with their parents for under ride reservations. advance

## ROCKPORT

In the 19th century, Rockport was just that: a sheltered harbor town from which granite blocks were shipped to construction sites up and down the Atlantic seaboard, and even across the ocean to Europe, often as ships' ballast. Cut at a half-dozen quarries just west of the Rockport Granite Quarry Wharf, the stone was also the favored local building material, and monuments, curbstones, building foundations, pavements and piers all remain as a testament to Rockport's past. The town's several granite buildings are particularly handsome, and sturdy to a fault.

A century ago, Winslow Homer, Childe Hassam, Fitz Hugh Lane and other acclaimed artists came to picturesque Rockport. They painted the hearty fisherfolk who wrested a hard, but satisfying, living from the sea.

The artists told their friends about this pretty town, and those friends told other friends, and today Rockport makes its living from tourists who come to look at the artists. The artists have long since given up looking for hearty fishermen because the descendants of the fishers are all running boutiques and B&Bs.

Rockport is just as visually appealing as it was a century ago. In summer it's mobbed with day-trippers. It's got beaches, boutiques, restaurants, nice walks and drives and a festive air about it. And there are still some artists in residence.

## Orientation

The center of town is Dock Square, at the beginning of Bearskin Neck. Most everything is within a 10-minute walk of it. The railroad station is less than a 15-minute walk west of Dock Square.

Parking is very difficult on summer weekends. Unless you get here in time for breakfast, you'd do well to park at one of the lots on MA 127 from Gloucester and take the shuttle bus to the center. The few lots in town charge $8 per day, but fill early. Meters (25¢ an hour) are policed vigorously every day; if you overstay your meter it'll cost you $10. Scrupulously observe the parking regulation signs everywhere.

## Information

The Rockport Chamber of Commerce (☎ 978-546-6575, 888-726-3922, fax 978-546-5997, www.rockportusa.com), 3 Pier Ave (PO Box 67), Rockport, MA 01966, is in the town center just off Main St, uphill from Dock Square. It's open from 9 am to 5 pm Monday to Saturday (10 am to 4 pm weekdays in winter). The Rockport Information Center, on MA 127 as you enter Rockport from Gloucester, is open in summer. They'll help you find a room if you need one.

Toad Hall Bookstore (☎ 978-546-7323), 51 Main St, is not only a good place to buy books, but some of its net income is donated to environmental projects.

## Walking Tours

Rockport is a wandering town. Start at Dock Square and flow with the crowds along Bearskin Neck, window-shopping, stopping for coffee, ice cream or a snack and finally emerging at the Breakwater, which overlooks Rockport Harbor to the south and Sandy Bay to the west.

For a guided tour, contact Footprints (☎ 978-546-7730), 3 North St on Bearskin Neck, which sponsors walking tours at 10 am daily.

The red fishing shack decorated with colorful buoys is 'Motif No 1.' So many artists of great and minimal talent have been painting and photographing it for so long that it well deserves its tongue-in-cheek name. Actually, it should be called Motif No 1-B, as the original shack was destroyed by a great storm in 1978 and a brand-new replica was erected in its place.

Follow Main St west and north from Dock Square to reach Back Beach on Sandy Bay, which is the nearest beach to the town center.

About a mile north of Dock Square on the water, Wharf Rd heads west from the Rockport Granite Company Wharf, the granite pier from which there are panoramic views of the pretty town and Sandy Bay.

Pigeon Cove, the neighborhood about 2 miles north of Dock Square, has been preserved as a working fishing and lobsterboat harbor (after escaping modern development as a site for luxury condominiums).

For excellent views of the town and the sea, walk southeast from Dock Square along Mt Pleasant St, then east along Atlantic Ave or Heywood Ave to the public footpath marked as the 'Way to the Headlands.' The walk from Dock Square takes only 10 or 15 minutes and you'll be rewarded with the view.

## Halibut Point State Park

Only a few miles north of Dock Square along MA 127, just northeast of the Old Farm Inn, is Halibut Point State Park (☎ 978-546-2997), open daily, for a fee of $2 per person or $5 per carload. A 10-minute walk through the forest brings you to yawning, abandoned granite quarries, huge hills of broken granite rubble and a granite foreshore of tumbled, smoothed rock perfect for picnicking, sunbathing, reading or painting. The surf can be strong here, making swimming unwise, but natural pools can be good for wading or cooling your feet.

Park rangers lead nature walks, explaining the marine life in tidal pools, the working of granite quarries, the local bird life and the area's edible plants. Call to learn about current programs.

## Paper House

Inland from Pigeon Cove is the Paper House (☎ 978-546-2629), 52 Pigeon Hill St, a curiosity begun in 1922 when Mr Elis F Stenman decided something useful should be done with all those daily newspapers lying about. He and his family set to work, folding, rolling and pasting the papers into suitable shape as building materials.

Twenty years and 100,000 newspapers later, the house was done. The walls are 215 layers thick, the furnishings – table, chairs, lamps, sofa, even a grandfather clock and a piano – are all made of newspapers. Some pieces even specialize: one desk is made from *Christian Science Monitor* reports of Charles Lindbergh's flight and the fireplace mantel is made from rotogravures drawn from the *Boston Sunday Herald* and the

*New York Herald Tribune.* On all of the papers in the house, the text is still readable.

The house is open 10 am to 5 pm from April through October, for a donation.

## Cruises

Rockport Schooner Company's *Appledore III* (☎ 978-546-9876) is a 56-foot, two-masted schooner built in 1984. It circumnavigated the globe, and now, in early retirement, it takes passengers on 1½-hour sailing cruises of the bay five times daily ($24, children under 10 half price). The sunset cruise from 7 to 8:30 pm is a favorite. Reserve in advance, then buy your tickets at least half an hour before sailing. Beer is sold on board.

You can go on a half-hour **lobstering cruise** (☎ 978-546-7730) in Sandy Bay each morning at 9:30 or 11:30 am from the T-wharf at the center of town. Hour-long island cruises depart at 1:30 and 3 pm.

Rockport Whale Watch (☎ 978-546-3377), 9 Tuna Wharf (off Bearskin Neck), will take you on a half-day whale-watching cruise. Adults pay $24, seniors $19, children 13 and under $15.

## Special Events

The Rockport Chamber Music Festival (☎ 978-546-7391), 2 Main St, sponsors internationally acclaimed performers who give concerts in the Rockport Art Association gallery from mid-June to early July.

## Places to Stay

Rockport has many small inns, B&Bs and a few motels, almost all of them within an easy walk of Dock Square. Many require two-night minimum stays on weekends (three nights on holiday weekends), some do not accept children under 12, and virtually all are nonsmoking and include at least a light breakfast in the room price.

**Motels** The 24-room *Captain's Bounty Motor Inn* (☎ 978-546-9557, *1 Beach St*) is right on the beach and only a few minutes' stroll from Dock Square. Its prime location allows it to set rates at $100 to $125 in high summer, without breakfast.

*Sandy Bay Motor Inn* (☎ 978-546-7155, *800-437-7155, 173 Main St*) is a modern motel with a restaurant and enclosed swimming pool less than 2 miles inland along Main St (MA 127). In summer, rooms cost $98 to $142 without breakfast.

**Inns & B&Bs** The Victorian *Linden Tree Inn* (☎ 978-546-2494, *800-865-2122, ltree@shore.net, 26 King St*) has a variety of double rooms (18 of them) for $85 to $100; there's one small single that rents for a low $65. Check out the view from the cupola.

Conveniently located *Lantana House* (☎ 978-546-3535, *800-291-3535, 22 Broadway*) has some of the least expensive rooms in Rockport: double or twin-bed rooms for $75 to $90. Some have kitchenettes and air-con.

*Rockport Lodge* (☎ 978-546-2090, *61 South St*) is a special lodging for women only. Founded in 1906 by the National League of Working Women, it was meant to be a place where women of low or moderate incomes could find a restful vacation from the drudgery of factory labor at affordable prices. It continues to fulfill that mission, offering beds and two meals for $50 single, $45 per person double or $40 per person triple. If you just stay the night and have no meals, the charge is $30. Weekly rates are equally reasonable. Linens are provided, but you bring your own towels and soap and tidy up your own room.

*Carlson's B&B* (☎ 978-546-2770, *43 Broadway*), the Victorian home of a prominent local artist, rents double rooms with a private bath, a private entrance, garage parking and full breakfast for $76 to $90.

*Sally Webster Inn* (☎ 978-546-9251, *877-546-9251, 34 Mt Pleasant St*) is a handsome brick colonial built in 1832, offering very nice rooms with bath for $80 to $94.

The beautiful Greek Revival *Addison Choate Inn* (☎ 978-546-7543, *800-245-7543, 49 Broadway*) is among the more charming and historic inns, with a swimming pool and a variety of rooms and suites priced from $115 to $140, including breakfast and afternoon tea.

*Tuck Inn* (☎ 978-546-7260, *800-789-7260, tuckinn@shore.net, 17 High St*) offers nine comfortable rooms priced from $80 to $100, with a four-person suite that goes for $120.

**The Inn on Cove Hill** (☎ 978-546-2701, 37 Mt Pleasant St) is an early-American house (1791) built, so they say, with pirates' gold discovered nearby. Their double rooms, furnished in Federal style with canopy beds, are priced at $49 with shared bath, $65 to $120 with private bath.

The Victorian **Pleasant Street Inn** (☎ 978-546-3915, 800-541-3915, 17 Pleasant St) has a hilltop location only a few blocks from the center. All of its rooms have private bath and are priced from $90 to $98 double.

## Places to Eat

Remember that Rockport is 'dry,' with no alcohol for sale at all, either in stores or restaurants (there are no bars). You can buy bottles in Gloucester or Lanesville, and most restaurants (but not fast-food places) will open and serve them for a corkage fee of about $1.50 per person. Lanesville Package Store, on MA 127 in Lanesville (4 miles from central Rockport), is open 8 am to 10 pm (10:30 pm on Friday and Saturday, closed Sunday). There are numerous liquor stores in Gloucester as well. In high summer, make reservations for dinner in the better restaurants.

Dock Square, at the beginning of Bearskin Neck, has several good cafes. **Dock Square Coffee & Tea House** (☎ 978-546-2525) is the town's fancy coffee purveyor, with excellent brew elaborately concocted and sold for $1.25 to $3.75 a cup. Coffee and pastry can cost less than $4. There are a few outdoor tables.

Bearskin Neck is crowded with ice cream shops, cafes and eateries. As you walk out, you'll pass several places good for a bowl of chowder, fish and chips, cheap lobster or a full and semi-elegant tuck-in.

**Roy Moore Lobster Company** (☎ 978-546-6696) has the cheapest lobster-in-the-rough on the Neck. Your beast comes on a tray with melted butter, a fork and a wet wipe for cleanup. Claws and shell are pre-cracked for convenience. If you'd like a bit more refinement, go upstairs right next door to **Roy Moore's Fish Shack Restaurant**

(☎ 978-546-6667), which still has fairly low prices given its upstairs water-view dining room. Bring your own wine or beer.

Off to the left (south) on a side street is the **Portside Chowder House** (☎ 978-546-7045), a tiny place specializing in chowders, sandwiches and pies. Because there's almost no water view and quarters are cramped (but cozy), prices are low, with good clam chowder for only $2.50 to $3.50. The corn chowder is equally good, and vegetarian. Sandwiches are a cheap $2 to $5; the most expensive item on the menu is only $10.

For a full-fledged restaurant, the **Hannah Jumper** (☎ 978-546-3600), on Tuna Wharf, has a long menu and water views from every table. Light meals like soup ($3 to $5) and sandwich ($6 to $10) compete with heavy eats like prime rib of beef. A trip to the varied salad bar costs $6, with one refill for free. The drinks list (all non-alcoholic, of course) is long and interesting.

The favorite Rockport restaurant is **My Place By the Sea** (☎ 978-546-9667, 68 Bearskin Neck), right out at the end. The location is the best in Rockport, with panoramic views of the bay, indoor and outdoor seating, excellent service and a concise, interesting menu. Lunch (about $8 to $12) is a good value, and the New American cuisine at dinner ($25 to $40) is very good; make reservations for dinner in high summer.

For coffee or tea and dessert, try **Helmut's Strudel** (☎ 978-546-2824, 49 Bearskin Neck), almost near the outer end, serving various strudels, filled croissants, pastries, cider and coffee. Four shaded tables overlook the yacht-filled harbor.

By the T-wharf in the center of town, **Ellen's Harborside** (☎ 978-546-2512, 1 Wharf Rd) is renowned for its simple but good old-time menu, decent portions, good food and low prices. It's open every day in summer 6 am to 9 pm. Bring your own bottle.

## Getting There & Away

**Train** Rockport is the terminus for MBTA Commuter Rail trains (☎ 617-722-3200, 800-392-6100, www.mbta.com) on the Rockport line. The trip from Boston takes you about

75 minutes and costs $4 for adults. Thirteen trains leave North Station daily (at least every two hours throughout the day).

**Car** If you're driving, MA 127 makes two loops around Cape Ann, both passing through Rockport. Driving details for Rockport are as follows:

| destination | mileage | hr:min |
|---|---|---|
| Boston, MA | 40 miles | 1:00 |
| Gloucester, MA | 7 miles | 0:15 |
| Portsmouth, NH | 57 miles | 1:10 |
| Salem, MA | 23 miles | 0:40 |

### Getting Around
The Cape Ann Transportation Authority (CATA; ☎ 978-283-7916) operates its bus routes among the towns of Cape Ann. On Saturday, Sunday and holidays from early June through mid-September, its Saltwater Trolleys make nine runs per day on a route connecting Essex, Gloucester, Rockport and outlying areas. For $4 for adults, $2 seniors and children five to 12, you can hop on and off anywhere along the route.

### IPSWICH
Famous for its clams, Ipswich is one of those New England towns that is pretty today because it was poor in the past. With no harbor, and no source of waterpower for factories, the commercial and industrial riches of the 18th and 19th centuries were produced elsewhere. As a result, Ipswich's old 17th-century houses were not torn down to build grander residences for the wealthy. Today, antique shops abound.

It's also famous as the home of novelist John Updike and the setting for some of his novels.

Beach-goers must try **Crane Beach**, at the end of Argilla Rd. It's 4 miles of fine-sand barrier beach on Ipswich Bay. Above the beach, on Castle Hill, is the estate built in 1928 by Chicago plumbing-fixture magnate Richard T Crane. The 59-room Stuart-style **Great House** (☎ 978-356-4351), 290 Argilla Rd, was the setting for the film *The Crucible* with Daniel Day-Lewis and is the site of summer concerts and special events.

For clams, the most famous spot is **Woodman's** (☎ *978-768-6057*), on Main St (MA 133) in neighboring Essex, on the way to Ipswich from MA 128 exit 14.

The MBTA trains (☎ 617-222-3200, 800-392-6100) on the Newburyport Line leave Boston's North Station for Ipswich (50 minutes, $3.50) 13 times each weekday, five times on Saturday, no trains Sunday.

# South Shore

## PLYMOUTH
Historic Plymouth, 'America's Home Town,' is synonymous with Plymouth Rock. Thousands of visitors come here each year to look at this weathered ball of granite and to consider what it was like for the Pilgrims who stepped ashore in this strange land in the autumn of 1620, seeking a place where they could practice their religion as they wished without interference from government.

You can see all there is to see of Plymouth Rock in a minute. But the rock is just a symbol of the Pilgrims' struggle, sacrifice and triumph, which are elucidated in many museums and exhibits nearby.

### Orientation & Information
'The rock,' on the waterfront, is on Water St at the center of Plymouth, within walking distance of most museums and restaurants. Main St, the main commercial street, is a block inland. Some lodgings are within walking distance, but others require a car.

'Destination Plymouth' (☎ 508-747-7533, www.visit-plymouth.com), the town's visitor information center at 225 Water St, Plymouth, MA 02360, is a half mile north of Plymouth Rock in the old Ocean Spray building. It is open 9 am to 4 pm weekdays year-round. There is also a seasonal information booth at the rotary on Water St and N Park Ave.

The Massachusetts Tourist Information Center (☎ 508-746-1150), MA 3 (exit 5), has information on many places in the region in addition to Plymouth. Look for special discount lodging coupons in the brochure racks. It's open (at a minimum) 8 am to 4:30 pm daily year-round.

## Plymouth Rock

Though the Pilgrims came from England, Plymouth Rock came from Pangaea, the gigantic continent that split in two to form Europe and Africa on the eastern side and North and South America on the western side, leaving the Atlantic Ocean in between. The boulder is of Dedham granite, a rock some 680 million years old. Most of the Dedham granite went to Africa when Pangaea split; bits were left in the Atlantica terrain, the geologic area around Boston. About 20,000 years ago, a glacier picked up Plymouth Rock, carried it and dropped it here.

We don't really know that the Pilgrims actually landed on Plymouth Rock; it's not mentioned in any early written accounts. But the colonial news media picked up the story and soon the rock was in jeopardy from its adoring fans. In 1774, 20 yoke of oxen were harnessed to the rock to move it and split it in the process. Half of the cloven boulder went on display in Pilgrim Hall from 1834 to 1867. The sea and wind lashed at the other half, and innumerable small pieces were chipped off and carried away by thoughtless souvenir hunters over the centuries.

By the 20th century, the rock was an endangered souvenir, and steps were taken to protect it. In 1921, the reunited halves were sheltered in the present granite enclosure designed by McKim, Mead & White. In 1989, the rock was repaired and strengthened to withstand weathering.

Plymouth Rock – relatively small, broken and mended, with the date '1620' cut into it – is a symbol of the quest for religious freedom. It's open to view all the time, for free.

## *Mayflower II*

If Plymouth Rock tells us little about the Pilgrims, *Mayflower II* (☎ 508-746-1622, www .plimouth.org), a replica of the small ship in which they made the fateful voyage, speaks volumes.

As you enter, you'll think it impossible that 102 people with all the household effects, tools, provisions, animals and seed to establish a colony could have lived together on this tiny vessel for 66 days, subsisting on

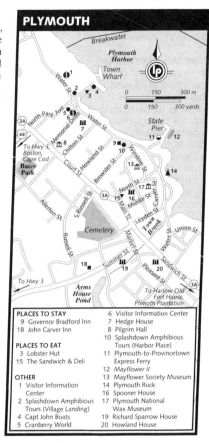

**PLYMOUTH**

| PLACES TO STAY | |
|---|---|
| 9 | Governor Bradford Inn |
| 18 | John Carver Inn |

| PLACES TO EAT | |
|---|---|
| 3 | Lobster Hut |
| 15 | The Sandwich & Deli |

| OTHER | |
|---|---|
| 1 | Visitor Information Center |
| 2 | Splashdown Amphibious Tours (Village Landing) |
| 4 | Capt John Boats |
| 5 | Cranberry World |
| 6 | Visitor Information Center |
| 7 | Hedge House |
| 8 | Pilgrim Hall |
| 10 | Splashdown Amphibious Tours (Harbor Place) |
| 11 | Plymouth-to-Provincetown Express Ferry |
| 12 | Mayflower II |
| 13 | Mayflower Society Museum |
| 14 | Plymouth Rock |
| 16 | Spooner House |
| 17 | Plymouth National Wax Museum |
| 19 | Richard Sparrow House |
| 20 | Howland House |

hard, moldy biscuits, rancid butter and brackish water, as the ship passed through the stormy north Atlantic waters. But they did, landing on this wild, forested shore in the frigid December of 1620 – eloquent testimony to their courage, spirit and the strength of their religious beliefs.

*Mayflower II*, moored at State Pier only a minute's walk north of Plymouth Rock, was built in England in 1955 and sailed the Atlantic to Plymouth in 1957. The ship is open to visitors 9 am to 5 pm daily from late March to late November. Admission costs $5.75

adults, $3.75 children; discounted combination tickets at $18.50 and $11 permit entrance to Plimoth Plantation as well.

## Plimoth Plantation

During the winter of 1620-21, half of the Pilgrims died of disease, privation and exposure to the elements. But the survivors were joined by new arrivals in 1621, and by 1627, just before an additional influx of Pilgrims founded the colony of Massachusetts Bay, Plymouth colony was sturdily built and on the road to prosperity.

The Plimoth Plantation (☎ 508-746-1622, ppcity@plimouth.org), a mile or so south of Plymouth Rock via MA 3A, is an authentic re-creation of settlements from 1627.

Everything in the 1627 Pilgrim Village – costumes, implements, vocabulary, artistry, recipes and crops – has been painstakingly researched and remade. Even the animals have been back-bred to be very similar to those which the Pilgrims had. You can see them in Nye Barn.

Hobbamock's (Wampanoag) Homesite replicates the life of a Native American community in this area at the same time: their crafts, costumes and huts are made of wattle and daub.

Costumed interpreters, acting in character, explain the details of daily life and answer your questions as you watch them work and play. In the Crafts Center, artisans weave baskets and cloth, throw pottery and build fine furniture using the techniques and tools of the early 17th century. Exhibits explain how these manufactured goods were shipped across the Atlantic in exchange for colonial necessities.

An interactive audio and video exhibit, 'Irreconcilable Difference,' illuminates the contrasts between a 'typical' Native American woman and a Pilgrim woman living between 1627 and 1690.

Tickets and hours are the same as to the *Mayflower II* and include entry to the 1627 Pilgrim Village, Hobbamock's Homesite, the Crafts Center and *Mayflower II*. A picnic area, bakery and several restaurants provide modern sustenance.

## Pilgrim Hall

This museum (☎ 508-746-1620), 75 Court St at Chilton St, boasts that it is the oldest continually operating public museum in the USA, having been built in 1824. Its exhibits are not reproductions, but the real things the Pilgrims and their Wampanoag neighbors used in their daily lives, right down to Miles Standish's sword. Monumental paintings in the museum's collection depict scenes of Pilgrim life.

Pilgrim Hall is open 9:30 am to 4:30 pm daily; closed in January. Admission costs $5 adults, $4.50 seniors, $3 children.

## Plymouth National Wax Museum

This museum (☎ 508-746-6468), 16 Carver St, across the street and up the hill from Plymouth Rock, is a good place to show children scenes of Pilgrim history. The life-sized wax figures – 180 in 26 scenes – recount the progress of the Pilgrims as they left England for Holland, then set sail for, and arrived in, America.

The museum is open 9 am to 5 pm daily (until 7 pm in May, June, September and October; until 9 pm in July and August); closed December through February. Admission costs $5.50 adults, $2.25 children.

## Historic Houses

As New England's oldest European community, Plymouth has its share of fine old houses, some very old indeed.

The **Richard Sparrow House** (☎ 508-747-1240), 42 Summer St, the oldest house in Plymouth, was built by one of the original Pilgrim settlers in 1640. It's open 10 am to 5 pm daily (except Wednesday) from May through November. Admission is $2 adults, $1 children.

The **Howland House** (☎ 508-746-9590), 33 Sandwich St, built in 1667, began as the residence for a family that came over on the *Mayflower*. You can take a tour between 10 am and 4:30 pm daily from late May to late November, for $3 adults, $2 seniors and college students, $1 children.

The **Mayflower Society Museum** (☎ 508-746-2590), 4 Winslow St, dates from 1754 and shows how wealthy a town Plymouth had become in a little over a century. Note especially the house's flying staircase. Visit 10 am to 4 pm daily from July to early September; in June and from early September to mid-October, visit Friday to Sunday at the same time.

The Plymouth Antiquarian Society (☎ 508-746-0012) maintains three historic houses and staffs them with costumed interpreters who can tell you all about Pilgrim life. The houses span 1½ centuries of Plymouth architectural history.

The **Harlow Old Fort House** (1677), 119 Sandwich St, shows you how the second generation of Plymouth colonists lived. The **Spooner House** (1747), 27 North St, was occupied by the same family for more than two centuries, which accounts in part for its very rich collection of period furnishings. **Hedge House** (1809), 126 Water St, is in the Federal style.

The houses are all open 10 am to 4 pm Thursday to Saturday, early June to mid-October. Tickets are $3 adults, $1 children; combo tickets to all three houses cost $6 adults, $2 children.

### Cranberry World

Soon after the Pilgrims arrived, they discovered the tart red berries that filled the sandy bogs near Plymouth and south to Cape Cod. Cranberries made it onto that first Thanksgiving menu and have been there ever since. You can learn all about the sour, yet appealing and healthful, fruit at Cranberry World (☎ 508-747-2350), Water St at the rotary, near the town wharf on the waterfront. It's open 9:30 am to 5 pm daily May through November. Admission is free, as are sample cranberry refreshments.

### Organized Tours

Whale-watching cruises on Capt John Boats (☎ 508-746-2643, 800-242-2469), at Town Wharf, leave the harbor at least once daily for a four-hour whale-watching cruise. Boats operate from early April to October. During the educational and fun trip, an onboard marine biologist illuminates the differences

MICHELLE GAGNÉ-BALLARD

**Massasoit, chief of the Wampanoags at the time of the Pilgrims' arrival**

between the humpback, finback, minke, right and pilot whales you may encounter. The outfit has a 99% sighting record. Tickets cost $25 for adults, $20 for seniors and $15 for children under 12.

Splashdown Amphibious Tours (☎ 508-747-7658, 800-225-4000), at Harbor Place (adjacent to the Governor Bradford Inn on Water St) and Village Landing (near the town wharf), utilize authentic WWII beach-assault vehicles to transport modern day out-of-towners. You can't miss the behemoths rolling through the town's historic district and plunging into the harbor for a continuation of the hour-long tour. Exact departure times are tide-dependent, so you'll have to call. Tours run daily mid-April through September and on weekends in October. Tickets cost $15 for adults, $9 for children under 12, $3 under three.

### Places to Stay

**Camping** The nearest state facility is ***Myles Standish State Forest*** (☎ *508-866-2526 for* *off season reservations, 877-422-6762 for reservations late May to early September)*. It is about 6 miles south of Plymouth. Take MA 3 exit 5 or MA 58 to S Carver. Within the 16,000-acre park are 16 miles of bike trails, hiking trails, nine ponds (two with beaches and bathhouses) and 450 campsites priced at $6 per site, $7 if you want to be right on water's edge. There is camping mid-April to mid-October, but the park is open year-round.

*Wompatuck State Park (☎ 781-749-7160, 877-422-6762 for reservations late May to early September)*, off MA 228 in Hingham, is 30 miles north of Plymouth. The 2900-acre park has 12 miles of paved biking trails, even more mountain biking trails, hiking trails and 250 campsites priced at $6 per site, $9 with electricity.

The private campgrounds in the area charge about twice the fees of the state parks and forests. *Pinewood Lodge Campground (☎ 508-746-3548, 190 Pinewood Rd)*, off US 44 in Plymouth, is among the closest to the town center.

*Sandy Pond Campground (☎ 508-759-9336, 834 Bourne Rd)* has 30 sites with electricity and sewer connections, 80 with only electricity, two sand beaches and hiking trails. Tenting for two people costs $20.

*Plymouth Rock KOA Kampground (☎ 508-947-6435)*, US 44 in Middleboro, is farther away.

**Motels** *Governor Bradford Inn (☎ 508-746-6200, 800-332-1620, fax 508-747-3032, djconnell@governorbradford.com, 98 Water St)* is convenient and charges $93 to $130 for its double rooms in summer; those with sea views are the more expensive ones. Off season it's $59 to $79 double.

*John Carver Inn (☎ 508-746-7100, 800-274-1620, fax 508-746-8299, 25 Summer St)* has three categories of rooms, smoking and nonsmoking, ranging from $99 to $129 in summer and fall.

*Pilgrim Sands Motel (☎ 508-747-0900, 800-729-7263, fax 508-746-8066, thebeach@pilgrimsands.com, 150 Warren Ave)*, across the street from the entrance to Plimoth Plantation, charges you $98 to $130 for its

rooms in the summertime. Rooms are $50 to $110 the rest of the year.

## Places to Eat
Fast-food shops line Water St opposite the *Mayflower II*. For better food at lower prices, walk a block inland to Main St, the attractive thoroughfare of Plymouth's business district.

*The Sandwich & Deli (☎ 508-746-7773, 65 Main St)*, at North St, has clam chowder and bacon, lettuce and tomato sandwiches for $3. Huge reuben and pastrami sandwiches are $4 and many other quick-lunch plates are priced in between.

For lunch ($3 to $7) or dinner ($6 to $18) with a view of the sea, try the *Lobster Hut (☎ 508-746-2270)*, on the town wharf five short blocks north of *Mayflower II*. Big plates of fried clams and fish and chips are priced at about $10. Seating is both indoors and out.

## Getting There & Away
**Bus** Plymouth & Brockton buses (☎ 508-746-0378, 778-9767, www.p-b.com) connect Boston and Logan Airport with Plymouth (one hour) and Hyannis (45 minutes), running over a dozen buses daily in summer. The P&B terminal is in North Plymouth's Industrial Park off MA 3 at exit 7, about 2 miles from the center of town. Some morning buses stop at the old post office in the center of town.

You can reach Plymouth from Boston by train (☎ 617-222-3200, 800-392-6100, www.mbta.com). From the station at Cordage Park, 'GATRA' buses connect to Plymouth Center. One-way tickets are $3.25.

**Car** Driving details for Plymouth are as follows:

| destination | mileage | hr:min |
| --- | --- | --- |
| Boston, MA | 41 miles | 0:55 |
| Hartford, CT | 141 miles | 3:00 |
| Hyannis, MA | 37 miles | 0:50 |
| New York, NY | 205 miles | 4:00 |
| Providence, RI | 39 miles | 0:50 |
| Provincetown, MA | 83 miles | 1:50 |

**Boat** The Plymouth-to-Provincetown Express Ferry (☎ 508-747-2400, 800-242-2469), State Pier, operated by the ubiquitous Capt John Boats, deposits you on the tip of the Cape faster than if you drove. No matter the day, the 90-minute journey departs Plymouth at 10 am and leaves Provincetown at 4:30 pm. During the summer (mid-June to early September), service is daily. Late May and late September, the ferry also runs on the weekends, with additional service on Tuesday and Wednesday in September. A roundtrip ticket costs $25 for adults, $20 for seniors and $16 for children under 12; bikes cost an additional $2.

## NEW BEDFORD

During its heyday as a whaling port (1765-1860), New Bedford commanded as many as 400 whaling ships. This vast fleet brought home hundreds of thousands of barrels of whale oil for lighting America's lamps. So famous was the town's whaling industry that Herman Melville set his great American novel, *Moby-Dick; or, The Whale* in New Bedford. (At the time, he lived in Pittsfield, Massachusetts.) If you're interested in whaling history, this is the place to find it.

When whale oil was supplanted by petroleum and electricity, New Bedford turned to fishing, scalloping and textile production for its wealth. In the early 20th century, the textile industry headed south, then offshore, in search of cheaper labor, and in recent years New England's Atlantic fishing grounds have been exploited to near extinction, so New Bedford is again in search of a source of wealth.

The city, with a population of 100,000, gets its share of bad press like any city its size. But the city center, complete with its cobblestone streets and gas lanterns and designated a National Historical Park in late 1996, is really worth a look.

### Orientation

The heart of the old city center is the restored historic district around Melville Mall. The area is about a mile south of I-195 via MA 18 (take Downtown exit 18S). At the first set of lights, take a right and park in the municipal garage on the right. Parking is cheap. The National Historical Park visitor center is one block away.

### Information

The New Bedford Whaling National Historical Park Visitor Center (☎ 508-996-4095, www.nps.gov/nebe), 33 William St, New Bedford, MA 02740, is open 10 am to 4 pm daily. Walking tours (highly recommended) are offered twice daily in July and August.

The New Bedford Office of Tourism (☎ 508-979-1745, 800-508-5353, www.ci .new-bedford.ma.us), Wharfinger Building, Pier 3, New Bedford 02740, is located on the waterfront. They will send information prior to your visit and provide accommodations information once you arrive, if you need it. Pick up a self-guided brochure for the 'dock walk' that orients you to the working harbor. The office is open 8:30 am to 4 pm weekdays and 9 am to 5 pm weekends, late May to mid-October.

Mid-July brings the Whaling City Festival. For more information on this and other special events, contact the New Bedford Area Chamber of Commerce (☎ 508-999-5231), 794 Purchase St, PO Box 8827, New Bedford, MA 02742. The office is open from 8:30 am to 5 pm weekdays.

### Whaling Museum

The New Bedford Whaling Museum (☎ 508-997-0046, www.whalingmuseum.org), at 18 Johnny Cake Hill, actually includes seven buildings situated between William and Union Sts. To learn what whaling was all about, you need only tramp the decks of the *Lagoda*, a fully rigged, half-size replica of an actual whaling bark. The onboard tryworks (a brick furnace where try-pots are placed) was where huge chunks of whale blubber were rendered to release the valuable oil. Old photographs and a 22-minute video of an actual whale chase bring this historic period to life.

Don't ignore the 100-foot-long mural depicting sperm whales or the exhibits of delicate scrimshaw, the carving of whalebone into jewelry, notions and beautiful household items.

The museum is open 9 am to 5 pm daily; tickets are $4.50 adults, $3.50 seniors, $3 children.

## Seamen's Bethel

This small chapel (☎ 508-992-3295), upon Johnny Cake Hill across from the Whaling Museum, was a refuge for sailors from the rigors and stresses of the maritime life. Melville, who suffered terrible conditions on a whaling ship, immortalized it in *Moby-Dick*. You can visit 10 am to 4 pm daily, except Sunday (1 to 4 pm), May to mid-October. Admission is free (donations accepted).

## New Bedford Fire Museum

Antique fire trucks and fire-fighting equipment fill this museum (☎ 508-992-2162) in a century-old building right next to a working New Bedford fire station on Bedford St at 6th St. Children love the old trucks, uniforms, pumps and fire poles, all on display 9 am to 4 pm daily, July to early September. Admission costs $2 adults, $1 children.

## Rotch-Jones-Duff House & Garden

New Bedford's grandest historic house (☎ 508-997-1401), at 396 County St, was designed in Greek Revival style in 1834 by Richard Upjohn (1802-1878), first president of the American Institute of Architects. The English-born architect later rebuilt New York's Trinity Church (1839). You can wander or tour the grand house 10 am to 4 pm daily year-round (except it's closed Monday January through March). Admission is $4 adults, $3 seniors, $2 children.

## Places to Stay & Eat

New Bedford is not thick with lodging possibilities, to put it mildly. The visitor center can provide you with additional information if you're in a jam.

Near the Rotch-Jones-Duff House, try the *1875 House* (☎ 508-997-6433, fax 991-5095, bandb1875newbedford@compuserve .com, 36 7th St), which has three rooms, all with private bath, for $55 to $65, expanded continental breakfast included.

The historic district contains several simple restaurants and snack shops that can fill the need for sustenance.

## Getting There & Away

**Bus** American Eagle (☎ 508-993-5040) operates buses between New Bedford and Boston's South Station ($8 one way) about every two hours on weekdays and Saturday; it runs every four hours on Sunday.

**Car** Driving details for New Bedford are as follows:

| destination | mileage | hr:min |
|---|---|---|
| Boston, MA | 57 miles | 1:10 |
| Fall River, MA | 15 miles | 0:25 |
| Hartford, CT | 103 miles | 2:10 |
| Hyannis, MA | 43 miles | 1:00 |
| New York, NY | 206 miles | 4:20 |
| Plymouth, MA | 38 miles | 0:50 |
| Providence, RI | 32 miles | 0:50 |
| Provincetown, MA | 93 miles | 2:00 |

**Boat** Cape Island Express Lines, Inc (☎ 508-997-1688) operates the passenger boat MV *Schamonchi* on the route between New Bedford and Vineyard Haven on Martha's Vineyard. In the summer, there are three voyages in each direction (1½ hours) daily for $17 to $19 adults, $8 to $11 children, $5 bikes. Fares are based on roundtrip passage.

## FALL RIVER

Fall River has a good harbor, rivers for water power and a humid climate well suited to working woolen thread, so it was natural that it became one of New England's most important textile production centers during the 19th century.

Thousands of tons of the local granite were hewn to build the huge textile mills that are still the most prominent feature of Fall River's cityscape.

But Fall River was the victim of its own success. Industrial wealth led to inflation and higher costs. After the turn of the century, the textile trade moved to cheaper labor markets in the southern states and then moved overseas, leaving Fall River's great textile mills empty.

Today, the great granite buildings are busy again. Fall River has become an off-price shopping mecca, the 'largest factory-outlet shopping center in New England,' as the signs say. Most of the spacious mills are again filled with textiles – goods not made here, but imported from the Far East and Latin America.

## Factory Outlet Stores

The concept of the factory outlet store began a century ago when flawed, but still usable, products would be sold at very low prices to locals. Today, in some factory stores, prices are much the same as in city department stores and specialty shops. But in Fall River, cheap rents in the old mills allow manufacturers to pass on savings to consumers.

Over 100 merchants have set up shop in the mills, selling everything from cut-price jeans to designer dresses that are only a little bit out of fashion. You'll find accessories, baskets, belts, books, candy and nuts, carpets, children's clothing, cosmetics, crystal and glass, curtains, furniture, gift wrap and greeting cards, handbags, kitchenware, leather goods, linens, lingerie, luggage, toys, raincoats and overcoats, shoes, sweaters, ties, towels and even wallpaper.

You can easily reach the outlets via I-195 (they are visible from the road).

## Battleship Cove

Take I-195 exit 5 at the Braga Bridge, then follow the signs to Battleship Cove (☎ 508-678-1100, 800-533-3194), a quiet corner of Mt Hope Bay that holds well-preserved WWII-era vessels, which you can visit. The exhibits are open 9 am to 5 pm daily; tickets cost $9 adults, $6.75 seniors, $4.50 children.

The 46,000-ton battleship USS *Massachusetts*, longer than two football fields and taller than a nine-story building, carried a crew of 2300 and was the first and last battleship to fire her 16-inch guns in WWII.

The USS *Joseph P Kennedy, Jr*, named for President John F Kennedy's older brother, did battle in the Korean and Vietnam Wars and is now a museum.

The USS *Lionfish* is a WWII submarine still in full working condition. There are also two PT boats, a landing craft, a Japanese attack boat and other craft.

Food is available at the site. You can even dine in the *Massachusetts'* wardroom if you like.

Just past the battleship, the **Marine Museum at Fall River** (☎ 508-674-3533), 70 Water St, is especially strong in intricate ship models, including a scale model of the *Titanic* used in the 1950s movie on the subject. Admission costs $4 adults, $3.50 children. The museum is open 9 am to 5 pm weekdays (noon to 5 pm Saturday, noon to 4 pm Sunday).

# Cape Cod

Mariner Bartholomew Gosnold (1572-1607) sailed the New England coast in 1602, naming natural features as he went. He gave the name Cape Cod to the sandy, 65-mile-long peninsula that juts eastward from mainland Massachusetts into the Atlantic.

When the Pilgrims first set foot in the New World in November 1620, it was at the site of Provincetown, at the tip of Cape Cod. They rested only long enough to draw up rules of governance (the Mayflower Compact) before setting sail westward in search of a more congenial place for their settlement, which they found at Plymouth.

After that first visit by the Pilgrims, later settlers founded fishing villages along the coasts. The fishing industry drew boatbuilders and salt makers. Soon there were farmers working the cranberry bogs as well, and whaling ships bringing home rich cargoes of oil and whalebone.

In the mid-19th century, Henry David Thoreau made a walking tour of Cape Cod, reporting on the peninsula just before it became a popular summer vacation destination for wealthy families from Boston and Providence.

In 1879, Cape Cod was connected to Europe by an undersea telephone cable, which ran from Orleans to Brest, France, a distance of 4000 miles. Early in the next century, Guglielmo Marconi (1874-1937) set up a wireless telegraph station on the beach in South Wellfleet to communicate with Great Britain.

At the beginning of the 20th century, the US government financed construction of the Cape Cod Canal (1909-14), which joined Buzzards Bay and Cape Cod Bay, cutting long hours off any voyage between Boston and Providence and New York. It also cut off Cape Cod from the mainland, making Cape Cod an island.

'The Cape,' as it is universally called by locals, is among New England's favorite summer vacation destinations and it thrives on tourism, but light industry and fishing

also contribute to the economy. Vacationers come for the beaches that cover much of its 400 miles of shore, though the seawater is usually chilly to downright cold. There is real New England beauty in the Cape's dune-studded landscapes cloaked in scrub oak and pine, its fine stands of tall sea grass and the grace and dignity of its colonial towns.

Cape-wide information may be procured at the Massachusetts Tourist Information

## Highlights

- Watching the sunrise over Nobska Lighthouse in Woods Hole
- Biking on the Cape Cod Rail Trail
- Clambering across Cape Cod National Seashore dunes
- Taking an airplane ride above the Outer Cape
- Eating oysters in Wellfleet
- People-watching and gallery-hopping in Provincetown
- Boating through Nauset Marsh in Orleans or to Chatham's Monomoy Island

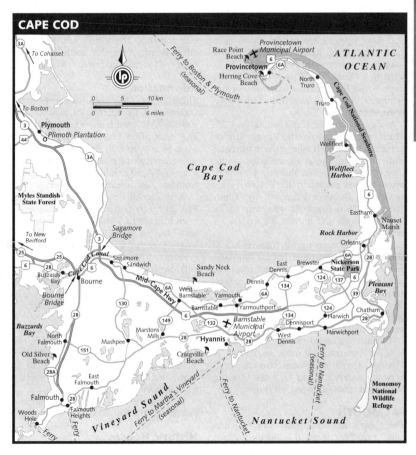

CAPE COD

Center (☎ 508-746-1150) in Plymouth at exit 5 off MA 3 (for those heading from Boston to Cape Cod). The well-stocked and staffed building is open roughly 8:30 am to 4:30 pm daily year-round. Coming from the south or west, the Cape Cod Chamber of Commerce's satellite office, 3 miles east of the Bourne Bridge on Route 25, is open 9 am to 5 pm daily year-round.

Once on Cape Cod, stop in at the Cape Cod Chamber of Commerce information office (☎ 508-862-0700, 800-332-2732, www .capecodchamber.com) just off of US 6 at exit 6 in Hyannis. (Write to PO Box 790, Hyannis, MA 02601.) In addition, all towns have their own information bureaus. In an emergency, call ☎ 911.

## Getting There & Around

The Sagamore (northeast) and the Bourne (southwest) Bridges span the Cape Cod Canal, linking the Cape to the mainland. Take the Bourne Bridge to Falmouth and Woods Hole (for Martha's Vineyard). Use the Sagamore Bridge for the rest of the Cape. The bridges are only 4 miles apart via US 6.

Locals use a somewhat confusing nomenclature for the various districts on Cape Cod. The 'Upper Cape' is the region near the canal and the mainland. 'Mid-Cape' is roughly from Barnstable and Hyannis eastward to Orleans. The 'Lower' (or 'Outer') Cape is the long, narrow extension of the peninsula north and east from Orleans to Provincetown.

Main roads on the Cape include MA 28, which heads south from the Bourne Bridge to Falmouth, where it takes a sharp turn east and runs along the southern edge of the Cape through Hyannis and into Chatham, where it takes a northern jog before it ends in Orleans. Between Falmouth and Chatham, MA 28 is overbuilt with strip malls, fast-food joints and motels; it's quite congested in summer.

The Cape's main transit route is US 6, also called the Mid-Cape Hwy, a four-lane divided highway that runs inland from the canal to Orleans, where the Cape begins to narrow as it heads north. US 6 is the only through-road to Provincetown, and traffic on this part of it is usually free-flowing, if heavy in summer.

The alternative to the Mid-Cape Hwy, highly recommended if you have the time, is MA 6A, a rural and scenic two-lane road between Sandwich and Orleans, offering occasional views of Cape Cod Bay.

## FALMOUTH

The Cape's second-largest town, which is quite spread out, is noted for its picturesque village green, attractive Main St area, beaches and nature preserves. Cape Cod doesn't get more quintessentially New England than the village green: A white picket fence surrounds a large triangle of grass bordered by fine 19th-century houses and a Congregational church with a white steeple. The church's bell was cast in 1796 by patriot Paul Revere. This is a nice place for a picnic.

### Orientation

MA 28 leads to Main St and the town green, the center of activity for inns, dining and shopping. Farther east on MA 28, college students flock to the Falmouth Heights area on Grand Ave and Falmouth Heights Rd, known for its inexpensive lodging and beachside activities. The town's best beach, Old Silver Beach, is 5 miles north of the town center, off scenic and tranquil MA 28A.

### Information

There are two locations for the Falmouth Chamber of Commerce (☎ 508-548-8500, 800-526-8532, www.falmouth-capecod.com). The main office at 20 Academy Lane, off Main St, is open 8:30 am to 5 pm weekdays year-round, plus the same time on Saturday from mid-April to mid-October and Sunday from late June to early September.

A smaller office at 320 Palmer Ave (on MA 28 barely north of the town center) is open 8:30 am to 5 pm Monday to Saturday mid-May to mid-October, with slightly longer hours on Friday night. It's also open 8:30 am to 5 pm on Sunday from late June to early September.

The Market Bookshop (☎ 508-548-5636), 15 Depot Ave, is the best in the area, bar none.

The year-round Falmouth Self-Service Laundromat (☎ 508-548-3911) is located at 32 Scranton Ave. The Maytag Self-Service Laundry (☎ 508-548-0776) is at 807 Main St.

Falmouth Hospital (☎ 508-548-5300), 100 Terheun Drive, off MA 28 just north of town, is open 24 hours a day.

In an emergency, call ☎ 911; for Falmouth police, call ☎ 508-457-2526.

### Historic Houses

The Falmouth Historical Society (☎ 508-548-4857) operates three historic buildings just off the town green.

In addition to scrimshaw carvings and 18th-century sailors' valentines, the **Conant House** has a room dedicated to Katherine Lee Bates, the town resident who wrote the popular patriotic hymn 'America the Beautiful.' Next door, the **Julia Wood House**, 55-65 Palmer Ave, features exhibits related to Falmouth's history. The **Hallet Barn**, behind the Wood House, contains 19th-century tools and farming equipment.

The houses are open 2 to 5 pm Wednesday to Sunday, mid-June to mid-September.

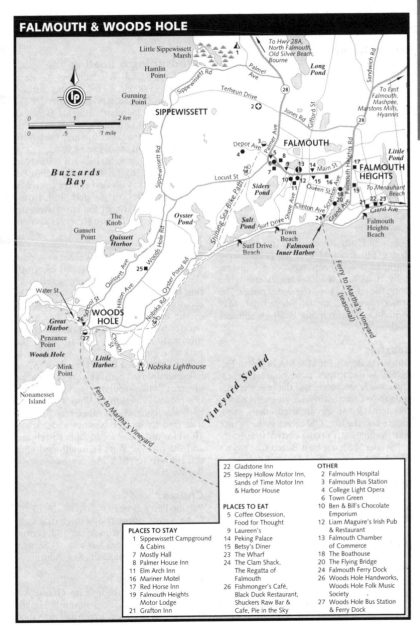

# FALMOUTH & WOODS HOLE

22  Gladstone Inn
25  Sleepy Hollow Motor Inn,
    Sands of Time Motor Inn
    & Harbor House

**PLACES TO EAT**
5   Coffee Obsession,
    Food for Thought
9   Laureen's
14  Peking Palace
15  Betsy's Diner
23  The Wharf
24  The Clam Shack,
    The Regatta of
    Falmouth
26  Fishmonger's Café,
    Black Duck Restaurant,
    Shuckers Raw Bar &
    Cafe, Pie in the Sky

**PLACES TO STAY**
1   Sippewissett Campground
    & Cabins
7   Mostly Hall
8   Palmer House Inn
11  Elm Arch Inn
16  Mariner Motel
17  Red Horse Inn
19  Falmouth Heights
    Motor Lodge
21  Grafton Inn

**OTHER**
2   Falmouth Hospital
3   Falmouth Bus Station
4   College Light Opera
6   Town Green
10  Ben & Bill's Chocolate
    Emporium
12  Liam Maguire's Irish Pub
    & Restaurant
13  Falmouth Chamber
    of Commerce
18  The Boathouse
20  The Flying Bridge
24  Falmouth Ferry Dock
26  Woods Hole Handworks,
    Woods Hole Folk Music
    Society
27  Woods Hole Bus Station
    & Ferry Dock

The admission to all of the buildings is $3 for adults and 50¢ for children.

## Nature Reserves

Ashumet Holly and Wildlife Sanctuary (☎ 508-563-6390), off of Route 151 from MA 28 in East Falmouth, is an Audubon bird sanctuary with eight nature trails and dozens of varieties of holly trees and bushes. The 45-acre sanctuary is open sunrise to sunset daily year-round; $3 adults, $2 children.

Waquoit Bay National Estuarine Research Reserve (☎ 508-457-0495), off MA 28 in East Falmouth, contains over 2500 acres of barrier beach and fragile estuary. Pick up a trail map and head out for a walk or simply spread out a picnic overlooking the estuary. The reserve is open during daylight hours daily.

Lowell Holly Reservation (no ☎), off of Route 130 from MA 28 in neighboring Mashpee, is a 130-acre oasis of woodlands, holly trees and wildflowers. A trail runs along the edge of two freshwater ponds. The preserve is open 9 am to 5 pm daily late May to mid-October; parking is $6 on summer weekends.

## Beaches

Old Silver Beach, off MA 28A in North Falmouth, is the town's most popular beach. The crowds are young and the beach is long and sandy. Facilities include changing rooms and a snack bar serving fried clams, sandwiches and the like. Old Silver makes a nice bike destination. Parking costs $10 daily.

Parking at Menauhant Beach (the town's best bay beach), off of Central Ave from MA 28 heading east, costs $5 weekdays and $8 weekends.

Town Beach, at the end of Shore St from Main St, is usually quite crowded because of its central location.

While Surf Drive Beach, off Main St, is popular with sea kayakers, it is also accessible from the Shining Sea Bike Path (see the Bicycling section). Parking costs $5 weekdays, $8 weekends.

The South Cape Beach State Park (☎ 508-457-0495), off Great Neck Rd from MA 28 in East Falmouth, has nature trails

and a snack stand, as well as a 2-mile-long sandy beach overlooking the Vineyard. Parking costs $2.

## Windsurfing & Boating

The Cape Cod Windsurfing Academy (☎ 508-495-0008), based at the Surfside Resort on Menauhant Rd, rents jet skis there and at Falmouth Heights Beach on Grand Ave. At Old Silver Beach, one of the Cape's best for windsurfing, they offer lessons and rent canoes and kayaks.

Waquoit Kayak at Edward's Boatyard (☎ 508-548-2216), 1209 MA 28 in East Falmouth, rents kayaks and canoes from May to mid-October to go paddling around Waquoit Bay National Estuarine Research Reserve (see the Nature Reserves section).

## Bicycling

Bicycling in Falmouth makes sense because the town is so spread out and car traffic slows to a snail's pace in summer. In addition, beach 'entrance' fees are usually nil for cyclists.

The chamber of commerce has a map with bicycling routes as well as detailed information on bike rental shops and parking regulations.

The Shining Sea Bike Path, which follows a former railroad bed, is a very popular and pleasant 7-mile (roundtrip) excursion from downtown Falmouth to Woods Hole. This path also connects to other bicycle routes that lead to smaller beaches and harbors. Head toward the wooded Sippewissett area and the tranquil West Falmouth and Quissett Harbors (off MA 28A north of town) to flee the crowds.

## Cruises

Patriot Party Boats (☎ 508-548-2626), 227 Clinton Ave, offers two-hour coastal sightseeing and sailing trips in an 18th-century replica schooner from July to early September. Tickets cost $20 adults, $14 children.

## Places to Stay

Guest houses and motels on Grand Ave, which runs alongside Falmouth Heights Beach, tend to be less expensive than those in the middle of town, but they're also noisier and often full in summer.

**Camping** The *Sippewissett Campground and Cabins* (☎ 508-548-2542, 836 Palmer Ave), off MA 28, about 2 miles north of town, has 100 wooded campsites and 11 camping cabins on 13 acres. Although the campground caters to RVs, you won't feel out of place in a tent. It's open mid-May to mid-October and features a free beach and Martha's Vineyard ferry shuttle. Rates for two people are $28 in summer, $20 off-season. Cabins cost $300 to $575 weekly in summer.

**Motels** *Falmouth Heights Motor Lodge* (☎ 508-548-3623, 800-468-3623, fax 508-548-2616, 146 Falmouth Heights Rd), a mile from the center of town and within walking distance of the beach and Vineyard ferry, has 24 standard motel rooms. Rates range from $79 to $120 in July and August, but are about $25 to $30 less off-season. It's open from May to mid-October.

The *Mariner Motel* (☎ 508-548-1331, 555 Main St), a five-minute walk from the center of town, has an outdoor pool and 30 motel-style rooms with refrigerators. Open year-round, rooms cost $89 to $119 in July and August, $49 to $69 in spring and fall.

The *Red Horse Inn* (☎ 508-548-0053, 800-628-3811, fax 508-542-6563, 28 Falmouth Heights Rd), just a five-minute walk to the island ferries, has 22 rooms with refrigerators that rent for $104 to $120 in July and August, $70 to $90 off-season. The motel is open May through October.

**B&Bs** The *Elm Arch Inn* (☎ 508-548-0133, 26 Elm Arch Way), off Main St in the center of town, offers 20 colonial-style guest rooms, many with shared bath and all with an in-room sink. The rambling inn, with lots of common rooms and a pool, dates to the early 19th century, but there's a modern annex too. The inn is open April through October; summer rates are $70 to $95, depending on the bath situation. The pricier rooms have TVs. Credit cards are not accepted here.

On the town green, the *Palmer House Inn* (☎ 508-548-1230, fax 540-1878, innkeepers@ palmerhouseinn.com, 81 Palmer Ave) is an early-19th-century Victorian house with 17 guest rooms decorated with period antiques. A full breakfast is included with these rates: $105 to $165 in the summer, $78 to $135 off-season.

*Mostly Hall* (☎ 508-548-3786, 800-682-0565, fax 508-457-1572, mostlyhl@cape.com, 27 W Main St), just off the town green, has six large and airy guest rooms. The B&B has a lot going for it: congenial innkeepers, full breakfasts, a comfortable living room and loaner bikes. Rooms cost $135 to $140 late May to mid-October; off-season they're $95 to $115. The inn is closed from January to mid-February.

Near Falmouth Heights Beach, a beach popular with college-age visitors southeast of the town center, is the *Gladstone Inn* (☎/fax 508-548-9851, 219 Grand Ave). The inn has 16 rooms renting for $65 to $85 for a double with shared bath, $120 up to $140 for a double with private bath, $45 for a single. A buffet breakfast is included. There is also a studio apartment over the garage renting for $150 nightly.

The *Grafton Inn* (☎ 508-540-8688, 800-642-4069, fax 508-540-1861, 261 Grand Ave), across from the beach, has 11 rooms with private bath and TV. Rates ($139 to $179) include a full buffet breakfast on the porch. The inn is open April to early December and off-season rooms cost $95 to $149.

## Places to Eat

*Coffee Obsession* (☎ 508-540-2233, 110 Palmer Ave) is a delightfully alternative place to hang out and get a cup of strong coffee. Jazz fills the rafters and the newspapers are communal.

*Laureen's* (☎ 508-540-9104, 170 Main St) is an upscale deli with fancy sandwiches, cold pasta salads, veggie burritos, rich desserts and good coffee.

*Food for Thought* (☎ 508-548-4498, 37 N Main St), open year-round for breakfast and lunch ($4 to $9), features burgers, soups and Mexican dishes. But there are plenty of vegetarian choices like eggplant parmesan.

*Betsy's Diner* (☎ 508-540-0060, 457 Main St), open for all meals year-round, is always crowded with locals who appreciate large portions of no-frills, inexpensive ($2 to $11), old-fashioned American fare.

*The Wharf* (☎ 508-548-0777, 228 Grand Ave), open May through October, is popular with the volleyball crowd that plays on the beach off the back porch. Fish and chips, sandwiches and burgers ($7 to $24) rule the lunch and dinner menu. The Dry Dock Bar, within the Wharf, is quite popular.

If you're tired of eating fish, the *Peking Palace* (☎ 508-540-8204, 452 Main St) serves remarkably good Cantonese, Szechuan and Mandarin dishes. It's open year-round, until 2 am nightly in summer.

*The Clam Shack* (☎ 508-540-7758, 227 Clinton Ave) is a classic of the genre: tiny, with picnic tables on the back deck and lots of fried clams for a few bucks. It's open from mid-May to early September.

*The Regatta of Falmouth* (☎ 508-548-5400, 217 Scranton Ave) has an enviable location overlooking the mouth of the inner harbor. Fortunately the food rivals the view: The creative continental cuisine is easily the finest in the area. Dishes might include grilled fish with a three-mustard sauce or boneless rack of lamb. Fancy but unstuffy, the restaurant is open mid-May to mid-September for dinner. Arrive before 5:45 pm for a $20 three-course special or spend about $40 per person for a complete dinner with wine.

The *Chapoquoit Grill* (☎ 508-540-7794, 410 MA 28A), a few miles north of town, has excellent pizzas loaded with garlic and even better nightly seafood and swordfish specials for $7 to $18 per dish. You'll wait in line in summer, but it's worth it.

## Entertainment

*Liam Maguire's Irish Pub & Restaurant* (☎ 508-548-0285, 273 Main St) is as authentic as it gets this side of the Atlantic. Between Guinness on draft, an Irish waitstaff and boisterous sing-alongs, you'll leave here looking for the Blarney Stone.

*The Flying Bridge* (☎ 508-548-2700, 220 Scranton Ave), with a prime harbor location, is better for appetizers and for grazing –

especially when accompanied by live entertainment in summer – than full meals.

For live music, *The Boathouse* (☎ 508-548-7800, 88 Scranton Ave), open from late May to mid-October, has festive crowds.

The *College Light Opera* (☎ 508-548-0668), Depot Ave, a collegiate company of singers and musicians, performs nine productions late June to late August. Call for schedules.

## Shopping

Main St, worth a stroll as you enjoy an ice cream from Ben & Bill's Chocolate Emporium (☎ 508-548-7878), 209 Main St, is lined with clothing stores and home-accessory shops.

## Getting There & Away

**Bus** Bonanza buses (☎ 800-556-3815, www .bonanzabus.com) serve Falmouth from Boston, Providence and New York City. At least 10 buses go from Boston to Falmouth daily; the ride takes 85 minutes and costs $13.50 one way. The bus stops on Depot Ave, near the center of town.

**Car** From the Bourne Bridge, take MA 28 South into town; in the center of Falmouth MA 28 makes a left turn and heads east toward Hyannis and Chatham. The directional names for MA 28 can be confusing: Even though you are heading due east toward Hyannis, West Dennis and Chatham, the road signs say MA 28 South.

The driving details for Falmouth are as follows:

| destination | mileage | hr:min |
|---|---|---|
| Boston, MA | 75 miles | 1:30 |
| Bourne Bridge, MA | 15 miles | 0:20 |
| Hyannis, MA | 23 miles | 0:45 |
| Providence, RI | 71 miles | 1:25 |
| Provincetown, MA | 71 miles | 1:15 |
| Woods Hole, MA | 4 miles | 0:12 |

**Boat** From Falmouth you can catch a passenger ferry (no cars) to Martha's Vineyard. (Car ferries to the Vineyard depart from nearby Woods Hole.)

See the Martha's Vineyard & Nantucket Island chapter for information on getting out to the Vineyard from Falmouth.

## Getting Around

The Whoosh Trolley, which operates 10 am to 9 pm daily late May to mid-October, costs $1 per ride. It makes a loop around the major points of interest in Falmouth and the Martha's Vineyard ferry in Woods Hole. Pick up a schedule of current locations and the departure times from the chamber of commerce.

For information on getting around by bicycle, see Falmouth's Bicycling section, earlier in this chapter.

## WOODS HOLE

Woods Hole is a world-famous center for marine research and exploration. The only places to visit in this picturesque village are a few small maritime exhibits. Most travelers passing through town are headed for the Steamship Authority's big car ferries to Martha's Vineyard.

## Orientation & Information

From MA 28 in Falmouth, Woods Hole Rd leads directly to the ferry terminal. Water St, the main road, branches off Woods Hole Rd and leads to restaurants and the research institutions.

The chamber of commerce in Falmouth has information on Woods Hole; see Information under Falmouth.

## Things to See & Do

The **National Marine Fisheries** (☎ 508-495-2001), Albatross St, was founded here in 1871 to study and promote the well-being of the USA's fisheries. Their aquarium, the country's first, is free and open 10 am to 4 pm weekdays year-round and on weekends mid-June to mid-September. Seals are fed twice daily in front of the aquarium.

The Marine Fisheries was followed in 1888 by the **Marine Biological Laboratory** (☎ 508-289-7623 for tour reservations), set up to do basic biology research based on marine life forms. Their tours are popular, so make reservations one week in advance.

Otherwise, the visitors center on Water St is open 10 am to 4 pm weekdays June through August.

In 1930, the **Woods Hole Oceanographic Institution** (☎ 508-289-2100), 15 School St, was established to pursue deep-sea research using funding from the Rockefeller Foundation. The exhibit center is open 10 am to 4:30 pm various days of the week April through December.

In the 1960s, these three were joined by the USGS's Branch of Marine Geography (☎ 508-548-8700). Most recently, the **Sea Education Association** (☎ 508-540-3954) was formed in 1975. If you want to know anything about the oceans, this is where to find it.

**Nobska Lighthouse**, Church St off Woods Hole Rd, is dramatically situated on a point overlooking Vineyard Sound. It's a great place for a picnic or to watch the sun slowly set or quickly rise.

The **Shining Sea Bike Path** runs between Falmouth and Woods Hole. See the Bicycling section under Falmouth.

## Places to Stay

The *Sleepy Hollow Motor Inn* (☎ 508-548-1986, fax 548-5932, 527 Woods Hole Rd), just out of town, has 24 basic rooms for $85 to $115 mid-June to mid-September, $65 to $95 off-season (closed November through April).

The *Sands of Time Motor Inn and Harbor House* (☎ 508-548-6300, 800-841-0114, fax 508-457-0160, susan@sandsoftime .com, 549 Woods Hole Rd), a 10-minute walk from town, overlooks the harbor. There are 20 modern motel rooms and 12 inn-style guest rooms (some with fireplaces) in the adjacent Victorian house that rent for $100 to $170 June through September, $75 to $125 in off-season (closed mid-November through March).

## Places to Eat

All of Woods Hole's eateries overlook the water. The first one you see as you enter the village along Water St is the *Fishmonger's Café* (☎ 508-548-9148, 56 Water St). It's just what you'd expect: rustic, atmospheric, with lots of good food for all three meals. Lunch ranges from $5 to $10, dinner from $8 to $20 (closed December and January).

The seasonal *Black Duck Restaurant* (☎ *508-548-9165, 73 Water St)*, just a few steps away on the opposite side of the street, also has a good menu and decent prices.

*Shuckers World Famous Raw Bar & Cafe* (☎ *508-540-3850, 91A Water St)*, behind the Woods Hole Oceanographic Institution's News and Information Offices, has fresh-shucked clams and oysters as well as a good selection of light meals and, in the evening, full dinners for $6 to $16; open seasonally.

*Pie in the Sky* (☎ *508-540-5475, 10 Water St)* is *the* year-round place to go for coffee, pastries and sandwiches while you wait for the ferry.

### Entertainment
The *Woods Hole Folk Music Society* (☎ *508-540-0320)*, in the Community Hall on Water St, hosts performances on the first and third Sunday of each month between October and May.

### Shopping
Woods Hole Handworks (☎ 508-540-5291), 68 Water St, carries a varied selection of creative items made by cooperative members.

### Getting There & Away
**Bus** Bonanza buses (☎ 800-556-3815, www .bonanzabus.com) discharge passengers at the ferry terminal in Woods Hole from Boston, Providence and New York City. In theory, bus schedules are designed to coincide with ferry departures and arrivals, but in practice, neither waits if the other is late. So it's better not to rely on the last connection of the day.

**Car** Driving details for Woods Hole are as follows:

| destination | mileage | hr:min |
| --- | --- | --- |
| Boston, MA | 81 miles | 1:45 |
| Bourne Bridge, MA | 21 miles | 0:32 |
| Falmouth, MA | 4 miles | 0:12 |
| Hyannis, MA | 29 miles | 1:00 |
| Provincetown, MA | 75 miles | 1:30 |

**Boat** See the Martha's Vineyard & Nantucket Island chapter for details on getting to the island from Woods Hole. Note that you will need advance reservations to take your car, and that the parking lots in Woods Hole fill up early and often in summer. There are satellite lots with shuttle bus service in Falmouth.

### Getting Around
Woods Hole is tiny, so your feet will serve you well. For a nominal fee, the Whoosh Trolley (see the Getting Around section under Falmouth) connects the ferry terminal to points of interest in Falmouth. See also Bicycling under Falmouth.

## SANDWICH
The Cape's oldest town (founded in 1637) is also the first one you'll encounter across the Bourne Bridge. Among its many attractions are a quaint village center complete with duck pond and grist mill, fine historic houses, a famous glass museum, a renowned horticultural park with indoor collections of Americana and an adequate town beach. After exploring the village, head east out of town on MA 6A, the prettiest road on the Cape.

### Orientation
Cross the Sagamore Bridge to US 6 East to Route 130 North (also called Water St) into the center of town. Or take MA 6A after crossing the bridge and take Main St into town.

Water, Main and Grove Sts converge in the small village center. Tupper Rd, off of MA 6A, leads to the marina and town beach.

### Information
The office of the Cape Cod Canal Region Chamber of Commerce (☎ 508-759-6000, www.capecodcanalchamber.org), 70 Main St (MA 6A), is in the village of Buzzards Bay, on the mainland side of the Bourne Bridge. The office (open 9 am to 5 pm weekdays year-round) contains information on Sandwich, the village of Bourne and activities along the Cape Cod Canal.

If you're visiting during summer, skip the main office and head to the seasonal booth (no ☎) on Route 130 North.

Titcomb's Book Shop (☎ 508-888-2331), 432 MA 6A, is the best on the north side of the Cape.

## Museums

The **Heritage Plantation of Sandwich** (☎ 508-888-3300), on Grove St, about a mile from the center, has a number of fine collections (vintage automobiles, crafts and folk art, firearms and miniatures) spanning various American periods. The lovely grounds include 76 acres of naturalized plantings and an outdoor cafe. The museum is open 10 am to 5 pm daily early May to late October; admission is $9 adults, $4.50 children.

The **Sandwich Glass Museum** (☎ 508-888-0251), 129 Main St, celebrates Sandwich's famous glassmaking heyday from 1825 to 1888. There are fine examples of molded, blown and etched glass, as well as dioramas that show how the glass was formed and a video that recounts the dramatic rise and fall of the industry. The museum is open 9:30 am to 5 pm daily April through October, 9:30 am to 4 pm Wednesday through Sunday November through March (closed in January). Admission is $3.50 adults, $1 children.

The **Dexter Mill** (no ☎), near Main and River Sts, stands at the edge of a picturesque mill pond. Originally built in 1654, the present one was rebuilt in 1961. Today, in addition to touring the small mill, you can purchase bags of freshly ground cornmeal. It's open 10 am to 4:45 pm Saturday and 1 to 4:45 pm Sunday mid-May to mid-October, plus 10 am to 4:45 pm weekdays mid-June to mid-September. Admission is $1.50 adults, 75¢ children.

The **Hoxie House** (☎ 508-888-1173), 18 Water St (Route 130), is the best of Sandwich's many historic houses. The restored circa-1675 house is filled up with period antiques. It's open 10 am to 5 pm Monday through Saturday and 1 to 5 pm on Sunday mid-June to mid-October. Admission is the same as at the mill; combination tickets are available for the Hoxie House and mill.

The **Thornton W Burgess Museum** (☎ 508-888-4668), 4 Water St, is dedicated to the Sandwich native, naturalist and children's book author (he wrote all the Peter Rabbit books). Children enjoy the 'see-and-touch' room, story hours and Peter Rabbit puzzles and games. It's open 10 am to 4 pm Monday through Saturday and 1 to 4 pm Sunday mid-April through October. A nominal donation is requested.

### Green Briar Nature Center

This conservation area (☎ 508-888-6870), a few miles east of town off MA 6A, offers 57 acres of land with walking trails and wildflower and herb gardens. The center hosts lectures and natural-history classes, but for some the big draw is the old-fashioned kitchen that makes and sells jams. The kitchen is open the same hours as the Burgess Museum; trails are accessible year-round.

### Cape Cod Canal

The canal, which effectively separates the Cape from mainland Massachusetts, took five years to dig and was opened in 1914, just a couple of weeks before the Panama Canal. Every year it saves thousands of ships from having to sail an extra 135 miles around the tip of the Cape at Provincetown, a treacherous route studded with constantly changing sandbars.

You can take a boat ride up the 17-mile-long canal with Cape Cod Canal Tours (☎ 508-295-3883), off US 6 and MA 28 at the Onset Bay Town Pier, a few miles west of the Bourne Bridge. Depending on the length of the trip, tours are $7 to $8 adults, $3.50 to $4 children.

### Beaches

Off Tupper Rd from MA 6A, Town Neck Beach is a long, pebbly beach, best visited at high tide if you want to swim. There are restrooms; parking costs $5.

### Bicycling

Each side of the Cape Cod Canal has a well-maintained bike trail. In Sandwich rent bicycles at Sandwich Cycles (☎ 508-833-2453),

40 MA 6A. Near the canal, try P&M Cycles (☎ 508-759-2830), 29 MA 6A, which is in Buzzards Bay.

## Places to Stay

For the money, Sandwich offers more value in its lodging than surrounding towns.

**Camping** *Shawme Crowell State Forest* (☎ 508-888-0351, 877-422-6762 for reservations), off Route 130 from MA 6A about 2 miles from the center of town, has 285 wooded sites scattered over almost 3,000 acres. Open year-round, camping costs $9 for two people.

*Scussett Beach State Reservation* (☎ 508-888-0859, 877-422-6762 for reservations), off MA 3 on the mainland side of the canal just before the Sagamore Bridge, has 98 sites adjacent to the Cape Cod Canal. Fees are similar to Shawme, and it is open year-round.

*Peter's Pond Park* (☎ 508-477-1775), Cotuit Rd off Route 130 South, is more developed than the other camping options. There are 480 sites (mostly shaded, some along the pond) on 100 acres with walking trails and a pond for swimming. It's open mid-April to mid-October and costs $24 to $36 for two. The campground also rents tents. Teepees rent for $225 weekly, $40 daily in-season.

**Motels** About 5 miles east of town, the well-maintained *Spring Garden Motel* (☎ 508-888-0710, 800-303-1751, fax 508-833-2849, springg@capecod.net, 578 MA 6A) has nine rooms and two efficiency apartments. Rooms overlook a tranquil salt marsh and tidal creek and rent for $79 to $99 in July and August, $67 to $89 off-season (closed December through March). There is also a pool.

The nicely landscaped and well-shaded *Shadynook Inn & Motel* (☎ 508-888-0409, 800-338-5208, fax 508-888-4039, thenook@capecod.net, 14 MA 6A) has 30 clean, simple and large rooms, some of which are efficiency units with a microwave. Doubles rent for $95 to $140 mid-June to early September; one suite sleeps four people for $175. The motel is open year-round and rooms rent for $65 to $140 off-season.

The *Sandy Neck Motel* (☎ 508-362-3992, fax 362-5170, snmotel@capecod.net, 669 MA 6A), at the entrance to Sandy Neck Beach (see the Beaches section under Barnstable), has 12 standard rooms that rent for $79 to $89 mid-June to early September, $65 to $75 off-season. The motel is closed January through March.

**B&Bs** The *Dillingham House* (☎ 508-833-0065, fax 833-4713, 71 Main St), a mile or so out of town, is a circa-1650 Cape house with three simple rooms and two living rooms. Both living rooms are comfortable, stocked with books, well-worn couches, a piano and a wood stove. A continental breakfast is included for $75 for a shared bath, $10 more for a private bath; the house is open June through October.

The *Summer House* (☎/fax 508-888-4991, sumhouse@capecod.net, 158 Main St), in the center of town, has five simple but nice guest rooms. Whimsical common space takes up the 1st floor, where a full breakfast is served. English tea is served on the back porch or in the garden. Rooms are $80 to $105 late May to mid-October, less in the winter.

The *Captain Ezra Nye House* (☎ 508-888-6142, 800-388-2278, fax 508-833-2897, 152 Main St) has six carpeted guest rooms, one with a working fireplace. One of the living rooms has a TV and VCR. A full breakfast is included in the rates of $85 to $110 mid-May through October; it's open year-round.

*Wingscorton Farm Inn* (☎ 508-888-0534, fax 888-0545, 11 Wing Blvd), an 18th-century farmhouse set well back from MA 6A, has been authentically restored and furnished with antiques and four-poster beds. Each suite can accommodate four. A separate carriage house has a complete kitchen and plenty of space to stretch out; it's great for longer stays. The farm is home to free-range chickens (breakfast eggs are fresh) and other small animals. Open year-round, suites rent for $115, the carriage house $150.

## Places to Eat

The *Sagamore Inn* (☎ 508-888-9707, 1131 MA 6A) is a friendly restaurant owned and staffed by locals. The interior is classic 'old Cape Cod' with tin ceilings, wooden floors, wooden booths and country curtains. In addition to a beloved Yankee pot roast, the kitchen serves hearty Italian and seafood dishes ($7 to $12) for lunch and dinner daily, except Tuesday, April through November.

The *Bee-Hive Tavern* (☎ *508-833-1184, 406 MA 6A*) is popular with the locals who come for value-conscious servings of pasta, fried seafood, burgers and sandwiches. You can also get more complete meals like chicken teriyaki. It's open for lunch and dinner daily ($5 to $16) and for breakfast on weekends year-round.

The *Dunbar Tea Shop* (☎ *508-833-2485, 1 Water St*), operated by a British couple, offers a ploughman's lunch (choice of three cheeses, baguette, side salad and pickled beets and onions), soup, quiche and Scottish shortbread at lunchtime. Otherwise, patrons come for an authentic English tea ($9.75 per person, plus tea) in a country setting. The place is usually packed. It's open 8 am to 8 pm daily late May through October and 11 am to 4:30 pm Thursday through Monday the rest of the year.

The *Marshland Restaurant* (☎ *508-888-9824, 109 MA 6A*), a small roadside place, serves coffee and muffins at breakfast and $6.50 lunch specials such as meatloaf or baked stuffed shells. Eat at a booth or take out. It's open for breakfast on Sunday, breakfast and lunch on Monday and all three meals the rest of the week.

*Captain Scott's* (☎ *508-888-1675, 71 Tupper Rd*) serves basic Italian dishes, fried seafood and simply prepared fish for $4 to $15 in casual surroundings that draw in the locals. It's open 11:30 am to 9:30 pm daily year-round.

The *Dan'l Webster Inn* (☎ *508-888-3622, 149 Main St*) is the fanciest place to eat in town. Have lunch ($7 to $14) in the sunny solarium filled with potted plants and retreat to the tavern for lighter meals and drinks in the evening. Or dress neatly but not formally for continental cuisine in the main dining room. The restaurant is open for lunch and dinner daily year-round, and for breakfast daily mid-April to mid-November.

## Shopping
Since 1837, Pairpoint Crystal (☎ 508-888-2344, 800-899-0953), 851 MA 6A, has been renowned for its glass-blowing techniques and original designs. You can watch artisans at work 9 am to 4:30 pm weekdays April through December. The sales showroom is open daily year-round.

## Getting There & Away
**Bus** Plymouth & Brockton buses (☎ 508-778-9767, www.p-b.com) do not serve Sandwich but they stop nearby in Bourne. Call for specifics about the inconvenient location.

**Train** Cape Cod Scenic Railroad (☎ 508-771-3788), Jarves St off MA 6A, makes a two-hour return journey to Hyannis, passing cranberry bogs, salt marshes and small villages along the way. At press time, the train was not running, but there are plans to resurrect it.

**Car** Driving details for Sandwich are as follows:

| destination | mileage | hr:min |
|---|---|---|
| Boston, MA | 64 miles | 1:10 |
| Chatham, MA | 32 miles | 0:45 |
| Hyannis, MA | 16 miles | 0:22 |
| Providence, RI | 68 miles | 1:20 |
| Provincetown, MA | 62 miles | 1:15 |
| Sagamore Bridge, MA | 4 miles | 0:08 |

## BARNSTABLE
Barnstable's section of MA 6A lives up to its reputation as the Cape's most picturesque road. It's a tranquil, winding route affording glimpses of the ocean and salt marshes. It's also dotted with antique stores, art galleries, craft shops and pricey B&Bs. Take practically any northern turn off of MA 6A and you'll reach the shores of Cape Cod Bay. Perhaps the best thing about Barnstable is Sandy Neck Beach, a 6-mile-long stretch of barrier beach and dunes.

## Orientation
MA 6A runs from Sandwich through Barnstable, Yarmouth, Dennis and Brewster. If

you're in a hurry, take US 6 to exit 5 for West Barnstable, exit 6 for Barnstable.

The town of Barnstable includes seven distinct villages and stretches the width of the Cape, from Cape Cod Bay on the north shore to Nantucket Sound on the south. But the most interesting section of town follows historic MA 6A, which is also referred to as Main St and Old King's Hwy.

## Information

Contact the Hyannis Area Chamber of Commerce (☎ 508-362-5230, 800-449-6647, www.hyannischamber.com), 1481 Route 132, in Hyannis, for information on all seven of Barnstable's villages. The office is open 9 am to 5 pm Monday through Saturday year-round, and on Sunday from late May to early September.

The conveniently located Cape Cod Chamber of Commerce (☎ 508-862-0700, 888-332-2732, www.capecodchamber.com), just off exit 6 from US 6, represents the entire Cape and certainly provides information on Barnstable. It's open 8:30 am to 5 pm weekdays year-round, with additional Saturday (10 am to 4 pm) and Sunday (10 am to 2 pm) hours from mid-May to mid-October.

## Things to See

The **West Parish Meetinghouse** (☎ 508-362-8624), on Route 149 between US 6 and MA 6A, dates to 1717. Its members belong to the oldest Congregational parish in the country and trace their origins back to London's First Congregational Church.

The **Donald Trayser Memorial Museum Complex** (☎ 508-362-2092), 3353 MA 6A, served as the Old Customs House from the mid- to late 19th century. At that time, Barnstable Harbor was the busiest port on the Cape. (It silted up in the early 20th century.) The museum contains a random assortment of items: the custom keeper's office, imported ivory, a collection of Sandwich glass, a bicycle dating to 1900 and a late 17th-century jail cell. It's open 1:30 to 4:30 pm Tuesday through Sunday mid-June to mid-October; donations are requested.

## Beaches

Sandy Neck Beach is Cape Cod Bay's best beach; it's 6 miles long and backed by a rather extensive network of high dunes. Facilities include a changing room, restrooms and a snack bar; parking is $10. To reach it take Sandy Neck Rd off MA 6A on the Sandwich-Barnstable town line.

A 9-mile (roundtrip) nature trail begins at the parking lot and heads into the dunes and salt marshes. It's well worth the four-hour walk.

## Whale-Watching Cruises

At Barnstable Harbor off MA 6A, Hyannis Whale Watcher Cruises (☎ 508-362-6088, 888-942-5392) offers trips with an onboard naturalist for $18 to $24 adult, $15 children, April through October.

## Places to Stay

MA 6A is lined with former sea captains' houses that have been converted into romantic B&Bs. If you have a bit of money to spare, you'll find a few places to spend it here.

The *Henry Crocker House* (☎ 508-362-6348, fax 375-0902, hnrycrokr@capecod.net, 3026 MA 6A), with three guest rooms and lots of common space, is a period timepiece operated by amicable hosts. Rooms, including a full breakfast, rent for $95 to $125 year-round.

The circa-1750 *Crocker Tavern Bed & Breakfast* (☎ 508-362-5115, 800-773-5359, fax 508-362-5562, crocktav@capecod.net, 3095 MA 6A), an historic hostelry, features five spacious but sparsely decorated period-style guest rooms. Rates are $100 to $125 year-round.

The *Charles Hinckley House* (☎ 508-362-9924, fax 362-8861), on Scudder Lane at MA 6A, is an 1809 Federal-style house with four lovely and comfortable rooms, each with a fireplace and period antiques. The full breakfast is one of the best on the Cape. Rates are $129 to $169 year-round.

## Places to Eat

*Mill Way Fish and Lobster Market* (☎ 508-362-2760), in Barnstable Harbor, is operated by a professional chef who packs up fish sandwiches, fried seafood and fish chowder for patrons to take to the harbor for $5 to $8. It's open April through October.

***Barnstable Tavern*** (☎ *508-362-2355, 3176 MA 6A*), in the center of the village, serves lunch ($5 to $10) and dinner ($11 to $20) year-round. You'll find standard pub fare such as burgers and sandwiches, but you can also get items such as hummus, stuffed grape leaves and grilled rainbow trout. The front patio is pleasant in warm weather.

***Four Seas*** (☎ *508-775-1394, 360 S Main St),* in Centerville, named after the four bodies of water that surround the Cape, is often regarded as the Cape's best home-made ice cream purveyor. The shop dispenses its ultra-fresh riches from mid-May to mid-September. The place is packed as densely as pints of beach plum ice cream. Don't think about the fat content, especially if you can visit only once.

### Entertainment

The ***Benefit Coffeehouse*** (☎ *508-775-5165, 428-1053),* on Main St in Liberty Hall in Marstons Mills, sponsors acoustic-folk and folk-rock benefit concerts. Call to see what's playing; tickets are $8 to $10. To reach the village of Marstons Mills, take Route 149 south from US 6.

The ***Barnstable Comedy Club*** (☎ *508-362-6333, 3171 MA 6A),* the country's oldest non-professional theater group, performs serious and hilarious plays year-round. Call for the schedule.

### Getting There & Around

The Plymouth & Brockton bus (☎ 508-778-9767, www.p-b.com) from Boston stops at the commuter lot on US 6 in Barnstable, a few miles from anything of interest in town.

Driving details for Barnstable are as follows:

| destination | mileage | hr:min |
| --- | --- | --- |
| Boston, MA | 77 miles | 1:25 |
| Hyannis, MA | 5 miles | 0:10 |
| Provincetown, MA | 53 miles | 1:15 |
| Sagamore Bridge, MA | 17 miles | 0:25 |
| Sandwich, MA | 12 miles | 0:15 |
| Yarmouth, MA | 4 miles | 0:08 |

MA 6A is winding and narrow, so it's not a road that's well-suited to bicycles.

## HYANNIS

Hyannis is the commercial and transportation hub of Cape Cod. The recently rejuvenated waterfront and Main St area make it a pleasant place to wait for a ferry or a bus. Hyannis draws crowds of summer college workers for their one night off per week, and also attracts Kennedy fans: Hyannisport is the summer home to this US political family.

### Orientation

From US 6, take Route 132 South (exit 6) to the airport rotary to Barnstable Rd to Main St. From Falmouth or Chatham, take MA 28 directly to Main St.

Main St (one way) is the principal shopping and dining thoroughfare. North and South Sts run parallel to it on either side. Ocean St runs south from Main St to a town park and beach.

Gosnold St connects Ocean St to Sea St, where there is another decent beach. Both ferry terminals (the Ocean St Dock and the South St Dock) are about a 10-minute walk from the bus station, which is just one block north of Main St.

### Information

The office of the Hyannis Area Chamber of Commerce (☎ 508-362-5230, 800-449-6647, www.hyannischamber.com), 1481 Route 132, about a mile south of US 6, is generally open 9 am to 5 pm Monday through Saturday year-round. From late May to early September it's also open on Sunday.

Borders Books, Music, Cafe (☎ 508-862-6363) and Barnes & Noble (☎ 508-771-1400), both on MA 132, are the big players in town.

Cape Cod Hospital (☎ 508-771-1800), 27 Park St, a few blocks from the center of town, is open 24 hours a day.

In an emergency call ☎ 911; for Hyannis police, call ☎ 508-775-0387.

The Laundry Room (☎ 508-771-5022), at 497 W Main St, is open 7 am to 10 pm daily.

MASSACHUSETTS

# HYANNIS

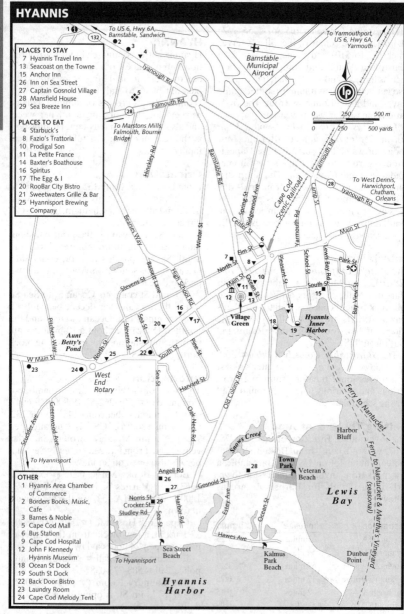

**PLACES TO STAY**
- 7   Hyannis Travel Inn
- 13   Seacoast on the Towne
- 15   Anchor Inn
- 26   Inn on Sea Street
- 27   Captain Gosnold Village
- 28   Mansfield House
- 29   Sea Breeze Inn

**PLACES TO EAT**
- 4   Starbuck's
- 8   Fazio's Trattoria
- 10   Prodigal Son
- 11   La Petite France
- 14   Baxter's Boathouse
- 16   Spiritus
- 17   The Egg & I
- 20   RooBar City Bistro
- 21   Sweetwaters Grille & Bar
- 25   Hyannisport Brewing Company

**OTHER**
- 1   Hyannis Area Chamber of Commerce
- 2   Borders Books, Music, Cafe
- 3   Barnes & Noble
- 5   Cape Cod Mall
- 6   Bus Station
- 9   Cape Cod Hospital
- 12   John F Kennedy Hyannis Museum
- 18   Ocean St Dock
- 19   South St Dock
- 22   Back Door Bistro
- 23   Laundry Room
- 24   Cape Cod Melody Tent

## John F Kennedy Hyannis Museum

This museum (☎ 508-790-3077), 397 Main St, celebrates John F Kennedy's life in Hyannis through an exhibition of more than 100 heart-warming photographs. John F Kennedy, the 35th president of the US, and his family summered in Hyannisport (an exclusive section of Hyannis) from the early 1930s until he was assassinated in 1963. Many Kennedy family members still have family homes here. The 'Kennedy Compound,' as it is called, is just a group of private houses (albeit lovely ones), surrounded in most cases by tall fences.

The museum is open 10 am to 3:45 pm Monday to Saturday and 1 to 4 pm Sunday from mid-April to mid-October. Off-season (except January to mid-February), it's open Wednesday to Saturday. Admission is $3 for all over age 16.

A simple JFK memorial was erected off Ocean St overlooking the harbor where he often sailed.

## Beaches

The Sea Street Beach, off Sea St from the western end of Main St, is a narrow but decent beach with restrooms and a bathhouse; parking is $8.

Kalmus Park Beach, off Ocean St, has a restroom, bathhouse and good windsurfing conditions; parking is $8.

Veteran's Beach, off Ocean St at the town park, is as much a park as it is a beach. Families come to picnic and barbecue (there's a snack bar too), play paddle ball and swim in shallow waters. Parking is $8.

West Hyannisport (technically Centerville) has Craigville Beach, the largest and one of the most popular on Cape Cod. It has restrooms and changing rooms; parking is $8.

## Activities

Eastern Mountain Sports (EMS; ☎ 508-362-8690), 1513 MA 132, rents kayaks and offers instructional clinics throughout the year on everything related to outdoor activities, from using a compass to discussing specific bicycling routes.

## Airplane Sightseeing

Cape Flight (☎ 508-775-8171), Barnstable Municipal Airport at the Route 132 rotary, offers 30- and 60-minute sightseeing trips in twin-engine propeller planes high above this fragile strip of land. Fly over the lighthouse at Chatham or the Cape Cod Canal ($69 up to three people) or out to Provincetown ($129 up to three people). It's a great way to fully appreciate the Cape's unique geology and topography. The grand tour ($200 up to three people) lasts two hours and includes the islands.

## Cruises

The boat *Eventide* (☎ 508-775-0222), at the Ocean St Dock, offers a variety of voyages designed to suit laid-back sailors who want to maximize wind power and minimize motor noise. It sails far into Nantucket Sound, around the bay at twilight and along the coast in front of the Kennedy compound. Tickets cost $20 adults, $5 children, mid-April to late November.

Hyannisport Harbor Cruises (☎ 508-778-2600), at the Ocean St Dock, offers hour-long sightseeing trips of the harbor and bay during the day and at sunset late April to late October. Tickets cost $10 to $14 adults, $5 to $7 children.

Cape Cod Duck Mobile Tours (☎ 508-362-1117), 448 Main St, utilizes amphibious vehicles on a 45-minute tour of Hyannis' harbor and side streets. If you take it, you'll finally understand the meaning of feeling like a 'duck out of water.' Tickets are $12 adults, $8 children.

## Places to Stay

**Motels** *Hyannis Travel Inn* (☎/fax 508-775-8200, 800-352-7190, 18 North St) has 83 rooms. They also have an indoor swimming pool as well as an outdoor pool. Doubles in July and August cost $50 to $99; off-season they are $36 to $69; closed December and January.

*Seacoast on the Towne* (☎ 508-775-3828, 800-466-4100, fax 508-771-2179, seacoast@capecod.net, 33 Ocean St) is right in the middle of the action. The 26 cheery rooms, some with refrigerator, cost $55 to $98 in

July and August, $42 to $68 off-season. Keep in mind that the motel is closed November through April.

The *Anchor Inn* (☎ 508-775-0357, fax 775-1313, info@anchorin.com, 1 South St), about a half mile from the ferries, rents 43 simple rooms, most of which have balconies overlooking the harbor. Rates are $90 to $145 mid-June to mid-September, $39 to $85 the rest of the year.

**Cottages** *Captain Gosnold Village* (☎ 508-775-9111, 230 Gosnold St), at Sea St, a block from Sea Street Beach, offers motel rooms, fully equipped cottages and efficiency apartments that can sleep up to eight people. This is a good place for longer stays and for families since there's a playground, a pool and plenty of wooded space between units. From mid-June to early September, rates begin at $90 for rooms, $105 for studios and $170 for cottages; prices increase with the size of the cottage. It's open year-round.

**B&Bs** The *Mansfield House* (☎/fax 508-771-9455, mansfldhse@aol.com, 70 Gosnold St), a short walk from a few beaches, has four rooms with TV and VCR; one room has a private deck. The rooms, which are constantly being upgraded, cost $75 to $90, including breakfast. It's closed mid-October to mid-May.

The *Sea Breeze Inn* (☎ 508-771-7213, fax 862-0663, seabreeze@capecod.net, 397 Sea St) has 14 clean and pleasant motel-style rooms (all with private bath) within a sandal shuffle of the beach. A few rooms have ocean views. Summertime rates are $75 to $140; $55 to $105 the rest of the year.

The *Inn on Sea Street* (☎ 508-775-8030, innonsea@capecod.net, 358 Sea St), within an easy walk of the beach, is very nice. Most of the nine rooms have private bath; all are decorated with tasteful Victorian or English country antiques. If you want to splurge, rent the simple, all-white cottage with a complete kitchen. A nice home-baked breakfast is included: $78 to $115 for rooms, $125 for the cottage. It's closed mid-November through March.

## Places to Eat
There are more than 60 places to eat in town, so you'll be able to find something that suits your wallet and taste buds.

The *Prodigal Son* (☎ 508-771-1337, 10 Ocean St), a laid-back coffeehouse more apropos of the West Coast than the Cape, has a limited but sufficient selection of lunch and dinner plates ($5 to $8) and a fine selection of microbrews and wine. The coffee is strong. The comfortable couches are perfect for listening to an extensive line-up of folk, blues and jazz. Stop in to check out the listings of up-coming events. The restaurant is open morning until late at night.

*Spiritus* (☎ 508-775-2955, 500 Main St) serves good strong coffee, pizza by the slice and filling sandwiches. The funky storefront cafe is a popular hang-out throughout the day and night.

*La Petite France* (☎ 508-771-4445, 349 Main St), presided over by a hands-on Frenchman, serves excellent onion soup and cold Mediterranean salads, as well as highly recommended clam chowder and sandwiches made with baguettes and home-roasted meats.

The *Hyannisport Brewing Company* (☎ 508-775-8289, 720 Main St) is a popular microbrewery where you can munch on onion rings, burgers and chili – all made with the same beer you'll be drinking. Dishes at lunch and dinner cost $6 to $12.

*The Egg & I* (☎ 508-771-1596, 521 Main St), open when other places aren't (11 pm to 1 pm), is probably the only place on the Cape where you can get a fried steak sandwich at 4 am. After sunrise, locals stop in for eggs, pancakes and corned beef hash. You won't have to spend more than $6 here.

While *Baxter's Boathouse* (☎ 508-775-4490, 177 Pleasant St), open for lunch and dinner mid-April to mid-October, serves the requisite fish and chips, it also boasts a raw bar and lively bar scene. Best of all, though, is its harborfront location with picnic tables on a floating dock.

*Starbuck's* (☎ 508-778-6767), on Route 132, open for lunch and dinner, serves a wide selection of dependable standbys: burgers, pasta, Tex-Mex, shrimp and chicken sandwiches. Starbuck's (which has nothing to do with the major coffee chain) is also known for frozen cocktails and other 20oz libations, but keep in mind that this pleasant, lively place serves as many families as it does drinks. Meals are in the $5 to $15 range.

*Fazio's Trattoria (☎ 508-775-9400, 294 Main St)* offers authentic and contemporary Italian dishes including thin-crust pizzas, homemade pasta and veal specialties. Dishes at this storefront bistro cost $10 to $16 at dinner.

*Sweetwaters Grille & Bar (☎ 508-775-3323, 644 Main St)* features Southwestern dishes such as black bean soup, burritos and chicken fajitas for $9.50 to $13.50 at dinnertime. It's hard to go wrong with ordering here. Lunch is also served on summer weekends.

The *RooBar City Bistro (☎ 508-778-6515, 586 Main St)*, open for dinner and known for its lively bar scene, is a hip place with an exposed kitchen, high ceilings and New American 'fusion' cuisine. If grilled swordfish served with sunflower seed and jalapeño pesto makes your mouth water, this is your place. Expect to spend $12 to $19 per main course.

### Entertainment

The *Cape Cod Melody Tent (☎ 508-775-9100)*, W Main St, hosts big-name musicians and comedians, such as Tony Bennett and Joan Rivers, under a giant outdoor tent from June through September.

The *Back Door Bistro (☎ 508-775-2386, 488 South St)* features jazz and piano nightly in summer and on weekends throughout the year.

Outdoor movies are often shown on the village green in July and August; check with the chamber of commerce.

Several restaurants also have lively bar scenes; see the Places to Eat section.

### Shopping

In addition to a number of used bookstores, Main St offers a few other places worth ducking into. The Spectrum (☎ 508-771-4554), 342 Main St, features handmade contemporary American crafts. Plush & Plunder (☎ 508-775-4467), 605 Main St, is a funky store with retro accessories. The Hyannis Antique Center (☎ 508-778-0512), 500 Main St, is part scavenger heaven, part antique co-op. For one-stop shopping, chances are that if you need it, you'll find it at the Cape Cod Mall (☎ 508-771-0200), at the intersection of MA 28 and Route 132.

### Getting There & Away

**Air** The Barnstable Municipal Airport (☎ 508-775-2020), at the rotary intersection of MA 28 and Route 132, is served by regional carriers of US Airways and Continental. You can get to Hyannis from Boston on Cape Air (☎ 508-790-1980, 800-635-8787, www.flycapeair.com), as well as from New York's La Guardia Airport on Colgan Air (☎ 800-272-5488).

See also the Getting There & Away sections in the Martha's Vineyard & Nantucket Island chapter.

**Bus** The Plymouth & Brockton bus (☎ 508-778-9767, www.p-b.com), at the corner of Center and Elm Sts, connects Boston to Hyannis and other Cape points between Hyannis and Provincetown. There are about 30 daily buses from Boston to Hyannis ($12 one way) and four daily buses from Hyannis to Provincetown ($9 one way).

Bonanza buses (☎ 508-775-6502, 800-556-3815, www.bonanzabus.com) carry passengers to Hyannis from New York City and Providence. From New York there are about six buses daily that make the six-hour trip ($45 one way, $79 return).

**Train** The Cape Cod Scenic Railroad (see Sandwich) is expected to begin running again between Hyannis and Sandwich.

**Car** Hyannis is one of the few places on Cape Cod where you can pick up a rental car. Hertz (☎ 800-654-3131), National (☎ 800-227-7368) and Avis (☎ 800-331-1212) are all at the airport. U-Save (☎ 508-790-4700) and Trek (☎ 508-771-2459) are just two blocks away.

Driving details for Hyannis are as follows:

| destination | mileage | hr:min |
|---|---|---|
| Boston, MA | 79 miles | 1:35 |
| Bourne Bridge, MA | 23 miles | 0:35 |
| Chatham, MA | 19 miles | 0:40 |
| Falmouth, MA | 23 miles | 0:45 |
| Provincetown, MA | 50 miles | 1:15 |
| Sandwich, MA | 17 miles | 0:25 |

**Boat** See the Martha's Vineyard & Nantucket Island chapter for information on getting to the islands via ferry service departing from Hyannis.

## Getting Around
Summertime traffic congestion can be time-consuming. From the town center, you can walk almost anywhere of interest in 20 minutes. Park for free (there are no meters) along North St.

The Hyannis Area Trolley (☎ 508-362-5230) runs along Main St and the waterfront area. Trolleys run every 30 minutes from mid-morning until 9 pm or so daily from late June to early September.

The Yarmouth Easy Shuttle (☎ 800-352-7155) runs from the Hyannis bus station along MA 28 (including to the beaches) and into neighboring Yarmouth from late June to early September.

Sea Line buses (☎ 800-352-7155) operate between Hyannis and Woods Hole, with stops along MA 28 in small Barnstable villages, Mashpee and Falmouth. Sea Line begins at the Plymouth & Brockton terminal (at Center and Elm Sts) in Hyannis and ends at the ferry terminal in Woods Hole. Fares vary ($1 to $4 one way) with the distance traveled.

The H2O (☎ 508-352-7155) bus travels west along MA 28 through West Yarmouth, South Yarmouth, West Dennis, Dennisport and Chatham to Orleans daily year-round.

In summer, the Hyannis Area Trolley stops at the airport rotary (walk out to the rotary from the airport) and heads to Main St and the waterfront. But at other times of the year, walk the mile into town or call a taxi.

## YARMOUTH
The north side of Yarmouth along MA 6A is quiet and dignified, lined with shady trees, antique shops and former sea captains' homes. Along MA 28 on the south side, Yarmouth is thick with low-slung motels built right on the narrow beaches.

## Orientation
Take US 6 exit 7 (Willow St) into Yarmouthport, or exit 8 for Yarmouth and South Yarmouth. Better yet, keep wending your way along MA 6A. The villages of Yarmouthport and Yarmouth are on MA 6A; South Yarmouth and West Yarmouth are on MA 28. Everything you'll need is on or just off these two roads.

## Information
For information, the Yarmouth Chamber of Commerce (☎ 508-778-1008, 800-732-1008, www.yarmouthcapecod.com), 657 MA 28 in South Yarmouth, is open 9 am to 5 pm daily (with slightly shorter hours on Sunday) early May to mid-October and 9 am to 5 pm on weekdays the rest of the year.

The Parnassus Book Service (☎ 508-362-6420), 220 MA 6A, is one of the Cape's best antiquarian and used bookstores. An outside wall is lined with shelves of books through which you can browse anytime of day or night; pay on the honor system when the store is closed.

## Things to See & Do
The **Winslow Crocker House** (☎ 508-362-4385, www.spnea.org), 250 MA 6A, is a lovely Georgian house filled with notable antiques from the 17th, 18th and 19th centuries. Tours of the Winslow Crocker House are offered on the hour 11 am to 4 pm on weekends June to mid-October; tickets cost $4 adults, $2 children.

The **Captain Bangs Hallet House** (☎ 508-362-3021), behind the post office off MA 6A, was once home to a prosperous sea captain who made his fortune sailing to China and India. After touring the house, take a walk on the short nature trails behind it. The house is open for tours 1 to 3 pm on Sunday June through October and for Thursday tours in July and August. Tickets cost $3 for adults and 50¢ for children.

The historic store **Hallet's** (☎ 508-362-3362), 139 MA 6A, has a revered place in Yarmouth's history. It began as an apothecary in 1889 and has also served as a post office and town meeting hall. It still boasts its original soda fountain, complete with swivel stools. Stop in for coffee, ice cream or a sandwich. Upstairs there is a wonderfully nostalgic little museum chockfull of items collected over the last 100 years.

**SLAM Paintball** (☎ 508-398-6919, 888-599-7526), 934 MA 28, in South Yarmouth, is catching on. You can use the practice target range before launching a full scale 'pursuit of the enemy' using air-powered pumps loaded with water-based paint. The course is open 10 am to dusk daily year-round.

## Beaches

Grey's Beach (also known as Bass Hole Beach), off Centre St from MA 6A, isn't known for great swimming but it does have a long boardwalk that stretches out into the tidal marsh and across a creek.

Seagull Beach, off of S Sea Ave from MA 28, is Yarmouth's best south-side beach. The lovely approach is alongside a tidal river. Parking is $8; there is a bathhouse.

## Places to Stay

**Motels** The *Beach 'n Towne Motel* (☎ 508-398-2311, 1261 MA 28), in South Yarmouth, has 21 standard rooms for $60 to $67 in summer, $44 to $54 the rest of the year; closed December and January.

Also in South Yarmouth, the *All Seasons Motor Inn* (☎ 508-394-7600, 800-527-0359, fax 508-398-7160, 1199 MA 28) is an attractive two-story place with 114 modern motel rooms (with refrigerators), two pools (one indoor), saunas and a whirlpool. Rooms rent for $99 to $125 in July and August, $39 to $89 the rest of the year.

*Tidewater* (☎ 508-775-6322, 800-338-6322, fax 508-778-5105, tidewater@tidewaterml .com, 135 MA 28), in West Yarmouth, offers 101 rooms located as close to the Nantucket ferry as you can get without being in Hyannis. From late June to early September

rooms are $85 to $99; the rest of the year (except closed in December and January) they're $39 to $79.

**B&Bs** The *Village Inn* (☎ 508-362-3182, 92 MA 6A), located in Yarmouthport, an old-fashioned, family-run hostelry with lots of common room, has 10 modest guest rooms of varying sizes. Expect to pay $95 for a private bath in-season, less for shared bath, including full breakfast.

The circa-1710 *Lane's End Cottage* (☎ 508-362-5298, 268 MA 6A), in Yarmouth-port, a small English-style B&B surrounded by flowers and tucked back in the woods, has three simple rooms, all with private bath. The brick patio, where a full breakfast is served, is ringed with potted plants. Rates are $100 to $110 year-round. No credit cards are accepted.

Also in Yarmouthport, *Wedgewood Inn* (☎ 508-362-5157, fax 362-5851, 83 MA 6A) is easily the loveliest B&B along MA 6A. Its nine rooms (some with private porches and fireplaces) are spacious and filled with antiques, oriental carpets and fireplaces. A full breakfast is included with the rates: $125 to $185 June through October, $105 to $145 the rest of the year.

## Places to Eat

*Jack's Outback* (☎ 508-362-6690, 161 MA 6A), in Yarmouthport, is a no-frills, pine-paneled place that serves good, cheap American food for all three meals daily year-round. Pour your own coffee, write your own order and pick up your plate when it's ready. Jack's has been doing things this way for years and patrons love it. You'll be well-fed and out the door for $3 to $7.

You can't miss the *Lobster Boat* (☎ 508-775-0486, 681 MA 28), in West Yarmouth, an overgrown and hybridized pirate-ship-cum-lobster-boat. Come for daily twin lobsters and early-bird specials for $10 to $15. It's open 4 to 10:30 pm daily early April to late October.

*Clancy's* (☎ 508-775-3332, 175 MA 28), in West Yarmouth, has a pleasant country-tavern atmosphere and has a more-than-adequate menu of burgers, sandwiches, peel-and-eat shrimp and chicken fingers. Prices range from $5 to $11 for lunch, double that for dinner.

The *Aardvark Cafe* (☎ 508-362-9866, 134 MA 6A), in Yarmouthport, a casually upscale and bustling bistro, is a great place for morning coffee, pastries and light lunches of creative hot and cold sandwiches. Tables on the front patio are available any time of day.

The *Inaho* (☎ 508-362-5522, 157 MA 6A), in Yarmouthport, an authentic Japanese restaurant with excellent sushi, also features traditional bento boxes, tempura and more exotic dishes for $12 to $23. If green tea ice cream doesn't strike your fancy, try the distinctly American flourless chocolate cake made by the Japanese owner.

For a creative meal served in sophisticated but unpretentious surroundings, head to *Abbicci* (☎ 508-362-3501, 43 MA 6A), in Yarmouthport. Contemporary Italian dishes like ravioli stuffed with game or duck breast with mustard sauce are served in a 1775 house modernized with track lighting, contemporary art and an upscale bar. The early-bird dinner specials are a bargain at $14 to $18; otherwise, you should expect to spend about $17 to $25 for main courses at dinner, half that at lunch.

### Spectator Sports
The *Cape Cod Crusaders* (☎ 508-790-4782) play professional soccer from early May to mid-August at the Dennis-Yarmouth High School (take exit 8 off MA 6). Tickets are $7 adults, $5 children; call for exact times and dates.

### Shopping
The length of MA 6A is riddled with antique shops. The one-block center of Yarmouthport boasts a few upscale home-accessories shops.

### Getting There & Around
The Plymouth & Brockton bus (☎ 508-778-9767, www.p-b.com) makes a stop at Hallet's on MA 6A in the center of Yarmouthport on its route from Boston and Hyannis to Provincetown.

The driving details from Yarmouth to other destinations are as follows:

| destination | mileage | hr:min |
| --- | --- | --- |
| Barnstable, MA | 4 miles | 0:08 |
| Boston, MA | 80 miles | 1:30 |
| Bourne Bridge, MA | 20 miles | 0:30 |
| Dennis, MA | 4 miles | 0:08 |
| Hyannis, MA | 4 miles | 0:10 |
| Provincetown, MA | 45 miles | 1:00 |

The Yarmouth Easy Shuttle (☎ 800-352-7155) runs from Yarmouth to the Hyannis bus station along MA 28 from late June to early September.

## DENNIS
Similar to Yarmouth's sprawl, Dennis stretches from Cape Cod Bay to Nantucket Sound. Along MA 6A you'll find cranberry bogs, salt marshes and lots of antique stores and artisans' shops. Dennis also has a museum dedicated to area artists, a highly regarded summer theater, an art cinema and a fine lookout point.

### Orientation
To reach most of the town, continue driving along MA 6A or take exit 9 from US 6 (north to MA 6A or south to MA 28). The villages of East Dennis and Dennis are on MA 6A; West Dennis and Dennisport are along MA 28. Route 134 runs north-south (through South Dennis), linking MA 6A to MA 28.

### Information
The office of the Dennis Chamber of Commerce (☎ 508-398-3568, 800-243-9920, www.dennischamber.com), at MA 28 and Route 134 in West Dennis, is open 9:30 am to 4 pm daily late June to early September (10 am to 2 pm on weekdays the rest of the year and 10 am to 2 pm on weekends in spring and fall).

Stop at the Arm Chair Bookstore (☎ 508-385-0900), 619 MA 6A, and Paperback Cottage (☎ 508-760-2101), 927 MA 6A, for all your reading needs. Since many summer visitors are voracious readers, Paperback Cottage also rents books by the week.

## Things to See

The **Cape Museum of Fine Arts** (☎ 508-385-4477), MA 6A, represents Cape artists, both living and dead, famous as well as up-and-coming, working in a variety of media. The airy museum, part of which is housed in an old barn, is open 10 am to 5 pm Tuesday through Saturday and 1 to 5 pm on Sunday year-round. Admission is $5 for everyone over 16.

From **Scargo Tower** (take MA 6A to Old Bass River Rd to Scargo Hill Rd) you can see all the way to Provincetown on a clear day. The high vantage point gives you a good idea of just how delicate the ecology of this little peninsula really is. Directly below is Scargo Lake, one of the Cape's 365 freshwater lakes.

The **Cape Cod Discovery Museum** (☎ 508-398-1600), 444 MA 28 in Dennisport, provides a nice alternative to bumper boats and trampolines. Interactive science and nature exhibits, do-it-yourself crafts areas, puzzles and lots more challenge children of all ages. Admission ($4.50 adults, $4 children) is valid 9:30 am to 5:30 pm daily year-round, until 7:30 pm in summer.

## Beaches

Chapin Memorial Beach, off MA 6A, is a long, dune-backed beach with a gently sloping grade. As with all bay-side beaches, at low tide you can walk for a mile out onto the tidal flats. Parking is $9.

West Dennis Beach, off MA 28 in West Dennis, is a narrow, mile-long beach on Nantucket Sound. It's quite popular (the parking lot holds 1000 cars); facilities include a snack bar and restrooms. Parking is $9.

## Bicycling & In-Line Skating

The paved **Cape Cod Rail Trail** follows the flat railroad bed of the Old Colony Railroad for 26 miles from Dennis to Wellfleet. Along the way you'll pass ponds, forests, a country store or two, ocean vistas, beaches and salt marshes. It's one of the most pleasant excursions on the Cape.

Park at the trailhead on Route 134 in South Dennis, just south of US 6. You can rent bikes and rollerblades (in-line skates)

at Barbara's Bike and Sports Equipment (☎ 508-760-4723), located on MA 134.

## Canoeing & Kayaking

Cape Cod Waterways (☎ 508-398-0080), on MA 28 near Route 134 in Dennisport, allows you to explore the small, but interesting, Swan River from the vantage point of a canoe or kayak from mid-May to mid-October.

## Cruises

The schooner *Freya* (☎ 508-385-4399), at Sesuit Harbor off MA 28 in East Dennis, takes two-hour sails into Cape Cod Bay and hour-long sunset trips for $16 to $18 adults, $10 children. Save $4 by going on the morning sail.

Water Safari's *Starfish* (☎ 508-362-5555), at the Bass River Bridge on MA 28 in West Dennis, offers narrated trips on flat-bottom boats up the largest tidal river on the East Coast. Tickets cost $12 adults, $7 children.

## Places to Stay

**Motels** *Holiday Hill Motor Inn* (☎ 508-394-5577, 352 MA 28), in Dennisport, has 56 large rooms with refrigerators for $59 to $79 in summer, $30 to $69 off-season; the motel is closed mid-October through April.

The *Huntsman Motor Lodge* (☎ 508-394-5415, fax 398-7852, huntsman@capecodramp .com, 829 MA 28), in West Dennis, has 17 simple rooms and nine efficiencies. From late June to early September rates are $79 to $89; the rest of the year they're $27 to $69.

**B&Bs** The *Isaiah Hall B&B Inn* (☎ 508-385-9928, 800-736-0160, fax 508-385-5879, isaiah@capecod.net, 152 Whig St), off of MA 6A, in Dennis, offers 11 unpretentious rooms with TV (one with a fireplace) in a 19th-century house and an attached, renovated barn. In addition to lovely gardens, an enthusiastic host and plenty of common space both inside and out, the inn is a 10-minute walk from the beach. Rates are $93 to $128 mid-June to early September, a little lower off-season; closed mid-October to mid-April.

Once a Victorian sea captain's mansion, and now called the *Captain Nickerson Inn*

(☎/fax 508-398-5966, 800-282-1619, captnick@ capecod.net, 333 Main St), in South Dennis, has four guest rooms that are delightfully off-the-beaten-path. A full breakfast is included with the rates: $82 to $97 double and $135 for four people in the family suite late May to mid-October. Off-season, rates drop to $70 to $75; the inn is closed late December through February.

**By The Sea** (☎ 508-398-8685, 800-447-9202, fax 508-398-0334, bythesea@capecod .net, 57 Chase Ave), at Inman Rd in Dennisport, smack on Inman Beach, has 12 spacious rooms with old-fashioned beach-house furnishings, TV and updated bathrooms. Rates are $85 to $142 July to early September, $60 to $110 off-season. The hostelry is closed December through April.

## Places to Eat

Of the Cape's ubiquitous clam shacks, **Captain Frosty's** (☎ 508-385-8548, 219 MA 6A), in Dennis, is better because it offers more than fried clams and burgers. You might also order a daily special such as grilled shrimp with a salad. It's open early April to mid-September; you'll spend $3 to $14 for a meal here.

If you want to eat indoors, try **Bob Briggs' 'Wee Packet'** (☎ 508-398-2181), on Depot St in Dennisport. The simple, diner-style place is usually packed with people who appreciate moderately priced meals ($3 to $13). The menu extends from broiled seafood, sandwiches and quiche to homemade desserts. The Wee Packet is open for lunch and dinner May through September and for breakfast during the height of summer.

The decor of the **Contrast Bistro and Espresso Bar** (☎ 508-385-9100, 605 MA 6A), in Dennis, is like no other place on MA 6A, alive with bold colors and large canvases. It's more affordable than you might imagine; you'll find large portions of such disparate dishes as a frittata, grilled chicken sandwich with sun-dried tomato pesto and Cornish game hens. The desserts are luscious and the coffee strong. Plan on a very well-spent $6 to $10 for breakfast and lunch, $13 to $19 for dinner.

**Gina's By The Sea** (☎ 508-385-3213, 143 Taunton St), off MA 6A in Dennis, is popular with locals. Arrive early (no reservations are taken), put your name on the waiting list and go to the beach, just steps away. The northern Italian menu features traditional, garlicky dishes for $9 to $22. The interior is pleasant, with knotty-pine paneling, exposed ceiling beams and a small bar. It's open for dinner April through November (nightly June through September).

Awash in polished wood and natural light, the **Scargo Café** (☎ 508-385-8200, 799 MA 6A), in Dennis, is open for lunch ($5 to $12) and dinner ($10 to $18) year-round. The pre-matinee and theater crowd munch on specials such as grilled lamb, shrimp and pasta and chicken with ginger sauce.

## Entertainment

The **Cape Playhouse** (☎ 508-385-3838, 385-3911, 820 MA 6A), in Dennis, is generally regarded as the Cape's best summer theater. Well-known actors and rising stars perform in a different production each week from mid-June to early September. Shows are nightly except Sunday, with matinees on Wednesday and Thursday. Musical theater for children is produced on Friday mornings in July and August. Tickets cost $15 to $28; children's shows are $6.

On the grounds of the Cape Playhouse, the **Cape Cinema** (☎ 508-385-2503), on MA 6A, shows foreign, art and independent films daily mid-April to mid-October. The exterior looks like a Congregational church, but it was built to be a cinema in 1930 and the art deco ceiling was painted with a huge mural depicting heaven.

**Christine's** (☎ 508-394-7333, 581 MA 28), in West Dennis, is the liveliest place outside of Hyannis on the Cape's southside. Look for the current line-up of dance bands, cabaret, jazz and comedy.

## Shopping

As a change from the ubiquitous antique shops, Scargo Pottery (☎ 508-385-3894), 30 Dr Lord Rd South, barely east of Scargo Lake beach, off MA 6A, features playful (and pricey) interpretations of architectural icons that double as birdhouses.

## Getting There & Away
The Plymouth & Brockton bus (☎ 508-778-9767, www.p-b.com) stops at the Dennis Post Office and at Player's Plaza in East Dennis, both on MA 6A, on its way from Boston and Hyannis to Provincetown.

Driving details for Dennis are as follows:

| destination | mileage | hr:min |
|---|---|---|
| Boston, MA | 86 miles | 1:40 |
| Bourne Bridge, MA | 26 miles | 0:35 |
| Brewster, MA | 6 miles | 0:10 |
| Hyannis, MA | 8 miles | 0:15 |
| Provincetown, MA | 45 miles | 1:00 |
| Yarmouth, MA | 4 miles | 0:08 |

## Getting Around
The section of MA 6A that passes through Dennis is only 3 miles long, and MA 28 is about the same, so there isn't much problem with navigation. From MA 6A, it's a mile east to Scargo Tower and 2 miles west to Chapin Memorial Beach.

The Coach of Dennis Trolley (☎ 800-352-7155), operating from late June to early September, provides a link between points on MA 28 and Route 134 and some beaches, as well as connections to Harwich, Yarmouth and Hyannis.

See the Getting Around section under Hyannis for information on the H2O bus.

## BREWSTER
Brewster, another tranquil little town on MA 6A, is home to an excellent natural history museum, a state park with camping and many fine restaurants worth a splurge.

## Orientation & Information
From US 6 take exit 10 (Route 124 North) into town or continue along MA 6A; everything of interest is on or just off of MA 6A.

The office of the Brewster Visitor Information Center (☎ 508-896-3500, www.capecod.com/brewster), 2198 MA 6A, a half-mile east of Route 124 and behind the town

offices, is open 9 am to 3 pm weekends May to mid-October and daily from mid-June to early September.

The Brewster Book Store (☎ 508-896-6543), 2648 MA 6A, is well-stocked with local titles as well as children's books.

## Things to See & Do
The mission of the **Cape Cod Museum of Natural History** (☎ 508-896-3867, 800-896-3867), 869 MA 6A, is to 'educate, enlighten, and entertain' people about the Cape's unique natural history. To that end, you'll find a series of photographs showing coastline erosion, fish tanks, whale displays and three short nature trails that cross cranberry bogs, salt marshes and beech groves. The museum ($5 adults, $2 children) is open from 9:30 am to 4:30 pm Monday to Saturday and 11 am to 4:30 pm on Sunday year-round.

With 2000 acres, **Nickerson State Park** was a local businessman's hunting and fishing estate in the early 1900s. It boasts eight ponds, a network of trails for **bicycling** and walking, picnic sites and sandy beaches. And it can all be enjoyed for free. The Cape Cod Rail Trail (see the Dennis Bicycling section) runs through here. The most convenient bike rental shop is Idle Times (☎ 508-896-9242), just west of the park's entrance on MA 6A. Rail Trail Bike & Blades (☎ 508-896-8200), 302 Underpass Rd off MA 6A, also rents in-line skates as well as bikes; it's open year-round.

The **Stony Brook Grist Mill and Herring Run** (☎ 508-896-6745), at Setucket and Stony Brook Rds (both off MA 6A), is one of the Cape's most tranquil and lush spots. If you visit mid-April to early May, you'll see thousands of herring migrating from the ocean to fresh water in order to spawn. As for the mill, the water wheel still turns the machinery that grinds cornmeal. The mill is open 2 to 5 pm Thursday through Saturday April through June, and 2 to 5 pm on Friday in July and August.

The **New England Fire & History Museum** (☎ 508-896-5711), 1439 MA 6A, arranged to resemble a 19th-century village, includes a blacksmith's shop, apothecary's shop and

30 working fire engines. There are no dalmatians. The museum is open 10 am to 4 pm weekdays and noon to 4 pm late May to mid-September, weekends until mid-October. Tickets are $5 adults, $2.50 children.

## Canoeing & Kayaking

The Cape Cod Museum of Natural History (☎ 508-896-3867, 800-896-3867) sponsors a variety of excellent naturalist-led canoe and kayak trips and seal-watching trips. Call for an exact schedule and prices.

Jack's Boat Rentals (☎ 508-896-8556), on Flax Pond within Nickerson State Park, rents canoes, kayaks and other flotation devices.

## Places to Stay

**Camping** *Nickerson State Park (☎ 877-422-6762 for reservations, 508-896-3491 for information, 3488 MA 6A)* has the best campsites on the Cape. There are 418 wooded sites, some with pond views, that cost $9 nightly. Advance reservations are taken for a limited number of sites; the rest are rented first-come, first-served. In the summer, don't get your hopes up. Although it's open year-round, there are no toilet facilities or running water in winter.

If Nickerson is full, try the **Shady Knoll** *Campground (☎ 508-896-3002)*, at MA 6A and Route 137. The 100 sites cost about $20 nightly mid-May to mid-October.

**Inns** A former girls' school, the **Old Sea Pines Inn** *(☎ 508-896-6114, fax 896-7387, seapines@C4.net, 2553 MA 6A)* has rooms that range from small to moderately roomy. Some have antique iron and brass beds; others in the rear annex are more motel-like but quite pleasant. The living room is spacious and the front porch set with rockers. Rooms range from $65 to $125 late May through October; family suites for three to four people cost $135 up to $145; closed January to mid-March.

The late-18th-century **Isaiah Clark House** *(☎ 508-896-2223, 800-822-4001, fax 508-896-2138, innkeeper@isaiahclarkhouse .com, 1187 MA 6A)* has seven unpretentious and homey guest rooms. Some have a fire-

place, perfect as the inn is open year-round. A full breakfast, served in the historic keeping room or on the back deck, is included in the rates: $98 to $140 mid-May to mid-October and $78 to $112 off-season.

**Captain Freeman Inn** *(☎ 508-896-7481, 800-843-4664, fax 508-896-5618, visitus@ capecod.net, 15 Breakwater Rd)*, off MA 6A, the most upscale place to stay in town, offers some rooms with TV, VCR, fireplace, refrigerator and whirlpool tub. A couple of the more 'simple' rooms have floor-to-ceiling windows and parquet floors. The innkeeper makes such exceptional low-fat breakfasts that you'd bet your guidebook they're laden with carbs and calories. (You'd lose the bet.) Rooms are $125 to $250 June through October; they are $120 to $200 the rest of the year.

## Places to Eat

For a hit of caffeine, a morning newspaper and something sweet, head to the **Sundae Times & Coffee** *(☎ 508-896-5991, 2655 MA 6A)*, in Foster's Square Marketplace.

Just off the Cape Cod Rail Trail, order the requisite fried seafood platter at **Cobie's** *(☎ 508-896-7021, 3260 MA 6A)* and crunch and munch it at outdoor picnic tables. Cobie's is open all afternoon and into the evening mid-May to mid-September.

**JT's** *(☎ 508-896-3355, 2689 MA 6A)*, an informal lunch and dinner eatery, offers up way-above-average fried seafood and sea food rolls. The evening's specials are always worthy. You'll spend about $10 per person here.

The **Brewster Fish House** *(☎ 508-896-7867, 2208 MA 6A)* is highly regarded for its simple, well-prepared seafood at moderate (for Cape Cod) prices in pleasant surroundings. Expect a serious wait if you arrive after 6:30 pm for dinner. It's open for lunch ($6 to $11) and dinner ($15 to $22 per main course) early April to early December.

**Chillingsworth** *(☎ 508-896-3640, 2449 MA 6A)* is perhaps the Cape's best French restaurant. Their seven-course, fixed-price dinner will set you back $49 to $59 per person, but there are ways to experience this place without losing your shirt. Come for an à la carte lunch ($8 to $11.50) or select from the bistro dinner menu in the less formal but still upscale Garden Room. It's open late May to late November.

The **Old Manse Inn** (☎ 508-896-3149, 1861 MA 6A), open for dinner April through December, offers an exceptional 'intercontinental bistro' menu of Szechuan salmon and curried coconut soup and lamb sausage. Dessert is not to be missed. As for atmosphere, the old sea captain's house is alive with modern art. Dishes are $18 to $25.

### Entertainment

The **Woodshed** (☎ 508-896-7771), MA 6A, just east of the town common, is a rustic bar and restaurant where the locals hang out. It has local bands most nights in summer.

The **Cape Repertory Theatre** (☎ 508-896-1888, 3397 MA 6A) stages creative, outdoor productions in a natural amphitheater surrounded by trees as well as indoors at the Old Sea Pines Inn. Tickets cost $10 to $14 adults, $7 children; less for daytime children's productions.

### Shopping

The Great Cape Cod Herb, Spice & Tea Co (☎ 508-896-5900), 2628 MA 6A, stocks almost 175 herbs and lots of New Age health books.

The Brewster Store (☎ 508-896-3744), at MA 6A and Route 124, is an old-fashioned country store that's managed to stay in operation since 1866. Upstairs there is a little museum of sorts: It has town memorabilia dating from the mid-19th to the mid-20th century.

The Sydenstriker Galleries (☎ 508-385-3272), at 490 MA 6A, whose craftspeople employ a glass-fusing technique developed by a Brewster local, are open year-round.

The Punkhorn Bookshop (☎ 508-896-2114), 672 MA 6A, and Kings Way Books and Antiques (☎ 508-896-3639), 774 MA 6A, will satisfy all your antiquarian needs.

Brewster has perhaps the most dense concentration of antique shops on MA 6A. But it also has fine potters. Stop at Clayworks (3820 MA 6A), Kemp Pottery (258 MA 6A) and Heart Pottery (1145 MA 6A).

### Getting There & Away

The Plymouth & Brockton bus (☎ 508-778-9767, www.p-b.com) stops at the Brewster Store, on MA 6A, on its way from Boston to Hyannis and Provincetown.

The driving details for Brewster are as follows:

| destination | mileage | hr:min |
| --- | --- | --- |
| Boston, MA | 90 miles | 1:45 |
| Bourne Bridge, MA | 30 miles | 0:45 |
| Chatham, MA | 9 miles | 0:15 |
| Dennis, MA | 6 miles | 0:10 |
| Orleans, MA | 5 miles | 0:10 |
| Provincetown, MA | 34 miles | 0:45 |

## HARWICH

There's not much to recommend here in Harwich, but if you're passing through from Hyannis to Chatham, you'll find a waterfront restaurant, a homey B&B, an alternative Nantucket ferry and one of the Cape's most picturesque harbors. Tranquil Wychmere Harbor, with a convenient grassy picnic spot overlooking it, sits right on MA 28.

The Harwich Chamber of Commerce (☎ 508-432-1600, 800-441-3199), on MA 28, is open 9 am to 4:30 pm daily mid-June to mid-September and on weekends for the month before and after.

Wychmere Book & Coffee (☎ 508-432-7868) as well as Sea Street Books (☎ 508-430-1816), both in the small center of Harwichport, have the market covered.

Cape Water Sports (☎ 508-432-7079), at MA 28 and Route 124, rents canoes for paddling on the Herring River.

The **House on the Hill** (☎ 508-432-4321, 968 MA 28), in South Harwich, is a homey throw-back to the 19th century. Set up on a knoll off the busy road, the farmhouse has three simple guest rooms with private bath that rent for $65 in summer, $55 off-season; open year-round.

**Mason Jar** (☎ 508-430-7600, 544 MA 28), open daily year-round, offers fancy sandwiches, cheeses and pâtés.

**Thompson's Farm Market** (☎ 508-432-5415, 710 MA 28), is more a grocery store than the name implies, but it has a great deli section and indoor tables.

The *Harwich Children's Theatre* (☎ 508-432-2002), at Division and Willow Sts in West Harwich, the oldest children's theater in the country, stages four shows in summer; tickets $8.

See Nantucket's Getting There & Away section (in the Martha's Vineyard & Nantucket Island chapter) for Nantucket ferry information.

## CHATHAM

Chatham is the patriarch of Cape Cod towns. A genteel, refined reserve is evident along its pretty Main St; the shops are upscale and expensive, the lodging-places tony. Though the bulk of the town's summer residents are regulars, there is an ardent tourist trade.

### Orientation

From US 6, take Route 137 South (exit 11) to Old Queen Anne Rd to MA 28 and Main St.

From Hyannis and points west, continue on MA 28 North (you're actually heading due east) into the center of town. From Orleans and points north, take MA 28 South into town to Shore Rd, which runs along the shore, past the Fish Pier, the lighthouse and onto Morris Island. Main St is about a mile long from the MA 28 rotary to Shore Rd.

Chatham is something of a peninsula, surrounded on three sides by water.

### Information

Conveniently located, the Chatham Information Booth (☎ 508-945-5199, 800-715-5567, chamber@chathamcapecod.org), 533 Main St, is a tiny little place with a knowledgeable staff and crammed with everything you could ever want to know about the town. The booth is open 10 am to 5 pm daily from late May to mid-October.

On Main St you'll find two independent bookstores: Cabbages and Kings (☎ 508-945-1603) and Yellow Umbrella Books (☎ 508-945-0144).

The Chatham Laundry Center (☎ 508-945-4122), at 22 Queen Anne Rd, is open daily year-round.

In an emergency call ☎ 911; for the Chatham police, call ☎ 508-945-1213.

## Things to See & Do

The **Railroad Museum** (no ☎), at 153 Depot Rd from Old Harbor Rd north off Main St, is fashioned from an 1887 depot and features a 1910 wooden caboose. The museum is open 10 am to 4 pm Tuesday to Saturday mid-June to mid-September; admission is free.

The **Old Atwood House** (☎ 508-945-2493), 347 Stage Harbor Rd (off the western end of Main St from the rotary) contains a historical collection of over 2000 items pertaining to Chatham's past. It's open 1 to 4 pm Tuesday through Friday mid-June through September; admission is $3 adults, $1 children.

The **Chatham Light** viewing area located on Shore Rd, with an expansive vista of sand and sea, is the town's most visited attraction. The break in Nauset Beach (the long spit of sand is now broken by a channel of water) was caused by a ferocious storm in 1987; residents still talk about the environmental consequences. The present light, by the way, dates to 1878 and is visible 15 miles out to sea. There is free parking and a fine beach below (see the Beaches section).

Head to the **Fish Pier** on Shore Rd mid-afternoon to watch the fishing fleet come in with its daily catch. Chatham's boats haul in some of the freshest fish around because they're too small to stay out overnight. On Chatham menus, the term 'daily catch' really has meaning!

The 2700-acre wildlife refuge on **Monomoy Island** is a haven for offshore birds, and only accessible by boat. You'll be well-rewarded for taking the additional effort to reach it. Call the Wellfleet Bay Wildlife Sanctuary (☎ 508-349-2615) or the Cape Cod Museum of Natural History (☎ 508-896-3867) to make a bird-watching tour reservation.

Harbor and gray seals summer and winter off the coast of Chatham. See Getting Around, below, for local boat operators who also offer seal trips.

## Beaches

Chatham Light Beach, directly below the lighthouse on Shore Rd, is a long, wide sandy beach. It's best to walk or bicycle here since parking at the lighthouse is limited to 30 minutes.

Desolate and long North and South Beaches are accessible only by shuttle boat. They're worth the added expense of getting there. See the Chatham Getting Around section.

## Bicycling

If you want to keep your feet on the ground (sort of), Chatham's side streets and shady lanes are well-suited to bicycling. Rent bikes at Bert & Carol's (☎ 508-945-0137), 347 MA 28, North Chatham.

## Surfing & Windsurfing

The waters off Chatham are great for surfing (though it's not the Banzai Pipeline) and windsurfing, and the friendly folks at Monomoy Sail & Cycle (☎ 508-945-0811), 275 MA 28, North Chatham, rent boards.

## Airplane Sightseeing

Open year-round, the Cape Cod Flying Circus (☎ 508-945-9000, 945-2363), at the Chatham Municipal Airport on George Ryder Rd off MA 28 in West Chatham, offers 20-minute sightseeing flights over the immediate coastline, bays and inlets for $60.

## Cruises

Chatham Harbor Tours (☎ 508-255-0619), at the Fish Pier on Shore Rd, offers four narrated cruises daily (mid-June through September) of Pleasant Bay and the North Beach area. Adults pay $15, children $10.

The Pleasant Bay Marsh Cruise (☎ 508-896-3867), in Ryders Cove, sponsored by the Cape Cod Museum of Natural History, operates narrated two-hour trips through the rich ecosystem of the bay and marsh. Call for departure times and reservations. Adults pay $25, children $18.

## Places to Stay

With the exception of the motels, Chatham's lodgings are both upscale and expensive.

**Motels** In addition to a private beach, the *Hawthorne Motel* (☎ 508-945-0372, sdwen@ capecod.net, 196 Shore Rd) has 27 standard rooms and efficiency units overlooking the ocean. There is a four-night minimum stay in summer. Rates are $100 to $150 nightly mid-May to mid-October; after that, it's closed.

Two miles west of town, the *Chatham Motel* (☎ 508-945-2630, 1487 MA 28) has 26 rooms set back from the highway in a pine grove. Rates are $105 to $145 in July and August, $75 to $115 off-season; it's closed November through April.

The *Chatham Highlander* (☎ 508-945-9038, highlander@capecod.net, 946 MA 28), just beyond the rotary and within walking distance of town, consists of 28 standard but very well-maintained motel rooms, each with TV and refrigerator. From mid-June to early September rooms are $104; off-season, they cost $58 to $79; the motel is closed December through March.

**B&Bs** The *Bow Roof House* (☎ 508-945-1346, 59 Queen Anne Rd), just off the rotary and within walking distance of the town and town beach, is delightfully old-fashioned in price and offerings. Within this late-18th-century house are six rooms that rent for $70 to $75 year-round.

*The Mooring's* (☎ 508-945-0848, 800-320-0848, fax 508-320-0848, 326 Main St), in the middle of town, features a great array of accommodations surrounded by immaculately landscaped private grounds. In addition to a few lovely B&B rooms, there are upgraded motel rooms and multi-bedroom efficiencies behind the renovated B&B. From mid-June to mid-September, rates are $148 to $225 for rooms (including a full breakfast), $170 to $230 efficiencies and $128 motel (aka 'carriage house') rooms. It's closed January to mid-February.

The gracious 19th-century *Cyrus Kent House* (☎/fax 508-945-9104, 800-338-5368, 63 Cross St) boasts 10 antique-furnished, canopy-bedded rooms in its beautifully restored sea captain's house. A block from the center of town, rooms rent for $135 to $280 mid-June to mid-October, $95 to $180 the rest of the year.

**Hotels** *Chatham Bars Inn (☎ 508-945-0096, 800-527-4884, fax 508-945-5491, salescbi@ chathambarsinn.com)*, Shore Rd, is the Cape's grande dame of hotels. Rooms and cottages are pricey at $190 to $400 in summer, but inquire about off-season packages starting at $130 nightly in winter. Facilities include an oceanside pool, tennis courts and a private beach. In any event, it's an impressive place to see, especially from a rocking chair on the expansive veranda.

## Places to Eat

The town's most popular all-purpose tavern, the *Chatham Squire (☎ 508-945-0945, 487 Main St)* dishes out a long and varied lunch menu ($5 to $13) year-round. At dinner, try the shrimp and chicken stir-fry or seafood stew ($16 to $17). The bar, to the left as you walk in, offers the same food served at a higher noise level.

Only a half block away, the *Impudent Oyster (☎ 508-945-3545, 15 Chatham Bars Ave)* is a bit more upscale and reserved, with an extensive seafood menu, fresh-shucked oysters and a loyal following. Lunch is reasonable ($6 to $13); dinner main courses are more than double that.

*Upstairs at Christian's (☎ 508-945-3362, 443 Main St)* serves home-style meals ($6 to $20 per main course) such as meatloaf with gravy and chicken with biscuits. But the pub-style place is fine for a beer and a large order of Cajun french fries.

At the *Beach House Grill (☎ 508-945-0096, 297 Shore Rd)*, just across from the Chatham Bars Inn, you might expect to pay through the nose for a privileged beachside perch. But you don't. The menu consists of burgers, salads and fried seafood for $7 to $16. It's open for breakfast and lunch mid-June to early September.

*Luscious Louie's (☎ 508-945-5223, 524 Main St)*, in the rear of the Chatham Cookware shop, has a wide selection of desserts and a more limited selection of good soups and gourmet sandwiches to take away or munch in the modest back room.

*Carmine's (☎ 508-945-5300, 595 Main St)* serves pizza and scoops of gelato in a faux old-fashioned ice cream parlor setting.

If you're tired of sandwiches, stop at *Marion's Pie Shop (☎ 508-432-9439, 2022 MA 28)* and pick up a chicken pot pie or breakfast baked goods.

## Entertainment

Most Cape towns have summertime outdoor concerts, but Chatham has the granddaddy of them all. Thousands of folks have gathered every Friday at 8 pm since the mid-1930s to listen and dance to big-band music from the gazebo in Kate Gould Park. Follow the crowds to Kate Gould Park off Main St from early July to early September.

The *Monomoy Theatre (☎ 508-945-1589)*, MA 28 toward Harwich, is a well-known Equity playhouse. A new production is staged weekly by Ohio University students late June to early September.

## Shopping

Main St is bursting at the seams with shops that could drain your pockets fast. Three galleries, in particular, are more like museums. Just west of the rotary, the Chatham Glass Company (☎ 508-945-5547), 758 Main St, displays brilliant glass pieces blown on the premises. Nearby, the Munson Gallery (☎ 508-945-2888), 880 Main St, within a renovated horse barn, is truly one of the best galleries on the Cape (unlike other galleries, there's not a trace of 'tourist art' here). Odell's Studio and Gallery (☎ 508-945-3239), 423 Main St, in the middle of town, features work by two exceptional artists, a metalsmith and a painter.

## Getting There & Away

See the Hyannis Getting Around section for information on the H2O bus.

The driving details for Chatham are as follows:

| destination | mileage | hr:min |
|---|---|---|
| Boston, MA | 95 miles | 1:50 |
| Brewster, MA | 9 miles | 0:15 |
| Hyannis, MA | 19 miles | 0:35 |
| Orleans, MA | 9½ miles | 0:15 |
| Provincetown, MA | 38 miles | 0:50 |
| Sagamore Bridge, MA | 35 miles | 0:50 |

## Getting Around

Chatham is best explored on foot; it's about a 30-minute walk from the western end of Main St to the lighthouse on Shore Rd and another 15 minutes from the lighthouse to the fish pier.

To reach Monomoy Island or South Beach, take the Monomoy Island Ferry (☎ 508-945-5450) from Wikis Way off Morris Island Rd.

The Beachcomber (☎ 508-945-5265, 680-5064), with boats docked at the fish pier, Ryder's Cove and Stage Harbor, takes passengers to desolate stretches of Nauset Beach (see Beaches in the Orleans section) or Monomoy.

Like all the others, Outermost Harbor Marine (☎ 508-945-2030), off Morris Island Rd, offers seasonal transportation to South Beach (from $9 adults, $4.50 children) and Monomoy (a bit more expensive). Call them when you're ready to depart and don't forget to schedule a pick-up time.

## ORLEANS

To some, Orleans is simply the place where MA 28 and US 6 converge and US 6 heads north to Provincetown. Others know that Nauset Beach is exceptional, that Nauset Marsh has a rich ecosystem worth exploring and that there are lots of good restaurants here. But fewer know that Orleans has a military history: The British fired upon Orleans during the War of 1812 and a German submarine fired a few torpedoes at it during WWI.

## Orientation

US 6, MA 6A and MA 28 all converge at the rotary on the northern edge of town.

Main St, which intersects with MA 6A and 28, runs northwest to picturesque Rock Harbor and east to East Orleans center and Nauset Beach (where it turns into Beach Rd). The stretch of MA 28 that heads south through Orleans, past Pleasant Bay, is particularly scenic.

## Information

The Orleans Chamber of Commerce (☎ 508-240-2484, www.capecod-orleans.com), on Eldredge Park Way off MA 6A just north of US 6, maintains a seasonal information booth that's open 9 am to 6 pm Monday to Saturday and 10 am to 3 pm Sunday late May to mid-October. Until late November, it is open Friday to Sunday.

The Compass Rose Bookshop (☎ 508-255-1545), on Main St, is the best in town, even before taking into consideration the selection of 40%-off bargain books.

## Things to See & Do

The French Cable Station Museum (☎ 508-240-1735), on MA 28 at Cove Rd, stands as testimony to late-19th-century technology. This former station contains equipment used to transmit the first communications via a 4000-mile underwater cable laid between Orleans and Brest, France. Among the messages relayed: Lindbergh's arrival in Paris and Germany's invasion of France. The museum is open 1 to 4 pm Monday through Saturday in July and August and Friday through Sunday in June and September; admission is free.

Although Rock Harbor consists of little more than a clam shack, charter fishing fleet and a small beach, it's quiet and picturesque and worth a detour.

You can rent bicycles to explore the quiet back roads at Orleans Cycle (☎ 508-255-9115), 26 Main St.

## Beaches

Nauset Beach, at the end of Beach Rd from Main St in East Orleans, is one of the best beaches on the Cape for walking, sunning and bodysurfing. It's a sandy 9-mile-long barrier beach on the Atlantic Ocean with good facilities, including restrooms, changing rooms and a snack bar; parking is $8, though it's usually free off-season.

## Canoeing

The Goose Hummock Outdoor Center (☎ 508-255-2620), off MA 6A at Town Cove, rents canoes and kayaks for use on the protected and calm waters of Pleasant Bay. They also have organized half-day tours and introductory paddling courses.

## Cruises

Nauset Marsh Cruise (☎ 508-255-4250), in back of the Goose Hummock Outdoor

Center near the US 6 and MA 28 rotary, offers narrated tours of Nauset Marsh and the barrier beach from mid-June to early September. Tickets cost $16 adults; kids (up to eight) are charged twice their age.

## Places to Stay

**Efficiencies** The *Kadee's Gray Elephant* (☎ 508-255-7608, fax 240-2976, 216 Main St), in East Orleans, has 10 fancifully painted, artsy efficiency apartments carved out of a 200-year-old sea captain's house. Each rents for $110 in summer, $85 nightly off-season; closed December and January. It's about a 30-minute walk to Nauset Beach from here.

**Motels** In the middle of town but apart from the bustle, *The Cove* (☎ 508-255-1203, 800-343-2233, fax 508-255-7736, 13 MA 28) has 47 very nice motel rooms. Some are right on Town Cove, and all have access to a bit of private shoreline. Outside are barbecue grills and a heated pool. The rooms have refrigerators, coffeemakers and free movies. Doubles rent for $99 to $124 in July and August and $59 to $89 the rest of the year. Four people can get an efficiency for $165 to $189 in summer.

The *Ole Tavern Motel & Inn* (☎ 508-255-1565, 800-544-7705, 151 MA 6A), about a half mile east of the rotary, has 28 of the least-expensive but nicest (albeit standard) motel rooms in town. Rates at the brick one-story motel are $79 to $110 mid-June to early September, $49 to $79 off-season; closed December through March.

**B&Bs** Of the 18 rooms at the *Ship's Knees Inn* (☎ 508-255-1312, fax 240-1351, 186 Beach Rd), in East Orleans, a few are nice inn-style rooms but more are plain motel rooms. Rooms with shared bath cost $55 to $90, while those with private bath cost $110 to $135 mid-June to mid-September. The rest of the year, doubles are $45 to $80 shared bath, $80 to $115 private bath.

The *Nauset House Inn* (☎ 508-255-2195, jvessell@capecod.net, 222 E Main St), at Beach Rd in East Orleans, is one of the best area B&Bs. The innkeepers are friendly, the rooms comfortable, the common areas plen-

tiful (including a greenhouse conservatory) and the location excellent – it's about a 10-minute walk to Nauset Beach. Afternoon snacks, drinks and an excellent breakfast are included in the rates: $75 to $135 April to late October. A few rooms have shared bath. A single rents for $55.

The rambling 18th-century *Parsonage Inn* (☎ 508-255-8217, 888-422-8217, fax 508-255-8216, innkeeper@parsonageinn.com, 202 Main St), in East Orleans, has eight simple rooms, all with private bath, that rent for $95 to $125 June through September and $70 to $105 the rest of the year. There is also a studio apartment that rents for a bit more.

## Places to Eat

Orleans has a remarkably diverse selection of high-quality eateries. If you're staying in a nearby town, chances are you'll be eating in Orleans.

Look for the *farmer's market* (19 West Rd), off MA 6A, 8 am to noon on Saturday in-season.

The *Hot Chocolate Sparrow* (☎ 508-240-2230), on MA 6A east of the rotary or on Old Colony Way adjacent to the Cape Cod Rail Trail (depending on when the shop moves), has the strongest and most consistent espresso around, bar none. They also hand-dip chocolate.

*New York Bagels* (☎ 508-255-0255, 125 MA 6A) has New York-style bagels and everything else you'd expect to find at a Jewish deli in Brooklyn.

Frequented by locals, *Land Ho!* (☎ 508-255-5165, 38 MA 6A), in the center of town, is part bar, part restaurant. Patrons come daily for inexpensive lunch and dinner sandwiches, fried seafood platters, barbecue ribs, clam pie and burgers ($9 to $15). The atmosphere is informal with wooden floors, old business signs on the walls and newspapers hanging on a wire that separates the tables from the bar.

*Cap't Cass Rock Harbor Seafood* (no ☎, 117 Rock Harbor Rd), a little harborside seafood shack that's more quaint than most, offers generous lobster rolls, clam chowder and daily blackboard specials. Lunch ($5 to $12) and dinner are served daily in summer and on weekends in spring and fall, mid-April to mid-October.

Filled with nautical paraphernalia, the **Lobster Claw** (*☎ 508-255-1800, 42 MA 6A*), near the rotary, is an informal family-friendly place. Lobsters, mixed-seafood plates and all kinds of fish: they're all on the menu. The portions don't generally allow room for dessert. The restaurant is open from 11:30 am to 9 pm daily April through November. Expect to spend about $7 at lunch, $9 to $17 at dinner.

The **Binnacle Tavern** (*☎ 508-255-7901, 20 MA 28*), a cozy tavern known for gourmet pizza, also offers Italian specialties ($6 to $11) such as eggplant parmigiana and home-made pasta. It's open nightly from April to mid-October and on the weekends the rest of the year.

**Joe's Beach Road Bar & Grille** (*☎ 508-255-0212*), on Beach Rd in East Orleans, a year-round rustic and boisterous hangout for locals and tourists, serves upscale lamb dishes in addition to pizza and pasta. They also have lobster cooked five different ways every night; expect to spend $7 to $17 per main dish.

At **Kadee's Lobster & Clam Bar** (*☎ 508-255-6184, 212 E Main St*), in East Orleans, prices are a bit high, but the seafood is fresh and outdoor tables draw 'em in after a day at Nauset Beach, just down the road. You know the choices by now: oysters, seafood stew, lobster, scallops. Kadee's is open for lunch ($6 to $14) and dinner (about $4 more per main course) late May to early September.

The **Nauset Beach Club** (*☎ 508-255-8547, 222 E Main St*), in East Orleans, serves the most creative cuisine (northern Italian and fish specials) to the most fashionable crowd in town. The restaurant, a former duck-hunting cottage, is small but the portions are enormous (no sharing is permitted). Main dishes are $14 to $21; closed December and January.

### Entertainment
The outdoor sundeck of the **Orleans Inn** (*☎ 508-255-2222*), at the MA 28 and US 6 rotary, is a great place for an après-beach or sunset drink.

**Academy Playhouse** (*☎ 508-255-1963, 120 Main St*) stages a variety of dramas, musicals and comedies in the 1873 former town hall.

### Shopping
For women's clothes, you can do no better than the casually chic Karol Richardson (*☎ 508-255-3944*) and Hannah (*☎ 508-255-8234*), which are next door to each other at 47 Main St.

Among the numerous art galleries in town, Tree's Place (*☎ 508-255-1330*), MA 6A at MA 28, has the most diverse line-up of art, from pricey oil paintings to hand-painted tiles to unusual gifts.

The Bird Watcher's General Store (*☎ 508-255-6974, 800-562-1512*), MA 6A near the rotary, is more devoted to our feathered friends than many people are to their mothers. The staffers are quite knowledgeable about where and when to spot the various species of birds that populate the Cape Cod area.

### Getting There & Around
The Plymouth & Brockton bus (*☎ 508-778-9767, www.p-b.com*) stops off at the CVS drugstore on MA 6A on its way from Provincetown to Hyannis and Boston.

Driving details for Orleans are as follows:

| destination | mileage | hr:min |
| --- | --- | --- |
| Boston, MA | 87 miles | 1:45 |
| Brewster, MA | 5 miles | 0:10 |
| Chatham, MA | 10 miles | 0:15 |
| Falmouth, MA | 42 miles | 1:00 |
| Provincetown, MA | 29 miles | 0:40 |
| Sagamore Bridge, MA | 37 miles | 0:45 |

It's about 3 miles from the center of Orleans to Nauset Beach, and about half that distance in the opposite direction to Rock Harbor.

### EASTHAM
Eastham, home to the Cape's oldest windmill, is one of the Cape's quietest, most compact towns, just 3 miles wide from bay to ocean, and 6 miles long. It's perhaps best known for what happened in 1620: The

Pilgrims first 'encountered' Native Americans on a stretch of land now aptly called First Encounter Beach. The meeting was less than amicable, though there were no fatalities, and the Pilgrims didn't return to the area for another 24 years.

## Information

The chamber of commerce in Eastham (☎ 508-255-3444, 240-7211, www.capecod .net/eastham/chamber), US 6 just north of the Fort Hill Area, is open 10 am to 5 pm daily late May through September, with slightly longer hours in July and August.

For more tourist information, go to the Cape Cod National Seashore Salt Pond Visitor Center (☎ 508-255-3421, www.nps .gov/caco), off US 6 in Eastham; see also the Cape Cod National Seashore boxed text.

## Things to See & Do

The **Fort Hill area**, east of US 6, is one of the Cape's most scenic spots. It commands a high position above the extensive and fragile Nauset Marsh, and boasts a short but lovely 1½ mile (roundtrip) walking trail that skirts the marsh and then heads inland and leads you through a red maple swamp.

Atop Fort Hill, the **Edward Penniman House** (☎ 508-255-3421), a mid-19th-century sea captain's house, is slowly being restored to its former grandeur by the National Park Service (NPS). Although visiting hours are erratic, you can always look in the windows. The Salt Pond Visitor Center has current opening times.

The **Old Schoolhouse Museum** (☎ 508-255-0788), across from the visitor center, houses the Eastham Historical Society. There is a small exhibit on Henry Beston's year spent in a cottage on Coast Guard Beach, the subject of *The Outermost House*. (Beston lived alone in 1928 on Coast Guard Beach and recorded the natural environment around him.) The museum entrance is marked by a huge set of whale jaw bones. Admission is free and it's open 1 to 4 pm weekdays in July and August.

The **bike trail** from the visitor center to Coast Guard Beach takes you across a dramatic salt marsh and through a pretty forest. You can rent bikes across from the Salt

---

## Cape Cod National Seashore

With the backing of President Kennedy, who appreciated the Cape's uniqueness and considered it his home, Congress established the Cape Cod National Seashore (CCNS) in 1961. The CCNS includes the whole eastern shoreline of the Lower (or Outer) Cape, from South Beach in Chatham all the way to Provincetown. It covers more than 42 sq miles in all, including at least half (and often more) of the land mass in Eastham, Wellfleet, Truro and Provincetown. The seashore is known for its pristine and virtually endless beaches, crashing waves, dunes, nature trails, ponds, salt marshes and forests.

Everything of interest is on or just off of US 6, the only highway that runs from Orleans to Provincetown.

The Salt Pond Visitor Center (☎ 508-255-3421, www.nps.gov/caco), off US 6 in Eastham, anchors the southern portion of the CCNS. There are excellent exhibits and films about the Cape's geology, history and ever-changing landscape. Check out the daily list of ranger- and naturalist-led walks and talks, which are usually free. There are two short walking trails that lead from the visitor center. The center is open 9 am to 4:30 pm daily from March through December (until 5 pm in summer) and on weekends in January and February.

The Province Lands Visitor Center (☎ 508-487-1256), Race Point Rd, in Provincetown, has similar services and exhibits; you can also pick up local trail and bike maps here. It's open 9 am to 5 pm daily from mid-April through November.

Pond Visitor Center at Little Capistrano Bike Shop (☎ 508-255-6515).

## Beaches

Coast Guard Beach, east of the visitors' center on the Atlantic Ocean, is a long sandy beach backed by tall, undulating dune grasses. Facilities include restrooms, showers and changing rooms. In summer, shuttles bus people from a parking lot near the visitor center to the beach for $7.

Nauset Light Beach, north of Coast Guard Beach, is also great. Its features and facilities are similar to Coast Guard Beach, but you can park at the beach for $7. **Nauset Lighthouse**, a picturesque red-and-white striped tower, guards the shoreline. (Threatened by an ever-encroaching shoreline, the lighthouse was moved about 250 feet from the current cliff in 1996.)

Both beaches are administered by the NPS, so the parking permits are transferable, which means that you can spend the morning at one beach and the afternoon at the other and not have to pay the parking fee again. Seasonal passes, valid at any National Seashore beach, are a bargain at $20.

## Places to Stay

**Hostels** Eastham has *Hostelling International, Mid-Cape* (☎ 508-255-2785, 800-909-4776 for reservations in-season, fax 508-240-5598, 75 Goody Hallet Drive), open mid-May to mid-September. The 50 beds in eight cabins cost $14 for members, $17 nonmembers. Reservations (by mail or by phone with credit card) are essential in July and August. Off-season, write to Hosteling International Boston, 12 Hemenway St, Boston, MA 02215 or call ☎ 617-779-0900 or fax 617-424-6558. From US 6 and the Orleans rotary, follow Harbor Rd to Bridge Rd to Goody Hallet Drive.

**Motels & Cottages** The *Captain's Quarters* (☎ 508-255-5686, 800-327-7769, fax 508-240-0280, info@captains-quarters.com), on US 6, about a half mile north of Brackett Rd, is a motel with 75 large rooms (many well-suited to four people), a heated pool

KIM GRANT

**Nauset Lighthouse**

and tennis courts. Bike use is complimentary. Rates are $96 to $126 in July and August, and $55 to $74 off-season; closed December through March.

The *Saltaway Cottages* (☎ 508-255-2182), Aspinet Rd off US 6, are thankfully well off the highway. The seven well-maintained and homey efficiency units rent for $470 to $695 per week in summer, $320 to $415 offseason; closed November through April.

The *Midway Motel & Cottages* (☎ 508-255-3117, 800-755-3117, fax 508-255-4235, inquire@midwaymotel.com, 5460 US 6) are set back from the highway and shaded by pine trees. The cottages are rented weekly in summer ($600 to $780); rooms are $78 to $84 nightly in summer and reduced to about half that off-season. The complex is closed November through March.

**Hotels** Sheraton's *Four Points Hotel at the National Seashore* (☎ 508-255-5000, 800-533-3986, fax 508-240-1870, sheraton@cape .com), US 6, less than a mile north of Salt Pond Visitor Center, is expensive ($199) in summer for what you get. But during the rest of the year, rates drop to $89 or so, depending on occupancy. Half the rooms overlook the indoor pool and some have refrigerators.

**B&Bs** The *Overlook Inn* (☎ 508-255-1886, fax 240-0345, winstonsc@aol.com), off US 6, across from the Salt Pond Visitor Center, is set back from the road and offers 10 airy guest rooms furnished with antiques and large modern canvases. The Scottish innkeepers have somewhat eccentric but charming common rooms, including a billiard room and a parlor devoted to Winston Churchill. The Cape Cod Rail Trail is right out the back door. Rates, including a full breakfast, are $95 to $165 in summer, $75 to $95 the rest of the year.

*Whalewalk Inn* (☎ 508-255-0617, fax 240-0017, whalewalk@capecod.net, 220 Bridge Rd), off the Orleans-Eastham rotary, is the best Outer Cape B&B. If you want to splurge, there are five private suites here (most with kitchen) and six luxurious carriage-house rooms. Rooms cost $150 to $250 late May to mid-October, $125 to $200 offseason. The common rooms are sophisticated country-elegant and the full breakfast, which is served on the flagstone patio, is a real eye-opener.

### Places to Eat
The *Eastham Lobster Pool* (☎ 508-255-9706, 4360 US 6) offers informal indoor and outdoor dining on lobsters (surprise!), tasty clam chowder ($2.50) and fish cooked practically any way you'd like ($14 to $18). It's open 11:30 am to 9 pm daily April through October.

*Arnold's Lobster & Clam Bar* (☎ 508-255-2575, 3580 US 6) is similar but also has a raw bar, great onion rings and weekday lunch specials as low as $3.

### Entertainment
The little yellow chapel known as the *First Encounter Coffee House* (☎ 508-255-5438), on Samoset Rd off US 6 from the windmill, hosts acoustic and folk performances on the second and fourth Saturday of each month. Tickets are $10 to $15.

### Getting There & Away
The Plymouth & Brockton bus (☎ 508-778-9767, www.p-b.com) stops at the Eastham Town Hall and the North Eastham village green (both on MA 6) on its way from Boston and Hyannis to Provincetown.

The driving details for Eastham are as follows:

| destination | mileage | hr:min |
|---|---|---|
| Boston, MA | 100 miles | 1:50 |
| Hyannis, MA | 24 miles | 0:35 |
| Orleans, MA | 5 miles | 0:10 |
| Provincetown, MA | 25 miles | 0:35 |
| Sagamore Bridge, MA | 40 miles | 0:50 |
| Wellfleet, MA | 11 miles | 0:15 |

## WELLFLEET
Like most Outer Cape towns, Wellfleet is relatively untouched by development and rampant commercialism. Although Wellfleet in summertime is full of professional people who have taken up residence for the season, day-trippers are lured by art galleries, fine beaches, quiet scenic roads and the famous Wellfleet oysters. The town is very quiet from early September to late June.

### Orientation & Information
Main and Commercial Sts run parallel to each other in the center of town. Continue west along either road to scenic Chequessett Neck Rd. West of US 6, Pilgrim Spring Rd is also scenic; there is a nice harbor view from its terminus. East of US 6, LeCount Hollow Rd leads to Ocean View Drive and Atlantic Ocean beaches.

The Wellfleet Chamber of Commerce (☎ 508-349-2510), just off US 6 in South Wellfleet, is open 9 am to 6 pm daily in July and August and 10 am to 4 pm Friday through Sunday in spring (from mid-May) and fall (until mid-October).

West Main Books (☎ 508-349-2095), on W Main St, is small but selective.

### Things to See & Do
The Massachusetts Audubon Society's scenic 1000-acre **Wellfleet Bay Wildlife Sanctuary**

(☎ 508-349-2615, www.wellfleetbay.org), west off US 6, boasts walking trails that crisscross tidal creeks, salt marshes and a Cape Cod Bay beach. There are excellent natural history day camps for children and field schools for adults. The visitors' center is open 8:30 am to 5 pm daily year-round (except closed Monday from November through April). Trails ($3 adults, $2 children) are open sunrise to sunset.

The **Marconi Wireless Station**, east off US 6 in South Wellfleet, was the first place in the US to transmit messages across the Atlantic Ocean. Little remains today except for interpretive plaques. There is an expansive vista from here, a walking trail and a fine beach.

### Beaches
Marconi Beach, off of US 6, is a narrow Atlantic beach backed by high sand dunes. Parking is $7; enter by foot or bicycle and pay $1; facilities include changing rooms and showers. See Beaches in Eastham for more parking details.

Cahoon Hollow and White Crest Beach, on the Atlantic Ocean, are excellent but parking is more expensive at $10 daily. White Crest is popular with hang gliders.

### Hiking
The 8-mile **Great Island Trail**, off Chequessett Neck Rd, requires four hours, lots of sunscreen, water and a bit of stamina since you'll be walking on soft sand out to a spit of sand that curves around into Wellfleet Bay. The lack of human presence more than compensates for the extra effort. The road to the Great Island Trail is narrow, hilly and winding.

### Bicycling
The **Cape Cod Rail Trail**, which begins in Dennis 26 miles southwest, ends at LeCount Hollow Rd, a couple miles from two good beaches. You can rent bikes at the Idle Times Bike Shop (☎ 508-349-9161), on US 6, or at the smaller Wellfleet Cycles (☎ 508-349-9322), 54 E Commercial St, mid-June to mid-September.

### Boating
Jack's Boat Rentals (☎ 508-349-7553), US 6 near Wellfleet Center, rents kayaks, canoes and sailboards. Inquire about their guided trips on local rivers and glacial ponds. They also have a location on Gull Pond if you want the ease of paddling where you pick up.

### Places to Stay
**Camping** *Maurice's Campground* (☎ 508-349-2029), on US 6 just north of the Eastham town line and on the Cape Cod Rail Trail, reserves about a quarter of its 180 sites for tents. They also have a few cottages and cabins. Open from mid-May until mid-October, tent sites cost $20 for two people, cabins $60 for three and cottages $375 weekly for four.

*Paine's Campground* (☎ 508-349-3007, 800-479-3017), on Old Colony Rd off US 6, open mid-May to mid-October, offers 150 sites, most of which are reserved for tenters: $18 to $24 for two people. It's a 20-minute walk to the beach.

**Motels & Cottages** *Ocean Pines Motel and Cottages* (☎ 508-349-2774, 935 US 6) has the cheapest beds in town at $72 to $79 double. Cottages rent by the week: $475 for two people in summer.

The *Even' Tide Motel* (☎ 508-349-3410, 800-368-0007 in Massachusetts only, fax 508-349-7804, eventide@capecod.net, 650 US 6) is about 4 miles north of the Salt Pond Visitor Center and set back in a grove of trees. There are 31 rooms ($82 to $140 nightly) and nine cottages ($640 to $1750 weekly for up to eight people). Other pluses include an indoor heated pool, a nearby 1-mile hiking trail to Marconi Beach and the Cape Cod Rail Trail, which runs right behind the motel.

The *Wellfleet Motel & Lodge* (☎ 508-349-3535, 800-852-2900, fax 508-349-1192), US 6, across from the wildlife sanctuary, north of the Wellfleet Drive-In, has two pools and 65 above-average rooms. Each has a refrigerator, coffeemaker and free movies for $125 to $145 in July and August, $60 to $75 the rest of the year.

**B&Bs** *Blue Gateways* (☎ 508-349-7530, bonnie@ma.ultranet.com, 252 Main St), a homey and completely renovated small B&B, has three tidy guest rooms within walking distance of many galleries. Fireplaces make the B&B appealing in the winter. Rates, including a light breakfast, are $90 to $110 late May to early September, $20 less the rest of the year.

The nicest rooms at *Inn at Duck Creeke* (☎ 508-349-9333, fax 349-0234 in the summer, duckinn@capecod.net, 70 Main St), near US 6, are in the cottage and carriage house. Otherwise the old-fashioned inn rooms are adequate for $70 to $95 in summer, depending on the bath situation, and about $20 less in spring and fall.

The decidedly old-fashioned *Holden Inn* (☎ 508-349-3450), on Commercial St, hasn't changed much since the current family purchased it in the mid-1920s. The sparsely furnished guest rooms are housed in three buildings. You can't beat the price, but you get what you pay for (namely, a roof over your head if it's raining): $58 to $68 double for an in-town location and a rocking chair on the front porch.

## Places to Eat

Start your day at *Beanstock Coffee Roasters* (☎ 508-349-7008, 70 Main St), a tiny shop where rich espresso is dispensed alongside homemade scones. Afternoon hours are unpredictable.

The *Box Lunch* (☎ 508-349-2178, 50 Briar Lane) serves deli meats and salads rolled up in pita bread ($4 to $7). Box Lunch is open daily year-round.

The *Lighthouse* (☎ 508-349-3681, 317 Main St) is one of the few places in town open year-round, and for all three meals too! It's nothing fancy, just decent food at good prices: omelets ($5), grilled codfish and other sandwiches at lunch (about $7), burgers and steaks at dinner ($9 to $15) and Guinness on tap. Off-season, Friday night is steak night. Try to get a table in the glassed-in dining room; it's quieter.

At *Moby Dick's* (☎ 508-349-9795), US 6, across from Gull Pond Rd, a self-service place where patrons dine on indoor picnic

tables, you'll dig into large portions of very fresh seafood. The clam chowder, onion rings and steamers (clams) are particularly good. Bring your own beer or wine if you wish. It's open 11:30 am to 10 pm daily early May to early October.

*Captain Higgins Seafood Restaurant* (☎ 508-349-6027), on the Town Pier, is an informal seafood place for lunch ($6 to $10) and dinner ($11 to $17), mid-June to mid-September. The outdoor deck is key. Try the lobster rolls, native bluefish and especially the Wellfleet oysters.

The 'in' crowd hangs out at *Painter's Restaurant & Studio Bar* (☎ 508-349-3003, 50 Main St), downing fresh oysters, Portuguese stew, cheeses baked in individual terra cotta dishes and New American seafood (pan-seared mustard-sesame tuna) for dinner ($10 to $23) mid-May to mid-November. It's also open for breakfast and lunch off-season. The Studio Bar menu is lighter and less expensive; Milo, the bar at Painter's Restaurant, is cozy and a good place to go if you are in the mood for a quiet conversation.

The *Upstairs Bar at Aesop's Tables* (☎ 508-349-6450, 316 Main St) has an old-world feel with velveteen chairs, comfortable couch groupings and low lighting. It's a nice place to go for a lighter meal (steak sandwiches or barbecue ribs cost about $10), dessert or an after-dinner drink and a quiet conversation. You can hear live music on Thursday evenings.

## Entertainment

The *Beachcomber* (☎ 508-349-6055), at Cahoon Hollow Beach off Ocean View Drive, is an indoor-outdoor, all-in-one restaurant, bar and nightclub on the beach. It's the best area hang-out for live music at night, but the club is also known for Sunday afternoon concerts and happy hours with drinks poured to a reggae beat. It's open daily May through September (until 1 am in July and August).

The *Tavern Room* (☎ 508-349-7369, 70 Main St) is a fine place to listen to live jazz, folk and Latin music. You can also get good burgers, pizzas and upscale but light bistro treats (roasted eggplant on focaccia, for instance) in this cozy place with beamed ceilings. It's open weekends May to mid-October and nightly in summer.

The **Wellfleet Drive-In** (☎ *508-349-7176, 800-696-3532)*, on US 6, one of the few remaining drive-in theaters in New England, shows first-run double features at dusk May through September.

The **Wellfleet Harbor Actors Theater** (*WHAT;* ☎ *508-349-6835, www.what.org, 1 Kendrick Ave)*, on the harbor off Commercial St, stages contemporary, experimental plays mid-May to mid-October. The productions are always lively, sometimes bawdy and usually the subject of animated conversation long after the curtain comes down. Purchase tickets at their box office on Main St, next to the pharmacy. Half-price student 'rush tickets' are available just before curtain time.

### Shopping

Wellfleet has over 20 galleries representing both fine art and tourist art. Most galleries host receptions (with free food and drink) on Saturday nights in July and August. It's best to just wander Main and Commercial Sts and look for the galleries that are open.

The Wellfleet Flea Market (☎ 508-349-2520, 800-696-3532), at the drive-in theater on US 6, is the Cape's biggest venue for both treasure and junk. It's open weekends mid-April to mid-October; in July and August it is also open on Wednesday and Thursday.

### Getting There & Around

The Plymouth & Brockton bus (☎ 508-778-9767, www.p-b.com) stops at the D&D Market in South Wellfleet (US 6) and the town hall in Wellfleet center (off US 6) on its way from Boston and Hyannis up the Cape to Provincetown.

The driving details for Wellfleet are as follows:

| destination | mileage | hr:min |
| --- | --- | --- |
| Boston, MA | 110 miles | 2:05 |
| Eastham, MA | 11 miles | 0:15 |
| Hyannis, MA | 36 miles | 0:45 |
| Provincetown, MA | 15 miles | 0:20 |
| Sagamore Bridge, MA | 51 miles | 1:05 |
| Truro, MA | 7 miles | 0:09 |

The center of Wellfleet is best explored by foot and by bike since there is very little parking.

## TRURO

An odd collection of elements coexist peacefully in Truro: strip motels and cookie-cutter cottage complexes, huge homes built in the hills and dales west of US 6 and undeveloped forests and beaches to the east. There's very little to do in this sleepy little town, but you'll find good camping and beaches.

### Orientation & Information

Truro is about 10 miles long and only a few miles wide, with no town center per se. Everything you'll need is on or just off US 6. In North Truro, MA 6A veers off US 6 and is filled with motels as it heads into Provincetown. Take any winding road east or west of US 6, get lost a bit and soak in the beautiful New England scenery.

The chamber of commerce in Truro (☎ 508-487-1288), on US 6 in North Truro, is open 10 am to 5 pm daily late June to early September, with additional weekend hours a month before and after that.

### Things to See & Do

The Highland Light, also known as **Cape Cod Light**, east of US 6 in North Truro, replaced the Cape's first lighthouse, which was built on this spot in 1798. Adjacent is the Cape's oldest public golf course.

Once a summer hotel, the **Highland House Museum** (☎ 508-487-3397), situated just before the lighthouse, is now an interesting local museum dedicated to Truro's farming and maritime past. It's open daily 10 am to 5 pm early June to late September; adults are charged $3.

The **Pilgrim Heights Area**, east of US 6, has two short trails with splendidly expansive views. One trail leads to the spot where the Pilgrims purportedly tasted their first spring water in the New World.

A 4-mile **bike path** runs along the ocean from Head of the Meadow Beach (see below), past the Pilgrim Heights Area, to the end of Highhead Rd.

## Beaches

Head of the Meadow Beach, east off US 6, is a wide, dune-backed beach with lots of parking for $7. There are restrooms and changing rooms. See Beaches in Eastham for more parking details.

Corn Hill Beach, off US 6 on Cape Cod Bay, is nice for walking at low tide and windsurfing at high tide. Head up the street above it for a great view of the rolling dunes. Parking is $5.

## Places to Stay

The *North of Highland Camping Area* (☎ 508-487-1191), on Head of the Meadow Rd, in North Truro, is open mid-May to mid-September and has 237 sites on 60 acres shared by tents and RVs. It's a short walk to the beach from here and costs $18 for two.

Open year-round, *North Truro Camping Area* (☎ 508-487-1847), on Highland Rd, reserves about 100 of its 350 mostly wooded sites for tents; $18 for two people in summer.

*Horton's Camping Resort* (☎ 508-487-1220, 800-252-7705, 71 S Highland Rd), North Truro, has 200 sites, about a third of which have RV hookups.

The *Hostelling International, Truro* (☎ 508-349-3889, 800-909-4776 for reservations in-season), at the very end of N Pamet Rd, abutting Ballston Beach, North Truro, is open late June to early September and costs $14 nightly for members, $17 nonmembers. Reserve by mail or by phone with credit card; off-season, write to Hosteling International Boston, 12 Hemenway St, Boston, MA 02215 or call ☎ 617-779-0900 or fax 617-424-6558. This former Coast Guard station (now with 42 beds) has a dramatic location amid dunes and marshes, just a five-minute walk from the beach.

The *Seaside Village* (☎ 508-487-1215, fax 240-2786, innkeep@capecod.net, 482 MA 6A), North Truro, has 32 above-average motel rooms with refrigerators ($75 to $115 double) and 18 studio and efficiency apartments rented weekly in-season ($655 to $860). The motel is closed mid-October to mid-May.

*East Harbour* (☎ 508-487-0505, fax 487-6693, sonja@eastharbour.com, 618 MA 6A), a beachfront complex of cottages and motel units, is one of the better colonies that line MA 6A in North Truro like ducks in a row. Considering the communal grills and in-room microwaves and refrigerators, this motel may suffice for longer stays. From mid-June to early September, cottages cost $800 to $900 weekly for two people, $100 more per child, $200 more per adult. Cottages rent for about $80 to $90 nightly in spring and fall, when they're not rented weekly ($500 to $610).

## Places to Eat

Open late May to early September, *Jams, Inc* (☎ 508-349-1616), off US 6, in 'downtown' Truro, has fancy picnic foods such as rotisserie chicken, salmon pâté and imported cheese. The espresso is both rich and strong.

The *Village Cafe* (☎ 508-487-5800, 4 Highland Rd), in the center of Truro, a pleasant little place with outdoor seating, offers bagels, sandwiches and soups from 7 am, mid-May through September (until 10 pm in summer).

*Adrian's* (☎ 508-487-4360), on US 6 in North Truro, has big picture windows that take advantage of a commanding view atop a bluff overlooking the dunes and ocean. Try the *huevos rancheros* or frittatas at breakfast ($3 to $7). An Italian menu ($7 to $15) with brick-oven pizzas and pasta dishes reigns at dinner. It's open nightly mid-May to mid-October and for breakfast on weekends in spring and fall, daily in summer.

Nondescript from the outside, *Terra Luna* (☎ 508-487-1019), MA 6A, North Truro, is a little bistro-style place gussied up with local art. Dishes ($10 to $19) lean toward New American and Italian with some vegetarian overtones. Terra Luna is open for breakfast and dinner mid-May to mid-October.

## Getting There & Away

The Plymouth & Brockton bus (☎ 508-778-9767, www.p-b.com) stops at Jam's in Truro center and at Dutra's Market in North Truro on its way from Boston and Hyannis to Provincetown. Both of these stops are just off MA 6.

Driving details for Truro are as follows:

| destination | mileage | hr:min |
|---|---|---|
| Boston, MA | 120 miles | 2:20 |
| Chatham, MA | 31 miles | 0:45 |
| Hyannis, MA | 44 miles | 0:50 |
| Provincetown, MA | 8 miles | 0:10 |
| Sagamore Bridge, MA | 60 miles | 1:20 |
| Wellfleet, MA | 7 miles | 0:09 |

## PROVINCETOWN

Provincetown is Cape Cod's most lively resort town and New England's gay mecca. Painters and writers, Portuguese American fishermen and solitude seekers and their families make up this tolerant year-round community of 3500. Walking down Commercial St on any given day, you may see cross-dressers, children eating saltwater taffy, leather-clad motorcyclists, barely clad rollerbladers, women strolling hand in hand and middle-Americans wondering what they've stumbled into on their way to a whale-watching ferry.

This outpost also appeals to those who appreciate long stretches of pristine beach, dramatic sand dunes, contemporary art and one-of-a-kind shops and boutiques. Beyond the main thoroughfare, there are also 4000 acres within the protected CCNS through which to bicycle, walk or gallop.

'P-town,' as it's known to outsiders but never to locals, is jam-packed from late June to early September as its seasonal population swells to 40,000. Even though there are hundreds of rooms to rent, it's essential to arrive with lodging reservations during summer. Because of special events, it also remains very crowded on weekends through the end of October. From January through March Provincetown becomes a desolate but hauntingly beautiful place to visit; just enough restaurants and guest houses remain open to service visitors.

### Orientation

Three exits off US 6 go into town: Snail Rd goes to the quieter East End, Conwell St leads to the town center and MacMillan Wharf, Shank Painter Rd leads to the West End.

There are two routes to the CCNS beaches and dunes: Take Race Point Rd north off US 6 or follow US 6 to its end and head north on Province Lands Rd.

Commercial St is the town's main drag, lined with shops, restaurants, places to stay, entertainment venues and a few museums and historic houses. About 3 miles long from end to end, the one-way street runs parallel to the shoreline and functions as the town's boardwalk. Bradford St runs parallel to Commercial St and receives less foot but more auto traffic. Quiet guest houses line the dozens of little streets that link Bradford and Commercial Sts. Parking within the center of town is difficult and the driving slow, but there are plenty of public parking lots. Commercial St is eminently strollable, as long as you are willing to share it with kamikaze rollerbladers and convertibles cruising the strip at 5mph.

### Information

The chamber of commerce (☎ 508-487-3424, fax 487-8966, www.ptownchamber.com) maintains an information office at 305 Commercial St on MacMillan Wharf, open 9 am to 5 pm daily April through October and 10 am to 4 pm daily (except Wednesday and Sunday) November through March.

The Province Lands Visitor Center (☎ 508-487-1256), at the end of Race Point Rd, is open 9 am to 5 pm daily mid-April through November. They have dozens of scheduled nature-oriented programs. By all means, stop in.

The Provincetown Business Guild (☎ 508-487-2313, 800-637-8696, www.ptown.org), 115 Bradford St, promotes gay-owned businesses, while the Women Innkeepers of Provincetown (☎ 800-933-1963) caters to women-owned businesses.

There are public toilets behind the chamber of commerce information office and on the 2nd floor of the town hall.

Ya Hootie Mobile Laundry Facilities (☎ 508-487-2258), Conwell St, can be a scene.

Outer Cape Health Services (☎ 508-487-9395), Harry Kemp Way off Conwell St from US 6, is open for walk-ins 8 to 8:30 am

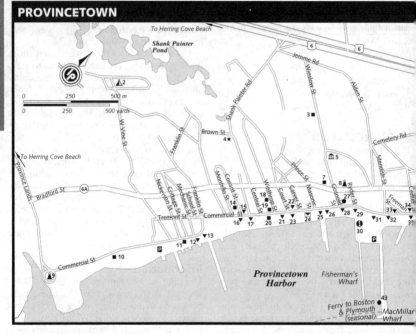

## PROVINCETOWN

Monday through Saturday and 9 to 11:30 am Sunday in summer. Otherwise, call for an appointment.

In an emergency, call ☎ 911. For Provincetown police, call ☎ 508-487-1212; the police station is at 26 Shank Painter Rd.

### Art Museums & Galleries

Provincetown began attracting artists in the early 1900s shortly after the Cape Cod School of Art was founded in 1899 by Charles Hawthorne. By the 1920s artists drawn to the clear light had created a fashionable art colony, much like those in Taos, New Mexico, East Hampton, New York and Carmel, California.

Provincetown remains a vital center on the American arts scene with more than 20 galleries representing artists of various persuasions, from avant-garde to representational.

The **Provincetown Art Association & Museum** (☎ 508-487-1750) at 460 Commercial St was organized in 1914 and is one of the country's foremost small museums. Paintings from the permanent collection are rotated throughout the year; exhibits may show works by Marsden Hartley and Milton Avery, as well as emerging local artists. The museum is open noon to 5 pm daily (and 8 to 10 pm Friday and Saturday) late June to early September. The rest of the year, hours are limited to noon to 5 pm weekends; admission is $3.

Pick up a copy of the *Provincetown Gallery Guide* for the very latest offerings. The town's well-established galleries include the following:

Berta Walker Galleries
 (☎ 508-487-6411) 208 Bradford St
Julie Heller Gallery
 (☎ 508-487-2169) 2 Gosnold St
Packard Gallery
 (☎ 508-487-4690) 418 Commercial St

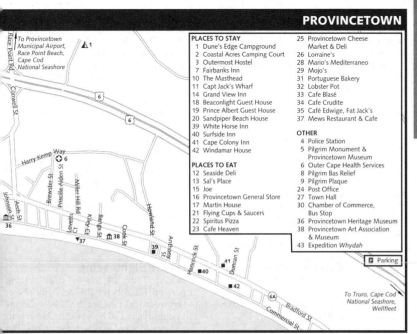

**PLACES TO STAY**
1 Dune's Edge Campground
2 Coastal Acres Camping Court
3 Outermost Hostel
7 Fairbanks Inn
10 The Masthead
11 Capt Jack's Wharf
14 Grand View Inn
18 Beaconlight Guest House
19 Prince Albert Guest House
20 Sandpiper Beach House
39 White Horse Inn
40 Surfside Inn
41 Cape Colony Inn
42 Windamar House

**PLACES TO EAT**
12 Seaside Deli
13 Sal's Place
15 Joe
16 Provincetown General Store
17 Martin House
21 Flying Cups & Saucers
22 Spiritus Pizza
23 Cafe Heaven

25 Provincetown Cheese
   Market & Deli
26 Lorraine's
28 Mario's Mediterraneo
29 Mojo's
31 Portuguese Bakery
32 Lobster Pot
33 Cafe Blasé
34 Cafe Crudite
35 Café Edwige, Fat Jack's
37 Mews Restaurant & Cafe

**OTHER**
4 Police Station
5 Pilgrim Monument &
   Provincetown Museum
6 Outer Cape Health Services
8 Pilgrim Bas Relief
9 Pilgrim Plaque
24 Post Office
27 Town Hall
30 Chamber of Commerce,
   Bus Stop
36 Provincetown Heritage Museum
38 Provincetown Art Association
   & Museum
43 Expedition *Whydah*

Provincetown Group Gallery
  (☎ 508-487-8841) 465 Commercial St
Rice/Polak Gallery
  (☎ 508-487-1052) 430 Commercial St

## Provincetown Heritage Museum

This museum (☎ 508-487-7098), at Commercial and Center Sts, is topped with a 162-foot steeple that has served since 1861 as a landmark for fishermen sailing into port. It houses the world's largest indoor model of a fishing schooner, which was built at Flyer's Boatyard down the road and assembled upstairs in the museum. Other artifacts celebrating Provincetown's maritime history include an offshore whaling boat, 19th-century fishing artifacts and a trap fishing boat. Open 10 am to 5:30 pm daily late May to mid-October, the museum costs $3 for adults.

## Pilgrim Sights

In their search for a place to settle and freely practice religion, the Pilgrims first set foot on American soil in 1620 at Provincetown. A plaque marks the spot at the western end of Commercial St near the Provincetown Inn. The Pilgrims anchored here for five weeks in search of fresh water and fertile ground; when they failed to find adequate supplies of either, they forged on to Plymouth.

In spite of their short stay, the Pilgrims did make history here. The **Pilgrim Bas Relief**, on Bradford St behind the Provincetown Town Hall, commemorates the Mayflower Compact, which the Pilgrims drew up while anchored in the harbor. The compact, a predecessor to the US Constitution, was designed to quell brewing insurrection by the indentured servants on board by granting them full rights in the new land.

The **Pilgrim Monument & Provincetown Museum** (☎ 508-487-1310, 800-247-1620), on High Pole Rd off Winslow St from Bradford St, is modeled after the Torre del Mangia in Siena, Italy. Climb the 116 stairs and 60 ramps for a great view of town, the beaches, the spine of the Outer Cape and even Boston on a clear day (it's 30 miles away as the crow flies).

The museum portrays the Pilgrims' early challenges of finding food and water as well as the lives of whaling captains who later settled here. A children's area features dioramas of a whaling captain's onshore life, the natural history of the Outer Cape and 18th-century toys and dolls. The museum ($5 adults, $3 children) is open 9 am to 5 pm daily April through November, until 7 pm in July and August.

### Pirate Sights

The Expedition *Whydah* (☎ 508-487-8899, www.whydah.org), 16 MacMillan Wharf, showcases booty and artifacts from the only pirate ship ever recovered from waters near Marconi Beach. It sank in 1500 feet of water off Wellfleet in 1717 and was recovered in 1984 by a team from Cape Cod. The museum is open 10 am to 5 pm daily April to mid-October and weekends through January; adults $5, children $3.50.

### Beaches

Race Point Beach, off US 6 within the CCNS, is known for its pounding surf and high dunes stretching as far as the eye can see. There are lifeguards on duty; facilities include restrooms and showers. Parking is $7 for cars, $2 bicycles.

The water at Herring Cove Beach, at the end of US 6, is calmer than Race Point and the sunsets more spectacular (this beach faces west). Facilities and parking are similar to Race Point. See Beaches in Eastham for more parking details pertaining to Race Point and Herring Cove.

Long Point Beach is reached via a water shuttle (see Getting Around) or a very long walk (about two hours one way along the stone jetty at the western end of Commercial St). There are no facilities out here; pack a picnic and lots of water and sunscreen before heading to Cape Cod's most remote grains of sand. It's well worth getting to because of the relative lack of fellow human beings.

### Horseback Riding

Nelson's Riding Stables (☎ 508-487-1112), 43 Race Point Rd, offers one-hour guided rides ($30 per person) on CCNS trails traversing the dunes and woods from April through October and off-season when the weather permits. More experienced riders can gallop along the beach at sunset ($60 per person, not available in July and August).

### Bicycling

There are 7 miles of great paved bike trails within the CCNS; two spur trails lead to the Herring Cove and Race Point Beaches. Rent bicycles at Arnold's (☎ 508-487-0844), 329 Commercial St, in the center of town, and at Galeforce Bicycle Rentals (☎ 508-487-4849), 144 Bradford St, on the western edge of town. Mountain bikes cost about $16 daily or $8 for two hours.

### Airplane Sightseeing

Willie Air Tours (☎ 508-487-0240), at the airport on Race Point Rd, gets you above the crowds to fully comprehend how narrow this peninsula is and how susceptible it is to the whims of wind and water currents. The 15-minute trips cost $50 for one person, $80 for four.

### Organized Tours

To get oriented, board the Provincetown Trolley (☎ 508-487-9483), on Commercial St in front of the town hall, for a 40-minute narrated sightseeing tour; $8 adults, $5 children. Tours depart on the half hour 10 am to 4 pm and on the hour 5 pm to 8 pm May through October. Hop on and off at various points including the Provincetown Art Association and the Province Lands Visitor Center.

Art's Dune Tours (☎ 508-487-1950), at Commercial and Standish Sts, offers hourlong, narrated, 4-WD dune tours within the CCNS from mid-April to mid-November. Fares are $10 to $12 per person; reservations are recommended for the sunset trip.

The *Schooner Hindu* (☎ 508-487-0659) and *Bay Lady II* (☎ 508-487-9308), both traditional schooners, depart from MacMillan Wharf mid-May to mid-October for two-hour bay sails. Adults pay $10 to $15, children $6.

Commemorating the first battle of the Revolutionary War at Old North Bridge, Concord, MA

Just about every fishing village in New England offers whale-watching and fishing cruises.

STEPHEN TRIMBLE

Leaves aren't the only fall color in Cape Cod.

MARKHAM JOHNSON

One of Cape Cod's many lighthouses

KIM GRANT

Long, pristine stretches of beach make up the Cape Cod National Seashore, MA.

## Whale-Watching Cruises

Of the half-dozen companies that offer trips departing from MacMillan Wharf, the Dolphin Fleet Whale Watch (☎ 508-349-1900, 800-826-9300) offers the best tours. On-board scientists and naturalists hail from the Center for Coastal Studies. Even on a warm day, bring a sweater for the 3½-hour voyage. Tickets cost for $18 adults, $15.50 children.

## Places to Stay

**Camping** As the name suggests, *Dune's Edge Campground* (☎ 508-487-9815, camp@dunes-edge.com) is just off US 6 on the edge of the dunes. Open May to late September, the 100 pine-shaded RV and tent sites go for $24 to $30 for two people, $8 each additional adult ($3 children).

*Coastal Acres Camping Court* (☎ 508-487-1700), on Blueberry Rd off Bradford St, on the western edge of town, is open April through October. Tent sites are $22.

**Hostels** The *Outermost Hostel* (☎ 508-487-4378, 26-28 Winslow St), off Bradford St, a privately run hostel, has five cabins housing six bunks ($15 nightly). Common space includes a kitchen and living room; barbecues and picnic tables are handy.

**Efficiencies** About a mile west of the town center, *The Masthead* (☎ 508-487-0523, 800-395-5095, fax 508-487-9251, 31-41 Commercial St) sits right on the bay. A variety of room configurations are available (have them fax you a listing): multi-room apartments, cottages, efficiencies and simple motel rooms. In July and August rooms and efficiencies begin at $567 weekly, while cottages and apartments start at $984. Off-season, you can get a bed for as little as $63 or as much as $218 nightly.

*Capt Jack's Wharf* (☎ 508-487-1450, 73A Commercial St) consists of a series of connected apartments and studios built on a wharf. In a few of them you can see right between the floor boards to the tide beneath you. They're as airy, funky and bohemian on the inside as their exterior suggests. The wharf is lined with bistro tables and draped with colorful buoys. Units rent for $750 to $1100 weekly, $600 to $880 off-season, $86 to $126 nightly with a three-night minimum; closed late September to late May. No credit cards are accepted.

**Motels** The *Cape Colony Inn* (☎ 508-487-1755, 280 Bradford St) has 54 rooms that rent for $85 to $144 per double in-season, $67 to $102 off-season; closed November through April.

*Surfside Inn* (☎/fax 508-487-1726, 800-421-1726, ourwhoopi@aol.com, 543 Commercial St) is perhaps the least-attractive building in town, and one of the only ones made of concrete. But since it has 84 rooms, it's likely to have a vacancy when others don't. Half the rooms have balconies overlooking the bay; others overlook the pool and Commercial St. Rooms cost $99 to $169 in summer, $20 less off-season; closed late October to mid-April.

**Guesthouses & B&Bs** Provincetown has perhaps a hundred small inns and guesthouses that provide the most interesting accommodations. Most guesthouses have a mix of rooms with private or shared bath. In summer, most will also be booked in advance. If you can't make an advance reservation, arrive early in the day and ask the chamber of commerce to help you find a vacant room for the night. Better yet, try to visit before June or after early September.

*Windamar House* (☎ 508-487-0599, fax 487-7507, windamar@tiac.net, 568 Commercial St), a former sea captain's house, has six lovely rooms (shared and private bath) and two even-better apartments. The house's manicured backyard is also one of the most tranquil in town. From late May to early September, rooms rent for $55 to $110, apartments for $775 or $895 weekly; in spring and fall they drop to $80 to $100; closed January through March. No credit cards are accepted.

The *Grand View Inn* (☎ 508-487-9193, fax 487-2894, vanbelle@capecod.net, 4 Conant St) is a clean and well-kept place on a quiet street, yet convenient to the center of town. In summer, the 12 rooms go for $65 to $125 (with shared and private bath). They cost $40 to $95 the rest of the year.

The *White Horse Inn* (☎ *508-487-1790, 500 Commercial St*) rents 12 simple rooms, each decorated with original local art and most with shared bath, for $70 to $75 double ($35 to $40 single) in summer, $50 off-season. There are also six far more interesting bohemian, bungalow-style apartments that rent for $125 in summer, but they have a three-night minimum. No credit cards are accepted.

The gracious *Fairbanks Inn* (☎ *508-487-0386, fax 487-3540, fairbank@capecod.net, 90 Bradford St*), an historic 18th-century hostelry with its integrity still intact, boasts restored wide-pine floors and fireplaces. It's also been upgraded with fine amenities and down comforters. The 13 rooms (a couple with shared bath) rent for $99 to $155 in July and August, and are an even better bargain off-season ($50 to $125).

Among Provincetown's other welcoming and elegant guesthouses, the *Beaconlight Guesthouse* (☎/fax *508-487-9603, 800-696-9603, beaconlite@capecod.net, 12 Winthrop St*) also rises to the top. Very comfortable, harmoniously decorated rooms and suites cost between $100 and $220 in summer, $55 to $155 the rest of the year. The innkeepers also run the *Oxford Guesthouse* (☎ *508-487-9103, 800-456-9103, www.capecodnet/oxford, 8 Cottage St*), which is nearby and equally lovely with similar rates.

*Prince Albert Guest House* (☎ *508-487-0859, 800-992-0859, palbert@capecod.net, 166 Commercial St*), facing the Sandpiper Beach House, has been completely renovated with a Victorian flair. The 10 rooms (most with private bath) rent for $100 to $160 in summer ($75 to $85 for a shared bath) and $80 to $100 off-season (less for shared bath). It's perfectly kept and congenial, complete with front and rear patios.

The *Sandpiper Beach House* (☎ *508-487-1928, 800-354-8628, fax 508-487-8828, 165 Commercial St*) is nicely kept and conveniently located. The frilly parlors are comfy, and the front porch is good for people-watching. Rooms cost $105 to $195 for a double in summer.

## Places to Eat

**Delis** No matter where you are on Commercial St, you'll never be far from one of these three delis. From east to west, they are the *Provincetown Cheese Market & Deli* (☎ *508-487-3032, 225 Commercial St*), the *Provincetown General Store* (☎ *508-487-0300, 147 Commercial St*) and the *Seaside Deli* (☎ *508-487-7179, 93 Commercial St*). The cheese market and the general store are open year-round.

**Cafes & Coffeehouses** Without a doubt, *Spiritus Pizza* (☎ *508-487-2808, 190 Commercial St*) is *the* place to go for a late-night slice. Strong coffee and a pastry will jump-start you in the morning.

*Joe* (☎ *508-487-6656, 148A Commercial St*) offers consistently excellent cappuccino.

Not only does *Flying Cups & Saucers* (☎ *508-487-3780, 205-209 Commercial St*) open before everyone else does (at 7:30 am), they also make protein drinks and exotic juice drinks along with espresso.

**Restaurants** While there are plenty of moderately priced eateries and take-out joints hawking sandwiches, burgers, pizza, pasta and seafood, Provincetown also has a surprising number of fine but pricey restaurants. Dining options range from Portuguese to fried seafood to Italian to New American.

Provincetown's favorite snack is a big wad of hot, sugar-dusted fried dough ($1.50) from the *Portuguese Bakery* (☎ *508-487-1803, 299 Commercial St*). This simple bakery-lunchroom, which has been here for a century, also sells the town's cheapest breakfasts and sandwiches.

Every town has one and Provincetown is no exception: *Mojo's* (☎ *508-487-3140*), on Ryder St, at MacMillan Wharf, is Provincetown's classic clam shack. It's open for lunch mid-May to mid-October and for dinner in summer.

Dark and cozy, *Fat Jack's* (☎ *508-487-4822, 335 Commercial St*) is a fine, year-round (well, almost, it's closed in December) standby for burgers, sandwiches and fish and chips. It's open for lunch and dinner; prices range from $5 to $13.

The principle activity for many at *Cafe Blasé* (☎ 508-487-9465, 328 Commercial St), the town's premier outdoor cafe for people-watching, is dishing people as they saunter by. But the cafe has some good dishes to eat, too: crabmeat salad, Caesar salad with grilled tuna, smoked turkey sandwiches and garden burgers for $7 to $15 at lunch and dinner.

Light and airy but small and crowded, *Cafe Heaven* (☎ 508-487-9639, 199 Commercial St) is an excellent three-meal-a-day sort of place. From fluffy omelets ($6) to cold salads and sandwiches ($4 to $8) to create-your-own pasta dishes served at night ($10 to $18), there is more value here than at most eateries.

*Cafe Crudite* (☎ 508-487-6237, 336 Commercial St), on a 2nd-floor deck overlooking the street, boasts a world-influenced vegan and vegetarian menu, a traditional Japanese macrobiotic menu and a veggie burger with upward of 28 ingredients. Filling your belly will cost about $5 at lunch, under $10 at dinner.

*Café Edwige* (☎ 508-487-2008, 333 Commercial St) is the most popular breakfast place among locals and repeat visitors. For $4 to $7.50 you can choose from frittatas, tofu casserole, broiled flounder and fruit pancakes. Expect to wait unless you arrive by 8:30 am. At dinnertime the cafe is transformed into a romantic bistro offering an eclectic menu with the likes of Thai stir-fry, crab cakes and Asian-style paella for $16 to $23. The solicitous service and creative cuisine make it a top place to dine.

*Sal's Place* (☎ 508-487-1279, 99 Commercial St) serves simple but good southern Italian dishes at outdoor tables on the bay or indoors in a classic trattoria. Dinner ($9 to $20 per main course) is served May through September.

There's a reason why lines form outside the *Lobster Pot* (☎ 508-487-0842, 321 Commercial St). Inside you'll find fresh seafood and fish, chowder, a bakery, tables overlooking the harbor and fast service. A filling lunch costs $7 to $13, dinner $13 to $19. It's open daily (closed December and January).

*Lorraine's* (☎ 508-487-6074, 229-R Commercial St), down an alley leading toward the harbor, is small but cozy and features Mexican cuisine with a slight New England accent. Local littleneck clams are served in a cilantro lime broth with roasted garlic, shallots and scallions; fresh sea scallops are served with tomatillos in a green chile sauce, flambéed with tequila. Dinner costs about $14 to $22.

*Mario's Mediterraneo* (☎ 508-487-0002, 265 Commercial St) will serve you an Italian sandwich, or a cup of soup and a slice of pizza for $4, which you can eat at one of the cafe tables in the front. Out back are tables overlooking the beach and a more expensive California-Mediterranean menu.

The *Martin House* (☎ 508-487-1327, 157 Commercial St), a rustic 18th-century house with fireplaces, is particularly well-suited to year-round dining. It's difficult to categorize the innovative menu ($15 to $28 for main dishes) except to say that some dishes are internationally inspired, some lean toward continental, others celebrate vegetarians. One thing is certain: Leave room for desserts like the caramelized banana and lime tart.

The waterfront *Mews Restaurant and Cafe* (☎ 508-487-1500, 429 Commercial St), the best place to splurge, offers less-expensive food upstairs than at the fancier downstairs dining room, but it's still from the same exceptional kitchen that thinks of food as an art form. Go all out with a mixed-seafood grill or *bouillabaisse* or hold back with a fancy pasta dish. Lunch, when you can enjoy the view, costs $6 to $12, while serious dinner entrees cost $17 to $24. (It could be the best $20 you spend on grilled tuna.)

## Entertainment

Look for posted playbills for the *Provincetown Repertory Theatre* (☎ 508-487-5600) and the *Provincetown Theatre Company* (☎ 508-487-9500), both of which produce fine plays in the great tradition of Provincetown's early days when Eugene O'Neill staged *Bound East For Cardiff*.

The *New Art Cinema* (☎ 508-487-9222, 214 Commercial St) shows new films.

*The Boatslip Beach Club* (☎ 508-487-1669, 161 Commercial St) is known for its wildly popular afternoon tea dances (from

3:30 to 6:30 pm). They rent pool chairs for $3 a day, although you must depart by 3 pm so they can set up for the tea dances. The Boatslip attracts a highly eclectic crowd, and in the summer, more often than not, the place is packed with people.

The waterfront *Pied Piper* (☎ 508-487-1527, 193A Commercial St) is the women's bar in town. They host 'post-tea' parties at 6:30 pm.

The *Atlantic House* (☎ 508-487-3821, 4 Masonic Place), referred to simply as the 'A-House,' features three distinct men's bars: leather, disco and an intimate bar with an off-season fireplace.

The *Crown & Anchor* (☎ 508-487-1430, 247 Commercial St) draws a gay and mixed crowd to its 'leather and Levi's' bar, disco, drag and cabaret shows. (The building was still under major post-fire reconstruction at press time.)

## Shopping

Commercial St is lined with the most creative specialty shops on the Cape. You'll find almost anything that could suit your fancy, from leather implements of torture to rubber stamps, from cutting-edge women's clothing to artsy T-shirts, from sculpture to hand-crafted jewelry. It's best to wander.

There are two shops you shouldn't miss. Marine Specialties (☎ 508-487-1730), 235 Commercial St, is a cavernous store filled to the rafters with random, surplus Army and Navy stuff and other odd items, all priced to sell. Shop Therapy (☎ 508-487-9387), 346 Commercial St, with its psychedelic exterior, carries retro and cutting-edge goods that tip the scales away from 'normal.'

## Getting There & Away

**Air** Cape Air (☎ 508-487-0241, 800-352-0714, www.flycapeair.com) provides daily year-round service from Boston to Provincetown's Municipal Airport, about 4 miles from town and reached via taxi. Summertime fares range from $160 to $180 roundtrip. The flight takes about half an hour.

**Bus** The Plymouth & Brockton bus (☎ 508-778-9767, www.p-b.com), which stops at the chamber of commerce, provides four daily buses (3½ hours; $21 one way) between Provincetown and Boston with stops in Truro, Wellfleet, Eastham, Orleans, Brewster, Dennis, Yarmouth, Hyannis and West Barnstable.

**Car** Following are the driving details for Provincetown (assuming that you don't get bogged down in heavy traffic):

| destination | mileage | hr:min |
|---|---|---|
| Boston, MA | 128 miles | 2:30 |
| Chatham, MA | 37 miles | 0:50 |
| Hyannis, MA | 46 miles | 1:00 |
| New York, NY | 300 miles | 6:00 |
| Providence, RI | 128 miles | 2:30 |
| Sagamore Bridge, MA | 63 miles | 1:15 |
| Woods Hole, MA | 71 miles | 1:30 |

**Boat** You can get to and from Provincetown by passenger ferry from Boston and from Plymouth.

Bay State Cruises (☎ 508-487-9284 in summer, 617-748-1428 for year-round information) links Provincetown's MacMillan Wharf and Boston's Commonwealth Pier on Northern Ave. The three-hour voyage costs $18 adults, $15 children, $5 bicycles one way. Boats depart once daily from Provincetown at 3:30 pm and from Boston at 9 am in summer and on weekends late May to mid-October. There's also a new high-speed ferry which takes two hours. It departs Boston at 8 am and 4 pm, and Provincetown at 10:30 am and 6:30 pm twice daily from mid-May to mid-October. It costs $39 one way, $75 roundtrip.

Cape Cod Cruises (☎ 508-747-2400, 800-242-2469), on State Pier next to the *Mayflower* in Plymouth, departs for Provincetown at 10 am and return at 6 pm weekends late May to late September and daily mid-June to early September. Return tickets are $25 adults, $16 children and $2 bicycles.

## Getting Around

A Summer Shuttle (☎ 508-240-0050) travels up and down Bradford St with a detour to MacMillan Wharf between 8:15 am and midnight in summer; flag the bus down and hop on and off anywhere along the 3-mile route. Another bus departs on the hour (between 10 am and 6 pm) from MacMillan Wharf for Herring Cove Beach. The fare is $1.25 for a one-way ticket.

Flyer's Shuttle (☎ 508-487-0898), 131A Commercial St, ferries sunbathers across the bay to remote Long Point mid-June to mid-September. The fare is $7 one way, $10 roundtrip.

# Martha's Vineyard & Nantucket Island

Islands are enchanting places – the geographical confinement lets people know neighbors better and have more community spirit.

In the 18th century, the islands off New England's coast were maritime vanguards, havens for whaling vessels and merchant fleets. With the coming of the Age of Steam in the 19th century, they became vacation resorts, charming places where city dwellers could escape the summer's heat and find a cool, constant sea breeze.

For most of the 20th century, Martha's Vineyard and Nantucket have been pleasure destinations for New Englanders of all social classes. But recently these two islands have gone noticeably upscale: President and Mrs Clinton chose Martha's Vineyard for their vacation in 1994, '95, '97 and '98, as did an increasing number of rich and famous celebrities. Generally, Martha's Vineyard tends to attract a more ethnically and economically diverse holiday crowd than Nantucket.

Nantucket, meanwhile, continues to see the construction of more and more $5 and $6 million 'trophy' homes, which raised the median home price to about $400,000 in 1999. No wonder the island's small airport experiences more takeoffs and landings of private jets in summer than most other places in the country. It has enjoyed that ultimate American chic: It was the setting for a TV sitcom *(Wings)*.

Almost everything is more expensive on Martha's Vineyard and Nantucket Island, even more expensive than on Cape Cod. But these two special places are beguiling, historic and beautiful, and there are ways to visit the islands without hemorrhaging money.

stopped at this island and named it Martha's Vineyard in honor of his daughter.

Today, the island boasts an actual working vineyard that you can visit. There are also lots of beaches, bike paths, charming towns, open spaces, restaurants and inns. To the residents of eastern Massachusetts, it's simply 'the Vineyard.'

## Highlights

- Watching the sunset from the clay cliffs of Aquinnah
- Touring the gingerbread Victorian houses of Oak Bluffs
- Walking deserted off-season beaches on Chappaquiddick Island
- Wandering up-island on Martha's Vineyard to buy farm-fresh produce
- Canoeing or kayaking on a quiet inlet
- Taking Nantucket's Great Point natural history tour
- Bicycling Nantucket's Polpis Rd
- Snapping pictures of the rose-covered cottages of 'Sconset

## Martha's Vineyard

In the early 17th century, mariner Bartholomew Gosnold cruised the coast of New England, charting it for later exploration. It is thought that he found wild grapes when he

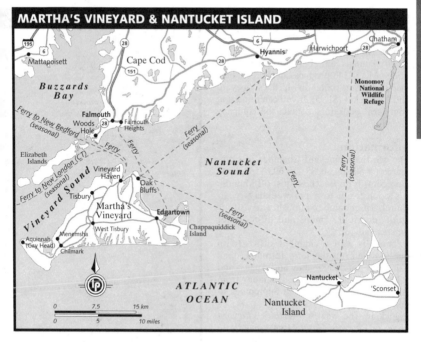

**MARTHA'S VINEYARD & NANTUCKET ISLAND**

## History

Prior to 1640, 3000 Wampanoag Indians lived on the island. Over the next century, English settlers colonized the Vineyard and converted the Wampanoags to Christianity. Many Wampanoags died from diseases imported by the English, and by the mid-18th century there were only 300 native islanders left. Today, many of their descendants live in Aquinnah (known as Gay Head until mid-1997).

Vineyarders are a proud, fiercely independent lot, relishing the fact that they're separate from the mainland. They have strong opinions on everything. Nevertheless, they've opened their island to a thriving tourist trade: The year-round population of 11,000 swells to 90,000 in July and August.

## Orientation

The main ports of entry are Vineyard Haven, the island's year-round commercial center,

and Oak Bluffs, a seasonal, somewhat honky-tonk town with ornate Victorian houses and a history of racial integration. It's 3 miles from Vineyard Haven to Oak Bluffs along Beach Rd.

Edgartown, the pricey grande dame of the Vineyard, is the island's other principal town. Its lovely back lanes are filled with houses built by whaling captains and separated by white picket fences. It's 5 miles along the shoreline from Oak Bluffs to Edgartown.

Chappaquiddick, a relatively tourist-free spit of land within a stone's throw of Edgartown, is reached via a five-minute ferry from Edgartown center. The small island has pristine beaches.

The other towns on Martha's Vineyard – West Tisbury, Chilmark, Menemsha and Aquinnah – are relatively undeveloped and collectively referred to as 'up-island.' The western tip of the island belongs to the colorful cliffs of Aquinnah, 21 miles from Edgartown or Vineyard Haven.

**Maps** Rubel Bike Maps (☎ 617-776-6567, info@bikemaps.com), PO Box 401035, Cambridge, MA 02140, produces an excellent bike map that covers routes on Martha's Vineyard and Nantucket ($1.95). If you can't find it at your local bookstore, contact the company directly.

## Information

The Martha's Vineyard Chamber of Commerce (☎ 508-693-0085, fax 693-7589, www .mvy.com) is on Beach Rd just off Main St. It's open 9 am to 5 pm weekdays year-round. The chamber publishes a visitor's guide, distributes maps and offers other practical advice.

There is also a chamber office (with public toilets) in the ferry terminal, open 8 am to 8 pm daily in July and August and 8:30 am to 5:30 pm Friday to Sunday from late May through June and September to mid-October.

Pick up the weekly *Martha's Vineyard Times* or *Vineyard Gazette* (www.mvgazette .com) for a current calendar of events.

For laundry facilities, try the Airport Laundromat (☎ 508-693-5005), off of the Edgartown-West Tisbury Rd, and Cottage City Spin Cycle (☎ 508-696-9116) on Hiawatha Ave.

The Martha's Vineyard Hospital (☎ 508-693-0410) is off the Vineyard Haven-Oak Bluffs Rd.

In an emergency, call ☎ 911. To reach the police, call these numbers:

| | |
|---|---|
| Edgartown | ☎ 508-627-4343 |
| Oak Bluffs | ☎ 508-693-0750 |
| Vineyard Haven | ☎ 508-696-4240 |

## Organized Tours

Gay Head Sightseeing, MV Sightseeing and Island Transport (☎ 508-693-1555) are operated by the same company. These buses depart from the ferry terminals in Vineyard Haven and Oak Bluffs from late May to late October. Buses are timed with ferry arrivals, more or less. The 2½-hour island-wide tour

**MARTHA'S VINEYARD**

takes in all the major towns and also stops at Aquinnah (Gay Head). Tickets costs $12.50 for adults, $5 for children.

See also the Chappaquiddick Island section, which describes tours by The Trustees of the Reservations.

## Getting There & Away

**Air** Cape Air (☎ 508-790-0300, 800-352-0714, www.flycapeair.com) flies throughout the year from Boston; Nantucket; Providence, Rhode Island; Hyannis; and New Bedford to Martha's Vineyard Airport in

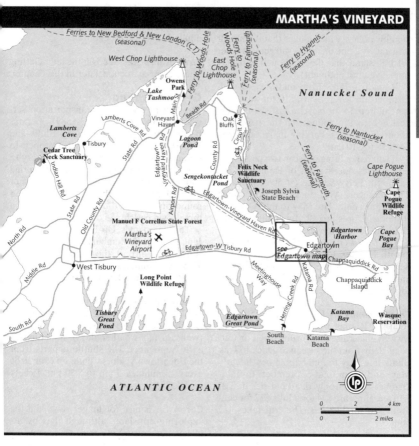

## MARTHA'S VINEYARD

Ferries to New Bedford & New London (CT)
(seasonal)

Ferry to Woods Hole

Ferry to Falmouth (seasonal)

Ferry to Hyannis (seasonal)

West Chop Lighthouse

East Chop Lighthouse

Nantucket Sound

Owens Park

Lake Tashmoo

Main St

Beach Rd

Ferry to Nantucket (seasonal)

Lamberts Cove

Lamberts Cove Rd

Vineyard Haven

Oak Bluffs

State Rd

Lagoon Pond

County Rd

Circuit Ave

Ferry to Falmouth (seasonal)

Cedar Tree Neck Sanctuary

Tisbury

Edgartown-Vineyard Haven Rd

Felix Neck Wildlife Sanctuary

Cape Pogue Lighthouse

Indian Hill Rd

Edgartown Haven Rd

Airport Rd

Sengekontacket Pond

Joseph Sylvia State Beach

Cape Pogue Wildlife Refuge

Lamberts Cove

State Rd

Manuel F Corellus State Forest

Edgartown-Vineyard Haven Rd

Edgartown Harbor

Cape Pogue Bay

North Rd

Martha's Vineyard Airport

Edgartown-W Tisbury Rd

see Edgartown map

Edgartown

Chappaquiddick Rd

Middle Rd

West Tisbury

Meetinghouse Way

Katama Rd

Chappaquiddick Island

Long Point Wildlife Refuge

Herring Creek Rd

South Rd

Tisbury Great Pond

Edgartown Great Pond

South Beach

Katama Beach

Katama Bay

Wasque Reservation

ATLANTIC OCEAN

0    2    4 km
0    1    2 miles

---

West Tisbury. Cape Air has joint ticketing with major airlines.

US Airways Express (☎ 800-428-4322) offers year-round service from Boston; New York (La Guardia Airport); Washington, DC; and Nantucket.

A taxi ride from the airport to either Vineyard Haven or to Edgartown costs approximately $10.

**Boat** Ferries run to the Vineyard from several points along the coast and from Nantucket Island.

***From Woods Hole & Falmouth*** The car ferries (which also take passengers) operated by the Steamship Authority (☎ 508-477-8600 for advance auto reservations, and 548-3788 for day-of-sail information, www.steamshipauthority.com) sail daily in summer from Woods Hole out to Vineyard Haven (10 trips) and to Oak Bluffs (four trips). In other seasons, all 13 daily trips go to Vineyard Haven. For the summer, make automobile reservations months in advance, especially if you are traveling on Friday or a weekend.

On Tuesday, Wednesday and Thursday in summer, the Authority has a 'guaranteed standby policy,' which means that if your car is in line by 2 pm, the boats will get you on or off the island that day (although you may not leave until midnight).

Roundtrip fares from mid-May to mid-October are $94 for cars, $10 for adults, $5 for children, $6 for bicycles. Off-season, cars cost $42 to $56 roundtrip. The trip takes about 45 minutes. Parking in Woods Hole costs $8 to $10 daily.

If you're not bringing a car, two passenger-only ferries operate out of Falmouth. The Falmouth Ferry Service (☎ 508-548-9400), 278 Scranton Ave, docks in Edgartown three times daily, late May to mid-October. Roundtrip fares are $22 for adults, $16 for children, $6 for bicycles.

The *Island Queen* (☎ 508-548-4800), Falmouth Heights Rd, docks in Oak Bluffs. Service operates late May to mid-October and costs $10 for adults, $5 for children, $6 for bicycles.

**From Hyannis** Hy-Line Cruises (☎ 508-778-2600 in Hyannis, 693-0112 in Oak Bluffs, www.hy-linecruises.com) runs three or four boats daily from the Ocean St Dock to Oak Bluffs, late May to mid-September. In early May and from mid-September to mid-October, there's only one boat per day, at 9:15 am. Fares are $24 for adults, $12 for children, $10 for bicycles. The trip takes 1½ hours.

**From New Bedford** The Martha's Vineyard Ferry *Schamonchi* (☎ 508-997-1688) operates mid-May to mid-October, running three boats per day during summer, but at other times there are only one or two boats. The trip to Vineyard Haven takes 1½ hours. Roundtrip tickets cost $17 to $19 for adults, $8 to $11 for children, $5 for bicycles.

**From New London, Connecticut** Fox Navigation's *Sassacus* (☎ 860-437-6928, 888-724-5369) operates a high-speed catamaran to Vineyard Haven at 8:30 am daily, May through October. The boat returns at 4 pm. The trip takes 2½ hours and avoids seriously aggravating traffic jams. The boat does not take cars. Return tickets cost $80 to $110 for adults, $40 to $56 for children.

**From Nantucket** See Nantucket's Getting There & Away section, later in this chapter.

## Getting Around

**Bus** Martha's Vineyard Transportation Services (☎ 508-693-0058, 693-1589) operates between Vineyard Haven, Oak Bluffs and Edgartown from May through October. In summer, buses are supposed to run every 15 minutes between 8 am and 11 pm. In spring and fall, they run every 30 minutes until 5 or 6 pm. Tickets are about $2 one way, $3 roundtrip, but you'd do well to purchase a three-town pass for $5 daily, $15 weekly.

The company's Up-Island shuttle (late June to early September) from Edgartown stops at the airport, the youth hostel, West Tisbury, Chilmark and Aquinnah (Gay Head). Roundtrip fare is $8.50.

**Beach Shuttle** The South Beach Trolley (☎ 508-627-7448), from Edgartown to South Beach (also known as Katama), runs daily (well, on fair weather days), mid-June to early September. The shuttle departs from the Edgartown Visitors Center on Church St every 15 minutes, 9 am to 5:30 pm. Tickets are $1.50 one way.

**Car** A car is nice for longer stays and for exploring up-island, although it is by no means necessary. Note that it's cheaper to bring your own car over for two days than to rent one for two days.

For rentals, Budget (☎ 508-693-1911, 800-527-0700) has offices in Oak Bluffs, Vineyard Haven and Edgartown and at the airport. The least-expensive cars cost about $70 for 24 hours. All-Island Rent-a-Car (☎ 508-693-6868) is based at the airport.

**Bicycle & Moped** Vineyard Haven, Oak Bluffs and Edgartown all have plenty of bike rental shops with competitive prices. (See the Activities or Bicycling sections under each town heading.) Expect to spend $16 to $20 per day for a bike. See Maps under Orientation, earlier in this chapter, for information about ordering bike maps in advance.

The only destination for which you might want a moped is Aquinnah (Gay Head); it's quite hilly out there and it is 20 or so miles from Edgartown or Vineyard Haven. Give yourself a day for that trip by bike.

Mopeds, by the way, are banned in Edgartown center. Sun 'n Fun (☎ 508-693-5457), on Beach Rd in Oak Bluffs, and Adventure Rentals (☎ 508-693-1959), on Beach Rd in Vineyard Haven, rent mopeds for about $35 to $40 daily.

## VINEYARD HAVEN

Although this is the island's commercial center, it isn't lacking in charm. Its harbor is filled with more wooden boats than any harbor of its size in New England. And its back streets, especially William St, are lined with lovely sea captains' homes. It's the most mellow of the three principal towns – the most 'real,' if you will. It's a year-round community, so if you're coming off-season, this is the place to stay.

### Orientation & Information

The principal part of Vineyard Haven is just four or five blocks wide by about a half mile long.

The Steamship Authority ships dock at the end of Union St, a block from Main St. From the terminal, Water St leads to Beach Rd and the infamous 'Five Corners' intersection: Five roads come together and no

one really has the right of way. Traffic here is generally a problem in the summertime.

From the Five Corners, Beach Rd heads to Oak Bluffs along the ocean. For a picnic place, head west on Main St to Owen Park, a nice patch of lawn that slopes down to the harbor.

Bunch of Grapes Bookstore (☎ 508-693-2263), 68 Main St, has a fine reputation for carrying a wide selection of books.

### Things to See & Do

Making wine is not easy in New England, but **Chicama Vineyards** (☎ 508-693-0309), about 3½ miles south of town off State Rd, does a credible job, and it only seems right that there be a working vineyard on the Vineyard. Stop by for a free tour and tasting 11 am to 5 pm Monday through Saturday, mid-May to mid-October (1 to 5 pm on Sunday), or on Saturday afternoon, mid-October to mid-May.

**Vineyard Seaman's Society/Seafaring Center** (☎ 508-693-9317), 110 Main St, is housed in a former little schoolhouse and is devoted to preserving mementos and artifacts that represent the clientele the society served for over 100 years: sailors. It's open 11 am to 3 pm weekdays in summer; donations are accepted.

**West Chop Lighthouse**, at the northern end of Main St, was built in 1817 with wood and replaced with brick in 1838.

If you're looking for beaches, head up-island or to Edgartown.

### Activities

Scooter & Bike (☎ 508-693-0782), near the ferry on Union St, rents bikes and Cycle Works (☎ 508-693-6966), 3512 State Rd, repairs them. Before heading out to Oak Bluffs (a flat route along the ocean), bicycle 2 miles northwest on Main St to see West Chop Lighthouse. For information on ordering bike maps in advance, see Maps in the Orientation section at the beginning of this chapter.

Wind's Up (☎ 508-693-4252 for instruction, 693-4340 for rentals), Beach Rd at the drawbridge, rents canoes and kayaks by the hour and half-day and gives lessons to beginners. The adjacent lagoon is perfect for 'intro to windsurfing,' so Wind's Up gives lessons and rents equipment for windsurfing, too. (Experienced windsurfers who want to harness stronger winds around the island will appreciate the staff's wisdom.)

Martha's Vineyard Kayak (☎ 508-627-0151) delivers kayaks to five great locations around the island. The equipment is perfect for a two- or three-hour paddle ($25 to $40 per person).

MV Parasail (☎ 508-693-2838), Pier 44 Marina on Beach Rd, offers lessons and rentals for waterskiing, wakeboarding, kneeboarding, parasailing and tubing for ages four and up. Mark, the owner, has never met anyone he couldn't teach.

Sports Haven (☎ 508-696-0456), 5 Beach St near the ferry, rents in-line skates by the half and full day, as well as by the week. In Vineyard Haven, skating is not permitted on Main St or at the Steamship Authority. You'll also have to remove the skates in downtown Edgartown and on Circuit Ave in Oak Bluffs.

## Cruises

Gosnold Cruises' *Andy Rosse* (☎ 508-693-8900) takes passengers on two-hour sails around the island and on a half-day sail to the neighboring Cuttyhunk Island.

## Places to Stay

All across the island, most places require a minimum stay during summer, so plan to settle in for a few days. Make reservations as far in advance as possible for summer and fall weekends. Better yet, go mid-week in May, June or October.

**Camping** At *Martha's Vineyard Family Camping* (☎ 508-693-3772, 569 Edgartown Rd) are wooded sites for campers with tents ($30) and cable TV hookups for RVs. Rustic cabins sleep five to six people for $80 to $90, mid-May to mid-October.

**Motels** At the *Vineyard Harbor Motel* (☎ 508-693-3334, fax 693-0320, 28 Beach Rd) are 40 uniformly modern rooms, each with air-con, TV and a refrigerator. Some rooms

have small kitchens, and since the motel's on the edge of the harbor (and town), some rooms also have water views. In-season rates are $90 to $105; you'll pay $45 to $75 the rest of the year. There are also two apartments for $110 in-season.

**B&Bs** The *Look Inn* (☎ 508-693-6893, 13 Look St), just a five-minute walk from the ferry, has a low-key, 19th-century farmhouse feel. The cost is $125 July through September and $100 in spring and fall. Rates for the three shared-bath guest rooms include breakfast.

*Nancy's Auberge* (☎ 508-693-4434, 98 Main St), in the center of town, has three unpretentious and homey rooms. One has a private bath; the others are perfect for a family or friends traveling together. A light breakfast is served on the private patio. Rates are $98 to $148 year-round.

The 1843 *Captain Dexter House* (☎ 508-693-6564, fax 693-8448, 92 Main St), also in the center of town, has eight large rooms (all with private bath), furnished with a mixture of Victorian, colonial and New England antiques. A couple of rooms have a fireplace; some have four-poster canopy beds. From late May through September, rooms go for $110 to $175 and drop down to $65 to $145 off-season.

## Places to Eat

Vineyard Haven has a surprising range of places to eat, many of which are open year-round. It's a 'dry' town, so no alcohol is served in restaurants or sold in stores, but you can 'bring your own bottle' (BYOB) to the restaurant and waiters will uncork it for you for a nominal charge.

The *Black Dog Bakery* (☎ 508-693-4786), on Water St, 100 yards east of the Steamship Authority terminal, is often the first place people go as they disembark from the ferry. Good coffee and freshly baked sweets are perfect any time of the day. The bakery's open daily year-round.

*90 Main St Market & Deli* (☎ 508-693-0041, 90 Main St) is dedicated to providing coffee, salads and sandwiches at decent prices year-round.

Across Main St, an upscale alternative is the *Vineyard Gourmet* (☎ 508-693-5181), which has pâté, smoked salmon and spiced asparagus spears year-round.

*Sandwich Haven* (☎ 508-696-8383, 32 Beach Rd) offers Middle Eastern specialties like hummus, falafel and baba ghanoush – a great alternative to the ubiquitous smoked turkey and lobster rolls.

*Louis' Tisbury Cafe & Take-Out* (☎ 508-693-3255, 350 State Rd), less than a mile out of town, is popular with the locals because it's a great value. Vegetarian dishes, pasta, pizza, lasagna and other Italian dishes, such as the shrimp *diavolo*, are the reason for coming. As the name suggests, everything is prepared for take-out, too, starting at 11 am. For dinner, try to arrive before 7 pm if you don't want to wait.

A visit to the *Black Dog Tavern* (☎ 508-693-9223), on Beach St Extension at the harbor, has become synonymous with a visit to the island. The food is good but pricey – about $22 to $27 for main courses. The American menu is weighted toward fresh seafood and locally grown vegetables. Desserts are made around the clock at the bakery next door. Reservations are not accepted, and the lines are usually quite long, so try to arrive before 6 pm for dinner. The tavern's open year-round for all three meals.

*Le Grenier* (☎ 508-693-4906, 96 Main St) is the loveliest place in town. It serves traditional and exceptional French cuisine for dinner year-round. Entrees range from $21 to $30.

## Entertainment

The volunteer-run *Wintertide Coffeehouse* (☎ 508-693-8830), Five Corners, is *the* place to go for live folk music and jazz. The coffeehouse sponsors a bit of improv and cabaret, too, in addition to serving light meals. It bills itself as a 'chemical free' (that is, no smoking or alcohol) spot, but that rule doesn't extend to coffee.

The *Capawock Movie House* (☎ 508-627-6689), on Main St, was built in 1912 and shows movies year-round. Off-season, this is a great place to pick up island gossip.

The *Vineyard Playhouse* (☎ 508-693-6450 for information, 696-6300 for tickets, 24 Church St) presents fine plays, musicals and other performances year-round (daily except Monday in summer) in a former Methodist meetinghouse. Tickets are $26 for adults, $15 for children, but there may be unsold 'rush' tickets available 10 minutes before the curtain goes up.

## Shopping

Among the art galleries in town, the year-round Shaw Cramer Gallery (☎ 508-696-7323), 76 Main St, on the 2nd floor, specializes in contemporary crafts.

The Vineyard Studio/Gallery (☎ 508-693-1338), 860 State Rd, a couple miles out of town opposite Lambert's Cove Country Rd, is a cooperative where artists are on hand to discuss their work. It's open seasonally, mid-June to mid-September.

## OAK BLUFFS

Oak Bluffs is the island's summer fun center: informal, downscale, even gaudy. Brightly colored Victorian 'gingerbread houses' line several streets, and there's an old-fashioned carousel that claims to be the oldest in the country.

## Orientation & Information

The *Island Queen* ferry from Falmouth docks at the end of Circuit Ave Extension, which is lined with inexpensive outdoor eateries. The Steamship Authority's ships dock at Sea View and Oak Bluffs Aves.

Oak Bluffs Ave (lined with bike and car rental shops) turns into Lake Ave, which runs parallel to the harbor. Keep going west to reach Vineyard Haven. Sea View Ave, also called the Oak Bluffs-Edgartown Rd, heads south out of town, along the shore, to Edgartown.

Circuit Ave is the main drag. To the left and right of it, on the side streets, are the gingerbread houses for which the town is famous.

The information booth (☎ 508-693-4266), behind the Flying Horses Carousel on Circuit Ave at Lake Ave, is open 9:30 am to 5 pm daily, June to mid-October.

Public rest rooms can be found across from the Steamship Authority off Water St; next to Our Market on the harbor; and on Kennebec Ave, a block west and parallel to Circuit Ave.

## Gingerbread Houses

Wesleyan Grove is bounded by Lake, Sea View and Dukes County Aves and sliced in the middle by Circuit Ave. The grove contains the renowned Victorian gingerbread cottages that look like they're dripping with icing. Bold colors and whimsical ornamental woodwork characterize what is known by architects as the Carpenter Gothic style.

In 1835, when the Methodist Campmeeting Association began holding summer revival meetings here, the congregation camped in tents. As the meetings grew, participants who returned year after year began putting up bigger tents. Then they pitched their tents on wooden platforms, which evolved into small cottages. Every year, they adorned their cottages with more and more fanciful wooden trim. *Voilà!* A Carpenter Gothic village.

This neighborhood is no museum: Members of the religious congregation still live here, so note the posted rules, especially no 'rude or loud behavior.' Services are still held in the 1879 wrought-iron Trinity Park Tabernacle.

The **Cottage Museum** (☎ 508-693-0525), 1 Trinity Park, is typical of the 300 or so tiny 19th-century cottages in Oak Bluffs. It's open 10 am to 4 pm daily except Sunday, mid-June to mid-September, and charges a nominal admission.

## Flying Horses Carousel

This merry-go-round, Circuit Ave at Lake Ave, is said to be the oldest operating carousel (1876) in the country. Rides cost $1 each (or $8 for a book of 10 tickets). More adults ride the merry-go-round than you might think.

## Joseph Sylvia State Beach

On Beach Rd (Oak Bluffs-Edgartown Rd), this narrow, 2-mile-long stretch of white sandy beach is backed by low dunes. It's also referred to as the Bend-in-the-Road Beach. You can park for free along the road.

## Bicycling

Since lots of ferries pull into town, discharging lots of passengers, there are lots of places renting lots of bicycles. Try Anderson Bike Rentals (☎ 508-693-9346), on Circuit Ave Extension, and Vineyard Bike & Moped (☎ 508-693-4498), across from the Flying Horses Carousel on Oak Bluffs Ave.

For information on ordering bike maps in advance, see Maps in the general Orientation section at the beginning of this chapter.

The Oak Bluffs-Edgartown Rd straddles the ocean, a good beach and a saltwater pond for much of the route. The 5-mile ride is scenic, but be prepared to inhale car exhaust, since the bike path runs parallel to the heavily traveled road.

Also, head up to the bluff where the East Chop Lighthouse is situated: Take Lake Ave toward Vineyard Haven, turn right on Commercial St (along the water) and continue on Highland Ave.

## In-Line Skating

In-line skating at the Correllus State Forest is great, and Jamaican Jam (☎ 508-693-5003), 154 Circuit Ave, rents skates. Despite the location of the rental shop, though, Circuit Ave is off limits to skaters.

## Special Events

The actual date of 'Illumination Night' is kept secret until about a week before it becomes obvious: Residents gather for a heartwarming community sing, then the town of Oak Bluffs shuts off all electrical lights, and the eldest resident lights a Japanese lantern. When the rest of the Methodist Campmeeting Association follows suit, an eerie glow illuminates the neighborhood.

## Places to Stay

Of the following lodgings, only Surfside is open year-round; most places in Oak Bluffs are open from April through mid-October.

**Motels & Hotels** *Surfside Motel* (☎ 508-693-2500, 800-537-3007, fax 508-693-7343,*

7 Oak Bluffs Ave) is right in the middle of things, so it can get noisy at times. Of the 32 rooms, the more expensive ones have refrigerators and water views. In-season, rooms go for $100 to $165; the rest of the year, they cost $40 to $125.

The **Wesley Hotel** (☎ 508-693-6611, 800-638-9027, fax 508-693-5389, 1 Lake View Ave) is a gracious, three-story, turn-of-the-century hotel. A long veranda dotted with rocking chairs faces the marina. Half of the 95 comfortably furnished rooms have water views. Doubles rent for $145 to $175 mid-June to mid-September, $95 to $110 off-season. The hotel's closed mid-October to April.

**B&Bs**  At the gingerbread-style **Attleboro House** (☎ 508-693-4346, 11 Lake Ave) are 11 basic rooms, all with shared bath. (A few rooms have a sink in them, and some can handle an extra person or two.) An attic room sleeps six. The house enjoys unobstructed views of the protected marina from the rocking chairs on the front porch. Open mid-May through September, the Attleboro House charges $65 to $95 for a regular double ($95 to $175 for the attic room).

The Victorian-style **Narragansett House** (☎ 508-693-3627, 46 Narragansett Ave), smack in the middle of the gingerbread-cottage community, has 13 well-kept rooms with private bath, two apartments that can accommodate larger groups of six and newly renovated rooms in the adjacent Iroquois Cottage. Many of these latter rooms are small but boast cathedral ceilings or little balconies. Rooms rent for $85 to $145, May through October; call for apartment rates.

The **Admiral Benbow Inn** (☎ 508-693-6825, fax 693-1131, 520 New York Ave) is on the edge of a well-traveled road into town. Its seven rooms, all with private bath, are decorated with Victorian furnishings and cost $100 to $150 in-season, $75 to $100 the rest of the year.

The **Oak Bluffs Inn** (☎ 508-693-7171, 800-955-6235, fax 508-693-8787, bmyguest@ oakbluffsinn.com, 64 Circuit Ave) has nine guest rooms and suites decorated with bright and fanciful cottage-style furniture.

Since the inn is on the edge of Wesleyan Grove, most rooms have picturesque views of the camp meetinghouses. When the inn is open (May to mid-December), rooms rent for $120 to $165. (Suites are more).

Rooms at **Oak House** (☎ 508-693-4187, fax 696-7293, inns@vineyard.net), Seaview Ave at Pequot Ave, have oak furniture, oak walls and oak ceilings. It's all quite Victorian: cozy, nicely put together and expensive. Most of the 10 rooms have water views, and some have private balconies. A big afternoon tea is included in the rates ($160 to $265). Subtract $40 to $60 in spring and autumn. The Oak House is closed late October to early May.

## Places to Eat
Oak Bluffs has more than inexpensive summer resort eateries offering the standard menu of burgers, sandwiches, shrimp and lobster. If you're ready to splurge, there are also some fine choices.

The **Juice Caboose** (☎ 508-693-3825, 14 Circuit Ave, rear) squeezes sunflower sprouts with fruit juices to cleanse your system after a few too many fried clams.

Java junkies follow their noses to **Mocha Mott's** (☎ 508-696-1922, 10 Circuit Ave), open daily all year-round. The basement hangout has newspapers and sweets, too.

**Linda Jean's** (☎ 508-693-4093, 25 Circuit Ave) is the town's best all-around inexpensive restaurant. A three-egg omelette filled with vegetables costs $6, a bowl of chowder $3, burgers $3.50, and a platter of fried seafood is as expensive as it gets at $12. Linda Jean's is open for breakfast, lunch and dinner year-round.

**Giordano's** (☎ 508-693-0184, 107 Circuit Ave), at Lake Ave, is doing something right: It's been in business since 1930. Large portions of homestyle Italian-American food, served 11 am to 11 pm, cost $8 to $16. Giordano's is also known for its salad bar, hefty cocktails and fried clams.

**Papa's Pizza** (☎ 508-693-1400, 158 Circuit Ave), a pleasant storefront eatery with a central location, is a nice place to sit down, but you can also get your pizza to go. (Take it to Ocean Park and listen to an old-fashioned band concert.) Luckily, this place is open daily year-round, even in the winter.

Within the shell of an old barn, the *Offshore Ale Co* (☎ 508-693-2626), Kennebec Ave, open for lunch and dinner ($7.50 to $15) year-round, brews its own beer and serves it alongside great burgers, brick-oven pizzas and beer-batter onion rings. Entertainment often accompanies the free-flowing supply of peanuts on each table.

*Jimmy Sea's Pan Pasta* (☎ 508-696-8550, 32 Kennebec Ave) serves fancy pasta dishes, cooked to order and served in the skillet. It's a small, casual place that offers up large portions to locals who know a good thing when they find it. Come to dinner with an appetite and be prepared to spend $15 to $23 per entree.

*Lola's Southern Seafood* (☎ 508-693-5007), on Beach Rd a bit out of town, is a hopping joint with authentic barbecue ribs, seafood jambalaya and other New Orleans-style dishes for $20 to $28. The $12 brunch is a steal, but if you just want access to the lively scene, you can easily make do with the lighter pub menu ($11 to $16). There's a varied lineup of entertainment throughout the year.

The chef-owned *Sweet Life Cafe* (☎ 508-696-0200, 168 Circuit Ave), easily the best food in town, features a changeable New American menu, but you can count on something along the lines of oven-roasted halibut with garlic mashed potatoes. The three-course menu ($35) is an island-style 'bargain'; otherwise you'll pay $20 to $28 per entree.

## Entertainment
Oak Bluffs is the island's most lively town; walking around after dark is sometimes entertainment enough.

There's always something going on (year-round) at the *Atlantic Connection* (☎ 508-693-7129, 124 Circuit Ave). Live reggae bands share the stage with DJs and comedy acts that appeal to a twenty-something, beer-guzzling crowd.

The *Ritz Cafe* (☎ 508-693-9851, 1 Circuit Ave) is a popular blues dive that's open year-round.

The *Lamppost* (☎ 508-696-9352), Circuit Ave, is a 2nd-floor dance club, while its 1st-floor sister (if you will), the *Rare Duck*, entertains patrons with frozen drinks.

## Shopping
The Firehouse Gallery (☎ 508-693-9025), 88 Dukes County Ave at Vineyard Ave, is the best in town. In summer, the gallery hosts weekly tri-artist member shows, when a whole range of media is explored, from quilts and sculpture to pastels, oils and watercolors. It's open year-round.

## EDGARTOWN
Patrician Edgartown is the island's architectural showpiece. Its 18th- and 19th-century whaling captains' houses are perfectly maintained, with clipped lawns, blooming gardens and white picket fences. Though it's crowded in summer, Edgartown is downright quiet between October and April.

## Orientation & Information
You'll probably come into town via Main St, which extends down to the harbor. Running parallel to the harbor is Water St, and N Water St leads out to the Edgartown Lighthouse. N Water St is lined with fine sea captain's houses.

The Edgartown Visitors Center (no ☎), around the corner from the Old Whaling Church on Church St, is open 9 am to 5 pm daily, June to early September. There are public rest rooms and a post office here. The South Beach Trolley (see Getting Around, near the beginning of this chapter) stops here.

Definitely stop in at the Bickerton and Ripley (☎ 508-627-8463) bookstore, Main St at S Summer St.

## Martha's Vineyard Historical Society
The Martha's Vineyard Historical Society (☎ 508-627-4441), Cooke St at School St, occupies several buildings, including the 1765 Thomas Cooke House. The island's most interesting museum contains whaling and maritime relics, scrimshaw and the huge Fresnel lens from the Gay Head Lighthouse.

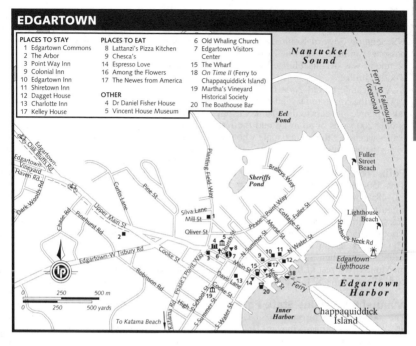

## EDGARTOWN

**PLACES TO STAY**
1 Edgartown Commons
2 The Arbor
3 Point Way Inn
9 Colonial Inn
10 Edgartown Inn
11 Shiretown Inn
12 Dagget House
13 Charlotte Inn
17 Kelley House

**PLACES TO EAT**
8 Lattanzi's Pizza Kitchen
9 Chesca's
14 Espresso Love
16 Among the Flowers
17 The Newes from America

**OTHER**
4 Dr Daniel Fisher House
5 Vincent House Museum

6 Old Whaling Church
7 Edgartown Visitors
  Center
15 The Wharf
18 On Time II (Ferry to
   Chappaquiddick Island)
19 Martha's Vineyard
   Historical Society
20 The Boathouse Bar

The Vineyard Museum is open 10 am to 5 pm Tuesday through Saturday, mid-June to mid-October, and 1 to 4 pm Wednesday through Friday the rest of the year. Adults pay $6, children $4.

### Historic Buildings

The **Dr Daniel Fisher House** (☎ 508-627-8619 for tours, 627-8017 for information), 99 Main St, is the magnificently preserved 1840s Federal-style house once owned by the founder of the Martha's Vineyard National Bank. It's yours for the touring at 11 am, noon, 1 and 2 pm daily, from late May to mid-October.

A combination ticket ($6) also gets you into the adjacent **Old Whaling Church**, constructed in 1843 using the same techniques as those employed in building whaling ships, and the 1672 **Vincent House Museum**, behind the church. Since the house was in the same family until 1977, its architectural

integrity has been well-guarded. Three rooms appear as they would have in the 17th, 18th and 19th centuries.

### Chappaquiddick Island

There are very few houses on the island and no shops or eateries. The prime attractions are the 500-acre **Cape Pogue Wildlife Refuge** (complete with a remote lighthouse) and the 200-acre **Wasque Reservation**, both unspoiled and unfrequented stretches of sand. In addition to its beautiful open space, the island contains the meditative 14-acre **Mytoi** Japanese garden.

The Trustees of the Reservations (☎ 508-627-3599) offer three-hour naturalist-led expeditions of Cape Pogue twice daily in summer ($40 for adults, $15 for children), as well as shorter trips that include a tour of the Cape Pogue lighthouse ($15 for adults, $6 for children). Call for exact departure times and reservations.

Chappaquiddick is perhaps most widely known for the tragic incident that involved US Senator Edward Kennedy in 1969. A passenger in his car drowned when the car Kennedy was driving plunged off a small wooden bridge.

A six-car ferry, *On Time II* (☎ 508-627-9427), at the corner of Daggett and Dock Sts, takes people and cars to the island. 'Chappy' is only 200 yards or so away, and the ferry leaves whenever there are people who want to go; that way, it's always 'on time.'

### Felix Neck Wildlife Sanctuary

This 350-acre Audubon sanctuary (☎ 508-627-4850, www.massaudubon.org), off the Edgartown-Vineyard Haven Rd, is criss-crossed with 6 miles of trails that traverse woods, meadows, marshes and the beach. The visitors' center is open 8 am to 4 pm daily, June through September, and closed on Monday the rest of the year. Trail access costs $3 for adults, $2 for children.

### Manuel F Correllus State Forest

The 4400-acre state forest (☎ 508-693-2540), also off the Edgartown-Vineyard Haven Rd, occupies a huge chunk of the island's mid-section. It has walking and biking trails. Park near the Barnes Rd exit.

### Beaches

South of Edgartown, Katama Beach (extending west as South Beach), off Katama Rd, is 3 miles long, with moderate surf. There's a big parking lot, which means there are usually a lot of people. A shuttle bus also ser-vices Katama (see Getting Around, earlier in this chapter).

Lighthouse Beach, at the end of N Water St, is a nice, easily accessible beach where you can watch boats put into Edgartown Harbor.

Fuller St Beach, at the end of Fuller St near Lighthouse Beach, is a hangout for college students and summer workers.

### Bicycling

RW Cutler Bike (☎ 508-627-4052), 1 Main St, and Wheel Happy (☎ 508-627-5928), S Water St at Main St, both rent bicycles. The Correl-lus State Forest has biking trails.

For information on ordering bike maps in advance, see Maps in the general Orienta-tion section at the beginning of this chapter.

### Cruises

The catamaran *Mad Max* (☎ 508-627-7500), on the harbor, takes daily two-hour excur-sions around the island at 2 and 6 pm, late May to mid-October; tours cost $45 for adults, $35 for children.

For a more old-fashioned and intimate sail (only six people at a time), climb aboard the sloop *Vela Daysails* (☎ 508-627-1963), at Memorial Pier next to the Chappy Ferry. The price is similar.

Edgartown Harbor Cruises (☎ 508-627-4388), Main St near the Edgartown Yacht Club, offers short narrated tours on the hour, late May to early September; tours cost $18 for adults, $5 for children.

### Special Events

Of all the Vineyard's various seasonal events, the 'Possible Dreams Auction,' usually held in Edgartown at the Harborside Hotel, is the most unique. Every August (early in the month), nationally known celebrities with second homes on the island throw a creative auction to benefit island community services. Highest bidders might win a tour of the *60 Minutes* studios in New York by anchor Mike Wallace or a personal performance by singer Carly Simon.

### Places to Stay

**Efficiencies** The *Edgartown Commons* (☎ 508-627-4671, 800-439-4671, fax 508-627-4271, 20 Pease's Point Way), at Planting Field Way, is suited to longer stays. Just a couple blocks from the town center, it's actually a complex of seven buildings with studios and multi-bed apartments. Guests (most of whom are families) also have access to outdoor barbecues and a pool. Rates (for two to six people, depending on the apart-ment size) are $135 to $205 in summer, $75 to $115 in spring and fall.

**Hotels** The hotel-like *Colonial Inn* (☎ 508-627-4711, fax 627-5904, 38 N Water St) is a three-story rambling inn right in the middle of the action. Its 43 rooms, all with private bath, are comfortable, with TVs and air-con. Price is based on size and view: $152 to $212 in summer, $77 to $160 the rest of the year (mid-week specials, too).

The *Kelley House (☎ 508-627-7900, 800-225-6005, fax 508-627-8417, 23 Kelley St)* has a pool and 59 nicely maintained modern rooms, each with air-con and TV, some with harbor views. It's right in the thick of things and can get loud at night. Doubles start at $245 in summer, $140 in spring and fall. Off-season packages are sometimes offered.

**Inns & B&Bs** The *Edgartown Inn (☎ 508-627-4794, 56 N Water St)* has 20 simple rooms, some of which share a bath. The two airy rooms in the Garden Cottage are the nicest. In the summer, doubles rent for $75 to $90 for a shared bath, $125 to $185 for a private bath. In the spring and fall, rooms range from $55 to $130. No credit cards are accepted.

The centrally located *Shiretown Inn (☎ 508-627-3353, 800-541-0090, fax 508-627-8478, holiday@shiretowninn.com)*, N Water St, has 34 simple but adequate rooms in the motel-like Carriage House behind the main house. There are also 'housekeeping units' (with kitchenette) and some rooms with period furnishings and private entrances. Doubles range wildly from $89 to $349 in summer.

The *Arbor (☎ 508-627-8137, 222 Upper Main St)* is a 10-minute walk from the harbor, so its location keeps the prices more reasonable. Most of the 10 guest rooms have a private bath, and rooms are furnished with a combination of antiques and modern pieces. Doubles cost $120 to $165 in-season, $90 to $125 off-season; the inn's closed late October through April.

The *Daggett House (☎ 508-627-4600, 800-946-3400, fax 508-627-4611, stephen@mvweb.com, 59 N Water St)* has 31 rooms and suites, with private bath, in four buildings. One cottage is right on the harbor; more modern rooms are across the street. (The lawn stretches down to the harbor, so wherever you stay you can sit on the harbor.) The main house served as the island's first tavern in the 17th century; a full

breakfast is served in this atmospheric, museum-style room. Rates start at $155 in-season, $85 the rest of the year.

The *Point Way Inn (☎ 508-627-8633, 888-711-6633, fax 508-627-3338, pointwayinn@vineyard.net, 104 Main St)*, at Pease's Point Way, formerly a whaling captain's house, has been transformed into a stylish enclave with 12 rooms and suites, many with four-poster canopy beds and fireplaces. The courtyard protects you from the hordes of tourists. The owners have an extra car that they loan to guests (on a first-come, first-served basis) for free. Doubles start at $190 from June through October, $110 in spring and fall.

The *Charlotte Inn (☎ 508-627-4751, fax 627-4652, 27 S Summer St)* caters to a well-heeled crowd. The 23 rooms, connected by English gardens and brick walkways, are furnished with practically priceless antiques. If you don't think you'll feel too out of place, the cheapest room rents for $295 June through October, $225 the rest of the year. The Charlotte Inn really does deserve its reputation as one of the finest inns in New England. If you're going to go all the way, it has an outstanding (and equally expensive) French restaurant, too: L'Étoile.

## Places to Eat

With the exception of our suggestions, the quality of food in Edgartown is generally lower than prices warrant.

*Espresso Love (☎ 508-627-9211, 2 S Water St)* boasts the richest cup o' joe in town.

At *Among the Flowers (☎ 508-627-3233, 17 Mayhew Lane)*, off N Water St, there are only a few tables outdoors. But don't let that deter you from getting an omelette, soup, salad or a quiche, especially since it will only cost you $4 to $10 for lunch, about double that for a moderately upscale dinner. The cafe is open May through October, but dinner is only available in July and August.

The *Newes from America (☎ 508-627-4397, 23 Kelley St)*, open 11 am to 11 pm daily year-round, has very good traditional pub grub, as well as the excellent burritos and burgers, for about $8 per person. (Don't order anything too fancy.) It's a dark and cozy place with a low-beamed ceiling. The clientele can be a bit preppy, but they're a fun-loving, boisterous crowd all the same.

*Lattanzi's Pizza Kitchen* (☎ 508-627-8854), Old Post Office Square, is the fashionable place for brick-oven pizzas, May to mid-October.

Quite pleasant and very popular, *Chesca's* (☎ 508-627-1234, 38 N Water St) features a far-ranging menu of mostly Italian dishes: mix-and-match pastas with sauces or vegetarian risotto or seafood creations like paella. The egalitarian range of prices is unusual for Martha's Vineyard: $9 to $30 per main dish. Chesca's is open mid-April through October for dinner.

## Entertainment

The house specialty at *The Newes from America* (see Places to Eat) is a 'rack of beer,' a sampler with five unusual brews. The entire microbrew menu, in fact, is worth a sample.

*Hot Tin Roof* (☎ 508-693-1137, www .mvhottinroof.com), at the airport, owned in part by islander Carly Simon and movie mogul Harvey Weinstein, draws crowds of celebrity watchers. As for the music, the entertainment centers on mostly hip reggae, R&B and blues performers, some of which are national acts.

*The Wharf* (☎ 508-627-9966), Dock St, is a popular wharf pub with live music on most summer evenings.

A similar place, *The Boathouse Bar* (☎ 508-627-4320, 2 Main St), is within the Navigator restaurant on the waterfront.

## UP-ISLAND

This is the truly pastoral side of island life. The landscape is a patchwork of rolling fields, lined with stone walls and private dirt roads and dotted with barns and grazing sheep. There's very little to do up-island, except enjoy the scenery by car or bicycle and head to the beach.

## Orientation

From West Tisbury, all roads – South, Middle and North – lead to Menemsha. But take South Rd (it's the prettiest) to 'Beetlebung Corner,' which is the center (just a cross-

roads, really) of Menemsha. To reach the harbor, follow Menemsha Cross Rd and look for signs to Dutcher's Dock.

Only South Rd leads to Aquinnah (Gay Head) from Menemsha. At one particularly high point, you can see Menemsha Harbor to the north.

There are public rest rooms near the parking area at the Clay Cliffs of Aquinnah (Gay Head) and at Dutcher's Dock, Menemsha Harbor.

## Alley's General Store

This local gathering place in West Tisbury has served up-island residents since 1858. It was in danger of succumbing to the pressures of modern retailing in 1994, but fortunately a group of locals created a foundation to both save it and overhaul it. In 1998, the Wampanoag Indians stepped up to the plate to operate it.

## Menemsha

This quaint little fishing village was used as the setting for the movie *Jaws*. There's a nice beach and good restaurant here and the sunsets are spectacular, too.

## Clay Cliffs of Aquinnah

The multicolored clay cliffs were formed by glaciers more than 100 million years ago. Rising 150 feet from the ocean, they're dramatic any time of day. The Wampanoag Indians own the cliffs, a National Historic Landmark, and it's illegal to bathe in the mud pools, which form at the bottom of the cliffs, and to remove clay from the premises. The brick lighthouse standing precariously at the edge of the bluff was built in 1844.

## Wildlife Sanctuaries

The **Cedar Tree Neck Sanctuary** (☎ 508-693-5207), off Indian Hill Rd in West Tisbury, has a few trails and covers over 300 acres of bogs, fields and forests.

The 600-acre **Long Point Wildlife Refuge** (☎ 508-693-7662), off the Edgartown-West Tisbury Rd, has just a few short trails, but one leads to a deserted stretch of South Beach. Parking costs $7, and each adult pays $3.

## Arboretum

The 20-acre Polly Hill Arboretum (☎ 508-693-9426), 809 State Rd in West Tisbury, celebrates local woodlands and protects endangered species. It's an oasis in summer, but beautiful in spring and fall, too; $5 for adults, $3 for children.

## Beaches

Aquinnah Public Beach (also known as Gay Head Beach) is 5 miles long. Head north for the cliffs; the further you go in this direction, the less clothing you'll see. To the south, the beach is wider, but it's technically restricted to residents only. Stick to the water's edge, and you'll have no problem. Parking costs $15 daily or $5 for two hours.

Menemsha Beach, northeast of Dutcher's Dock and the harbor, is pebbly, but the water is calm. Across the 'cut' of water, to the southwest, is Lobsterville Beach, popular with families because of the gentle and shallow water. In summer, there's usually a little ferry (☎ 508-645-3511) that takes people and their bikes ($7 roundtrip, $4 one way) across the cut. (It's a good thing, because parking at Lobsterville is restricted to residents.)

Lucy Vincent Beach, off South Rd about a half mile before the junction with Middle Rd, is open to Chilmark residents only. That's unfortunate because it's the loveliest stretch of sand (complete with dune-backed cliffs) on the island. You shouldn't have trouble using the unmarked beach off-season.

## Bicycling

It's a long and hilly ride from Edgartown to Aquinnah (21 miles one way), but you'll be rewarded with expansive vistas and the quiet, intimate details of island life. With the exception of the path that borders the state park, you'll be riding on narrow winding roads with all the other traffic.

For information on ordering bike maps in advance, see Maps in the general Orientation section at the beginning of this chapter.

## Cruises

The catamaran *Arabella* (☎ 508-645-3511), docked in Menemsha Harbor, makes a daily run to nearby Cuttyhunk Island (11 am to 5 pm; $60) and an evening sunset trip around the cliffs ($40). Captain Hugh Taylor is singer James Taylor's brother, but he doesn't like to make a big deal about it.

## Places to Stay

Unless you stay at the hostel, it's impractical to stay up-island without a car.

**Hostels** The *Manter Memorial AYH Hostel* (☎ 508-693-2665, 800-909-4776 in-season, 617-779-0900 off-season, fax 508-693-2699, marthasvineyardhostel@juno.com), on the Edgartown-West Tisbury Rd in West Tisbury, has 78 beds ($14 to $17) and is open April to mid-November. The building was designed to be a hostel, so it's got a great kitchen.

In summer, the hostel sponsors a couple of weekly programs on such topics as stargazing, the environment, budget travel and the Wampanoags. Advance reservations are essential in summer. Bike or hitch to the hostel; although you can use the Gay Head shuttle (see Getting Around, earlier in this chapter), don't rely on it. It's an 8-mile ride (via State Rd, then Old County Rd) from Vineyard Haven. To make reservations before the hostel opens for the season, write to Hostelling International Boston, at 12 Hemenway St, Boston, MA 02215, or fax them at 617-424-6558.

**Inns, B&Bs & Cottages** The 17th-century *Captain Flanders' House* (☎ 508-645-3123), on North Rd between Menemsha Cross and Tabor House Rds in Chilmark, enjoys a tranquil setting on 60 acres of rolling farmland overlooking a pond. Accommodations include four very modest guest rooms (two with private bath) in the main house and two snug, romantic cottages. From late May to mid-October, rates (including a coveted pass to Lucy Vincent Beach) are $60 single, $125 to $150 double, $205 cottage. The rest of the year, rates drop to $50 single, $75 to $85 double, $110 cottage.

*Menemsha Inn and Cottages* (☎ 508-645-2521), on North Rd between Menemsha Cross Rd and Menemsha Harbor in Menemsha, offers 12 simple and tidy one- and two-bedroom cottages, each with a kitchen and fireplace, that go for $1300 to $1700 weekly in summer, $875 to $1000 off-season. There are also 15 rooms and suites that rent for $140 to $220 in summer, $85 to $125 off-season. If you can't reserve far in advance, you can always hope someone cancels. Guests get passes to Lucy Vincent Beach. No credit cards are accepted; the inn's closed early November through April.

The **Duck Inn** (☎ 508-645-9018), off State Rd in Aquinnah, sits on a bluff practically overlooking Philbin Beach (adjacent to Aquinnah Public Beach). The 1st floor, draped in kilims (Middle Eastern rugs) and Native American carpets, is devoted to bohemian-style common space. A large wood stove sits in the middle of the room, and plenty of picture windows offer scenic views. Rooms are individually decorated, to say the least, with perhaps a feather duvet or marble wash basin or French door for the toilette. Rates include breakfast: $105 to $205 in summer, $85 to $125 the rest of the year.

## Places to Eat

The **West Tisbury Farmer's Market** takes place at the Old Agricultural Hall (in the center of West Tisbury – you can't miss it) 9 am to noon every Saturday from June through September (with additional Wednesday afternoon hours in July and August).

Inexpensive take-out shacks litter the route to the Clay Cliffs of Aquinnah.

The **Chilmark Store** (☎ 508-645-3739), on State Rd in the center of Chilmark, will satisfy your need for a quick energy fix and a thirst quencher if you're bicycling to Aquinnah (Gay Head). You can also assemble a picnic, though it will cost a bit more than if you'd done it in Edgartown.

**The Galley** (☎ 508-645-9819), on Menemsha Harbor, a little shack with picnic tables, sells meaty lobster rolls, chowder and burgers.

**Home Port** (☎ 508-645-2679), on Menemsha Harbor, is very good; make reservations or be prepared to wait. Better yet, go to the back door and order the same food that everyone else is getting – fresh seafood and surf-and-turf combos – and take it to the

dock and watch the sunset. Inside, dinners cost $20 to $36; à la carte from the back door will be less. Home Port is open for dinner mid-April to mid-October.

Just so you're not out of the loop, the **Red Cat** (☎ 508-693-9599), on State Rd in North Tisbury, is the most see-and-be-seen restaurant these days. The ultra-creative, albeit limited, menu changes daily and is served in a deliberately low-brow, small roadside joint. Entrees cost $24 to $30, and the tasting menu is even more ($68 per person). But you can save by bringing your own bottle of wine.

## Shopping

A flea market at the Chilmark Community Church, in the center of Menemsha, is held from about 7 am to 2 pm every Wednesday and Saturday during summer.

The modest-appearing Craven Gallery (☎ 508-693-3535), State Rd at the Middletown Exchange, is a delight. Big-name artists like Milton Avery and Edward Hopper hang alongside, or are stacked behind, lesser-known artists who will probably be known in due time, if the eagle-eye owner is any judge. And she is.

If you're conscious, you can't miss the Field Gallery and Sculpture Garden (☎ 508-693-5595), State Rd in the center of West Tisbury. Large white sculptures, playfully posing while tourists dance around them, direct your attention to the otherwise quiet field. There's an indoor gallery, too.

The island's rutted dirt roads lead to many potters, but Chilmark Pottery (☎ 508-693-6496), off State Rd in West Tisbury, is one of the better known.

Martha's Vineyard Glass Works (☎ 508-693-6026), on State Rd in West Tisbury, offers the opportunity to watch master craftspeople at work as they turn sand into fragile and colorful creations.

# Nantucket Island

Thirty miles south of the Cape Cod coast lies Nantucket, a beautiful island of grassy moors, salt bogs, blueberry fields, warm-water beaches and charming villages.

# History

The Pilgrims landed at Plymouth in 1620 after a brief stop at the tip of Cape Cod, and within 40 years there were white settlers living on Nantucket, going out in boats and hunting whales. By 1686, one of these whalers, a certain Jethro Coffin, had made a fortune large enough to afford a grand house built of brick. The house still stands.

Throughout the 18th century, Nantucket grew ever richer from the whaling trade. The wealthy island's contribution to the Revolutionary War effort was exemplary: Around 2000 Nantucketers lost their lives and more than 100 whaling vessels were lost in battle.

Though ultimately victorious in the war, Nantucketers were economically defeated by the peace. Before the island could recover from these huge losses, the War of 1812 began and robbed them of yet more men and ships. By the mid-19th century, the great age of the sailing ship was over, supplanted by steam. With the advent of coal and petroleum as fuels, the trade in whale oil suffered a fatal decline.

The same steamships that robbed Nantucket of its whaling wealth brought a new means of prosperity: tourism. Nantucket's mariners abandoned whaling and took up cruising, shuttling visitors between the coast and the island. In the late 19th century, huge, rambling, wood-frame hotels were built to house vacationers, and the island settled into a comfortable, seasonal trade. In the early 1960s, islander and developer Walter Beinecke, Jr, began to revitalize the waterfront. He convinced merchants, restaurateurs and innkeepers that since the island had finite resources, it was far better to attract a moneyed crowd than folks with just a few dollars to spend. The theory continues to drive the island: You'll see far more jewelry stores and galleries than T-shirt shops.

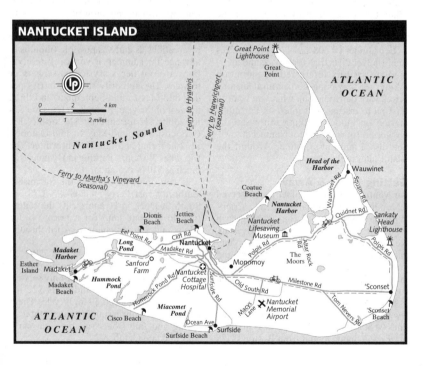

MASSACHUSETTS

The brash, booming 1980s saw the advent of direct jet flights from New York City to Nantucket, allowing the chic and trendy to fly up for the week, the weekend or just for dinner before returning to the city.

## Organized Tours

There's no better way to orient yourself and get a quick overview of the island's main attractions than to take one of these 90-minute tours.

Gail's Tours (☎ 508-257-6557) offers the unique perspective of a seventh-generation islander. Gail is full of interesting island trivia and also allows guests to hop out of the van to take photos. Tours ($12) depart year-round at 10 am, 1 and 3 pm in front of the Visitor Services & Information Bureau, 25 Federal St. Call ahead off-season.

Barrett's Tours (☎ 508-228-0174), at 20 Federal St, and Nantucket Island Tours (☎ 508-228-0334), on Straight Wharf, offer five or six daily tours from April to early December. Many buses are timed to depart after the ferry arrives. These tours are a tad shorter than Gail's.

Eco Guides (☎ 508-228-1769) customizes island 'adventure' trips for novice and intermediate visitors interested in mountain biking, sea kayaking and natural history. Prices vary depending on what you want to do. Call to discuss your interests. For information on guided walking tours, see the Organized Tours section for Nantucket town. See also Lighthouses, under Around the Island, later in this chapter.

## Getting There & Away

**Air** Nantucket's Memorial Airport is served by a number of national and local carriers. With the exception of the evening rush hour, just show up at the airport in Hyannis, New Bedford, Providence or Martha's Vineyard, buy a ticket for the next flight and you'll be on the island in less than 45 minutes. The taxi ride into Nantucket town costs $7.

Cape Air (☎ 508-790-0300, 800-352-0714, www.flycapeair.com) and Nantucket Airlines (☎ 508-790-0300, 800-635-8787 in state) offer daily flights to and from Boston ($138 up to $224 roundtrip in summer), Hyannis ($58), New Bedford ($104 to $125) and Martha's Vineyard ($71).

Island Air (☎ 508-228-7575, 800-248-7779) also operates from Hyannis; flying time is 20 minutes.

Colgin Air (☎ 508-325-5100, 800-272-5488) flies from La Guardia airport in New York City ($250 to $415 roundtrip in summer).

Among the national carriers, Business Express/Delta Connection (☎ 800-345-3400) and Northwest Airlink (☎ 800-225-2525) offer connecting flights from Boston, while Continental Express (☎ 800-272-5488) flies from La Guardia.

**Boat** Nantucket is served by ferries departing from the Cape Cod coast and Martha's Vineyard.

*From Hyannis* The Steamship Authority (☎ 508-477-8600 for advance car reservations, 771-4000 for day-of-sailing information, www.steamshipauthority.com), South St Dock in Hyannis, carries people and autos to Nantucket year-round. Make car reservations as early as possible (months in advance for summer, if you can); reservations are not necessary for passengers or bicycles. The authority runs six ferries per day, mid-May to mid-September, and three the rest of the year. Roundtrip fares are $24 for adults, $12 for children, $10 for bicycles. Cars cost $230 mid-May to mid-October, $162 in spring and fall, $118 in winter. The trip takes 2¼ hours. Parking in Hyannis is as much as $10 per calendar day.

If you don't have a car, the Steamship Authority Fast Ferry (☎ 508-495-3278), at South St Dock in Hyannis, cuts the sailing time to just one hour for a price: $42 for adults and $30 for children, April through September.

Hy-Line (☎ 508-778-2600, 888-778-1132 for advance sales, www.hy-linecruises.com), Ocean St Dock, has passenger-only service, which takes 2¼ hours and costs $22 for adults, $11 for children, $9 for bicycles. There are six boats daily in summer, one to three in spring and fall. Boats run between early May and late October.

Hy-Line's *Grey Lady* (☎ 508-778-0404, 800-492-8082), Ocean St Dock in Hyannis, also has a 'hi-speed' passenger service that reaches Nantucket from Hyannis in about one hour. Since the boat accommodates only 40 passengers, advance reservations are recommended. The boat makes six trips a day in summer, five the rest of the year. A roundtrip ticket costs $52 for adults, $39 for children, $10 for bicycles.

***From Harwichport*** Freedom Cruise Line (☎ 508-432-8999), on Route 28 at Saqua-tucket Harbor in Harwichport, offers daily morning, noon and evening ferries, mid-May to mid-October. The first two ferries permit you to explore the island for about six hours before catching the return boat. The trip takes 2¼ hours and costs $34 for adults, $28 for children, $10 for bicycles. Advance reservations are recommended for the first two boats. Parking is free for the first 24 hours, then it's $10 per day. The advantage of this boat is that you can avoid the traffic in Hyannis.

***From Martha's Vineyard*** Hy-Line Cruises (☎ 508-693-0112) operates three daily inter-island passenger ferries in each direction, early June to mid-September. The trip takes 2¼ hours; one-way tickets cost $11 for adults, $5.50 for children, $5 for bicycles. The ferry docks in Oak Bluffs on the Vineyard and on Straight Wharf in Nantucket (☎ 508-228-3949).

There is no inter-island car ferry.

## Getting Around

**Bus** The NRTA Shuttle (☎ 508-228-7025) delivers its passengers to major points of interest from about 7 am to 11:30 pm, June through September. The Madaket bus ($1) departs on the hour from 15 Broad St. The bus to Surfside (50¢) departs from here, too, but leaves on the quarter hour. The bus to 'Sconset ($1) departs on the hour from Washington and Main Sts. Some of the buses have bike racks. Consider purchasing a three-day ($10) or a weekly ($15) pass at the Visitor Services & Information Bureau, 25 Federal St.

**Car** In summer, the center of town is choked with automobiles. You don't need a car unless you're staying a week or longer.

Nantucket Windmill Auto Rental (☎ 508-228-1227, 800-228-1227) is based at the airport but offers free pick-up and delivery. In town, head to Young's (☎ 508-228-1151) on Steamboat Wharf or Affordable Rental (☎ 508-228-3501) on S Beach St. Expect to pay $85 to $100 daily for a car in summer, half that off-season. If you can find one for a day (most companies rent by the week), a 4WD vehicle could cost $219 daily in summer ($189 daily if renting for two or more days), $995 weekly.

**Taxi** Taxis are plentiful, especially on Lower Main St and at Steamboat Wharf. Fixed rates to every point on the island are posted in the taxi. Rides cost $3 for one person within Nantucket town limits, $11 to 'Sconset. A nominal charge is added for each additional person in the taxi, and another charge is added after dark. Most taxi drivers can give you a personal tour of the island; you'll have to negotiate a price.

**Bicycle & Moped** Virtually every able-bodied person takes a bicycle or moped ride while on the island. Bicycling is the best way to get away from summertime crowds (don't try it on the cobblestones of Main St), savor the island's natural beauty and reach much of the protected conservation land. Besides, the generally flat island has honest-to-goodness bike paths, which are a rarity on the mainland.

For the location of bicycle rental shops, see Bicycling under Nantucket town, later in this chapter. Rent mopeds at the Nantucket Bike Shop (☎ 508-228-1999).

For information on ordering bike maps in advance, see Maps under Orientation, later in this chapter.

## NANTUCKET

The only town of any size on this eponymous island, Nantucket town boasts quaint cobblestone streets shaded by towering elms and lined with gracious 19th-century homes. The whole town is, in fact, a National

# NANTUCKET

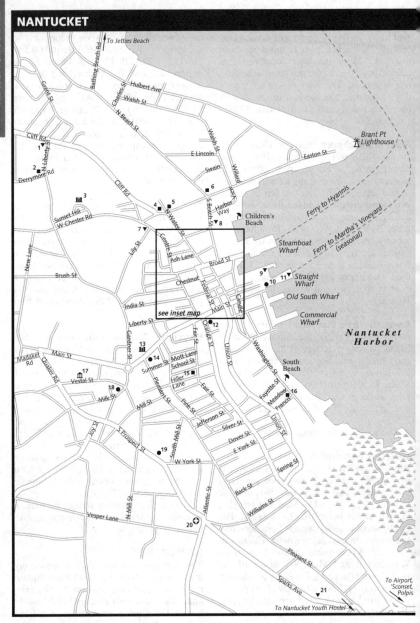

To Jetties Beach

Bathing Beach Rd

Grant St

Hulbert Ave

Charles St

Walsh St

N Beach St

Cliff Rd

Liberty St

1

2

Derrymore Rd

Sunset Hill
W Chester Rd

3

Cliff Rd

New Lane

Brush St

Lily St

N Water St

4   5

7

Centre St

Ash Lane

Chestnut

Broad St

Federal St

India St

Liberty St

see inset map

E Lincoln

Swain

Willard

S Beach St

Harbor Way

6

8

Children's
Beach

Brant Pt
Lighthouse

Easton St

Ferry to Hyannis

Steamboat
Wharf

Ferry to Martha's Vineyard
(seasonal)

9

10   11   Straight
Wharf

Old South Wharf

Commercial
Wharf

Nantucket
Harbor

Main St

Madaket
Rd

Quaker Rd

Gardner St

Main St

Vestal St

17

Milk St

18

Joy St

S Prospect St

N Mill St

Vesper Lane

13

14

Summer St

Mott Lane

School St

15

Hiller
Lane

Pleasant St

Mill St

South Mill St

Fair St

Orange St

12

Union St

Washington St

Fayette St

Meadow

Francis St

16

South
Beach

Jefferson St

Silver St

Dover St

E York St

19

W York St

Back St

Atlantic St

Williams St

Union St

Spring St

20

Pleasant St

Sparks Ave

21

To Nantucket Youth Hostel

To Airport,
'Sconset,
Polpis

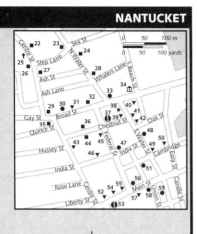

**NANTUCKET**

Historic Landmark, holding the country's largest concentration of houses built prior to 1850. In summer, Nantucket's Main St is always busy with shoppers, strolling day-trippers and cyclists walking their wheels (riding over cobbles is uncomfortable).

## Orientation

There are two ferry terminals, Steamboat Wharf and Straight Wharf, both a block or two off Main St in the center of town. Both terminals are within walking distance of most of the town's lodgings.

The majority of tourist/visitor facilities – restaurants, inns, bicycle rental shops and stores – are within a 10-minute radius of Main St and the wharves. These principal areas are bounded by Main, Centre, Broad and S Water Sts. If you walk 30 minutes in any direction from the wharves, you will be on the outskirts of town.

**Maps** Rubel Bike Maps (☎ 617-776-6567, PO Box 401035, Cambridge, MA 02140, info@bikemaps.com) produces an excellent bike map covering routes on Martha's Vineyard and Nantucket for $1.95. If you can't find it at your local bookstore, contact the company directly.

## Information

The tourism industry on Nantucket is a well-oiled machine. The official Nantucket Chamber of Commerce (☎ 508-228-1700, www.nantucketchamber.org), 48 Main St, is stocked with plenty of information on seasonal activities and special events. The office is open 9 am to 5 pm weekdays year-round. Call for the free *Official Guide*.

The Nantucket Visitor Services & Information Bureau (☎ 508-228-0925), 25 Federal St, is the place to go for up-to-the-minute information on room availability and bus schedules. The bureau is open from 9 am to 5:30 pm daily year-round (until 9 pm, late May to mid-October). The bureau also maintains seasonal kiosks at both of the island's ferry terminals.

At the Internet Cafe (☎ 508-228-6777, www.nantucket.net), 2 Union St, you can access the Net for $10 per hour.

Nantucket Bookworks (☎ 508-228-4000), 25 Broad St, and Mitchell's Book Corner (☎ 508-228-1080), 54 Main St, have very good selections. The Hub (☎ 508-228-3868), at the corner of Main and Federal Sts, is *the* source for magazines and newspapers.

There are public rest rooms at the information bureau, the Steamship Authority ferry terminal and the end of Straight Wharf.

Nantucket Cottage Hospital (☎ 508-228-1200), S Prospect St at Vesper Lane, is on the edge of town. It's open 24 hours.

In an emergency, call ☎ 911; for Nantucket police, call ☎ 508-228-1212.

For further information, including pictures from a live video camera on Main St, look up www.nantucketonline.com.

## Walking Tours

To enjoy a self-guided walking tour, pick up the brochure of the Nantucket Historical Association (☎ 508-228-1894), available at the Visitor Services & Information Bureau, 25 Federal St.

For information on guided walking tours, see the Organized Tours section later in this chapter.

## Historic Houses & Museums

The Nantucket Historical Association (☎ 508-228-1894), 15 Broad St, oversees eight of the island's most important historic buildings. Together, these buildings and their contents represent island life from its farming beginnings to its prosperous whaling days. A special combination pass ($10 for adults, $5 for children) allows you unlimited visits during your stay. Most buildings are open 10 am to 5 pm daily, mid-June to early September; off-season hours, late May to mid-June and early September to mid-October, are changeable.

The most deservedly famous property, the **Nantucket Whaling Museum** (☎ 508-228-1736), Broad St, memorializes the island's principle industry, the original source of its prosperity. By all means, stop in; it's open late April through October.

Other buildings worth a look include the island's **oldest house**, which was built in 1686 on Sunset Hill Rd as a wedding present for Jethro Coffin and Mary Gardner Coffin. On the corner of S Mill and Prospect Sts stands a working **windmill** built in 1746. The **Old Gaol**, 15R Vestal St, was the island prison from 1805 to 1933. The first prisoner to escape was also the last.

Stroll Upper Main St, west of Orange St, to see some of the island's most beautiful (mostly private) houses, including brothers Henry and Charles Coffin's houses at 75 and 78 Main St; the three identical Georgian mansions known as the 'Three Bricks' at 93, 95 and 97 Main St; and the 'Two Greeks' at 94 and 96 Main St.

Of these, the only one that may be toured is the **Hadwen House** (96 Main St), a Nantucket Historical Association property and a rarefied example of privileged life in the 19th century. Individual tickets (as opposed to the combination pass) are $3 for adults, $2 for children.

Climb to the top of the **First Congregational Church** (☎ 508-228-0950), 62 Centre St, for an eagle-eye view of town. The steeple is open 10 am to 4 pm daily except Sunday, from mid-June through September. The suggested donation is $2 for adults and 50¢ for children.

## Atheneum

The Greek Revival town library (☎ 508-228-1110), on Lower India St, is one of the town's greatest cultural resources. It's filled with whaling-ship records, island genealogy, scrimshaw and other historical articles dating back to 1816. One feels a great sense of history just reading the morning newspaper here. Often there are special events in the Great Hall on the 2nd floor, where notables such as Frederick Douglass and Ralph Waldo Emerson (to name but two of dozens) once spoke.

## Maria Mitchell Association

This association (☎ 508-228-9198), consisting of five buildings headquartered at 2 Vestal St, is devoted to Maria Mitchell (1818-1889), the island's foremost astronomer.

In 1847, Mitchell discovered an uncharted comet and went on to become the first woman ever admitted into the American

Academy of Arts and Sciences and the country's first female professor of astronomy.

The association consists of the Science Library; the Hinchman House, a natural science museum where naturalists lead walks and talks; an observatory open only on clear Monday, Wednesday and Friday evenings in summer; Mitchell's birthplace, which has lovely wildflower and herb gardens; and a waterfront aquarium. Check in at the headquarters for a complete schedule of opening times and offerings. A combination ticket ($7 for adults, $4 for children) allows entry to all buildings, but tickets may also be purchased separately.

### Brewery

Cisco Brewers (☎ 508-325-5929), 5 Bartlett Farm Rd, makes excellent porters, stouts and ales that are sold here and at the liquor store on Main St. The brewery offers tastings, too. (It's all as fresh as can be.) Follow Hummock Pond Rd south of town for about 2½ miles.

### Beaches

You'll have to pedal, hitch or take a bus to the island's prime beaches, but to feel sand between your toes as quickly as possible, head to Children's Beach, off S Beach St just north of Steamboat Wharf, and South Beach, a few blocks south of the wharf.

Jetties Beach, a 20-minute walk or a short bus ride away, is popular because of its location, off Bathing Beach Rd (accessible from N Beach Rd). It's good for walking, as well as activities like volleyball, tennis and sailing.

### Bicycling

There are thousands of bikes to rent from at least a half-dozen shops. Try either the Nantucket Bike Shop (☎ 508-228-1999) or Young's Bicycle Shop (☎ 508-228-1151), on Steamboat Wharf, which rents bikes for about $20 to $25 per day in-season ($15 off-season).

All bicycle rental shops have good, free island maps with routes highlighted. For information on ordering maps in advance, see Maps under Orientation, earlier in this chapter.

The **Cliff Road Bike Path** is a short, in-town route that takes you past big summer houses on the edge of town.

The island's pace and terrain are well-suited to bicycling (see Getting Around). The 3-mile **Surfside Bike Path** to the beach is flat; the ride takes 15 minutes. The 7-mile **'Sconset (or Milestone) Bike Path** begins east of the historic district and passes forests, bogs and moors. It takes 30 minutes if you're cruising. **Polpis Road Bike Path** is lined with millions of daffodils in the springtime. The circular loop from town to 'Sconset and back via Polpis is about 17 miles.

To reach the western end of the island, take the **Madaket Bike Path**, a hilly and winding 6-mile path that passes beautiful terrain.

### Boating

Sea Nantucket (☎ 508-228-7499), Washington St Extension, offers half- and full-day tours of the scallop-shaped harbor on non-rollable sea kayaks and canoes. Don't want a tour? Half-day kayak rentals cost $30 for a single and $50 for a double, $50 for a canoe. Full-day rentals are only $10 more. On choppy days, kayaks and canoes can be delivered to quieter inland ponds.

Astronomer Maria Mitchell

Indian Summer Sports (☎ 508-228-3632), 6 Steamboat Wharf, rents boogie boards and windsurfers in summer.

The Sunken Ship (☎ 508-228-9226), at Broad St and S Water St, is a full-service, year-round dive shop.

Striped bass and bluefish 'run' off of Nantucket's shores. A half-dozen or so charter boats dock at Straight Wharf, including the *Herbert T* (☎ 508-228-6655).

## Organized Tours

Since practically every building in Nantucket town is a historical showpiece with a story to tell, take an organized walking tour to get the most out of a visit. Dirk Gardiner Roggeveen (☎ 508-221-075), who is a 12th-generation islander, offers delightfully informative tours around the core of town for $10 per person. It's well worth it.

The Maria Mitchell Association (☎ 508-228-9198), 2 Vestal St, offers birding walks around the island, depending on where the birds are at any given time, mid-June to mid-September. Tours cost $10 for adults, $6 for children.

## Cruises

Nantucket Whalewatch (☎ 978-283-0313, 800-322-0013), on Straight Wharf, offers daylong trips with an on-board naturalist. The boat departs every Tuesday morning, mid-July to mid-September, and costs $75 for adults, $40 for children. If this is your only chance to take a whale-watching trip, do it. Otherwise, Boston, Provincetown, Plymouth and Gloucester are all closer to the whale's habitat.

The Friendship Sloop *Endeavor* (☎ 508-228-5585), Slip 15, Straight Wharf, offers three daily harbor sails and a sunset cruise May through October. Prices, from $15 to $30, vary with the length of the sail.

## Places to Stay

Staying overnight in Nantucket is generally not cheap. To get around this, it's best to visit in spring or fall (or even winter if you don't mind gray, windy days). It's difficult to find a room in July and August without advance reservations. In addition, many places require a two-night minimum and do not accept credit cards. Although not all places are open all year-round, enough places are. Camping or sleeping under the stars, or even in your car, is not permitted on the island. This policy is strictly enforced.

**Hostels** The *Nantucket Youth Hostel* (☎ 508-228-0433, 617-779-0900 for off-season information, fax 508-228-5672, 31 Western Ave) is about 3 miles from the center of town on Surfside Beach. The island's first lifesaving station, an architectural gem, now has bunk rooms accommodating a total of 50 people. The hostel is open mid-April to mid-October. Advance reservations are absolutely essential in summer, but there is usually plenty of room in spring and fall. Beds cost $14 to $17. To make reservations before the hostel opens, write to Hostelling International Boston, 12 Hemenway St, Boston, MA 02215, or send a fax to 617-424-6558.

**Hotels** The *Overlook Hotel* (☎ 508-228-0695, 3 Step Lane), a three-story summer hotel with wraparound porches, has 25 serviceable rooms (some with private bath) priced at $105 to $150. There is one single for $95. Open late May through October, the hotel has slightly lower rates after late September.

The *Point Breeze Hotel* (☎ 508-228-0313, 800-365-4371, fax 508-325-6044, ptbreeze@nantucket.net, 89 Easton St), a 10-minute walk from Main St, was built in 1893. It's a rambling summer hotel with 23 simple but clean rooms, suites and cottages well-suited to families. Mid-June to mid-September, rooms rent for $165 up to $175; two-bedroom cottages that sleep six rent for $375. Off-season, they rent for $99 to $150 and $240 to $300, respectively. The hotel is closed mid-October to late May.

**B&Bs** The centrally located *Nesbitt Inn* (☎ 508-228-0156, fax 325-4476, 21 Broad St) has 14 rooms with shared bath that rent for $55 to $65 single, $65 to $75 double, $105 for a quad. A real bargain and a favorite among Europeans, the 1872 house has many original Victorian furnishings. This is a real find!

Mrs Ven Johnson's **Hungry Whale** (☎ 508-228-0793, 8 Derrymore Rd), in a quiet residential neighborhood about 12 minutes' walk from the center, is a pleasant, traditional Nantucket house. The three rooms (one with private bath) rent for $60 to $85, which includes a good breakfast served on the umbrella-shaded deck. It's an excellent value if you can get a room!

The **Periwinkle Guest House** (☎ 508-228-9267, 800-673-4559, fax 508-325-4046, rhinn@aol.com, 7-9 N Water St) has 16 rooms just a few minutes from Steamboat Wharf. Rooms come in a variety of sizes and shapes; singles and doubles, with and without bath, go for $65 to $225 in-season, $35 to $125 off-season. The Periwinkle's closed mid-December to mid-April.

The **White House** (☎ 508-228-4677, fax 228-1934, marantqs@nantucket.net, 48 Centre St), a simple and inexpensive guest house in the center of the historic district, has three rooms and a suite with private bath that rent for $95 to $130 in-season and $75 to $85 in the off-season.

The best bargains at **Beachway Guests** (☎ 508-228-1324, 3 N Beach St), a few blocks from the center, are the shared-bath rooms that rent for $90; otherwise, you'll pay $150 for a private bath.

Elegantly furnished, the **Martin House Inn** (☎ 508-228-0678, martinn@nantucket.net, 61 Centre St), has canopy beds, antiques and fireplaces in many of its 13 rooms. A few bargain rooms have shared bath ($90); otherwise, the range is $125 to $195 in-season. Singles cost $60. The rest of the year, doubles cost $85 to $165.

The antique-filled **Corner House** (☎ 508-228-1530, cornerhs@nantucket.net, 49 Centre St) has 17 lovely historic rooms and suites, all with bath. The least-expensive, smaller rooms on the 3rd floor are quite nice. Afternoon tea is served on the brick patio or sun porch. In-season rates ($120 to $195) drop to $65 to $145 off-season; the inn's closed early January to early April.

The **Hawthorn House** (☎ 508-228-1468, 2 Chestnut St) has nine modest, but still quiet comfortable, guest rooms (most with private bath) in the middle of the historic

district. It's homey and old-fashioned, and rates include breakfast at a bona-fide nearby restaurant: $130 to $150 in summer, $78 to $80 the rest of the year.

The **Brass Lantern Inn** (☎ 508-228-4064, 800-377-6609, fax 508-325-0928, grthbr@nantucket.net, 11 N Water St), a few blocks from the waterfront, has 17 traditionally furnished and modern rooms (some with bath) that rent for $132 to $194 double in-season, $87 to $150 the rest of the year.

Across the street from the Corner House, the **Anchor Inn** (☎ 508-228-0072, anchorin@nantucket.net, 66 Centre St) is a sea captain's house built in 1806. Its 11 nicely appointed rooms (all with tiled bath) cost $140 to $185 in summer, $65 to $135 off-season; the inn's closed January and February.

The **Cliff Lodge** (☎ 508-228-9480, fax 228-6308, 9 Cliff Rd) is a converted 1771 sea captain's house 10 minutes from Straight Wharf. Its 11 fresh, light and airy rooms and an apartment ($300) are decorated in an English-country style. In-season, rooms rent for $105 single, $140 to $180 double. The rest of the year, rooms cost $85 to $110 double.

The **Ship's Inn** (☎ 508-228-0040, 13 Fair St) is a 10-minute walk from Straight Wharf on a quiet residential street. This 1831 whaling captain's house has 10 large, airy and comfortable rooms for $65 to $90 single with shared bath, $145 to $175 double with private bath.

Right in the middle of Nantucket is the **Chestnut House** (☎ 508-228-0049, fax 228-9521, 3 Chestnut St). It has four suites and one room, all with private bath and refrigerator, that rent for $150 to $195 double. Most can sleep four people for an additional $15 to $20 per person. A four-person cottage with a complete kitchen rents for $300. A full breakfast is included at three recommended restaurants nearby.

**Inns** The centrally located **Jared Coffin House** (☎ 508-228-2405, 800-248-2405, fax 508-228-8549, jchouse@nantucket.net, 29 Broad St) is the island's most famous and historic lodging place. There are sixty rooms, all with private bath, housed in an 1845

Federal-style brick mansion and five adjacent buildings. Colonial-style reproduction furniture is the norm; most rooms have a TV. In-season rates range from $90 to $150 single, $160 to $210 double. For historical value, it can't be beat, but for the price, there are more elegant places in Nantucket town to stay. It's a better value off-season, year-round, at $95 to $110 double.

**Cottages** An absolute bargain, the *Harbor Cottages* (☎ 508-228-4485, fax 228-2451, nisda@nantucket.net, 71 Washington St), about a 10-minute walk from 'downtown' and across from a kayaking beach, are rustic by island standards, downright princely by our standards. The simple studios and one-bedroom cottages have painted floorboards, exposed rafters and white-washed walls. From June through September, studios go for $675 weekly or $100 to $115 nightly; cottages go for $775 to $875 weekly or $125 to $150 nightly. The larger cottages sleep up to six people. The tidy complex is open year-round.

## Places to Eat
Nantucket town has plenty of inexpensive sandwich and bistro-style places, all generally creative and inventive. Nantucket is also renowned for its dense concentration of exceptional restaurants, so if you've been waiting to splurge, this may be the place to do it, but you'll have to be careful not to burn a hole through your pocket. Reservations are advised for the moderate and expensive restaurants in summer. Unless noted, most places are open mid-May to mid-October, but you won't go hungry in the off-season.

**Farmer's Markets** Locally grown produce is sold on Main St from the backs of trucks daily except Sunday during the growing season (about May through October).

**Cafes** The *Espresso Cafe* (☎ 508-228-6930, 40 Main St) serves strong coffee, breakfast pastries, vegetarian dishes, hearty soups and cold salads year-round for less than $9. If it wasn't so popular, it would be more of a find. There's a quiet rear patio.

*Provisions* (☎ 508-228-3258), Straight Wharf, open mid-April to mid-December, makes huge sandwiches, such as a smoked turkey sandwich with cranberries, that are large enough to share.

The tiny *Downy Flake* (☎ 508-228-4533, 18 Sparks Ave), known for doughnuts and blueberry pancakes, has been a local institution since the 1960s.

*Dave's Soda Fountain* (☎ 508-228-4549, 47 Main St), inside Congdon's Pharmacy, and the *Nantucket Pharmacy* (☎ 508-228-0180), next door, are classic drugstore soda fountains with swivel stools and cheap coffee, peanut butter and jelly sandwiches and the like for a few bucks. Both are open year-round.

*Something Natural* (☎ 508-228-0504, 50 Cliff Rd), on the way to Madaket Beach, prepares sandwiches and natural snacks mid-April to mid-October.

The *Juice Bar* (☎ 508-228-5799, 12 Broad St), purveyors of fruit and veggie drinks, also serves delicious ice cream and nonfat yogurt concoctions.

**Restaurants** The family-friendly *Vincent's Restaurant* (☎ 508-228-0189, 21 S Water St) offers plain and fancy pasta dishes, pizzas and seafood for lunch ($7 to $12) and dinner ($10 to $19). The decor is classic Italian-American, with Chianti bottles hanging from the ceiling and red-and-white-checked tablecloths. Vincent's is closed mid-October to mid-April.

*Atlantic Cafe* (☎ 508-228-0570, 15 S Water St) is a casual and fun year-round place that gets louder and louder as the night wears on. The 'AC' serves generous portions of noshing food like nachos, buffalo wings, chowder and burgers for $5 to $18.

The pub-style *Rose & Crown* (☎ 508-228-2595, 23 S Water St), open mid-April to mid-December, is similar. Its large, barn-like room was formerly a livery stable.

The *Brotherhood of Thieves* (no ☎, 23 Broad St), a dark tavern lit by candles even during the day, is a friendly and boisterous place frequented by locals. They come to chow on chowder, burgers and sandwiches for $8 to $15. There's always a long line in

Weathervane, Martha's Vineyard

The remote and stately Great Point Light, Nantucket, MA

Replica of old-fashioned lightship, MA

Cheery flowers are all over Nantucket.

Bicycling is a popular way to tour Martha's Vineyard, MA.

Just another friendly New Englander

When in Maine, be sure to have some blueberries.

Farm stands are a common New England sight.

Church on the Hill, Lenox, MA

summer (and during the rest of the year), so you'll be seated at tables with fellow patrons for lunch and dinner.

The name says it all: ***Sushi by Yoshi*** (☎ *508-228-1801, 2 E Chestnut St)*. Here a transplanted Japanese chef prepares fresh sashimi, sushi and more exotic creations. In winter, this shop closes, but you can still get Yoshi's sushi at his other restaurant, Nantucket Tapas.

***Nantucket Tapas*** (☎ *508-228-2033, 15 Beach St)*, open for lunch and dinner year-round, offers a delightfully innovative concept to battle the high cost of island dining: There are dozens of appetizers ($7 to $10) from which to choose. Yes, the bill can add up, but for grazing or sharing among many people, this spot can't be beat. Not only are communal tables fun, but the management is fine with patrons simply enjoying a Cisco beer and an appetizer, too.

The ***Centre Street Bistro*** (☎ *508-228-8470, 29 Centre St)* is usually open for breakfast and lunch year-round. Dine at a few tables indoors, a quiet back patio or the front patio, which is great for people-watching. Get poached eggs with pan fried grits (a trademark) for breakfast ($4 to $8). The changing dinner menu ($14 to $23) is hard to pin down, but if we mention warm goat cheese tarts or seared salmon with crispy wontons, do you get the idea? For the money and quality, this is one of Nantucket's better places. BYOB.

***Arno's 41 Main*** (☎ *508-228-7001, 41 Main St)* is open throughout the day (April to mid-December) and serves decent portions of well-priced food in a pleasant storefront eatery with high ceilings. Sandwiches, Thai peanut noodles, fish and chips and a few vegetarian dishes will set you back $8 to $23; breakfasts of banana pancakes and eggs Benedict cost less.

***Cambridge Street Victuals*** (☎ *508-228-7109, 12 Cambridge St)*, with a dim and boisterous interior that you can glimpse before going inside, specializes in over-the-top portions of barbecue, but you'll also get good *schwarma* (roasted lamb on a spit), thin-crust pizza and tandoori-style chicken. Microbrews reign. Dinner costs about $12 to

$22 per main dish. This spot is closed in winter from mid-December to mid-April.

The ***Tap Room*** (☎ *508-228-2400, 29 Broad St)*, in the basement of the Jared Coffin House, is a cozy 19th-century tavern serving hearty and traditional American dishes like cod cakes with molasses baked beans year-round. You can also dine on the shaded terrace. Lunch dishes hover around $6 to $13, while dinner costs $14 to $20.

For mingling with the locals, there's no better place than ***Hutch's*** (☎ *508-288-5550)*, at the airport. Starving after a day at the beach? Hutch's will get you in and out in minutes. Since Jamaicans work the short-order line, you can safely assume the Friday-night homeland specials are great. Year-round, you can count on seafood omelettes, chicken fingers and fish and chips for $5 to $11.

Although it might look too pricey, the harborfront ***Ropewalk*** (☎ *508-228-8886)*, Straight Wharf, offers Nantucket-style bargains at lunch ($7 to $13). Focaccia pizza, oysters and assorted shellfish from the raw bar, frozen drinks and fine seafood rope the patrons in every time.

The ***Ship's Inn*** (☎ *508-228-0040, 13 Fair St)*, on the ground floor of an old sea captain's house, is well known for healthy and creative California-French cuisine. Off-season, it also has less expensive dishes in its Dory Bar; these are a bargain from $11 to $17. The inn's closed January through April.

***American Seasons*** (☎ *508-228-7111, 80 Centre St)* celebrates the four corners of the country with an eclectic menu that highlights jazzed-up dishes inspired by the Wild West, the Pacific Coast, the South and New England. The dining room features lots of folk art, and the artfully presented entrees range from $23 to $30. It may be pricey, but you won't have to eat again for another day. Better yet, don't eat anything the day preceding your visit.

The ***Boarding House*** (☎ *508-228-9622, 12 Federal St)*, which consistently rises to the top of 'must eat' places, offers innovative American cuisine for lunch and dinner. Entrees like grilled lobster tail and pan-roasted salmon ($23 to $32) are served in a cozy basement setting or outdoors on a brick patio, great for people-watching. The bar, where a less-expensive bistro-style menu is served, is very popular with locals. The restaurant's open almost year-round.

The *Company of the Cauldron* (☎ 508-228-4016, 7 India St) offers a table d'hôte, fixed-price dinner for $46 to $50 per person, plus wine. The creative New American menu, served at two seatings in a romantic setting, changes nightly and might go like this: roasted red-and-yellow-pepper soup, Nantucket greens, baked jumbo shrimp stuffed with crab and a chocolate tart to finish up.

### Entertainment

*Nantucket Map & Legend* and *Yesterday's Island* (www.yesterdaysisland.com), two free weeklies, have up-to-the-minute listings of concerts, theater productions and festivals on the island.

Many restaurants provide entertainment as well as food. You'll find live music and dancing at the boisterous *Rose & Crown* (☎ 508-228-2595, 23 S Water St), live folk music at the *Brotherhood of Thieves* (no ☎, 23 Broad St) and live piano or guitar at the Jared Coffin House's *Tap Room* (☎ 508-228-2400, 29 Broad St). The *Atlantic Cafe* (☎ 508-228-0570, 15 S Water St) is a popular place to hang out later in the evening.

At the *Gaslight Theatre* (☎ 508-228-4435, 1 N Union St), they concentrate on art films, while the *Dreamland Theater* (☎ 508-228-5356, 19 S Water St) shows first-run movies.

*Nantucket Filmworks* (☎ 508-228-3783), Centre St at Main St, a slide show at the Methodist church, features fine, year-round photographic images by islander Cary Hazlegrove. Adults pay $4.50, children $2.50.

### Shopping

There are dozens and dozens of pricey antique shops, clothing boutiques, jewelry stores, art galleries and specialty shops that carry the island's trademark woven 'lightship baskets,' which can cost between $300 and $3000. The Sailor's Valentine Gallery (☎ 508-228-2011), 12 Straight Wharf, has one of the most eclectic collections of contemporary art. The Spectrum (☎ 508-228-4606), 26 Main St, features high-quality contemporary American crafts.

## AROUND THE ISLAND

The island measures 14 miles by 3 miles and is ringed by sandy beaches, almost all of which are open to the public. Great Point and Coatue Point are narrow strips of beach only accessible by 4WD vehicle. Because over one-third of the island is protected as conservation land, there is plenty of space in the interior of the island to walk and enjoy nature.

The only other town of note besides Nantucket town is Siasconset, always referred to locally as 'Sconset; the four or five other towns you'll see on the map are really just residential communities with very little going on except new home construction. To get to 'Sconset, head out of Nantucket town on Milestone Rd, which will take you directly to the village.

You'll definitely want to balance the history that seeps from the town's cobblestones with the natural open spaces around the island. In fact, it would be a travesty not to get out of town and explore the island. Head west from town to reach the largest tracts of conservation land or head east to Polpis Rd, where you can detour to the Lifesaving Museum, The Moors, the remote settlement of Wauwinet and Sankaty Head Lighthouse before reaching the eastern shore. Beaches, of course, ring the entire island.

### 'Sconset

The charming residential village of 'Sconset is definitely worth a detour. In the summertime, the houses are awash with blooming roses. In the 17th century, fishermen and whalers lived in the tiny weathered cottages, adding 'warts' (equally tiny rooms) when their families came out to stay with them. By the late 1800s, 'Sconset was fashionable with New York City actors who summered here. 'Sconset is 7 miles from Nantucket town; the best way to reach it is by bicycle, although you can take a bus (see Getting Around under Nantucket Island).

'Sconset Beach is long and narrow (it's suffered much erosion in recent years), with a good deal of surf and undertow. It's just south of 'Sconset on the island's eastern shore.

If you're looking for places to eat, there are a few options. The *Siasconset Market* (☎ 508-257-9915) and *Claudette's* (☎ 508-257-6622), both next to the post office in the tiny center of town and open seasonally, have picnic supplies and sandwich fixings for those recovering from the long bike ride or preparing for an afternoon at the beach.

The *'Sconset Cafe* (☎ 508-257-4008), Post Office Square, serves an eclectic lunch menu with creative soups and salads ($5 to $14). If you pedal out for breakfast, you'll be rewarded with cranberry and blueberry pancakes ($5). The cafe also serves fancier New American dinners ($16 to $26) in the same airy setting, surrounded by local artwork.

The *Chanticleer* (☎ 508-257-6231, *9 New St)* is arguably the island's best restaurant. The setting is elegant and romantic, in the courtyard of a rose-covered cottage or in small dining rooms overlooking the courtyard. The exquisite French cuisine is even pricey at lunch ($20 to $25), while the more memorable fixed-price dinner costs $65 per person. Expect to pay $25 to $35 for à la carte entrees.

### Nantucket Lifesaving Museum

The museum (☎ 508-228-1885), on Polpis Rd about 5 miles east of Nantucket town, displays lifesaving boats, as well as photographs and accounts of dramatic sea rescues. On the edge of a pond, it's nicely situated for a picnic. It's open to visitors 9:30 am to 4 pm daily, mid-June to mid-October; admission is $3 for adults, $2 for children.

### The Moors

Off Polpis Rd to the south is the island's highest point, Altar Rock, which offers expansive views of the moors, heather and cranberry bogs. The Moors, crisscrossed with walking trails and rutted dirt roads, are spectacular in autumn and are lovely at dawn or dusk throughout the year.

### Conservation Land

Much of the island's wetlands, moors and grasslands are protected from development and are a naturalist's delight. If you plan to be on the island for any length of time, stop by the Nantucket Conservation Foundation (☎ 508-228-2884), 118 Cliff Rd, in Nantucket town, for an up-to-date map ($3) of the foundation's ever-expanding holdings.

Sanford Farm, Ram Pasture and the Woods, off Madaket Rd, are collectively a former 900-acre farm with walking and biking trails.

### Lighthouses

As you might expect, the island is ringed with working lighthouses. Brant Point Light guards the entrance to the harbor.

Around the island, Great Point Light is accessible only by 4WD vehicle. Its remote location, worth the expense it takes to get there, makes it all the more stately and lonesome. The Trustees of the Reservations (☎ 508-228-6799) offer a three-hour natural history tour of Great Point that culminates in climbing to the top of the lighthouse. Tickets cost $40 for adults, $15 for children; tours are offered at 10 am and 2 pm each day, mid-May to mid-October. Ara's Tours (☎ 508-228-1951) leads a similar expedition that's slightly more geared toward bird watchers and photographers.

'Sconset's Sankaty Head Lighthouse, visible 30 miles out to sea, stands on the edge of a rapidly encroaching 90-foot bluff.

### Wauwinet

*The Wauwinet* (☎ *508-228-0145, fax 325-0657, 120 Wauwinet Rd)* is the ultimate island splurge when price is no object. Set on a dramatic and narrow strip of land between the harbor and Atlantic Ocean, 8 miles from Nantucket town, The Wauwinet's 35 luxuriously appointed guest rooms start at $240 in spring, $210 in fall and $350 in summer. A free jitney service shuttles guests to and from town. Service is exceptional here, and lots of extras are included.

Within the inn, *Topper's* (☎ *508-228-8768)*, also open early May through October, vies for the title of 'best island dining.' Again, when

MASSACHUSETTS

price is no object, you are sure to depart with memories that will last for years. Skillful New American cuisine, utterly gracious service and a wine list to knock your socks off could set you back as little as $130 for two people (if you're careful).

## Beaches

Dionis Beach, about 3 miles from Nantucket town off Eel Point Rd (accessible from the Madaket Bike Path), is the island's only beach with dunes. It's good for swimming (the water is relatively calm) and shelling.

Surfside Beach, 3 miles from Nantucket town and accessible by frequent shuttle bus, is popular with the college and twenty-something crowd. It's a wide beach with moderate-to-heavy surf.

Madaket Beach, at the end of the name-sake bike path, is the most popular place to watch sunsets. Strong currents and heavy surf here make for less-than-ideal swimming conditions.

Cisco Beach, 4 miles from Nantucket town off Hummock Pond Rd (accessible from Milk St), is popular with surfers.

# Central Massachusetts & the Berkshires

To many visitors, Massachusetts means Boston and Cape Cod to the east, and the Berkshires to the west. In fact, central Massachusetts saw some of the region's earliest settlement and, during the 19th century, some of its most explosive industrial growth.

The Connecticut River, navigable from Long Island Sound to Vermont in colonial times, was the early settlers' highway into the interior, and the route out for the ships full of the crops and products they produced. The Pioneer Valley, as it's called in Massachusetts, has an interesting mix of colonial, early American and 19th-century industrial villages and towns. It is home to five colleges and universities, bringing a youthful, cosmopolitan spirit to several of its towns.

## Getting There & Around

**Air** Worcester Regional Airport (☎ 888-359-9672) receives flights by US Airways Express as well as by commuter and regional airlines, though the air traffic hub of the region is Boston's Logan International Airport. Springfield and the Pioneer Valley towns are served by Bradley International Airport, across the state line in Windsor Locks, Connecticut.

**Bus** Peter Pan Bus Lines (☎ 617-426-7838, 800-343-9999, www.peterpan-bus.com), a Trailways affiliate, has its hub in Springfield, and runs buses daily to Albany, New York; Amherst, Massachusetts; Bennington, Vermont; Boston and Logan Airport; Deerfield; Hartford, Connecticut; Holyoke; Hyannis; Lee; Lenox; New Haven, Connecticut; North Adams; Northampton; Pittsfield; Providence, Rhode Island; South Hadley; Sturbridge; Toronto, Ontario; Williamstown; Windsor Locks; and Worcester.

Bonanza Bus Lines (☎ 212-947-1766, 800-556-3815, www.bonanzabus.com) runs buses daily between New York City's Port Authority Bus Terminal and Bennington via Great Barrington, Stockbridge, Lee, Lenox, Pitts-field and Williamstown. There's service between Albany and Pittsfield connecting with the service between Pittsfield and New York City. Another service connects Providence with Springfield, the Berkshire towns and Albany.

**Train** The Boston section of Amtrak's (☎ 800-872-7245, www.amtrak.com) *Lakeshore Limited* departs from Boston's South

## Highlights

- Scouring the stalls for treasures at the Brimfield Antique Show
- Getting a taste of early American life at Historic Deerfield Village
- Discovering the bucolic pleasures of the Berkshires, including Stockbridge, Lenox and Lee
- Taking in a performance at the renowned Jacob's Pillow Dance Festival in Lee
- Exploring the enormous new Massachusetts Museum of Contemporary Art in Williamstown

Station (☎ 617-482-3660) in the afternoon, stopping at Framingham, Worcester, Springfield and Pittsfield before reaching Albany-Rensselaer in the evening. There it links up with the *Lakeshore* section from New York City (☎ 212-582-6875), and the full train continues to Chicago.

The *Vermonter* runs daily during daylight hours between New York City and St Albans, Vermont, via Springfield, with connecting bus service to Montreal from St Albans.

The *Adirondack* runs between Montreal and New York City's Grand Central Station daily during daylight hours. The closest it gets to Massachusetts is Albany-Rensselaer, where you must continue to the Berkshires by bus.

**Car** The Massachusetts Turnpike (or Mass Pike, I-90) and MA 2 are the major east-west roads connecting Boston with central and western Massachusetts. It takes about three hours to drive all the way across Massachusetts from Boston to Lenox on the Mass Pike, which is a toll road between Boston and Springfield.

The MA 2, between Boston and Williamstown, is mostly four lanes between Cambridge and I-91 at Greenfield (but not always limited access, so some parts of the road have lower speed limits and the drive can take longer). West of Greenfield to Williamstown it's a scenic two-lane road.

# Central Massachusetts

If you have a few days to spend, Central Massachusetts will reward you with beautiful landscapes, excellent, little-known museums, and a delightful absence of tourist crowds.

## WORCESTER

Though blessed with several fine museums, one of America's best concert halls and numerous institutions of higher learning, Worcester (pronounced 'woosta' by locals)

suffers from being in the shadow of Boston, only an hour's drive to the east. It was not always so.

## History

Once the home of the Nipmuck Indians, Worcester was incorporated as a town in 1722, and as a city in 1848. During the 19th century, Worcester was one of the inland cities and towns of Massachusetts and Connecticut that boomed with industry and invention. All sorts of new devices, implements and conveniences were thought up in these cities' small workshops and passed on to the water-powered mills nearby for large-scale manufacture. Worcester produced machines that were the first to weave carpets, fold envelopes and turn irregular shapes on a lathe. Worcester citizen Esther Howland (1828-1904) was the first person to produce and market Valentine's Day cards in quantity. And in 1887 Sam Jones made the

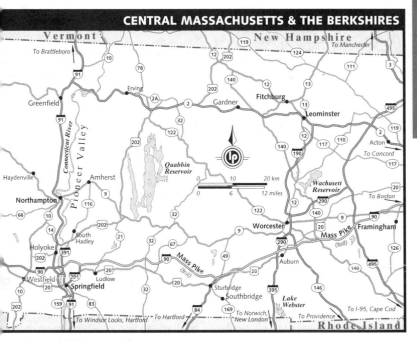

CENTRAL MASSACHUSETTS & THE BERKSHIRES

first lunch wagon big enough for customers to step inside – the precursor to that American culinary icon, the diner.

During its heyday, Worcester hosted the first national convention on women's suffrage (1850) and saw the foundation of several colleges and universities including Clark, Holy Cross and Worcester Polytechnic Institute, as well as several significant museums. One of its native sons, Dr Robert Goddard (1882-1945), for whom the Goddard Space Flight Center in Greenbelt, Maryland, is named, launched the first liquid-fuel rocket from Pakachoag Hill in 1926, inaugurating the age of American rocketry.

But the genius of invention moved on to other parts of the country and manufacturing largely moved to the Far East, leaving Worcester behind, reminiscing about its lost prosperity.

Nonetheless, Worcester has sights worth seeing, among them the Worcester Art Museum and the Higgins Armory Museum. Don't make your stop in Worcester on a Monday as the museums will be closed.

## Orientation

Appropriately named Commercial St, a block south of Main St, is the city's center of commerce. The Centrum concert hall is here as well.

## Information

The Worcester County Convention and Visitors Bureau (☎ 508-753-2920, fax 754-8560, www.worcester.org), 33 Waldo St, Worcester, MA 01608, on a short street parallel to and between Main and Commercial Sts, should be able to help with questions or problems. The CVB also administers the Central Massachusetts Tourist Council (☎ 800-231-7557). They operate a Visitor Center in the Worcester Common Outlets (☎ 508-754-0305), 110 Front St, as well.

## Worcester Art Museum

During Worcester's golden age, its captains of industry bestowed largesse upon the town and its citizens. The Worcester Art Museum (☎ 508-799-4406), 55 Salisbury St, off Park and Main Sts (follow the signs), is one of the most generous and impressive bequests.

This small regional museum has a surprisingly comprehensive collection, ranging from ancient Chinese, Egyptian and Sumerian artifacts through European masterworks and those of Japanese *ukiyo-e* (17th- to 19th-century woodcut) painters to great American paintings and primitives. The museum's collection of more than 2000 photographs spans the history of the medium, from Matthew Brady to Gary Winogrand.

The museum boasts a good number of world-famous masterpieces. Edward Hick's *Peaceable Kingdom* is perhaps the most easily recognizable piece, but you can also see Mary Cassatt's *Woman Bathing*, Paul Gauguin's *Brooding Woman* and Rembrandt's *St Bartholomew*.

The museum is open 11 am to 4 pm Tuesday through Friday (until 8 pm Thursday), until 5 pm Saturday and 1 to 5 pm Sunday. Admission costs $6 for adults, $4 for seniors, full-time college students and youth ages 13 to 18; it's free for children 12 and under. Admission is free on Saturday between 10 am and noon. The Museum Café makes a convenient place to eat before moving on; see the listing under Places to Eat.

## Salisbury Mansion

Very near the art museum, the Salisbury Mansion (☎ 508-753-8278), 40 Highland St, was built in 1772 and was the Salisbury family home until 1851. It was moved to its present site in 1929 and is now preserved as a museum, decorated in the style of the early 19th century. It's open 1 to 4 pm Thursday through Sunday for $2 per person.

## Worcester Historical Museum

The Worcester Historical Society (☎ 508-753-8278), 30 Elm St, just around the corner from the art museum, preserves the record of Worcester's history, particularly its 19th-century golden age. The museum is open

from 10 am to 4 pm, Sunday 1 to 4 pm, and is closed Monday. Admission is $2.

## American Antiquarian Society

If you're interested in doing research in the largest single collection of printed source materials relating to the first 250 years of US history, the American Antiquarian Society (☎ 508-755-5221), 185 Salisbury St, a few blocks from the art museum, is a must-see. The society was founded in 1812, and the documents in its library cover all aspects of colonial and early American culture, history and literature. It's open for research 9 am to 5 pm weekdays; free tours are given each Wednesday at 2 pm.

## Higgins Armory Museum

John Woodman Higgins, president of the Worcester Pressed Steel Company at the beginning of the 20th century, loved good steel. Medieval armorers made good steel, so he collected it: over 100 full suits of armor for men, women, children and even dogs. His collection got so big that in 1929 he built a special armory to house it – this art deco building with interior neo-gothic accents is the Higgins Armory Museum (☎ 508-853-6015, www.higgins.org), 100 Barber Ave off W Boylston St (MA 12). Children will like the Quest Gallery where they can try on 'castle clothing' and replica suits of armor. It's open 10 am to 4 pm (Sunday noon to 4 pm); it's closed Monday except in July and August. Admission costs $4.75 for adults, $4 seniors, $3.75 children six to 16.

## Mechanics Hall

Mechanics Hall (☎ 508-752-5608), 321 Main St, was constructed in 1857 on the orders of the Worcester County Mechanics Association, a group of artisans and small business owners who typified Worcester's inventive and industrial strength in the mid-19th century. The hall boasts superb acoustics and is regarded as America's finest standing pre-Civil War concert hall. Thoreau and Emerson spoke here, as did Dickens, Twain and Theodore Roosevelt.

Restored in 1977, the hall is still used for concerts, lectures and recording sessions.

Call for information on visiting hours, or call the box office (☎ 508-752-0888) for tickets to a lecture or performance.

## Worcester Common Outlets

Built as part of a plan to draw people to a revitalized city center, the huge Worcester Common Outlets (☎ 508-798-2581) shopping complex is right in the city center, with acres of parking and all of the usual shops, such as Saks Fifth Avenue, Polo, Ann Taylor, London Fog, Media Play and Sports Authority.

## Places to Stay

Worcester has a number of business hotels. Most of the tourist lodgings in this area are about 20 miles southwest, in and around Sturbridge. The biggest concentration of motels is near I-290 exit 20, 3 miles northeast of the city center. Ask about special offers when you call for reservations.

The *Days Inn Days Lodge* (☎ 508-852-2800, 800-932-3297, 50 Oriol Drive (I-290 exit 20)) has 114 comfortable rooms amid landscaped grounds in a quiet setting for $73.

The *Holiday Inn Worcester* (☎ 508-852-4000, 800-465-4329, 500 Lincoln St (I-290 exit 20)) charges $89 to $109 for its very good rooms, $10 for every additional adult.

The *Hampton Inn* (☎ 508-757-0400, 800-426-7866, 110 Summer St (I-290 exit 16)) serves a free breakfast to guests, with rooms priced at $89 to $125. It's right next to I-290; look for the Aku-Aku sign.

The 73-room *Beechwood Hotel* (☎ 508-754-5789, 800-344-2589, fax 508-752-2060, 363 Plantation St), east of the city center along MA 9 near the Massachusetts Biotechnology Park, is a cylinder-shaped hotel with a good reputation, friendly service and luxury rooms priced from $109 to $149.

*Crowne Plaza-Worcester* (☎ 508-791-1600, 800-465-4329, 10 Lincoln Square) is well placed between the Centrum (see Entertainment, below) and the art museum, within walking distance to most of the city's

## Johnny Appleseed

John Chapman (1774-1845), later known as Johnny Appleseed, was born in Leominster, Massachusetts, a few months before his father was to fight with the minutemen at Concord. Around 1797 he began his legendary westward journey, planting apple seeds as he went.

Popular legend portrays Johnny Appleseed as a happy, barefoot hobo wearing a saucepan for a hat and scattering seeds from a sack over his shoulder, providing free apple trees – and apples – for the good of one and all.

The true story is no less fascinating. Early American land law required settlers to establish their claims by planting at least 50 apple trees on their claimed property, both to ensure the settler's nutrition and survival, and to discourage claims made without intention of settlement.

Chapman was a pioneer, setting out ahead of the waves of westbound settlers. He bought apple seeds in bulk from cider mills in Pennsylvania, and traveled west as far as Indiana, staking many claims, gaining title to the land, and cultivating the land as nurseries for the apple trees that would be required by the settlers.

For 50 years he sold seedlings to the settlers, donated others, and preached the tidings of the Swedenborgian Church of the New Jerusalem to one and all.

In March 1845, Chapman arrived in Fort Wayne, Indiana, to find someone damaging one of his nurseries. In the altercation that followed, Chapman died, putting an end to the planting, but giving a beginning to the legend.

In the early 1990s, the owners of Harvey Farm in Nova, Ohio, identified a huge, ancient apple tree on their property as one planted by Chapman. Soon after arborists took cuttings from it, the tree was destroyed in a storm. The cuttings survive, however, and have been propagated to produce 30,000 new trees, which will carry on the legend of Johnny Appleseed.

attractions, with luxury rooms priced at $119 for a single and $149 for a double.

## Places to Eat

The *Museum Café* (☎ 508-799-4406, 55 Salisbury St), in the Worcester Art Museum, is a good choice for light meals and moderate prices at a location you'll probably visit in any case. It serves soups, salads and sandwiches for $6 to $18. It is open daily for lunch, except Monday, and open for dinner on Thursday.

In the city center, many small shops and eateries offer food you can take out to the shady park in front of City Hall for an impromptu picnic during nice weather.

The amusingly named *Woosta Pizza* (☎ 508-791-3333, 8 Franklin St) has imaginative pizza toppings, such as asparagus and other seasonal produce. A slice and a soda can cost as little as $3.

*La Patisserie Bakery-Cafe* (☎ 508-756-1454, 250 Commercial St), just a half block northeast of the City Hall park, advertises 'gourmet sandwiches' that sell for $5 to $8.

*Brick Oven Bakery* (☎ 508-757-1611, 80 Franklin St), at Portland St, features good coffee and baked goods, as well as sandwiches and roll-ups for $4 to $9.

The light, attractive *Cafe Abba* (☎ 508-799-9999, 535 Main St), at Franklin St, serves up a medley of American southwest, New Orleans, Italian and Asian cuisines. Soup and a sandwich at lunch go for $7 to $12; main courses at dinner are slightly more.

*Applebee's Neighborhood Grill & Bar* (☎ 508-831-9911, 100 Front St), in the Worcester Common Outlets, is a family-oriented restaurant with main courses priced reasonably from $6 to $11. It's open until 11 pm.

The *Firehouse Cafe* (☎ 508-753-7899, 1 Exchange Place) has a full menu of pub grub, which you eat within view of an antique fire engine or, in good weather, outside in the brick courtyard. Expect to spend $7 to $10 for lunch, somewhat more at dinner.

## Entertainment

Worcester has made a name for itself by attracting big-name musical performers to its three high-quality venues: *Mechanics Hall* (☎ 508-752-0888) for classical and jazz performers, the huge *Centrum* (☎ 508-798-8888; for tickets 617-931-2000) for rock and other big-crowd acts and the *New Aud* (☎ 508-799-1250), formerly the Worcester Memorial Auditorium, for some of each and more. Check newspapers or call for current offerings.

## Getting There & Away

**Air** Worcester Regional Airport (☎ 508-799-1741, 888-359-9672), several miles due west of the city center along MA 122 (Chandler St), is served by US Airways Express and several smaller lines.

**Bus** Peter Pan Bus Lines (☎ 508-753-1515, 754-4600, 800-343-9999, www.peterpan-bus.com), 75 Madison St, has direct services between Worcester and Albany, Amherst, Bennington, Boston (and Logan Airport), Deerfield, Hartford, Holyoke, Hyannis, New York City, Northampton, Pittsfield, Plymouth, South Hadley, Springfield, Sturbridge, Toronto and Williamstown.

**Train** The daily *Lakeshore Limited*, operated by Amtrak (☎ 508-755-0356, 800-872-7245, www.amtrak.com), 45 Shrewsbury St, stops here on its route between Boston and Chicago. MBTA Commuter Rail (☎ 617-722-3200, 800-392-6099, www.mbta.com) operates five trains from Boston to Worcester on weekdays, all in the afternoon and evening; and five trains from Worcester to Boston, all in the morning and early afternoon. The three trains in each direction on weekends are in the morning, early afternoon and evening.

**Car** Driving details for Worcester are:

| destination | mileage | hr:min |
| --- | --- | --- |
| Boston, MA | 40 miles | 1:00 |
| Hartford, CT | 63 miles | 1:30 |
| Lenox, MA | 90 miles | 1:45 |
| New York, NY | 172 miles | 3:30 |
| Northampton, MA | 54 miles | 1:15 |
| Springfield, MA | 51 miles | 1:00 |
| Sturbridge, MA | 22 miles | 0:30 |

## STURBRIDGE

The small, central Massachusetts town of Sturbridge kept much of its colonial character until after WWII. When the Mass Pike (I-90) and I-84 were built just south of the town, change came all at once.

Sturbridge reclaimed its past in a unique manner. To take advantage of the handy highway transport, the town became host to one of the country's first 'living museums.' Old buildings were moved here from throughout the region, and others were replicated, as needed, to recreate a typical 1830s New England village. Rather than exhibit labels, this museum has 'interpreters' – people who dress in costume, ply the trades and occupations of their ancestors and explain to visitors what they are doing and why.

The concept of the living museum was new when Old Sturbridge Village was built. It has now spread throughout New England and the world, but this remains one of its best exemplars.

Sturbridge is very busy with visitors in summer and the autumn foliage season. Traffic increases exponentially during the three times per year (early May, early July and early September) when the Antiques and Flea Market is held in Brimfield, 5 miles east along US 20.

### Orientation

There are actually three Sturbridges. The first one you see is the least attractive, the commercial strip along US 20 (Main St) just south of I-90 exit 9, which has most of the town's motels and restaurants. The second is Sturbridge as it used to be, best seen at the town common, backed by the historic Publick House Inn, on MA 131, a half mile southeast of US 20. The third is Old Sturbridge Village, entered from US 20.

### Information

The Sturbridge Area Tourist Association information office (SATA, ☎ 508-347-7594, 800-628-8379), is opposite the entrance to Old Sturbridge Village at 380 Main St (US 20). The Peter Pan/Trailways bus stop is here as well. The SATA is a division of the Tri-Community Area Chamber of Commerce, whose name you will see on the sign.

### Old Sturbridge Village

During the first half of the 20th century, two brothers, Albert Wells and J Cheney Wells, lived in Southbridge and carried on a very successful optics business. They were enthusiastic collectors of antiques – so enthusiastic, in fact, that by the end of WWII their collections left no free space in their homes.

They bought 200 acres of forest and meadow in Sturbridge and began to move old buildings to this land. Opened in 1946, Old Sturbridge Village (OSV; ☎ 508-347-3362, www.osv.org) is an authentically recreated New England town of the 1830s, with 40 restored structures filled with the Wells' antiques.

Authenticity is the key watchword here: the country store is stocked with products brought from throughout the world by New England sailing ships. Trades and crafts are carried out with authentic tools and materials. The livestock has even been back-bred to approximate the breeds of animals – smaller, shaggier, thinner – that lived on New England farms a century and a half ago. The OSV library has more than 20,000 manuscripts and books describing various aspects of early-19th-century life in the region.

Plan at least a day for your visit. OSV is open every day from April to early November from 9 am to 5 pm; in March, the rest of November and in December it's closed Monday, but open other days from 10 am to 4 pm. Admission costs $16 for adults, $15 for seniors 65-plus, $8 for children ages six to 15; under six are free. Admission is good for two consecutive days. Food services in the village include the Bullard Tavern, with buffet and à la carte service for full meals, light meals and snacks. There is also a picnic grove with grills and a play area.

### St Anne Shrine

Monsignor Pie Neveu, a Roman Catholic Assumptionist bishop, ministered to a diocese in Russia from 1906 to 1936. While at his post, Bishop Neveu collected valuable

Russian icons, a hobby no doubt made easier by the fall of the old order and the advent of secularist communism. Bishop Neveu's collection was further augmented by acquisitions brought to the USA by the Assumptionist fathers who served as chaplains at the US embassy in Moscow between 1934 and 1941. The collection was installed at the St Anne Shrine in 1971.

Since WWII, it has been illegal to export icons from Russia, so the collection of 60 rare works preserved at the St Anne Shrine (☎ 508-347-7338), 16 Church St, is a treasure. The icon museum, open daily from 9 am to 6 pm (free, donations accepted) is one building in the shrine complex just off US 20 at the western end of Sturbridge, in the neighborhood sometimes called Fiskdale. Watch for the sign just east of the intersection of US 20 and MA 148.

## Winery & Brewery

Ten miles southeast of town along MA 131 in West Dudley, just north of the Connecticut state line, is Mellea Winery (☎ 508-943-5166), 108 Old Southbridge Rd.

Joe Compagnone, who is a local chemist-industrialist, has planted his vinifera and French-American hybrid vines on a gravelly south-facing hillside and produces a variety of wines, from table-grade to premium, using his own grapes and others imported from southeastern Massachusetts, Long Island and Oregon. White wines are favored, but there are drinkable reds as well. Come for a free tour and tasting from late May through December, Wednesday through Sunday from noon to 5 pm.

If beer is your beverage, visit the Hyland Orchard & Brewery (☎ 508-347-7500), a 150-acre farm with its own craft brewery producing Sturbridge Amber Ale. To find Hyland, go west on Main St (US 20) to Arnold Rd, turn right and go 2 miles north on Arnold Rd to the farm.

## Brimfield Antique Shows

Six miles west of Sturbridge along US 20 is Brimfield, a mecca for collectors of antique furniture, toys, tools and collectibles. Up to 5000 sellers and 35,000 buyers come from a dozen states and beyond to do business in 23 farmers' fields here, the largest outdoor antiques fair in the USA. The town has numerous shops open year-round, but the major antiques and collectibles shows are held in early to mid-May, early July and early September, usually on the second weekends in those months. Actually, there are 20 separate fairs set up in fields surrounding the town. Admission into the grounds costs $3 on weekdays, $5 on the weekend.

If you're interested, contact the Brimfield Antique Show Promoters' Association (☎ 203-763-3760, www.brimfieldshow.com) or the SATA (☎ 508-347-7594, 800-628-8379) for dates and details. Be sure to have advance hotel reservations.

## Places to Stay

Many lodgings fill on weekends in summer and, especially, in autumn. When the Brimfield Antiques and Flea Market is in progress (see above), local lodging prices rise substantially and advance reservations are necessary.

**Camping** *Wells State Park* (☎ 508-347-9257), MA 49 (Mountain Rd), Sturbridge, north of I-90, offers 59 wooded sites on its 1470 acres at $8 to $10 for up to five people, the higher price being for a lakefront site. You can reserve your site in advance with a two-night deposit.

*Yogi Bear's Sturbridge Jellystone Park* (☎ 508-347-9570), River Rd (I-84 exit 2), has 400 sites and many amusements, including two pools, a hot tub, waterslide and other entertainment. It's close to Sturbridge, but fairly expensive. Rates range from $38 to $42, depending upon hookups. Rustic cabins capable of sleeping up to five people are rented for $58 to $74 per night. For cheaper sites, try *Outdoor World Resort* (☎ 508-347-7156, 19 Mashapaug Rd), Sturbridge; *Quinebaug Cove Campground* (☎ 413-245-9525, 49E Brimfield Holland Rd), Brimfield; or the *Village Green Campground* (☎ 413-245-3504, 228 Sturbridge Rd), Brimfield.

There are also several private campgrounds in Charlton, south of US 20 about

8 miles east of Sturbridge. Try *Applewood Campground* (☎ 508-248-7017, 44 King Rd) with 60 sites.

**Motels** If you don't have a reservation when you arrive in Sturbridge, go to the SATA information office (see the Information section for Sturbridge, above) and look through the motel brochures. Some include coupons that are good for special rates or discounts.

The cheapest lodgings are the smaller motels off US 20 (Main St) such as the *Sturbridge Heritage Motel* (☎ 508-347-3943, 499-501 Main St), a mile west of OSV across from the Whistling Swan restaurant, charging $45 to $50 for its eight relatively quiet rooms. The family-run *Village Motel* (☎ 508-347-3049), on Main St (more or less across the road from Sturbridge Heritage and down an unpaved lane), is almost as cheap ($55) and even quieter.

*Super 8 Motel* (☎ 508-347-9000, 800-800-8000, 358 Main St) is not far off I-84 exit 3B, close to OSV. It has a pool and charges $79, breakfast included.

Three other budget motels are about 2 miles from OSV on MA 131 southeast of the Publick House, up the hill and past the Sturbridge Plaza shopping center: *Green Acres Motel* (☎ 508-347-3496, 888-545-3510, fax 508-347-2021), on MA 131, just past Rom's Restaurant at Shepard Rd, has rooms for $68 to $76; *Rodeway Inn* (☎ 508-347-9673, 800-228-2000, fax 508-347-2475), on MA 131, for $58 to $85; and the most basic of the lot, the *Sir Francis Motel* (☎ 508-347-9514, 140 Main St), a bit farther along, charging $50 for a double room.

*Sturbridge Motor Inn* (☎ 508-347-3391), on Haynes St, via I-84 exit 2 then MA 15, between the common and OSV, has a variety of rooms priced from $75 to $85; the more expensive rooms are larger and quieter, with king-size beds.

*Holiday Inn Express* (☎ 508-347-5141, fax 347-2034, 478 Main St), less than a mile west of OSV, has 64 comfortable rooms at $99, light breakfast included.

*Econo Lodge* (☎ 508-347-2324, 800-446-6900, 682 Main St), 2 miles west of OSV,

charges $75 to $80 for its 48 rooms, with pool, playground and coin-operated laundry.

*Best Western American Motor Lodge* (☎ 508-347-9121), on US 20 just off I-90 exit 9 and I-84 exit 3B, a half mile east of OSV, has 55 rooms for $95 in summer. Services include a heated pool, saunas and coin-operated laundry.

*Old Sturbridge Village Lodges & Oliver Wight House* (☎ 508-347-3327, 800-733-1830, fax 508-347-3018, www.osv.org), on Main St, next to the entrance to OSV and administered by it, is a modern 47-unit motel in updated colonial style. Rooms cost $75 to $110 per night in the lodges, and $90 to $130 per night in the Oliver Wight House (an adjacent white clapboard inn built in 1789) and Dennison Cottage.

*Sturbridge Coach Motor Lodge* (☎ 508-347-7327, fax 347-2954, 408 Main St), a pristine, attractive and quiet motel on a hill above the highway just west of OSV, has 54 rooms priced at $70 to $80.

**Inns & B&Bs** The SATA (☎ 508-347-7594, 800-628-8379) can direct you to B&Bs that are members of its association, and it can help you make same-day reservations if you stop in at the information office.

*Publick House Inn* (☎ 508-347-3313, 800-782-5425, fax 508-347-1246), on MA 131 along the common, is Sturbridge's most famous historic inn (1771), now a mini-industry with frequent weekend theme programs, several dining rooms and 17 comfortable guest rooms for $90 to $155. The *Colonel Ebenezer Crafts Inn*, an eight-room B&B operated by the Publick House, costs the same. Adjoining the Publick House (and run by it) is *Country Motor Lodge*, with lower-priced rooms and suites for $70 to $130.

*Commonwealth Cottage* (☎ 508-347-7708, 11 Summit Ave) is a big Queen-Anne-style Victorian in a quiet location with three guest rooms (one with private bath) priced at $95, breakfast included. Follow US 20 West and, just past the MA 148 intersection, turn left onto Commonwealth Ave. Bear left at the Heritage Green sign.

Other Sturbridge B&Bs with rooms going for $75 to $95 include *Bethany B&B*

**MASSACHUSETTS**

*(☎ 508-347-5993, 9 McGregory Rd)* and ***The Birch Tree** (☎ 508-347-8218, at 522 Leadmine Rd)*.

**Sturbridge Country Inn** *(☎ 508-347-5503, fax 347-5319, 530 Main St)* is a stately Greek Revival mansion about a mile west of OSV on US 20 in the commercial district. Its nine sybaritic rooms all have fireplaces, whirlpool baths, TV and air-con, and cost $79 to $169. There's a bit of traffic noise in front.

## Places to Eat

US 20 is sprinkled with the usual fast-food outlets. Most of the local independent restaurants are on the same road.

For low prices and good food, escape the tourist crowds by following US 20 to the east side of I-84, where you'll find the **Heritage Family Restaurant & Pizza** *(☎ 508-347-7673)*, on Charlton Rd, where you can fill up with a pizza, grinder, calzone, salad or fish and chips for $7 or so.

**Annie's Country Kitchen** *(☎ 508-347-2320, 140 Main St (MA 131))* is the place for an early breakfast – it's open at 5 am – such as the lumberjack special of ham and three eggs, toast, homefries, juice and coffee for under $5. Lunch is served every day but Saturday, and simple early suppers Wednesday through Saturday.

For a complete meal, try **Rom's** *(☎ 508-347-3349)*, on MA 131, a mile or so southeast of the Publick House, across from the shopping center. This Sturbridge institution serves up big portions of its traditional Italian-American fare (and drinks) for moderate prices – plan on about $15 to $20 for a full meal.

The much-advertised **Publick House** *(☎ 508-347-3313)*, on the common, has a decent dining room with traditional American dishes; try the lobster pie. Full three-course dinners with drinks can be had for $32 to $50, less for lunch. **Ebenezer's Tavern** is the venue for less formal meals. Lighter meals are served on the terrace in good weather, where, if you're lucky, there may be a musician to serenade you.

The **Whistling Swan** *(☎ 508-347-2321, 502 Main St)*, in a Greek Revival mansion (1855) and about a mile west of OSV, serves a menu of traditional American and continental dishes with inventive twists. A full dinner with wine might cost $35 to $60 per person. The restaurant's **Ugly Duckling** loft is less formal, offering both lighter dishes and lower prices.

Just west of the Sturbridge Coach Motor Lodge, off US 20, **Cedar Street Restaurant** *(☎ 508-347-5800, 12 Cedar St)* offers innovative, delicious New American preparations of filet mignon, rack of lamb, pork loin and seafood. The menu includes a good number of tasty vegetarian dishes as well. Prices are moderate for the quality: $25 to $40 for a full dinner. It opens for dinner – the only meal served – at 5 pm. The Cedar Street Restaurant is closed Sunday.

**The Casual Cafe** *(☎ 508-347-2281, 538 Main St)* serves popular Italian dishes such as linguine in white clam sauce and *tortellini con carciofi* (artichokes) at very moderate prices: $8 to $12 for main courses. Dinner is the only meal served here, Tuesday through Saturday.

If you're up for taking a drive, follow US 20 (2 miles west of OSV) to MA 148 North; 7 miles along, turn left (west) onto MA 9 and go 5 miles to the **Salem Cross Inn** *(☎ 508-867-2345)*, Ware Rd, West Brookfield. The tranquil inn, built in 1705 and set on 600 acres of farmland, is a welcome respite from the vehicular and commercial fury of Sturbridge. Traditional New England meals are served noon to 9 pm Tuesday through Friday, 5 to 10 pm Saturday, noon to 8 pm Sunday and holidays, closed Monday (except holidays). A typical dinner costs $40 up to $60 per person, drinks, tax and tip included.

## Getting There & Away

**Bus** Peter Pan Bus Lines *(☎ 508-347-7594, 800-343-9999, www.peterpan-bus.com)* runs one-day excursion buses right to OSV from Boston *(☎ 617-426-7838)*, via Worcester and from New York City *(☎ 212-564-8484)* via Hartford and Springfield. For other bus routes you must connect at Boston or Springfield. The Peter Pan bus stop is opposite the entrance to OSV, at the SATA information office.

MASSACHUSETTS

**Car** Driving details for Sturbridge are:

| destination | mileage | hr:min |
|---|---|---|
| Boston, MA | 65 miles | 1:20 |
| Hartford, CT | 42 miles | 0:55 |
| Lenox, MA | 73 miles | 1:30 |
| New York, NY | 165 miles | 3:30 |
| Springfield, MA | 32 miles | 0:45 |
| Worcester, MA | 18 miles | 0:25 |

# Pioneer Valley

The Connecticut River valley is known as the Pioneer Valley because of its early settlement. Within a few years after the Pilgrims landed at Plymouth in 1620, fur-traders and settlers were making their way up the great river, deep into the center of New England. Springfield and other valley towns later became pioneers of technical advancement.

For information on the Connecticut River Valley in Massachusetts, check out www .virtual-valley.com or www.valleyvisitor.com.

## SPRINGFIELD

Springfield, the largest city in western Massachusetts, is at the region's transportation nexus, where the traditional east-west route from Boston to Albany crosses the Connecticut River valley. Its 19th-century industrial might brought its residents the wealth to build several excellent museums (closed Monday and Tuesday), a library and a grand symphony hall. Basketball players all over the world pay tribute to Springfield with every shot: the game was conceived here. Springfield's eventful history is typical of most New England crossroads towns.

Like nearby Hartford, Springfield is a city of commuters. The stately Romanesque buildings around Court Square and the nearby modern office blocks are populated with workers who flee the city center in cars at the end of the workday. There is little nightlife, making Springfield perfect for a day stop on your way to Northampton, Amherst or the Berkshires. You may also choose to stay in Northampton or Amherst and visit Springfield on a day trip.

## History

By 1636, pioneers and settlers had come up the Connecticut River to Springfield to trade for furs with the Omiskandoagwiak ('Wolf People,' the Connecticut River Valley Indians) and to farm the valley's fertile alluvial soil. Later, industry sprang up here because the river provided cheap waterpower and transport to the markets of Hartford, New York and Philadelphia.

Springfield's prosperity was assured in 1777 when General George Washington and his chief of artillery, Colonel Henry Knox, decided upon this spot for the USA's first arsenal. Though centrally located and easy to access, it was safely distant from the major theaters of the Revolutionary War. Muskets, cannons, and other arms were stored here and paper cartridges were manufactured for them. After independence was won, Springfield continued to be the new nation's major arsenal.

**Shays' Rebellion** In 1786, the American Revolutionary War had been won, but the new nation found itself suffering a severe economic depression. The paper money issued to fund the war was still in circulation, but rarely accepted at face value.

The Boston merchants and traders, for whom 'sound money' was essential, led a movement to adopt a gold standard. Public officials with fat salaries and Boston lawyers acting on behalf of the rich went along. But farmers in western Massachusetts, who could pay in kind, were opposed to a gold standard. Country people were burdened with heavy land and poll taxes, the foreclosure of mortgages on their farms and debtors' prison; those without property could not vote at all.

The discontent broke out in rebellion on August 29, 1786 when Daniel Shays (1747?-1825), formerly a captain in the Revolutionary army, led armed men to prevent the sitting of the courts in Northampton that were handing down judgments against debtors. Shays and his followers planned their moves in an Amherst tavern. Their action forced even the state supreme court to adjourn its session in Springfield.

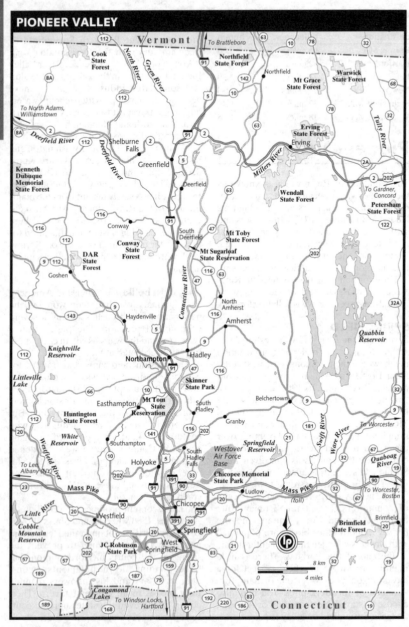

# PIONEER VALLEY

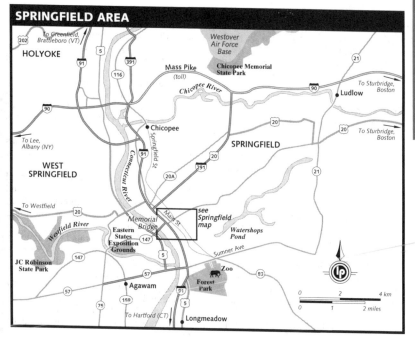

**SPRINGFIELD AREA**

Early in 1787, Governor Bowdoin sent General Benjamin Lincoln and 4400 men to put down the rebellion. As they marched to Springfield, Daniel Shays and his 1200 men attacked the federal armory on January 25, but were repulsed by the Massachusetts state militia and suffered several casualties.

Put on the defensive, they retreated to Petersham, where Lincoln's troops routed them in February, capturing many. Shays himself escaped to Vermont.

Shays' Rebellion alerted Boston to the dire conditions in the western part of the state. Bowdoin was driven from office, and the senate became more sensitive to the needs of the rest of the state. Governor John Hancock later pardoned Daniel Shays and other rebellion leaders. Similar rebellions in other states influenced public opinion in the direction of a strong federal government capable of preserving public order.

## Orientation

Take I-91 exit 6 northbound or exit 7 southbound, follow it to State St (east) then Main St (north), and you'll be at Court Square in the heart of Springfield, a good place to start your explorations. Museum Quadrangle is a few blocks east, and the Tower Square complex, which includes the Marriott Hotel, is two blocks north. The Springfield Armory is a 10-minute walk east and the Basketball Hall of Fame is a 10-minute walk southwest.

## Information

The Greater Springfield Convention and Visitors Bureau (☎ 413-787-1548, 800-723-1548, www.valleyvisitor.com), 1441 Main Street, Springfield, MA 01103, is a half block north of Court Square.

There's a brochure and map rack next to the snack stand (and near the public toilets) in the lower lobby of City Hall, the grand

Corinthian palace with the tall campanile on the north side of Court Square. For more information, visit the city's own website at www.ci.springfield.ma.us.

The post office is on Main St at the corner of Liberty St, eight blocks north of Court Square.

## Court Square

Court Square is surrounded by fine buildings, including Symphony Hall and City Hall on its north side and, to the west, the First Congregational Church (1819) and the granite Hall of Justice (Hampden County Superior Courthouse) by Henry Hudson Richardson, inspired by Venice's Palazzo Vecchio. William Pynchon, who led the group of Puritans who settled here in 1636, and incorporated the town five years later, is honored with a statue.

## Museum Quadrangle

The Springfield Library and Museums (☎ 413-263-6800, www.spfldlibmus.org), 220 State St, are gathered around Museum Quadrangle, two blocks northeast of Court Square. Look for Merrick Park, at the entrance to the quadrangle, and Augustus Saint-Gaudens' statue *The Puritan*. All of these museums are open noon to 4 pm Wednesday through Sunday. Admission costs $4 for adults, $1 for children aged six to 16, free for children under six.

The **George Walter Vincent Smith Art Museum** was established by a man who amassed a fortune manufacturing carriages, and then spent his money on works of art and artifacts. There are fine 19th-century American and European paintings, textiles, ceramics and works in several other media. The Japanese armor collection is among the finest outside of Asia.

The **Museum of Fine Arts** has more than 20 galleries filled with lesser paintings of the great European masters and the better works of lesser masters. Among the masterworks here is Erastus Salisbury Field's *The Rise of the American Republic*, hung above the main stairway. In the impressionist and expressionist galleries, look for Monet's *Haystacks* and artworks by Degas, Dufy,

Gauguin, Pissarro, Renoir, Rouault and Vlaminck. In the contemporary gallery there are works by George Bellows, Lyonel Feininger, Georgia O'Keeffe and Picasso. Modern sculptors featured include Leonard Baskin and Richard Stankiewicz.

The **Springfield Science Museum** is a good place for children. The Dinosaur Hall has a full-size replica of a Tyrannosaurus rex. The African Hall has many exhibits about Africa's peoples, animals and ecology. The historic Seymour Planetarium has eight weekly shows (which cost a few dollars).

At the **Connecticut Valley Historical Museum** are exhibits on the decorative and domestic arts of the Connecticut River valley from 1636 to the present. There are collections of furniture, pewter and glass, as well as four rooms decorated authentically in period styles: a 17th-century kitchen, a Federal-period dining room and two rooms from an early-19th-century tavern.

The **Springfield City Library**, at the corner of State and Chestnut Sts, is open noon to 5 pm (closed Monday), and has more than a million books, records and videos in its system.

## Springfield Armory

The Springfield Armory National Historic Site (☎ 413-734-8551, www.nps.gov/spar), 1 Armory Square, Federal St at State St, preserves what remains of the USA's greatest federal armory. During its heyday in the Civil War, 3400 people worked in the armory, turning out 1000 muskets a day. Springfield Technical Community College now occupies many of the former firearm factories and officers' quarters, but exhibits in several of the old buildings recall the armory's golden age quite effectively.

The Armory is a 10-minute walk eastward from Court Square along State St past Museum Quadrangle. It's open from 10 am to 4:30 pm, closed Monday and Tuesday. Take I-291 exit 3 to Armory St and follow it to Federal St. Admission is free.

On the site, the **Small Arms Museum** holds one of the world's largest collections of firearms, including lots of Remingtons,

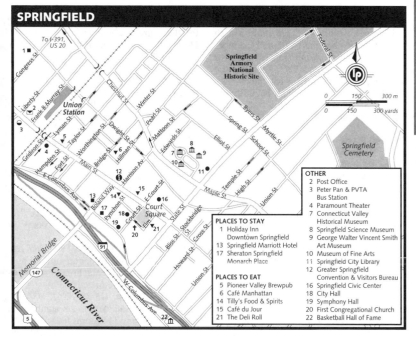

SPRINGFIELD

To I-391,
US 20

Springfield
Armory
National
Historic Site

Union
Station

Springfield
Cemetery

0        150        300 m
0        150        300 yards

**OTHER**
2  Post Office
3  Peter Pan & PVTA
   Bus Station
4  Paramount Theater
7  Connecticut Valley
   Historical Museum
8  Springfield Science Museum
9  George Walter Vincent Smith
   Art Museum
10 Museum of Fine Arts
11 Springfield City Library
12 Greater Springfield
   Convention & Visitors Bureau
16 Springfield Civic Center
18 City Hall
19 Symphony Hall
20 First Congregational Church
22 Basketball Hall of Fame

**PLACES TO STAY**
1  Holiday Inn
   Downtown Springfield
13 Springfield Marriott Hotel
17 Sheraton Springfield
   Monarch Place

**PLACES TO EAT**
5  Pioneer Valley Brewpub
6  Café Manhattan
14 Tilly's Food & Spirits
15 Café du Jour
21 The Deli Roll

Colts, Lugers and even weapons from the 1600s. Don't miss the Organ of Rifles.

## Basketball Hall of Fame

The Naismith Memorial Basketball Hall of Fame (☎ 413-781-6500, www.hoophall.com), 1150 W Columbus Ave at Union St, is one mile south of I-91 exit 7, on the east side of I-91. The hall of fame is an active place where you can shoot baskets, feel the center-court excitement in a wraparound cinema and learn about the sport's history and great players. Plan at least an hour's stop, though you could easily stay all morning. It's open 9:30 am to 5:30 pm daily (9 am to 7 pm in July and August). Admission costs $8 for adults, $5 seniors and children seven to 14.

## Indian Motorcycle Museum Hall of Fame

Springfield claims the birth of the gasoline-powered motorcycle, invented here in 1901.

Motorcycles were produced here until 1953 by the Indian Motorcycle Company, which once had a sprawling factory complex that turned out motorbikes, large motorcycles, armored police motorcycles, military cycles with rifle holsters and motorcycles with side-cars for sweeping the streets, putting out fires, carrying paying passengers and delivering merchandise. The company also made cars, aircraft engines, air-conditioners and, in 1947, the 'snowboat,' a precursor of the snowmobile.

The last of the company's buildings, once the engineering division, is now the museum (☎ 413-737-2624, www.sidecar.com .indian/), 33 Hendee St, with the largest and finest collection of Indian motorcycles and memorabilia in the world. There are other makes as well, and lots of funky period mementos. All of the machines are in working order (note the oil-drip pans underneath), and are taken out and run every three months. If you like bikes, don't miss this place. It's fascinating.

It's open 10 am to 5 pm daily March through November and 1 to 4 pm December through February. Admission costs $4 for adults, $1 for children six to 12. To find the museum, take I-291 exit 4 (St James Ave) then follow the signs north on Page Blvd to Hendee St. The museum is a low brick building in an industrial area.

## Forest Park

Forest Park (☎ 413-787-6440), 2 miles south of the Springfield shopping center off of Sumner Ave (MA 83), is an 800-acre swath of lawns, woods, gardens, ponds, fountains, walking and horse trails, swimming pools and tennis courts. Walkers and bikers are admitted free; cars must pay a small admission charge. The Zoo at Forest Park (☎ 413-733-2251), open daily from 10 am to 5 pm for a small fee, has more than 200 animals, a miniature train and educational field trips.

## Cruises

Springfield's Peter Pan Bus Lines operates the Peter Pan River Bus (☎ 413-746-6679, 877-746-6679, www.peterpan-bus.com) that departs Springfield's River Front Park off W Columbus Avenue at the foot of State St. The Connecticut River cruises are held May through October. The 1½-hour cruises cost $10 for adults, $6 for children three to nine; families enjoy special discounts.

## Special Events

In mid-September, sleepy West Springfield, on the west bank of the river, explodes into activity with the annual 'The Big E,' the Eastern States Exposition (☎ 413-737-2443, 800-334-2443 for ticket orders only, fax 413-787-0271, www.thebige.com), 1305 Memorial Ave (MA 147). The fair goes on for two weeks, with farm exhibits, horse shows, carnival rides, regional and ethnic food, parades, Wild West and high-diver shows, a circus, a petting zoo and country and pop music performances. Each of the six New England states hosts a large pavilion with its own exhibits as well.

There's an admission charge that changes annually. Once you're in the fairgrounds, all the shows are free; carnival rides cost extra. Hotels fill up when the Big E is in session, particularly on weekends.

## Places to Stay

*Berkshire Bed & Breakfast* (☎ 413-268-7244, fax 268-7243) will help you make a reservation at a small B&B in a historic neighborhood of Springfield such as Maple Hill or Forest Park. Rooms cost $70 to $120 double, breakfast included.

Most of Springfield's inexpensive motels are actually in West Springfield on or near Riverdale St off I-91 exit 13, near the intersection with US 5 and I-391.

*Red Roof Inn* (☎ 413-731-1010, 800-843-7663, 1254 Riverdale St) has 111 rooms for $67 to $84.

*Hampton Inn* (☎ 413-732-1300, 800-426-7866, 1011 Riverdale St) has an outdoor pool and offers free continental breakfast with its 126 rooms, which are priced at $99.

*Quality Inn* (☎ 413-739-7261, 800-228-5151, 1150 Riverdale St) has a restaurant, an outdoor pool, and 114 rooms for $65 to $95.

The hotels in downtown Springfield tend to be large and luxurious.

*Holiday Inn Downtown Springfield* (☎ 413-781-0900, 800-465-4329, 117 Dwight St), at Congress St, just over a half mile north of Court Square, has 245 rooms for $109 to $139.

The city's top two hotels are right in the city center facing one another across Boland Way, at I-91 exit 6 northbound or exit 7 southbound, a block north of Court Square. The 304-room *Sheraton Springfield Monarch Place* (☎ 413-781-1010, 800-426-9004) offers rooms priced at $119 to $139 per night, and the 265-room *Springfield Marriott Hotel* (☎ 413-781-7111, 800-228-9290) has rooms for $124 to $174.

## Places to Eat

Because it is a commuter town, downtown Springfield has few good restaurants. Other than those in the big hotels, there are only small lunch places facing Court Square or on nearby streets.

*The Deli Roll* (☎ 413-827-7007, 17 Elm St), on the south side of Court Square, sells sandwiches and light luncheon plates for $5 to $8. Most customers come for take-out, but there are several tables inside, and more on the sidewalk in front during nice weather.

For other luncheon fare, walk north on Main St from Court Square.

*Café du Jour* (1369 Main St) is just north of Court St, serving good coffee and light meals to the office workers in the towers nearby.

*Tilly's Food & Spirits* (☎ 413-732-3613, 1390 Main St) is an Irish pub serving soups, pasta, steaks and American favorites at moderate prices: you can get a filling lunch for $10 to $15.

*Pioneer Valley Brewpub* (☎ 413-732-2739, 51-59 Taylor St), at Main St four blocks north of Court Square, is Springfield's art deco brewpub and bistro, serving its own beer and full lunch ($6 to $12) and dinner ($10 to $20) menus inside the dining room and at the courtyard tables.

A bright spot in the food picture is *Café Manhattan* (☎ 413-737-7913, 301 Bridge St), at Barnes St, an upscale storefront bistro 2½ blocks north of Court Square serving traditional American and continental cuisine for lunch and dinner daily except Sunday. Special luncheon plates are priced around $8 to $11, dinners about twice as much.

## Entertainment

Pick up a copy of *The Valley Advocate* (www.valleyadvocate.com), a free weekly newspaper, for entertainment listings.

Recitals and concerts by the members of the *Springfield Symphony Orchestra* (☎ 413-787-6600) are held year-round in the grand Symphony Hall, just off Court Square.

For theater, try *Stage West* (☎ 413-781-2340), on Bridge St (off Main St) in Columbus Center.

## Pioneers of Invention

In 1794, President George Washington selected Springfield as a location for one of two federal armories that would manufacture muskets for the US Army. The first musket produced here in 1795 was a copy of the French 'Charleville,' popular with US soldiers during the Revolutionary War.

During the 19th century, Yankee ingenuity went to work at Springfield. In 1819, Thomas Blanchard invented a wood-turning lathe to produce identical gun stocks quickly and cheaply. Percussion ignition replaced the flintlock, and breech-loaders replaced muzzle-loaders. The Model 1903 Springfield rifle was what American doughboys carried into battle in WWI, and the M-1 Garand, built in Springfield, armed the troops in WWII.

After WWII, the armory evolved into a design and testing laboratory for small arms, machine guns, grenade launchers and similar armaments, but these were built elsewhere by private contractors. Finally, in 1968, the Department of Defense decided to close down the armory. It had served the military needs of the nation for almost two centuries.

Arms were not Springfield's only contribution to American life and world culture. It was here, in 1891, that Dr James Naismith conceived the game of basketball, now played and loved around the world. Appropriately, Springfield is home to the Naismith Memorial Basketball Hall of Fame.

Springfield's impressive list of inventions goes on: the monkey wrench, steel-bladed ice skates, the USA's first planetarium and the gasoline-powered motorcycle (1901). Another invention was the first practical internal-combustion engine automobile, built in 1894 on the top floor of the building at 41 Taylor St by the Duryea brothers, Charles and Frank. For a short time in the 1930s the world's most elegant auto, the Rolls-Royce, was also assembled in this city.

The modern building east of Court Square is the **Springfield Civic Center** (☎ *413-787-6600, 1277 Main St*), a venue for exhibits, rock concerts and athletic events. A smaller venue for musical and stand-up comedy performances is the restored old **Paramount Theater** (☎ *413-734-5874, 1700 Main St*).

**Pioneer Valley Brewpub** (see Places to Eat) serves up its own brews.

## Getting There & Away

**Air** Springfield is served by the Bradley International Airport (☎ 860-292-2000, www.bradleyairport.com) in Windsor Locks, Connecticut, 18 miles to the south. See Getting There & Away under Hartford in the Connecticut chapter for details.

**Bus** Springfield is the home of Peter Pan Bus Lines (☎ 413-781-2900, 800-343-9999, www.peterpan-bus.com), which serves Massachusetts, New England, New York City, Philadelphia, Baltimore and Washington, DC. The bus station is at 1776 Main St at Liberty St, a 10-minute walk north of Court Square. There are daily buses from Springfield to Albany, Amherst, Bennington, Boston, Deerfield, Hartford, Holyoke, Lee, Lenox, New Haven, New York City, North Adams, Pittsfield, South Hadley, Williamstown and Worcester.

Peter Pan's service connecting the college towns of the Pioneer Valley (Amherst, Holyoke, Northampton and South Hadley) with Springfield and Boston is frequent, with 15 buses daily. Buses run from each of these towns to Springfield almost hourly from 5 am to 6 pm, with two additional late-evening buses. From Springfield, frequent connecting buses go on to Boston. There is also direct service via Boston between the Pioneer Valley towns, Springfield and Hyannis.

The Pioneer Valley Transportation Authority (PVTA; ☎ 413-781-7882), 1776 Main St in the Peter Pan terminal, runs 43 routes to 23 communities in the region.

---

## Having a Ball

The Pioneer Valley seems to be the cradle of big-ball games: both basketball and volleyball were invented here.

Born in Canada, James Naismith (1861-1939) graduated from McGill University in Montreal, then came to Springfield to work as a physical education instructor at the International YMCA Training School (later Springfield College). He wanted to develop a good, fast team sport that could be played indoors during the long New England winters. About December 1, 1891, he took two empty wooden half-bushel peach baskets and nailed them to opposite walls in the college gymnasium. He wrote down 13 rules for the game (12 of which are still used), and basketball was born.

Students at the college took to the new game enthusiastically. News of the game's invention spread fast and far, as students carried their enthusiasm with them when they went home for Christmas vacation that year.

Naismith went on to become basketball coach at the University of Kansas. His successor in that post, Forrest Allen (1885-1974), worked to have basketball included in the Olympic Games, and was successful in 1936.

Volleyball was invented in nearby Holyoke by William G Morgan, who worked for the Holyoke YMCA. It was intended to be an indoor game for businessmen who found basketball too strenuous. Morgan named his new game 'mintonette,' but a professor at Springfield College thought 'volleyball' more appropriate, because of the back-and-forth movement of the ball.

The rules of the game were first published in 1897, and the United States Volleyball Association was formed in 1922.

Bonanza Bus Lines (☎ 800-556-3815, www.bonanzabus.com) runs a route connecting Providence, Springfield, Lee, Lenox, Pittsfield, Williamstown and Bennington.

**Train** Amtrak's (☎ 800-872-7245, www.amtrak .com) *Lakeshore Limited* between Boston and Chicago stops at Springfield's Union Station (☎ 413-785-4230), 66 Lyman St, a 10-minute walk north of Court Square. See the beginning of this chapter for details on trains.

**Car** Driving details for Springfield are:

| destination | mileage | hr:min |
| --- | --- | --- |
| Albany, NY | 82 miles | 1:40 |
| Amherst, MA | 24 miles | 0:40 |
| Boston, MA | 87 miles | 1:45 |
| Hartford, CT | 25 miles | 0:30 |
| Holyoke, MA | 9 miles | 0:15 |
| Lenox, MA | 40 miles | 0:55 |
| New York, NY | 134 miles | 2:45 |
| Northampton, MA | 18 miles | 0:25 |
| South Hadley, MA | 15 miles | 0:23 |
| Sturbridge, MA | 32 miles | 0:45 |
| Worcester, MA | 52 miles | 1:00 |

## Getting Around

For airport transport, contact Valley Transporter (☎ 413-733-9700, 413-253-1350) or Peter Pan Bus Lines (☎ 413-781-2900).

## SOUTH HADLEY

North of Springfield is Hampshire County, the central region of the Pioneer Valley, sometimes known as the Five College area because it is home to Amherst College, Hampshire College, Mount Holyoke College, Smith College and the University of Massachusetts at Amherst.

The quiet town of South Hadley, 15 miles north of Springfield on MA 116, is the most southerly of the Five College towns, with the USA's oldest college for women, Mount Holyoke College, at its center.

With views of hills, fields and old tobacco barns, MA 116 between South Hadley and Amherst, and MA 47 between South Hadley and Hadley, are among the prettiest drives in the Pioneer Valley. For bicycling

information, see the Activities section under Amherst, later in this chapter.

## Information

The South Hadley Chamber of Commerce (☎/fax 413-532-6451) is at 362 N Main St, South Hadley, MA 01075. Worth a stop out of your way is the Odyssey Book Shop (☎ 413-534-7307), 9 College St.

## Mount Holyoke College

Founded in 1837 by teacher Mary Lyon, Mount Holyoke College (www.mtholyoke .edu) is the country's oldest women's college, with a current enrollment of about 2000 students. Campus tours (☎ 413-538-2222) can be arranged any day.

The great American landscape architect Frederick Law Olmstead laid out the center of Mount Holyoke's parklike 800-acre campus in the latter part of the 1800s. Among the college's other 19th-century legacies is the chapel's hand-crafted organ, one of the last built by New England's master organmaker, Charles B Fisk.

In the present century the college has added a multi-million-dollar sports complex, a Japanese garden and teahouse and an equestrian center.

Besides a walk around the lovely campus, you can enjoy the **College Art Museum** (☎ 413-538-2245), open year-round.

## Skinner State Park

This park (☎ 413-586-0350), north of South Hadley off MA 47 in Hadley, is at the summit of Mt Holyoke. The Summit House affords panoramic views of the Connecticut River, its oxbow curve and its fertile valley. There are hiking trails and a picnic area as well.

## Holyoke Range State Park

Just a few miles north of South Hadley on MA 116, Holyoke Range State Park (☎ 413-253-2883) has trail walks ranging from 0.75 to 5.4 miles on the Metacomet-Monadnock Trail (see the boxed text) and side trails.

## Places to Stay & Eat

Lodgings are in Amherst, Northampton and Springfield. For a very satisfying meal, try

*Woodbridge's Restaurant* (☎ 413-536-7341), right at the intersection of MA 47 and 116, on the common in the center of South Hadley. Main courses at dinner range from $13 to $19; Sunday brunch (10:30 am to 2 pm) is $13. The front terrace tables are the best in good weather.

## Entertainment

The *Mount Holyoke Summer Theater* (☎ 413-538-2406) stages outdoor evening performances. All performances are held Tuesday through Saturday on the common.

## Getting There & Away

Springfield is the long-distance transportation center for the region. PVTA buses (see Getting There & Away in Springfield) can bring you to South Hadley.

Driving details for South Hadley are:

| destination | mileage | hr:min |
|---|---|---|
| Amherst, MA | 7 miles | 0:12 |
| Northampton, MA | 11 miles | 0:18 |
| Springfield, MA | 15 miles | 0:25 |

## NORTHAMPTON

Northampton, settled in 1654, is both an eminently livable and visitable place, described by 'The Swedish Nightingale,' Jenny Lind, as the 'Paradise of America' during her visit in 1850. As the Hampshire County seat and the home of highly regarded Smith College, it has a sophistication, a low crime rate and a list of services that might be envied by cities twice its size. Northampton is also the dining center of the region, with a gratifying array of moderately priced restaurants.

The presence of college students and staff give the town a liberal political and sexual atmosphere, with an active and outspoken lesbian community. The strong influence adds a female sensibility to the college-town lineup of shops, banks, bookstores, cafes, copy shops and pizza parlors.

For information on bicycling, see the Activities listing under Amherst.

### Orientation

The center of town is at the intersection of Main St (MA 9) and Pleasant St (MA 5). Restaurants, banks, shops and other services are within a few blocks' walk, although lodgings are on the outskirts.

### Information

Check in with the Greater Northampton Chamber of Commerce (☎ 413-584-1900, www.chamber.northampton.ma.us), 99 Pleasant St, Northampton, MA 01060. The Town

---

## Metacomet-Monadnock Trail

The Metacomet-Monadnock Trail is part of a 200-mile greenway footpath that extends from Connecticut along the Connecticut River valley to New Hampshire's Mt Monadnock and beyond.

In Connecticut, the trail is named for Metacomet (the Indian commander who waged war on the colonists in 1675). It enters Massachusetts near the Agawam/Southwick town line to become Massachusetts' Metacomet-Monadnock Trail, 177 miles long. From the state line, the trail proceeds north up the river valley through public and private lands, ascends Mt Tom, then heads east along the Holyoke Range, through Skinner State Park and Holyoke Range State Park, before bearing north again.

After entering New Hampshire, the trail ascends Mt Monadnock, where it joins the Monadnock-Sunapee Greenway.

The easiest access to the trail for day hikes is in the state parks, where leaflets and simple local trail maps are available. For longer hikes, it's good to have the *Metacomet-Monadnock Trail Guide* (8th edition, 1995), published by the Berkshire Chapter Trails Committee of the AMC, PO Box 9369, North Amherst, MA 01059. It's also available through the AMC's main office (☎ 800-262-4455), at 5 Joy St, Boston, MA 02108, and at bookshops and outdoor stores.

of Northampton has a less useful website, which you can find at www.noho.com.

## Smith College

Smith College (www.smith.edu), at the western end of the downtown area, was founded 'for the education of the intelligent gentlewoman' in 1875 by Sophia Smith. The student body, numbering about 2700, continues to consist largely of women, with a sprinkling of men. The wooded 125-acre campus along Elm St holds an eclectic architectural mix of nearly 100 buildings, as well as Paradise Pond.

Visitors are welcome at the **Lyman Plant House** (☎ 413-585-2740), a collection of Victorian greenhouses that are the venue for the Bulb Show and Chrysanthemum Show (see below). You should also take a look at the **Smith College Museum of Art** (☎ 413-585-2770), Elm St at Bedford Terrace, which has a good collection of 17th-century Dutch and 19th- and 20th-century European and American paintings, including fine works by Degas, Winslow Homer, Picasso and Whistler. It's open 9:30 am to 4 pm Tuesday through Sunday, except that it is open until 8 pm on Thursday and it opens at noon on Sunday. Admission is free.

Guided campus tours can be arranged through the Office of Admissions (☎ 413-585-2500), or you can guide yourself using the good campus folder available for free at the college switchboard in College Hall, or from the Office of Admissions.

## Special Events

Flower-lovers should check out Smith College's renowned Annual Bulb Show in mid-March and the Chrysanthemum Show in November, held at the Lyman Plant House.

Springfield has the Big E, but Northampton has the Three-County Fair (☎ 413-584-2237) starting on the Friday of Labor Day weekend. The fair, first held in 1818, features agricultural and livestock exhibits, horse races, food and rides. The Three-County Fairgrounds, on MA 9 just west of I-91 exit 19 North and US 20 South, is also the site of the New England Morgan Horse Show, held annually in July.

## Places to Stay

It's usually easy to find a room during the summer. At other times of year, room price and availability depend on the college's schedule of ceremonies and sporting events.

Cheapest is the ***Econo Lodge*** (☎ 413-584-9816, fax 586-7512, 237 Russell St (MA 9)), in Hadley, 4 miles northeast of central Northampton. Rooms (some with kitchenettes) cost $60 to $89 in summer. There's a swimming pool.

***Valley Inn*** (☎ 413-586-1500, 117 Conz St), at I-91 exit 18, 2 miles south of the town center, has an outdoor pool and 60 rooms priced at $69 to $99, continental breakfast included.

***Autumn Inn*** (☎ 413-584-7660, 413-586-4808, 259 Elm St (MA 9)) has a swimming pool and an innlike ambiance despite its motel-like layout. The 34 rooms cost $80 single, $108 double.

The 72-room ***Hotel Northampton*** (☎ 413-584-3100, fax 584-9455, 36 King St), behind the county courthouse, has been receiving Northampton's important guests since 1916. It charges $95 to $215 for its comfortable, centrally located rooms.

## Places to Eat

Compared to the high prices of Boston and Cape Cod, Northampton's restaurant prices are a joy. Surveying the restaurants, on and off Main St, reveals American, Chinese, French, Greek, Indian, Italian, Japanese, Mediterranean, Mexican, Moroccan, Persian, Thai and Turkish cuisine, not to mention a handful of cafes. In addition, most Northampton restaurants offer some vegetarian fare and alcoholic drinks.

***Java Net Café*** (☎ 413-587-3400, 241 Main St) is Northampton's cybercafe, serving up coffee, tea, baked goods and the Internet.

***Bart's*** (☎ 413-584-0721, 235 Main St) specializes in custom-made ice cream (you pick the 'add-ins'), but also serves coffee, pastries and light lunches.

***Tailgate Picnic*** (☎ 413-584-4458, 159 Main St) is pleasant and popular, serving great picnic comfort food such as meat loaf, corned beef and turkey sandwiches for low prices: many dishes cost $4.

*Haymarket Café & Juice Joint* (☎ 413-586-9969, 185 Main St) is a popular place for soups, salads, sandwiches and vegetarian dishes priced from $2 to $6.

*Bakery Normand* (☎ 413-584-0717, 192 Main St), across from Haymarket, serves rich pastries, cakes, tarts and coffee mostly to go, but there are two small tables as well.

Playing on Northampton's nickname of Paradise, *Pizzeria Paradiso* (☎ 413-586-1468, 12 Crafts Ave), off Main St, is a wine bar masquerading as a traditional wood-fired, brick-oven pizza restaurant. Dinner, the only meal served, can cost from $8 to $16.

*Paul and Elizabeth's* (☎ 413-584-4832, 150 Main St), in Thornes Marketplace, is the town's premier natural foods restaurant, serving lunch and dinner every day. The cuisine is vegetarian, but seafood is served as well. A three-course dinner with wine can cost $22 to $26, less at lunch.

*La Veracruzana* (☎ 413-586-7181, 31 Main St) has down-home Mexican food such as tamales, enchiladas, tostadas and taco plates for $3 to $8. It's open for lunch and dinner every day.

At *La Taqueria Cha Cha Cha!* (☎ 413-586-7311, 134 Main St), Northampton's other centrally located Mexican eatery, the mood is young, hip and informal, and a meal of burritos or quesadillas with a glass of wine costs about $10.

For fancier Mexican fare, head for *La Cazuela* (☎ 413-586-0400, 7 Old South St), off Main, a good Southwest/Mexican restaurant and cantina, with a pleasant terrace dining area for good weather and two types of salsa on every table – hot and very hot. Dinners cost $16 to $30, including your margaritas.

*Northampton Brewery* (☎ 413-584-9903, 11 Brewster Court), with the main entrance actually on Hampton Rd, one long block south of Main St, is a modern brewpub with excellent beer, a good menu of light meals and nouvelle cuisine entrees. A pint and a sandwich costs under $12. Dine in the pretty beer garden in good weather.

*Mulino's Trattoria* (☎ 413-586-8900, 21 Center St) is a storefront bistro with a long list of homestyle Italian dishes, including

pizza from a wood-fired oven ($8 to $10), panini (Italian sandwiches, $5 to $7) and pasta, meat and fish for $12 to $16. It's open daily for dinner only; there's a cozy piano bar downstairs.

*Eastside Grill* (☎ 413-586-3347, 19 Strong Ave), a half block south of Main St, has a vast and eclectic menu listing everything from Louisiana fried oysters and chicken étouffée to steaks and pecan pie. The tenderloin costs $18; everything else is several dollars less. The clientele is well dressed. Lunch and dinner are served daily; the wine list is good and reasonably priced.

Many people rate *Spoleto* (☎ 413-586-6313, 50 Main St) as Northampton's best restaurant. The classic dishes such as veal scaloppini and chicken saltimbocca are prepared with California accents. Vegetarians should try the eggplant rollatini. A full dinner (the only meal served) costs from $25 to $40 per person, drinks included.

## Entertainment

Northampton is the center of nightlife in the Five College area. For listings of what's happening throughout the Pioneer Valley, pick up a copy of *The Valley Advocate* (www .valleyadvocate.com), which is a free weekly newspaper.

**Theater** The *New Century Theatre at Smith College* (☎ 413-585-3220) stages modern works in July and August at the Hallie Flanagan Studio Theatre in the Mendenhall Center for Performing Arts, on Green St on campus.

**Music** The *Iron Horse Music Hall* (☎ 413-584-0610, 20 Center St), a half block off Main St, is the prime folk and jazz venue. Call for the current program, then look for the small storefront with the line of people waiting to get in.

*Pearl St* (☎ 413-584-7771, 10 Pearl St), at the corner with Strong Ave, is the best dance club, drawing local, regional and national performers and enough loyal patrons to produce a line any weekend night. Wednesday is gay night, Thursday is 18+, Friday is retro and Saturday is for modern rock.

*Fire & Water Vegetarian Café & Performance Space (☎ 413-586-8336, 5 Old South St)* features folk, jazz, blues and new talent in a funky atmosphere.

The *Academy of Music (☎ 413-584-8435, 274 Main St)* is a cinema but also hosts performers who draw the big crowds when they come to town.

**Pubs** *Northampton Brewery (☎ 413-584-9903, 11 Brewster Court)* has a lively pub atmosphere every evening, and live music some evenings.

*Packard's (☎ 413-584-5957, 14 Masonic St)*, off Main St, is a lively pub. Billiard tables on the 3rd floor can be rented by the hour.

*FitzWilly's (☎ 413-584-8666, 23 Main St)*, at Strong Ave, is a longtime favorite, a lively, centrally located tavern and restaurant with an extensive menu of burgers, salads and pizzas for $5 to $8.

### Getting There & Away
See Springfield for information on air, bus and train service.

Driving details for Northampton are as follows:

| destination | mileage | hr:min |
| --- | --- | --- |
| Amherst, MA | 7 miles | 0:12 |
| Boston, MA | 108 miles | 2:20 |
| Deerfield, MA | 16 miles | 0:25 |
| Lenox, MA | 61 miles | 1:25 |
| South Hadley, MA | 8 miles | 0:16 |
| Springfield, MA | 18 miles | 0:25 |

## AMHERST
The town of Amherst is best known as the home of prestigious Amherst College, but the major academic presence here is the University of Massachusetts at Amherst, and the smaller Hampshire College on the outskirts. The town has produced its share of famous people, among whom poet Emily Dickinson, 'the belle of Amherst,' is perhaps the best known.

### Orientation & Information
At the center of Amherst is the town common, a broad New England green that is framed by churches, inns and a number of other grand buildings.

The Amherst Area Chamber of Commerce (☎ 413-253-0700), 409 Main St at Railroad St, Amherst, MA 01002, is less than a half mile east of Pleasant St. The chamber maintains a summer information booth on the common facing S Pleasant St, directly across from the Peter Pan bus station (which is at 79 S Pleasant St). The post office (☎ 413-549-0418) is on N Pleasant St at Kellogg Ave. There's a Council Travel agency (☎ 413-256-1261) at 44 Main St. For books, the Jeffrey Amherst Bookshop (☎ 413-253-3381) at 55 Pleasant St is recommended.

### Dickinson Homestead
Emily Dickinson (1830-86) was raised in the strict Puritan household of her father, a prominent lawyer. When he was elected to Congress she traveled with him to Washington and Philadelphia, then returned to Amherst and this house to live out the rest of her days in near seclusion. Some say she was in love with Reverend Charles Wadsworth, a local married clergyman. Unable to show her love, she withdrew from the world into a private realm of pain, passion and poignancy.

Dickinson wrote finely crafted poems on scraps of paper and old envelopes and stuffed them in her desk. She published only seven poems during her lifetime, and no one recognized her then as a major talent. After her death, more than 1000 of her exquisite poems were discovered and published. These verses on love, death, nature and immortality made her one of America's most important poets.

Emily Dickinson's former home (☎ 413-542-8161), 280 Main St, has several rooms open for touring May through October, Wednesday through Saturday from 1:30 to 3:45 pm; in April and from November to mid-December, it's open on Wednesday and Saturday only. The guided tour costs $3; call for reservations.

### Hampshire College
The region's newest and perhaps most innovative center of learning, Hampshire College

MASSACHUSETTS

(www.hampshire.edu) is 3 miles south of Amherst center on MA 116. It has a lovely campus, and you can schedule a tour through the Admissions Office (☎ 413-582-5471).

## Amherst College
Founded in 1821, Amherst (www.amherst .edu) has retained its character and quality partly by maintaining its relatively small size (1575 students); thus its prestige has grown. The main part of the campus is just south of the town common. The information booth has a map and brochure for self-guided walking tours, or you can ask questions at Converse Hall (☎ 413-542-2000).

## University of Massachusetts at Amherst
The University of Massachusetts at Amherst (☎ 413-545-0111, www.umass.edu), founded in 1863 as the Massachusetts Agricultural College, is now part of the official university system of the Commonwealth of Massachusetts. About 24,000 students study at UMass' sprawling Amherst campus, to the northwest of the common. A free PVTA bus line serves the campus, which allows for easy local transport.

## Atkins Farms Fruit Bowl
This recently expanded farm-produce center (☎ 413-253-9528) offers maple sugar products in spring, garden produce in summer and apple-picking in autumn. Other activities, such as a scarecrow-making workshop in October, take place throughout the year. A deli and bakery sells picnic supplies; Atkins Farms will also ship gift baskets.

## Activities
See the South Hadley section for information on hiking in the Holyoke Range, south of Amherst.

The **Norwottuck Rail Trail** (nor-WAH-tuk) is a foot and bike path that follows the former Boston & Maine Railroad right-of-way from Amherst to Hadley and North-ampton, a distance of 8.5 miles. For much of its length, the trail parallels MA 9. Parking and the access to the trail are on Station Rd in Amherst, the Mountain Farms Mall on

Emily Dickinson, the 'belle of Amherst'

MA 9 in Hadley and Elwell State Park on Damon Rd in Northampton.

Biking the trail is particularly enjoyable. Bicycles can be rented for the day (about $15) from Valley Bicycles (☎ 413-256-0880), 319 Main St, less than a half mile east of Pleasant St; and Laughing Dog Bikes (☎ 413-253-7722), at 63 S Pleasant St in Amherst.

## Places to Stay
There aren't many campgrounds in this region. The **White Birch Campground** (☎ 413-665-4941, 122 North St), in Whately, has 40 sites, all of which are open May through November. Follow MA 116 North through North Amherst and Sunderland to South Deerfield, then go southwest to Whately.

**Motels & Hotels** *Amherst Motel* (☎ 413-256-8122, 408 Northampton Rd (MA 9)), on the south side of MA 9, a mile west of the Amherst town common, and just over the town line in Hadley, charges $54 to $68 for a room in summer, light breakfast included.

A bit farther along MA 9 is *Howard Johnson* (☎ 413-586-0114, 800-654-2000, fax 413-584-7163, 401 Russell St (MA 9)), in Hadley, under 2 miles from the Amherst town common, with a pool, restaurant, and rooms for $75 to $115 per night.

*University Lodge (☎ 413-256-8111, 345 North Pleasant St (MA 116))*, only a few blocks north of the town common, has rooms for $75 to $95.

*Campus Center Hotel (☎ 413-549-6000, fax 545-1210)* is inside the high-rise tower of the Murray D Lincoln Campus Center at UMass off N Pleasant St. Rooms rent for $69 to $89.

**Inns & B&Bs** The Amherst Area Chamber of Commerce (see Information, above) has a list of member B&Bs that includes phone numbers and prices.

*Allen House (☎ 413-253-5000, 599 Main St)*, over a half mile east of Pleasant St, is a prim Queen-Anne-style Victorian cottage charging $85 to $135 for its air-conditioned, bath-equipped rooms, with a full breakfast included. Main St has some traffic noise during the day.

*Lincoln Avenue B&B (☎ 413-549-0517, 242 Lincoln Ave)*, a half mile west of Pleasant St in a quiet residential neighborhood, has three bedrooms with shared baths for $65 to $95, breakfast included.

The 49-room *Lord Jeffrey Inn (☎ 413-253-2576, 800-742-0358, fax 413-256-6152, 30 Boltwood Ave)*, facing the town common, is the classic college-town inn: colonial, collegiate, cozy and comfortable. Rooms are priced at $69 to $158, and the location couldn't be better.

## Places to Eat

As a college town, Amherst has lots of places serving pizza, sandwiches, Mexican *antojitos* (appetizers), Chinese take-out and fresh-brewed coffee. The fast-food and restaurant zone is on N Pleasant St north of Main St to Kellogg Ave. Here you'll find *Bruegger's Bagels*, *D'Angelo's Sandwich Shops*, *Papa Gino's*, *Starbucks* and the like, as well as local efforts.

*La Veracruzana (☎ 413-253-6900, 63 S Pleasant St)* is convenient to the common and the bus station, with burritos, quesadillas, enchiladas, tacos and various other Mexican staples for $2.50 to $7.

*Antonio's Pizza by the Slice (☎ 413-253-0808, 31 N Pleasant St)* is Amherst's most popular pizza place, which is saying a lot. No cheap cheese-on-cardboard here: the variety of toppings, flavorings and spices is vast, and prices are low: $1.50 to $3 per slice.

*Judie's (☎ 413-253-3491)*, in a converted house at 51 N Pleasant St, has an eclectic menu of original – some would say odd – dishes, such as a chicken 'sandwich' with apple butter, bananas, peanuts, coconut, raisins, cranberry sauce and a curry glaze, served in a popover. A full lunch can cost $12 to $18, dinner $16 to $35, but there's usually a luncheon special priced around $5.50. Alcohol is served.

*Rao's Coffee Roasting Company (☎ 413-253-9441, 17 Kellogg Ave)*, a half-block east of Pleasant St along Boltwood Walk, serves specialty coffees ($1 to $3) and appropriate nibbles at its indoor and outdoor cafe tables.

*Panda East (☎ 413-256-8923, 103 N Pleasant St)*, on Boltwood Walk at Kellogg Ave, serves Chinese and Japanese cuisine at very reasonable prices in attractive surroundings. Choose from the long list of luncheon specials, which come with soup and steamed rice, for only $5 to $6.

*Amherst Chinese Food (☎ 413-253-7835, 62 Main St)*, one long block east of Pleasant St, has been serving Chinese dishes for decades. Main courses are $6 to $12 at dinner, less at lunch.

*The Windowed Hearth* at the Lord Jeffrey Inn *(☎ 413-253-2576, 30 Boltwood Ave)*, facing the common, is where parents go when they need a fancy meal. Pecan-crusted duck breast and venison *osso buco* typify the offerings. Full dinners cost from $40 to $60. *Elijah Boltwood's Tavern* downstairs is less fancy and pricey, serving breakfast and light meals.

For a meal and a view, try the *Top of the Campus Restaurant (☎ 413-545-0636)* inside the Murray D Lincoln Campus Center at UMass. The food is traditional, prices are moderate and the view of the campus and the countryside is impressive. Lunch is served on weekdays and dinner is served Tuesday through Saturday.

## Entertainment

UMass' *Fine Arts Center* (☎ 413-545-2511) has a full program of concert programs, shows, folk, jazz and rock. *Amherst Brewing Company* (☎ 413-253-4400, 24-36 N Pleasant St) has a full calendar of jazz, blues, rock and reggae groups performing, usually with no cover charge. *Black Sheep* (☎ 413-253-3442, 79 Main St) is the most popular folk club.

## Getting There & Away

See the Springfield section for air, bus and train information. Amherst's connection to the outside world is through the Peter Pan Amherst Center Bus Terminal (☎ 413-256-0431), 79 S Pleasant St, just south of Main St. Tickets are also sold at the Campus Center Hotel and the Southwest Hampden Dining Common on the UMass campus.

The driving details for Amherst are as follows:

| destination | mileage | hr:min |
|---|---|---|
| Boston, MA | 80 miles | 2:00 |
| Deerfield, MA | 16 miles | 0:30 |
| Hartford, CT | 49 miles | 1:10 |
| Lenox, MA | 64 miles | 1:25 |
| New York, NY | 158 miles | 3:25 |
| Northampton, MA | 7 miles | 0:15 |
| Springfield, MA | 24 miles | 0:40 |

## Getting Around

UMass Transit Service (☎ 413-586-5806) runs free buses along MA 116 (Pleasant St) between the town center and the UMass campus.

## DEERFIELD

During the mid-17th century, pioneers settled at Deerfield in the fertile Connecticut River Valley (16 miles northwest of Amherst). But this was the borderlands of colonial settlement and it was open to attack by the area's Native Americans.

Massasoit (1580?-1661), great *sachem* of the Wampanoags, signed a treaty of peace with the Pilgrims at Plymouth in 1621 and he scrupulously observed it until his death. In the four decades after the founding of Plymouth, English settlers poured into the region.

The Wampanoags and other native peoples became dependent on English goods and found themselves yielding their lands in exchange for English cloth, kitchen utensils and firearms.

Upon Massasoit's death, his son Metacomet (called 'King Philip' by the English) became sachem, and though he preserved peace for several years, he and his people became increasingly agitated by the colonists' steady encroachment.

In 1671, the English government, suspicious of Metacomet's motives, brought him in for questioning, levied a fine and demanded that the Wampanoags give up their arms. They did.

Still, friction increased, and in 1675, when three Wampanoags were tried and executed for the murder of a Christian Indian who had been an informer for the English, war broke out.

King Philip's War, as it was called by the English, brought devastation to frontier settlements such as Deerfield. In the autumn of 1675, an Indian force a thousand strong massacred 64 residents here.

The survivors rebuilt the town, only to have the Indians attack again in 1704. Nearly 50 residents were killed and the rest marched off to Canada; many others died along the way. But the survivors returned and rebuilt the town once again.

Later in the 18th century, when the region had returned to peace, settlers returned to farm the rich bottomlands.

## Orientation & Information

The modern commercial center is in South Deerfield, and the original settlement of Deerfield, 6 miles to the north, has been preserved and restored to something like its appearance in those earlier, dangerous times.

To get information before you arrive, contact Historic Deerfield (☎ 413-774-5581, www.historic-deerfield.org), PO Box 321, Deerfield, MA 01342; or the Franklin County Chamber of Commerce (☎ 413-773-5463, www.co.franklin.ma.us), 395 Main St, Greenfield, MA 01302. When you arrive in Deerfield, inquire at the information desk in

Metacomet (King Philip), *sachem* of the
Wampanoags

the museum across from the Deerfield Inn.
It has maps, brochures and a short audiovisual presentation that gives you an overview
of Historic Deerfield Village.

## Historic Deerfield Village

The main street of Historic Deerfield Village
escaped the ravages of time and change and
now presents a noble prospect: a dozen
houses dating from the 1700s and 1800s, well
preserved and open to the public.

The **Wright House** (1824) has collections
of American period paintings, Chippendale
and Federal furniture and Chinese export
porcelain. The **Flynt Textile Museum** (1872)
has textiles, costumes and needlework from
Europe and the US. There's also the Henry N
Flynt Silver and Metalwork Collection
(1814). Furnishings in **Allen House** (1720)
were made in the Pioneer Valley and Boston.

The **Stebbins House** (1799-1810) was the
home of a rich land-owning family, and is
furnished with typical luxury items of the
time. In the **Barnard Tavern**, many of the
exhibits are touchable, which makes this a
favorite with children. The rooms of the

**Wells-Thorn House** (1717-51) are furnished
according to period from colonial times to
the Federal period.

The **Dwight House**, built in Springfield in
1725, was moved to Deerfield in 1950. It now
holds locally made furniture and an 18th-
century doctor's office. **Sheldon-Hawks House**
(1743) was the 18th-century home of the Sheldons, wealthy Deerfield farmers. Contrast its
furnishings with those in the Stebbins House,
built and furnished a half century later.

The local parsonage, or minister's residence, was the **Ashley House** (1730). The
**Ebenezer Hinsdale Williams House**, which
took 22 years to build, has recently been
restored to its original appearance (it was
built between 1816 and 1838).

The Memorial Hall Museum (☎ 413-774-
7476), at the corner of Memorial St and US
5 and 10, was the original building (1798) of
Deerfield Academy, the prestigious preparatory school. It's now a museum of Pocumtuck Valley life and history. Puritan and
Indian artifacts include carved and painted
chests, embroidery, musical instruments and
glass-plate photographs (1880-1920).

When visiting the museum, don't miss the
Indian House Door, a dramatic relic from
the French and Indian Wars. In February
1704, the house of the Sheldon family was
attacked by Indians. The attackers chopped
and bashed at the door, but it wouldn't yield.
Finally, they hacked a hole through its center
and did in the inhabitants with musket fire.

The museum is open 9:30 am to 4:30 pm
daily from May through October. It costs
nothing to stroll along the street; for a half-
hour tour of the buildings, the fee is $12 for
adults, $6 for children six to 17. Guides in the
houses provide commentary.

## Cruises

The *Quinnetukut II* (☎ 413-659-3714) glides
along the Connecticut River on 12-mile, 1½-
hour cruises daily in summer. A lecturer fills
you in on the history, geology and ecology of
the river and the region. It's a good idea to
call for reservations. Tickets ($7 for adults, $6
for seniors, $3 for children 14 and under) are
on sale at the Northfield Mountain Recreation and Environmental Center on MA 63

north of MA 2, open 9 am to 5 pm Wednesday through Sunday. Take I-91 north to exit 27, then MA 2 east, then MA 63 north.

## Places to Stay

*Erving State Forest* (☎ 413-544-3939), on the north side of MA 2A in Erving, has 32 campsites about 16 miles east of Greenfield.

*Barton Cove Campground* (☎ 413-659-3714), off MA 2 in Gill, has 23 family tent sites on a mile-long wooded peninsula on the Connecticut River. The nature trail takes you to dinosaur footprints and nesting bald eagles. Take I-91 exit 27, then MA 2 East for 4 miles and look for the sign on the right.

The Franklin County Chamber of Commerce (☎ 413-773-5463) can recommend any of dozens of B&Bs in the region.

The *Deerfield Inn* (☎ 413-774-5587, 800-926-3865, fax 413-773-8712), The Street, Deerfield, has 23 modernized, comfortable rooms right at the head of Historic Deerfield's main street. Rooms cost $150 to $225 double with breakfast and afternoon tea. The inn, built in 1884, was destroyed by fire and rebuilt in 1981.

## Getting There & Away

Air, rail and bus service connects to Springfield (see that section), and Peter Pan bus service goes to Greenfield.

The driving details for Deerfield are as follows:

| destination | mileage | hr:min |
|---|---|---|
| Amherst, MA | 16 miles | 0:30 |
| Boston, MA | 90 miles | 2:10 |
| Greenfield, MA | 3 miles | 0:07 |
| Hartford, CT | 60 miles | 1:15 |
| Lenox, MA | 79 miles | 2:00 |
| New York, NY | 165 miles | 3:20 |
| Northampton, MA | 16 miles | 0:25 |
| Springfield, MA | 39 miles | 0:55 |

# The Berkshires

Few places in America can combine culture with rural countryside as well as the Berkshire hills in western Massachusetts. Extending from the highest point in the state – Mt Greylock (3491 feet), near North Adams – southward to the Connecticut state line, the Berkshires have been a summer refuge for more than a century. On summer weekends when the sidewalks are scorching in Boston, New York and Hartford, crowds of city-dwellers jump in their cars and head for the cool shade and breezes of the Berkshires to hike, bike, canoe and swim.

In the evenings, culture beckons. The Boston Symphony Orchestra's summer concert series at Tanglewood, near Lenox, draws the biggest crowds. The Williamstown Theatre Festival attracts many well-known New York and Hollywood actors who also want to escape the city. Nearby, the Clark Art Institute's collection of impressionist works rivals any big-city museum.

Most visitors congregate in the southern half of the Berkshires, from Great Barrington to Lenox. Williamstown, to the north, is far less crowded, resembling the pastoral setting of its neighbor state, Vermont.

## GREAT BARRINGTON

No town in the Berkshires has undergone more of a change in the past five years than the southernmost village, Great Barrington. Great Barrington's Main St used to consist of Woolworth's, Grant's, several hardware stores, thrift shops and a rundown diner. They have been replaced by artsy boutiques, antique shops, coffeehouses, and restaurants. The industrial-looking Union Bar & Grill could easily fit into Manhattan's SoHo district. Indeed, locals are beginning to call their town 'Little SoHo,' perhaps to attract the many city travelers that are now stopping here to shop and eat at the best selection of restaurants in the region.

If you are put off by the SoHo label, don't worry. Barringtonians are down-to-earth and highly independent – traits that stem from their past. In 1774 local citizens, chafing under the abuses of the king's governors in Boston, prevented the royal judges from meeting in the local courthouse. Great Barrington also saw the birth of the great African American teacher and civil rights leader William Edward Burghardt DuBois

# THE BERKSHIRES

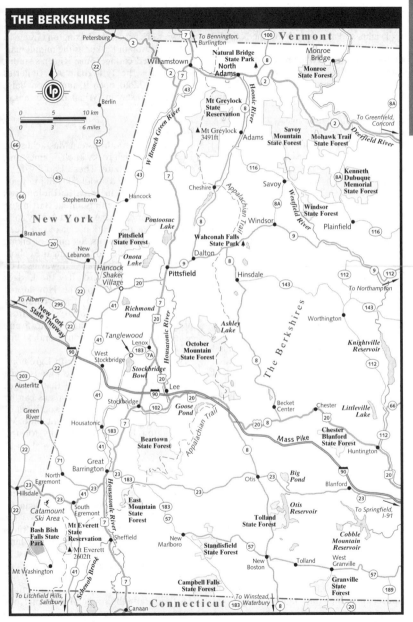

(1868-1963). After receiving a PhD from Harvard, Dr DuBois became a pioneer for civil rights and a co-founder of the NAACP.

## Orientation & Information

The Housatonic River flows through the center of town just east of Main St (US 7), the main thoroughfare. Most lodgings and restaurants are on Main St in the town center, or on heavily congested US 7 North, or MA 23/41 south of the town. However, the finest accommodations (usually B&Bs) are on small roads outside of town in the farmlands.

The Southern Berkshire Chamber of Commerce (☎ 413-528-1510, www.bcn.net/commerce/southern), 362 Main St, Great Barrington, MA 01230, has lots of good maps, brochures, restaurant menus and other materials on the area attractions and businesses.

## Searles Castle

Mr and Mrs Edward Searles were Great Barrington's most wealthy and prominent citizens in the late 19th century. Mrs Searles, the widow of railroad tycoon Mark Hopkins, built an imposing mansion here in 1886. Now called Searles Castle, it stands behind high walls on Main St at the southern end of the town center. It must have seemed out of place in a town otherwise populated by sturdy peasants. Today the great house is the home of John Dewey Academy, a private school.

## Monterey & Tyringham

Take MA 23 East out of Great Barrington 8 miles to the village of Monterey. Its general store is much like it was when it opened a half-century ago. If you buy lunch at its deli, try the local Rawson Brook Farm goat cheese.

The village of Tyringham, several miles north of Monterey via the back road, is the perfect destination for an excursion deep into the heart of the countryside. Once the home of a Shaker community (1792-1870s), the village is now famous for its **Gingerbread House,** an architectural fantasy designed at

the beginning of the 20th century by sculptor Henry Hudson Kitson. Kitson's best-known work graces the Lexington Green – a statue of Captain Parker as the minuteman. The thatched cottage, once Kitson's studio, now houses the **Tyringham Art Galleries** (☎ 413-243-3260), open 10 am to 5 pm daily. For places to stay in Tyringham, see Inns & B&Bs, below.

## Hiking

To residents of southwestern Massachusetts, a 'cobble' is a high rocky knoll of limestone, marble or quartzite. These knobby hills, which were formed about 500 million years ago, are now a curiosity. **Bartholomew's Cobble**, 10 miles south of Great Barrington along US 7 and MA 7A toward Ashley Falls, is a 277-acre reservation cloaked in trees, ferns, flowers and moss. Six miles of hiking trails provide routes for enjoying the cobble and the woods set beneath a flyway used by over 200 species of birds. Try the Ledges Trail that weaves along the Housatonic River. This property of the Trustees of Reservations (☎ 413-229-8600) is open from mid-April to mid-October, 9 am to 5 pm. Admission costs $3 for adults and $1 for children.

Twelve miles south of South Egremont, right on the New York state line, is **Bash Bish Falls**, a scenic waterfall that plunges down a 1000-foot gorge. Two paths can be used to reach it. Follow MA 41 south out of Great Barrington and turn right onto Mt Washington Rd, following signs for the Catamount Ski Area. Then follow signs to the falls, taking East St, then West St and finally Bash Bish Falls Rd, deep in the Mt Washington State Forest.

On US 7, less than 5 miles north of the town center, **Monument Mountain** can be climbed by either of two trails. Writer Nathaniel Hawthorne wrote that Monument's summit resembled 'a headless sphinx wrapped in a Persian shawl.' On August 5, 1850, Hawthorne climbed up Monument Mountain with Oliver Wendell Holmes and Herman Melville. It was the first time Hawthorne and the young Melville met, but they quickly became good friends and kept in touch throughout their lives.

## Special Events
The Aston Magna Festival (☎ 413-528-3595) celebrates classical (especially Baroque) music each summer in July and August. If you like Bach, Brahms and Buxtehude, buy your tickets ($19) well in advance. Concerts are held in the St James Church, on Main St (US 7) at Taconic Ave, near the Town Hall.

## Places to Stay
A good half-hour drive to Lenox and Tanglewood, Great Barrington is nonetheless a popular place for people to stay in the summer. Unless otherwise stated, rates quoted are for weekends in the high-peak months of July and August (when Tanglewood is in session). Prices for rooms midweek and off-season are substantially lower.

**Camping** *Beartown State Forest* (☎ 413-528-0904), on Blue Hill Rd in Monterey, 8 miles east of Great Barrington via MA 23, has 12 simple sites that overlook Benedict Pond. RVs have trouble getting up the winding road so most sites are rented by backpackers. At the *Mt Washington State Forest* (☎ 413-528-0330), on East St, in the village of Mt Washington to the southwest of South Egremont, there are 15 wilderness sites for hikers.

*Tolland State Forest* (☎ 413-269-6002), on MA 8 in Otis, 16 miles east of Great Barrington along MA 23, has 90 sites. *Prospect Lake Park* (☎ 413-528-4158), on Prospect Lake Rd in North Egremont, has 140 sites open May through mid-October. Most of the other campgrounds are in or near Otis, including *Laurel Ridge Camping Area* (☎ 413-269-4804), in East Otis, with 140 sites.

**Motels** On the southern side of the town center, the conveniently located *Days Inn* (☎ 413-528-3150, 372 Main St), right behind the chamber of commerce, has rooms for $89 midweek, $135 weekends.

*Lantern House Motel* (☎ 413-528-2350, 254 Stockbridge Rd (US 7)), just north of the center, is the best deal in terms of value. Rooms cost $60 to $70 Sunday through Wednesday, $85 Thursday through Saturday. There's a nice swimming pool.

The *Barrington Court Motel* (☎ 413-528-2340, 400 Stockbridge Rd) costs $75 midweek, $115 on weekends.

*Monument Mountain Motel* (☎ 413-528-3272, 249 Stockbridge Rd) charges $70 to $80 midweek, $95 to $110 Thursday through Saturday.

*Briarcliff Motor Lodge* (☎ 413-528-3000, 506 Stockbridge Rd) is on a far more scenic stretch of Route 7 than the motels in town. Located directly across from Monument Mountain, its rooms cost $55 to $125.

**Inns & B&Bs** *Littlejohn Manor* (☎ 413-528-2882, 1 Newsboy Monument Lane) is a nice big Victorian house perched above a pond and cornfields. The four double rooms with shared baths cost $80 to $95 in summer, including a full English breakfast and afternoon tea.

*Manor Lane B&B* (☎ 413-528-8222, 145 Hurlburt Rd) is nestled between horse farms, a five-minute drive from the center of town. The large house has three spacious rooms, a cozy sitting room with requisite piano and Turkish carpets, and a glassed-in breakfast area. Outside are a pool, tennis courts and trails into the woods. Rooms cost $125 to $140.

*The Wainwright Inn* (☎ 413-528-2062, 518 S Main St) bills itself as 'a country bed and breakfast,' although it's a short walk from the center of town. The big house has eight guest rooms with private baths ranging from $100 to $150, depending on the day of the week.

*The Pink House* (☎ 413-528-6680, 42 East St) is an apt name for this rosy-colored house located in a quiet residential neighborhood. Owner Barbara Beach has created a charming garden where guests are served home-cooked breakfasts and fresh fruit. The three rooms cost $85.

*Baldwin Hill Farm B&B* (☎ 413-528-4092, 121 Baldwin Hill Rd), off MA 71 in South Egremont, has four rooms priced from $89 to $110, a fine pool and exquisite views of the surrounding mountains.

***Race Brook Lodge*** (☎ 413-229-2916, *864 S Undermountain Rd (MA 41)*), in Sheffield, sits at the base of Mt Race. Take the strenuous trail behind the lodge to Race's summit, where the Appalachian Trail will lead you on a sky-high ridge walk. The 21 guest rooms in this 200-year-old converted barn start at $75 midweek.

If you fall in love with Tyringham, you can spend the night at ***The Golden Goose*** (☎ 413-243-3008, *123 Main Rd*). The two rooms rent for $125 to $180, breakfast included. There's also the ***Sunset Farm B&B*** (☎ 413-243-3229), on Main Rd, with four rooms priced from $80 to $100.

## Places to Eat

The restaurants in the town center are remarkably diverse, with offerings that range from Middle Eastern food to sushi to old-time diners.

***Berkshire Coffee Roasting Company*** (*286 Main St*) is a good place to meet locals in the morning over a cup of joe.

***Baba Louie's*** (☎ 413-528-8100, *284 Main St*) is known for wood-fired pizzas with organic sourdough crust. A large vegetable pizza costs $11.50.

Also at 284 Main St, ***Helsinki Tea Company*** (☎ 413-528-3394), in the back of the small arcade, is a good place to plop down on an overstuffed sofa and order a pot of green tea. Their eclectic menu features such fare as the Moroccan-style lamb and the Sibelius Barbecue, a honey-orange-roasted half-chicken named for Finland's most famous composer. They plan to open a bar and dance club next door by the time this book is published.

***The Neighborhood Diner*** (☎ 413-528-8226, *282 Main St*) is an inexpensive place for breakfast (tasty blueberry pancakes) or sandwiches for lunch. Meals won't cost more than $10 per person.

***Castle St Café*** (☎ 413-528-5244, *10 Castle St*), just off Main St, has doubled in size and now features a piano bar. The piano in the back once belonged to Nat King Cole, who

owned a summer home in Tyringham. Chef/owner Michael Ballon uses lots of fresh local ingredients, like Hillsdale chèvre cheese and Pittsfield fettuccine, to create his innovative menu. Main courses average $17. It's closed on Tuesday.

***Bizen*** (☎ 413-528-4343, *17 Railroad St*) is a Japanese restaurant featuring a small sushi bar, sashimi and tempura. All the meals are served on pottery created during owner Michael Marcus' four years in Japan.

***Union Bar & Grill*** (☎ 413-528-6228, *293 Main St*) is considered one of the hottest new restaurants in the Berkshires, but don't come here expecting an intimate candlelight dinner. Intriguing entrees like portobello lasagna and duck quesadillas are served on aluminum tables against a backdrop of metallic walls. The trendy, yet moderately priced, restaurant is one of the few places open until 11 pm, so you can venture here after going to Tanglewood. It's closed on Wednesdays.

***Viviani's*** (☎ 413-528-3843, *177 Main St*) is a small Northern Italian restaurant on the outskirts of town and is known for chicken and veal dishes. Expect to spend $20 per person. It's closed Wednesdays.

The ***Captain Toss Seafood Restaurant*** (☎ 413-528-3512, *485 Main St*) is one of the best places in the region to find fresh fish.

***Cheesecake Charlie's*** (☎ 413-528-7790, *271 Main St*) has 50 varieties of cheesecake and an espresso bar. It also offers extremely affordable pastas and sandwiches, starting at $4.95.

Outside of the center of town, ***Jodi's Country Cookery*** (☎ 413-528-6064, *327 Stockbridge Rd*) is a homey 'old farmhouse' set on a commercial street. The menu features everything from burgers to fettuccine puttanesca to grilled duck sausage with apple brandy. Dinners average $15 to $30 per person.

In South Egremont, ***The Old Mill*** (☎ 413-528-1421, *53 Main St*) is a 1797 grist mill and blacksmith's shop turned into a highly praised restaurant serving American and continental cuisine. Dinner with dessert will cost you $30.

## Getting There & Away
Driving details for Great Barrington are as follows:

| destination | mileage | hr:min |
|---|---|---|
| New York City | 150 miles | 3:00 |
| Boston, MA | 146 miles | 3:00 |
| Lenox, MA | 13 miles | 0:25 |
| Litchfield, CT | 33 miles | 1:00 |
| South Egremont, MA | 4 miles | 0:11 |
| Stockbridge, MA | 7 miles | 0:15 |
| Williamstown, MA | 42 miles | 1:20 |

## STOCKBRIDGE
Stockbridge is the quintessential New England picture-postcard town, absolutely beautiful, almost too perfect – the way Norman Rockwell might have seen it.

In fact, Rockwell *did* see it, because he lived here. Whether it has always been this beautiful, or whether it has remade itself in Rockwell's image, we will never know.

Both the town and the artist attract the summer crowds. They come to stroll its streets, inspect its shops and sit in the rockers on the porch of the grand old Red Lion Inn. And they come (by the busload) to visit the Norman Rockwell Museum on the town's outskirts.

Also of interest in this pretty town are Chesterwood, the country home and studio of sculptor Daniel Chester French; Naumkeag, a lavish early-20th-century 'Berkshire cottage' and the Berkshire Theatre Festival.

### Orientation & Information
Stockbridge's Main St is MA 102. The central district is only a few blocks long.

Volunteers sometimes staff an information kiosk on Main St in the summertime months. For accommodations information, you can get in touch with the Stockbridge Lodging Association (☎ 413-298-5327, www.stockbridgechamber.org), PO Box 224, Stockbridge, MA 01262.

### Norman Rockwell Museum
Norman Rockwell (1894-1978) was born in New York City, and he sold his first magazine cover illustration to the *Saturday Evening Post* in 1916. In the following half century he did another 321 covers for the *Post*, as well as illustrations for books, posters and many other magazines. His clever, masterful, insightful art made him the best-known and most popular illustrator in US history. His wonderful sense of humor can be seen in his painting *Triple Self Portrait* (1960), where an older Rockwell looks in a mirror, only to paint a much younger version of himself.

Rockwell lived and worked in Stockbridge for the last 25 years of his life. This new, modern museum has the largest collection of his original art. His studio was moved here from behind his Stockbridge home. The museum (☎ 413-298-4100) is open every day from 10 am to 5 pm May to October and 10 am to 4 pm on weekdays from November to April. Admission costs $20 per family, $9 for adults, $2 for children over five; under five are free. Picnic tables are set in a grove near the museum.

The museum is on MA 183 to the south of MA 102. Follow MA 102 west from Stockbridge, turn left (south) on MA 183, and look for the museum on the left side.

### Chesterwood
Daniel Chester French (1850-1931) is best known for his statue *The Minute Man* (1875) at the Old North Bridge in Concord, Massachusetts, and his great statue of Abraham Lincoln sitting in the Lincoln Monument in Washington, DC (1922).

French's work was mostly monumental sculpture. He created more than 100 great public works and became a wealthy man as a result. His home was in New York City, but he spent most summers after 1897 at Chesterwood (☎ 413-298-3579), his gracious Berkshire estate. He continued work on his sculptures here while enjoying the society of the other 'cottage' owners.

The sculptor's house and studio are substantially as they were when he lived and worked here, with nearly 500 pieces of sculpture, finished and unfinished, in the barnlike studio.

Chesterwood is open to the public 10 am to 5 pm daily May through October. The museum is on Williamsville Rd near the village of Glendale, off of MA 183 south of the Norman Rockwell Museum. Follow MA 102 west from Stockbridge and turn left onto Glendale Middle Rd, proceed through Glendale to Williamsville Rd and turn left; the museum is on the right. Admission costs $17 for a family, or $7.50 per adult, $4.50 for youths 13 to 18, $2 for children six to 12, under six free.

### Naumkeag

This grand Berkshire 'cottage' on Prospect Hill is well worth a visit. It was designed in 1885 by Stanford White for attorney and diplomat Joseph Hodges Choate. Choate was a noted collector of art, so his summer house is filled with Oriental carpets, Chinese porcelain and other luxury goods. The gardens are the work of 30 years of devotion on the part of prominent landscape architect Fletcher Steele and the Choate family.

You can take a guided tour of the house (☎ 413-298-3239) and a stroll through the gardens 10 am to 4:15 pm daily (except Monday) from late May through early September. From early September through mid-October the house is open on weekends and holidays. Admission costs $7 for adults ($5 for the gardens only), $2.50 for children six to 12; under six free. Follow Pine St from the Red Lion Inn to Prospect St.

### Mission House

This historic residence (☎ 413-298-3239) on Main St was the home of the Reverend John Sergeant, the first missionary to the native peoples in this area. He built the original part of the house in 1739. It's furnished with 17th- and 18th-century effects and houses a small museum of Native American artifacts. It's open from late May through early September from 11 am to 3:30 pm. Admission costs $5 for adults, $2.50 for children six to 12.

### Merwin House

At 14 Main St, this late-Federal-style brick residence (☎ 413-298-4703) is furnished with an eclectic mix of European and American

pieces. There are tours at noon, 1, 2, 3 and 4 pm on Tuesday, Thursday, Saturday and Sunday, June through mid-October. Admission costs $4 for adults, $3.50 seniors, $2 children 12 and under.

### Berkshire Botanical Garden

Two miles from the center of Stockbridge the 15-acre Berkshire Botanical Garden (☎ 413-298-3926), at 5 W Stockbridge Rd (MA 102), is within walking distance of the Norman Rockwell Museum. Wildflowers herbs, perennials, water plants, an alpine forest and rock gardens are yours to enjoy 10 am to 5 pm daily. Admission costs $5 for adults, $4 seniors; children 12 and under are free.

### West Stockbridge

Though not nearly as picturesque as Stockbridge, West Stockbridge still retains its historic charm. Old country stores and the 19th-century train station stand next to new galleries and art studios. This is a great place to stay during Tanglewood season, because Lenox is less than a 15-minute drive away on rarely used backcountry roads.

### Places to Stay

There are numerous inns and B&Bs in and around Stockbridge. The following are among the least expensive.

***Williamson Guest House*** (☎ 413-298-4931, 32 Church St), a mile from the Stockbridge town center, is a large yellow house on a scenic road. The four rooms with shared baths are priced from $75 to $90. The inn is only open in the summer.

***Red Lion Inn*** (☎ 413-298-5545, fax 298-5130, 30 Main St) is the very heart of Stockbridge. A huge 108-room white frame hotel, it dominates the town center both by its size and activity. Founded in 1773, it was completely rebuilt after a fire in 1897. Rooms are a bit pricey, from $165 to $255. However, rooms with shared baths are only $87.

***Card Lake Inn*** (☎ 413-232-0272, 29 Main St), in West Stockbridge, is owned by a young family with twins, so this is a good place for families. The eight rooms range from $80 to $95, and include a hearty breakfast.

*The Williamsville Inn* (☎ 413-274-6118), on MA 41, in West Stockbridge, is a 1797 farmhouse 5 miles from the center of West Stockbridge. The 16 rooms range from $130 to $150, but are worth the splurge to stay in a room that reeks and creaks with history. Thick wood floors, exposed beams, and red brick fireplaces are de rigueur.

## Places to Eat
The *Red Lion Inn* (see Places to Stay, above) is also Stockbridge's premier place for dining. Besides the elegant formal dining room, there's the *Widow Bingham Tavern*, a rustic colonial pub. The *Lion's Den*, downstairs, is the cocktail lounge with a sandwich and salad menu. On weekends, they have good jazz and folk music. Plan to spend about $35 or $40 per person for a luxurious continental dinner. In summer, you can dine in the pretty courtyard in back.

*Once Upon a Table* (☎ 413-298-3870, 36 Main St), in the Mews not far away, serves upscale fare such as pan-seared sea bass or sweet potato-filled ravioli, on its glass-enclosed porch. Dishes range from $12 to $18 for dinner. An assortment of soups and sandwiches are available for lunch. It is closed Tuesdays.

*Main Street Café* (☎ 413-298-3060, 40 Main St) is a fine place for sandwiches and salads in the $5 to $8 range.

*Daily Bread Bakery* (☎ 413-298-0272, 31 Main St), 'on the sunny side of Main St,' sells cakes, cookies, bread and rolls that are good for snacks or picnics.

*Caffe Pomodoro* (☎ 413-232-4616), in West Stockbridge, in the 1838 railroad station right next to the post office, is where the local artisans lunch on large sandwiches and freshly made soups.

*Berkshire Ice Cream*, (☎ 413-232-4111, 4 Albany Rd), in West Stockbridge, recently won over big boys Haagen-Dazs and Ben & Jerry's in a taste test sponsored by the *Boston Globe*. The increasingly popular ice cream, now featured at Tanglewood, is made with pure Golden Guernsey milk, from the owner's farm. Try a scoop of the sublime black raspberry.

*The Williamsville Inn* (☎ 413-274-6118, 286 Great Barrington Rd), on MA 41 in West Stockbridge, is the ideal choice for couples looking for an intimate candlelit dinner. Book a table in the private Library Room, and while away the hours dining on salmon, steak or chicken dishes. Expect to spend about $30 per person.

## Entertainment
The *Berkshire Theatre Festival* (☎ 413-298-5576, PO Box 797, Stockbridge, MA 01262-0797) stages new and innovative plays from late June through early September at its Mainstage and smaller Unicorn Theatre. Tickets are priced from $18 to $31. There's a Children's Theatre ($5) as well. Call or write for current offerings.

## Getting There & Away
The driving details for Stockbridge are as follows:

| destination | mileage | hr:min |
| --- | --- | --- |
| Great Barrington, MA | 7 miles | 0:15 |
| Lee, MA | 5 miles | 0:15 |
| Lenox, MA | 7 miles | 0:20 |
| West Stockbridge, MA | 8 miles | 0:17 |

## LEE
Lee, incorporated in 1777, is a historic town like many of its neighbors. Though there is nothing wrong with Lee, most people go barreling through it, forgetting that they're no longer on the turnpike, heading for some other town. Some of those who go to Lenox end up back in Lee looking for a vacant motel or B&B room.

### Orientation & Information
The town of Lee, at I-90 exit 2, is the gateway to Lenox, Stockbridge and Great Barrington. US 20 is Lee's main street, and leads to Lenox.

The Lee Chamber of Commerce (☎ 413-243-0852, www.leelodging.org), PO Box 345, Lee, MA 01238-0345, maintains an information booth on the town green in front of the town hall in summer. The chamber of commerce can help visitors out with accommodations recommendations.

## Jacob's Pillow Dance Festival

Founded by Ted Shawn in an old barn in 1932, Jacob's Pillow has developed into one of the USA's premier summer dance festivals. Through the years Alvin Ailey, Merce Cunningham, the Martha Graham Dance Company, the Bill T Jones/Arnie Zane Dance Company and other leading interpreters of the dance have taken part. The theaters are in the village of Becket, 7 miles east of Lee along US 20 and MA 8. For a brochure, call, fax or write Jacob's Pillow (☎ 413-243-0745, fax 243-4744), PO Box 287, Lee, MA 01238-0287. Performances take place from mid-June through early September. Tickets are priced from $15 to $50.

## October Mountain State Forest

Remarkably, most out-of-towners who venture to the Berkshires head to the Mt Greylock State Reservation to see the state's highest peak and thus leave this 16,500-acre state park (☎ 413-243-1778), the largest tract of green space in Massachusetts, to the locals. Canoe Buckley Dunton Reservoir, a small body of water stocked with bass and pickerel and hidden amidst the hardwoods. For hikers, a nine-mile stretch of the Appalachian Trail pierces the heart of the forest through copses of hemlocks, spruces, birches and oaks. To get there from Lee, follow Route 20 West for 3 miles and look for signs.

### Places to Stay

For campers, the *October Mountain State Forest (☎ 877-422-6762, for reservations)* has 45 sites with hot showers available near the shores of the Housatonic River. Cost is $6. To find the campground, turn east off US 20 onto Center St and follow the signs.

There's also a wonderful cabin on the shores of scenic Upper Goose Pond run by the Berkshire chapter of the Appalachian Mountain Club (☎ 413-499-4262). To get there, follow MA 20 West from Lee for 2 miles until you see signs for the Appalachian Trail. Park the car and continue on foot 2 miles south on the AT. This cabin in the woods has bunks for eight campers and is only open in the summer. First come, first served. Cost for a bunk bed is $3.

Lee's motels are clustered around I-90 exit 2, on heavily trafficked Route 7. They include the *Super 8 Motel (☎ 413-243-0143, 170 Housatonic St)*, the 22-room *Sunset Motel (☎ 413-243-0302, 114 Housatonic St)* and the *Pilgrim Motel (☎ 413-243-1328, 127 Housatonic St)*. Prices range from $65 to $145.

*Inn at Laurel Lake (☎ 413-243-1436, 615 Laurel St)* is one of the few lodgings in the Berkshires that sits on the shores of a lake and thus features swimming and boating. Ideal for families, the 19 rooms cost $95 to $195.

### Places to Eat

For a meal, there's no better slice of Americana in the Berkshires than *Joe's Diner (☎ 413-243-9756, 63 Center St)*. Norman Rockwell's famous painting of a policeman sitting at a counter talking to a young boy, *The Runaway* (1958), was partly inspired by this diner. Indeed, every politician who's ever run for office in Massachusetts, including Senator Ted Kennedy and former Governor Michael Dukakis, has stopped at Joe's to get his or her picture taken and put on the wall. Open 24 hours, Joe's is about as cheap as you get in the Berkshires.

To stock up on sandwiches and beverages before heading out to hike in October Mountain State Forest, head to *Juice and Java (60 Main St)*.

### Getting There & Away

Driving details for Lee are as follows:

| destination | mileage | hr:min |
| --- | --- | --- |
| Boston, MA | 134 miles | 3:00 |
| Great Barrington, MA | 11 miles | 0:25 |
| Lenox, MA | 5 miles | 0:12 |
| Springfield, MA | 45 miles | 1:00 |

## LENOX

Originally named Yokuntown after a local Native American leader, Lenox took its current name in honor of Charles Lenox, Duke of Richmond, who had been sympathetic to the American Revolution.

This gracious, wealthy town is an historical anomaly: its charm was not destroyed by the Industrial Revolution, and then, prized for its bucolic peace, the town became a summer retreat for those wealthy families (like Andrew Carnegie's) who had made their fortunes by building factories in other towns.

Today, Lenox is home to the Tanglewood Music Festival, an incredibly popular summer event since its inception in 1934.

## Orientation & Information

It's easy to get around Lenox on foot, though some of the many inns are a mile or two from the center. Tanglewood is located 1½ miles west of Lenox's center along West St (MA 183).

The Lenox Chamber of Commerce (☎ 413-637-3646, www.lenox.org), 75 Main St (PO Box 646), Lenox, MA 01240, is the local source of information, open Tuesday through Saturday from 10 am to 6 pm, Sunday until 2 pm, Monday until 4 pm. They'll help you with same-day room reservations. Pick up a copy of the pamphlet *Walking through Lenox History,* detailing the interesting buildings from Lenox's past.

Simply called The Bookstore (☎ 413-637-3390), 9 Housatonic St, this is the place to stop for that map, atlas or summer novel you need.

## Berkshire Scenic Railway Museum

This museum (☎ 413-637-2210), on Willow Creek Rd, 1½ miles east of Lenox center, is a nonprofit museum of railroad lore set up in Lenox's 1902 railroad station.

The museum's two elaborate model railroad displays are favorites with children, as is the short train ride in a full-size train on the museum grounds. Admission is free; the train ride costs $2 for adults, $1 for children.

## The Mount

Almost 50 years after Nathaniel Hawthorne left his home in Lenox (now part of the Tanglewood estate), another writer found inspiration in the Berkshires. Edith Wharton (1862-1937) came to Lenox in 1899 and proceeded to build her palatial estate, the Mount. Wharton summered at the Mount

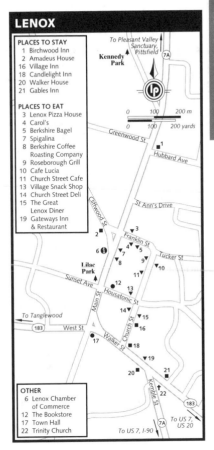

**LENOX**

**PLACES TO STAY**
1 Birchwood Inn
2 Amadeus House
16 Village Inn
18 Candlelight Inn
20 Walker House
21 Gables Inn

**PLACES TO EAT**
3 Lenox Pizza House
4 Carol's
5 Berkshire Bagel
7 Spigalina
8 Berkshire Coffee Roasting Company
9 Roseborough Grill
10 Cafe Lucia
11 Church Street Cafe
13 Village Snack Shop
14 Church Street Deli
15 The Great Lenox Diner
19 Gateways Inn & Restaurant

**OTHER**
6 Lenox Chamber of Commerce
12 The Bookstore
17 Town Hall
22 Trinity Church

for a decade before moving permanently to France. When not writing, she would entertain friends such as Henry James.

The dramatic conclusion of *Ethan Frome* (1911) was based on an actual sleigh ride accident on Lenox's Courthouse Hill.

Today, the Mount stages plays by the acting troupe Shakespeare & Company (see below). You can tour The Mount (☎ 413-637-1899), at Plunkett St and US 7 on the outskirts of Lenox, hourly 10 am to 2 pm daily, except Monday, in summer, and on weekends through mid-October. Admission costs $6 for adults, $5.50 seniors, $4.50 children 13 to 18 (12 and under free).

## Pleasant Valley Sanctuary

The 1112-acre wildlife sanctuary (☎ 413-637-0320), at 472 W Mountain Rd, has several pleasant walking trails through forests of maples, oaks, beeches and birches. It's not uncommon to see beavers here if you come at dawn or dusk. To find the sanctuary, go north on US 7 or MA 7A. Three-quarters of a mile north of the intersection of US 7 and MA 7A, turn left onto W Dugway Rd and go 1½ miles to the sanctuary.

## Tanglewood Music Festival

In 1934, Boston Symphony Orchestra conductor Serge Koussevitzky's dream of a center for serious musical study came true with the acquisition of the 400-acre Tanglewood estate in Lenox. Young musicians – including Leonard Bernstein, Seiji Ozawa and many others – came to Tanglewood to study at the side of the great masters. Along with the lessons came musical performances: concerts by masters and students together.

Today, the Tanglewood Music Festival is among the most esteemed music events in the world. Symphony, pops, chamber music, recitals, jazz and blues are performed from late June through early September. Performance spaces include the coyly named 'Shed,' a simple 6000-seat concert shelter with several sides open to the surrounding lawns. The newest space is the Seiji Ozawa Concert Hall. Electronic amplification systems boost the music's volume for those seated on the lawn, making it easier to hear, but less worth hearing.

The Boston Symphony Orchestra concerts on weekends in July and August are the most popular events at Tanglewood. Most casual (as opposed to devoted) attendees – up to 8000 of them on a typical summer weekend evening – arrive three or four hours before concert time. They stake out good listening spots on the lawn outside the Shed or the Concert Hall, then relax and enjoy elaborate picnic suppers until the music starts. The event is for everyone, including young families, many of whom come with their babies in tow.

Contemporary star performers include greats such as Midori, Itzhak Perlman, Anne-Sophie Mutter, Yo-Yo Ma and André Watts. Besides classical stars, such notable popular performers as Frank Sinatra, James Taylor, Wynton Marsalis (in jazz mode), The Manhattan Transfer, Joshua Redman Quartet and Ray Charles have given Tanglewood concerts.

**Tickets** Tickets range from $13 to $14 per person for picnic space on the lawn to $79 for the best seats at the most popular concerts. If you pay for general admission to the lawn and it rains during the concert, you get wet. (Sorry, no refunds or exchanges.)

For information, call ☎ 617-266-1492 in Boston; ☎ 413-637-5165 in Lenox (after June 5) or ☎ 413-637-1666 for weekly program information. Tickets may be purchased at the box office at Tanglewood's main entrance, or through the Ticketmaster service (subject to a service fee). Ticketmaster's numbers are ☎ 617-931-2000 in Boston; ☎ 413-733-2500 in the Berkshires; ☎ 212-307-7171 in New York City; and ☎ 800-347-0808 from other areas.

If you arrive two or three hours before concert time, you can often get lawn space; Shed and Concert Hall seats should be bought in advance.

**Parking** Ample concert parking is available. Keep in mind that parking – and, more importantly, *unparking* – 6000 cars can take time. It's all organized very well and runs smoothly, but you will still have to wait a while in your car during the exodus.

**Organized Tours** You can take a walking tour of the Tanglewood grounds on Wednesday at 10:30 am or Saturday at 1:15 pm, starting from the visitors' center.

Several tour companies operate special Tanglewood concert buses that take you directly to the concert, then back home. In Boston, call K&L Tours (☎ 617-267-1905); in New York City, call Biss Tours (☎ 718-426-4000).

## Other Concerts

The renown of Tanglewood has drawn other musicians and audiences to Lenox. The Armstrong Chamber Concert series (☎ 860-868-0522) performs in Lenox's National Music Center from April through October. The National Music Center (☎ 413-637-4718 for schedules and tickets, 413-637-1800 for information), 70 Kemble St, also presents pop, folk, blues, country and jazz concerts in its 1200-seat state-of-the-art theater.

The Berkshire Opera Company (☎ 413-528-4420) stages full-dress productions of classic and modern operas in the Cranwell Opera House on US 20.

## Shakespeare & Company

Among the most enjoyable cultural events of a Lenox summer are the performances of the Bard's great plays staged on the grounds of Edith Wharton's lavish mansion, The Mount (see above), by Shakespeare & Company (☎ 413-637-1199, fax 637-4274). There are several performance spaces, including small theaters in the mansion itself and in the stables, but for the 'Mainstage,' the lawn is the stage, the forest the backdrop, and plays such as *A Midsummer Night's Dream* really come to life. Plays are staged daily except Monday. Tickets cost $12.50 to $35.

## Activities

Kennedy Park in downtown Lenox is popular with mountain bikers in the summer and cross-country skiers in the winter. The Arcadian (☎ 413-637-3010), 91 Pittsfield Rd (US 7), rents mountain, road, and children's bikes ($25), cross-country skies and snowshoes ($11). They also rent tents ($15) and sleeping bags ($15).

## Places to Stay

Lenox has no hotels and only a few motels, including the *Susse Chalet* (☎ 413-637-3560, fax 637-3218) and the *Quality Inn* (☎ 413-637-4244, 130 Pittsfield Rd), on US 7, 2 miles north of the town center. Rooms range from $95 to $179. However, there are lots of wonderful inns.

Because of Tanglewood's weekend concerts, many inns require a two- or three-night minimum stay on summer weekends. When you add the 5.7% state room tax and 4% Lenox room tax to weekend rates, that means a Lenox weekend can cost $280 to $500 just for lodging. Faced with such prices, many thrifty travelers opt to sleep in lower-priced communities such as Great Barrington. But if you can afford them, Lenox's inns provide charming digs and memorable stays.

Most inn rooms have a private bath, and include a full breakfast and perhaps even afternoon tea. Prices are always quoted per double room. Very few Lenox inns accept children under 10 or 12, or pets.

*Walker House* (☎ 413-637-1271, 74 Walker St), convenient to everything in the town center, looks relatively modest from the front. Behind the classic façade are three acres of gardens and the friendliest innkeepers in town. The eight rooms with private bath cost $90 to $150 midweek, $110 to $200 weekends.

*Amadeus House* (☎ 413-637-4770, 800-205-4770, 15 Cliffwood St) is modest compared to some of Lenox's great houses, but very comfortable and reasonably priced at $65 to $115 midweek, $85 to $175 weekends. The owner of this homey eight-room inn is a former classical music correspondent on National Public Radio who enjoys chatting with his guests about the previous night's performance.

*The Village Inn* (☎ 413-637-0020, fax 637-9756, 16 Church St) was built in 1771. The Federal-style inn has 32 rooms with bath priced from $90 to $225, a dining room serving breakfast, afternoon tea and dinner, and a tavern featuring English ales, draft beer and light meals.

The *Candlelight Inn* (☎ 413-637-1555, 35 Walker St) is well known for its candlelit restaurant. The guest rooms, at $80 to $175, are simple but comfy and well located.

*The Gables Inn* (☎ 413-637-3416, 103 Walker St) was originally known as Pine Acre. Built in 1885, the Queen-Anne-style 'cottage' was the summer home of Mrs William C Wharton, whose son Teddy married Edith Newbold Jones (see The Mount, above). The house has been nicely restored, and now rents its 17 rooms for $90 to $210.

*The Birchwood Inn* (☎ *413-637-2600, 800-524-1646, 7 Hubbard St*) dates from 1767. The mansard-roofed house is now quite a gracious inn enjoying fine views of the town. The 12 rooms cost $60 to $210 per night.

If money is no object, the place for you is *Blantyre* (☎ *413-637-3556, fax 637-4282*), 3 miles west of I-90 exit 2 along US 20. An imitation Scottish Tudor mansion built in 1902, Blantyre sits on 85 acres of grounds equipped with four tennis courts, croquet lawns, a swimming pool, hot tub and sauna. The 23 rooms, suites and cottages are priced from $290 to $685 per night, continental breakfast included.

Shadowbrook, the former summer home of Andrew Carnegie, is now one of America's finest yoga centers, *Kripalu Center* (☎ *413-448-3400*), on MA 183. Their spectacular 300-acre grounds, within walking distance of Tanglewood, overlook Stockbridge Bowl (a small lake). Kripalu accommodates some 300 students who come to study yoga and meditation in peaceful surroundings. Rates for their most popular program, 'Retreat & Renewal,' including a variety of workshops and good vegetarian meals, start at $75 per day for a dormitory room.

## Places to Eat

The chamber of commerce has a collection of menus from local restaurants. Because many people take picnics to the Tanglewood concerts, most eateries can prepare your chosen food for take out. Start your restaurant roamings on Church St, which is lined with eateries.

**Breakfast & Lunch**  Because of Lenox's city-sophisticate clientele, it's easy to find balsamic vinegar this and three-mustard that. So where does one find cheap, good food? At the old-time diner, *Village Snack Shop* (☎ *413-637-2564, 35 Housatonic St*), at Church St, breakfast and lunch are served at the lunch counter and won't break your budget.

*Church Street Deli* (☎ *413-637-0979, 37 Church St*) is a simple place to grab a decent sandwich for lunch.

The *Berkshire Bagel* (☎ *413-637-1500, 18 Franklin St*) has reasonable bagels and bagel-sandwiches for $1 to $4.

The *Lenox Pizza House* (☎ *413-637-2590, 7 Franklin St*) serves pan pizza (whole pie or by the slice), grinders, Greek salads and pasta.

*Carol's* (☎ *413-637-8948*), across from the Lenox Pizza House on Franklin St, has a long menu of light meals and snacks priced around $6, plus lots of take-out items.

*The Berkshire Coffee Roasting Company* (☎ *413-637-1606, 52 Main St*) is where locals linger over steaming bowls of cafe au lait.

**Dinner**  Though some of these restaurants serve lunch and dinner, most do only the evening meal.

*The Great Lenox Diner* (☎ *413-637-3204, 30 Church St*) is your best bet for a cheap dinner in town. They serve typical diner fare such as meat loaf, Yankee pot roast and rotisserie chicken for $6.95 to $9.95.

*Church Street Cafe* (☎ *413-637-2745, 69 Church St*) has made customers happy for years with its reasonably priced lunches (under $10) and inventive dinners ($17.50 to $25.50 for entrees), served in a large festive dining room and on the deck.

*Roseborough Grill* (☎ *413-637-2700, 83 Church St*), just down from the Church Street Cafe and similar in price, is a converted house with tables set out on the front porch. The emphasis here is on fresh local produce, home-baked goods and grilled meats, poultry, fish and vegetables.

*Cafe Lucia* (☎ *413-637-2640, 90 Church St*) serves classic, though somewhat pricey, Italian dinners (it's closed on Sunday and Monday), as does *Antonio's* (☎ *413-637-9894*), around the corner on Franklin St.

One restaurant in town that local inn owners rave about is *Spigalina* (☎ *413-637-4455, 80 Main St*). Tantalizing pasta, fish and meat dishes are served in a room where dim lighting and yellow walls create a Mediterranean ambience. Expect to spend $25 per person.

A number of inns in Lenox serve elegant dinners: *The Village Inn* has a good dining room with moderate prices. The *Candlelight Inn* has four dining rooms decorated in early 20th-century style. Come for dinner (you can sit outside in good weather), or to get after-performance drinks and desserts. See Places to Stay in the Lenox section for contact information.

The *Gateways Inn & Restaurant* (☎ 413-637-2532, 51 Walker St) was the mansion of Harley T Procter (of Procter & Gamble). He supposedly wanted the house to look like a bar of Ivory Soap (not even close). Its elegant dining room is known as the place to go in town for an anniversary or birthday dinner and its chef won high acclaim from the food magazine *Gourmet*. Prices for main dishes range from $17 to $27.

### Getting There & Away
The nearest airports are in Windsor Locks and in Albany. Peter Pan Bus Lines (☎ 800-343-9999) operates buses between Lenox and Boston. See the Tanglewood Music Festival section, above, for organized tours information. Trains stop in nearby Pittsfield (see that section for details).

Driving details for Lenox are as follows:

| destination | mileage | hr:min |
|---|---|---|
| Albany, NY | 45 miles | 1:00 |
| Boston, MA | 138 miles | 3:10 |
| Great Barrington, MA | 16 miles | 0:30 |
| Hartford, CT | 78 miles | 1:30 |
| Lee, MA | 5 miles | 0:12 |
| Litchfield, CT | 46 miles | 1:15 |
| New York, NY | 147 miles | 3:20 |
| Pittsfield, MA | 7 miles | 0:15 |
| Springfield, MA | 40 miles | 0:55 |
| Stockbridge, MA | 5 miles | 0:12 |
| West Stockbridge, MA | 9 miles | 0:20 |
| Williamstown, MA | 29 miles | 0:50 |

## PITTSFIELD
Pittsfield is the service city of Berkshire County and the least attractive part of the region. This is where the trains stop and where one finds the biggest stores. For tourists, there are only two or three things worth stopping for.

### Orientation & Information
Park Square, at the intersection of North, South, East and West Sts, is the center of Pittsfield. North and South Sts are also US 7.

The RSVP tourist information booth in Park Square is open daily in summer. The Central Berkshire Chamber of Commerce (☎ 413-499-4000, www.bcn.net/commerce/central/), a half block west of Park Square in the Tierney Building, also provides information. The Berkshire Visitors Bureau (☎ 413-443-9186), inside the Berkshire Common building by the Crowne Plaza Hotel, has lots of information. Pittsfield Central (☎ 413-443-6501), 141 North St (US 7), 1½ blocks north of Park Square, can give you a brochure for a self-guided architectural walking tour of central Pittsfield.

### Hancock Shaker Village
The Shakers were among the earliest and most admirable of the numerous millennial Christian sects that flourished in the fertile climate of religious freedom in the New World. Hancock Shaker Village, 5 miles west of Pittsfield on US 20, gives you a studied look at their peaceful, prayerful way of life.

Twenty of the original Shaker buildings are carefully restored at Hancock Shaker Village and are open to view. Most famous is the Round Stone Barn (1826), but other structures, including the Brick Dwelling (1830), the laundry and the machine shop (1790), the trustees' office (1830-1895), the meetinghouse (1793) and the sisters' and brethren's shops (1795) are of equal interest.

The Hancock Shaker Village (☎ 413-443-0188), on US 20 and southwest of Pittsfield center near the intersection with MA 41 (*not* in the village of Hancock), was known as the 'City of Peace,' and was occupied by Shakers until 1960. At its peak in 1830, the community numbered some 300 souls. Preserved as a historic monument, the village still gives you a good look at what the excellent principles of Shakerism could accomplish.

Interpreters in the historic buildings demonstrate the quiet, kindly, hard-working Shaker way of life 9:30 am to 5 pm May through October; there are guided tours at 10 am and 3 pm in April and November.

Admission costs $33 for a family, $13.50 adults, $5.50 children six to 17; under six are free. On Saturday evening, you can feast on a bountiful Shaker candlelit dinner while being entertained by Shaker music. Call for details and reservations.

## Berkshire Museum

Pittsfield's major repository of art, history and natural science is the Berkshire Museum (☎ 413-443-7171), 39 South St (US 7), just south of Park Square. The museum's painting collection holds the works of 19th-century masters such as Bierstadt, Church, Copley, Inness and Peale. The history collections are strong in regional artifacts, tools, firearms, dolls and costumes. The natural science section highlights the ecology, flora and fauna of the Berkshires and has a rock and mineral collection numbering over 3000 pieces.

It's open 10 am to 5 pm daily in July and August (Sunday 1 to 5 pm) and Tuesday through Sunday the rest of the year. Admission costs $6 for adults, $5 seniors and students, $4 youths 12 to 18; under 12 are free.

## Melville's Arrowhead

The novelist Herman Melville (1819-1891) lived in Pittsfield at 780 Holmes Rd from 1850 to 1863. Melville moved to Pittsfield to work on a farm so he could support himself while he wrote. It was here, in the house he called Arrowhead (☎ 413-442-1793), that he wrote his masterwork, *Moby Dick*.

Inspired by the view of Mt Greylock in winter, which supposedly reminded him of a whale, Melville completed the 600-plus pages of *Moby Dick* in less than a year. The house is now a museum maintained by the Berkshire County Historical Society and is open for visits or guided tours. It is open

---

### Shakes of Ecstasy

The United Society of Believers in Christ's Second Appearing, or the Millennial Church, popularly known as the Shakers, an offshoot of Quakerism, began in 1747 in England. Followers of the sect believed in, and strictly observed the principles of, communal possessions, pacifism, open confession of sins and equality – but celibacy – of the sexes.

Shakers believed that God had both a male and a female nature. Ann Lee, an ardent follower of the sect, proclaimed that she had been blessed with the 'mother element' of the spirit of Jesus. Calling herself Mother Ann, she pressed her claim so zealously that she was imprisoned.

On her release, she set sail with a handful of followers for New York. They founded the first Shaker community in the New World near Albany, in 1774.

Mother Ann died in 1784, but her followers went on to found other Shaker communities in northern New England. In addition to Hancock, there are surviving Shaker communities at Canterbury, New Hampshire (near Concord), and Sabbathday Lake, Maine (north of Portland).

With celibacy as a tenet, Shakerism depended upon conversion for its growth and sustenance. Converts to the church turned over all their worldly possessions to the movement and worked selflessly on its behalf, but members were free to leave at any time. Shaker worship services were characterized by a communal dancelike movement, during which some congregants would be overcome with religious zeal and suffer tremors ('shakes') of ecstasy.

Each community was organized into 'families' of 30 to 90 members who lived and worked together. Though there was equality of the sexes, there was also a good deal of segregation. Communities were largely self-sufficient, trading produce and handicrafts with the rest of the world for the things they could not produce themselves. Work, among Shakers, was considered a consecrated act, an attitude reflected in the high quality of workmanship and design of Shaker furniture and crafts. In effect, every product was a prayer.

10 am to 5 pm (last tour at 4:30 pm) weekdays. Admission costs $4.50 adults, $4 senior, $3 children six to 16; $15 for a family.

## Places to Stay & Eat

Pittsfield has the usual selection of business-oriented hotels and motels for a city of its size. Most visitors prefer to stay in one of the more picturesque communities such as Lenox, Great Barrington or Williamstown.

There are plenty of places to pick up a quick meal on North and South Sts (US 7) as you pass through or around Park Square, if you plan to stop. But there's one place here, *Elizabeth's* (☎ *413-448-8244, 1264 East St)*, to which innkeepers in Lenox have no qualms about sending their clientele. Don't be put off by the locale of this nondescript pink building that sits across the street from a vacant General Electric plant. Chefs travel from New York and Boston to sample Tom and Elizabeth Ellis' innovative pasta dishes.

Start with the *insalata mista*, a house salad overflowing with crisp greens, veggies, fruits and cheeses. Then choose the special pasta of the day, often something as imaginative as linguine with clam sauce infused with Thai spices (lemongrass and ginger). Pastas are priced from $8.95 to $13.95, including the house salad.

## Getting There & Away

**Air** The nearest airports are in Windsor Locks and in Albany. For airport transportation, contact Peter Pan Bus Lines (see Bus, below).

**Bus** The Pittsfield Bus Terminal (☎ 413-442-4451) is at 57 S Church St.

Peter Pan Bus Lines (☎ 800-343-9999) operates routes connecting Pittsfield with Albany, Bennington, Boston, Hartford, Lee, Lenox, North Adams, Springfield, Toronto, Williamstown and Worcester. Many other destinations, including Amherst, Hyannis, New Haven, New York City, Philadelphia and Washington, are available via Peter Pan's Springfield hub.

Bonanza Bus Lines (☎ 800-556-3815) runs buses daily between New York City and Bennington through Great Barrington, Stockbridge, Lee, Lenox, Pittsfield (with

connecting service to Albany) and Williamstown. The ride between New York City and Pittsfield takes about four hours.

**Train** For Amtrak information, see the Train section at the beginning of this chapter.

**Car** The driving details for Pittsfield are as follows:

| destination | mileage | hr:min |
|---|---|---|
| Albany, NY | 38 miles | 0:50 |
| Bennington, VT | 36 miles | 0:50 |
| Boston, MA | 145 miles | 3:20 |
| Hartford, CT | 85 miles | 1:40 |
| Lenox, MA | 7 miles | 0:15 |
| Litchfield, CT | 53 miles | 1:25 |
| New York, NY | 154 miles | 3:30 |
| Springfield, MA | 47 miles | 1:10 |
| Williamstown, MA | 22 miles | 0:40 |

## WILLIAMSTOWN

After all the domestic architectural extravagances of the central Berkshires area, Williamstown comes as something of a surprise. The big buildings here are not palatial mansions, but marble-faced college halls. The northwestern corner of Massachusetts, though far from university-strewn Boston or the college-crowded Pioneer Valley, has its own prestigious institution of higher learning in Williams College. Bennington College is only 30 minutes north, in Vermont, making this area of the Berkshires something of a find.

## History

Ephraim Williams Jr, born in 1714, was a soldier in the British colonial army. He worked at surveying this area until he was given command of the line of British frontier forts facing the French North American territories. Fort Massachusetts, in North Adams, was one of these forts. Six miles to the west was the town of West Hoosuck.

In 1755, Williams led a column of Massachusetts troops toward Lake George and the French positions there. He died in the fighting. His will provided a substantial amount of money for the founding of a college in West Hoosuck, if the town would rename itself after him. Luckily for future Hoosuckers, it did. Williams College, in Williamstown, enrolled its first students in 1793. The college is now, and has been for two centuries, the lifeblood of the town.

## Orientation

US 7 and MA 2 (Main St) intersect at the western corner of the town center. The small central commercial district is off Main St on Spring St. Other businesses, including motels, are on US 7 and MA 2 on the outskirts of town. The marble-and-brick-faced buildings of Williams College fill the town center.

## Information

In summer, the Williamstown Board of Trade (☎ 413-458-9077), PO Box 357, Williamstown, MA 01267, operates its self-service information booth at the intersection of MA 2 and US 7, a short distance from the Williams Inn. You can pick up a copy of 'Williamstown: A Walk along Main Street,' a brochure that details a self-guided tour of the town's interesting old buildings.

For information about Williams College, contact the Office of Public Information (☎ 413-597-3131), Williams College, PO Box 676, Williamstown, MA 01267.

The Northern Berkshire Chamber of Commerce (☎ 413-663-3735, www.bcn.net/ commerce/northern), in the Windsor Mill, Union St (MA 2), North Adams, MA 01247, is another information source.

## Clark Art Institute

The Sterling and Francine Clark Art Institute (☎ 413-458-9545), 225 South St, is a gem among American art museums.

Robert Sterling Clark (1877-1956), a Yale engineer whose family had made money in the sewing machine industry, began collecting art in Paris in 1912. He and his French wife, Francine, eventually housed their wonderful collection in Williamstown, in a white marble temple built expressly for the purpose.

The collection and its needs soon outgrew the original building. In 1973, the museum's space was greatly expanded.

The Clarks' collections are particularly strong in the impressionists, their academic contemporaries in France and the mid-century Barbizon artists, including Millet, Troyon and Corot. Contemporary American painting is represented by Cassatt, Homer, Remington and Sargent. From earlier centuries, there are excellent works by Piero della Francesca, Memling, Gossaert, Jacob van Ruisdael, Fragonard, Gainsborough, Turner and Goya. There are some sculptures, including Degas' famous *Little Dancer of Fourteen Years*, as well as prints, drawings and noteworthy collections of silver and porcelain.

Even if you are not an avid art lover, you should not miss this museum. It is less than a mile south of the information booth at the intersection of US 7 and MA 2. It's open 10 am to 5 pm, closed Monday; admission is free.

## Williams College Museum of Art

The Clark Art Institute's sister museum in Williamstown is the very highly regarded Williams College Museum of Art (☎ 413-597-2429), in Lawrence Hall, the Greek Revival building on Main St backed by a big modern addition. The college museum hosts traveling exhibits and stages its own with works from community and regional artists. Call for current offerings. It's open daily from 10 am to 5 pm (Sunday 1 to 5 pm), and admission is free.

## Massachusetts Museum of Contemporary Art

The MASS MoCA (☎ 413-662-2111) is no ordinary gallery museum. It's housed in the former Sprague Electric Company factory; more than 31 million dollars were spent to modernize 'the largest gallery in the United States.' The museum includes 220,000 sq feet of space in five buildings, with 19 galleries, art construction areas and performance centers. The spaces are huge, large enough to exhibit Robert Rauschenberg's '*The ¼ Mile or 2 Furlong Piece*,' which was exhibited at the museum's opening.

Large, audacious works in mixed media, some even with moving or performance com-

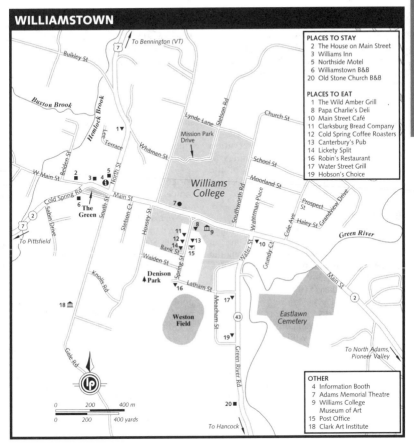

**WILLIAMSTOWN**

To Bennington (VT)

Bulkley St

Buxton Brook

Hemlock Brook

Lynde Lane

Church St

Mission Park Drive

Stetson Rd

Terrace

Whitman St

School St

Belden St

North St

W Main St

Moorland St

Williams College

Waterman Place

Prospect St

Cole Ave

Haley St

Grandview Drive

Cold Spring Rd

Main St

Green River

Sabin Drive

To Pittsfield

6 The Green

Stetson Ct

South St

Hoxsey St

Spring St

Bank St

Walden St

11
12
14
15

8
13
9

Water St

10

Grundy Ct

Knolls Rd

Denison Park

Latham St

16

17

Meacham St

Main St

18

Weston Field

43

Green River Rd

Eastlawn Cemetery

19

20

To North Adams, Pioneer Valley

To Hancock

**PLACES TO STAY**
2  The House on Main Street
3  Williams Inn
5  Northside Motel
6  Williamstown B&B
20  Old Stone Church B&B

**PLACES TO EAT**
1  The Wild Amber Grill
8  Papa Charlie's Deli
10  Main Street Café
11  Clarksburg Bread Company
12  Cold Spring Coffee Roasters
13  Canterbury's Pub
14  Lickety Split
16  Robin's Restaurant
17  Water Street Grill
19  Hobson's Choice

**OTHER**
4  Information Booth
7  Adams Memorial Theatre
9  Williams College Museum of Art
15  Post Office
18  Clark Art Institute

0    200    400 m
0    200    400 yards

ponents, fit right in. Indeed, the museum itself is very much a work in progress. Another 350,000 sq feet of space is marked for renovation as funds become available.

The museum is open 10 am to 5 pm daily June through October (until 7 pm on Friday and Saturday); 10 am to 4 pm Tuesday through Sunday, from November through May.

## Mt Greylock State Reservation

Mt Greylock (3491 feet) is Massachusetts' highest peak. It sits in an 18-sq-mile forest reservation of balsam fir, beech, birch, maple, red oak and red spruce that also includes Mt Prospect, Mt Fitch, Mt Williams and Saddle Ball Mountain.

Wildlife in the reserve includes bears, bobcats, deer, porcupines, raccoons and birds such as hawks, grouse, thrushes, ravens and wild turkeys.

The **Hopper** is a stunning V-shaped wedge of trees that forms a valley between Mts Greylock, Williams and Prospect and Stoney Ledge. Its forests have some old-growth trees (more than 150 years old).

There's an access road to the summit that begins in North Adams, 6 miles east of Williamstown along MA 2. Several miles up the road, as you reach the summit, you'll see the 92-foot-high War Veterans Memorial Tower (1932), restored in 1975, and Bascom Lodge (☎ 413-743-1591), a mountain hostelry built by the CCC in the 1930s. Bascom Lodge is administered by the AMC; it can provide beds for 32 people from mid-May through mid-October. Reservations are essential.

The Mt Greylock State Reservation (☎ 413-499-4262) has some 45 miles of hiking trails, including a portion of the Appalachian Trail. Several state parks have campsites (see Camping, below).

### Bicycling

Williamstown and environs, with its rolling farmland and quiet country roads, are an excellent place to bike. Route 43, along the Green River, is one of the prettier routes. The Spoke (☎ 413-458-3456), 618 Main St (US 2), rents bikes ($10).

### Special Events

From the third week in June to the third week in August, the Williamstown Theatre Festival (☎ 413-597-3399, tickets 597-3400), PO Box 517, Williamstown, MA 01267, mounts the region's major theatrical offerings, and tickets are usually inexpensive. This is one of the most renowned stages in the country for summer-stock theater. Kevin Kline, Richard Dreyfuss and Gwyneth Paltrow are but a few of the many well-known thespians who have performed here. The main works are presented in the 500-seat Adams Memorial Theatre on Main St. Plays in the 96-seat Other Stage are new and experimental. There are also cabaret performances in area restaurants. On Sundays, the Clark Art Institute is the scene for special dramatic events.

### Places to Stay

**Camping** The 35 campsites ($4) at *Mt Greylock State Reservation* (☎ 413-499-4262) should be your first choice. The sites are near scenic Stoney Ledge.

If you follow MA 8 north from North Adams, you'll pass *Natural Bridge State Park* (☎ 413-663-6392), a day-use area for picnicking; a bit farther along MA 8 is *Clarksburg State Park* (☎ 413-664-8345), on Middle Rd, with 47 campsites ($4) and pit toilets, but no showers.

*Savoy Mountain State Forest* (☎ 413-663-8469), on Central Shaft Rd, has 45 sites, some of which may be reserved in advance, priced at $6. There are showers and flush toilets. This is one of the top state parks for mountain biking.

**Motels & Hotels** There are hotels and motels on MA 2 East and US 7 North, as well as in the town center.

*Northside Motel* (☎ 413-458-8107, 45 North St), very near the information booth, charges $60 to $84 for its 33 rooms. It has a small pool and is near the museums.

*Williams Inn* (☎ 413-458-9371, 1090 Main St), on the green, is the major hotel in the center of town, with a restaurant and indoor pool. Its 100 rooms have the standard luxury hotel comforts and cost $100 to $175.

Out on US 7 North, *Cozy Corner Motel* (☎ 413-458-8006, 284 Sand Springs Rd), 1½ miles north of the information booth, charges $68 to $93 for its rooms, depending upon season, and prides itself on the fish and chips served in the adjoining restaurant.

The *Green Valley Motel* (☎ 413-458-3864, 1216 Simonds Rd), just to the south of the Vermont-Massachusetts state line, has 18 rooms with bathtubs and a swimming pool. Cost is $80. A light breakfast is included.

Going east from the town center along MA 2, you pass the following lodgings. *Four Acres Restaurant & Motel* (☎ 413-458-8158, 213 Main St) has 31 neat rooms for $60 to $115.

*The Orchards* (☎ 413-458-9611, 222 Adams Rd) is the area's most expensive place to stay, a modern hotel decorated as an old inn. The luxurious 47 rooms are priced from $165 to $230; the dining room is very good.

*Chimney Mirror Motel* (☎ 413-458-5202, 295 Main St), a mile east of the center, charges $65 to $90 for its 18 rooms with one or two double beds, serves a continental breakfast and has a picnic area.

***Willows Motel*** *(☎ 413-458-5768, 480 Main St)* has completely renovated its 16 rooms and is under new management. Prices range from $65 to $95.

The small, 15-room ***Maple Terrace Motel*** *(☎ 413-458-9677, 555 Main St)*, on the outskirts, has a big old house with motel units behind it, priced from $63 to $98, light breakfast included. There's a secluded pool.

There are additional inexpensive motels in North Adams, the next town to the east of Williamstown along MA 2.

**Inns & B&Bs** Most of these have a two-night minimum on weekends, and some require a three-night stay on holidays and during special college events. Breakfast is included in the rates.

The favorite of all is ***River Bend Farm*** *(☎ 413-458-3121, 643 Simonds Rd)*, just off US 7 on the north side of the little bridge over the Hoosic River. A Georgian tavern since revolutionary times, it has been carefully and authentically restored. Rooms with bath cost $90 to $115 double.

***Field Farm Guest House*** *(☎ 413-458-3135, 554 Sloan Rd)* was the country estate of art collectors Lawrence and Eleanore Bloedel. Built in spare, clean-lined post-WWII style on 296 wooded acres, the estate was willed to the Trustees of Reservations, which now operates it. The five modern rooms with bath are priced from $100 to $125. There's a pond, 4 miles of walking trails, a tennis court, a swimming pool and blissful quiet. Follow US 7 South to MA 43 West, and, just past the intersection, turn on Sloan Rd. Field Farm is just over a mile down Sloan Rd.

***Old Stone Church B&B*** *(☎ 413-458-9506, 1213 Green River Rd)* is nestled between the farmlands on a scenic road. As the name implies, the inn was a former Baptist church built in 1832. Purchased by an art history professor who specialized in Islamic art at Williams College in the 1970s, this large open space is now owned by a folk singer and her daughter. The three spacious bedrooms in the back, all with private bath, cost $80.

***The House on Main Street*** *(☎ 413-458-3031, 1120 Main St)*, just down from the Williams Inn, is a nice Victorian once owned by the daughter of President Woodrow Wilson, with six rooms (three with private baths) priced from $65 to $85.

***Williamstown B&B*** *(☎ 413-458-9202, 30 Cold Spring Rd (US 7 South and MA 2 West))*, right in the center of town just off the green, charges $90 for its three rooms with private baths.

***The Harbor House Inn*** *(☎ 413-743-8959, 725 N State Rd (US 8))*, in Cheshire, is about 15 miles from Williamstown and 17 miles from Lenox, but it's worth mentioning because of its spectacular location, on the back side of Mt Greylock. Part of a 200-year-old farm, the Harbor House is run by a family whose two young daughters are the ideal hosts. The five rooms range from $85 to $125.

## Places to Eat

Visitors to the Berkshires think nothing of driving 30 miles to reach a favorite restaurant, but there are a number of good eating places right in Williamstown itself. Many serve vegetarian dishes.

For pizza, a sandwich or a light meal, wander along Spring St, the main shopping street. The sandwiches ($4 to $5) at ***Papa Charlie's Deli*** *(☎ 413-458-5969, 28 Spring St)* are named after stars who've performed in Williamstown.

***Clarksburg Bread Company*** *(☎ 413-458-2251, 37 Spring St)* has fresh-baked biscuits, breads, coffee cakes, cookies, muffins, pies, rolls, scones and squares, as well as coffee, tea and juices. It's open Tuesday through Saturday 7 am to 4 pm.

***Canterbury's Pub*** *(☎ 413-458-2808, 46 Spring St)* features an Olde English decor, foreign beers, Guinness on tap, a salad bar, soups and sandwiches.

***Cold Spring Coffee Roasters*** *(☎ 413-458-5010, 47 Spring St)*, roasts, grinds, brews and serves its premium coffees in elaborate preparations, complemented by baked treats, daily.

***Lickety Split*** *(☎ 413-458-1818, 68 Spring St)* is the place to get homemade ice cream, along with soups and sandwiches.

*Robin's Restaurant* (☎ *413-458-4489, 117 Latham St)*, at the south end of Spring St, serves California-style cuisine with New England's seasonal ingredients in white-tablecloth style. Prices tend to be on the high side for the size of the portions; lunch costs $10 to $15, dinner $28 to $45. Closed Monday; call ahead in the off-season.

*Water Street Grill* (☎ *413-458-2175, 123 Water St)* is a large restaurant that features moderately priced steaks, seafood and salads. It's open until 11 pm nightly, so it's a good choice in summer after a play.

Just down the street, *Hobson's Choice* (☎ *413-458-9101, 159 Water St)* has a country home feel that's popular with students. Soups and sandwiches for lunch are served in cozy booths. Main dishes at dinner such as grilled chicken or seafood pasta cost from $12 to $18.

*The Wild Amber Grill* (☎ *413-458-4000)*, on US 7 North, just down the hill from the information booth, serves contemporary American cuisine like seared tuna with sesame seeds at an average price of $17 a plate (dinner). Lunch is served every day except Sunday, dinner nightly.

The other choice for fine dining is the new *Main Street Café* (☎ *413-458-3210, 16 Water St)*. Walk though their small garden to a vibrant yellow room that features continental cuisine. Expect to spend around $30 for dinner.

## Entertainment

During the academic year, call Concertline (☎ 413-597-3146) of the Williams College Department of Music for information on concerts, recitals and performances. In the summer, *Williamstown Chamber Concerts* (☎ *413-458-8273)* stages concerts at the Clark Art Institute.

For pub action, head for *Canterbury's*, described above in Places to Eat. Or try the *Mezze Bistro & Bar* (☎ *413-458-0123, 84 Water St)*, where many of the actors from the Williamstown Theatre go for a drink after performances. Sit on the patio outside overlooking a small waterfall on the Green River.

## Getting There & Away

North Adams has a small airport and the Mohawk Soaring Club, but no scheduled air service.

Williamstown's bus station is in the lobby of the Williams Inn (☎ 413-458-2665), on Main St near the intersection of US 7 and MA 2.

Peter Pan Bus Lines (☎ 800-343-9999) runs daily buses between Bennington and Boston via Williamstown, Pittsfield, Lee and Springfield. The trip between Boston and Williamstown takes slightly over four hours.

Bonanza Bus Lines (☎ 800-556-3815) runs its daily buses between New York City and Bennington via Great Barrington, Stockbridge, Lee, Lenox, Pittsfield and Williamstown. The bus ride between New York and Williamstown takes about five hours.

Driving details for Williamstown are as follows:

| destination | mileage | hr:min |
| --- | --- | --- |
| Amherst, MA | 61 miles | 1:20 |
| Bennington, VT | 14 miles | 0:30 |
| Boston, MA | 145 miles | 3:30 |
| Deerfield, MA | 45 miles | 1:10 |
| Hartford, CT | 107 miles | 2:30 |
| Lenox, MA | 29 miles | 1:05 |
| Litchfield, CT | 75 miles | 2:00 |
| New York, NY | 165 miles | 3:45 |

# Rhode Island

Although the 'Ocean State,' as Rhode Island is known, is the smallest state in the USA, that distinction doesn't do justice to its beauty and variety. This corner of New England has its own special character and charm.

Providence, the state capital and third-largest city in New England, is a pleasant, historic, manageable city that's recently undergone an ambitious facelift. Newport, the famed 19th-century summer playground of the colossally wealthy, is now the region's yachting capital and summer home to the merely inordinately wealthy. Block Island is a junior version of Nantucket or Martha's Vineyard, perfect for a day trip or overnight. The hundreds of miles of seacoast ringing the convoluted shoreline of Narragansett Bay provide ever-changing scenery. The coast of southwestern Rhode Island is laced with good, long and sandy beaches.

The Rhode Island Tourism Division (☎ 401-222-2601, 800-556-2484, fax 401-222-2102, www.visitrhodeisland.com) is at 7 Jackson Walkway, Providence, RI 02903. The Rhode Island Travelers Aid Society, also based in Providence, provides a helpline (☎ 401-351-6500, 800-367-2700) that can help you with accommodations emergencies and directions.

Bed & Breakfast of Rhode Island (☎ 401-849-1298, 800-828-0000), PO Box 3291, Newport, RI 02840, can make reservations at more than 200 B&Bs and inns in the state for a $5 postage and handling fee.

There's a Rhode Island Welcome Center as you head north on I-95, between exits 2 and 3; it's open 8 am to 5 pm daily year-round, and until 6:30 pm from Memorial Day to Columbus Day.

## Getting There & Around

See the Providence section, below, for this information. Rhode Island law requires you to wear automobile seat belts; violators are subject to a fine of $30.

## PROVIDENCE

Providence is a compact, walkable city of some 160,000 people. In size, it vies with Worcester, Massachusetts, for the distinction of being the second-largest city in New England (after Boston).

While it is neither as populous or cosmopolitan as New England's hub city, nor as fun-loving and tourist-oriented as seaside Newport, Providence does offer the discriminating visitor a sense of history and a wealth of fine architecture. For its size, the city is also well-endowed with excellent restaurants in all price ranges.

Providence's high-profile universities and colleges (Brown; the Rhode Island School of

### Highlights

- Strolling through the college campuses and museums of Providence
- Touring the opulent mansions of Newport
- Relaxing on a beautiful South County beach
- Biking the narrow roads and trails of Block Island

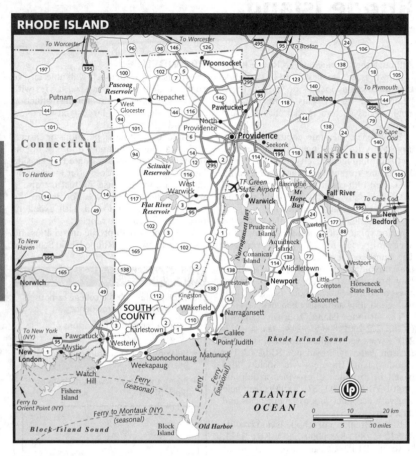

**RHODE ISLAND**

Design, or RISD; Johnson & Wales) keep the city's social and arts scenes lively by providing a student population of nearly 20,000.

For such a historic city, Providence is looking shiny and new these days. A billion-dollar downtown renovation project under the guidance of architect Bill Warner, begun in 1983, is now completed after more than 15 years of construction.

The city's skyline is punctuated by the art deco lines of the Fleet Bank building (often referred to as 'the Superman building' because of its resemblance to the structure

in the old TV show, which the Caped One was able to 'leap over in a single bound'). The skyline now sports a towering Westin Hotel, part of the Rhode Island Convention Center complex in the heart of the new downtown.

Taking a cue from San Antonio, Texas, Providence has been busily reclaiming its long-neglected waterfront. The Waterplace Park project and its Riverwalk extensions have moved the city's two central rivers – the Moshassuck and the Woonasquatucket Rivers, which merge into the Providence

River – back to their historic positions after more than a century of filling and dredging had reduced them to near-invisibility.

Lining the riverbanks are curvy, landscaped parks that invite strollers to see Providence's historic downtown from a new perspective. You can even rent kayaks and canoes for a paddle on the rivers themselves.

## History

Ever since it was founded in 1636 by Roger Williams (1603-83), a religious outcast from Boston, Providence has been a city with an independent frame of mind. The gilded statue atop the Rhode Island State House is called, appropriately, *The Independent Man.*

Williams' guiding principle, the one that got him ostracized from the Puritan Massachusetts Bay Colony, was that all people should have freedom of conscience. He was an early advocate of separation between civil and religious authorities. With his new settlement of Providence, he put these core beliefs into practice, remaining on friendly terms with the local Narragansett Indians after purchasing from them the land for his bold experiment in tolerance and peaceful coexistence.

So it should perhaps not be surprising that Rhode Island became the first colony to declare independence from England, in May 1776. From that time until 1900, the state's two big cities – Providence and Newport – alternated as state capital, but Providence was the state's premier port city following the devastation wrought on Newport by the British during the Revolutionary War.

The most significant name in Providence history (after that of Roger Williams) is Brown. John Brown, whose magnificent mansion on the East Side is now a museum, was a slave-trader who also opened trade with China to establish the family's wealth. John's brother Joseph was an architect whose excellent buildings, including John Brown's mansion, the First Baptist Meeting House and Market House, are among the most distinguished in the city. And Moses Brown, who unlike his slave-trader brother was an abolitionist and a pacifist, founded the Quaker school in Providence, which is

named for him. The last of the Brown brothers, Nicholas, was the founder of Brown University, which was founded in 1764 in the town of Warren as a Baptist institution named Rhode Island College.

Like many small East Coast cities, Providence went into a precipitous decline in the 1940s and '50s as its manufacturing industries (textiles and costume jewelry) faltered. In the 1960s, preservation efforts led by Antoinette Downing salvaged the historic architectural framework of the city, and following a few stalls and starts in the decades since, a new and much finer Providence has arisen.

## Orientation

Providence is situated at the head of Narragansett Bay astride two rivers, the Moshassuck and the Woonasquatucket, which merge to form the Providence River at Waterplace Park. Surrounding Providence are the populous bedroom suburbs of Warwick, Cranston, Johnston, Pawtucket and East Providence.

I-95 is the primary north-south artery through Providence, with I-195 splitting from it eastward toward Cape Cod. Take exit 22 (Downtown) from I-95 or the Wickenden St exit from I-195 to reach Kennedy Plaza and the Amtrak train station. For the Italian neighborhood and restaurant district of Federal Hill, take exit 21 (Atwells Ave/Broadway).

Kennedy Plaza, with the Providence Biltmore hotel and City Hall on its southwestern side, is the center of the city. To the west of the Biltmore are the Westin Hotel and the Rhode Island Convention Center. The old Union Station building is on the northwestern side of Kennedy Plaza, and beyond it, across the river, are the new Providence (Amtrak) Station (☎ 800-872-7245) and the Rhode Island state capitol, called the State House, on its hilltop perch. The huge new Providence Place Mall is to the west between Kennedy Plaza and the State House. The Greyhound Bus Terminal is on Fountain St, five blocks southwest of Kennedy Plaza.

East of the Providence River is the East Side, marked by College Hill and its wealth of 18th- and 19th-century buildings, plus RISD and Brown University. Federal Hill, the Italian neighborhood to the west, has dozens of good restaurants, pastry shops and taverns along its main axis, Atwells Ave.

The heart of the city is a surprisingly compact area, and you'll get more of the flavor of Providence on foot than you will in a car. Remember to look up! Many of downtown's most architecturally interesting building facades are several stories above street level.

## Information

**Tourist Offices** The Rhode Island Tourism Division (☎ 401-222-2601, 800-556-2484), at 1 W Exchange St, Providence, RI 02903, will send you booklets and maps on the whole state, and update you on special events.

The Travelers Aid Society of Rhode Island (☎ 401-521-2255) is at 177 Union St, Providence, RI 02903. Call their helpline (☎ 401-351-6500, 800-367-2700) for aid in finding a room or getting directions.

The Providence-Warwick Convention & Visitors Bureau (☎ 401-274-1636, 800-233-1636) is at 1 W Exchange St, Providence, RI 02903.

**Bookstores** Brown University Bookstore (☎ 401-863-3168), 244 Thayer St, and College Hill Bookstore (☎ 401-751-6404), 252 Thayer St, near each other on College Hill, are the city's most comprehensive bookstores.

For maps and a good selection of guidebooks, The Map Center (☎ 401-421-2184), 671 N Main St, is a gold mine.

For a quality selection of used books, try Cellar Stories (☎ 401-521-2665), 190 Mathewson St downtown, and Seward's Folly (☎ 401-861-6271), 139 Brook St, on the East Side.

**Newspapers** The daily newspaper for Providence and indeed all of Rhode Island is the *Providence Journal*. 'Lifebeat,' a daily arts and entertainment section, includes listings of performances and events; the Friday edition carries an expanded listings section. Visitors should also have a look at its website at www.providencejournal.com.

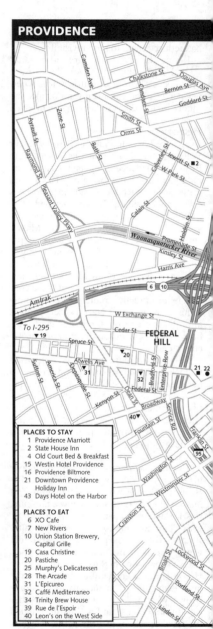

**PROVIDENCE**

To I-295

FEDERAL HILL

PLACES TO STAY
1  Providence Marriott
2  State House Inn
4  Old Court Bed & Breakfast
15 Westin Hotel Providence
16 Providence Biltmore
21 Downtown Providence Holiday Inn
43 Days Hotel on the Harbor

PLACES TO EAT
6  XO Cafe
7  New Rivers
10 Union Station Brewery, Capital Grille
19 Casa Christine
20 Pastiche
25 Murphy's Delicatessen
28 The Arcade
31 L'Epicureo
32 Caffé Mediterraneo
34 Trinity Brew House
39 Rue de l'Espoir
40 Leon's on the West Side

# PROVIDENCE

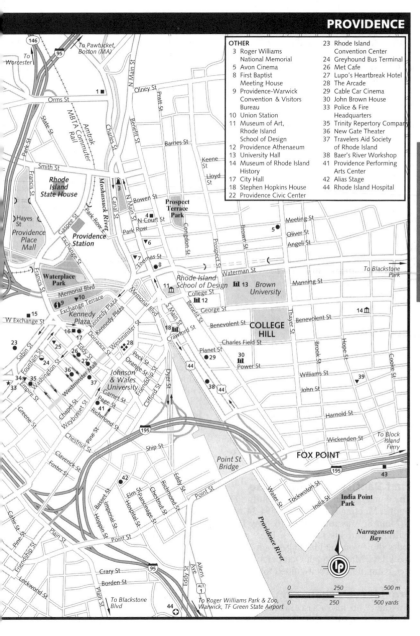

**OTHER**

3 Roger Williams
  National Memorial
5 Avon Cinema
8 First Baptist
  Meeting House
9 Providence-Warwick
  Convention & Visitors
  Bureau
10 Union Station
11 Museum of Art,
   Rhode Island
   School of Design
12 Providence Athenaeum
13 University Hall
14 Museum of Rhode Island
   History
17 City Hall
18 Stephen Hopkins House
22 Providence Civic Center

23 Rhode Island
   Convention Center
24 Greyhound Bus Terminal
26 Met Cafe
27 Lupo's Heartbreak Hotel
28 The Arcade
29 Cable Car Cinema
30 John Brown House
33 Police & Fire
   Headquarters
35 Trinity Repertory Company
36 New Gate Theater
37 Travelers Aid Society
   of Rhode Island
38 Baer's River Workshop
41 Providence Performing
   Arts Center
42 Alias Stage
44 Rhode Island Hospital

The Providence *Phoenix,* which appears Thursday, is the city's alternative weekly, with nightclub listings and reviews.

**Medical Services** If you need medical attention, go to Rhode Island Hospital (☎ 401-444-4000), 593 Eddy St, south of the center near I-95 exit 19.

## Rhode Island State House

The Rhode Island State House (☎ 401-222-2357) rises above the Providence skyline, easily visible from the highways that pass through the city. It's a beautiful building of Georgia marble that was modeled in part on St Peter's Basilica in Vatican City. Inside the public halls are the battle flags of Rhode Island military units and a curious Civil War cannon, which sat here for a century loaded and ready to shoot until someone thought to check whether it was disarmed. Luckily, the hot air of politics hadn't set it off.

Visitors are welcomed for free guided tours at the Smith St (US 44) entrance 8:30 am to 4:30 pm weekdays (last tour at 3:30 pm).

## The Arcade

This imposing 1828 Greek Revival building (☎ 401-598-1199), at 65 Weybosset St, connecting Weybosset and Westminster Sts, bustles at lunchtime with the downtown business crowd. The 1st floor of the Arcade has several good, inexpensive lunch spots, such as Jensen's, Villa Pizza and the Providence Cookie Co, and the 2nd and 3rd floors have gift and clothing boutiques. It's open daily except Sunday. There is parking across Weybosset St in the Arcade garage.

## First Baptist Meeting House

The congregation now resident in the First Baptist Meeting House (☎ 401-454-3418), 75 N Main St, was founded in 1638 by Roger Williams and his followers. Free guided tours show you the building 10 am to 3 pm weekdays, May through October; or use the free pamphlet for a self-guided tour.

## Providence Athenaeum

Anyone who has a visceral attraction to books will enjoy a visit to the Athenaeum

(☎ 401-421-6970), the private subscription library at 251 Benefit St. It's one of the oldest libraries in the country (1831). In these stacks poet Edgar Allan Poe carried on his courtship of Providence's Sarah Helen Whitman, who was the inspiration for his poem *Annabel Lee.*

This is a library of the old school: The card catalog is kept in old-fashioned wooden drawers rather than in a computer, and plaster busts and oil paintings on the walls give the place a feeling of closeness with the past. It's open every day except Sunday; admission is free.

## Brown University

Occupying the crest of the College Hill neighborhood on the East Side, the campus of Brown University (☎ 401-863-2378, www .brown.edu) has Ivy League charm. University Hall, a 1770 brick edifice that was used as a barracks during the Revolutionary War, is at its center. To explore the campus, start at the wrought-iron gates opening from the top of College St and make your way across the green toward Thayer St.

Free tours of the campus are conducted five times daily on weekdays, and on Saturday mornings from mid-September to mid-November, beginning from the College Admission Office in Corliss Brackett House, 45 Prospect St.

## John Brown House

Called the 'most magnificent and elegant mansion that I have ever seen on this continent' by John Quincy Adams, this brick residence at 52 Power St was built in 1786 for Providence merchant John Brown by his brother Joseph. It is now operated as a museum house by the Rhode Island Historical Society (☎ 401-331-8575). It's open 10 am to 5 pm (noon to 4 pm Sunday) daily except Monday; admission is $6 for adults, $4 for students and seniors, $2.50 for children. Tours run every half-hour between 11 am and 3:30 pm.

## Museum of Rhode Island History

The Aldrich House (☎ 401-331-8575), 110 Benevolent St, was built in 1822 and is now the headquarters of the Rhode Island Historical Society and its museum. Exhibits teach about Rhode Island history, and the Hall of Fame holds portraits of famous Rhode Islanders. Visit 9 am to 5 pm (noon to 4 pm Sunday); it's closed Saturday and Monday. Admission to the exhibit area costs $2 for adults, $1 for seniors and students.

## Museum of Art, Rhode Island School of Design

Exhibits in the small but select Museum of Art, Rhode Island School of Design (☎ 401-454-6500), 224 Benefit St, include 19th-century French paintings, classical Greek, Roman and Etruscan art, medieval and Renaissance works, European and Oriental decorative arts, and examples of 19th- and 20th-century American painting, furniture and decorative arts. It's open 10 am to 5 pm (until 8 pm Friday); closed Monday and Tuesday. Admission costs $5 for adults, $4 for seniors, $2 for college students with ID,

$1 for youth five to 18. Children younger than five are admitted for free.

## Neighborhoods

**Federal Hill** Among the most colorful of Providence's neighborhoods is Federal Hill, which is fervently Italian. It is always a great place to wander, taking in the aromas of sausages, peppers and garlic from a multitude of neighborhood groceries such as Tony's Colonial Market, Providence Cheese and Roma Gourmet. Scialo Bakery on Atwells is the prototypical Italian pastry shop, with sweet confections tantalizingly displayed atop paper doilies in its glass cases. Many of Providence's best restaurants are on Atwells Ave as well.

**Fox Point** The city's substantial Portuguese population still resides in this waterfront section of the city, though gentrification has taken place with influxes of Brown University professors and students and artists from

RHODE ISLAND

### Providence Architecture

Even though much of Providence is new, the city's main appeal is its historic buildings. Its colorful colonial history is reflected in the multihued 18th-century houses that line Benefit St on the East Side. These are, for the most part, private homes, but many are open for tours one weekend in mid-June during the annual Festival of Historic Homes, organized by the Providence Preservation Society (☎ 401-831-7440), 21 Meeting St.

Benefit St is a fitting symbol of the Providence renaissance. Rescued by local preservationists in the 1960s from misguided urban-renewal efforts that would have destroyed it, the street today offers the richest concentration of colonial houses in the nation. Its treasures range from the 1708 Stephen Hopkins House, 1 Hopkins St at Benefit St (open Wednesday and Saturday from April through October; donations accepted), to the clean Greek Revival lines of the 1838 Providence Athenaeum, a privately operated subscription library and rare books collection that is a must-see for bibliophiles. The Rhode Island Historical Preservation & Heritage Commission (☎ 401-222-2678) is at 150 Benefit St.

Downtown, the beaux-arts style of the city hall makes an imposing centerpiece to Kennedy Plaza, and the stately white dome of the Rhode Island State House (designed by McKim, Mead & White in 1904) is visible from many corners of the city. The USA's first indoor shopping mall – the 1828 Greek Revival Arcade – is an airy, tile-floored space with shops and cafes on three floors.

Victorian and Queen Anne-style houses line Broadway and Elmwood Ave in an area of Providence that fell into decay for several decades before reclamation in the early 1980s. These once-grand houses, though, are still jewels in the rough.

RISD. But you can still find an Old World-style grocery like the Friends Market on Brook St tucked in among the trendy coffee-houses, salons and galleries. Most of the action in Fox Point centers around Wicken-den St.

**Blackstone Boulevard** The boulevard is not so much a neighborhood as an address that says you've arrived. Along this 2-mile avenue, divided by a parklike central strip of green space on Providence's East Side, are some of Providence's most imposing residences, most dating to the 1920s and '30s and surrounded by lush landscaping. Joggers favor Blackstone Park, and it's also worthwhile to explore the lovely grounds of Swan Point Cemetery on the banks of the See-konk River.

## Waterplace Park & Riverwalk
Cobblestone paths lead along the Woonas-quatucket River to this central pool and fountain, overlooked by a stepped amphitheater where outdoor performance artists liven up the scene in warm weather. Virtually all of what you see is new, the result of decades of urban renewal. Take a look at the historical maps and photos mounted on the walls of the walkway beneath Memorial Blvd.

## Prospect Terrace Park
A great spot from which to get an overview of the city, Prospect Terrace is a small pocket of green space off Congdon St on the East Side. In warm weather, you'll find students throwing Frisbees, office workers picnicking and people just gazing at the view, which is particularly good at sunset. The monumental statue facing the city is that of Providence founder Roger Williams, whose remains were moved to this site in 1939.

## Roger Williams Park & Zoo
In 1871, Ms Betsey Williams, great-great-great granddaughter of the founder of Providence, donated her farm to the city as a public park. Today this 430-acre expanse of greenery, only a short drive south of Providence at 1000 Elmwood Ave, includes lakes and ponds, forest copses and broad lawns, picnic grounds, the Planetarium and the Museum of Natural History, a boathouse, greenhouses and Ms Williams' cottage.

Perhaps the park's most significant attraction is the Roger Williams Park Zoo (☎ 401-785-3510). The zoo, home to more than 600 animals, is open 9 am to 5 pm daily (until 4 pm in winter; until 6 pm on summer weekends). Admission costs $6 for adults, $3.50 for children and seniors, and is free for those younger than three. To reach the park, go south from Providence on I-95 to exit 17 (Elmwood Ave). If you are heading north from Connecticut or from the Rhode Island beaches, take exit 16.

## East Bay Bicycle Path
Starting at India Point Park on the Narragansett Bay waterfront in Providence, the scenic East Bay Bicycle Path wends its way for 14½ miles south along a former railroad track. The mostly flat, paved path follows the shoreline to the pretty seaport of Bristol. State parks along the route make good spots for picnics.

## Boating
Kayaks and canoes may be rented from Baer's River Workshop (☎ 401-453-1633) at 222 Water St downtown. Baer's offers an urban boating experience, with paddlers heading into the heart of the city along the landscaped riverways.

## Places to Stay
**Camping** Camping areas are outside the city, but since Rhode Island is small, they aren't all that far away.

*George Washington Management Area* (☎ *401-568-2013*), on US 44, 2 miles east of the Connecticut state line in West Glocester, has 45 simple tent and RV sites ($12 for out-of-staters/$8 residents) and two shelters ($20 per night) in a wooded area overlooking the Bowdish Reservoir.

If the state-operated campground is full, try the neighboring private *Bowdish Lake Camping Area* (☎ *401-568-8890*), with 450 sites priced from $16 to $26, depending upon the location and facilities. You'll also find

*Camp Ponagansett* (☎ 401-647-7377), 2 miles north of RI 102 on Rustic Hill Rd, with 40 RV sites open from mid-April to mid-October.

**Motels** As usual, inexpensive motels ($60 to $85 double, depending upon the room and the season) are on the outskirts near interstate exits, about 3 to 5 miles from the city center. Go north to neighboring Pawtucket for the *Comfort Inn* (☎ 401-253-6700, 2 George St), at I-95 exit 28. Go south to Warwick for the *Motel 6* (☎ 401-467-9800, 20 Jefferson Blvd) and the *Susse Chalet* (☎ 401-941-6600, 800-524-2538, fax 401-785-1260, www.sussechalet.com, 36 Jefferson Blvd), at I-95 exit 15.

**Hotels** Luxury hotels are in the city center.

The 274-room *Downtown Providence Holiday Inn* (☎ 401-831-3900, 800-465-4329, fax 401-751-0007, 21 Atwells Ave), at I-95 exit 21, is right next to the Civic Center between downtown and Federal Hill, runs its free shuttles to TF Green State Airport in Warwick, and charges $100 to $116 per room.

The *Providence Marriott* (☎/fax 401-272-2400, www.marriott.com), at Charles and Orms Sts, has 345 deluxe rooms and suites, an indoor/outdoor pool, whirlpool, sauna and fitness center. Room rates range from $109 to $174.

With 244 rooms, the *Providence Biltmore* (☎ 401-421-0700, 800-294-7709, fax 401-331-0830, www.grandheritage.com), on Kennedy Plaza, is a classic grand hotel of the 1920s, with rooms for $120 to $170.

The *Westin Hotel Providence* (☎ 401-598-8000, fax 598-8200, www.westin.com, 1 W Exchange St) is the city's newest high-rise, opened in 1994. Its 363 rooms are priced from $175 and up.

The *Days Hotel on the Harbor* (☎/fax 401-272-5577, www.travelnow.com/usa, 220 India St) is just north of India Point Park off I-195 near Wickenden St. Many of its 136 rooms, priced from $79 to $149, have views of the harbor.

**Inns & B&Bs** Bed & Breakfast of Rhode Island (☎ 401-849-1298, 800-828-0000, fax 401-849-1306), 175 Spring St (PO Box 3291), Newport, RI 02840, has listings for the entire state, including Providence.

The *State House Inn* (☎ 401-351-6111, fax 351-4261, www3.edgenet.net/statehouseinn, 43 Jewett St) is a restored 1880s house close to the Rhode Island State House. The 10 simple rooms are decorated with tasteful colonial and Shaker-style furnishings and priced from $109 to $139 with private bath, TV and phone.

*Old Court Bed & Breakfast* (☎ 401-751-2002, fax 272-4830, reserve@oldcourt.com, 144 Benefit St) has 10 rooms in an elegant 1863 Italianate building in the heart of Providence's historic area priced from $115 to $135, with discounts in the winter.

## Places to Eat

Providence is a great place to find a good meal in almost any price range. Both RISD and Johnson & Wales University have culinary programs that annually turn out creative new chefs who liven up the city's restaurant scene. The large student population assures that there are always plenty of good, inexpensive places.

**Kennedy Plaza Area** For a quick, light meal, don't forget *The Arcade*, described in the section by that name, above.

For a sandwich and a beer right in the city center, head straight for *Murphy's Delicatessen* (☎ 401-621-8467, 55 Union St), in the back of the Biltmore parking garage. Murphy's has been serving up standard deli sandwiches such as hot pastrami and Swiss cheese ($5.25) since 1929.

A favorite college hangout in the evenings is the *Trinity Brew House* (☎ 401-453-2337, 186 Fountain St), which makes its own hop-heavy Irish/British-style beer. There's entertainment most nights, and the kitchen is open until midnight. Sandwiches and burgers cost $3.50 to $7, pizzas $8 or $9.

A worthy alternative is the *Union Station Brewery* (☎ 401-274-2739, 36 Exchange Terrace), on the north side of the former Union Station at Kennedy Plaza. Luncheon sandwiches and platters cost $6 to $8, fancier dinner main courses $10 to $16. The beer made here is more in the American style. Malted grains used in the brewing process are recycled to make the pizza. In good weather, outdoor tables have fine views of the State House.

Next to the Union Station Brewery is the **Capital Grille** (☎ 401-521-5600, 1 Cookson Place), more upscale and refined with its dry-aged steaks ($9 to $22), fish and lobster ($20 to $30).

**College Hill** You can park your car for free on the residential back streets near Prospect Terrace Park and walk downhill to two restaurants. **XO Cafe** (☎ 401-273-9090, 125 N Main St) is an artsy, trendy little bistro serving dinner only (after 5 pm). The menu changes with the seasons, but besides the New American cuisine there's always wood-oven-baked pizza. Full dinners cost $30 to $55 per person.

**New Rivers** (☎ 401-751-0350, 7 Steeple St) serves dinner only and specializes in 'contemporary American cooking,' which is to be interpreted as novel, innovative and fancy, using organic and locally grown produce when possible. 'Small meals,' including pastas and polentas, cost $12 to $19 per plate, grilled and baked main courses $18 to $23 and full dinners $20 to $55.

The city's long-running favorite, **Rue de l'Espoir** (☎ 401-751-8890, 99 Hope St), is not as French as it sounds. The menu is eclectic and ever-changing; prices are moderate, with main courses priced from $13 to $20.

**Federal Hill** The Italian district is just west across the bridge from the Holiday Inn. Look for the huge concrete arch with a big pineapple marking Atwells Ave, which has dozens of eateries.

Good food at the best prices is the specialty at **Leon's on the West Side** (☎ 401-273-1055, 166 Broadway), two blocks south of Atwells. Inventively prepared Italian classics, salads, pizzas and pastas priced from $10 to $20 are served nightly (except Monday). There's no lunch on weekdays, but great brunches are offered weekends.

You'd never stumble across it, but locals in the know find their way to **Casa Christine**

(☎ 401-453-6255, 145 Spruce St), a family-run dining room on a drab back street a block north of Atwells Ave. Come for lunch (Tuesday to Friday) or dinner (Tuesday to Saturday) in a cozy atmosphere with home-cooked food; dinners cost about $18 to $35 per person.

**Caffé Mediterraneo** (☎ 401-331-7760, 134 Atwells Ave) is a favorite with ladies at lunchtime, a traditional Italian-American trattoria serving full and filling dinners for $30 to $50 per person.

Farther up the price scale, the elegant **L'Epicureo** (☎ 401-454-8430, 238 Atwells Ave) features Italian-influenced New American cuisine, including wood-grilled meats and inventive pasta dishes for $13 to $25, for dinner only.

For dessert and coffee, **Pastiche** (☎ 401-861-5190, 92 Spruce St), a block north of Atwells, is awash in soothing colors and warmed by a fire in winter; closed Monday.

## Entertainment

The **Providence Civic Center** (☎ 401-331-6700, 1 LaSalle Square) is the place to see touring rock groups as well as sporting events (see Spectator Sports, below).

**Theater** The **Trinity Repertory Company** (☎ 401-351-4242, 201 Washington St) performs classic and contemporary plays in the historic Lederer Theater downtown. Trinity is a favorite try-out space for Broadway productions, and it's not unusual for well-known stars to turn up in a performance. Over several decades, Trinity Rep has earned a reputation for adventurous productions, but mainstream audiences are satisfied as well.

Contemporary and avant-garde productions are staged by several smaller theater companies in Providence. Check local listings in the newspaper or call **Alias Stage** (☎ 401-831-2919, 31 Elbow St) or **New Gate Theater** (☎ 401-421-9680, 134 Mathewson St) for upcoming performances. **Leeds Theatre at Brown University** (☎ 401-863-2838) stages traditional and contemporary productions featuring student actors.

The **Providence Performing Arts Center** (☎ 401-421-2787, 220 Weybosset St) is a popular venue for touring Broadway shows. The former Loew's Theater building, which dates from 1928, has a lavish art deco interior that has been restored to its original splendor.

**Cinemas** The *Cable Car Cinema (☎ 401-272-3970, 204 S Main St)*, specializing in offbeat and foreign films, invites its patrons to sit on couches and enjoy all-you-can-eat popcorn while they enjoy the show. Local talent often perform to warm up the audience before the movie.

The *Avon Cinema (☎ 401-421-3315, 260 Thayer St)*, on College Hill, also has foreign films, cult classics and experimental movies.

**Nightclubs** With its large population of students, Providence has a lively nightclub scene. Refer to the 'Lifebeat' section in the daily *Providence Journal* for listings of performers, venues and schedules.

Legendary in the city is *Lupo's Heartbreak Hotel (☎ 401-272-5876, 239 Westminster St)*, which is host to national acts (progressive rock, R&B and blues, with tickets from $10 to $18) in an intimate space that usually accommodates some dancing. Nearby is the smaller *Met Cafe (☎ 401-861-2142, 130 Union St)*.

## Spectator Sports

The *Pawtucket Red Sox (☎ 401-724-7300)*, a Triple-A (minor league) farm team for the Boston Red Sox, play all spring and summer at McCoy Stadium in Pawtucket, just north of Providence. A night here, complete with hot dogs and peanuts, is a favorite way for baseball addicts to get a fix without the hassle and cost of driving to and parking at Fenway Park in Boston.

The *Providence Bruins* hockey team, another farm team for Boston, plays a regular schedule at the Civic Center in the fall and winter.

## Getting There & Around

**Air** TF Green State Airport (☎ 401-737-8222) is in Warwick, about 20 minutes south of central Providence. Green is served by American Airlines, Continental, Delta, Southwest, United and US Airways. There is no airport bus, though some luxury hotels have shuttle buses. Taxi services include Airport Taxi (☎ 401-737-2868) and Checker Cab (☎ 401-273-2222).

**Bus** Rhode Island Public Transit Authority (RIPTA; ☎ 401-781-9400, 800-221-3797, www.ripta.com) links Providence's Kennedy Plaza with the rest of the state for fares ranging from $1 to $3.

RIPTA bus No 11 (Broad St) takes you from Kennedy Plaza to Broad and Montgomery Sts, from which you can walk to Roger Williams Park & Zoo. Bus No 60 (Providence-Newport) makes 24 trips from Kennedy Plaza to Newport on weekdays, 15 on Saturday and 10 on Sunday and holidays.

Bonanza Bus Lines (☎ 401-751-8800, 888-751-8800, www.bonanzabus.com) connects Providence and TF Green State Airport with Boston and Boston's Logan Airport with 18 express buses daily from its terminal 2 miles north of the Kennedy Plaza at I-95 exit 25 (Route 126/Smithfield Ave). The Providence-Boston fare is $8.75 one way. There's shuttle service between Kennedy Plaza and the Bonanza terminal.

The Greyhound Bus Terminal (☎ 401-454-0790) is at 100 Fountain St at Mathewson. Buses depart for Boston (seven daily, 1¼ hours, $6); New York City (four hours by the two daily expresses, 5¼ hours by local, $19); New London (six daily, 1½ hours, $15.50) and New Haven (seven daily, 2½ hours, $21), Connecticut; and Foxwoods Resort Casino ($15 roundtrip), among other destinations.

**Train** Eleven daily Amtrak trains connect Providence (Amtrak) Station with Boston (one hour) and New York (four hours). Call ☎ 800-872-7245 for details.

For information on Amtrak's *Cape Codder* trains between New York City and Hyannis, Massachusetts, via Providence, see the Getting There & Away chapter at the front of this book.

Boston's MBTA Commuter Rail (☎ 617-222-3200, 800-392-6099) trains also run between Providence and Boston's South Station.

**RHODE ISLAND**

**Car** With hills, two interstates and two rivers defining its downtown topography, finding your way around in Providence can be confusing. Parking can be difficult in the city center as well. Be patient and allow time.

All of the major car rental companies have offices at TF Green State Airport in Warwick. Avis (☎ 401-521-7900) has an office downtown as well.

Driving details for Providence are as follows:

| destination | mileage | hr:min |
| --- | --- | --- |
| Boston, MA | 45 miles | 1:00 |
| Hyannis, MA | 50 miles | 1:10 |
| Mystic, CT | 40 miles | 0:50 |
| New Bedford, MA | 32 miles | 0:45 |
| New Haven, CT | 104 miles | 2:10 |
| New London, CT | 55 miles | 1:10 |
| New York, NY | 185 miles | 4:00 |
| Newport, RI | 30 miles | 0:45 |

**Boat** Interstate Navigation Co runs summer ferries to Block Island from its terminal at the southern end of Water St, at the India St Dock west of India Point Park. See the Block Island section, later in this chapter, for additional details.

## NEWPORT

Perfectly situated for access by sea, Newport was an important commercial port, a conquered war prize and a wealthy summer resort before becoming one of New England's busiest and most entertaining tourist destinations. The town is packed all summer by young day-trippers, older bus tourists, foreign visitors and families whose cars pack the narrow colonial streets, bringing traffic to a standstill.

Once the home of the America's Cup race, Newport is still one of the East Coast's premier yachting ports, with an enthusiasm for the sport that borders on mania. The plethora of yachts and tippling aristocrats led one wag to comment that 'Newport is a drinking town with a yachting problem.'

Much of Newport is beautiful, with restored colonial buildings, cobbled streets and surprising sea views. The rest is hum-drum, a collection of crowded residential areas, cheerless condominium developments and decaying maritime industry facilities.

Most people visit Newport to look at the many sumptuous mansions – disingenuously called 'summer cottages' by their fabulously wealthy owners – ranged along Bellevue Ave, with peerless views of the sea. Others come by yacht to visit friends, who may still live in some of the more secluded mansions. Still other tourists come to the music festivals – classical, folk, jazz – which are among the most important in the USA. In addition, Newport boasts several of New England's most beautiful and oldest religious buildings.

July and August are the busiest months. If you come in late April, May, late October or early November, you'll enjoy lower prices, smaller crowds and easier parking. Whenever you come, you'll enjoy Newport more if you carefully plan where to park your car and your body.

### Orientation

Newport occupies the southwestern end of Aquidneck Island. Adjoining it to the north is Middletown, which holds many of the services, less-expensive residential areas and unsightly commercial strips not allowed in (but needed by) Newport. Most cheap motels and guest houses are in Middletown, several miles north of the center, while the more expensive inns, B&Bs and hotels are in Newport proper.

Downtown Newport's main north-south commercial streets are America's Cup Ave and Thames (that's 'thaymz,' not 'temz') St, just in from the harbor. There are public toilets at the entrance to the parking lot at Bowen's Wharf.

Your initial destination in Newport should be the Newport Gateway Transportation & Visitors Center (see Information, below), which holds the bus station, tourist office and public toilets. Walking or biking around town is probably the best way to go; see Bicycling, later in this section, for bike rentals.

**Parking** Parking is particularly difficult and expensive. The cheapest is at the Newport

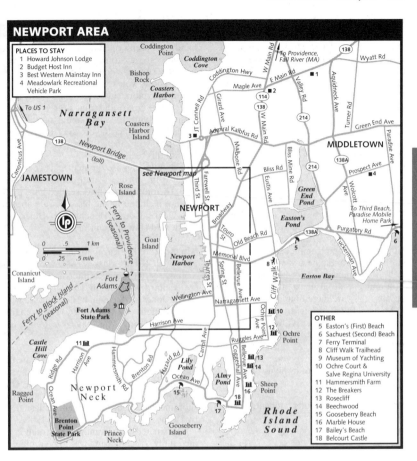

**NEWPORT AREA**

**PLACES TO STAY**
1 Howard Johnson Lodge
2 Budget Host Inn
3 Best Western Mainstay Inn
4 Meadowlark Recreational
   Vehicle Park

**OTHER**
5 Easton's (First) Beach
6 Sachuest (Second) Beach
7 Ferry Terminal
8 Cliff Walk Trailhead
9 Museum of Yachting
10 Ochre Court &
   Salve Regina University
11 Hammersmith Farm
12 The Breakers
13 Rosecliff
14 Beechwood
15 Gooseberry Beach
16 Marble House
17 Bailey's Beach
18 Belcourt Castle

**RHODE ISLAND**

Gateway Transportation & Visitors Center, which gives you the first half-hour for free, the next for $1 and each additional half-hour for 75¢, to a maximum of $10 per day. If you park at a meter (25¢ for 15 minutes, up to two hours), scrupulously observe its time limit or you'll end up with a ticket.

## Information

The Newport County Convention & Visitors Bureau (☎ 401-849-8048, 800-326-6030, fax 401-849-0291, www.gonewport.com) operates the information office inside the Newport

Gateway Transportation & Visitors Center, 23 America's Cup Ave. In summer it's open 9 am to 6 pm (until 7 pm on Friday and Saturday); in winter it's open until 5 pm. Information personnel won't make room reservations, but they post a list of B&Bs, inns and hotels with vacancies, and you can call them for free from a bank of special phones.

For books on Newport and Rhode Island and especially the New England coast, look for the Armchair Sailor bookstore (☎ 401-847-1219), 543 Thames St at Dean St, which has an extensive nautical collection.

## Walking Tours

The Newport Historical Society (☎ 401-846-0813) will take you on a walking tour of Historic Hill, the Cliff Walk and Bellevue Ave for $7 on Thursday, Friday or Saturday from mid-May through mid-October. Tours begin at the Museum of Newport History, on Thames St.

If you'd rather go on your own, the Historical Society has erected a system of 26 self-guided walking-tour signs on the sidewalks of Historic Hill describing many of the prominent and historic buildings found there.

## Newport Mansions

During the 19th century, the wealthiest New York bankers and business families chose Newport as their summer resort. This was pre-income tax America, their fortunes were fabulous and their 'summer cottages' – actually mansions and palaces – were fabulous as well. Most mansions are on Bellevue Ave. You must visit at least a few of them, because they are incredible.

Many of the mansions are under the management of the Preservation Society of Newport County (☎ 401-847-1000, fax 847-1361), 424 Bellevue Ave, which offers combination tickets that save you money if you intend to visit several of its mansions. Here's a fee schedule:

| ticket | adults | students | children |
| --- | --- | --- | --- |
| The Breakers | $10 | $6 | $4 |
| The Breakers Stable | $3.50 | $2 | free |
| The Elms, etc* | $8 | $5 | $3.50 |
| Any 2 buildings | $14 | $8.50 | $5.50 |
| Any 3 buildings | $19 | $11.50 | $7.50 |
| Any 4 buildings | $24 | $14.50 | $9.50 |
| Any 5 buildings | $27 | $16 | $10.50 |
| Any 6 buildings | $30 | $18 | $11 |
| Any 7 buildings | $33 | $20 | $13 |
| Any 8 buildings | $35.50 | $21 | $14 |

*The Elms, Château-sur-Mer, Chepstow House, Green Animals, Hunter House, Isaac Bell House, Kingscote, Marble House or Rosecliff

Most of the Preservation Society's mansions are open 10 am to 5 pm daily from late March through October.

Several mansions are operated by other interests. A few mansions are still in private hands and aren't open to visitors.

The best way to see the mansions is by bicycle. Cruising along Bellevue Ave at bike speed allows you to enjoy the view of the grounds, explore side streets and paths and ride right up to the mansion entrances without having to worry about parking or holding up traffic. If you can't bring your own bike, you can rent one (see Bicycling, later in this section).

The following are the mansions you pass going from north to south along Bellevue Ave. The only mansions described here that are not included in the fee schedule above are Ochre Court, Beechwood, Belcourt Castle and Hammersmith Farm.

**Kingscote**  This Elizabethan fantasy, complete with Tiffany glass, was Newport's first 'cottage' strictly for summer use, designed by Richard Upjohn in 1841 for George Noble Jones of Savannah, Georgia. It was later bought by China-trade merchant William H King, who gave the house its name.

**The Elms**  Edward J Berwind, a graduate of the US Naval Academy and a Navy officer, made his fortune by selling coal to the US Navy after his retirement. He had this supremely graceful summer house designed by Horace Trumbauer and built in 1901.

Threatened with imminent destruction – incredibly – the mansion was to be replaced with a housing project. However, thanks to the efforts of the Preservation Society, good sense prevailed. The Elms, nearly identical to the Château d'Asnieres built near Paris in 1750, is now exquisitely furnished with pieces on loan from major museums.

**Château-sur-Mer**  Originally designed by Seth Bradford and built of granite for retired banker William S Wetmore in 1852, this Victorian neo-Gothic house was remodeled by Richard Morris Hunt during the 1870s and '80s for the original owner's son. Compared to the others, it has a more 'lived-in' feel.

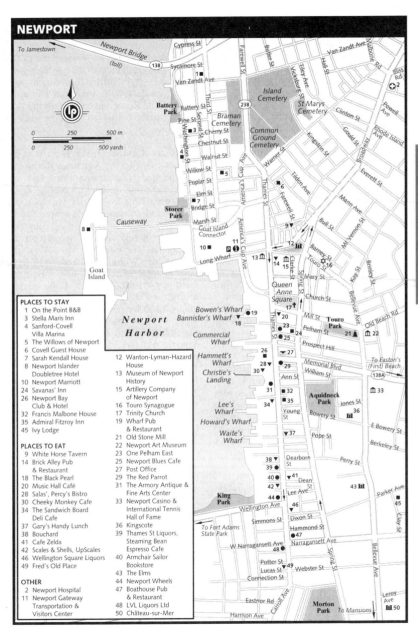

# NEWPORT

To Jamestown

Newport Bridge
(toll)

138

To Easton's
(First) Beach

138A

RHODE ISLAND

**Ochre Court** Designed by Richard Morris Hunt and built in 1892, Ochre Court is now the administration building of Salve Regina University. You can visit much of the main floor anytime between 9 am to 4 pm weekdays. In summer, there are guided tours. Admission is free.

**The Breakers** Most magnificent of all the Newport mansions is The Breakers, a 70-room Italian Renaissance palace designed by Richard Morris Hunt for Cornelius Vanderbilt II and completed in 1895 at Ochre Point, a prime oceanside site next to Ochre Court. Sumptuous is the only way to describe it. The furnishings, most made expressly for The Breakers, are all original. Don't miss the Children's Cottage on the grounds.

The Breakers' grand **Stable & Carriage House**, also designed by Hunt, is inland several blocks, on the west side of Bellevue Ave. It is now a museum of Vanderbilt family memorabilia, much of which provides a detailed look at the lifestyle of one of the USA's wealthiest families at the turn of the century.

**Rosecliff** Rosecliff was designed by Stanford White to look like the Grand Trianon at Versailles – but in some respects it is even grander. Its Marie Antoinette was Mrs Hermann Oelrichs (née Theresa Fair), an heiress of the Comstock Lode silver treasure. Mrs Oelrichs liked to entertain, so she saw to it that her house had Newport's largest ballroom.

**Beechwood** William B Astor built this home (☎ 401-846-3772, www.astors-beechwood .com), 580 Bellevue Ave, in 1856. Today, it is occupied by Beechwood Theater Company actors, who bring the house to life by portraying a 'typical' summer's houseful of family, staff and guests. It's open from 10 am to 5 pm daily in summer; until 4 pm November to mid-December; 10 am to 4 pm February to mid-May. It is closed from mid-December through January. The cost of admission is $8.75, $6.50 for seniors and children 12 and under.

**Marble House** Designed by Richard Morris Hunt and built in 1892 for William K Vanderbilt, the younger brother of Cornelius II, Marble House was inspired by the palace of Versailles, complete with original Louis XIV-style furnishings which were custom-made for the mansion. The aptly named Gold Room was created for the Vanderbilt's grand balls. Don't miss the Chinese Teahouse.

**Belcourt Castle** Oliver Hazard Perry Belmont, heir to the American Rothschild fortune, had Hunt design him a 60-room castle according to the 17th-century tastes of France's King Louis XIII. He stocked it with period art, tapestries, furniture, glassware and suits of armor from 32 countries. Staffed by 30 servants, it even had a private menagerie. He and his wife, Alva, the former Mrs William K Vanderbilt, lived here in regal splendor. Tours of Belcourt Castle (☎ 401-846-0669), 657 Bellevue Ave, are offered daily. Admission costs $8 for adults, $6.50 for seniors and recent college grads, $5.50 for students 13 to 18 and $3.50 for children six to 12. Hours are 9 am to 5 pm from late May to mid-October; call for other times.

**Hammersmith Farm** This 'farm' (☎ 401-846-0420), on Ocean Ave southwest of Fort Adams State Park, differs from other Newport mansions. The 28-room mansion, built in 1887, was the summer residence of the Auchincloss family. Mrs Hugh Auchincloss' daughter, Jacqueline Bouvier, was married to John F Kennedy in Newport. The reception was held here. When Jack became president of the US and Jackie the First Lady, they visited the farm occasionally. It's now open to the public, with many of its original furnishings, 10 am to 5 pm mid-April to mid-November, until 7 pm in summer. Admission costs $8.50 for adults, $3.50 for children six to 12.

## Museums

For an island, Newport has more than its share of museums, from the ponderous to the sublime to the ridiculous.

The Breakers is a Newport 'cottage' built for the Vanderbilts.

The Griswold Mansion (1864), a vast Victorian frame summer cottage at 76 Bellevue Ave, houses the **Newport Art Museum** (☎ 401-848-8200). It has changing exhibits of paintings, sculpture, metalwork, ceramics, photography, etc. Call for current shows. It's open 10 am to 5 pm (4 pm in winter; noon to 4 pm Sunday; closed Wednesday). The admission fee depends upon the exhibit, but is usually $8 for adults, $5 for seniors and students 13 to 18; and children 12 and younger get in free.

In Newport's historic Brick Market building, the **Museum of Newport History** (☎ 401-846-0813), run by the Newport Historical Society (☎ 401-846-0813), traces the town's eventful history. The museum is open 10 am to 5 pm (1 to 5 pm Sunday; closed Tuesday). Admission costs $5, $4 for seniors and children older than five.

The **Wanton-Lyman-Hazard House**, 17 Broadway, constructed in 1675, is the oldest restored house in the city. Used as a residence by colonial governors and well-to-do residents, it's now a museum of colonial Newport history operated by the Newport Historical Society. Call the society (see number above) for hours of operation.

The **Old Stone Mill**, off Bellevue Ave in Touro Park, is a curious stone tower of uncertain provenance. Some people believe it was built by Norse mariners before the voyages of Columbus; others say it was built by an early governor of the colony.

The **International Tennis Hall of Fame** (☎ 401-849-3990), 194 Bellevue Ave just south of Memorial Blvd, is in the historic Newport Casino building (1880), once the wealthy Newporters' summer club. The forerunners of today's US Open Tennis Tournament were held here in 1881. Admission costs $8 for adults, $6 for seniors, $4 for children younger than 16 ($20 per family). Playing on one of its 13 grass courts costs $25 per person per hour. The hall is open 10 am to 5 pm every day of the year, though the grass courts close for winter.

For decades, Newport was the home port for America's Cup races, which is why it has a **Museum of Yachting** (☎ 401-847-1018) in Fort Adams State Park. It's open 10 am to 5 pm daily mid-May to October.

The **Artillery Company of Newport** (☎ 401-846-8488), at 23 Clarke St, has an extensive collection of military uniforms, paraphernalia and other memorabilia on view 10 am to 4 pm daily except Tuesday, June to September (noon to 4 pm Sunday), and at other times by appointment. Admission costs $3 for adults, $2 for children.

## Touro Synagogue

This house of worship (☎ 401-847-4794), on Touro St near Spring St, was designed by Peter Harrison (who did King's Chapel in Boston) and built by the nascent Sephardic Orthodox Congregation Yeshuat Israel in 1763, and it has the distinction of being North America's oldest Jewish synagogue. Inside, a letter to the congregation from President George Washington, written in 1790, hangs in a prominent spot. There's an historic cemetery just up the street.

The synagogue is open for worship only on Saturday. Visitors may see it 10 am to 5 pm daily (except Saturday) in summer. In spring and fall, it's open 11 am to 3 pm (1 to 3 pm Sunday); in winter, 1 to 3 pm Sunday and by appointment.

## Trinity Church

This Episcopal church (☎ 401-846-0660), at Spring and Church Sts on Queen Anne Square, follows the design canon of Sir Christopher Wren's Palladian churches in London. Built between 1725 and 1726, it has a fine wineglass-shaped pulpit, tall windows to let in light and traditional box pews to keep out drafty air. It's open 10 am to 4 pm daily mid-June to early September; 1 to 4 pm in May and from the early part of September to mid-October; and 10 am to 1 pm the rest of the year.

## Cliff Walk

The Cliff Walk is a footpath that runs along the eastern edge of the peninsula, with vast views of the sea to one side and the mansions along Bellevue Ave to the other. It starts at the inn called Cliff Walk Manor, just west of Easton's Beach, and goes south and then west almost to Bailey's Beach. Strolling its entire length takes about an hour.

## Beaches

Newport's public beaches are on the eastern side of the peninsula along Memorial Blvd.

All are open 9 am to 6 pm in summer and charge a parking fee of $10 per car ($15 on weekends).

Easton's Beach (☎ 401-848-6491), also called First Beach, is the largest, with an attractive Victorian-style pavilion with bath houses and showers, a snack bar and a small aquarium where children can see and touch a variety of tidepool creatures and fish. It's within walking distance of Newport's center.

East of Easton's Beach along Purgatory Rd is Sachuest (Second) Beach (☎ 401-846-6273), named for the nearby wildlife sanctuary. It's prettier and cleaner than Easton's Beach and has showers, a snack bar and a lovely setting, overlooked by the neo-Gothic tower of St George's prep school.

A short distance east of Second Beach is Third Beach (☎ 401-847-1993). Popular with families because it is protected from the open ocean, Third Beach also appeals to windsurfers because the water is calm and the winds steady.

Other 'pocket' beaches exist along Ocean Ave, but most of these, such as Bailey's Beach, are private. An exception is Gooseberry Beach, open to the public for a fee of $10 per car, $3 for pedestrians and cyclists.

## State Parks

Fort Adams, built between 1824 and 1857, crowns a rise at the end of the peninsula, which juts northward into Newport Harbor. Like many American coastal fortresses, it had a short, practical life as a deterrent and a long life as a tourist attraction. It's the centerpiece of **Fort Adams State Park** (☎ 401-847-2400), the venue for the Newport Jazz and Folk Festivals and special events. A beach, picnic and fishing areas and a boat ramp are open 6 am to 11 pm daily. The Museum of Yachting (see Museums, above) and the ferry to Block Island are here as well.

At the opposite end of the peninsula, **Brenton Point State Park**, due south of Fort Adams on Ocean Ave, is a prime place for gazing at the ocean and flying kites.

## Bicycling

Newport is a fine town for bicycling, with only a few gentle slopes. Observe traffic laws just as you would in a car: Ride in the direction of traffic and don't ride on sidewalks.

Perhaps the most beautiful and satisfying ride is the 10-mile loop around Ocean Ave, which includes Bellevue Ave and its many beautiful mansions.

Rent your wheels at Newport Wheels (☎ 401-849-4400), 561 Thames St at Wellington Ave, where bikes – including mountain bikes – cost $5 per hour, $20 for the first day and $10 for each additional day (you can get one with a baby seat for $7.50 per hour). Motor scooters cost $35/45/65/95 for one/two/four/eight hours, or $125 for 24 hours (which is about three times what a four-person rental car would cost). You can also rent bikes at Ten Speed Spokes (☎ 401-847-5609), 18 Elm St, really on America's Cup Ave next to the Newport Gateway Transportation & Visitors Center.

### Special Events

Newport has a crowded calendar of community celebrations. During your visit, you may find special events involving polo, flowers and horticulture, Irish music, clam chowder, traditional crafts, soapbox racers, tennis, beer and of course yachts, yachts, yachts. There's even a winter festival (☎ 800-976-5122, 401-847-7666) in mid-February. For the full schedule, see www.gonewport.com.

If you plan to attend any of the major events described below, make sure you reserve accommodations and tickets in advance (tickets are usually on sale in mid-May).

**Newport Music Festival** – In mid-July, this includes classical music concerts in many of the great mansions for $28 to $44 per ticket. For a schedule, write to the Newport Music Festival, PO Box 3300, Newport, RI 02840, or call ☎ 401-846-1133.

**International Tennis Hall of Fame Championships** – In July, this event hosts top professionals. Contact the Hall of Fame (☎ 401-849-3990), 194 Bellevue Ave, Newport, RI 02840.

**Ben & Jerry's Folk Festival/Newport** – In early August, big-name stars and up-and-coming groups perform at Fort Adams State Park and other venues around town. Call ☎ 401-847-3700 for information; tickets cost $25 to $39.

**JVC Jazz Festival/Newport** – This event (☎ 401-847-3700) usually takes place on a mid-August weekend, with concerts at the Newport Casino (International Tennis Hall of Fame) and Fort Adams State Park.

**Newport International Boat Show** – The boat show (☎ 401-846-1115), held in late September, is the biggest and best-known of Newport's many boat and yacht shows.

### Places to Stay

Newport's lodgings are expensive. The cozy inns and harborside hotels in the center of town generally charge $125 to $200 and up for a double room with breakfast in summer. Rhode Island sales tax of 7% and Newport lodging tax of 5% will be added to your bill.

On Friday and Saturday, prices are highest; during the music festivals, they're higher still. Sunday through Thursday, rates fall as much as 30%. Many lodgings require a two-night minimum on summer weekends, and a three-night minimum on holidays.

As rooms can be scarce in summer, you might want to use a reservation service. Anna's Victorian Connection (☎ 401-849-2489, 800-884-4288, fax 401-847-7309, annas@wsii.com), 5 Fowler Ave, Newport, RI 02840, will make a reservation at any one of 250 hostelries in Rhode Island and southeastern Massachusetts at no cost to you.

Bed and Breakfast of Newport Ltd (☎ 401-846-5408, fax 846-1828), 33 Russell Ave, Newport, RI 02840, represents 350 establishments in the Newport area. Taylor-Made Reservations (☎ 800-848-8848, fax 401-848-0301, www.Enjoy-Newport.com) represents a full range of lodgings as well.

If you arrive without a reservation, go to the visitors center and ask to see its list of vacancies. Except in summer, you may find handbills in the brochure racks that entitle you to special reduced rates.

**Camping** The *Paradise Mobile Home Park* (☎ *401-847-1500, 459 Aquidneck Ave (RI 138A))*, in Middletown northeast of Easton's Beach, takes self-contained RVs only, with full hookups, charging $30 to $40 per night. Reserve in advance.

The *Meadowlark Recreational Vehicle Park* (☎ *401-846-9455, 132 Prospect Ave)*, off

RI 138A in Middletown, has 40 RV sites open from mid-April through October for $24 per night.

There's also the *Melville Ponds Campground* (☎ *401-849-8212, 181 Bradford Ave*), off RI 114, a municipal campground in Portsmouth, about 10 miles north of Newport's center. It has 57 tent sites ($15) and 66 RV sites ($21 to $24) open April through October. To find it, take RI 114 to Stringham Rd, go to Sullivan Rd, then head north to the campground.

Across the Newport Bridge on Conanicut Island in Jamestown is *Fort Getty State Park* (☎ *401-423-7264*), with 25 tent sites ($20) and 100 RV sites ($25). From RI 138, go south on North Rd, cross Narragansett Ave and continue on Southwest Ave, then merge into Beaver Tail Rd and turn right onto Fort Getty Rd.

**Motels** Compared to Newport's many wonderful inns, its motels lack character, but they make up for it with modern amenities and lower prices. Most are in Middletown on RI 114 (W Main Rd) and RI 138 (E Main Rd). RIPTA bus No 63/Purple Line will take you to downtown Newport, saving you the expense and bother of parking.

The *Best Western Mainstay Inn* (☎ *401-849-9880, 800-528-1234, fax 401-849-4391, 151 Admiral Kalbfus Rd (RI 138)*), near the Newport Bridge, is a bit closer to downtown Newport and charges $119 to $159 for a room with two double beds on Friday and Saturday, but only $95 the rest of the week.

The *Budget Host Inn* (☎ *401-849-4700, 800-862-2006*), on W Main Rd (RI 114) in Middletown, charges only $68 Sunday to Thursday, $115 on weekends.

*Howard Johnson Lodge* (☎ *401-849-2000, 800-446-4656, fax 401-849-6047, 351 E Main Rd (RI 138)*), in Middletown, charges $99 on weekdays, $149 on weekends.

**Hotels** Newport's downtown hotels are convenient, elegant, beautiful and pricey.

The *Newport Bay Club & Hotel* (☎ *401-849-8600, fax 846-6857, 337 Thames St*) is a beautiful stone building right at the foot of Memorial Blvd upon the waterfront. One-

bedroom suites cost $179 on weekdays. On weekends the suites cost $299.

The posh 317-room *Newport Marriott* (☎ *401-849-1000, 888-634-4498, fax 401-849-3422, 25 America's Cup Ave*) charges $209 to $229 during the week, $249 to $289 on summer weekends.

The 253-room *Newport Islander Doubletree Hotel* (☎ *401-849-2600, 800-222-8733*), right out in the harbor on Goat Island (connected to the mainland via a causeway), has all the amenities, which can be yours for $219 on weekdays, $279 on weekends.

**Inns & B&Bs** Unless otherwise mentioned, all inn and B&B rooms have private baths and come with breakfast.

North of the Newport Gateway Transportation & Visitors Center is the quiet residential district called The Point, with a good collection of small inns and B&Bs. Prices here are generally a bit lower than at lodgings south of the visitors center.

*On the Point B&B* (☎ *401-846-8377, 102 3rd St*), between Sycamore and Van Zandt, is comfy (rooms have color TV) and a bit farther than most from Newport's center, so rooms are reasonably priced at $115 on weekends, $90 on weekdays.

*Sarah Kendall House* (☎ *401-846-3979, 47 Washington St*), at Elm, is homey and nice. The rooms, for $145 to $225, have aircon and cable TV, and most have water views.

*Stella Maris Inn* (☎ *401-849-2862, 91 Washington St*), near Pine, is a big, quiet stone-and-frame inn with numerous fireplaces. Its rooms with garden view rent for $150, with water view for $175 on summer weekends; during the week rates fall to $110 and $125.

Victorian 'Stick-style' *Sanford-Covell Villa Marina* (☎ *401-847-0206, 72 Washington St*), at Walnut, was perhaps Newport's most lavish house when it was built in 1869. With a saltwater swimming pool and spa and a marvelous wraparound veranda right over the water with wonderful sunset views, it's still pretty lavish. Rooms range in price from $105 (small, no water view, shared bath) to $235 (large, lavish, grand water views). Some mid-price rooms have a toilet and sink but share showers with other rooms.

***The Willows of Newport*** (☎ 401-846-5486, 8 Willow St) has four delicately, lavishly decorated rooms for $188 to $228 and up in-season, $128 to $158 off-season, breakfast in bed included.

***Covell Guest House*** (☎ 401-847-8872, 43 Farewell St), several blocks to the east of The Point, was built in 1805 and renovated in 1982. Its five rooms cost $75 to $85 for summer weekdays and $110 to $130 for the weekends.

South of the visitors center, on Historic Hill and off lower Thames St, are many more inns and B&Bs, at slightly higher prices. Here are a few of the better-value, quieter ones.

***Savanas' Inn*** (☎ 401-847-3801, 888-880-3764, fax 401-841-0994, 41 Pelham St), at Spring, is a lovely, centrally located Second Empire-style house built around 1865 and recently restored to its original splendor. Each of its four rooms is individually decorated; an English garden and hot tub are ideal places to relax, and several cats are effective lap-warmers on chilly days. Rooms cost $185 to $275 on summer weekends, $150 to $235 weekdays.

***Francis Malbone House*** (☎ 401-846-0392, 800-846-0392, fax 401-848-5956, 392 Thames St), at Brewer, is a grand brick mansion designed by the Touro Synagogue's architect and built in 1760 for a shipping merchant. Now beautifully decorated and immaculately kept, with a fine garden in back, it is one of Newport's finest inns. Some guest rooms have working fireplaces, as do the public rooms. Rates are $175 to $285 double in summer, $155 to $225 in winter, breakfast and afternoon tea included. The location on lower Thames St puts a dozen restaurants within a few minutes' walk.

On the south side of the Francis Malbone House, ***Admiral Fitzroy Inn*** (☎ 401-848-8000, 800-343-2863, fax 401-848-8006, 5star@admiralsinns.com, www.admiralsinns.com, 398 Thames St), between Brewer and Dennison, is set back from the street, which means it's relatively quiet. Each of the 17 large rooms has some period furnishings, a

mini-fridge, electric tea kettle, color TV and hair dryer. There's an elevator and ample parking behind the inn (a valuable asset in Newport!). Its rates from May through October are $125 to $225; $85 to $165 the rest of the year.

***Ivy Lodge*** (☎ 401-849-6865, 12 Clay St) is a block east of Bellevue Ave along Parker Ave, east of The Elms. Though not quite as grand as other Bellevue mansions, it is an impressive place, with guest rooms renting for $135 to $185, buffet breakfast included.

## Places to Eat

From June through September, reserve your table for dinner in advance, then show up on time or cancel. Some of the most popular restaurants do not take reservations, in which case you must get in line early. Many Newport restaurants don't accept credit cards; you must pay with cash, traveler's checks or by personal check with sufficient identification. Ask about payment when you reserve.

The centrally located, ever-popular ***Brick Alley Pub & Restaurant*** (☎ 401-849-6334, 140 Thames St), at Broadway, has a huge menu of snacks, sandwiches, bar food, Mexican specialties and full meals, as well as Newport's most elaborate drinks list. Try the all-you-can-eat soup, salad and bread bar for $7 before 5 pm, $9 afterward. There is an outdoor eating area and billiards and pinball in the back room.

***The Black Pearl*** (☎ 401-846-5264), on Bannister's Wharf, is Newport's 'old reliable,' offering three types of dining. The Tavern's sandwich board and seafood menu ($8 to $20) are long and varied, the atmosphere suitably nautical; have a big bowl of clam chowder and a beer for less than $10. For traditional swordfish, steaks and rack of lamb ($20 to $38) in fancier surroundings, there's the Commodore's Room. The Hot Dog Annex supplies cheap snacks ($2.50). In our informal survey of clam chowder throughout New England, the Black Pearl's comes in first.

The richest selection of restaurants in all price ranges is undoubtedly along lower Thames St, south of America's Cup Ave.

Some allow you to 'BYO' (bring your own wine or beer), which you can buy at **Thames St Liquors** (☎ 401-847-0017, 517 Thames St), between Dearborn and Holland; at **LVL Liquors Ltd** (☎ 401-842-0800, 651 Thames St), at Narragansett; or at **Wellington Square Liquors** (☎ 401-846-9463, 580 Thames St).

**Percy's Bistro** (☎ 401-849-7895, 341 Thames St), just off Memorial Blvd, is a good, moderately priced storefront place for a quiet, romantic dinner. Low lights, main courses priced from $13 to $20 and daily specials as low as $10 are the attractions.

**Salas'** (☎ 401-846-8772, 345 Thames St), above Percy's but with a separate entrance, is a Newport institution for the hearty, hungry and thrifty. The Italian, American, 'Oriental' and seafood dishes – and the children's menu – are simple but tasty: a meatball sandwich for $3, baked cod for $9. And the huge plates of pasta in red clam sauce are sold by weight! Come Friday and Saturday for prime rib of beef.

From Percy's Bistro and Salas', walk west toward the water and you'll find the **Cheeky Monkey Cafe** (☎ 401-845-9494, 14 Perry Mill Wharf), the posh, chic, cool place popular with the BMW and SUV sets. Salads for $7, pasta plates for $18 and fancier fare for $20 to $24 keep them happy except on Sunday and Monday, when it's closed.

**The Sandwich Board Deli Cafe** (☎ 401-849-5358, 397 Thames St) has breakfast bagels, luncheon salads and cheap sandwiches ($1.75 to $5) that can be consumed at sidewalk tables.

Cheap and popular, **Gary's Handy Lunch** (☎ 401-847-9480, 462 Thames St) is between Pope and Milburn Court. Locals crowd the booths from early morning into the evening for big plates of spaghetti and meatballs for $4.50, steak sandwiches and french fries for $5, or clam, scallop and shrimp plates priced at $9 or $10. For a *big* breakfast, try the prime rib and eggs for $6.25.

**Scales & Shells** (☎ 401-846-3474, 527 Thames St), at Holland, is a moderately priced, plainly decorated retro seafood place with an open kitchen and a blackboard menu. Have your squid or lobster grilled for a change, with a glass of chardonnay from

Greenvale, a local Rhode Island vineyard. Full meals cost $28 to $45, or more for elaborate dishes such as lobster *fra diavolo*. Come early – there's often a two-hour wait in summer – or make a reservation at **UpScales** (☎ 401-847-2000), Scales & Shells' more genteel 2nd-floor dining room with slightly higher prices.

**Cafe Zelda** (☎ 401-849-4002, 528 Thames St) is an elegant little bistro with low lights and a romantic atmosphere. Chef Marjorie Knerr prepares innovative dishes drawing on international cuisines for ideas. Full dinners cost $35 to $50 per person. The very popular bar is in a separate space next door.

**Bouchard** (☎ 401-846-0123, 505 Thames St) is great for a splurge. American chef Albert Bouchard prepares fine, solid, artful nouvelle cuisine that's not prissy. A great, fancy three-course dinner costs about $50 or $60 per person, wine, tax and tip included.

For more traditional fare, the historic **White Horse Tavern** (☎ 401-849-3600), Marlborough St, has been the place since 1687. The menu is traditional American and continental and includes local ingredients when possible. Dinner (at which men must wear a jacket) costs $30 to $40 per person; lunch (Thursday, Friday and Saturday only) is somewhat less.

**Music Hall Café** (☎ 401-848-2330, 250 Thames St) is a Tex-Mex place that serves tacos, burritos, barbecue pork ribs and – incongruously – Italian pastas and vegetarian plates, all priced from $10 to $18, with sandwiches from $6 to $8.

The farther you walk, the more you save: **Fred's Old Place** (☎ 401-847-7949, 677 Thames St), at Potter, serves lots of beef, from $7 burgers to $20 filets – and that price includes bread, salad, vegetables and potato, rice or pasta. Bring your own wine or beer (this also keeps the price down). Breakfast and dinner are served daily in summer; dinner only in off-season.

## Entertainment

This is a resort town, and in July and August it rocks at night (see Special Events, earlier in this section). But really, any day is a good one for finding a congenial cafe, pub or music club. For what's going on, consult the website www.cityentertainment.com.

The **Steaming Bean Espresso Cafe** (☎ *401-849-5255, 515 Thames St)*, at Coddington Wharf, is a great place to grab some fine java. Soup and salad cost $7 at lunch.

**The Red Parrot** (☎ *401-847-3140, 348 Thames St)*, at Memorial Blvd, is huge, with tables on two floors and jazz most nights. The menu lists burgers starting at $6 and other bar dishes up to $18. The **Boathouse Pub & Restaurant** (☎ *401-846-7700, 636 Thames St)* is heavy on 'Ye Olde Newporte' nautical decor, with music many nights.

Stop in at **One Pelham East** (☎ *401-847-9460, 1 Pelham St East)*, at Thames, opposite Bannister's Wharf, for an Irish theme and live music (not all Irish) on many nights. Pelham St, by the way, was the first street in the USA to be illuminated by gas (1805), and it's still lit that way today.

The nearby **Newport Blues Cafe** (☎ *401-841-5510, 286 Thames St)*, at Green, is just that: a popular rhythm and blues bar with a program posted on the door a month in advance. Six to 10 pm, when the music's on, there's a $10-per-person minimum in the dining room.

The **Wharf Pub & Restaurant** (☎ *401-846-9233, 37 Bowen's Wharf)* specializes in microbrew beer.

## Shopping

The Armory Antique & Fine Arts Center (☎ 401-848-2398), 365 Thames St at Ann, has more than 125 antique dealers in one building, an ivy-covered, castlelike former armory now stuffed with pottery, porcelain, paintings, estate jewelry and furniture.

## Getting There & Away

Bonanza Bus Lines (☎ 401-846-1820, 888-751-8800, www.bonanzabus.com), at the Newport Gateway Transportation & Visitors Center, operates a half-dozen buses daily between Newport and Boston (1¾ hours, including Logan Airport) via Fall River, Massachusetts.

The Rhode Island Public Transit Authority (RIPTA; ☎ 401-781-9400, 800-244-0444, www.ripta.com) runs its buses on RI 60

between Newport (Gateway Center) and Providence (Kennedy Plaza, Francis St Terminus) at least every hour from around 5:30 am to 9:30 pm for $4. There's also a shuttle service to TF Green State Airport (☎ 401-737-8222).

From late May through mid-October, RIPTA operates buses connecting Newport with the Amtrak railroad station in Kingston for $3. Express buses make the trip in 35 minutes.

A summer ferry (☎ 401-783-4613) from Providence stops at Fort Adams Dock, taking passengers to Block Island (a two-hour trip); see the Block Island section, below, for details.

## Getting Around

RIPTA runs several bus routes from the Newport Gateway Transportation & Visitors Center every 30 minutes: Bus No 61/Orange Line runs to First and Second Beaches; bus No 62/Red Line runs along Thames St to Fort Adams; bus No 63/Purple Line runs to Middletown and the motels described earlier in Places to Stay; and bus No 67/Yellow Line runs along Bellevue Ave to the mansions.

See Bicycling, earlier in this section, for bike-rental information.

## GALILEE & POINT JUDITH

Rhode Island's port for car ferries to Block Island is at Galilee State Pier, at the southern end of RI 108 in the village of Galilee, near Point Judith. Galilee – sometimes called Point Judith in ferry schedules – is a real workaday fishing town with docks for fishing craft, a dock for the ferries, Roger W Wheeler Memorial Beach, and Fishermen's Memorial State Park (see South County Beaches, later in this chapter, for camping information).

RIPTA (☎ 401-781-9400, 800-244-0444) bus No 65 connects the Kingston Amtrak railroad station with Galilee State Pier eight times each weekday, four times on Saturday and two on Sunday. Some buses connect at Wakefield Mall with bus No 64 for Newport and bus No 66 for Providence and TF Green State Airport.

All-day parking in Galilee costs about $5 in any of several lots. The ***Portside Restaurant & Chowder House***, the ***Top of the Dock Restaurant*** and other eateries are good for a drink, snack or meal while you're waiting for the boat. (See the following Block Island section for ferry details.)

## BLOCK ISLAND

This 11-sq-mile island, shaped something like a pork chop, doesn't have the celebrity cachet of Martha's Vineyard or Nantucket. Instead, it seems content to be just what it is, a sleepy little island 13 miles off the Rhode Island coast with a few Victorian-era hotels and guest houses, and a Brigadoon-like air of otherworldliness. Its self-satisfied somnolence seems broken only during Block Island Race Week in early summer, when yachters come from all over the East Coast to compete in a series of races around the island.

### History

In 1614, before the Pilgrims founded their settlement at Plymouth, Massachusetts, a mariner named Adriaen Block stopped at this island and gave it his name.

When colonists came to the region a decade later, relations with the local Pequot Indians were not particularly cordial. But by 1672, the thriving fishing town of New Shoreham had received a royal charter.

Fishing and farming were mainstays of the island's economy for almost two centuries. In the mid-19th century, the development of fast, dependable steam-powered vessels and the wealth of the New England economy made it possible for mainlanders to take affordable summer vacations on the island.

Block Island had its heyday as a summer resort in the 1890s, when steamboats made regular trips from New York and Boston, and the hotels were full of long-skirted ladies and men in straw boaters.

Today, the island landscape has the spare, haunted feeling of an Andrew Wyeth painting, with stone walls demarcating centuries-old property lines, and few trees to interrupt the ocean views.

Not much changes on Block Island from one year to the next. The row of gingerbread Victorian inns along the Old Harbor landing shows the same face to visitors that it did 50 or even 100 years ago, and the island's simple attractions remain much the same as well. In a nutshell (or a clamshell), these are the 'four Bs': beaches, boating, bicycling and birds.

### Orientation & Information

It's confusing: All of Block Island is incorporated as the town of New Shoreham, but the main settlement is known as Old Harbor, or sometimes as the town of Block Island.

Most of the boating activity is centered in New Harbor, the island's other main settlement, on the shore of Great Salt Pond.

For tourist information, contact the Block Island Chamber of Commerce (☎ 401-466-2982, 800-383-2474, www.blockisland.com), PO Drawer D, Water St, Block Island, RI 02807.

### Southeast Light

You'll likely recognize this red-brick lighthouse building from postcards of the island. Set dramatically atop 200-foot red-clay cliffs called **Mohegan Bluffs**, the lighthouse actually had to be moved back from the eroding cliff edge in 1993. With the waves crashing below and the sails moving across the Atlantic offshore, it's probably the best place on the island to watch the sunset.

### North Light

At **Sandy Point**, the northernmost tip of the island, scenic North Light is at the end of a long, sandy path lined with beach roses. The 1867 lighthouse contains a small maritime museum with information about famous island wrecks. Also at Sandy Point is **Settlers Rock**, a boulder that bears the names of the island's original settlers, who arrived at this spot in 1661. The boulder was erected as a memorial in 1911.

### Beaches

The island's east coast to the north of Old Harbor is lined with 2 miles of glorious beach, the Block Island State Beach. The southern part, closest to town, is Benson

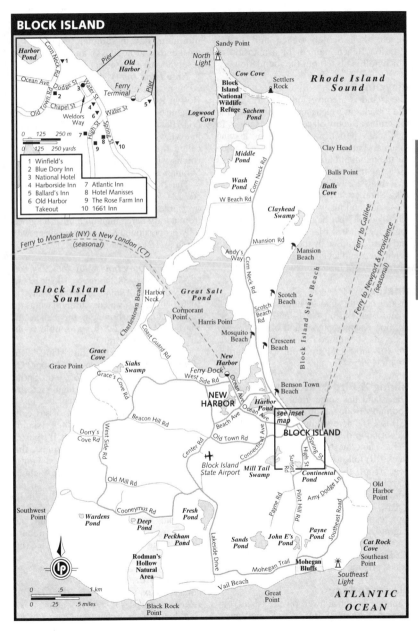

# BLOCK ISLAND

**Inset map (Old Harbor area):**

Harbor Pond

Corn Neck Rd
Ocean Ave
Dodge St
Old Town Rd
Chapel St
Weldors Way
Water St
High St
Spring St
Water St
Pier
Old Harbor
Ferry Terminal

1 Winfield's
2 Blue Dory Inn
3 National Hotel
4 Harborside Inn
5 Ballard's Inn
6 Old Harbor Takeout
7 Atlantic Inn
8 Hotel Manisses
9 The Rose Farm Inn
10 1661 Inn

0   125   250 m
0   125   250 yards

**Main map labels:**

Sandy Point
North Light
Cow Cove
Settlers Rock
*Rhode Island Sound*

Block Island National Wildlife Refuge
Logwood Cove
Sachem Pond
Clay Head
Balls Point
Balls Cove

Middle Pond
Corn Neck Rd
Wash Pond
W Beach Rd
Clayhead Swamp

Ferry to Montauk (NY) & New London (CT) (seasonal)

Mansion Rd
Mansion Beach

Andy's Way
Corn Neck Rd

Ferry to Newport & Providence (seasonal)
Ferry to Galilee

*Block Island Sound*

Harbor Neck
Great Salt Pond
Cormorant Point
Harris Point
Mosquito Beach
Scotch Beach Rd
Scotch Beach
Crescent Beach

Block Island State Beach

Grace Cove
Grace Point
Siahs Swamp
Grace's Cove Rd
Charlestown Beach
Coast Guard Rd

New Harbor
Ferry Dock
West Side Rd
Ocean Ave

NEW HARBOR
Benson Town Beach

Harbor Pond
Ocean Ave
see inset map

BLOCK ISLAND

Beacon Hill Rd
Beach Ave
Old Town Rd
Center Rd
Connecticut Ave
Sunset Rd
High St
Spring St

Dorry's Cove Rd
West Side Rd

Block Island State Airport
Mill Tail Swamp
Continental Pond

Old Mill Rd

Old Harbor Point

Southwest Point
Wardens Pond
Deep Pond
Cooneymus Rd
Fresh Pond
Peckham Pond
Lakeside Drive
Sands Pond
John E's Pond
Payne Rd
Pilot Hill Rd
Amy Dodge Ln
Payne Pond
Southeast Road

Cat Rock Cove
Southeast Point

Rodman's Hollow Natural Area

Mohegan Trail
Mohegan Bluffs
Southeast Light

Vail Beach
Great Point
Black Rock Point

*ATLANTIC OCEAN*

0   .5   1 km
0   .25   .5 miles

Town Beach, which has a pavilion for changing and showering. North of that is Crescent Beach, then Scotch Beach and finally Mansion Beach, named for a mansion of which nothing is left but the foundation.

## Bicycling

The island is a convenient size for biking, and bicycles as well as mopeds are available for rental at many places in Old Harbor. In fact, many people save money by leaving their cars parked at the ferry dock in Galilee on the mainland and bring only their bikes for a day trip.

Rentals are available from the Old Harbor Bike Shop (☎ 401-466-2029), Esta's (☎ 401-466-2651), and many other places. Expect to pay about $17 per day for bikes, $45 per day for mopeds. Most islanders resent the noise and hazards caused by tourists on mopeds, so you'll get friendlier greetings (and more exercise) if you opt for a bicycle.

## Boating

Fishing charters may be booked from Block Island Boat Basin (☎ 401-466-2631) in New Harbor. Kayaks, canoes and other types of boats may be rented from Oceans & Ponds (☎ 401-466-5131) or from Twin Maples (☎ 401-466-5547).

## Hiking & Bird-Watching

The island has some great places to hike: **Rodman's Hollow** (entrance off Cherry Hill Rd) is a 100-acre wildlife refuge laced with trails that end at the beach – perfect for a picnic. The **Clay Head Nature Trail** (off Corn Neck Rd) follows high clay bluffs along the beachfront, then veers inland through a mazelike series of paths cut into low vegetation that attracts dozens of species of bird.

Bird-watching opportunities are excellent, especially in spring and fall when migratory species make their way north or south along the Atlantic Flyway. The island's verdant landscape and many freshwater ponds provide ample habitat.

## Places to Stay

Camping is not allowed on the island, but there are some 35 B&Bs and small guest house-style inns. You should know, however, that many places have a two- or three-day minimum stay in summer (especially on weekends and holidays), and that advance reservations are essential.

**Rose Farm Inn** (☎ 401-466-2034, fax 466-2053, rosefarm@blockisland.com), Box E, Roslyn Rd, Block Island, RI 02807, is convenient both to Old Harbor and the beach (via High St). The older part of the inn has fine views of the ocean; a newer addition called the Captain Rose House has nine rooms with more modern accoutrements. Summer rates are $105 to $200 per room.

The 1879 **Atlantic Inn** (☎ 401-466-5883, 800-224-7422), on High St in Old Harbor, overlooks the activities at the ferry landing from a lofty perch high on a hill. The gracefully proportioned Victorian inn has a wide porch and 21 rooms priced at $125 to $235 double.

The **Blue Dory Inn** (☎ 401-466-2254, 800-992-7290), Box 488, Dodge St, Block Island, RI 02807, has 14 small rooms decorated in Victorian style. It's a cozy little place at the edge of Old Harbor near the beach and charges $135 to $225 for a double room; large suites cost more.

The fanciest hotel on the island is the **Hotel Manisses** (☎ 401-466-2063, 466-2421, 800-626-4773, fax 401-466-2858), on Spring St in Old Harbor. With its high Victorian 'widow's walk' turret and small but lushly furnished guest rooms, the Manisses combines sophistication with Block Island's relaxed brand of country charm. It's part of a family accommodations business that includes the 1661 Inn, 1661 Guest House, Dewey Cottage, Dodge Cottage, Nicholas Ball Cottage and Sheffield House, so one call gets you information on dozens of rooms ranging in price from $55 to $335 depending upon the room, the building and the season. Buffet breakfast, wine and cheese hour, an island tour and service (but not tax) are included.

## Places to Eat

For an inexpensive meal, **Old Harbor Takeout** (☎ 401-466-2935), Water St, is a good bet for sandwiches to take on a picnic.

The *1661 Inn* (☎ *401-466-2421*), Spring St, serves an excellent – if somewhat pricey – outdoor buffet brunch on a grassy hillside overlooking the Atlantic.

For lunch, the *Harborside Inn* (☎ *401-466-5504*), Water St, is a good choice. You can't miss the red umbrellas of its outdoor patio as you step off the ferry at Old Harbor. Expect to spend $10 to $20 per person for lunch, almost twice that at dinnertime.

*Ballard's Inn* (☎ *401-466-2231*), in Old Harbor near the ferry landing, is popular with young people and the boating crowd. Lobster, seafood and standard fare are served in a cavernous dining room draped with flags.

For a classier dining experience, one of the best dining rooms on the island is at the *Hotel Manisses* (☎ *401-466-2421*), Spring St. Vegetables come from the hotel's garden, and the style of cooking is creative, often featuring fresh local seafood. Full dinners cost around $40 to $50 per person.

Another classy place is *Winfield's* (☎ *401-466-5856*), Corn Neck Rd, with exposed wooden ceiling beams, white tablecloths and a menu that features such classics as rack of lamb and filet mignon at prices similar to those at the Hotel Manisses.

## Entertainment

No one goes to Block Island for the nightlife, but there are a couple of places that might keep you up past 10 pm. *McGovern's Yellow Kittens* (☎ *401-466-5855*), on Corn Neck Rd just north of Old Harbor, has live music on weekends and jukebox music on weeknights. It's been an island mainstay for decades, attracting New England-area bands and keeping patrons happy with pool, table tennis and darts.

The elevated porch of the *National Hotel* (☎ *401-466-2901*), on Water St across from the ferry landing, has a relaxed 'Margaritaville' atmosphere, with live music on most summer evenings.

There are two places to catch first-run movies on Block Island: *Oceanwest Theater* (☎ *401-466-2971*), in New Harbor, and the *Empire* (☎ *401-466-2555*), in a former roller-skating rink in Old Harbor.

## Shopping

Opportunities for shopping are limited. Most shops are small, seasonal boutiques along Water and Dodge Sts in Old Harbor. Worth a look are the Ragged Sailor (crafts, paintings and folk art), the Scarlet Begonia (jewelry and craft items for the home) and the Star Department Store, a wood-floored classic that calls itself 'Block Island's general store.' This is the place to go for saltwater taffy and corny island souvenirs.

## Getting There & Away

**Air** New England Airlines (☎ 401-596-2460, 800-243-2460) provides air service between Westerly State Airport, on Airport Rd off RI 78, and Block Island State Airport (25 minutes) for $65 per person, roundtrip.

**Boat** Interstate Navigation Co and Nelseco Navigation Co (for reservations ☎ 401-783-4613, for offices 203-442-7891, 442-9553, www.blockislandferry.com), based in New London, Connecticut, operate the ferry services to Block Island.

Interstate operates the car-and-passenger ferries from Galilee State Pier, Galilee, to Old Harbor, Block Island, a voyage of just over an hour. Adults pay $13.50 for a same-day roundtrip ticket, children half-price. Cars are carried for $26.30 each way; reserve your car space in advance. See the Galilee & Point Judith section, earlier in this chapter, for transportation information for Galilee State Pier.

A daily Interstate passenger boat runs in summer (late June to mid-September) from Providence's India St Dock (four hours, $13.70) via Newport's Fort Adams Dock (two hours, $7.65) to Old Harbor, Block Island; children pay half of these same-day roundtrip adult fares. This boat takes bikes but not cars; finding safe, inexpensive parking in Providence and Newport can be difficult.

Nelseco runs a daily car-and-passenger ferry from early June to early September. It leaves New London at breakfast time and it returns from Old Harbor, Block Island, in the late afternoon. The two-hour voyage (same-day roundtrip) costs $17.50 for adults,

$11 for children, $50 for a car (make your reservations in advance).

Viking Star (☎ 516-668-5709) runs passenger ferries between Montauk, Long Island, and Old Harbor (1¾ hours) from mid-May through mid-October.

## Getting Around
Block Island Car Rental (☎ 401-466-2297) rents cars, or you can hire a taxi. There are usually several taxis available at the ferry dock in Old Harbor and in New Harbor. See Bicycling, above, for moped and bicycle rentals.

## WATCH HILL
One of the toniest summer colonies in the Ocean State, Watch Hill occupies a spit of land at the southwesternmost point of Rhode Island, just south of Westerly. Drive into the village along winding RI 1A, and the place grabs you: Huge shingled and Queen Anne summer houses command the rolling landscape from their perches high on rocky knolls. These houses show the wealth of their owners with subtle good taste; though they were built around the turn of the century, contemporaneously with Newport's mansions, they aren't flashy palaces. Perhaps partly because of that, Watch Hill's houses are still in private hands, while Newport's became white elephants, rescued only as tourist attractions.

Visitors not lucky enough to own a summer house here spend their time at the beach and browsing in the shops along Bay St, the main street. An ice cream cone from St Clair's Annex and a twirl on the Flying Horses Carousel provide immediate gratification and fodder for fond memories.

Watch Hill is at the end of Watch Hill Rd, 6 miles south of Westerly and 12 roundabout miles east of Stonington, Connecticut, by car.

## Flying Horses Carousel
The antique merry-go-round at the end of Bay St dates from 1883. Besides being among the few historic carousels still in operation in the country, it boasts a unique design: Its horses are suspended on chains so that they really do 'fly' outward as the carousel spins around. Rides cost $1 apiece.

## Beaches
For a long, leisurely beach walk, the half-mile stroll to **Napatree Point**, at the westernmost tip of Watch Hill, is unbeatable. With the Atlantic on one side and the yacht-studded Little Narragansett Bay on the other, Napatree is a protected conservation area, so walkers are asked to stay on the trails and off the dunes.

The nearest state beach to Watch Hill is **Misquamicut State Beach**, 3 miles to the east along RI 1A, but there is a fine beach, Ocean House Beach, right in Watch Hill, in front of the Ocean House Hotel. Access to the beach is by a right-of-way off Bluff Ave, but there is no parking nearby, and neighboring property owners are vigilant about restricting beachgoers to the public area below the high tide line. There's also small **Watch Hill Beach**, open to the public for a fee, behind the Flying Horses Carousel.

## Places to Stay
The *Ocean House Hotel* (☎ *401-348-8161, 2 Bluff Ave*), open only late June to early September, is the grand old lady of hotels in Watch Hill, the lone survivor of a series of fires and hurricanes that had destroyed its Victorian sisters by about 1950. While it's true that the imposing, yellow-clapboard Ocean House is looking a bit less spiffy inside these days, the place does have the authentic ambience of bygone days. The oceanfront porch is a great spot to sit with a drink after a day at the beach. Double rooms cost about $200, breakfast and dinner included.

More modern and comfortable is the *Inn at Watch Hill* (☎ *401-596-0665*), with motel-style rooms priced from $130 to $150 set above the row of shops on Bay St.

## Places to Eat
The most atmospheric restaurant is the *Olympia Tea Room* (☎ *401-348-8211*), on Bay St. The Olympia is an authentic 1918 soda fountain turned into a classy bistro, open in-season for breakfast, lunch and

dinner. Varnished wooden booths, black-and-white checkered tiles on the floor and the antique marble-topped soda fountain all give the place an air of authenticity. Light lunch platters and sandwiches cost about $10 or $12 with a drink, dinners at least twice as much.

For more inexpensive food, including good take-out for picnics, there's the *Bay Street Deli* (☎ *401-596-6606, 110 Bay St*). The *St Clair's Annex* ice-cream shop across the street, run by the same family for more than a century, features more than 30 flavors of homemade ice cream.

# Rhode Island Beaches

It's not by accident that Rhode Island is nicknamed the Ocean State. It's the little state with 400 miles of coastline – though most of those miles are actually on Narragansett Bay (which is better for boaters than for beachgoers).

Most public beaches in Rhode Island charge parking fees ranging from $5 to $15 for the day from mid-June to Labor Day. The best deals are the state beaches, where state residents pay just $5 to $7, and out-of-staters $10 to $12, to park. Reasonably priced season passes (which may be used at any state beach) are a good option if you're going to spend more than a few days at the beach during your stay.

Below is a selective look at some of the best beaches the Ocean State has to offer.

## SOUTH COUNTY BEACHES

Rhode Island's topography means that it has two very different styles of ocean beaches. The best-known beaches in the state are those in what is known as South County, the colloquial name for the southwestern coastline towns from Narragansett to Watch Hill. The other beaches are on Narragansett Bay; see that section below.

These beaches, which trace the coast like a necklace looped with tidal salt ponds, are similar in nature and, geologically speaking,

are all the same beach: a wide apron of pristine sand separating huge salt ponds such as Quonochontaug and Ninigret from the surfy, generally seaweed-free open ocean.

The salt ponds are home to multitudes of waterfowl and shellfish, and some (such as Trustom Pond in South Kingstown) have been designated as national wildlife refuges. If you're the type of person who gets bored just lying in the sun, take a bird-watching walk around the salt ponds instead. You're likely to see herons, egrets and sandpipers hunting for lunch, and, at low tide, clams squirting from beneath the muddy sand.

For information on the South County beaches and attractions, contact the South County Tourism Council (☎ 401-789-4422, 800-548-4662, www.southcounty.com), 4808 Tower Hill Rd, in Wakefield.

### Roger W Wheeler Memorial Beach

Colloquially known as Sand Hill Cove, this has long been a favorite of families with small children. Not only does it have a playground and other facilities, it also has an extremely gradual drop-off and little surf because it is protected by the rocky arms of a breakwater called the Point Judith Harbor of Refuge. Roger W Wheeler Memorial Beach is just south of Galilee.

### South Kingstown Town Beach

A fine, sandy beach that epitomizes the South County model, South Kingstown also has an attractive pavilion and convenient parking in nearby Wakefield.

### Blue Shutters Town Beach

A Charlestown-managed beach, this is also a good choice for families. There are no amusements other than nature's, but there are convenient facilities, a watchful staff of lifeguards and generally mild surf.

### Misquamicut State Beach

Misquamicut is one of the busiest beaches in the state because it's the closest to the Connecticut state line. It has a lot to offer families: It's inexpensive, it has convenient facilities for changing, showering and eating,

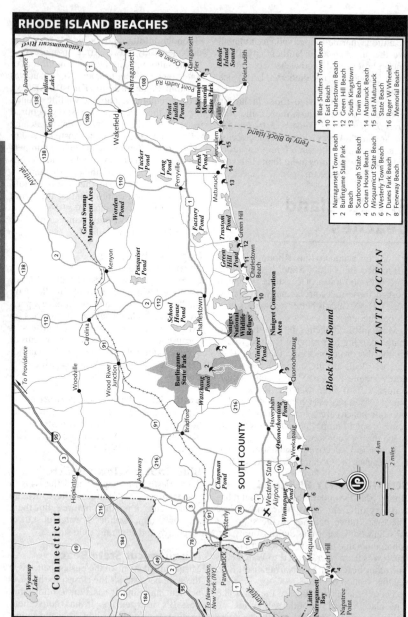

# RHODE ISLAND BEACHES

1  Narragansett Town Beach
2  Burlingame State Park
3  Scarborough State Beach
4  Ocean House Beach
5  Misquamicut State Beach
6  Westerly Town Beach
7  Dunes Park Beach
8  Feneway Beach
9  Blue Shutters Town Beach
10  East Beach
11  Charlestown Beach
12  Green Hill Beach
13  South Kingstown Town Beach
14  Matunuck Beach
15  East Matunuck State Beach
16  Roger W Wheeler Memorial Beach

and it's close to a charmingly old-fashioned amusement area, Atlantic Beach Park. Here you'll find plenty to enjoy – waterslides, miniature golf, bumper cars, kiddie rides and arcade games. Misquamicut is just south of Westerly.

## Places to Stay

**Camping** The state-managed campgrounds in South County are among the prettiest spots in the state. The fee to camp at these campgrounds is $12, $16 for hookups.

The **Burlingame State Park Campsites** (☎ 401-322-7994, 322-7337), off US 1 in Charlestown, have more than 750 wooded sites near crystal-clear Watchaug Pond for $12. First-come, first-served is the rule, but you can call ahead to check on availability.

There's also **Charlestown Beachway** (☎ 401-364-7000, 322-8910), off Charlestown Beach Rd, with 75 RV sites (running water only) open from mid-April through October for $12.

At the **Legrand G Reynolds Horsemen's Camping Area** (☎ 401-539-2356, 277-1157) in Exeter, you must be on horseback to camp in one of the 20 sites ($3). To get there, take I-95 exit 5S, then follow RI 102, then take RI 3 to RI 165 west, and go north on Escoheag Hill Rd.

The **Ninigret Conservation Area** (☎ 401-322-0450), off E Beach Rd in Charlestown, has 20 RV sites, but you need a special summer-long permit ($50).

Private campgrounds include **Wakamo Park Resort** (☎ 401-783-6688), on Succotash Rd in South Kingstown, with 30 RV sites open from mid-April through mid-October for $40 each. From I-95 south, take RI 2 to RI 78 to US 1, then follow signs for East Matunuck.

**Worden's Pond Family Campground** (☎ 401-789-9113, 416A Worden's Pond Rd), in South Kingstown, has 75 tent sites ($17) and 125 RV sites ($20). From US 1, follow RI 110 to the second left (Worden's Pond Rd); from there, it's less than a mile to the campground.

**Hotels** Near the beachy town of Matunuck, the **Admiral Dewey Inn** (☎ 401-783-2090,

*668 Matunuck Beach Rd)*, in South Kingstown, is an 1898 National Historic Register building whose 10 rooms range in price from $100 to $130.

At the upper end of the price scale in South County is the **Weekapaug Inn** (☎ 401-322-0301), on Spring Ave in Weekapaug. The vast shingled inn, with its wraparound porch and lawn sloping down to Quonochontaug Pond, is a classic shore hotel that caters to a rather sedate crowd, many of whom have been regulars for decades. The inn's setting, with its own private ocean beach, is one of the loveliest in New England. Double rooms cost about $300, including all meals.

**B&Bs** Within the town limits of Westerly, yet close to the beach town of Weekapaug, the **Grandview Bed & Breakfast** (☎ 401-596-6384, 212 Shore Rd) is a simply furnished

### Beach Activities

South County's salt ponds and tidal rivers are ideal for **kayaking** and **canoeing**. It's even possible to venture out into the surf in a sea kayak. Outfitters in the area include Narragansett Kayak Co (☎ 401-364-2000), 2144 Matunuck Schoolhouse Rd, Charlestown; and Quaker Lane Bait & Tackle (☎ 401-294-9642), 4019 Quaker Lane, North Kingstown.

Narragansett Town Beach is considered to be among the top spots on the East Coast for **surfing**. You can rent surfboards, sailboards and any other water-sports gear you might need at The Watershed (☎ 401-789-3399), 396 Main St, Wakefield. The owner offers surfing lessons as well.

For the adventurous, **deep-sea fishing** trips – for a whole or a half day – can be arranged with the Frances Fleet (☎ 401-783-4988, 800-662-2824), 2 State St, Galilee. The Frances fleet also runs whale-watching cruises in summer. If you want to charter a boat for a longer trip, contact Snug Harbor Marina (☎ 401-783-7766), Gooseberry Rd, Galilee.

**RHODE ISLAND**

but comfortable small guest house that's moderately priced for the area at $75 to $95 per night in summer.

## Places to Eat

Not surprisingly, seafood is the order of the day in South County. Most spots are casual and beachy; shorts and T-shirts are far more common than suits and ties.

*Aunt Carrie's* (☎ 401-783-7930, 1240 Ocean Rd), at RI 108, near Point Judith, has been a Rhode Island landmark for more than 60 years. Within a stone's throw of the ocean itself, the place is noted for its traditional shore dinners (steamed clams, corn on the cob and lobster), clamcakes and chowder.

*Champlin's Seafood* (☎ 401-783-3152), in Galilee's port, is similarly casual, with an outdoor deck that overlooks the activity of the port. *George's of Galilee* (☎ 401-783-2306), on Sand Hill Cove Rd, also at the port, has a take-out window where hordes of sandy people line up on summer afternoons for clamcakes that are crisp on the outside, doughy on the inside and studded with bits of clam.

## Entertainment

Quiet, seaside South County is not noted for its nightlife, but there are a couple of places in the area that keep some folks up past 9 pm.

*Theatre-by-the-Sea* (☎ 401-782-8587), on Cards Pond Rd in South Kingstown, offers a summer schedule of likable musicals and plays in a simple, barnlike building in a scenic area close to the beaches of Matunuck.

For live rock music geared to a younger crowd, there's *Ocean Mist* (☎ 401-782-3740, 145 Matunuck Beach Rd), in South Kingstown, which is set so close to the beach that if it weren't for the crashing bass, you might hear the crashing surf.

## Shopping

Unusual is a mild way of describing The Fantastic Umbrella Factory (☎ 401-364-6616), RI 1A, Charlestown. The place is a throwback to the '60s with a series of sheds filled with a wide variety of gift items: everything from flower bulbs and perennials to greeting cards, toys and handmade jewelry. You enter the place through a lush, unkempt garden and farm area where exotic birds and farm animals add to the communelike ambience.

## Getting There & Away

Though the *Shore Route* Amtrak trains between Boston and New York stop in Westerly, you really need a car to get to the beaches. Distances are not great (this is Rhode Island): from Westerly to Wakefield is only about 21 miles.

## NARRAGANSETT BAY BEACHES

Though South County's beaches are more famous, there are also presentable if smaller ones along the shores of Narragansett Bay. Many are in coves surrounded dramatically by huge boulders. These are particularly lovely early and late in the day when the sun slants on the granite, stage-lighting the scene.

To get Narragansett area information, contact the Narragansett Chamber of Commerce (☎ 401-783-7121), The Towers, RI 1A (PO Box 742), Narragansett, RI 02882.

## Goosewing Beach

Lovely, remote Goosewing is the only good public beach in Little Compton, on the east shore of Narragansett Bay, but access can be tricky. Due to an ongoing wrangle between the town and the Nature Conservancy over control of the beach, parking and lifeguard coverage are perennially in question. Still, year after year since the dispute began, it has been possible to get onto Goosewing by the unusual means of parking at the town beach called South Shore and walking across a small tidal inlet to the more appealing Goosewing. What makes it so appealing will be immediately apparent: The long sand beach with its wide-open ocean view is backed by rolling farmland that seems a throwback to another era. With no facilities to speak of, Goosewing can't be called convenient, but it is a lovely place to spend a summer's day.

## Scarborough State Beach

Scarborough (sometimes written as 'Scarboro') is the prototypical Rhode Island beach, and many consider it the best in the state. A lovely, castlelike pavilion, generous boardwalks, a beachfront that is both wide and long, and great, predictable surf make Scarborough special. It tends to attract a lot of teenagers, but it's large enough that other people can take them or leave them.

## Narragansett Town Beach

Narragansett tends to be crowded because it is within an easy walk of the beachy town of Narragansett Pier. It is the only beach in Rhode Island that charges a per-person admission fee ($4) on top of a parking fee ($5). Still, people – surfers in particular – adore it.

## Places to Stay

**Camping** In the fishing port of Galilee, *Fishermen's Memorial State Park* (☎ 401-789-8374), off RI 108, is so popular that many families return year after year to the same site. There are only 180 campsites at Fishermen's, so it's wise to reserve early by requesting the necessary form from the park management at 1011 Point Judith Rd, Narragansett, RI 02882, or the Division of Parks and Recreation (☎ 401-222-2632), 2321 Hartford Ave, Johnston, RI 02919. Sites cost $12 for a tent ($8 for Rhode Island residents), $14 to $16 for sites with hookups.

**B&Bs** *The Richards* (☎ 401-789-7746, 144 Gibson Ave), in Narragansett, is built of locally quarried granite, and its Gothic English-manor look sets it apart from other B&Bs. Rooms range in price from $85 to $135.

## Places to Eat

Every beach has its collection of clam shacks and snack shops good for a quick lunch. Here are some of the better, less obvious places to dine.

For a fancy night out, *The Coast Guard House* (☎ 401-789-0700, 40 Ocean Rd), in Narragansett, has traditional American favorites such as steak, veal and seafood. It also occupies a dramatic seaside site – one that has made it vulnerable to hurricanes in recent years.

Another good place is *Ginger's* (☎ 401-789-0914, 333 Main St), in Wakefield. Lunch and dinner are served in a comfortable, bistro-style atmosphere. Main courses at dinner cost a moderate $10 to $20.

## Getting There & Around

Transportation around Narragansett Bay is by car. Ferries connect Block Island (see that section) to the mainland at Galilee, Newport and Providence.

RHODE ISLAND

# Connecticut

Connecticut has a surprising variety of landscapes and cityscapes. The southeastern region looks to New York City. The coast is a varied mix of historic towns and villages and booming high-tech cities. Hartford, the capital, is an oasis of skyscrapers amid miles of farmers' fields. The northwestern corner is a more sedate, low-key version of Massachusetts' Berkshires.

Bisecting the state is the Connecticut River, called by the area's original inhabitants the Quinnehtukqut, or 'long tidal river.' Navigable all the way to Hartford, the great river was one of the reasons the colony, and then the state, prospered in the days before good highways and air transport.

Most of Connecticut's visitors come to visit Mystic Seaport, the historic re-creation of a 19th-century working coastal town; to visit the campus and museums of Yale University at New Haven or the US Coast Guard Academy at New London; to relax in a historic inn along the coast or on the banks of the Connecticut River; and to enjoy the scenery of the Litchfield Hills and their lakes.

The Connecticut Office of Tourism (☎ 800-282-6863, www.state.ct.us), 505 Hudson St, Hartford, CT 06106-7106, will send you a free, comprehensive *Connecticut Vacation Guide*, or you can pick one up at a Welcome Center.

The Connecticut Welcome Centers are located at Bradley International Airport (Terminals A and B) and on major highways entering the state. Coming from New York City, look for one on I-95 at Darien, the Merritt Parkway at Greenwich and farther along the coast upon I-95 at Westbrook. Coming from Rhode Island, there's one on I-95 at North Stonington, just east of Mystic. Coming from New York State on I-84, look for one at Danbury and another at Southington. Coming from Massachusetts along I-84, there's one at Willington. On I-91 northbound, there's one at Middletown; southbound, there's one at Wallingford.

A 12% hotel tax is levied on all accommodations charges. Figure it in when calculating your lodging costs.

## Getting There & Around

**Air** Bradley International Airport (☎ 860-292-2000, www.bradleyairport.com), about 12 miles north of Hartford in Windsor Locks (I-91 exit 40), serves the Hartford, Connecticut, and Springfield, Massachusetts area. Direct flights by American, Continental,

### Highlights

- Wine-tasting at a vineyard in Litchfield County
- Cruising aboard the *Charles W Morgan* at Mystic Seaport Museum
- Admiring the high-Victorian splendor of Mark Twain's mansion in Hartford
- Exploring the charming towns of the Lower Connecticut River Valley
- Trying your luck at the Indian gambling casinos north of Mystic
- Having fun with the children at Lake Compounce Theme Park

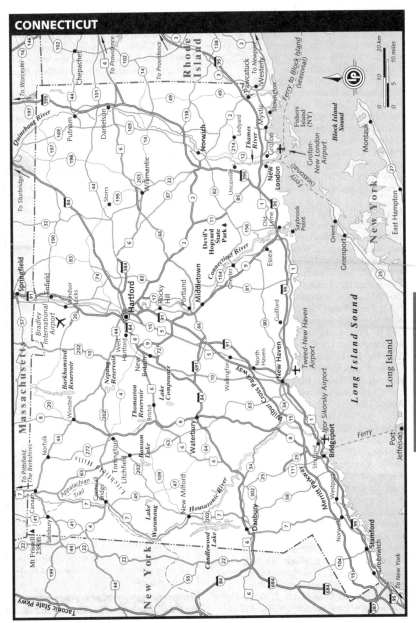

CONNECTICUT

Delta, Northwest, TWA, United and US Airways connect Bradley with about 60 other US airports. Bus and shuttle services transport passengers between the airport and major towns and cities in central Connecticut and Massachusetts.

Tweed-New Haven Airport (☎ 203-787-8283), in New Haven, serves the southeastern part of the state with flights by United, US Airways and others. See New Haven's Getting There & Away section.

Groton-New London Airport (☎ 860-445-8549), in Groton, and Igor Sikorsky Memorial Airport (☎ 203-576-7498), closer to New York City in Bridgeport-Stratford, also serve the coast with commuter flights.

**Bus** Peter Pan Bus Lines (☎ 413-781-3320, 800-343-9999, www.peterpan-bus.com), with its hub in Springfield, operates routes connecting Bridgeport, New Haven, Middletown and Hartford with New York City, Springfield and Boston.

Bonanza Bus Lines (☎ 401-331-7500, 800-556-3815, www.bonanzabus.com), with its hub in Providence, Rhode Island, runs buses from New York City via Danbury and Hartford to Providence; and via New Milford, Kent and Canaan, Connecticut, to Massachusetts' Berkshire hills and Bennington, Vermont. Connect at Providence with buses to Newport, Rhode Island, and to Boston and Cape Cod's Falmouth, Hyannis and Woods Hole.

**Train** Metro-North trains (☎ 212-532-4900, 800-638-7646, www.mta.nyc.ny.us) make the 1½-hour run between New York City's Grand Central Station and New Haven almost every hour from 7 am to midnight on weekdays, with more frequent trains during the morning and evening rush hours. On weekends, trains run about every two hours. There are frequent stops.

Other branches of Metro-North service also have frequent stops and go north to Danbury (connect at South Norwalk), New Canaan (connect at Stamford) and Waterbury (connect at Bridgeport).

Connecticut Commuter Rail Service's *Shore Line East* service (☎ 800-255-7433,

www.rideworks.com/rwsl.htm) travels along the shore of Long Island Sound, connecting New London, Old Saybrook, Westbrook, Clinton, Madison, Guilford, Branford and New Haven. At New Haven, the *Shore Line East* trains connect with Metro-North and Amtrak routes.

Amtrak (☎ 800-872-7245, www.amtrak .com) trains depart New York City's Pennsylvania Station for Connecticut on three lines: New Haven, Hartford, Springfield;

---

## Outdoor Connecticut

New England's three northern states – Vermont, New Hampshire and Maine – are justly noted for their outdoor activities, but that doesn't mean that Connecticut can't compete.

Northwest Connecticut's Housatonic River is particularly good for canoeing, kayaking, rafting and tubing. With the spring floods, the white water can reach Class III; in summer, it's Class I and II.

Riverrunning Expeditions, Ltd (☎ 860-824-5579, fax 824-5286), 85 Main St, Falls Village (Canaan), CT 06031, can set you up with equipment, training and river guides for an adventure on the Housatonic River. They will rent you a two-person canoe ($45), a raft ($25 per person), a kayak ($35 per person) or a tube ($10) to run the Housatonic, as well as a guide ($80 per day for up to eight canoes), and they also provide shuttle service.

Clarke Outdoors (☎ 860-672-6365), 163 US 7, West Cornwall, CT 06796, can also equip you for a run down the Housatonic River.

Farmington River Tubing (☎ 860-693-6465), in New Hartford, Connecticut, a division of North American Canoe Tours, Inc (☎ 860-739-0791) of Niantic, will take you tubing down the Farmington River at Satans Kingdom State Recreation Area, which is only a dozen miles west of Hartford on US 44.

New Haven, Hartford, Windsor Locks, Boston; and New Haven, New London, Mystic, Providence, Boston. Most tickets and trains allow stopovers along the way at no extra charge, so a ticket on the shore route between New York City and Boston may allow you to see New Haven, New London, Mystic and Providence for the same fare.

**Car** Drivers and front-seat passengers are required to wear safety belts in Connecticut. Children younger than one must be in a child safety seat; children ages one to four must sit in a back seat and wear a safety belt.

The use of radar detectors is illegal in Connecticut, and the fines are in the hundreds of dollars.

The maximum fine for a *first* speeding offense is $350, or $700 in a work zone. Connecticut state police patrol the highways in marked and unmarked cars and routinely use radar to catch speeders.

Connecticut fuel prices are usually at least 10% higher than in neighboring New England states and increase as you approach New York City.

**Boat** For information on ferry travel, see the Getting There & Away sections under New Haven and New London & Groton.

## HARTFORD

It's a rare person who goes to Hartford on vacation – it's a workaday city rather than a tourist destination – but once you're here, for whatever reason, you'll be surprised at how much Connecticut's capital city has to offer visitors, with particular strengths in history and art. If you plan your visit for a weekend, you can take advantage of surprisingly reasonable lodging prices.

With a population of about 124,000, Hartford's main business, aside from the state government, is insurance. In fact, the city has long been known as the insurance capital of the nation, home to some 35 major insurance companies.

## History

The earliest settlement of Hartford was by the local Saukiog Indians. Then in 1633, a trading post called the House of Good Hope was established on the shore of the Connecticut River by the Dutch, venturing north from New York. At the same time, a second group of Europeans came west to the Hartford area from the Massachusetts Bay Colony under the leadership of the Reverend Thomas Hooker.

The Hartford Colony, named for a town in England, became the Colony of Connecticut under the charter granted by King Charles II in 1662. A watershed event in the city's history took place 25 years later when the charter's provisions were threatened by the English governor, Sir Edmund Andorra. In defiant response, the citizenry hid the charter in the trunk of a large oak tree in Hartford, and never afterward surrendered it. A plaque at Charter Oak Place now marks the spot where the tree stood until 1856.

The insurance industry got its start in Hartford as early as the late 18th century as a means of guaranteeing the profitability of the shipping trade. In 1794, the Hartford Fire Insurance Co was founded. Eventually, fire and disaster insurance became the mainstay of Hartford insurance companies. (In 1996, mergers and 'reorganizations' left quite a few insurance workers unemployed; however, insurance is still the major industry here.)

Trinity College, with its beautiful campus overlooking Hartford, was established in 1823. The 96-acre campus has fine examples of University Gothic architecture.

By the late 19th century, Hartford was an established city, and its location between New York and Boston made it appealing to writers and artists. Samuel Clemens (better known as Mark Twain) first visited the city in 1869, calling it 'the best built and handsomest town I have ever seen. They have the broadest, straightest streets, and the dwelling houses are the amplest in size, and the shapeliest, and have the most capacious ornamental grounds about them.'

Twain eventually made Hartford his home, building his dream house in the pastoral area of the city then called Nook Farm and living in it from 1874 to 1891, years he

# HARTFORD

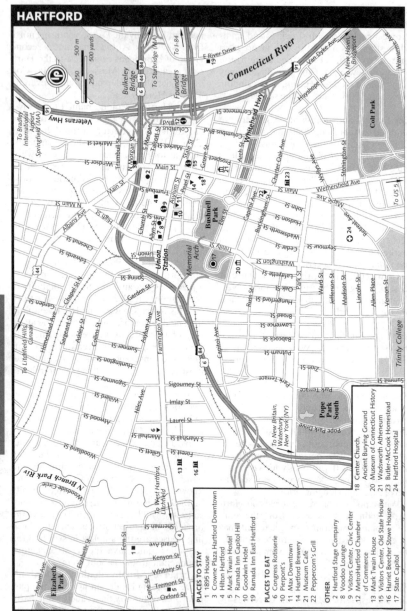

**PLACES TO STAY**
1  1895 House
3  Crowne Plaza Hartford Downtown
4  Hilton Hartford
5  Mark Twain Hostel
7  Ramada Inn Capitol Hill
10 Goodwin Hotel
19 Ramada Inn East Hartford

**PLACES TO EAT**
6  Congress Rotisserie
8  Pierpont's
11 Max Downtown
14 Hartford Brewery
21 Museum Cafe
22 Peppercorn's Grill

**OTHER**
2  Hartford Stage Company
9  Voodoo Lounge
12 Visitors Center, Civic Center
    MetroHartford Chamber
    of Commerce
13 Mark Twain House
15 Visitors Center, Old State House
16 Harriet Beecher Stowe House
17 State Capitol
18 Center Church,
    Ancient Burying Ground
20 Museum of Connecticut History
21 Wadsworth Atheneum
23 Butler-McCook Homestead
24 Hartford Hospital

later called the happiest of his life. Among the famous author's neighbors were Harriet Beecher Stowe and William Dean Howells.

Hartford entered a decline in the first half of the 20th century from which it has only partly recovered. In the 1960s, an urban planning project gave the city Constitution Plaza, a complex of office buildings in the heart of downtown, and in the '70s, the city opened its Civic Center, a venue for concerts and sporting events with associated shops and a hotel. But Hartford today suffers from an excess of commuters: people who drive in to work in the insurance towers, but who live – and pay taxes – in smaller towns. Urban renewal will not bring back the prosperous city of Twain's day until the people who work here live here.

## Orientation

On its hilltop perch, the pseudo-Gothic Connecticut State Capitol is visible from most of the interstate highways entering the city. The tallest building, with a brilliant laser beacon shining atop it at night, is the Travelers Tower. The Georgian-style, red-brick, gold-domed Old State House, dwarfed by insurance company skyscrapers, is in the city center. It has an information office but no place to park. The Hartford Civic Center is the huge building complex at the city's heart, with plenty of parking.

The easiest way to take in most of the Hartford attractions – the Wadsworth Atheneum, Old State House, Center Church and Butler-McCook Homestead – is on foot. The houses of literary figures Mark Twain and Harriet Beecher Stowe are a mile or so west of the town center off Farmington Ave.

Continue west on Farmington Ave and it becomes the main street of surprisingly lovely West Hartford, a 10-minute drive from downtown. It's lined with shops and cafes.

## Information

**Tourist Offices** The Greater Hartford Tourism District (☎ 860-244-8181, 800-793-4480, www.enjoyhartford.com), 234 Murphy Rd (I-91 exit 27), Hartford, CT 06114, and the Greater Hartford Convention & Visitors Bureau (☎ 860-728-6789, 800-446-7810,

www.grhartfordcvb.com) provide information as well as a good walking-tour pamphlet. Other visitors' centers are in the Old State House (☎ 860-522-6766), the Civic Center (☎ 860-633-6890) and the State Capitol (☎ 860-240-0222).

The MetroHartford Chamber of Commerce (☎ 860-525-4451, www.metrohartford .com), 250 Constitution Plaza, has an information office as well.

Hartford Guides (☎ 860-522-0855) offers guided walking tours. You may also see these friendly types on the street as you stroll. Feel free to ask them for directions, hotel and restaurant suggestions or other visitor information.

**Bookstores** The Reader's Feast is a unique environment for book shopping – see the listing under Entertainment, later.

Also look for the Gallows Hill Bookstore (☎ 860-297-5231), 300 Summit St. Bookworm (☎ 860-233-2653) is at 968 Farmington Ave, on the charming main street of West Hartford.

**Medical Services** The city's major medical facility is Hartford Hospital (☎ 860-524-2525), 80 Seymour St. Walk-in service is available at the Immediate Medical Care Center (☎ 860-296-8330), 423 Franklin Ave.

## State Capitol

The Connecticut State Capitol (☎ 860-240-0222), Capitol Ave and Trinity St, on Capitol Hill, is an imposing white marble building with Gothic details and a gold-leaf dome. Because of the variety of architectural styles it reflects, it has been unkindly dubbed 'the most beautiful ugly building in the world.' Designed by Richard Upjohn in 1879, it's open for free visits 8 am to 5 pm weekdays. One-hour guided tours, also free, depart from the Legislative Office Building, on Capitol Ave near Broad St, at 9:15, 10:15 and 11:15 am and 12:15 and 1:15 pm on weekdays (also 2:15 pm in July and August). On Saturday from April through October, they depart from the southwest (Capitol Ave) entrance to the capitol at 10:15 and 11:15 am and 12:15, 1:15 and 2:15 pm.

CONNECTICUT

## Museum of Connecticut History

While you're up on Capitol Hill, have a look at this museum (☎ 860-566-3056), 231 Capitol Ave, housed in the State Library and Supreme Court Building just across from the State Capitol. Nationally known for its genealogy library, it also holds Connecticut's royal charter of 1662, a prime collection of Colt firearms (which were manufactured in Hartford), clocks and the table at which Abraham Lincoln signed the Emancipation Proclamation. The museum is open 9:30 am to 4 pm weekdays, and admission is free.

## Bushnell Park

Hartford's 37-acre Bushnell Park (☎ 860-522-3668), spreading down the hill from the capitol, was designed by Jacob Weidenmann in the 1850s. The Tudor-style Pump House Gallery (1947) in the park features art exhibits and a summer concert series.

Children will enjoy the Bushnell Park Carousel (☎ 860-987-5900), a 1914 merry-go-round designed by Stein and Goldstein with 48 horses and a Wurlitzer band organ. The carousel operates 11 am to 5 pm daily except Monday from mid-May through August, and on weekends from mid-April to mid-May and in September. Rides cost 50¢.

The Gothic Soldiers and Sailors Memorial Arch (☎ 860-522-3668), which frames the Trinity St entrance, was designed by George Keller and dedicated in 1886. It commemorates Civil War veterans and offers fine views from its turrets – after you've climbed the 97 steps to the top.

## Wadsworth Atheneum

The nation's oldest continuously operating art museum, the Wadsworth Atheneum (☎ 860-278-2670, www.wadsworthatheneum .org), 600 Main St, houses more than 40,000 pieces of art in a castlelike Gothic Revival building. Included are paintings by members of the Hudson River School, including some by Hartford resident Frederic Church; 19th-century impressionist works; 18th-century furniture; and the mobile and stabile sculptures of the Connecticut artist Alexander Calder. The Amistad Foundation Gallery has an outstanding collection of African American art and historical objects; the Matrix Gallery features works by contemporary artists. The Atheneum is open 11 am to 5 pm daily except Monday. Admission costs $7 for adults, $5 for seniors and students, $3 for youth aged six to 17.

You can have lunch here, too; see Places to Eat, below. If you visit on weekends, there's free parking in Travelers Lot No 7 on Prospect St.

## Old State House

Connecticut's Old State House (☎ 860-522-6766), 800 Main St, boasts that it is the oldest state capitol in the country. Designed by Charles Bulfinch – who also did the Massachusetts State House in Boston – it was the site of the trial of the *Amistad* prisoners (see the boxed text later in this chapter); reenactments of the trial are held periodically. Gilbert Stuart's famous portrait of George Washington hangs in the senate chamber. Children will like the blasts from antique cannons at 10 am and 4 pm daily. There's a tourist information office as well. Free tours of the building are conducted 10 am to 4 pm weekdays, 11 am to 4 pm Saturday (closed the last two weeks in August).

## Center Church

This church (☎ 860-249-5631), 675 Main St, was established by the Reverend Thomas Hooker when he came to Hartford from the Massachusetts Bay Colony in 1636. The present building dates from 1807 and was modeled on St Martin's-in-the-Fields in London. In the **Ancient Burying Ground** behind the church lie the remains of Hooker and Revolutionary War patriots Joseph and Jeremiah Wadsworth. Some headstones date from the 17th century.

## Butler-McCook Homestead

A single family occupied the Butler-McCook Homestead (☎ 860-247-8996, 522-1806), 396 Main St, for four generations, from 1782 to 1971. The museum house contains its original 18th- and 19th-century furnishings, a collection of Japanese armor, toys, pewter plates and stoneware. A Victorian garden is part of the grounds. The house (required) costs $9 for adults, $8 for seniors, $5 for children six to 12. The last tour leaves at 4 pm.

## Harriet Beecher Stowe House

Next door to the Twain house is this author's home (☎ 860-525-9317), 73 Forest St. Stowe was the woman whom Abraham Lincoln said started the Civil War with her book *Uncle Tom's Cabin*. Built in 1871, the Stowe house reflects the author's strong ideas about decorating and domestic efficiency as she expressed in her best-seller *American Woman's Home*, which was nearly as popular as the phenomenal *Uncle Tom's Cabin*. The house is light-filled, with big windows draped in plants.

Adjoining the Stowe house is the Katharine S Day House, named for Stowe's grandniece, who sought to preserve the memory of her great-aunt's community spirit and works. The house has splendid 1884 interior decoration as well as changing exhibits.

Both houses are open 9:30 am to 4 pm daily from June to mid-October and in December (noon to 4 pm Sunday); Stowe house is closed Monday the rest of the year.

Mark Twain

is undergoing extensive renovations at this writing but will probably be open by the time you arrive. Hours may be Tuesday, Thursday and Sunday afternoons from mid-May to mid-October; admission costs $6 (children younger than 18 get in for $2).

## Mark Twain House

One of the premier attractions in Hartford is this eccentric home (☎ 860-493-6411), 351 Farmington Ave, in an area once called Nook Farm. For 17 years, Samuel Langhorne Clemens (1835-1910) lived in this striking orange-and-black brick Victorian house that architect Edward Tuckerman Potter lavishly embellished with turrets, gables and verandas. Some of the interiors were done by Louis Comfort Tiffany. Here, the author penned some of his most famous works, including *The Adventures of Tom Sawyer*, *The Adventures of Huckleberry Finn*, *The Prince and the Pauper* and *A Connecticut Yankee in King Arthur's Court*. The house is open 9:30 am to 5 pm daily (11 am to 5 pm Sunday); it's closed Tuesday from mid-October to late May. The guided tour

---

### A Trashy Museum

For all but the most recent fraction of recorded history, humankind didn't think about trash at all. It barely existed. Since the end of WWII, however, trash has become one of the planet's most vexing and expensive problems.

The Trash Museum (☎ 860-247-4280), 211 Murphy Rd (I-91 exit 27), at the Connecticut Resources Recovery Authority Visitors Center, examines the advent of trash, follows its creation and disposal and educates the public on what can be done to reuse and recycle it. Don't miss the Temple of Trash – recycling at its best. The museum is open 10 am to 4 pm Wednesday, Thursday and Friday (also Tuesday and Saturday in July and August); admission is free.

**CONNECTICUT**

The required guided tour costs the same amount as at the Mark Twain House.

## Elizabeth Park Rose Gardens

Known for its fine collection of roses, Elizabeth Park (☎ 860-722-6514), Prospect Ave at Asylum Ave, is a 100-acre preserve on the Hartford-West Hartford town line. More than 14,000 rose plants – 900 varieties including climbers, American Beauties, ramblers and heavily perfumed damasks – cover the grounds. June and July are the months to see the roses in full flower, but they bloom, if less profusely, well into fall. Elizabeth Park also has greenhouses, landscaped walking paths and a pretty gazebo. Park greenhouses are open 10 am to 4 pm daily.

## Places to Stay

Hartford's city center luxury hotels charge high rates on weekdays and surprisingly low rates (less than half the weekday rates) on weekends. The suburban motels charge very reasonable rates all the time.

The 42-bed *Mark Twain Hostel* (☎ 860-523-7255, 800-909-4776 code 21, fax 860-233-1767, 131 Tremont St), at I-84 exit 46, charges only $18 for a clean bed and use of the fully equipped kitchen and laundry facilities. It's in the city's West End off Farmington Ave, a 25-minute walk from Union Station; or call for pick-up service.

Just outside the center of Hartford are many of the usual chain motels, usually offering the best accommodation value.

Ten miles south of the city center in Wethersfield at I-91 exit 24 (Silas Deane Hwy) is a 146-room *Motel 6* (☎ 860-563-5900, 800-466-8356, 1341 Silas Deane Hwy). Rooms are comfortable and clean for $46, morning coffee included. There's a coin-operated laundry in the building and a restaurant next door.

At I-91 exit 27 (Brainerd Rd), the *Grand Chalet Inn & Suites* (☎ 860-525-9306, 800-524-2538, 185 Brainerd Rd) has 130 units (60 of them suites) for $70 to $80, continental breakfast included. There's a fitness room and outdoor swimming pool as well.

The *Howard Johnson Motor Lodge* (☎ 860-875-0781, 451 Hartford Turnpike), at

I-84 exit 65, is northeast of the city in Vernon, on the way to Boston. The 64 rooms cost $50 to $70, light breakfast included. There's a swimming pool as well.

In the city center, there's not much in the way of B&Bs, but one standout is the *1895 House* (☎ 860-232-0014, 97 Girard Ave), on the west side of the city, close to the West Hartford line. The graceful Victorian house has just three guest rooms. A suite on the 3rd floor is in what was originally a billiard room. Rooms cost $85 for two people, breakfast included.

Overlooking the State Capitol grounds is the *Ramada Inn Capitol Hill* (☎ 860-246-6591, 800-272-6232, 440 Asylum St), close to train and bus connections at Union Station. The Ramada is relatively small, with 96 rooms, many of which offer good views of the Capitol, for $70 to $80. There's another, the *Ramada Inn East Hartford* (☎ 860-528-9703, 100 E River Drive), across the river in East Hartford, on the east side (I-84 West exit 54, I-84 East exit 53, I-91 North exit 29, I-91 South exit 30, CT 2 exit 4).

For convenience of location, the high-rise *Hilton Hartford* (☎ 860-728-5151, 800-325-3535, 315 Trumbull St) is hard to beat. The 22-story, 388-room hotel is connected to the Hartford Civic Center and within easy walking distance of everything downtown. Weekday rates are about $179, but on weekends they can go as low as $79.

Also close to the Civic Center is the *Crowne Plaza Hartford Downtown* (☎ 860-549-2400, 50 N Morgan St), at I-91 exit 32B, I-84 exit 50. With 350 guest rooms, this is a typical chain hotel with many guest services, including shuttle service to Bradley Airport, an outdoor pool, an on-site restaurant and baby-sitting services. Rooms start at $70 on weekends, $170 on weekdays.

The fanciest hotel address in Hartford is the *Goodwin Hotel* (☎ 860-246-7500, 800-922-5006, fax 860-247-4576, 1 Haynes St), facing the Civic Center. This five-story, 124-room, 1881 red-brick building looks historic on the outside, but inside it has been entirely remodeled to appeal to modern preferences for large, light-filled rooms. Decor is traditional, with antique reproduction furniture.

Afternoon tea is served in the lobby. Rooms cost $99 on weekends, $229 on weekdays.

## Places to Eat

A convivial atmosphere is on tap at Hartford's first brewpub, the ***Hartford Brewery*** *(☎ 860-246-2337, 35 Pearl St)*, around the corner from the Old State House. The place has inexpensive pub-style food for lunch or dinner ($7 to $11), as well as pool, darts and backgammon to pass the time.

The favorite spot of the downtown 'in' crowd is the classy and urbane ***Max Downtown*** *(☎ 860-522-2530, 185 Asylum St)* at Haynes St. Serving a wide selection of American bistro dishes and creative interpretations of regional classics, Max is open for lunch and dinner on weekdays, and for dinner on Saturday as well. Full dinners cost $20 to $30 per person; you'll pay less at lunch.

The ***Museum Cafe*** *(☎ 860-728-5989, 600 Main St)*, in the Wadsworth Atheneum, serves lunch daily except Monday. It's casual, but menu offerings tend to be light and sophisticated, with main courses for about $11.

The top choice for a romantic dinner on the town is ***Pierpont's*** *(☎ 860-522-4935, 1 Haynes St)*, in the Goodwin Hotel. Named for financier J Pierpont Morgan, a sometime Hartford resident, Pierpont's offers expert preparation and service of traditional continental dinners for $30 to $50, less at lunch.

Modern American interpretations of traditional Italian dishes are the specialty of the house at ***Peppercorn's Grill*** *(☎ 860-547-1714, 357 Main St)*, between Capitol and Buckingham. In this family-run place, you might find anything from veal saltimbocca to a zesty dish of ravioli with scallops and lobster. Lunch ($12 to $20) is served weekdays, dinner ($30 to $48) weekdays and Saturday; it's closed Sunday.

For vegetarian fare, see the ***Reader's Feast*** bookstore and cafe, below.

For picnic fare to eat among the roses at Elizabeth Park, the ***Congress Rotisserie*** *(☎ 860-278-7711, 274 Farmington Ave)* is a wholesome deli with creative sandwiches, soups and salads.

## Entertainment

The ***Hartford Civic Center Coliseum*** *(☎ 860-727-8010)* is the venue for big shows; historic ***Bushnell Memorial Hall*** *(☎ 860-246-6807, 166 Capitol Ave)* is where you go for most ballet, symphony and chamber music performances. For the rundown on current performances, contact the Hartford Downtown Council *(☎ 860-522-6400, www.hartford-hdc.com)* or the Greater Hartford Arts Council *(☎ 860-525-8629, www.connectthedots.org)*. For events in Bushnell Park, call ☎ 860-722-6500.

The ***Hartford Symphony*** *(☎ 860-244-2999)* and ***Hartford Ballet*** *(☎ 860-987-5999)* have full winter performance seasons with very reasonable ticket prices.

Contemporary as well as classic plays are presented by the ***Hartford Stage Company*** *(☎ 860-527-5151, 50 Church St)* from September through June. The theater building is striking, designed by Venturi & Rauch of red brick with darker red zigzag details.

A gallery that combines contemporary works on paper and canvas with works in video, poetry and musical events, ***Real Art Ways*** *(☎ 860-232-1006, 56 Arbor St)* is consistently offbeat and adventurous. Admission is free; performances usually cost $5 to $10. The gallery is open 10 am to 5 pm weekdays, noon to 5 pm Saturday.

If you want to catch a movie, the gorgeous, velvet-seated ***Cinestudio*** *(☎ 860-297-2463 for show times, 297-2544 for office, 300 Summit St)*, at Trinity College, shows first-run and art films at lower-than-average prices.

For casual live music, check out the cafe culture at ***Reader's Feast*** *(☎ 860-232-3710, 529 Farmington Ave)*, near Whitney St. It's a cozy environment to grab a book, sip latte, munch vegetarian food and see a band.

The ***Voodoo Lounge*** *(☎ 860-525-3003, 191 Ann St)*, at Allyn St on the west side of the Civic Center, is the cool place to go for dancing and drinking, with music supplied by the in-house DJ.

## Getting There & Away

See this chapter's introductory Getting There & Around section for more information on transport options.

CONNECTICUT

**Air** Bradley International Airport (☎ 860-292-2000, www.bradleyairport.com), about 12 miles north of Hartford in Windsor Locks, is central Connecticut's regional airport, with service by AirTran, American, Continental, Delta, Delta Express, MetroJet, Midway, Midwest Express, Northwest, Shuttle America, TWA, United, US Airways and eight regional airlines.

**Bus** Greyhound (☎ 860-247-3524), Peter Pan Trailways (☎ 860-724-5400, 800-343-9999, www.peterpan-bus.com) and Bonanza (☎ 800-556-3815, www.bonanzabus.com) provide bus links from Hartford's Union Station to other Northeast cities. See the beginning of this chapter for details.

**Train** Amtrak (☎ 800-872-7245) trains connect Hartford to New York and Boston at Union Station (☎ 860-247-5329).

**Car** Driving details for Hartford are as follows:

| destination | mileage | hr:min |
| --- | --- | --- |
| Boston, MA | 102 miles | 2:10 |
| Litchfield, CT | 34 miles | 1:00 |
| Mystic, CT | 54 miles | 1:00 |
| New Haven, CT | 36 miles | 0:50 |
| New London, CT | 52 miles | 1:00 |
| New York, NY | 117 miles | 2:30 |
| Providence, RI | 71 miles | 1:30 |

### Getting Around

The bus service within the city is by Connecticut Transit (☎ 860-525-9181, www.cttransit.com), which has an information booth at State House Square and Market St.

Taxis are available outside Union Station downtown, or call Yellow Cab Co (☎ 860-666-6666).

## AROUND HARTFORD

The environs of Hartford hold many things to see and do. Here are several of the best.

### Old Wethersfield

The historic town of Wethersfield, 5 miles south of Hartford off I-91 exit 26, boasts that George Washington stayed here while planning the final victorious campaign of the Revolutionary War. The town's historic district, known as Old Wethersfield, has many fine colonial and Revolutionary-era houses. Three 18th-century houses comprise the **Webb-Deane-Stevens Museum** (☎ 860-529-0612), 211 Main St. Exhibits in all the houses bring to life the America of more than two centuries ago. In the Webb House, grand murals commissioned in 1916 depict the strategy conference between Generals Washington and Rochambeau, held right here to plan what became the victorious American campaign against the British-held Yorktown. The museum is open 10 am to 4 pm daily except Tuesday from May through October; in winter, it's open weekends only. Admission costs $8 for adults, $7 for seniors, and $4 for students and children five or older.

### Dinosaur State Park

Two hundred million years ago, dinosaurs traipsed across mudflats near Rocky Hill, 10 miles due south of Hartford along I-91. Their tracks hardened in the mud and remained safely buried until the 20th century when road-building crews serendipitously uncovered them. Connecticut's answer to Jurassic Park is Dinosaur State Park (☎ 860-529-8423), 400 West St (I-91 exit 23, then 1 mile east), where you can view the hundreds of footprints preserved beneath a geodesic dome, tour an 80-foot-long diorama that shows how – and by what – the tracks were made, and view other dinosaur-related exhibits. The park also has a picnic area and 2 miles of nature trails.

If you're driving along I-91 and you have children and a spare hour, this makes a great detour. The park is free and open daily. The domed Exhibit Center – the park's main attraction – is open 9 am to 4:30 pm (closed Monday); admission to the center costs $2 for adults, $1 for children six to 17.

### Lake Compounce Theme Park

Connecticut's answer to Disneyland is a delightful 100-acre theme and amusement park set on the shores of a pretty lake in the

KIM GRANT

Rosecliff mansion, a Newport, RI 'cottage'

ANDRE JENNY

Providence, RI skyline

RANDY WELLS

Colonial architecture on Providence's Benefit St

KIM GRANT

Slater Mill, north of Providence in Pawtucket, RI

The *Joseph Conrad*, Mystic Seaport Museum, CT

Clipper ship mural, South Norwalk, CT

A tranquil spot near Bridgewater, CT

town of Bristol, 18 miles southwest of Hartford. Lake Compounce Theme Park (☎ 860-583-3300), 822 Lake Ave, at the junction of CT 61 and CT 132, has two roller coasters, a whitewater raft ride, a historic steam train, an interactive haunted house and many other amusements. Splash Harbor Water Park, with its pools, jets and waterslides, is perfect for a hot summer's day, and the 180-foot free-fall 'swing' will thrill even the most jaded of extreme sports enthusiasts – not to mention the rest of us. Every member of the family will find something fun to do here.

The park is open from late May through late September; call for days and times. Admission (including unlimited use of most rides and amusements) costs $22 for adults and $16 for children under 52 inches tall. Admission to the park alone (no rides) costs $6; there's a $4 parking charge as well. Thus a day's amusements here cost a family of four $80 – a decent value for the money.

# Lower Connecticut River Valley

Unlike New York's Hudson River and New London's Thames, the Connecticut River has escaped the bustle of industry and commerce that so often mar the heavily used rivers of the Northeast. The Connecticut is the longest river in New England (with its headwaters near New Hampshire's Canadian border), but it is surprisingly shallow near its mouth at Long Island Sound. This lack of depth led burgeoning industry to look for better harbors elsewhere, and thus the lower end of the Connecticut has luckily preserved much of its alluring 18th-century appearance.

Fine old Connecticut towns grace the river's banks, including Old Lyme, Old Saybrook, Essex, Ivoryton, Chester, Hadlyme and East Haddam. Each is charming on its own, and together they offer visitors a combination of attractions that include fine dining, theater, river excursions, art museums and more. The sections below on places to stay and places to eat include information on all these towns as a group.

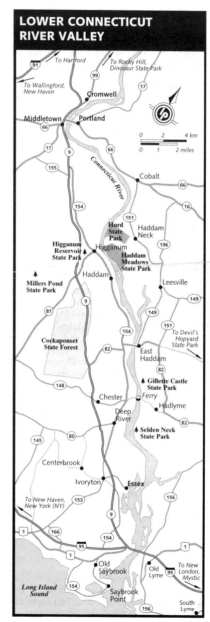

If possible, plan to visit this area during the week. Lodging prices are substantially higher on weekends (Friday and Saturday nights), and campgrounds fill up early on those days.

## Information

For information on the towns of the Connecticut River Valley, contact the Connecticut River Valley and Shoreline Visitors Council (☎ 860-347-0028, 800-486-3346, www.cttourism.org), 393 Main St, Middletown, CT 06457.

For information about Old Lyme, contact the Lyme and Old Lyme Chamber of Commerce (☎ 860-434-1665), 70 Lyme St, PO Box 268, Old Lyme, CT 06371.

## OLD LYME

Near the mouth of the Connecticut River, on the east bank, is Old Lyme (I-95 exit 70), which in the 19th century was home to some 60 sea captains. Since the early 20th century, however, Old Lyme has been better known as a center for the American impressionist art movement. Artists such as Charles Ebert, Childe Hassam, Willard Metcalfe, Henry Ward Ranger and Guy and Carleston Wiggins came here to paint, staying in the mansion of local art patron Florence Griswold. The house (which her artist friends often decorated with murals in lieu of paying rent) is now a museum containing a good selection of both impressionist and Barbizon paintings. The **Florence Griswold Museum** (☎ 860-434-5542), 96 Lyme St, is closed Monday in summer, Monday and Tuesday the rest of the year. Admission is $4 for adults, $3 for seniors and students.

The neighboring **Lyme Academy of Fine Arts** (☎ 860-434-5232), 84 Lyme St, and the **Lyme Art Association Gallery** (☎ 860-434-7802), 90 Lyme St, regularly feature recent works by local artists. Both are closed on Monday.

## OLD SAYBROOK

A colony was founded at Old Saybrook, at the mouth of the Connecticut River on the west bank, in 1635. Exhibits at **Fort Saybrook Monument Park** (☎ 860-395-3123), Saybrook Point (CT 154, CT 9 exit 2), tell the story. The park, open for free daily from sunrise to sunset, also offers panoramic views of the mouth of the mighty Connecticut River.

For even better views, hop aboard a boat run by the **Deep River Navigation Company** (☎ 860-526-4954, www.deeprivernavigation .com) for a cruise up the river. Mid-June through early September, boats leave at noon and 2:30 pm daily on two-hour cruises ($10), at 5 and 6 pm on one-hour cruises ($6).

## ESSEX

Essex, the chief town of the region, was established in 1635 and is now well endowed with lovely Federal-period houses that are the legacy of rum and tobacco fortunes made in the 19th century. Essex today has the genteel, aristocratic air of self-conscious historical beauty evident in other fine old New England towns. Everything from landscaping to street signage is scripted to look good, and it does.

Coming into the town center from CT 9, you'll eventually find yourself on Main St. The social centerpiece of Essex is the 1776 **Griswold Inn** (☎ 860-767-1776), 36 Main St, a hostelry since the time of the Revolutionary War (see Places to Stay, below). 'The Gris,' as the natives call it, is today both an inn and a restaurant, and its taproom is the obvious place to meet the townfolk. Sunday morning 'Hunt Breakfasts' are a renowned tradition dating to the War of 1812, when British soldiers occupying Essex demanded to be fed well and in quantity.

Down past The Gris at the eastern end of Main St is the riverfront and the **Connecticut River Museum** (☎ 860-767-8269), next to Steamboat Dock. Its exhibits recount the history of the area. Included among them is a replica of the world's first submarine, the *Turtle*, a wooden barrel-like vessel built here by Yale student David Bushnell in 1776. Admission costs $4 for adults, $3 for seniors, $2 for children six to 12; it's open 10 am to 5 pm (closed Monday).

North of The Gris along Ferry St is the Essex marina, crowded with yachts both huge and sleek. You can lunch here (see the Places to Eat section).

One of the most enjoyable activities here is the Essex Steam Train & Riverboat Ride on the **Valley Railroad** (☎ 860-767-0103, 800-377-3987), 1 Railroad Ave (CT 9 exit 3), on the west side of CT 9 from the main part of Essex. An authentic coal-fired steam engine powers the train, which rumbles slowly north to the town of Deep River. There passengers may connect with a riverboat for a cruise on the Connecticut up to the Goodspeed Opera House and CT 82 swing bridge before heading back down to Deep River and returning to Essex via a train. The roundtrip train ride takes about an hour, covering about 12 miles; with the riverboat ride, the complete excursion takes 2½ hours. Trains leave the Railroad Ave station five times daily in summer, six times on weekends. Fall foliage runs are usually scheduled as well. Combination tickets for the train and riverboat cruise are $15; $10 for the train ride alone. Children pay half-price.

## IVORYTON

A mile west of Essex, on the west side of CT 9, is the sleepy town of Ivoryton. Named for the African elephant tusks imported during the 19th century by the Comstock-Cheney piano manufacturers for use in making piano keys, it is also the home of Witch Hazel, a traditional folk medicine. Today, the ivory industry is long gone, and most people visit relaxed, quiet Ivoryton to dine at the Copper Beech Inn (see Places to Stay, below).

## CHESTER

Yet another lovely, slow old river town is Chester, cupped in the valley of Pattaconk Brook. A general store, post office, library and a few shops pretty much account for all the activity in town.

Most visitors come either for fine dining (see Places to Eat) or to browse in the antique shops and boutiques on the town's charming main street.

## HADLYME

From Chester, a small car ferry (☎ 860-566-7635) crosses the Connecticut River to Hadlyme. The trip takes just five minutes; the ferry – which carries just eight cars – is the second-oldest in continuous operation in the state, operating daily from April through mid-December. Crossing eastbound, the ferry drops you at the foot of Gillette Castle in East Haddam.

## EAST HADDAM

East Haddam is the only town in Connecticut to span the river. Looming on one of the Seven Sisters hills above the east-bank ferry dock is **Gillette Castle** (☎ 860-526-2336), 67 River Rd, East Haddam, a turreted, 24-room riverstone mansion that is one of Connecticut's curiosities. Built between 1914 and 1919 by eccentric actor William Gillette, it was modeled on the medieval castles of Germany's Rhineland. Gillette made his name and his considerable fortune on stage in the role of Sherlock Holmes. He created the part himself, based on the famous mystery series by Sir Arthur Conan Doyle. In a sense, he made his castle/home part of the Holmes role as well: An upstairs room replicates Conan Doyle's description of the sitting room at 221B Baker St, London.

Following Gillette's death in 1937, his dream house and its surrounding 117 acres were designated a Connecticut state park. The castle is open 10 am to 5 pm Friday to Sunday from late May to early September. Admission costs $4 for adults, $2 for children six to 11.

North of Gillette Castle, on the east bank of the river just south of the CT 82 swing bridge, stands the **Goodspeed Opera House** (☎ 860-873-8668, www.goodspeed.org), a Victorian music hall renowned as the only theater in the country dedicated to both the preservation of old and the development of new American musicals.

The shows *Man of La Mancha* and *Annie* premiered at the Goodspeed before going on to national fame. The six-story, Victorian-style theater, built in 1876, enjoyed a huge reputation before the Great Depression. It was saved from demolition in 1959 by a group of concerned citizens, then refurbished and reopened in 1963. Its schedule of performances runs Wednesday to Sunday from April through December.

CONNECTICUT

Also in East Haddam is the **Nathan Hale Schoolhouse** (☎ 860-873-9547), on Main St behind St Stephen's Church in the center of town. Hale taught in this one-room building from 1773 to 1774 when it was called the Union School. He was a peripatetic pedagogue, and numerous other one-room Connecticut schoolhouses bear his name, and corresponding museum status. Hale (1755-1776) is famous for his patriotic statement, 'I only regret that I have but one life to lose for my country,' as he was about to be hanged for treason by the British without trial. Today it is a museum of Hale family memorabilia and local history. The museum is open 2 to 4 pm weekends and holidays in summer.

## STATE PARKS & FORESTS

The Lower Connecticut River Valley has a half dozen state parks and forests good for outdoor activities. For information on any park, contact the Bureau of Outdoor Recreation (☎ 860-424-3200), 79 Elm St, Hartford, CT 06106-5127.

**Cockaponset State Forest**, in Haddam, has fishing, hiking and swimming.

**Devil's Hopyard State Park** (☎ 860-566-2304), just off CT 82 in East Haddam, has 860 acres of parkland for camping and hiking, including the 60-foot Chapman Falls.

**Haddam Meadows State Park**, in Haddam, is good for boating and fishing. **Hurd State Park**, in East Hampton, has camping, fishing, hiking and picnicking.

**Selden Neck State Park**, in Lyme, has camping places for those making canoe trips on the river, as well as hiking trails.

## PLACES TO STAY
## Camping

There are simple, inexpensive campsites in *Devil's Hopyard State Park* (☎ 860-566-2304), East Haddam; *Hurd State Park*, East Hampton; and *Selden Neck State Park*, Lyme.

More elaborate facilities are available at *Wolf's Den Campground* (☎ 860-873-9681, 256 Town St (CT 82)), in East Haddam, with 235 sites; *Little City Campground* (☎ 860-345-4886, 741 Little City Rd), in Higganum,

with 50 sites; *Markham Meadows* (☎ 860-267-8012, 7 Markham Rd), in East Hampton, with 75 sites; and *Nelson's Family Campground* (☎ 860-267-5300, 71 Mott Hill Rd), also in East Hampton, with 300 sites.

## Motels

Moderately priced motels are found along the Boston Post Rd (US 1) in Old Saybrook, reached via I-95 exit 66.

Try the *Days Inn* (☎ 860-388-3453, 800-329-7466, 1430 Boston Post Rd), which has 52 rooms for $78 on weekdays, $118 on weekends; the *Saybrook Motor Inn* (☎ 860-399-5926, 1575 Boston Post Rd), with 24 rooms for $65 on weekdays, $85 on weekends; the *Super 8 Motel* (☎ 860-399-6273, 800-800-8000, 37 Spencer Plain Rd), with 44 rooms going for $70 on weekdays, $95 on weekends.

There's another cluster of motels near I-95 exits 67 North and 68 South.

## Inns & B&Bs

The *Griswold Inn* (☎ 860-767-1776, 36 Main St), in Essex, is the town's landmark lodging and dining place. Despite The Gris' antiquity (it has been serving travelers since the Revolutionary War), its 25 guest rooms have modern conveniences, and cost $90 to $115 (more for suites), light breakfast included. Hint: Room No 24 costs only $70. The inn's famous all-you-can-eat Hunt Breakfasts (11 am to 2:30 pm Sunday) cost $13. Otherwise, lunch in the dining room costs $10 to $20, full dinners $30 to $50.

A farmhouse built in 1776 was the original *Inn at Chester* (☎ 860-526-9541, 800-949-7829, 318 W Main St (CT 148)), in Chester. Several buildings have been added during the 20th century to produce a colonial-style inn with modern conveniences in its 42 air-conditioned rooms priced from $105 to $145 (more for suites). In the spacious dining room, dinner main courses tend to the traditional and gamey (venison, duck) with nouvelle-cuisine touches, and cost $17 to $26, with full dinners for about twice as much. To reach the inn from the center of Chester, follow CT 148 west for 4.4 miles and go past CT 9 exit 6 and pretty Killingworth Reservoir to the inn, which is right on the Chester-Killingworth town line.

The **Bee & Thistle Inn** (☎ 860-434-1667, 100 Lyme St), in Old Lyme, is a 1756 Dutch Colonial farmhouse with 11 rooms ($79 to $159), some of which share baths. The dining room (closed Tuesday) is renowned for its innovative cuisine and romantic ambience, so it's a very good idea to reserve your table in advance. Expect to spend $35 to $60 for a full meal.

The **Copper Beech Inn** (☎ 860-767-0330, 888-809-2056, 46 Main St), in Ivoryton, follows the model of the Connecticut River Valley: fine old inns with sophisticated restaurants. Built in the 1890s as the residence of ivory importer AW Comstock, the inn has four guest rooms in the main house and nine more luxurious rooms in the Carriage House, priced from $105 to $175. The updated French classic dishes served in the dining room are both superb and in high demand. Reserve well in advance and expect to pay $50 to $65 per person for dinner. To find the inn, take CT 9 exit 3 and follow the signs on to Ivoryton, going west 1.6 miles through Center Brook to the inn on the left-hand side of the road.

### PLACES TO EAT

Most experienced travelers know that hotel dining rooms often suffer in comparison to independent restaurants. But in the Connecticut River Valley, some of the best restaurants are in gracious old inns, such as the **Copper Beech** in Ivoryton, the **Griswold** in Essex, the **Bee & Thistle** in Old Lyme and the **Inn at Chester**. For details, see Places to Stay, above.

For inexpensive but good sandwiches and picnic fare in pricey Essex, you need go no farther than **Olive Oyl's Carry-out Cuisine** (☎ 860-767-4909, 77 Main St), behind the Strong Real Estate office. Good breads, cheese, pâtés, pastries, sandwiches ($5) and snacks fill the display cases and will fill you as well.

The aptly named **Crow's Nest Gourmet Deli** (☎ 860-767-3288), on Pratt St in Essex, overlooks the boatyard and marina from its perch at Brewer's Shipyard. Breakfast and

lunch are served every day to the yachting crowd here. Follow Ferry St from The Gris to reach it.

The delightful village of Chester has several good places to dine. At **Fiddler's** (☎ 860-526-3210, 4 Water St), the specialty is seafood, such as bouillabaisse and inventive lobster dishes. Lunch ($9 to $17) and dinner ($20 to $35) are served daily except Monday. The **Wheat Market Deli**, next door, provides picnic supplies.

**Restaurant du Village** (☎ 860-526-5301, 59 Main St), also in Chester, is like a little piece of Provence in the Connecticut countryside. With its flower-filled windowboxes set beneath multipaned windows, the blue-painted restaurant features country French cuisine, with main courses priced between $21 and $27 at dinner.

### SHOPPING

The Connecticut River Artisans Cooperative (☎ 860-526-5575), 4 Water St, Chester, features one-of-a-kind art and craft pieces including clothing, folk art, furniture, jewelry, paintings, photographs and pottery. The shop is open 10 am to 5 pm daily except Monday and Tuesday; from January to mid-March, it's open Friday through Sunday.

# Connecticut Coast

Connecticut's coastline on Long Island Sound is long and varied. The western coast is crowded with industrial and commercial cities and suburban bedroom communities, all within the magnetic influence of New York City. The central coast, from New Haven to the mouth of the Connecticut River, is less urban, with historic towns and villages. The eastern coast includes New London and Groton, both important in naval history, and Mystic, where the Mystic Seaport Museum brings maritime history to life.

Here are the most interesting points along the coast, from west to east.

### NEW HAVEN

Although it is home to one of the USA's most prestigious universities, this is no mere college town. Both business and industry – shipping, manufacturing, health care, telecommunications – power New Haven's economy more than student dollars.

As you roll into town along I-91 or I-95, New Haven appears bustling and muscular – it's still an important port, as it has been since the 1630s. But at the city's center is a tranquil core: New Haven Green, decorated with graceful colonial churches and venerable Yale University.

## History

The Puritan founders of New Haven established their colony in 1637-38 at a spot where the Quinnipiac and other small rivers enter Long Island Sound. The new town was to be no haven of religious freedom: This was a theocracy, so only believers could be citizens, and the Bible was the law.

The strictness of religious law was softened somewhat in 1665 when New Haven reluctantly joined the larger province of Connecticut. It served as joint provincial capital (along with Hartford) from 1701 to 1875, testifying to its prominence during that time.

Its prominence first came from the town's port, but by the late 18th and early 19th centuries, Yankee ingenuity had made New Haven an important manufacturing city as well.

In 1702, a collegiate school was founded in nearby Clinton by James Pierpont. It soon moved to Old Saybrook, and in 1717 went to New Haven in response to a generous grant of funds by Elihu Yale. In 1718, the name was changed to Yale in honor of the benefactor.

Re-chartered in 1745, Yale grew extensively during the following century, adding

### Amistad

On July 2, 1839, the slave ship *Amistad* was sailing along the coast of Cuba with its 'cargo' of 55 Africans who had been abducted and forced into slavery. One of the captives, known to history as Joseph Cinque, managed to remove his shackles surreptitiously and led a rebellion of other captives against the European crew. The captain and cook were killed, but the mutineers spared the Spanish navigator so that he could guide the ship back to Sierra Leone for them.

The navigator had other plans, however. Though he headed the ship eastward during the day when the sun's position made its course evident to the mutineers, at night he used the stars to head west, hoping to bring the ship to a port where he could get help.

For two months the *Amistad* sailed back and forth, exhausting its supplies of food and water. Finally it was sighted by a US Coast Guard ship, seized off Long Island and towed to New London, Connecticut. The Africans were accused of rebellion, transported to New Haven and imprisoned awaiting trial.

The plight of the *Amistad* abductees became a *cause célèbre* among abolitionist forces in the state and the nation. A committee of concerned Christian abolitionists was formed to aid in their legal defense. The *Amistad* abductees' case went all the way to the US Supreme Court, and former President John Quincy Adams was persuaded to emerge from retirement to plead their case. The court found that they had been abducted illegally and therefore could not be held liable for mutiny when they sought their own freedom. The decision was a powerful moral and legal victory for the antislavery forces.

The *Amistad* abductees were repatriated to Africa, and the committee formed to help them was incorporated in 1846 as the American Missionary Association. The AMA went on to found more than 500 schools for those emancipated by the Civil War and, later, many noted institutions of higher learning, including Atlanta University, Fisk University and Howard University.

schools of medicine, divinity, law, art and architecture, music, forestry, engineering and drama and a graduate school. By 1887 it was time to rename it Yale University. Now a member of the Ivy League, Yale has one of the finest libraries in the country, with many rare manuscripts.

Yale may be the best-known school in the vicinity, but New Haven is also home to the University of New Haven and Southern Connecticut State College.

## Orientation

Entering New Haven along I-95 or I-91 (which joins I-95 right in the city), take I-95 exit 47 for CT 34, the Oak St Connector, to reach New Haven Green, the city center, with Yale to its west. From the Wilbur Cross Parkway, take exit 57, 59 or 60 and follow the signs to the center.

Most hotels and sights are within a few blocks of the green. The bus and train stations are near I-95 in the southeast part of the city.

## Information

**Tourist Offices** The Greater New Haven Convention & Visitors Bureau (☎ 203-777-8550, 800-332-7829, www.newhavencvb.org) is at 59 Elm St, New Haven, CT 06510.

Yale University has a Visitor Information Center (☎ 203-432-2300), 149 Elm St at Temple St, on the north side of the green, where you can get free campus maps and a self-guided walking-tour pamphlet. Guided tours depart the center at 10:30 am and 2 pm weekdays, at 1:30 pm weekends.

**Travel Agencies** There's a Council Travel office (☎ 203-562-5335) at 320 Elm St.

**Bookstores** To get in touch with the student population, the Yale Co-Op (☎ 203-772-0670), 77 Broadway, has not only a great number of books but also Yale sweatshirts and souvenirs. The Atticus Bookstore Café is a huge favorite; see Places to Eat, below.

**Dangers & Annoyances** As a working city, New Haven has urban pleasures and problems, including street crime. You should

meet with no problems during the day in the city center, but avoid run-down neighborhoods and empty streets after dark, and don't leave *anything* visible in your parked car to tempt thieves.

## New Haven Green

New Haven's traditional town green, the spiritual center of the city, is spacious and framed by its beautiful churches. The Trinity Church (Episcopal), on Chapel St, resembles England's Gothic York Minster. The Georgian-style Center Church on the Green (UCC), a good example of New England's interpretation of Palladian architecture, harbors many colonial tombstones in its crypt. At the northeastern corner of the green is United Church (UCC), another Georgian-Palladian work.

Grove Street Cemetery, at 227 Grove St three blocks north of the green, has the graves of several famous New Havenites behind its grand Egyptian-Revival gate (1845), including rubber magnate Charles Goodyear, the telegraph inventor Samuel Morse, lexicographer Noah Webster and cotton gin inventor Eli Whitney.

## Yale University

Established in 1702 by Connecticut's colonial government as the Collegiate School, this institution was first at Killingworth, then at Saybrook. It finally moved to New Haven in 1717. A year later it was renamed in honor of Elihu Yale (1649-1721), a wealthy British businessman, philanthropist and benefactor whose donations of books and capital allowed the school to construct a college building.

The third-oldest university in the nation, Yale can boast many distinguished alumni and alumnae, including Presidents Bill Clinton, George Bush, Gerald Ford and William Howard Taft, as well as Hillary Rodham Clinton, Noah Webster, Eli Whitney and Samuel FB Morse.

Crowded with University Gothic buildings, Yale's old campus dominates the northern and western portions of downtown New Haven. Tallest of its Gothic spires is Harkness Tower, from which a carillon peals at

# NEW HAVEN

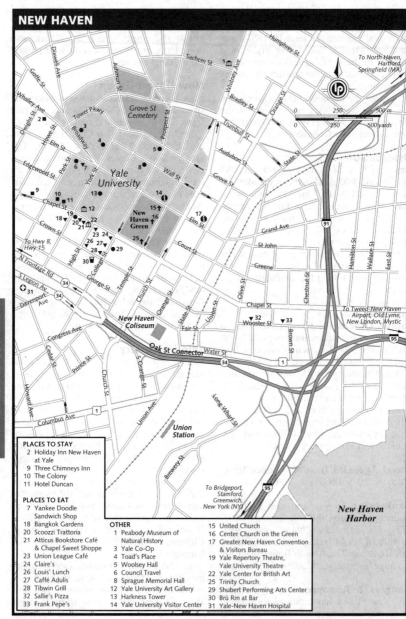

CONNECTICUT

appropriate moments throughout the day. On the south side of the Oak St Connector is an extensive modern campus holding the Yale-New Haven Hospital and many other medical science buildings.

Stop at the Visitor Information Office at Elm St and Temple St (see Information, above) and pick up a free campus map and a walking-tour brochure. For a free one-hour student-guided walking tour, arrive slightly before 10:30 am or 2 pm weekdays or at 1:30 pm weekends.

Yale's museums have outstanding collections, and the art museums are free.

**Peabody Museum of Natural History** The museum (☎ 203-432-5050), 170 Whitney Ave, five blocks northeast of the green along Temple St, has a vast collection of animal, vegetable and mineral specimens, including dinosaur fossils, wildlife dioramas, meteorites and minerals. It's open 10 am to 5 pm daily (noon to 5 pm Sunday). Admission costs $5 for adults, $3 for seniors and children from three to 15.

**Yale Center for British Art** This museum (☎ 203-432-2800), 1080 Chapel St, at the corner of High St a block west of the green, holds the most comprehensive collection of British art outside the UK. The collections cover the period from Queen Elizabeth I to the present, with special emphasis on the period from Hogarth (born 1697) through Turner (died 1851). It's open 10 am to 5 pm (noon to 5 pm Sunday) and is closed Monday; admission is free.

**Yale University Art Gallery** Masterworks by Frans Hals, Peter Paul Rubens, Manet, Picasso and van Gogh fill the Yale Gallery (☎ 203-432-0600), 1111 Chapel St between High and York, opposite the Yale Center for British Art. Besides the masterworks, there are important collections of American silver from the 18th century and art from Africa, Asia, the pre- and post-Colombian Americas and Europe: 75,000 objects in all. It's open 10 am to 4:45 pm (2 to 4:45 pm Sunday); closed Monday. Admission to the gallery is free.

## Places to Stay

**Camping** There are no campgrounds near New Haven. The closest are 21 miles east along I-95 near Clinton. *Hammonasset Beach State Park* (☎ 203-566-2304), on the coast between Madison and Clinton (I-95 exit 62), has 558 sites for $12 each and, despite its size, is often full in high summer.

Private campgrounds are more expensive than state park campgrounds (such as Hammonasset Beach). The *Riverdale Farm Campsites* (☎ 203-669-5388), on River Rd in Clinton, has 250 sites open mid-April through September. The nearby *River Road Campground* (☎ 203-669-2238, 13 River Rd) has 50 sites that are open from mid-April to mid-October.

**Motels** The *Motel 6 New Haven* (☎ 203-469-0343, 800-466-8356, 270 Foxon Blvd), I-91 exit 8, is a few miles north of the city, with 58 rooms for $58 to $64. The *Quality Inn & Conference Center* (☎ 203-387-6651, 800-228-5151, 100 Pond Lily Ave), just off the Wilbur Cross Parkway (exit 59), several miles to the northeast, offers its 125 rooms for $99, light breakfast included.

**Hotels & Inns** *Hotel Duncan* (☎ 203-787-1273, 1151 Chapel St), at York, is New Haven's classic hostelry, a period piece more than a century old. The decor and facilities of fin-de-siècle New Haven have been preserved (rooms have fans rather than aircon). Prices also seem from an earlier time: $48 single, $68 double, $79 for a suite.

Only a few steps from the Duncan is *The Colony* (☎ 203-776-1234, 800-458-8810, fax 203-772-3929, 1157 Chapel St), a modernish hotel with 86 comfortable rooms within walking distance of everything, going for $99 single, $109 double. Ask about special discounted rates.

*Holiday Inn New Haven at Yale* (☎ 203-777-6221, 30 Whalley Ave) has 160 rooms (the higher rooms have good views) only a few minutes' walk from the green. Rooms are priced around $99, depending upon the exact date and room.

*Three Chimneys Inn* (☎ 203-777-1201, 800-443-1554, fax 203-776-7363, 1201 Chapel St), at Howe, is an 1870 Victorian townhouse that's been well restored. The 10 rooms, decorated in period style (mostly Victorian), rent for $160 per night, full breakfast included.

## Places to Eat

For some reason, New Haven has one of the most changeable restaurant scenes in New England. Places pop up and go out of business rapidly.

**Cafes & Diners** *Atticus Bookstore Café* (☎ *203-776-4040, 1082 Chapel St),* between High and York, has been serving coffee, soups, sandwiches and pastries amid the stacks for almost two decades. Mocking McDonald's, it proclaims 'Millions of scones served since 1981.' Prices are not low, and a slice of choice pastry or cheesecake might cost as much as $5, though there are things for less. The bookstore adjoins, and both are open true college-town hours: 8 am to midnight daily.

*Louis' Lunch* (☎ *203-562-5507, 261-263 Crown St),* between College and High, claims to be the place where the hamburger was invented – well, almost. Around 1900, when the vertically grilled ground beef sandwich was first introduced at Louis', the restaurant was in a different location. It still uses the historic vertical grills, and serves other sandwiches as well, most for less than $4.50. It's open 11 am to 4 pm (until 1 am Friday and Saturday); closed Sunday.

*Yankee Doodle Sandwich Shop (258 Elm St),* at York, is a classic hole-in-the-wall American lunch counter – Formica countertop, chrome and plastic stools – with prices to match: hamburgers for $1.75, ham and cheese sandwiches for $3. It's open for breakfast and lunch daily except Sunday.

**Restaurants** *Claire's* (☎ *860-562-3888, 1000 Chapel St),* at College, is the local favorite for vegetarian cuisine, eat-in or take-out. Bright and airy, it's always busy with students picking up healthy light meals ($5 to $7) or gooey desserts. Clear your own table when you're done.

*Bangkok Gardens* (☎ *203-789-8684, 172 York St),* just off Chapel, is the center's most popular Thai eatery. At lunch, big plates of pork, beef and chicken with vegetables cost only $5 to $6, and the special three-course lunch is only $7. At dinner, main courses range from $9 to $11. It's open daily.

*Tibwin Grill* (☎ *203-624-1883, 220 College St),* at the corner of Crown, is an upscale New American bistro just a short stroll from the green. Grilled beef, lamb, pork and fowl turn on the spits as diners nibble exotic appetizers and quaff select wines and beers. Lunch comes to around $15 to $18, dinner $25 to $40. Despite the red-meat emphasis, it does have a few vegetarian dishes (this is a college town). It's open daily for lunch and dinner, Sunday for brunch only (noon to 3 pm).

Want to try something different? New Haven is one of the few cities in New England with an Ethiopian-Eritrean restaurant. It's *Caffé Adulis* (☎ *203-777-5081, 228 College St),* a few doors north of the Tibwin Grill. Eritrean cooking is distinguished by the use of sun-dried hot peppers called *berbere,* which are simmered in some dishes. An exotic dinner might cost $25 to $40 here, lunch half that.

*Scoozzi Trattoria* (☎ *203-776-8268, 1104 Chapel St),* at York next to the Yale Repertory Theatre, serves trendy Italian fare with strong New American cuisine accents. Their little pizzettes and other appetizers are favorites with the before- and after-theater crowd, who combine them with wine by the glass to make a light supper. More substantial fare includes creative pasta combinations and new variations on traditional Italian meat courses. Lunches cost $12 to $18, dinners $20 to $40. Scoozzi is closed Sunday.

The *Union League Café* (☎ *203-562-4299, 1032 Chapel St)* is an upscale European bistro in the historic Union League building. Expect a menu featuring continental classics along with those of nouvelle cuisine for about $15 to $22 per person at lunch, twice that at dinner. On weekends, only dinner is served, and the Sunday dinner is a fixed-price ($24) repast.

Wooster Square, six blocks east of the green, is a mostly residential neighborhood, but it's famous for its pizza parlors.

*Frank Pepe's* (☎ *203-865-5762, 157 Wooster St*) serves good pizza, just as it has for decades, in spartan surroundings. Prices range from $5 to $20 per pie, depending on size and toppings.

A nearby challenger to Pepe's is *Sallie's Pizza* (☎ *203-624-5271, 237 Wooster St*), younger but even more highly regarded by many New Havenites.

**Sweets** *Chapel Sweet Shoppe* (☎ *203-624-2411, 1042 Chapel St*), at High, is every candy lover's pearly gates. High-quality sweets, chocolate and coffee beans fill the windows, the display cases and the loyal customers. It's almost impossible for children to walk by without walking in.

## Entertainment

As a college town and a city of some size, New Haven has a lively evening entertainment scene.

**Theater & Ballet** The well-regarded *Yale Repertory Theatre* and the *Yale University Theatre* companies both perform in a converted church (☎ *203-432-1234, 222 York St*), at the corner of Chapel, with a full and varied program of performances from October to May.

The famous *Long Wharf Theatre* (☎ *203-787-4282, 222 Sargent Drive*), at I-95 exit 46, is down on the waterfront near the Howard Johnson, with a season extending from October through June.

The *Shubert Performing Arts Center* (☎ *203-562-5666, 800-228-6622, 247 College St*) is the venue for ballet and many musical performances from September through May.

For shows that draw a large audience, it's the *New Haven Coliseum* (☎ *203-772-4200, 275 S Orange St*).

**Classical Music** The *New Haven Symphony Orchestra* (☎ *203-776-1444, 800-292-6476*) holds concerts at 8 pm each Tuesday evening from October through June in Yale's Woolsey Hall.

The *Chamber Music Society* at Yale (☎ *203-432-4158, 470 College St*) sponsors concerts at 8 pm Tuesday evenings from September through April in the Morse Recital Hall of Sprague Memorial Hall, 470 College St.

Other concerts are hosted by the *Yale School of Music* (☎ *203-432-4157*) and by the *Yale Collection of Musical Instruments* (☎ *203-432-0822*).

**Folk & Rock Music** *Toad's Place* (☎ *203-624-8623 recording, 562-5589 office, 300 York St*) is a hot, very well-known nightclub worth checking out. Performers such as Black 47, Johnny Cash, Michael Bolton and The Dave Matthews Band headline there. Cover is free to $25, depending upon the act.

The *Greater New Haven Acoustic Music Society* (☎ *203-468-1000*) hosts folk concerts and performances in the summer in the Eli Whitney 1816 Barn, and in the winter in Dodds Hall, 300 Orange Ave, on the University of New Haven (not Yale) campus.

**Dance Clubs** Check out the *Brü Rm at Bar* (☎ *203-495-1111, 254 Crown St*), facing Louis' Lunch. The Brew Room (as its name translates) serves up brewpub beer, brick-oven pizza and dancing till midnight on most nights, till 1 am on Friday and Saturday.

## Getting There & Away

**Air** Connecticut Transit (☎ 203-785-8930) can shuttle you to Tweed-New Haven Airport (☎ 203-787-8283), I-95 exit 50, from where several commuter airlines can take you to Boston or New York.

**Bus** Peter Pan Bus Lines (☎ 800-343-9999, www.peterpan-bus.com) connects New Haven with New York City, Hartford, Springfield and Boston, as does Greyhound Bus Lines (☎ 203-772-2470, 800-221-2222, www.greyhound.com), inside New Haven's Union Station.

New Connecticut Limousine (☎ 800-472-5466) runs buses between New Haven and New York City's airports (La Guardia, JFK and Newark).

**Train** Metro-North trains (☎ 212-532-4900, 800-223-6052, 800-638-7646, www.mta.nyc.ny.us) make the 1½-hour run between New

York City's Grand Central Station and New Haven's Union Station, I-95 exit 47, almost every hour from 7 am to midnight on weekdays, with more frequent trains during the morning and evening rush hours. On weekends, trains run about every two hours. Commuter Connection buses (☎ 203-624-0151) run at peak morning hours and during the afternoon/evening commuter times to shuttle passengers from Union Station to New Haven Green.

There are also several daily Amtrak trains (☎ 800-872-7245, www.amtrak.com) from New York's Pennsylvania Station, but at a higher fare.

See the beginning of this chapter for information on *Shore Line East* trains from New Haven east to New London.

**Car** Avis, Budget and Hertz rent cars at Tweed-New Haven Airport. Driving details for New Haven are as follows:

| destination | mileage | hr:min |
|---|---|---|
| Boston, MA | 141 miles | 3:25 |
| Hartford, CT | 36 miles | 0:50 |
| Litchfield, CT | 36 miles | 1:00 |
| Mystic, CT | 55 miles | 1:15 |
| New London, CT | 46 miles | 1:00 |
| New York, NY | 75 miles | 1:30 |
| Providence, RI | 101 miles | 2:15 |

**Boat** The Bridgeport & Port Jefferson Steamboat Company (☎ 203-367-3043, 516-473-0286, www.portjeff.com/pjferry.html), 102 W Broadway, Port Jefferson, NY 11777, operates its daily car ferries year-round between Bridgeport, 10 miles southwest of New Haven, and Port Jefferson on Long Island about every 1½ hours. The 1½-hour voyage costs $10 to $12 per adult one way, $9 to $11 for seniors, $5 to $6 for children six to 12. The higher prices are for peak periods, which include certain times on weekends and holidays; most weekdays are off-peak. In peak periods, the fee for a car and driver is $28 to $33, with each passenger subject to an additional fare; off-peak, a car, its driver and all its passengers go for $37. Call to reserve space for your car.

## NEW LONDON & GROTON

Stretching 6 miles along the west bank of the Thames (pronounced 'Theymz') River, New London is an industrial, commercial and military city with a small tourist trade. During its golden age in the mid-19th century, New London was home port to some 200 whaling vessels, more than twice as many as were based at all other Connecticut ports combined. Its whaling commerce rivaled that of Massachusetts' great whaling ports of Nantucket and New Bedford. Unlike Nantucket, however, New London is short on charm and long on industrial bustle.

On the east bank of the Thames, Groton is known for the General Dynamics Corporation, a major naval defense contractor, and for the US Naval Submarine Base, the first (1881) and now the largest in the country. It's a fitting place for these establishments, because the world's first submarine was launched in 1776 just down the coast in Old Saybrook.

### Orientation

For New London, take I-95 exit 84, then go north on CT 32 (Mohegan Ave) for the US Coast Guard Academy, or take I-95 exits 82, 83 or 84 and go south for the city center. New London's transportation center is the Amtrak train station on Water St at State St; the bus station is in the same building and the ferry terminal (for boats to Long Island, Block Island and Fishers Island) is next door. The center of the commercial district is just southwest of the Amtrak station along Bank St. Follow Ocean Ave (CT 213) to reach Ocean Beach Park and Harkness Memorial State Park.

For Groton, take I-95 exits 85, 86 or 87.

### Information

Contact the Chamber of Commerce of Southeastern Connecticut (☎ 860-443-8332), 105 Huntington St, New London, CT 06320, or the Southeastern Connecticut Tourism District (☎ 860-444-2206, 800-863-6569, www.mysticmore.com), 470 Bank St (PO Box 89), New London, CT 06320, also called Connecticut's Mystic & More! Convention & Visitors Bureau.

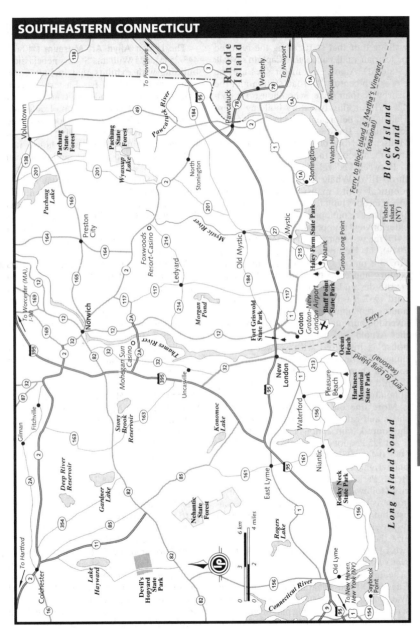

# SOUTHEASTERN CONNECTICUT

CONNECTICUT

## Things to See & Do

**New London** This town has a well-laid-out walking tour that starts along the restored pedestrian mall called the **Captain's Walk** (State St). Among the major sites are the city's 19th-century railroad station and the nearby Nathan Hale Schoolhouse (☎ 860-426-3918), a tiny two-story building where Hale taught before enlisting in the Connecticut militia. There is also the 1833 Custom House, the front door of which was made from the wood of the USS *Constitution*.

Between Federal St and Governor Winthrop Blvd, **Whale Oil Row** features four identical white mansions with imposing Doric façades built for whaling merchants in 1830. They're not open to the public, but the exterior view is impressive.

Of the two **Hempsted Houses** (☎ 860-443-7949), 11 Hempstead St, the older one (1678) is one of the best-documented 17th-century houses in the country. Maintained by the descendants of the original owners until 1937, it is one of the few 17th-century houses remaining in the area, having survived the burning of New London by Benedict Arnold and the British in 1781. (The house is insulated with seaweed, of all things.) The houses are open to visitors noon to 4 pm Thursday to Sunday from mid-May to mid-October, and at other times by appointment.

More fine old houses are on Starr St; shops and cafes line Bank St southwest of the Amtrak train station near the waterfront.

At 325 Pequot Ave, **Monte Cristo Cottage** (☎ 860-443-0051) was the boyhood home of playwright Eugene O'Neill. Near Ocean Beach Park in the southern districts of the city (follow the signs), the Victorian-style house is now a research library for dramatists, but many of O'Neill's belongings are on display, including his desk. You might recognize the living room: It was the setting for two of O'Neill's most famous plays, *Long Day's Journey into Night* and *Ah, Wilderness!* (Theater buffs should be sure to visit the Eugene O'Neill Theater Center in nearby Waterford, which hosts an annual summer series of readings by young playwrights.) The house is open 10 am to 5 pm (1 to 5 pm on

Sunday) from late May to early September; closed Monday. Admission costs $4.

The **Lyman Allyn Art Museum** (☎ 860-443-2545), 625 Williams St, is a neoclassical building with exhibits that include early American silver and Far Eastern, Greco-Roman, European and ethnic art of many cultures, as well as a collection of dolls and dollhouses. Included on the grounds of the museum is the Deshon-Allyn House, a whaling captain's Federal-style house, furnished with period antiques and American regional fine art. It is open 10 am to 5 pm (1 to 5 pm Sunday); closed Monday. Admission costs $4, $3 for seniors and students.

At the southern end of Ocean Ave is **Ocean Beach Park**, 1225 Ocean Ave, a popular beach and amusement area with waterslides, a picnic area, miniature golf, an arcade, a swimming pool and an old-fashioned boardwalk.

Visitors can tour the grounds of the **US Coast Guard Academy** (☎ 860-444-8270), on Mohegan Ave, one of the four US military academies, any day. From May through October, the visitors pavilion boasts a multimedia show on cadet life; the academy's interesting museum is open year-round. You can climb aboard the tall ship *Eagle*, used for cadet training and boat parades, when it's in port (usually on Sunday).

## Groton

At the **Historic Ship Nautilus & Submarine Force Museum** (☎ 860-694-3174, 800-343-0079, www.ussnautilus.org), 1 Crystal Lake Rd on the Naval Submarine Base, visitors can board the world's first nuclear-powered submarine, the *Nautilus*, launched on January 21, 1954. Other exhibits chronicle the history of the US submarine force and feature working periscopes and minisubs. The museum is open 9 am to 5 pm daily (1 to 5 pm Tuesday) from mid-May through October. In winter, it's open 9 am to 4 pm; closed Tuesday. Admission is free.

At **Fort Griswold State Park** (☎ 860-445-1729), at Monument St and Park Ave in Groton, a 130-foot obelisk marks the place where colonial troops were defeated and massacred by Benedict Arnold and the British in 1781, in a battle that saw the death of colonial Colonel William Ledyard and the

British burning of Groton and New London. Monument House features the Daughters of the American Revolution's collection of Revolutionary and Civil War memorabilia. It's open 10 am to 5 pm daily from late May to early September. From that time until mid-October, it's open weekends. Admission is free.

## Places to Stay

In high summer, rates are highest on Friday and Saturday nights and usually substantially lower from Sunday through Thursday.

**Motels & Hotels** As usual, several of I-95's exits have clusters of motels. On the New London side of the river, the *Red Roof Inn* (☎ 860-444-0001, 800-843-7663, 707 Colman St), I-95 North exit 82A, I-95 South exit 83, has 108 rooms for about $90 in summer. New London also has a pricier 136-room *Holiday Inn* (☎ 860-442-0631, 800-465-4329), at I-95 and Frontage Rd, and the 120-room *Radisson Hotel New London/Mystic* (☎ 860-443-7000, 800-333-3333, 35 Governor Winthrop Blvd), both of which offer shuttle bus service to Foxwoods Resort Casino. A bit farther west, the new 93-room *Motel 6* (☎ 860-739-6991, 800-466-8356, www.motel6 .com) should be open in Niantic by the time you arrive.

On the Groton side of the river, the *Econo Lodge* (☎ 860-445-6550, 800-424-4777, 425 Bridge St) has 50 rooms for $85 to $95 in summer; the *Thames Inn & Marina* (☎ 860-445-8111, 193 Thames St) has 26 rooms with fully equipped kitchens (and a coin-operated laundry on the premises) for $69 to $89 midweek, or $110 on weekends. The *Clarion Inn* (☎ 860-446-0660, 156 Kings Hwy (US 1)) has 69 rooms for $99 to $159, and the *Groton Inn and Suites* (☎ 860-445-9784, 800-452-2191, 99 Gold Star Hwy (CT 184)), at I-95, has 115 rooms priced from $120 to $180 in summer.

**Inns** The *Queen Anne Inne* (☎ 860-447-2600, 800-347-8818, 265 Williams St), in New London, is a high-Victorian 1903 mansion with an art gallery as well as 10 guest rooms priced from $145 to $175 in summer, full

breakfast and an afternoon tea included. A 20th-century hot tub is also available.

Close to the beach is the *Lighthouse Inn* (☎ 860-443-8411, 888-443-8411, fax 860-437-7027, www.lighthouseinn-ct.com, 6 Guthrie Place), also in New London, just inland from Guthrie Beach at the southern end of Montauk Ave. The 51 deluxe rooms in the huge, finely restored 1902 mansion are priced from $120 to $150 in summer (suites cost more), but in the Carriage House you pay $90 to $120. The lower prices apply Sunday through Thursday.

## Places to Eat

New London and Groton are short on fancy restaurants, but most motels and inns have dining rooms, and there are a number of cafes and bars along Bank St in New London. For great, inexpensive pizza (said to rival New Haven's famous Pepe's), New London has the *Recovery Room* (☎ 860-443-2619, 443 Ocean Ave), a family-run place near the beach. Medium-size pizzas cost $8 to $12.

In Groton, try *G Williker's* (☎ 860-445-8043, 156 King's Hwy (US 1)) and the *Fun 'n' Food Clam Bar* (☎ 860-445-6186, 283 CT 12).

## Getting There & Away

**Air** The Groton-New London Airport (☎ 860-445-8549) is served by several small commuter airlines that connect with the major airlines in Boston and New York City.

**Train** Amtrak (☎ 800-872-7245, www.amtrak .com) trains between New York and Boston on the shore route stop at New London.

**Car** Driving details for New London and Groton are as follows:

| destination | mileage | hr:min |
| --- | --- | --- |
| Boston, MA | 101 miles | 2:00 |
| Hartford, CT | 52 miles | 1:00 |
| Hyannis, MA | 104 miles | 2:00 |
| Mystic, CT | 9 miles | 0:15 |
| New Haven, CT | 46 miles | 0:55 |
| New York, NY | 121 miles | 2:30 |
| Providence, RI | 54 miles | 1:00 |

CONNECTICUT

**Boat** Cross Sound Ferry (☎ 860-443-5281, 516-323-2525, www.longislandferry.com), at 2 Ferry St (PO Box 33), New London, CT 06320, operates car ferries year-round between Orient Point, Long Island (New York) and New London, a 1½-hour run. From late June through Labor Day, ferries depart each port every hour on the hour from 7 am to 9 pm (last boats at 9:45 pm). Weekend voyages in June and September are almost as frequent. Off-season, boats tend to run every two hours. For one-way/same-day roundtrip, adults pay $9/14 and children two to 12 pay $4.50/7. Cars are charged $31, bicycles $2 one way. Call for car reservations. Another ferry service goes to Fishers Island, New York.

In summer, there are daily boats between New London and Block Island, Rhode Island, as well. See the Rhode Island chapter for details.

## MYSTIC

Southeastern Connecticut is the most-touristed region of the state because it is here that one finds the famous Mystic Seaport Museum and Foxwoods Resort Casino (see the 'Foxwoods' boxed text).

Mystic was a fine old seaport town centuries before the Seaport Museum became such a popular tourist attraction, and the town is still a pleasant place to stroll, shop and dine.

### Orientation

Take I-95 exit 90 for the Mystic Seaport Museum and Mystic town center. Motels are both north and south of I-95; Mystic Seaport Museum is a mile south of the highway on CT 27 (Greenmanville Ave); the center of the town is less than a mile south. Old Mystic is a separate town to the north of I-95. The Foxwoods Resort Casino is north of I-95 off CT 2 and 214.

The appealingly old-fashioned Mystic River Bascule Bridge (1922), known locally as 'the drawbridge,' carries US 1 across the Mystic River at the center of the town of Mystic. It's a familiar ritual in Mystic to wait while the drawbridge is raised for river traffic. There are shops and restaurants on both sides of the bridge, but most of the ice cream shops are on the west side.

### Information

Contact the Mystic Chamber of Commerce (☎ 860-572-9578, www.mysticchamber.org), 16 Cottrell St (PO Box 143), Mystic, CT 06355, south of the drawbridge on the east bank of the river.

### Mystic Seaport Museum

From simple beginnings in the 17th century, the village of Mystic grew to become one of the great shipbuilding ports of the East Coast. In the mid-19th century, Mystic's shipyards launched clipper ships, many from the George Greenman and Co Shipyard, which is now the site of Mystic Seaport Museum, inaugurated in 1929.

Today, the Mystic Seaport Museum (☎ 860-572-0711, www.mystic.org), 75 Greenmanville Ave (CT 27), covers 17 acres and includes more than 60 historic buildings, four ships and many smaller vessels. Some buildings in the Seaport are original to the site, but as at Old Sturbridge Village in Massachusetts, many were transported to Mystic from other parts of New England and arranged to re-create the look of the past. Seaport buildings are staffed by costumed interpreters who talk with visitors about their crafts and trades.

Visitors can board the *Charles W Morgan* (1841), the last surviving wooden whaling ship in America; the *LA Dunton*, a three-masted fishing schooner; or the *Joseph Conrad*, a square-rigged training ship. 'Fishermen' interpreters on the *Dunton* show how cod was salted and demonstrate some other skills essential to life at sea in the 19th century. The museum's latest exhibition is a replica of the 77-foot schooner *Amistad*, the slave ship on which 55 kidnapped Africans cast off their chains and sailed to freedom. In the Steven Spielberg movie *Amistad,* Mystic Seaport Museum was used to stage many of the scenes like took place in colonial New London. See the boxed text in the New Haven section.

At the Henry B duPont Preservation Shipyard, visitors can watch large wooden boats being restored. In the Small Boat

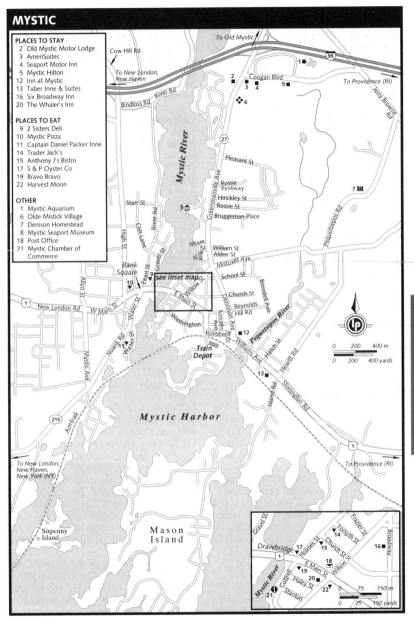

# MYSTIC

**PLACES TO STAY**
2  Old Mystic Motor Lodge
3  AmeriSuites
4  Seaport Motor Inn
5  Mystic Hilton
12  Inn at Mystic
13  Taber Inne & Suites
16  Six Broadway Inn
20  The Whaler's Inn

**PLACES TO EAT**
9  2 Sisters Deli
10  Mystic Pizza
11  Captain Daniel Packer Inne
14  Trader Jack's
15  Anthony J's Bistro
17  S & P Oyster Co
19  Bravo Bravo
22  Harvest Moon

**OTHER**
1  Mystic Aquarium
6  Olde Mistick Village
7  Denison Homestead
8  Mystic Seaport Museum
18  Post Office
21  Mystic Chamber of
    Commerce

**CONNECTICUT**

Shop, smaller-scale wooden boats are hand-built by skilled craftsmen using authentic 19th-century techniques, then either sold or used along the waterfront at the museum. The Seaport includes a general store, chapel, school, sail loft, shipsmith and the ship chandlery – all the sorts of places that you'd expect to find in a real shipbuilding town of 150 years ago. The Wendell Building has a display of ships' figureheads and carvings.

The *Sabino* (☎ 860-572-5315), a 1908-era steamboat, takes visitors on excursion trips up the Mystic River from May through October.

The museum is open 9 am to 5 pm daily in summer. All-day admission is $16 for adults, $8 for children six to 15; if you order your tickets in advance from the museum's website (www.mystic.org), you may get a discount.

## Mystic Aquarium

Family-oriented Mystic Aquarium (☎ 860-572-5955, www.mysticaquarium.org), 55 Coogan Blvd (CT 27; use I-95 exit 90), has more than 6000 species of sea creatures – including a great white shark – an outdoor viewing area for seals and sea lions, a penguin exhibit and a 1400-seat Marine Theater where dolphin acts are presented. It's open 9 am to 6 pm daily (till 5 pm in winter). Admission is $13 for adults, $12 for seniors, $8 for children ages three to 12.

## Denison Homestead

The displays in this 1717 home (☎ 860-536-9248), on Pequotsepos Rd to the east of Mystic Seaport Museum, illustrate life in New England from the colonial period through the 1940s. The house contains memorabilia from 11 generations of the Denison family arranged in a series of rooms: a colonial kitchen, a Revolutionary-era bedroom, a Federal parlor, a Civil War bedroom and an early-20th-century living room. It's open 10 am to 4 pm Friday to Monday from mid-May through mid-October. Admission is $4 for adults, $3 for seniors and students, $1 for those younger than 16.

## Places to Stay

As the major attraction on Connecticut's coast, Mystic has many motels and a few inns, many of which post photographs on www.visitmystic.com. In July and August, most lodgings fill up every day. Prices on Friday, Saturday and Sunday nights are typically higher than on other nights. When you call for reservations, consider alternatives in nearby communities such as New London, Groton and Stonington.

**Camping** Though there are several state parks nearer, the closest with camping is *Rocky Neck State Park* (☎ 860-424-3200), south of I-95 in East Lyme. *The Island* (☎ 860-739-8316, 20 Islanda Court) has another 35 sites in East Lyme. The *Seaport Campgrounds* (☎ 860-536-4044, www .seaportcampground.com), on CT 184 in Old Mystic, has 130 RV sites ($27 to $31) with or without hookups, a separate tenting area, and services from free hot showers to miniature golf. It's open from March through November.

**Motels & Hotels** Most of Mystic's motels are clustered near I-95 exit 90, most on CT 27 (Greenmanville Ave/Whitehall Ave) north and south of the interstate.

*AmeriSuites* (☎ 860-536-9997, 800-833-1516, fax 860-536-9686), on CT 27 just south of I-95, is the newest lodging in this cluster, charging $139 to $179 for its up-to-date suites, many of which sleep four or six people.

You can't miss the *Seaport Motor Inn* (☎ 860-536-2621, 800-447-0764, fax 860-536-4493), on Coogan Blvd just south of I-95. It has 117 clean, simple rooms with motel conveniences and an outdoor pool. Prices in summer are a reasonable $95 to $129.

Across CT 27, the *Old Mystic Motor Lodge* (☎ 860-536-9666, fax 536-2044, 251 Greenmanville Ave (CT 27)) is a local effort with a nice pool and 56 rooms on two floors, all equipped with refrigerators and microwaves and priced from $99 to $139 in summer.

The *Mystic Hilton* (☎ 860-572-0731, 800-445-8667, fax 860-572-0328, 20 Coogan Blvd) has predictably comfortable accommodations in a convenient location across from Mystic Aquarium. Summer rates are $169 to

$225, but special packages may give you more for less – call and ask about them.

North of I-95 along CT 27 you'll find the ***Days Inn of Mystic*** *(☎ 860-572-0574, 800-329-7466, fax 860-572-1164, 55 Whitehall Ave)*, charging $139 to $149 for its 122 rooms around a nice swimming pool. The neighboring ***Comfort Inn*** *(☎ 860-572-8531, 800-228-5150, fax 860-572-9358, 48 Whitehall Ave)* has 120 rooms for similar rates.

***Best Western Mystic Sovereign Hotel*** *(☎ 860-536-4281, 800-528-1234, fax 860-536-4802, 9 Whitehall Ave)* has an indoor heated pool, children's playground and 150 comfy rooms for $119 on weekdays and $129 on weekends.

Several other good choices are east of the center of Mystic along US 1.

The ***Inn at Mystic*** *(☎ 860-536-9604, 800-237-2415, fax 860-572-1635)*, at US 1 and CT 27, has a variety of accommodations from $115 to $210 on weekdays, $165 to $265 on weekends. Rooms range from simple, clean motel-style units to luxury chambers in the hilltop Georgian mansion decorated with colonial-style furniture and antiques. From the inn's hilltop setting, lawns sweep down to a boat dock, tennis court and swimming pool. The Flood Tide restaurant is well regarded.

***Taber Inne & Suites*** *(☎ 860-536-4904, fax 572-9140, 66 Williams Ave)*, a minute's drive east of Mystic center along US 1, is popular with families. There's quite a range of comfortable accommodations here, from 28 motel-type rooms to luxurious one- and two-bedroom townhouses. Prices in summer range from $145 to $340.

**Inns & B&Bs** Right in the center of Mystic by the drawbridge, ***The Whaler's Inn*** *(☎ 860-536-1506, 800-243-2588, fax 860-572-1250, whalersinn@riconnect.com, 20 E Main St)* consists of an 1865 Victorian house, a contemporaneous inn and a more modern motel-like structure known as Stonington House. Rooms cost $99 to $149 in summer, depending upon the number and size of beds and the building they're in.

***Six Broadway Inn*** *(☎/fax 860-536-6010, 6 Broadway)* is a fine old Victorian house a short distance from the center of Mystic. European-style luxury is the aim for guests in its five rooms priced from $150 to $195 weekdays, $180 to $225 on weekends (two-night minimum). You'll pass the inn as you drive south from Mystic Seaport Museum to the center of Mystic.

Perhaps the finest of Mystic's inns is the ***Whitehall Mansion*** *(☎ 860-572-7280, 800-572-3993, fax 860-572-4724, 42 Whitehall Ave (CT 27))*, a grand colonial house built in 1771, restored in 1970 and converted to a luxury B&B in 1996. Each of the five luxury rooms has a fireplace, whirlpool bath and individual climate control and costs $169 to $249, breakfast and evening wine and cheese included.

***The Old Mystic Inn*** *(☎ 860-572-9422, fax 572-9954, omysticinn@aol.com, 52 Main St)*, in Old Mystic, has eight guest rooms (three with working fireplaces, two with whirlpool tubs) named for New England authors and priced at $125 midweek, $155 on weekends.

The ***House of 1833*** *(☎ 860-536-6325, 800-367-1833, 72 N Stonington Rd (CT 201))*, in Mystic, is a Greek Revival mansion with five luxury guest rooms furnished in antiques, a swimming pool, a Har-Tru tennis court and 18-speed bikes for touring. Rooms are priced from $115 to $165 on weekdays, $155 to $225 on Friday, Saturday and Sunday (two-night minimum).

Cow Hill Rd, the road going north from I-95 exit 89, has a number of nice inns.

The ***Adams House B&B*** *(☎ 860-572-9551, fax 572-9552, 382 Cow Hill Rd)* is only 1½ miles from the center of Mystic and offers cozy rooms with queen beds and private baths for $115 on weekdays, $145 on weekends, breakfast and afternoon tea included.

Also on Cow Hill Rd in Mystic is the ***Pequot Hotel B&B*** *(☎ 860-572-0390, fax 536-3380, 711 Cow Hill Rd)*, once a stagecoach stop. The Greek Revival house, built in 1840, now has three luxury guest rooms with bath (two with fireplaces) for $95 to $135 on weekdays, $110 to $150 on weekends.

At the ***Red Brook Inn*** *(☎ 860-572-0349, fax 572-0146)*, near the intersection of Cow Hill Rd and CT 184 (Gold Star Hwy), you

**CONNECTICUT**

## Foxwoods

Rising above the verdant forest canopy of Great Cedar Swamp 7 miles north of Mystic, the gleaming 18-story towers – and soon 38-story towers – of the mammoth *Foxwoods Resort Casino* (☎ *800-752-9244*) seem to have been dropped from outer space into this placid rural Connecticut countryside. The impression is heightened by the lack of clues to its existence: no billboards tout it, and no highway signs direct you to it.

All the same, more than 50,000 visitors make their way here daily, eager to tempt Lady Luck and to enjoy Las Vegas-style entertainment 24 hours a day, 365 days a year. What's going on here?

Under treaties dating back centuries, many native peoples claim important territorial and legal rights separate from those enjoyed by other citizens of the US. In recent times, these aboriginal ethnic 'nations' have successfully used the courts and the Congress to elaborate these treaty rights into a potent vehicle for solving their longstanding problems of poverty and ethnic discrimination.

One such group, the 700-member Mashantucket Pequot Tribal Nation, known as 'the fox people,' kept a tenuous hold on a parcel of ancestral land in southeastern Connecticut. The tribe had dwindled to insignificant numbers through assimilation and dispersion in search of work and careers, but a few hardy souls refused to abandon the reservation. Living in decrepit trailers dragged onto the land, they fought a dispiriting legal battle against attempts to declare the reservation abandoned.

Their tenacity paid off in 1986 when they reached an agreement with the Connecticut state government that allowed the Pequots to open a high-stakes bingo hall. It prospered. In 1992, again under an agreement with the state, the tribe borrowed $60 million from a Malaysian casino developer and began to build Foxwoods. With no casino gambling allowed in any other New England state, and New York City within a 2½-hour drive, Foxwoods now brings in more than a billion dollars annually. The tribe is poor no more. The reservation now

have your choice of two buildings: the Haley Tavern (1740), with seven guest rooms, and the Crary Homestead (1770), with three guest rooms. Rooms cost $109 to $169 in summer.

### Places to Eat

There are several places to grab a snack or sit down to a full meal within Mystic Seaport Museum, but most of the town's restaurants are in or near the town center, close to the drawbridge.

For huge, good sandwiches, fruit, bottled drinks and other picnic supplies, try *Harvest Moon*, on US 1 (Main St) at Willow across from the post office. *2 Sisters Deli* (☎ *860-536-1244, 4 Pearl St*), on the west side of the drawbridge, offers a huge selection of even cheaper ($3.50 to $5.25) sandwiches, as well as vegetarian meals and beer, and you can sit down right there to consume them.

Most of the town's excellent *ice cream shops*, by the way, are on the west side of the drawbridge.

*Mystic Pizza* (☎ *860-536-3737, 56 W Main St*) calls its pizzas 'little slices of heaven' and also serves salads, hearty grinders and beer. If the name sounds familiar, it may be because it was the title of a low-budget comedy film starring Julia Roberts (one of her first movies). The movie was inspired by the pizza parlor, which is now more popular than ever.

Several full-service restaurants are right in the center of town, east of the drawbridge. *Bravo Bravo* (☎ *860-536-3228, 20 E Main St*), at Holmes, serves nouvelle Italian food – flavorful and inventive pastas, seafood and beef (each about $15) – in a bright, sophisticated setting. Across the street on the riverbank, *S&P Oyster Co* (☎ *860-536-2674,*

## Foxwoods

has its own police and fire departments, tribal government and, presumably, a large and ultramodern accounting department to keep track of the flood of tribal money.

The agreement with the State of Connecticut apportions some of the gambling proceeds to the state in lieu of taxes and also stipulates that the casino cannot be advertised and publicized in certain ways – such as on billboards and road signs. This hilarious legal figleaf serves to hide the existence of Foxwoods only from the surpassingly clueless.

Take I-95 to exit 92 ('North Stonington,' east of Mystic), then follow CT 2 West; or take I-395 to exit 79A, 80, 81 or 85 and follow the signs for the 'Mashantucket Pequot Reservation' (you won't see the word 'Foxwoods' anywhere) – or just follow the heavy stream of traffic.

There's lots of bus transport as well. South East Area Transit (SEAT; ☎ 860-886-2631) runs buses from New London's Amtrak train station to Foxwoods, and there are direct buses from Providence (see that section).

The resort complex, tasteful compared to those in Las Vegas, has the world's largest gambling casino, with 370 table games, 5750 slot machines and a 3700-seat bingo hall; 30 food and beverage outlets; three nightclubs with free entertainment (no cover, no minimum); cinemas, rides, video-game and pinball parlors for the children; and 1400 luxury guest rooms (☎ 800-369-9663 for reservations) in three hotels (the **Grand Pequot Tower**, **Great Cedar Hotel** and **Two Trees Inn**).

Even if you're not a gambler, you may want to come for the $193-million **Mashantucket Pequot Museum & Research Center** (☎ 860-396-6838, www.mashantucket.com), a beautiful, ultramodern museum for an ancient people, open 10 am to 7 pm daily (last admission at 6 pm) for $10 ($8 for seniors, $6 for children six to 15).

**Mohegan Sun** (☎ 888-226-7711), at I-395 exit 79A, is a smaller version of Foxwoods operated by the Mohegan tribe on its reservation.

If you've come to gamble, keep in mind that these lavish pleasure palaces in the countryside were not built with money from the winners, but from the losers.

*1 Holmes St)* boasts 'the best view in Mystic.' Luncheon sandwiches cost $6 or $7, seafood plates $8 or $9, or at dinner $14 to $18. There's a children's menu, too.

Just a block up Holmes St is **Anthony J's Bistro** (☎ *860-536-0448, 6 Holmes St)*, a classy trattoria serving pizzas for $8 to $11 and a full menu of Italian specialties (pastas for $9 to $12, grills for $16 to $20). A block farther north, **Trader Jack's** (☎ *860-572-8550, 14 Holmes St)*, a tavern at the corner of Church St, often has the very best deals at lunch.

On the west side of the drawbridge, then south on Water St (CT 215; a five-minute walk) is the **Captain Daniel Packer Inne** (☎ *860-536-3555, 32 Water St)*, in a historic building dating from 1754. The food here is prepared with flair. A special favorite is Steak Blackjack, a 16oz slab of beef in a

sauce laced with whiskey. Expect to spend $35 to $60 for a very filling dinner.

Lobster lovers should check out **Abbott's Lobster in the Rough** (☎ *860-536-7719, 117 Pearl St)*, on the waterfront in neighboring Noank, just west of Mystic. Abbott's is as simple as it gets: Order your lobster (or other seafood) at the window, get a number, pick out a picnic table by the water and, when your number is called, pay ($15 to $22 per meal) and eat. It doesn't get much better than this on a warm summer night. Abbott's is open daily for lunch and dinner, May through October.

### Shopping

Olde Mistick Village, on CT 27 just south of I-95, is a pseudocolonial village green centered on a Congregational church and surrounded by shops selling sportswear, gifts, crafts, jewelry and Lladró porcelain. Nearby is Mystic Factory Outlets (☎ 860-443-4788), with 24 outlets for men's and women's clothes, leather, handicrafts, shoes and more. The town's best shops are on Main St west of the drawbridge.

## Getting There & Away

**Train** Amtrak (☎ 800-872-7245, www.amtrak .com) trains between New York and Boston on the shore route stop at Mystic's train depot on Roosevelt St, less than a mile south of Mystic Seaport Museum.

**Car** Driving details for Mystic are as follows:

| destination | mileage | hr:min |
| --- | --- | --- |
| Boston, MA | 108 miles | 2:00 |
| Hartford, CT | 54 miles | 1:00 |
| Hyannis, MA | 95 miles | 1:50 |
| New Haven, CT | 55 miles | 1:05 |
| New London, CT | 9 miles | 0:15 |
| New York, NY | 130 miles | 2:40 |
| Providence, RI | 45 miles | 1:00 |
| Stonington, CT | 5 miles | 0:10 |

## Getting Around

The Mystic Trolley circulates through the town and among the major points of interest, charging $2 per ride or $5 for unlimited rides all day.

## STONINGTON

Five miles east of Mystic on US 1 is Stonington, unquestionably one of the most appealing towns on the Connecticut coast. Many of the town's 18th- and 19th-century houses were once the homes of sea captains. One of the finest of these belonged to Captain Nathaniel Palmer, who earned fame at the very tender age of 21 by discovering the continent of Antarctica.

It's best to explore this historic town – actually a 'borough,' Connecticut's oldest – on foot. Compactly laid out on a peninsula that juts into Long Island Sound, Stonington has wonderful streetscapes of period architecture. The short main thoroughfare, Water St, is lined with interesting shops, many featuring high-end antiques, colorful French

Quimper porcelain and upscale gifts. There are also a couple of good waterfront restaurants and delis. At the southern end of Water St is the 'point' or tip of the peninsula, with a park and tiny beach.

## History

Settled in 1752 and chartered in 1801, tiny Stonington was a whaling village until the advent of steam power fated it to become a major transfer point on the rail-and-steamship route between New York and Boston. At one time in the mid-19th century, some 17 rail lines converged on the town from Boston and other New England points, bringing passengers and cargo to continue on to New York by steamboat.

Ironically, when the era of the steamships ended in the 1880s and the Northeast Corridor trip could be made entirely by rail, the once-vital connection at Stonington was no longer needed. Then, a new railroad viaduct across the main north-south road into Stonington had the effect of cutting off the village from the commercial highway corridor of US 1. Many longtime Stonington residents credit (or blame, depending on their point of view) the railroad viaduct for consigning the mile-long peninsula and its little village to a time warp in which it has remained ever since.

In the first half of the 19th century, the borough's two main north-south streets, Water and Main, were lined with the fine houses of successful shipping merchants as well as bustling commercial buildings. Some of Stonington's earliest buildings were destroyed in the Battle of Stonington during the War of 1812, but many more remain, including the sweet little Greek Revival arcade.

The battle was a moment of high drama for the village: On August 9, 1814, four British ships used 158 Royal Navy guns to batter the town, which was suspected of harboring torpedoes. Forty buildings were destroyed, but miraculously there was only one human casualty on the American side. The Brits didn't fare so well, as Stonington men successfully defended the town with all they had in their arsenal: a pair of 18-pound cannons and one 6-pounder hastily set up at the end of the point and aimed out to sea.

The Battle of Stonington is memorialized in the village's Cannon Square, where the cannons that served Stonington so well are on perpetual display. A plaque mounted at the end of the point bears the simple statement 'This is To Remember.' British cannonballs, recovered from all over the village after the battle, are fixed atop granite gateposts and hitching posts around town.

## Things to See

Stonington has had its share of famous residents over the years. Drive or walk down Water St (one-way southbound) to its southern end for a good look at the town, and then drive north on Main St, the other major north-south street, one block east of Water St.

The **Colonel Amos Palmer House** (1780), on Water St at Wall St, was the home of artist James McNeill Whistler and later of poet Stephen Vincent Benét. (The house is not open to the public.)

At the southern end of Water St, close to the point, the houses become plainer and simpler, many dating from the 18th century. These were the residences of ships' carpenters and fishermen.

At the end of the point, near the small shingle DuBois Beach, is the **Old Lighthouse Museum** (☎ 860-535-1440), 7 Water St. The octagonal-towered granite lighthouse, built in 1823 as the first government lighthouse in Connecticut, was moved to its present location in 1840 and deactivated 50 years later. In 1925, it was remodeled as a museum with exhibits on whaling, Native American artifacts, curios from the China trade, wooden boats, weaponry, 19th-century oil portraits, toys and decoys. The museum is open 10 am to 5 pm (closed Monday) May to October. Adults pay $4; children six to 12 pay $2.

Heading back north, the **Portuguese Holy Ghost Society** building on Main St is a reminder of the contributions made to Stonington by the Azoreans who signed onto Stonington-bound whalers during the 19th century and eventually settled in the village. Today, their descendants still form a signifi-

cant part of Stonington's population, though the small village's ever-increasing appeal to wealthy New Yorkers seeking summer homes has had the effect of driving the locals out of the real estate market. Nearby is the old Custom House, from the days when Stonington was a major port.

## Places to Stay

Stonington is the area's quaintest place to stay; see Mystic or New London & Groton for cheaper or chain motels.

**Camping** *Highland Orchards Resort Park* (☎ 860-599-5101, 800-624-0829), in North Stonington, has 260 sites for $29 to $39. It's open all year.

The *MHG RV Park* (☎ 860-535-0501), on CT 184 in North Stonington, is also open all year.

**Motels** Budget motels – some of the cheapest in the area – are northeast of the center of Stonington along US 1 on the way to Pawcatuck. The *Sea Breeze Motel* (☎ 860-535-2843, 812 Stonington Rd) has 30 rooms from $65 to $75 on weekdays, $95 to $105 on weekends in summer. The nearby 16-room *Cove Ledge Resort Motel* (☎ 860-599-4130), on Whewell Circle, US 1, in Pawcatuck, is similar, with prices from $70 to $90. The simple *Stonington Motel* (☎ 860-599-2330, 901 Stonington Rd (US 1)), in Stonington, has 12 rooms priced from $65 to $79 on weekends, with a 10% discount during the week.

**Inns & B&Bs** Calling itself 'a quiet guest house' – the only one found in the heart of Stonington – *Lasbury's* (☎ 860-535-2681, 41 Orchard St), off Church St (turn left off of Water St at Noah's restaurant), is simple, unpretentious and also conveniently within walking distance of everything in town. Double rooms cost $85 (no breakfast).

*Randall's Ordinary* (☎ 860-599-4540, www.randallsordinary.com), on CT 2 in North Stonington, is a centuries-old farmhouse (1685) that is now an inn and restaurant (see Places to Eat, below). As you enter the farm, it's easy to believe you've gone back in time: Authenticity of the exterior appearance is a strong point here, even though on the inside, the inn and converted barn have all modern conveniences. In the main house are three guest rooms; nine more are in the barn. All rooms have private baths and are priced from $140 to $175 in summer; the four suites cost $175 to $250. The inn is 8.4 miles northeast of the center of Stonington along CT 2, three-tenths of a mile north of I-95 exit 92.

### Places to Eat

Stonington's few restaurants are revealed to you as you proceed south on Water St.

The *Water St Cafe* (☎ 860-535-2122, 142 Water St), north of Grand St, boasts a menu that is creative and moderately priced – a rare combination. Recent dishes included escargot pot pie, tuna tartare and a pork empanada. Lunch can cost as little as $10; dinner is more like $20 to $30. They serve Sunday brunch as well.

Across the street, the *Water St Market & Deli* (☎ 860-535-0797, 143 Water St) is perfect for picnic supplies – have your picnic in the park at the southern end of Water St.

Breakfast, lunch and dinner are served at *Noah's* (☎ 860-535-3925, 115 Water St), at Church St. A pretty, informal place with two small rooms topped with original stamped-tin ceilings, Noah's has local art on the walls and an authentic old-fashioned atmosphere. Dinners cost about $16 to $24 per person; it's closed Monday.

Off Water St to the right is *Skipper's Dock* (☎ 860-535-2000), a casual seafood restaurant with a waterside deck. This is the place to order steamers, lobster or what is locally known as a clam boil – the works, including clams, corn, lobster, fish and sausage, for $25 to $35 per person at dinner, about half that at lunch.

Hearth cooking in the authentic colonial manner is the specialty at *Randall's Ordinary* (☎ 860-599-4540), on CT 2 in North Stonington (see Places to Stay, above). Breakfast and lunch are à la carte, but there is just one dinner seating, at 7 pm, for a fixed-price menu of slow-simmered soups, beef, fish, chicken or venison, hearth-baked

cornbread and colonial-style desserts. Dinner costs $39 per person, plus drinks, tax and tip. Reservations are essential.

### Shopping

Stonington is one of only two towns in the USA (the other is Alexandria, Virginia) with an official shop for Quimper Faïence (☎ 860-535-1712, 800-470-7339, www.quimperfaience .com), 141 Water St. Pronounced 'kamm-PEHR,' this is the colorfully painted dinnerware handmade in France since the 17th century. The folk-art plates, cups, mugs, platters, figurines and utensils are avidly collected by their fans. Prices are not low, but then, each Quimper piece is one of a kind by definition. The shop is closed Sunday.

# Litchfield Hills

The gently rolling hills in the northwestern corner of Connecticut are named for the historic town of Litchfield at their center. Sprinkled with lakes and dotted with state parks and forests, this beautiful, tranquil area offers an abundance of natural beauty but a paucity of accommodations. Only a handful of inns and campgrounds provide for travelers, an intentional curb on development that guarantees the preservation of the area's exceptional rural beauty.

### LITCHFIELD

The centerpiece of the region is Litchfield, which is Connecticut's best-preserved late-18th-century town.

Founded in 1719, Litchfield prospered from 1780 to 1840 on the commerce brought through the town by the stagecoaches en route between Hartford and Albany. In the mid-19th century, railroads did away with the coach routes, and industrial water-powered machinery drove Litchfield's artisans out of the markets, leaving the town to retreat into a torpor of faded gentility.

This proved to be its salvation. Its grand 18th-century houses were not torn down to build factories or Victorian mansions or malls. With the advent of the automobile, Litchfield's economy was saved by tourism.

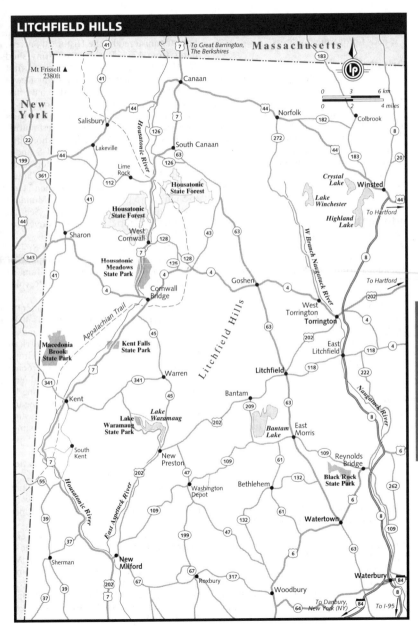

# LITCHFIELD HILLS

Massachusetts

Mt Frissell ▲ 2380ft

New York

Salisbury

Lakeville

Lime Rock

Sharon

Housatonic River

Housatonic State Forest

Canaan

South Canaan

Housatonic State Forest

West Cornwall

Housatonic Meadows State Park

Cornwall Bridge

Appalachian Trail

Macedonia Brook State Park

Kent Falls State Park

Warren

Kent

Lake Waramaug State Park

Lake Waramaug

South Kent

New Preston

Washington Depot

New Milford

Sherman

Roxbury

Norfolk

Colbrook

Crystal Lake

Lake Winchester

Winsted

Highland Lake

To Hartford

W Branch Naugatuck River

Goshen

West Torrington

Torrington

To Hartford

East Litchfield

Litchfield Hills

Litchfield

Bantam

Bantam Lake

East Morris

Reynolds Bridge

Black Rock State Park

Bethlehem

Watertown

Woodbury

Waterbury

To Danbury, New York (NY)

To I-95

Naugatuck River

Housatonic River

East Aspetuck River

CONNECTICUT

0    3    6 km
0    2    4 miles

But it is mostly day-trip tourism. By plan, Litchfield and surrounding towns have very few beds for overnight visitors.

## Orientation

US 202 goes right through the center of Litchfield along West St, the town's main street. CT 63 passes east of the center along North and South Sts. The town green is at the intersection of US 202 and CT 63. An 18th-century milestone stands on the green as it has since stagecoach days, when it informed passengers that they had another 33 miles to ride to Hartford, or 102 to New York City. Several restaurants face the green.

## Information

From June through mid-September, an information booth on the town green is staffed daily by helpful locals; it's open weekends from mid-September through October.

Litchfield Hills Travel Council (☎ 860-567-4506, www.litchfieldhills.com), PO Box 968, Litchfield, CT 06759, can send you an excellent booklet with precise route details on touring the Litchfield Hills by car, by boat, by bike or on foot.

Barnidge & McEnroe, described below in Places to Eat, is the place to find books.

## Things to See & Do

A walk around town starts at the information kiosk on the town green. Just north across West St is the town's historic jail. Stroll along North St to see the fine houses.

More of Litchfield's well-preserved 18th-century houses are along South St. Set well back from the roadway across broad lawns and behind old trees, the houses take you back visually to Litchfield's golden age.

The **Litchfield Historical Society** (☎ 860-567-4501), 7 South St, has set up a museum in its headquarters, open 11 am to 5 pm (1 to 5 pm Sunday; closed Monday) from mid-April to mid-November. Admission costs $5 for adults, $3 for seniors, nothing for children younger than 16, and allows admission both to the museum and to the Tapping Reeve House.

The **Tapping Reeve House** (☎ 860-567-4501), 82 South St at the corner of Wolcott, now administered by the Historical Society, dates from 1773. Beside it is a tiny shed (1784) that once housed America's first school of law, established by Tapping Reeve in 1775. Lest it look too modest to have had any effect, you should know that John C Calhoun and 130 members of Congress were trained here. The school's most notorious graduate was Aaron Burr who, while serving as vice president of the US under Jefferson, shot Alexander Hamilton in an upstate New York duel in 1804. The house and the historical law school are open 11 am to 5 pm (1 to 5 pm Sunday; closed Monday) from mid-May through November. See the Litchfield Historical Society (above) for ticket information.

At the southern end of South St is a house that may have been the birthplace of Ethan Allen, leader of Vermont's famous 'Green Mountain Boys' during the Revolutionary War.

One mile southeast of the town center off CT 118, **Haight Vineyards** (☎ 860-567-4045, 800-325-5567), 29 Chestnut Hill Rd, makes wines from vinifera and French-American hybrid grapes grown on the property. Grape varieties include Chardonnay, Maréchal Foch, Seyval Blanc, Vidal Blanc and Vignoles. They even make a sparkling wine by the *méthode champenoise*, hand-riddling the bottles and disgorging by hand after resting on the lees. Winery tours and free tastings are available 10:30 am to 5 pm (1 to 5 pm Sunday) year-round.

At the **White Memorial Conservation Center** (☎ 860-567-0857), 2½ miles west of town along US 202, are 35 miles of hiking and nature trails on 6¼ sq miles, open year-round. The Natural History Museum is open 9 am to 5 pm (noon to 4 pm Sunday).

Two miles east of the town green via CT 118, **Topsmead State Forest** was once the estate of Ms Edith Morton Chase. You can visit Ms Chase's grand Tudor-style summer home, complete with its original furnishings, spread a blanket on the lawn and have a picnic while enjoying the view from this perch at 1230 feet. There are hiking trails as well.

You can hike the trails and swim in the lake at Mt Tom State Park (☎ 860-868-2592), 6½ miles west of Litchfield green, for $5 per car on weekdays, $8 on weekends; it's free off season.

## Places to Stay

**Camping** The simple *Looking Glass Hill Campground* (☎ 860-567-2050), 5 miles west of the Litchfield green on US 202 in Bantam, is the most appealing, with 30 sites for $20 to $24, open April to mid-October. The elaborate *Hemlock Hill Camp Resort* (☎ 860-567-2267), on Hemlock Hill Rd, has 125 pine-shaded sites open from May through late October. From Litchfield, go west along US 202 for a mile, then right on Milton Rd.

*Valley in the Pines* (☎ 860-491-2032) has 35 sites open all year. Go west on US 202 almost to Bantam, turn north on Maple St and go 5½ miles to the campground.

## Inns & B&Bs

*Abel Darling* (☎ 860-567-0384, 102 West St), at Spencer, opposite the lower end of the green, is an early American house (1782) with two rooms to rent for $95 and $105, continental breakfast included.

The *Tollgate Hill Inn* (☎ 860-567-4545, 800-445-3903), at US 202 and Tollgate Rd, was built in 1745 and now offers 20 rooms with private bath (eight with fireplaces) for $110 to $140. It has a restaurant popular in the summer (closed in winter).

The *Litchfield Inn* (☎ 860-567-4503, 800-499-3444, fax 860-567-5358), set in extensive grounds 2 miles west of the town green on US 202, has 30 luxury rooms priced from $115 to $130 and 'theme' rooms with special decor and working fireplaces for $180; continental breakfast is included. The more expensive rooms can sleep three or four people.

## Places to Eat

Most of the town's restaurants are lined up on West St facing the green.

*Barnidge & McEnroe* (☎ 860-567-4670, 7 West St), facing the flagpole on the green, serves up great coffee ($1 to $3), good sweet buns and intellectual satisfaction – it's a bookstore cafe.

The *Litchfield Food Co* (☎ 860-567-3113, 37 West St) and *Superior Foods* (☎ 860-567-8731, 31 West St) are grocery store-delis good for picnic supplies.

The *Difranco's Restaurant & Pizzeria* (☎ 860-567-8872, 19 West St) is traditional and inexpensive, offering veal marsala for $12, pasta and sandwiches for $4 to $6. Wine and beer are served.

*Aspen Garden* (☎ 860-567-9477, 51 West St), facing the green, serves a good selection of light meals ($5 to $8) with Greek accents: salads, sandwiches, baklava and tiramisu. There's beer as well. Sit at an umbrella-shaded terrace table in good weather.

The *West Street Grill* (☎ 860-567-3885, 41 West St), facing the green, is a sophisticated city grill and tavern serving creative New American cuisine, with full dinners going for about $30 per person, hamburger platters for $9. The wine and drink list is extensive.

The *Village Restaurant* (☎ 860-567-8307, 25 West St) features gourmet sandwiches and similar lighter fare, served with wine and beer.

## Getting There & Away

**Bus** Bonanza Bus Lines (☎ 800-556-3815) runs four buses between New York City and Bennington, Vermont, via Danbury, Kent and Cornwall Bridge, Connecticut. No buses stop in Litchfield; these come the closest.

**Car** Driving details for Litchfield are as follows:

| destination | mileage | hr:min |
|---|---|---|
| Boston, MA | 136 miles | 2:00 |
| Great Barrington, MA | 33 miles | 1:00 |
| Hartford, CT | 34 miles | 1:00 |
| Lake Waramaug, CT | 15 miles | 0:25 |
| Lenox, MA | 46 miles | 1:15 |
| New Haven, CT | 36 miles | 1:00 |
| New York, NY | 99 miles | 2:30 |
| Springfield, MA | 58 miles | 1:25 |

## LAKE WARAMAUG

Of the dozens of lakes and ponds in the Litchfield Hills, Lake Waramaug, north of New Preston, is perhaps the most beautiful.

Gracious inns dot its shoreline, parts of which are protected as a state park.

As you make your way around the northern shore of the lake on North Shore Rd, you'll come to the **Hopkins Vineyard** (☎ 860-868-7954), on Hopkins Rd in Warren. The wines, made mostly from French-American hybrid grapes, are eminently drinkable. Right next door, the *Hopkins Inn* (☎ 860-868-7295) has a fine restaurant with a traditional continental and American menu. In good weather, the views from the terrace are very fine. Full dinners cost $30 to $40.

The lake's newest restaurant is the *Lakeview Inn* (☎ 860-868-1000, 107 N Shore Rd), in New Preston. 'Casual fine dining' in a hilltop estate set in expansive grounds is the theme. The menu has a number of creative, innovative New American cuisine dishes as well as the more traditional pheasant and Black Angus steaks. Dinner might cost $45 to $65 per person. Reservations are recommended on weekends.

Around the bend in the lake is *Lake Waramaug State Park* (☎ 860-868-0220, 30 Lake Waramaug Rd), with 88 beautiful lakeside campsites that are usually booked well in advance.

*The Boulders* (☎ 860-868-0541), E Shore Rd (CT 45) in New Preston, was a grand summer house and now makes a fine inn with a highly regarded restaurant. Rooms cost $275 up to $320 on weekends, breakfast included, about $50 less during the week. For $35 more per room per night, you can have a full dinner as well.

## NORTH TO SALISBURY

Almost every town in the northwest corner of Connecticut has a historic inn or two, a main street with a few antique and handicraft shops and an art gallery.

From Lake Waramaug, go north on CT 45 via Warren to **Cornwall Bridge**, stopping for a look at its famous namesake covered bridge.

North of Cornwall Bridge, flanking US 7, is **Housatonic Meadows State Park** (☎ 860-927-3238), famous for its 2-mile-long stretch

of Carse Brook set aside exclusively for fly fishing. The *campground* (☎ 860-672-6772) has 102 sites and is open from mid-April to mid-October.

The town of **Lime Rock**, west of US 7 along CT 112, is famous for its automobile racetrack, the Lime Rock Park Raceway (☎ 860-435-0896).

The *Inn at Iron Masters* (☎ 860-435-9844), on CT 44 in nearby Lakeville, can provide moderately priced lodging for $95 on weekdays, $135 on Friday and Saturday nights, breakfast included.

## SALISBURY

This pristine New England village is Connecticut's answer to the gracious towns of Massachusetts' Berkshire hills, just to the north across the state line. Salisbury prides itself on its beautiful inns, its good restaurants and its wealthy real estate brokers.

The 23-room *White Hart Inn* (☎ 860-435-0030), on the village green right where CT 41 and US 44 meet, has the perfect front porch for watching the minimal activity in the town, and frilly chintz-filled rooms for $119 to $199. The dining room, called *Julie's New American Sea Grill*, serves all three meals.

Just across US 44 is the 10-room *Ragamount Inn* (☎ 860-435-2372), open from May through October, which also has a good restaurant.

*Under Mountain Inn* (☎ 860-435-0242, 482 Under Mountain Rd) is an 18th-century farmhouse that's perfect for a country getaway. Rates for the seven rooms are $350 to $410 double for two nights, breakfast and dinner included.

Tea-lovers will want to know about Mary O'Brien's *Chaiwalla* (☎ 860-435-9758, 1 Main St (US 44)), which serves many varieties of tea, especially unblended Darjeelings (unblended teas are a tea-drinker's equivalent to estate-bottled wines, brewpub beer and single-malt scotches). Traditional accompaniments such as open-faced sandwiches, scones and shortbread are also served 10 am to 6 pm daily.

# Vermont

Vermont is one of the most rural states in the union. We're talking rolling farmlands as green as billiard felt and littered with cows; backcountry roads where the only traffic is the local farmer's tractor; and the backbone of the Green Mountains standing tall. (In fact, the name Vermont is drawn from the French *vert mont,* which means 'green mountain.')

Vermont is small, with a population of only about half a million people. It has only one city worthy of the name – Burlington – with a population of a mere 50,000. It's a land of towns and villages, self-sufficient in the way of the old-fashioned USA before jet planes and interstate highways.

Some of its towns bear the scars of the Industrial Revolution: Once-proud 19th-century brick factories sit by the riverside now somewhat forlorn and dispirited, recycled for storage or retail space. But many Vermont towns and villages are proud inheritors of the New England traditions of hard, honest work, good taste and staunch patriotism. Some could be virtual museums of pristine New England architecture and town planning.

Vermont is busiest with visitors in winter, when its many ski slopes draw enthusiasts from Albany, New York; New York City; Boston; Hartford, Connecticut; and Montreal, Canada. But if you want to see lush green pastures, summer is the more splendid time, and fall foliage is positively glorious.

To enjoy Vermont properly, you must get out of your car and hike into the forests or canoe down a rushing stream. Don't rush it. Enjoy the land and the friendly people.

## Information

Information on the state is available from the Vermont Dept of Tourism and Marketing (☎ 802-828-3236, 800-837-6668, www .travel-vermont.com), 6 Baldwin St, Montpelier, VT 05633-1301, open weekdays during business hours. Contact them in advance for a free detailed road map. This organization maintains Vermont Welcome Centers on I-91 near the Massachusetts state line, on VT 4A near the New York state line and on I-89 near the Canadian border.

For information on the best spots to see colorful foliage (fall only), call the state's Autumn Foliage Hotline (☎ 802-828-3239).

## Highlights

- Driving VT 100 from Killington to Waterbury
- Strolling through the historic villages of Newfane, Grafton and Craftsbury Common
- Biking a rural route through fall foliage
- A day hike on Vermont's Long Trail
- Crossing Lake Champlain by ferry from Burlington
- Touring the Shelburne Museum
- Seeing Vermont cheese being made at the Plymouth Cheese Company in Plymouth
- Sampling the fare at the Ben & Jerry's Ice Cream Factory in Waterbury

# VERMONT

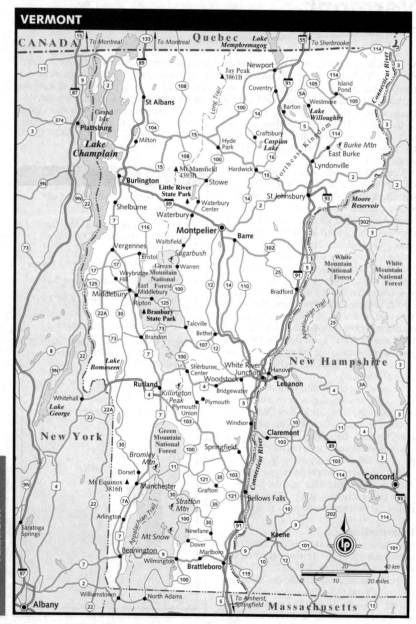

The Vermont Chamber of Commerce (☎ 802-223-3443, www.vtchamber.com), PO Box 37, Montpelier, VT 05601, offers information on Vermont businesses, including hotels, restaurants and other tourist services. It's open 8:30 am to 5 pm weekdays.

The Vermont Ski Areas Association (☎ 802-223-2439, www.skivermont.com), PO Box 368, 26 State St, Montpelier, VT 05601, can provide you with helpful information on planning a ski trip to the area. For daily reports on skiing conditions (in winter only), call ☎ 802-229-0531.

## Getting There & Around

**Air** Vermont's major airport is in Burlington, which is served by large and small planes, but there is also a commercial airport in Rutland. Delta, Continental, Northwest and US Airways service these airports. Other gateways to Vermont include Albany, New York; Montreal, Canada; Hartford, Connecticut; and Boston.

**Bus** Based in Burlington, Vermont Transit (☎ 802-864-6811, 800-451-3292 New England, www.vermonttransit.com) provides land transport to major towns in Vermont as well as to Manchester, New Hampshire; Keene, New Hampshire; Boston; and Albany.

Greyhound Lines (☎ 800-231-2222, www .greyhound.com) operates five buses daily between Burlington and Montreal. The three-hour trip costs $18 one way.

**Train** Taking Amtrak's (☎ 800-872-7245, www.amtrak.com) *Ethan Allen Express* or *Vermonter* is the relaxing way to travel around the state. The *Ethan Allen* departs from New York City and makes stops in Fair Haven and Rutland, with continuing bus service to the Killington and Okemo ski resorts in winter. Space for storing skis and snowboards is available at no additional charge. The *Vermonter* originates in New York, makes two stops in Connecticut (New Haven and Hartford) and nine in Vermont (Brattleboro, Bellows Falls, Windsor, White River Junction, Randolph, Montpelier, Waterbury-Stowe, Burlington and St Albans) before ending its journey in Montreal.

If you're a biker, you can buy one ticket on the *Vermonter* and get on and off as many times as you like, as long as you reserve a space for you and your bike ahead of time.

**Car** Though Vermont is not a particularly large state, it is mountainous. The I-89 and I-91 provide speedy access to certain areas of the state, but the rest of the time you must plan to take it slow and enjoy the winding roads and mountain scenery.

VT 100 is the state's scenic highway, snaking its way north from the Massachusetts border right through the center of Vermont, almost to Quebec. Along the way it passes through, or near, many of the things you've come to see. If time allows, take VT 100, not one of the interstate highways.

**Boat** Ferries crossing Lake Champlain carry passengers, bikes and cars between New York state and Vermont. Service is seasonal, so call for the latest schedules.

Ferries operated by the Lake Champlain Transportation Company (☎ 802-864-9804) run between Plattsburgh, New York, and Grand Isle; Port Kent, New York, and Burlington; and Essex, New York, and Charlotte. They also operate cruises and charters.

The Fort Ti Ferry (☎ 802-897-7999) runs from Larrabees Point (reached via VT 74) in Shoreham to Ticonderoga Landing (also known as Ferry Rd), three-quarters of a mile from the center of Fort Ticonderoga, New York. The trip takes about seven minutes, and the ferry runs 8 am to 6 pm daily, except in July and August, when it runs 7 am to 8 pm. People ride for 50¢; bicycles and motorcycles are $3; cars are $6 one way and $10 roundtrip. Recreational vehicles (RVs) cost $7 to $30 one way.

# Southern Vermont

Tidy white churches and inns surround village greens throughout historic southern Vermont, home to several towns that predate the Revolutionary War. In summer, the roads between the three 'cities' of Brattleboro,

## A Taste of Vermont

Vermont is famous for its dairy farms, especially for Vermont cheddar cheese. Ben Cohen and Jerry Greenfield, founders of the Ben & Jerry's premium ice cream company, established themselves in Vermont because of its good dairy industry. You can visit their factory in Waterbury Center near Stowe.

The large number of dairy cattle has also given rise to another Vermont institution: the cow shop. A cow shop may be an elaborate store or a simple pushcart that sells jokey gear based on the black-and-white mottle of the Holstein. The first time you see a cow shop it's funny, the second time boring, the third time depressing.

Vermont maple syrup and maple sugar candy are also big exports, even though maple trees can be tapped well into Canada and as far south as Pennsylvania and west to Wisconsin.

Perhaps the best of Vermont products are its crafts: textiles, carvings of wood and stone, wrought ironwork and pottery. The Vermont State Craft Center organizes exhibits and sales at outlets, the foremost of which is at Frog Hollow in Middlebury.

**Tom Brosnahan**

Bennington and Manchester roll over green hills; in winter, they wind their way toward the ski slopes of Mt Snow, southern Vermont's cold-weather playground. For those on foot, the Appalachian Trail passes through the Green Mountain National Forest here, offering a colorful hiking experience during the fall foliage season.

## BRATTLEBORO

The site of Vermont's first colonial settlement (1724), Brattleboro is the first town you're likely to encounter if you drive straight to Vermont from Boston or New York.

Brattleboro is one of Vermont's larger towns (population 12,000), a pleasant and workaday sort of place with an interesting ambience: This is where the USA's 1960s 'alternative' lifestyle settled down to live. You'll see lots of bookstores, art galleries and male facial hair. Don't be put off by the harsh red brick exterior of Brattleboro's buildings. This might not be quintessential Vermont, but those buildings house some of the finest restaurants in the state, as well as a welcoming community.

### History

Fort Dummer, a wooden stockade, was built on Whetstone Brook in 1724 to defend the local settlers against Indian raids. The town received its royal charter a year later and took its name from Colonel William Brattle, Jr, of the King's Militia, who never got the chance to visit his namesake.

Despite its country-town ambience, Brattleboro has seen its share of history. The first postage stamp used in the USA was made here in 1846. Jubilee Jim Fisk, the partner of railroad robber baron Jay Gould, was born here and was buried here after he died in a quarrel over a woman. Dr Robert Wesselhoeft developed the Wesselhoeft Water Cure using the waters of Whetstone Brook and treated such luminaries as Harriet Beecher Stowe and Henry Wadsworth Longfellow from 1846 to 1871.

The Mormon leader Brigham Young was born in nearby Windham County in 1801. Rudyard Kipling married a Brattleboro girl in 1892 and lived for a time in a big Brattleboro house he named Naulaukha. While living there, he wrote *The Jungle Book*.

The Green Mountain National Forest, VT

Old First Church, Old Bennington, VT

Canoeing in Vermont on a crisp fall day

Tapping for maple syrup in Vermont

The Holstein cow, a familiar sight in Vermont

The Vermont countryside is dotted with bright-red barns.

## Orientation

Brattleboro proper is east of I-91; West Brattleboro is west of the highway. Downtown Brattleboro's commercial district is surprisingly compact, with most of the good restaurants clustered around the landmark Latchis Hotel.

## Information

A Vermont Information Booth (☎ 802-257-1112) sits on VT 9 on the western outskirts of West Brattleboro, near the town's covered bridge. The Brattleboro Chamber of Commerce (☎ 802-254-4565, fax 254-5675, www.sover.net/~bratchmb) is at 180 Main St, Brattleboro, VT 05301. It's open 8:30 am to 5 pm weekdays.

Beneath the 2nd-floor restaurant Common Ground (see Places to Eat, below) is Everyone's Books, a store that sells political literature and T-shirts with phrases such as, 'Discover Columbus's legacy – 500 years of racist oppression and stolen land.'

## Things to See & Do

At the center of the town's commercial district – and of its history in this century – is the pure art deco **Latchis Building**, which

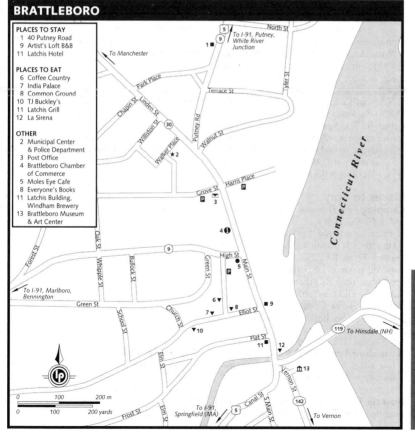

**BRATTLEBORO**

PLACES TO STAY
1   40 Putney Road
9   Artist's Loft B&B
11  Latchis Hotel

PLACES TO EAT
6   Coffee Country
7   India Palace
8   Common Ground
10  TJ Buckley's
11  Latchis Grill
12  La Sirena

OTHER
2   Municipal Center & Police Department
3   Post Office
4   Brattleboro Chamber of Commerce
5   Moles Eye Cafe
8   Everyone's Books
11  Latchis Building, Windham Brewery
13  Brattleboro Museum & Art Center

houses the Latchis Theatre, Latchis Hotel and Latchis Grille. Built in the 1930s by Demetrius Latchis, a Greek immigrant successful in the fruit business, the building has been nicely restored and still serves its original purposes. You can stay and dine in the hotel and see first-run movies in the theater.

The **Brattleboro Museum & Art Center** (☎ 802-257-0124), in the Union Railroad Station, is right in the center of town near the intersection of VT 119 and VT 142. In addition to the permanent collection of Estey reed organs made in Brattleboro during the late 19th century, the museum displays changing art and history exhibitions. It's open 10 am to 6 pm daily except Monday from mid-May through October. Adults pay $4, seniors and students $2; children under 18 are free.

Windham County has 30 **covered bridges**. For a free driving guide that will lead you to them, contact the Brattleboro Chamber of Commerce (see Information, above).

Vermont Canoe Touring (☎ 802-257-5008, 254-3908), Veterans Memorial Bridge, 451 Putney Rd (US 5), north of Brattleboro, offers guided **canoe** jaunts down the Connecticut or West Rivers. To find this outfitter, go north on US 5 (Putney Rd) to the bridge where the West River meets the Connecticut River.

## Places to Stay

**Camping** *Fort Dummer State Park* (☎ 802-254-2610, 483-2001) has 61 sites for $13 (10 of them lean-to shelters), hot showers and hiking trails. It's open late May to early September. From I-91 exit 1, go north a few hundred yards on US 5, then a half mile east on Fairground Rd, then a mile south on Main St to Old Guilford Rd.

*Hidden Acres Campground* (☎ 802-254-2098, 254-2724) has lots of services, even miniature golf, for a base rate of $16. It's on US 5 about 2½ miles north of I-91 exit 3. *Brattleboro North KOA* (☎ 800-468-8562) is a few miles farther north and even more elaborate, with sites for $18 to $26.

**Hostels** Run by Hostelling International/American Youth Hostels, the nearest hostel, the *HI/AYH – Vagabond* (☎ 802-874-4096), VT 30, Box 224, East Jamaica, VT 05343, is in a stunning locale 25 miles north of Brattleboro along VT 30. Vagabond serves as a hostel from late May through mid-October, and a ski lodge-hostel the rest of the year. Office hours are 5 to 9 pm; the 20 beds are priced at $14. Couples can request one of the few private rooms. Reserve your place at least 24 hours ahead.

**Motels** Motels line Putney Rd (US 5) north of Brattleboro and VT 9 west of town. The *Molly Stark Motel* (☎ 802-254-2440), on VT 9, 3 miles west of I-91, has 14 nice units for $42.

The small *West Village Motel* (☎ 802-254-5610, 480 Western Ave), also on VT 9, is simple, just as cheap and a bit closer to the center of town.

**Hotels** One of the better places to stay today, as it was in the 1930s, is the *Latchis Hotel* (☎ 802-254-6300, 50 Main St), with comfortable renovated rooms for $75 to $95.

**Inns** One of the most unique places to stay in Vermont is the *Artist's Loft B&B* (☎ 802-257-5181, 103 Main St) in the heart of town. Gracious innkeepers and renowned artists Patricia Long and William Hays only have one room, but what a room! Situated in a 125-year-old building, this spacious 3rd-floor suite, the size of a large one-bedroom apartment, overlooks the expanse of the Connecticut River and the mountains in the background. The room costs $88 to $98.

On scenic Putney Rd, bordering the West River, sits *40 Putney Road* (☎ 802-254-6268, 800-941-2413). This 70-year-old estate has four bedrooms, all with private bath, in the $90 to $175 range. Canoe rentals on the river are a five-minute walk away.

## Places to Eat

*Coffee Country* (☎ 802-257-0032, 1 Harmony Place) attracts everyone from tongue-studded teenagers to 65-year-old farmers. Drop in for a cup of good java and hot baked goods.

***Common Ground*** (*☎ 802-257-0855, 25 Elliot St*), just off Main St, is perhaps New England's purest expression of 1960s alternative dining. Its 2nd-floor location continues to thrive, and for good reason: excellent, healthy food (fish and vegetarian) for low prices. Luncheon specials usually cost less than $6, and dinner is a bargain as well. It's closed Tuesday.

***La Sirena*** (*☎ 802-257-5234*), Main St, right by Whetstone Brook, serves organic Mexican food, with lots of brown rice and fresh veggies, at low prices ($7 or $8). Lunch is served Tuesday, Friday and Saturday, with dinner Tuesday through Sunday.

If you're in the mood for Indian food, try ***India Palace*** (*☎ 802-254-6143, 65 Elliot St*). At lunchtime, the affordable curries cost $4.50 to $5.95.

The ***Marina Restaurant*** (*☎ 802-257-7563*), Putney Rd, offers lunch and dinner in a glassed-enclosed patio with wonderful views of the West River. Food is reasonably priced, with fish and chips for $6.75, pastas for $7.25 to $8.75 and chicken dishes for $8.95.

***Latchis Grille*** (*☎ 802-254-4747, 6 Flat St*), in the Latchis Hotel, features views over Whetstone Brook and serves top-notch New American cuisine, including roasted chicken breast stuffed with fresh greens, fennel, walnuts and currents, with a black currant *velouté* ($14). The Windham Brewery is here as well. (See Entertainment, below.) Both establishments are open for lunch and dinner every day.

***TJ Buckley's*** (*☎ 802-257-4922, 132 Elliot St*) seats just 18 in a classic old diner, and the lucky 18 are in for an exceptional dinner. The menu of four entrees changes nightly, and locals rave about the food being the best in town.

## Entertainment

The oak-paneled ***Moles Eye Cafe*** (*☎ 802-257-0771*), at the corner of Main and High Sts in the former Brooks Hotel, has live entertainment Wednesday through Saturday and a well-stocked bar, as well as good meals at moderate prices.

The ***Windham Brewery*** (*☎ 802-254-4747, 6 Flat St*) is in the Latchis Hotel. Try a pint of Olde Guilford Porter, a dark, medium-bodied ale ($2.75).

## Getting There & Away

**Bus** Vermont Transit (*☎ 802-864-6811, 800-451-3292* in New England) runs four buses daily between Hanover, New Hampshire, and Springfield, Massachusetts, with connections to Hartford, New York City, Burlington and Montreal.

**Train** Amtrak's *Vermonter* (*☎ 800-872-7245*, www.amtrak.com) stops in Brattleboro. See the introductory Getting There & Around section of this chapter for more details on the *Vermonter*'s route.

**Car** Driving details for Brattleboro are as follows:

| destination | distance | hr:min |
|---|---|---|
| Bennington, VT | 40 miles | 1:10 |
| Marlboro, VT | 8 miles | 0:20 |
| Springfield, MA | 65 miles | 1:15 |
| Wilmington, VT | 21 miles | 0:45 |

## MARLBORO

Upon first sight, the village of Marlboro appears pretty but unremarkable: a white church, a white inn, a white village office building and a few white houses, all a short distance off the Molly Stark Trail (VT 9), 8 miles west of Brattleboro.

However, to lovers of chamber music, Marlboro looms large as the home of the Marlboro Music Fest, founded and directed for many years by the late Rudolf Serkin and attended by Pablo Casals. On weekends from mid-July to mid-August, the small Marlboro College is alive with music students and concertgoers, who pack the small, 700-seat auditorium.

Many concerts sell out almost immediately, so it's essential to reserve your seats in advance. Write to Marlboro Music, 135 S 18th St, Philadelphia, PA 19103, for information; after June 20, call *☎ 802-254-2394*. Tickets cost $5 to $20.

Heading west from Marlboro on VT 9 brings you to the top of **Hogback Mountain** (2410 feet). At the high point, there's a lookout and the *Skyline Restaurant (☎ 802-464-3536)*, a moderately priced place to stop for a snack or a meal, with its marvelous '100-mile' view.

For camping, *Molly Stark State Park (☎ 802-464-5460)*, on VT 9, 3 miles east of Wilmington, has 34 sites (10 lean-tos) for $14 to $16, hot showers, and hiking trails with panoramic views. It's open late May through mid-October.

## NEWFANE & GRAFTON

Vermont has dozens of pretty villages, but Newfane and Grafton are near the top of everyone's list. All the picturesque sights you expect in a Vermont town are here: tall old trees, white, high-steepled churches, excellent inns and gracious old houses. In spring, both villages are busy making maple sugar; in summer come the yard sales; fall sees the arrival of 'leaf peepers'; and winter brings couples seeking good food and cozy rooms in a cold-weather hideaway.

### Orientation

Newfane is on VT 30, 12 miles northwest of Brattleboro, 19 miles northeast of Wilmington and 15 miles south of Grafton. Grafton is at the junction of VT 121 and VT 35.

### Things to See & Do

A short stroll shows you all of Newfane – you'll see the stately Congregational Church (1839) and the Windham County Courthouse (1825), built in Greek Revival style, and a few antique shops.

Graceful Grafton is not that way by accident. In the 1960s, the Windham Foundation, a private foundation, established a program for the restoration and preservation of the entire village, and it has been eminently successful. It is virtually an open-air museum. The real museum, however, is the **Grafton Historical Society** (☎ 802-843-2584), on Main St near the post office and south of the Old Tavern. It's open on weekend afternoons in summer.

The **Grafton Village Cheese Company** (☎ 802-843-2221), a half mile south of the village on Townshend Rd, makes Covered Bridge Cheddar, which you can sample while you watch it being made. The Cheese Company is open 8 am to 4 pm weekdays and 10 am to 4 pm weekends.

### Places to Stay & Eat

**Newfane** Tucked into the deep forest, *Townshend State Park (☎ 802-365-7500)*, on VT 30, 3 miles north of Newfane, is one of the better places to camp in the state. The 34 tent sites ($13) are open from early May through mid-October. Hiking trails include the sometimes steep, challenging path to the summit of Bald Mountain (1680 feet), a rocky climb that rises 1100 feet in less than a mile. Other trails are easier. There's swimming and boating at the nearby Army Corps of Engineers' Recreation Area at Townshend Dam. The West River is good for canoe trips.

Most people stop in Newfane just long enough for a meal or a night at the *Four Columns Inn (☎ 802-365-7713, 21 West St)*, located in the town center. The 1830s Greek Revival inn has a fine dining room serving New American cuisine with Vermont ingredients, and 15 guest rooms priced from $100 to $205.

The *West River Lodge (☎ 802-365-7745)*, just outside of town, features English riding workshops (it has its own stables) and farmhouse accommodations for $80 to $90, breakfast included.

Just north of Newfane is one of the region's very finest restaurants, *Mezzanotte (☎ 802-365-4545, 117 Hill Rd)*, off VT 30. Innovative pasta and Italian dishes cost $10 to $17 at dinner.

**Grafton** The central landmark here is *The Old Tavern at Grafton (☎ 802-843-2231, 800-843-1801)*, at VT 35 and Townshend Rd. The original inn is quite formal, the tavern restaurant in the adjoining barn less so. The 65 rooms cost $125 to $185.

*The Inn at Woodchuck Hill (☎ 802-843-2398)*, outside Grafton on Middletown Rd, s a 1790s farmhouse on 200 acres with its own hiking and cross-country ski trails. The antique-filled guest rooms cost $110 to $140, full breakfast included.

## WILMINGTON/MT SNOW

Wilmington is the gateway to Mt Snow/ Haystack, one of New England's best ski resorts in the winter and an excellent spot for mountain biking and golfing in the summer. Many of the restaurants and stores in town cater to families, the resort's predominant clientele.

### Orientation

The state's central north-south highway, VT 100, goes north from Wilmington past Haystack and Mt Snow, and VT 9, the main route across southern Vermont, is Wilmington's main street.

Wilmington is 21 miles west of Brattleboro (45 minutes on the winding road) and 20 miles east of Bennington (40 minutes).

### Information

The Mt Snow/Haystack Chamber of Commerce (☎ 802-464-8092, www.visitvermont com), PO Box 3, Wilmington, VT 05363, maintains an information booth on the eastern outskirts of Wilmington at the junction of VT 100 and VT 9. It is open 10 am to 5 pm weekdays and 11 am to 4 pm weekends, May through October.

### Mt Snow/Haystack

The terrain at Mt Snow (☎ 802-464-3333, 800-245-7669) is diverse, making it popular with the whole family. The resort features 134 trails (20% beginner, 60% intermediate, 20% expert) and 26 lifts, plus a vertical drop of 1700 feet and the snowmaking ability to blanket 80% of the trails. Cross-country routes cover more than 60 miles. Come summer, Mt Snow hosts one of the best mountain-biking schools in the country.

### Places to Stay

**Camping** See Marlboro, earlier in this chapter, for information on *Molly Stark State Park*.

**Motels** The *Vintage Motel* (☎ 802-464-8824, 800-899-9660), on VT 9 a mile west of the town center, has 18 tidy units open all year and a heated pool. Rooms cost $70, light breakfast included.

The *Nutmeg Inn* (☎ 802-464-3351), also on VT 9 west of Wilmington, is a larger, fancier motel with 14 rooms for $89 to $199.

**Inns** Built in 1885, the red, rambling *Deerfield Valley Inn* (☎ 802-464-6333), on VT 100 in West Dover, offers nine antique-filled rooms priced $69 to $109. Ask about ski and golf packages.

The *Red Shutter Inn* (☎ 802-464-3768), on VT 9 in Wilmington, is a grand old house dating from 1894. The seven rooms and two suites, each with a unique decor and private bath, range from $105 to $145.

Only a mile from the slopes of Mt Snow is the elegant *Snow Goose* (☎ 802-464-3984, 888-604-7964), VT 100, West Dover. Twelve large rooms, priced $110 to $210, have large Jacuzzis and private decks overlooking the forest.

*Trail's End* (☎ 802-859-2585), on Smith Rd about 4 miles north of Wilmington, has a country-home feel and 15 cozy rooms with private bath for $110 to $170, full breakfast included. Take VT 100 north to East Dover Rd, which leads to Smith Rd.

The *White House of Wilmington* (☎ 802-464-2135, 800-541-2135, fax 802-464-5222), on VT 9, crowns a hill on the eastern outskirts of the town. This grand, white Federal mansion has an indoor pool, a large outdoor pool, great cross-country trails and luxury rooms for $138 to $208 a double, full breakfast included.

### Places to Eat

Judging from the muddy pickup trucks in the parking lot, *Cup N' Saucer* (☎ 802-464-5813), VT 100 in Wilmington, is where locals go for breakfast and lunch. Sit around the circular counter and order a burger for $1.85 or a hot open-faced turkey sandwich for $4.50. It's open 6 am to 2:30 pm daily.

*Dot's* (☎ 802-464-7284, 464-5476) has two locations: on Main St in the village and on

VT 100 near the slopes of Mt Snow. Both places are popular with skiers in search of incredibly cheap breakfasts and lunches ($2 to $4.50). Dot's is also known for quick service.

The **Silo** (☎ 802-464-2553), across VT 100 in West Dover, is a bit more upscale but also a good choice for pasta, pizza and sandwiches at lunch.

A devoted flock of locals venture to **Julie's Café** (☎ 802-464-2078), VT 100 in West Dover, for large salads and veggie pasta dishes.

During ski season, you'll find a line at **The Roadhouse** (☎ 802-464-5017), VT 100 in Wilmington, served from 6 to 10 pm nightly, features rack of lamb, baked salmon filet and fresh Vermont trout ($15.95 to $22.95, including salad and dessert).

**Mother's Deli** (☎ 802-464-3354), on W Main St in Wilmington, gets rave reviews for its chili. An 8oz bowl with tortilla chips costs $3.50.

**Alonzo's** (☎ 802-464-2355), W Main St in Wilmington, is the place to go for Italian food. Dinner prices range from $7.95 to $14.95. It's open 4 to 10 pm daily.

Since 1972, **Poncho's Wreck** (☎ 802-464-9320, 10 S Main St), Wilmington, has been a favorite with the après-ski crowd. The menu is extensive, but don't stray too far from the seafood dishes.

### Getting There & Around

On weekends in winter, Absolute Adventures (☎ 212-921-9161, 802-464-2810) offers a shuttle service from New York's Upper West Side to Mt Snow. Shuttles depart Manhattan at 7 pm Friday night and arrive at Mt Snow at 11:30 pm (drop-off at your accommodation).

On Sunday, they leave Mt Snow at 5 pm and arrive in Manhattan at 10 pm. The cost is $65 roundtrip. Advance reservations are recommended.

To reach Mt Snow/Haystack from Wilmington, travel 10 miles north on VT 100. Free bus service, called the Moover (☎ 802-464-8487), transports skiers from Wilmington to the slopes of Mt Snow every 30 minutes between 7 am and 10 pm.

## BENNINGTON

Bennington, a felicitous mix of picture perfect Vermont village (Old Bennington) and workaday town (Bennington proper), is the more refined of Vermont's two large southern towns. Home to Bennington College and the famous Bennington Museum, it is a historic place, famed for its tall monument commemorating the crucial Battle of Bennington during the Revolutionary War. Robert Frost, one of the most famous American poets of the 20th century, is buried in Bennington.

### History

In August of 1777, during the Revolutionary War, British General John ('Gentleman Johnny') Burgoyne, his supplies depleted during the battle at Fort Ticonderoga, sent two units toward Bennington to seize military supplies held by the colonials. He misjudged the size of the American defenses and was unaware that General John Stark, a veteran of Bunker Hill and a commander under Washington at the battles of Trenton and Princeton, was leading the defense.

Stark headed off the British advance in Walloomsac, New York, 6 miles west of Bennington. 'There are the Redcoats!' he exclaimed. 'They will be ours tonight or Molly Stark sleeps a widow!'

The two sides clashed on August 16, 1777. The ferocious battle lasted two hours, with the Americans victorious, but British reinforcements still posed a threat to Stark's troops. The American victory was assured by Colonel Seth Warner and his Green Mountain Boys, who arrived in time to counter the British resurgence. The Americans captured more than 800 British regulars, about one-sixth of Burgoyne's total force. (Every year Arlington, Vermont, re-enacts the exploits of the Green Mountain boys with Ethan Allan Days – 'Fun with the Green Mountain Boys,' held in mid-June. See the boxed text 'Ethan Allen & Vermont' in the Facts about New England chapter.)

Unable to procure supplies in Bennington and suffering badly from the loss of soldiers, Burgoyne's forces were greatly weakened when they went into the Battle of

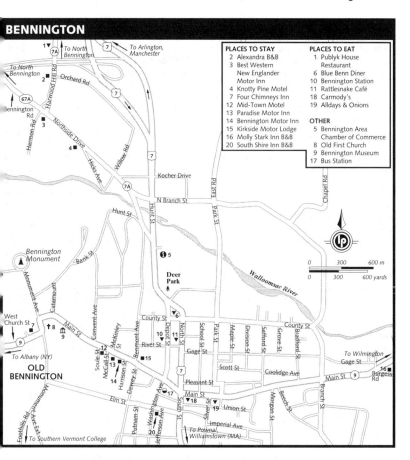

## BENNINGTON

**PLACES TO STAY**
2 Alexandra B&B
3 Best Western New Englander Motor Inn
4 Knotty Pine Motel
7 Four Chimneys Inn
12 Mid-Town Motel
13 Paradise Motor Inn
14 Bennington Motor Inn
15 Kirkside Motor Lodge
16 Molly Stark Inn B&B
20 South Shire Inn B&B

**PLACES TO EAT**
1 Publyk House Restaurant
6 Blue Benn Diner
10 Bennington Station
11 Rattlesnake Café
18 Carmody's
19 Alldays & Onions

**OTHER**
5 Bennington Area Chamber of Commerce
8 Old First Church
9 Bennington Museum
17 Bus Station

aratoga later that fall. After a disastrous defeat there, General Burgoyne surrendered his entire command to the Americans, ending his drive down the Hudson Valley, which, if successful, would have cut the colonies in two.

### Orientation

Converging in Bennington are US 7, VT 7A and VT 9, making the city an important crossroads. Most businesses, lodgings and restaurants are in downtown Bennington, but the Bennington Monument, Bennington

Museum and prettiest houses are in Old Bennington, a mile from the center of town, at the western end of Main St on the way to New York state. The actual site of the Battle of Bennington is in Walloomsac, New York, 6 miles west of the monument.

### Information

The Bennington Area Chamber of Commerce (☎ 802-447-3311, www.bennington .com), Veterans Memorial Drive (US 7), maintains an information office that's open 9 am to 5 pm weekdays.

## Bennington Museum

Heading west from downtown Bennington via W Main St (VT 9), you climb the hill to the Bennington Museum (☎ 802-447-1571), a mile from the town center.

The museum holds an outstanding collection of early Americana: furniture, glassware and pottery (made in Bennington), sculpture, paintings, dolls, toys and military memorabilia.

The museum is especially noted for its rich collection of paintings by **Anna Mary Moses** (1860-1961), a New York farm wife. At the age of 70, when she could no longer keep up with the heavy physical demands of farm labor, 'Grandma Moses' began to paint pictures. Her lively, natural depictions of farm life were eagerly sought out, and she painted until she was 100 years old.

The museum is open 9 am to 5 pm daily from March to December 23 and on weekends only in January and February. Admission costs $6 for adults and $5.50 for seniors and children aged 12 to 17; younger children are free.

## Old Bennington

A few hundred yards west of the museum is the charming hilltop site of the colonial town of Old Bennington, with 80 substantial Georgian and Federal houses (dating from 1761 – the year Bennington was founded – to 1830) arranged along a broad mall.

The **Old First Church**, towering over the village center, was built in 1806 in Palladian style. Its churchyard holds the remains of five Vermont governors, numerous Revolutionary War soldiers and poet **Robert Frost** (1874-1963). Frost was born in California of New England stock and lived and wrote in England for a time, but he is famous for his poems of the New England experience, inspired by his life on several New England farms. Although never successful at farming, Frost became the best-known, and perhaps best-loved, American poet of the 20th century. Near Franconia, New Hampshire, is the Frost Place, one of his farms (see the White Mountains section of the New Hampshire chapter). Another of the poet's farms is in Ripton, Vermont, near Middlebury Col-

lege's Bread Loaf School of English (se Ripton, later in this chapter).

Across from the church, the ramshackl **Walloomsac Inn** (1764) was a workin hostelry up until the 1980s, complete wit Victorian-era plumbing and spartan appoint ments. It's now closed.

Up the hill to the north is the **Benningto Monument** (☎ 802-447-0550). The impressiv obelisk, built between 1887 and 1891, is th loftiest structure in Vermont. The origina staircase has been replaced by an elevator, s you can ride the 306 feet to the top. The ele vator is open 9 am to 5 pm daily from Apr through October; admission costs $1/50¢ fo adults/children. Purchase tickets at th nearby gift shop. The view is quite nice.

To reach the actual site of the Battle c Bennington, which is 6 miles away, follo the 'Bennington Battlefield' signs from th monument, along back roads, through a his toric covered bridge (there are two other nearby) to North Bennington, then go wes on VT 67 to the **Bennington Battlefield His toric Site**. Admission is free, and picnic table are provided under welcome shade.

Just off VT 67A, at the corner of West an Park Sts in North Bennington, is the **Park McCullough House Museum** (☎ 802-442 5441). The 35-room mansion was built i 1865 for Trenor and Laura Hall Park of Nev York City as their summer 'cottage.' Today, holds period furnishings and a fine collec tion of antique dolls, toys and carriages. It open 10 am to 4 pm (last tour at 3 pm) from May through October. Admission is $5/4/ for adults/seniors/students.

## Canoeing

Batten Kill Canoe Ltd (☎ 802-362-2800, 800 421-5268), on VT 7A, 20 minutes away i Arlington, can outfit you for a day trip ($4 per canoe) on the Batten Kill River, a lovel stream that winds through a Vermont fores down to the Hudson River. The staff als arranges longer trips, from two to 10 days combined with stays at inns.

## Cross-Country Skiing

The Prospect Mountain Cross-Country Sk Touring Center (☎ 802-442-2575), VT 9

Woodford, in the Green Mountains about 20 minutes east of Bennington, always seems to be covered in snow. More than 20 miles of groomed trails wind through the area.

## Maple Sugaring

Farms in Bennington County produce lots of delicious maple syrup. Shops in town sell it, but it's much more interesting to visit one of the farms during maple sugaring (March and April), when the sap is collected and boiled in the sugar house to yield maple syrup. For a list of the farms that give demonstrations, tastings and tours, contact the Bennington County Conservation District (☎ 802-442-2275), 118 South St, Bennington, VT 05201.

## Places to Stay

**Camping** *Woodford State Park* (☎ *802-447-7169)*, on VT 9, 10 miles east of Bennington, has 102 sites (20 lean-tos) for $14 to $16, hot showers, a beach, boat and canoe rentals and hiking trails.

Several other campgrounds are off US 7 south of Bennington, near Pownal and the Massachusetts state line. *Shady Acres* (☎ *802-442-4960)*, on Jackson Cross Rd, less than a half mile from Pownal, charges $15. *Pine Hollow* (☎ *802-823-5569)* charges $18 to $20 for its 50 sites. To reach the campground from Bennington, follow US 7 south 6½ miles, turn left on Barbers Pond Rd, drive 1½ miles, and then turn right on Old Military Rd, proceeding for a half mile.

*Lake Shaftsbury State Park* (☎ *802-375-9978)*, on VT 7A, 2 miles south of Arlington, has 15 sites, all lean-tos, for $14. There's a beach, boat and canoe rentals, and a nature trail. It's open from late May through early September.

Nearby Arlington, north of Bennington, also has campgrounds. *Howell's* (☎ *802-375-6469)*, on School St, 1 mile off VT 7A/313, rents 70 sites for $16 each. *Camping on the Batten Kill* (☎ *802-375-6663)*, on VT 7A, also charges $16, with more than 100 sites open from mid-April through October.

**Hostels** Nestled in the Green Mountains, *Greenwood Lodge & Campsites* (☎ *802-442-*

*2547)*, in Woodford, 8 miles east of Bennington on VT 9 at Prospect Mountain, boasts one of the best sites for an HI/AYH hostel in Vermont. Accommodations include budget dorms ($14 to $17 per person) and guest rooms (singles/doubles cost $30/$36), as well as 20 campsites ($14) on 120 acres. Greenwood is open from mid-May to mid-October and during ski season. Office hours are 8 to 10 am and 5 to 10 pm. Reserve by phone; no credit cards are accepted.

**Motels** *Harwood Hill Motel* (☎ *802-442-6278)*, on VT 7A, 2 miles north of Bennington, features fine views of the Bennington Monument and the town and charges an agreeable $40 to $64 for its 18 rooms.

*Mid-Town Motel* (☎ *802-447-0189, 107 W Main St)* has 17 rooms, economy units as well as deluxe efficiencies, for $45. The facilities include a pool and hot tub.

*Kirkside Motor Lodge* (☎ *802-447-7596, 250 W Main St)*, very near the marble church of St Francis de Sales, has 25 tidy rooms right in the center of town for $54 to $85.

*Knotty Pine Motel* (☎ *802-442-5487, 130 Northside Drive)*, on VT 7A, in a commercial strip just off US 7, has a fairly convenient location and decent rooms for $56 to $58.

*Paradise Motor Inn* (☎ *802-442-8351)* is the big, fancy place in town, with 76 rooms and suites ($61 to $96), a restaurant and all the amenities.

*Bennington Motor Inn* (☎ *802-442-5479, 800-359-9900, 143 W Main St)* is within walking distance of most sights and charges $62 to $68 for its 16 rooms.

*Best Western New Englander Motor Inn* (☎ *802-442-6311, 220 Northside Drive)*, near the Knotty Pine Motel, contains 58 rooms in a variety of styles, priced at $67 to $85.

Many other motels are south of Bennington, along US 7 on the way to Williamstown, Massachusetts.

**Inns** The following listings are all located in Bennington.

*Molly Stark Inn B&B* (☎ *802-442-9631, 800-356-3076, 1067 Main St)* is a big Victorian house (built in 1890) with an equally large sign and four comfy guest rooms

**VERMONT**

priced $70 to $95, some with private bath. In the backyard, a recently added honeymoon cottage, complete with Jacuzzi, rents for $145. The very gracious innkeepers serve an excellent breakfast.

*Alexandra B&B* (☎ 802-442-5619), VT 7A at Orchard Rd, is a tidy house about 2 miles north of Bennington. The six guest rooms cost $85 to $125, breakfast included.

*South Shire Inn B&B* (☎ 802-447-3839, 124 Elm St) is a Victorian inn furnished in antiques. Nine rooms all have private bath and air-con, and some have fireplaces; they cost $105 to $160.

*The Four Chimneys Inn & Restaurant* (☎ 802-447-3500, 21 West Rd) is the only B&B in Old Bennington. This grand white mansion, set amid verdant manicured lawns, has 11 comfortable rooms with private bath for $125 to $185.

Many more cozy inns and B&Bs lie north of Bennington in nearby Arlington; call the chamber of commerce (see Information, above) for further information.

### Places to Eat

*Alldays & Onions* (☎ 802-447-0043, 519 Main St) encourages you to create your own sandwich from its bewilderingly long blackboard menu of ingredients. Salads, soups, quiches and other light fare rule at breakfast and lunch. It's also popular in the evening, with entrees such as grilled swordfish and prime rib, priced from $11.95 to $17.95. Despite its name, Alldays is not open on Sunday.

For a longer menu with several international dishes, try the *Blue Benn Diner* (☎ 802-442-5140) on North St. The standard diner fare is supplemented with Mexican, Asian and vegetarian dishes. An average meal costs around $10. Breakfast begins at 6 am and is served all day.

*Rattlesnake Café* (☎ 802-447-7018, 230 North St) is the local Mexican joint. A hefty bean-and-cheese burrito will set you back $6.95. Try one of the strong margaritas ($4.25).

*Carmody's* (☎ 802-447-5847, 421 Main St), a large, bright restaurant, serves basic American fare: burgers, fries, pasta, seafood.

Set in an authentic 100-year-old train station, *Bennington Station* (☎ 802-447-1080, 150 Depot St) features an extensive menu of prime rib, fish, pasta, salad and children's dishes. Entrees range from $11.95 to $17.95.

The menu at the *Publyk House Restaurant* (☎ 802-442-8301), on VT 7A a mile or so north of the town center, offers traditional American food, including lots of sirloin, shrimp, crab and chicken, priced from $10 to $20 per entree. The setting is exceptional: Enjoy great views of Mt Anthony and the lofty Bennington Monument through the greenhouse glass.

### Getting There & Away

Vermont Transit (☎ 802-864-6811, 800-451-3292 in New England) runs three buses daily between Albany and Burlington, stopping in Bennington. See the general Getting There & Around section earlier in this chapter.

Driving details for Bennington are as follows:

| destination | distance | hr:min |
|---|---|---|
| Boston, MA | 140 miles | 3:10 |
| Brattleboro, VT | 40 miles | 1:10 |
| Manchester, VT | 19 miles | 0:30 |
| Williamstown, MA | 14 miles | 0:25 |
| Wilmington, VT | 20 miles | 0:40 |

## MANCHESTER

For almost two centuries, Manchester has been a resort. Formerly, it was the mountain scenery, equable summer climate and the Batten Kill River, one of Vermont's best trout streams, that drew the crowds.

Now the draw is mostly winter skiing and shopping, but Manchester is still busy in summer with hikers, golfers and shoppers. From mid-September to mid-November, one of Vermont's biggest fall festivals, the Stratton Arts Festival, takes place at nearby Stratton Mountain.

Two families put Manchester on the map. The first was that of native son Franklin Orvis (1824-1900), who became a New York businessman but then returned to Manchester to found the Equinox House Hotel

(1849). Orvis did much to beautify Manchester with the laying of marble sidewalks, the construction of public buildings and the opening of roads in the forest for excursions. Franklin's brother, Charles, founded the Orvis Company, makers of fly-fishing equipment, in 1856. The Manchester-based company now has a worldwide following.

The second family was that of Abraham Lincoln (1809-1865), 16th president of the USA. His wife, Mary Todd Lincoln (1818-1882), and their son Robert Todd Lincoln (1843-1926) came here during the Civil War,

and Robert returned to build a mansion, Hildene, a number of years later.

## Orientation

US 7 bypasses the town to the east; VT 7A goes right through the town's center.

Manchester has a split personality. When the locals say 'Manchester' or 'Manchester Village,' they're referring to the southern part of the town, a beautiful, dignified, historic Vermont village centered on the huge, venerable, posh Equinox Hotel. There are several other charming, expensive inns as well.

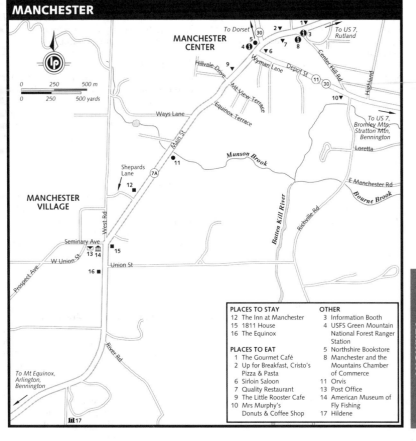

MANCHESTER

PLACES TO STAY
12 The Inn at Manchester
15 1811 House
16 The Equinox

PLACES TO EAT
1 The Gourmet Café
2 Up for Breakfast, Cristo's Pizza & Pasta
6 Sirloin Saloon
7 Quality Restaurant
9 The Little Rooster Cafe
10 Mrs Murphy's Donuts & Coffee Shop

OTHER
3 Information Booth
4 USFS Green Mountain National Forest Ranger Station
5 Northshire Bookstore
8 Manchester and the Mountains Chamber of Commerce
11 Orvis
13 Post Office
14 American Museum of Fly Fishing
17 Hildene

VERMONT

'Manchester Center,' a few miles north along VT 7A, used to be called Factory Point, but this name did not fit well with Manchester's resort image, and so it was changed. Manchester Center has several moderately priced inns and inexpensive-to-moderate restaurants, but the area is devoted mostly to upscale outlet stores – Mark Cross, Giorgio Armani, Polo, etc – and ye olde Vermont-type shops.

## Information

The Manchester and the Mountains Chamber of Commerce (☎ 802-362-2100, www .manchesterandmtns.com) maintains an information office on the village green in Manchester Center (open 9 am to 5 pm weekdays, 10 am to 4 pm Saturday, 10 am to 2 pm Sunday), a few hundred yards north of the main intersections in town along VT 7A. The chamber also helps visitors find hotel rooms.

The Northshire Bookstore (☎ 802-362-2200), on Main St in Manchester Center, is a good stop.

## Hildene

The wife and children of Abraham Lincoln, one of the USA's greatest presidents, had tragic lives. His wife went mad, and only one of his four sons lived to adulthood. That son was Robert Todd Lincoln, who served on General Grant's staff during the Civil War. He later became a corporate lawyer in Chicago, president of the Pullman Palace Car Company, Secretary of War and minister (ambassador) to Great Britain.

Robert Todd Lincoln built a 24-room Georgian Revival mansion, which he named Hildene, on VT 7A a short distance south of Manchester. He enjoyed the house until his death, and his great-granddaughter lived in the house until her death in 1975. Soon after, it was converted to a museum by the Friends of Hildene.

Many of the Lincoln family's personal effects and furnishings are still in the house, which has been authentically restored. Guided tours are offered 9:30 am to 4 pm daily, mid-May through October. Admission is $8/4 for adults/children. Call Friends of

Hildene (☎ 802-362-1788) for more information about tours of the house.

## American Museum of Fly Fishing

This museum (☎ 802-362-3300), at VT 7A and Seminary Ave, just north of Manchester Village, has perhaps the world's best display of fly-fishing equipment, including historic rods used by novelists Ernest Hemingway and Zane Grey and several US presidents. It's open 10 am to 4 pm daily, May through October, and on weekdays November to April. Admission is $3 for adults and free for children.

To examine the new stuff, go farther north, about a half mile, to the Orvis store (☎ 802-362-3750), on the west side of VT 7A, open 9 am to 6 pm daily. Try out a rod in the trout ponds on the grounds.

## Mt Equinox

A 5-mile drive takes you from Manchester to the summit of Mt Equinox (3835 feet). Follow VT 7A south out of Manchester and look for Sky Line Drive, a private toll road. Sky Line Drive (☎ 802-362-1114) is open 8 am to 10 pm daily, May through October. At the summit is the Equinox Mountain Inn (see Places to Stay, below, for details).

## Activities

For skiers, there's the Bromley Mountain (☎ 802-824-5522, 800-865-4786), VT 11 in Manchester, approximately 10 minutes from town. The small family resort features 42 downhill ski runs, nine chairlifts, and 84% snowmaking capacity. In summer, there's an Alpine Slide, and the chairlifts take hikers up to the trails that lead even higher – or back down the mountain. Vermont's Long Trail goes right through Bromley.

Well-known Stratton Mountain (☎ 802-297-2200, 800-843-6867), on VT 30 about 16 miles east of Manchester, is larger, with 90 trails, 12 lifts (including a 57-person summit gondola) and a vertical drop of more than 2000 feet on a 3875-foot mountain. The longest downhill skiing trail is 3 miles, and there are 10 miles of cross-country trails. In summer, there's lots of golf, tennis and hiking. The gondola will take you

## A Month in the Woods

America's first long-distance hiking trail, Vermont's Long Trail is a 264-mile mountainous corridor that runs the length of the state from Massachusetts to Canada.

Backpackers have been hiking the south-to-north ridge of the Green Mountains since 1930, when the Green Mountain Club finished clearing the length of the trail. Today, the Green Mountain Club has approximately 6200 members who maintain the trail system, 440 miles altogether when you include the 175 miles of side-trails.

And what an impressive network of trails it is. Often only 3 feet wide, the Long Trail crosses over streams, skirts every hidden pond from Massachusetts to Canada, weaves up and down mountains on open ridges to bare summits offering exceptional vistas of the entire state. Wave after wave of hillside gently rolls back to a sea of green dotted with the occasional

pasture or meadow. A little less than half of the trail is located inside the Green Mountain National Forest.

The trail is best taken from south to north so you don't have to read the *Guide Book of the Long Trail* backwards. Also recommended is *The Long Trail End-to-Ender's Guide*, packed with nitty-gritty details on equipment sales and repairs, mail drops and B&Bs that provide trailhead shuttle services. Both guides are published by the Green Mountain Club.

For shelter, the Green Mountain Club maintains more than 60 lodges, camps and lean-tos along the trail. Hikers can easily walk from one shelter to the next in a day because the rest stops were built at 5- to 7-mile intervals. However, it is imperative that you bring a tent in case a shelter is full. Although the trail is wonderful for a trip of several days, many hikers use it for day hikes.

For more information, contact the Green Mountain Club (☎ 802-244-7037), VT 100, PO Box 650, Waterbury Center, VT 05677.

and your mountain bike to the summit for an adventurous ride down.

The **Appalachian Trail** passes just east of Manchester, and in this area it is the same as Vermont's **Long Trail**. Shelters pop up about every 10 miles; some are staffed. The good day hikes here include one to the summit of Bromley Mountain and another to Stratton Pond. For details and maps, contact the USFS Green Mountain National Forest (☎ 802-362-2307) at the corner of VT 11 and VT 30 in Manchester Center.

The Batten Kill Sports Bicycle Shop (☎ 802-362-2734, 800-340-2734), on VT 11 and VT 30 between VT 7A and US 7, rents road, mountain and hybrid bikes for as little

as $18 per day, including helmet, lock, trail recommendations and map. The shop does repairs and is open daily in summer.

Green Mountain Adventures (☎ 802-362-1202, 375-2448), PO Box 1711, Manchester, VT 05255, organizes outdoor activities, including hiking, mountain biking, river tubing and canoe trips.

### Places to Stay

**Camping** At the *Emerald Lake State Park* (☎ *802-362-1655*), on US 7 just north of the village of East Dorset, there are 105 sites, including 32 lean-tos. Sites cost $14 to $16 and are open from late May on through mid-October. There's both swimming and canoeing on the 80-foot-deep lake and hiking through the mountains; some trails connect with the Long Trail.

Camping on the Batten Kill River, described earlier in the Bennington section, is not too far south of Manchester on VT 7A.

**Motels** *Wedgewood North Motel* (☎ 802-362-2145), north of Manchester on VT 7A, has 12 cozy little cottages trimmed with Wedgewood blue for $52 to $68, light breakfast included. Also on VT 7A, the *Stamford Motel* (☎ 802-362-2342) has 14 tidy units with the standard comforts for $60 to $70.

The *Aspen Motel* (☎ 802-362-2450), on VT 7A in Manchester, is a sprawling place with 25 rooms priced from $60 to $85.

The *Chalet Motel* (☎ 802-362-1622, 800-343-9900), on VT 11 and VT 30 east of the town center, is also very reasonably priced.

If the above motels are full, try the *Eyrie Motel* (☎ 802-362-1208), on US 7 in East Dorset, 7 miles north of Manchester Center. Eleven rooms cost $75.

*Palmer House Motel* (☎ 802-362-3600, 800-917-6245), VT 7A north of the Barnumville intersection, is a lavish resort motel with lots of services and 42 guest rooms priced from $90 to $120.

**Inns** *Seth Warner Inn* (☎ 802-362-3830,), on VT 7A, features a country decor and five rooms priced at $90.

*The Inn at Manchester* (☎ 802-362-1793, 800-273-1793), on VT 7A, has 18 rooms and four suites in a restored house and carriage house. Rates range from $100 to $150, with breakfast, tea and Saturday wine and cheese included. The clientele is loyal.

*Barnstead Innstead* (☎ 802-362-1619, 345 Bonnet St), in Manchester Center, is among the town's best inns for charm, location and price. The 14 rooms are in a renovated 1830s hay barn and have all the usual comforts for $100 to $150 in summer, somewhat more in foliage season.

*1811 House* (☎ 802-362-1811), VT 7A, is a grand Federal house built in the 1770s and surrounded by 7 acres of lawns and gardens. It's been an inn since 1811. The 14 antique-filled rooms cost $120 to $230.

**Resorts** You'll want to know about *The Equinox Mountain Inn* (☎ 802-362-4700, 800-362-4747), Manchester's, and arguably Vermont's, top place to stay. The property contains 183 rooms, an 18-hole golf course, indoor and outdoor pools and three tennis courts. Other activities include falconry, off-road driving and snowmobiling. Elegant rooms cost $189 to $329, depending upon the season. The original building here, the Marsh Tavern, dates from 1769.

## Places to Eat

The *Quality Restaurant* (☎ 802-362-9839, 735 Main St) has been here since 1920 and was run by the same family for over half a century. Normal Rockwell used it for the setting of his painting *War News*. The Quality has a long menu of breakfast items, salad plates and sandwiches for lunch, and dinner specials in the evening (until 9 pm), all at very good prices. *Christo's Pizza & Pasta* (☎ 802-362-2408), across the street, is a modern alternative.

*Up for Breakfast* (☎ 802-362-4204), above Christo's, is open for dinner five nights a week. Every breakfast dish, from huevos rancheros to wild turkey hash, is available for $4 to $8. Climb one flight of steps to reach the restaurant on the upper floor.

Manchester's down-home favorite for breakfast is *Mrs Murphy's Donuts & Coffee Shop* (☎ 802-362-1804), on VT 30 and VT 11, a few blocks east of Main St (look for the pickup trucks). Come for fresh doughnuts, decent coffee and more substantial bacon-and-egg 'tuck-ins' (think Egg McMuffin) at the lowest prices in town.

*The Gourmet Café* (☎ 802-362-1254), in the Green Mountain Village Shops, which are on VT 7A, is a casual place for cheap sandwiches ($4 to $6).

A wee bit more upscale is *The Little Rooster Cafe* (☎ 802-362-3496), on VT 7A. A flatbread sandwich with Vermont goat cheese or chicken *satay* costs $6.95.

The *Sirloin Saloon* (☎ 802-362-2600), on VT 30 and VT 11, east of VT 7A, claims to be Vermont's oldest steak house, and that's still the specialty, though there's good seafood, too. Wines are reasonably priced, and a full dinner might cost $20 with drinks. It's open for dinner every day.

A favorite with families is the very large *Laney's* (☎ 802-362-4456), on VT 30 and VT 11, east of VT 7A. Wood-fired pizzas cost $6.95 to $8.95, and pasta dishes start at $8.95.

Manchester's many inns have excellent (though pricey) dining rooms. *The Restaurant at Willow Pond* (☎ 802-362-4733), in the Inn at Willow Pond on VT 7A north of Manchester Center, serves northern Italian cuisine, with a long list of Italian wines. The signature dish is a half rack of lamb for $21.95.

Nestled deep in the woods and overlooking a stream is *Mistral's* (☎ 802-362-1779), on the Toll Rd off VT 30 and VT 11 (toward Bromley). Enjoy the scenery before dark and then dine on Norwegian salmon or roast duck for $21 to $28 in an incredibly intimate setting.

### Entertainment

The *Southern Vermont Art Center* (☎ 802-362-1405), on West Rd, has a full program of summer concerts. Other concerts are organized by Hildene (☎ 802-362-1788), the Manchester Music Festival (☎ 802-362-1956) and Barrows House (☎ 802-867-4455), in Dorset.

### Getting There & Away

Trains and stagecoaches brought early vacationers to Manchester. Now it's buses and cars. Vermont Transit's (☎ 802-864-6811, 800-451-3292 in New England) Montreal line (three runs daily) includes a stop in Manchester, as well as stops in Bennington, Rutland and Burlington. There's connecting service to and from New York City; connections from Boston go through Rutland or Albany.

Driving details for Manchester are as follows:

| destination | distance | hr:min |
|---|---|---|
| Bennington, VT | 19 miles | 0:30 |
| Brattleboro, VT | 46 miles | 1:15 |
| Rutland, VT | 32 miles | 0:55 |

### DORSET

Dorset, 6 miles north of Manchester along VT 30, is a perfect Vermont village like many others, with its village green, stately inn and lofty church. The difference, however, is that in Dorset the sidewalks, the church and lots of other things are made of creamy marble.

Settled in 1768, Dorset became a farming community with a healthy trade in marble. The quarry, about a mile south of the village center, supplied much of the marble for the grand New York Public Library building and numerous other public edifices, but it's now filled with water.

Much like Manchester, Dorset became a summer playground for well-to-do city folks more than a century ago. Today, in addition to the village's pristine beauty, the draw is the **Dorset Playhouse** (☎ 802-867-5777) on Cheney Rd, past the marble United Church of Christ. In summer, the actors are professionals; at other times, community players.

### Places to Stay & Eat

Dorset's lodging and dining places are upscale. The restored *Dorset Inn* (☎ 802-867-5500), at Church and Main Sts, just off VT 30, faces the village green. Its 31 guest rooms cost $75 per person, breakfast and dinner in the excellent restaurant included.

Also facing the village green, the *Dovetail Inn* (☎ 802-867-5747, fax 867-0246), on VT 30, offers tidy, well-kept rooms for $90 to $185, including good fresh-baked breakfast breads and muffins.

*Cornucopia B&B* (☎ 802-867-5751), on VT 30, has five perfectly kept guest rooms for $125 to $175, full breakfast included.

# Central Vermont

The heart of Vermont, the state's center features some of the most bucolic countryside in New England. Just north of Rutland, Vermont's second-largest city, cows begin to outnumber people. Outdoor lovers make frequent pilgrimages to central Vermont, especially to the resort area of Killington, which attracts countless skiers in winter and hikers in summer. For those interested in indoor pleasures, antique shops and art galleries dot the back roads between picturesque covered bridges.

VERMONT

## WOODSTOCK

Woodstock, Vermont, is the antithesis of that symbol of 1960s hippie living, Woodstock, New York. Vermont's Woodstock, chartered in 1761, has been the highly dignified seat of Windsor County since 1766.

It prospered in this role. The townspeople built many grand houses surrounding the town common, and Woodstock's churches boast no fewer than four bells cast by Paul Revere. Senator Jacob Collamer, a friend of President Abraham Lincoln's, once said, 'The good people of Woodstock have less incentive than others to yearn for heaven.'

In the 19th century, other New England towns built smoky factories, but the only pollution from Woodstock's main industry, county government, was hot air, and it quickly rose out of sight.

Today, Woodstock is still very beautiful and very rich. Spend some time walking around the beautiful village green, where you can admire the Federal and Greek Revival houses and public buildings. Both the Rockefellers and the Rothschilds own estates in the surrounding countryside, and the well-to-do come to stay at the grand Woodstock Inn & Resort. Despite its high-tone reputation, the town does offer lodgings and meal possibilities at decent prices for those who want to enjoy the interesting activities nearby.

### Orientation

Woodstock, off US 4, is part of the Upper Connecticut River Valley community that includes Hanover and Lebanon, in New Hampshire, and Norwich and White River Junction, Vermont. People think nothing of driving from one of these towns to another to find a bed, a meal or an amusement.

### Information

The Woodstock Area Chamber of Commerce (☎ 802-457-3555, www.woodstockvt .com), 4 Central St, PO Box 486, Woodstock, VT 05091, operates a small information booth on the village green in summer. Parking places are at a premium in this town, and enforcement is strict, so obey the regulations.

For local guidebooks, maps and books in general, stop in at the Yankee Bookshop (☎ 802-457-2411), 12 Central St.

### Billings Farm & Museum

After your walk, pay a visit to the Billings Farm & Museum (☎ 802-457-2355), less than a mile north of the village green, along VT 12 at River Rd.

The railroad magnate Frederick Billings founded the farm in the late 19th century and ran it on sound 'modern' principles of conservation and animal husbandry. In 1871, he imported cattle directly from the Isle of Jersey in Britain, and the purebred descendants of these early bovine immigrants still give milk on the farm today.

Life on the working farm is a mix of 19th- and 20th-century methods, all of which delight curious children. Call for details about the daily demonstrations, audio-visual shows and special programs. The farm is open 10 am to 5 pm daily, May through October, and 10 am to 4 pm on weekends in November and December. Admission costs $7 for adults, $1 to $5.50 for children.

### Quechee Gorge

Eight miles east of Woodstock along US 4, the highway passes over Quechee (KWEE-chee) Gorge, a craggy chasm cut by the Ottauquechee River. Though it's less than 170 feet deep, the gorge provides romantic views, and Quechee Gorge State Park, on the east side of the gorge, has camping, hiking trails and picnic facilities (see Places to Stay, below). The walk through the gorge down to the river takes only 15 minutes.

### Breweries

Halfway between Killington and Woodstock, at the junction of US 4 and VT 100A, is the **Long Trail Brewing Company** (☎ 802-672-5011). Sit down at the Visitor's Center (open 10 am to 6 pm daily), order a sandwich or burger and wash it down with a Long Trail Ale, 'Vermont's No 1 Selling Amber.' Other beers include a hearty stout and a fruity blackberry wheat ale. Tours are free.

In Windsor, southeast of Woodstock along US 5, **Catamount Brewing Company**

(☎ 800-540-2248), Ruth Carney Drive, offers free tours and tastings. It is open 9 am to 5 pm Monday through Saturday (Saturday only in winter).

## Vermont Raptor Center

Learn all about raptors and other birds of prey at the Vermont Raptor Center (☎ 802-457-2779), in the Vermont Institute of Natural Science, 1½ miles southwest of the village green in Woodstock, along Church Hill Rd.

The two dozen species of raptors that live at the site range from the tiny, 3oz saw-whet owl to the mighty bald eagle. The birds have sustained permanent injuries that do not allow them to return to life in the wild. In good weather, the three self-guided nature trails are a delight.

The center is open 10 am to 4 pm daily; closed Sunday from November through April. Admission costs $6 for adults, $2 to $3 for children aged five to 18.

## Summer Activities

The **Billings Park Trails** start on the far side of the Ottauquechee River from the village green, along the east edge of the cemetery. Stop at the Woodstock Inn & Resort (see Places to Stay, below) for maps. Be sure to look out for Woodstock's three covered bridges over the Ottauquechee.

There are also hiking trails and lakes good for swimming, boating and canoeing at nearby state parks. See Camping under Places to Stay for locations.

Bike Vermont (☎ 800-257-2226, www .bikevt.com), PO Box 207, Woodstock, VT 05091, operates two-, three- and five-day bike tours, including inn-to-inn tours. Local bicycle shops, including Woodstock Sports (☎ 802-457-1568), 30 Central St, and Cyclery Plus (☎ 802-457-3377), 490 Woodstock Rd (VT 4), rent bicycles and provide maps of good local routes. Expect to pay $20 for full-day rentals.

Green Mountain Horse Association & Youth Center (☎ 802-457-1509), in South Woodstock, has steeds and knows the riding trails. Check also with Kedron Valley Stables (☎ 802-457-1480).

Bald eagles live at the Vermont Raptor Center.

## Skiing

**Downhill** In 1934, Woodstockers installed the first mechanical ski-tow in the USA, and skiing is still important here. **Suicide Six** (☎ 802-457-6661, 800-448-7900), 3 miles north of town on VT 12 in Pomfret, is known for its challenging downhill runs. The lower slopes are fine for beginners, though. There are 22 trails and three lifts (30% beginner, 40% intermediate, 30% expert).

**Cross-Country** Just south of town, the **Woodstock Ski Touring Center** (☎ 802-457-6674), on VT 106, rents equipment and has 50 miles of groomed touring trails.

## Places to Stay

**Camping** The Woodstock area has lots of state parks and many private campgrounds as well.

*Quechee Gorge State Park* (☎ 802-295-2990, 886-2434, 190 Dewey Mills Rd), in White River Junction, is 8 miles east of Woodstock and 3 miles west of I-89, along US 4. The 54 pine-shaded sites (six lean-tos) are only a short stroll from Quechee Gorge and cost $13.

*Silver Lake State Park* (☎ 802-234-9451, 886-2434), off VT 12 in Barnard, is 10 miles north of Woodstock. It has 47 sites (seven lean-tos) for $13 to $16, as well as a beach, boat and canoe rentals, and fishing.

***Ascutney State Park*** *(☎ 802-674-2060, 886-2434)*, Windsor, is about 22 miles southeast of Woodstock off I-91. The 49 sites (10 lean-tos), at an elevation of 3144 feet, cost $13 to $16, panoramic views included. The park also features a playground, hiking trails and cliffs for hang gliding. It's open late May to mid-October.

***Wilgus State Park*** *(☎ 802-674-5422, 866-2434)* is 2 miles south of I-91 exit 8, along US 5 in Ascutney. The 29 sites (nine lean-tos) next to the Connecticut River cost $13 to $16. There are hiking trails and possibilities for fishing and canoeing.

***Thetford Hill State Park*** *(☎ 802-785-2266)*, in Thetford, has 16 sites (two lean-tos) for $13 to $18, plus hiking trails and a playground. From I-91 exit 14, go a mile west on VT 113 to Thetford Hill, then a mile south on Academy Rd.

**Motels** The ***Woodstock Motel*** *(☎ 802-457-2500)*, on US 4 on the east side of town, has 15 comfortable rooms for $48 to $78.

The ***Braeside Motel*** *(☎ 802-457-1366)*, on US 4 east of town, has a nice location, a swimming pool and 12 good rooms for $68 to $78, light breakfast included.

***Shire Motel*** *(☎ 802-457-2211, 46 Pleasant St)*, on US 4 on the east side of town, is within walking distance of the town center and charges $88 to $145 for its 33 comfy rooms.

Farther out of town is the ***Quality Inn*** *(☎ 802-295-7600)*, on US 4 just east of the Quechee Gorge, with 70 rooms for $80 to $100. And the ***Pleasant View Motel*** *(☎ 802-295-3485)*, a few miles farther east in Hartford, just west of White River Junction, has 16 rooms for $66.

**B&Bs** The ***Barr House*** *(☎ 802-457-3334, 55 South St)*, on VT 106, a five-minute walk south of the green, is a handsome B&B with two rooms sharing a bath. A room with a large country breakfast costs $45 to $60 single, $65 to $75 double.

***Rosewood Inn*** *(☎ 802-457-4485, 674 Bartlett Brook Rd)*, South Pomfret, is a small six-room B&B 2 miles north of Woodstock. For a room with shared bath and country breakfast, you pay $70 to $125.

The ***1830 Shire Town Inn*** *(☎ 802-457-1830, 31 South St)* is a cozy, family B&B with three rooms, all with private bath, for $75 to $95.

***Woodstocker B&B*** *(☎ 802-457-3896, 800-457-3896, 61 River St)* offers nine spacious rooms for $90 to $125 (breakfast included) in a house dating from the 1830s.

***Canterbury House*** *(☎ 802-457-3077, 800-390-3077, 43 Pleasant St)* is a restored 1880s Victorian B&B with eight charming guest rooms priced from $90 to $155, full breakfast included.

**Inns** ***Village Inn of Woodstock*** *(☎ 802-457-1255, 800-722-4571, 41 Pleasant St)* is a Victorian mansion owned by the chef who presides in the cozy dining room, where roast turkey dinners are the specialty. The eight guest rooms cost $85 to $130, full breakfast included.

The Victorian-style ***Parker House Inn*** *(☎ 802-295-6077, 16 Main St)*, in Quechee, was built in 1857 for a former Vermont senator. Just 100 yards from the Ottauquechee River's covered bridge and waterfall, the antique-laden inn features seven large rooms, all with private bath, at $100 to $125.

Just 3 miles to the east of Woodstock is the ***Applebutter Inn*** *(☎ 802-457-4158)*, on Happy Valley Rd in Taftsville. Set on 12 wonderful acres with one of the most picturesque barns in Vermont, the Applebutter is housed in a Federal gabled house, circa 1850. The six rooms, all with private bath, cost $70 to $135, including an immense breakfast in a wonderful old kitchen.

**Resorts** ***Woodstock Inn & Resort*** *(☎ 802-457-1100, 800-448-7900, fax 802-457-6699, 14 The Green)* is one of the most luxurious hotels in the state, with extensive grounds, a formal dining room, indoor sports center and 144 rooms priced from $165 to $312.

## Places to Eat

You'll find authentic Italian pastries and the best cup of espresso this side of the Connecticut River at ***Pane e Salute*** *(☎ 802-457-4882,*

*61 Central St)*. Expect buttery *panettone*, rolls filled with ricotta, pear and chocolate, and Florentine coffee cake.

If you have a picnic lunch, take it to the George Perkins Marsh Man and Nature Park, a tiny hideaway right next to the river on Central St, across the street from Pane e Salute. You can get a sandwich or other yummy picnic fare at the *Mountain Creamery* (☎ *802-457-1715)*, a few steps west along Central St. This spot serves breakfast and lunch, as well as the most scrumptious apple pie in Woodstock.

Perhaps the best value in town is the roast turkey dinner served at the *Village Inn of Woodstock* (☎ *802-457-1255, 41 Pleasant St)*. For under $15, you get turkey, apple-sausage bread stuffing, gravy, homemade cranberry sauce, popovers and tasty maple-bourbon candied yams, as well as a vegetable, potato, bread and salad. Several other entrees are available à la carte.

*The Prince & the Pauper* (☎ *802-457-1818, 24 Elm St)* is Woodstock's elegant New American bistro, serving a sublime three-course prix-fixe menu for $35. You can order things like applewood-smoked ruby trout with griddled corn cake and *crème fraîche* from the à la carte menu if you like. Also ask about their early-dinner specials.

Expect tranquillity, exquisite views of Mt Tom and the premier cuisine in Woodstock at the *Jackson House Inn* (☎ *802-457-2065, 37 Old Route 4 West)*. The $45 prix-fixe menu includes a first course of oysters, scallops or duck in phyllo. Then you can opt for a main dish of pepper-crusted tuna or a juicy little squab lightly caramelized with maple syrup. End with the cheese sampler or *tarte Tatin*. For a special occasion, this place is worth the splurge.

*Simon Pearce Restaurant* (☎ *802-295-1470)*, in the Mill on Main St in Quechee (a 10-minute drive from Woodstock), enjoys a dramatic setting in an old brick mill overlooking a waterfall and a covered bridge. Influenced by New American cuisine, the menu nevertheless maintains a refreshing simplicity: try sweet potato soup, hickory-smoked coho salmon, beef-and-Guinness stew and grilled leg of lamb with garlic, rosemary and balsamic vinaigrette. Lunch (from 11:30 am to 2:45 pm) costs about $10 to $15, dinner (6 to 9 pm) $20 to $40. The beautiful stemware used at the restaurant was blown by hand in the Simon Pearce Glass workshops, also located in the mill and open for tours 9 am to 9 pm daily.

Right next door in Quechee is the *Parker House Inn* (☎ *802-295-6077, 16 Main St)*. As locals will attest, the food here is just as tasty as at Simon Pearce, but at a far better price. However, you don't get views of the waterfall or opportunities to use Simon Pearce stemware.

Eight miles south of Woodstock on VT 12, in Hartland Four Corners, is the 200-year-old *Skunk Hollow Tavern* (☎ *802-436-2139)*. The worn wooden floors of this tiny abode reek of history. You can have burgers or fish and chips for $6.95 at the bar, or venture upstairs for a more intimate feel and higher prices ($21 for rack of lamb). It's a treat when there's live music – the band takes up half the room. The tavern's closed Monday and Tuesday.

## Getting There & Away
**Air** The nearest airports are at Lebanon, New Hampshire (15 miles), and Rutland, Vermont (35 miles), served by Delta, Northwest and US Airways.

**Bus** Vermont Transit (☎ 802-864-6811, 800-451-3292 in New England) offers direct bus service from downtown Boston, Boston's Logan Airport and Springfield, Massachusetts, plus connecting service from New York City; Hartford, Connecticut; and Montreal. All buses stop at nearby White River Junction. One late-morning bus travels the route between White River Junction, Quechee, Woodstock, Sherburne (Killington) and Rutland. If you take the bus to White River Junction on your way to Woodstock, you might find it easiest to take a taxi (drivers wait at the bus station) from there to Woodstock, a distance of 16 miles.

**Train** Amtrak's daily *Vermonter* (☎ 800-872-7245, www.amtrak.com), which runs between New York and St Albans, stops at nearby

**VERMONT**

White River Junction. (See Bus, above, for information on continuing on to Woodstock.) For more details on the *Vermonter's* route, see the Getting There & Around section at the beginning of this chapter.

**Car** Driving details for Woodstock are as follows:

| destination | distance | hr:min |
|---|---|---|
| Boston, MA | 155 miles | 3:10 |
| Burlington, VT | 89 miles | 2:00 |
| Hanover, NH | 22 miles | 0:35 |
| Plymouth, VT | 14 miles | 0:25 |
| Rutland, VT | 31 miles | 0:45 |
| Sherburne (Killington), VT | 20 miles | 0:35 |
| White River Junction, VT | 16 miles | 0:25 |

## PLYMOUTH

The small farming village of Plymouth, 14 miles southwest of Woodstock, is known for two things: the Coolidge Homestead and the Plymouth Cheese Company, run by Coolidge descendants.

### History

'If you don't say anything, you won't be called on to repeat it,' said Calvin Coolidge (1872-1933), 30th president of the USA. Coolidge was born in Plymouth, Vermont. He attended the nearby Amherst College in Massachusetts, opened a law practice in Northampton, Massachusetts, ran for local office, and then served as state senator, lieutenant governor and governor of Massachusetts. Elected as vice president of the USA on the Warren Harding ticket in 1920, he assumed the presidency upon Harding's sudden death in 1923.

Vice President Coolidge was visiting his boyhood home in Plymouth when word came of Harding's death, and his father, Colonel John Coolidge, the local justice of the peace, administered the presidential oath of office by kerosene lamp at 2:47 am on August 3, 1923.

Known for his simple, forthright New England style and his personal honesty, Coolidge had the good fortune to preside over a time of great prosperity – the Roaring Twenties. His laissez-faire business policies were well accepted but contributed to the stock market crash of 1929. With wonderful *après-moi-le-déluge* luck, he declined to run for another term as president in 1928, although he probably would have won. Instead, he retired to Northampton to write articles for newspapers and magazines.

Thus, the burden of blame for the Great Depression fell hard on the shoulders of the 31st president, Herbert Hoover, who had engineered many of the Coolidge Administration's successes as its Secretary of Commerce. Hoover had only been in office a matter of months when the stock market crashed. In 1931, with many banks failed and a quarter of the nation's workers unemployed, former President Coolidge understatedly reflected, 'The country is not in good shape.'

### Coolidge Homestead

Here you can tour the Coolidge birthplace, homestead and Wilder Barn, a farmers' museum. Wilder House, once the home of Coolidge's mother, has now become a lunchroom. Calvin Coolidge is buried in the local cemetery.

The Coolidge Homestead (☎ 802-672-3773), on VT 100A, is open 9:30 am to 5 pm daily from late May through mid-October. Admission for adults is $5, children under 14 are free and family (two adults and two children) tickets cost $17.

### Plymouth Cheese Company

A good Vermont cheese can melt in your mouth like butter or it can have the sharpness of a dry chardonnay. At the Plymouth Cheese Company (☎ 802-672-3650), on VT 100A at the Coolidge Homestead, you can see how some of the state's finest cheeses are made, and taste the yummy results. Try the granular-curd cheddar that's made from creamy Vermont milk. Watch the process 11:30 am to 1 pm weekdays; the shop is open for tasting and selling 8 am to 5:30 pm daily.

### Places to Stay
**Camping** *Coolidge State Park* (☎ 802-672-3612, 886-2434), PO Box 105, is on VT 100A,

3 miles northeast of Plymouth Union, and even closer to Plymouth itself. The 60 sites (35 lean-tos), in a 25-sq-mile state forest at an elevation of 2100 feet, cost $13 to $16 and are open from late May to early October. There's a backcountry camping area, as well as hiking and fishing.

*Sugarhouse Campground* (☎ *802-672-5043), Plymouth*, is on the west side of VT 100, a half mile north of the junction with VT 100A. The 45 sites have full hookups and cost $14 and up.

**Hostels** *HI/AYH – Trojan Horse Hostel* (☎ *802-228-5244, 800-547-7475, 44 Andover St)* is on VT 100 just south of Plymouth, 11 miles south of Plymouth. It's open every month except April and charges $15 for its 18 beds in summer, $23 in winter, when it's crowded with skiers from the nearby Okemo Mountain ski area. Reserve in advance by phone December through March. Office hours are 8 to 10 am and 5 to 9 pm.

**B&Bs** Innkeepers Micki Smith and Paul Darnauer have made *The Golden Stage Inn* (☎ *802-226-7744)*, VT 103 in Proctorville, one of the coziest overnight stays in the Okemo area. Paul is a gracious and genuine host, and Micki is known for her exemplary cooking. The former 18th-century stagecoach stop is now an 11-room inn with views of Okemo. Rooms cost $99.

## KILLINGTON
Killington (☎ 802-422-3261, 800-621-6867) is Vermont's prime ski resort, with 205 runs on seven mountains, a vertical drop of more than 3000 feet, and 32 lifts, including the Skyeship gondola that lifts up to 3000 skiers per hour in heated cars with closed-circuit radio along a 2½-mile cable. The experts attempt to ski Outer Limits, the steepest mogul run in the East.

The area has facilities for most winter activities, from ice skating to snowboarding. Ski season typically runs from mid-October through late May.

In summer, the Killington facilities are used for hiking, biking and other outdoor activities.

The Merrell Hiking Center (☎ 802-422-6708, 800-372-2007), in the Killington Base Lodge on Killington Rd, offers guided and self-guided nature interpretation hikes. For $10, you can ride the Skyeship gondola to the summit and hike down the mountain with a trail map and pocket field guide.

The Mountain Bike Center (☎ 802-422-6232, 800-372-2007) rents mountain bikes for $25 to $50 per day (helmet and trail map included). You can take a 1¼-mile chairlift ride to the 4241-foot summit of Killington Mountain and ride your bike down, finding your way among 37 miles of trails.

### Places to Stay
There are well over 100 lodging places in the Killington area. The best way to find a bed is to call the Killington Travel Service at ☎ 800-372-2007. Package deals with sports activities and lodgings can be attractively priced, so ask about them when you call.

*Gifford Woods State Park* (☎ *802-775-5354, 886-2434)*, in Killington, has 48 campsites (21 lean-tos) on 114 acres, just a half mile north of the intersection of US 4 and VT 100. Rates are $13 to $16, and the season lasts from late May through early October. There's a playground, hiking trails and fishing in Kent Pond.

### Places to Eat & Drink
With 25 clubs and more than 100 restaurants, Killington is a place where the après-ski scene rages. Many of these nightspots lie along the 4-mile Access Rd, which is Killington's version of a town. Check out these: *Wobbly Barn* (☎ *802-422-3392)*, *The Nightspot* (☎ *802-422-9855)* and the *Pickle Barrel* (☎ *802-422-3035)*.

### Getting There & Away
**Air** The nearest airport to Killington is in Rutland, Vermont, 15 miles away. It is served by Delta, Northwest and US Airways.

**Bus** Vermont Transit (☎ 802-864-6811, 800-451-3292 in New England) offers direct service from downtown Boston, Boston's Logan Airport and Springfield, Massachusetts, plus connecting service from New York

City, Hartford and Montreal. Buses arrive in nearby Sherburne (Killington).

**Train** Amtrak's daily *Ethan Allan Express* (☎ 800-872-7245, www.amtrak.com) runs between New York and Rutland. A late-night bus continues on to Sherburne, but you can also take a taxi.

## RUTLAND

Rutland is Vermont's second-largest city (Burlington is larger and more charming). US 7 bypasses the center of Rutland, and you should probably do the same. If you need to find a big hardware store, automobile dealership, airport or hospital, Rutland will do. Otherwise, move on.

In the 19th century, Rutland was important as a railroad town. The trains shipped Vermont marble out and the manufactured goods of the world in. But the city's main railroad station was torn down in the 1960s and replaced by a nondescript shopping mall, leaving Rutland without even a visual memory of its heyday.

The Vermont State Fair takes place here in early September. For more information on Rutland, contact the Rutland Region Chamber of Commerce (☎ 802-773-2747), 256 N Main St (US 7), Rutland, VT 05701.

## MIDDLEBURY

Prosperity lives at the crossroads, and Middlebury obviously has its share. Aptly named, Middlebury stands at the nexus of eight highways, and as a result the center of town is always busy with traffic.

Despite Middlebury's history of marble quarrying, most buildings in the town's center are built of brick, wood and schist (a stone). Middlebury College, however, contains many buildings made with white marble and gray limestone.

### History

Middlebury was permanently settled at the end of the 18th century. In 1800, Middlebury College was founded, and it has been synonymous with the town ever since.

The establishment of this renowned liberal arts college was not Middlebury's only educational milestone. In 1814, education pioneer Emma Willard (1787-1870) founded the Middlebury Female Seminary, a college-preparatory boarding school that was designed to prepare women for college admission – a radical idea in early-19th-century America. The school later moved to nearby New York state.

John Deere was an apprentice blacksmith in Middlebury during the 1820s. He soon moved to Illinois, where he discovered that conventional plows had a hard time with the black prairie soils of the Midwest. He fashioned a plow with a one-piece steel plowshare and moldboard, which proved to be a major advance in plow technology.

Robert Frost (1874-1963) owned a farm in nearby Ripton, and he co-founded the renowned Bread Loaf School of English at nearby Middlebury College. (For more information on Robert Frost, see the White Mountains section of the New Hampshire chapter.)

If you're in the area during the first week of July, Brandon, just south of Middlebury, offers self-guided tours of the cellars and hiding places once used by slaves fleeing to Canada on the Underground Railroad.

### Orientation

Middlebury, in the western part of the state, stands on hilly ground straddling Otter Creek. Main St (VT 30) crosses the creek just above the Otter Creek Falls. The town green, Middlebury Inn and the Addison County Chamber of Commerce information office are on the north side of the creek; Frog Hollow (a shopping complex in an old mill) and Middlebury College are to the south.

### Information

The Addison County Chamber of Commerce (☎ 802-388-7951, fax 388-8066, www .midvermont.com), 2 Court St, Middlebury, VT 05753, maintains an information office in a grand mansion facing the town green across from the Middlebury Inn.

The Vermont Book Shop (☎ 802-388-2061, 800-287-2061), 38 Main St, features a good selection of books.

VERMONT

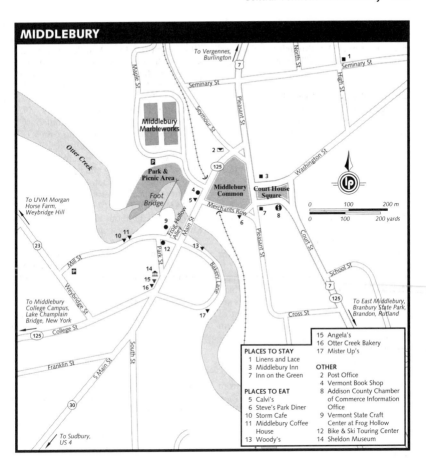

# MIDDLEBURY

PLACES TO STAY
1  Linens and Lace
3  Middlebury Inn
7  Inn on the Green

PLACES TO EAT
5  Calvi's
6  Steve's Park Diner
10  Storm Cafe
11  Middlebury Coffee House
13  Woody's
15  Angela's
16  Otter Creek Bakery
17  Mister Up's

OTHER
2  Post Office
4  Vermont Book Shop
8  Addison County Chamber of Commerce Information Office
9  Vermont State Craft Center at Frog Hollow
12  Bike & Ski Touring Center
14  Sheldon Museum

## Middlebury College

For tours of Middlebury College, contact the Admissions Office (☎ 802-443-3000), in the Emma Willard House, on the south side of S Main St (VT 30). The **Middlebury College Museum of Art** (☎ 802-443-5007), on S Main St (VT 30), southwest of Porter Field Rd, has good collections of Cypriot pottery, 19th-century European and American sculpture, and modern prints. It is open 10 am to 5 pm Tuesday through Friday, noon to 5 pm on weekends; admission is free.

## Vermont State Craft Center

The Vermont State Craft Center at Frog Hollow (☎ 802-388-3177), 1 Mill St, has an exhibition and sales gallery showing the works of many excellent Vermont artisans.

## Sheldon Museum

This museum (☎ 802-388-2117), 1 Park St, is the work of Henry Sheldon, an town clerk, church organist, storekeeper and avid collector of 19th-century Vermontiana. His collection of folk art, paintings, furniture and bric-a-brac is housed in a brick Federal-style mansion (1829), open 10 am to 5 pm week-days and 10 am to 4 pm Saturday. Tours are given from mid-May through October, and admission costs $4/3.50/1 for adults/seniors/children.

## University of Vermont Morgan Horse Farm

In 1789, Justin Morgan and his thoroughbred Arabian colt Figure came to Vermont from Springfield, Massachusetts. The colt grew to a small bay stallion, and the hardy farmers and loggers of Vermont looked upon him as pretty but not particularly useful.

Morgan, however, proved to them the horse's surprising strength, agility, endurance and longevity. Renamed Justin Morgan after his owner, the little horse became the USA's first native breed, useful for heavy work, carriage draft, riding and even war service.

The quarter horses of the Southwest have Morgan blood, as do the American Albino and the Palomino breeds. Pure Morgans are still raised today, surprisingly with most of the excellent qualities that made them famous two centuries ago.

You can see 70 registered Morgans and tour their stables and the farm grounds at the University of Vermont's Morgan Horse Farm (☎ 802-388-2011), about 3 miles from Middlebury. Drive west on VT 125, then north (right) onto Weybridge St (VT 23) to the farm, open 9 am to 4 pm daily, May through October.

## Activities

Bike & Ski Touring Center (☎ 802-388-6666), 74 Main St at Frog Hollow Alley, has equipment and information on camping, biking and skiing in the region.

## Places to Stay

Middlebury has plenty of lodgings. If you don't find what you want in Middlebury proper, try looking in East Middlebury, 5 miles southeast along US 7.

**Camping** There is little camping in or very close to Middlebury, but several places are within an easy drive.

*Lake Dunmore Kampersville* (☎ 802-352-4501, 388-2661), VT 53 in Salisbury (a 10-minute drive from Middlebury), has 210 sites with hookups and two swimming pools (one heated), as well as many other services, and it's open year-round. The sites start at $18.

*Branbury State Park* (☎ 802-247-5925, 483-2001), 10 miles south of Middlebury, is on the east side of Lake Dunmore on VT 53, between Brandon and Middlebury. With 44 sites (five lean-tos) on 96 acres, it charges $13 to $16 for camping and is open from late May through early October. Hiking trails lead to spectacular views.

*DAR State Park* (☎ 802-759-2354, 483-2001), on VT 17 about 17 miles northwest of Middlebury, enjoys a choice location on the shores of Lake Champlain between West Addison and Chimney Point. The park has 71 campsites (21 lean-tos) priced from $13 up to $16, as well as boating, fishing and a playground.

*Elephant Mountain Camping Area* (☎ 802-453-3123), on VT 116 between East Middlebury and Bristol, has 50 sites with hookups priced from $13 to $18 and is open year-round.

*Smoke Rise Family Campground* (☎ 802-247-6472), 2 miles north of Brandon on US 7, has 50 sites, most with hookups, for $14 and up. It's open from mid-May through mid-October.

*Ten Acre Camping* (☎ 802-759-2662), in Addison, has 90 sites (78 with hookups), a large tenting area, a pool and lots of amusements, for $14 and up. Ten Acre is 15 miles west of Middlebury on VT 125, a mile south of the Lake Champlain Bridge to New York. It's open May to mid-October.

**Hostels** *Covered Bridge Home Hostel* (☎ 802-388-0141, 62 Seymour St) is a six-bed hostel right next to the Green Mountain National Forest and Otter Creek. Beds cost $13 to $15.

**Motels** Some rooms at the *Sugarhouse Motel* (☎ 802-388-2770), 2 miles north of the town center on US 7, have kitchens. Rates range from $40 to $75. Pets are welcome.

The ***Greystone Motel*** (☎ *802-388-4935*), just 2 miles south of the town center on US 7, has 10 rooms for $60 to $70.

The ***Blue Spruce Motel*** (☎ *802-388-4091*), on US 7, 3 miles south of the town center, charges $58 to $145 for its 24 comfortable rooms.

**B&Bs** Liz Hunt's ***Middlebury Bed & Breakfast*** (☎ *802-388-4851*) has four rooms (one with private bath) for $55 to $85, continental breakfast included. It's within walking distance of the town center, along Washington St Extension.

***Linens & Lace*** (☎ *802-388-0832, 29 Seminary St*) is in a quiet residential neighborhood and within easy walking distance of Middlebury College and the village. The five simple rooms cost $89 to $119.

***The Annex B&B*** (☎ *802-388-3233*), on VT 125 (5 miles from Middlebury), has six rooms, some with shared bath, in the $60 to $70 range.

**Inns** The ***Waybury Inn*** (☎ *802-388-4015*), on VT 125 in East Middlebury, is a former stagecoach stop with a popular pub. Its 14 rooms cost between $85 and $120.

The ***Inn on the Green*** (☎ *802-388-7512, 888-244-7512, 19 S Pleasant St*) is an 1803 Federal-style home offering seven spacious rooms in the house and four more rooms in the adjoining carriage house. Rates range from $125 to $175 and include a full country breakfast.

The ***Middlebury Inn*** (☎ *802-388-4961, 800-842-4666, fax 802-388-4563, 14 Court House Square (VT 7)*) has a fine old main building (1827) with formal public rooms. Many of the inn's guest rooms are modern motel units in the back, but there are rooms in the Porter House section of the inn as well. Rates are $68 to $144 single, $84 to $250 double. Pets are welcome in the motel.

***Swift House Inn*** (☎ *802-388-9925, fax 388-9927*), on US 7 at Stewart Lane, is a grand white Federal house built in 1814, plus a large gatehouse and carriage house surrounded by fine lawns and gardens. Amenities include a steam room, a sauna and Middlebury's best dining room. The luxury accommodations at the Swift House Inn are priced from $80 to $195.

## Places to Eat

***Steve's Park Diner*** (☎ *802-388-3297, 66 Merchants Row*) is the cheapest place in town for breakfast and lunch. Sit at small wooden booths and order sandwiches ($2.95 to $3.75).

***Middlebury Coffee House*** (☎ *802-388-8204*), Frog Hollow Mill, is a cozy place to sink into the sofas and warm up with a cup of joe.

***Storm Cafe*** (☎ *802-388-1063*), in the basement of the stone Frog Hollow Mill, is popular with artists and artisans. Soups, salads, sandwiches and some organic fruits and vegetables are available for $3 to $6. In good weather, find a table outdoors on the terrace overlooking Otter Creek.

***Calvi's*** (☎ *802-388-9338, 42 Main St*) has been in this early 20th-century building since the 1950s and has changed little. The authentic mid-century decor includes a real soda fountain. A balcony dining area overlooks Otter Creek. Deli sandwiches cost $4 to $5.

***Angela's*** (☎ *802-388-0002, 86 Main St*) offers decent Italian fare at very affordable prices. Pasta dishes cost $4.95 to $6.95. It's closed on Sunday.

***Otter Creek Bakery*** (☎ *802-388-3371, 14 College St*) is popular for take-out pastries, coffee and sandwiches.

***Woody's*** (☎ *802-388-4182, 800-346-3603, 5 Bakery Lane*) has a fine location overlooking the creek just east of Main St. Innovative international cuisine is featured for lunch (11:30 am to 3 pm) and dinner (5 to 10 pm). At lunch, try the cup of soup and half a sandwich for under $5; main courses at dinner run from $11 to $17. The bar stays open until midnight.

Nearby is ***Mister Up's*** (☎ *802-388-6724, 4 Bakery Lane*), also overlooking the creek, with a vibrant international menu at similar prices.

***Fire & Ice*** (☎ *802-388-7166, 26 Seymour St*) is known for its prime rib, steak and stir-fried dishes, as well as the good salad bar.

***Swift House Inn*** (☎ *802-388-9925*), at the corner of Stewart Lane and US 7, boasts

**VERMONT**

Middlebury's finest and most expensive dining room. The menu changes daily and usually focuses on classic dishes with a nouvelle twist. Dinner costs $30 to $50.

## Getting There & Away

**Air** There are two airports: one in Rutland (32 miles away) and one in Burlington (34 miles). The Burlington airport is much busier, with many national connections (see Burlington, later in this chapter, for details).

**Bus** Vermont Transit (☎ 802-864-6811, 800-451-3292 in New England) operates three buses daily on the Burlington-Rutland-Albany route, stopping at Middlebury. You can connect at Albany with buses for New York City and at Burlington with buses for Montreal.

**Car** Driving details for Middlebury are as follows:

| destination | distance | hr:min |
|---|---|---|
| Boston, MA | 210 miles | 5:00 |
| Burlington, VT | 34 miles | 0:50 |
| Rutland, VT | 32 miles | 0:45 |
| Stowe, VT | 55 miles | 1:30 |
| Warren, VT | 36 miles | 0:55 |
| Woodstock, VT | 63 miles | 1:30 |

## RIPTON

Ten miles east of Middlebury on VT 125 lies the village of Ripton, a beautiful little hamlet set in the Vermont mountains. Two white churches, a few houses and the ***Chipman Inn*** *(☎ 802-388-2390)*, a big old country house turned into an inn – that's Ripton. Sit on the lawn in the sun, go down to the river and pitch stones, read, walk, think, talk. The inn, a beautiful Federal house built in 1828, is big on Frostiana and also on the peace and quiet that Robert Frost sought. The eight guest rooms, all with private bath, cost $85 to $125, full breakfast included.

Frost spent 23 years on a farm nearby, and just east of Ripton is the **Robert Frost Wayside Recreation Area**. A forest trail, less than a mile in length, is marked with signs quoting the poet's works. From Ripton, take VT 125 east for 2 miles, and look for the trail on the right side of the road.

For information on the Bread Loaf School of English and Writers' Conference in Ripton, contact Middlebury College (☎ 802-443-3000).

## SUGARBUSH, WARREN & WAITSFIELD

North of Killington, VT 100 is one of the finest stretches of road in the country – a bucolic mix of rolling hills, farmland so fertile you feel like jumping out of the car and digging your hands in the soil, covered bridges and the ubiquitous Vermont white steeple. An hour north of Killington, you'll reach Waitsfield and Warren, towns you might have seen in the advertisements for Vermont tourism. They're places where nothing ever changes. This is especially true of Sugarbush and the nearby Mad River ski area, both popular with locals. Mad River still has a chairlift for single skiers, and both mountains feature the New England skiing of yore, a time when trails were cut by hand and weren't much wider than a hiking path.

### Orientation

The gap roads that run east to west over the Green Mountains offer some of the most picturesque views of the region. VT 73 crosses the Brandon Gap (2170 feet) from Brandon to Rochester and Talcville. VT 125 crosses the Middlebury Gap from East Middlebury (2149 feet) to Hancock. A narrow local road crosses Lincoln Gap (2424 feet) from Bristol to Warren. (The Lincoln Gap road is closed in wintertime due to heavy snowfall.)

VT 17 crosses the Appalachian Gap (at 2356 feet) from Bristol to Irasville and Waitsfield, offering the best views of all.

### Information

There's an information office for the Sugarbush Chamber of Commerce (☎ 802-496-3409, 800-828-4748, www.madrivervalley .com), PO Box 173, Waitsfield, VT 05673, on VT 100. It's open 9 am to 5 pm weekdays and 10 am to 5 pm weekends during the summer, fall and winter tourism seasons.

Local telephone calls from public phones are free in Warren and Waitsfield, courtesy of the Waitsfield-Fayston Telephone Company.

## Skiing

**Downhill** The nature of New England skiing is flying down serpentine trails around corners, down quick dips, through tight slots, always in the company of trees. On the best trails, the woods surround you as you whiz by a rolling tapestry of maple, oak, birch, spruce, pine and balsam. That's exactly what happens at **Sugarbush** (☎ 802-583-2381). Paradise, Castlerock and the backcountry runs in between braid through the forest like a crazed snake.

Subaru wagons with Vermont license plates often have bumper stickers that offer this dare, 'Mad River Glen, Ski It If You Can.' Bumper stickers don't lie. **Mad River Glen** (☎ 802-496-3551) is the nastiest lift-served ski area in the East, a combination of rocks, ice, trees – and snow, of course. It's truly a place where the ski slope seems little removed from a mountain's gnarled primal state.

**Cross-Country** Five local ski touring centers feature more than 100 miles of groomed trails. Call the Sugarbush Chamber of Commerce (see above) for information. The two biggest ski touring centers are Blueberry Lake Cross Country Ski Center (☎ 802-496-6687) and the Inn at Round Barn Farm (☎ 802-496-2276); see Places to Stay, below, for more information on the inn. Blueberry Lake rents equipment.

## Bicycling

Mad River Cyclers (☎ 802-496-9996), on VT 100 just south of VT 17 in Waitsfield, and Blueberry Lake Cross Country Ski Center (☎ 802-496-6687) organize tours and races and can advise you about rentals and routes, including excellent mountain-bike routes. Rentals cost $20 for a full day, $14 for a half day.

## Canoeing & Kayaking

Canoeing and kayaking are good on the Mad River (along VT 100) and White River (along VT 100 near Hancock) in April, May and early June, and on the larger Winooski River (along I-89) all spring, summer and fall.

Clearwater Sports (☎ 802-496-2708), on VT 100 in Waitsfield, rents canoes, kayaks, river-floating tubes, in-line skates, bicycles and many other types of sports equipment and organizes one-day guided canoe and kayak trips.

By the way, Waitsfield is home to Mad River Canoe (☎ 802-496-3127), New England's premier maker of canoes, open for factory tours 10 am to 4 pm weekdays.

## Soaring

You take off from Warren-Sugarbush Airport in a glider towed by a conventional aircraft. After gaining altitude, you cast off the tow rope and soar quietly through the skies above the mountains and river valleys, kept aloft by updrafts of warm air. A glider can accommodate one or two passengers.

Rides last 20 to 40 minutes, depending upon the weather, and cost $69 to $95 for one person, $99 to $129 for two. For information, contact Sugarbush Soaring (☎ 802-496-2290).

## Horseback Riding

Vermont Icelandic Horse Farm (☎ 802-496-6707) in Waitsfield, 1000 yards south of the town common, can take you on half-day or full-day rides in the summertime. In the wintertime, they offer skijoring rides (a skier is drawn over the snow by a horse). Icelandic horses are fairly easy to ride, even for novice riders.

## Places to Stay

Because the Sugarbush area is primarily active in the winter ski season, there are no campgrounds nearby. Many of the accommodations in the area are condominiums marketed to the ski trade. The largest selection of condos is rented by **Sugarbush Village** (☎ 800-451-4326), located right at the ski area. Rentals cost $90 to $550 per day, depending on condo size, location, date of arrival and length of stay.

**Hyde Away** (☎ 802-496-2322, 800-777-4933), on VT 17 in Waitsfield, is an 1830 farmhouse, sawmill and barn with its own mountain-bike touring center and 12 rooms priced from $39 to $89, breakfast included.

**John Egan's Big World Pub, Grill, & Lodge** (☎ 802-496-3033), on VT 100 in Waitsfield, is close to the slopes at Sugarbush. Twelve rooms, all with private bath, cost $60 to $70.

**The Garrison** (☎ 802-496-2352, 800-766-7829), on VT 17 in Waitsfield, is mainly a condo complex, but the motel section has rooms for $48 in summer, $70 in winter.

The **Inn at Mad River Barn** (☎ 802-496-3310, 800-834-4666), on VT 17 in Waitsfield, is an old-time Vermont lodge containing 15 rooms with private bath, some with queen-size beds and TVs, priced at $55 to $75.

**Beaver Pond Farm Inn** (☎ 802-583-2861), RD Box 306, Warren, is a restored 1840 farmhouse very near the Sugarbush Golf Course, charging $82 to $118.

**The Inn at Round Barn Farm** (☎ 802-496-2276), Waitsfield, is one of the premier lodgings in this area. The inn gets its name from the adjacent round barn that was built in 1910, one of the few round barns that remain in Vermont. The lower level of the barn now has an indoor 60-foot lap pool. In addition, the inn features a large cross-country ski touring center. The 11 rooms cost $135 to $225, including a huge country breakfast.

## Places to Eat

Skiers' taverns abound in this area. Restaurants are quite busy in ski season, a bit sleepy at other times.

**The Warren Store** (☎ 802-496-3864), in Warren village, serves the biggest and best sandwiches in the area. Eat on the deck overlooking the waterfall in the summer.

**Miguel's Stowe Away** (☎ 802-253-7574), Sugarbush Access Rd, Warren, serves Americanized Mexican recipes for $6.50 (tacos) to $13 (mole poblano). Miguel's opens at 4 pm; dinner is served 5:30 to 10 pm daily.

**Georgio's Café** (☎ 802-496-3983), at Tucker Hill Lodge on VT 17 in Waitsfield, features a traditional Italian stone oven that keeps a steady temperature of 700°F to cook pizza just right. The signature dish is an old family recipe, scallops Venetian style ($15).

Another excellent choice for pizza is **American Flatbread** (☎ 802-496-8856), on VT 100 in Waitsfield. Cooked in a primitive wood-fired oven, the Revolution Flatbread is so good that it's sold in the frozen foods section of grocery stores throughout New England.

Don't let the decor outside of **John Egan's Big World Pub and Grill** (☎ 802-496-3033), on VT 100 in Waitsfield, fool you. Extreme skier John Egan hired a renowned chef from Montpelier's New England Culinary Institute, and the venison and lamb dishes are arguably the finest in the Green Mountain State.

The locals rave about the **Spotted Cow** (☎ 802-496-5151), in Waitsfield Village. It's owned by a Bermudian, so you can't go wrong with a bowl of the Bermudian fish chowder ($4.50).

Among the area's fancy places, a long-time favorite is **The Common Man** (☎ 802-583-2800), on German Flats Rd in Warren, in a beautifully restored 19th-century barn. Despite its proletarian name, the restaurant specializes in New American cuisine and has a fine wine cellar. Dinner, the only meal served, costs $25 to $40 per person.

## Getting There & Away

Driving details for the Sugarbush area are as follows:

| destination | distance | hr:min |
| --- | --- | --- |
| Boston, MA | 190 miles | 4:00 |
| Burlington, VT | 40 miles | 1:00 |
| Middlebury, VT | 36 miles | 0:55 |
| Montpelier, VT | 20 miles | 0:35 |
| Montreal, Canada | 140 miles | 3:00 |
| Stowe, VT | 22 miles | 0:40 |
| Woodstock, VT | 55 miles | 1:35 |

# Northern Vermont

Home to the state capital, Montpelier, northern Vermont also contains the state's largest city, Burlington. The most 'cosmopolitan' of Vermont's regions, this area still features all of the rural charms found elsewhere. Even within the city of Burlington, cafe-lined streets coexist with scenic paths along Lake Champlain. Farther north, the pastoral Northeast Kingdom offers a full range of outdoor activities, from skiing to biking, in the heart of the mountains.

## MONTPELIER

Montpelier (mont-PEEL-er), with its population of 8000 souls, would qualify as a large village in some countries. But in sparsely populated Vermont, it is the capital city, complete with a gold-domed State House built of granite that was quarried in nearby Barre in 1836. You might want to visit Montpelier if you are intensely interested in Vermont history and affairs.

### Orientation & Information

Montpelier is small. Look for the golden dome of the State House to find the three major sights.

There's an information kiosk on State St, opposite the post office, open in the summer months. The Vermont Chamber of Commerce (☎ 802-223-3443, fax 229-4581, www .vtchamber.com), PO Box 37, Montpelier, VT 05601, issues information by phone, fax and mail.

You'll find Bear Pond Books (☎ 802-229-0774) well worth a stop at 77 Main St.

### State House

The front doors of the State House (☎ 802-828-2228), on State St, are guarded by a massive statue of Revolutionary War hero Ethan Allen. (See the boxed text 'Ethan Allen & Vermont' in the Facts about New England chapter.) You can wander about the building on your own from 8 am to 4 pm weekdays, or take one of the free tours given on the half-hour, 10 am to 3:30 pm (11 am to 2:30 pm Saturday) from July through mid-October. The State House is closed on Sunday.

### Vermont Historical Society

Next door to the State House, the Pavilion Building is home to state offices and the Vermont Historical Society and its museum (☎ 802-828-2291), open 9 am to 4:30 pm Tuesday through Friday, 9 am to 4 pm Satur-

day, and noon to 4 pm Sunday. Admission costs $2/1 for adults/seniors and students.

### TW Wood Art Gallery

This gallery (☎ 802-828-8743), on College St at E State St, on the Norwich University campus, was founded in 1895 by Thomas Waterman Wood (1823-1903), a native of Montpelier who gained a regional reputation for his portraits and genre paintings. The museum has a large collection of Wood's art, as well as Depression-era paintings. Changing exhibits, especially of arts made in Vermont, fill the main gallery. The gallery is open noon to 4 pm Tuesday to Sunday. Admission is $2, and children under 12 are free.

If you enjoy crafts shows, the Festival of Vermont Crafts takes place in Montpelier the first weekend of October. The show affords an opportunity to enjoy local crafts and good fall foliage simultaneously.

### Places to Stay

Two refurbished Federal houses right in the heart of town make up *The Inn at Montpelier (☎ 802-223-2727, 147 Main St)*. Nineteen rooms cost $89 to $155.

### Places to Eat

Home to the New England Culinary Institute (NECI; ☎ 802-223-6324), one of the finest cooking schools in the country, Montpelier is an excellent place to stop for a meal. NECI runs three restaurants in town. Depending on the student chefs of the day, you can either have one of the best meals in New England at an affordable price or a damn good attempt. Be a guinea pig and support someone's education. *Main Street Grill & Bar (☎ 802-223-3188, 118 Main St)*, run by first-year students, offers breakfast, lunch and dinner. Dinners are reasonably priced at $9.25 to $11.25 and include such fun fare as almond-crusted trout and bouillabaisse.

Upstairs, *Chef's Table (☎ 802-229-9202, 118 Main St)* is run by second-year students. The food is far more innovative and more expensive. Entrees change nightly but include bacon-stuffed rabbit loin ($17.50) and pan-seared rare tuna ($17.95).

NECI's third restaurant is a casual bakery and cafe, **La Brioche** (☎ 802-229-0443, 89 Main St). Soups and sandwiches on home-made bread cost $3.95 to $5.95.

If you don't feel like tossing the dice and risking a meal made by students, go to an old Montpelier standby, **Sarducci's** (☎ 802-223-0229, 3 Main St). In an old railroad station overlooking the Winooski River, Sarducci's features Italian fare such as pastas, wood-oven pizza and eggplant parmesan in the $6.50 to $13.95 range.

### Getting There & Away
**Bus** Vermont Transit (☎ 802-864-6811, 800-451-3292 in New England) runs four buses daily between Boston and Burlington, stopping at Montpelier.

**Train** Amtrak's *Vermonter* (☎ 800-872-7245, www.amtrak.com), which begins in New York, stops in Montpelier on its way to St Albans. See the Getting There & Around section at the beginning of this chapter for more details on the *Vermonter*'s route.

**Car** Driving details for Montpelier are as follows:

| destination | distance | hr:min |
| --- | --- | --- |
| Boston, MA | 182 miles | 3:30 |
| Burlington, VT | 38 miles | 0:45 |
| Montreal, Canada | 142 miles | 3:00 |
| St Johnsbury, VT | 39 miles | 1:00 |
| Stowe, VT | 22 miles | 0:30 |
| Waitsfield, VT | 20 miles | 0:35 |

## BARRE
Montpelier's smaller neighbor Barre (pronounced 'barry') touts itself as the 'granite capital of the world.'

### Rock of Ages Quarries
The Rock of Ages Quarries (☎ 802-476-3119), 4 miles southeast of Barre off I-89 exit 6, on VT 14, are the largest granite quarries in the world, covering 50 acres and mining a vein that's 6 miles long, 4 miles wide and 10 miles deep. The beautiful, durable, granular stone, formed more than

330 million years ago, is used for tombstones, building facades, monuments, curbstones and tabletops.

The Rock of Ages Visitor Center is open 8:30 am to 5 pm daily; it's closed Sunday mornings, except during foliage season. You can see granite products being made – some with an accuracy that approaches 25 millionths of an inch – at the Rock of Ages Manufacturing Division, open 8 am to 3:30 pm weekdays. Follow a self-guided tour around the quarry or take a guided tour for a small fee.

### Hope Cemetery
Where do old granite carvers go when they die? In Barre, they end up in Hope Cemetery, just a mile north of US 302 on VT 14.

To granite carvers, tombstones aren't dreary reminders of mortality but artful celebrations of the carver's life. And what celebrations! A carver and his wife sit up in bed holding hands and smiling at eternity; a granite cube balances precariously on one corner; a carver's favorite armchair is reproduced, larger than life and tellingly empty. If a cemetery can ever be fun, this one is. It's open all the time.

## STOWE
Stowe, in a cozy valley where the West Branch River flows into the Little River, has a certain Vermont-style charm. Its small center is pretty without being prim. Its inns and hotels, ranged along Mountain Rd up to

the ski slopes of Mt Mansfield (4393 feet), have adopted central European names to go with their architecture. Stowe also has central European weather, with a lavish amount of rain and snowfall. Despite occasional storms, though, the town's visitors, who come from all over, find plenty to do.

## History

Founded in 1794, Stowe was a simple, pretty, backwoods farming town until 1859, when the Summit House was built as a summer resort atop Mt Mansfield. Skiing was introduced around 1912, and in the early 1930s Civilian Conservation Corps (CCC) workers cut the first real ski trails in the mountain's slopes.

In the late 1930s, the Mt Mansfield Corporation was established, and after it installed the longest and highest chairlift in the USA, skiing really took off in Stowe.

An Austrian ski champion named Sepp Ruschp was hired as the resort's first ski school director, and he eventually rose to become head of the corporation. At the time of Ruschp's death in 1990, Stowe was among

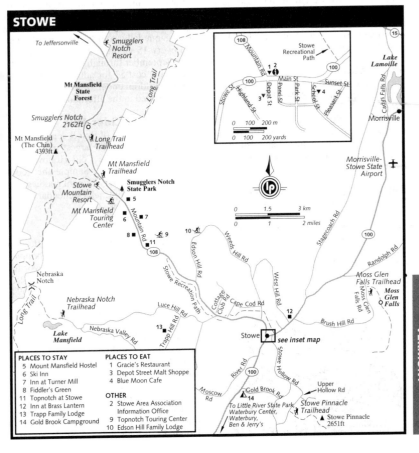

STOWE

PLACES TO STAY
5  Mount Mansfield Hostel
6  Ski Inn
7  Inn at Turner Mill
8  Fiddler's Green
11 Topnotch at Stowe
12 Inn at Brass Lantern
13 Trapp Family Lodge
14 Gold Brook Campground

PLACES TO EAT
1  Gracie's Restaurant
3  Depot Street Malt Shoppe
4  Blue Moon Cafe

OTHER
2  Stowe Area Association Information Office
9  Topnotch Touring Center
10 Edson Hill Family Lodge

VERMONT

the best-regarded ski resorts in the eastern USA, a reputation it still maintains.

## Orientation

Stowe is 10 miles north of I-89 exit 10, on VT 100. Waterbury, just 3 miles north of I-89 on the way to Stowe, is the home of Ben & Jerry's premium ice cream company.

Stowe village, at the intersection of VT 100 and VT 108, is small and easily negotiated on foot. However, many of the town's hotels and restaurants are spread out along Mountain Rd (VT 108, officially named the 10th Mountain Division Memorial Hwy), which goes northwest from the town past Mt Mansfield and through the rocky gorge known as Smugglers Notch to Jeffersonville (18 miles). Smugglers Notch is closed by snow in the winter months.

## Information

There is an information office for the Stowe Area Association (☎ 802-253-7321, 800-247-8693, fax 802-253-2159, www.stoweinfo.com), PO Box 1320, Stowe, VT 05672, on Main St in Stowe village. It is open every day. The association is well organized and can make reservations for air travel, rental cars and local accommodations.

## Ben & Jerry's Ice Cream Factory

Worked up an appetite and feel you deserve a treat? Head to Waterbury, just south of Stowe, and the prominent Ben & Jerry's Ice Cream Factory (☎ 802-882-1266, www.benjerry.com). Take exit 10 off I-89 and go north on VT 100 toward Stowe. The factory is on a hilltop beside the road.

Many years ago, childhood buddies Ben Cohen and Jerry Greenfield sent away $5 for information about how to make ice cream. They opened up shop in a disused gas station in downtown Burlington, and the ice cream shop-cum-luncheonette prospered – partly because of their unorthodox flavor combinations. As the super-premium (full-cream) ice creams became wildly popular, the partners abandoned the gas station location and took to shipping their tasty product nationwide.

You can tour the factory and eat free ice cream. The tour schedule varies: every 15 minutes, 10 am to 5 pm daily from November through May; every 20 minutes, 9 am to 5 pm daily in June; every 10 minutes from 9 am to 8 pm daily from July through August; and every 15 minutes, 9 am to 6 pm daily from September through October. The half-hour tours cost $2 for adults and $1.75 for seniors; children under 12 are free. Tours are most crowded in the afternoon.

## Cold Hollow Cider Mill

Several miles north of Ben & Jerry's, on VT 100, is New England's largest producer of fresh apple cider, the Cold Hollow Cider Mill (☎ 802-244-8771). Sample the goods and stock up on other Vermont goodies such as maple syrup, apple jellies, cheddar cheese and honey mustards.

## Skiing

**Downhill** You're new to the sport, your wife's an expert and the kids love bopping down the intermediate slopes. No worries. Visit **Stowe Mountain Resort** (☎ 802-253-7311). With 47 trails (16% beginner, 59% intermediate, 25% expert), the variety of terrain at Stowe is unparalleled in the East. Beginning skiers can chute through the scenic 3.7-mile Toll Road or venture to Spruce Peak; middle-of-the-roadies can glide down Tyro or Lullaby Lane; the hardcore can tackle the Front Four or more coveted spots such as the Chin or the Birthday Bowls (off Big Spruce).

'The family that skies together, stays together' should be the motto for **Smuggler's Notch Resort** (☎ 800-451-8752), situated just outside of Stowe. The resort's fully equipped condos cater extensively to families, and the lineup of activities for children is longer than a child's wish list for Santa. The complex, spread out over three mountains, includes indoor pools, outdoor skating rinks, a tube-sliding hill that is lighted at night, 14 miles of cross-country trails and a magic learning trail, where young children ski up to exhibit panels that teach them about various winter animals. Other activities include horse-drawn sleigh rides and nightly family entertainment. Junior won't get bored here, nor will his parents.

**Cross-Country** With four of the top ski touring centers in the state, including the **Trapp Family Lodge** (☎ 802-253-8511), made famous by Maria von Trapp, Stowe is easily the premier cross-country skiing destination in the Northeast. The other centers, linked by some 250 miles of trails, are the **Mt Mansfield Ski Touring Center** (☎ 802-253-7311), the **Edson Hill Nordic Center** (☎ 802-253-8954) and the **Topnotch Touring Center** (☎ 802-253-8585). The centers connect via some tough backcountry ski runs, like the Bruce and Teardrop Trails, two of the earliest downhill trails in the country (they were cut by the Civilian Conservation Corps in the early '30s).

Within this wide network of trails that traverse mountains and skirt lakes is one 280-mile-long route that runs the length of Vermont. Called the **Catamount Trail**, it starts in southern Vermont at Readsboro and ends at North Troy on the Canadian border. In between lies some of the finest skiing in the East, from backcountry trails that are etched in Mt Mansfield to ski touring centers located in the Green Mountain National Forest, such as Blueberry Hill and Mountain Top. Contact the Catamount Trail Association for more information (☎ 802-864-5794).

## Hiking

The **Stowe Recreation Path** is the obvious choice for a short walk. It follows the course of the Waterbury River (and Mountain Rd) for 5.3 miles from the village northwest to

the Stowe Mountain Resort. The path is for bicycle, roller-skate and foot traffic only.

The Green Mountain Club (☎ 802-244-7037), RR 1, Box 650, Waterbury Center, VT 05677, with offices on the 1836 May Farm, on VT 100 a few miles south of Stowe, was founded in 1910 to maintain the Long Trail. The club also publishes some excellent hikers' materials, available from the Green Mountain Club's offices or by mail. For more information on the Long Trail, plus trail guidebooks, see the boxed text 'A Month in the Woods' in the Manchester section, earlier in this chapter.

The Green Mountain Club recommends the following day hikes around Stowe:

Moss Glen Falls
Half mile, half-hour, an easy walk. Follow VT 100 for 3 miles north of Stowe Center and bear right onto Randolph Rd. Go 0.3 mile and turn right for the parking area, then walk along the obvious path to reach a deep cascade and waterfalls.

Stowe Pinnacle
2.8 miles, two hours, moderate difficulty. Follow VT 100 south of Stowe and turn east onto Gold Brook Rd, proceeding for 0.3 miles; cross a bridge and turn left to continue along Gold Brook Rd. About 1.6 miles later, you come to Upper Hollow Rd; turn right and go to the top of the hill, just past Pinnacle Rd, to find the small parking area on the left. The hike to Stowe Pinnacle, a rocky outcrop offering sweeping mountain views, is short but steep.

Nebraska Notch
3.2 miles, 2¼ hours, moderate difficulty. Take VT 100 south of Stowe, then turn west onto River Rd, which becomes Moscow Rd. Continue for 5.8 miles to the Lake Mansfield Trout Club. The trail follows an old logging road for awhile and then ascends past beaver dams and grand views to join the Long Trail at Taylor Lodge.

Mt Mansfield
7 miles, five hours, a difficult hike. Follow VT 108 west from Stowe to the Long Trail parking area, 0.7 miles past Stowe Mountain Resort ski area. Mt Mansfield is thought by some to resemble a man's profile in repose. Follow the Long Trail to the 'chin,' then go south along the summit ridge to Profanity Trail; follow that aptly named route to Taft Lodge, then take the Long Trail back down.

**VERMONT**

## Bicycling

Several bike shops can supply you with wheels for cruising along the Stowe Recreation Path. Mountain Bike Shop (☎ 802-253-7919), on Mountain Rd, rents bikes for $7 per hour, $25 per day. There's also AJ's Mountain Bikes (☎ 802-253-4593), which rents in-line skates as well.

## Canoeing & Kayaking

Umiak Outdoor Outfitters (☎ 802-253-2317), Gale Farm Center, 1880 Mountain Rd, rents canoes for $35 per day and offers lake and river shuttle trips (canoeists and canoes are shuttled to the river and then picked up at the put-out) for $25 per person. The full moon canoe tours ($35) are unforgettable. Guides also lead three-hour snowshoeing jaunts in the winter for $30.

## Soaring

Stowe Soaring (☎ 802-888-7845, 800-898-7845), at Morrisville-Stowe State Airport on VT 100, will take two people up in a glider for 10 minutes ($48) to an hour ($169).

## Special Events

If you are lucky enough to be in Waterbury on a Thursday night in summer (mid-June to mid-August), the town hosts free concerts in the park – with free ice cream!

## Places to Stay

Stowe has a wide variety of lodging choices, with about 75 inns, motels and B&Bs; many are along Mountain Rd. The Stowe Area Association (☎ 802-253-7321, 800-247-8693, fax 802-253-2159) can help you make your reservations.

**Camping** *Little River State Park* (☎ 802-244-7103, 479-4280), on RD 1 in Waterbury, just north of I-89, has 101 campsites (20 lean-tos) open late May through early September for $13 to $16. The park is next to Waterbury Reservoir, which has boating, fishing and swimming. To find the park, go 1½ miles west of Waterbury on US 2, then 3½ miles north on Little River Rd.

*Smugglers Notch State Park* (☎ 802-253-4014, 7248 Mountain Rd), 8 miles northwest

of Stowe, is a small park with 35 sites (14 lean-tos) on 25 acres; it's priced from $13 to $16 and open late May to mid-October.

*Gold Brook Campground* (☎ 802-253-7683), on VT 100, 7½ miles north of I-89, has 100 campsites (half with hookups), free hot showers and many services. The rate for two in a tent is $16. It's open year-round; you may need to reserve in advance for the busy summer months.

**Hostels** A mere 400 yards from the ski lifts of Stowe and the hiking trails of Mt Mansfield, the location of the *Mount Mansfield Hostel* (☎ 802-253-4010, 6992 Mountain Rd) is hard to beat. Built in 1933 to house the members of the Civilian Conservation Corps (CCC) while they cut the first ski trails, the bunk rooms now cost $12 to $24. Add $12 for breakfast and dinner.

**Motels** *Die Alpenrose Motel* (☎ 802-253-7277, 800-962-7002, 2619 Mountain Rd) has two rooms and three efficiency units for $48 to $69.

*Innsbruck Inn* (☎ 802-253-8582, 800-225-8582, 4361 Mountain Rd) is a modern interpretation of a traditional Alpine inn. Rooms are comfy and well-equipped and cost $79 to $129 in summer.

*Northern Lights Lodge* (☎ 802-253-8541, 800-448-4554), on Mountain Rd, has 40 rooms and seven efficiencies, a dining room, indoor and outdoor swimming pools, a sauna, whirlpool and game room. Rooms cost $58 to $78.

*Stowe Motel* (☎ 802-253-7629, 800-829-7629, 2043 Mountain Rd) has 16 efficiencies priced from $86 to $94 in summer. Amenities include a swimming pool, tennis court, badminton and lawn games. You can also borrow bicycles to ride on the recreation path.

**Inns** A favorite is the simple, traditional, reasonably priced *Ski Inn* (☎ 802-253-4050) on Mountain Rd. Only a mile from the ski area, the Ski Inn opened in 1941, just after the first chairlift was built. It has clean and simple rooms (some with private bath; others share) and a family atmosphere.

## Vermont: Alive with the Sound of Music

Stowe has a more famous Austrian connection than ski champion Sepp Ruschp: the Trapp family, immortalized in *The Sound of Music*.

In Austria in the 1920s, Maria Augusta Kutschera (1905-87) was hired as governess to the seven children of Baron Georg von Trapp, a widower. The baron, who loved children and music, married the governess in 1927 and sired three more children, bringing the family to a neat dozen, just enough for a good choir.

By the mid-1930s the young ones were old enough to sing, and by 1937 they had made a European singing tour. When Hitler took Austria, they fled to the USA, making singing tours around the country from 1940 to 1947, when Baron von Trapp died. Baroness von Trapp wrote the family history, *The Story of the Trapp Family Singers* (1949), and continued touring until 1955.

The Trapp story came to the attention of composer Richard Rodgers and lyricist Oscar Hammerstein II, who romanticized it and made it into a wildly successful Broadway show (1959), followed by the movie *The Sound of Music*, starring Julie Andrews as Maria.

The Trapp family, aglow with fame and royalties, retired to the hills above Stowe on a 2000-acre farm. They built an Austrian-style inn, the Trapp Family Lodge, which has become a large, luxurious country hotel and condominium resort.

**Tom Brosnahan**

---

Rates range from $55 to $65 (including breakfast and dinner) in winter and $30 to $40 in summer (including breakfast).

*Fiddler's Green Inn* (☎ 802-253-8124, 800-882-5346, 4859 Mountain Rd), near the Ski Inn, has rustic pine walls, a fieldstone fireplace and seven guest rooms priced from $40 to $60. Meals are served in the dining room.

Hidden in the forest next to a raging creek, a mile from Stowe's lifts, *The Inn at Turner Mill* (☎ 802-235-2062 ), on Mountain Rd, offers an assortment of clean efficiencies in a rambling wood building. Ask owner Greg Speer, an avid outdoorsman, about the special winter adventure weekends that include snowshoeing, cross-country skiing and ice climbing. Apartments range from $48 (one bedroom, shared bath) to $335 (four bedrooms, 2 private baths, with full kitchen and fireplace).

All 12 rooms at *The Buccaneer Country Lodge* (☎ 802-253-4772, 3214 Mountain Rd) enjoy excellent views of Mt Mansfield, only a 3-mile drive away. Most of the rooms have full kitchens. Rates range from $75 to $95 and include a full breakfast.

*The Siebeness Inn* (☎ 802-253-8942, 800-426-9001, 3681 Mountain Rd) is an 11-room family country inn with a swimming pool and lots of other activities. Rooms cost $90 to $165 in summer, but ask about special package rates.

*Andersen Lodge* (☎ 802-253-7336, 800-336-7336, 3430 Mountain Rd) is a 17-room Tyrolean-style inn with a good dining room, swimming pool, tennis courts and sauna. Rooms cost $96 for two, breakfast included.

The dramatically rustic 46-room *Stowehof Inn & Resort* (☎ 802-253-9722l, 800-932-7136), on Edson Hill Rd, has a hillside location, a good dining room, many amenities and guest rooms priced from $140 to $250, breakfast included.

With 92 rooms, *Topnotch at Stowe* (☎ 802-253-8585, 800-451-8686, fax 802-253-9263), on Mountain Rd, is Stowe's most lavish resort. Prices range from $150 to $300.

*The Riverside Inn* (☎ 802-253-4217, 800-966-4217, 1965 Mountain Rd) has 10 cozy rooms in a lodge and six motel units. Prices range from $45 to $85.

*Nichol's Lodge* (☎ 802-253-7683), on Stowe St south of the town center, is a basic

**VERMONT**

place with eight rooms and two dorms. Rooms cost a low $32 to $55.

The **Bittersweet Inn** (☎ 802-253-7787), on Stowe St just southwest of the town center, is a homey eight-room B&B with a swimming pool, lawn games and rooms priced from $56 to $66.

Just north of town on VT 100, **The Inn at the Brass Lantern** (☎ 802-253-2229) has spacious rooms with fireplaces in the $90 to $150 range.

## Places to Eat

Food in Stowe, for the most part, is expensive and mediocre. However, there are several places, such as the Blue Moon Cafe, that excel.

The locals traditionally take breakfast at **McCarthy's** (☎ 802-253-8626). The breakfasts are hearty and reasonably priced ($3 to $4). Choices include french toast, apple pancakes with maple syrup and lots of different omelettes. Look for McCarthy's in the shopping center near the Stowe Cinema, across Mountain Rd from Ye Olde England Inne.

For lighter breakfast fare and a good cup of coffee, check out **The Bagel** (☎ 802-253-9943) in the Baggy Knees Shopping Center on Mountain Rd.

**Thompson's Flour Stop** (☎ 802-253-9044), on Main St, is a good place to grab a quick muffin, sandwich or snack ($1.50 to $5). There are tables inside and outside.

**Depot Street Malt Shoppe** (☎ 802-253-4269, 57 Depot St), in the center of town, is where the locals go for a burger and an old-fashioned ice cream soda. Prices for lunch range from $2.70 to $4.95.

**Brown Bag Deli and Donuts** (☎ 802-253-4600), in the Baggy Knees Shopping Center on Mountain Rd, has the best selection of sandwiches in town ($4.25 to $5.75).

**Gracie's Restaurant** (☎ 802-253-8741), off Main St and behind Carlson Real Estate, is becoming so popular that supermarkets around the country now carry Gracie's sauces. Specialties include Thai chicken flatbread ($8.95) and the garlic-laden shrimp scampi. It's open until 12:30 am, a plus for late-night eaters.

A local favorite for pizza and pasta is **Pie in the Sky** (☎ 802-253-5100, 492 Mountain Rd), with affordable prices that are generally in the $5.95 to $10.95 range.

**Trattoria La Festa** (☎ 802-253-8480, 4080 Mountain Rd), near the Topnotch at Stowe mountain resort, has great Italian fare made by authentic Italian chefs. Try the spaghetti pescatore, chock-full of mussels, clams and shrimp ($15.95). Open nightly, the trattoria serves dinner only.

**Mr Pickwick's Pub & Restaurant** (☎ 802-253-7064, Mountain Rd), in Ye Olde England Inne, is heavy on the British decor and features 120 beers and ales, including rare Scottish malts. Menu highlights include beef Wellington, bangers and mash, and steak and kidney pie. Dinner costs $12 to $30.

**Whiskers** (☎ 802-253-8996), on Mountain Rd, is a steakhouse specializing in prime rib, including an 18oz to 20oz monster portion for $19; a bowl of soup and salad bar can be had for under $10. The outdoor dining is nice in summer.

**Blue Moon Cafe** (☎ 802-253-7006, School St), a half block off Main St in a converted house with a little sunporch, is among New England's top restaurants. This intimate cafe changes entrees nightly, and whatever is on the menu is usually sublime. Expect Maine crabs, salmon dishes, oysters, rabbit and an extensive wine list. Dinner for two costs $60 to $80.

## Entertainment

**Matterhorn** (☎ 802-253-8198), at the top of Mountain Rd, is always hopping at 5 pm, when skiers start to hobble off the slopes.

If you're searching for an après-ski scene with a bit more class, check out **Charlie B's** (☎ 802-253-7355, 1746 Mountain Rd) at the Stoweflake Inn and Resort.

**The Mountain Road House** (☎ 802-253-2800, 1677 Mountain Rd) is a casual setting (peanut shells on the floor) that offers the best R&B music in town.

**The Shed** (☎ 802-253-4364, 1859 Mountain Rd) is a cozy microbrewery with six tasty beers always on tap.

## Getting There & Away

**Air** See the Burlington section, later in this chapter, for details.

**Bus** The Vermont Transit (☎ 802-864-6811, 800-451-3292 in New England) buses that travel between Boston and Burlington (with connections for Montreal) stop at Waterbury, 10 miles south of Stowe, two or three times daily. From Waterbury, you can call Peg's Pick Up at ☎ 800-370-9490 for the short drive into Stowe ($15 per person).

**Train** Amtrak's daily *Vermonter* (☎ 800-872-7245, www.amtrak.com) stops at Waterbury, 10 miles away. Some hotels and inns will arrange to pick up guests at the station. For more details about the *Vermonter's* route, see the Getting There & Around section at the beginning of this chapter.

**Car** Driving details for Stowe are as follows:

| destination | distance | hr:min |
|---|---|---|
| Boston, MA | 205 miles | 4:05 |
| Burlington, VT | 36 miles | 0:45 |
| Middlebury, VT | 55 miles | 1:30 |
| Montpelier, VT | 22 miles | 0:35 |
| Montreal, Canada | 140 miles | 3:15 |
| New York, NY | 330 miles | 7:00 |
| Waitsfield, VT | 22 miles | 0:40 |
| Woodstock, VT | 73 miles | 2:00 |

## Getting Around

If you don't have your own vehicle, look for the Stowe Trolley, a bus that runs every half hour daily during ski season from Stowe village, along Mountain Rd, to the ski slopes. For a schedule and list of stops, ask at your inn or at the Stowe Area Association's information office.

## BURLINGTON

Vermont's largest city (population 55,000) would be a small city in most other states, but Burlington's small size is one of its charms. With the University of Vermont's (UVM) student population and a vibrant cultural and social life, Burlington has a spirited, youthful character. As far as nightlife goes, Burlington is Vermont's center, often offering the only big-name acts in the state.

The city's location adds more charm. Perched on the shore of Lake Champlain,

Burlington is less than an hour's drive from Stowe and other Green Mountain towns. Burlington can be used as a base for exploring much of northern Vermont, where each season brings its own festivals and events. In early April, the town of St Albans hosts the Vermont Maple Festival. The state's proud dairy heritage is celebrated at the Vermont Dairy Festival, held in Enosburg Falls in early June. The first week of October brings the annual Applefest to South Hero.

Burlington is not without its own special events: The Discover Jazz Festival is in June; a popular reggae fest is held in the summer; the Fourth of July brings a patriotic civic celebration; the Bard is back from July through August for the Champlain Shakespeare Festival; and the city celebrates New Year's Eve with a festive First Night celebration – a winter festival featuring a parade, an ice- and snow-sculpture exhibition, music and more. Contact the chamber of commerce for more details.

Perhaps the best way to enjoy Burlington is to stroll along Church St Marketplace, have lunch or dinner, then spend the night. The next day, tour the famous Shelburne Museum of Americana and Shelburne Farms (both south of the city) before leaving town.

## Orientation

Take I-89 exit 14 to reach the city center; or take exit 13 to I-189 west to go straight to Shelburne and the motel strip that runs along US 7, south of Burlington.

Downtown Burlington is easily negotiated on foot. Parking is usually not a big problem. The heart of the city is the Church St Marketplace and the adjacent pedestrian mall.

Four blocks west along College St is the city's nice Waterfront Park.

## Information

The Lake Champlain Regional Chamber of Commerce (☎ 802-863-3489, www.vermont .org), Main St, Burlington, VT 05401, provides information, as does the information kiosk at Church and Bank Sts.

In the nearby town of Williston, east of Burlington on I-89, you'll find one of the

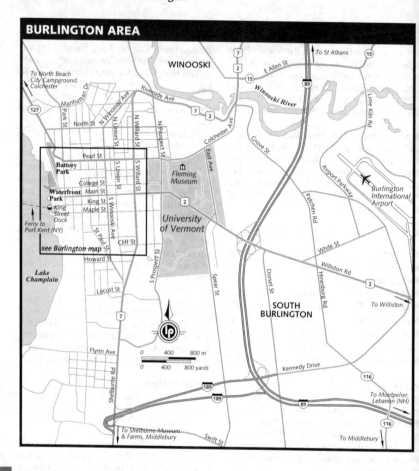

## BURLINGTON AREA

great outdoor adventure stores, Adventurous Traveler Bookstore (☎ 800-282-3963).

### Shelburne Museum

The Shelburne Museum (☎ 802-985-3346), approximately 9 miles south of Burlington off US 7, is a 45-acre estate once owned by the Havemeyer family. HO and Louisine Havemeyer were patrons of the arts and collectors of European and Old Masters paintings. Their daughter Electra's interests, however, tended toward the more familiar and utilitarian. Electra Havemeyer (1888-

1960) amassed a huge, priceless collection of American works of art and craft that she put on display in the numerous buildings of the museum. Indeed, the buildings themselves are exhibits. Many were moved here from other parts of New England in order to assure their preservation.

The collections, 80,000 objects housed in 37 buildings, include exhibits on folk art, decorative arts, Vermont history, tools and trades, transportation and New England houses. There's also a classic round barn (1901), a railroad station complete with locomotive (1915) and luxury private rail coach (1890), a Circus Building and 1920s carousel, a sawmill (1786), a covered bridge (1845), a lighthouse (1871) and even the Lake Champlain side-wheeler steamboat called the SS *Ticonderoga* (1906).

The museum is open 10 am to 5 pm daily from late May through late October; at other times, a 90-minute guided tour of selected buildings starts at 1 pm daily, except holidays. Admission tickets, good for two consecutive days, cost $15 for adults and $6 for children aged six to 14; children five and under are free. A minimal visit takes three hours, and you can easily (and pleasantly) spend all day here. Food is available at the refreshment stand and the more elaborate Dog Team Cafe restaurant, as well as in Shelburne village.

A local bus (CCTA) runs from Burlington's Cherry St terminal along US 7 south to the Shelburne Museum 10 times on weekdays and four times on Saturday, with no Sunday service. The fare is 75¢ for adults, 35¢ for seniors and 50¢ for children.

## Shelburne Farms
In 1886, William Seward Webb and Lila Vanderbilt Webb made a little place for themselves in the Vermont countryside on Lake Champlain. The 1400-acre farm, designed by landscape architect Frederick Law Olmsted (who also designed New York's Central Park), was both a country house for the Webbs and a working farm.

The grand, 24-bedroom English country manor (1899), now an inn, is surrounded by working farm buildings inspired by European romanticism. You can visit Shelburne Farms (☎ 802-985-8686, 985-8442), buy some of the cheese, maple syrup, mustard and other items produced here, hike the walking trail and visit the animals in the Children's Farmyard.

The farm, 8 miles south of Burlington, is open 10 am (9 am in summer) to 5 pm. (The walking trail and the Children's Farmyard close at 4 pm.) Guided tours lasting 90 minutes begin at 9:30 and 11 am, 12:30, 2 and 3:30 pm, mid-May through mid-October. A tour of the farm is $5/4/3 for adults/seniors/children. A ticket good for both the walking trail and the Children's Farmyard costs $4 for adults and $3 for children.

## University of Vermont
The University of Vermont (☎ 802-656-3131, www.uvm.edu), with its 10,400 students, gives Burlington its youthful vigor. East of the town center, the green campus features a number of 18th-century buildings. It's said that the students here drink more than the students do at Dartmouth, which might be hard to actually prove, but if true is something of an accomplishment. If you go out at night, you'll no doubt run into a few of them.

From fall to spring, the main event at the Guterson Field House is UVM hockey, which consistently draws sellout crowds; call ahead for information on getting tickets to these thrillers. The university's website includes a campus calendar of events, including appearances by public speakers, art exhibitions and sporting events.

## Fleming Museum
The Robert Hull Fleming Museum (☎ 802-656-2090), 61 Colchester Ave, is UVM's art museum. Its collections of more than 17,000 objects include African masks, Indian drums, Samurai armor, an Egyptian mummy and Vermont paintings.

The museum is open 9 am to 5 pm Tuesday to Friday, and 1 to 5 pm on weekends. Admission is free, but the suggested donation is $2.

## Hiking & Bicycling
The Burlington Recreation Path (☎ 802-864-0123) runs along the waterfront through the Waterfront Park and Promenade, as does the 9-mile Burlington Bikeway, a popular route for walking, biking and in-line skating. You can rent bikes at the Community Boathouse (see Boating, below).

## Boating
Approximately 120 miles long and 12 miles wide, Lake Champlain is the largest freshwater lake in the country after the Great Lakes. Consistently good wind, sheltered bays, hundreds of islands and scenic anchorages combine to make this immense body of

VERMONT

water one of the top cruising grounds in the Northeast. Winds of Ireland (☎ 802-863-5090) charters five Hunters (30 to 40 feet) at a daily or weekly rate. Prices start at $145 per day. A captain costs extra. McKibben Burlington's Community Boathouse (☎ 802-865-3377), on the lakeshore at the foot of College St, rents rowboats, sailboats, canoes and kayaks.

## Diving

Ever since the French and Indian War in the 18th century, 120-mile long Lake Champlain

has been a major thoroughfare from the S\ Lawrence Seaway to the Hudson River During the Revolutionary War and the Wa\ of 1812, numerous historic battles were fought on the lake to control this navigational stronghold. In the latter half of the 19th-century, commercial vessels replaced gunboats. Many of these military and merchant ships sank to the lake's deep dark bottom as a result of the cannonball or of temperamental weather.

These vessels' misfortunes are lucky finds for the scuba diver. Two hundred wrecks

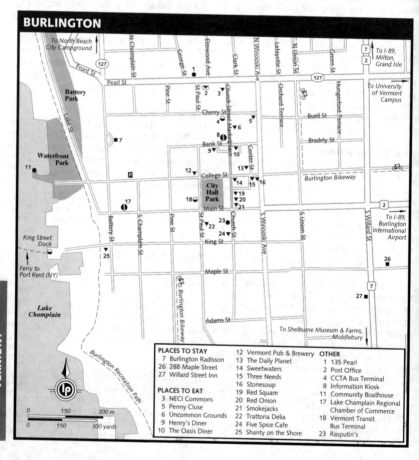

**BURLINGTON**

To North Beach City Campground
Front St
127
Pearl St
Battery Park
Cherry St
Bank St
Waterfront Park
College St
City Hall Park
Main St
King Street Dock
Ferry to Port Kent (NY)
King St
Lake Champlain
Maple St
Burlington Bikeway
Adams St
Burlington Recreation Path
To Shelburne Museum & Farms, Middlebury

To I-89, Milton, Grand Isle
To University of Vermont Campus
Bueli St
Bradely St
Burlington Bikeway
To I-89, Burlington International Airport

0   150   300 m
0   150   300 yards

| PLACES TO STAY | 12 Vermont Pub & Brewery | OTHER |
|---|---|---|
| 7 Burlington Radisson | 13 The Daily Planet | 1 135 Pearl |
| 26 288 Maple Street | 14 Sweetwaters | 2 Post Office |
| 27 Willard Street Inn | 15 Three Needs | 4 CCTA Bus Terminal |
| | 16 Stonesoup | 8 Information Kiosk |
| PLACES TO EAT | 19 Red Square | 11 Community Boathouse |
| 3 NECI Commons | 20 Red Onion | 17 Lake Champlain Regional |
| 5 Penny Cluse | 21 Smokejacks | Chamber of Commerce |
| 6 Uncommon Grounds | 22 Trattoria Delia | 18 Vermont Transit |
| 9 Henry's Diner | 24 Five Spice Cafe | Bus Terminal |
| 10 The Oasis Diner | 25 Shanty on the Shore | 23 Rasputin's |

VERMONT

have already been discovered, including the 54-foot Revolutionary War boat *Philadelphia*, pulled from the waters in 1935 (and now sitting in the Smithsonian Institution in Washington, DC). Unfortunately, many of the earlier wrecks are far too deep for scuba divers, but six of the commercial vessels that lie on the lake's floor have been preserved by the state of Vermont as an underwater historical site.

There are no special permit fees, but all divers must register with the Vermont Division for Historic Preservation (☎ 802-828-3051). In return, you get a nifty little book that details all six wrecks. Register at any dive shop in the state. Waterfront Diving Center (☎ 802-865-2771), 214 Battery St in Burlington, offers rentals, charters and instruction.

## Places to Stay

**Camping** The *North Beach Campground* (☎ 802-862-0942, 60 Institute Rd) is operated by the city of Burlington. With 137 sites (mostly for tents) on 45 acres near the city center, but right on Lake Champlain, it's the first choice for tent campers. The tent sites cost $18. To find it, go to the lakeshore in Burlington, then head north along Battery St and North Ave (VT 127), turning left on Institute Rd.

The *Shelburne Camping Area* (☎ 802-985-2540, 985-2296, 2056 Shelburne Rd), near the prominent Dutch Mill Motel, a mile north of the Shelburne Museum on the east side of US 7, has 76 sites in a pine grove off the highway. The base rate is $18; it's open from mid-May to mid-October.

**Hostels** *Mrs Farrell's Home Hostel* (☎ 802-865-3730) has six beds priced at $15. Reservations are essential; call at least 24 hours in advance, and before 8 pm. Nancy Farrell will give you directions to the hostel when you call.

**Motels** Burlington's budget and mid-range motels are on the outskirts of town. It's not usually necessary to reserve in advance, but if you call ahead on the day you intend to stay and ask for the 'same-day rate,' you may get a discount.

The *Susse Chalet* (☎ 802-879-8999), I-89 exit 12, offers a 'same-day rate' under $50, continental breakfast included.

Many of the chain motels (Econo Lodge, Comfort Inn, Anchorage Inn, etc) lie on Williston Rd east of I-89 exit 14. There is another collection of lodgings that are along US 7 north of Burlington in Colchester (take I-89 exit 16).

Perhaps the best selection of budget and mid-range places is along Shelburne Rd (US 7) in South Burlington on the way to Shelburne. Here are some suggestions, listed in the order you'll come to them as you drive south from central Burlington.

The 37-room *Colonial Motor Inn* (☎ 802-862-5754, 462 Shelburne Rd) has the advantage of being near central Burlington and is moderately priced at $58 per room.

The *Town & Country Motel* (☎ 802-862-5786, 490 Shelburne Rd) and the wonderfully named *Ho Hum Motel* (☎ 802-658-1314, 1200 Shelburne Rd) are nearby, in the same price range.

The *Howard Johnson Motel & Suites* (☎ 802-860-6000, 800-874-1554, fax 802-864-9919, 1720 Shelburne Rd) is a step up in both price and comfort. Its 121 rooms cost $89 to $99. There's a nice swimming pool, whirlpool bath, sauna and a free airport shuttle.

The *Northstar Motel* (☎ 802-863-3421, 2427 Shelburne Rd), Shelburne, advertises rates of $28.50/$38.50 for a single/double. Look at your room before you decide.

*Yankee Doodle Motel* (☎ 802-985-8004, 3972 Shelburne Rd), Shelburne, only 2 miles north of the Shelburne Museum, offers 15 very clean and tidy rooms for $45/$55, continental breakfast included, the latter price being for a room with two double beds.

The *Countryside Motel* (☎ 802-985-2839, 6475 Shelburne Rd), just south of Shelburne Museum, charges $72.

**Hotels** Downtown hotels in Burlington are very comfortable and somewhat higher in price than the motels above. The 255-room *Burlington Radisson* (☎ 802-658-6500, 800-333-3333, fax 802-658-4659, 60 Battery St) has the best location and offers rooms for $159 to $179.

**VERMONT**

**Inns** *The Hartwell House B&B* (☎ *802-658-9242, 170 Ferguson St)* is only a five-minute drive from the center of town in a quiet residential neighborhood. Owner Linda Hartwell has three clean rooms with shared bath and a small outdoor pool. Prices, including breakfast, are a bargain at $45 to $65.

*The Willard Street Inn* (☎ *802-651-8710, 800-577-8712, 349 South Willard St)* is perched on a hill within easy walking distance of the University of Vermont and the Church St Marketplace. This Queen-Anne-style home was built in the late 1880s. Many of the 16 guest rooms (13 with private bath) overlook Lake Champlain. Prices range from $85 to $175 and include a full breakfast, such as the sublime cranberry-walnut french toast.

Close by are two other small B&Bs that are popular with parents bringing their kids to UVM. At *288 Maple Street* (☎ *802-863-2033)* there are three rooms, two with private bath, in the $70 to $100 range. For a view of the lake, ask for the aptly named Lake Room, the uppermost room in this cozy Victorian house. *Burlington Redstone* (☎ *802-862-0508, 497 S Willard St)* is a wonderful old stone house owned by an avid gardener. Stroll through her perennial gardens on a hill overlooking the lake. Two rooms with shared bath cost $85, and a room with private bath and lake views costs $115.

If you've always dreamed of being lord of the manor, you can indulge your fantasies at the sumptuous *Inn at Shelburne Farms* (☎ *802-985-8498)*, 8 miles south of Burlington off US 7. The inn was once the summer mansion of the wealthy Webb family. Rooms vary in size and appointments and are priced from $95 to $175 (shared bath) or $190 to $350 (private bath). Meals are available for an additional charge. The inn is open from mid-May to mid-October.

## Places to Eat

Burlington is perhaps the only place in Vermont that has a full range of restaurants. There are dozens in and near the Church St Marketplace.

*Uncommon Grounds* (☎ *802-865-6227, 42 Church St)* is a good local place for coffee.

Take your newspaper, order a cup of joe and a muffin and blend into the woodwork, or take over one of the sidewalk tables (in good weather).

In the original home of Ben & Jerry's ice cream, *Penny Cluse* (☎ *802-651-8834, 169 Cherry St)* serves one of the best breakfasts in town, including Southwestern selections such as the breakfast burrito ($5). Indeed, local chefs rave about the innovative breakfasts served here.

*Henry's Diner* (☎ *802-862-9010, 115 Bank St)* is a Burlington fixture, having opened in 1925. The daily special meal of soup, main course, dessert and beverage costs only around $5. (Compare this to $3.50 for a bratwurst with sauerkraut from a pushcart in the Church St Marketplace.) Everything on Henry's menu is priced under $8. The food is simple, the atmosphere homey and pleasant, the prices unbeatable.

Another old-time place is *The Oasis Diner* (☎ *802-864-5308, 189 Bank St)*. Just off Church St, this is a stainless steel diner with an old-time feel serving cheap breakfast and lunch from 5:30 am to 4:30 pm. Try it for Sunday brunch, 8 am to 3 pm.

*The Daily Planet* (☎ *802-862-9647, 15 Center St)* has big sandwiches for $6 and, in the evening, main courses such as potato-crusted salmon with Moroccan vegetable sauté, or Thai shrimp salad, for $11 to $16.

*Stonesoup* (☎ *802-862-7616, 211 College St)* is a big lunch hit with local vegetarians. Popular items include homemade soups ($2.50 to $3.25) and sandwiches on homemade bread ($4 to $5).

Next door, *Three Needs* (☎ *802-658-0889, 207 College St)* is a pleasant microbrewery that has wons awards year after year for its brews.

Expect lines at lunch, even in the blustery days of winter, at the popular *Red Onion* (☎ *802-865-2563, 140½ Church St)*. Hot open-faced turkey sandwiches or veggie lentil soup are a few of the tempting treats.

*Sweetwaters* (☎ *802-864-9800, 120 Church St)*, heavily nouveau Victorian in decor, is a local watering hole for the young and upwardly mobile. In the evening the glass-enclosed patio is loud with chatter and redoent of nachos and chicken wings; the beverage of choice is an exotic beer.

*Vermont Pub & Brewery* (☎ *802-865-0500, 144 College St*) has pints for $3 and an assortment of specialty and seasonal brews made on the premises, such as Burly Irish Ale, Dogbite Bitter, Dr Walther's Wunder Pils and Vermont Smoked Porter. There's plenty of bar food to go with the pints.

For dim sum brunch on Sunday, you've got to go to *Five Spice Café* (☎ *802-864-4045, 175 Church St*), which serves excellent dishes from China, India and Indonesia, as well as Thailand and Vietnam.

*NECI Commons* (☎ *802-862-6324, 25 Church St*) is run by students from Montpelier's New England Culinary Institute. Dishes such as rotisserie chicken, roasted turkey breast and sea bass are served at the long, welcoming wooden counter or at quiet tables. Entrees at dinner run from $9.95 to $13.50. Stop by for coffee and freshly baked pastries in the morning.

Don't be fooled by the small bar at the entrance of *Red Square* (☎ *802-859-8909, 136 Church St*). This restaurant is a maze of rooms, where tables are always filled with locals excited to know what special entree chef Lenny Williams is whipping up that day. Williams, who has worked at some of the top restaurants in New England, including the Chanticleer and Summer House in Nantucket, serves delectable goodies such as crab cakes wrapped in banana leaves served with a peanut sauce ($10) or sautéed shrimp with Cajun spices ($10).

Down the block, *Smokejacks* (☎ *802-658-1119, 156 Church St*) is known for its fresh fish dishes, including crispy Chilean sea bass on a bed of soba noodles. Main courses cost $12.75 to $18.50. The locally famous cheese list features some of America's finest small farm cheeses.

*Trattoria Delia* (☎ *802-864-5253, 152 St Paul St*) is consistently rated the top Italian restaurant in the city by *Vermont Magazine*. Expect homemade pastas or specialties like *osso bucco*. Dinner, priced $9 to $18.50, is served from 5 pm to 10 pm daily.

For lakefront dining, try *Shanty on the Shore* (☎ *802-864-0238, 181 Battery St*). It faces the car ferry dock and enjoys a fine view of the lake. This combined seafood market and eatery serves fresh lobster, fish and shellfish lunches and dinners for $8 to $20.

## Entertainment

The *Burlington Free Press*, the local newspaper, carries a special weekend entertainment section in its Thursday issue. This is perhaps the town's best source for up-to-date concert, theater, cinema, lecture and other program information.

Church St Marketplace, with its many restaurants and sidewalk cafes, is also the center of Burlington nightlife.

*Red Square* (☎ *802-859-8909, 136 Church St*) has a stylish Soho-like ambience. This is where Vermonters in the know go to sip martinis or wine, listen to Burlington's best roadhouse music and dine on the excellent food (see Places to Eat).

The *Daily Planet* (☎ *802-862-9647, 15 Center St*) is for the young and hip. Thirtysomethings who have 'made it' (or hope they have) go to *Sweetwaters* (☎ *802-864-9800, 120 Church St*) to eat the free snacks on weekday afternoons from 5 to 7 pm, though the action doesn't pick up until after 9:30 pm.

*Rasputin's*, on Church St, is a popular college hangout with loud music and fast dancing. *135 Pearl* (☎ *802-864-9800, 135 Pearl St*) is the center of the gay scene.

## Getting There & Away

**Air** The Burlington International Airport is located east of the city center. Delta, Continental, Northwest and US Airways serve Burlington's airport, as do small commuter operations.

**Bus** Vermont Transit buses (☎ 802-864-6811, 800-451-3292 in New England), based in Burlington, provides transport to major towns in Vermont, as well as to Manchester and Keene, New Hampshire; Albany and Boston. The Vermont Transit terminal, at 135 St Paul St, faces City Hall Park.

Greyhound Lines (☎ 800-231-2222) operates one bus daily between Burlington and Montreal. The three-hour trip costs $23.50 one way.

**VERMONT**

**Train** Amtrak's *Vermonter* (☎ 800-872-7245, www.amtrak.com) stops in Burlington. For additional train details, see the Getting There & Around section at the beginning of this chapter.

**Car** Driving details for Burlington are as follows:

| destination | distance | hr:min |
| --- | --- | --- |
| Boston, MA | 230 miles | 4:35 |
| Middlebury, VT | 34 miles | 0:50 |
| Montreal, Canada | 102 miles | 2:15 |
| New York, NY | 345 miles | 7:00 |
| Plattsburgh, NY | 26 miles | 0:40 |
| Stowe, VT | 36 miles | 0:50 |

**Boat** Lake Champlain Transportation Co (☎ 802-864-9804), King St Dock in Burlington, runs car ferries across the lake to connect Burlington with Port Kent, New York, 14 times daily in summer. There are fewer trips in spring (eight) and fall (11), and there's no service from mid-October to mid-May. The fare for the one-hour voyage is $12 for a car and driver, $3/1 additional for each adult/child aged six to 12. Ferries depart from the dock at the foot of King St.

The company also operates ferries connecting Charlotte, Vermont, with Essex, New York (south of Burlington); and Grand Isle, Vermont (north of Burlington), with Plattsburgh, New York. The latter service runs year-round.

## Getting Around

**To/From the Airport** The Chittenden County Transportation Authority (☎ 802-864-0211) operates buses from its Cherry St Terminal (at the corner of Church St) to Burlington Airport. Buses run about every half-hour, departing Cherry St at quarter past and quarter to the hour. There is no service on Sunday. Normal adult fare is 75¢; 50¢ if you're younger than 18; and 35¢ if you're 60-plus.

**Bus** The local bus is the CCTA, or the Chittenden County Transportation Authority (☎ 802-864-0211). CCTA buses depart from the Cherry St Terminal (at the corner of Church St). There is no service on Sunday. The fare is 75¢ for adults, 50¢ for children under 18, and 35¢ for those over 60.

A free College St shuttle bus runs a loop route from the Waterfront Park near the Community Boathouse, stopping at Battery St, St Paul St, Church St Marketplace, Winooski Ave, Union St, Willard St and ending at the UVM campus. In summer, shuttles run every 10 minutes from 11 am to 6 pm.

## NORTHEAST KINGDOM

Speaking to a small group of his constituents in Lyndonville, Vermont, in 1949, Senator George Aiken noted that 'this is such beautiful country up here. It ought to be called the Northeast Kingdom of Vermont.' The locals took the wise senator's advice. The Northeast Kingdom now consists of Essex, Orleans and Caledonia counties – a large tract of land wedged between the Quebec and New Hampshire borders.

In a state that's known for its rural setting (only Wyoming and Alaska contain fewer people), this is Vermont putting on its finest pastoral dress, with a few holes here and there. Wave after wave of unspoiled hillside form a vast sea of green, and small villages and farms spread out in the distance under a few soaring summits. Here, inconspicuous inns and dairy cows have replaced the slick resorts and Morgan horses found in the southern part of the state, and the white steeples are chipped, not freshly painted. Indeed, it is the most authentic area in Vermont, a region that doesn't put on any airs about attracting tourists.

## History

It was the 1830s when the Fairbanks family of St Johnsbury, the Kingdom's largest community, began manufacturing weight scales. The Fairbanks clan soon became one of America's wealthiest families and, fortunately for St Johnsbury, began pouring their money into the village. They would open one of the finest libraries in America, where leather-bound books would share space with a 19th-century art gallery. They also opened one of the first natural history museums in the country. The two sites, the St Johnsbury Athenaeum and the Fairbanks Museum & Planetarium, have remained relatively unaltered and are still open to the public.

## Orientation

While St Johnsbury is easily reached by I-91 or I-93 (a three-hour drive from Boston through New Hampshire), the rest of the Northeast Kingdom is incredibly spread out. Use I-91 as your north-south thoroughfare, and then use smaller routes like VT 5A to find stunning Lake Willoughby or VT 14 to find Craftsbury Common, a town of white clapboard houses perfectly set around a village green. Other favorite villages include Greensboro, nestled upon the shores of Caspian Lake, and Barton, near pristine Crystal Lake.

## Information

Contact the office of the Northeast Kingdom Chamber of Commerce (☎ 802-748-3678, www.vermontnekchamber.org), 30 Western Ave, St Johnsbury, VT 05819, for information on lodging, dining and sightseeing in the region.

## St Johnsbury Athenauem

The St Johnsbury Athenauem (☎ 802-748-8291), 1171 Main St, was founded in 1871, when Horace Fairbanks gave the town a library. He hired bibliographer WF Poole to select some 8000 finely bound copies of the world's classic literature. In addition, Fairbanks added an art gallery to the back of the building and installed works by such noted Hudson River School painters as Asher B Durand, Worthington Whittredge and Jasper Crospey.

His crowning achievement was the purchase of Albert Bierstadt's 10-foot-by-15-foot *Domes of the Yosemite*. Bierstadt is said to have returned to the gallery every summer until his death to touch up his masterpiece occasionally. Today, the Athenaeum's art collection is the oldest art gallery still in its original form in the USA. You can visit these artworks 10 am to 8 pm Monday and Wednesday; 10 am to 5:30 pm Tuesday,

Thursday and Friday; and 9:30 am to 4 pm Saturdays. Admission is free.

## Fairbanks Museum & Planetarium

In 1891, when Franklin Fairbanks' collection of stuffed animals and cultural artifacts from across the globe grew too large for his home, he built the **Fairbanks Museum of Natural Science** (☎ 802-748-2372), 1302 Main St. This massive stone building with a 30-foot-high barrel-vaulted ceiling still displays more than half of Franklin's original collection. More than 3000 preserved animals in glass cases can be seen, including a 1200lb moose shot in Nova Scotia in 1898, an American bison from 1902 and a Bengal tiger. The museum is open 10 am to 4 pm Monday through Saturday, 1 to 5 pm Sunday. Admission is $5/3 for adults/children. Admission to the planetarium is $2 per person.

## Activities

Not surprisingly, this sylvan countryside is the perfect playground for outdoor activity in New England. Almost any outdoor activity is at its best in this region.

**Skiing** The Northeast Kingdom has downhill skiing, and when it's balmy in Boston in winter, you can still expect a blizzard at Vermont's northernmost ski resort, **Jay Peak** (☎ 802-988-2611), on VT 242, 8 miles north of Montgomery Center. Bordering Quebec, Jay gets more snow than any other ski area in New England (about 350 inches of powder). Being so far north, Jay also accommodates far more Quebecois than New Yorkers. Black-diamond lovers enjoy the steeper tree runs off the tram, while novices find the trails in Bonaventure Basin to their liking. Add the natural off-piste terrain, and you have some of the most challenging backcountry snowboarding and skiing runs in America.

**Burke Mountain** (☎ 802-626-3305), off of US 5 in East Burke, is relatively unknown to anyone outside the Northeast Kingdom. Locals enjoy the challenging trails and the lack of lift lines. Burke has 33 trails (30% beginner, 40% intermediate, 30% expert), and four lifts, including one quad chair and one lift with a vertical drop of 2000 feet.

If you are a cross-country skier, you're bound to find snow at **Craftsbury Outdoor Center** (☎ 802-586-7767), on Lost Nation Rd, 3 miles from Craftsbury Common. The 80 miles of trails, 50 of them groomed, roll over meadows and weave through forests of maples and firs, offering an ideal experience for all levels. Even if you don't plan on skiing, you should take a drive over to Craftsbury Common, where you'll find what may be Vermont's most spectacular village green. White clapboard buildings surround a rectangular lawn that hasn't changed one iota from the mid-19th century.

Nearby, **Highland Lodge** (☎ 802-533-2647), on Craftsbury Rd, has 40 miles of trails that slope down to the shores of Caspian Lake.

**Hiking** Lake Willoughby's stunning beauty will leave even a jaded visitor in awe. Sandwiched between Mt Hor and Mt Pisgah, cliffs plummet over 1000 feet to the glacial waters below and create, in essence, a landlocked fjord. The scenery is best appreciated on the three-hour hike to the summit of **Mt Pisgah**.

From West Burke, take VT 5A for 6 miles to a parking area on the left-hand side of the road, just south of Lake Willoughby. The 1.7-mile (one-way) South Trail begins across the highway. (It's about a 30-minute drive from St Johnsbury to Mt Pisgah.)

**Mountain Biking** East Burke, on VT 114 off I-91, is a terrific place to start a mountain bike ride. In the summer of 1997, John Worth, co-owner of East Burke Sports, and several other dedicated locals linked together more than 150 miles of single tracks and dirt roads to form a network they call the **Kingdom Trails**. Riding on a soft forest floor dusted with pine needles and through century-old farms makes for one of the best mountain-biking experiences in New England. East Burke Sports (☎ 802-626-3215), on VT 114 in East Burke, rents bikes and can supply maps.

## Places to Stay

The Northeast Kingdom offers some of the most affordable lodging in the state. The best accommodations are at small inns on family-run farms or by the shores of a hidden lake.

**Camping** *Brighton State Park* (☎ 802-723-4360), off VT 105 not far from the town of Island Pond, has 84 sites near the shores of Lake Willoughby. Sites cost $13 to $16.

Two other campsites lie on VT 232 south of St Johnsbury and near Lake Groton. *Stillwater Campground* (☎ 802-584-3822) has 79 sites and a prime swimming spot on the northwestern shores of Lake Groton. *Ricker Pond State Park* (☎ 802-584-3821) has 55 sites on the shores of Ricker Pond.

**Inns** *The Wildflower Inn* (☎ 802-626-8310), on Darling Hill Rd in Lyndonville, is a perennial favorite among Boston families. Maybe it's because owners Jim and Mary O'Reilly have eight children and their home is littered with toys. Or perhaps it's the hay rides, mountain bike trails, a petting zoo with sheep and goats, a playground, pool, tennis courts, batting cage, basketball courts, skating rink, sleigh hill and sleigh rides. Did we forget to mention the exquisite views of the region from atop Darling Hill? Rooms range from $115 up to $230 and include an breakfast.

Just down the road from The Wildflower Inn, you'll see the splendid *Mountain View Creamery* (☎ 802-626-9924), on Darling Hill Rd in East Burke. Built in 1883 as the quintessential gentleman's farm, Mountain View once housed 100 Jersey cows, pigs and Morgan horses in impressive and very large red barns . The farm is set on 440 acres, ideal for mountain biking, cross-country skiing or simply a long stroll on the hillside. Situated in the former creamery, the 10 rooms, all with private bath, range from $90 to $120.

*The Village Inn* (☎ 802-626-3161), VT 114 in East Burke, is conveniently located at the base of Burke Mountain's ski area. Five very clean rooms, all with private bath, cost a mere $60. In the wonderful garden out back, you can follow a trail that leads to a water-fall. (If only life could be this simple.)

Overlooking the majestic granite cliffs of Mt Hor and Mt Pisgah, the ***Willoughvale Inn*** (☎ *802-525-4123*), VT 5A in Westmore, sits on the northern shores of Lake Willoughby. In the summer, cast off from the small beach and kayak on the cool waters of the lake; in the winter, rent snowmobiles and head up into the hills. The eight rooms and four cottages range from $79 to $129.

***The Anglin B&B*** (☎ *802-525-4548, 202 Lakeside Land*), Barton, is an apt name for the clapboard house that sits on the shores of Crystal Lake. You can wake up in the morning and throw your line off the dock. You can also rent canoes. The 4 rooms, all with private bath, cost $65, including a full breakfast.

Rarely will you ever come across more gracious innkeepers than Jack and Louise Smith, owners of ***Heermansmith Farm Inn*** (☎ *802-754-8866*) in Coventry. The farm, off VT 16, has been in their family since 1807. They offer six neat, modest rooms, three with private bath, in their 1860s farmhouse for $65. They also own one of the region's best restaurants. See Places to Eat, below.

Not far from the shores of Shadow Lake is ***Rodgers Country Inn*** (*802-525-6677*) in Glover. Jim and Nancy Rodgers offer six rooms in their 1840s farmhouse. Hang out on the front porch and read, or take a stroll on this 350-acre former dairy farm. Smack dab in the middle of farm country, this inn is for people who really want to feel what it's like to live in rural Vermont. Daily rates are $45 per person, including breakfast and supper. Weekly rates are $250 per person, including breakfast and supper.

***Craftsbury Bed & Breakfast*** (☎ *802-586-2206*), Craftsbury Common, is just down the road from the historic village green and close to the Craftsbury Outdoor Center for mountain biking and cross-country skiing. Set in a farmhouse atop Wylie Hill, this B&B offers expansive views of the rolling farmland. Six rooms with shared bath cost $55 to $70.

***The Highland Lodge*** (☎ *802-533-2647*) is perched on a hill over Caspian Lake, down the road from one of the best country stores in the state, Willey's. A trail leads to a private beach and canoe rental shop. Guests can enjoy an extensive cross-country skiing network in the winter. Rates for the 11 rooms, all with private bath, range from $102 to $250, including breakfast and dinner.

***Inn at Trout River*** (☎ *802-326-4391*), Main St in Montgomery Center, is one of the better places to stay if you plan on skiing Jay Peak. Built by a lumber baron over a century ago, the inn features 10 guest rooms, one suite and a top-notch restaurant. Rooms cost $43 per person, including a full breakfast.

## Places to Eat

You'll be surprised at the fine food served in these parts and even more surprised at the cheap tab.

***Anthony's Restaurant*** (☎ *802-748-3613, 50 Railroad St*), St Johnsbury, is a good place to sit around the large counter and have breakfast. Try the mountain-size Vermont cheddar burger.

The area's best bookstore, ***Northern Lights Bookshop and Cafe*** (☎ *802-748-4463, 79 Railroad St*), St Johnsbury, is also known for its tasty salads and sandwiches ($3.95 to $6.95). The cafe stays open for dinner Thursday, Friday and Saturday.

***The Bagel Depot*** (☎ *802-748-1600, 213 Railroad St*), in the Creamery Building in St Johnsbury, serves the freshest bagel in the Northeast Kingdom.

***Cucina di Gerardo*** (☎ *802-748-6772*), also in the Creamery Building in St Johnsbury, serves hearty Italian fare and pizzas.

***Miss Lyndonville Diner*** (☎ *802-626-9890*), VT 5 in Lyndonville, 5 miles north of St Johnsbury, is popular with locals, as evidenced by the numerous cars and trucks that always pack the parking lot. Large breakfasts cost $1 to $3, and sandwiches fall in the $4.95 to $5.95 range, but the affordable and tasty dinners are a real steal. Expect to spend $6.25 for roast turkey with all the fixings or $6.75 for a half-pound baked Vermont ham. The service is friendly and prompt.

***Avery's Café*** (☎ *802-626-3017, 60 Depot St*), Lyndonville, is a good place for soups, sandwiches and standard veggie fare, such as burgers and burritos. Prices range from $3.95 to $4.95.

*The River Garden Café* (☎ 802-626-3514), on VT 114 in East Burke, is a local favorite for its salads, stir-fried dishes and pizzas. Sample the Green Mountain Pizza, topped with Vermont goat cheese, mozzarella, pesto and tomato sauce for $5.50.

If you don't stay at *The Willoughvale Inn* (☎ 802-594-9102), VT 5A in Westmore, then at least have a meal in its glass-enclosed dining room overlooking Lake Willoughby. Hearty American fare, including prime rib, turkey and chicken, costs $10.95 to $15.95.

*Pierce Pharmacy* (☎ 802-525-3400), in Barton, is a malt shop that hasn't changed much since the 1950s. Sit down at the counter and order an old-fashioned frappe and a sandwich for a couple of dollars.

*Heermansmith Farm Inn* (☎ 802-754-8866), Coventry, might be in the middle of nowhere, but it serves one of the finest dinners in the Kingdom. Try the signature dish, oven-roasted Duck à la Heerman-smith, topped with homemade strawberry *chambord* sauce ($16.95). From I-91, take exit 26 and head north on VT 5 for 5 miles. Take a left across from a school and head into Coventry, then make the next left onto Heermanville Rd. The farm and its sign are on the right side of the road.

## Getting There & Away

**Air** See the Burlington section, earlier in this chapter, for details.

**Bus** Vermont Transit (☎ 802-864-6811, 800-451-3292 in New England) runs its buses between Boston and St Johnsbury.

**Car** Driving details for St Johnsbury are as follows:

| destination | distance | hr:min |
|---|---|---|
| Boston, MA | 200 miles | 3:30 |
| Burlington, VT | 76 miles | 1:30 |
| Montpelier, VT | 39 miles | 0:45 |
| Montreal, Canada | 130 miles | 2:15 |
| New York, NY | 320 miles | 6:00 |

# New Hampshire

New Hampshire, like neighboring Vermont, is mountainous and beautiful. The state's White Mountain Range includes Mt Washington (6288 feet), one of the highest peaks east of the Mississippi River. The state's symbol is the 'Great Stone Face' (also called the Old Man of the Mountain), a natural 'profile' of a man formed by the granite of a rocky hillside at Franconia Notch in the White Mountain National Forest.

New Hampshire's earliest recorded inhabitants were the Abenakis, an eastern woodland people of the Algonquian group. In 1622, the Council for New England awarded the territory from the Merrimack to the Kennebec Rivers (named 'the Province of Maine') to Captain John Mason and Sir Ferdinando Gorges. A year later, the first English settlers arrived and set up home at Portsmouth.

In 1629, Mason's land grant, which he renamed New Hampshire, was extended from the Merrimack to the Piscataqua River. Later, it was enlarged even further, though these early borders were often in dispute. In 1641, four New Hampshire towns placed themselves under the protection of the royal governor of Massachusetts, but in 1679, New Hampshire received its own royal charter from King Charles II. The border disputes between the two provinces were only settled by royal decree in 1740. The following year, Benning Wentworth of Portsmouth was appointed the colony's first royal governor. By this time, white settlers had long since penetrated the 211-mile-long Connecticut River Valley and the 100-mile-long Merrimack River.

Four months before the 'shot heard round the world' rang out in Lexington, Massachusetts, on April 19, 1775, the farmer-soldiers of New Hampshire captured Fort William and Mary from the British, signaling the start of the troubles. They seized the fort's military stores and sent them south to the Boston area, where they were later used at the Battle of Bunker Hill.

New Hampshirites provided important supplies, manpower and navy vessels for the Revolutionary War. The sloop *Ranger*, made famous through the exploits of Captain John Paul Jones, was both built and launched at Portsmouth.

On January 5, 1776, New Hampshire's provincial assembly adopted a constitution, and within a half year, the colony proclaimed its independence from Britain. On June 21, 1788, New Hampshire ratified the US Constitution and provided the ninth and final vote necessary to inaugurate the radically different form of government it described.

## Highlights

- Camping and hiking in the White Mountain National Forest
- Sampling restaurants in Portsmouth
- Driving the beautiful Kancamagus Highway
- Hiking in the Presidential Range
- Swimming and boating on Lake Winnipesaukee
- Riding the Cog Railway to the top of Mt Washington

By 1790, New Hampshire had a population of almost 142,000. In the mid-19th century, the Industrial Revolution brought considerable wealth to New Hampshire, which was blessed, like much of New England, with abundant water power. The great Amoskeag mills along the river at Manchester are an impressive relic of this era. Perhaps because of its industrial wealth (in part), New Hampshire produced two of America's best 19th-century sculptors: Daniel Chester French (1850-1931) and Augustus Saint-Gaudens (1848-1907).

At the beginning of the 20th century, during the great migration to the eastern US, large numbers of immigrant workers settled in New Hampshire. In 1905, Portsmouth was the venue for the signing of the treaty ending the Russo-Japanese War. And in 1944, a United Nations conference at Bretton Woods designed the world's postwar economic model, resulting in the creation of the World Bank and the International Monetary Fund.

Today, New Hampshire's farms produce part of the state's wealth, but tourism is a bigger industry. There's some light industry as well, but many New Hampshirites head south to Massachusetts to find work.

Known as the most politically conservative of the New England states, New Hampshire suffers the barbs and insults of its liberal neighbors in Vermont and Massachusetts. New Hampshirites take comfort in the words of native General John Stark, victor at the crucial Battle of Bennington (1777): 'Live free or die.' They also live by their tourism slogan: 'It's *right* in New Hampshire.'

The state is a lake-lover's paradise. Among the 1300 lakes and ponds scattered across New Hampshire, the largest is vast Lake Winnipesaukee. New Hampshire even has a seacoast for beach fun. If you like the outdoors, you'll love New Hampshire.

In addition to its natural charms, the state has several cities, some good small museums and Dartmouth College in Hanover, one of the nation's most prestigious institutions of higher education.

The New Hampshire Office of Vacation Travel (☎ 603-271-2666, www.visitnh.gov), PO Box 856, Concord, NH 03301, is the statewide information source, but you'll get more complete information from the regional tourism offices. These offices, operated by local chambers of commerce or tourism councils, are mentioned below in each regional section.

## Getting There & Around

**Air** Manchester Airport (☎ 603-624-6556, www.flymanchester.com), the state's largest airport, has enjoyed exponential growth in recent years as a 'relief airport' for Boston's overburdened Logan International Airport. Low-fare airlines favor Manchester. There is frequent daily nonstop service to Boston, New York and Washington, DC, provided by Business Express, COMAIR Delta Connection, Continental, MetroJet, Northwest, Southwest, United and US Airways.

Keene and several smaller New Hampshire cities are served by Colgan Air (☎ 703-368-8880, 800-272-5488, www.colganair.com), with connections to national and international airlines at Boston, Manchester and Newark.

The Lebanon Municipal Airport serves Hanover (and Dartmouth College), as well as Woodstock, Vermont.

**Bus** Concord Trailways (☎ 603-228-3300, 800-639-3317, www.concordtrailways.com) operates a bus route to and from Boston and Logan International Airport, with stops in Manchester, Concord, Laconia, Meredith, Conway, Jackson, Gorham and Berlin, New Hampshire. There's also another route through Plymouth, North Woodstock/Lincoln, Franconia, Littleton and some other points along the way.

In addition, Vermont Transit (☎ 802-864-6811, 800-451-3292 in New England, www.vermonttransit.com) operates a route connecting Boston and Portsmouth, with continuing service to Portland, Bangor and Bar Harbor, Maine.

**Train** There is no scheduled rail passenger service in New Hampshire, although the Amtrak *Vermonter* runs up the Connecticut River Valley and stops off at White River

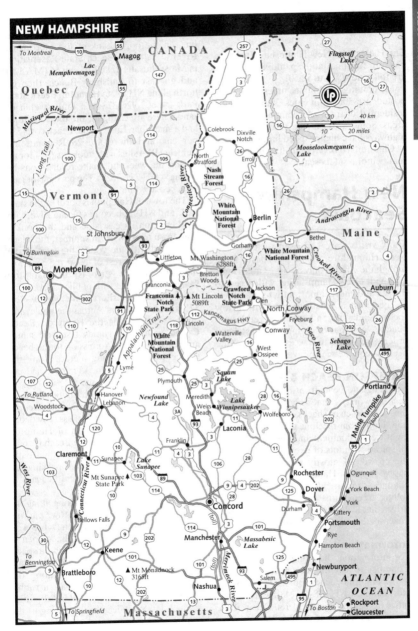

**NEW HAMPSHIRE**

Junction, Vermont, a town that is near Hanover, New Hampshire.

**Car** The eastern New Hampshire Turnpike, Everett Turnpike and Spaulding Turnpike are toll roads (75¢ to $2.50).

Maximum speed limits, unless otherwise posted, are 30mph in cities, 35mph in rural residential districts and 55mph in all other areas. Some areas of the state's interstate highways have higher speed limits posted.

Children younger than five must use a seat belt or a safety seat.

# New Hampshire Seacoast

Many visitors are surprised to learn that New Hampshire has a seacoast. Even though the coast is only about 18 miles long, it provides New Hampshirites with access to the sea and, more importantly, to the beach.

The coast is mostly beach, with a few rocky headlands and coves. Several state beaches and parks along the coast have orderly, well-regulated access. The rest of the beach is commercially developed.

## HAMPTON BEACH & RYE

New England beachfront honky-tonk at its best (or worst) – that's Hampton Beach. In the summer, clam shacks, cheap motels, hot dog stands, coin-machine game arcades, free nightly entertainment and weekly fireworks, all spiced with lots of neon and noise, keep the crowds of mostly young sun seekers happy. North of Hampton Beach, the mood changes dramatically. Rye is a town of rolling greenswards and serpentine private drives that lead to oceanfront mansions and dozen-bedroom 'summer cottages.'

## Information

For information, the Hampton Beach Area Chamber of Commerce (☎ 603-926-8718, www.hamptonbeaches.com), 836 Lafayette Rd, Hampton, NH 03842-1248, has a summer office in the town center at 180 Ocean Blvd. Also, check www.seacoastnh.com.

## Beaches

The beach actually begins south of the state line, on the north bank of the Merrimack River at **Salisbury Beach State Reservation** in Massachusetts. Take I-95 exit 56 (MA 1A) and go east to Salisbury Beach, then go north along NH 1A to **Hampton Beach State Park** (☎ 603-926-3784), a long stretch of sand. There are changing and toilet facilities and a snack bar. Entry to the beach costs $10 per car, and there are 28 Recreational Vehicle (RV) sites with hookups ($14 for an RV on the weekend; make reservations by calling ☎ 603-271-3628). The parking lot gate is locked at 8 pm.

The town of Hampton is north of the state park, and NH 1A becomes Ocean Blvd, with the beach on its east side and the honky-tonk town on its west. In summer, the beach is crowded with the young, the tanned, the beautiful and the rest of us. At the center of the long seaside strip is the **Hampton Seashell**, a building with public toilets, a first aid station and a **visitors' center** (☎ 603-926-8717) for beach users. Across the boulevard, on its west side, is the **Hampton Beach Casino**, with video games, fast-food stands and souvenir shops. Admission to the beach is free, but the parking meters along the boulevard charge 25¢ for 15 minutes ($1 per hour) for up to eight hours.

In the residential neighborhoods north of Hampton Beach, you'll find less spectacular, serviceable beaches that are less crowded.

A 10-minute drive north of Hampton Beach, **North Hampton State Beach** (☎ 603-436-9404) is not nearly as wide. It has bathhouses, lifeguards and a small parking lot, and it's quieter than the grand beaches to the south.

As NH 1A enters Rye, parking along the road is restricted to those with town parking stickers, but **Jenness State Beach** (☎ 603-436-9404) has a small parking lot that's open to the general public – if you can find a space. However, farther north at **Rye Harbor State Park**, you're allowed to park along the roadway. Climb over the seawall of rubble and riprap to get to the gravel beach, which is much less crowded than anything to the south.

**Wallis Sands State Beach** (☎ 603-436-9404) has a large parking lot and nice grass lawns for children's games.

At **Odiorne Point State Park** (☎ 603-436-7406), you can enjoy seaside strolls, picnicking and fishing, but there's no beach.

## Places to Stay

Most of the accommodations in Hampton Beach are rental rooms and apartments that are booked well in advance (people start calling in February and March), with two- or three-night minimum stays in July and in August. Contact *Preston Real Estate* (☎ 603-926-2604, 63 Ocean Blvd) in Hampton Beach for examples. Weekly rates range from $600 for a small apartment to $750 or $800 for a three-bedroom apartment to $2500 for a big apartment with ocean views and lots of amenities.

As for hotels, during beach season it's very difficult, if not impossible, to find a room for a single night. Hotel rooms tend to be booked well in advance for multi-night stays.

The *Nautical Motel* (☎ 603-929-3522, 147 Ashworth Ave), near the center of town and just a short stroll from the casino and the beach, is typical of the town's lodgings. An apartment with a microwave oven, refrigerator and two double beds that will sleep two adults and two children costs $89 in high season and about 20% less in June and late September.

North of Hampton Beach, *Ashworth By the Sea* (☎ 603-926-6762, 800-345-6736, 295 Ocean Blvd) is a tidy hotel with luxury rooms renting for $150 to $210, depending upon the view. Next door, *Kentville on the Ocean* (☎ 603-926-3950, 800-992-4297, 315 Ocean Blvd) is somewhat less expensive.

## PORTSMOUTH

The New England coast is dotted with graceful old cities that grew to importance during the great days of New England's maritime ascendancy, when local merchants made fortunes trading with the world. Portsmouth (population 26,000) is New Hampshire's only such city, but it's one of the region's most attractive and has much of historical interest.

Portsmouth's checkered history has left it with a particularly impressive and eclectic array of historic buildings from all periods. It is neither a prissy, perfectly preserved 'museum town,' nor a modernized city, but more of an architectural museum of real life as lived on the New Hampshire seacoast from 1623 to the present day.

Because of its position (an hour's drive north of Boston, an hour's drive south of Portland and an hour's drive east of Manchester), Portsmouth has become something of a 'restaurant resort.' The selection of places to eat is excellent for a town of its size. People from other cities zoom here on I-95 or NH 101 for a leisurely lunch and a stroll through town.

## History

In 1623, only three years after the Pilgrims landed at Plymouth Rock, another band of

---

### Nuclear Seabrook

In 1976, construction began on a controversial nuclear electricity plant on the coast at Seabrook. Despite vociferous protests from local and regional groups and charges of inappropriate use of governmental powers, construction progressed. In 1989, the Nuclear Regulatory Commission approved emergency evacuation plans for the plant despite the strenuous objections of many citizens' groups and the governor of nearby Massachusetts.

The plant began generating electricity commercially in 1990, after 14 years of construction and testing. Today, New Hampshirites pay some of the highest electricity rates in the USA, due largely to the folly of Seabrook. Meanwhile, the plant contains tons of high-level radioactive waste that will be a danger to the environment for thousands of years, with no plan for permanent storage, no permanent storage facility available and no budget to build one.

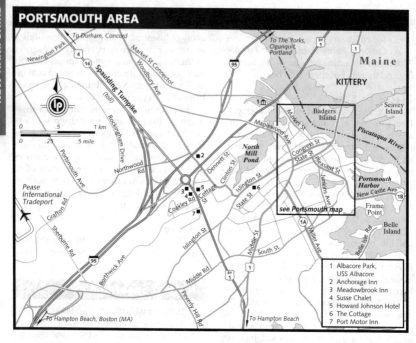

**PORTSMOUTH AREA**

To Durham, Concord

Newington Park

To The Yorks, Ogunquit, Portland

**Maine**

**KITTERY**

Market St Connector

Woodbury Ave

Spaulding Turnpike (toll)

Rockingham Drive

Badgers Island

Seavey Island

Maplewood Ave

Piscataqua River

0   .5   1 km
0   .25   .5 mile

North Mill Pond

Congress St
State St
Pleasant St

Portsmouth Harbor

New Castle Ave

Portsmouth Ave

Northwood Rd

Dennett St
Clinton St
Islington St

State St

Junkins Ave

Frame Point

Pease International Tradeport

Grafton Rd

Coakley Rd
Cottage St

see Portsmouth map

Miller Ave

Belle Island

Sherburne Rd

Islington St

Middle St

South St

Belle Isle Rd

Borthwick Ave

Middle Rd

Beverly Hill Rd

To Hampton Beach, Boston (MA)

To Hampton Beach

1 Albacore Park,
   USS *Albacore*
2 Anchorage Inn
3 Meadowbrook Inn
4 Susse Chalet
5 Howard Johnson Hotel
6 The Cottage
7 Port Motor Inn

---

intrepid settlers sailed to the mouth of the Piscataqua River. They landed and scrambled up a bank covered with wild strawberries – a good omen to hungry seafarers. They decided to stay and named the place Strawbery Banke, but the name changed to Portsmouth in 1653.

The purpose of this colony was fishing. The early settlers caught and sold fish and built and sold fishing boats. By the time of the American Revolution, Portsmouth was among the dozen largest cities in the English colonies. Its streets were lined with handsome houses (many of which remain today) that were built by merchants and ship captains.

The War of 1812 was the beginning of the end for Portsmouth's greatness, as trading and shipping dropped off drastically during the war and other ports grew to take up the slack in the postwar years. But the graceful houses, fine churches and other great buildings from Portsmouth's heyday remain.

Today, Portsmouth makes its living from tourism and from manufacturing such things as computers and fiber-optic cable.

## Orientation

Historic Portsmouth is surrounded on three sides by water. To the northeast is the Piscataqua River, to the northwest is the North Mill Pond and the South Mill Pond is to the southeast. Market St, reached via I-95 exit 7, is the main commercial street and has shops, restaurants and two information centers. Motels are clustered around I-95 exits 5 and 6.

## Information

The Greater Portsmouth Chamber of Commerce (☎ 603-436-1118, fax 436-5118, www .portcity.org), 500 Market St, PO Box 239, Portsmouth, NH 03802-0239, can help to answer your questions about the area. Stop at its information office on Market St just east of I-95 exit 7 (follow the signs) or at its

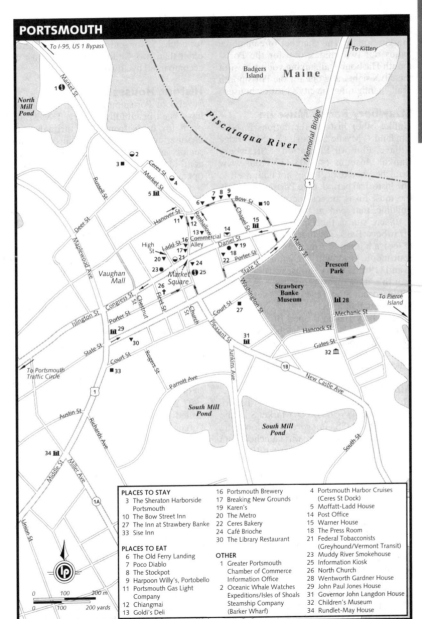

# PORTSMOUTH

information kiosk at the corner of Market and Daniel/Congress Sts in the city center at Market Square. The chamber of commerce hands out two guides: one for the Portsmouth Harbour Trail, taking you to most of the city's sights, and one for the Portsmouth Trail, highlighting the city's historic houses.

## Strawbery Banke Museum

Unlike other historic recreations in New England – Mystic Seaport, Old Sturbridge Village, Plimoth Plantation – Strawbery Banke Museum (☎ 603-433-1100, www.strawberybanke.org) does not limit itself to one historical period. Like Portsmouth itself, the museum is an eclectic gathering of 35 buildings that span the town's history. Set on a 10-acre site in the Puddle Dock section, Strawbery Banke includes the Pitt Tavern (1766), a hotbed of American revolutionary sentiment, Goodwin Mansion and other grand 19th-century houses from Portsmouth's most prosperous time, Abbott's Little Corner Store (1943) and several other interesting buildings.

Strawbery Banke is open 10 am to 5 pm daily, mid-April through October. An admission ticket good for two consecutive days costs $12 for adults, $11 for seniors, $8 for children seven to 17 and $28 for families.

## Albacore Park

The city's maritime museum in Albacore Park (☎ 603-436-3680), 600 Market St, is the home of the USS *Albacore*, a 205-foot-long submarine. The *Albacore* was launched from the Portsmouth Naval Shipyard in 1953, and with a crew of 55 men, it was piloted around the world for 19 years without firing a shot. The sub was then retired to Portsmouth, where it became the centerpiece of the maritime museum. You can tour the 27-foot-wide sub, located off Market St near I-95 exit 7 (before the chamber of commerce), from 9:30 am to 5:30 pm, May through mid-October. The cost is $4 for adults, $3 for seniors and $2 for children seven to 17.

## Children's Museum

The Children's Museum of Portsmouth (☎ 603-436-3853), 280 Marcy St, has chang-

ing exhibits, toys and experiments for children one to 10 years old. Admission costs $4 for adults, $3 for seniors and $4 for children older than two. Children under 12 must be accompanied by an adult.

## Historic Houses

Several of Portsmouth's grand old houses have been beautifully preserved. Most are open for tours from June through mid-October; tours cost $4 for adults, $3.50 for seniors and $2 for children under 12. It's a good idea to call and confirm the hours of operation.

**Governor John Langdon House** (☎ 603-436-3205), 143 Pleasant St, built in 1784, was the home of a prosperous merchant who later served as the state's governor.

The **John Paul Jones House** (☎ 603-436-8420), 43 Middle St at State St, built in 1758, was a boarding house when the naval hero lodged here during the outfitting of the *Ranger* (1777) and the *America* (1781). It's now the headquarters of the Portsmouth Historical Society and is open 10 am to 4 pm Monday to Saturday, noon to 4 pm Sunday.

The **Wentworth Gardner House** (☎ 603-436-4406), 50 Mechanic St, built in 1760, is one of the finest Georgian houses in the USA. It's open 1 to 4 pm Tuesday to Sunday.

The Federal-style **Rundlet-May House** (☎ 603-436-3205), 364 Middle St, was built in 1807 by a wealthy merchant, and it's furnished with many pieces that were made in Portsmouth.

The **Warner House** (☎ 603-436-5909), built in 1716, is a fine brick residence at the corner of Daniel and Chapel Sts.

The **Moffatt-Ladd House** (☎ 603-436-8221), 154 Market St, was owned by an influential ship captain and was later the home of General William Whipple, a signer of the Declaration of Independence. The gardens, which overlook the Piscataqua River, are particularly fine.

The 18th-century **Wentworth-Coolidge Mansion** (☎ 603-436-6607), on Little Harbor Rd south of the town center, was the home of New Hampshire's first royal governor. The 42-room mansion served as the colony's government center from 1741 to 1767. The lilacs on its grounds are descendants of the first lilacs planted in America, which were brought over from England by Governor Benning Wentworth.

## Prescott Park

The city's major waterfront park (☎ 603-431-8748) is at the northeastern end of the peninsula, just up Marcy St from Strawbery Banke. The large formal garden with fountains features more than 500 varieties of annuals. Musical performances, part of the Prescott Park Arts Festival, take place throughout the summer. The park is open all day for free and provides a haven of shade, flowers and quiet, along with fine views of the river mouth and harbor.

## Cruises

Portsmouth Harbor Cruises (☎ 603-436-8084, 800-776-0915), Ceres St Dock, takes visitors on cruises upriver, through the harbor, along the coast and out to the Isles of Shoals. Cruises last one to 2½ hours and cost $7.50 to $15 for adults, $6.50 to $14 for seniors and $5 to $8 for children older than two.

Oceanic Whale Watch Expeditions (☎ 603-431-5500, 800-441-4620, www.islesofshoals.com), 315 Market St (at Barker Wharf off Market St), in affiliation with the Isles of Shoals Steamship Company, runs a variety of whale-watching, harbor and music cruises. The cost is $10 to $25 for adults. Call for details.

## Places to Stay

**Camping** Most camping areas are privately run and are inland from the seacoast. They're also very busy in the summer season, usually filled by RVs. Some campgrounds do not accept tents, only RVs.

### John Paul Jones

Born in Scotland, the son of a gardener, John Paul Jones (1747-92) was America's first great naval commander.

At the age of 12, John Paul (his full name then) signed on as an apprentice aboard a merchant vessel bound for America. He later joined the British navy but soon saw that a working man could not get ahead there. He worked on a slave ship, then as an actor in the West Indies. On a trip back to Britain, the ship's captain and first mate both died of typhoid fever, leaving Paul the only man aboard who could navigate. He brought the ship safely to port, and the ship's owners made him its captain.

Troubled by several incidents in which he disciplined sailors severely, Paul left his ship and, adding 'Jones' to his name, disappeared into the colonies and set himself up as a planter.

When the Revolutionary War began, Jones rode to Philadelphia and signed on as first lieutenant aboard the *Alfred*, later becoming commander of the *Providence*. In 1777, he outfitted the sloop *Ranger* in Portsmouth, New Hampshire, and took it to Europe, where he set about sinking British coastal ships.

In France, he took command of the *Bonhomme Richard* and chased a British convoy in the North Sea. On September 23, 1779, his ship was engaged by HMS *Serapis*, a 44-gun frigate escorting the convoy. The crews fired at each other at close range for several hours. His ship in tatters, Jones had the bowsprit of the *Serapis* lashed to his own mizzenmast so the enemy ship could not get away. The British commander called for Jones' surrender, to which Jones replied, 'I have not yet begun to fight!'

The battle continued. When an American sailor lobbed a grenade into the *Serapis'* gunpowder magazine, Jones gained the victory.

After independence, he served the new American government as an agent in Europe. Later, he was an admiral in the imperial Russian navy for a short time. He died in Paris in 1792.

**NEW HAMPSHIRE**

*Great Bay Camping* (☎ 603-778-0226, 56 NH 108), in Newfields, has 115 sites best suited to RVs. Family-oriented *Ferndale Acres* (☎ 603-659-5082, 132 Wednesday Hill Rd), off NH 155 in Lee, has 150 sites for both tents and RVs for $22. *Wellington Camping Park* (☎ 603-659-5065), Lee Hook Rd off Bennett Rd in Lee, is a bit cheaper.

**Hotels & Motels** Many of Portsmouth's motels and hotels are clustered at I-95 exits 5 and 6, around the Portsmouth (or Interstate) Traffic Circle. Prices are generally lower during the week (Sunday to Thursday), rising by about 25% for Friday and Saturday. The low prices given here are for weekdays in summer, the high prices for weekends.

*Susse Chalet* (☎ 603-436-6363, 800-524-2538, 650 Borthwick Ave Extension), just off the Interstate Traffic Circle and the US 1 bypass, has 105 simple rooms for $84, continental breakfast included.

The *Anchorage Inn* (☎ 603-431-8111, 800-370-8111, 417 Woodbury Ave) is very close to the Interstate Traffic Circle. It has 93 rooms, an indoor swimming pool and a sauna. Rates are $99 to $109.

The 122-room *Meadowbrook Inn* (☎ 603-436-2700, 800-370-2727, fax 603-433-2700), near the Interstate Traffic Circle, has an older section with rooms for $60 to $90. In the newly renovated section, rooms cost $89 to $105. There's a swimming pool, fitness room, restaurant and lounge.

The *Port Motor Inn* (☎ 603-436-4378, 800-282-7678), just southeast of the Interstate Traffic Circle on the US 1 bypass, has 56 rooms for $110 to $130. Its many amenities include an outdoor heated pool, free HBO movies and continental breakfast.

There's also a 135-room *Howard Johnson Hotel* (☎ 603-436-7600, 800-654-2000) at the Interstate Traffic Circle. The hotel restaurant is open 24 hours. Rooms cost $111 to $145.

The *Sheraton Harborside Portsmouth* (☎ 603-431-2300, 800-235-3535, 250 Market St) offers the city's grandest accommodations, conveniently located across from the Isles of Shoals Steamship Company docks and only a three-block stroll from Market Square. Rooms cost $140 to $175.

**Inns & B&Bs** Breakfast is included in all the rates that are listed below.

*The Cottage* (☎ 603-431-3353, 442 Islington St) is a simple B&B a half mile southwest of Market Square. A double room with shared bath costs $60.

*The Inn at Strawbery Banke* (☎ 603-436-7242, 800-428-3933, 314 Court St) has seven rooms with private bath priced from $115 to $120. It is in a convenient location among historic houses and is just a five-minute walk from Market Square.

*The Bow Street Inn* (☎ 603-431-7760, 121 Bow St), just a few blocks from Market Square, is in a converted red-brick brewery overlooking the river. Rates are $114 for a regular room, $135 for a room with a river view and $149 for a mini-suite.

*Sise Inn* (☎ 603-433-1200, 800-232-4667 in New Hampshire, 40 Court St) is a large, elegant, Queen Anne-style inn dating from 1881. It has 28 rooms ($145 to $165) and six suites ($165 to $210). The town center is only a short walk away.

## Places to Eat

**Near Market Square** *Café Brioche* (☎ 603-430-9225, 14 Market Square) is a nice, upscale coffee, pastry and light-meal cafe overlooking Market Square. Coffees and pastries cost $1 to $3, and sandwiches cost $5 to $6. For picnicking, try one of the box lunches for $11.

At *Breaking New Grounds* (☎ 603-436-9555, 16 Market St), coffee is the main item, and there are numerous choices. The roasting and grinding machines are in full view. Order your brew, then sit and talk or read. There are a few pastries as well.

*Portsmouth Brewery* (☎ 603-431-1115, 56 Market St) is a brewpub with a long menu of lunch dishes, pastas, hot and cold sandwiches ($7 to $9), main-course dinners ($9 to $14) and even vegetarian fajitas. If you just want a pint and a bite, there are many appetizer plates priced from $5 to $8.

*Portsmouth Gas Light Company* (☎ 603-430-9122, 64 Market St) is in the historic building once occupied by its namesake. The specialty here is brick-oven pizza ($9 to $14), but there are more elaborate dishes as well. In fine weather, you can dine in back on the umbrella-shaded terrace.

**Bow & Penhallow Sts** The area that is around Bow and Penhallow Sts, down from Market St, has many restaurants.

*Poco Diablo* (☎ 603-431-5967, 37 Bow St) is a restaurant-cantina serving Tex-Mex dishes, such as fajitas, quesadillas and chiles rellenos, to a young, fun-loving crowd. The menu also includes lobster rolls and hamburgers ($5.50 to $8). Poco Diablo has nice views of the harbor and a waterside dining area that is pleasant in good weather.

*The Stockpot* (☎ 603-431-1851, 53 Bow St) advertises 'good food cheap,' and it delivers on the promise. If you want a table with a view of the water while you enjoy soup and half a sandwich for $5, this is the place. After 5 pm, more substantial plates are served, but nothing on the menu is over $14.

*Portobello* (☎ 603-431-2989, 67 Bow St) is Portsmouth's traditional Italian restaurant, with full dinners for $30 to $48. *Harpoon Willy's* (☎ 603-433-4441, 67 Bow St), behind Portobello, has fine water views, 'lobster in the rough' (simple steamed lobster), large plates of fish and chips for $9, fried clams and peel-and-eat shrimp at good prices. It's open in warm weather only.

*The Old Ferry Landing* (☎ 603-431-5510, 10 Ceres St), next to the tugboats, is an inexpensive seafood restaurant in the former terminal for ferries connecting Portsmouth with other coastal points. Lunch plates cost $8 to $11, and dinner plates run $9 to $15. Be sure to notice the live lobster tank – always a good sign – just inside the door. It's open in warm weather only.

*Chiangmai* (☎ 603-433-1289, 128 Penhallow St), just off Bow St, serves good Thai cuisine for lunch and dinner every day. The three-course luncheon specials cost a mere $6 to $9. Chicken satay is $6, pad Thai only a bit more. Try the Gourmet Madness: shrimp, scallops, mussels and squid stir-fried with mushrooms and vegetables in a very hot chili sauce.

*Goldi's Deli* (☎ 603-431-1178, 106 Penhallow St), just up from Chiangmai, is an attractive deli with a long menu of cheap

sandwiches such as sausage for $3.50 and, of course, lots of bagels. *Ceres Bakery* (☎ 603-436-6518, 51 Penhallow St) is a good place to pick up fresh bread or pastry for a snack or picnic.

*Karen's* (☎ 603-431-1948, 105 Daniel St) specializes in healthy breakfasts and in lunches, including, but certainly not limited to, vegetarian dishes. It's especially popular with local women. Breakfast is served daily; weekend brunch from 8 am to 2 pm is a specialty ($7 to $11). Dinner is not served on Monday and Tuesday.

**Upscale Dining** A short half-block off of Congress St at Market Square, *The Metro* (☎ 603-436-0521, 20 High St) is among the city's posh places to dine. The New American menu is appealing and is substantially cheaper at lunch ($10 to $22) than at dinner ($30 to $55). There's live jazz on Friday and Saturday evenings.

*The Library Restaurant* (☎ 603-431-5202, 401 State St) is housed in a palatial home built by a prominent judge in 1785. The menu highlights traditional, classic dishes, and the surroundings are opulent. In addition to the wood-paneled dining room, there's an English pub. The Library's open every day for lunch ($12 to $20) and dinner ($30 to $50).

## Entertainment

Portsmouth is a local mecca for evening entertainment as well as for dining. Several local clubs feature ever-changing schedules of local and national talent playing rock, folk, jazz, R&B, etc. Try *The Press Room* (☎ 603-431-5186, 77 Daniel St). It has live music most nights and a long menu of bar food with most items costing less than $8.

Another lively venue is the *Muddy River Smokehouse* (☎ 603-430-9582, 21 Congress St), at Market Square, where the barbecue competes with the bands. *The Metro*, mentioned above under Places to Eat, has live jazz on Friday and Saturday evenings.

## Getting There & Away

**Bus** Greyhound/Vermont Transit runs three or four buses daily on a route connecting

Boston and Portsmouth with Portland, Bangor and Bar Harbor, Maine. It is an 80-minute ride from Portsmouth to Boston. The bus station is at Federal Tobacconists (☎ 603-436-0163), 7 Congress St, just off Market Square.

C&J Trailways (☎ 603-742-5111, 800-258-7111), at Pease International Tradeport (Portsmouth's airport) also has service to Boston's Logan International Airport. The fare (for either company) is $22.

**Car** Driving details for Portsmouth are as follows:

| destination | mileage | hr:min |
| --- | --- | --- |
| Boston, MA | 57 miles | 1:10 |
| Concord, NH | 47 miles | 1:00 |
| Kennebunkport, ME | 28 miles | 0:45 |
| Manchester, NH | 47 miles | 1:00 |
| New York, NY | 275 miles | 5:45 |
| Portland, ME | 55 miles | 1:10 |

# Manchester & Concord

Although New Hampshire is noted for its mountains and forests rather than its cities, Manchester, a historic mill city, and Concord, the state's tidy capital, are worth a look.

## MANCHESTER

Exploiting the abundant water power of the Merrimack River, Manchester (population 102,000) became the state's manufacturing and commercial center in the early 19th century. It's now the banking center as well. In addition, students crowd the campuses of New Hampshire Technical College, Notre Dame College and the University of New Hampshire.

### Orientation

Manchester stretches along the east bank of the Merrimack River; West Manchester is on the river's west side. If you enter Manchester from I-93, you miss the view that defines the city's history: the red-brick swath of the great Amoskeag textile mills stretch-

ing along the east bank of the river for over a mile. To get the view, follow I-293 along the west bank of the river. After you've passed the mills, exit via the Amoskeag Bridge or the Queen City Bridge to enter the town.

The heart of Manchester lies along Elm St (US 3), which runs north-south through the business and commercial district. The Currier Gallery of Art is six blocks east of Elm St along Beech St (there are signs). Hotels and motels are at the interstate exits.

### Information

The Manchester Chamber of Commerce (☎ 603-666-6600, www.manchester-chamber .org), Manchester, NH 03101, is a good information source, as is the Southern New Hampshire Convention & Visitors Bureau (☎ 603-635-9000, 800-932-4282, www.snhcvb .com), Windham, NH 03087. The City of Manchester also operates a website, which is at ci.manchester.nh.us.

### Currier Gallery of Art

The state's premier fine arts museum is the Currier Gallery of Art (☎ 603-669-6144, www.currier.org), 201 Myrtle Way near Beech St. It has an excellent collection of 19th- and 20th-century European and American glass, English and American silver and pewter and colonial and early American furniture. As for European painters, Degas, Jan Gossaert and a follower of Meliore are represented. The museum is open 11 am to 5 pm Sunday, Monday, Wednesday and Thursday; 11 am to 8 pm Friday; 10 am to 5 pm Saturday. Admission costs $5 for adults, $4 for seniors and nothing for children under 18. Everyone gets in free from 10 am to 1 pm Saturday. To reach the museum from Elm St (US 3), go east on Orange St for six blocks.

### Amoskeag Mills

The great brick buildings with hundreds of tall windows are former textile mills, and they stretch along Commercial St on the Merrimack riverbank for almost 1½ miles. Other mills face the buildings from across the river in West Manchester. For almost a century, from 1838 to 1920, the Amoskeag

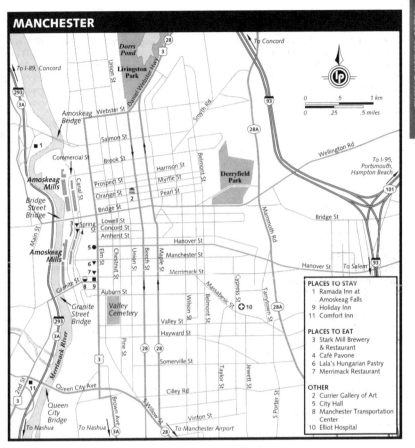

MANCHESTER

**PLACES TO STAY**
1 Ramada Inn at Amoskeag Falls
9 Holiday Inn
11 Comfort Inn

**PLACES TO EAT**
3 Stark Mill Brewery & Restaurant
4 Café Pavone
6 Lala's Hungarian Pastry
7 Merrimack Restaurant

**OTHER**
2 Currier Gallery of Art
5 City Hall
8 Manchester Transportation Center
10 Elliot Hospital

Manufacturing Company was the world's largest manufacturer of textiles. The mills employed up to 17,000 people a year (out of a city population of 70,000). Many of the mill employees lived in the trim-brick tenements that stretch up the hillside eastward from the mills. The tenements have been restored and are still used as housing.

As for the mills themselves, the company abandoned them in 1935, after going bankrupt during the Great Depression. Since that time, the city has been searching for tenants. Many have been found, and there are now offices, college classrooms, restaurants, warehouses, and broadcasting studios where noisy looms were once driven by water-power and steam. But much of the vast extent of space still remains empty.

Unless you have business in the buildings, just view them from the outside.

### Anheuser-Busch Brewery

The Anheuser-Busch Company (☎ 603-595-1202, www.budweisertours.com), 221 Daniel Webster Hwy, has a large brewery in nearby Merrimack, one of a dozen throughout the

USA. The company, which brews Budweiser and Michelob, is the world's largest brewer of beer, making 86 million barrels annually.

You can tour the plant for free, watch the foamy stuff being made, then lift a sample glass yourself. Tours, departing from the alpine-looking building, run 9:30 am to 5 pm daily, May to October, and 10 am to 4 pm Wednesday to Sunday, November to April.

Animal lovers should not miss a visit to the **Clydesdale Hamlet,** home of a dozen huge and majestic draft horses that are Anheuser-Busch's trademark (you may have seen their advertisements with the Clydesdales pulling an old-fashioned brewer's wagon).

To get to the brewery, go south on I-293 to the Everett Turnpike (US 3) and then take exit 10 (Industrial Drive).

## Places to Stay

**Camping** Although there are no camping places in greater Manchester, southern New Hampshire has a number of nice state parks. If you're willing to drive a bit, you can camp at *Pawtuckaway State Park* (☎ 603-895-3031), NH 156 in Nottingham, halfway between Manchester and Portsmouth. It has 193 sites on 6500 acres. Take NH 101 east to Raymond and follow the signs.

*Bear Brook State Park* (☎ 603-485-9869), NH 28 in Allenstown, halfway to Concord, has 96 sites. Follow US 3 north, turn right onto NH 28 at the town of Suncook and follow the signs. You can reserve a site (at least seven days in advance; two night minimum) by calling ☎ 603-271-3628.

**Hotels** Most of the city's lodging is for business travelers. Discounts for hotels are often available when business is slow, so be sure to ask.

Most central is the 250-room *Holiday Inn* (☎ 603-625-1000, 800-465-4329, 700 Elm St). It is right in the middle of the business district at The Center of New Hampshire. Rooms normally cost $119 to $129, but call the toll-free number and ask about special weekend packages.

*Ramada Inn at Amoskeag Falls* (☎ 603-669-2660, 800-272-6232, 21 Front St), off

I-293 exit 6, on the west side of the river, has 120 comfortable rooms for $95.

The *Comfort Inn* (☎ 603-668-2600, 800-228-5150, 298 Queen City Ave), off I-293 exit 4, has 100 new, comfortable rooms for $80 to $85. While it's in a commercial district on the west side of the highway and the river, the hotel is still convenient to the Queen City Bridge.

The 120-room *Susse Chalet Inn* (☎ 603-625-2020, 800-258-1980, 860 S Porter St), off I-293 exit 1, is about 2 miles southeast of the city center and not far from the airport. It has simple but adequate rooms for $77.

## Places to Eat

There are several good restaurants on Elm St (US 3) in the center of the business district (take I-293 exit 5 and cross the Granite St Bridge). The *Merrimack Restaurant* (☎ 603-669-5222, 786 Elm St), at W Merrimack St, has familiar American fare – salads, sandwiches, seafood, chicken and steaks – at low prices, with most main course plates for $8 to $14. The daily specials often cost as little as $5. It's closed Sunday afternoon but otherwise open for breakfast, lunch and dinner.

A block north, *Lala's Hungarian Pastry* (☎ 603-647-7100, 836 Elm St), opposite Manchester St, has wondrous central European delights to spoil your diet, as well as savory luncheon specials, including goulash and Wiener schnitzel, for prices as low as $4.

For fancier fare in old-time surroundings, try *Cafe Pavone* (☎ 603-622-5488, 75 Arms Park Drive), down near the river and the Amoskeag mills (go west down Spring St (off Elm St), turn right, then left). In warm weather, the vine-shaded terrace, with views of the river, is set with tables. A menu of moderately priced Italian dishes is served at lunch ($12 to $20) and dinner ($25 to $40). No lunch on weekends.

Just north of the Cafe Pavone, the *Stark Mill Brewery & Restaurant* (☎ 603-622-0000, 500 Commercial St) has a basement brewery and grill, with live music on most weekends. Among the attractions here are the house beers, including Mt Uncanoonuc Golden Cream Ale, General Stark Dark, and Molly's Oatmeal Stout. Sandwiches and pizzas are priced from $5 to $10.

## Getting There & Away

**Air** Manchester Airport (☎ 603-624-6556, www.flymanchester.com), off US 3 south of Manchester, is only an hour's drive northwest of Boston. As a result, it is becoming a relief airport for the greater Boston area. You may find it advantageous to fly into Manchester instead of Boston and take a bus (see below) or rent a car to continue your travels.

Manchester has daily nonstop service to Baltimore, Boston, Chicago, Cincinnati, Detroit, Nashville, New York City, Orlando, Philadelphia, Pittsburgh and Washington, DC, with connecting service to many other cities. Business Express, COMAIR Delta Connection, Continental, MetroJet, Northwest, Southwest, United and US Airways provide service.

**Bus** Concord Trailways (☎ 603-647-6900, 800-639-3317, www.concordtrailways.com), at the Manchester Transportation Center, 119 Canal St at the corner of Granite St (just east of the Granite St Bridge), runs 11 buses daily to and from Boston (one hour) and Logan International Airport (80 minutes). An equal number of buses go north to Concord (30 minutes).

**Car** Driving details for Manchester are as follows:

| destination | mileage | hr:min |
| --- | --- | --- |
| Boston, MA | 53 miles | 1:00 |
| Concord, NH | 19 miles | 0:25 |
| Laconia, NH | 42 miles | 0:55 |
| Lincoln, NH | 92 miles | 1:45 |
| Portsmouth, NH | 51 miles | 1:00 |

## CONCORD

The New Hampshire state capital (population 38,000) is a well-rounded town. Its citizens work at government, light manufacturing, crafts, education and retail sales, as you'll see immediately when you approach the gigantic shopping mall beside I-93.

They also quarry granite, a suitable occupation in the Granite State. The stone facade of the Library of Congress in Washington, DC, was quarried at nearby Rattlesnake Hill. The State House and many of the buildings surrounding it are also cut from the local stone.

Despite its modest charms, Concord will not grip you, and after a visit of several hours, you may be on your way again.

## Orientation & Information

I-93 passes just to the east of the city center, and US 3 is Main St, where you'll find everything worth visiting. Take I-93 exit 14 or 15 for Main St.

In summer, the Greater Concord Chamber of Commerce (☎ 603-224-2508, www .concordnhchamber.com), 244 N Main St, Concord, NH 03301, maintains a small information kiosk in front of the State House on N Main St (closed Sunday).

## State Capitol

The handsome State House (☎ 603-271-2154), 107 N Main St, was built in 1819. The state legislature still meets in the original chambers, the longest such tenure in the USA.

Inside, the Hall of Flags holds the standards that state military units carried into battle. Portraits and statues of New Hampshire leaders, including the great orator Daniel Webster, line its corridors and stand in its lofty halls. A statue of Franklin Pierce (see Pierce Manse, below) stands in front of the building.

The State House Visitors Center has brochures for self-guided tours, but you can also make advance reservations for a guided tour. The center's open 8 am to 4:30 pm weekdays (and weekends, July to October).

## Museum of New Hampshire History

The New Hampshire Historical Society's museum (☎ 603-225-3381, www.newww.com/org/nhhs), 30 Park St, is across from the State House and behind the first block of buildings. The museum can fill you in on such Granite State topics as the Concord

Coach, the stagecoach that provided transport to much of America's western frontier.

There are also beautiful 19th-century landscape paintings of the state's White Mountains. The building itself – granite again – is a good place for a stroll. There is a small park with a fountain and sidewalk cafe.

The museum is open 9:30 am to 5 pm weekdays, noon to 5 pm Sunday. Admission costs $4 for adults, $2 for children six to 18 and $12 for families. Thursday evenings, from 5 to 8:30 pm, are free.

### Pierce Manse

The home of Franklin Pierce (1804-69), 14th president of the US, is now a museum. The Pierce Manse (☎ 603-225-2068, 224-7668), 14 Penacook St, at the end of N Main St, was built in 1838-39 and saved from destruction a decade ago by the Pierce Brigade.

Pierce was the son of a two-term New Hampshire governor, a member and later Speaker of the New Hampshire General Court (legislature) and a representative and senator in Congress. He retired from the US Senate to practice law in Concord, maintaining an interest in politics but having little interest in further public service. But during the Democratic party's convention of 1852, there were so many strong candidates for the presidency that none could achieve a majority vote. On the 49th ballot, Pierce, a compromise candidate, became the party's nominee, and he went on to win the presidential election.

The manse was his family home from 1842 to 1848. It's open for visits 11 am to 3 pm weekdays from mid-June through mid-September. Admission costs $3 for adults, 50¢ for children.

### Christa McAuliffe Planetarium

This planetarium (☎ 603-271-7827, www .starhop.com), just northeast of I-93 exit 15 (follow the signs), is named in honor of the New Hampshire schoolteacher chosen to be America's first teacher-astronaut. McAuliffe and her fellow astronauts died in the tragic explosion of the *Challenger* spacecraft on January 28, 1986. Call for a schedule of shows, many of which are open to the public.

### Places to Stay

There are several good highway hotels and motels to serve those visiting Concord on government business. Most tourists rocket through to the mountains or lakes. A full range of camping and lodging choices is available in the nearby towns of Laconia, Gilford and the other towns around Lake Winnipesaukee.

The 100-room *Comfort Inn* (☎ 603-226-4100, 71 Hall St), off I-93 exit 13 in the center of town, charges $89 to $139 in the summer. The 122-room *Holiday Inn* (☎ 603-224-9534, 172 N Main St) is similarly comfortable for $95 to $103.

### Places to Eat

Most of Concord's restaurants are across from the State House on N Main St at Park St, where they catch the legislative lunch crowd. *Forefathers' Taverne* (☎ 603-223-9770, 132 N Main St) is the main schmoozing place, and prices are pleasing: only $5 or $6 for the daily special plates. A few doors away, the *Brown Bag Deli* (☎ 603-225-9110, 1 Eagle Square (100 N Main St)) and the *Coffee Mill* (☎ 603-224-8081, 124 N Main St) offer less formality and good picnic fare at even lower prices.

Perhaps the most interesting place to dine is the *Capital City Diner* (☎ 603-228-3463), off I-93 exit 13. This authentic diner from the 1950s serves breakfast, lunch, dinner and drinks at low prices: about $7 for the dinner specials.

### Getting There & Away

Concord Trailways (☎ 603-228-3300, 800-639-3317, www.concordtrailways.com), at the Trailways Transportation Center, 30 Stickney Ave (I-93 exit 14), runs 11 buses daily between Manchester and Boston and Logan International Airport.

Driving details for Concord are:

| destination | mileage | hr:min |
| --- | --- | --- |
| Boston, MA | 72 miles | 1:30 |
| Laconia, NH | 23 miles | 0:35 |
| Lincoln, NH | 73 miles | 1:20 |
| Manchester, NH | 19 miles | 0:25 |
| North Conway, NH | 73 miles | 2:00 |

## CANTERBURY SHAKER VILLAGE

Members of the United Society of Believers in Christ's Second Appearing were called 'Shakers' because of the religious ecstasies they experienced during worship. (For a history of Shakers, see the Facts about New England chapter or the Pittsfield, Massachusetts, section of this book.)

The Shaker community at Canterbury was founded in 1792 and was actively occupied for two centuries. Sister Ethel Hudson, last member of the Shaker colony here, died in 1992 at the age of 96. Now Canterbury Shaker Village (☎ 603-783-9511, 800-982-9511, www.shakers.org), 288 Shaker Rd, is preserved as a nonprofit trust to present the history of the Shakers. The lone surviving Shaker community, at Sabbathday Lake, Maine, still accepts new members.

Canterbury Shaker Village has 'interpreters' in period dress who still perform the tasks and labors of community daily life: fashioning Shaker furniture and crafts (for sale in the gift shop) and growing herbs and producing herbal medicines. The guided tour takes you to an herb garden, Meetinghouse (1792), apiary (bee house), ministry, 'Sisters' shop (a crafts shop run by Shaker women), laundry, horse barn, infirmary and schoolhouse (1826).

On Thursday, Friday and Saturday evenings, you can join in a traditional four-course candlelight dinner. There's one seating per evening, and it begins at 7 pm sharp. Dinner is served family style at long tables, and you can choose from a poultry, meat or fish main course. Recipes, ingredients and cooking methods are all true to Shaker form and philosophy. After dinner, you'll be guided through the village by candlelight, or if it's off-season and the village is closed, you'll be treated to an evening of folk singing. Dinner costs about $40 per person.

Alternatively, *The Creamery* restaurant is open for lunch 11:30 am to 2 pm daily and 11 am to 2 pm Sunday.

Canterbury Shaker Village is open for guided tours 10 am to 5 pm Monday to Saturday and noon to 5 pm Sunday (last tour is at 4 pm) from May to October. In April, November and December, the village is open 10 am to 5 pm weekends; it's closed January to March. Admission costs $9.50 for adults and $4 for children six to 12.

To find the village, take I-93 exit 18 and follow the signs, or go 15 miles north of Concord on MA 106.

# Lakes Region

New Hampshire's Lakes Region, centered on vast Lake Winnipesaukee, is an odd mix of wondrous natural beauty and commercial tawdriness.

The forest-shrouded lakes have beautiful, sinuous coastlines stretching for hundreds of miles. The roads skirting the shores and connecting the lakeside towns are a riotous festival of popular culture, lined with a mindless hodgepodge of shopping malls, gas stations, miniature golf courses, amusement arcades, auto dealerships, go-cart tracks, motels, private zoos, clam shacks, tourist cottages, junk food outlets and boat docks.

Most visitors to the Lakes Region are New England families who have cottages on or near the lakeshore or who take their annual vacations in one of the roadside motels.

If you're heading north on your way to the White Mountains or south to Boston, you can spend a day or two pleasantly enough here. Lake Winnipesaukee, the euphonious Indian name of New Hampshire's largest lake, means 'smile of the Great Spirit.' Winnipesaukee has 183 miles of coastline, more than 300 islands and, despite being landlocked, excellent salmon fishing.

Stop for a swim or a picnic at one of the two state parks on the lake. Take a ride on one of the several lake-cruising motor launches. Better yet, take a seaplane ride to view all the lakes from the air. Visit a museum. And, if you have children, don't miss a chance to prowl the video arcades, bowladromes and junk-food cafes of Weirs Beach.

## Orientation & Information

Laconia is the population center of the Lakes Region and the place you go to find a hospital, auto parts store or other service.

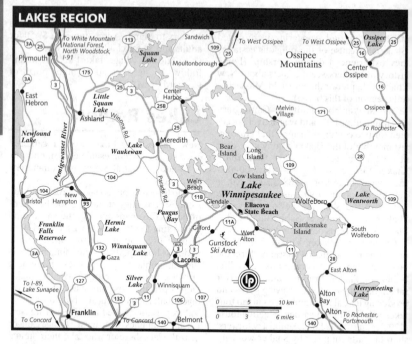

## LAKES REGION

Most visitors to the area stay in the small towns near the lake.

Meredith is a largish town with many lodging and dining possibilities. Weirs Beach is the place to go for honky-tonk game arcades and boat rides. Glendale is sedate, with small hotels, motels and cottages shaded by pines. Wolfeboro, on the southeastern shore, is aristocratic.

Each of the larger towns has its own chamber of commerce information office. See the Information section for each destination. You can also try the Lakes Region Association (☎ 603-744-8664, 800-605-2537, lakesregion.org), PO Box 430, NH 104, New Hampton, NH 03256, or visit the site www.winnipesaukee.com.

## LACONIA, GILFORD & GLENDALE

The largest town of the Lakes Region, Laconia occupies itself with light manufac-

turing of shoes and electrical components. Neighboring Gilford, in the shadow of Belknap Mountain (2384 feet, pronounced 'BELL-nap'), is joined at the hip to Laconia and is indistinguishable from Laconia to the casual visitor. Glendale, north of Gilford, is a sedate lakeside area where you'll find Ellacoya State Park and its fine beach.

## Information

The Greater Laconia & Weirs Beach Chamber of Commerce (☎ 603-524-5531, 800-531-2347, www.laconia-weirs.org), 11 Veterans Square, Laconia, NH 03246, maintains an information office in the old railroad station in the center of Laconia.

## Lake Winnipesaukee

The lake is the big attraction of the region, of course. The area around Glendale is much prettier and less commercial than Laconia itself. To get there, follow NH 11 south from

Gilford. Watch for signs for Belknap Point Rd, which is the narrower shoreline drive (NH 11 is well back from the shore).

Most lakeshore lodgings have access to the water. If yours does not, head for Ellacoya State Park (☎ 603-293-7821), just southeast of Glendale. There's a 600-foot-wide beach, picnic area and campground. Open from late May to Columbus Day, the park charges $3.50 for adults (12 to 55 years old); it's free for others.

### Hiking
A few miles south of West Alton on NH 11, a sign points right for the Mt Major Trail, which is in the Belknap Mountain State Forest. Park just off the road and make the 2-mile trek up Mt Major (1780 feet).

### Skiing
When the snows of winter cover the ground, a different kind of play begins on Belknap Mountain. **Gunstock** (☎ 603-293-4318, 800-486-7862, www.gunstock.com), on NH 11A in Gilford, is a ski area run by the county. It has no lodging other than its campground (see Places to Stay).

Gunstock sports 45 downhill runs on a vertical drop of 1400 feet. There are seven lifts, including a quad and two triples, as well as a ski school and day care facilities. Most of the mountain trails are intermediate, with a larger percentage of advanced than beginner trails.

Over 30 miles of cross-country trails follow the wooded paths around Gilford. Of the trails, 25 are tracked, 37 are skate-groomed and 13 are left ungroomed for backcountry skiing.

Downhill and cross-country skis are available for rental, as well as snowboards, snowskates (boots attached to shortened skis) and telemark skis. Call the main number to connect with the ski shop.

### Special Events
The area's annual Motorcycle Week (www.weirsbeach.com/mcweek.html), from June 12 to 18 or thereabouts, draws two-wheeled crowds to the New Hampshire International Speedway (☎ 603-783-4931, nhis.com), on NH 106 in Loudon, south of Laconia. There are races, shows and other events, and bikers are everywhere. Lodgings, particularly campgrounds and motels, are expensive and can be difficult to find, so reserve ahead.

### Places to Stay
**Camping** The *Ellacoya State Park* (☎ 603-293-7821, 436-1552 for reservations), off of NH 11, has 35 unshaded sites with full hookups for RVs. Sites cost $30, and the park is open mid-May to mid-October.

*Gunstock* (☎ 603-293-4344, 800-486-7862), NH 11A in Gilford, is a ski area with a campground. The campground operates summer and winter but is closed from October to late November. The basic rate is $22 to $30, with electricity hookups at the site. There are heated bathrooms, but no water, at the sites.

*Clearwater Campground* (☎ 603-279-7761), NH 104 in Meredith, charges $22 to $32 for its sites. *Twin Tamarack Family Camping & RV Resort* (☎ 603-279-4387), NH 104 in New Hampton, is a bit more expensive at $30 to $35.

**Motels** One of the cheaper motels in the area is the 63-room *Super 8 Motel* (☎ 603-286-8882, 800-800-8000), off I-93 exit 20 in Tilton. Rooms with a king bed or two double beds cost $56 to $62.

Along Belknap Point Rd, just northwest of Ellacoya State Park, is the *Belknap Point Motel* (☎ 603-293-7511, www.bpmotel.com, 107 Belknap Point Rd). This good lodging choice has excellent views of the lake and mountains, with motel rooms and efficiencies right near the water for $88 to $98 in-season.

### Places to Eat
*Las Piñatas* (☎ 603-528-1405, 9 Veterans Square), in the old railroad station in downtown Laconia, has lots of traditional Mexican specialties, as well as some Tex-Mex dishes. A full dinner need cost only $12 to $18.

### Getting There & Away
**Bus** Concord Trailways (☎ 603-524-0530, 800-639-3317, www.concordtrailways.com),

NEW HAMPSHIRE

at Week's Restaurant, 331 S Main St, runs three buses daily between Boston and Logan International Airport and the New Hampshire towns of Tilton Junction, Concord and Manchester. There are one or two extra buses on weekends from Tilton Junction. The bus stop is 6 miles southwest of Laconia at the Irving fuel station (☎ 603-286-3532), at the junction of US 3 and I-93 exit 20.

**Car** The driving details for Laconia are as follows:

| destination | mileage | hr:min |
| --- | --- | --- |
| Boston, MA | 95 miles | 2:15 |
| Concord, NH | 23 miles | 0:35 |
| Lincoln, NH | 45 miles | 1:10 |
| Manchester, NH | 42 miles | 0:55 |
| Meredith, NH | 8 miles | 0:18 |
| North Conway, NH | 49 miles | 1:25 |
| Wolfeboro, NH | 27 miles | 0:55 |

## Getting Around
The Greater Laconia Transit Agency (☎ 603-528-2496, 800-294-2496) runs shuttle trolleys and double-decker buses through town ($1) to Weirs Beach and Meredith ($2).

## WEIRS BEACH
Called Aquedoctan by its Native American settlers, Weirs Beach (www.weirsbeach.com) takes its English name from the Indian weirs (enclosures for catching fish) that the first white settlers found along the small sand beach that still draws swimmers.

Weirs Beach is the honky-tonk heart of Lake Winnipesaukee's childhood amusements. It's famous for its video game arcades and the great variety of junk food available. But there's also a nice lakefront promenade, a small state park and beach, the dock for the MS *Mount Washington* cruise boat and a train station for the local scenic railroad. Above the town on US 3, you'll find a water slide and a drive-in theater.

In addition, the town has a surprising amount of evocative, Victorian-era, lakeside-vacation-cottage fantasy architecture. It's as though Weirs Beach found its cultural and commercial niche a century ago and has stayed there ever since that time.

For information on getting to and from the area, see the Laconia, Gilford & Glendale section, above.

## Information
The Greater Laconia & Weirs Beach Chamber of Commerce (☎ 603-524-5531, 800-531-2347, www.laconia-weirs.org) has an information booth a mile south of Weirs Beach on US 3. The staff can help you find same-day accommodations.

## Winnipesaukee Scenic Railroad
The Winnipesaukee Scenic Railroad (☎ 603-745-2135, www.hoborr.com) has its terminus in Weirs Beach. Its season runs from March 15 to December 31. Trains run hourly 11 am to 5 pm daily, mid-June to early September, and on weekends in spring and autumn. A one-hour ride costs $7.50 for adults, $5.50 for children four to 11.

## Cruises
To see the lake up close, hop aboard one of the boats that depart Weirs Beach daily for scenic cruises. The MS *Mount Washington* (☎ 603-366-2628, www.msmountwashington.com) steams out on two- and 2½-hour scenic cruises several times daily. The cost is $14 to $16 for adults, $7 to $8 for children four to 12. In the evening, there are dinner cruises with entertainment (ask what the night's theme will be).

Other motor cruisers run by the same company include the MV *Sophie C*, the US Mail boat that takes the mail out to many of the lake's islands on 1½-hour morning and evening runs ($12 for adults, $6 for children), and the MV *Doris E*, making one-hour ($8) and two-hour ($13) cruises from Weirs Beach and Meredith (children pay half fare).

## Places to Stay
**Camping** The town's campgrounds, open from mid-May to mid-October, are north of Weirs Beach along US 3 (Daniel Webster Hwy). Rates are generally $20 for a tent site and $22 to $28 for an RV site with hookups. Reserve well in advance if you can.

*Hack-Ma-Tack Campground* (☎ 603-366-5977), 1½ miles north of Weirs Beach on US 3, has 75 sites (45 with hookups) going for $20 to $23. It's open from early May to early October. *Pine Hollow Camping World* (☎ 603-366-2222) is a mile north of town. *Paugus Bay Campground* (☎ 603-366-4757), on Hilliard Rd off US 3, has 130 wooded sites overlooking the bay.

At the *Weirs Beach Tent & Trailer Park* (☎ 603-366-4747), semipermanent trailers fill many of the 175 sites, but there are usually some spots available for transients; some have hookups.

**Motels** The *Half Moon Motel & Cottages* (☎ 603-366-4494), on the hillside overlooking the town center, features convenient motel rooms and cottages for $73 to $83. The complex is only a few steps from the arcade action.

Some of the nicer, moderately priced motels in this area lie on the stretch of US 3 (Weirs Blvd) that runs north from Gilford to Weirs Beach. The 24-room *Birch Knoll Motel* (☎ 603-366-4958, 867 Weirs Blvd), in Laconia, is among the better ones, with rooms for $84 to $98. Also, try the *Bay Top Motel* (☎ 603-366-2225, 1025 Weirs Blvd), in Laconia, which has regular rooms and efficiencies priced from $65 to $95.

## Places to Eat

Weirs Beach is all about eating: burgers, hot dogs, fried dough, lobsters, ice cream, doughnuts and anything sweet and fatty. Stroll Lakeside Drive for the snack shops. For more substantial fare, try *Elvio's Pizzeria & Restaurant* in the center of town. Italian-American meals cost $8 to $18. *Weirs Beach Lobster Pound* (☎ 603-366-5713), above the town on US 3 (across from the Weirs Beach Water Slide), serves local seafood and steaks. There's a children's menu as well.

## MEREDITH

More sedate and upscale than Weirs Beach, Meredith is still a real Lakes Region town, with a long lakeside commercial strip of restaurants, shops and places to stay.

For information on getting to and from the area, see the Laconia, Gilford & Glendale section, earlier.

## Orientation & Information

US 3, NH 25 and NH 104 meet in Meredith, which is spread along the lakeshore. The main Meredith Chamber of Commerce (☎ 603-279-6121, www.meredithcc.org), 272 Daniel Webster Hwy (US 3), Meredith, NH 03253, at Mill St, maintains an information office at the southern end of Meredith's business district (on the inland side of US 3).

## Places to Stay

**Camping** The *Harbor Hill Camping Area* (☎ 603-279-6910), on NH 25, 1½ miles east of Meredith, has 140 sites, mostly wooded and with hookups, for $20 to $28.

The *Long Island Bridge Campground* (☎ 603-253-6053), 13 miles northeast of Meredith near Center Harbor, has a private beach and very popular tent sites for $19 to $23. In July and August, you must rent a site for three days minimum; reservations are accepted from May to September. Follow NH 25 east for 1½ miles from Center Harbor, then go south on Moultonboro Neck Rd for 6½ miles.

*White Lake State Park* (☎ 603-323-7350), West Ossipee, is 22 miles northeast of Meredith on the shores of White Lake. It has 200 tent sites priced at $16 ($22 for waterfront sites), plus swimming and hiking trails.

**Inns** *Tuckernuck Inn* (☎ 603-279-5521, 888-858-5521, 25 Red Gate Lane) has five cozy, quiet guest rooms for $90 to $100, breakfast included. To find the inn, from Main St go inland along Water St, then turn right (uphill) onto Red Gate Lane. It's a five-minute walk from the center of town.

The *Meredith Inn B&B* (☎ 603-279-0000), Main St at Waukegan St, is a delightful Victorian inn charging $99 to $139 for eight guest rooms, all of which have whirlpool baths (six of which have whirlpool tubs).

The *Red Hill Inn* (☎ 603-279-7001, 800-533-4455, fax 603-279-7003), NH 25B at College Rd in Center Harbor, commands a fine view of the lakes region from its hilltop perch north of Meredith. Rooms in a farm-house and in cottages that surround the main lodge cost $105 to $175. The dining room is excellent.

### Places to Eat

Locals flock to the **Meredith Bay Bakery & Cafe** (☎ 603-279-2279, 7 Main St) for break-fast and lunch. Huge sandwiches made from fresh-baked bread cost $5 or $6. The bakery faces the big Mill Falls Marketplace, which is just inland from the main intersection in town.

## WOLFEBORO

Named for General Wolfe, who died van-quishing Montcalm on the Plains of Abra-ham in Quebec, Wolfeboro (founded in 1770) claims to be 'the oldest summer resort in America.' Whether that's true or not, Wolfe-boro is now the most pleasant resort town on the lake, with a fine lakefront location, an agreeable bustle and plenty of services.

### Information

The Wolfeboro Chamber of Commerce Information Booth (☎ 603-569-1817) is on S Main St at the intersection of NH 28 and NH 109, opposite the Citgo and Mobil gas stations. To reach the chamber's main office (☎ 603- 569-2200), follow Main St down the hill into the business district, then turn right (east) onto Railroad Ave and go one block. Public toilets can be found here and at PJ's Dockside Restaurant (see Places to Eat).

For additional information, visit the web-site www.wolfeboro.com.

### Walking Tours

Wolfeboro is a pretty town with some good examples of New England's architectural styles, from Georgian through Federal, Greek Revival and Second Empire.

The information office has several good suggestions (and pamphlets) for walks, including the half-mile-long Bridge Falls Path, which runs along the southern shore of Back Bay; the 10-minute walk to Abenaki Tower; and the Wolfeboro-Sanbornville Recreational Trail, which follows an aban-doned railroad bed for 12 miles.

### Libby Museum

At the age of 40, Dr Henry Forrest Libby, a local dentist, began collecting things. Start-ing with butterflies and moths, the amateur naturalist built up a private natural history collection. In 1912, he built a home for his collections, the Libby Museum (☎ 603-569-1035), on NH 109 in Winter Harbor, 3 miles north of Wolfeboro. Other collections fol-lowed, including Abenaki relics and early-American farm and home implements.

The museum is open 10 am to 4 pm Tues-day to Sunday, June to early September. Admission is $3 for adults.

### Clark House

The Clark House (☎ 603-569-4997) is on S Main St (south of the information booth) opposite Huggins Hospital. It's Wolfeboro's eclectic historical museum and has colonial artifacts, fire engines and equipment dating back to 1872, and a one-room schoolhouse from 1868.

### Cruises

The Wolfeboro Inn's 65-foot, 75-passenger diesel-powered launch, the MV *Judge Sewall* (☎ 603-569-3016), takes inn guests and others on tours of the lake daily in summer. You can board the quaint vessel, built in 1946, at the town dock off Main St. The cost is $8.

The MV *Mount Washington* also has a daily 3½-hour cruise from Wolfeboro. See Weirs Beach, above, for details and fares.

### Places to Stay

**Camping** Go north on NH 28 to find these places: **Willey Brook Campground** (☎ 603-569-9493), on NH 28, 3 miles north of Wolfe-boro and north of the junction with NH 109, has tent ($16) and RV ($18) sites only a mile from the Lake Wentworth State Beach. **Wolfeboro Campground** (☎ 603-569-9881, 569-4029, 61 Haines Hill Rd), off NH 28, 4½ miles north of Wolfeboro, has 40 RV sites and 10 tent sites priced at $16 to $18 for a family of four. It's open from mid-May to mid-October.

**Inns** The best-known spot here is the **Wolfe-boro Inn** (☎ 603-569-3016, 800-451-2389, 44

N Main St), the town's main lodging house since 1812, with 43 very comfortable rooms priced from $119 to $179.

A few hundred yards north is the *Tuc' Me Inn B&B* (☎ 603-569-5702, 118 N Main St), a conveniently located B&B charging $85 to $95 for its rooms, country breakfast included.

More or less across the street is the *123 North Main B&B* (☎/fax 603-569-9191, 800-577-9506, 123 N Main St), an 1850 colonial-style house with three guest rooms (private baths) priced at $135, breakfast included.

Farther north along N Main (NH 28) are several good motels. The *Lakeview Inn* (☎ 603-569-1335, 200 N Main St), less than a mile north of Wolfeboro center, has very nice rooms priced from $80 to $90, breakfast included. The dining room here is a local favorite.

The 43-room *Allen 'A' Motor Inn* (☎ 603-569-1700, 800-732-8507), on NH 28, 2 miles north of Wolfeboro, is set on 7 acres bordering Lake Wentworth. The comfortable rooms cost $69 to $89.

## Places to Eat
For breakfast or a light lunch, try the *Strawberry Patch* (☎ 603-569-5523, 30 N Main St). The menu includes pancakes, eggs and sandwiches priced from $3 to $8.

For a light breakfast or snack, the nearby *Yum Yum Shop* (☎ 603-569-1919) serves all sorts of baked goods, from doughnuts to wedding cakes, as well as good, strong coffee for low prices.

In the middle of the shopping district, *Rumors Cafe* (☎ 603-569-1201, 6 N Main St) is the locals' favorite tavern-hangout, and for good reason. The eclectic menu ranges from a basket of chicken or teriyaki steak sandwiches ($5 to $8) to more substantial platters and steaks for $9 to $14. The bar and rear terrace have fine lake views.

*PJ's Dockside Restaurant*, just off Main St in the center of town (by the docks for the MV *Judge Sewall* and the MV *Mount Washington*), serves good seaside fare, such as clam rolls and seafood combo plates, for $10 to $15.

For a full restaurant, try the Wolfeboro Inn. In front of the rustic, colonial inn is

*Wolfe's Tavern*, with a bar and menu that ranges from sandwiches to substantial 'tuck-ins' for $8 to $20. In front of the tavern, terrace tables are set outside in good weather. The inn's *Dining Room* is more modern and formal, serving American and continental fare for $20 to $35 per person.

## Getting There & Around
Driving details for Wolfeboro are as follows:

| destination | mileage | hr:min |
| --- | --- | --- |
| Boston, MA | 114 miles | 2:50 |
| Laconia, NH | 30 miles | 0:45 |
| Lincoln, NH | 75 miles | 1:55 |
| Manchester, NH | 54 miles | 1:35 |
| North Conway, NH | 43 miles | 1:20 |
| Portland, ME | 60 miles | 1:50 |
| Portsmouth, NH | 51 miles | 1:25 |

Molly the Trolley (☎ 603-569-5257) trundles along Main St each hour, 10 am to 4 pm daily. An all-day pass costs $1.

# White Mountains

New England's greatest range, the White Mountains have become one of the region's prime outdoor playgrounds. Most of the range is protected from overdevelopment as part of the White Mountain National Forest. Activities include hiking, rustic and backwoods camping, canoeing, kayaking and skiing.

Highlights of the White Mountain Range include Waterville Valley, a planned mountain resort community; the Kancamagus Hwy, a beautiful wilderness road over Kancamagus Pass; North Conway and Jackson, centers for downhill and cross-country skiing, canoeing and kayaking; Mt Washington, with Bretton Woods and its famous Mount Washington Hotel, and the Franconia Notch area, which has several ski areas and many dramatic geological formations (including New Hampshire's symbol, the Old Man of the Mountain).

## Information
For information about this area, the headquarters of the White Mountain National

# WHITE MOUNTAINS

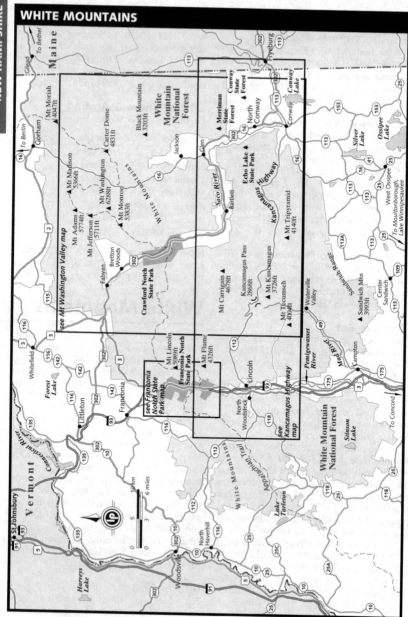

Forest (☎ 603-528-8721), PO Box 638, Laconia, NH 03247, is the nerve center, but the office in Lincoln, just off I-93 exit 32, can help you as well.

## WATERVILLE VALLEY

The Waterville Valley, in a beautiful mountain valley, was developed to be a complete mountain resort community.

As early as 1829, there was an incorporated town here in the shadow of Mt Tecumseh, on the banks of the Mad River, but the valley took its present shape during the last decades of the 20th century. Hotels, condominiums, vacation villas, golf courses, ski runs, roads and services were all laid out according to plan by the Waterville Company. The result is a harmonious, although somewhat sterile, resort with lots of organized sports activities.

Sports facilities include downhill and cross-country ski trails, hiking trails, tennis courts, a golf course, road and mountain-bike routes and in-line skating paths.

### Orientation & Information

Waterville Valley (☎ 800-468-2553, www .waterville.com) is reached from I-93 exit 28 (Campton). For information the Waterville Valley Regional Chamber of Commerce (call ☎ 603-726-3804, 800-237-2307, www .watervillevalleyregion.com), RR 1, Box 1067, Campton, NH 03223, is easily visible from the main road (NH 49). The road continues 13 miles northeast into the valley and to Waterville Valley resort.

Tripoli Rd (unpaved, closed in winter) goes northwest from Waterville Valley to I-93 exit 31 and north to Lincoln.

Town Square is the main service facility, with the post office, bank, information office, laundry, restaurants and shops.

### Places to Stay & Eat

**Camping** Two national forest campgrounds in Plymouth, on I-93 south of Waterville Valley, are convenient to the valley. *Waterville Campground (☎ 603-536-1310)*, open all year, has 27 very basic sites for $11; some can be reserved in advance.

*Campton Campground (☎ 603-536-1310)* has 58 sites near the Mad River for $14; some can be reserved in advance. There are pay showers and flush toilets.

**Hotels** The Waterville Valley resort has no cheap lodging, though there are economical lodgings in Campton, 13 miles to the southwest near I-93. Reservations for resort lodgings may be made through the central reservations service (☎ 800-468-2553, fax 603-236-4174). If you call a hotel directly to make reservations, you may be asked if you've ever stayed there before. A 'yes' answer (regardless of your previous lodging history) will probably get you a 'previous-guest' discount of up to 10%. Don't be bashful.

The *Black Bear Lodge (☎ 603-236-4501, 800-349-2327, 3 Village Rd)* has 107 one-bedroom suites that can sleep up to six people. Each suite has a fully equipped kitchen, and there's an indoor pool – it's great for families. Suites rent for $109 to $131 in summer.

The 85-room *Snowy Owl Inn (☎ 603-236-8383, 800-766-9969)* has a variety of accommodations. The simplest is modestly called Superior and it goes up from there to Deluxe, Premium, Loft/Studio and Fireside. Prices range from $106 to $213 in the summer.

*The Valley Inn (☎ 603-236-8336, 800-343-0969, fax 603-236-4294, www.valleyinn.com)*, on Tecumseh Rd, has hotel rooms for $84 to $121 and condominiums that sleep up to six people for $145 to $165. All prices include use of the many resort facilities, from tennis courts and health club to mountain-bike trails and golf course.

For Waterville Valley condominium rentals, call ☎ 800-556-6522.

Most of the hotels in Waterville Valley have decent dining rooms, and there are a number of theme restaurants in the Town Square complex.

### Getting There & Away

Waterville Valley is easy to reach by car. Driving details follow.

| destination | mileage | hr:min |
|---|---|---|
| Boston, MA | 139 miles | 3:00 |
| I-93 exit 28 | 13 miles | 0:25 |
| Laconia, NH | 44 miles | 1:15 |
| Lincoln, NH | 27 miles | 0:45 |

## KANCAMAGUS HIGHWAY

The Kancamagus Hwy is a stretch of NH 112 between Lincoln and Conway, through the White Mountain National Forest and over Kancamagus Pass (2868 feet). It's a beautiful, paved road unspoiled by commercial development, and many USFS campgrounds are reached by this road.

### History

About 1684, Kancamagus, 'the fearless one,' assumed the powers of *sagamon* (leader) of the Penacook Confederacy of Native American peoples in this region. He was the third and the final sagamon, succeeding his grandfather, the great Passaconaway, and his uncle Wonalancet.

Kancamagus worked to keep the peace between the indigenous peoples and European explorers and settlers. But provocations by the whites pushed his patience to the breaking point. Kancamagus resorted to battle to rid the region of the whites but lost. By 1691, he and his followers were heading north to escape them.

### Hiking

White Mountain National Forest (☎ 603-744-9165) is laced with excellent hiking trails of varying difficulty. For detailed trail-by-trail information, stop at the Lincoln/Woodstock Chamber of Commerce Information Center (☎ 603-745-6621) in Lincoln, just east of I-93 exit 32.

If you're the kind who plans ahead, get a copy of the *AMC White Mountain Guide* from the Appalachian Mountain Club (☎ 617-523-0636, www.outdoors.org), 5 Joy St, Boston, MA 02108, or from an outfitter or local bookshop. Here are some hiking suggestions:

Lincoln Woods Trail
The trailhead (elevation 1157 feet) is at the Lincoln Woods Trail parking lot on the Kancamagus Hwy, 5 miles east of I-93. The 2.9-mile-long trail ends at the Pemigewasset Wilderness Boundary (elevation 1450 feet). This, along with the Wilderness Trail, is among the easiest and most popular trails in the national forest.

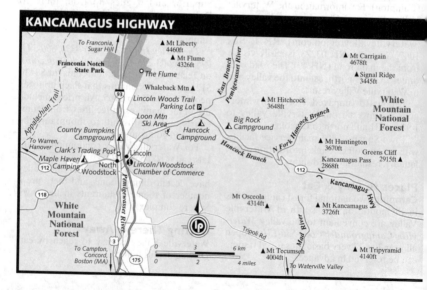

### KANCAMAGUS HIGHWAY

Wilderness Trail

This trail begins where the Lincoln Woods Trail ends, and it continues for 6 miles to Stillwater Junction (elevation 2060 feet). You can, if you like, follow the Cedar Brook and Hancock Notch Trails to return to the Kancamagus Hwy, which is some miles east of the Lincoln Woods Trailhead parking lot.

## Places to Stay

The beautiful, heavily wooded national forest campgrounds east of Lincoln along the Kancamagus Hwy offer primitive sites (pit toilets only) for $12; a few campgrounds have flush toilets and charge $14 per site. These campgrounds are in heavy demand in the warm months. Arrive in the morning to get a site and on Thursday or Friday morning to pin one down for the weekend. Call ☎ 603-536-1310 or 603-447-5448 for more information on camping in the White Mountain National Forest.

The following campground recommendations are listed from west to east (Lincoln to Conway).

Four miles east of Lincoln, *Hancock Campground*, has 56 sites near the Pemigewasset River and Wilderness Trail. Hancock is open all year.

*Big Rock Campground*, 6 miles east of Lincoln, has 28 sites near the Wilderness Trail and is open all year.

*Passaconaway Campground*, 12 miles west of Conway, has 33 sites on the Swift River, which is good for fishing. Camping season runs from mid-May through November.

*Jigger Johnson Campground*, 10 miles west of Conway, has 75 sites, flush toilets and nature lectures on summer weekends. It's open mid-May to mid-October.

Six miles west of Conway, the *Covered Bridge Campground* has 49 sites for $9; some can be reserved. And yes, you do cross the Albany Covered Bridge to reach the campground. The season runs from mid-May to mid-October.

The *Blackberry Crossing Campground*, 6 miles west of Conway on the south side of the Kancamagus Hwy, is a former Civilian Conservation Corps (CCC) camp with 26 sites going for $8 each. It's open all year.

## NORTH WOODSTOCK & LINCOLN

The twin towns of North Woodstock and Lincoln serve a diverse clientele. Outdoorsy types in heavy boots stop here for provisions

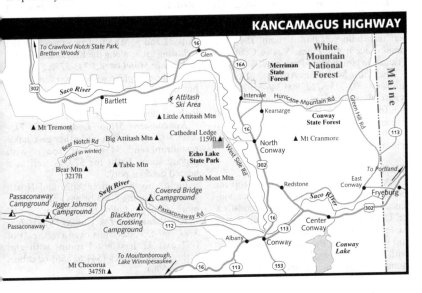

**KANCAMAGUS HIGHWAY**

**NEW HAMPSHIRE**

on their way to camp and hike along the Kancamagus Hwy (NH 112). Retirees in huge peach-colored road cruisers stop for cocktails after photographing the Old Man of the Mountain in Franconia Notch State Park.

If you've come as far as North Woodstock and Lincoln, you must see the Old Man of the Mountain and enjoy the other natural wonders of the park. See the Franconia Notch State Park section, later in this chapter, for more details.

### Orientation

The Pemigewasset River springs just south of Franconia Notch and runs south parallel to I-93. It is joined by its east branch at North Woodstock, which is west of I-93 exit 32. Lincoln, on the east branch, is east of I-93. Both are pretty much one-street towns and the Kancamagus Hwy comes into them from Conway, which is 18 miles east of Kancamagus Pass (286 feet).

### Information

The Lincoln/Woodstock Chamber of Commerce (☎ 603-745-6621, 800-227-4191 for lodging reservations, www.linwoodcc.org), PO Box 358, Kancamagus Hwy, Lincoln, NH 03251, is in The Depot shopping center on the eastern side of the town. The chamber staff can help you find a room. There's a small office in the Flume Visitor Center in Franconia Notch State Park as well.

The White Mountains Attractions Association (☎ 603-745-8720, 800-346-3687, www.visitwhitemountains.com) operates the White Mountain Information Center in Lincoln, just east of I-93 exit 32. Pick up brochures that detail the hiking trails in the national forest.

### Clark's Trading Post

Clark's Trading Post, a traditional stop for families traveling in the White Mountains since 1928, is just north of North Woodstock on US 3 and just south of Franconia Notch State Park. If the children are bored from too much time in the car, Clark's can help with its old-fashioned photo parlor, water-bumper boats, magic house, narrow-gauge

steam locomotive and a gift shop that sells moccasins. Commercial? You bet, but fun.

### Places to Stay

**Camping** For the USFS campgrounds along the Kancamagus Hwy east of Lincoln, see Camping in the Kancamagus Highway section, earlier.

There's a fine, state-run campground at Lafayette Place in Franconia Notch State Park (see that section, later in this chapter) with 97 tent sites ($14) in a wooded location. It's in very heavy demand in summer, so arrive early in the day to claim a site.

As for commercial campgrounds, *Maple Haven Camping* (☎ 603-745-3350), a mile west of North Woodstock on NH 112, charges $20 to $25 for tent and RV sites. *Lost River Valley Campground* (☎ 603-745-8321), 3 miles farther west, covers 200 acres (100 wooded), with lots of tent and RV sites near streams for $22 to $28. *Country Bumpkins* (☎ 603-745-8837), near the Pemigewasset River and Bog Brook, has 46 sites for $20 to $26. Take I-93 exit 33, then go south on US 3 and look for the campground on the east side of the road, north of Lincoln.

**Motels** A few motels are in the center of Lincoln and east along the Kancamagus Hwy, but most are on US 3 between I-93 exits 32 and 33. The first two motels in the following list lie along the Kancamagus Hwy.

*Lincoln Motel* (☎ 603-745-2780, *5 Church St*) is a homey place with only seven rooms, but it's convenient and priced well at $55. Look for it on the north side of the highway in the center of Lincoln.

*Kancamagus Motor Lodge* (☎ 603-745-3365, 800-346-4205), a bit farther east, has a restaurant and 34 modern rooms with private steam baths for $79, as well as a heated outdoor pool.

Going north from Lincoln and North Woodstock along US 3 brings you to many more motels, including those below.

*Riverbank Motel & Cabins* (☎ 603-745-3374, 800-633-5624), just over a mile east of I-93 exit 32, has motel rooms with and without kitchenettes ($44 to $56) or cabins ($66 to $96).

*Cozy Cabins* (☎ 603-745-8713) has passable little cabins for $42 to $48 with two bedrooms and, in the more expensive units, a full kitchen.

*Red Doors Motel* (☎ 603-745-2267) does indeed have red doors on its plain but comfy rooms, which rent for $44 to $66.

*Drummer Boy Motor Inn* (☎ 603-745-3661, 800-762-7275) is a fairly luxurious place with nice indoor and outdoor pools, sauna, playground and comfortable rooms for $68 to $90, light breakfast included.

*Woodward's Motor Inn* (☎ 603-745-8141, 800-635-8968) is the class act here with lots of facilities: an indoor pool, sauna, hot tub, racquetball court, tennis court and game room, as well as 80 good rooms for $79 to $108.

*Franconia Notch Motel* (☎ 603-745-2229) is very tidy, well-kept and attractive, with rooms for $45 to $70.

**Inns** The *Woodstock Inn* (☎ 603-745-3951, 800-321-3985), on Main St in North Woodstock, consists of three restored houses with lodging and dining rooms. The Victorian Main House has six rooms sharing three hall baths. Riverside has 11 rooms with private bath, and Deachman House has two rooms sharing a hall bath. Rates for bed and breakfast for two range from $90 to $150.

## Places to Eat

The Kancamagus Hwy (NH 112), which runs through Lincoln, bears the usual assortment of fast food emporia – *Burger King, McDonald's* and the other franchise shops. *Gordi's Fish & Steak House* (☎ 603-745-6635), in The Depot shopping center, is a big place with a hearty menu to suit appetites sharpened by outdoor exercise. Big steaks ($13 to $18) are featured, as is fish ($11 to $18), but there's also a pub menu of cheaper fare ($5 to $12).

*The Italian Garden Restaurant* (☎ 603-745-2626), in the Millfront Marketplace section of the Mill at Loon Mountain shopping center, has a good selection of lighter meals (antipasti, pizzas, calzones for $5 to $15) and a few Italian classics. Its bar is a gathering place in the evening.

## Geography of New Hampshire

Southern New Hampshire is a region of glacial lakes and low mountains, many of which are batholiths – huge rounded granite domes formed deep underground and brought to the surface by upheavals and erosion. Mt Monadnock (3166 feet), southeast of Keene, is the most famous of New Hampshire's batholiths.

The Merrimack River Valley drains the central and southern portions of the state. The river itself is easily traceable on any road map because it shares its valley with I-93 and I-293. Springing at Newfound Lake, the river flows southeastward through Concord, Manchester, Merrimack and Nashua-Hudson before turning northeastward and entering the Atlantic at Newburyport, Massachusetts.

South-central New Hampshire's major feature is vast Lake Winnipesaukee, with 183 miles of shoreline. Surrounding lakes, which would be large in most other places, look small by comparison.

North-central New Hampshire has the White Mountain Range and the northern end of the Appalachian Mountains, including the famous Presidential Range, which has peaks named after many US presidents. Mt Washington (6288 feet) is the highest, of course.

Most of the White Mountain Range is included in the vast White Mountain National Forest. Several 'notches' (narrow passes) provide passage between major mountains. The most famous of these is Franconia Notch, a 5-mile-long gap that is within the serene and unwavering gaze of the Old Man of the Mountain (also known as the Great Stone Face).

In general, eating possibilities improve west of the highway on Main St (US 3) in North Woodstock.

**The Chalet Restaurant** (☎ 603-745-2256), right at the junction of US 3 and NH 112, is the touristy place. Its perennial lobster-special dinners (boiled or broiled) costs $13 to $19. Many other dishes are served as well.

Right next door, **Peg's Family Restaurant** (☎ 603-745-2740) is where the locals go for hearty, early breakfasts (from 5:30 am; $2.30 to $6) and late luncheon sandwiches (it closes at 4 pm) at low prices. Have the meat loaf sandwich with gravy for $7.

North of all these places on US 3 is the **Sunny Day Diner** (☎ 603-745-4833), an authentic American diner serving breakfast and lunch 6 am to 2 pm (closed Tuesday). The food is classic diner fare: peanut butter and jelly sandwiches and blue plate specials such as meat loaf. The bakery in the basement supplies all the bread, rolls and pies. Full meals (including the dinners served from 4:30 to 8 pm on Thursday and Friday) cost $8 to $10 – an unbeatable value.

**Truant's Taverne & Restaurant** (☎ 603-745-2239), facing the aforementioned Chalet Restaurant but entered around the back via Depot St, has a long list of bar food ($5 to $8), such as spare ribs, chicken fingers and peel-and-eat shrimp, but there's also vegetarian stir-fry and a children's menu. Most main-course dishes cost less than $12. There's live entertainment on weekends, including blues bands on Sunday night.

**Woodstock Station & Stock Room** (☎ 603-745-3951, Main St), in the Woodstock Inn, can probably satisfy any food craving you may have. The menu includes fish, pasta, steaks, Mexican food, sandwiches – just about everything. Most main courses cost $12 to $18. The restaurant's upscale Clement Room offers perhaps the most elegant dining in the area and features such continental favorites as roast rack of lamb ($24) and steak Diane ($21).

**Govoni's Italian Restaurant** (☎ 603-745-8042), 1½ miles west of North Woodstock along NH 112, has been serving traditional Italian fare each summer since 1914. The menu lists such standards as linguine with clam sauce, veal parmigiana and manicotti, priced from $8 to $16. Reservations are not accepted, so arrive early (particularly on summer weekends) or plan to wait.

## Getting There & Away

Driving details for Lincoln/North Woodstock are as follows:

| destination | mileage | hr:min |
|---|---|---|
| Boston, MA | 140 miles | 3:10 |
| Franconia, NH | 11 miles | 0:20 |
| Laconia, NH | 45 miles | 1:10 |
| Montpelier, VT | 65 miles | 1:40 |
| North Conway, NH | 42 miles | 1:05 |

## FRANCONIA NOTCH STATE PARK

Franconia Notch, a narrow gorge that was shaped over the eons by a wild stream cutting through craggy granite, is among the most dramatic of the state's several notches (mountain passes).

The symbol of the Granite State is the natural rock formation called the Great Stone Face, or Old Man of the Mountain. The Old Man gazes across Franconia Notch from his lofty perch high on the west wall of the gorge, not even blinking as thousands of tourists pass by daily and look up at him. Southeast of the Old Man lies the undulant crest of Mt Liberty, which some people think resembles George Washington lying in state. This is, after all, the Presidential Range.

## Orientation

The most scenic parts of the notch are encompassed and protected by Franconia Notch State Park. Lodging, meals and services are available in Lincoln and North Woodstock, south of the park, and, to a lesser extent, in Franconia and Littleton to the north.

Franconia Notch is narrow. Reduced to two lanes, I-93 (renamed the Franconia Notch Parkway) squeezes through the gorge. Stopping on the narrow road is not permitted; you must exit the road and park in a designated parking lot.

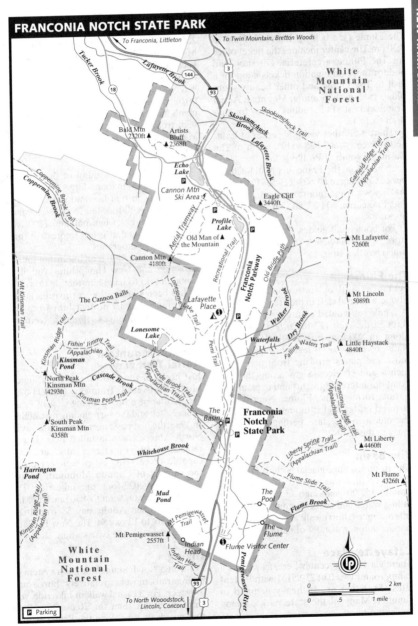

# FRANCONIA NOTCH STATE PARK

To Franconia, Littleton

To Twin Mountain, Bretton Woods

Tucker Brook

Lafayette Brook

144

3

93

18

White Mountain National Forest

Skookumchuck Brook

Skookumchuck Trail

Lafayette Brook

Garfield Ridge Trail (Appalachian Trail)

Coppermine Brook Trail

Coppermine Brook

Bald Mtn 2320ft

Artists Bluff 2368ft

Echo Lake

Cannon Mtn Ski Area

Eagle Cliff 3440ft

Aerial Tramway

Profile Lake

Old Man of the Mountain

Cannon Mtn 4180ft

Recreational Trail

Mt Lafayette 5260ft

Franconia Notch Parkway

Old Bridle Path

Mt Kinsman Trail

The Cannon Balls

Lonesome Lake Trail

Lafayette Place

Mt Lincoln 5089ft

Kinsman Ridge Trail (Appalachian Trail)

Fishin' Jimmy Trail (Appalachian Trail)

Kinsman Pond

Lonesome Lake

Cascade Brook Trail (Appalachian Trail)

Pemi Trail

Walker Brook

Waterfalls

Dry Brook

Little Haystack 4840ft

Falling Waters Trail

North Peak Kinsman Mtn 4293ft

Cascade Brook

Kinsman Pond Trail

South Peak Kinsman Mtn 4358ft

Franconia Ridge Trail (Appalachian Trail)

Harrington Pond

The Basin

Franconia Notch State Park

Whitehouse Brook

Liberty Spring Trail (Appalachian Trail)

Mt Liberty 4460ft

Kinsman Ridge Trail (Appalachian Trail)

Mud Pond

Flume Slide Trail

The Pool

Mt Flume 4326ft

Flume Brook

Mt Pemigewasset Trail

Mt Pemigewasset 2557ft

Indian Head

Indian Head Trail

The Flume

Flume Visitor Center

Pemigewasset River

White Mountain National Forest

93

3

To North Woodstock, Lincoln, Concord

0    1    2 km

0    .5    1 mile

P Parking

## Information

There's a visitors' center (☎ 603-745-8391) at The Flume (see below). It's open 9 am to 4:30 pm. The center includes the ticket office for The Flume, a cafeteria, gift shop and auditorium. Combination tickets good for a visit to The Flume and other beauty spots, plus a ride on the Cannon Mountain Aerial Tramway, cost $14 for adults and $7 for children six to 12.

There's another visitors' center at Lafayette Place (☎ 603-823-9513), north of The Basin and south of Profile Lake.

In addition, the Franconia Notch Chamber of Commerce (☎ 603-823-5661, 800-237-9007, www.franconianotch.org), PO Box 780, Franconia, NH 03580, can answer your questions.

For books and guides, the Village Bookstore (☎ 603-444-5263), 81 Main St in Littleton, is worth a stop.

## The Flume

Four miles north of North Woodstock is The Flume, a natural cleft in the granite bedrock. A 2-mile self-guided nature walk takes you through the cleft (12 to 20 feet wide) and along an 800-foot boardwalk. The granite walls tower 70 to 90 feet above you, with moss and plants growing from precarious niches and crevices. Signs along the way point out interesting sights and explain how nature formed The Flume. Nearby is a covered bridge that is thought to be one of the oldest in the state, perhaps erected as early as the 1820s.

## The Basin

The Basin is a huge glacial pothole 20 feet in diameter that was carved deep into the granite 15,000 years ago by the action of falling water and swirling stones. The Basin offers a nice (short) walk and a cool spot to ponder a minor wonder of nature.

## Lafayette Place

There's a visitors' center here, as well as a campground (☎ 603-823-9513) with 97 tent sites ($14) that are in heavy demand in summer. Many of the state park's hiking trails start here.

## Old Man of the Mountain

At the beginning of the 19th century, after 200 million years in the making, the Old Man of the Mountain (or the Great Stone Face, as he's also known), a rock outcrop high up on the west wall of Franconia Notch, was 'discovered' by white settlers passing through the notch. The striking profile of a man's face (à la Picasso, perhaps) can be seen from the north (follow signs for 'Old Man Viewing'). From the parking lot, a path leads down to Profile Lake, and plaques tell you all about the Old Man.

Marketed as the symbol of the Granite State, the Old Man looms larger in the imagination than in real life, and some viewers find it small. A 40-foot-tall, 25-foot-wide face is indeed big, but when perched 1200 feet above the ground, it is less impressive than its close-up photographs.

Since the Old Man is an important tourist attraction and New Hampshire symbol, it would not do to have him tumble down, so he has been stabilized with (invisible) concrete and rebar to protect him from the natural consequences of earth tremors, wind, water and ice.

## Cannon Mountain Aerial Tramway

Just north of the Old Man is the Cannon Mountain Aerial Tramway (☎ 603-823-5563), offering a breathtaking view of Franconia Notch and the surrounding mountains. In 1938, the first passenger aerial tramway in North America was installed here. It was replaced in 1980 by a larger cable car that is capable of carrying 80 passengers up to the summit of Cannon Mountain in five minutes – a 2022-foot, one-mile ride. The tramway operates 9 am to 4:30 pm, late May to mid-October. Adults pay $8 roundtrip; children six to 12 pay $4. The New England Ski Museum is in the base station.

## Hiking

Franconia Notch State Park has a system of hiking trails; most are relatively short, some are steep. For a casual walk or bike ride, you can't do better than the Recreation Path that wends its way along the Pemigewasset

River and through the notch for 8 miles. Other hikes include the following:

Mt Pemigewasset Trail
  This trail begins at The Flume Visitor Center and climbs for 1.4 miles to the 2557-foot summit of Mt Pemigewasset (Indian Head), offering excellent views. You can return by the same trail or the Indian Head Trail, which joins US 3 after 1 mile. From there, it's a 1-mile walk north to The Flume Visitor Center.

Lonesome Lake Trail
  Departing from Lafayette Place and its campground, this trail climbs 1000 feet in 1½ miles to Lonesome Lake. Various branch trails lead farther up to the several summits of The Cannon Balls and Cannon Mountain (3700 to 4180 feet) and south to The Basin.

Kinsman Falls
  On the Cascade Brook, these falls are a good goal for a short, half-mile hike from The Basin via The Basin Cascade Trail.

Bald Mountain and Artists Bluff Trail
  Just north of Echo Lake, off NH 18, this 1½-mile loop skirts the summit of Bald Mountain (at 2320 feet) and Artists Bluff (2368 feet), with short spur trails to the summits.

## Skiing

**Downhill** The state operates the **Cannon Mountain Ski Area** (☎ 603-823-5563), off I-93 exit 2. In addition to the three cafeterias and the base station and lounges nearby, you'll find a ski school, a nursery and a ski shop where you can buy and rent equipment.

The vertical drop is 2145 feet, and the slopes are positioned so they naturally receive and retain more than the average amount of white stuff. The ski area also makes its own snow.

Cannon Mountain has an aerial tramway, one triple and two double chairlifts, one quad chair and a pony lift. There are 26 miles of trails and slopes.

If Cannon Mountain gets too crowded, **Mittersill** (☎ 603-823-5511), its junior cousin on I-93, has a vertical drop of 1600 feet, with one double chairlift and one T-bar lift.

Along the Kancamagus Hwy east of Lincoln, **Loon Mountain** (☎ 603-823-5563, 823-8100 for daily snow updates) is another option.

**Cross-Country** Thanks to the extensive national forest, there are more than a few cross-country trails available, both at the downhill areas and elsewhere. Contact the Lincoln/Woodstock Chamber of Commerce (☎ 603-745-6621) for details on rentals and directions.

## FRANCONIA

Franconia, a few miles north of Franconia Notch via I-93, is a pleasant, tranquil New England town with splendid mountain views and a poetic attraction: Robert Frost's farm. Franconia is a fine place to stay: prettier, more tranquil and a bit cheaper than the lodgings south of Franconia Notch, but most places are open only from late May through mid-October.

### Orientation

NH 18, NH 116 and NH 117 meet at the center of town, marked by a prominent, pale yellow building topped by a cupola with clock – the home of the local prep school, Dow Academy. NH 18 is Main St. Nearby Sugar Hill, a few miles west along NH 117, has several fine country inns.

### Information

The Franconia Notch Chamber of Commerce (☎ 603-823-5661, 800-237-9007, www .franconianotch.org), PO Box 780, Franconia, NH 03580, maintains an information office on NH 18 just southeast of the town center.

### The Frost Place

Robert Frost (1874-1963) was America's most renowned and best-loved poet in the middle of the 20th century. Born in San Francisco, Frost moved to Massachusetts with his mother after his father's death. He attended – but didn't graduate from – Dartmouth, then Harvard. He bought a small farm near Derry in southern New Hampshire but didn't do well as a farmer.

After a sojourn of several years in England, Frost lived with his wife and children on this farm near Franconia. The years spent here were some of the most productive and inspired years of his life. He wrote

## Frost's Accomplishments

In addition to writing very popular poetry, Robert Frost (1874-1963) garnered critical acclaim. In 1923, he won a Pulitzer Prize for his collection *New Hampshire*. He won the same prize twice more for *Collected Poems* (1930) and *A Further Range* (1936).

In 1958, Frost was appointed the Poetry Consultant to the Library of Congress, and he later received honorary doctorates from Oxford and Cambridge. At John F Kennedy's inauguration as president of the US (1961), Frost read his poem 'The Gift Outright.' At the time of his death in 1963, Frost was considered the unofficial poet laureate of the US. Not bad for a college dropout.

many of his best and most famous poems to describe life on this farm and the scenery surrounding it, including 'The Road Not Taken' and 'Stopping by Woods on a Snowy Evening.'

The farmhouse has been kept as faithful to the period as possible, with numerous exhibits of Frost memorabilia. In the forest behind the house, there is a half-mile-long nature trail. Frost's poems are mounted on plaques in sites appropriate to the things the poems describe; in several places, the plaques have been erected at the exact spots where Frost composed the poems.

The Frost Place (☎ 603-823-5510), marked on some signs as the Frost Museum, has been preserved as a memorial to the poet's life and work. It's open 1 to 5 pm weekends, late May through June; 1 to 5 pm Wednesday to Monday, July through mid-October. The price of admission ($3 for adults, $2 for seniors, $1.25 for children six to 15) includes a 20-minute slide show about Frost's early life and work and about the countryside here.

To find Frost's farm, follow NH 116 south from Franconia. After exactly a mile, turn right onto Bickford Hill Rd, then left onto unpaved Ridge Rd and you'll find it a short distance along on the right.

### Places to Stay

**Camping** Camping is available in nearby Lafayette Place in Franconia Notch State Park – see that section, earlier in this chapter. There's also the *Fransted Family Campground* (☎ 603-823-5675), on NH 18 between Franconia and Franconia Notch, with sites for $14 to $17.

**Motels** Most of the lodgings listed below have their own restaurants.

*Gale River Motel & Cottages* (☎ 603-823-5655, 800-255-7989, 1 Main St) in the center of town, is a classic roadside motel with heated pool, hot tub and Jacuzzis. Rooms cost $55 to $85.

The most prominent lodging place, on Wallace Hill Rd in the town center, is the *Red Coach Inn* (☎ 603-823-7422, 800-262-2493), with an indoor pool, Jacuzzi and health club, as well as guest rooms priced at $85.

*Hillwinds* (☎ 603-823-5551, 800-473-5299), south of the town center on the riverbank (follow the road south by the Dow Academy), is a comfortable motel with a riverside location, rooms for $65 to $75 and a restaurant with moderate prices.

*Raynor's Motor Lodge* (☎ 603-823-9586, 800-634-8187), less than a mile south of town along NH 18, has 30 comfortable rooms for $60 to $75 and a heated swimming pool.

Just south of Raynor's, *Stonybrook Motel & Lodge* (☎ 603-823-8192, 800-722-3552), on NH 18 just over a mile south of town, has heated indoor and outdoor pools and tidy, comfortable rooms for $64 to $89.

**Inns** There are several dozen inns near Franconia. Here are some of the more interesting ones.

*Pinestead Farm Lodge* (☎ 603-823-8121), on NH 116, is a working family farm with nine clean, simple rooms for rent; each set of three rooms shares a bath and kitchen/sitting room. The cost is $20 per person, double. You'll share your farm experience with Bob and Kathleen Sherburn, as well as assorted cattle, pigs, chickens, ducks and horses. If you come in late winter, you can help with the maple sugaring. The family's been renting rooms since 1899.

The 34-room *Franconia Inn* (☎ *603-823-5542, 800-473-5299; fax 603-823-8078*), on NH 116 just over 2 miles south of Franconia, is a fine old inn set on 107 acres in a broad, fertile, pine-fringed river valley. The estate has prime cross-country ski possibilities in winter and hiking and horseback riding in summer. In summer, rooms cost $83 to $128, breakfast included.

*Sugar Hill Inn* (☎ *603-823-5621, 800-548-4748*), a mile west of Franconia on NH 117 in Sugar Hill, is a restored 1789 inn with lots of activities, an excellent dining room and 11 guest rooms with private bath priced from $85 to $145, breakfast included. There are cottages as well.

*Lovett's Inn* (☎ *603-823-7761*), on Profile Rd (NH 18) 2 miles south of Franconia, is known for its dining, which is open to non-guests, as well as its good rooms that rent for $110 to $150, breakfast included.

### Places to Eat

Many of Franconia's inns offer fine dining, including the *Franconia Inn*, *Hillwinds*, *Lovett's Inn* and the *Sugar Hill Inn*. See Places to Stay, above, for their location information.

In addition, there's *Polly's Pancake Parlor* (☎ *603-823-5575*), Hildex Farm in Lisbon (2 miles west of Franconia on NH 117). Attached to a farmhouse, this local favorite offers pancakes made with home-ground flour and topped with the farm's own maple syrup, eggs from the chickens and sausages from the hogs, as well as sandwiches and quiches, all priced from $5 to $15. It's open 7 am to 3 pm daily from Mother's Day to mid-October and on weekends off-season.

### Getting There & Away

Concord Trailways buses (☎ 603-228-7266, 800-639-3317, www.concordtrailways.com) stop at Kelly's Foodtown in the center of Franconia.

If you're coming by car, driving details for Franconia are as follows:

| destination | mileage | hr:min |
|---|---|---|
| Boston, MA | 151 miles | 3:30 |
| North Conway, NH | 44 miles | 1:15 |
| Lincoln, NH | 11 Miles | 0:20 |
| St Johnsbury, NH | 25 miles | 0:40 |

# Mt Washington Valley

The Mt Washington Valley, stretching north from the eastern end of the Kancamagus Hwy, includes the towns of Bartlett, Conway, Glen, Intervale, Jackson and North Conway. The valley harbors a myriad of outdoor sports possibilities. The hub of the valley is the town of North Conway.

## NORTH CONWAY

The Kancamagus Hwy's eastern terminus is the town of Conway, at the intersection of NH 16, NH 113, NH 153 and US 302. But the activities capital of the region is North Conway, 5 miles north along NH 16 and US 302.

### Orientation

North Conway is at the center of the Mt Washington Valley, an area that offers a great variety of hiking, camping, canoeing and kayaking. Within a few miles' drive of the town are several alpine ski areas such as Attitash, Black Mountain and Cranmore. Nearby Jackson and Intervale have miles and miles of cross-country ski trails.

Most of the time, the glut of auto traffic on Main St (NH 16 and US 302) moves at a glacial pace. If your aim is to get around North Conway, not into it, take West Side Rd, which follows the west bank of the Saco River between Conway and Glen. River Rd connects NH 16 to West Side Rd (see map).

### Information

The Mt Washington Valley Chamber of Commerce & Visitors Bureau (☎ 603-356-3171, 800-367-3364 for lodging reservations,

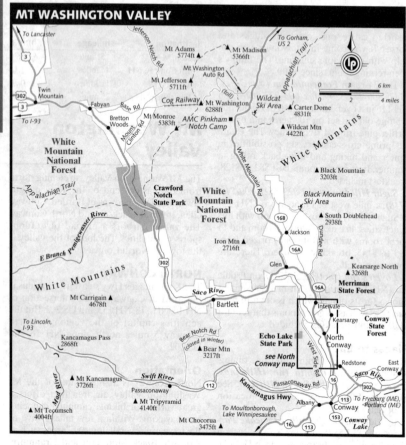

## MT WASHINGTON VALLEY

www.4seasonresort.com), PO Box 2300, North Conway, NH 03860, is the local information source. The chamber maintains an office on Main St (NH 16 and US 302), on the south side of the town center.

The State of New Hampshire runs an information office in the rest area on NH 16 and US 302 at Intervale, 2 miles north of the center of North Conway.

EMS (☎ 603-356-5433, www.emsonline .com), on Main St in North Conway, is an outfitter that sells maps and guides to the White Mountain National Forest. EMS also rents camping equipment and, in the winter, cross-country skis. A climbing school operates year-round (it requires reservations). Call EMS to connect to the 'weather phone,' a report updated daily.

The various ski areas – Attitash, Mt Cranmore, Black Mountain, Wildcat – can help you make lodging reservations. See those sections, below, for contact information.

### Conway Scenic Railroad

Conway Scenic Railroad (☎ 603-356-5251, 800-232-5251, www.conwayscenic.com) has

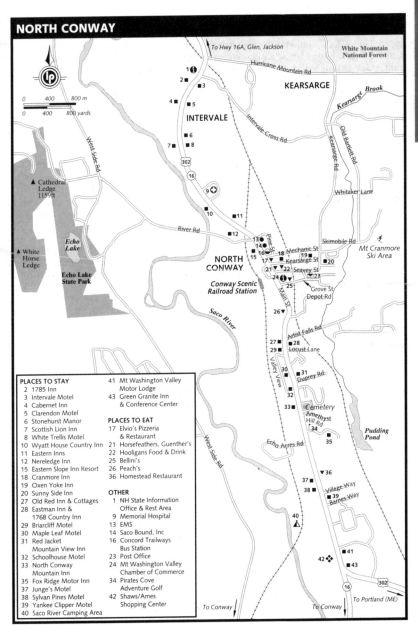

# NORTH CONWAY

To Hwy 16A, Glen, Jackson

White Mountain National Forest

Hurricane Mountain Rd

KEARSARGE

Kearsarge Brook

INTERVALE

Intervale Cross Rd

Old Bartlett Rd

Kearsarge Rd

Whitaker Lane

West Side Rd

Cathedral Ledge 1159ft

White Horse Ledge

Echo Lake

Echo Lake State Park

River Rd

Skimobile Rd

Mt Cranmore Ski Area

NORTH CONWAY

Mechanic St

Kearsarge St

Seavey St

Conway Scenic Railroad Station

Pine St

Main St

Grove St

Depot Rd

Saco River

Artist Falls Rd

Locust Lane

Valley View

Duprey Rd

Cemetery

Amethyst Hill Rd

Pudding Pond

Echo Acres Rd

West Side Rd

Village Way

Barnes Way

To Conway

To Conway

To Portland (ME)

**PLACES TO STAY**
2 1785 Inn
3 Intervale Motel
4 Cabernet Inn
5 Clarendon Motel
6 Stonehurst Manor
7 Scottish Lion Inn
8 White Trellis Motel
10 Wyatt House Country Inn
11 Eastern Inns
12 Nereledge Inn
15 Eastern Slope Inn Resort
18 Cranmore Inn
19 Oxen Yoke Inn
20 Sunny Side Inn
27 Old Red Inn & Cottages
28 Eastman Inn &
   1768 Country Inn
29 Briarcliff Motel
30 Maple Leaf Motel
31 Red Jacket
   Mountain View Inn
32 Schoolhouse Motel
33 North Conway
   Mountain Inn
35 Fox Ridge Motor Inn
37 Junge's Motel
38 Sylvan Pines Motel
39 Yankee Clipper Motel
40 Saco River Camping Area

41 Mt Washington Valley
   Motor Lodge
43 Green Granite Inn
   & Conference Center

**PLACES TO EAT**
17 Elvio's Pizzeria
   & Restaurant
21 Horsefeathers, Guenther's
22 Hooligans Food & Drink
25 Bellini's
26 Peach's
36 Homestead Restaurant

**OTHER**
1 NH State Information
   Office & Rest Area
9 Memorial Hospital
13 EMS
14 Saco Bound, Inc
16 Concord Trailways
   Bus Station
23 Post Office
24 Mt Washington Valley
   Chamber of Commerce
34 Pirates Cove
   Adventure Golf
42 Shaws/Ames
   Shopping Center

a station in the center of town, a prominent feature on Main St. Built in 1874 and restored in 1974, the station is the departure point for its one-hour, 11-mile antique steam train rides through the Mt Washington Valley.

Trains run twice daily on weekends from April to mid-May, several times daily from mid-May to late October, and then again on weekends only until mid-December. Fares are $8.50 (coach) or $10.50 (1st class) for adults, $6 to $7.50 for children four to 12. Children younger than four ride free in coach class or for $4.50 in 1st class.

### Echo Lake State Park
Two miles west of North Conway via River Rd is Echo Lake State Park (☎ 603-356-2672), with its placid mountain lake at the foot of the sheer rock wall called White Horse Ledge. There's a scenic road up to the 700-foot-high Cathedral Ledge and panoramic views of the White Mountains. You can swim in the lake and use the picnic area, but there's no camping. Admission costs $3.

### Skiing
**Attitash** This ski area (☎ 603-374-2368, 374-0946 for snow report, 800-223-7669 for lodging reservations), on US 302 west of Glen, has a vertical drop of 1750 feet, six lifts and 28 ski trails. Half of them are intermediate level, 25% are beginner and 25% are expert. The resort can make 98% of its own snow. Lift-ticket prices are the highest in the valley but not unreasonable.

**Mt Cranmore** Cranmore Ski Resort (☎ 603-356-5543, 800-786-6754 for snow report, 800-543-9206 for lodging reservations), right on the outskirts of North Conway, has a vertical drop of 1200 feet, 30 trails (40% beginner, 40% intermediate and 20% expert), five lifts and 100% snowmaking ability. The resort also has 40 miles of groomed cross-country trails, half of them tracked.

**Black Mountain** Black Mountain Ski Area (☎ 603-383-4490, 800-698-4490 for snow report, 800-677-5737 for lodging reservations), on NH 16B in Jackson, has a vertical

drop of 1100 feet, 22 trails (three for teaching, six beginner, nine intermediate, four expert), three lifts and 98% snowmaking capacity, making this a good place for beginners and families with small children.

### Summer Activities
In summer, the chairlifts keep working at the Attitash ski area to take you to the top of the Alpine Slide, a long track that you schuss down on a little cart – an exhilarating ride safe for all ages.

### Canoeing & Kayaking
Saco Bound Inc (☎ 603-447-2177, 800-677-7238, www.sacobound.com), 2 miles east of Center Conway on US 302, rents canoes and kayaks and organizes guided trips. The trips range in length from a few hours to four days on the Saco River and other nearby rivers and ponds. Inquire at the information center (summer only) set up on Main St in North Conway (across from the Eastern Slope Inn). Rates for daily canoe rental range from $20 to $25. The season runs April through October.

Kayak Jack Fun Yak Rentals (☎ 603-447-5571), on NH 16 next to Eastern Slope Campground in Conway, rents kayaks for $22 a day.

### Places to Stay
**Camping** There are commercial campgrounds in Conway, North Conway and Glen. Here is a partial listing.

In Conway, look for **Beach Camping Area** (☎ *603-447-2723*), NH 16 on the Saco River, and **Cove Camping Area** (☎ *603-447-6734*), off Stark Rd on Conway Lake. The **Eastern Slope Camping Area** (☎ *603-447-5092*), in Conway on NH 16, has 260 sites for $20 to $30 and long beaches on the Saco River.

In North Conway, try the **Saco River Camping Area** (☎ *603-356-3360*), on the Saco River off NH 16, which charges $20 to $22 for its 140 sites.

**Hostels** New Hampshire's only youth hostel is the 43-bed **Albert B Lester Memorial HI/AYH Hostel** (☎ *603-447-1001, fax 603-447-3346, 36 Washington St*), off Main St

(NH 16), in Conway – not *North* Conway. This 'sustainable living center' focuses on environmentally friendly practices and conservation. The hostel is big on recycling and gives out information on how to apply 'green' technologies to your daily life.

More importantly, the facility offers six bedrooms with bunk beds ($16 per person) and three family-size rooms ($45, regardless of number). The cost includes linens and continental breakfast. Excellent hiking and bicycling opportunities are just outside the door, and canoeists can easily portage to two nearby rivers. Phone reservations are accepted if you have a credit card.

**Motels** Lodging prices are highest on weekends in late July and August, lower on weekdays and surprisingly low – less than half of high-season prices – in winter. You may face two- or three-night minimum stay requirements in the high season.

Most of North Conway's motels range for 3 miles along Main St (NH 16 and US 302) south of the town center. It can be difficult to find a place in this strip, as street numbers are rarely used. Therefore, on the map we've included motels, restaurants and other businesses as landmarks, even though they aren't mentioned in the text. Here are some of the better choices for lodging (presented from south to north).

The *Yankee Clipper Motel* (☎ 603-356-5736) has standard rooms for $69 to $79. The *Sylvan Pines* (☎ 603-356-2878), set on spacious grounds, is nicer and a bit more expensive at $79 to $99.

*Junge's Motel* (☎ 603-356-2886) is a tidy family-run hostelry set back from the busy roadway, with a heated pool and rooms priced at $75 to $80.

The tidy and comfortable *North Conway Mountain Inn* (☎ 603-356-2803) charges $109 to $119 for its rooms on August weekends.

*School House Motel* (☎ 603-356-6829, 800-638-6050) has a heated outdoor pool, as well as comfy rooms priced at a very reasonable $70 in high season.

*Best Western Red Jacket Mountain View Inn* (☎ 603-356-5411, 800-752-2538, fax 603-356-3842) has resort-style facilities: heated indoor and outdoor swimming pools, saunas, whirlpool baths, tennis courts and a restaurant and lounge. Rooms cost $139 to $159 on August weekends.

The *Maple Leaf Motel* (☎ 603-356-5388) is reasonably priced, with rooms for $62 up to $72. The neighboring *Briarcliff Motel* (☎ 603-356-5584, 800-338-4291) has rooms for $79 to $89.

There are also a few motels along NH 16 on the north side of North Conway, including *Eastern Inns* (☎ 603-603-356-5447, 800-628-3750), a tidy place and a good-value at $89 to $105. The slightly less expensive *White Trellis Motel* (☎ 603-356-2492) is nearby. The *Clarendon Motel* (☎ 603-356-3551, 800-433-3551) has rooms for $72 to $79, and the *Intervale Motel* (☎ 603-356-9776) rents rooms for $65.

**Inns & B&Bs** There are dozens of inns in this region, many of them affordable B&Bs. The rates given below are for the most expensive periods: mid-July through August and foliage season (late September through mid-October). Expect substantial discounts off-season.

A dozen inns, including several mentioned below, have formed an organization called Country Inns in the White Mountains. It has its own reservations line to help visitors find lodging: ☎ 603-356-9460.

Along Main St (NH 16 and US 302) south of North Conway's town center are several inns, including the attractive and aptly named *Old Red Inn & Cottages* (☎ 603-356-2642, 800-338-1356, fax 603-356-6626), which charges $65 to $150 for its 10 cottages (half of which have kitchenettes) and its seven inn rooms with private baths. A full breakfast is included in the rates.

*Sunny Side Inn* (☎ 603-356-6239), on Seavey St, a quiet back street one block east of Main St, is a nice old house with nine rooms, all with private baths, for $60 to $90, breakfast included.

*Cranmore Inn* (☎ 603-356-5502, 800-526-5502), on Kearsarge St a block east of Main St, has been among North Conway's most reliable values for decades. Rooms with private bath cost $74, full breakfast included.

The **Oxen Yoke Inn** (☎ 603-356-6321, 800-862-1600), a block farther east along Kearsarge St, has guest rooms in an old village house and barn. There is also an outdoor pool. The rooms cost $80 to $177 in the high season. Because the inn is under the administration of the Eastern Slope Inn Resort, guests at the Oxen Yoke get to use all of the larger inn's many facilities at no additional charge.

**Eastern Slope Inn Resort** (☎ 603-356-6321, 800-258-4708) is the poshest of the town's inns. It is just north of the central business district on NH 16 and US 302 and charges $119 to $305.

**Nereledge Inn** (☎ 603-356-2831), on River Rd, has nice rooms for $59 to $99 (full breakfast included) and a warm, helpful family atmosphere.

There are several more inns along NH 16 and US 302 north of the town center, including the **Wyatt House Country Inn** (☎ 603-356-7977, 800-527-7978). You'll be pampered with fresh-baked goods at breakfast, sherry in the evening and lots of antique decor. Rooms range from $85 to $139, depending upon views and amenities; the most expensive rooms have two-person Jacuzzis.

Spacious, gracious **Stonehurst Manor** (☎ 603-356-3113, 800-525-9100) has 24 rooms in a manor house and annex set on 33 acres. Luxury rooms (many with fireplaces) cost $106 to $176. The 11 rooms at the romantic **Cabernet Inn** (☎ 603-356-4704, 800-866-4704) have queen beds and fireplaces or Jacuzzis for $75 to $135, breakfast included.

The 17 rooms at the colonial **1785 Inn** (☎ 603-356-9025) are individually decorated and priced at $69 to $119; the cheapest rooms share baths. The inn's dining room is well regarded and has a good wine list. There's a swimming pool too.

## Places to Eat

Many inns – especially those north of the town center and in Jackson (see below) – have good, elegant dining rooms.

**Guenther's**, Main St at Seavey St, is like your mother's kitchen: simple and homey, with big portions of straightforward food such as steak and eggs ($7.50). Come for breakfast or lunch ($5 to $13), which is served 7 am to 3 pm. It's up one flight from Campbell's Bookstore. A good alternative is **Peach's** (☎ 603-356-5860), south of the commercial center on Main St.

**Horsefeathers** (☎ 603-356-2687), on Main St in the center of town, tries to humor everyone with its encyclopedic, eclectic, jokey menu featuring pasta, salads, sandwiches, burgers, bar snacks and main-course platters from $6 to $18.

**Elvio's Pizzeria & Restaurant** (☎ 603-356-3307), on Main St at Kearsarge St, has indoor and outdoor dining, lots of white lattice and white wine and Italian-American cuisine. An average meal costs $8 to $18.

**Bellini's** (☎ 603-356-7000, 33 Seavey St) is the place to go for classic Italian cuisine served in huge portions at moderate prices, from eggplant parmigiana ($13) to a 1lb sirloin steak ($24). Drinks tend to be on the expensive side.

## Getting There & Away

**Bus** Concord Trailways (☎ 603-228-7266, 800-639-3317, www.concordtrailways.com) runs a daily route between Boston and Berlin, stopping at Manchester, Concord, points near Lake Winnipesaukee, Conway, Glen, Jackson, Pinkham Notch and Gorham. The trip between Boston and the Mt Washington Valley takes about 3½ hours.

The bus from Boston will drop you in North Conway on Main St across from the Eastern Slope Inn. The bus to Boston, however, will only pick you up in Jackson (Ellis River Grocery Store, ☎ 603-383-9041, on NH 16), Glen (Storybook Motor Inn, ☎ 603-383-6800, at the intersection of NH 16 and US 302) or Conway (First Stop Convenience Store, ☎ 603-447-8444, on W Main St).

**Car** Distances and travel times to North Conway are as follows:

| destination | dileage | hr:min |
| --- | --- | --- |
| Boston, MA | 144 miles | 3:40 |
| Bretton Woods, NH | 32 miles | 0:50 |
| Franconia, NH | 44 miles | 1:15 |
| Laconia, NH | 49 miles | 1:25 |
| Lincoln, NH | 39 miles | 1:00 |

## JACKSON

Seven miles north of North Conway, just east of NH 16 and across the Ellis River via a red covered bridge, is the village of Jackson, the Mt Washington Valley's premier cross-country ski center. Jackson has many inns that provide charming accommodations in summer or winter, but prices are fairly high.

For details on getting to Jackson, see the North Conway section, earlier in this chapter.

## Orientation & Information

NH 16A circles from NH 16 through the center of Jackson and back to NH 16, and NH 16B heads into the hills.

The Jackson Area Chamber of Commerce (☎ 603-383-9356, 800-866-3334, www .jacksonnh.com), PO Box 304, Jackson, NH 03846, covering the villages of Jackson, Bartlett, Glen and Intervale, can help with lodging reservations. The chamber's information office is south of the covered bridge on NH 16.

## Storyland

On NH 16 in nearby Glen, Storyland (☎ 603-383-4186, www.storylandnh.com) is a delightful 30-acre theme and amusement park for children from three to nine years old. The rides, activities and shows are small-scale and well done – a refreshing break from the mega-amusements and crowds of parks such as Walt Disney World and Universal Studios.

Storyland is open mid-June to mid-October. Admission costs $17 per person (children three and under get in for free). For best value, pay and enter after 3 pm, and you'll receive a pass good for the next day as well.

## Cross-Country Skiing

Jackson is famous for its 93 miles of trails. Each of the downhill ski areas in the valley (see Ski Areas in the North Conway section, earlier in this chapter) has some cross-country trails ranging from easy to expert. There is a small fee for the use of the trails. Clinics, tours and rentals are available in Jackson and North Conway.

## Places to Stay

**Motels** You can't miss the ***Covered Bridge Motor Lodge*** (☎ 603-383-6630, 800-634-2911) just south of Jackson's covered bridge on NH 16. Comfortable rooms go for $78 to $88, breakfast included.

**Inns** Jackson's inns have character, charm, lots of activities and quite substantial price tags. One charming inn quotes prices from $125 to $270, breakfast included, but the small print adds 8% tax and 15% service charge, resulting in a daily price tag of $154 to $332. If you call for reservations, ask that prices be quoted with these extras added.

***The Village House*** (☎ 603-383-6666, 800-972-8343), on NH 16A in Jackson, is the large house on the left just after you go east across the covered bridge. Ten comfy rooms with private bath cost $60 to $80 with breakfast; some have kitchenettes. There's a swimming pool, hot tub and tennis court.

***The Forest, A Country Inn*** (☎ 603-356-9772, 800-448-3534), NH 16A in Intervale, has 11 rooms in a mansard-roofed Victorian for $95 to $120, full breakfast included. There's a heated pool as well.

The *Wildcat Inn & Tavern* (☎ 603-383-4245, 800-228-4245), on Main St in the village center, has a dozen rooms, most with private bath for $82, but a few rooms sharing a hall bath cost a bit less.

## Places to Eat

Many of Jackson's inns have excellent (and expensive) dining rooms. For a simpler meal or snack, try *As You Like It* (☎ 603-383-6425), a bakery in Jackson next to the post office. Enjoy a hot buffet breakfast from 8 to 11 am and deli lunches with a salad bar from 11:30 am to 5 pm.

## PINKHAM NOTCH

In the 1820s, a settler named Daniel Pinkham attempted to build a road north from Jackson through the narrow notch on the eastern slope of Mt Washington. Torrential rains in 1826 caused mud slides that buried his best efforts, but not his name. The place is still called Pinkham Notch. It was almost a century later before an auto road was built in the narrow mountain gap and Pinkham's dream of easy transit was finally realized.

Today, this area is still known for its wild beauty even though useful facilities for campers and hikers make it among the most popular activity centers in the White Mountains. Wildcat Mountain and Tuckerman's Ravine offer good skiing, and an excellent system of trails provides access to the natural beauties of the Presidential Range, especially Mt Washington. For the less athletically inclined, the Mt Washington Auto Road provides easy access to the summit.

## Orientation & Information

NH 16 goes north 11 miles from North Conway and Jackson to Pinkham Notch (2032 feet), then past the Wildcat Mountain ski area and Tuckerman's Ravine, through the small settlement of Glen House and past the Dolly Copp Campground to Gorham and Berlin. The Appalachian Mountain Club (AMC) maintains a hikers' cafeteria and dormitory facilities at its excellent Pinkham Notch Camp.

The Pinkham Notch Camp is the intelligence center in these parts (see Pinkham Notch Camp section, below). The AMC's main office (☎ 617-523-0636, www.outdoors.org) is at 5 Joy St, Boston, MA 02108.

## Mt Washington

Mt Washington's summit is at 6288 feet, making it the tallest mountain in the Northeast. The mountain is renowned for its frighteningly bad weather. The average temperature on the summit is 26.5°F. The mercury has fallen as low as -47°F, but only risen as high as 72°F. About 256 inches (over 21 feet) of snow fall each year (one year, it was 47 feet). At times, the climate can mimic Antarctica's, and hurricane-force winds blow every three days or so, on average.

If you attempt the summit, pack warm, windproof clothes and shoes, even in high summer, and always consult with AMC personnel at the huts. Don't be reluctant to turn back if the weather changes for the worse. On a typical August day, those who set out on Tuckerman Ravine Trail in T-shirts and shorts could suffer hypothermia (and worse) at the summit, where snow, ice and 115mph winds rage in 20°F weather. Dozens of hikers who ignored such warnings and died are commemorated by trailside monuments and crosses. For more information on visiting the mountain, contact **Mt Washington State Park** (☎ 603-466-3347) or visit www.mountwashington.com.

In good weather, the hike up Mt Washington is an exhilarating experience. If you're in good physical condition and you start early, you can make it to the top and back down in a day. You can do several good, short hikes from Pinkham Notch Camp, including the short walk to Crystal Cascade and the equally easy one to Glen Ellis Falls.

The Tuckerman Ravine Trail starts at the Pinkham Notch Camp and it continues for 4.2 miles to the summit. It's the shortest hike to the top, taking just over four hours going up and slightly less going down.

Other trails to the peak are described in the Crawford Notch section, later in this chapter.

The restored Tip Top House hotel no longer provides overnight lodging, but hikers and patrons of both the Mt Washington Auto Road (see below) and the Mt Washington Cog Railway (described in the Bretton Woods section, later in this chapter) can now find food, souvenirs and historical exhibits at the top of the mountain.

## Mt Washington Auto Road
The Mt Washington Summit Road Company (☎ 603-466-2222, www.mt-washington.com) operates an 8-mile-long alpine toll road from Pinkham Notch to the summit of Mt Washington. Look for the entrance off of NH 16, 2½ miles north of the AMC Pinkham Notch Camp.

Private cars (trucks and campers aren't allowed) pay a toll of $15 for car and driver and $6 for each passenger ($4 for children five to 12,); this includes an audio cassette tour. For information on vehicle limitations, see the company's website.

If you'd rather not drive, vans operated by the company will take you to the top and back down again (1½ hours) for $20 per person ($10 for children). The auto road is open 7:30 am to 6 pm, mid-May to mid-October; van tours run 8:30 am to 4:30 pm. In severe weather, the road may be closed (even in-season).

## Pinkham Notch Camp
Guided nature walks, canoe trips, cross-country ski and snowshoe treks and other outdoor adventures out of Pinkham Notch Camp are organized by the AMC (☎ 603-466-2727, 800-262-4455, www.amc-nh.org).

The *AMC White Mountain Guide*, on sale here, includes detailed maps and the vital statistics of each trail: how long and how difficult it is, the vertical rise, the average walking time, reference points along the way and information on what to look at as you walk. Individual trail maps and guides are available as well. You can also purchase the guide online from the main AMC site, www.outdoors.org.

The AMC also maintains two hikers' huts providing meals and lodging. Carter Notch Hut is on Nineteen-Mile Brook Trail, and Lakes of the Clouds Hut is on Crawford Path (for more information, see Crawford Notch, later in this chapter).

For lodging and meal information at the camp, see Places to Stay, below.

## Skiing
**Wildcat Mountain** This ski area (☎ 603-466-3326, 800-255-6439, 800-643-4521 for snow report), whose mountain tops off at 4415 feet, is on NH 16 in Pinkham Notch north of Jackson. Its downhill skiing facilities sport a vertical drop of 2100 feet, 31 ski trails (30% beginner, 40% intermediate, 30% expert), six lifts and 90% snowmaking capacity.

**Tuckerman Ravine** The cirque at Tuckerman Ravine has several ski trails for ski purists. What's pure about it? No lifts. You climb up the mountain, then ski down. Purists say that if you climb up, you have strong legs that won't break easily in a fall on the way down.

Tuckerman is perhaps best in spring, when most ski resorts are struggling to keep their snow cover, since nature conspires to keep the ravine in shadow much of the time and in deep natural snow.

Park in the Wildcat Mountain lot for the climb up the ravine.

## Summer Activities
The Gondola Skyride at the Wildcat Mountain ski area, which was the first in the USA, operates in summer as well as winter – just for the fun of the ride and the view. Adults pay $8, children five to 12 pay $4. Rides take place 9 am to 5 pm daily (twilight rides 6 to 8:30 pm on Sunday and Wednesday), late May through mid-October.

## Soaring
Mt Washington Sky Adventures (☎ 603-466-5822, 466-3374), 289 Main St in Gorham, at the junction of NH 2 and NH 16, will take you soaring over the summit of Mt Washington in a three-seat glider. Call for prices, wind conditions and reservations.

## Places to Stay
The *Dolly Copp Campground* (☎ 800-283-2267), off NH 16, is a USFS campground 6 miles north of the AMC camp. Its 176 simple

sites, priced at $12, are open all year. Call for reservations during the summer and autumn.

The AMC *Pinkham Notch Camp* (☎ 603-466-2727, 800-262-4455, www.amc-nh.org) includes the Joe Dodge Lodge, with dorms that house more than 100 beds. The cost is $30 for adults, $20 for children 12 and younger. You must reserve your bunks in advance and pay a non-refundable deposit.

## CRAWFORD NOTCH

US 302 travels west from Glen, then north to Crawford Notch (1773 feet), through some beautiful mountain scenery. Crawford Notch State Park has a system of shorter trails (half mile to 3 miles) for hikes to the summit of Mt Washington.

### Crawford Notch State Park

In 1826, torrential rains in this steep valley caused massive mud slides that descended on the home of the Willey family. The house was spared, but the family was not – they were outside at the fatal moment and were swept away by the mud.

The dramatic incident made the newspapers and fired the imaginations of painter Thomas Cole and author Nathaniel Hawthorne. Both men used the incident for inspiration, thus unwittingly putting Crawford Notch on the tourist maps. Soon, visitors arrived to visit the tragic spot, and they stayed for the bracing mountain air and healthy exercise.

In 1859, the Crawford family opened the Crawford House hotel and set to work grooming mountain trails so their guests could penetrate the trackless wilderness. Their work was the basis for today's excellent system of trails. (The hotel was razed in 1977.) Crawford Notch State Park (☎ 603-374-2272) now occupies this beautiful, historic valley.

From the Willey House site, now used as a state park visitors' center, you can walk the easy half-mile Pond Loop Trail, the 1-mile Sam Willey Trail and the Ripley Falls Trail, a 1-mile hike from US 302 via the Ethan Pond Trail. A half mile south of the Dry River Campground on US 302 is the trailhead for Arethusa Falls, a 1.3-mile hike.

## Mt Washington Hiking Trails

There is general information – and live webcam views from the summit – at www.mountwashington.com. Please read the warnings about severe weather (under Mt Washington in the Pinkham Notch section, earlier in this chapter) and consult with AMC personnel before attempting a hike to the summit of Mt Washington. If you're in shape and properly equipped, try the trails below.

**Ammonoosuc Ravine Trail** This trail, via the AMC's Lakes of the Clouds Hut (elevation 5000 feet), is one of the shortest hiking routes to the summit. It's one of the best routes to take in inclement weather because it is protected from the worst of the winds, and, if the weather turns very nasty, you can take shelter in the AMC hut. For overnight lodging and meals, you must reserve in advance through the Pinkham Notch Camp (☎ 603-466-2727, 800-262-4455).

The trail starts at a parking lot on Base Station Rd, which is near the entrance to the Mount Washington Cog Railway (elevation 2560 feet), and climbs easily for 2 miles up the dramatic ravine to Gem Pool. From Gem Pool, however, the climb is far more strenuous and demanding, with a sharp vertical rise to the AMC hut.

From the Lakes of the Clouds Hut, other trails ascend to the summit and the Tip Top House, a hotel that doesn't provide lodging but does have other services.

**Jewell Trail** This trail is more exposed than the Ammonoosuc Ravine Trail and should be used only in good conditions. The last 0.7 mile is above the tree line and very windy.

The Jewell Trail starts at the same parking lot as the Ammonoosuc Ravine Trail but follows a more northeasterly course up a ridge. At 2.8 miles, the trail rises above the timberline and climbs 3½ miles by a series of switchbacks to meet the Gulfside Trail. The Gulfside continues to the summit.

### Places to Stay

*Dry River Campground*, just east of US 302 near the southern end of Crawford Notch State Park, has 30 tent sites for $11 each.

You can also stay at AMC's **Lakes of the Clouds Hut**. See the Ammonoosuc Ravine Trail section, above, for details.

## BRETTON WOODS

Before 1944, the name Bretton Woods (www.brettonwoods.com) was known only to locals and the wealthy summer visitors who patronized the grand Mount Washington Hotel. When President Roosevelt chose the hotel as the site of the conference to establish a new world economic order after WWII, the whole world learned about Bretton Woods.

The mountainous countryside is still as beautiful now as it was during those historic times, the hotel is almost as grand (if a bit past its prime) and the name still rings with history. At the very least, stop to admire the view of the great hotel set against the mountains. You may want to stay a night or two. Ascending Mt Washington in a train pulled by a cog-driven steam locomotive is fun for all and a must for railroad buffs.

### History

WWII devastated both Europe and Japan, causing the world economy to go into an economic tailspin. Even before the war ended, world leaders realized that rebuilding these war-torn areas and restoring the world economy would be a principal concern once the fighting stopped.

From July 1 to 22, 1944, world leaders and financial experts gathered in Bretton Woods for the United Nations Monetary and Financial Conference. Their purpose was to develop a model for the world's postwar economy. The conference's results included the creation of the International Monetary Fund and the World Bank. The experts also formulated plans for stable currency exchange rates and temporary assistance to member nations with balance-of-payments problems.

The Bretton Woods conference paved the way for the conference at Dumbarton Oaks in Washington, DC, in September and October 1944, at which time a prototype for the United Nations charter was written. At Yalta, in February 1945, the shape of the new organization was refined, setting the

stage for the United Nations' founding conference, which was held in San Francisco from April to June 1945.

Though some elements of the economic world order that emerged at Bretton Woods – such as the gold standard – have been superseded, much of the conference's work has proven to be remarkably durable.

### Information

The Twin Mountain Chamber of Commerce (☎ 603-846-5407, 800-245-8946) has an information booth at the intersection of US 302 and US 3 in the center of Twin Mountain, several miles northwest of Bretton Woods.

### Mt Washington Cog Railway

Purists walk, those out of shape drive, but certainly the quaintest way to reach the summit of Mt Washington is to take the Mt Washington Cog Railway (☎ 603-846-5404, 800-922-8825, www.mtwashingtoncograilway .com). A coal-fired, steam-powered locomotive follows a 3½-mile track along a steep trestle up the mountainside.

A cog, or gear wheel, on its undercarriage engages pins between the rails to pull the locomotive and a single passenger car up the mountainside, burning a ton of coal and blowing a thousand gallons of water into steam along the way. Up to seven locomotives may be huffing and puffing at one time, all with boilers tilted to accommodate the grade, which at the 'Jacob's Ladder' trestle is a 37% grade – the second-steepest railway track in the world.

In operation since 1869, the three-hour, roundtrip scenic excursion costs $44 for adults, $40 for seniors and $30 for children six to 12 (free for children under six who sit on a parent's lap). The first train puffs off at 8:30 am, the last at 4:30 pm. Trains operate on weekends from early May to early June, then daily through late October and on weekends until early November.

To be sure of a seat and to avoid a long wait, reserve in advance by phone. Also, remember that the average temperature at the summit is 40°F in summer (it may be lower) and the wind is always blowing, so bring a sweater and windbreaker.

**NEW HAMPSHIRE**

The base station is 6 miles east of US 302. Turn east at the town of Fabyan, just northwest of the Mount Washington Hotel and between Bretton Woods and Twin Mountain.

### Places to Stay

**Camping** The *Cherry Mountain KOA* (☎ 603-846-5559, 800-743-5819), on US 3 north of Twin Mountain but south of the junction with NH 115, has lots of facilities and charges $23 to $28 and up for a site.

**Motels** Run by the Mount Washington Resort, *The Bretton Woods Motor Inn* (☎ 603-278-1000, 800-258-0330, fax 603-278-3457) enjoys the best view of the Mount Washington Hotel and its mountain backdrop. The modern motel is the least expensive of the resort's four accommodations, with rooms priced at $89 to $139.

*Boulder Motor Court* (☎ 603-846-5437, 800-352-4556) on US 302 (east of US 3) in Twin Mountain, has rooms for $68. *Patio Motor Court* (☎ 603-846-5515) on US 3 north of Twin Mountain, has rooms for $55, two-bedroom and duplex units for somewhat more. *Carlson's Lodge* (☎ 603-846-5501, 800-348-5502), on US 302 (a half mile west of US 3), has rooms for $51 to $80, the latter equipped with microwave oven and refrigerator.

**Hotels** The *Mount Washington Hotel* (☎ 603-278-1000, 800-258-0330, fax 603-278-3457, www.mtwashington.com), on US 30, is the prime choice. The hotel has grand public rooms, thousands of acres of grounds, 27 holes of golf, 12 clay tennis courts, an equestrian center, indoor and outdoor heated pools and other amenities. The 170 rooms cost $249 to $389, breakfast and dinner included. Add 8% for service and another 8% for tax.

**Inns** On the same estate as the Mount Washington Resort, *The Bretton Arms Inn* (☎ 603-278-1000, 800-258-0330, fax 603-278-3457) was built as a grand summer cottage in 1896, but it has been an inn since 1907. It was restored extensively in 1986. Rooms cost $99 to $169.

### THE BALSAMS

The great north woods of New Hampshire – north of Berlin – are less populated and have fewer tourists than the rest of the state, with one exception: *The Balsams (☎ 603-255-3400, 800-255-0800 in New Hampshire, 800-255-0600 in US and Canada, fax 603-255-4221, www.thebalsams.com)*, on NH 26 in Dixville Notch. Nestled in a narrow valley, this elegant, 15,000-acre resort has been hosting guests since 1866. The 212 guest rooms cost $195 single, $390 to $450 double in summer, slightly lower in spring and autumn. The price includes all three meals (available to you in any of the resort's several dining rooms and taverns), unlimited use of two golf courses, putting greens, tennis courts, swimming pool, lake, boats, hiking and mountain-biking trails and all other resort services. Other activities include shuffleboard, badminton, croquet, horseshoes, ping-pong and billiards.

# Upper Connecticut River Valley

Hanover is part of the larger community of the Upper Connecticut River Valley, which includes Lyme and Lebanon, New Hampshire, as well as Norwich, White River Junction and Woodstock, in Vermont. When looking for services (including accommodations and dining possibilities), consider all of these places, not just Hanover.

### HANOVER

Chartered in 1761 and settled in 1765, Hanover was named after Britain's reigning dynasty. It was a frontier farming outpost with little to set it apart from others.

Hanover's future was determined when Reverend Eleazar Wheelock moved his Christian school for Native American youth from Connecticut to Hanover. The new school was funded with money raised in England by one of Reverend Wheelock's former students, and the Earl of Dartmouth, King George III's colonial secretary, lent it his noble patronage and name.

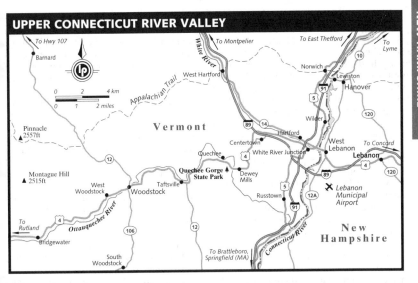

UPPER CONNECTICUT RIVER VALLEY

Dartmouth College was chartered in 1769 primarily 'for the education and instruction of Youth of the Indian Tribes.' The school was located deep in the forests where its prospective students lived. Although teaching 'English Youth and others' was only its secondary purpose, in fact Dartmouth graduated few Indian youths and was soon attended almost exclusively by colonists. Daniel Webster (1782-1852), who graduated in 1801 and went on to become a prominent lawyer, US senator, secretary of state and, perhaps, the USA's most esteemed orator, is the college's most illustrious alumnus.

Though it declines to call itself a university, Dartmouth is far more than a New England liberal arts college. It has well-regarded schools of medicine, engineering and business administration. The BASIC computer language was developed in its mathematics department. Today, despite its graceful Georgian buildings and ivy-covered campus, Dartmouth is very high-tech.

## Orientation

To visit Hanover is to visit Dartmouth College, for the college dominates the town.

Hanover is fairly easily negotiable. Many services (including restaurants) are along Main St. The central reference for everything is the green, the broad lawn bounded by Wheelock, N Main, Wentworth and College Sts.

## Information

The Hanover Area Chamber of Commerce (☎ 603-643-3115, www.hanoverchamber.org), 37 S Main St (PO Box 5105), Hanover, NH 03755, has maps, brochures and answers to your questions about Hanover and adjoining Norwich, Vermont. The Hanover Area Chamber of Commerce also maintains an information booth near the village green in summer.

The Dartmouth Bookstore (☎ 603-643-3616), 33 S Main St, with a large selection, comes highly recommended.

## Dartmouth College

Free guided walking tours of the campus are offered at various times throughout the year. Consult the tour schedule at www.dartmouth.edu or call the admissions office (☎ 603-646-2875).

For a look at Dartmouth's prettiest and most historic buildings, start from the green. To the north is Baker Memorial Library (☎ 603-646-2560), the college's central library. In the basement reading room, you'll find a series of murals by José Clemente Orozco (1883-1949), the renowned Mexican muralist who taught and painted at Dartmouth from 1932 to 1934. The series follows the course of civilization in North America from the time of the Aztecs to the present.

Along the east side of the green on College St is picturesque Dartmouth Row, four harmonious Georgian buildings named Wentworth, Dartmouth, Thornton and Reed. Dartmouth Hall was the original college building, constructed in 1791. After it burned in 1904, it was wisely rebuilt using brick.

The Hopkins Center for the Arts (☎ 603-646-2422) is Dartmouth's outstanding venue for the performing arts. A long way from such cosmopolitan centers as Boston, New York and Montreal, Dartmouth must make its own entertainment to fill the long winter nights. Much of the entertainment takes place at the Hopkins.

South of the Hopkins Center is the Hood Museum of Art (☎ 603-646-2808), with fine collections that range from ancient Greece and Rome through the European Renaissance and up to modern times.

### Special Events

Each February, Dartmouth celebrates its weeklong Winter Carnival. The winter's major fun-and-social event features special art shows, drama productions, concerts, an ice sculpture contest and other amusements. Call the chamber of commerce (see the Information section, earlier) for dates and details.

### Places to Stay

Hanover's economy has a split personality: Eating places are designed and priced for students, while lodgings are designed for the (mostly) well-heeled parents who come to visit. Thus, meals are cheap, but accommodations are surprisingly expensive.

Accommodations in this region (Hanover, Lebanon, White River Junction, Woodstock) are in greatest demand during foliage season, when virtually all the rooms are reserved in advance; there is also high demand in summer and at special college times. Sometimes visitors find themselves driving for hours to find a room, so it's a good idea to reserve in advance if you can.

**Camping** The *Storrs Pond Recreation Area* (☎ 603-643-2134) is a private campground with 35 sites ($12 to $17) on a 15-acre pond. There's an Olympic-size pool and two sandy beaches for swimming. It's open mid-May to mid-October. From I-89 exit 13, take NH 10 north and look for signs.

**Motels** The *Airport Econo Inn* (☎ 603-298-8888, 7 Airport Rd), in West Lebanon, doesn't have a country setting, but prices are low at $59.50.

*Chieftain Motor Inn* (☎ 603-643-2550, 800-845-3557, 84 Lyme Rd (NH 10 North)), in a country setting, has large, clean, comfortable rooms for $79 single, $89 double, including continental breakfast.

*Holiday Inn Express* (☎ 603-448-5070, 800-465-4329), at I-89 exit 18 in Lebanon, charges $99, including continental breakfast.

**Inns** Just across the Connecticut River in Norwich, Vermont, the *Norwich Inn* (☎ 802-649-1143), on Main St, features 14 rooms in the inn for $99 and 7 rooms in the motel for $69. There's a good dining room here as well.

In New Hampshire, *Two Mile Farm* (☎ 603-643-6462, 2 Ferson Rd), off Etna Rd, is a farmhouse built in the late 1700s, now a B&B with three rooms that cost $85 (shared bath) to $110 (private bath).

Ten miles north of Hanover via NH 10 is the town of Lyme, and facing its common are the *Alden Inn* (☎ 603-795-2222) and *Dowds' Country Inn* (☎ 603-795-4712). The Alden Inn, built in 1809, has 15 colonial guest rooms with modern facilities for $130 to $145. The Alden also boasts a very good restaurant and tavern. Dowds' has 22 rooms for $125 to $165, breakfast included.

The most prominent lodging is the *Hanover Inn* (☎ 603-643-4300, 800-443-7024, fax 603-646-3744), at the corner of Wheelock and Main Sts, which faces the

Mt Washington Cog Railway, NH

Hike the Appalachian Trail in New Hampshire.

A snowy day in the White Mountains, NH

Fall brings blazing colors to the White Mountain National Forest, NH.

Canterbury Shaker Village, NH

Covered bridge over the Pemigewasset River, NH

The Canterbury Shaker Village in New Hampshire presents the history of the Shaker community.

town green. Owned by Dartmouth College, the inn has colonial decor, upscale ambience and high prices, with rooms going for $227.

Four miles east of Dartmouth, the ***Trumbull House B&B*** (☎ *603-643-2370, 40 Etna Rd)* is a wonderful alternative to staying in town. With a pond and a hiking trail that links to the Appalachian Trail, the inn has a country feel. This colonial house, built in 1919, has five rooms ranging from $100 to $250. The owner has five children, so it's a family-friendly B&B.

## Places to Eat

Hanover's eateries compete to invent new ways of preparing the student classics – sandwiches, burgers, pizza, pasta – and still keep prices low. There's not a lot of fancy food in town, but there aren't fancy prices either.

***Murphy's on the Green*** (☎ *603-643-4075, 11 S Main St)*, opposite the Hanover Inn, is

where students and faculty meet over pints of ale ($2.50) and big, satisfying plates of hearty bar food.

***Molly's Bar & Grill*** (☎ *603-643-2570, 43 S Main St)*, has gourmet burgers, salads and pastas for $5 to $8 at lunchtime. In the evening, the menu goes upscale a bit with pepper chicken linguine and similarly trendy fare, but prices stay put at about $9 to $15 per dish.

***Mai Phai*** (☎ *603-643-9980, 44 S Main St)* has five different types of pad Thai for $6.95 to $9.95.

***Lou's*** (☎ *603-643-3321, 30 S Main St)* is the oldest establishment in town, opened in 1947. Sit in a booth or at the formica-topped counter and order typical diner food such as eggs, sandwiches and burgers. Lou's is open 6 am to 3 pm.

For a student hangout, try ***Patrick Henry's*** (☎ *603-643-2345, 39 S Main St)* They serve lots of sandwiches ($5 to $7) and

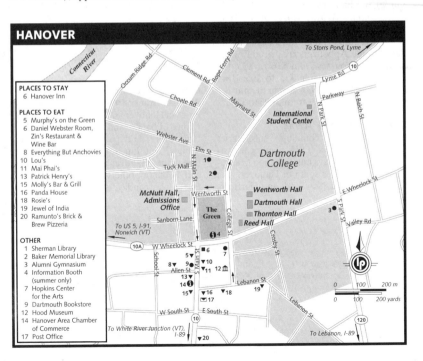

### HANOVER

**PLACES TO STAY**
6 Hanover Inn

**PLACES TO EAT**
5 Murphy's on the Green
6 Daniel Webster Room, Zin's Restaurant & Wine Bar
8 Everything But Anchovies
10 Lou's
11 Mai Phai's
13 Patrick Henry's
15 Molly's Bar & Grill
16 Panda House
18 Rosie's
19 Jewel of India
20 Ramunto's Brick & Brew Pizzeria

**OTHER**
1 Sherman Library
2 Baker Memorial Library
3 Alumni Gymnasium
4 Information Booth (summer only)
7 Hopkins Center for the Arts
9 Dartmouth Bookstore
12 Hood Museum
14 Hanover Area Chamber of Commerce
17 Post Office

old-time American favorites such as turkey pot pie ($8).

***Everything But Anchovies** (☎ 603-643-6135, 5 Allen St)*, between Main and School Sts, has luncheon sandwiches, salads and pastas to eat on the premises or to take out. It's a great place to pick up ready-made picnics.

***Rosie's** (☎ 603-643-5282, 15 Lebanon St)* has good veggie sandwiches, such as eggplant with feta, pesto, tomato and fresh basil for $5.95. It's also a good place to hang out with students and have a cup of coffee.

***Ramunto's Brick & Brew Pizzeria** (☎ 603-643-9500, 68 S Main St)* is the best pizza joint in town. Prices start at $5.95.

***Jewel of India** (☎ 603-643-2217, 27 Lebanon St)* adds some variety to the gustatory map by bringing in a whiff of curry. Try the Sunday brunch with lots of curry and 10 kinds of bread. For Chinese cuisine, head to the ***Panda House** (☎ 603-643-1290, 3 Lebanon St)*, two blocks away.

The ***Daniel Webster Room** at the Hanover Inn (☎ 603-643-4300)*, Main and Wheelock Sts, is perhaps the town's most elegant place to dine. Appetizers are priced from $6 to $9, main courses from $16 to $23, full dinners with wine from $35 to $65. ***Zin's Restaurant & Wine Bar***, also in the inn, is a lot cheaper, with dishes from $8.95 to $15.25.

## Getting There & Away

**Air** The short-haul 'commuter' subsidiaries of Delta, Northwest, TWA, American Airlines and US Airways link Lebanon Municipal Airport, 6 miles south of Hanover, with Boston, Montreal, New York and Hartford, Connecticut.

**Bus** Vermont Transit (☎ 802-864-6811, 800-451-3292 in New England) has direct buses from Boston, Logan International Airport and Springfield, Massachusetts. There's also connecting service from New York, Hartford and Montreal to White River Junction, Vermont. You can travel by taxi or Advance Transit bus (see Getting Around, below) from White River Junction to Hanover.

Dartmouth Mini Coach (☎ 603-448-2800, 448-1184) operates three shuttles daily between Hanover and the Manchester airport and Boston's Logan International Airport. The fare is $35, and reservations are required.

**Car** The driving details for Hanover are as follows:

| destination | mileage | hr:min |
| --- | --- | --- |
| Boston, MA | 135 miles | 3:00 |
| Burlington, VT | 111 miles | 2:35 |
| Concord, NH | 59 miles | 1:10 |
| Hartford, CT | 155 miles | 3:10 |
| Laconia, NH | 63 miles | 1:35 |
| Lebanon, NH | 5 miles | 0:10 |
| Woodstock, VT | 20 miles | 0:40 |

## Getting Around

Advance Transit (☎ 802-295-1824) operates buses in Hanover and between Hanover and Lyme, Lebanon and West Lebanon, New Hampshire; and Norwich, Hartford and White River Junction, Vermont. Rides are free within Hanover and between Hanover and Lebanon; otherwise, the fare is $1.25. Bus stops are indicated by a blue-and-yellow AT symbol.

# Maine

Maine is a study in contrasts. It has the largest land area of the six New England states (there are over 500,000 acres of state and national parks) but the sparsest population of any state east of the Mississippi River.

The rockbound coast of Maine is about 228 miles long as the crow flies, but a tall-masted schooner sailing its tortuous course would cover almost 3500 miles. Bays, islands, inlets, peninsulas, isthmuses and coves make up the granite-strewn coast, along with a few stretches of sand beach.

When European explorers discovered Maine, it was populated by an Algonquian people known as the Abenaki, many of whom belonged to the Penobscot and Passamaquoddy tribes.

John and Sebastian Cabot, a father and son from England, sailed the coast of Maine at the end of the 15th century. It was not until 1607 that a permanent English colony was founded, at Popham Beach, but it was short-lived. Many of the first European settlers were French who came south from Quebec. English, Scots-Irish and German colonists from Europe followed. In 1614, British explorer John Smith (also famous as the man whose life was saved by Pocahontas) charted the Maine coast, and in less than a decade there were settlements at Monhegan (1622), Saco (1623) and York (1624). In 1641, York became the first chartered city in English America.

In the 17th century, a series of wars raged on between Maine's English colonists and Quebec's French colonists who were aided by Native American tribes. The first war was King Philip's War (1675-78); next was King William's War (1689-97); Queen Anne's War (1702-13) followed; and last was King George's War (1744-48). In 1759, when the British defeated the French on the Plains of Abraham at Quebec, there was finally peace among Maine's English, French and Native American inhabitants.

During the Revolutionary War, Benedict Arnold started out from Augusta on his expedition to capture Quebec. In 1775, British forces burned Portland.

Maine was governed from Boston, Massachusetts, until 1820. At that time, as part of the Missouri Compromise, Maine became the 23rd state admitted to the union. Portland was the original capital, but the capital was moved to Augusta in 1827, and the State Capitol building was completed in 1832.

## Highlights

- Biking the Carriage Roads in Acadia National Park

- Taking a windjammer cruise out of Camden's picturesque harbor

- Dining on lobsters and steamers at a lobster pound

- Shopping at LL Bean and the outlets in Freeport

- Picnicking at the Portland Head Light and Museum

- Admiring the fine old mansions in Kennebunkport

- Canoeing in the remote ponds and lakes of Baxter State Park

# MAINE

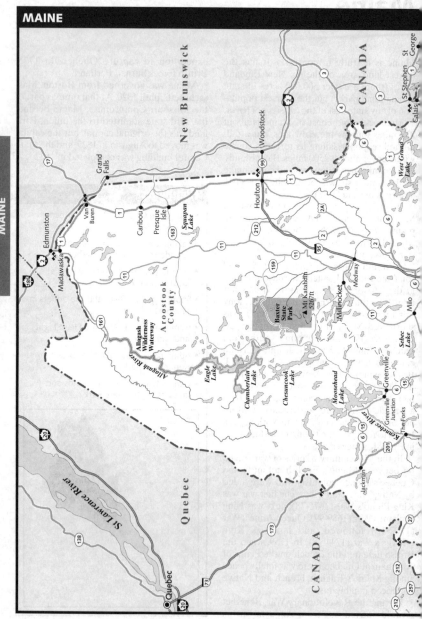

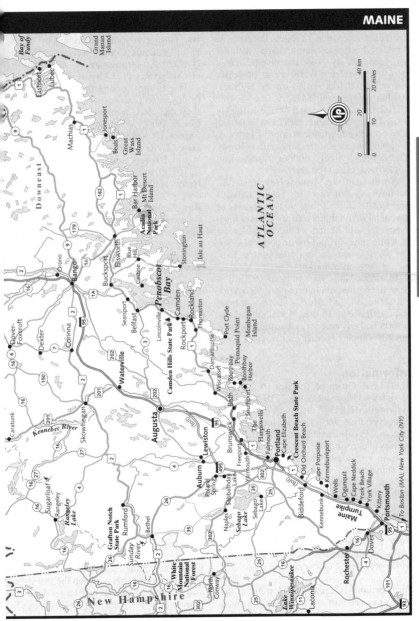

In 1783, the St Croix River was established as the border between Maine and the Canadian province of New Brunswick; however, both sides were unhappy with the arrangement. By 1838, the dispute flared into the Aroostook War – a war of words, not bullets. It was settled by the Webster-Ashburton Treaty in 1842.

Today, southern coastal Maine is thickly settled. The settlements vary from beautiful, well-preserved historic towns to miles of shopping malls and 'factory outlet' stores. There are genteel summer resorts and honky-tonk beach resorts.

Northern inland Maine is New England's wilderness, with vast (for New England) areas of trackless forest and thousands of glacial lakes inhabited only by fish and fowl. About 89% of Maine is covered by forests of white pine, fir and hardwood trees. See the North Woods section, later in this chapter, for more information.

In winter, Maine feels isolated and distant from the cosmopolitan centers of New York City, Boston and Montreal. In summer, those cities seem to invade Maine's coastal resorts, and city accents and attitudes crowd out the simpler speech and ways of local folk.

## Information

The Maine Office of Tourism (☎ 207-623-0363, www.visitmaine.com), 325B Water St, Hallowell, ME 04347, maintains information centers on the principal routes into the state (Calais, Fryeburg, Hampden, Houlton, Kittery and Yarmouth). Each facility is open 9 am to 5 pm daily, with extended hours in the summer.

In an emergency, call ☎ 800-482-0730 for Maine state police.

## Getting There & Around

A project is under way to revive Amtrak train service between Boston and Portland, but as of this writing, you are limited to transport by air, bus, car and ferryboat.

**Air** Portland International Jetport is the state's main airport, but a number of airlines also serve Bangor International Airport.

Smaller airports served by commuter or charter aircraft include the Augusta Airport; Bar Harbor Airport; Caribou; Fort Kent; Houlton; Knox County Regional Airport; Northern Aroostook Airport; and the Northern Maine Regional Airport in Presque Isle.

The airlines serving these airports vary from year to year, but at the time of writing, they include Continental Express, run by Colgan Air (☎ 800-272-5488), and Business Express (☎ 800-345-3400). In addition to the above, Delta Airlines, United Airlines, Trans World Express and US Airways Express serve Portland and Bangor (see the Toll-Free Numbers directory at back of the book).

**Bus** Concord Trailways (☎ 800-639-3317, www.concordtrailways.com) operates daily buses between Logan International Airport in Boston and numerous towns in Maine (Bangor, Bath, Belfast, Brunswick, Camden/Rockport, Damariscotta, Lincolnville, Portland, Rockland, Searsport, Waldoboro, Ellsworth and Bar Harbor). Some Concord Trailways buses connect with the Maine State Ferry Service to islands off the coast.

SMT Line (☎ 207-767-9500) buses carry passengers from Bangor to St Stephen, New Brunswick, Canada.

Cyr Bus Lines (☎ 207-942-3354) runs from Bangor to Caribou via Orono, Houlton, Presque Isle and other towns in between.

**Car** Except for the Maine Turnpike (I-95 and I-495), Maine has no fast, limited-access highways. Roads along the coast are often very crowded with traffic during the summer tourist season. As a result, you must plan for more driving time when traveling in Maine.

*Note:* Moose are a particular danger to drivers in Maine, even as far south as Portland – they've been known to cripple a bus and walk away. Be especially watchful in spring and fall and around dusk and dawn, when the animals are most active.

**Boat** Maine State Ferry Service (☎ 207-596-2202) operates boats between the mainland and several of the state's larger islands. Marine Atlantic (☎ 800-341-7981) offers car and passenger ferry service from Portland

and Bar Harbor (see those sections) to Yarmouth, Nova Scotia, Canada.

# Southeast Maine

Many people associate the Maine coast with the works of the American artist Winslow Homer, who spent his summers in Prout's Neck. His powerful watercolors depict the boulder-strewn coastline, the battering surf of the North Atlantic and the merciless Maine climate, complete with dense fog and forceful gales. Well, that Maine coast does exist – to the north of Prout's Neck (just south of Portland).

South of Prout's Neck are long stretches of beach inundated with tourists, taffy and T-shirt shops. This is especially true in towns like Ogunquit, Wells and Old Orchard Beach, where the commercialism can be daunting. Kennebunkport, former President George Bush's hideaway, is far more serene.

## KITTERY

Entering Kittery from New Hampshire via US 1 or I-95 can be less than thrilling – unless you're going shopping. Kittery is famous for its shopping malls and outlet stores, all of which claim to offer deep discounts on everything from apparel to china to camping gear.

If shopping is not your bag, you can head straight through Kittery, fast on I-95, or much more slowly on US 1. Keep in mind that US 1 from Kittery to Portland is the Maine coast's commercial artery, lined with motels, campgrounds, fuel stations, restaurants, shops and other businesses. If you find yourself in need of a room, a tent site, a meal or any other service or product, just get on US 1 and cruise until you find it.

## THE YORKS

York Village, York Harbor, York Beach and Cape Neddick make up the Yorks. York Village, the first city chartered in English North America, has a long and interesting history and well-preserved colonial buildings in the village center. York Harbor was developed more than a century ago as a posh summer resort, and it maintains some of that feeling today. York Beach was where

hoi polloi came in the summer, and its working-class roots still show in its large number of campgrounds and humdrum commercial development.

Historic York was called Agamenticus by precolonial Indian inhabitants. British colonials settled York in 1624, and it was chartered as a city in 1641. The Old York Historical Society (☎ 207-363-4974) is proud of the town's historic buildings and has preserved several of them as a museum of town history.

All the museum's buildings are open 10 am to 5 pm Tuesday to Saturday, 1 to 5 pm on Sunday; closed Monday. The museum is open mid-June through September. Admission tickets good for all buildings cost $6/2.50 for adults/children six to 16; no family pays more than $16. Admission tickets for the museum are sold at Jefferds Tavern Visitor Center, off US 1A, on Lindsay Rd.

The School House is a mid-18th-century school building. The Old Gaol (jail) gives a vivid impression of crime and punishment two centuries ago. The Emerson-Wilcox House is a museum of New England decorative arts and the Elizabeth Perkins House is a wealthy family's summer home. The John Hancock warehouse preserves the town's industrial and commercial history; the George Marshall Store now houses a research library.

## OGUNQUIT & WELLS

Ogunquit ('Beautiful Place by the Sea') is a small town (population 1000) famous for its 3-mile-long sand beach that affords swimmers the choice of chilly, pounding surf or warm, peaceful back-cove waters. The beach is special enough to draw hordes of visitors from as far away as New York City, Montreal and Quebec City, increasing the town's population exponentially in summer.

Many visitors come to stay for a week or more in efficiency units (room with kitchen). Many accommodations require minimum two- or three-night stays in summer, particularly on weekends.

Neighboring Wells, to the northeast, has the eastward continuation of Ogunquit Beach and several camping areas. To drive US 1 through Wells is to subject yourself to

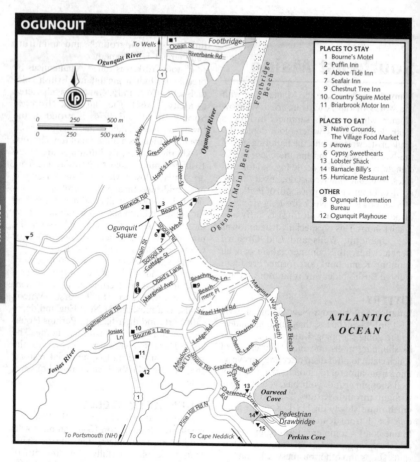

# OGUNQUIT

**PLACES TO STAY**
1  Bourne's Motel
2  Puffin Inn
4  Above Tide Inn
7  Seafair Inn
9  Chestnut Tree Inn
10 Country Squire Motel
11 Briarbrook Motor Inn

**PLACES TO EAT**
3  Native Grounds,
   The Village Food Market
5  Arrows
6  Gypsy Sweethearts
13 Lobster Shack
14 Barnacle Billy's
15 Hurricane Restaurant

**OTHER**
8  Ogunquit Information
   Bureau
12 Ogunquit Playhouse

the usual visual assault perpetrated by American commercial strip development. But for all its commercial tawdriness, Wells has good beaches, as well as lots of useful and relatively inexpensive motels and campgrounds.

## Orientation & Information

The center of Ogunquit, called Ogunquit Square, is the intersection of Main St (US 1), Shore Rd and Beach St. The town, which seems to be mostly comprised of tourist services, stretches southeast down Shore Rd to

Perkins Cove, and northeast to the neighboring town of Wells. Parking in town lots costs $6 per day during the busy summer months.

You'll find the Ogunquit Information Bureau (☎ 207-646-5533, www.ogunquit.org) on US 1, east of the prominent Playhouse and a third of a mile south of the town's center.

## Marginal Way

Marginal Way, Ogunquit's famous coastline footpath, starts southeast of Beach St at Shore Rd and ends near Perkins Cove.

It follows the 'margin' of the sea, hence its name. The path and right-of-way were ceded to the town in the 1920s after its owner, Josiah Chase, sold off his valuable sea-view property. The scenic walk is slightly more than a mile. If you don't want to walk back, you can take the trolley that runs in the summer.

## Wells Auto Museum
In 1946, a resident of Wells was given a Stanley Steamer that his uncle found in the cellar of his barn in Vermont. The new owner restored the antique car, built early in the century, and soon had a burgeoning collection of restored classic cars powered by steam, electricity and gasoline. The museum, a nonprofit organization, now has 70 cars of 45 different makes, including Rolls-Royce, Stutz, Cadillac, Packard, Pierce Arrow and Knox.

The Wells Auto Museum (☎ 207-646-9064), on US 1, is open 10 am to 5 pm daily mid-June to mid-September. Admission is $4/2 for adults/children; children under six are free.

## Ogunquit Playhouse
The Ogunquit Playhouse, on Main St, lit up for the first time in 1933. It has been at its present site, south of the town center, since 1937. The season begins in late June and offers three musicals and two plays each year in the 750-seat theater. Occasionally, there are well-known performers in the cast – or in the audience.

Call the box office (☎ 207-646-5511, www.ogunquitplayhouse.org) for schedules (usually available in mid-May) and ticket prices .

## Beaches
Ogunquit Beach (or Main Beach to the locals) is only a five-minute walk along aptly named Beach St, east of US 1. Walking to the beach is a good idea in the summer, because you must pay $2 per hour to park and the lot often fills up early. The 3-mile-long beach fronts Ogunquit Bay to the south; on the west side of the beach are the warmer waters of the tidal Ogunquit River.

There are toilets, changing rooms, restaurants and snack shops.

Footbridge Beach, 2 miles to the north near Wells, is actually the northern extension of Ogunquit Beach. It's reached from US 1 by Ocean St and a footbridge across the Ogunquit River. There's yet another way to access the beach via Eldridge Rd in Wells – follow the sign for Moody Beach.

Little Beach is near the lighthouse on Marginal Way and is best reached on foot.

## Cruises
Perkins Cove is the spot to climb aboard the *Finestkind* (☎ 207-646-5227) lobster boat for a 50-minute voyage to pull up the traps and collect the delicious beasts. Trips leave every hour on the hour, 9 am to 3 pm. The cost is $8.50/6.50 for adults/children. There are 90-minute cruises, cocktail cruises in the late afternoon and evening, and even a 9 pm starlight cruise as well.

You can take sailing yacht cruises aboard the *Silverlining* (☎ 207-361-9800), a 42-foot Hinckley sloop that departs from Perkins Cove four times daily. The two-hour cruise costs $28 per person in high season. The *Cricket* (☎ 207-646-5227), a locally built catboat (a sailboat), sails away from Barnacle Billy's dock in Perkins Cove on 1³/₄-hour cruises; cruises depart four times daily for $20.

## Places to Stay
Though a few places stay open all year, most open in mid-May and close by mid-October. Room rates, which are low at the start of the season, double in July and August and on holiday weekends (see Public Holidays & Special Events in the Facts for the Visitor chapter).

**Camping** As you might imagine, the campgrounds fill up early in the day in July and August.

*Dixon's Campground* (☎ *207-363-2131, 1740 US 1*), in Cape Neddick south of Ogunquit, has 100 sites for tents and RVs on its 40 acres. The fee for two people is $23 in high summer. There's free transport to Ogunquit Beach from late June to early September.

MAINE

**MAINE**

*Pinederosa Camping Area* (☎ 207-646-2492) is on Captain Thomas Rd, which goes north from US 1 a mile north of Ogunquit center (turn just south of the Captain Thomas Motel). You pay $20 for a site in high summer.

Wells has several other campgrounds (mostly on US 1), including *Ocean View Cottages & Campground* (☎ 207-646-3308) on ME 109, west of the Maine Turnpike Wells exit, as well as the following:

| campground | phone |
| --- | --- |
| *Beach Acres* | ☎ 207-646-5612 |
| *Gregoire's Campground* | ☎ 207-646-3711 |
| *Ocean Overlook* | ☎ 207-646-3075 |
| *Riverside Park Campground* | ☎ 207-646-3145 |
| *Sea Breeze Campground* | ☎ 207-646-4301 |
| *Sea-Vu Campground* | ☎ 207-646-7732 |
| *Stadig Campground* | ☎ 207-646-2298 |
| *Wells Beach Resort* | ☎ 207-646-7570 |

**Motels** *Briarbrook Motor Inn* (☎ 207-646-7571), south of the center of town on US 1, adjacent to the Ogunquit Playhouse, charges $85 to $93 for rooms in high summer.

*Bourne's Motel* (☎ 207-646-2823, 646-9093), US 1 at Ocean St, is not far from Footbridge Beach and charges $85. The *Studio East Motor Inn* (☎ 207-646-7297) on US 1 is similar. The *Country Squire Motel* (☎ 207-646-3162), US 1 at Bourne's Lane, is also good.

**Inns & B&Bs** The *Cape Neddick House B&B* (☎ 207-363-2500, 1300 US 1), Cape Neddick, is a late-19th-century Victorian that rents double rooms with private bath and full breakfast. The summer rate is $95.

*Seafair Inn* (☎ 207-646-2181, 14 Shore Rd), Ogunquit, is a Victorian summer house on the way to the beach, charging $70 for rooms with shared bath; $95 with private bath. Continental breakfast is included.

*Chestnut Tree Inn* (☎ 207-646-4529, 800-362-0757, 93 Shore Rd), on the way to Perkins Cove, was built in 1870 and has 22 guest rooms going for $50 to $85, continental breakfast included.

*Puffin Inn* (☎ 207-646-5496, 233 US 1), just north of the center of town, is another

big Victorian with a convenient location and 10 rooms with private bath and breakfast for $65 to $125.

The aptly named *Above Tide Inn* (☎ 207-646-7454, 26 Beach St) is perched on piles above the Ogunquit River, only a stone's throw from Ogunquit Beach. It advertises 'spectacular views.' During high season, the price is $115, with a three-night minimum.

## Places to Eat

*Native Grounds* (☎ 207-646-4118), on US 1 near Shore Rd, serves soups, sandwiches and similar light fare, which you can eat on the terrace at umbrella-shaded tables right next to the busy intersection. This is Ogunquit's prime place to see and be seen. The pastries and confections are wonderful ($3 to $6 with coffee).

Nearby, *The Village Food Market* (☎ 207-646-4118) is also a good bet for lunch, especially pizzas and soups.

*Gypsy Sweethearts* (☎ 207-646-7021, 10 Shore Rd) serves the catch of the day and other seafood at moderate prices. Dinner with wine costs around $20 to $35 per person. Breakfast, served 7:30 am to noon, includes fresh-ground coffee and just-baked bread.

For lunch or dinner with a view, try the *Hurricane Restaurant* (☎ 207-646-6348) at Perkins Cove. It features Maine lobster chowder, but the menu always includes special items like lobster spring rolls or chocolate martinis. Expect to spend $25 to $45 for dinner with wine.

Another perennial favorite in Perkins Cove is *Barnacle Billy's* (☎ 207-646-5575). Once a rough-and-ready eatery, it is now more refined, with prices to match. Lobsters are priced according to the season, but a big lunch or dinner usually costs $20 to $30 with wine or beer. An alternative is the *Lobster Shack* (☎ 207-646-2941) on Oarweed Ave, just down the road from Perkins Cove. It has been serving lobsters for 40 years.

*Arrows* (☎ 207-361-1100), on Berwick Rd, is one of the two finest restaurants in this section of Maine (the other being White Hart Inn in Kennebunkport). Located in a wonderfully restored 18th-century farmhouse, the two owners are chefs from San Francisco, where they picked up Far Eastern culinary influences. One of their signature dishes is grilled lobster stewed in a Thai-style curry sauce. Expect to spend more than $100 per couple. Make reservations.

## Getting There & Away
Driving details for Ogunquit are as follows:

| destination | mileage | hr:min |
| --- | --- | --- |
| Bar Harbor, ME | 196 miles | 4:30 |
| Boothbay, ME | 94 miles | 2:25 |
| Boston, MA | 70 miles | 1:30 |
| Freeport, ME | 51 miles | 1:05 |
| Kennebunkport, ME | 11 miles | 0:30 |
| Portland, ME | 35 miles | 0:50 |
| Portsmouth, NH | 17 miles | 0:25 |

## Getting Around
'Trolleys' (disguised buses, 50¢) circulate through Ogunquit every 10 minutes, 8 am to midnight in the summer months. They take you from the center of town to the beach or to Perkins Cove.

## THE KENNEBUNKS
Together, the towns of Kennebunk, Kennebunkport and Kennebunk Beach make up the Kennebunks. Kennebunkport, the most famous of the three towns, is beautiful, historical and absolutely packed in the summer. Walk anywhere in the town to see the pristine 100- and 200-year-old houses and mansions, manicured lawns and sea views. Even in the autumn, when beach resorts such as Old Orchard Beach have closed down, visitors throng to Kennebunkport to shop in its boutiques, stay in its gracious inns and drive along the ocean to admire the view.

Ocean Ave presents the most dramatic vistas, but the back streets, inland from the Kennebunk River and the sea, are less busy.

## Orientation
The epicenter of Kennebunkport activity is Dock Square, just over the bridge on the east side of the Kennebunk River. South of Dock Square is the historic district, with many fine old mansions, some of which are now inns. Ocean Ave goes south from Dock Square to the sea, then northeast to Walker's Point and the Bush compound (the vacation residence of President George W Bush). It's not all that exciting, but every visitor to Kennebunkport makes the drive out there. Continue northeast on Ocean Ave to reach Cape Porpoise, a charming hamlet.

On the west side of the Kennebunk River Bridge is Kennebunk Lower Village, virtually part of Kennebunkport.

## Information
The Kennebunkport Information & Hospitality Center (☎ 207-967-8600), just southeast of Dock Square, has toilets, brochures and maps; the staff can help you find accommodations for the same night. It's open 10 am to 9 pm in summer only, 11 am to 4 pm in fall.

The Kennebunk-Kennebunkport Chamber of Commerce Information Center (☎ 207-967-0857, www.kkcc.maine.org) is on Port Rd (ME 35) in Kennebunk Lower Village. It's open 10 am to 6 pm daily (to 4 pm on Sunday); in September and October, it's open 10 am to 5 pm weekdays.

## Seashore Trolley Museum
Trolleys, the light rail systems that provided most urban transport a century ago, are the focus of the Seashore Trolley Museum (☎ 207-967-2800) on Log Cabin Rd. (Take North St north from Dock Square to reach Log Cabin Rd.) Founded as the Seashore Electric Railway, the museum now holds a variety of streetcars (including one named *Desire*), antique buses and public transit paraphernalia. The museum is open May to October, but has a complicated schedule of business hours. Call before you go.

## Beaches
Kennebunkport proper has only Colony Beach, dominated by the Colony Hotel. But Beach St and Sea Rd (west of the Kennebunk River and then south of Kennebunk Lower Village) lead to three good public beaches: Gooch's Beach, Middle Beach and Mother's Beach, known collectively as Kennebunk Beach.

MAINE

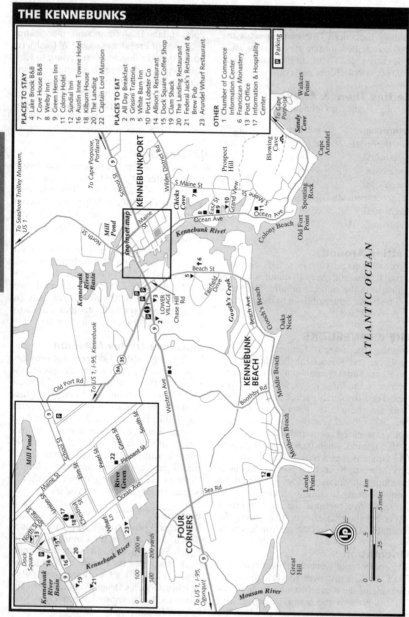

# THE KENNEBUNKS

**PLACES TO STAY**
4   Lake Brook B&B
7   Cove House B&B
8   Welby Inn
9   Green Heron Inn
11  Colony Hotel
12  Sundial Inn
16  Austin Inne Towne Hotel
18  Kilburn House
20  The Landing
22  Captain Lord Mansion

**PLACES TO EAT**
2   All Day Breakfast
3   Grissini Trattoria
5   White Barn Inn
10  Port Lobster Co
14  Allison's Restaurant
15  Dock Square Coffee Shop
19  Clam Shack
20  The Landing Restaurant
21  Federal Jack's Restaurant & Brew Pub
23  Arundel Wharf Restaurant

**OTHER**
1   Chamber of Commerce Information Center
6   Franciscan Monastery
13  Post Office
17  Information & Hospitality Center

P  Parking

## Bicycling

Bicycling is a good way to get around Kennebunkport. The Cape-able Bike Shop (☎ 207-967-4382, 800-220-0907), at Town House Corners and Arundel Rd (follow North St from Dock Square), rents bikes. Fees range from $8 for a three-speed or child's bike to $25 for a new 21-speed.

## Cruises

You can go out on the *Second Chance* (☎ 207-967-5507, 800-767-2628), a 45-foot Downeast lobster boat, for a 1½-hour cruise. Boats leave port at 10 am, noon, 2, 4 and 7 pm; cost is $12.50/6 for adults/children six to 12. Board the boat at 4-A Western Ave in Kennebunk Lower Village, south of the Kennebunk River Bridge.

The schooner *Eleanor* (☎ 207-967-8809) takes passengers on two- or four-hour sailing cruises in the waters off Kennebunkport for $30 to $50 per person. Call Captain Rich Woodman or stop by Schooner's Wharf, near the southern end of Ocean Ave, for schedules and reservations, and feel free to bring a picnic.

## Places to Stay

Accommodations in Kennebunkport are not cheap, but there are many beautiful inns.

**Camping** The campgrounds here are open mid-May through mid-October.

*Salty Acres Campground* (☎ 207-967-2483), on ME 9 north of Cape Porpoise on Goose Rocks Beach, has 225 sites going for $18 to $25. There's also *Kennebunkport Camping* (☎ 207-967-2732), just past the Seashore Trolley Museum, off of Log Cabin Rd, offering 82 sites; and the *Mousam River Campground* (☎ 207-985-2507), on Old Alford Rd in West Kennebunk, with 115 sites.

**Motels** The *Beachwood Motel* (☎ 207-967-2483), on ME 9, 5 miles northeast of Dock Square, has 76 rooms (some are efficiencies) priced from $45 to $95. There's a swimming pool, children's pool, tennis court and shuffleboard. Not all rooms are air-conditioned.

The 20-room *Turnpike Motel* (☎ 207-985-4404), off I-95 exit 3 in Kennebunk, charges $69 for a room in high summer.

**Hotels** *Austin Inne Towne Hotel* (☎ 207-967-4241, 800-227-3809), just steps from Dock Square, couldn't be more centrally located. It's modern, but done in traditional style, with rooms priced from $49 (off-season weekday) to $109 (Saturday night during the high season).

*The Landing* (☎ 207-967-4221), on Ocean Ave, is a big, old wooden summer hotel right over the water in a prime location in the high-rent district. It's most famous for its restaurant, but there are some guest rooms going for $90 double.

**Inns & B&Bs** *Green Heron Inn* (☎ 207-967-3315, 126 Ocean Ave) is a dependably comfy inn. Its 11 rooms, all with private bath, color TV and air-conditioning, cost $90 to $145.

*Kilburn House* (☎ 207-967-4762, 6 Chestnut St) is a turn-of-the-century B&B with four rooms on the 2nd floor ($75/115 for shared/private bath); and a suite on the 3rd floor for $195.

*Cove House B&B* (☎ 207-967-3704, 11 S Maine St) has 3 rooms in an 18th-century home for $75 to $95 per night, full breakfast included.

The *Lake Brook B&B* (☎ 207-967-4069, 57 Western Ave), Kennebunk Lower Village, is a nice turn-of-the-century farmhouse at the edge of a salt marsh and tidal brook. Four rooms with private bath and full breakfast are priced from $65 to $120.

The *Welby Inn* (☎ 207-967-4655, 92 Ocean Ave) is a large gambrel-roofed house with seven guest rooms (all with private bath) priced from $90 to $115 (open in summer only), full breakfast included.

The *Sundial Inn* (☎ 207-967-3850, fax 967-4719, 48 Beach Ave), facing Kennebunk Beach, was built around 1891 and fully renovated in 1987. Summer rates for bright, sunny rooms are $139 to $161, continental breakfast included. The price depends on the room size, the view and the date.

If cost is no object, the *Mansion* (☎ 207-967-3141, fax 967-3127, 6 Pleasant St) is the

**MAINE**

place for you. This great sea captain's house has been meticulously restored and is, if anything, more plush and beautiful than when lived in by its original occupants. Rooms are priced $159 to $299 double, full breakfast included. On weekends, you must stay at least two nights.

## Places to Eat

The tiny **Dock Square Coffee House** (☎ 207-985-4070) is usually packed. It's open 7 am to 3 pm. In addition to the usual array of fancy coffees, teas and pastries, they offer one or two lunch items each day: hand-cut sandwiches, chilis or stews, priced at $6 or $7.

As the name implies, **All Day Breakfast** (☎ 207-967-5132, 55 Western Ave (US 9)) is open for breakfast on weekdays to 1 pm, weekends to 2 pm. The blueberry pancakes are $5.50.

On the west side of the bridge in Kennebunk Lower Village, the **Clam Shack** has hamburgers for $2 and fried-clam-and-fish plates for $6 to $10. You can eat standing up on their deck over the water, but beware of seagulls, which will snatch your food.

**Grissini Trattoria** (☎ 207-967-2211, 27 Western Ave) serves Northern Italian fare in an informal and very airy room. Expect fresh fish and pastas in the $8 to $14 range.

**Allison's Restaurant** (☎ 207-967-4841, 5 Dock Square), at the center of town, is crowded all day because of its decent pub food at very good prices. Lunch selections include fried shrimp basket ($7), shepherd's pie ($5.50) and the extra-long lobster roll ($9). It's open daily for lunch and dinner.

**Arundel Wharf Restaurant** (☎ 207-967-3444), on Arundel Wharf just south of Dock Square, is moderately priced at about $5 to $15 for lunch; $30 to $45 for dinner. Try the coastal paella or a seafood skewer for $16. The location, overlooking the Kennebunk River, is pleasant.

**Port Lobster Co** (☎ 207-967-5411, 122 Ocean Ave) is a lobster pound and fish market that also sells crab meat, shrimp and lobster rolls, as well as boiled lobster. Dining is decidedly informal, and prices are good.

**The Wayfarer** (☎ 207-967-8961, 1 Pier Rd), in Cape Porpoise, is a casual and affordable place to head for lunch. A large bowl of haddock chowder costs $4.50.

**The Landing Restaurant** (☎ 207-967-4221, 201 Ocean Ave), in the hotel by the same name, is a comfy old favorite among longtime residents of Kennebunkport. Seafood is the specialty, of course, and prices are moderate.

**Federal Jack's Restaurant & Brew Pub** (☎ 207-967-4322, 8 Western Ave) is in the Shipyard complex in Kennebunk Lower Village, above the Kennebunkport Brewing Co. It has a good menu of pub food, salads, sandwiches, pizzas and some heartier main courses to go with its selection of 'hand-crafted' ales on draft. The microbrews here are excellent. A meal may cost anywhere from $6 to $20.

The **White Barn Inn** (☎ 207-967-2321, fax 967-1100, 37 Beach St) is Kennebunkport's most renowned restaurant. The decor and ambience are 'country-elegant,' and the food is New American. The menu changes weekly and features local seafood complemented by locally grown herbs, fruits and vegetables and California greens. Dinner is served nightly. Make reservations, dress well and expect to pay $50 to $75 per person.

## Getting There & Away

Driving details for Kennebunkport are as follows:

| destination | mileage | hr:min |
|---|---|---|
| Bar Harbor, ME | 187 miles | 4:20 |
| Boothbay, ME | 88 miles | 2:15 |
| Boston, MA | 80 miles | 1:45 |
| Freeport, ME | 45 miles | 1:00 |
| Ogunquit, ME | 11 miles | 0:30 |
| Portland, ME | 29 miles | 0:40 |
| Portsmouth, NH | 28 miles | 0:40 |

## Getting Around

The In-Town Trolley (☎ 207-967-3686) circulates through Kennebunkport all day. Your ticket ($5 adult, $2 child) is good all day. You can stay on for the 45-minute narrated tour of the whole route, or hop on and off as you like at the designated stops, including along Beach Ave.

## OLD ORCHARD BEACH

Old Orchard Beach is the quintessential New England beach playground, alive with lights, music and noise. Skimpily clad crowds of fun-loving sun worshippers make the rounds of fast-food emporiums, mechanical amusements and gimcrack shops selling trinkets. Palace Playland, on the beach at the very center of town, is a fitting symbol, with its carousel, Ferris wheel, children's rides, fried-clam and pizza stands, T-shirt and souvenir shops.

Old Orchard Beach has long been a favorite summer resort of Quebecois, who flock south in July and August. Many signs are bilingual (English and French) to accommodate the friendly Canadians.

Dozens of little motels and guest houses line the beaches to the north and south of town center, and all are full from late June through Labor Day. Before and after that, Old Orchard Beach slumbers. If you're driving by, you can spend a pleasant afternoon here.

## PORTLAND

Portland is a small, manageable, safe, pleasant, relatively prosperous city of 65,000 people. It is Maine's largest city, largest port and largest commercial center. If you include the suburbs, Greater Portland has a population of about 241,000.

Like London, Portland offers many surprising urban perspectives: turn a corner, look down a street and a grand building or view is framed neatly at the end of it. It also has similarities to San Francisco's port area. Walk down the old cobblestones of Portland's narrow Wharf St at twilight and you'll feel as if a tough fisherman might pop out of nowhere to shanghai you. (Don't worry, this won't happen – Wharf St is far too upscale these days for drunken sailors.)

The city center's architectural unity stems in part from tragedy. The city was ravaged by fire several times in its history, the latest and worst being the great fire of 1866. Built mostly of wood, the port area's buildings were reduced to ashes.

Portlanders resolved not to let it happen again, so they rebuilt their city in the style of the time, using brick and stone. A providential lack of booming prosperity kept its old buildings from being torn down and replaced by sterile modern structures. Today, the Old Port section of Portland is a charming area for a stroll.

### Orientation

Portland is set on a ridge of hills along a peninsula surrounded by the Fore River, Casco Bay and Back Cove. Portland Harbor, where the Fore River meets Casco Bay, is its historical heart, and is where you'll want to spend your time. Known as the Old Port, it holds most of the city's good restaurants, hotels, galleries and shops.

Atop the hills at the southwestern end of the peninsula is the Western Promenade, a long stretch of green park framing a neighborhood of grand stone and brick houses. At the opposite end of the peninsula, the Eastern Promenade serves the same function, with much finer views of Casco Bay and its islands, though the neighborhood is not quite so plush.

Downtown Portland, with its business district, museums, shops and galleries, is centered between the promenades. Congress St is the main thoroughfare along the top of the ridge, passing Portland's most imposing buildings: city hall, banks, churches and hotels. Commercial St is the fitting name of the main business street in the Old Port where tourists spend most of their time.

The I-95 skirts the city to the west, while I-295 makes a detour into the city and hooks back up with I-95 north of Back Cove. Approaching Portland from the south, follow I-95 to exit 6A, then take I-295 to exit 4, then take US 1 to US 1A North, which is Commercial St. Stay on Commercial St and it will take you right into the Old Port.

From the north, follow I-295 to exit 7, then US 1A South (Commercial St).

### Information

The Convention & Visitors Bureau of Greater Portland (☎ 207-772-4994, www .visitportland.com), 305 Commercial St at Foundry Lane, has an information office on the south side of the Old Port. It's open

# PORTLAND

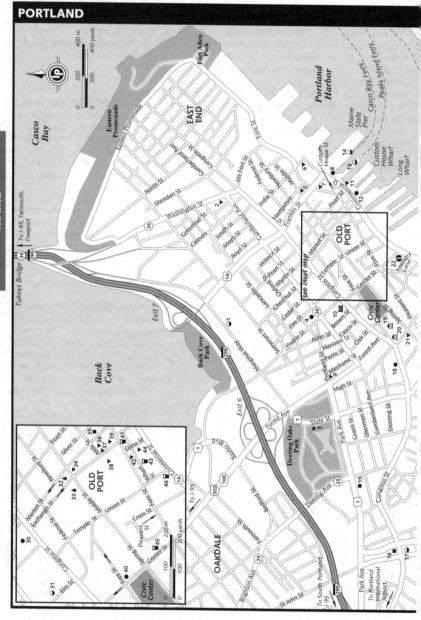

MAINE

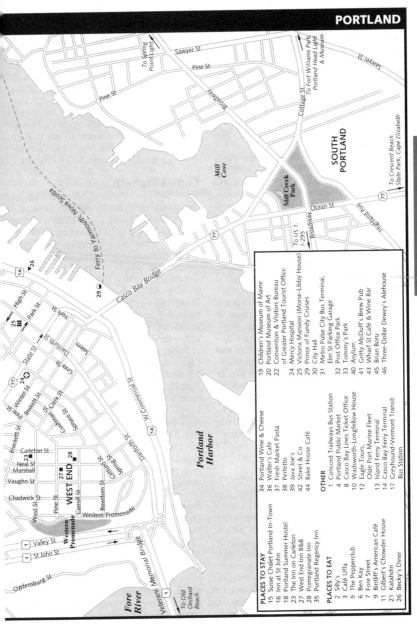

**PORTLAND**

To Spring Point Light

Sawyer St
Pine St
Pine St
Broadway
Cottage St
To Fort Williams Park
Portland Head Light
& Museum
Sawyer St

Mill Cove

SOUTH
PORTLAND

Mill Creek
Park
Ocean St

To US 1,
I-295
Broadway
Highland Ave

To Crescent Beach
State Park, Cape Elizabeth

77

**MAINE**

Ferry to Yarmouth, Nova Scotia

Casco Bay Bridge

26
29
77

High St
Park St
Fox St

25

State St
Danforth St
Salem
Gray St
Winter St
Weymouth St
Brackett St
Gilman St
Carleton St
Clark St
Spruce St
Cushman St
Vaughan St
Chadwick St
West St
Pine St
Carroll St
Bowdoin St
Clifford St
W Commercial St
Danforth St

1A

Portland
Harbor

Blackett St
Carleton St
23
Neal St
Marshall
28
27
WEST END
Western Promenade

1   Valley St
1   St John St
Western
Promenade

Veterans Memorial Bridge

1
To Old
Orchard
Beach

Ogdensburg St

Fore
River

**PLACES TO STAY**
15  Susse Chalet Portland In-Town
16  Inn at St John
18  Portland Summer Hostel
23  The Inn on Carleton
27  West End Inn B&B
28  Pomegranate Inn
35  Portland Regency Inn

**PLACES TO EAT**
2   Silly's
3   Café Uffa
5   The Pepperclub
6   Ben Kay
7   Fore Street
9   Bintliff's American Café
11  Gilbert's Chowder House
21  Katahdin
26  Becky's Diner

34  Portland Wine & Cheese
36  Walter's Cafe
37  Fresh Market Pasta
38  Perfetto
39  Java Joe's
42  Street & Co
44  Bake House Café

**OTHER**
1   Concord Trailways Bus Station
4   Portland Public Market
8   Casco Bay Lines Ticket Office
10  Wadsworth-Longfellow House
12  Eagle Tours,
    Olde Port Marine Fleet
13  Island Ferry Terminal
14  Casco Bay Ferry Terminal
17  Greyhound-Vermont Transit
    Bus Station

19  Children's Museum of Maine
20  Portland Museum of Art
22  Convention & Visitors Bureau
    of Greater Portland Tourist Office
24  Mercy Hospital
25  Victoria Mansion (Morse-Libby House)
29  Prince of Fundy Cruises
30  City Hall
31  Metro Pulse City Bus Terminal,
    Elm St Parking Garage
32  Post Office Park
33  Tommy's Park
40  Asylum
41  Gritty McDuff's Brew Pub
43  Wharf St Café & Wine Bar
45  Brian Boru
46  Three-Dollar Dewey's Alehouse

8 am to 6 pm weekdays and 10 am to 6 pm weekends and holidays, mid-May to mid-October. During the rest of the year, it's open to 5 pm weekdays and 3 pm weekends and holidays.

Books Etc (☎ 207-774-0626, 38 Exchange St) is an inviting store to browse for books.

In an emergency, call ☎ 911; for Portland police, call ☎ 207-874-8300; to reach the Maine State Police, call ☎ 207-624-7076.

## Museums

The **Portland Museum of Art** is the city's fine arts museum (☎ 207-773-2787, 800-639-4067), 7 Congress Square, at Congress and High Sts, has an outstanding collection especially rich in the works of Maine painters Winslow Homer, Edward Hopper, Rockwell Kent and Andrew Wyeth. There are works by European masters such as Degas, Picasso and Renoir as well, though exhibit space is limited compared to the size of the collection. From time to time, there are very good special shows (call for current offerings). The museum ($6) is open 10 am to 5 pm (until 9 pm Thursday and Friday, noon to 5pm Sunday). Friday nights are free.

The **Children's Museum of Maine** (☎ 207-828-1234), 142 Free St, near Congress and High Sts, gives children the opportunity to try such adult activities as hauling in lobster traps on a child-sized boat, broadcasting the news and making stained glass. If you have kids, head for the Children's Museum (especially on rainy days). It's open 10 am to 5 pm (noon to 5 pm Sunday) in summer. Winter hours vary, so call first. Admission costs $5 (children younger than one enter free).

## Historic Houses

The **Victoria Mansion** (☎ 207-772-4841), 109 Danforth St, at Park St, a few blocks southeast of the art museum, is also known as the Morse-Libby House. This Italianate palace was built in 1859 and decorated sumptuously with rich furniture, frescoes, paintings, carpets, gilding and exotic woods and stone. It's open to visitors 10 am to 5 pm (noon to 5 pm Sunday), Tuesday to Sunday from late May through early September; closed on weekends early September through mid-

October. Admission costs $5 and includes a 45-minute guided tour.

**Wadsworth-Longfellow House** (☎ 207-879-0427), 485 Congress St, was built of brick (1786) in the Federal style. The builder was General Peleg Wadsworth, a hero in the Revolutionary War and also the grandfather of poet Henry Wadsworth Longfellow. Longfellow grew up here, and the house's furnishings recall his 19th-century surroundings. The museum is open 10 am to 4 pm daily, late May through mid-October. Admission is $5 for adults, $1 for children.

## Cape Elizabeth

Southeast from Portland, across the bay via the Casco Bay Bridge, are the towns of South Portland and Cape Elizabeth. Fort Williams Park, 4 miles from central Portland in Cape Elizabeth, is worth a visit for its panoramas and picnic possibilities.

The vast rolling lawns of the park are dotted with WWII bunkers and gun emplacements. Fortification of Portland Head began in 1873, and the installation was named Fort Williams in 1899. The fort guarded the entrance to Casco Bay and was active until 1964.

Right next to the park is Portland Head Light, the oldest of Maine's 52 functioning lighthouses. It was commissioned by President George Washington in 1791 and staffed until 1989, when machines took over. The keeper's house is now the **Museum at Portland Head Light** (☎ 207-799-2661), which traces the maritime and military history of the region. It's open 10 am to 4 pm from June through October; 10 am to 4 pm weekends April through May and November on through mid-December.

## Portland Public Market

Opened in October 1998, the **Portland Public Market** (☎ 207-228-2000), 25 Preble St, is a 37,000-sq-foot open food hall that features 22 locally owned businesses, a half block from Monument Square. It's a great place to stock up on picnic food, such as fresh-baked bread, local produce, Maine cheeses and regional wines. Several of the vendors also serve food at lunch, and there are numerous tables for sitting. The Pantry sells a wide assortment of Maine salsas, salad dressings, honey, jams and granolas. The New England Bison Company serves ground bison, a daily bison stew ($4.50) and bison jerky. Stone Soup features a variety of hot and cold soups to enjoy at the market.

## Jogging

Back Cove, northwest of the city's center on the other side of I-295, is surrounded by a 2-mile jogging trail. Take I-295 exit 6 and follow US 1 North; or take bus No 2 to Forest Ave Plaza, Bus 6 to Payson Park or bus No 8 to the Shop n' Save and you'll be near Back Cove.

## Sea Kayaking

Just outside of Portland, there is a slew of islands in Casco Bay that are ideal for sea kayaking. Casco Bay Lines (☎ 207-774-7871) leaves every hour in the summer for a 15-minute cruise to Peaks Island. Once there, you can hook up with Maine Island Kayak Company (☎ 800-796-2373), a reputable outfitter that offers daily instruction and tours of the area.

## Organized Tours

Mainely Tours (☎ 207-774-0808) has 90-minute tours of the city that start in front of the Convention & Visitors Bureau of Greater Portland, 305 Commercial St. The fun trip gives you an overview of the city's history as you make your way around Old Port, Eastern Prom, Western Prom, and the Portland Head Light. Cost is $12.

While not exactly an organized tour, a ride on bus No 1 ($1) is a good and inexpensive way to see the Eastern and Western Promenades, Congress St and the heart of downtown Portland. You can ride until you've had enough. You can catch the No 1 bus on Congress St.

## Cruises

The motorboats of Casco Bay Lines (☎ 207-774-7871, www.cascobaylines.com) cruise the Casco Bay islands delivering mail, freight and visitors. These are working boats, but they're comfortably outfitted. The cruises vary: a roundtrip cruise to the Diamond Islands (1¾ hours) costing $8.50/7/3.50 for adults/seniors/children from five to nine; a roundtrip nature cruise, complete with lecture, to Bailey Island (5¾ hours) for $14.50/13/6.50. Two of the six cruises operate daily year round. All cruises depart from the Casco Bay Ferry Terminal at 56 Commercial St, at Franklin St.

You can also cruise Casco Bay under sail aboard the *Palawan* (☎ 207-773-2163), which is a 58-foot ocean racing yacht designed by Sparkman & Stevens. There are cruises in the morning ($20 for three hours), afternoon ($30 for three hours) and evening ($20 for two hours). Seniors and children 12 and under pay half price.

Eagle Tours (☎ 207-774-6498), at Long Wharf on Commercial St, runs tours of Casco Bay, including trips to Eagle Island and Portland Head Light.

The Olde Port Marine Fleet (☎ 207-775-0727, 800-437-3270) has three boats departing from Long Wharf for deep-sea fishing trips, whale watching, lobstering trips and one-hour harbor cruises. Call for details, or stop by the blue ticket booth next to the Key Bank on Commercial St.

## Places to Stay

**Camping** There are no camping places in Portland, but there are several near Freeport, only 16 miles to the northeast. See the Freeport section for details.

**Hostels** From June through August, the University of Maine's Portland Hall becomes the local HI/AYH hostel, called the ***Portland Summer Hostel*** (☎ 207-874-3281, off-season 617-735-1800, 645 Congress St). Rooms are $15 per person. Most have two beds, so if you come alone, there's a chance you'll be sharing. The price includes linens and a continental breakfast, as well as free parking in their gated lot – a plus in downtown Portland. There's no age limit.

**Motels** Motels outside the city's center are moderately priced. There are several at I-95 exit 7, near the Maine Mall (Comfort Inn, Portland Marriott, Days Inn), and at exit 8.

For these chain motels' numbers, see the Toll-Free Numbers directory at the back of this book.

***Susse Chalet Portland/Westbrook*** (☎ 207-774-6101, 800-258-1980), off I-95 exit 8, charges $59.70 for up to four people, even less if you call and ask for the same-day rate.

***Howard Johnson*** (☎ 207-774-5861, 800-654-2000, 155 Riverside St), off I-95 exit 8, has 120 rooms, a restaurant and indoor pool. Cost is $104.95 to $119.95.

The ***Holiday Inn West*** (☎ 207-774-5601, 800-465-4329, fax 207-774-2103, 81 Riverside St) is at exit 8 as well. They have 200 rooms for $131 a night.

**Hotels** The Inn at St John (☎ 207-773-6481, 939 Congress St), at St John St, advertises itself as Portland's 'low-fat' hotel, with rooms starting at $34.70 per night and going up to $124.70. It's somewhat noisy, but it's right across the street from the Greyhound/Vermont Transit bus station, and on city bus routes 1 and 3. Continental breakfast is included.

The ***Susse Chalet Portland In-Town*** (☎ 207-871-0611, 800-258-1980, 340 Park Ave) charges $89.70 for a double room. Rooms with two double beds can sleep up to four. The hotel sometimes offers a same-day rate that's substantially less. From I-95, take exit 6A to I-295 exit 5A (Congress St); at the end of the ramp turn right, then left at the signs for Stroudwater/Westbrook.

The ***Portland Regency Inn*** (☎ 207-774-4200, 800-727-3436, fax 207-775-2150, 20 Milk St) is in a great location in the Old Port, a block from the waterfront. The inn's 95 very comfortable rooms, housed in the Port's substantial red-brick armory, are priced $189 to $199.

**Inns & B&Bs** Portland's West End, near the Western Promenade, is a quiet residential neighborhood with many grand Victorian houses, some of which have been converted to inns.

Few innkeepers can mix modern art with antiques as skillfully as Isabel Smiles has done in the ***Pomegranate Inn*** (☎ 207-772-1006, 800-356-0408, www.innbook.com/pome.html,

49 Neal St). A former antiques dealer and interior designer, Smiles' eclectic taste runs the gamut from faux marble columns in the living room to hand painted walls and century-old dressers in the guest rooms. Large contemporary sculpture and collages are displayed in the hallways. Remarkably, they all seem to fit together. She has eight rooms priced $95 to $175, full breakfast included.

The ***West End Inn B&B*** (☎ 207-772-1377, 800-338-1377, 146 Pine St) was built in 1871. It has only five rooms, all with TV and private bath, for $79 to $169, depending on when you stay.

***The Inn on Carleton*** (☎ 207-775-1910, 46 Carleton St) is a restored 1869 Victorian house with six rooms, all with private bath, priced at $135 to $165.

## Places to Eat

If you think every restaurant in Portland serves lobster, steamers and a cute plastic bib, you're in for a big surprise. Bostonians think nothing of making the two-hour drive to Portland for an exceptional meal. Many of these fine dining establishments focus on Maine's abundant goodies – treasures from the sea, as well as locally farmed chickens, venison and organically grown produce. Most of the best restaurants are in the Old Port section of town on Wharf, Exchange and Fore Sts.

If you want to meet working fishermen, opt for breakfast or lunch at ***Becky's Diner*** (☎ 207-773-7070, 390 Commercial St) on the waterfront. Sit at the counter and hobnob with the salty dogs and order one of the cheapest meals in town. The diner offers fresh muffins in the morning and steak sandwiches ($5) in the afternoon. It's open 4 am to 9 pm daily.

***Java Joe's*** (☎ 207-761-5637, 13 Exchange St), near Fore St, is the favored place for a good cup of joe, plain or fancy, for 85¢ to $3. They serve a selection of sandwiches, cookies and pastries as well. There's cool, live music some evenings, and lots of whispered intellectual discussion.

Head to ***Bintliff's American Café*** (☎ 207-774-0005, 98 Portland St), for the best brunches in town (served 7 am to 2 pm daily). Choices include salmon Benedict for $9 or banana-pecan pancakes for $6.

***Portland Wine & Cheese*** *(☎ 207-772-4647)*, Middle St at Exchange St, has high-quality sandwiches and salads for lunch.

The ***Bake House Café*** *(☎ 207-773-2217)*, Dana St at Commercial St, is good for baked goods, pastries, sandwiches, soups and salads.

***Gilbert's Chowder House*** *(☎ 207-871-5636, 92 Commercial St)*, at Pearl St, is a simple diner with a lunch counter and tables, good for a load of fish and chips ($8) or a big bowl of their renowned thick clam chowder ($4).

The freshest sushi in town can be found at ***Ben Kay*** *(☎ 207-773-5555, 2 India St)*, across from the Casco Bay Wharf. The specialty is lobster *sashimi*, the whole tail, for $19.50.

Away from the Old Port area, but worth the walk or short drive, is a funky little place called ***Silly's*** *(☎ 207-772-0360, 40 Washington Ave)*. Locals travel across town to gobble one of their tasty abdullahs (sandwiches rolled in bakery-fresh tortillas) for lunch ($2.25 to $4.75). Dinners, such as jerk chicken or fish and chips, are also cheap. It's open 10 am to 10 pm Monday to Saturday.

Serving innovative seafood at affordable prices is ***Café Uffa*** *(☎ 207-775-3380, 190 State St)*. Choices of main dishes in this casual and spacious setting include grilled Chilean sea bass ($14.50). Expect long lines at Sunday brunch.

For the best selection of veggie fare, head over to ***The Pepperclub*** *(☎ 207-772-0531, 78 Middle St)*, just northeast of Franklin Artery. Dinner is served every night and the place is usually packed shortly after 6 pm. The reason is the eclectic menu – a Middle Eastern *meze* plate for starters, then Thai-lime vegetables with *udon* noodles and sesame tofu, or mushroom and fresh basil lasagna. Most main courses cost $8 to $10, making possible an excellent, interesting dinner, with wine, for about $20 per person. Service is friendly and good.

***Katahdin*** *(☎ 207-774-1740, 106 High St)*, at Spring St, is a local secret. It is in a non-descript red building, somewhat off the beaten path. The menu puts a new twist on old American favorites, as in the pot roast with vegetables braised in red wine gravy, or wild mushroom ravioli in seasonal vegetable broth. The decor is artsy, with hand-painted tables and patchwork quilts hanging from the walls. Entrees are reasonably priced from $7.95 to $12.95, but the best deal is the 'Blue Plate Special.' It includes soup, salad and main course for $10.95. Save room for a slice of peach raspberry cobbler.

The menu at ***Street & Company*** *(☎ 207-775-0887, 33 Wharf St)* might be simple – chalked on a blackboard that's carted from table to table, but you can rest assured that the seafood is the best in town. There's grilled, broiled or Cajun-style fish (tuna, salmon, swordfish), plus various sea critters like mussels, clams or shrimp that are steamed or sautéed. You can have your choice served over pasta or in a broth that's perfect for dipping with a hunk of fresh bread. The cramped but congenial dining rooms are usually packed for dinner, so reserve in advance. Entrees range from $14.95 to $21.95.

Across the street, ***Wharf Street Café and Wine Bar*** *(☎ 207-773-6667, 35 Wharf St)* is another of these industrial buildings converted for fine dining: rough brick walls and smooth cuisine. You might start dinner with a crab and avocado quesadilla, then go on to the spicy shrimp and scallop *fra diavolo*. The wine list is good, and they serve local beers. Total, the bill will be about $22 to $32.

For a bowl of affordable and tasty pasta, head to ***Fresh Market Pasta*** *(☎ 207-773-7146, 43 Exchange St)*. You can have a large bowl of pasta with any sauce you want, from marinara to bolognese to pesto, for as little as $3.75 to $4.50. There's a child's menu for $2.50.

***Walter's Café*** *(☎ 207-871-9258, at 15 Exchange St)* is one of Portland's best-loved bistros, a narrow storefront dining room with a high ceiling and even higher culinary aspirations. Maine ingredients are frequently featured, as in the grilled salmon in a blueberry basil oil over mixed greens. Vegetarians should try the Rasta Pasta, a combination of linguine and julienne vegetables. This is a good place for a hot lunch. Closed Sunday.

**MAINE**

Across the street is another one of the top restaurants in town, **Perfétto** (☎ 207-828-0001, 28 Exchange St). This Italian bistro, in a building with an attractive brick façade, features such specialties as the sun-dried tomato encrusted haddock or salmon osso bucco for $15.

If you have just one night in Portland to dine, head to **Fore Street** (☎ 207-775-2717, 288 Fore St). The airy, exposed-brick and pine panel room – a former wartime storage area – features an open-air kitchen that practically the entire restaurant can view. Chefs busily sauté food and finish plates on three long tables, but the real spectacle is the food itself. Owner and chef Sam Hayward has made apple-wood grilling and roasting his forte, and, whenever possible, he uses local meats. Start with roasted Blue Hill bay mussels with pistachios, served in a broth that will leave you craving more ($7.95). Then choose the roasted pork loin ($16) or the incredibly tender Atlantic striped bass ($20). To complete this memorable meal, finish with the maple crème brûlée ($5).

## Entertainment

Fore St, between Union and Exchange Sts, is lined with restaurants and bars. Those near Union, such as **Three Dollar Dewey's Alehouse**, at Commercial and Union Sts, tend to be sports bars with large-screen TVs and pinball machines or billiard tables clicking nearby.

The most popular spot for a pint of award-winning beer is **Gritty McDuff's Brew Pub** (☎ 207-772-2739, 396 Fore St). The half-dozen beers, ales and stouts served here are all brewed downstairs.

Another favorite hangout is the Irish pub, **Brian Ború** (☎ 207-780-1506), on Center St between Spring and Fore Sts.

If you want to sip martinis and act hip, head to **Una** (☎ 207-828-0300, 505 Fore St).

**Wharf St Café and Wine Bar** (☎ 207-773-6667, 38 Wharf St), on a wonderful street in town, has a long list of wines by the glass.

For live music, there's no better choice than **Asylum** (☎ 207-772-8274, 121 Center St).

This small and very popular bar often attracts widely known bands.

## Getting There & Away

**Air** Portland International Jetport (☎ 207-874-8877) is Maine's largest and busiest air terminal. The 'International' in the airport's name refers mostly to flights to and from Canada. For long-distance international flights, you must connect through Boston or New York City (JFK airport).

Airlines serving the airport include Continental, Delta, Northwest, United and US Airways (see the Toll-Free Numbers section at the back of the book).

City buses can take you from the airport to the center of town for $1 (see Getting Around, below).

**Bus** Vermont Transit (☎ 207-772-6587, 802-864-6811, 800-451-3292, www.vermonttransit.com), in the Greyhound Terminal, 950 Congress St at St John St, is near I-295 exit 5. They run six buses daily to and from Boston (2½ hours), connecting with buses to Hartford (3¼ hours more) and New York City (4½ hours more).

Vermont Transit also runs three buses northeastward to Brunswick, and four up the Maine Turnpike to Lewiston, Augusta, Waterville and Bangor (3¼ hours), with one bus continuing to Bar Harbor (four hours from Portland).

Concord Trailways (☎ 207-828-1151, 800-639-3317, www.concordtrailways.com) has its terminal at 161 Marginal Way (the street running parallel to I-295), just southwest of Franklin Artery. They run six nonstop buses daily between Portland, Boston and Boston's Logan Airport.

From Portland, three Concord Trailways buses go northeast to Bangor; one bus connects at Bangor with a Cyr bus headed north to Medway, Sherman, Houlton, Presque Isle and Caribou. There's also local service from Portland that runs along the coast, stopping at the towns of Brunswick, Bath, Wiscasset, Damariscotta, Waldoboro, Rockland, Camden/Rockport, Lincolnville, Belfast, Searsport and Bangor. On this bus route, the Portland-to-Bangor trip takes approximately four hours.

**Train** Plans are in the works to restore daily train service between Boston and Portland. Contact Amtrak (☎ 800-872-7245, www.amtrak.com) for details.

**Car** Driving details for Portland are as follows:

| destination | mileage | hr:min |
| --- | --- | --- |
| Bar Harbor, ME | 161 miles | 4:00 |
| Boothbay, ME | 59 miles | 1:15 |
| Boston, MA | 108 miles | 2:15 |
| Freeport, ME | 16 miles | 0:22 |
| Kennebunkport, ME | 29 miles | 0:40 |
| Ogunquit, ME | 35 miles | 0:50 |
| Portsmouth, NH | 52 miles | 1:05 |

**Boat** For passenger ferry cruises between Portland and Bailey Island, see Cruises, above.

Prince of Fundy Cruises' MF *Scotia Prince* (☎ 207-775-5616, 800-341-7540, www.princeoffundy.com) departs Portland for Yarmouth, Nova Scotia, Canada, each evening at 9 pm. It arrives the next morning at breakfast time after cruising for 11 hours. The return trip departs Yarmouth at 10 am for Portland, arriving after dinner. You must have proof of citizenship (US citizens may use a passport or US citizen's birth certificate; non-US citizens need a passport or alien registration (green) card; travelers may be asked to present a driver's license) to enter Canada at Yarmouth.

The cruises operate daily (with some exceptions) from early May through late October. From mid-June to mid-September, Portland-to-Yarmouth overnight fares for one-way for two adults in an economy cabin range from $344 to $418, including shipment of a car. The day trip from Portland to Yarmouth costs $80/40 for each adult/child (plus $98 for a car); off-season rates are $60/30 ($80 for your car). Children under five sail free. If you'd like a day-use cabin on the Portland-to-Yarmouth run, prices start

at $22. Meals and port tax ($3) are not included in the price.

Car fares are reduced by half on certain days (mostly Tuesday and Wednesday); call for details. Thus, for a couple with two children aged five to 14, with a car, traveling in-season in two moderately priced cabins (at night, Portland to Yarmouth), the roundtrip cost can reach about $1000, with meals, taxes and tips included. Off-season, the same family, staying in the most inexpensive cabin, sailing at night and bringing their own food, can go roundtrip for about $400 minimum.

## Getting Around

Portland's Metro (☎ 207-774-0351) is the local bus company, with its main terminus ('Metro Pulse') at the Elm St parking garage (Elm St at Congress St). The fare is $1.

Here are some useful routes serving the city center:

| destination | bus nos |
| --- | --- |
| Airport | 5 |
| Back Cove | 2, 3, 6 |
| Casco Bay Ferry Terminal | 8 |
| Concord Trailways Bus Terminal | 8 |
| Eastern Promenade | 1 |
| International Ferry Terminal | 8 |
| Old Port | 8 |
| Portland Museum of Art | 1, 3, 8 |
| Vermont Transit/<br>Greyhound Bus Terminal | 1, 3, 5 |
| Western Promenade | 1, 8 |

## FREEPORT

Here, amid the natural beauties of Maine's rockbound coast, is a town devoted almost entirely to city-style shopping. Tony luggage, expensive china, trendy clothes and perfumed soaps are all available in its more than 100 shops that are backed by a maze of parking lots. The town's mile-long Main St (US 1) is a perpetual traffic jam of cars from all over the country and Canada – all visiting Freeport in the name of nature.

Freeport's fame and fortune began a century ago when Leon Leonwood Bean opened

## Shopping

It's all around you, as are the shoppers.

Why should prices for luxury goods be lower here than in the major cities? The answer is rent and middlemen. The rent in Freeport is a fraction of that on Fifth Ave in Manhattan or Newbury St in Boston. And by establishing their own shops in this small Maine town, major purveyors of luxury goods avoid paying 50% or more of the retail price to the big-city department stores and specialty shops.

The car license plates seen here are from Connecticut, Massachusetts, New York, Ontario, Pennsylvania, Quebec and even farther afield. As for the shoppers themselves, many look to be outdoorsy types, but most seem to have more interest in the outdoors as a romantic idea than as a place to work up a sweat.

It's ironic that LL Bean, a store that built its fame on supplying outdoor sports enthusiasts, has led the transformation of Freeport into a mecca for urban shopping sophisticates.

a shop to sell equipment and provisions to hunters and fishers heading north into the Maine woods. LL Bean gave good value for money, and his customers were loyal. One foundation of their loyalty was his Maine Hunting Shoe, a rugged rubber bottom molded to a leather upper. It kept feet dry and warm in the chill air of dawn as hunters crouched in their duck blinds.

Over the years, the store added lots of other no-nonsense, good-quality outdoor gear and some engaging retailing practices: a catalog operation, perpetual open hours (the store *never* closes) and an iron-clad returns policy that allows shoppers to send items back any time they prove unsatisfactory. Though the store fell on hard times in the 1960s, a shot of big-city marketing expertise soon boosted it to nationwide fame.

In summer, the LL Bean store (☎ 800-341-4341 ext 7801), and indeed most of Free-port's shops, are busy with shoppers all day and into the night. Don't miss visiting the Delorme Mapping Company, just south of Freeport on US 1 (☎ 207-846-7100). Makers of the essential *Maine Atlas and Gazetter*, Delorme also creates maps and software for almost any destination on earth.

### Orientation

Take I-95 exit 19 or 20 to reach downtown Freeport. The downtown shopping district along Main St (US 1) is easily negotiated on foot, but you might have to drive a short distance to your lodgings if you plan to stay the night.

The epicenter of Freeport shopping is the big LL Bean store that made Freeport what it is today. It is right on Main St.

South Freeport, south along US 1, is a sleepy residential community, but its town dock has a good local eatery and bay cruises.

### Information

The State of Maine has a large information center at I-95 exit 17. It can provide you with information on Freeport and all of Maine. The Freeport Chamber of Commerce (☎ 207-865-1212, www.freeportusa.com) maintains information centers on Main St at Mallet St, and on Mill St a block south of Main St. Both of the centers are open 9 am to 5 pm weekdays.

### Hiking

Bradbury Mountain State Park on ME 9, 6 miles west of Freeport and just north of Pownal, has several miles of forested hiking trails, including an instant-gratification 10-minute hike from the picnic area uphill to the summit for a spectacular view that reaches all the way to the ocean. There's camping as well (see below). Surprisingly, one sees very few Freeport shoppers testing their new outdoor gear in this pretty park.

Follow ME 125 and ME 136 north from Freeport, but turn left just after crossing I-95, following the state park signs.

### Hot-Air Balloon Rides

Freeport Balloon Co (☎ 207-865-1712), 41 Tuttle Rd, Pownal, ME 04069, boasts 'fair winds, soft landings and good crew.' They'll take you aloft for a little over an hour for about $150 per person. Reserve in advance.

## Cruises

In South Freeport, a few miles south of the shopping frenzy, is the Freeport Town Wharf, the departure point for several boats offering cruises around Casco Bay. Freeport Sailing (☎ 207-865-9225, 756-1230) will take you on a four-hour morning cruise for $30 per person. Atlantic Seal Cruises (☎ 207-865-6112) offers three-hour cruises for $20. Remember to pack a picnic lunch or ask about catered picnics when you make reservations.

## Places to Stay

**Camping** Camping is available at a half-dozen campgrounds within a 6-mile radius of Freeport. Choicest is the *Delia B Powers Winslow Memorial Park* (☎ 207-865-4198), on Staples Point Rd. It is a town park right on the ocean with water-view sites for $15 and non-view for $13. There are no hookups. It opens Memorial Day weekend and closes after early September. Head south from Freeport along US 1, take a left at the towering Native American statue and go toward South Freeport, then right onto Staples Point Rd (there's a park sign) and go about 2 miles to the park.

Next best is *Bradbury Mountain State Park*, with 41 forested sites ($15). It is on ME 9 north of Pownal. See Hiking (above) for details.

Closest to Freeport's center is *Sandy Cedar Haven Campground* (☎ 207-865-6254, 19 Baker Rd (ME 125 North)), with 58 mostly wooded sites. On this same road is the *Florida Lake Campground* (☎ 207-865-4874), with 40 sites renting for $14 to $16 per day, 3 miles north of Freeport. A good alternative is *Blueberry Pond Campground* (☎ 207-688-4421, 355 Libby Rd), in Pownal, 4 miles northeast of Freeport. It's a private place a few miles northeast of Bradbury Mountain (head for Bradbury Mountain, then follow the signs). *Flying Point Campground* (☎ 207-865-4569) has 38 sites on Lower Flying Point Rd, 4 miles southeast of LL Bean via Bow St.

**Motels** Motels are mostly south of the city center on US 1 near I-95 exit 19. The highly visible *Super 8 Motel* (☎ 207-865-1408, 800-800-8000) is priced at $81.88 to $95.88 double. The *Eagle Motel* (☎ 207-865-4088, 800-334-4088, 291 US 1 South) is a handsome, classic American motel charging $80 per double, breakfast included. *Casco Bay Motel* (☎ 207-865-4925, 317 US 1 South), a few minutes' drive south of the town center, right next to the 40-foot Native American statue, charges $79 to $89 for a room with a double bed.

**Inns & B&Bs** Several B&Bs are on Main St just north of the big Harraseeket Inn. Others are within an easy walk of the city center. In summer, most charge from $70 to $100 for a double room with bath and breakfast.

The *Captain Josiah A Mitchell House* (☎ 207-865-3289, 188 Main St) is a historic house with Victorian furnishings. It once belonged to a ship captain. Seven rooms, with full- or half-bath, cost $95, breakfast included.

*Holbrook Inn* (☎ 207-865-6693, 7 Holbrook St) charges $95 to $135 for one of its four spacious rooms with private bath and breakfast.

*Bayberry Bed & Breakfast* (☎ 207-865-1868, 8 Maple Ave) dates from the mid-19th century. The very friendly owners feature six rooms with private baths for $87 to $110, breakfast included.

*Country at Heart B&B* (☎ 207-865-0512, 37 Bow St) is 2½ blocks from LL Bean and charges $85 for a double with bath and breakfast.

Only a ten-minute drive from downtown Freeport, in rural Durham, the *Bagley House* (☎ 207-865-6566) dates from pre-Revolutionary War times. The owners, two former nurses from Boston, definitely know how to cater to the whims of tired shoppers, who are often found lounging in the acres of open fields and gardens. The $95 room price includes breakfast.

There are also some nice, quiet B&Bs on Main St in South Freeport, near the town dock. The *Atlantic Seal B&B* (☎ 207-865-6112, 25 Main St) features three rooms with

MAINE

harbor views at $105 to $175 a night. They offer boat cruises as well as lodging.

After shopping all day in town, it's wonderful to know that you only have to walk a block back to the ***Harraseeket Inn*** *(☎ 207-865-9377, 800-342-6423, 162 Main St)* where you can enjoy afternoon tea and cakes and then soak your weary bones in an oversized Jacuzzi. Owner Nancy Gray is a native Mainer who grew up on a sporting camp. When she was 10 years old, her father bought her a gun, just in case she got caught on the way home from school between a mother bear and her cub. She charges $180 to $235 a night for her 84 elegant rooms.

### Places to Eat
Freeport's Main St (US 1) has a dozen places to eat. Unfortunately, most of them serve standard tourist fare. Try the ***Lobster Cooker*** *(☎ 207-865-4349, 39 Main St)*. It's a fast-food place with excellent clam chowder ($4), good coleslaw and boiled lobster lunches ($15). Dine inside or on the deck.

Hidden away from the throngs of shoppers, ***The Village Store*** *(☎ 207-865-4230, 97 South Freeport Rd)* is where workers in the area have their lunch. The nondescript storefront serves large sandwiches for $3.75 to $7. There are several tables if you want to eat on the premises.

***Harraseeket Lunch & Lobster Co*** *(☎ 207-865-4888)*, on the Town Dock in South Freeport, serves a full menu of lunch items to be eaten at shaded picnic tables overlooking the bay. Get twin 1lb lobsters for $10, a clambake for $13 or a good lobster roll with french fries for $10. Live and cooked lobsters to take out are sold as well.

***Gritty McDuff's*** *(☎ 207-865-4321)*, on Lower Main St, is a popular place for a pint.

***15 Independence*** *(☎ 207-865-1515, 15 Independence Drive)*, south of town just off US 1, is run by the same people who own the highly touted Perfétto in Portland. New American cuisine, such as gorgonzola-encrusted filet mignon ($18) or rotisserie chicken ($13.50), is served in a 19th-century farmhouse.

The ***Broad Arrow Tavern*** *(☎ 800-342-6423, 162 Main St)*, in the Harraseeket Inn,

has a good selection of microbrews and moderately priced brick-oven specialties. A bowl of hearty lobster stew costs $5.50.

Far more upscale, and also in the Harraseeket Inn, is the ***Maine Dining Room*** *(☎ 207-865-1085, 162 Main St)*. Fresh tuna, rack of lamb and Maine coast bouillabaisse are but a few of their tempting offers. Dessert crepes, made at the table, provide the perfect ending. Entrees are pricey, $19 to $28. The restaurant is also known for its extravagant Sunday brunch buffet.

### Getting There & Away
For bus transport, see the Portland section; buses do not stop in Freeport. Driving details for Freeport are as follows:

| destination | mileage | hr:min |
| --- | --- | --- |
| Bar Harbor, ME | 145 miles | 3:45 |
| Kennebunkport, ME | 45 miles | 1:00 |
| Ogunquit, ME | 51 miles | 1:10 |
| Portland, ME | 16 miles | 0:22 |
| Portsmouth, NH | 73 miles | 1:20 |

## AUGUSTA
Maine's capital city is small (population 22,000). Founded as a trading post in 1628, it was later abandoned, then resettled in 1724 at Fort Western (later Hallowell). Lumber, shingles, furs and fish were its early exports to the world, sent down the Kennebec River in sloops built right here. Augusta became Maine's capital in 1827, but was only chartered as a city in 1849.

Augustans do the work of running the government in this rural state, but for excitement, they head for Portland. But if you're passing by, stop for a look at the Maine State Museum, admire the state capitol and browse the antique shops in neighboring Hallowell.

### Orientation
Memorial Circle, near the state capitol, is this city's traffic nexus. (US 202, US 201, ME 11, ME 12, ME 27 and ME 1 all intersect in this large traffic circle.)

Augusta's traditional commercial district is just across the Kennebec River, on its east bank. Western Ave goes from Memorial Circle due west 1½ miles to I-95 exit 30; most of Augusta's motels are on Western Ave or west of the Interstate exit. Three miles northwest of the center, at I-95 exit 31, you'll find the University of Maine at Augusta, the Augusta Civic Center, the Mall at Augusta, the Kennebec Valley Chamber of Commerce and a couple more chain motels. Water St (US 201/ME 27) runs south from Memorial Circle, past the capitol, to Hallowell. With attractive shops, cafes and restaurants, Hallowell is virtually an appendage of Augusta.

### Information
You can call the office of the Kennebec Valley Chamber of Commerce (☎ 207-623-4559, www.augustamaine.com), University Drive (I-95 exit 31), Augusta, ME 04332-0192, with questions.

### Things to See
The granite **State House** was designed, as was Boston's, by Charles Bulfinch. It was built in 1832 and remodeled and enlarged in 1909 under the direction of another Boston architect, C Henri Desmond. Park in the lot on the southwest side of the building, near the Department of Education and Maine State Museum, enter the capitol through the southwest door and pick up a leaflet for a self-guided tour; or pick up a red courtesy phone and request a free guided tour (9 am to 1 pm weekdays).

You should have a look at the **Maine State Museum** (☎ 207-289-2301), in the Maine State Library and Archives, next to the State House on State St. The museum traces Maine's history through an astounding 12,000 years and includes prehistoric arrowheads and tools, as well as artifacts from more recent centuries. It's open 9 am to 5 pm weekdays, 10 am to 4 pm Saturday, 1 to 4 pm Sunday.

Located in its own riverside park, **Old Fort Western** (☎ 207-626-2385) is across the river. Originally built as a frontier outpost in 1754, the restored 16-room structure is now a museum. It is open 10 am to 4 pm daily during the summer. Admission is $5 for adults and $2.50 for children six to 16.

The **Blaine House** (☎ 207-287-2121), State St at Capitol St, in the city center, was once the family home of US presidential candidate James G Blaine. It's now Maine's governors' mansion, and is worth a look. Call for tour times.

### Places to Stay
Lodging prices are wonderfully low in this non-touristy town.

The *Motel 6* (☎ 207-622-0000, 18 Edison Drive) is the best value, with rooms for $38 single, $44 double; children 17 and under stay for free with their parents. The nearby *Super 8 Motel* (☎ 207-626-2888, fax 623-8468, 395 Western Ave) is similar, though a few dollars more expensive. The *Susse Chalet* (☎ 207-622-3776, fax 622-3778, 65 Whitten Rd), just up from the Sears shopping center, is also similar in price and amenities. It even has a small swimming pool.

The class act is the *Best Western Senator Inn & Conference Center* (☎ 207-622-5804, 800-528-1234, 284 Western Ave): Big, comfortable, luxurious rooms (there's even a TV and refrigerator in the bathrooms) are priced at $89 to $99 single, $99 to $119 double.

For more attractive surroundings, take I-95 exit 30 for US 202 West, then immediately turn left onto Whitten Rd and follow the signs to *Maple Hill Farm* (☎ 207-622-2708, 800-622-2708, fax 207-622-0655, www.maplebb.com), Outlet Rd, Hallowell. It is a late-Victorian B&B set upon 62 acres of rolling fields. Rooms have shared or private baths and cost $55 to $115 single, $65 to $125 double.

### Places to Eat
There's a cluster of fast-food chain restaurants at I-95 exit 30, and the motels here have restaurants serving formula food (except for the dining room at the Senator Inn). For more interesting food, cruise Water St (US 201/ME 27), south of the capitol, in Hallowell.

The motto at *Louise's Bakery* (☎ 207-623-9850, 345 Water St) is 'Get your buns in here!' No matter how good your buns may be, Louise's also serves good cakes, doughnuts, pastries, breakfast and lunch.

**MAINE**

*CJ's Pizza* (☎ 207-626-2906, *339 Water St*) serves the cheapest sandwiches, pasta plates and pizzas for $3.60 to $14.

At *Delirious Dave's* (☎ 207-621-4981, *130 Water St*), Hallowell, you 'build your own' sandwich by circling items on a menu slip. The cost is $4 and up – it depends on the number of items you choose. Build your own pizza the same way.

For fancier fare, *Slate's Restaurant & Bakery* (☎ 207-622-9575, *169 Water St*), Hallowell, has a cozy bar-lounge and lighter, airier dining rooms where you can order from an extensive, interesting menu: fish, quiche, sandwiches and crêpes for $6 to $12 at lunch, more at dinner; good vegetarian dishes, too.

### Getting There & Away
Augusta, 23 miles north of Wiscasset, is best visited on a day excursion, or while passing through along I-95. Colgan Air (☎ 207-623-1684, 800-272-5488) flies between Augusta and Boston. Greyhound buses stop at 312 Water St (US 201/ME 27).

# Midcoast Maine

The English first settled this region in 1607 (the same time as the Jamestown settlement in Virginia). The early settlers, however, returned to England within a year. British colonization resumed in 1620. After suffering the long years of the French and Indian wars, the area became the home of a thriving shipbuilding industry, a tradition that continues today.

Midcoast Maine is a region celebrated for its exceptional natural beauties and down-to-earth residents. You will find a dramatic coastline dotted with friendly seaside villages, thick pine forests and numerous opportunities for biking, hiking, sailing kayaking and other adventures.

## BRUNSWICK
Settled in 1628 and incorporated in 1738, Brunswick was named in honor of the British royal house. Today, the town is most famous as the home of highly regarded Bowdoin College.

A short drive through the city center reveals stately Federal and Greek Revival houses and mansions built by wealthy sea captains. At 63 Federal St, Harriet Beecher Stowe wrote *Uncle Tom's Cabin*. This story of a runaway slave, published in 1852, was hugely popular. The poignant story fired the imagination of people in the northern states, who saw the book as a powerful indictment against slavery. It was translated into numerous foreign languages.

Brunswick's green, called the Town Mall, is along Maine St. Farmer's markets are set up on Tuesday and Friday, and there are band concerts on Wednesday evenings in summer. In early August, the four-day Maine Arts Festival is held a short distance east of Brunswick in Cooks Corner at Thomas Point Beach.

### Orientation & Information
To one driving along US 1, the commercial center of Brunswick does not present a very attractive prospect. In fact, as the home of Bowdoin College, Brunswick is the cultural center for this part of the state. Turn off of US 1 onto aptly named Pleasant St for a completely different view of Brunswick.

The Brunswick Area Chamber of Commerce (☎ 207-725-8797, www.midcoastmaine.com), 59 Pleasant St, can provide you with a map and help you with a room reservation if you need one.

### Bowdoin College
Founded in 1794, Bowdoin is among the oldest colleges in the USA, and is the alma mater of Henry Wadsworth Longfellow, Nathaniel Hawthorne and US President Franklin Pierce. For general campus information, call ☎ 207-725-3375. For a campus tour, follow the signs from Maine St to Moulton Union.

Smith Union is the student center, with an information desk on the mezzanine level, as well as a cafe, pub, small convenience store, lounge and small art gallery. There's also the requisite bookstore where you can buy a

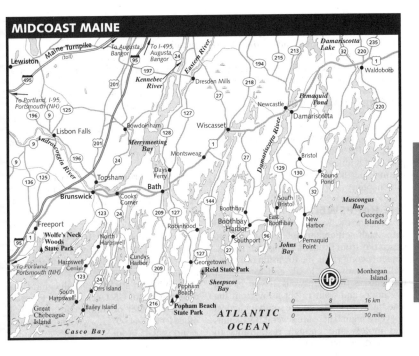

## MIDCOAST MAINE

sweatshirt, and a mailroom where you can get stamps and send off your letters. There's also a bulletin board with information on local events, concerts and potential inexpensive transportation: ride shares.

Among the sites to visit on campus is the Bowdoin College Museum of Art (☎ 207-725-3275), strong in the works of 19th- and 20th-century European and American painters. It is open 10 am to 5 pm Tuesday to Saturday, 2 to 5 pm on Sunday. Admission is free.

The Peary-MacMillan Arctic Museum (☎ 207-725-3416), in Hubbard Hall, holds memorabilia from the expeditions of Robert Edwin Peary and Donald Baxter MacMillan, Bowdoin alumni who were among the first explorers to reach the North Pole.

### Pejepscot Museums

Local history is preserved in the museums of the Pejepscot Historical Society.

The Pejepscot Museum (☎ 207-729-6606), 159 Park Row, has exhibits and displays old photographs of Brunswick, Topsham and Hartwell. The Skolfield-Whittier House, 161 Park Row, a grand 17-room brick mansion adjacent to the museum, is a virtual time capsule, having been closed up from 1925 to 1982. Even the receipts for the building's construction and the spices in the kitchen racks are authentic. The museum is open 9 am to 5 pm Tuesday to Friday (until 9 pm Thursday), 9 am to 4 pm Saturday. Admission is free.

The Joshua L Chamberlain Museum, 226 Maine St, holds artifacts from the late owner's eventful life as college professor, Civil War hero, president of Bowdoin College and four-term governor of Maine. The museum is open 10 am to 4 pm Tuesday to Saturday, June 1 to Columbus Day (second Monday in October).

## Entertainment

During the summer months, Bowdoin's Pickard Theater hosts the *Maine State Music Theater* (☎ 207-725-8769), a summer musical comedy series that runs eight performances a week, June through August.

## Getting There & Away

Brunswick is the point at which I-95 heads north and inland toward Augusta, Waterville and Bangor, and US 1 heads northeast along the coast. It's about 9 miles away from Freeport, and 8 miles from Bath. For bus information, see the Portland section, earlier in this chapter.

## THE HARPSWELLS

Several narrow, wooded peninsulas dotted with small settlements jut southward into Casco Bay from Brunswick. Together the settlements, comprising the township of Harpswell, are known to locals and to summer residents as the Harpswells. If you have a few hours and want to get away from the mad traffic on US 1, venture south for a meal or even a night. There are several B&Bs, inns and motels and enough restaurants to provide dependable sustenance.

Want to go the distance? Head all the way south on ME 24 to Bailey Island, reached from Orrs Island over a granite bridge (1927) that allows the tides to flow right through it.

The village dock on Bailey Island is a stop on the Casco Bay cruise circuit. It can be more crowded than one expects when the cruise boats are tied up for their lobster bakes. If you want a lobster lunch, try *Cook's Lobster Pound* (☎ 207-833-2818) on ME 24.

## BATH

In colonial times, the forested coasts of Maine were thick with tall trees just right for making masts for the king's navy. Indeed, for a time the king forbade anyone to cut the trees in Maine for anything else.

In 1607, the pinnace *Virginia*, one of the earliest vessels built by Europeans on this coast, was launched into the Kennebec River at Phippsburg, south of Bath. Later, the shipyards on the Kennebec turned to building coastal freighters, then tall clipper ships and grand multi-masted schooners.

Today, Bath continues the tradition by building steel frigates, cruisers and other navy craft at the Bath Iron Works (BIW), one of the largest and most active shipyards in the USA. The Maine Maritime Museum, south of the shipyard, is Bath's biggest attraction. The other half of town is the picturesque Historic District, with long stretches of 19th-century Victorian homes.

## Orientation & Information

The ironworks sprawls to the south of US 1. At 3:30 pm on weekdays, when the workshift changes at the ironworks, US 1 chokes with cars, and traffic throughout the town comes to a virtual halt. It's best to prepare for this, and be on your way past Bath by 3:15 pm, or be parked downtown for a walk around.

Bath has an attractive, small commercial district north of US 1, centered on Front St.

The chamber of commerce information office (☎ 207-443-9751, www.midcoastmaine.com) is at 45 Front St. It is open 8:30 am to 5 pm weekdays.

## Maine Maritime Museum & Shipyard

The Maine Maritime Museum (☎ 207-443-1316), 243 Washington St, south of the ironworks on the western bank of the Kennebec, preserves the Kennebec's long shipbuilding tradition.

In summer, the preserved 19th-century Percy & Small Shipyard still has boatwrights hard at work building wooden boats. The Maritime History Building holds paintings, models and hands-on exhibits that tell the tale of the last 400 years of maritime history. In the apprentice shop, boat builders restore and build wooden boats using traditional tools and methods.

In summer, there's a cruise boat called the *Hardy II* that takes visitors for a 50 minute ride on the Kennebec.

There's a play ship and picnic area, as well as the museum's Mariners' Fare restaurant. The museum is open 9:30 am to 5 pm daily.

Admission costs $8.50/5.75/25 for adults/ children/family; but the river cruise is not included in the price.

## Places to Stay

**Camping** The *Ocean View Park Campground* (☎ 207-389-2564), on ME 209 at Popham Beach, is south of Bath and at the end of the peninsula near Popham Beach State Park.

**B&Bs** Bath has a number of reasonably priced B&Bs in nice 19th-century houses.

*Packard House* (☎ 207-443-6069, 45 Pearl St), a late-18th-century Georgian house, charges $75 to $85 for double rooms with semi-private bath.

*The Fairhaven Inn* (☎ 207-443-4391, 118 N Bath Rd), near the Bath Country Club, is a bit out of the city center, set on spacious grounds. You pay $60 to $90 for a double with full breakfast.

Bath's most splendid B&B is simply called the *Inn at Bath* (☎ 207-443-4294, 969 Washington St). The early-19th-century Greek Revival home is in the heart of Bath's Historic District. Owner Nick Bayard, a former Wall St broker, has poured all of his profits into the nine elegant rooms and common spaces. Maybe it's his ancestry – the Bayards have been in America since the days of George Washington – that gives rise to Nick's impeccable taste for antiques. Rooms are priced from $85 to $165 (the two higher-end rooms have Jacuzzis).

The Federal style *1774 Inn* (☎ 207-389-1774), Phippsburg, is 4 miles south of Bath and 4 miles from the ocean. Five rooms, with private bath, cost $90 to $130.

South of Bath, and near three of Maine's loveliest midcoast beaches, is the *Edgewater Farm B&B* (☎ 207-389-1322), ME 216, Small Point. Six rooms, most with private bath ($75 to $130), are set in a restored 19th-century farmhouse. Many of the ingredients for their large country breakfasts come from their 4 acres of organic gardens.

## Places to Eat

*The Starlight Café* (☎ 207-443-3005, 15 Lambard St), across from the Custom House, has great homemade scones, muffins and other baked goods for breakfast.

Across from the Bath Iron Works is one of Bath's longtime favorites, *The Cabin* (☎ 207-443-6224, 552 Washington St). Sit down in one of the small wooden booths or outdoors at picnic tables during the summer, and order pizzas, pastas and affordably priced subs ($2 to $4).

For fine dining, head to *Kristina's* (☎ 207-442-8577, 160 Centre St), at the corner of High St. Once known only for their baked goods, the restaurant has expanded to offer reasonably priced seafood and steak dishes. This is also popular destination for Sunday brunch.

## Getting There & Away

For bus information, see the Portland Getting There & Away section, earlier in this chapter. Bath is 8 miles east of Brunswick and 10 miles southwest of Wiscasset.

## WISCASSET

'Welcome to Wiscasset, the Prettiest Village in Maine.' That's what the sign says as you enter Wiscasset from the west along US 1.

Other villages may dispute this claim, but certainly Wiscasset's history as a major shipbuilding port in the 19th century has left it with a legacy of exceptionally grand and beautiful houses.

Like Bath, Wiscasset was a shipbuilding and maritime trading center. Great four-masted schooners sailed down the Sheepscot River bound for England and the West Indies – a route known as the Triangle Trade. They carried items such as timber, molasses, rum, salt and salt fish. Two relics of Wiscasset's vanished maritime importance are the wrecked and weather-beaten hulks of the schooners *Hesper* and *Luther Little*. Built to haul lumber to Boston and bring coal back to Wiscasset, they ran aground in 1932 and have been slowly dissolving in the mud along the Sheepscot's west bank ever since.

Any town with lots of old houses is also bound to have a thriving antiques trade, and Wiscasset does. You can admire the houses and shops as you pass through along US 1, or better, stop for a meal or the night.

MAINE

## Orientation & Information

The village straddles US 1 and most of it is easily accessible on foot. If you're just passing through by car, you'll still get to see quite a bit of the village, as traffic is normally very slow in summer.

The Wiscasset Regional Business Association (☎ 207-882-4600), PO Box 150, Wiscasset, ME 04578, serves as the local chamber of commerce.

## Things to See

The **Old Jail Museum** (☎ 207-882-6817), on Federal St (ME 218 North) about a half mile north of US 1, is a hilltop structure of granite, brick and wood built in 1811 to house Wiscasset's rowdier citizens. It's now a museum open 11 am to 4 pm Tuesday to Sunday in July and August.

Wiscasset's grandest and best-situated mansion is **Castle Tucker** (☎ 207-882-7364), at High and Lee Sts, a five-minute uphill walk that starts opposite the Bailey Inn. Judge Silas Lee had the house built to resemble a mansion in Dunbar, Scotland. He moved into it in 1807, then moved on to that great mansion in the sky a mere seven years later. Acquired by Captain Richard Tucker in 1858, it is still owned by his descendants. The house commands beautiful views, which you can enjoy whether you tour the house or not. It's open 11 am to 4 pm Tuesday to Sunday in July and August, and open by request in June, September and October. Admission is $4.

On the way to Tucker Castle, stop at the **Musical Wonder House** (☎ 207-882-7163), 16-18 High St. An outstanding collection of antique music boxes, player pianos and early talking machines are displayed in period rooms. Guided tours are given 10 am to 5 pm daily, May 31 to October 15; the gift shop stays open until 6 pm.

The **Nickels-Sortwell House** (☎ 207-882-6218), on US 1 at the corner of Federal St (ME 218), just downhill from the Bailey Inn, is one of the town's finest Federal mansions (1807). It is open afternoons Wednesday to Sunday, June through September. Tours, given on the hour, start at noon; the last tour

is at 4 pm. Admission costs $4 for adults, $3.50 for seniors and $2 for children six to 12.

**Fort Edgecomb** (☎ 207-882-7157) is an octagonal wooden blockhouse built in 1808 to protect the valuable shipbuilding trade of Wiscasset. It sits a half mile south of the eastern end of the bridge that spans the Sheepscot River. Commanding the riverine approach to the town, the fort is now the area's prime picnic site ($1).

## Maine Coast Railroad

Rail service, both for freight and passengers, is slowly being restored on some sections of the old Maine Central Railroad that used to run along the coast from Portland to Rockland, with a spur up to Augusta.

The Maine Coast Railroad (☎ 207-882-8000, 800-795-5404, fax 207-563-5261) runs restored 1930s coaches that are hauled by a diesel locomotive from Wiscasset to Newcastle (40 minutes) and back (1½ hours). Trains depart Wiscasset at 11 am and 1 pm on weekends, late May through mid-June; 11 am, 1 and 3 pm daily in summer; 11 am and 1 pm daily, with an extra 3 pm train on weekends, early September through mid-October. Cost is $10 adults, $9 seniors, $5 children five to 14 and $25 for families. The station is at Wiscasset Harbor, at the southern end of the town.

## Places to Stay

Forty-three campsites are available for $16 to $22 at the ***DownEast Family Camping*** (☎ 207-882-5431). It is on ME 27, 4 miles north of Wiscasset.

***Wiscasset Motor Lodge*** (☎ 207-882-7137, 800-732-8168), on US 1, west of the city center, charges $50 to $70 for its comfy rooms and cottages. A light breakfast is included.

***Highnote B&B*** (☎ 207-882-9628, 36 Lee St) is one of the best-kept secrets on Maine's midcoast. For $65, you get a spacious room and shared bath in a Victorian home built in 1876. The price includes a European-style breakfast with fruits, meats, bread and homemade scones. It is within walking distance of all the major sites, antique shops and restaurants in Wiscasset. The name of the inn, by

Moose taking a dip in Baxter State Park, ME

Atlantic puffins, Machias Seal Island, ME

Breeching humpback whale, Maine coast

Harbour seal pup enjoying the beach, ME

One of Maine's 61 lighthouses, 'The Nubble Light' (Cape Neddick Lighthouse) is in York, ME.

A majestic windjammer sailing along the Maine coastline

The way to Footbridge Beach, Ogunquit, ME

Three salty dogs from Maine

the way, was inspired by the owner's occupation – an opera singer.

The *Edgecomb Inn* (☎ 207-882-6343) is on US 1 in Edgecomb. It is on the east side of the bridge and has inn rooms ($79 to $99), motor lodge suites ($99 to $119) and tidy little frame cottages ($79 to $89) in a pine grove overlooking the river.

The *Squire Tarbox Inn* (☎ 207-882-7693) is on Westport Island, 4 miles southwest of Wiscasset on US 1 and another 8 miles south on US 144. This rambling 18th-century farmhouse and carriage house, perched atop a hill not far from the ocean, feature 11 rooms, all with private bath. Rooms cost $112 to $179, including breakfast. If you want to add a five-course dinner for two at the inn, prices for rooms run from $174 to $241.

### Places to Eat

Open only in the summetime, *Red's Eats* (☎ 207-882-6128), on Main St at Water St, is a simple red take-out stand serving some of the tastiest lobster and clam rolls in Maine.

*Sarah's Café* (☎ 207-882-7504), in the center of town, on US 1 at Middle St, is known for its large sandwiches, homemade soups and pizza.

*Sea Basket* (☎ 207-882-6581), on US 1, 2 miles southwest of town, is the local lobster in-the-rough joint, featuring large bowls of lobster stew and buckets of fried clams and fried scallops.

*Le Garage* (☎ 207-882-5409), overlooking the wrecks of the wooden schooners *Hesper* and *Luther Little*, is perched at the end of Water St. This is the place for a filling, reasonably priced lunch ($5 to $10) or dinner ($10 to $25). Try the sautéed Maine shrimp with herbs and garlic ($14) or the finnan haddie (salt cod in a cream sauce). Come for lunch or dinner any day except Monday; Le Bar is open every day in summer.

### Getting There & Away

Wiscasset is 10 miles northeast from Bath, 7 miles west of Damariscotta, 13 miles north of Boothbay Harbor and 23 miles south of Augusta. For bus transport, see the Portland section.

## BOOTHBAY HARBOR

A beautiful little seafarers' town on a broad fjord-like harbor – that's Boothbay Harbor. Large, well-kept Victorian houses crown its many small hills, and a wooden footbridge ambles across the harbor to the far side.

From Wiscasset, cross the Sheepscot River on US 1, turn right onto ME 27 and head south to reach Boothbay Harbor.

Boothbay Harbor is a beautiful town, which is why in summer its narrow, winding, hilly streets are choked with cars and its sidewalks are thronged with visitors boarding boats for a coastal cruise or browsing Boothbay's boutiques.

It's definitely a walking town. After you've strolled the waterfront along Commercial St, and the business district along Todd and Townsend Aves, walk along McKown St to the top of McKown Hill for a fine view. Then, take the footbridge across the harbor to the town's East Side, where there are several huge seafood restaurants.

### Orientation

There are several towns with similar names, for example, Boothbay and East Boothbay. Boothbay Harbor is the largest and busiest. Follow ME 27 south to the town, which you will enter along Oak St (one way). Oak St runs into Commercial St, the main street.

Parking can be very difficult in the summer months. It's best to park farther out and shuttle (free) into the city center rather than get caught in the slow-moving river of cars that flood the narrow, hilly streets. You can catch the shuttle at the small mall on Townsend Ave.

### Information

The Boothbay Chamber of Commerce (☎ 207-633-4743, www.boothbayharbor.com), ME 27, Boothbay, ME 04537, maintains an information office on ME 27 in the town of Boothbay. A short distance to the south, along ME 27, is another office that's run by the Boothbay Harbor Region Chamber of Commerce (☎ 207-633-2353), PO Box 356, Boothbay Harbor, ME 04538. During the summer, it is open every day.

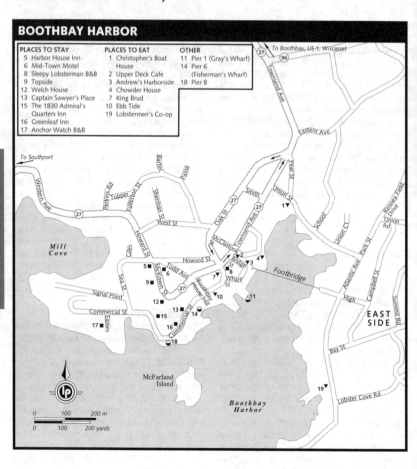

# BOOTHBAY HARBOR

**PLACES TO STAY**
5  Harbor House Inn
6  Mid-Town Motel
8  Sleepy Lobsterman B&B
9  Topside
12 Welch House
13 Captain Sawyer's Place
15 The 1830 Admiral's
   Quarters Inn
16 Greenleaf Inn
17 Anchor Watch B&B

**PLACES TO EAT**
1  Christopher's Boat
   House
2  Upper Deck Cafe
3  Andrew's Harborside
4  Chowder House
7  King Brud
10 Ebb Tide
19 Lobstermen's Co-op

**OTHER**
11 Pier 1 (Gray's Wharf)
14 Pier 6
   (Fisherman's Wharf)
18 Pier 8

## Boothbay Railway Village

On ME 27 in Boothbay, the Railway Village (☎ 207-633-4727) is an historical replica of a New England village. It has 27 buildings and a narrow-gauge (2-foot) steam train line running through it. This nonprofit educational park also has a collection of more than 60 antique steam- and gasoline-powered motor vehicles.

## Cruises

Boothbay's fine natural harbor features many possibilities for maritime excursions.

You can take a 2½-hour sail-powered cruise around the harbor aboard the 64-foot windjammer *Appledore* (☎ 207-633-6598) for $20 per person. There are four trips daily in summer that depart from Fisherman's Wharf.

The *Bay Lady* (☎ 207-633-2284, 800-298-2284) is a 31-foot friendship sloop, the kind of small sailboat once favored by lobstermen. The *Bay Lady* departs four times daily from Pier 8.

*Sylvania W. Beal* (☎ 207-633-1109) is an 84-foot windjammer that was built in Boothbay Harbor in 1911. The 2-hour trip costs $22 for adults, $14 for children.

Cap'n Fish's Boat Trips (☎ 207-633-3244, 633-2626), in the red ticket booth at Pier 1, sails a variety of routes along the coast and among the islands in search of whales, puffins, seals and other wildlife. Voyages last from one to three hours. And yes, the owner's name really is Cap'n Bob Fish.

Balmy Days Cruises (☎ 207-633-2284, 800-298-2284) will take you out to Monhegan Island (see Monhegan Island, later in this chapter) for a day's visit, leaving after breakfast and returning before supper, for $29 adult, $18 child. They also run one-hour harbor tours ($8.50 and $4.25), night lights tours and supper cruises, all from Pier 8.

## Places to Stay

Boothbay has campgrounds, motels, inns and B&Bs for every taste. Many places are only open from early May through mid-October, so call in advance at other times of the year.

**Camping** Several large campgrounds are north of Boothbay Harbor along ME 27. Most campgrounds in the area cater to gigantic land yachts in need of 30-amp electricity and metered LP gas hookups, but all accept tent campers as well.

*Little Ponderosa Campground* (☎ 207-633-2700), on ME 27, 6 miles north of Boothbay Harbor, has big open fields for games and 97 campsites ($17 to $23) among tall pine trees, as well as 30 sites along the shore. There's a shuttle bus from the campground into Boothbay Harbor.

Smaller and quieter is *Camper's Cove Campground* (☎ 207-633-5013), 3¼ miles west of Boothbay, with 56 sites on Back River Rd. *Gray Homestead* (☎ 207-633-4612), in Southport, south of Boothbay Harbor, has 40 oceanfront sites for $17 to $24.

**Motels** Boothbay and Boothbay Harbor also have many comfortable motels. Those on Townsend Ave (ME 27) north of the town are less expensive than the elaborate places on Atlantic Ave on the east side of the harbor.

*Mid-Town Motel* (☎ 207-633-2751) is a tidy place in the very center of town near the intersection of Todd Ave and McKown St. Open May through October, its simple but adequate rooms rent for $65 double.

*Seagate Motel* (☎ 207-633-3900, 800-633-1707, 124 Townsend Ave (ME 27)), at the north entrance to Boothbay Harbor, is well kept and in a fairly good location. Rooms have all the comforts, including refrigerators, and cost $80 to $90. Free trolley service is available to shuttle you to the city center, so you don't have to deal with the frightful parking (it stops in front of the motel).

The *Howard House B&B Motel* (☎ 207-633-3933, 633-6244), also on Townsend Ave, is modern, attractive, comfortable and reasonably priced at $65 to $82 double in summer, breakfast included.

**Inns & B&Bs** Boothbay Harbor has dozens of small inns and B&Bs. Some have only two or three rooms, others have up to a dozen. From mid-July through early September, reservations are a must. The chamber of commerce will help you with same-day reservations if you have trouble finding a room.

*Harbor House Inn* (☎ 207-633-2941, 44 McKown St), near the top of McKown Hill, is a homey place renting nine simple rooms for $55 to $90.

*Sleepy Lobsterman B&B* (☎ 207-633-5565, 57 Oak St) gets the best-name award. It's a nice old house, north of the Thistle Inn, charging $65 double for either of its two rooms with semi-private bath, or $80 for the queen-bed room with private bath. It's a pleasant five-minute walk to the city center.

Atop McKown Hill, *Topside* (☎ 207-633-5404) has unparalleled views of the town and the harbor. The 24 rooms, in the original sea captain's house or the adjoining motel, cost $45 to $150. All have private baths and refrigerators.

*Welch House* (☎ 207-633-3431, 36 McKown St) is another charming inn with fine views. Its 16 rooms with private baths cost $55 to $125.

*Captain Sawyer's Place* (☎ 207-633-2290, 87 Commercial St) is the big yellow house overlooking the harbor, right in the midst of

MAINE

everything. All rooms have private baths, and the captain's suite ($95) has its own deck. Rooms at the back without the sea view cost $60, those in the front cost $85.

Right next to Captain Sawyer's Place, the **Greenleaf Inn** (☎ *207-633-7346, 91 Commercial St)* has five recently refurbished rooms for $95 to $135.

Overlooking Commercial St and the harbor, **The 1830 Admiral's Quarters Inn** (☎ *207-633-2474, 105 Commercial St)* is a large quaint clapboard house on the side of McKown Hill. The house has six rooms that rent for $75 to $145.

**Anchor Watch B&B** (☎ *207-633-7565, 3 Eames Rd)* is in a superb location, at the western end of Commercial St, past Sea St, right out on Signal Point. It has four rooms for $75 to $135.

If you don't mind staying outside of town, there are several very fine choices.

The village of East Boothbay, 2 miles from Boothbay Harbor, is not as touristy or commercialized as Boothbay Harbor. It's a lot more like the real Maine. The **Linekin Bay B&B** (☎ *207-633-9900, 771 Ocean Point Rd)* is owned by an extremely amicable former police officer. The four rooms, including full breakfast and private bath, cost $69 to $149.

**Five Gables Inn** (☎ *207-633-4551, 800-451-5048,),* Murray Hill Rd, just off ME 96, is a 125-year-old summer hotel with wraparound porch and 15 rooms with private bath for $100 to $170, double, breakfast included.

The **Lawnmeer Inn** (☎ *207-633-2544, 800-633-7645)* is on Southport Island, southwest of Boothbay Harbor, via ME 27. The nice old inn, set on spacious lawns, is at the water's edge far away from the hustle and bustle of town. The 35 rooms cost $90 to $140 in summer and have private baths.

## Places to Eat

Most Boothbay Harbor restaurants are open from early May through mid-October.

**King Brud** has been selling hot dogs ($1) in the center of Boothbay Harbor for more than 50 years. In summer, you'll see his cart every day at the corner of McKown and Oak Sts. Veterans, ladies and others who ask politely may get a free autographed King Brud color picture postcard.

**Ebb Tide** (☎ *207-633-5692)*, on Commercial St, is always packed in the summer with locals and tourists. They're popular for their breakfasts, fish chowder ($5.95) and fresh peach shortcake ($4.95).

**Andrew's Harborside** (☎ *207-633-4704)*, just down Townsend Ave toward the footbridge, has country-style chicken pie for $10, scallops for $14, lots of sandwiches and great views of the traffic on the footbridge. If you'd rather have something lighter (and cheaper), the adjoining **Upper Deck Cafe** has a long sandwich and salad menu ($6 to $10) and some water views.

Walk down the hill and toward the footbridge, but before reaching the bridge, bear left through the parking lot to find the **Chowder House** (☎ *207-633-5761)*, fraught with nautical paraphernalia and serving gallons of its namesake daily. A simple chowder-based lunch can be had for about $5, a more elaborate tuck-in for three or four times as much.

**Christopher's Boat House** (☎ *207-633-6565, 25 Union St)* is Boothbay's best bistro, serving innovative seafood dishes and wood-fired meats in the $14 to $24 range. It's open for lunch and dinner.

There's no place like Maine for seafood dinners. On the east side of the bay, the **Lobstermen's Co-op** (☎ *207-633-4900)*, on Atlantic Ave, serves the traditional shore dinners of steamed soft-shell clams, boiled lobster and corn on the cob for $14 to $20, depending on the seasonal price of the catch. This is an informal place with lots of outdoor seating. For a full sit-down restaurant, also with outdoor tables, try the **Lobsterman's Wharf** (☎ *207-633-3443)*. It is on ME 96 in East Boothbay.

To experience the full nautical ambience, try **Cabbage Island Clambakes** (☎ *207-633-7200)*. You sail out of Boothbay Harbor from Pier 6 at Fisherman's Wharf aboard the motor vessel *Argo*. When you arrive at Cabbage Island, the captain and crew prepare a traditional clambake with steamed lobsters and clams, clam chowder, corn on the cob, onions and Maine potatoes, followed by Maine blueberry cake and coffee. The four hour voyages depart at 12:30 and 5 pm Monday through Saturday and 11:30 am and 1:30 pm Sunday from late June through early September. The cost is $37.50 per person, all included.

## Getting There & Away

Driving details for Boothbay Harbor are as follows:

| destination | mileage | hr:min |
|---|---|---|
| Bar Harbor, ME | 125 miles | 2:45 |
| Boston, MA | 167 miles | 4:00 |
| Camden, ME | 48 miles | 1:10 |
| Freeport, ME | 43 miles | 1:00 |
| Portland, ME | 59 miles | 1:20 |
| Wiscasset, ME | 13 miles | 0:25 |

## DAMARISCOTTA

Damariscotta is a pretty Maine town with numerous fine churches and an attractive downtown commercial district that serves the smaller towns and villages of the Pemaquid Peninsula to the south.

West of the town center, on US 1, is a tourist information center operated by the Damariscotta Region Information Bureau (☎ 207-563-3176). Follow US 1B ('Business') to reach the center of town. There's another tourism information office run by the Damariscotta Region Chamber of Commerce (☎ 207-563-8340, www.drcc.org) at the southern end of the town, just after ME 129/130 veers off to the right.

Try also the Maine Coast Book Shop (☎ 207-563-3207), which is on Main St, for additional information on the area.

## PEMAQUID PENINSULA

ME 130 goes south from Damariscotta through the heart of the Pemaquid Peninsula to Pemaquid Neck, the southernmost part of the peninsula. On the west side of Pemaquid Neck are Pemaquid Beach and Fort William Henry, a relic of the colonial period. At the southern tip of Pemaquid Neck is Pemaquid Point, one of the most picturesque locales in Maine.

### Pemaquid Beach & Trail

Yes! There are a few stretches of sand beach along this rockbound coast, and Pemaquid Beach is one of them. As ME 130 approaches Pemaquid Neck, watch for signs on the right (west) for Pemaquid Beach and make a right onto Huddle Rd (which turns into Snowball Hill Rd). The Pemaquid Trail, a paved dead-end road, heads south from Snowball Hill Rd just east of the Pemaquid Beach access road.

The beach is set in a park, and both are open in summer for a small fee. The water is usually very cold for swimming (this is Maine).

### Fort William Henry

A quarter mile north of Pemaquid Beach are the remains of Fort William Henry (☎ 207-677-2423), a reconstructed circular stone fort with commanding views (off to the left as you enter), many old foundations, an old burial ground with interesting tombstones, an archaeological dig and a small museum. The fort and museum are open 9 am to 5 pm daily, Memorial Day to Labor Day. Admission is $1 for adults, seniors free and 50¢ for children five to 11.

This area was well explored in the early 17th century. English explorers set foot on the Pemaquid Peninsula early in the 1600s, then Weymouth in 1605 and Popham in 1607. But France claimed the land as well, because the great Samuel de Champlain came here in 1605. Captain John Smith (English) came for a look in 1614. By the 1620s, there was a thriving settlement here with a Customs House.

The first fortress to be built, Fort Pemaquid was overcome and looted by pirates in 1632. In 1689, its replacement, Fort Charles, fell to the allied French and Indians. The fort was later restored and renamed Fort Frederick (1729). During the Revolutionary War, it was torn down. In 1908, it was partially rebuilt as a historic site and called Fort William Henry. The nearby Old Fort House was built about this time and still stands.

### Pemaquid Point

Along a 3500-mile coastline famed for its natural beauty, Pemaquid Point stands out because of its tortuous, grainy igneous rock formations pounded by restless, treacherous seas.

Perched atop the rocks in Lighthouse Park ($1 for adults, 50¢ for seniors) is the 11,000-candlepower Pemaquid Light, built in 1827. It's one of the 61 surviving lighthouses along the Maine coast, 52 of which are still in operation. The keeper's house now serves as the Fishermen's Museum at Pemaquid Point, open 10 am to 5 pm (11 am on Sunday); donations accepted. Lighthouse and fishing paraphernalia and photos are on display, as well as a nautical chart of the entire Maine coast with all the lighthouses marked.

By all means, take photographs here at Pemaquid. But also take a few minutes to fix the view in your mind, because no photo can do justice to its wild beauty. If you clamber over the rocks beneath the light, do so with great care. Big waves sweep in unexpectedly, and periodically, tourists are swept back out with them, ending their Maine vacations in a sudden, dramatic and fearfully permanent manner.

## Places to Stay & Eat

Near Pemaquid Beach is *Sherwood Forest Campsite & Log Cabins* (☎ 207-677-3642), New Harbor. It is on the Pemaquid Trail, about a quarter mile inland. Tent and RV sites cost $16 to $18. There's a swimming pool, and they'll sell you live lobsters and clams for your own private clambake.

On Pemaquid Point, the *Hotel Pemaquid* (☎ 207-677-2312), US 130, New Harbor, is a century-old frame hotel with a grand front porch, period guest rooms and housekeeping cottages priced from $55 to $125. It's just 100 yards from Lighthouse Park.

The *Bradley Inn* (☎ 207-677-2105, 800-942-5560, 3063 Bristol Rd), New Harbor, a few hundred yards inland, has 16 luxury rooms decorated with Victorian and nautical antiques. Rooms are priced $125 to $185, and there is a restaurant and pub.

If you need refreshments, the *Sea Gull Restaurant and Gift Shop* (☎ 207-677-2374) is right next to the lighthouse park, serving breakfast ($5), lunch ($15) and dinner ($15) with those same beautiful views.

## THOMASTON & PORT CLYDE

Once among the wealthiest communities in New England, Thomaston's wood shipbuilding business faded away with the coming of ironclad vessels. The town's stately homes, dating from the mid-19th century, have fallen into dowdiness, though it's still possible to imagine their former glory.

Just east of Thomaston, ME 131 goes south from US 1 to St George, Tenants Harbor and Port Clyde.

The village of Port Clyde is the mainland port for the Monhegan Boat Company's (☎ 207-372-8848) vessels out to Monhegan Island (see below).

## MONHEGAN ISLAND

This rocky outcrop off the Maine coast, due south of Port Clyde, is a popular destination for summer excursions. The small island (just 1½ miles long by a half mile wide) was known to Basque and Portuguese fishers and mariners before the English cruised these waters, but it came into its own as a summer resort in the early 19th century. When the cities of the eastern seaboard were sweltering in summer's heat, cool sea breezes bathed Monhegan and those fortunate enough to have taken refuge here. (Be sure to bring a sweater and windbreaker, as the voyage and the coast can be chilly even in August.)

Early in its history as a resort, Monhegan became popular with artists who admired its dramatic views and agreeable isolation. The island village is small and very limited in its services. The few unpaved roads are lined with stacks of lobster traps. This is definitely not a cutesy Manhattanized celebrities' island like Nantucket; rather, plain living, high thinking and traditional village life are the attractions here.

Adding to the island's Victorian charm is the near-total absence of motor vehicles. The island is really too small to need many cars; the ones it has for essential jobs are few and old. Thus, Monhegan is laid out for walking, with 17 miles of trails. Children, in particular, enjoy the southern tip of the island, with its wrecked ship rusting away, lots of rocks to climb and cairn-art (stacks of stones and driftwood made into fantasy sculptures). The views from the lighthouse are excellent, its little museum ($2) amusing.

The island's environments – natural, social and commercial – are fragile and thus subject to strict rules: smoking and fires are prohibited outside the village; and mountain biking is not allowed. In addition, all telephones require credit cards (there are no coin phones).

Unless you've made reservations well in advance at one of the island's few lodgings, you should not plan on finding a room upon arrival. Plan to take a day excursion from Port Clyde or Boothbay Harbor, and allow yourself at least a half day (four hours or more) to walk the trails over the rocks and around the shore. Stop at the **lighthouse** (1824) for a look at the museum in the keeper's former house.

Browse www.monhegan.com for more information

## Places to Stay

Accommodations are simple and basic; few rooms have private baths. To reserve by mail, send your letter to the lodging, Monhegan, ME 04852, and it'll get there.

The **Island Inn** (☎ 207-596-0371, www.midcoast.com/~islandin) is a typical Victorian mansard-roofed summer hotel with 45 small, simple rooms, eight of them with private bath. The big front porch offers marvelous views, and the dining room serves three meals a day. Also, full breakfast is included in the room rates of $98 to $210. Reserve early in the spring for dates in July and August.

**Monhegan House** (☎ 207-594-7983, 800-599-7983, fax 207-596-6472) has been a guest house since 1870. Its 32 rooms share the common bathroom facilities on the second floor, and cost $57 single, $90 double. The Monhegan House Café serves all three meals, featuring baked goods made fresh in the inn's kitchen. Meals are not included in the rates, so you can dine as you wish.

**The Trailing Yew** (☎ 207-596-0440) has been hosting guests in pretty much the same manner since 1926: 40 very simple guest rooms lighted by kerosene lamps, simple but nutritious meals served family style and prices of $65 per person, with both breakfast and dinner included.

**Shining Sails** (☎ 207-596-0041, fax 596-7166, PO Box 346) has fine ocean views from several of its seven rooms and kitchen-equipped apartments, all with private bath, priced $70 to $125 per night, breakfast included.

**Tribler Cottage** (☎ 207-594-2445) has one room with bath and four efficiency apartments (room with kitchen and bath) priced from $65 to $110 double. No meals are served.

**Hitchcock House** (☎ 207-594-8137), on Horn's Hill, has several rooms and small apartments with kitchens.

## Places to Eat

Right by the wharf is **The Barnacle Cafe & Bakery** (on your left as you leave the boat). The pasta and veggie salads are good here, as are the pies and pastries. It's open 8 am to 5 pm.

**The Periwinkle**, farther inland, has good, cheap, simple lunches, such as clam chowder and a grilled cheese sandwich, or grilled hummus and tomato sandwich and french fries, for $5 or $6. There's sheltered open-air seating. Across from it, **North End Pizza-NOT!** (☎ 207-594-5546) serves its namesake at umbrella-shaded picnic tables. The **Monhegan Store** sells picnic supplies.

**Monhegan House Cafe** (☎ 207-594-7983) features a daily blue plate special for about $15, including dessert and coffee; and huge sandwiches, such as their ½lb hamburger for about $6.

## Getting There & Away

**From Port Clyde** Monhegan Boat Line (☎ 207-372-8848, www.monheganboat.com) vessels to Monhegan Island depart Port Clyde, south of Thomaston, year round, with schedules and fares varying according to the season. You must make advance reservations to journey on these boats.

In high summer, boats depart Port Clyde at 7 and 10:30 am and 1:30 and 4:30 pm daily. Return trips depart Monhegan at 9 am, noon and 3 and 6 pm daily. The first voyage of the day takes 70 minutes, the later ones, in the

*Laura B*, take 50 minutes. The roundtrip fare is $25 for adults, $12 for children 12 and under. Parking in Port Clyde costs $4 per day.

**From New Harbor** During the warm months, the motor vessel *Hardy III* (☎ 207-677-2026, www.hardyboat.com) departs from New Harbor, on the east side of the Pemaquid Peninsula, at 9 am daily bound for Monhegan. It returns to New Harbor at 4 pm. The roundtrip fare is $26 for adults, $15 for children under 12; parking is free.

**From Boothbay Harbor** You can also visit Monhegan on a day excursion from Boothbay Harbor aboard one of the boats run by Balmy Days Cruises (☎ 207-633-2284, 800-298-2284, www.anchorwatch.com/balmy). See Cruises in the Boothbay section, earlier in this chapter.

# Acadia National Park Region

The best-known feature of the coastal area south of Bangor is Acadia National Park, the only US national park in New England. Acadia is the centerpiece of the 'Downeast' region, and it is quintessential Maine.

Penobscot Bay, to the west of Acadia, is world famous for its yachting ports: Camden, Rockport and Rockland, from which tall-masted windjammers take passengers on cruises of the beautiful coast. Blue Hill Bay and Frenchman Bay frame Mt Desert Island, a choice summer resort area for a century, and now the center of Acadia National Park.

To the east of Acadia, the coast of Downeast Maine is less traveled, but all the more scenic and unspoiled, all the way to the town of Lubec, where the USA meets New Brunswick, Canada.

## ROCKLAND

Rockland is the birthplace of poet Edna St Vincent Millay (1892-1950), who grew up in neighboring Camden. Today, Rockland is,

along with Camden, at the center of Maine's very busy windjammer sailing business. In the summer, windjammers, the tall-masted sailing ships descended from those long built on these shores, cruise up and down the Maine coast to the delight of their paying passengers. For details on windjammer cruises and places to stay in the area, see the Camden section, below.

### Farnsworth Art Museum
Rockland is also famous for its Farnsworth Art Museum (☎ 207-596-6457), on Elm St, one of the best small regional museums in the country. Its collection of 5000 works is especially strong in landscape and marine artists who have worked in Maine, such as NC, Andrew and Jamie Wyeth; Louise Nevelson; Rockwell Kent; John Marin; and others. The museum is open 10 am to 5 pm (1 to 5 pm Sunday) daily in summer; closed on Monday off-season.

### Places to Stay & Eat
*The Lime Rock Inn* (☎ 207-594-2257, 800-546-3762, 96 Limerock St) is an eight-room mansion built in 1890 for a local congressman. Now decorated with the finest mahogany furniture, rugs and king-size beds the owners could find, the rooms cost $95 to $185, including breakfast.

*Jessica's* (☎ 207-596-0770, 2 South Main St (US 73)) is one of the finest restaurants in the state. Set in a Victorian home, this European bistro features creative veal, lamb and seafood dishes that are in the $15 to $22 price range.

### Getting There & Away
**Air** Rockland is served by Continental Connection, operated by Colgan Air (☎ 207-596-7604, 800-272-5488), via its route from Boston to Bar Harbor.

**Bus** Concord Trailways (☎ 800-639-3317) runs buses from Boston and Logan Airport to Rockland via Portland (terminating at the Maine State Ferry Service docks for boats to Vinalhaven). The trip from Boston to Rockland takes 4½ hours.

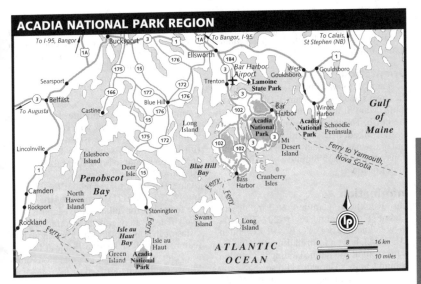

ACADIA NATIONAL PARK REGION

**Car** Driving details for Rockland are as follows:

| destination | mileage | hr:min |
|---|---|---|
| Camden, ME | 8 miles | 0:15 |
| Damariscotta, ME | 26 miles | 0:40 |
| Port Clyde, ME | 19 miles | 0:45 |
| Portland, ME | 81 miles | 2:00 |

**Boat** Rockland is the port for the Maine State Ferry Service (☎ 207-596-2203) to the islands of Vinalhaven and North Haven. Ferries depart Rockland three times daily year round on the one-hour trip to North Haven. For Vinalhaven, boats depart six times daily, April through October, with at least three boats daily at other times of the year.

## CAMDEN

Camden and its picture-perfect harbor, shadowed by the mountains of Camden Hills State Park, is one of the prettiest sites in the state. Home to Maine's large and justly famed fleet of windjammers (sailing ships), Camden continues its historic close links with the sea. Most vacationers come to sail on their boats, or on somebody else's boats, or just to look at boats. But Camden is popular with landlubbers too, who come into town to shop and dine at its excellent seafood restaurants. Camden Hills State Park, adjoining the town to the north, has hiking, picnicking and camping.

Like many communities along the Maine coast, Camden has a long history of shipbuilding. The mammoth six-masted schooner *George W Wells* was built here, setting the world record for the most masts on a sailing ship.

Camden was the girlhood home of Edna St Vincent Millay (1892-1950), who was one of America's most popular poets during the first half of the 20th century. Camden figures in some of the poet's work, as in these lines from 'Renascence':

All I could see from where I stood
Was three long mountains and a wood;
I turned and looked another way,
and saw three islands in a bay.

Alas, beauty comes at a price. The cost of Camden's lodgings and food during the summer are higher than in less posh Maine communities.

## Orientation

US 1 snakes its way through Camden, and is the town's main street, named Elm St to the south, Main St in the center and High St to the north. Though the downtown section is easily walked, it is several miles from one end of town to the other. Some accommodations are up to a 15 minutes' walk from the center of town.

## Information

The Rockport, Camden & Lincolnville Chamber of Commerce (☎ 207-236-4404, www.camdenme.org), PO Box 919, Camden, ME 04843, has an information office on the waterfront at the public landing in Camden, behind Cappy's Chowder House.

The Owl & Turtle Bookshop (☎ 207-236-4769), 8 Bayview St, is the place to stop for books.

## Camden Hills State Park

Far less crowded than Acadia National Park, Camden Hills State Park has its own set of mountains along the sea, offering some exquisite views of Penobscot Bay. The entrance is just over 1½ miles northeast of Camden center on US 1. The park has an extensive system of well-marked hiking trails, from the half-mile, 45-minute climb up Mt Battie to the 3-mile, two-hour Ski Shelter Trail.

Admission to the park costs $2 for adults, 50¢ for children five to 12. Simple trail maps are available at the park entrance. The picnic area is on the south side of US 1, with short trails down to the shore.

## Sea Kayaking

To cruise the coast at your own speed, contact the Mt Pleasant Canoe & Kayak Co (☎ 207-785-4309), in West Rockport. The outfit offers guided sea-kayaking trips for $45 a half day, $80 a day and $25 for a sunset paddle.

Ducktrap Sea Kayak Tours (☎ 207-236-8608), on US 1 in Lincolnville Beach, will take you on a 2½-hour coastal tour in a sea kayak for $25-$30 per person. They also offer custom-tailored full-day trips. Call for reservations.

## Bicycling

From Camden, it's a 5-minute drive to Lincolnville Beach where you catch the 20-minute ferry ride to the island of Islesboro (for Islesboro ferry schedule, call ☎ 207-789-5611). You'll want to bring your bike, because Islesboro is one of finest places to ride in Maine. Rentals are available at the Spouter Inn (☎ 207-789-5171), across the street from the ferry; $15 for full day. The island is relatively flat, yet hilly enough to offer majestic vistas of Penobscot Bay and long enough to feature a 28-mile bike loop. Picnic at Pendleton Point, where harbor seals and loons often lounge on the long, striated rocks.

## Cruises

Camden is at the center of windjammer cruise country. Many boats dock at Rockport and Rockland as well. Cruise itineraries vary with the ship, the weather and the length of the cruise.

Daysailers are windjammers that take passengers out for two- to four-hour cruises in Penobscot Bay. Usually you can book your place on a daysailer the same day, even the same hour. The following boats depart from Camden's Town Landing or adjoining Sharp's Wharf (across from the Chamber of Commerce:

*Appledore* (☎ 207-236-8353) $20 per adult for two hours

*Olad* (☎ 207-236-2323) $20 per adult, $10 for children six to 12, for a two-hour sail

*Surprise* (☎ 207-236-4687) $25 per adult, includes snacks; no children under 12 accepted

If you don't want to go out on a windjammer, you can take a two-hour lobster-fishing trip on the *Lively Lady Too* (☎ 207-236-6672), for $20 ($5 for children under 15), from Sharp's Wharf.

For overnight adventures, there are a few boats out of Rockland, such as the schooner *Wendameen* (☎ 207-594-1751, www.midcoast .com/wendameen), that take passengers cruising for a day and a night. The cost is $160 per person, all meals included, for this good taste of a Maine coastal cruise.

Longer cruises last from three to six days. Many six-day cruises visit points along the Maine coast from Boothbay Harbor in the southwest to Mt Desert Island (Acadia National Park) in the northeast. Stops may be made at Stonington, at the tip of Deer Isle; at the village of Castine; at various small islands offshore and at points in and around Acadia National Park.

Three-day cruises cover less of the coast, but are still delightful. Many three- to six-day cruises are priced $300 to $700 per person, accommodations and all meals on board included.

Reservations are a must for overnight cruises. For information on the vessels available, call the numbers on the next page.

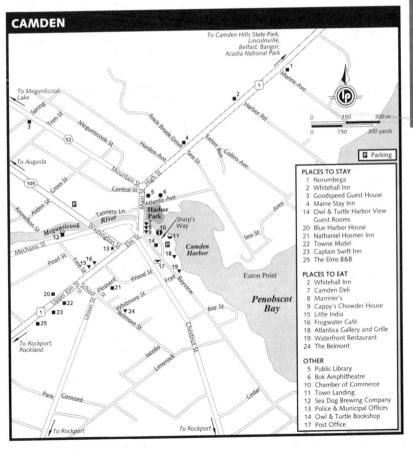

**CAMDEN**

To Camden Hills State Park,
Lincolnville,
Belfast, Bangor,
Acadia National Park

To Megunticook Lake

To Augusta

To Rockport, Rockland

To Rockport

To Rockport

*Penobscot Bay*

Eaton Point

Camden Harbor

Harbor Park

Megunticook River

**P** Parking

**PLACES TO STAY**
1 Norumbega
2 Whitehall Inn
3 Goodspeed Guest House
4 Maine Stay Inn
14 Owl & Turtle Harbor View Guest Rooms
20 Blue Harbor House
21 Nathaniel Hosmer Inn
22 Towne Motel
23 Captain Swift Inn
25 The Elms B&B

**PLACES TO EAT**
2 Whitehall Inn
7 Camden Deli
8 Marriner's
9 Cappy's Chowder House
15 Little India
16 Frogwater Café
18 Atlantica Gallery and Grille
19 Waterfront Restaurant
24 The Belmont

**OTHER**
5 Public Library
6 Bok Amphitheatre
10 Chamber of Commerce
11 Town Landing
12 Sea Dog Brewing Company
13 Police & Municipal Offices
14 Owl & Turtle Bookshop
17 Post Office

Maine Windjammer Association
(☎ 207-374-2955, 800-807-9463,
fax 207-374-5272,
www.midcoast.com/~sailmwa)
PO Box 1144, Blue Hill, ME 04614

North End Shipyard Schooners
(☎ 207-594-8007, 800-648-4544,
fax 207-594-8015)
PO Box 482, Rockland, ME 04841

Windjammer Wharf
(☎ 800-999-7352)
PO Box 1050, Rockland, ME 04841

## Places to Stay

**Camping** *Camden Hills State Park* (☎ 207-236-3109) has a camping area with hot showers, flush toilets and 112 forested tent and RV sites (no hookups) for $15 each. Reservations are advised for high summer. A few sites cannot be reserved and are held on a first-come, first-served basis. Plan to arrive by noon to claim one.

If the park is full (as it often is), try *Megunticook by the Sea* (☎ 207-594-2428, 800-884-2428), 3 miles south of Camden off US 1, which rents sites on the coast for $16 to $22. There's also *Camden Rockport Campground* (☎ 207-236-2498), 2 miles west of Rockport on ME 90, charging $16 to $24 for a site.

*Old Massachusetts Homestead Campground* (☎ 207-789-5135), at Lincolnville Beach, is 7 miles north of Camden on US 1. The 60-acre forested site includes rental cabins with decks and private baths, as well as 68 sites for tents and RVs starting at $19.

Farther to the north, *Searsport Shores Camping Resort* (☎/fax 207-548-6059), a mile south of Searsport on US 1, has 100 RV sites in a waterfront location. Rates range from $15 for a tent site to $29 for a humongous motor home site.

**Motels & Hotels** Most of the area's motels are along US 1. There's a large concentration in Lincolnville Beach, the next town to the north of Camden. Rates range from $30 for the cheapest places off-season to about $100 for the choicest rooms in-season.

*Birchwood Motel & Cottages* (☎ 207-236-4204), Belfast Rd (US 1)), north of Camden, has 15 motel rooms for $70.

*Towne Motel* (☎ 207-236-3377, 68 Elm St), has 19 rooms priced $89 to $99, light breakfast included, right in the center of town.

The *Strawberry Hill Motor Inn* (☎ 207-594-5462, 800-589-4009, 886 Commercial St (US 1)), Rockport, is set on a hillside with wonderful views of the sea. The 20 rooms are $50 to $105.

There are several good motels north of Camden, on the less commercial stretch of US 1 to Lincolnville Beach. *Sunrise Motor Court* (☎ 207-236-3191), on US 1, is just a mile from Lincoln Beach. All of the 13 cottages have bay views and cost just $40 to $69. *High Tide Inn* (☎ 207-236-3724, 800-778-7068), on US 1, has an assortment of accommodations from cottages to hotel units to a house. Cost ranges from $65 to $175, including breakfast and use of the beach.

**Inns & B&Bs** Camden has over 100 places to stay, most of them small inns or B&Bs, with prices ranging from $75 to over $300 for a double room. If you want help in making reservations, call Camden Accommodations & Reservations (☎ 207-236-6090, 800-236-1920), PO Box 858, Camden, ME 04843. Like travel agents, they don't charge you for this service; the inns and hotels pay a commission to Camden Accommodations.

*Goodspeed Guest House* (☎ 207-236-8077, 60 Mountain St (ME 52)), a half mile uphill from the city center, has eight nicely decorated rooms, six with bath, for $55 to $95, breakfast included.

*Owl & Turtle Harbor View Guest Rooms* (☎ 207-236-9014, 8 Bayview St), above the Owl & Turtle Bookstore, has three rooms overlooking the harbor, for $90 to $105, with bath. This is a great deal.

Elm St (US 1), just south of the city center, has a number of nice B&Bs.

*Captain Swift Inn* (☎ 207-236-8113, 72 Elm St) is an 1810 Federal house with four rooms, all with bath, for $85 to $110, breakfast included.

*Blue Harbor House* (☎ 207-236-3196, 800-2348-3196, 67 Elm St) is a cozy New England Cape Cod-style house built in 1810 with 10 guest rooms, all with private baths, for $85 to $145, breakfast included.

## All about Windjammers

**Windjammer Facts** A windjammer is an ocean-going sailing ship such as a schooner, ketch or yacht, usually 60 to 135 feet in length, with two or three masts. These graceful vessels crowd the coves and harbors around Rockland, Rockport and Camden in summer, waiting for passengers for cruises. They are sometimes joined by several motor-powered yachts that, though not windjammers, make for comparable cruises.

A windjammer normally sleeps between 20 and 45 passengers in single, double, triple and quad cabins. Many have sinks with hot and cold water. Showers are usually shared.

Passengers dine aboard, and the prices for cruises usually include all three meals. Often, one of these meals is a traditional clambake or lobster bake on a coastal island.

Seasickness is rarely a problem on windjammer cruises, as the ships sail mostly in protected waters and do not encounter the heavy wave action of the high seas.

Windjammers welcome passengers of all ages, except for young children. Usually a child must be at least 10 or 12 years of age to sail on a cruise.

**When to Cruise** The cruising season actually starts on Memorial Day weekend (last weekend in May), and it continues right through the autumn foliage season.

The month of **June** is good because the days are very long, the harbors uncrowded, the fog rare and light and the rates are low. However, days can be cool and nights even chillier. Forget swimming, unless you're a polar bear.

**July** is warmer, with daytime temperatures in the 70s; cruise rates are highest in July and August.

In **August**, the sea water gets as warm as it's going to, as does the air. Rates are at their highest and ports at their busiest, but while city dwellers are sweltering, cruisers are cool and happy.

After early **September**, the coastline begins to show signs of autumn color. Days are shorter, rates are lower and the crowds have gone. With luck, the weather in early September can be as good as it is in August.

In **October**, you can count on the shortest days, the coolest weather and the coldest water, but the upside is that you will have the best foliage color and lowest rates of the season. The season usually ends after the Columbus Day weekend in mid-October.

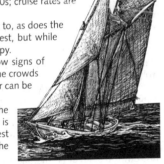

---

***The Elms B&B*** (☎ *207-236-6250, 84 Elm St*), built in 1806, has six rooms with bath and breakfast for $85 to $95.

***Maine Stay Inn*** (☎ *207-236-9636, 22 High St*) is a fine Greek Revival house and carriage house. The eight guest rooms, six with bath, cost $75 to $140, with full breakfast included.

***Nathaniel Hosmer Inn*** (☎ *207-236-4012, 800-423-4012, 4 Pleasant St*) is a block off the main street in a quiet residential neighborhood. The seven rooms, with bath, rent for $95 to $125, full breakfast included.

***Whitehall Inn*** (☎ *207-236-3391, 800-789-6565, 52 High St*) has an traditional, proper New England ambience behind the Ionic columns on its broad front porch. Most of the 50 rooms in the main inn, the Maine House and the Wicker House have private baths and are priced $75 to $170. Breakfast and dinner are served in the elegant dining room.

Luxury accommodations in a coastal setting are available at the **Inn at Oceans Edge** (☎ *207-236-0945*), on US 1. Nestled among 7 oceanfront acres of gardens and woods, just five minutes north of downtown Camden, the owners couldn't have chosen a better spot. The inn features 15 spacious rooms, 14 with waterfront views, two-person Jacuzzis, fireplaces and four-poster king-size beds. Rooms are priced $220 to $250, including breakfast outside on the deck.

A listing of Camden lodgings would not be complete without a mention of **Norumbega** (☎ *207-236-4646, 61 High St*), a fantastic, castlelike stone Victorian mansion with 13 rooms renting for $185 to $450. The inn's brochure uses such words as 'exceptional,' 'sumptuous' and 'magnificent,' which, for the prices, it should be – and is.

## Places to Eat

As with its lodgings, so it is with its restaurants: Camden prices tend to be higher than in most other towns.

Many places in Maine bill themselves as 'the place for chowder,' but **Cappy's Chowder House** (☎ *207-236-2254, 1 Main St*), at Bayview St, right in the very center of town, is probably telling the truth. A huge mug of thick, creamy chowder, chock-full of clams and potatoes, is served with a buttermilk biscuit for $4.95. The long menu lists just about everything, from sandwiches and light meals to hearty tuck-ins, but go with their namesake.

Just down the street, in the midst of the shopping district, is **Marriner's** (☎ *207-236-2647, 35 Main St*), an old-fashioned, inexpensive lunchroom serving a big plate of fish and chips for $6, a bowl of chili with biscuits and salad for $5 and a huge plate of fried clams with potato, salad, bread and butter for $10.

For a picnic down by the water or atop Mt Battie, pick up a substantial sandwich at the **Camden Deli** (☎ *207-236-8343, 37 Main St*). Sandwiches are priced $3.60 to $6; there are several vegetarian choices.

The chef at **Frogwater Café** (☎ *207-236-8998, 31 Elm St*) likes to use local produce to create venison stews, salmon filets and

Caesar salads. Main dishes, including soup and salad, are reasonably priced at $6.95 to $14.95. They're open for lunch and dinner.

If you're in the mood for curry, **Little India** (☎ *207-230-0434, 31 Elm St*) is next door. Lunch specials, served with *nan* (flat bread), cost $3.95 to $5.95.

**Atlantica Gallery and Grille** (☎ *207-236-6019, 1 Bayview Landing*) is right on the water with good views of the bay. Its international fare includes a Thai-peanut curry with vegetables or seafood Provençale. A dinner for two will cost $30 to $40. The restaurant also has a good children's menu.

**Waterfront Restaurant** (☎ *207-236-3747*), on Bayview, has atmospheric waterfront dining rooms and a spacious deck right next to the boats. Try the *salade niçoise* ($8) for a light lunch, or the Penobscot Bay seafood platter (including clams, crabs and lobster) for $16. There's a raw bar for fresh clams and oysters as well. Lunch is served 11:30 am to 2:30 pm; dinner 5 to 10 pm.

For every type of lobster imaginable, steamers, shrimp, fish and all the other critters in the sea, head to the large **Lobster Pound Restaurant** (☎ *207-789-5550*), US 1, Lincolnville Beach. It's perfectly placed on the shores of the Atlantic. Lobsters start at $11.75.

Several of Camden's inns have fine dining rooms serving fancy fare. Try the **Whitehall Inn** (☎ *207-236-3391, 800-789-6565, 52 High St*) for an excellent dinner in formal surroundings. Meals cost $30 to $60 per person. There is also Jerry Clare's **The Belmont** (☎ *207-236-8053, 6 Belmont Ave*), serving its 'late 20th-century cuisine in late 19th-century surroundings.'

## Entertainment

The **Sea Dog Brewing Company** (☎ *207-236-6863, 43 Mechanic St*), inside the Knox Mill, is a spacious restaurant/pub/nightspot serving sophisticated bar food ($5 to $10) and locally made beer and brown and pale ales. One lofty wall, all glass, looks out on the crashing waterfall of the old mill race. This is one of Camden's coolest places to see and be seen.

## Getting There & Away

Driving details for Camden are as follows:

| destination | mileage | hr:min |
|---|---|---|
| Bangor, ME | 53 miles | 1:15 |
| Bar Harbor, ME | 77 miles | 1:45 |
| Boothbay, ME | 48 miles | 1:10 |
| Boston, MA | 195 miles | 4:00 |
| Portland, ME | 85 miles | 2:00 |

## BELFAST & SEARSPORT

North of Camden, near Belfast and Searsport, motels, campgrounds, restaurants, antique shops and flea markets dot the road, providing dining, lodging and shopping opportunities. The establishments along here are considerably cheaper, and more likely to have vacancies in high summer, than comparable tourist meccas such as Camden, Blue Hill and Bar Harbor.

For example, *The Penobscot Bay Hostel (☎ 207-548-2506, 132 West Main St)*, Searsport, has 10 beds available for $15 each. The Penobscot Museum is nearby and the hostel often has lectures on area history, lighthouses and astronomy.

If you're looking for a bite to eat in Belfast, you won't be disappointed with *Darby's (☎ 207-338-2339, 105 High St)*. The eclectic menu at this reasonably priced restaurant and pub features everything from pad Thai to fish and chips to Moroccan lamb. Wash it down with a local microbrew beer.

## BUCKSPORT

A crossroads for highways and rail lines, Bucksport is a workaday town with light industry and a big Champion paper mill. Look a little closer and you'll also find an artsy community, somewhat similar to Brattleboro in Vermont. There are numerous motels, restaurants and other services. The Bucksport Chamber of Commerce has an information office (☎ 207-469-6818) next to the municipal offices in the center of town.

### Fort Knox

Just out of town, on ME 174 just north of the bridge, on the west side of the river, is the Fort Knox State Historic Site (☎ 207-469-7719). This huge granite fortress dominating the Penobscot River narrows comes as a surprise in peaceable rural Maine, but only until you learn the spot's history.

This part of the Penobscot River Valley was the riverine gateway to Bangor, the commercial heart of Maine's rich timber industry. It was held by the British in the Revolutionary War and the War of 1812.

In 1839, it appeared that the US and the UK might once again go to war over the disputed boundary between Maine and New Brunswick, and the US government feared that Bangor might once again fall into British hands. To protect the river approach to Bangor, construction was begun on Fort Knox in July 1844. Work continued for almost a decade.

The elaborate fortress mounted 64 cannons, with an additional 69 defending the outer perimeter. Though it was garrisoned from 1863 to 1866 during the Civil War, and in 1898 during the Spanish-American War, it never had to use its firepower. Fort Knox was either a great waste of money or an effective deterrent, depending on your point of view.

Like so many of the world's elaborate military constructions, it is now a tourist attraction, open 9 am to sunset in summer and to 6:30 pm in spring and autumn. Admission costs $2 for adults, 50¢ for children five to 11 and is free for toddlers and those 65-plus. Bring a flashlight if you plan a close examination, as the fort's granite chambers are unlit. There's a nice picnic area outside the admissions gate.

## CASTINE

At Orland, a few miles east of Bucksport along US 1, ME 175/166 goes south to the dignified and historic seaside village of Castine. Following an eventful history, Castine today is charming, quiet and refreshingly off the beaten track. It's the home of the Maine Maritime Academy and its big training ship, the *State of Maine* (1952), which you can visit.

Both Castine and Blue Hill are good places to get the feel of pre-tourist boom Maine – these are gorgeous villages with none of the kitsch you might stumble across in Boothbay or Bar Harbor.

## History

It was the great French explorer Samuel de Champlain who, in 1604, first mapped the peninsula, then called Pentagoët.

His countryman, Sieur Claude de Turgis de la Tour, founded Fort Pentagoët here in 1613. His goal was to trade with the Tarratine Indians of the region, which he did until the English came and conquered this part of the Maine coast in 1628, renaming Pentagoët as Majabagaduce. The village was back in French hands in 1635, put there by treaty, but would change hands many times between then and 1674, when the Dutch took it for two years.

In 1676, Jean Vincente d'Abbadie de St Castin, the second son of a French nobleman, claimed the land after military service in Quebec and reopened the trading station. He maintained excellent relations with the Native Americans, moving upriver to live with them and marrying the daughter of the Tartan Sagamore Madockawando. Castin returned to France in 1701 to claim the baronial title left vacant by his older brother's death.

By 1760, however, the British ruled throughout these former French lands, and 'Castin's Fort' was in their hands.

During the Revolutionary War, Majabagaduce's citizens were split between those loyal to the British crown and those supporting the American cause. In 1779, a British naval force from Nova Scotia occupied the town and built a fortress, taunting the Americans by naming it Fort George, after the King George III. They hoped to force the fledgling USA to set its northern boundary here, at the Penobscot River, leaving eastern Maine to the Crown.

Rising to the challenge, the Great and General Court (legislature) of the Commonwealth of Massachusetts, which then controlled Maine, outfitted an expedition force at the enormous cost of $8 million and sent it off to take Fort George. Bad leadership and bad luck doomed the expeditionary force to ignominious defeat,

and the Commonwealth to near-bankruptcy. The Brits held on.

What bullets could not claim, diplomacy gained, however. The Treaty of Paris that ended the Revolutionary War set the boundary at the St Stephen River, where it remains. The Crown's zealously loyal Bagaducians became rebel Americans. So distasteful was this prospect that many loyalists put their houses onto rafts and sailed them to New Brunswick, plunking their homes down safely in British Canada. (A few of these houses still exist in and near St Andrews, New Brunswick, Canada.)

In 1796, Majabagaduce became Castine, and in 1814, during the War of 1812, British forces occupied it yet again, though there was little military action. They left in April 1815, and Castine set to work once more as a farming and shipbuilding town.

## Orientation & Information

Castine, at the southern end of ME 166, is small enough to be walked easily. A free map entitled *A Walking Tour of Castine* is readily available at establishments in town.

## Castine's Forts

After such an embattled history, you'd expect Castine to have old forts, but there are no great stone citadels like Fort Knox at Bucksport. Rather, the forts in Castine are low earthworks, now parklike and planted with grass.

Close to the Maine Maritime Academy campus, **Fort George** is near the upper (northern) end of Main St where it meets Battle Ave and Wadsworth Cove Rd. **Fort Pentagoët** is on Perkins Rd at Tarratine St. The American **Fort Madison** (earlier Fort Porter, 1808) is farther west along Perkins St, opposite Madockawando St.

Take a look also at the **Wilson Museum** on Perkins St near Fort Pentagoët. It holds a good collection of Native American artifacts, historic tools and farm equipment and other relics from Maine's past.

## Places to Stay

The *Castine Inn* (☎ 207-326-4365), on Main St, is a 20-room Victorian summer hotel that is beautifully maintained as an inn. Rooms with private bath cost $85 to $135, full breakfast included. From July through early September, you must stay at least two nights.

*The Pentagoët Inn (☎ 207-326-8616, 800-845-1701)*, on the other side of Main St, has 16 rooms with bath at similar rates. Other gracious inns include *The Castine Harbor Lodge (☎ 207-326-4335)* on Perkins St. The 15 rooms go for $65 to $125. *The Village Inn (☎ 207-326-9510)*, Main St at Water St, has four rooms for $65 to $85.

### Getting There & Away
Castine is 18 miles south of US 1 at Orland; 56 miles northeast of Camden; 23 miles west of Blue Hill; and 56 miles west of Bar Harbor.

## BLUE HILL
Blue Hill is a dignified, small Maine coastal town with tall trees, old houses and lots of culture. Many outstanding handicrafts artisans live and work here, and a summer chamber music series draws fine musicians.

### Orientation & Information
Blue Hill, at the junction of ME 15, ME 172, ME 175, ME 176 and ME 177, is small enough for easy walking, with a few inns, a few restaurants, a few antique stores and lots of lofty trees. You can tour Blue Hill on foot in 1½ or two hours, as you wish, though a few inns and restaurants are on the outskirts.

The Blue Hill Chamber of Commerce (no ☎), PO Box 520, Blue Hill, ME 04614, issues a map available for free at establishments in town.

### Special Events
From early July through mid-August, the annual Kneisel Hall Chamber Music Festival (☎ 207-374-2811) attracts visitors from Portland, Bar Harbor and beyond. Concerts are held in Kneisel Hall on Pleasant St (ME 15) on Friday evenings and Sunday afternoons.

The Blue Hill Fair (first week in September), held at the fairgrounds northeast of the town center on ME 172, has oxen and horse pulls, sheepdog trials, livestock shows, fire-

works, auto-thrill shows, a petting zoo and other countrylike things to do.

### Places to Stay
Blue Hill is decidedly charming and decidedly upscale. Accommodations in town are wonderful, but pricey.

**Camping** For camping, you must travel some distance. The *Gatherings Family Campground (☎ 207-667-8826)*, on ME 172, 4 miles southwest of Ellsworth, has tent sites for $14 and RV hookups for $18 on a wooded lakefront.

The *Balsam Cove Campground (☎ 207-469-7771, 800-469-7771)*, off ME 15 south of East Orland, is a mile south of US 1, then another mile east along an unpaved road. Tent campers in particular are welcome at this forested lakefront campground.

**Inns** The *Mountain Road House (☎ 207-374-2794)*, on Mountain Rd, offers three rooms with private bath ($55 to $85) in a fine 1890s farmhouse with views of the bay. It is a few miles outside of the village. Mountain Rd runs between ME 15 and ME 172; look for the inn's signs.

The long-time favorite lodging place is the *Blue Hill Inn (☎ 207-374-2844)*, on Union St. It is a few steps from the village center and across from the George Stevens Academy. It has ten rooms and two suites, dating from 1840, which cost $140 to $190 double, with breakfast and dinner included. Reduce the price by $40 if you don't want to have dinner.

*Captain Isaac Merrill Inn (☎/fax 207-374-2555, 1 Union St)* is right in the center of things. Though only opened in 1994, it has the feel of a 19th-century hostelry. Rates are $85/95 with a shared/private bath.

### Places to Eat
*Jean-Paul's Bistro (☎ 207-374-5852)*, Main St, serves lunch and tea in an early-19th-century Federal-style house. Sit on the harborfront terrace and take in the waterfront views as you dine on lite French food.

The *Left Bank Bakery & Café (☎ 207-374-2201)*, on ME 172, northeast of the village, has reasonably priced baked goods, sandwiches and spinach pies.

Blue Hill's best restaurants are very busy at dinner, and reservations may be necessary.

*Firepond* (☎ 207-374-9970), on Main St by the creek, opens at 10 am for muffins and coffee, serves lunch (quiche, quesadillas) from 11 am and dinner from 5 pm. The dinner menu is classic, but with a modern twist: veal with morel mushrooms or Black Angus sirloin with peppercorn sauce. Full dinners cost $30 to $40. The choicest tables are on the screened porch at creekside.

*Jonathan's Restaurant* (☎ 207-374-5226), on Main St right in the town's center, has an equally interesting and similarly priced menu featuring Maine crab cakes and lamb shanks braised in beer and bourbon.

### Getting There & Away
Blue Hill is 23 miles east of Castine; 13 miles southwest of Ellsworth; 18 miles southeast of Bucksport.

## DEER ISLE & STONINGTON
Travel south along ME 15 for views of pristine farms and stretches of rocky Maine coast with sailboats moored offshore. Deer Isle is a collection of islands joined by causeways and connected to the mainland by a picturesque, tall and narrow suspension bridge near Sargentville.

### Information
The Deer Isle-Stonington Chamber of Commerce (☎ 207-348-6124) maintains an information booth a quarter mile south of the suspension bridge, open 10 am to 4 pm (11 am to 5 pm Sunday) in summer.

Stonington is a departure point for Isle au Haut; see that section, later in this chapter.

### Deer Isle Village
The small village of Deer Isle is a collection of shops and services near the Pilgrim Inn. Seven miles to the east of the village is the **Haystack Mountain School of Crafts** (☎ 207-348-2306), founded in 1950 and now open for public tours at 1 pm on Wednesday, June through August. The several galleries in Deer Isle and neighboring Stonington testify to the fascination this beautiful seaside area has for fine artists.

### Stonington
At the southern tip of Deer Isle, Stonington is a granite-quarrying, fishing and tourist town, the three industries thriving close together but separately. Signs warn tourists not to park on the town dock, because it is reserved for pickups hauling lobster traps and refrigerated trucks laden with fish. On the main street, art galleries and other nice shops alternate with auto parts stores and ship chandleries.

Stonington got its name and its early prosperity from the pink granite quarried here. The rocky islets in the harbor show you the color of the stone, and small-scale quarrying continues today. Stonington calls itself 'the ideal coastal Maine village,' and is proud that it is 'a real place, with a real working harbor,' rather than a fantasy tourist village.

There's not much to do in Stonington but enjoy Stonington, which is easy enough, as a short walk around town will prove.

### Places to Stay
*Sunshine Campground* (☎ 207-348-6681), RR 1, is nearly 6 miles east of Deer Isle, off ME 15, with tent sites for $12, RV hookups for $15.

Well off the beaten path is *Goose Cove Lodge* (☎ 207-348-2508), US 15, Sunset. On a spruce-clad, granite-ledge cliff, Goose Cove is a tranquil hideaway where the sea rolls in over the ledges and the sounds of foghorns wake you up in the morning. The lodge has modern cottages and main lodge rooms are spread out over 20 acres. Cost is $95 to $153 per person, including breakfast and a dreamy four-course dinner.

*Pilgrim's Inn* (☎ 207-348-6615), on Main St in Deer Isle, dates from 1793 and has 13 quite elegant guest rooms, all with baths and water views. Two parlors have 8-foot-wide fireplaces, the library is well stocked and the barn has been converted to a rustic dining room where nonguests can also reserve space for dinner. Room rates run from $185 a double, breakfast and dinner included.

*Boyce's Motel* (☎ 207-367-2421, 800-224-2421), on Main St in Stonington, is a cedar-shake-covered hostelry that looks more like an inn. It rents simple but suitable rooms for $44 double, up to $95 for apartments.

*Près du Port B&B* (☎ 207-367-5007), in Stonington, just up the hill at the west end of Main St, has three harbor-view rooms, two with shared bath, for $60 to $80 each, breakfast included.

*Burnt Cove B&B* (☎ 207-367-2392) on Whitman Rd, is a short distance northwest of the Stonington center. They have three charming rooms (two with shared bath), with waterfront views for $60 to $90, breakfast included.

Right in the center of Stonington, on Main St, the recently refurbished *Inn on the Harbor* (☎ 207-367-2420) has 13 rooms for $100 to $125, all with private bath. The cheaper rooms face the street. The seaside terrace, which serves breakfast, coffee and snacks, has the best harbor view in town.

## Places to Eat

*Pilgrim's Inn* (☎ 207-348-6615), on Main St in Deer Isle, has a barn that has been converted to a rustic dining room. It serves a prix-fixe selection ($31.50). Nonguests are welcome for dinner.

*Lily's Café* (☎ 207-367-5936), US 15 at the corner of Airport Rd, is a good place to dine for lunch, or grab sandwiches, salads and homemade soups for a picnic.

*Downtown Diner* (☎ 207-367-5099), on Main St in Stonington, serves breakfast from 5 am (7 am on Sunday) and it features a welcome list of sandwiches for around $2. It closes at 2 pm.

Across the street, the *Atlantic Café* (☎ 207-367-2420), in the Inn on the Harbor, features broiled and grilled seafood for breakfast and lunch.

*Fisherman's Friend Restaurant* (☎ 207-367-2442), north up the hill on School St in Stonington, is a general purpose dining spot with a full menu.

## Getting There & Away

Deer Isle and Stonington are just about 5 miles apart. Stonington is 23 miles south of Blue Hill, 36 miles southwest of Ellsworth and 78 miles east of Camden.

Boats depart Stonington for Isle au Haut. See below.

## ISLE AU HAUT

Much of Isle au Haut (that's 'aisle-a-ho'), a rocky island 6 miles long, is in the keeping of Acadia National Park. More remote than the park lands near Bar Harbor, it is not flooded with visitors in summer. Serious hikers can tramp the island's miles of trails and camp for the night in one of the five shelters maintained by the National Park Service.

For information on hiking and camping on Isle au Haut, contact Acadia National Park (☎ 207-288-3338, www.nps.gov/acad), PO Box 177, Bar Harbor, ME 04609. Reservations for shelters must be accompanied by a fee of $5; reservations for the summer season are not accepted before April 1.

### Getting There & Away

The Isle au Haut Company (☎ 207-367-5193, evenings 367-2355) operates daily mail-boat trips from Stonington's Atlantic Ave Hardware Dock to the village of Isle au Haut year round. In summer, except for Sunday and major holidays, there are at least three trips a day on the 45-minute crossing, for $9 per adult, $4.50 per child under 12 ($11 and $5 on Sunday). On Sunday and major holidays, there is only one boat a day. Bicycles, motorcycles, boats and canoes (no cars) can be carried to the village of Isle au Haut.

From late June through mid-September, the company also makes the one-hour crossing to Duck Harbor, the entrance to the Isle au Haut territory of Acadia National Park. No bicycles, canoes or kayaks are transported on this run; no dogs are allowed in the Acadia campground.

## MT DESERT ISLAND

Samuel de Champlain, the intrepid French explorer, sailed along this coast in the early 17th century. Seeing the bare, windswept granite summit of Cadillac Mountain, he called the island on which it stood *L'Île des Monts Déserts*. The name is still pronounced duh-ZERT almost 400 years later.

MAINE

MAINE

Mt Desert Island holds Bar Harbor, Maine's oldest summer resort, and Acadia National Park, the only national park in New England. Because of its dramatic Maine scenery and outdoor sports possibilities, it's one of the state's most popular and busiest summer resorts. Acadia is among the most heavily visited national parks in the country.

Visitors come, first and foremost, for the beautiful coastal scenery. They hike the island's 120 miles of trails , bike the 50 miles of unpaved carriage roads, camp in the park's 500-plus campsites or stay in country inns and seek out the 200 species of plants, 80 species of mammals and 273 kinds of birds that live here.

## Orientation

The resort area of Bar Harbor and Acadia extends from the town of Ellsworth, on US 1, to the southern tip of the large mountainous island of Mt Desert. The island's major town, Bar Harbor, is on its northeast side, 20 miles southeast of Ellsworth. Acadia National Park covers much (but not all) of the land on the island. It includes large tracts of land on the Schoodic Peninsula south of Winter Harbor, across the water to the east and on Isle au Haut, far to the southwest. The Schoodic Peninsula and Isle au Haut areas are not easily accessible from Mt Desert Island.

## Information

In summer, the Thompson Island Information Center (☎ 207-288-3411), a joint effort of the NPS and three area chambers of commerce, is about 7½ miles south of Ellsworth. Acadia National Park's Hulls Cove Visitor Center (☎ 207-288-3338) is 16 miles south of Ellsworth and 3 miles north of Bar Harbor; it is open May through October. Follow the signs. In the off-season, go to Park Headquarters for information. It is 3 miles west of Bar Harbor on ME 233.

The Bar Harbor Chamber of Commerce (☎ 207-288-5103, 800-345-4617, fax 207-288-2565, www.barharborinfo.com), PO Box 158, Bar Harbor, ME 04609, maintains a small information office at the Bluenose Ferry Terminal on ME 3 on the northern outskirts of Bar Harbor.

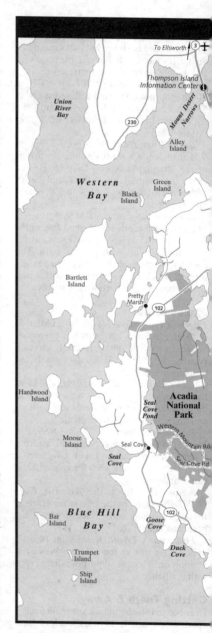

# ACADIA NATIONAL PARK (MT DESERT ISLAND)

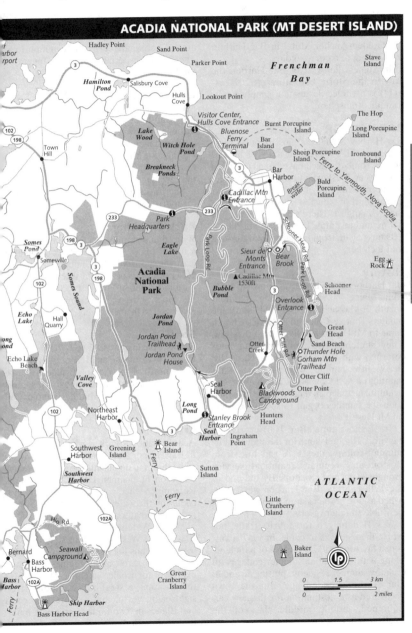

MAINE

Hadley Point
Sand Point
Parker Point
*Frenchman Bay*
Stave Island

Harbor
rport
Hamilton Pond
Salisbury Cove
Hulls Cove
Lookout Point
The Hop
Long Porcupine Island

102
198
Town Hill
Lake Wood
Witch Hole Pond
Visitor Center, Hulls Cove Entrance
Bluenose Ferry Terminal
Burnt Porcupine Island
Bar Island
Sheep Porcupine Island
Ironbound Island

Breakneck Ponds
Bar Harbor
Bald Porcupine Island
Breakwater
Ferry to Yarmouth, Nova Scotia

Cadillac Mtn Entrance
233
Park Headquarters
233

Somes Pond
198
3
Somesville
198
3

Eagle Lake
Park Loop Rd
Sieur de Monts Entrance
Bear Brook
Schooner Head Rd
Egg Rock

102
198
3
**Acadia National Park**
Cadillac Mtn 1530ft
Bubble Pond
Schooner Head

Echo Lake
Hall Quarry
Jordan Pond
Overlook Entrance
Great Head

ong ond
Echo Lake Beach
Jordan Pond Trailhead
Jordan Pond House
Otter Creek
Otter Cliff Rd
Sand Beach
Thunder Hole
Gorham Mtn Trailhead
Otter Cliff

Valley Cove
Seal Harbor
Blackwoods Campground
Otter Point

Northeast Harbor
Long Pond
Stanley Brook Entrance
*Seal Harbor*
Hunters Head
Ingraham Point

102
3
Southwest Harbor
Greening Island
Bear Island
Ferry
Sutton Island
*ATLANTIC OCEAN*

*Southwest Harbor*
Little Cranberry Island

Hio Rd
102A
Ferry

Bernard
Seawall Campground
Baker Island

*Bass Harbor*
Bass Harbor
102A
Great Cranberry Island

Ferry
*Ship Harbor*
Bass Harbor Head

0   1.5   3 km
0   1   2 miles

The Acadia Area Association has an 'official lodging office' at 55 West St, near the Golden Anchor Motel in Bar Harbor, open 10 am to 6 pm weekdays.

In Somesville, west of Bar Harbor, the Port in the Storm bookstore (☎ 207-244-4114) is a choice destination simply for its tranquil atmosphere.

## BAR HARBOR

Bar Harbor is Maine's most popular summer resort. It's a pleasant town of big old houses, some of which have been converted into inns and restaurants, creating a relaxed, but purposeful, way of life.

Bar Harbor's busiest season is late June through August. There's a bit of a lull just before and just after Labor Day, but then it gets busy again from foliage season through mid-October.

### History

Bar Harbor was chartered as a town in 1796, while Maine was still part of the Commonwealth of Massachusetts. In 1844, landscape painters Thomas Cole and Frederick Church came to Mt Desert and liked what they saw. They sketched the landscape and later returned with their art students. Naturally, the wealthy families who purchased their paintings asked Cole and Church about the beautiful land depicted in their paintings, and soon the families began to spend summers on Mt Desert.

In a short time, Bar Harbor rivaled Newport, Rhode Island, for the stature of its summer-colony guests. A rail line from Boston and regular steamboat service brought even more visitors. By the end of the 19th century, Bar Harbor was established as one of the eastern seaboard's most desirable summer resorts.

WWII damaged the tourist trade, but worse damage was to come. In 1947, a vast forest fire torched 17,000 acres of park land, along with 60 palatial 'summer cottages' of wealthy summer residents, putting an end to Bar Harbor's gilded age. But the town recovered as a destination for the new car-equipped, mobile middle class of the postwar years.

Although Mt Desert Island still has a number of wealthy summer residents, they are far outnumbered by the common folk. There is an especially large contingent of outdoor-sports lovers.

### Orientation & Information

ME 3 approaches Bar Harbor from the north and the west, and it passes right through the town. Main St is the town's principal commercial thoroughfare, along with Cottage St. Mt Desert St has many of the town's inns, just a few minutes' walk from the town green.

See Information under Mt Desert Island for tourist facilities.

### Rock Climbing

With all that granite, Acadia National Park is a mecca for rock climbers. If you'd like to learn the sport, Atlantic Climbing (☎ 207-288-2521) offers guide and instruction services. Acadia Mountain Guides (☎ 207-288-8186), 119 Main St, also gives instruction and can guide you to the best climbs.

### Soaring

Island Soaring (☎ 207-667-7627), at the Hancock County-Bar Harbor Airport, on ME 3 north of the Trenton Bridge, will take you in a glider for a soar above Mt Desert Island for as little as $100 per couple. Call for reservations.

### Cruises

Acadia National Park is what lures visitors to Bar Harbor, but there are several worthwhile things to do outside the park as well. A cruise on Frenchman Bay is one of them. Remember, when you cruise, it is often 20°F cooler on the water than on land, so bring a jacket or sweater and windbreaker.

Whale Watcher (☎ 207-288-3322, 800-508-1499), 1 West St at Main St, next to the town pier, runs the *Atlantis*, a 116-foot steel vessel with three main engines, designed expressly for whale watching. There's also the *Acadian*, a steel-hulled, motor-driven sightseeing vessel that explores the coast and islands on two-hour cruises with a naturalist aboard.

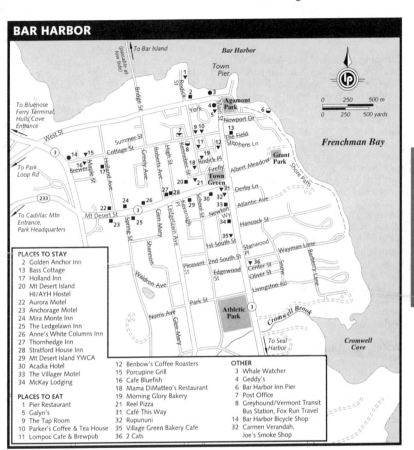

**BAR HARBOR**

To Bar Island

Bar Harbor

Town Pier

To Bluenose
Ferry Terminal,
Hulls Cove
Entrance

West St

To Park
Loop Rd

To Cadillac Mtn
Entrance,
Park Headquarters

Frenchman Bay

Agamont Park

Newport Dr

The Field

Stephens Ln

Grant Park

Albert Meadow

Town Green

Firefly

Derby Ln

Atlantic Ave

Hancock St

1st South St

Stanwood Pl

2nd South St

Edgewood St

Pleasant St

Waldron Ave

Park St

Norris Ave

Glen Mary

Athletic Park

To Seal Harbor

Cromwell Brook

Cromwell Cove

Wayman Lane

Barberry Lane

Center St

Oliver St

Livingston Rd

0    250    500 m
0    250    500 yards

Summer St

Cottage St

Bridge St

Rodick St

Main St

York St

Greely Ave

Roberts Ave

Kennebec St

School St

Kavanaugh

Ledgelawn Ave

Cottage St

Holland Ave

Maple St

Brewer

Mt Desert St

Spring St

Glen Mary

Shannon

Shore Path

**MAINE**

**PLACES TO STAY**
2  Golden Anchor Inn
13  Bass Cottage
17  Holland Inn
20  Mt Desert Island
    HI/AYH Hostel
22  Aurora Motel
23  Anchorage Motel
24  Mira Monte Inn
25  The Ledgelawn Inn
26  Anne's White Columns Inn
27  Thornhedge Inn
28  Stratford House Inn
29  Mt Desert Island YWCA
30  Acadia Hotel
33  The Villager Motel
34  McKay Lodging

**PLACES TO EAT**
1  Pier Restaurant
5  Galyn's
9  The Tap Room
10  Parker's Coffee & Tea House
11  Lompoc Café & Brewpub

12  Benbow's Coffee Roasters
15  Porcupine Grill
16  Cafe Bluefish
18  Mama DiMatteo's Restaurant
19  Morning Glory Bakery
21  Reel Pizza
31  Café This Way
32  Rupununi
35  Village Green Bakery Cafe
36  2 Cats

**OTHER**
3  Whale Watcher
4  Geddy's
6  Bar Harbor Inn Pier
7  Post Office
8  Greyhound/Vermont Transit
   Bus Station, Fox Run Travel
14  Bar Harbor Bicycle Shop
32  Carmen Verandah,
    Joe's Smoke Shop

Downeast Windjammer and Lighthouse Cruises (☎ 207-288-4585, 288-2373) depart from the Bar Harbor Inn Pier on two-hour cruises on the majestic 151-foot, four-masted schooner *Margaret Todd*. Cruises cost from $15 to $20 for adults and $8 to $10 for children under 12. Buy your tickets on the pier.

Bay Ferries' ultrafast car ferry *The Cat* (☎ 207-288-3395, 888-249-7245) provides a maritime link between Bar Harbor and Yarmouth, Nova Scotia, Canada. On board, there are buffets, bars, duty-free shops and gambling devices such as slot machines. The

voyage between Bar Harbor and Yarmouth takes just 2½ hours, so in a long day, you can cruise there and back, though an overnight stay makes more sense.

## Places to Stay

Bar Harbor has 2500 guest rooms in dozens of motels and inns. Many lodgings close mid-October to mid-May.

The nicest places to stay are the campgrounds of Acadia National Park, or in one of Bar Harbor's Victorian inns. The first is cheap, the second expensive, and in July and August, if you have not made reservations in advance, finding a place in either can be difficult.

**Camping** For camping in Acadia National Park, see the 'Acadia National Park' boxed text. Commercial campgrounds are located along ME 3 from Ellsworth, and they are clustered near the entrances to the park.

There's also good camping at *Lamoine State Park* (☎ 207-667-4778), in Lamoine Beach at the southern end of ME 184, about 30 miles away by road but only a few miles over the water. From Ellsworth, follow US 1 East past ME 3 to ME 184 South. Lamoine is open mid-May to mid-October.

**Hostels** The *Mt Desert Island HI/AYH Hostel* (☎ 207-288-5587, 27 Kennebec St), in the parish hall of St Saviour's Episcopal Church, has 20 beds going for $13 each. It's open 7 to 9 am and 4:30 to 11 pm, mid-June through August.

The *Mt Desert Island YWCA* (☎ 207-288-5008, 36 Mt Desert St) offers lodging to women only for $20/25/30 in a dorm/shared double/single, with reductions for longer stays.

**Motels** The *Anchorage Motel* (☎ 207-288-3959, 800-336-3959, 51 Mt Desert St) is amidst the inns on the town's grandest street. Modern rooms cost $67 to $96.

The nearby *Aurora Motel* (☎ 207-288-3771, 800-841-8925, 51 Holland Ave) is small, simple and well located, charging $80 to $96, with discounts if they're not busy.

*The Villager Motel* (☎ 207-288-3211, 207 Main St), charging $69 to $98 in high summer, is a block south of the town green and within walking distance to everything. Rates drop on August 25.

Among the best situated and most expensive is the *Golden Anchor Inn* (☎ 207-288-5033, 800-328-5033), on West St, convenient to everything. Rates range from $120 to $185 double, with water views starting at $145.

On ME 3 from Ellsworth to Bar Harbor, there are numerous inexpensive motels, some charging as little as $40 double in summer. If everything in Bar Harbor is full, which happens sometimes on weekends in high summer, you should be able to locate a motel room along ME 3 without prior reservation. However, start your search by early afternoon on weekends.

**Inns** Most of the huge old 'summer cottages' along Mt Desert St in Bar Harbor have been converted to inns. Prices are usually the same for one or two persons.

*Bass Cottage* (☎ 207-288-3705, 14 The Field) offers 10 simple rooms, some with shared bath, in a 113-year-old Victorian estate. Rooms go for $55 to $95.

Also, check out the cheap cottages, right on the water, north of Bar Harbor in the Salisbury Cove section of the island. *Emery's* (☎ 207-288-3432), *Edgewater* (☎ 207-288-3491) and *Bay Meadow* (☎ 207-288-4859) all rent cottages by the day or week in summer.

*McKay Lodging* (☎ 207-288-3531, 800-866-2529, 243 Main St) is a short hop south of the town green, with 23 rooms, some with shared bath, in a Bar Harbor house for $60 to $120.

The *Acadia Hotel* (☎ 207-288-5721, 20 Mt Desert St) is just off the green. Rooms in this well-kept old house cost $65 to $135 in high summer, and they're usually all reserved in advance; call early.

Just as affordable, and also within walking distance of town, is the *Holland Inn* (☎ 207-288-4804, 35 Holland Ave). In a restored 1895 farmhouse, the young and extremely personable innkeepers offer four rooms with private bath, large breakfast included, for $79 to $119.

*Mira Monte Inn* (☎ 207-288-4263, 800-553-5109, fax 288-3115, 69 Mt Desert St) is particularly well kept and gracious, with 13 rooms for $135 to $159 per night, suites for more.

Nearby, *Anne's White Columns Inn* (☎ 207-288-5357, 800-321-6379, 57 Mt Desert St) and the *Thornhedge Inn* (☎ 207-288-5398, 800-580-0800, 47 Mt Desert St) are under related management and charge $80 to $140 double for grand Victorian accommodations. Both inns are just a short walk from the park.

The aptly named *Stratford House Inn* (☎ 207-288-5189, 800-550-5189, 45 Mt Desert St) is a Tudor fantasy in the midst of Bar Harbor. Built by a wealthy Boston publisher, it now rents rooms for $75 to $175.

Bar Harbor's grandest downtown inn is *The Ledgelawn Inn* (☎ 207-288-4596, *66 Mt Desert St*), a vast Colonial Revival summer 'cottage' built in 1904 for a Boston shoe magnate. Well kept to this day, it exudes charm and grandeur, which can be yours for $75 to $225 (more for suites), depending on the day and the room.

Five miles out of downtown, and just 2 miles from the main entrance to Acadia National Park, is the oldest surviving lodging establishment in the area, the *Coach Stop Inn* (☎ 207-288-9886), on ME 3. Built in 1804, this five-room inn is set on 3 acres of pastoral gardens. Rooms cost $69 to $129.

Just outside of Bar Harbor, away from the crowds in a tranquil setting, lies the *Mill Brook House* (☎ 207-288-3860, *59 Old Norway Drive*). This traditional New England 'salt box' has three rooms with private baths and large breakfast for $95 to $125.

## Places to Eat

Try *Parker's Coffee & Tea House* (☎ 207-288-2882, *37-1/2 Cottage St*), next to the Criterion Theater, for a tasty cappuccino, latte or mocha. ($1 to $3). Also good are *Benbow's Coffee Roasters* (☎ 207-288-5271, *99 Main St*), right in the center of town, and *2 Cats* (☎ 207-288-2808, *318 Main St*), a few blocks south of the green. All three places serve muffins and other pastries as well as java, but no liquor or large meals.

Several bakery-cafe-deli places are good for breakfast, lunch and box lunches for your picnic in Acadia. *Morning Glory Bakery* (☎ 207-288-3041, *39 Rodick St*) serves good pastries to go. *Village Green Bakery Cafe* (☎ 207-288-9450, *195 Main St*) serves fresh baked goods, sandwiches, salads, pasta and, as the menu says, 'lobster, of course.'

*Jordan Pond House* (☎ 207-276-3316), in Seal Harbor, is the only restaurant in Acadia National Park. It carries on the long tradition of teahouses, serving tea and delectable popovers with strawberry jam ($6.75). It is open 11:30 am to 5:30 pm.

The best place for a lobster picnic is at one of the lobster pounds clustered north of Trenton Bridge on ME 3, about 6½ miles

south of Ellsworth on the road to Bar Harbor. The oldest and best is *Trenton Bridge Lobster Pound* (☎ 207-667-2977), with a pretty water-view picnic area, at the north end of the causeway that leads to Mt Desert Island. Just down the road is another good choice, *Lunt's* (☎ 207-582-4240). At either place, a lobster dinner with steamed clams and corn or coleslaw should cost only $9 or so. Prices are usually posted on highway signboards.

On Mt Desert Island, check out *Docksider* (☎ 207-276-3965), on Sea St in Northeast Harbor and *Beal's* (☎ 207-244-7178) in Southwest Harbor.

Bar Harbor's most interesting dining possibilities are on Rodick St and on Cottage St. *Café This Way* (☎ 207-288-4483, *14½ Mt Desert St*) is a casual, quirky place that locals love for its consistently good and affordable fare. Sit back, listen to smooth jazz and order hefty salads at lunch ($6) or fresh seafood at dinner ($9 to $15 for entrees).

At the top of Rodick St, *Mama DiMatteo's Restaurant* (☎ 207-288-3666) serves nouveau Italian cuisine: smoked chicken ravioli, shrimp sautéed with prosciutto, capers and olives and the like. Early bird specials (slightly smaller portions) are served from 4:30 to 6 pm.

Across the street, *Reel Pizza* (☎ 207-288-3828, *33B Kennebec St*) serves good pizza ($9 to $15) with a nightly flick.

*The Tap Room* (☎ 207-288-4914, *21A Cottage St*) only has about eight stools, but this popular brewpub can sure pack 'em in during lunch and dinner.

On Rodick, south of Cottage, is the *Lompoc Cafe & Brewpub* (☎ 207-288-9392, *36 Rodick*), with a short but eclectic, international menu – Indonesian peanut chicken, shrimp étouffée ($10 to $13) and ingenious pizzas (Greek, goat cheese, etc, $6 to $8) and a glass of Bar Harbor Real Ale. (There's also blueberry ale for the intrepid.) On most evenings, there's live entertainment (see Entertainment, below).

*Rupununi* (☎ 207-288-2886, *119 Main St*) is a good spot for families, serving standard American fare, such as burgers and pasta, at affordable prices. They also have the hottest

MAINE

## Acadia National Park

Acadia National Park, the only national park in all of New England, covers over 62 sq miles and offers activities that appeal to everyone from the couch potato to the hyperactive sports enthusiast.

### History

Mt Desert Island was a booming summer resort for the wealthy by the late 19th century, but it was a more industrial development that caused the creation of Acadia National Park. The invention of the 'portable sawmill' meant that the forests of Acadia could be stripped of trees for cheap lumber.

In 1901, as a result of this threat, summer residents, led by Harvard University President Charles W Eliot, formed a land trust. Wealthy landowners donated land to the trust, and Acadia's extents grew. By 1916, the trust was a national monument, and in 1919, it became a national park.

John D Rockefeller donated 10,000 acres of land to the park. Alarmed at the prospect of its being overrun with automobiles (and some would say that it is now is overrun anyway), he ordered construction of 50 miles of one-lane, gravel-topped carriage roads throughout the park. The carriage roads, built between 1918 and 1940, were meant to provide park access to more remote areas by horse-drawn carriage rather than by automobile. Today, they're popular with hikers and bikers as well.

### Orientation & Information

The park's main entrance is at Hulls Cove, northwest of Bar Harbor via ME 3. The visitor center (☎ 207-288-3338) is here and opens at 8 am in summer. From the visitor center, the 20-mile-long Park Loop Rd circumnavigates the northeastern section of the island. It is a one-way road for much of its length.

The admission fee to the park is $5 per vehicle and is good for seven consecutive days. The fee is collected at a booth on the Park Loop Rd, just north of Sand Beach. If you enter the park by bike or on foot, the fee is $2 per person.

Other entrances to the park and the Park Loop Rd are the Cadillac Mountain entrance just west of Bar Harbor; the Overlook Entrance, south of the town; and the Stanley Brook Entrance, east of Northeast Harbor.

Cadillac Mountain (1530 feet), the highest point in the park, is a few miles southwest of Bar Harbor. The summit can be reached by auto road, which is a pity. Most of the carriage roads (closed to motor vehicles) are between Bubble Pond and Somes Sound, to the west of Cadillac Mountain. Call the visitor center for camping, road and weather information. For park emergencies, call ☎ 207-288-3369.

bar in town upstairs, a cigar den downstairs, pool tables and dancing with live music (see Entertainment, below).

If you're really not sure what you want to eat, head to *Galyn's* (☎ 207-288-9706, 17 Main St). Set in a restored late-19th-century boarding house near the waterfront, they have an extensive menu of meats, chicken, pasta and lobster for $12.95 to $18.95 at dinner.

Down by the harbor, the *Pier Restaurant* (☎ 207-288-5033, 55 West St), in the Golden Anchor Inn, is usually busy because of its pier location, which commands a spectacular sunset view of the water and the pine-fringed coast. Have a drink in the open-air Topsider bar while you wait for a table. Fish courses cost around $13, vegetable lasagna is $10. The Pier opens for breakfast at 7 am and stops serving dinner at 9:30 pm.

## Acadia National Park

### Maps & Guides

Free NPS maps of the park are available at the information and visitor centers. The *AMC Guide to Mt Desert Island & Acadia National Park* by the Appalachian Mountain Club (available from Globe Pequot publishers) has descriptions of all the trails, as well as a good trail map. *Acadia's Biking Guide*, by Tom St Germain, has descriptions of numerous good bike tours to be taken along the park's carriage roads. These guides and others, as well as a variety of maps, are sold at the Hulls Cove Visitor Center and at bookshops in Bar Harbor.

### Touring Highlights

Start your tour with a drive along the Park Loop Rd. On the portion called Ocean Drive, stop at Thunder Hole, south of the Overlook Entrance, for a look at the surf crashing into a cleft in the granite (the effect is best with a strong incoming tide). Otter Cliffs, not far south of Thunder Hole, is a wall of pink granite rising up from the sea.

At Jordan Pond, there's a self-guided nature trail. Here, you're in the midst of the trail and carriage road systems. Stop for tea and popovers at *Jordan Pond House* (☎ 207-276-3316); see Places to Eat in the Bar Harbor section.

For swimming, try either Sand Beach or Seal Harbor for chilly salt water, or Echo Lake for fresh water.

Bikers should park near Eagle Lake, off Route 233, and pedal on the carriage paths around this body of water.

Finish your first explorations with a stop at the windy summit of Cadillac Mountain.

### Outfitters

Acadia is great for all sorts of outdoor activities, including hiking, rock climbing, mountain biking, canoeing and sea kayaking. Numerous outfitters in Bar Harbor provide guide service, equipment for rent or sale and sports lessons. Many are found at the west end of Cottage St near ME 3, including Acadia Bike & Canoe (☎ 207-288-9605, 800-526-8615), 48 Cottage St, across from the post office; Acadia Outfitters (☎ 207-288-8118), 106 Cottage St, across from the Exxon station; Bar Harbor Bicycle Shop (☎ 207-288-3886), 141 Cottage St; National Park Kayak Center (☎ 207-288-0342), 39 Cottage St; and Acadia Mountain Guides (☎ 207-288-8186), 137 Cottage St.

### Campgrounds

There are two campgrounds in the park. *Blackwoods Campground* (☎ 207-288-3338), open all year, requires reservations in summer; *Seawall Campground*, open May through September, rents sites on a first-come, first-served basis. No backcountry camping is allowed. There are private campgrounds outside the park. See the Places to Stay section in Bar Harbor for details.

The *Cafe Bluefish* (☎ 207-288-3696, 122 Cottage St) is an intimate storefront bistro offering tasty seafood choices such as curry-crusted salmon ($17.95) and Cajun-crusted swordfish ($18.95).

Across the street, the *Porcupine Grill* (☎ 207-288-3884, 123 Cottage St) is adored by locals who rave about the innovative menu and extensive wine list. It opens at 6 pm, and main dishes cost $17 to $24.

### Entertainment

The festive atmosphere of *Carmen Verandah* (☎ 207-288-2886, 119 Main St), on the 2nd floor terrace of Rupununi, is the place to grab a drink in Bar Harbor. They have pool tables, darts and a large dance floor to groove to the live music. Downstairs, there's *Joe's Smoke Shop*, an upscale cigar bar that often can be as crowded as Carmen Verandah.

MAINE

*Lompoc Cafe & Brewpub* (☎ 207-288-9392, 36 Rodick) is a homey place with a variety of performers playing jazz, blues, folk and classical. Check the signboard at the corner of Rodick and Cottage Sts for who's on and when. The cover charge varies.

Another festive spot with live music is *Geddy's* (19 Main St).

### Getting There & Away

**Air** Continental Connection, operated by Colgan Air (☎ 207-667-7171, 800-272-5488) connects Bar Harbor and Boston with daily flights year round. The Hancock County-Bar Harbor Airport is at Trenton, off ME 3, just north of the Trenton Bridge.

**Bus** Vermont Transit/Greyhound (☎ 207-288-3366, 802-864-6811, 800-451-3292) runs an early morning bus daily from Bar Harbor to Boston and New York City via Bangor and Portland. (Buses stop at Fox Run Travel, 4 Kennebec St.) Likewise, a bus starts out from New York at breakfast time, reaches Boston by lunchtime and arrives in Bar Harbor by dinnertime.

Also, Concord Trailways (☎ 888-741-8686) recently introduced an airport shuttle from Bangor to Bar Harbor.

The Bar Harbor bus stop is at Fox Run Travel, 4 Kennebec St at Cottage St. You can also flag the bus down in the parking lot of the McDonald's at the junction of US 1 and ME 3 in Ellsworth.

**Car** Driving details for Bar Harbor are as follows:

| destination | mileage | hr:min |
|---|---|---|
| Bangor, ME | 34 miles | 0:50 |
| Boothbay, ME | 125 miles | 2:45 |
| Boston, MA | 269 miles | 6:30 |
| Calais, ME | 132 miles | 3:15 |
| Camden, ME | 77 miles | 1:45 |
| Freeport, ME | 145 miles | 3:50 |
| Lubec, ME | 103 miles | 2:30 |
| New York, NY | 470 miles | 12:00 |
| Portland, ME | 161 miles | 4:00 |
| Northeast Harbor, ME | 13 miles | 0:30 |
| Southwest Harbor, ME | 15 miles | 0:35 |

**Boat** For details on the Bay Ferries to Yarmouth, Nova Scotia, see Cruises, above.

## NORTHEAST HARBOR

The aptly named vacation village of Northeast Harbor has a marina full of yachts, a main street populated with art galleries and boutiques and back streets dotted with comfortable summer hideaways that are good for a short stay.

Information is available at the marina, as is a shop selling soft drinks and snacks.

On Sea St, the *Docksider* (see Places to Eat in the Bar Harbor section, above, for details) is a beloved lobster house, especially known for its crab cakes and crab sandwiches.

Far more upscale, and always rated one of the best dining experiences on the island, is *Redfields* (☎ 207-276-5283), on Main St. Lamb, and of course, seafood, are this restaurant's specialties.

## SOUTHWEST HARBOR

More laid-back, and less wealthy than Northeast Harbor, Southwest Harbor also offers lots of things to do.

### Cruises

From the Upper Town Dock – a quarter mile along Clark Point Rd from the flashing light in the center of town – boats venture out into Frenchman Bay to the Cranberry Isles and on whale-watching expeditions. Cranberry Cove Boating Co (☎ 207-244-5882) operates the 47-passenger *Island Queen* on four cruises daily in summer. The voyage to and from the Cranberry Isles costs $12 per adult, half-price for children three to 12.

### Places to Stay & Eat

*Penury Hall* (☎ 207-244-7102), Southwest Harbor, will put you up for the night (two nights minimum in summer) and give you breakfast for $85. *Island House* (☎ 207-244-5180), on Clark Point Rd, is comparably priced, as is *Heron House* (☎ 207-244-0221), at ME 102 and Fernald Point Rd.

For sustenance, everyone heads to *Beal's Lobster Shack* (☎ 207-244-3202) on Clark

Point Rd. Grab a picnic table and dine on chowder, crabmeat rolls and, what else, lobster.

*Restaurant XYZ* (☎ 207-244-5221), Shore Rd, Manset, serves authentic Mexican food in a fabulous waterfront setting. Order dishes such as chicken in a mole sauce and Yucatecan-style pork (both $10), washed down with lime margaritas ($4.50).

## BANGOR

Though Bangor figures largely in present-day Maine, it is off the normal tourist routes. A boomtown during Maine's 19th-century lumbering heyday, Bangor was largely destroyed by a disastrous fire in 1911. Today Bangor is mostly a modern, workaday town, famous as the hometown of best-selling novelist Stephen King (look for his appropriately spooky mansion – complete with bat-and-cobweb fence – among the grand houses along Broadway). Bett's Bookstore (☎ 207-947-7052), 26 Main St, specializes in Stephen King's books.

The Bangor Historical Society (☎ 207-942-5766) has a museum in the Thomas A Hill House at 159 Union St (closed mid-December through February). The Cole Land Transportation Museum (☎ 207-990-3600), 405 Perry Rd, has exhibits of antique vehicles and photographs.

The Bangor Mall, off I-95 exit 49, is the shopping mecca for this part of the Penobscot River valley.

### Information

The Bangor Region Chamber of Commerce (☎ 207-947-0307, www.bangorregion.com), 519 Main St, Bangor, ME 04402, and the Bangor Convention & Visitors Bureau (☎ 207-947-5205, www.bangorcvb.org), in the same building, can answer questions and provide information. Both are open 8 am to 5 pm weekdays.

### Places to Stay

**Camping** The *Pleasant Hill Campground* (☎ 207-848-5127), with 105 spaces for everything from tents to giant motor homes, is 5½ miles northwest of I-95 exit 47, along Union St (ME 222). The 52 campsites at the *Paul Bunyan Campground* (☎ 207-941-1177, 1862 Union St) are available year-round.

**Hotels** The 35-room *Phenix Inn* (☎ 207-947-0411, fax 947-0255, 20 Broad St) is in the city center in the West Market Square Historic District, a row of buildings dating from 1837, when Bangor was Maine's lumber capital. Tidy rooms in this charming, renovated hotel cost $75/85; buffet breakfast is included. To find it, look for the little park with the fountain and stainless steel sculpture at the intersection of Maine St at Broad and Hammond Sts.

Otherwise, there are lots of motels off I-95, close to the Maine Mall. You'll save money if you drive beyond the obvious places that are right by the exit. For example, the *Scottish Inn* (☎ 207-945-2934, 1476 Hammond St) is a mile west of I-95 exit 45B, along US 2/ME 100. It charges only $55 to $65 for rooms with one or two double beds.

Of the places near the highway, the *Bangor Motor Inn* (☎ 207-947-0355, 800-244-0355 in Maine only, 701 Hogan Rd), opposite the Bangor Mall, offers the best value for money, with 115 rooms priced around $58, continental breakfast included. They'll even grant discounts if business is slow.

The fanciest modern hotel is the *Country Inn* (☎ 207-941-0200, 800-244-3961, 936 Stillwater Ave), at Hogan Rd, up on the hill above Crossroads Plaza and the Comfort Inn. The location is convenient, yet quietish, and the price of $70 is reasonable.

Bangor's other motels charge about the same or a bit more. Ask for a discount, if they have plenty of vacancies: *Best Western White House Inn* (☎ 207-862-3737, 800-528-1234, fax 207-862-6465, 155 Littlefield Ave) is at I-95 exit 44. *Super 8 Motel* (☎ 207-945-5681, 800-800-8000, 462 Odlin Rd) is at I-95 exit 45.

*Comfort Inn* (☎ 207-942-7899, 800-221-2222, 750 Hogan Rd) is at I-95 exit 49. *Econo Lodge* (☎ 207-945-0111, 800-393-0111, 327 Odlin Rd) is at I-95 exit 45B. *Fairfield Inn* (☎ 207-990-0001, 800-228-2800, 300 Odlin Rd) is at I-95 exit 45. The *Hampton Inn*

MAINE

(☎ *207-990-4400, 800-998-7829, 10 Bangor Mall Blvd*) is at I-95 exit 49. **Days Inn** (☎ *207-942-8272, 800-325-2525, 250 Odlin Rd*) is at I-95 exit 45B.

**B&Bs** *Hamstead Farm* (☎ *207-848-3749, RD 3, Box 703*) is an 1846 Cape Cod-style farmhouse on 150 acres of woods and pastures that are home to a small herd of black Angus cattle, as well as pigs and turkeys. Three guest rooms share two baths and cost $45 to $50, full breakfast included.

### Places to Eat

Dining options are limited. There are numerous national chain restaurants near I-95 exit 49. You can also order from restaurants that deliver, such as *China Wall* (☎ *207-941-9331, 930 Stillwater Ave*) at Crossroads Plaza.

*Intown Internet Cafe* (☎ *207-942-0999, 56 Main St*), near Broad and Hammond Sts, serves up java, as well as surprisingly cheap pastries, sandwiches and sausages for you to munch while you surf the net.

*City Limits* (☎ *207-941-9888, 737 Main St*) serves good and varied fare – Italian dishes, seafood, chicken – at moderate prices. Lunch might cost you $10 to $14, dinner $20 to $35.

### Getting There & Away

**Air** Bangor International Airport (☎ 207-947-0384) is the air transportation hub of the region. It is served by regional carriers associated with Continental, Delta and US Airways.

**Bus** For bus routes, see Getting There & Away in the Portland section. Vermont Transit (☎ 207-945-3000, 802-864-6811, 800-451-3292, www.vermonttransit.com), at the Bangor Bus Terminal, 158 Main St, runs four direct buses daily between Bangor and Boston via Portland and Portsmouth, New Hampshire. Concord Trailways (☎ 800-639-3317, www.concordtrailways.com), Trailways Transportation Center, 1039 Union St, has three more, as well as service south along the Maine coast to Portland, and connecting service north and east to Calais and St Stephen, New Brunswick, Canada.

# Downeast Maine

The 'Sunrise Coast' is the name given by Maine's tourism promoters to the area east of Ellsworth to Lubec and Eastport. To Mainers, this is Downeast Maine, the area downwind and east of the rest of the state. It's sparsely populated, slower-paced and more traditional than the Maine to the south and west. It also has more frequent and denser coastal fog.

If you seek quiet walks away from the tourist throngs, coastal villages with little impact from tourism and lower travel prices, explore the 900-plus miles of coastline east of Bar Harbor. But be mindful of the weather.

## SCHOODIC PENINSULA

Surrounded by islands, the Schoodic Peninsula juts south into the Atlantic. At its southern tip is a portion of Acadia National Park, with a 7.2-mile shore drive called the Schoodic Point Loop Road. It offers splendid views of Mt Desert Island and Cadillac Mountain. The loop road, a one-way road with a smooth surface and relatively gentle hills, is excellent for biking. At the Fraser's Point entrance to the park is a picnic area. Farther along the loop, at the end of a short walk from the road, is Schoodic Head, a 400-foot-high promontory with fine ocean views.

North of the peninsula, the towns of Gouldsboro and Winter Harbor provide the peninsula's stores, restaurants and other businesses.

This is the quieter part of Acadia, with fewer crowds – but also fewer activities. For information on local businesses, contact the Schoodic Peninsula Chamber of Commerce (☎ 207-963-7658, 800-231-3008).

There's camping at *Ocean Wood Campground* (☎ *207-963-7194*), south of Birch Harbor and ME 186, for $15 to $30 per site.

## JONESPORT & BEALS ISLAND

Jonesport and Beals Island are traditional Maine fishing and lobstering villages. Even the street signs show it: each one is topped with a carving of a Maine lobster boat.

The towns get a smattering of the more discerning tourists during the season, most of whom come to take photographs, paint pictures and walk on Great Wass Island. Follow ME 187 to find most of these towns' services, including restaurants and lodgings.

**Great Wass Island**, at the southern tip of the peninsula, just over 4 miles from Jonesport, is a 1540-acre nature reserve that is under the control of the Nature Conservancy (☎ 207-729-5181, www.tnc.org). In order to keep the reserve for those who appreciate it the most, the way to it is not well marked, and parking at the trailhead is severely limited – but the cars parked there bear license plates from many different states. This is a bird-watching reserve for the cognoscenti.

To find it, follow ME 187 into Jonesport. Look for the Union Trust Bank on the left and Tall Barney's Restaurant on the right. Turn left here onto Bridge St, cross the bridge and turn left. A little more than a mile farther on, cross the small, inconspicuous bridge that connects Beals Island to Great Wass Island and turn right; a small sign ('Nature Conservancy') points the way. A mile later, the paved road ends, and after another 1.5 miles on an unpaved road, you come to the Great Wass Island parking lot. It is capable of holding about a dozen cars. A sign advises that if the parking lot is full, you should not park on the road, but go away and come back some other time.

The reserve's attraction is its rocky coastal scenery, a large stand of jack pines, peat bogs and bird life, including the amusing puffins. If time permits, take the 2-mile hike to Little Cape Point (about 1½ to 2 hours roundtrip).

### Places to Stay

*Henry Point Campground*, on the point in Jonesport, is simple, with only portable toilets, picnic tables and one big stone fireplace, but it's surrounded by water and the semi-shaded sites have fine Maine coast views. Tent campers pay $8, RVs $10. To find

it, from ME 187 go southeast on Kelly Point Rd, and thereafter, when in doubt, bear right. If you reach the Jonesport shipyard, you've gone too far; go back 0.3 mile and turn right.

*Jonesport By-the-Sea B&B* (☎ 207-497-2590), Main St (ME 187), across from the post office, has five homey, comfortable rooms, some with private bath, for $40 to $65.

*Raspberry Shores B&B* (☎ 207-497-2463), on ME 187 in Jonesport, is a private home holding a combination B&B and antique shop, renting simple rooms with shared baths from April through October for $58 double.

*Harbor House on Sawyer Cove* (☎ 207-497-5417), Sawyer Square, Jonesport, has two rooms overlooking the harbor for $85, and an old-time-Maine cafe and curiosity shop.

## MACHIAS

The county seat of Washington County, Machias has a branch of the University of Maine, thereby making it the center of commerce and culture Downeast.

The Machias Bay Area Chamber of Commerce (☎ 207-255-4402), PO Box 606, US 1, Machias, ME 04654-0606, provides information. It is in a trailer on US 1 across from Helen's Restaurant (see below).

The *Maineland Motel* (☎ 207-255-3334), US 1, East Machias, has 30 simple, comfortable rooms for $45 single, $48 to $54 double. The nearby *Margaretta Motel* (☎ 207-255-6500), US 1, charges prices similar to those at the Maineland. *Machias Motor Inn* (☎ 207-255-4861), US 1, has 35 rooms overlooking the Machias River for $70, and an indoor heated pool. The *Bluebird Motel* (☎ 207-255-3332), US 1, on the west side of Machias, has 40 rooms for only slightly more.

Right next to the Mainland is *Joyce's Lobster House* (☎ 207-255-3015), US 1, tidy and popular, with brisk, friendly service. Lobster is served boiled, sautéed or stuffed. Simpler dishes, such as spaghetti with homemade meat sauce, are cheaper, but in any case, a dinner need cost only $10 to $20. Bring your own wine or beer.

**MAINE**

At *Helen's Restaurant* (☎ 207-255-8423), on US 1, there's a long menu of standard American fare, including many meat and seafood dinners for $7 to $10. Sandwiches cost as little as $2, and there's even a special weight-watchers plate.

The *Riverside Inn & Restaurant* (☎ 207-255-4134), on US 1, East Machias, less than 5 miles east of Machias' center, is a large house with four guest rooms (with private baths) for $70 to $78, breakfast included. The restaurant has a good dinner menu. Full dinners cost $17 to $22; bring your own wine or beer.

## LUBEC

Lubec, a small town with lots of churches, makes its living on the transborder traffic, a bit of tourism and fish processing. The last operating traditional herring smokehouse is here. There's a small **information office** in the Lubec Historical Society building that is on the left-hand side of ME 189 as you come into town from the west.

Lubec is about as far east as you can go and still be in the USA. People like to watch the sun rise at **Quoddy Head State Park** ($1 per person) so they can say they were the first in the country to see it. The 531-acre park's trademark red-and-white-banded West Quoddy Light (1858) is its most photographed feature, but the volcanic bedrock, the subarctic bogland and extreme tides – almost 16 feet in six hours – are really more interesting. Its four hiking trails vary in length from a few hundred feet to 4 miles.

Beyond Lubec, you're in Canada, specifically on Campobello Island, home to **Roosevelt Campobello International Park** (☎ 506-752-2922, www.fdr.net). Franklin Roosevelt's father, James, bought land here in 1883 and built a palatial summer 'cottage.' The future US president spent many boyhood summers here, and he was later given the 34-room cottage. Franklin and Eleanor made brief, but well-publicized, visits during his long tenure as president.

The park is open 9 am to 5 pm daily, Maine time (10 am to 6 pm New Brunswick time). Admission is free. Border formalities are quick and easy for US citizens in cars with US license plates who are crossing into Canada just to visit the park. Travelers from other countries should have their passports (and may need visas) to cross into Canada. The Campobello Island Chamber of Commerce (☎ 506-752-2233) can provide information on island services.

If you're going farther in Canada, pick up Lonely Planet's *Canada*.

### Places to Stay & Eat

*Sunset Point Trailer Park* (☎ 207-733-2150), on ME 189 toward Campobello Island, has 25 sites (some for tents).

The *Eastland Motel* (☎ 207-733-5501), a mile west of Lubec on ME 189, has simple but serviceable rooms with two double beds or a queen bed for $52 to $62.

The hilltop *Home Port Inn* (☎ 207-733-2077, 800-457-2077, 45 Main St) dates from 1880, and it has been an inn since 1982. Its seven fine rooms, each with private bath, are priced from $65 to $85 double, breakfast included. The dining room serves fine dinners for $20 to $30.

The *Peacock House* (☎ 207-733-2403, 27 Summer St) was built in 1860 by an English sea captain. Restored in 1989, it's now a fine B&B charging $60 to $70 single, $70 to $80 double for its five rooms with private bath and breakfast.

If you are up early, the *43 Water St Restaurant* is the place to go for breakfast, because it opens at 5:30 am (and closes at 2 pm) weekdays. For lunch and dinner, try the *Waterside Restaurant* by the public boat access and municipal marina. *Ivy's Place* (☎ 207-733-4440), on the way into town on ME 189 and on the east side of the cemetery, serves all three meals in homey surroundings, with no dish priced more than $10.

## CALAIS

At the northern end of US 1, Calais (pronounced 'callous') is a twin town to St Stephen, New Brunswick, Canada. During the War of 1812, when the USA and Britain (including Canada) were at war, these two remote outposts of nationalism ignored the distant battles. Their citizens were so closely linked by blood and strong family ties that politics – even war – was ignored.

St Stephen is the gateway to Atlantic Canada, which is covered in Lonely Planet's *Canada*.

# Western Lakes & Mountains

Western Maine is far less visited than coastal Maine. This suits the outdoorsy types who love western Maine the way it is. The fine old town of Bethel and the outdoor pleasures of the Rangeley Lakes are relatively accessible to city-dwellers in Boston, Providence and New York, and even closer to the outdoor playground of the White Mountain National Forest in New Hampshire and in Maine.

The mountains of western Maine yield an abundance of gemstones, such as amethyst, aquamarine and tourmaline. Keep your eye open for **gem shops**, or pick up their brochures at the Chamber of Commerce information office.

## SEBAGO LAKE

Sebago, a mere 15 miles northwest of Portland, is among Maine's largest and most accessible lakes. There are some small settlements along the eastern shore of the lake, best reached by US 302 from Portland. The town of Sebago Lake, at the lake's south end, is small and sleepy. Along the western shore, at East Sebago, are a few inns and cabins for rent.

At the northern tip of the lake, southeast of Naples, is *Sebago Lake State Park (☎ 207-693-6615)*, with camping, picnicking, swimming, boating and fishing.

## SABBATHDAY LAKE

Take I-495 exit 11, then ME 26 to reach the town of Sabbathday Lake, 30 miles north of Portland, near the lake of that name. Sabbathday has the nation's only active Shaker community. It was founded in the 18th century, and a small number of devotees (perhaps four or five) keep the Shaker tradition of prayer, simple living, hard work and fine artistry alive.

Among the plain white, well-kept buildings of the community are a welcome center, museum and shop selling the community's crafts. Most other buildings, including the impressive Brick Dwelling House, are not open to visitors.

A few miles to the north is the village of Poland Spring, famous for its mineral water, which is now sold throughout the USA. In the early 19th century, a visitor was miraculously cured by drinking water from Poland Spring. Not known to miss a good thing, the locals opened hotels to cater to those wanting to take the waters.

## BETHEL

For a small town in the Maine woods, Bethel, 63 miles northwest of Portland via ME 26, is surprisingly beautiful and refined. Part of its backwoods sophistication comes from its being the home of Gould Academy, a well-regarded prep school founded in 1836.

### Orientation & Information

The town is small enough that you can find your way around easily. The Bethel Area Chamber of Commerce (☎ 207-824-2282, www.bethelmaine.com) maintains an information office in the Bethel Station building near the big Norway Savings Bank. The Maine Information Office and the National Park Information Office are on US 2, opposite the Norway Savings Bank.

### Dr Moses Mason House

Stop by the Dr Moses Mason House (☎ 207-824-2908), 15 Broad St, for a look at the house of Dr Mason (1789-1866), a prominent local physician and state representative. The house is now the museum and research library of the Bethel Historical Society, and is open 1 to 4 pm Tuesday to Sunday in July and August.

### Summer Activities

There's golf at the Bethel Inn (see below), scenic drives and hiking in the nearby forests. The **Mt Will Trail** starts from US 2, east of Bethel, and ascends to mountain ledges with fine views of the Androscoggin Valley. **Grafton Notch State Park**, north of

Bethel via ME 26, has hiking trails and pretty waterfalls, but no camping. Try the 1½-mile trail up to Table Rock Overlook, or the walk to Eyebrow Loop and Cascade Falls, with excellent picnic possibilities right by the falls.

If you head west on US 2 toward New Hampshire, be sure to admire the **Shelburne birches**, a high concentration of the white-barked trees that grow between Gilead and Shelburne.

Bethel Outdoor Adventures (☎ 207-836-3607, 800-533-3607, fax 207-836-2708), 121 Mayville Rd (US 2), at the Riverside Campground, can rent you a canoe, kayak or bicycle and arrange lessons, guided trips and shuttles to and from the Androscoggin River. Wild River Adventures (☎ 207-824-2608), 288 Vernon St, offers similar services.

The Great American Renting Company (☎ 207-824-3092), on Sunday River Rd, rents tandems and mountain bikes for excursions into the countryside.

## Skiing

The mountains near Bethel are home to several major New England ski resorts. For information on cross-country skiing opportunities, contact the Maine Nordic Ski Council (☎ 207-824-3694).

Mt Abram (☎ 207-875-5003), Howe Hill Rd, Locke Mills, is a small, reasonably priced ski area (35 trails) just southeast of Bethel. It is good for families.

Sunday River Ski Resort (☎ 207-824-3000), Sunday River Rd, Bethel, 6 miles north of Bethel along ME 5/26, boasts eight mountain peaks and 120 trails. It's regarded as one of the best family ski destinations in the region.

## Places to Stay

For its small size, Bethel has a surprising number of places to stay, which testifies to its importance as a crossroads town at the junction of routes between the Maine coast, northern Maine and New Hampshire. The Bethel Chamber of Commerce operates the Bethel Area Reservations Service (☎ 800-442-5826), which will help you find a room if you need one.

**Camping** There are five simple public campgrounds, with well water and toilets, in the Maine portion of the White Mountains National Forest: *Basin Pond*, *Cold River*, *Crocker Pond*, *Hastings* and *Wild River*. Sites cost $10 per day ($12 at Basin Pond). For information, contact the Evan's Notch Visitor Center (☎ 207-824-2134), 18 Mayville Rd (US 2).

*Riverside Campground* (☎ 207-824-4224, 800-533-3607), 121 Mayville Rd (US 2), is right in Bethel and offers sites for tents ($15) and RVs ($20).

*Pleasant River Campground* (☎ 207-836-3000), US 2, West Bethel, has sites beneath fragrant pines.

*Stony Brook Recreation* (☎ 207-824-2836), US 2, Hanover, with 50 acres of forest, is north of Bethel and just east of Newry.

**Motels** The *Bethel Spa Motel* (☎ 207-824-2989, 800-882-0293), Main St, has inexpensive rooms for $46. The *Rostay Motor Inn* (☎ 207-824-3111), US 2, has simple, but adequate, rooms for $55 to $58 double.

*The Norseman Inn & Motel* (☎ 207-824-2002), US 2, in a 200-year-old inn and a renovated century-old barn, offers rooms for $68, or for $58 in the more modern (and air-conditioned) motel.

*The River View* (☎ 207-824-2808, 357 Mayville Rd) has 32 very comfortable, modern, two-bedroom suites with fully equipped kitchens, a tennis court, Jacuzzi, sauna and game room. The suites can sleep up to five people and are priced at $85 for two people, plus $10 for each extra person.

**Inns & B&Bs** Breakfast is included at the following places, and the prices given are for the summer. In winter during the ski season, prices are higher; ask about ski and meal packages when you call to make your winter reservations.

The *Douglass Place* (☎ 207-824-2229, 162 Mayville Rd (US 2)) has four guest rooms that share 2-1/2 baths. The cost is $50 for a single, $60 for a double.

Among the nicest, most economical and best-located lodgings is *The Chapman Inn* (☎ 207-824-2657), Main and Broad Sts, on the common, with a 24-bed dormitory and nine rooms for singles, couples and families; priced at $59 to $69, the cheaper rooms having shared bath.

*Holidae House B&B* (☎ 207-824-3400), on Main St, has two rooms with private bath, a studio apartment, and a three-bedroom apartment. Rates are $65 to $75.

The 16-room *Sudbury Inn & Sudz Pub* (☎ 207-824-2174, 800-395-7837, fax 207-824-2329), Main St, is the town's unofficial social center, with 16 guest rooms, a restaurant and pub in a late-19th-century Victorian house. The simple, but attractive, rooms in the inn and adjacent carriage house have private baths and cost $65 to $95.

The *Briar Lea B&B* (☎ 207-824-4717, 150 Mayville Rd (US 2)) is a 150-year-old Georgian farmhouse with a variety of rooms priced from $73 to $83, including a full gourmet breakfast.

*Abbott House* (☎ 207-824-7600, 800-240-2377, 170 Walkers Mills Rd), off ME 26, is more than two centuries old It charges $70 double for its four rooms, sharing two baths, full breakfast included.

**Resorts** The *Bethel Inn & Country Club* (☎ 207-824-2175, 800-654-0125, www.bethelinn .com), on Broad St, dominates the town common. It has full-resort facilities, including an 18-hole golf course designed by Geoffrey Cornish, a golf school, tennis, an outdoor heated swimming pool, saunas, workout and game rooms, a lake boathouse and numerous other facilities all set on manicured grounds. Rates depend on when you come, how long you stay and which of the several degrees of luxury you choose, but all rates include breakfast and dinner. The 57 inn rooms go for about $218 to $258 per night, the luxury suites for $338 to $398, with a variety of choices in between these.

## Places to Eat

Bethel doesn't have a large number of restaurants, but surprisingly good vegetarian dishes are available at almost all of them.

*Mother's* (☎ 207-824-2589), Upper Main St, is the best in town, with an innovative menu, decent prices and even nice outdoor seating in good weather. Full lunches cost $7 to $12; dinners with drinks cost $18 to $35. It's open for lunch and dinner daily.

The *Sudbury Inn* (☎ 207-824-2174), Main St, has a cozy dining room and a more limited menu, but good food. Expect to pay $20 to $40 for dinner. The *Suds Pub*, downstairs from the dining room, has a tavern menu, a selection of draft and bottled beers (many from small New England breweries) and live entertainment some nights.

For a formal crystal-and-linen breakfast, head for the *Briar Lea B&B* (☎ 207-824-4717, 150 Mayville Rd (US 2)), where breakfast is the main event as far as meals are concerned.

*Cafe di Cocoa* (☎ 207-824-5282), Lower Main St, features good coffee (and espresso), whole-grain baked goods and vegetarian lunches ($7 to $11) that are also available in a box to go. It opens early for breakfast.

*Sunday River Brewing Company* (☎ 207-824-4253), US 2 at Sunday River Rd, is Bethel's brewpub, featuring a half dozen of its own brews (from a light golden lager to a black porter), as well as a variety of sandwiches, steaks, barbecued meats and vegetarian plates for lunch and dinner. Expect to spend $8 to $12 at lunch, $14 to $25 at dinner.

## Getting There & Away

Bethel has a small airport (☎ 207-824-4321) with a paved 3150-foot runway, if you want to fly in with your own plane.

The rest must drive or use the Bethel Express Corp Taxi Shuttle Service (☎ 207-824-4646). Its 11-passenger vans will take you to or from Augusta for $60 or Portland for $70.

Driving details for Bethel are as follows:

| destination | mileage | hr:min |
| --- | --- | --- |
| Bangor, ME | 133 miles | 3:30 |
| Bar Harbor, ME | 179 miles | 4:30 |
| Boston, MA | 180 miles | 3:30 |
| Caratunk, ME | 128 miles | 3:15 |
| Laconia, NH | 106 miles | 3:00 |
| North Conway, NH | 57 miles | 1:30 |
| Rangeley, ME | 67 miles | 1:30 |
| Portland, ME | 63 miles | 1:20 |

MAINE

## RANGELEY LAKES

Driving the 67 miles from Bethel via US 2 and ME 17 to Rangeley Lake, the road climbs through country that's exceptionally beautiful – even for Maine. During the early 20th century, the lakes in this region were dotted with vast frame hotels and peopled with vacationers from Boston, New York and Philadelphia. Though most of the great hotels are gone, victims of changed economics and vacation preferences, the reasons for spending time here remain.

The Rangeley Lakes Chamber of Commerce (☎ 207-864-5571, 800-685-2537), on Main St in Rangeley, can answer questions.

In winter, Sugarloaf/USA (☎ 207-237-2000, 800-843-5623), in nearby Kingfield, is good for family ski vacations and for snowboarders. It features lifts that take you above the tree line. The nearby Sugarloaf Ski Touring Center has 85km of groomed trails.

In the village of Rangeley proper, a few vestiges of the region's early-20th-century heyday remain. The *Rangeley Inn* (☎ 207-864-3341, 800-666-3687, fax 207-864-3634, rangeinn@rangeley.org, www.rangeleyinn .com, 51 Main St) was built in 1907, and it still hosts guests in its 35 inn rooms and 15 motel rooms for $89 to $99.

The *Country Club Inn* (☎ 207-864-3831), right next to the public golf course, charges $105 for its rooms, with breakfast.

*Northwoods B&B* (☎ 207-864-2440), on Main St, will put you up for $60/75 double with shared/private bath.

# North Woods

On the map, the farther north you go in Maine, the fewer roads there are. It looks as though this is trackless wilderness. In fact, this vast area is owned by large paper companies that harvest timber for their paper mills. The land is crisscrossed by a matrix of rough logging roads. Logs used to be floated down the region's many rivers, but this practice increased the tannin levels in the rivers and threatened the ecological balance. With the advent of the internal combustion engine came the roads.

Now that the logs are out of the rivers, white-water rafters are in them. The **Kennebec River,** below the Harris Hydroelectric Station, passes through a dramatic 12-mile gorge that's among the country's prime rafting places. Outflow from the hydroelectric station is controlled, which means that there is always water, and the periodic big releases make for more exciting rafting.

The Kennebec Valley Tourism Council (☎ 800-778-9898), 179 Main St, Waterville, ME 04901, will help with information.

Maine sporting camps, those remote forest outposts for hunters, fishers and other deep-woods types, still flourish in the remotest regions. For information, contact the Maine Sporting Camp Association, PO Box 89, Jay, ME 04239.

## CARATUNK & THE FORKS

These villages, south of Jackman via US 201, are both at the center of the Kennebec rafting area. White-water rafting trips down the Kennebec and nearby rivers are wonderful adventures. Trips cost from $80 to $115 per person and are suitable for everyone from children (eight and older) to seniors in their 70s. No experience is necessary for many trips (see the boxed text 'White-Water Rafting' in the Facts for the Visitor chapter).

Reserve your rafting trip in advance, and bring a bathing suit, wool or polar fleece sweater, windbreaker or rain suit. Avoid cotton clothing (such as T-shirts and jeans), because cotton dries slowly and will make you feel cold; synthetics are better. Wear more clothing than you think you'll need, and bring a towel to dry with and a dry change of clothes for the end of the trip. Sneakers or other soft-soled footwear are required in the inflatable rafts. Before June 30th and after September 1st, you may be required to have a wetsuit for the trip because of the cold water temperature. Rafting companies often rent the suits and booties.

The rafting company supplies the raft, paddles, life vest, helmet, life preserver and first-aid kit. There will be a pre-trip orientation meeting with instruction about rafting and white-water safety. Your rafting company usually provides lunch (often grilled on the riverbank) as well.

Numerous companies will make arrangements for your rafting trip and for lodging on the Kennebec, Dead or Penobscot Rivers. Trips range in difficulty from Class II (easy enough for children age eight and older) to Class V (intense, difficult rapids, minimum age 15).

Most rafting companies have agreements with local lodgings (inns, dormitories and campgrounds) for your accommodation. Ask about their inclusive rafting packages.

The *Inn by the River* (☎/fax 207-663-2181), US 201, HCR 63, Box 24, West Forks, ME 04985, is a modern lodge overlooking the river. The very comfortable rooms all have large beds and private baths, and cost $90 to $120, breakfast included.

Here are some rafting companies to contact:

Crab Apple Whitewater
(☎ 207-663-4491, 800-553-7238, crabappleinc.com)
HC 63, Box 25, The Forks, ME 04985
Runs trips on rivers in western Massachusetts as well

Downeast Rafting, The Forks
c/o Saco Bound & Downeast Whitewater
(☎ 603-447-3002, 447-3801, www.sacobound.com)
PO Box 119, Center Conway, NH 03813
Runs rafting trips on the Rapid River as well

Maine Whitewater
(☎ 207-672-4814, 800-345-6246, www.mainewhitewater.com)
PO Box 633, Bingham, ME 04920

New England Outdoor Center
(☎ 207-672-5506, 800-766-7238, www.neoc.com)
PO Box 21, Caratunk, ME 04925

Northern Outdoors
(☎ 207-663-4466, 800-765-7238, www.northernoutdoors.com)
PO Box 100, The Forks, ME 04985
Runs rafting, mountain biking, fishing and sea kayaking trips in Maine and other areas

Professional River Runners of Maine
(☎ 207-663-2229, 800-325-3911, www.proriverrunners.com)
PO Box 92, West Forks, ME 04985
Runs rafting trips on these and other rivers in the eastern US

See the Activities section and the boxed text 'White-Water Rafting' in the Facts for the Visitor chapter for additional details on rafting.

## ONWARD TO QUEBEC CITY

North of the Kennebec Valley, US 201 heads through Jackman to the Canadian border. Continuing as QC 173, the road makes its way directly through the lush farm country of the St Lawrence Valley to Quebec City, 111 miles from Jackman; 280 miles from Portland. For travel in Canada, get a copy of Lonely Planet's *Canada*.

## MOOSEHEAD LAKE

Moosehead Lake, which is north of the town of Greenville, is huge. In fact, it is the largest lake completely contained within any one New England state (Lake Champlain is bigger, but shares a border with New York). This is lumber and backwoods country, which is what makes Greenville the region's largest seaplane station. The pontoon planes will take you even deeper into the Maine woods for fishing trips or on lumber company business.

For information about the region, contact the Moosehead Lake Region Chamber of Commerce (☎ 207-695-2702, fax 207-695-3440, www.moosehead.net/moose/chamber.html), PO Box 581, Greenville, ME 04441.

Though once a bustling summer resort, Greenville has since reverted to a backwoods outpost. A few of the old summer hotels survive, but most of the visitors today are camping or heading through on their way to Baxter State Park and Mt Katahdin, making only a brief visit to the famous *Road Kill Cafe* (☎ 207-695-2230) in Greenville Junction.

The SS *Katahdin* (☎ 207-695-2716), which is a 115-foot steamboat built in 1914, is owned and maintained by the Moosehead Marine Museum. It still makes the rounds of the lake from Greenville at 10 am and 2 pm daily in summer, just as it did in Greenville's heyday. The three-hour cruise costs $12 for adults, $10 seniors, $6 children five to 15. The lake's colorful history is preserved in the museum.

## Moose on the Loose

Although moose roam most of the New England states, Maine seems to have the largest herd.

The largest member of the deer family, the moose may weigh more than 1000lb, reach a body length of 8 to 10 feet and stand 6 or 7 feet high at the shoulder.

These dark-brown gentle giants are vegetarians. They mate from September through December, and the calves are born in the spring after an eight-month gestation. They stay with the mother cow until the following spring. The bull's horns drop off in the winter and begin growing anew into a rack that will be used during mating battles in the fall.

Moose antlers collected from the forests are valued at about $6 to $8 per pound, and are used to make all sorts of souvenirs, from 50¢ pencils to $5000 chandeliers. Moose droppings are also collected, lacquered and made into personal adornments for coprophiles and the aesthetically challenged.

Each year in the state of Maine, about 600 drivers pile their cars into moose. Most accidents occur at dawn and dusk when the animals are most active and visibility is poor; and in spring and early summer when the animals come out of the forest to lick up leftover road salt at the sides of the highways. Often, the car hits the moose broadside as it crosses the road, knocking out its long legs and sending a half-ton of hot moosemeat across the hood and into the windshield – altogether a closer acquaintance with a moose than anyone could want.

Tom Brosnahan

## BAXTER STATE PARK

Mt Katahdin (5267 feet), Maine's tallest mountain and the northern terminus of the 2000-mile-long Appalachian Trail, is the centerpiece of Baxter State Park, which has 46 other mountain peaks, 1200 campsites and 180 miles of hiking trails as well. It offers the wildest, most unspoiled wilderness adventures in New England, and Katahdin has a reputation as being a real rock climber's mountain.

Despite its relative inaccessibility – deep in the Maine woods over unpaved roads – Baxter hosts over 100,000 visitors annually, mostly during its summer season from mid-May through mid-October. It's open December through March for winter activities as well.

To fully enjoy Baxter State Park (www.mainerec.com/baxter1.html), you must arrive at the park entrance early in the day (only so many visitors are allowed in on any given day), and you should be well equipped for camping and perhaps for hiking and canoeing. Campsites in the park must be reserved well in advance by contacting Baxter State Park (☎ 207-723-5140), 64 Balsam Drive, Millinocket, ME 04462. You might also want to get some information from the Maine Appalachian Trail Club (www.matc.org), PO Box 283, Augusta, ME 04330 and the Katahdin Area Chamber of Commerce (☎ 207-723-4443), 1029 Central St, Millinocket, ME 04462.

If you are unable to get a reservation at one of the park's campsites, you can usually find a site at one of the private campsites just outside the Togue Ponds and Matagamon gates into the park. There are several campgrounds in Medway (just off I-95 exit 56), in Millinocket and in Greenville.

### Getting There & Away

Medway is at I-95 exit 56; Millinocket is about 11 miles northeast; and the southern border of Baxter State Park is about 20 miles northeast from Millinocket. Driving details for Medway follow.

| destination | mileage | hr:min |
|---|---|---|
| Bangor, ME | 58 miles | 1:15 |
| Boston, MA | 311 miles | 7:00 |
| Houlton, ME | 68 miles | 1:30 |
| Presque Isle, ME | 111 miles | 3:15 |
| New York, NY | 512 miles | 12:30 |
| Portland, ME | 203 miles | 4:30 |
| Montreal, Canada | 346 miles | 8:30 |
| Quebec City, Canada | 284 miles | 7:00 |
| Halifax, Canada | 359 miles | 9:30 |

## AROOSTOOK COUNTY

Aroostook County is huge, covering over 6400 sq miles, which makes it substantially larger than the entire state of Connecticut. 'The County,' as it's called, has more than 2000 lakes, ponds, streams and rivers. The western half of the county is deep forest owned by the timber and paper companies. The long eastern half, however, is good farming country, though the growing season is short – perfect for raising potatoes. The people of Aroostook County take advantage of this fact by producing 1½ million tons of potatoes every year.

If you're into potatoes or forests, Aroostook is heaven. Sit down at a restaurant in Houlton, Presque Isle or Madawaska and you'll find potatoes on the menu in all sorts of original ways. The names of the many varieties of the noble spud *(Solanum tuberosum)* – Kennebec, Katahdin, Norchip, Superior, Ontario, Russet Burbank, Norgold Russet – are bandied about by the locals over breakfast.

Unless you're in the business, the fascination provided by tubers fades fast. You may well find Aroostook to be just a pretty place to pass through on your way to somewhere else.

The I-95 ends at Houlton, on the border with the Canadian province of New Brunswick. NB 95 continues on the other side and links you to CN 2, the Trans-Canada Hwy.

From Houlton, US 1 goes north to Presque Isle, Caribou and Van Buren before crossing into New Brunswick. You can continue on NB 17 to Campbellton and Quebec's beautiful Gaspé Peninsula, or head northwest on CN 185, the Trans-Canada, to Rivie`re-du-Loup, Quebec, then southwest up the St Lawrence to Quebec City; though the fastest route from Maine to Quebec City is to take I-95 to Fairfield, just north of Winslow, then US 201 north via Skowhegan, Bingham, the Kennebec Valley and Jackman. But this way you don't get to see several thousand square miles of potatoes.

There are various local information offices, including the Aroostook County Tourist Hotline (☎ 800-487-1369, www.thecounty.com). There are also the chambers of commerce in most towns, including the following:

Caribou
  (☎ 207-498-6156,
  www.mainerec.com/caribou.html)
Houlton
  (☎ 207-532-4216,
  www.mainerec.com/houlton.html)
Presque Isle
  (☎ 207-764-6561, www.presqueisle.net)
Van Buren
  (☎ 207-868-5059)

MAINE

# New York City

Famed for its frenetic pace and notorious for its temperamental population, New York City can be a daunting destination. Here are some tips on surviving and enjoying the Big Apple (as it's popularly known) on your way to or from your New England vacation.

## ORIENTATION

New York City proper is divided into five boroughs: Manhattan, Queens, Brooklyn, the Bronx and Staten Island. The whole urban area, known as greater New York City, includes Manhattan Island, the western tip of Long Island, the southern end of the peninsula bounded by the Hudson River and Long Island Sound, Staten Island and neighboring parts of New Jersey.

In order to negotiate this urban sprawl, you've got to be familiar with these travelers' landmarks:

**John F Kennedy International Airport** – on Long Island; the major terminus for transcontinental and intercontinental flights

**La Guardia Airport** – in Queens; a major terminus for US domestic and Canadian flights

**Newark International Airport** – west of New York City in neighboring New Jersey; a busy international and domestic airport

**Grand Central Station** – E 42nd St and Park Ave; the major terminus for suburban and regional trains (take subway lines 4, 5, 6, 7 or S; bus Nos M1, M2, M3, M4, M5, M42, M98, M101, M102, M103 or M104)

**Pennsylvania Station (Penn Station)** – W 32nd St and Seventh Ave, 11 blocks south of Times Square; the terminus for Amtrak intercity trains to New England and other US regions (subway lines 1, 2, 3, 9, A, C or E; bus Nos M4, M10, M16 or M34)

**Port Authority Bus Terminal** – W 42nd St and Eighth Ave, four blocks west of Grand Central Station and one block west of Times Square; the USA's largest bus terminal, with buses to all parts of New England, other US regions and Montreal; has a special section for buses serving New York's three major airports (subway lines A, C or E; bus Nos M10, M11, M16, M27, M42 or M104)

See the Getting Around section, later in this chapter, for details on transport to and from the major airports.

Within Manhattan, the heart of the city, the avenues run north-south and the streets run east-west. Broadway, which slices diagonally across the city, was once a woodland path used by Native Americans.

**Midtown** refers to the largely commercial district from 23rd St north to 59th St (the southern boundary of Central Park), an area that includes the Empire State Building, United Nations headquarters, Rockefeller Center, Madison Square Garden, Times Square and the Broadway theater district, as well as many hotels and the offices of numerous airlines.

You are most likely to arrive in Manhattan in Midtown, at or near one of the three major transportation hubs (see above): Grand Central Station, the Port Authority Bus Terminal or Penn Station.

**Uptown**, north of 59th St (also called Central Park South), contains Lincoln Center and most of the city's major museums. Central Park divides the generally prosperous residential areas of the Upper

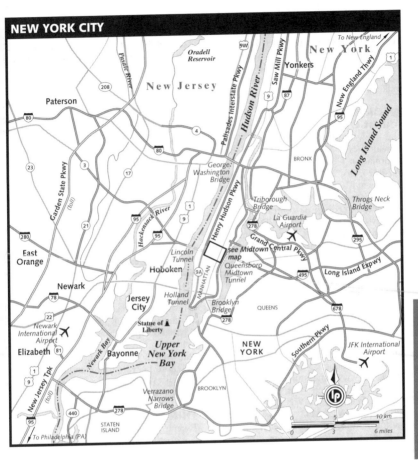

# NEW YORK CITY

East Side and Upper West Side. Above 59th St (Central Park South), Eighth Ave is called Central Park West. Fifth Ave borders the east side of the park, which ends at Harlem's southern border on 110th St, only a few blocks south of Columbia University.

**Downtown**, south of 23rd St, includes Greenwich Village, Washington Square Park, New York University, City Hall, Chinatown, Wall St and the Financial District, the World Trade Center, the Brooklyn Bridge and the docks where you can board ferries to the Statue of Liberty.

Running north from Washington Square Park, Fifth Ave divides Manhattan's East Side and West Side. Buildings on the cross streets are numbered east and west from Fifth Ave; thus, the Hard Rock Cafe, at 221 W 57th St, is just over two blocks west of Fifth Ave.

When looking for an address, be sure you know both the street and the avenue – 'There's a great little restaurant at 33rd and Third' ('toity-toid 'n' toid' in Brooklynese). If anyone directs you to the Avenue of the Americas, head for Sixth Ave.

New Yorkers routinely measure walking distances in city blocks. A city block in New York is typically 90 yards long from north to south and 350 yards wide from east to west. If you walk north or south for 20 blocks or east or west for five blocks, you will have walked about a mile.

## INFORMATION
### Tourist Offices

The New York Convention & Visitors Bureau's (NYCVB) state-of-the-art Visitor Information Center (☎ 212-397-8222, 800-692-8474, fax 212-245-5943, www.nycvisit .com) is at 810 Seventh Ave, New York, NY 10019, between 52nd and 53rd Sts at the southwestern corner of Central Park. (Take subway lines 1, 9, A, B, C or D.) It's open 9 am to 6 pm weekdays, 10 am to 3 pm weekends; for help and information in languages other than English, call ☎ 212-484-1222.

The NYCVB's free 150-page *Official NYC Guide* is excellent – almost essential – in its coverage of transportation, hotels, sights, restaurants, entertainment and shopping. The booklet, which contains discount coupons for hotels, restaurants, shops and tours, is available at hotels and major bus and train stations.

The Times Square Visitors Center (☎ 212-768-1560, www.timessquarebid.org), 1560 Broadway between 46th and 47th Sts (subway lines 1, 2, 3, 7, 9, N, R or S; bus Nos M6, M7, M10, M27, M42 or M104), has information booths, automated teller machines (ATMs), self-changing currency machines and Internet terminals. Visitors can also purchase Broadway theater tickets and subway MetroCards here (see the Getting Around section, later in this chapter, for more details on public transportation). The center is open 8 am to 8 pm daily.

### Money

Manhattan has thousands of ATMs, most of which charge about $3 for withdrawals. The alternative is to change foreign currency or traveler's checks at a bank branch (Chase Manhattan has 500 branches, American Express 14) or a currency exchange office, which may charge higher fees.

### Post

The General Post Office (☎ 212-967-8585, 421 Eighth Ave), at W 33rd St just west of Penn Station, is open 24 hours a day. It has a general delivery (ie, *poste restante*) service, but it's neither reliable nor recommended.

### Media

Several free pocket magazines, such as *City Guide* (weekly) and *New York Quick Guide* (monthly), have city maps; look for them in hotel brochure racks. CitySearch NY (www .newyork.citysearch.com) is a comprehensive commercial website that lists hotels, restaurants, amusements and shops.

### Dangers & Annoyances

Despite the city's widespread (but mostly undeserved) reputation for urban danger, you are unlikely to run into trouble in New York if you use common sense; follow the standard rules of urban defense and stick to the busier areas.

Avoid dark or deserted streets and empty subway cars. Guard against pickpockets at all times: on sidewalks, in buses and subways, and especially in crowds. Carry valuables securely, preferably covering them with your clothing.

Ignore beggars ('panhandlers') and hustlers (people who approach you for a variety of reasons, none of them good).

## THINGS TO SEE & DO

Even if you only have a day or two in New York before you head up to New England or return home, you can still dip into the delights of this fascinating city. Admission and tour prices quoted below are for adults; seniors, students and children usually pay 10% to 50% less. Some museums offer free or reduced-rate admission for several hours on a certain day each week; see the NYCVB's *Official NYC Guide* or call the museum.

### Midtown

Start your explorations right at the heart of Midtown. **Grand Central Station** (☎ 212-340-2345), the beaux arts palace on E 42nd St at Park Ave, was built in 1913 as a fitting railroad terminus for the great and growing

## MIDTOWN

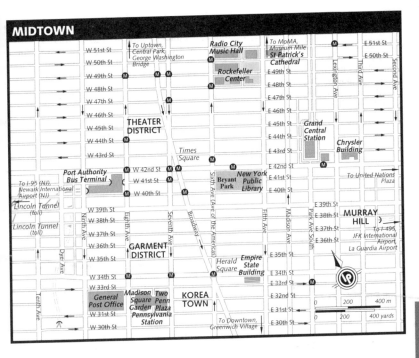

American metropolis. Grand it is, with a Romanesque facade and a recently restored vaulted ceiling boasting a map of the constellations with illuminated stars. Today, Grand Central Station serves mundane commuter trains while the long-distance trains arrive at Penn Station, between 31st and 33rd Sts near Eighth Ave.

A short block away from Grand Central Station at E 43rd St near Lexington Ave, the art deco **Chrysler Building** (1930) is one of New York's signature skyscrapers, its exterior decorated with motorcar motifs.

Four blocks east of the train station is the headquarters of the **United Nations** (☎ 212-963-7713), between E 42nd and E 48th Sts east of First Ave, which is built on land donated by the Rockefellers. Guided tours (45 minutes, $7.50) depart about every 30 minutes between 9:15 am and 4:45 pm daily except weekends in winter; enter at E 46th St and First Ave.

Two blocks west of Grand Central Station, the entrance to the main branch of the **New York Public Library** (☎ 212-930-0800), at E 42nd St at Fifth Ave, is framed by stone lions. The cavernous main reading room on the 3rd floor (closed Sunday) retains its original century-old Tiffany lamps, and several galleries hold manuscripts by famous authors. Shady **Bryant Park**, on the library's west side, is a good place for a rest or a picnic.

A block east of Bryant Park and the library is **Times Square**, the center of the theater and entertainment district. Look for all the neon signs in the triangle created by W 42nd St, Broadway and Seventh Ave.

Six blocks south of the library, the **Empire State Building** (☎ 212-736-3100), E 34th St at Fifth Ave, was the world's tallest building (1454 feet) from 1931 to 1977 and is still one of the most famous landmarks on the New York skyline. Open 9:30 am to midnight daily, the observatories ($6) on the 86th and 102nd floors are very popular, so come either early or late in the day to avoid the midday crowds.

Six blocks north of the library along Fifth Ave is **Rockefeller Center** (☎ 212-315-3544), 666 Fifth Ave, set off by a bronze sculpture of Atlas. Begun in 1931, this complex of fine art deco buildings stretches from 48th St to 52nd St. At its center, Rockefeller Plaza, with its signature gilded statue of Prometheus, is a welcome patch of open space amid the skyscrapers. In summer, the plaza is a terrace cafe-restaurant; in winter, it turns into an ice-skating rink.

Across Fifth Ave from the Rockefeller Center, **St Patrick's Cathedral** (☎ 212-753-2261) is the historic church where the Roman Catholic bishop of New York presides. Located at E 50th St, the spiritual landmark has been standing since the Civil War.

The stretch of **Fifth Ave** that runs north from Rockefeller Center to Central Park features a dense collection of airline offices and posh shops, including Saks Fifth Avenue, at E 50th St.

The **Museum of Modern Art** (☎ 212-708-9480), 11 W 53rd St between Fifth and Sixth Aves, is commonly known as 'MoMA' (MOH-mah). Its superb collection of paintings, sculpture, art objects, photographs and films spans the past century, from the early impressionists to artists of the moment. MoMA is open 10:30 am to 5:45 pm Sunday through Tuesday, Thursday and Saturday, until 8:15 pm Friday. It's closed Wednesday; $9.50.

## Uptown

For information about summer concerts in the 843-acre **Central Park**, ask at the visitors' center (☎ 212-794-6564) in the Dairy building along the 65th St pathway (off Fifth Ave), open 11 am to 4 pm daily except Monday.

The vast **Metropolitan Museum of Art** (☎ 212-879-5500), E 82nd St at Fifth Ave, is among the world's finest. It's open 9:30 am to 5:15 pm Sunday and Tuesday through Thursday, until 8:45 pm Friday and Saturday. It's closed Monday; $8.

The mammoth **American Museum of Natural History** (☎ 212-769-5100), W 79th St at Central Park West, holds more than 30 million artifacts, including enough dinosaur bones to fill three of the museum's most popular exhibit halls. It's open 10 am to 5:45 pm Sunday through Thursday, until 8:45 pm Friday and Saturday; $8.

Fifth Ave above 57th St, east of Central Park, is called **Museum Mile** because of the area's many fine museums, which include the **Frick Collection** (☎ 212-288-0700), 1 E 70th St. Built in 1914, the opulent former millionaire's mansion contains works by Bellini, Constable, Gainsborough, Titian and Vermeer. The Frick is open 10 am to 6 pm Tuesday through Saturday, 1 to 6 pm Sunday. It's closed Monday; $7.

Nearby, the **Whitney Museum of American Art** (☎ 212-570-2676), 945 Madison Ave at 75th St, houses 20th-century works by de Kooning, Hopper, Johns, O'Keeffe, Pollock, Rothko and other artists inside a massive concrete-and-stone building. The museum is open 11 am to 6 pm Sunday, Tuesday, Wednesday, Friday and Saturday, 1 to 8 pm Thursday. It's closed Monday; $8.

The sweeping spiral of the **Solomon R Guggenheim Museum** (☎ 212-423-3500), 1071 Fifth Ave at E 89th St, boasts an excellent collection of 20th-century paintings by Cézanne, Chagall, Picasso, Pollock and especially Kandinsky. It's open 10 am to 6 pm Sunday through Wednesday, until 8 pm Friday and Saturday. It's closed Thursday; admission is $12.

In 1901, steel magnate Andrew Carnegie built the 64-room mansion that has become the **Cooper-Hewitt National Design Museum** (☎ 212-849-8300), at 2 E 91st St at Fifth Ave. The museum is a must for anyone interested in architecture, engineering, jewelry, textiles or domestic design. The museum is open 10 am to 9 pm Tuesday, 10 am to 5 pm Wednesday through Saturday, noon to 5 pm Sunday. It's closed Monday; $5.

## Downtown

Everyone wants to see **Greenwich Village**, the legendary haunt of jazz greats, beat poets, soon-to-be-famous artists and, more recently, yuppies. Greenwich Village is bounded by 14th, Lafayette and Houston Sts and the Hudson River. **Washington Square Park**, at the southern end of Fifth Ave, is a good place to begin your explorations.

The society architect Stanford White designed the **triumphal arch** (1889) and **Judson Memorial Church** to the south. The row of town houses on the park's north side was the setting for *Washington Square*, Henry James' novel about late-19th-century social mores. Today, New York University owns most of the property around the park.

**The Financial District** Wall St, the metaphorical center of US banking and finance, takes its name from the wooden palisade (the 'wall') built by Dutch settlers in 1653 to protect their village, Nieuw Amsterdam, from attacks by the British and Native Americans.

At the intersection of Wall St and Broadway stands **Trinity Church** (1846), which once ranked as the tallest building in the city. From the church, walk east along Wall St to **Federal Hall**, distinguished by a huge statue of George Washington. In an earlier building on this spot, the first US Congress convened, and Washington was sworn in as the fledgling republic's first president.

Across the street is the Roman temple of the **New York Stock Exchange**. Come before noon if you want one of the free tickets for admission to the visitors' gallery overlooking the trading floor (weekdays only). Ask for tickets at the booth at 20 Broad St, around the corner from Wall St.

Walk south along Broad St for several blocks and turn left on Pearl St to see some of the few remaining colonial-era buildings in the city. Continue along Pearl St and turn right at Fulton St to **South Street Seaport**, an 11-block enclave of restored buildings and modern shops with **South Street Seaport Museum** (☎ 212-748-8600) as its centerpiece.

## ORGANIZED TOURS

With two locations, Gray Line (☎ 212-397-2620, www.graylinenewyork.com), in the Port Authority Bus Terminal and the Times Square Visitors Center, offers 29 different

---

### Miss Liberty

Officially named *Liberty Enlightening the World*, the Statue of Liberty (☎ 212-363-7620) was a gift from the people of France to the people of the USA. It is New York City's best-known landmark, the USA's signature symbol and the most famous work of French sculptor Frédéric-Auguste Bartholdi.

Begun in 1875, the statue took shape over 10 years as workers hammered massive copper sheets and attached them to the four huge iron supports designed by Alexandre-Gustave Eiffel (he of the tower) and Eugène-Emmanuel Viollet-le-Duc.

The 225-ton statue was disassembled, shipped from Paris to New York, erected on a small island in New York Harbor and dedicated by President Grover Cleveland on October 26, 1886. A century later, the copper cladding had become badly corroded, but a $100 million repair job by French and American workers was finished in time for the statue's gala centennial celebration in 1986.

If you want to climb the 354 steps – the equivalent of 22 stories in a skyscraper – to the top and enjoy the view from Miss Liberty's crown, you should breakfast early, take the subway to South Ferry or Bowling Green and catch the first ferry (☎ 212-269-5755) from Battery Park at 8:30 am. The ferries run every 30 minutes until 4 pm (7 pm in summer), offering spectacular views of the Manhattan skyline along the way. After Liberty Island, the ferry stops at Ellis Island, home to the Immigration Museum (☎ 212-269-5755).

---

tours priced from $25 to $55, including a hop-on, hop-off loop route through Manhattan ($33) with narration in English, French, German, Italian and Spanish. New York Apple Tours (☎ 212-944-9200, 800-876-9868), 53rd St at Eighth Ave, has double-decker buses that follow a similar loop. Hop on and off as you like for two days ($39).

The popular three-hour, 35-mile cruise around Manhattan with Circle Line (☎ 212-563-3200) costs $34 and departs Pier 83, at the western end of W 42nd St on the Hudson River, daily (except Tuesday and Wednesday in January and February). No subways run to the dock, so you'll have to walk or take a taxi.

## PLACES TO STAY

New York has a surprising range of accommodations and prices. Reserve your budget room well in advance, or you may have to settle for something more expensive.

### Hostels

Run by Hostelling International/American Youth Hostels, the *New York International Hostel* (☎ 212-932-2300, fax 932-2574, www.HInewyork.org, 891 Amsterdam Ave), at W 103rd St, west of the northern part of Central Park near Columbia University, has 624 beds ($22 to $24) and private rooms that sleep four to six people ($120); family rooms with shared bath cost $90. The hostel is open 24 hours a day. From June through October and during the Christmas and New Year's holiday, you must make reservations at least 24 hours in advance with a credit card. Subway trains 1 and 9 (also known as the Broadway local) stop at 103rd St, one block west of the hostel.

Fifteen blocks south, the *International Student Center* (☎ 212-787-7706, 38 W 88th St), at Central Park West, rents its beds for $15 to non-US residents between the ages of 18 and 30. Even closer to Midtown, *Banana Bungalow* (☎ 212-769-2441, 250 W 77th St), at Broadway, has beds for $18; the current renovation may improve this oft-criticized place and, perhaps, increase the price.

In Midtown, the basic *Big Apple Hostel* (☎ 212-302-2603, 119 W 45th St), at Sixth Ave, a block east of Times Square, stays open all day and has $28 beds and laundry facilities.

The *Chelsea Center Hostel* (☎ 212-643-0214, fax 473-3945, 313 W 29th St), between Eighth and Ninth Aves, has 22 beds ($25), which it prefers to rent to foreign travelers. You can make a reservation without a credit card, and later reconfirm that reservation 48 hours before your arrival.

### Hotels

There are some good hotels between Central Park and Greenwich Village. Unless otherwise stated, the prices below are 'rack' (walk-in) rates for double rooms in summer and are guidelines only; the price you are quoted will depend upon when you want to stay, when you call to reserve and how full the hotel is at that time. Single rooms are usually a few dollars cheaper. Breakfast and parking (if available) usually cost extra.

Package deals and astute haggling may bring the price down. If you are a student, auto club member, senior citizen, government worker, sports fan or theatergoer, mention it when you call and you may receive a discount.

Some of these hotels belong to hotel groups with websites; browse these sites for hints on special deals.

Be warned: A hefty 13.25% sales tax and a $2-per-night hotel room tax will be added to your bill, so a three-night stay in a $100-per-night hotel room will actually cost almost $350.

Just south of Columbus Circle, near the Visitor Information Center, is the *Westpark Hotel* (☎ 212-246-6440, fax 246-3131, 308 W 58th St), at Eighth Ave. Popular with European travelers, this hotel is conveniently located between the Uptown museums and the Midtown theaters. Rooms cost $110 to $130.

The *Best Western Woodward Hotel* (☎ 212-247-2000, 210 W 55th St), at Broadway, is quiet and efficient but pricey at $239. The nearby *Wellington Hotel* (☎ 212-247-3900, 800-652-1212, fax 212-581-1719, www.wellingtonhotel.com, 871 Seventh Ave), at 55th St, has 700 ordinary but serviceable rooms that are popular with tourists who don't mind the $160 to $180 price. The 57th St subway station is right across the street.

The *Ameritania* (☎ 212-247-5000, fax 247-3313, 230 W 54th St), at Broadway, a favorite with European bus tours, asks about $150, but try for a 10% discount by saying you saw a listing in this guidebook.

Nearby, and also managed by the Amsterdam Hospitality Group (☎ 888-664-6835, www.nycityhotels.net), is the *Amsterdam Court* (☎ 212-459-1000, fax 265-5070, 226 W 50th St), at Broadway, a stylish hotel in a somewhat downscale but convenient neighborhood. Double rooms cost $115 to $135.

*Days Hotel Midtown* (☎ 212-581-7000, 800-572-6232, fax 212-974-0291, 790 Eighth Ave), at 49th St, is a bustling, bland but comfortable chain hotel that charges $155 to $220. It's popular with bus tours, sports fans and school groups.

For a real New York experience, *Hotel Edison* (☎ 212-840-5000, 800-637-7070, fax 212-596-6850, www.edisonhotelnyc.com, 228 W 47th St), at Seventh Ave, is a wonderful art deco place right in the midst of the Broadway theaters and only two blocks north of Times Square. The rooms are adequate, if not fancy, and they are also well priced at $140.

Nearby, the clean but spartan *Portland Square Hotel* (☎ 212-382-0600, 800-388-8988, fax 212-382-0684, www.portlandsquarehotel .com, 132 W 47th St), between Broadway and Sixth Ave near Times Square, has singles with shared bath for $60, singles with private bath for $95 and doubles for $109 to $119. Larger rooms sleep three ($130) or four ($140) in two beds.

More or less across the street, the *Hampshire Hotel & Suites* (☎ 212-768-3700, 800-334-4667, fax 212-768-3403, 157 W 47th St) is a step up in comfort and price and a good value at $150 to $180.

The *Comfort Inn Midtown* (☎ 212-221-2600, fax 764-7481, 129 W 46th St), between Sixth and Seventh Aves east of Times Square, offers clean and presentable rooms for about $160. The owner, Apple Core Hotels (☎ 800-567-7720), also runs the Quality Hotel Eastside (see below) and three other Manhattan hotels.

The huge *Milford Plaza Ramada* (☎ 212-869-3600, 800-221-2690, fax 212-944-8357, 270 W 45th St) fills the entire block of Eighth Ave between W 44th and W 45th Sts. Its 1300 rooms, renovated in 1995, rent to tour groups, airline crews and Broadway show fans for $149 to $200.

The clean, modern, 189-room *Quality Hotel Fifth Avenue* (☎ 212-447-1500, 800-228-5151, fax 212-210-0972, 3 E 40th St), at Fifth Ave two blocks southwest of Grand Central Station, attracts lots of business travelers but offers heavy discounts on weekends and in summer, when rooms cost $200.

Photos of Greta Garbo grace the classy (if small) lobby of the *Hotel Metro* (☎ 212-947-2500, fax 279-1310, 45 W 35th St), between Fifth and Sixth Aves. The adjoining Metro Grill is also nice. The rooms ($165 to $200) are plain but adequate.

Right across the street, the *Comfort Inn Manhattan* (☎ 212-947-0200, fax 594-3047, www.comfortinnmanhattan.com, 42 W 35th St) includes a light breakfast and weekday newspaper in the price of its decent rooms ($150 to $190). The 34th St subway station is only a half-block to the west.

The *Herald Square Hotel* (☎ 212-279-4017, 800-727-1888, fax 212-643-9208, www .heraldsquarehotel.com, 19 W 31st St), in between Fifth and Sixth Aves, is a bright spot on a drab street of tailors, travel agents and parking garages. Under the same management as the aforementioned Portland Square Hotel, the Herald Square charges $55 for a single with shared bath, $80 for a single with private bath and $110 to $125 for a double with private bath.

A half-block east, the *Hotel Wolcott* (☎ 212-268-2900, fax 563-0096, www.wolcott .com, 4 W 31st St), at Fifth Ave, is a beaux art building with 280 rooms that cost $100 to $140.

The *Quality Hotel Eastside* (☎ 212-545-1800, 800-567-7720, fax 212-481-7270, 161 Lexington Ave), at E 30th St, is clean, reasonably priced ($120) and located in a nice neighborhood.

*Howard Johnson on Park Ave* (☎ 212-532-4860, 800-258-4290, fax 212-545-9727, 429 Park Ave S), at E 29th St, 13 blocks south of Grand Central Station, has a classy address in a good middle-class neighborhood, with comfortable rooms priced at $130.

In the Flatiron District, the outrageous *Gershwin Hotel* (☎ 212-545-8000, fax 684-5546, www.gershwinhotel.com, 7 E 27th St), between Fifth and Madison Aves, has huge glass 'horns' on its facade, a trendy art-filled lobby and – in a typical New York triumph of style over substance – spartan rooms favored by young, hip, international travelers. Dorm beds cost $27, private rooms $95 to $147; reservations are a must.

## PLACES TO EAT

New York offers all sorts of meals at every possible price. Street vendors near major tourist attractions and transportation stations supply cheap, quick snacks. In addition to the traditional hot dog with onions ($2), vendors offer fruit, soups, sandwiches, falafel, focaccia and even Thai cuisine for $3 to $8.

Most of the larger museums have cafes that serve lunch. Though relatively expensive, museum cafes usually have fairly good upscale cuisine, and your patronage supports the arts.

At lunchtime, Midtown office workers flock to more than two dozen delis, pubs and moderately priced restaurants on 55th and 56th Sts between Fifth and Sixth Aves. Avoid the noon to 1:30 pm crush by lunching early or late in the day.

The streets around Times Square (W 42nd St at Seventh Ave) are filled with hamburger joints and mid-range ethnic restaurants of varying quality; it's a good idea to stick to basic menu items. There are plenty of choices on **Restaurant Row**, the block of W 46th St between Eighth and Ninth Aves, and on nearby streets.

The East Village (between E 14th and Houston Sts east of Third Ave) offers the best prices and widest range of choices for budget travelers.

## ENTERTAINMENT

*Time Out* is the best guide to the city's nightlife. The Sunday and Friday editions of the *New York Times* and each weekly issue of the *New Yorker* cover opera and theater performances, classical music concerts, museum shows and other forms of 'high culture,' while dance clubs and smaller music venues advertise in the *Village Voice*. NYC On Stage (☎ 212-768-1818) is a 24-hour information line for music and dance.

ClubFone (☎ 212-777-2582) provides information on nightclubs and cabarets.

TeleCharge (☎ 212-563-2929) sells tickets to plays and musicals, both on and off Broadway, to anyone with a credit card. Ticketmaster (☎ 212-307-7171 for concerts, 307-4100 for other performing arts events, www.ticketmaster.com) has a lock on sales for most major concerts and sporting events.

The TKTS booth in Times Square (☎ 212-768-1818) sells same-day tickets to Broadway and off-Broadway musicals and plays at a 25% to 75% discount. You must pay with cash or traveler's checks; credit cards are not accepted. A line starts forming at 2 pm, and evening tickets are sold from 3 to 8 pm, with the best seats (if any are left) not available for sale until 7 pm. On Wednesday and Saturday, matinee tickets go on sale at 10 am. On Sunday, the booth opens at 11 am.

There is another TKTS outlet downtown, at 2 World Trade Center, on the mezzanine level (subway lines 1, 9, A, E, N or R; bus Nos M1, M2, M3 or M4). Purchase evening tickets here from 11:30 am to 5:30 pm Monday through Friday and 11:30 am to 3:30 pm Saturday. Tickets for Wednesday, Saturday and Sunday matinees are sold the day before the performance, beginning at 11:30 am.

## GETTING AROUND

For information on air, train and bus services to and from New York City, see the Getting There & Away chapter at the beginning of the book.

### To/From the Airport

Although New York City has seven airports, you will most likely pass through John F Kennedy International Airport, La Guardia Airport or Newark International Airport.

### John F Kennedy International Airport

JFK (☎ 718-656-4520, www.panynj.gov), 15 miles southeast of Manhattan on the southern shore of Long Island, has a richly deserved reputation for being difficult and confusing. Despite the airport's shortcomings, though, more than 31 million travelers pass through the terminals every year, most of them on international flights. In order to accommodate so many passengers, JFK has planned major renovations to terminals and roadways, including the construction of a link to the Long Island Railroad (LIRR). Expect plenty of inconvenience and delay until the project's completed in 2001.

For airport transportation information, call the Port Authority's hotline (☎ 800-247-7433) or ask at the Ground Transportation Information desk in the baggage claim area of any terminal. During rush hours (7 to 9:30 am and 3:30 to 7 pm weekdays), it may take you longer to travel between the airport and the city than the times cited below.

The easiest way to reach Midtown Manhattan is aboard a New York Airport Service Express Bus (☎ 718-706-9658), which runs every 15 to 30 minutes from 6 am to midnight. The bus stops at Grand Central Station, E 42nd St at Vanderbilt Ave (where passengers can board trains to the suburbs and to New Haven, Connecticut), and at the Port Authority Bus Terminal Airport Bus Center, W 42nd St at Eighth Ave (where buses depart for Boston and many other New England and US cities). The 45- to 70-minute ride to either of these destinations costs $13. To connect with Amtrak trains at Penn Station, between W 31st and W 33rd Sts at Seventh Ave, take an Airport Service Express Bus to the Jamaica Station of the LIRR, then a train to Penn Station. This service operates every hour from 6 am to midnight, takes 60 to 70 minutes and costs $13 for the bus plus $3.50 to $5 for the train.

Trans-Bridge Lines (☎ 800-962-9135) operates buses to the Port Authority Bus Terminal's Gate 8 three times daily, departing JFK at 3:20, 5:20 and 6:50 pm ($10).

Two minibus operators take passengers from JFK to almost any address in Manhattan, including all the hotels. The shuttle ride typically lasts at least 45 to 60 minutes and costs $19. The Gray Line Air Shuttle (☎ 212-315-3006, 800-451-0455) operates 7 am to 11 pm; Super Shuttle Manhattan Shared Ride Service (☎ 800-258-3826, www.supershuttle.com) operates 24 hours a day. This is good if

you're alone, but a taxi is cheaper and more convenient for two or more. These companies also offer transportation to JFK from Manhattan.

Numerous other shuttle van, bus and limousine services take passengers to New York's other boroughs and to Long Island, Westchester County and suburban Connecticut, New Jersey and Pennsylvania. For details, call the Port Authority's transportation hotline (☎ 800-247-7433).

A taxi from JFK to Manhattan takes 40 to 60 minutes and costs $30 (a fixed rate for the whole car, not per passenger) plus tolls and tip. Only take taxis indicated by the official uniformed dispatcher; ignore the hustlers who may approach you with offers of taxis, limos or other ground transportation.

The cheapest way to get into Manhattan is also the longest: Take the free yellow, white and blue Long-Term Parking Lot Bus to Howard Beach Station, then get on an 'A' subway train (☎ 718-330-1234), connecting with other subway lines to reach your final destination in Manhattan. Trains ($1.50 – cash, token or MetroCard) run every 15 minutes, 24 hours a day. On the return trip to JFK, take the 'A' train from Manhattan to the Far Rockaway station.

Another inexpensive option is to board a Q10 Green Bus (☎ 718-995-4700) for Lefferts Blvd and Kew Gardens, connecting to the A, E, F, J, R and Z subway lines. Green Buses depart JFK every 15 minutes, 24 hours a day, and cost $1 to $1.50. The subway fare is an additional $1.50. Also, the Q3 New York City Transit Authority bus to 169th St and Hillside Ave connects to the F and R trains. These are good routes if you know something about the New York City subway system.

At the end of your visit, your hotel can reserve a luxury sedan (limo) to take you to JFK for $40, but you can save money by calling a limo company and making the reservation yourself (see the NYCVB's *Official NYC Guide,* described in the Information section of this chapter, for a list of reliable limo companies). If you make your own arrangements, a chauffeur-driven luxury

**NEW YORK CITY**

sedan may cost about the same as a rattly, beat-up taxi driven by a maniac, the difference being that you can catch a taxi on the street, but you must telephone to get a limo.

**La Guardia Airport** La Guardia (LGA; ☎ 718-533-3400, www.panynj.gov), 8 miles northeast of Manhattan on the northern shore of Long Island, in the borough of Queens, handles mostly domestic US flights and flights to and from Canada.

The most convenient way to reach Midtown Manhattan is aboard a New York Airport Service Express Bus (☎ 718-706-9658), which runs every 15 to 30 minutes from 6:40 am to 11:40 pm. The bus stops just outside Grand Central Station at the corner of E 41st St and Park Ave and at the Port Authority Bus Terminal Airport Bus Center. The 20- to 45-minute ride costs $10. To connect with Amtrak trains at Pennsylvania Station, take the bus to the Jamaica Station of the LIRR, then take a train to Penn Station. The trip takes 60 to 70 minutes and costs $5 for the bus plus $3 to $4.25 for the train.

Two minibus operators also shuttle passengers from La Guardia to almost any location in Manhattan (45 to 60 minutes, $16). The Gray Line Air Shuttle (☎ 212-315-3006, 800-451-0455) and Super Shuttle (☎ 800-258-3826, www.supershuttle.com) offer good rates for anyone traveling alone, but a taxi is cheaper for two or more passengers. These shuttle services also transport passengers to the airport.

The Delta Water Shuttle (☎ 800-543-3779) departs La Guardia's Marine Air Terminal/Delta Shuttle and stops at docks along the East River side of Manhattan at E 90th St, E 62nd St, E 34th St and Wall St (Pier 11). The trip takes 30 to 45 minutes and costs $15. Call for exact schedules.

Call the Port Authority's transportation hotline (☎ 800-247-7433) for details on buses, minivans and taxis to the suburbs.

A taxi from La Guardia to Manhattan takes 20 to 30 minutes or more and costs $16 to $26 plus tolls and tip. Only take taxis indicated by the official uniformed dispatcher. For a chauffeur-driven limousine,

expect to pay about $30 (see advice about limos under John F Kennedy International Airport, above).

For the cheapest transportation into Manhattan, take the Q33 or Q47 Triboro Coach (☎ 718-335-1000) and then connect to subway trains E, F, R or 7. The buses depart every 10 to 20 minutes, 24 hours a day. The bus costs $1.50; the subway fare is an additional $1.50.

**Newark International Airport** Newark (EWR; ☎ 201-961-6000, www.panynj.gov), 16 miles southwest of Manhattan, handles both domestic and international flights.

The quickest, most comfortable and most convenient way to reach Manhattan is via the Olympia Airport Express Bus (☎ 212-964-6233, 908-354-3330) to the Port Authority Bus Terminal. Departing every 20 to 30 minutes between 6 am and 1 am and every 30 to 60 minutes between 1 am and 6 am, the ride lasts 30 to 40 minutes and costs $10. Between 6:15 am and midnight, other Olympia buses go to Grand Central Station, stopping at 120 E 41st St (30 to 60 minutes, $10), and to Pennsylvania Station (30 to 40 minutes, $10). Some Olympia buses running between 8 am and 9 pm will drop you right at your Midtown Manhattan hotel for $15 to $20 or at a downtown location for $10.

The Gray Line (☎ 212-315-3006, 800-451-0455) and Super Shuttle (☎ 800-258-3826, www.supershuttle.com) services also run to and from Newark for $19 per passenger, a good way to go if you're traveling alone.

Call the Port Authority's transportation hotline (☎ 800-247-7433) for details on buses, minivans and taxis to the suburbs.

A taxi from Newark International Airport to Manhattan costs about $34 to $38 plus tolls; the ride takes 40 minutes or more. From Manhattan to the airport, you pay the metered rate plus $10, as well as tolls and tip. For a chauffeur-driven limousine, expect to pay about $48 (see advice about limos under John F Kennedy International Airport, above).

**Inter-Airport Transfers** You can get from one airport to another by taking the New

York Airport Service Express Bus or the Olympia Airport Express Bus (see numbers above) into Manhattan and then transferring to another bus, but airport-to-airport buses and vans are faster and sometimes even cheaper.

The New York Airport Service Express Bus runs between JFK and La Guardia every 30 minutes from 6 am to midnight. The trip takes about 45 minutes and costs $11. A taxi is a bit faster, costs $19 to $22 and makes sense if you share the fare with someone else – better yet, with two or three someones.

Between JFK and Newark, the Princeton Airporter Van (☎ 609-587-6600, 800-385-4000) runs frequently from 9 am to 10 pm. The ride lasts about 90 minutes and costs $21. Taxi drivers charge $65 to $70 plus tolls.

Between La Guardia and Newark, the ETS Air Shuttle (☎ 888-467-4996) runs vans every 60 to 90 minutes between 7 am and 9 pm. The 75- to 90-minute trip costs $20. Alternately, you can take a New York Airport Service Express Bus or Olympia Bus into Manhattan and then another one out to the airport.

You must carry your baggage with you. There are no automatic baggage transfer services among airports.

## Bus & Subway

Obsolescent but functional subway trains and modern buses operated by the Metropolitan Transit Authority (MTA; ☎ 718-330-1234, www.mta.nyc.ny.us) run 24 hours a day. The 26 subway lines were not built as part of a master plan, so the system is confusing but useful. Maps are available at subway and train stations; subway clerks and other New Yorkers can usually tell you which subway train you need to take, or you can call the MTA for information.

The fare of $1.50 can be paid in cash (you must have exact change to board a bus), token or MetroCard (see below). Transfer tickets allow you to change from subway to bus or bus to bus during the same journey at no additional fare. Ask for a transfer when you begin your trip; it's good for two hours.

Plastic MetroCard debit cards with no time limit cost $6 for four rides or $15 for 11 rides; they're sold at most stations. Metro-Card Fun Passes, good for unlimited rides on MTA buses and subways, cost $4 for one day (good until 3 am the next morning) or $17 for one week. You can purchase the passes at many shops and visitors' centers.

Many visitors new to Manhattan make the mistake of boarding an express train, which speeds past most of the stations without stopping.. On official subway maps, local stops are shown as black dots, while express stops are white circles.

## Car

Avoid driving in Manhattan, as traffic is slow and perilous and parking is scarce and expensive. If you plan to rent a car, do it somewhere else, such as Providence, Rhode Island, or Boston.

## Taxi

The yellow cabs licensed by the city's Taxi & Limousine Commission (☎ 212-302-8294) charge $2 plus 30¢ per ⅕ mile and 20¢ a minute while sitting in traffic, with a 50¢ surcharge for rides after 8 pm. Tip 10% to 15% (minimum 50¢). During the morning and evening rush hours and in rainy weather, an empty taxi may be difficult to find, so allow extra time.

# Glossary

For a hilarious and informative look at Boston dialect, browse Adam Gaffin's site at www.boston–online.com/wickedv.html.

**Abenaki** – a New England Native American tribe

**Alpine Slide** – a concrete chute navigated for fun on a simple wheeled cart or, if it's a water slide, in an inflatable cushion

**AMC** – Appalachian Mountain Club

**ayuh** – locution pronounced by some people in New Hampshire and Maine during pauses in conversation; perhaps a distant variant of 'yes'; vaguely positive in meaning

**Back Bay** – a district of Boston west of Beacon Hill and Boston Common developed during the 19th century by filling in a bay in the Charles River

**batholith** – a mass of rock formed deep in the earth, later perhaps thrust to the surface; they are customarily of large crystalled rock (such as granite) and appear as mountainous domes of rock above surrounding terrain of softer material (as Mt Monadnock in southern New Hampshire)

**boondocks** or **boonies** – a city-dweller's derogatory term for the countryside, especially a remote rural place, as in 'The inn is nice, but it's way out in the boonies'

**Brahmin** – member of Boston's wealthy, well-educated, 19th-century class; now, any wealthy, cultured Bostonian

**BYO** or **BYOB** – 'bring your own' or 'bring your own bottle'; designates a restaurant that allows patrons to bring their own wine or beer; see *dry town*

**Cape, the** – Cape Cod

**CCC** – Civilian Conservation Corps, the Depression-era federal program established in 1933 to employ unskilled young workers, mainly on projects aimed at the conservation of US wildlands

**CCNS** – Cape Cod National Seashore

**chandlery** – retail shop specializing in yachting equipment

**cobble** – a high rocky knoll of limestone, marble or quartzite that is found in western Massachusetts

**cod cheeks** – soft oysterlike bits of meat found on the sides of a codfish's 'face'; a delicacy, along with cod tongues, in some parts of New England and Atlantic Canada

**common** – see *green*

**DAR** – Daughters of the American Revolution, a patriotic service organization for women

**Downeast** – the Maine coast, especially its more easterly reaches, roughly from Mount Desert Island to Eastport

**drumlin** – a low, elongated hill formed of glacial till (earth and rock debris) during the most recent Ice Age; a common feature of the terrain in New England

**dry town** – a town in which municipal ordinances prohibit the sale (but usually not the possession, consumption or service of) alcoholic beverages

**efficiency** (unit) – a hotel or motel room with cooking and dining facilities (hot plate or range, refrigerator, sink, utensils, crockery and cutlery); see also *housekeeping cabin/unit, kitchenette*

**Equity playhouse** – 'Actors' Equity' is the US actors' union; Equity actors are professionals, members of the union

**gap** – mountain pass with steep sides; called a notch in New Hampshire

**gimcrack** – a small item of uncertain use, perhaps frivolous; a gizmo

**glacial pond** – a deep, round freshwater pond formed by glacial gouging action during the Ice Age; a common feature of the New England terrain (as Walden Pond in Concord, Massachusetts)

**green** – the grass-covered open space typically found at the center of a traditional New England village or town, originally used as common pastureland ('the common'), but now serving as a central park; the green is often surrounded by community service buildings such as the town hall, library, court house and churches

**grinder** – a large sandwich of meat, cheese, lettuce, tomato, dressing, etc, in a long bread roll; also called a 'sporkie' or, in other parts of the US, a 'submarine,' 'po' boy,' 'Cuban' or 'hoagie'

**hidden drive** – a driveway entering a road in such a way that visibility for approaching drivers is impaired; signs warn of them
**hookup** – a facility at an RV camping site for connecting (hooking up) a vehicle to electricity, water, sewer or even cable TV
**housekeeping cabin/unit** – a hotel or motel room or detached housing unit equipped with kitchen facilities, rented by the day, week or month; see *efficiency, kitchenette*

**Indian summer** – a brief warm period, usually in late autumn, before the cold weather sets in for the winter
**ironclad** – a 19th-century wooden warship with iron sheathing
**Islands, the** – Martha's Vineyard and Nantucket off Cape Cod

**kitchenette** – a small, but adequately equipped, food preparation area in an efficiency or housekeeping unit; see *efficiency, housekeeping cabin/unit*

**leaf peeping** – recreational touring (by 'leaf peepers') to enjoy autumn foliage colors
**lean-to** – a simple shelter for camping, usually without walls, windows or doors, with a steeply slanting roof touching the ground on one side
**lobster roll** – a hot dog bun or other bread roll filled with lobster meat in a mayonnaise sauce and sometimes dressed with celery and lettuce
**Lower (or Outer) Cape** – the long, narrow extension of Cape Cod north and east from Orleans to Provincetown

**maple** – a tree of the genus *Acer* having lobed leaves, winged seeds borne in pairs and close-grained wood, well suited to making furniture and flooring; the sap of the sugar maple *(Acer saccharum)* is gathered, boiled and reduced to make maple syrup; see *sugar bush, sugaring off*
**Mid-Cape** – region of Cape Cod roughly from Barnstable and Hyannis eastward to Orleans
**minuteman** – a colonial militiaman pledged to be ready at a moment's notice to defend his home and village; first organized against Native American attacks, the minutemen provided the first organized American military force in the Revolutionary War against British troops
**mud time** – springtime in New England when the snow melts and the earth thaws

**NPS** – National Park Service, a division of the Dept of the Interior that administers US national parks and monuments

**OSV** – Old Sturbridge Village, Massachusetts

**P-Town** – Provincetown, on Cape Cod, Massachusetts
**package store** – liquor store
**pitched battle** – fighting without respite; the periods in a military engagement when both sides are actively fighting rather than resting, maneuvering or regrouping

**raw bar** – a counter where fresh uncooked shellfish (clams, oysters, etc) is served
**rush tickets** – sometimes called 'student rush' or 'rush seats,' these are discounted tickets bought at a theater or concert hall box office usually no more than an hour or two before a performance

**sachem** – Native American chieftain; Massasoit was sachem of the Wampanoag tribe
**sagamon** – similar to *sachem*
**shire town** – county seat, town holding county government buildings
**shopping center** – a collection of stores bordering a huge parking lot; stores usually include a large department or food store, plus smaller ones such as hairdressers, Laundromat/dry cleaners and fast-food restaurant(s)
**shopping mall** – or just 'mall,' a large, climate-controlled building surrounded by

parking lots or built above a parking garage and sheltering several large stores, many small shops and a few restaurants

**soaring** – term for glider (sailplane) rides

**Southie** – South Boston, a neighborhood inhabited largely by Bostonians of Irish descent with a strong sense of Irish identity

**sugar bush** – a grove of sugar maple trees; see *maple*

**sugaring off** – the springtime (March) harvest of sap from maple trees, which is collected and boiled to reduce it to maple syrup

**T, the** – official nickname for the Massachusetts Bay Transportation Authority (MBTA) Rapid Transit System

**tall ships** – tall-masted sailing vessels

**tin ceiling** – late 19th- to early-20th-century decorative feature consisting of thin steel sheets ('tinplate') embossed with decorative patterns, painted and used to cover ceilings

**tuck-in** – a substantial, satisfying sandwich-like meal

**UMass** – University of Massachusetts

**Upper Cape** – Cape Cod region near the Cape Cod Canal and the mainland

**USFS** – United States Forest Service, a division of the Dept of Agriculture that implements policies on federal forest lands on the principles of 'multiple use,' including timber cutting, wildlife management, camping and recreation

**USGS** – United States Geological Survey, an agency of the Dept of the Interior responsible for, among other things, detailed topographic maps of the entire country (USGS maps are particularly popular with hikers and backpackers)

**UVM** – University of Vermont

**Vineyard, the** – (pronounced 'VIN-yerd'), the island of Martha's Vineyard

**weir** – fishnet of string, bark strips, twigs, etc, placed in a river current to catch fish; using weirs is the oldest known method of fishing in the world

**windjammer** – a tall-masted sailing ship

**Yankee** – perhaps from *Jan Kees* (John Cheese), a derogatory term for English settlers in Connecticut used by 17th-century Dutch colonists in New York; an inhabitant or native of New England; one from the northeastern USA; a person or soldier from the northern states during the Civil War; and an American

# Toll-Free Numbers

Toll-free number information
☎ 800-555-1212

## Accommodations

| | |
|---|---|
| Baymont Inns and Suites | ☎ 800-428-3438 |
| Best Western | ☎ 800-528-1234 |
| Choice | ☎ 800-424-6423 |
| Clarion | ☎ 800-252-7466 |
| Comfort Inn | ☎ 800-221-2222 |
| Courtyard by Marriott | ☎ 800-321-2211 |
| Days Inn | ☎ 800-329-7466 |
| EconoLodge | ☎ 800-424-4777 |
| Embassy Suites Hotels | ☎ 800-362-2779 |
| Fairfield Inns | ☎ 800-228-2800 |
| Fairmont | ☎ 800-527-4727 |
| Four Seasons | ☎ 800-332-3442 |
| Hampton Inns | ☎ 800-426-7866 |
| HI-AYH | ☎ 800-909-4776 |
| Hilton | ☎ 800-445-8667 |
| Holiday Inn | ☎ 800-465-4329 |
| Howard Johnson | ☎ 800-446-4656 |
| Hyatt | ☎ 800-233-1234 |
| Inter-Continental Hotels | ☎ 800-327-0200 |
| ITT Sheraton | ☎ 800-325-3535 |
| La Quinta Motor Inns | ☎ 800-531-5900 |
| Loews | ☎ 800-235-6397 |
| Marriott | ☎ 800-228-9290 |
| Meridien | ☎ 800-543-4300 |
| Motel 6 | ☎ 800-466-8356 |
| Omni | ☎ 800-843-6664 |
| Radisson | ☎ 800-333-3333 |
| Ramada | ☎ 800-272-6232 |
| Red Lion Inns | ☎ 800-547-8010 |
| Red Roof Inns | ☎ 800-843-7663 |
| Rodeway Inn | ☎ 800-424-4777 |
| Sheraton | ☎ 800-325-3535 |
| Sleep Inns | ☎ 800-424-4777 |
| Super 8 | ☎ 800-800-8000 |
| Susse Chalet | ☎ 800-524-2538 |
| Travelodge | ☎ 800-578-7878 |
| Vagabond Hotels | ☎ 800-522-1555 |
| Westin | ☎ 800-228-3000 |
| Wyndham | ☎ 800-822-4200 |

## Airlines (Domestic)

| | |
|---|---|
| Airtran | ☎ 800-825-8538 |
| Alaska | ☎ 800-426-0333 |
| American | ☎ 800-433-7300 |
| America West | ☎ 800-235-9292 |
| Big Sky | ☎ 800-237-7788 |
| Continental | ☎ 800-525-0280 |
| Delta | |
| (Domestic) | ☎ 800-221-1212 |
| (International) | ☎ 800-241-4141 |
| Hawaiian | ☎ 800-367-5320 |
| Northwest | |
| (Domestic) | ☎ 800-225-2525 |
| (International) | ☎ 800-447-4747 |
| Skywest- | |
| Delta Connection | ☎ 800-453-9417 |
| Southwest | ☎ 800-435-9792 |
| Tower | ☎ 800-348-6937 |
| TWA | |
| (Domestic) | ☎ 800-221-2000 |
| (International) | ☎ 800-892-4141 |
| United | |
| (Domestic) | ☎ 800-241-6522 |
| (International) | ☎ 800-538-2929 |
| US Airways | ☎ 800-428-4322 |

## Airlines (International)

| | |
|---|---|
| Aer Lingus | ☎ 800-223-6537 |
| AeroLitoral | ☎ 800-237-6639 |
| Aeroméxico | ☎ 800-237-6639 |
| Air Canada | ☎ 800-776-3000 |
| Air France | ☎ 800-237-2747 |
| Air New Zealand | ☎ 800-262-1234 |
| Aviateca | ☎ 800-327-9832 |
| British Airways | ☎ 800-247-9297 |
| Canadian | ☎ 800-426-7000 |
| Grupo TACA | ☎ 800-535-8780 |
| Japan Air | ☎ 800-525-3663 |
| KLM | ☎ 800-374-7747 |
| Lufthansa | ☎ 800-645-3880 |
| Mexicana | ☎ 800-531-7921 |
| Qantas | ☎ 800-227-4500 |
| Virgin Atlantic | ☎ 800-862-8621 |

## Car-Rental Agencies

| | |
|---|---|
| Advantage | ☎ 800-777-5500 |
| Alamo | ☎ 800-327-9633 |
| Avis | ☎ 800-831-2847 |
| | 800-331-1212 |
| Budget | ☎ 800-527-0700 |
| | 800-472-3325 |
| CruiseAmerica (RV rental) | ☎ 800-327-7799 |
| Dollar | ☎ 800-800-4000 |
| Enterprise | ☎ 800-325-8007 |
| | 800-736-8222 |
| Hertz | ☎ 800-654-3131 |
| National | ☎ 800-227-7368 |
| | 800-328-4567 |
| | 800-227-3876 |
| National (TDD) | ☎ 800-328-6323 |
| Rent-a-Wreck | ☎ 800-535-1391 |
| Thrifty | ☎ 800-367-2277 |

## Money

| | |
|---|---|
| Western Union | ☎ 800-325-6000 |

## State & Federal Agencies

| | |
|---|---|
| National Park Service | ☎ 800-365-2267 |
| US Forest Service | ☎ 800-280-2267 |
| US Postal Service | ☎ 800-275-8777 |

## Transportation

| | |
|---|---|
| AAA | ☎ 800-272-2155 |
| Amtrak | ☎ 800-872-7245 |
| Green Tortoise | ☎ 800-227-4766 |
| Greyhound | ☎ 800-231-2222 |
| Greyhound International | ☎ 800-246-8572 |
| SuperShuttle | ☎ 800-258-3826 |

## Travel Agencies

| | |
|---|---|
| Carlson-Wagonlit Travel | ☎ 800-510-4703 |
| Council Travel | ☎ 800-226-8624 |
| STA | ☎ 800-777-0112 |

# Acknowledgements

## THANKS
Many thanks to the travelers who used the last edition and wrote to us with helpful hints, useful advice and interesting anecdotes:

Mary Aldington, Jacquie Ashmore, Peter Backwell, Connie Baker & John Sabo, Andrew Ball, Brian & Elaine Bates, MA Benson, Jessica Brown, Jennifer Burke, Agustin Cot, A Cuthbertson, Gareth Dark, Nicola Duckworth, Victor C Emmerson, Keith Geddes, Andy Hay, Carla Hoekendijk, Roxanne Horbett-Benton, TC & ML Hughes, Kari Jackson-Klönther, Joachim Jacobs, Katherine Kalweit, Brian Lew, Mole Lewis, Claudia Maarschalkerweerd, Zahid Malik, Christine J Mannetta, Robert McCarroll, Stuart Michael, Stephanie Mueller, Tom Murtha, Clare Napier, Paul Nickodem, M Norman, Gwyneth Parker, René Potvin, Andrew Reger, Christina Ricci, Annemarie Schellens-Ward, Daniela Schnider, Michael Schramm, Gabi Schwarz, Tim Scull, Tim Searle, Greg & Katherine Slay, Dan Smith, Samuel Solomon, Donald Somers, Mrs Stevens, Devin Taylor, Sue Thompson, Denise Travaillew, Maria & John Trimboli, BR Van Meurs, Mike & Greta White, Rob & Delyn Williams, Ryan Wright, Geoff Yeates.

# LONELY PLANET

## Guides by Region

**L**onely Planet is known worldwide for publishing practical, reliable and no-nonsense travel information in our guides and on our Web site. The Lonely Planet list covers just about every accessible part of the world. Currently there are ten series: travel guides, shoestring guides, walking guides, city guides, phrasebooks, audio packs, city maps, travel atlases, diving and snorkeling guides and travel literature.

---

**AFRICA** Africa – the South • Africa on a shoestring • Arabic (Egyptian) phrasebook • Arabic (Moroccan) phrasebook • Cairo • Cape Town • Central Africa • East Africa • Egypt • Egypt travel atlas • Ethiopian (Amharic) phrasebook • The Gambia & Senegal • Kenya • Kenya travel atlas • Malawi, Mozambique & Zambia • Morocco • North Africa • South Africa, Lesotho & Swaziland • South Africa, Lesotho & Swaziland travel atlas • Swahili phrasebook • Trekking in East Africa • Tunisia • West Africa • Zimbabwe, Botswana & Namibia • Zimbabwe, Botswana & Namibia travel atlas
**Travel Literature:** The Rainbird: A Central African Journey • Songs to an African Sunset: A Zimbabwean Story • Mali Blues: Traveling to an African Beat

**AUSTRALIA & THE PACIFIC** Australia • Australian phrasebook • Bushwalking in Australia • Bushwalking in Papua New Guinea • Fiji • Fijian phrasebook • Islands of Australia's Great Barrier Reef • Melbourne • Melbourne city map • Micronesia • New Caledonia • New South Wales & the ACT • New Zealand • Northern Territory • Outback Australia • Papua New Guinea • Papua New Guinea (Pidgin) phrasebook • Queensland • Rarotonga & the Cook Islands • Samoa • Solomon Islands • South Australia • South Pacific Languages phrasebook • Sydney • Sydney city map • Tahiti & French Polynesia • Tasmania • Tonga • Tramping in New Zealand • Vanuatu • Victoria • Western Australia
**Travel Literature:** Islands in the Clouds • Sean & David's Long Drive

**CENTRAL AMERICA & THE CARIBBEAN** Bahamas and Turks & Caicos • Bermuda • Central America on a shoestring • Costa Rica • Cuba • Dominican Republic & Haiti • Eastern Caribbean • Guatemala, Belize & Yucatán: La Ruta Maya • Jamaica • Mexico • Mexico City • Panama • Puerto Rico
**Travel Literature:** Green Dreams: Travels in Central America

**EUROPE** Amsterdam • Andalucía • Austria • Baltic States phrasebook • Berlin • Berlin city map• Britain • Brussels, Bruges & Antwerp • Central Europe • Central Europe phrasebook • Corsica • Czech & Slovak Republics • Denmark • Dublin • Eastern Europe • Eastern Europe phrasebook • Edinburgh • Estonia, Latvia & Lithuania • Europe • Finland • France • French phrasebook • Germany • German phrasebook • Greece • Greek phrasebook • Hungary • Iceland, Greenland & the Faroe Islands • Ireland • Italian phrasebook • Italy • Lisbon • London • London city map • Mediterranean Europe • Mediterranean Europe phrasebook • Norway • Paris • Paris city map • Poland • Portugal • Portugal travel atlas • Prague • Prague city map • Romania & Moldova • Rome • Russia, Ukraine & Belarus • Russian phrasebook • Scandinavian & Baltic Europe • Scandinavian Europe phrasebook • Scotland • Slovenia • Spain • Spanish phrasebook • St Petersburg • Switzerland • Trekking in Spain • Ukrainian phrasebook • Vienna • Walking in Britain • Walking in Italy • Walking in Switzerland • Western Europe • Western Europe phrasebook
**Travel Literature:** The Olive Grove: Travels in Greece

**INDIAN SUBCONTINENT** Bangladesh • Bengali phrasebook • Bhutan • Delhi • Goa • Hindi/Urdu phrasebook • India • India & Bangladesh travel atlas • Indian Himalaya • Karakoram Highway • Nepal • Nepali phrasebook • Pakistan • Rajasthan • South India • Sri Lanka • Sri Lanka phrasebook • Trekking in the Indian Himalaya • Trekking in the Karakoram & Hindukush • Trekking in the Nepal Himalaya
**Travel Literature:** In Rajasthan • Shopping for Buddhas

# LONELY PLANET

## Mail Order

L onely Planet products are distributed worldwide. They are also available by mail order from Lonely Planet, so if you have difficulty finding a title please write to us. North and South American residents should write to 150 Linden St, Oakland, CA 94607, USA; European and African residents should write to 10a Spring Place, London NW5 3BH, UK; and residents of other countries to PO Box 617, Hawthorn, Victoria 3122, Australia.

**ISLANDS OF THE INDIAN OCEAN** Madagascar & Comoros • Maldives • Mauritius, Réunion & Seychelles

**MIDDLE EAST & CENTRAL ASIA** Arab Gulf States • Central Asia • Central Asia phrasebook • Iran • Israel & the Palestinian Territories • Israel & the Palestinian Territories travel atlas • Istanbul • Jerusalem • Jordan & Syria • Jordan, Syria & Lebanon travel atlas • Lebanon • Middle East on a shoestring • Syria • Turkey • Turkish phrasebook • Turkey travel atlas • Yemen
**Travel Literature:** The Gates of Damascus • Kingdom of the Film Stars: Journey into Jordan

**NORTH AMERICA** Alaska • Backpacking in Alaska • Baja California • California & Nevada • Canada • Chicago • Chicago city map • Deep South • Florida • Hawaii • Honolulu • Las Vegas • Los Angeles • Miami • New England USA • New Orleans • New York City • New York city map • New York, New Jersey & Pennsylvania • Pacific Northwest USA • Puerto Rico • Rocky Mountain States • San Francisco • San Francisco city map • Seattle • Southwest USA • Texas • USA • USA phrasebook • Vancouver • Washington, DC & the Capital Region
**Travel Literature:** Drive Thru America

**NORTH-EAST ASIA** Beijing • Cantonese phrasebook • China • Hong Kong • Hong Kong city map • Hong Kong, Macau & Guangzhou • Japan • Japanese phrasebook • Japanese audio pack • Korea • Korean phrasebook • Kyoto • Mandarin phrasebook • Mongolia • Mongolian phrasebook • North-East Asia on a shoestring • Seoul • South-West China • Taiwan • Tibet • Tibetan phrasebook • Tokyo
**Travel Literature:** Lost Japan

**SOUTH AMERICA** Argentina, Uruguay & Paraguay • Bolivia • Brazil • Brazilian phrasebook • Buenos Aires • Chile & Easter Island • Chile & Easter Island travel atlas • Colombia • Ecuador & the Galapagos Islands • Latin American Spanish phrasebook • Peru • Quechua phrasebook • Rio de Janeiro • Rio de Janeiro city map • South America on a shoestring • Trekking in the Patagonian Andes • Venezuela
**Travel Literature:** Full Circle: A South American Journey

**SOUTH-EAST ASIA** Bali & Lombok • Bangkok • Bangkok city map • Burmese phrasebook • Cambodia • Hanoi • Hill Tribes phrasebook • Ho Chi Minh City • Indonesia • Indonesian phrasebook • Indonesian audio pack • Jakarta • Java • Laos • Lao phrasebook • Laos travel atlas • Malay phrasebook • Malaysia, Singapore & Brunei • Myanmar (Burma) • Philippines • Pilipino (Tagalog) phrasebook • Singapore • South-East Asia on a shoestring • South-East Asia phrasebook • Thailand • Thailand's Islands & Beaches • Thailand travel atlas • Thai phrasebook • Thai audio pack • Vietnam • Vietnamese phrasebook • Vietnam travel atlas

**ALSO AVAILABLE:** Antarctica • Brief Encounters: Stories of Love, Sex & Travel • Chasing Rickshaws • Not the Only Planet: Travel Stories from Science Fiction • Travel with Children • Traveller's Tales

# LONELY PLANET

## Phrasebooks

**L**onely Planet phrasebooks are packed with essential words and phrases to help travellers communicate with the locals. With color tabs for quick reference, an extensive vocabulary and use of script, these handy pocket-sized language guides cover day-to-day travel situations.

- handy pocket-sized books
- easy to understand Pronunciation chapter
- clear & comprehensive Grammar chapter
- romanization alongside script to allow ease of pronunciation
- script throughout so users can point to phrases for every situation
- full of cultural information and tips for the traveller

'...vital for a real DIY spirit and attitude in language learning'
*– Backpacker*

'the phrasebooks have good cultural backgrounders and offer solid advice for challenging situations in remote locations'
*– San Francisco Examiner*

Arabic (Egyptian) • Arabic (Moroccan) • Australian *(Australian English, Aboriginal and Torres Strait languages)* • Baltic States *(Estonian, Latvian, Lithuanian)* • Bengali • Brazilian • Burmese • Cantonese • Central Asia • Central Europe *(Czech, French, German, Hungarian, Italian, Slovak)* • Eastern Europe *(Bulgarian, Czech, Hungarian, Polish, Romanian, Slovak)* • Ethiopian (Amharic) • Fijian • French • German • Greek • Hill Tribes • Hindi/Urdu • Indonesian • Italian • Japanese • Korean • Lao • Latin American Spanish • Malay • Mandarin • Mediterranean Europe *(Albanian, Croatian, Greek, Italian, Macedonian, Maltese, Serbian, Slovene)* • Mongolian • Nepali • Papua New Guinea • Pilipino (Tagalog) • Quechua • Russian • Scandinavian Europe *(Danish, Finnish, Icelandic, Norwegian, Swedish)* • South Pacific Languages • South-East Asia *(Burmese, Indonesian, Khmer, Lao, Malay, Tagalog Pilipino, Thai, Vietnamese)* • Spanish (Castilian; *also includes Catalan, Galician and Basque)* • Sri Lanka • Swahili • Thai • Tibetan • Turkish • Ukrainian • USA *(US English, Vernacular, Native American languages, Hawaiian)* • Vietnamese • Western Europe *(Basque, Catalan, Dutch, French, German, Greek, Irish)*

# Lonely Planet Journeys

**J**OURNEYS is a unique collection of travel writing – published by the company that understands travel better than anyone else. It is a series for anyone who has ever experienced – or dreamed of – the magical moment when they encountered a strange culture or saw a place for the first time. They are tales to read while you're planning a trip, while you're on the road or while you're in an armchair in front of a fire.

These outstanding titles explore our planet through the eyes of a diverse group of international writers. JOURNEYS books catch the spirit of a place, illuminate a culture, recount a crazy adventure or introduce a fascinating way of life. They always entertain, and always enrich the experience of travel.

## FULL CIRCLE
### A South American Journey
*Luis Sepúlveda (translated by Chris Andrews)*
'A journey without a fixed itinerary' with Chilean writer Luis Sepúlveda. Extravagant characters and extraordinary situations are memorably evoked: gauchos organising a tournament of lies, a scheming heiress on the lookout for a husband, a pilot with a corpse on board his plane ... *Full Circle* brings us the distinctive voice of one of South America's most compelling writers.

**WINNER 1996 Astrolabe – Etonnants Voyageurs award for the best work of travel literature published in France.**

## GREEN DREAMS
### Travels in Central America
*Stephen Benz*
On the Amazon, in Costa Rica, Honduras and on the Mayan trail from Guatemala to Mexico, Stephen Benz describes his encounters with water, mud, insects and other wildlife – and not least with the ecotourists themselves. With witty insights into modern travel, *Green Dreams* discusses the paradox of cultural and 'green' tourism.

## DRIVE THRU AMERICA
*Sean Condon*
If you've ever wanted to drive across the USA but couldn't find the time (or afford the gas), *Drive Thru America* is perfect for you. In his search for American myths and realities – along with comfort, cable TV and good, reasonably priced coffee – Sean Condon paints a hilarious road-portrait of the USA.

**'entertaining and laugh-out-loud funny'**– *Alex Wilber, Travel editor, Amazon.com*

## SEAN & DAVID'S LONG DRIVE
*Sean Condon*
Sean and David are young townies who have rarely strayed beyond city limits. One day, for no good reason, they set out to discover their homeland, and what follows is a wildly entertaining adventure that covers half of Australia.

**'a hilariously detailed log of two burned out friends'** – *Rolling Stone*

## Lonely Planet On-line
**www.lonelyplanet.com** *or* AOL keyword: lp

**W**hether you've just begun planning your next trip, or you're chasing down specific info on currency regulations or visa requirements, check out Lonely Planet On-line for up-to-the minute travel information.

As well as mini-guides to more than 250 destinations, you'll find maps, photos, travel news, health and visa updates, travel advisories, and discussion of the ecological and political issues you need to be aware of as you travel. You'll also find timely upgrades to popular guidebooks, which you can print out and stick in the back of your book.

There's also an on-line travellers' forum where you can share your experience of life on the road, meet travel companions and ask other travellers for their recommendations and advice.

And of course we have a complete and up-to-date list of all Lonely Planet travel products, including travel guides, diving and snorkeling guides, phrasebooks, city maps, travel atlases, travel literature and videos, and a simple on-line ordering facility if you can't find the book you want elsewhere.

---

## Lonely Planet Diving & Snorkeling Guides

**B**eautifully illustrated with full-color photos throughout, Lonely Planet's **Pisces Books** explore the world's best diving and snorkeling areas and prepare divers for what to expect when they get there, both topside and underwater.

Dive sites are described in detail with specifics on depths, visibility, level of difficulty, special conditions, underwater photography tips, and common and unusual marine life present. You'll also find practical logistical information and coverage on topside activities and attractions, sections on diving health and safety, plus listings for diving services, live-aboards, dive resorts and tourist offices.

# LONELY PLANET

## Lonely Planet Travel Atlases

onely Planet has long been famous for the number and quality of its guidebook maps. Now we've gone one step further and produced a handy companion series: Lonely Planet travel atlases – maps of a country produced in book form.

Unlike other maps, which look good but lead travellers astray, our travel atlases have been researched on the road by Lonely Planet's experienced team of writers. All details are carefully checked to ensure the atlas corresponds with the equivalent Lonely Planet guidebook.

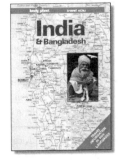

- full-colour throughout
- maps researched and checked by Lonely Planet authors
- place names correspond with Lonely Planet guidebooks
- no confusing spelling differences
- legend and travelling information in English, French, German, Japanese and Spanish
- size: 230 x 160 mm

**Available now:** Chile & Easter Island • Egypt • India & Bangladesh • Israel & the Palestinian Territories • Jordan, Syria & Lebanon • Kenya • Laos • Portugal • South Africa, Lesotho & Swaziland • Thailand • Turkey • Vietnam • Zimbabwe, Botswana & Namibia

## Lonely Planet TV Series & Videos

onely Planet travel guides have been brought to life on television screens around the world. Like our guides, the programs are based on the joy of independent travel, and look honestly at some of the most exciting, picturesque and frustrating places in the world. Each show is presented by one of three travellers from Australia, England or the USA and combines an innovative mixture of video, Super-8 film, atmospheric soundscapes and original music.

Videos of each episode – containing additional footage not shown on television – are available from good book and video shops, but the availability of individual videos varies with regional screening schedules.

**Video destinations include:** Alaska • American Rockies • Australia – The South-East • Baja California & the Copper Canyon • Brazil • Central Asia • Chile & Easter Island • Corsica, Sicily & Sardinia – The Mediterranean Islands • East Africa (Tanzania & Zanzibar) • Ecuador & the Galapagos Islands • Greenland & Iceland • Indonesia • Israel & the Sinai Desert • Jamaica • Japan • La Ruta Maya • Morocco • New York • North India • Pacific Islands (Fiji, Solomon Islands & Vanuatu) • South India • South West China • Turkey • Vietnam • West Africa • Zimbabwe, Botswana • Namibia

**The Lonely Planet TV series is produced by:** Pilot Productions
The Old Studio
18 Middle Row
London W10 5AT, UK

# FREE Lonely Planet Newsletters

**W**e love hearing from you and think you'd like to hear from us.

## Planet Talk

Our FREE quarterly printed newsletter is full of tips from travellers and anecdotes from Lonely Planet guidebook authors. Every issue is packed with up-to-date travel news and advice, and includes:

- a postcard from Lonely Planet co-founder Tony Wheeler
- a swag of mail from travellers
- a look at life on the road through the eyes of a Lonely Planet author
- topical health advice
- prizes for the best travel yarn
- news about forthcoming Lonely Planet events
- a complete list of Lonely Planet books and other titles

**To join our mailing list, residents of the UK, Europe and Africa can email us at go@lonelyplanet.co.uk; residents of North and South America can email us at info@lonelyplanet.com; the rest of the world can email us at talk2us@lonelyplanet.com.au, or contact any Lonely Planet office.**

## Comet

**O**ur FREE monthly email newsletter brings you all the latest travel news, features, interviews, competitions, destination ideas, travellers' tips & tales, Q&As, raging debates and related links. Find out what's new on the Lonely Planet Web site and which books are about to hit the shelves.

Subscribe from your desktop: www.lonelyplanet.com/comet

# Index

## Abbreviations

Can – Canada
CT – Connecticut
MA – Massachusetts
ME – Maine
NH – New Hampshire
NYC – New York City
RI – Rhode Island
VT – Vermont

## Text

### A

Abenaki people 25, 465, 515
Acadia National Park (ME) **564-5**, 570-1
Acadia National Park region (ME) 552-74, **553**
accommodations 73-7
activities 67-72. *See also specific activities*
AIDS. *See* HIV/AIDS
air tours 229, 241, 256
air travel
   air travel glossary 86-7
   airfares 85-91
   airlines 88, 98
   airports 85-8, 98, 166, 592-5
   around New England 98
   to/from New England 85-93
alcohol 80-2. *See also* breweries; wineries
Alcott, Louisa May 29, 177-8, 179, 180
Algonquian people 25
Allen, Ethan 19, 410, 422
Allenstown (NH) 478
American Automobile Association 49, 64-5, 103
American Museum of Fly Fishing (VT) 428
American Museum of Natural History (NYC) 588
Amherst (MA) 315-8
Amherst College (MA) 316
*Amistad* 380, 390

Amoskeag Mills (NH) 476-7
amusement parks 189, 371, 384-5, 398, 505, 527
animals 23-4
antiques & antique shows 38, 39, 40, 165, 206, 231, 234, 239, 300, 363
Appalachian Gap (VT) 442
Appalachian Mountain Club 111, 506
Appalachian Trail 65, 68, 328, 429, 582
Appleseed, Johnny 297
aquariums 132, 285, 402
Aquidneck Island (RI) 352
Aquinnah (Gay Head; MA) 263, 276
arboretums. *See* gardens
architecture 27-8, 347
Aroostook County (ME) 583
art galleries 164-5, 197, 242, 245, 251, 254-5, 269, 272, 278, 290, 322, 386
arts 26-30. *See also specific type*
Ashumet Holly and Wildlife Sanctuary (MA) 218
atlases 43
ATMs 50
Augusta (ME) 538-40

### B

Back Bay (MA). *See* Boston (MA)
Bailey Island (ME) 531, 542
balloon rides 536-7
Balsams, the (NH) 510
Bangor (ME) 573-4

Bantam (CT) 411
Bar Harbor (ME) 566-72, **567**
Barnstable (MA) 225-7
Barre (VT) 446
bars 83-4, 161-2
Bartholomew's Cobble (MA) 322
Barton (VT) 461
baseball 84, 130, 162, 351
Bash Bish Falls (MA) 322
Basin, the (NH) 496
basketball 162, 307, 310
Bath (ME) 542-3
battlefields 123-4, 174, 398, 424
Battleship Cove (MA) 213
Baxter State Park (ME) 582-3
beaches 70
   Connecticut 398
   Maine 521, 523, 527, 549
   Massachusetts 198, 206, 218, 223, 226, 229, 233, 235, 241, 243, 247, 249, 252, 256, 270, 274, 277, 285, 291, 292
   New Hampshire 468-9, 483
   Rhode Island 358, 364-6, 368, 369-73
Beacon Hill (MA). *See* Boston (MA)
Beals Island (ME) 574-5
bed & breakfasts. *See* accommodations
beer 81-2. *See also* breweries
Belfast (ME) 559

---

**Bold** indicates maps.

## D

Bold indicates maps.

**Bold** indicates maps.

# Y

# Z

**Bold** indicates maps.

# Boxed Text

# MAP LEGEND

## BOUNDARIES

| | |
|---|---|
| ·-·-·-·-·- | International |
| ···-··-··- | State, Province |

## HYDROGRAPHY

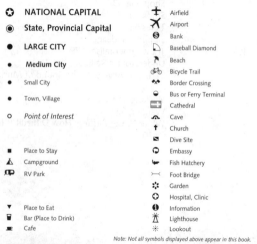

| | |
|---|---|
| | Water |
| | Coastline |
| | Beach |
| | River, Waterfall |
| ◎ | Swamp, Spring |

## ROUTES & TRANSPORT

| | |
|---|---|
| | Freeway |
| | Toll Freeway |
| | Primary Road |
| | Secondary Road |
| | Tertiary Road |
| ===== ----- | Unpaved Road |
| | Pedestrian Mall |
| —————— | Trail |
| ·················· | Walking Tour |
| — — — — | Ferry Route |
| +++++ | Railway, Train Station |
| Ⓜ Ⓣ | Mass Transit Station |

## ROUTE SHIELDS

| | | | |
|---|---|---|---|
| 🛡80 | Interstate | 55 | Canadian Highway |
| 1 | US Highway | | |
| 10 | State Highway | 40 | Trans-Canada Highway |

## AREA FEATURES

| | |
|---|---|
| | Park |
| | Forest |
| | Cemetery |
| | Building |
| | Plaza |
| | Golf Course |

## MAP SYMBOLS

| | | | |
|---|---|---|---|
| ✪ | **NATIONAL CAPITAL** | ▲ | Monument |
| ◉ | **State, Provincial Capital** | ▲ | Mountain |
| ● | **LARGE CITY** | 🏛 | Museum |
| ● | **Medium City** | ⌂ | Observatory |
| • | Small City | ← | One-Way Street |
| • | Town, Village | ♣ | Park |
| ○ | *Point of Interest* | 🅿 | Parking |
| | | )( | Pass |
| ■ | Place to Stay | 🌲 | Picnic Area |
| ▲ | Campground | ★ | Police Station |
| 🚐 | RV Park | 🛏 | Pool |
| | | ✉ | Post Office |
| ▼ | Place to Eat | ❖ | Shopping Mall |
| 🍶 | Bar (Place to Drink) | ⛷ | Skiing (Alpine) |
| ☕ | Cafe | ⛷ | Skiing (Nordic) |

| | | | |
|---|---|---|---|
| ✈ | Airfield | 🏛 | Stately Home |
| ✈ | Airport | ✡ | Synagogue |
| ⑂ | Bank | 🚶 | Trailhead |
| ⬡ | Baseball Diamond | 🍷 | Winery |
| ⚑ | Beach | 🐾 | Zoo |
| 🚲 | Bicycle Trail | | |
| ✦ | Border Crossing | | |
| ⛴ | Bus or Ferry Terminal | | |
| ⛪ | Cathedral | | |
| ⌒ | Cave | | |
| ✝ | Church | | |
| ⚓ | Dive Site | | |
| ℗ | Embassy | | |
| 🐟 | Fish Hatchery | | |
| ⤞ | Foot Bridge | | |
| ❀ | Garden | | |
| ✚ | Hospital, Clinic | | |
| ❶ | Information | | |
| 🕯 | Lighthouse | | |
| ☀ | Lookout | | |

*Note: Not all symbols displayed above appear in this book.*

# LONELY PLANET OFFICES

### Australia
PO Box 617, Hawthorn 3122, Victoria
☎ 03 9819 1877 fax 03 9819 6459
email talk2us@lonelyplanet.com.au

### USA
150 Linden Street, Oakland, California 94607
☎ 510 893 8555, TOLL FREE (800) 275 8555
fax 510 893 8572
email info@lonelyplanet.com

### UK
10A Spring Place, London NW5 3BH
☎ 0171 428 4800 fax 0171 428 4828
email go@lonelyplanet.co.uk

### France
1 rue du Dahomey, 75011 Paris
☎ 01 55 25 33 00 fax 01 55 25 33 01
email bip@lonelyplanet.fr
3615 lonelyplanet *(1,29 F TTC/min)*

**World Wide Web: www.lonelyplanet.com *or* AOL keyword: lp**
**Lonely Planet Images: lpi@lonelyplanet.com.au**